The
Good Food
Guide 2000

D1824342

WHICH? BOOKS

Which? Books is the book publishing arm of Consumers' Association, which was set up in 1957 to improve the standards of goods and services available to the public. Everything Which? publishes aims to help consumers, by giving them the independent information they need to make informed decisions. These publications, known throughout Britain for their quality, integrity and impartiality, have been held in high regard for four decades.

Independence does not come cheap: the guides carry no advertising, and no restaurant or hotel can buy an entry in our guides, or treat our inspectors to free meals or accommodation. This policy, and our practice of rigorously re-researching our guides for each edition, helps us to provide our readers with information of a standard and quality that cannot be surpassed.

The
Good Food
Guide 2000

Edited by Jim Ainsworth

CONSUMERS' ASSOCIATION

Which? Books are commissioned and researched by
Consumers' Association and published by
Which? Ltd, 2 Marylebone Road,
London NW1 4DF

Distributed by The Penguin Group:
Penguin Books Ltd, 27 Wrights Lane,
London W8 5TZ

British Library Cataloguing in Publication Data
A catalogue record for this book is
available from the British Library

ISBN 0 85202 777 X

For a full list of Which? books, please write to:
Which? Books, Castlemead, Gascoyne Way,
Hertford X, SG14 1LH
or access our web site at http://www.which.net

Photoset by Tradespools Ltd, Frome, Somerset
Printed in England by Clays Ltd, St Ives plc

Cover typography by Kysen
Cover design by Sarah Watson
Cover photography by Ginette Chapman
Typographic design by Tim Higgins

Contents

Telephone changes

On 22 April 2000 there will be changes to telephone codes and numbers in six geographic areas across the UK. They are Cardiff, Coventry, London, Northern Ireland, Portsmouth and Southampton. In the case of London, we have noted the relevant changes at the very beginning of the main-entry and Round-up sections; for the other areas we have listed both old and new numbers in the entries themselves.

The *Good Food Guide* voucher scheme £5

Again this year the *Guide* includes three £5 vouchers that readers will be able to redeem against the price of meals taken in participating restaurants. (Look for the £5 symbol at the very end of entries to locate those participating.) Only one voucher may be used per booked table, for a minimum of two people. Remember that your intention to use the voucher MUST be mentioned at the time of booking. Some restaurants may restrict use of the voucher at some sessions or for some menus (usually 'special offer' or lower-cost set meals); it is best to ask when booking. Actual vouchers (not photocopies) must be presented. The vouchers will be valid from 1 October 1999 to 30 September 2000, and may not be used in conjunction with any other offers.

The *Guide* online

Internet users can find *The Good Food Guide* online at the Which? Online web site http://www.which.net. (You will need to be a Which? Online subscriber to make full use of the *Guide* online.) For a free CD that will give you more details about Which? Online and how to be connected to the Internet, phone 0645 830254 (quoting IJ166).

Update service

Written details of restaurant sales, closures, chef changes and so on since this edition of the *Guide* was published will be available free of charge from 1 December 1999 to 1 May 2000. Readers should write to: FREEPOST, Update, *The Good Food Guide*, 2 Marylebone Road, London NW1 4DF (no stamp is required if you post your request in the UK). Alternatively, you may email *guidereports@which.co.uk* (remember to include your full name and address when you email), or phone 0171-830 7551 (020-7770 7551 from 22 April 2000). As always, readers who send in reports on meals will automatically be sent an Update Sheet.

How to use the *Guide*

FINDING A RESTAURANT

If you are seeking a restaurant in a particular area: *first go to the maps* at the centre of the book. Localities where *Good Food Guide* restaurants can be found are indicated on the maps (the London maps give the name of the restaurant). Once you know the locality (or, for London, the restaurant name), go to the relevant section of the book to find the entry for the restaurant. The *Guide*'s main entries are divided into seven sections: London, England, Scotland, Wales, Channel Islands, Northern Ireland, and Republic of Ireland. In the London section, restaurants are listed alphabetically by name; in all other sections, they are listed by locality (usually the name of the town or village).

In addition to the main entries are the Round-ups (a range of restaurants, cafés, bistros and pubs that are worth a visit but do not merit a full entry): those for London can be found just after the London main-entry section, and those for everywhere else are towards the back of the book just after the Republic of Ireland main-entry section.

If you know the name of the restaurant: *go to the index* at the back of the book, which lists both main and Round-up entries.

If you are seeking award-winning restaurants, those offering a particular cuisine, etc.: *make use of the lists* starting on page 11, which feature the top-rated restaurants, restaurants with outstanding wine cellars, restaurants of the year, new entries in the *Guide*, closures (since the last edition), restaurants that charge 15 per cent for service, London restaurants by cuisine, London party bookings, London restaurants with no-smoking rooms, and budget eating. There is also a page giving an eclectic selection of good places to go if you are looking for breakfast/brunch, vegetarian food, a child-friendly atmosphere, a pre-theatre meal, organic or free-range ingredients, a top-notch pub or a waterside setting.

HOW TO READ A GUIDE ENTRY

A sample entry is set out overleaf. At the top of the entry you will find the restaurant's name, map number, address, telephone and fax numbers, its email address if it has one, any symbols that may apply to the establishment, the mark awarded by the Editor for cooking, and the cost range for a three-course meal. (Full explanations of symbols, the cooking mark and the cost range follow the sample entry.) The middle part of the entry describes food, wines, atmosphere and so on, while the final section gives a wealth of additional information (explained in greater detail on pages 9-10).

LOCALITY County   map 4

▲ *Restaurant Name* ♟ ▮✑ ❊ £ | NEW ENTRY |
Address   COOKING 6
TEL: (01234) 111111   FAX: (01234) 222222   COST £15 to £100
EMAIL: restaurant@place.co.uk

This is where you will find information about the restaurant – cuisine, service, décor, wine list, and any other points of interest not covered by the details at the foot of the entry. Each entry in the *Guide* has been re-researched from scratch, and is based on information taken from readers' reports received over the past year, confirmed where necessary by anonymous inspection. In every case, readers and inspectors have been prepared to endorse the quality of the cooking. The text usually concludes with a description of the wines offered.

CHEFS: John and Mary Smith   PROPRIETOR: Mary Smith   OPEN: Mon to Fri L 12 to 2, Mon to Sat D 7 to 10   CLOSED: 25 and 26 Dec, Easter, 2 weeks July, bank hols   MEALS: alc (main courses £9 to £15). Set D £16 (2 courses) to £20. Cover £1.50. Light L available. BYO £5   SERVICE: not inc, card slips closed; 10% for parties of 6 or more   CARDS: Amex, Delta, Diners, MasterCard, Switch, Visa   DETAILS: 50 seats. 15 seats outside. Private parties: 25 main room, 15 private room. Car park. Vegetarian meals. Children's helpings. No children under 7. Jacket and tie. No smoking in dining-room. Wheelchair access (also WC). No music. Air-conditioned   ACCOMMODATION: 5 rooms, all with bath/shower. TV. Phone. B&B £35 to £80. Rooms for disabled. Baby facilities. Swimming pool. (*The Which? Hotel Guide*) ⊖ (£5)

● For an explanation of symbols, see inside front cover.

Cooking mark

Marks are given out of 10, and are for cooking only, as perceived by the *Guide* and its readers. They signify the following:

1–2 COMPETENT COOKING Cafés, pubs, bistros and restaurants which offer sound, basic, capable cooking. Those scoring 2 use better ingredients, take fewer short-cuts, please more reporters, and make good neighbourhood restaurants.

3–4 COMPETENT TO GOOD COOKING These restaurants use fine ingredients and cook them appropriately, although some inconsistencies may be noted. They please reporters most of the time. Those scoring 4 show greater skill in handling materials, and are worthy of special note in the locality.

5–6 GOOD TO VERY GOOD COOKING These restaurants use high-quality ingredients, achieve consistently good results, and are enthusiastically reported. Those scoring 6 show a degree of flair, and are among the best in the region.

7–8 VERY GOOD TO EXCELLENT COOKING A high level of ambition and achievement means that the finest ingredients are consistently treated with skill and imagination. Those scoring 8 are worth a special effort to visit.

9–10 THE BEST These are the top restaurants in the country. They are few in number, and can be expensive, but are highly individual and display impressive artistry. Those scoring 10 are the A-team, and can comfortably stand comparison with the stiffest international competition.

Cost

The price range given is based on the cost of a three-course meal (lunch and/or dinner) for one person, including coffee, house wine, service and cover charge where applicable, according to information supplied by the restaurant. The lower figure is the least you are likely to pay, from either à la carte or set-price menus, and may apply only to lunch. The higher figure indicates a probable maximum cost, sometimes based on a set-price meal of more than three courses, if that is what is offered. This figure is inflated by 20 per cent to reflect the fact that some people may order more expensive wine, extra drinks and some higher-priced 'special' dishes, and that price rises may come into effect during the life-time of this edition of the *Guide*.

Meals

At the bottom of entries information on the types of meals offered is given, with any variations for lunch (L) and dinner (D), and details of availability. An à la carte menu is signified by the letters *alc*. This is followed by a range of prices for main courses, rounded up to the nearest 50p. *Set L* denotes a set-price lunch; *Set D* means set-price dinner. Set meals usually consist of three courses, but can include many more. If a set meal has fewer than three courses, this is stated. If there is a cover charge, this is also indicated. *BYO* signifies that you may bring your own bottle of wine, and the corkage charge (if any) is given.

Service

Net prices means that prices of food and wine are inclusive of service charge, and this is indicated clearly on the menu and bill; *not inc*, that service is not included and is left to the discretion of the customer; *10%*, that a fixed service charge of 10 per cent is automatically added to the bill; *10% (optional)*, that 10 per cent is added to the bill along with the word 'optional' or similar qualifier; and *none*, that no service charge is made or expected and that any money offered is refused. *Card slips closed* indicates that the total on the slips of credit cards is closed when handed over for signature.

Other details

Information is also given on *seating*, *seating outside* and *private parties*. We say *car park* if the restaurant provides free parking facilities for patrons, and say *vegetarian meals* only if menus list at least one vegetarian option as a starter and one as a main course (if this is not noted, a restaurant may still be able to offer vegetarian options with prior notice – it is worth phoning to check). Any restrictions on children are given, such as *no children* or *no children under 6 after 8pm*; otherwise, it can be assumed that children are welcome. In addition, *children's helpings* are noted if smaller portions are available at a reduced price; *jacket and tie* if it is compulsory for men to wear a jacket and tie to the restaurant; *wheelchair access* if the proprietor has confirmed that the entrance is at least 80cm wide and passages at least 120cm wide in accordance with the Royal Association for Disability and Rehabilitation (RADAR) recommendations, and *also WC* if the proprietor has assured us that toilet facilities are suitable for disabled people (*not WC* means these are not available or the proprietor is not sure). *Music* indicates that live or recorded music is usually played in the dining-room; *occasional music* that it sometimes is; *no music* that it never is.

Accommodation

For establishments offering overnight accommodation, the number of rooms, along with facilities provided in the rooms (e.g. bath/shower, TV, phone), is set out. Prices are given usually for bed and breakfast (*B&B*). *D,B&B* indicates that the price also includes dinner. The first figure given is the lowest price for one person in a single room, or single occupancy of a double, the second is the most expensive price for two people in a double room or suite. *Rooms for disabled* means the establishment has stated that its accommodation is suitable for wheelchair-users. Restrictions on children, and facilities for guests with babies, are indicated. *The Which? Hotel Guide* means the establishment is also listed in the 1999 edition of our sister guide to over 1,000 hotels in Britain.

Miscellaneous information

At the end of London entries, the nearest Underground station is given after the symbol ⊖. For restaurants that have elected to participate in the *Good Food Guide* £5 voucher scheme, a £5 symbol appears at the very end of entries (see page 6 for further details).

The top-rated restaurants

(See pages 8–9 for explanation of marking system.)

Mark **10** for cooking

London
Chez Nico at Ninety Park
  Lane, W1

Mark **9** for cooking

London
Gordon Ramsay, SW3

England
Le Manoir aux Quat' Saisons,
  Great Milton
Waterside Inn, Bray

Winteringham Fields,
  Winteringham

Scotland
Altnaharrie Inn, Ullapool

Mark **8** for cooking

London
Oak Room Marco Pierre
  White, W1
Pied-à-Terre, W1
The Square, W1
La Tante Claire, SW1

England
Box Tree, Ilkley
Croque-en-Bouche,
  Malvern Wells

Fat Duck, Bray
Fischer's Baslow Hall, Baslow
Gidleigh Park, Chagford
Hambleton Hall, Hambleton
Merchant House, Ludlow
L'Ortolan, Shinfield
21 Queen Street, Newcastle

Scotland
La Potinière, Gullane

Restaurants with outstanding wine cellars
marked in the text with a ⚱

London
Bibendum, SW3
Chez Bruce, SW17
Clarke's, W8
Fifth Floor, SW1
Leith's, W11
Odette's, NW1
Oxo Tower Restaurant, SE1
Prism, EC3
Ransome's Dock, SW11
RSJ, SE1
The Square, W1
Tate Gallery Restaurant, SW1

England
Bowness-on-Windermere, Porthole
    Eating House
Bristol, Harveys
Bristol, Markwicks
Buckland, Buckland Manor
Chagford, Gidleigh Park
Chinnor, Sir Charles Napier
Corse Lawn, Corse Lawn House
Dartmouth, Carved Angel
Dedham, Le Talbooth
East Grinstead, Gravetye Manor
Elland, La Cachette
Epworth, Epworth Tap
Evershot, Summer Lodge
Faversham, Read's
Grasmere, Michael's Nook
Grasmere, White Moss House
Great Milton, Le Manoir aux Quat'
    Saisons
Great Yeldham, White Hart
Hambleton, Hambleton Hall
Hastings, Röser's
Hetton, Angel Inn
Horton, French Partridge
Ilkley, Box Tree
Keyston, Pheasant Inn
Leeds, Leodis
Leeds, Sous le Nez en Ville
Madingley, Three Horseshoes
Malvern Wells, Croque-en-Bouche
Middleham, Waterford House
New Milton, Chewton Glen, Marryat
    Restaurant
Norwich, Adlard's

Oxford, Cherwell Boathouse
Padstow, Seafood Restaurant
Ramsbottom, Village Restaurant
Romsey, Old Manor House
Ross-on-Wye, Le Faisan Doré
Shepton Mallet, Bowlish House
Southwold, The Crown
Stockcross, Vineyard at Stockcross
Tunbridge Wells, Hotel du Vin & Bistro
Ullswater, Sharrow Bay
Wareham, Priory Hotel
Waterhouses, Old Beams
Williton, White House
Winchester, Hotel du Vin & Bistro

Scotland
Achiltibuie, Summer Isles Hotel
Anstruther, Cellar
Dunkeld, Kinnaird
Edinburgh, Valvona & Crolla Caffè Bar
Fort William, Inverlochy Castle
Glasgow, Ubiquitous Chip
Gullane, Greywalls
Gullane, La Potinière
Kingussie, The Cross
Linlithgow, Champany Inn
Nairn, Clifton House
Peat Inn, Peat Inn
Port Appin, Airds Hotel
Ullapool, Altnaharrie Inn

Wales
Aberdovey, Penhelig Arms Hotel
Cardiff, St David's Hotel & Spa
Llandewi Skirrid, Walnut Tree Inn
Llandudno, St Tudno Hotel
Llansanffraid Glan Conwy, Old
    Rectory
Portmeirion, Hotel Portmeirion
Pwllheli, Plas Bodegroes
Reynoldston, Fairyhill

Republic of Ireland
Dublin, Le Coq Hardi
Dublin, Thornton's
Howth, King Sitric
Kenmare, Park Hotel Kenmare
Kenmare, Sheen Falls Lodge, La
    Cascade
Newport, Newport House

Restaurants of the year

This award does not necessarily go to the restaurants with the highest mark for cooking, but rather to ones which have shown particular merit or achievement during the year, whether as all-rounders or in a particular field. It may go to an old favourite or to a new entry, but in either case the places listed below are worth visiting in their own right, and have enhanced the eating-out experience in some way.

London
Club Gascon, EC1
Le Gavroche, W1
Inter-Continental, Le Soufflé, W1
Mirabelle, W1
St John, EC1
Zafferano, SW1
Zaiko, SW3

England
Bath, Green Street Seafood Café
Biddenden, West House
Brockenhurst, Le Poussin
Carlton-in-Coverdale, Forresters Arms
Cheesden, Nutters
Cheltenham, Le Champignon Sauvage
Corscombe, Fox Inn
Erpingham, Ark
Horton, French Partridge
Hunstrete, Hunstrete House
Kington, Penrhos Court
Ludlow, Merchant House
Lydford, Dartmoor Inn
Marsh Benham, Water Rat
Melksham, Toxique
Milton Ernest, Strawberry Tree
Morston, Morston Hall

Northleach, Old Woolhouse
Old Burghclere, Dew Pond
Portloe, Tregain
Romsey, Old Manor House
Rowde, George & Dragon
St Mawes, Tresanton Hotel
Staddlebridge, McCoy's Bistro
Swaffham, Strattons
Twickenham, McClements
Whitby, Magpie Café

Scotland
Achiltibuie, Summer Isles Hotel
Alyth, Drumnacree House
Gullane, Golf Inn Hotel, Daniel's Restaurant
Kingussie, The Cross
Lochinver, The Albannach
Spean Bridge, Old Pines
Troon, Lochgreen House

Wales
Fishguard, Three Main Street
Llandewi Skirrid, Walnut Tree Inn
Llanfihangel Nant Melan, Red Lion Inn
Pwllheli, Plas Bodegroes
Talsarnau, Maes-y-Neuadd

The *Guide's* longest-serving restaurants

The *Guide* has seen many restaurants come and go. Some, however, have stayed the course with tenacity. (Qualification for this list is that the restaurant has been in each edition of the *Guide* subsequent to its first entry.)

Connaught, W1	47 years
Gay Hussar, W1	43 years
Porth Tocyn Hotel, Abersoch	43 years
Gravetye Manor, East Grinstead	39 years
Sharrow Bay, Ullswater	39 years
French Partridge, Horton	35 years
Walnut Tree Inn, Llandewi Skirrid	35 years
Black Bull Inn, Moulton	33 years
Chez Moi, W11	31 years
Rothay Manor, Ambleside	31 years
Sundial, Herstmonceux	31 years
Le Gavroche, W1	30 years
Summer Isles Hotel, Achiltibuie	30 years
The Capital, SW3	29 years
Miller Howe, Windermere	29 years
Cringletie House, Peebles	28 years
Old Fire Engine House, Ely	28 years
Ubiquitous Chip, Glasgow	28 years
Peat Inn, Peat Inn	27 years
Plumber Manor, Sturminster Newton	27 years
Druidstone, Broad Haven	27 years
Waterside Inn, Bray	27 years
White Moss House, Grasmere	27 years
Carved Angel, Dartmouth	26 years
Isle of Eriska, Eriska	26 years
Old Woolhouse, Northleach	25 years
Airds, Port Appin	24 years
La Potinière, Gullane	24 years
Blostin's, Shepton Mallet	23 years
Farlam Hall, Brampton	23 years
Langan's Brasserie, W1	23 years
Croque-en-Bouche, Malvern Wells	22 years
Gidleigh Park, Chagford	22 years
Le Suquet, SW3	22 years
White House, Williton	22 years

New Entries

These restaurants are new main entries in the *Guide* this year, although some may have appeared in previous years, or in the Round-ups last year.

London
Amandier, W2
Arancia, SE16
Aroma II, W1
Asakusa, NW1
Aubergine, SW10
Babur Brasserie, SE23
Bali Sugar, W11
Cactus Blue, SW3
Cantaloupe, EC2
Chapter Two, SE3
Le Chardon, SE22
Club Gascon, EC1
Le Coq d'Argent, EC2
Fish!, SE1
Floriana, SW3
Frith Street Restaurant, W1
Gaudí, EC1
The Globe, SE1
Gordan Ramsay, SW3
Grano, W4
Great Eastern Dining Room, EC2
Idaho, N6
Itsu, SW3
Kulu Kulu Sushi, W1
Lomo, SW10
Love, W1
Lundum's, SW7
New Tayyab, E1
Offshore, W11
Old Delhi, W2
1 Lombard Street, EC3
One-O-One, SW1
L'Oranger, SW1
Passione, W1
Pétrus, SW1
Prism, EC3
Purple Sage, W1
Roussillon, SW1
Saigon Thuy, SW18
Salt House, NW8
Sheekey's, WC2
Soho Spice, W1
Spread Eagle, SE10
Tajine, W1
La Tante Claire, SW1
Teca, W1
Terrace, W8
Titanic, W1
Townhouse Brasserie, WC1
The Vale, W9
Zaika, SW3

England
Aymestrey, Riverside Inn
Bath, Bath Priory

Bath, Green Street Seafood Café
Bath, Richmond Arms
Biddenden, West House
Birmingham, Hyatt Regency, Number 282
Bishop's Waltham, Wine Bar
Brighton, Gingerman
Burrington, Northcote Manor
Coln St Aldwyns, New Inn
Cottesmore, Sun Inn
Dargate, Dove
Dartmouth, Carved Angel Café
Doncaster, Hamilton's
East Chiltington, Jolly Sportsman
East End, East End Arms
Elstree, Edwarebury Hotel
Fletching, Griffin Inn
Foss Cross, Hare & Hounds
Hexham, Hexham Royal Hotel
Ilkley, Farsyde
Kew, The Glasshouse
Liverpool, Ziba
Ludlow, Overton Grange
Lund, Wellington Inn
Lydford, Dartmoor Inn
Manchester, Bridgewater Hall
Manchester, Lincoln
Manchester, New Emperor
Manchester, Rhodes & Co
Manchester, Yang Sing
Manningtree, Stour Bay Café
Marsh Benham, Water Rat
Melbourn, Sheene Mill
Milton Ernest, Strawberry Tree
New Alresford, Hunters
Newcastle upon Tyne, Courtney's
Norton, Hundred House Hotel
Nottingham, Merchants
Ombersley, Venture In
Padstow, Brock's
Padstow, Rick Stein's Café
Padstow, St Petroc's
Peter Tavy, Peter Tavy Inn
Richmond, Canyon
St Ives, Alfresco
Sheffield, Milano
Skipton, Le Caveau
Standlake, Bell
Storrington, Fleur de Sel
Titley, Stagg Inn

Twickenham, TW1
Warwick, Findons
West Ilsley, Harrow Inn
Whitchurch, Red House
Wickham, Old House Hotel and Brasserie
Wokingham, Rose Street

Scotland
Aberfeldy, 7 the Square
Ballater, Balgonie Country House
Blair Atholl, Loft
Edinburgh, Blue Bar Café
Edinburgh, The Bonham
Edinburgh, Restaurant Martin Wishart
Edinburgh, Tower Restaurant
Edinburgh, Tuscan Square
Ednam, Edenwater House
Glasgow, Buttery
Gullane, Golf Inn Hotel, Daniel's Restaurant
Lochinver, The Albannach
Perth, Kinfauns Castle Hotel
Perth, Let's Eat Again
Troon, MacCallums' Oyster Bar

Wales
Cardiff, Gilby's
Cardiff, Pied-a-Terre
Cardiff, St David's Hotel & Spa
Cardiff, Woods Brasserie
Swansea, Hanson's
Wolf's Castle, The Wolfe

Channel Islands
Gorey, Jersey Pottery Restaurant
Gorey, Suma's
St Brelade, Sea Crest

Northern Ireland
Belfast, Crescent Townhouse, Metro
Holywood, Fontana

Republic of Ireland
Bantry, Larchwood House
Dublin, Lloyds Brasserie
Dublin, Mermaid Café
Lisdoonvarna, Sheedy's

London restaurants by cuisine

Boundaries between some national cuisines – British, French and Italian particularly – are not as marked as they used to be. Therefore, the restaurants listed below are classified by the predominant influence, although there may be some crossover.

American
Bradleys, NW3
Cactus Blue, SW3
Christopher's, WC2
Dakota, W11
Idaho, N6
Montana, SW6

Belgian
Belgo Noord, NW1

British
Alfred, WC2
Butlers Wharf Chop House, SE1
City Rhodes, EC4
Connaught, W1
French House Dining Room, W1
Greenhouse, W1
Quality Chop House, EC1
Rhodes in the Square, SW1
R.K. Stanleys, W1
Rules, WC2
St John, EC1
Savoy, Grill Room, WC2
Tate Gallery Restaurant, SW1
Wilsons, W14
Wiltons, SW1

Chinese
Aroma II, W1
Cheng-Du, NW1
Four Seasons, W2
Fung Shing, WC2
Golden Dragon, W1
Jenny Lo's Teahouse, SW1
Lee Fook, W2
Mandarin Kitchen, W2
Mr Kong, WC2
New Hoo Wah, W1
Royal China, W1 and W2
Zen Central, W1

Danish
Lundum's, SW7

Fish
Back to Basics, W1
Brady's, SW18
Café Fish, SW1
Fish!, SE1
Livebait, SE1 and WC2
Lobster Pot, SE11
Lou Pescadou, SW5
Offshore, W11
One-O-One, SW1

Sheekey's, WC2
Le Suquet, SW3
Two Brothers, N3
Upper Street Fish Shop, N1

French
Alexandra, SW20
Amandier, W2
Aubergine, SW10
Balzac Bistro, SW3
Brasserie St Quentin, SW3
Le Chardon, SE22
Chez Nico at Ninety Park Lane, W1
Club Gascon, EC1
Le Coq d'Argent, EC2
Criterion Brasserie, W1
La Dordogne, W4
L'Estaminet, WC2
Gordon Ramsay, SW3
Le Gavroche, W1
Inter-Continental Hotel, Le Soufflé, W1
Mirabelle, W1
Mon Plaisir, WC2
Oak Room Marco Pierre White, W1
L'Oranger, SW1
Pétrus, SW1
Pied-à-Terre, W1
Roussillon, SW1
755 Fulham Road, SW6
Spread Eagle, SE10
La Tante Claire, SW1

Greek
Daphne, NW1

Hungarian
Gay Hussar, W1

Indian/Pakistani
Babur Brasserie, SE23
Café Spice Namaste, E1 and SW11
Chor Bizarre, W1
Chutney Mary, SW10
Mem Saheb, E14
Mirch Masala, SW16
New Tayyab, E1
Old Delhi, W2
Sarkhel's, SW18
Salloos, SW1
Soho Spice, W1
Tamarind, W1
Veeraswamy, W1
Zaika, SW3

Indian Vegetarian
Kastoori, SW17
Rani, N3
Rasa, N16 and W1
Sabras, NW10
Sree Krishna, SW17

Indonesian/ Straits
Gourmet Garden, NW4
Melati, W1
Singapore Garden, NW6

Italian
Al San Vincenzo, W2
Arancia, SE16
Assaggi, W2
Bertorelli's, WC2
Cicoria, NW6
Como Lario, SW1
Daphne's, SW3
Del Buongustaio, SW15
Floriana, SW3
Grano, W4
Great Eastern Dining Room, EC2
Green Olive, W9
Halkin Hotel, SW1
Ibla, W1
L'Incontro, SW1
Neal Street Restaurant, WC2
Olivo, SW11
Orsino, W11
Osteria Antica Bologna, SW11
Passione, W1
Purple Sage, W1
Red Pepper, W9
Riva, SW13
River Café, W6
Sartoria, W1
Spiga, W1
Teca, W1
Zafferano, SW1

Japanese/sushi bars
Asakusa, NW1
Café Japan, NW11
Inaho, W2
Itsu, SW3
Kulu Kulu Sushi, W1
Matsuri, SW1
Mitsukoshi, SW1
Miyama, W1
Moshi Moshi Sushi, EC2, EC4 and E14
Nobu, W1
Sushi-Say, NW2

Tokyo Diner, WC2
Wagamama, WC1 and W1

Mauritian
Chez Liline, N4

**North African/
Middle Eastern**
Adams Café, W12
Al Bustan, SW1
Al Hamra, W1

Istanbul Iskembecisi, N16
Iznik, N5
Laurent, NW2
Tajine, W1

Peruvian
Fina Estampa, SE1

Spanish
Cambio de Tercio, SW5
Gaudí, EC1
Lomo, SW10

Moro, EC1

Thai
Blue Elephant, SW6
Mantanah, SE25
Sri Siam Soho, W1
Thai Garden, E2
Thailand, SE14

London party bookings for 25 or more in private rooms

Aroma II, W1
Asakusa, NW1
Atlantic Bar and Grill, W1
Balzac Bistro, W12
Belair House, SE21
Bistrorganic, W10
Blakes Dining Room, NW1
Cactus Blue, SW3
Café du Jardin, WC2
Cambio de Tercio, SW5
Chinon, W14
Chor Bizarre, W1
Chutney Mary, SW10
Coast, W1
Como Lario, SW1
County Hall Restaurant, SE1
Dakota, W11
Delfina Studio Café, SE1
La Dordogne, W4
L'Escargot, W1
Euphorium, N1
First Floor, W11

Fung Shing, WC2
Gaudí, EC1
The Globe, SE1
Golden Dragon, W1
Grano, W4
Halkin Hotel, SW1
L'Incontro, SW1
Ivy, WC2
Launceston Place, W8
Leith's, W11
Lobster Pot, SE11
Maison Novelli, EC1
Mem Saheb, E14
Mezzo, W1
Mirabelle, W1
Montcalm Hotel, Crescent,
    W1
New Hoo Wah, W1
Nobu, W1
Odette's, NW1
1 Lombard Street, EC3
Orsino, W11

Prism, EC3
Quaglino's, SW1
Quo Vadis, W1
Red Pepper, W9
Roussillon, SW1
Royal China (Queensway),
    W2
RSJ, SE1
Salt House, NW8
Sartoria, W1
755 Fulham Road, SW6
Singapore Garden, NW6
Soho Soho, W1
Soho Spice, W1
Spread Eagle, SE10
Sree Krishna, SW17
Sri Siam Soho, W1
Le Suquet, SW3
Townhouse Brasserie, WC1
The Vale, W9
Veeraswamy, W1

London restaurants with no-smoking rooms

Bali Sugar, W11
Bertorelli's, WC2
Clarke's, W8
Itsu, SW3
Love, W1
Mem Saheb, E14
Museum Street Café, WC1

Rasa N16 and W1
Soho Spice, W1
Sotheby's Café, W1
Stepping Stone, SW8
Sugar Club, W1
La Tante Claire, SW1
Teca, W1

Thai Garden, E2
Thailand, SE14
Tokyo Diner, WC2
The Vale, W9
Villandry, W1
Wagamama, WC1 and W1

Budget eating £

At the restaurants below, it is possible to have a three-course meal, including coffee, half a bottle of house wine and service, for £25 or less per person, at any time the restaurant is open, i.e. at dinner as well as lunch. It may be possible to spend considerably more than this, but by choosing carefully you should find £25 or less achievable.

London
Adams Café, W12
Anglesea Arms, W6
Arancia, SE16
Aroma II, W1
Asakusa, NW1
Back to Basics, W1
Brackenbury, W6
Brady's, SW18
Café Japan, NW11
Le Chardon, SE22
Cicoria, NW6
Daphne, NW1
Eagle, EC1
Four Seasons, W2
Gourmet Garden, NW4
Inaho, W2
Istanbul Iskembecisi, N16
Iznik, N5
Jenny Lo's Teahouse, SW1
Kastoori, SW17
Kulu Kulu Sushi, W1
Lansdowne, NW1
Laurent, NW2
Lomo, SW10
Love, W1
Mandarin Kitchen, W2
Mantanah, SE25
Mem Saheb, E14
Mesclun, N16
Mirch Masala, SW16
Mr Kong, WC2
Moshi Moshi Sushi, EC2, EC4 and E14
Museum Street Café, WC1
New Hoo Wah, W1
New Tayyab, E1
Osteria Antica Bologna, SW11
Purple Sage, W1
Rani, N3
Red Pepper, W9
Saigon Thuy, SW18
Sree Krishna, SW17
Sri Siam Soho, W1
Thai Garden, E2
Tokyo Diner, WC2
Townhouse Brasserie, WC1
Two Brothers, N3
Upper Street Fish Shop, N1
The Vale, W9
Wagamama, WC1 and W1

England
Aldeburgh, Lighthouse
Aldeburgh, Regatta
Aymestrey, Riverside Inn

Bath, No. 5 Bistro
Beverley, Wednesdays
Birmingham, Chung Ying
Birmingham, Maharaja
Birtle, Normandie
Bishop's Waltham, Wine Bar
Brighton, Terre à Terre
Brimfield, Roebuck
Bristol, Bell's Diner
Buckland, Lamb Inn
Burnham Market, Fishes'
Carterway Heads, Manor House Inn
Caunton, Caunton Beck
Cheltenham, Le Petit Blanc
Cockermouth, Quince & Medlar
Corscombe, Fox Inn
Cottesmore, Sun Inn
Dartmouth, Carved Angel Café
Diss, Weavers
East End, East End Arms
Elland, La Cachette
Emsworth, Spencers
Foss Cross, Hare & Hounds
Foulsham, The Gamp
Great Yeldham, White Hart
Harrogate, Drum and Monkey
Haworth, Weavers
Hexham, Hexham Royal Hotel
Huddersfield, Bradley's
Ilkley, Farsyde
Keyston, Pheasant Inn
Lavenham, Angel
Leeds, Salvo's
Leicester, Welford Place
Lincoln, Wig & Mitre
Liverpool, Far East
Liverpool, Tai Pan
Ludlow, Courtyard
Lydford, Dartmoor Inn
Manchester, Koreana
Manchester, Kosmos Taverna
Manchester, New Emperor
Manchester, Tai Pan
Marsh Benham, Water Rat
Masham, Floodlite
Newcastle upon Tyne, Metropolitan
Oxford, Al-Shami
Paxford, Churchill Arms
Portreath, Tabb's

Ramsbottom, Village Restaurant
Ramsgill, Yorke Arms
Richmond, Chez Lindsay
Rye, Landgate Bistro
Sale, Hanni's
Sawley, Spread Eagle
Scarborough, Lanterna
Shelf, Bentley's
Shepton Mallet, Blostin's
Skipton, Le Caveau
Snape, Crown Inn
Southall, Gifto's Lahore Karahi
Standlake, Bell
Sudbury, Brasserie Four Seven
Sudbury, Red Onion Bistro
Tadcaster, Singers
Taunton, Brazz
Titley, Stagg Inn
West Bay, Riverside Restaurant
Whitby, Magpie Café
Whitchurch, Red House
Winkleigh, Pophams
Woodbridge, Captain's Table

Scotland
Alyth, Drumnacree House
Auchmithie, But 'n' Ben
Cairndow, Loch Fyne Oyster Bar
Canonbie, Riverside Inn
Edinburgh, Blue Bar Café
Edinburgh, Fishers
Edinburgh, Kalpna
Edinburgh, Shore
Edinburgh, Tuscan Square
Edinburgh, Valvona & Crolla Caffè Bar
Fort William, Crannog
Glasgow, Café Gandolfi
Gullane, Golf Inn Hotel, Daniel's Restaurant
Milngavie, Gingerhill
Swinton, Wheatsheaf Hotel

Wales
Bassaleg, Junction 28
Broad Haven, The Druidstone
Cardiff, Armless Dragon
Colwyn Bay, Café Niçoise
Creigiau, Caesar's Arms
Dolgellau, Dylanwad Da

Hay-on-Wye, Pavement
Llanfihangel Nant Melan,
  Red Lion Inn
Mathry, Ann FitzGerald's
  Farmhouse Kitchen
Rosebush, Tafarn Newydd

St George, Kinmel Arms
Swansea, La Braseria

Northern Ireland
Belfast, La Belle Epoque
Belfast, Nick's Warehouse
Limavady, Lime Tree

Republic of Ireland
Cork, Crawford Gallery Café

Closures

Whatever happended to that restaurant? Those listed below have closed
since the last edition of the *Guide*, though one or two may still be open under
new owners or have re-opened under a different name.

London
Au Jardin des Gourmets, W1
Chavot, SW3
Interlude, W1
Snows by the Pond, SW13
33 St James's, SW1
Zujuma's, SW19

England
Oceanic, Birmingham
Warehouse Brasserie,
  Colchester
Fox & Hounds, Vistro,
  Crawley

Bear & Ragged Staff,
  Cumnor
Maypole Inn, Halifax
Bistro, Harrogate
Le Petit Canard, Maiden
  Newton
Rochers, Milford on Sea
Churche's Mansion,
  Nantwich
Stane Street Hollow,
  Pulborough
Pig'n'Fish, St Ives
Old Boot House, Shotley

Table, Torquay
Crahan, Trevenen
Rogers, Windermere

Scotland
Braeval, Aberfoyle
Stockbridge Restaurant,
  Edinburgh

Wales
Chandlers, Trefriw
Number One Wind Street,
  Swansea

Service charges

Restaurants still charging 15% for service (sometimes 'optional')

London
Belgo Noord, NW1
Café du Jardin, WC2
The Collection, SW3
The Connaught, W1
Daphne's, SW3
L'Escargot (Picasso Room),
  W1

Lou Pescadou, SW5
Maison Novelli, EC1
Mitsukoshi, SW1 (D only)
Miyama, W1
Neal Street Restaurant, WC2
Old Delhi, W2
Le Suquet, SW3
Zen Central, W1

England
Warminster, Bishopstrow
  House
Woodstock, Feathers Hotel

Republic of Ireland
Adare, Adare Manor

Themed listings

These lists are not comprehensive, but we hope that the few, sometimes quirky, suggestions will guide readers (whether out of necessity or curiosity) towards restaurants that they might not otherwise have considered. Please check entries for further details.

Al fresco dining

London
Butlers Wharf Chop House, SE1
Le Coq d'Argent, EC2

England
Clitheroe, Auctioneer
Edenbridge, Honours Mill
Goring, Leatherne Bottel
Moulsford, Beetle & Wedge
Oxford, White House
St Ives, Alfresco
Windermere, Holbeck Ghyll

Scotland
Blair Atholl, Loft

Breakfast/brunch

London
Bank, WC2
Bluebird, SW3
Cactus Blue, SW3
Chiswick, W4
Mash, W1
Ransome's Dock, SW11

England
Caunton, Caunton Beck
Lincoln, Wig & Mitre
Oxford, Le Petit Blanc

Scotland
Edinburgh, Valvona & Crolla
Caffè Bar

Cheese

London
La Dordogne, W4
L'Estaminet, WC2
Pied-à-Terre, W1

England
Bath, Bath Priory
Carlton-in-Coverdale,
Foresters Arms
Exeter, Lamb's
Langley Marsh, Langley
House

Scotland
Edinburgh, Martins

Wales
Llanddeiniolen, Ty'n Rhos
Mathry, Ann FitzGerald's
Farmhouse Kitchen

Food Pubs

England
Asenby, Crab & Lobster
Bath, Richmond Arms
Britwell Salome, Goose
Broadhembury, Drewe Arms
Crosthwaite, Punch Bowl Inn
Epworth, Epworth Tap
Harome, Star Inn
Paxford, Churchill Arms
Standlake, Bell
Sutton Gault, Anchor Inn

Pre-theatre meals

London
Café du Jardin, WC2
L'Estaminet, WC2
The Globe, SE1
Leith's Soho, W1
Magno's, WC2
Mon Plaisir, WC2
Palais du Jardin, WC2
Rules, WC2
Stephen Bull St Martin's
Lane, WC2
Terrace, W8

Sensible sourcing

London
Bistrorganic, W10

England
Bristol, Markwicks
Erpingham, Ark
Faversham, Read's
Golcar, Weavers Shed
Mawnan Smith, Nansidwell

Sheffield, Smith's of
Sheffield
Swaffham, Strattons

Scotland
Fort William, Crannog

Wales
Harlech, Castle Cottage

Vegetarian

London
Lanesborough, The
Conservatory, SW1
Mantanah, SE25

England
Brighton, Terre à Terre
Cockermouth, Quince &
Medlar
Diss, Weavers
Little Shelford, Sycamore
House
Ulverston, Bay Horse

Scotland
Glasgow, Rogano

Wales
Cardiff, Armless Dragon
Rosebush, Tafarn Newydd

Waterside views

London
Oxo Tower, SE1

England
Bristol, Glass Boat
Leeds, Rascasse
Maenporth, Pennypots
Maidencombe, Orestone
Manor
Sandgate, La Terrasse
Sutton Gault, Anchor Inn

Scotland
Achiltibuie, Summer Isles
Hotel
Stonehaven, Tolbooth

Wales
Portmeirion, Hotel
Portmeirion

Introduction

'We use local and organic ingredients wherever possible.'

This is a typical response to the *Guide*'s questionnaire, sent each year to all restaurants shortlisted as potential main entries, in the section where we ask for information about their food and cooking.

A rapidly growing number (yet still a minority) are making a genuine effort in this direction, while for others it remains more of an aspiration: sure, they use locally sourced materials (Tesco is just round the corner), and sure, they use organic carrots for a few weeks in the year, but otherwise they are jumping on the buzzword bandwagon without making any real commitment to organic food or sustainable agriculture. It is all very well for restaurateurs to crow about organically produced chicken (and for want of anything better, it is a good start), but the effect can be spoiled by their use of hothouse tomatoes, battery eggs, commercial bread and unseasonal imported strawberries.

Any progress in this direction is, of course, to be welcomed, since fewer and fewer people now take food safety for granted. But if restaurants are to convince customers that they are serious about it, they will have to devote greater effort to the cause. We know that only 1.5–2 per cent of British produce is organic – and that Britain imports approximately 70 per cent of the organic produce it uses – so where is all this local organic stuff suddenly coming from?

In order to be persuaded that claims are genuine, restaurant customers need more specific information, without having to ask for it. The menu is the obvious vehicle to convey it: some helpfully list the producers of all their meat, fish and vegetables, others spell out that a given dish is made from a particular rare breed. Proper sourcing must not just be done: it must be seen to be done.

Food sources: time for common sense?

Last year we made the point that the 'growing of GM foods was a dangerous experiment'. This year, their future seems uncertain. Perhaps if the idea been packaged differently, if independent research had been carried out over a sufficiently long period and adequate safeguards put in place, people might have given them a warmer reception: the idea of preventing cancers and promoting physical well-being through the food we eat is not such a terrible prospect *per se*. But the industry's failure to understand legitimate concerns about personal choice, the environment and the crops' unknown and potentially irreversible effects has provoked such deep mistrust that few people now, apart from those with vested interests, believe that GM foods are anything other than a way of boosting corporate profits at the expense of innocent consumers.

Thanks to a loud shout from the British public, supermarkets have wisely cleared their shelves, and many restaurateurs have publicly expressed their misgivings. Since processed foods are the worst culprits (an estimated 60–80 per cent of them contain GM products), it is to be hoped that very few restaurants in the *Guide* will be affected. But since tomato paste and soya oil, for example, may contain GM products, it can be difficult to get away from them. Significantly, when Consumers' Association conducted a survey in spring 1999, some three-quarters of respondents said they would like to know whether the food they were eating in a restaurant contained GM ingredients. Sadly, nobody can tell them, because nobody really knows.

Agricultural science, which has given us enormous benefits over the past fifty years (albeit at a well-documented price), recently seems to have lost the plot altogether. The mix of scientists, legislators and regulators who control our food and its processing makes for a lethal cocktail without the input of ordinary common sense. Consider just one issue: the question of size.

The common-sense view maintains that small can be beautiful. At least some crops and animals should serve the locality, selling through farmers' markets, box schemes, local butchers and greengrocers, and at the farm gate. Not all small producers (of chickens, for example) are whiter than white, but small flocks increase the chances of raising standards of quality and welfare; and if a health problem does develop, at least it is localised.

Abattoirs, of course, must adhere to high standards of cleanliness, but current policy has resulted in just a few very large abattoirs, replacing thousands of perfectly good and, by any ordinary measure, hygienic, small ones.

'Support your local abattoir' may not sound like much of a rallying call, so why does it matter? It matters because:

- we prefer animals not to be transported for long distances, which stresses them and lowers the quality of the meat

- we prefer them to be processed in a more humane way

- we would like to benefit from all the cuts, including insides and extremities, not merely fillets and chops

- and, not least, we welcome the employment opportunities such establishments offer and their impact on local economies.

On these and other important matters of food policy, a great gulf remains between what ordinary consumers want, and what out-of-touch legislators, regulators and agribusiness jointly deliver.

Better value for money

Regular readers may notice that a number of restaurants have scored less well this year than last. Indeed the cooking marks for some 100 restaurants (not counting those with a different chef from last year) have dropped, while only around 50 have increased.

This was not a deliberate plan, it is just the way things have turned out, following our analysis of thousands upon thousands of separate and individual assessments of meals from reporters and inspectors across the country, covering all kinds of restaurants. To that extent, it represents a genuine ground swell of opinion. Whether this signifies a real drop in standards, as chefs become complacent after a period of general acclamation, or whether reporters and inspectors are simply becoming more critical and demanding, is difficult to say. Most likely it is a combination of both.

Either way, feedback to the *Guide* indicates that disappointments are common. Sometimes this can be quite specific: for example, in the tiny handful of restaurants run by celebrity chefs. Having seen their icon cook wonderful food in some exotic location on television, readers promise themselves a treat, save up and look forward to a memorable meal cooked by the great man himself (it is usually men). What they get – more often than not, judging by reports – is a second-rate meal cooked by somebody else, in a high-turnover dining room ('We need the table back by 8.30'), served by arrogant or off-hand staff, at inflated prices. Is it any wonder they complain?

If dashed expectations generally cause the greatest disappointment, then one of the principal contributory factors – and one easily remedied by restaurants – is the mis-match between the quality of food and the prices asked.

The *Guide* does not exclude restaurants on grounds of price, since quality of cooking is the criterion for entry. Nor do we set ourselves up as an authority on how much money you should spend. We recognise that our wide reader-spectrum includes some people for whom £10 a head is pushing the boat out, others for whom £100 a head is no problem. But in several cases, where a restaurant achieves a low cooking mark, yet charges £60 or £70 a head for dinner, we find that reporters are generally reluctant to eat there. If they don't eat, they don't send us reports, so we send an inspector along to check it out. This is perfectly acceptable – it is what we are here for – but it can mean that after two or three years we end up with only our own inspections to go on, so the question arises: for whose benefit are we investigating and reporting on this restaurant? We seem, in other words, to be talking to ourselves rather than engaging with our readership.

That is why, this year, we have axed a number of restaurants on these grounds (country-house hotels are among the principal culprits), and why some otherwise promising newcomers (especially in London) have simply not made it into the *Guide*. Not all these places produce bad food, they just do not produce food that is good enough for the prices they are asking, which are 'absurd for this level of cooking', in the words of one reporter whose views are shared by many. Paying huge sums to be bored by food is not what they are looking for. Add ignorant service (at 12.5 per cent), and the package is not just unattractive, it is an insult. The comment 'I would not return' tells us all we need to know. If a restaurant cannot do better than that for the price, then of what use is it to anybody?

By contrast, places making the running in the present climate tend to serve smaller portions in generally informal style, especially in London. Sushi and other affordable Japanese-derived snacks continue in popularity; Spanish and North African tapas and raciones are coming into their own, proving that the Mediterranean still has a lot to offer; and there is an example based on the cooking of south-west France as well. Since dishes are priced individually, it is up to the customer how much to spend; given a degree of self-control, these restaurants need not be expensive.

What comes out of them may not be 'authentic' – although it may still be quite specific to a country or region – but that has never bothered British chefs, who have a long and distinguished history of adapting ideas to suit our own circumstances. Such adaptation is different from fusion food, which continues to have a small number of expert practitioners and many imitators. Fish, meanwhile, is still enthusiastically sold and eaten, perhaps indicating that converts from meat during the BSE crisis are retaining their new-found loyalty, or that lighter foods are more in tune with the times: a couple of new fish restaurants have swum into the London section this year.

Developments in this year's Guide

Wine awards – shown by a 'bottle' symbol given to restaurants with top lists (see page 12) and a 'glass' to those with very good ones – are intended to direct readers to places where they can really enjoy the wine. The awards have undergone refinement this year and, since high mark-ups seriously detract from enjoyment, many restaurants with otherwise good lists are not signposted in this way.

We have also tried to take more account in the narrative of the circumstances in which wines are served. For example, white gloves and decanting cradles are less useful than correct serving temperature and suitable glasses; offering good choice by the glass should not be difficult; passive smoking ruins the smell and taste of wine. Furthermore, if a restaurant sees fit to keep the bottle out of reach (a practice which does not endear itself to our readers in the first place), then it should make sure that glasses are topped up appropriately: not once in a blue moon, not after every sip, and not just at the whim of passing waiters, but when the customer is ready. If staff are not capable of divining when this might be, they should return the bottle to the customer's control.

Other changes this year to *Guide* entries concern those two oppressed minorities, children and vegetarians. In the former case most restaurateurs have become aware (and not before time) that tomorrow's customers deserve a bit of encouragement. Once upon a time we noted, in the details below entries, 'children welcome' in the few restaurants where they were. Now, it is assumed that children are welcomed everywhere happily ever after, unless there are some restrictions, in which case we mention them. Thus are great social upheavals absorbed into the mainstream.

Over the past few years vegetarians have also had an increasingly easier time, especially in large towns and cities. In other cases, where they still have difficulty, there is something that can be done to improve matters. A reporter typically writes to us, saying that he took a party of four to restaurant A, and that one of them, a vegetarian, was disappointed to be offered only an omelette or a boring selection of vegetables in a cream sauce, with a salad on the side. Then, on the other hand, a restaurateur tells us that, with only a short menu in a rural area, he cannot always offer a vegetarian main course, just on the off chance that a veggie might turn up. If only vegetarians would give him a day or two's notice, he complains, then he would go out of his way to produce something suitable.

Advance notice seems eminently reasonable to him: after all, he says, 'It is not as if the customer has decided to go on a special diet in the last 24 hours'. The *Guide*'s request to restaurateurs is: please have at least some materials, and a few ideas, that can be turned into an interesting vegetarian meal at the last moment, even if you do not publish it on the menu.

And our request to reporters is: please find out if any member of your party has any special needs or requirements, and tell the restaurant when booking. We all know from experience that this is not a foolproof system, but it might help to avoid a few disappointments and hot-tempered exchanges, and further improve the quality of life for vegetarians. In any case, this year we have been stricter about adding 'vegetarian meals' to the details of an entry, which should improve the prospects for those who seek them out.

Finally, an oppressed majority: when BBC2's *Food & Drink* did a telephone survey in 1999, 86 per cent of callers said they thought smoking should be banned in restaurants. One of our reporters notes that the 'tradition' of smoking in public places began long before it was established that smoking kills people. Now that the 'smoking kills you' message is beyond any doubt, it would surely be sensible to separate smokers from those who value their health, and from those who like to enjoy the taste of their food and wine. In Scotland, paradoxically (it is not renowned for healthy eating habits), some 68 per cent of restaurants in the *Guide* have either banned smoking or have a separate no-smoking room. In London, by contrast, it is only twenty restaurants (23 per cent); see page 17 for a list of them.

Tell us about it

The strength of the *Guide* is that readers and reporters share their information for the benefit of others. While some might rate a restaurant highly, others cannot see why it appeals; some hit the chef on a good day, others on his day off. It is the editorial responsibility to weigh the pros and cons, find the best balance that the available information can supply, and make a judgement on the strength of it. Many entries and scores are therefore a compromise. We know in some cases that the chef can do better, but experience shows that he is not consistent. There is no point assigning a cooking mark to reflect the best possible Oscar-winning performance when we know that some readers are going to invest time and money in a visit, only to be disappointed by a display of B-movie food.

As a result of reader recommendations and our own inspections we have listed close to 950 main entries and well over 300 Round-up entries. In fact, readers have reported on many more restaurants than appear in the *Guide*. They and our inspectors have jointly filtered out a significant number that do not make the grade, and which we do not list. The result is as reliable as we can make it. Please use the *Guide* to boost your daily enjoyment of life: it is too short to spend eating bad food. Examine the details carefully, and you will find some real gems and bargains waiting to be discovered.

If you keep reports coming, you will help others to avoid the disappointments you have experienced, and help them to share your discoveries. You could have a *Guide* with just a team of professional inspectors to eat on your behalf – they exist – but where's the fun in that? This way you can have your own say and help to change the world, or at least a small but significant part of it: a part on which you spend your own hard-earned money, and which therefore matters.

Interest in food and cooking, and in the sourcing and production of food, are at an all-time high. We all have a right to a say in how our food gets on the plate, and to comment on its cooking. This *Guide* is your opportunity to have a say in whether you have been ripped off, surprised, delighted, let down, restored, enchanted, brassed off, exhilarated, bored, stimulated, upset or bowled over by what you have eaten. If you tell us about it, then the next edition will be all the better because of it.

The past fifty years: progress, of a sort

In the 1960s **Derek Cooper** wrote *The Bad Food Guide*, a wry account of the British attitude to eating out. Forty years on, he surveys the restaurant scene to see how our tastes have changed.

In the late 1940s the Gallup Poll asked a cross-section of the British public what they would choose as a perfect meal. The answer was tomato soup, Dover sole, roast chicken, roast potatoes with peas and sprouts, followed by trifle and cheese and biscuits. In the early 1960s a similar survey was undertaken, and the choice was identical with the single exception of the dessert – top of the list was fruit salad. Black forest gâteau and tiramisù were still over the horizon.

We were, and to an extent remain, deeply conservative when it comes to food; hence the enduring popularity of that national roadside institution the 'all-day breakfast'. In aspirational circles fettuccini may be preferred, but a big fry-up defines the real genius of the nation.

Connoisseurs of the past can still enjoy cut-off-the-joint-and-two-veg at Simpson's in the Strand or poached egg on toast in a village teashop. All this may suggest that our national food preferences are inelastic, unadventurous. We're certainly still supporting an impressive number of fish 'n' chip shops despite inroads made by Indian takeaways and pizza deliveries, but compared with the rest of Europe the postwar years in UK have been marked by a frenzy of activity in the world of catering.

The industrialisation of food has made it possible, courtesy of the freezer truck, for the most remote hotel or restaurant in the land to serve an instant replica of alien dishes with the minimum of fuss and cost. Why bother with a chef when you can order forty different 'gourmet' items from a factory?

The fact that convenience foods bear little resemblance to the real thing goes largely unnoticed by the customers or kitchen staff who may never have encountered the real thing anyway. The 'meal experience' is more about fashion and style than about taste and flavour. Some years ago a chef who had worked for a big hotel chain told me how he found it difficult to motivate his staff. 'To start with, they were grossly underpaid. I would call it exploited. Most of them had been brought up in homes where little cooking took place. I asked one of these youngsters to taste the stock and tell me if it was a good one. It wasn't until he gave me a blank look that I realised that he had never seen a stockpot. To make a gravy, his mother had always used Oxo cubes or Bisto – there was no food culture in his background at all.'

Themes and variations

The last few decades have been marked by the emergence of the themed restaurant where the décor skilfully diverts attention from the shortcomings of the food. Some are got up to resemble an Italian trattoria or a French bistro. Greek tavernas in Britain can look more authentic than they do in Greece, and you are often left with the feeling that the message is not so much the meal as the surroundings in which it is eaten or takes place.

Even as I write, an invitation comes through the letterbox to attend the UK launch party of a new Italian restaurant to be sited in a leisure park. 'A large open kitchen, a bustling bar, strolling opera singers, make [the restaurant] a culinary innovator in great Italian dining. With over one hundred branches in the USA, [the restaurant] is set,' runs the handout, 'to awaken a new eating-out culture within the ever growing casual dining market.' Is it possible to awaken a new eating-out culture? Where have these strolling opera singers come from? Maybe they are taking time off as Covent Garden is rebuilt or perhaps they have been flown in from La Scala in Milan. No mention of that and no mention of what the menu will offer. One must assume it will be financially viable just as fast-food chains such as McDonald's, Kentucky Fried Chicken, Burger King and Wimpy have been financially viable, but will the food be worth eating?

The last twenty years have seen a massive wave of innovation in the catering industry. Terence Conran was among the first to perceive that big is beautiful and expansion is essential in order to stay ahead of the competition. The economies of scale have in his case created a gastro-empire where the cuisine is reliable and the design is seldom less than stunning.

Today there is intense pressure for talented restaurateurs to clone themselves, and there is no shortage of venture capital in the City to help them start their own small chains. Sometimes, as with Stephen Bull, it works without any lowering of standards. In other cases, the flair and expertise cannot survive the transition.

The right way to do it

With a few notable exceptions, eating out in brewery-owned pubs is a joyless experience. Where enterprising managers are given a free hand to use local fresh ingredients and there is a good cook to prepare them, miracles can occur, but if you look for pubs where that kind of food exists you may have a long drive. A few years ago I went to Worcestershire where on the banks of the River Teme a farming family runs a sixteenth-century inn called the Talbot Hotel. They brew their own beer and grow their own hops. In the kitchen garden the fruit and vegetables are organic. Their salmon comes from the River Wye and their game from neighbouring estates. In this paragon of pubs there are no gaming machines and no piped music. On the menu, besides meat and fish there are plenty of meatless dishes, and the whole atmosphere reflects the enthusiasm of the family and their pride in being able to present good food and drink in an unpretentious way. They told me about the training manager of a neighbouring brewery who regularly brought his recruits to the Talbot to show them how not to run a pub. 'You see, there's not a big profit doing things our way but then we're not looking for a big profit.'

The power of television in moulding the expectations of those who eat out should not be underestimated. Cooking has become peak viewing entertainment. The act of eating has more to do with aspiration than nutrition. However remote the hamlet in which we dwell, we all know how to fan out a breast of chicken and decorate a plate with baby vegetables air-freighted from the Third World. Polenta, lime leaves, mango salsa and pesto are the stuff of everyday conversation. When we eat out we're likely to encounter hand-assembled offerings from the Masterchef school of cookery. The gulf between good food and unnecessarily complicated food seems to grow ever wider.

What gives me hope for the future is the growing number of hotels, restaurants, cafés and pubs where there is an obvious concern for the integrity and quality of raw materials which come into the kitchen. It is no longer possible for people who spend their professional lives cooking to be indifferent to the way in which their raw materials are produced. Just as we expect librarians to be knowledgeable about books, so we are entitled to expect that a responsible chef should know about and, more importantly, care about the technologies of food production, the way in which animals are reared and soybeans are grown, and other food-related issues of the day.

'Take two eggs' is no longer enough. What sort of eggs? How were the chickens fed and in what poultry system were they reared? And so with the fruit and vegetables, the milk and the cheese. Where does it come from? There is a need to know. The power and the obligations of the chef have been compellingly summarised by John Ash, who runs a cookery school in Mendocino, California. 'I used to say,' he told me, 'that a chef should spend as much time sourcing his raw materials as he spends cooking them. These days I believe he should spend twice as much time!'

The future: restaurant renaissance or catering calamity?

Drew Smith, editor of *The Good Food Guide* from 1983 to 1989, reads the lapsang leaves for the next decade.

Heartening as the past ten years may have been for anyone enthusiastic about the development of a restaurant culture in the UK, one suspects that the seeds of its own destruction may already have been sown.

Although I cannot think of anyone better qualified to run Granada's food operation than Marco Pierre White, nor anyone more suited to inherit the mantle of Lyons Corner House than Sir Terence Conran, I feel a selfish regret that both have crossed the line from restaurateur to caterer.

Restaurant culture is still in its infancy in this country, and the fear is that it cannot survive the Neanderthal values paraded by some of the brewers, landlords and other large players. This guide, I am sure, will continue to seek out and find small independent chef/patrons over the next decade, but these may already have become an endangered species. The era of the independent is passing as restaurants become increasingly professional and business-like.

Why the odds are stacked against a restaurant culture

To open a restaurant is beyond the means of most young chefs, indeed of anyone without £500,000 to risk. Privately, estate agents will tell you that their preferred customers are (a) McDonalds, (b) publicly quoted companies, and (c) other American food chains. That commercial reality may come home to roost in the years ahead: it seems the UK is embarked on a foolhardy mission to replicate the American high street, although we have on our doorstep other models – from France, Italy or even Hong Kong – where a food culture is more solidly engrained.

London, we jingoistically claim, is the restaurant capital of the world. Oh yes? I have my doubts. And the cost of eating out remains prohibitive in this country compared with France or America, not least because of property costs.

Other elements also conspire against achieving a true restaurant culture:

- **lack of training and skills** If there is one major brake on the renaissance of London restaurants, it is that too many are erratic because basic skills do not run through the whole kitchen.

- **the destruction of small-scale supply trades** Supermarkets are already encouraging larger suppliers to move in on the domestic catering universe, with knock-on effects for restaurant provisions.
- **food safety** This is a serious issue for the independent sector, as bigger companies lobby government and opinion formers, in order to secure legislation and codes of practice to the detriment of smaller suppliers and craftsmen.

Will the restaurateur triumph over the chef?

Against that, one could claim that a new generation of chefs who have worked in high-class operations has yet to emerge and make an impact: Patrick Williams at Green's, for example, or James Kirby, formerly at Che. I enjoy their style of cooking, which combines the very British sense of letting good ingredients speak for themselves with French technical disciplines, which for me seems the logical direction in which modern British cooking should go.

Enslavement to the Michelin star system and its myopic understanding of gastronomy will do these kitchens no good. It remains a continued insult to the very restaurants that have brought about this huge improvement in standards – Alastair Little, Sally Clarke, Bibendum, I could supply a very long list – that Michelin chooses to ignore what is demonstrably a serious and important movement. Nobody takes pleasure from the kind of financial difficulties that some three-star restaurants have got into in France, but it is worth asking which of these restaurants are full and which are empty, M Michelin. The customer does not lie. I am not intent on attacking a rival publication, except to say that I regard its influence in the UK as pernicious and its values misguided.

One suspects, however, that the next few years may see the return of the restaurateur rather than the chef to the fore. One of the best examples of this is Claudio Pulze, Svengali behind the Frith Street Restaurant (and Zaika in Fulham Road, plus other new ventures in the pipeline). There will be others too, offering welcome relief after the last few years of TV-induced chef frenzy.

There is also money about. I have given up counting the number of press releases that pass across my desk announcing that former financier XYZ has given up banking and gone into the restaurant and bar world with young chef ABC. While the great British institutions have been inactive, anyone it seems with enough nous, vision and access to raising money has jumped ship. Many may fall flat on their faces, but enough will at least have established proper foundations upon which a professional restaurant culture could be built.

THE FUTURE

Where the trends are taking us

It is hard to see whether the motivation of these entrepreneurs is really to roll out identikit fast-food chains, or whether they might be content to provide a high-class neighbourhood restaurant, and encourage the development of kitchen and front-of-house skills like, say, Nigel Platts-Martin at The Square, Chez Bruce and Glasshouse. Ultimately it may be that we have to accept that the summit of any restaurant's achievement must be seen in the context of its local area, to reflect that culture, and to provide a service for the people who live and work there.

On that basis the big West End destination restaurants like Mezzo or Belgo are probably all one can expect in inner-city areas; unless, like Marco Pierre White, you have the ambition to enfranchise the whole of Piccadilly, or, in the case of Whitbread, the whole of Wimbledon. I recall with a certain amount of ambivalent pride that, as editor of this guide in the early '80s, I included the first incarnations of Chez Gérard and Pizza Express, which have since expanded, and which I predict will be the king-makers of the next ten years. Everyone has ideas, but it will need operators as professional as these to execute them.

Even if we are to be rocked by recession, the underlying trend, especially in cities, is that people want to eat out, and I don't see any sign of a reversal in that process. Historically customers rarely trade back down once they have been exposed to good food. Just how discriminating they are may prove to be a defining factor, especially for hotels where standards have been going backwards for years. It is noteworthy that those in control of British catering – brewers, hotel groups, planners – have for the most part lagged behind the renaissance in restauration. Brilliant at numbers some of their executives may be, but more than one or two would struggle to cook their own dinner. Inspiration has come instead from the kitchens, from the side street and from people with no previous catering experience.

As to the direction they are taking us, I feel that the Asian influence must get stronger, the French weaker, because already, even in France, the French restaurant seems mortally wounded and increasingly parochial. Even now in London the Italians would rightly claim to have eclipsed the French. Ultimately we will, I hope, all come to value the simple combustion of a kitchen that cooks fresh food to order, which is perhaps the principle on which this guide was founded. Virtually any restaurant in this edition scoring over 6/10 is probably a better restaurant than nearly anything I got to review in the '80s: so the seeds of renaissance are already there. All they need is our support.

So who's having the mullet?

Andrew Purvis, food writer and *Observer* columnist, asks why it is that restaurants often attract cooks who can't cook, bottle-washers who can't wash bottles, and waiters who just can't wait ....

My estranged wife always said I was a bit of a Sod, and at the time I misunderstood completely. What she meant, I'm sure, is that I have a knack for inventing neat philosophical Laws. Like the sunny-natured Sod (who, along with Murphy, lays claim to the phrase, 'If something can go wrong, it will'), I have come up with an observation which we shall call Odd-Bod's Law. In my view, it is incontrovertibly true that 'people gravitate towards the job that suits them least'. I have worked with dyslexic sub-editors, colour-blind illustrators, even a photographer with a glass eye, and everyone knows therapists are dysfunctional and GPs hate the sight of blood. My father-in-law, who trained as an eye surgeon, is so squeamish about body parts that he can't carve a chicken without wearing rubber gloves.

Nowhere is Odd-Bod's Law more apparent than in restaurants. Though there are exceptions, the business seems to attract cooks who can't cook, bottle-washers who don't wash bottles, glass-polishers who can't polish, cleaners who won't clean, and waiters who just can't wait. By far the most conspicuous are the non-waiters, but only because they are the quaking interface between customer and kitchen. Even if it is the foul-mouthed, bullying, cleaver-wielding celebrity chef who fails to deliver, it is the waiter or waitress who gets it in the neck.

In his short story 'The Boys',* Ethan Coen recounts the tale of a man in a Dakota diner who orders an omelette for his son. In this isolated Hicksville spot, the waitress doesn't know what an 'almlet' is, but goes away to ask. 'Well, the cook knows what it is,' she reports, 'but we don't have it on the menu.' 'OK, but can he make one?' the father suggests. 'I'm sorry, it's not on the menu,' the waitress persists, at which point her customer virtually combusts. 'All right,' he snaps. 'He'll have two scrambled eggs. And just ask the cook not to squish them around in the pan.'

When the eggs arrive, however, they aren't scrambled – they are fried. 'Bart looked up from his Sesame Street catalogue,' Coen writes chillingly, 'and stared at the two glistening eggs. They vibrated slightly as a truck rumbled by outside. The father watched with a cold clutch of fear, bracing himself for Bart's tantrum. He pictured himself muscling the waitress back through the swinging doors into the kitchen and, with one hand bending her arm behind her, forcing her face-down into a panful of frying eggs. He imagined giving her neck a vigorous whisking motion so her nose whipped the eggs while she loudly blubbered. But then, that would not be an omelette either.'

Take it or leave it

Though I may have cuddled a waitress or two, I don't think I have ever coddled one in this way. The desire to grill a chef, however, is all too familiar. Once, at a discreet restaurant in London (so discreet it looks like a house, and you have to ring the doorbell to be let in), I noticed how the attitude towards good service begins in the kitchen. I was with a food-critic friend, who eyed the menu wearily. It was awash with offal, black pudding and game, but it didn't feature anything remotely green. 'Why not?' my friend asked. The chef answered simply that customers didn't go there to eat leaves. 'They know our style of cooking,' he protested, 'and that's what they get.'

At another bustling shrine to the Old Millennium (expensive, meaty, robust food), a friend was again heretical enough to ask for a mixed salad. This threw the kitchen into confusion. 'What do you mean, exactly?' the waiter asked. 'Well, a few green leaves and something colourful like, er, a tomato.' After a determined search, the waiter returned: 'The chef doesn't have a tomato,' he said. Still, he did his best. It was the chef, with his recalcitrant refusal to keep a properly stocked kitchen, who typified Odd-Bod's Law. It seemed that he was temperamentally unsuited to a job where the customer comes first.

A waiter with a memory

In other countries, notably America, people can order whatever they like. Men always marvel at Meg Ryan's faked orgasm in the film *When Harry Met Sally*, but I find the way she orders diner-food far more impressive. Loads of women can simulate ecstasy, but only a New Yorker can specify what she wants in her salad, with or without six kinds of dressing, with the mustard (whether French, or American, or Dijon, or wholegrain, or low-cal, or low-chol, or sugar-free) squirled in the middle of her pastrami, rather than on the side. What's more, the kitchen will actually provide it.

The best story I have heard about service comes, of course, from the USA. At Georgia Brown's in Washington DC (reputedly the Clintons' favourite restaurant), a group gave their order to a waiter with no notepad. One wanted rare steak, the other medium. One asked for a Caesar salad with no Parmesan, her friend for a starter as a main course. The least hungry said she didn't want a starter, but – as the waiter retreated out of earshot – whispered to her boyfriend that she'd have one of his fish cakes. When the food arrived, it was delivered (and this is important) by another waiter. Without asking a single question, he put each dish down in the right place including two – side by side – with a fish cake on each!

Service like this is the exception that proves the rule of Odd-Bod's Law. A waiter with an extraordinary memory is perfectly suited to his job – physically, temperamentally, even genetically. If I'd been serving that group, it would have been a different kettle of fish. When a waiter brings food to the table, I can seldom remember what I ordered – let alone what anybody else asked for. 'The pan-fried mullet?' asks the waiter. Silence. 'Is anyone having the mullet?' he repeats. The atmosphere is thick with static embarrassment. 'Oh,' I say lamely, 'that must be me.' Had I been working at Georgia Brown's that night, every diner would have been fantasising about shoving me face-down into a panful of simmering poultry pieces and boiling blackeye beans. But then, that would not be spicy creole chicken wings either.

* From *Gates of Eden*, Transworld Publishers Ltd, London 1998; available as an Anchor paperback.

Vintage chart

In order to retain earlier vintages of note, some later, lesser vintages have been omitted.

SYMBOLS:

△ = immature

● = mature

▽ = drink up

□ = wines unlikely to be found in Britain, or undeclared vintages for port and champagne, which come from regions where only certain years are 'declared' or marketed as vintage wines.

★ = vintages not yet 'declared' or marketed (port, champagne)

All figures and symbols apply to the best wines of each vintage in each region.

Vintages have been rated on a 1 to 20 point scale (20 being the best).

	1	2	3	4	5	6	7	8	9	10	11
1998	13△	16△	17△	14△	13△	15△	14△	15△	17△	14△	13△
1997	16△	16△	16△	15△	17△	14△	16△	14●	19△	18△	16△
1996	18△	16△	16△	14△	13△	15△	15△	16●	16△	15△	14△
1995	17△	17△	15△	14△	16△	17△	15△	15●	16●	17△	16△
1994	14△	13△	15●	12●	13△	15●	17△	13●	16△	15△	13●
1993	15△	14△	12●	8△	14△	14△	13△	13●	13●	14△	13●
1992	12△	12△	13●	8●	15△	15●	14△	14●	18△	16△	15△
1991	14△	12△	13●	12△	14△	14●	13●	12▽	14●	16△	13●
1990	17△	18△	14●	19△	19△	19●	19△	19●	19△	18△	18●
1989	19△	19△	17●	19●	17●	19●	20△	18●	18●	16●	18●
1988	18△	19△	16●	18△	18●	15●	16△	17●	19●	18●	17●
1987	14▽	13▽	15▽	10●	13●	15▽	8●	12▽	12▽	14●	11▽
1986	19△	18△	14▽	17△	14▽	18▽	16▽	18▽	16▽	15●	16●
1985	18▽	18▽	18▽	15▽	19●	16▽	18●	16▽	17●	18▽	19●
1984	13▽	10▽	12▽	13●	11▽	12▽	8▽	10▽	12▽	14▽	13▽
1983	18●	17●	18▽	18△	14▽	17●	16▽	14▽	18●	19●	17●
1982	19●	19●	16▽	14●	13▽	15▽	13●	13▽	13▽	16▽	15▽
1981	16●	15▽	15▽	13●	11▽	8▽	16●	17▽	16▽	13▽	12▽
1980	11▽	10▽	11▽	12●	13▽	11▽	13●	12▽	8▽	14▽	14▽
1979	16●	18●	17▽	14●	14▽	16▽	14●	14▽	10▽	15▽	14▽
1978	17●	17●	17▽	12●	18●	17●	15●	18▽	12▽	19●	18●
1977	9▽	9▽	7▽	6▽	7▽	10▽	5▽	8▽	7▽	8▽	7▽
1976	16▽	14▽	16▽	17●	14▽	14▽	18●	16▽	18▽	18▽	14▽
1975	16●	17●	17▽	18●	4▽	6▽	16●	15▽	14▽	10▽	9▽
1971	15▽	16▽	18▽	16●	18●	17▽	16●	18▽	19●	17▽	17▽
1970	18●	17●	16▽	14●	13▽	13▽	16▽	16▽	11▽	16▽	18▽
1969	11▽	9▽	8▽	13▽	16▽	17▽	18●	16▽	13▽	18▽	17▽
1966	17●	18●	16▽	14▽	13▽	14▽	15●	18▽	16▽	17▽	18▽
1963	5▽	5▽	3▽	□	11▽	14▽	□	□	8▽	7▽	8▽
1962	14▽	15▽	16▽	17●	16▽	18▽	15●	14▽	14▽	17▽	16▽
1961	20●	20●	18▽	16▽	14▽	16▽	14●	16▽	18▽	20▽	19▽

1 = Red Bordeaux: Médoc & Graves
2 = Red Bordeaux: St-Emilion & Pomerol
3 = Dry white Bordeaux
4 = Sweet white Bordeaux: Sauternes & Barsac
5 = Red Burgundy
6 = White Burgundy
7 = Loire (sweet)
8 = Loire (dry)
9 = Alsace
10 = Northern Rhône
11 = Southern Rhône
12 = Midi
13 = Champagne
14 = Rioja
15 = Vintage port
16 = Red Portuguese
17 = Barolo & Barbaresco
18 = Tuscany
19 = Mosel–Saar–Ruwer
20 = Rhinelands
21 = Australia (red wines)
22 = New Zealand (white wines)
23 = California (red wines)

12	13	14	15	16	17	18	19	20	21	22	23	
14△	★	15△	★	15△	13△	15△	13△	14△	18△	14●	18△	1998
13△	★	17△	17△	17△	16△	16△	17△	17△	18△	16●	17△	1997
14△	★	16△	□	16△	14△	16△	13△	14△	17△	17●	15△	1996
17△	★	16△	15△	16△	17△	16△	17△	18△	15△	13●	17△	1995
16△	★	17△	19△	16△	14△	13●	15△	15△	15△	19●	17△	1994
13△	15△	14△	□	13●	17△	14△	19△	14△	13●	14●	15△	1993
15△	13△	16●	18△	16●	14△	13●	18●	17●	16△	15●	19△	1992
16△	13△	16●	18△	16●	13△	14△	13●	14●	18△	18●	19△	1991
19●	17△	18●	□	17●	18△	20△	20●	20●	17●	15●	18△	1990
18●	16●	18●	□	17●	18△	13●	19●	18●	10●	19●	14●	1989
18●	19△	17●	□	11▽	17△	19△	17●	17●	16●	□	15●	1988
14▽	□	16●	15△	15▽	14●	14▽	6▽	7▽	18●	□	12●	1987
16▽	15●	17▽	□	9▽	15●	17●	11▽	13▽	19●	□	14●	1986
18●	19▽	19●	18●	19▽	20●	19●	15▽	15▽	17●	□	19●	1985
□	□	13▽	□	14▽	8▽	9▽	3▽	5▽	18▽	□	13●	1984
18●	16▽	15●	18●	18▽	13▽	15▽	16▽	14▽	14▽	□	12▽	1983
□	17●	16▽	13●	15▽	19●	17▽	7▽	8▽	19●	□	15▽	1982
□	16▽	17▽	□	10▽	13▽	14▽	8▽	10▽	13▽	□	14▽	1981
□	10▽	16▽	16●	16▽	11▽	13▽	3▽	4▽	18▽	□	17▽	1980
□	17●	14▽	□	14▽	14▽	17▽	11▽	12▽	16▽	□	14▽	1979
□	12▽	19●	□	15▽	18●	16▽	9▽	9▽	18▽	□	16▽	1978
□	□	6▽	20△	16▽	11▽	16▽	5▽	8▽	14▽	□	12▽	1977
□	18●	13▽	□	12▽	14▽	13▽	19●	17●	17▽	□	14▽	1976
□	14▽	15▽	13▽	13▽	12▽	17▽	17▽	18▽	19▽	□	14▽	1975
□	17▽	9▽	□	9▽	18▽	18▽	20●	19●	20▽	□	14▽	1971
□	16▽	19▽	18●	17▽	17▽	16▽	12▽	11▽	14▽	□	17▽	1970
□	14▽	12▽	□	9▽	14▽	14▽	16▽	13▽	□	□	16▽	1969
□	16▽	15▽	18●	19▽	15▽	16▽	16▽	16▽	19▽	□	16▽	1966
□	□	12▽	20●	16▽	□	□	12▽	12▽	17▽	□	16▽	1963
□	15▽	13▽	□	□	13▽	16▽	14▽	16▽	18▽	□	13▽	1962
□	16▽	10▽	□	□	18▽	15▽	10▽	12▽	□	□	15▽	1961

London

Note that on 22 April 2000 London telephone codes and numbers will change, as follows: the code (0171) will become (020) followed by a 7, and the code (0181) will become (020) followed by an 8. For example: (0171) 222 1234 will change to (020) 7222 1234, and the number (0181) 333 1234 will change to (020) 8333 1234.

Adams Café £   map 12

77 Askew Road, W12 9AH   COOKING 3
TEL/FAX: (0181) 743 0572   COST £22–£30

Although now a shade more sophisticated – brighter paint, less crowded tables, cotton napkins in place of paper – there is no change in the warm hospitality at the Boukraas' ten year old North African restaurant. It deals in a host of staples including skewers of grilled meat and fish, couscous half a dozen ways, and slightly more involved tagines of lamb with artichokes, peas and limes, or rich, sweet, and filling chicken with dates and almonds. Set meals range from 'Rapide' (main course and mint tea) via 'Gourmet' (add a starter or dessert) to 'Gastronomique' (the works). Begin with crisp brik a l'oeuf, harrira soup, or ungreasy, spicy seafood briouats filled with 'tiny shrimps and mussels and who knows what else', and finish with baklava, lemon tart, or honey-soaked pancakes. Appetisers live up to their name, service is charming, and a handful of Moroccan wines turns up on the otherwise French wine list, where prices start at £8.

CHEF: Abdel Boukraa   PROPRIETORS: Abdel and Frances Boukraa   OPEN: all week D only 7 to 11   CLOSED: 1 week Christmas, 1 week Aug, bank hol Suns and Mons   MEALS: Set D £9.95 (1 course) to £14.95   SERVICE: not inc   CARDS: Amex, Delta, Diners, MasterCard, Switch, Visa
DETAILS: 60 seats. Private parties: 36 main room, 24 private room. Vegetarian meals. Wheelchair access (not WC). Music   ⊖ Shepherd's Bush, Ravenscourt Park (£5)

Alastair Little ✎   map 15

49 Frith Street, W1V 1TP   COOKING 3
TEL: (0171) 734 5183   FAX: (0171) 792 4504   COST £35–£53

The frontage remains unassuming – big windows, Venetian blinds, slate-coloured paint – giving it a somewhat reserved presence amid the surrounding Soho brashness. Inside, though, walls are festooned with paintings of outsized fruit and vegetables, tempering the legendary minimalism. The food's traditional allegiance to Italy still predominates, although it is now shared with a few other countries, producing grilled squid chermoula, tiger prawn 'pot stickers' with black bean salsa, and crisp-skinned duck breast with chorizo and sweet braised butter beans.

At inspection, however, it was Italy that came up trumps, in the shape of a thin-based pizzetta bianca with creamy mozzarella, tomato, Parmesan and a big clump of rocket. A summery example, significant for its freshness and compatibility of flavours, combined fine-textured pasta with a pale green sauce made from puréed broad beans mixed with peas and asparagus. While the simplicity that was a hallmark of the food seems to have been overtaken, the kitchen has turned out a smooth, wobbly pannacotta with raspberries, and a poached pear in a subtly spiced red wine syrup, with a scoop of tangy lemon and mascarpone ice cream. 'Exemplary' service is efficient and genuinely helpful, and a compact yet wide-ranging wine list starts with house Italian red and white at £13 and £14 respectively.

CHEFS: Alastair Little and James Rix   PROPRIETORS: Mercedes André-Vega, Kirsten Tormod Pedersen and Alastair Little   OPEN: Mon to Fri L 12 to 3, Mon to Sat D 6 to 11   CLOSED: bank hols   MEALS: Set L £25, Set D £33   SERVICE: not inc, 12.5% for parties of 8 or more   CARDS: Amex, Delta, Diners, MasterCard, Switch, Visa   DETAILS: 55 seats. Private parties: 10 main room, 20 private room. Vegetarian meals. Children's helpings. Wheelchair access (not WC). No music. Air-conditioned   ⊖ Tottenham Court Road

Alastair Little Lancaster Road

map 12

136A Lancaster Road, W11 1QU |NEW CHEF|
TEL: (0171) 243 2220   COST £29–£49

Just as the *Guide* went to press we learned that Edwin Lewis had left this 'elegant but plain' restaurant with its long, narrow dining room, although since his successor has spent some time working under the Alastair Little umbrella, the continuity of style is not surprising. As before, simplicity rules, and the Mediterranean sun still shines on salt cod brandade, mixed seafood bourride, and roast lamb chump with couscous and ratatouille. Casually dressed staff set a relaxed pace, and the same wine list is offered as at the Soho branch (see entry, above). Reports are particularly welcome.

CHEF: Tony Abarno   PROPRIETORS: Alastair Little, Kirsten Tormod Pedersen and Mercedes André-Vega   OPEN: Mon to Sat 12.30 to 2.30 (3 Sat), 7 to 11   CLOSED: bank hols   MEALS: alc L (main courses £8 to £12). Set D £27.50   SERVICE: not inc; 12.5% for parties of 8 or more   CARDS: Amex, Delta, Diners, MasterCard, Switch, Visa   DETAILS: 40 seats. 10 seats outside. Private parties: 16 main room. Vegetarian meals. Children's helpings. Wheelchair access (not WC). No music. Air-conditioned   ⊖ Ladbroke Grove

Al Bustan

map 14

27 Motcomb Street, SW1X 8JU   COOKING 1
TEL: (0171) 235 8277   FAX: (0171) 235 1668   COST £25–£58

Bringing a splash of greenery to its opulent environs, Al Bustan ('garden' in Arabic) has a bright, elegant interior, with trees painted on one wall, and trellis screens dividing the room into nooks. A cover charge provides raw vegetables, olives and an appetising garlic and chilli dip to nibble as you peruse the menu's plentiful choice of hot and cold starters: among meze, lahem bil agine (Lebanese pizza with a mincemeat and pine kernel topping) stands out. Main courses encompass offal and raw meat dishes, but less adventurous souls can choose from a variety of chargrilled meats and fish, such as lamb fillet marinated in garlic sauce. 'Fluffy' bread is an ideal accompaniment. For pudding you might choose hot pancakes stuffed with sweet cheese and walnuts and served with syrup. Service has been praised, but single diners could be better catered for.

Lebanese Ch. Musar is a highlight of the French-dominated wine list. House wine costs £12.

CHEF: Inam Atalla   PROPRIETORS: Mr and Mrs Atalla   OPEN: all week noon to 11 (10.30 Sun) CLOSED: Christmas   MEALS: alc (main courses £7 to £16). Set L £13. Cover £2   SERVICE: not inc   CARDS: Amex, Diners, MasterCard, Switch, Visa   DETAILS: 70 seats. 20 seats outside. Private parties: 10 main room, 8 and 12 private rooms. Occasional music. Air-conditioned
⊖ Sloane Street, Knightsbridge

Alexandra   map 12

507 Kingston Road, SW20 8SF
TEL: (0181) 542 4838   FAX: (0181) 540 7711   COOKING 1
EMAIL: alexandra@which.net   COST £21–£37

Eric Lecras's unpretentious bistro in residential Raynes Park is steadfastly French. The chef/patron sources ingredients and wine from his homeland, and the results can be seen on a regularly changing fixed-price menu offering half a dozen starters, main courses and puddings plus a couple of specials. A tartlet of goats' cheese and tomato with 'crisp, biscuity pastry' might kick off a meal, but thereafter vegetarians may have a fruitless search. Instead there are classic dishes such as 'tender, flavoursome' confit of duck with cep sauce, or grilled red mullet on an 'interesting, nicely dressed' salad. Desserts get much praise – one diner found raspberry crème brûlée 'staggeringly good' – and 'warm, attentive service' is also singled out. Alexandra occupies two small rooms, which have been newly decorated in apricot yellow. Most wines on the concise, exclusively French list are less than £20, with house wine £9.95.

CHEF/PROPRIETOR: Eric Lecras   OPEN: Sun L 12 to 2, Tue to Sat D 7 to 9.30   CLOSED: 2 weeks from 26 Dec, 1 week Apr, 2 weeks Aug   MEALS: alc Sun L (main courses £10.50 to £12.50). Set L Sun £11.95, Set D £17.95   SERVICE: 12.5% (optional), card slips closed   CARDS: Delta, MasterCard, Visa   DETAILS: 58 seats. 16 seats outside. Private parties: 25 main room, 20 private room. No children under 12. Music

Alfred   map 15

245 Shaftesbury Avenue, WC2H 8EH
TEL: (0171) 240 2566   FAX: (0171) 497 0672   COOKING 3
EMAIL: manager@alfred.co.uk   COST £28–£48

In a bit of a no-man's land between Soho and Bloomsbury, Alfred attempts to overcome its location not by faddy cooking or striking décor, but by a sincere attempt to offer real British food at reasonable prices. Both menu and drinks list fly the flag, one boasting potted duck, Welsh lamb shank with garlic mash, and roast Scottish salmon with baby seasonal vegetables; the other giving as much prominence to obscure bottled beers and ciders as to French wines. If the kitchen's output is not consistent, it is never less than agreeable. Dishes drawing praise include undyed smoked haddock with poached egg and salad leaves; 'moist and flavoursome' cod with pea purée on a potato pancake; and 'rich and creamy' chocolate tart with malt ice cream that 'the Ovalteenies would have loved'. Service is informal and laid back, melding appropriately with a plain dining room described by one as 'utilitarian' and by another as 'pleasantly modern, without any of the usual overkill'. House wines are naturally English, and priced from £11.75.

CHEF: Andrew Flitney PROPRIETOR: Fred Taylor OPEN: Mon to Fri L 12 to 3.30, Mon to Sat D 6 to 11 CLOSED: 25 Dec, 1 Jan, bank hols MEALS: alc (main courses £11 to £15). Set L and D £13.90 (2 courses) to £17 SERVICE: not inc, 12.5% for parties of 6 or more CARDS: Amex, Delta, Diners, MasterCard, Switch, Visa DETAILS: 45 seats. 20 seats outside. Private parties: 20 main room, 16 private room. Vegetarian meals. Children's helpings. No cigars/pipes in dining room. Wheelchair access (not WC). No music. Air-conditioned ⊖ Tottenham Court Road

Al Hamra

map 15

31–33 Shepherd Market, W1Y 7HR
TEL: (0171) 493 1954 FAX: (0171) 493 1044

COOKING 6
COST £40–£61

When this well-established Lebanese restaurant gets crowded in summer, tables are set up outside on the pavement; in the square dining room, meanwhile, with windows on two sides, mirrors on another, traditional Arabic music adds to the distinctly Middle Eastern ambience. Almost everything on the lengthy classical Lebanese menu is predictable – from macho raw meats and offal, to crisp falafel with herby yoghurt sauce – but the fifty-strong meze list also offers a couple of unusual items: sojuk (Armenian spiced sausages fried with eggs), and moujadar (lentils and coarse semolina). While there is no shortage of meat dishes, including charcoal-grilled skewers of chicken or lamb, vegetables play an essential role. Leeks, for example, are cooked in olive oil and garlic; broad beans come in a 'rich yet light' sauce with coriander; and aubergines are deployed in several ways: stuffed with walnuts and pickled (looking like 'a trio of shiny eggs'), or as moutabal (chargrilled and puréed with oil). Pastries from the sweets trolley include osmaliyeh, a crisp vermicelli sandwich layered with white cream cheese and pistachios. Thrice-boiled Lebanese coffee with cardamom is the business, and dark-suited men serve 'smoothly and confidently'. Nakad house wines from the Bekaa valley are £16.50.

CHEFS: Mahir Abboud and A. Rafiey Batah PROPRIETOR: Hassan Fansa OPEN: all week 12 to 11.30 CLOSED: 25 Dec to 1 Jan MEALS: alc (main courses £12 to £17.50). Set L and D £25. Cover £2.50 SERVICE: not inc CARDS: Amex, Delta, Diners, MasterCard, Switch, Visa DETAILS: 80 seats. 30 seats outside. Private parties: 80 main room. Vegetarian meals. Children's helpings. Wheelchair access (not WC). Music. Air-conditioned ⊖ Green Park

Al San Vincenzo

map 13

30 Connaught Street, W2 2AF
TEL: (0171) 262 9623

COOKING 4
COST £37–£60

This tiny, cream-painted converted shop, with print-covered walls and high-backed chairs, is the setting for some uncompromising Italian cooking. Vincenzo Borgonzolo's linguine with fresh clams, the menu tells us, is 'served without Parmesan cheese', while a dish of zampone (stuffed pig's trotter) and cotechino sausage with lentils makes a defiantly rich main course. Perhaps the absence of crowd-pleasing concessions, plus an attractively varied repertoire, explain why the food and cooking mark divide reporters quite sharply. One who ate a red mullet starter, braised ox tongue with Savoy cabbage, and a trio of sorbets (mango, pear and raspberry) rated it all extremely highly; another, who dined on cannellini bean soup, and capon with chestnut sauce, found that 'it promised more than it gave'. A third, meanwhile, enjoyed 'simple but excellent' spaghetti with porcini, line-caught sea bass baked with herbs and olive oil, and marzipan-stuffed dates with bitter chocolate sauce, and felt that 'the *Guide* has this restaurant just about right'. Just under twenty Italian wines start with house red and white from Puglia at £13.

CHEF: Vincenzo Borgonzolo PROPRIETORS: Elaine and Vincenzo Borgonzolo OPEN: Mon to Fri L 12.30 to 2, Mon to Sat D 7 to 9.45 CLOSED: Christmas MEALS: alc (main courses £14 to £21) SERVICE: not inc CARDS: Delta, MasterCard, Visa DETAILS: 24 seats. Private parties: 8 main room. No children under 12. No cigars/pipes in dining room. Music ● Marble Arch

Amandier   NEW ENTRY   map 13

26 Sussex Place, W2 2TH   COOKING 3
TEL: (0171) 262 6073   FAX: (0171) 723 8395   COST £32–£63

Opened at the end of 1998, Daniel Gobet's narrow, pale green and cream dining room (he previously owned La Ciboulette in King's Road) is described as a 'small and elegant French restaurant'. In fact its Mediterranean approach gives it a rather broader perspective, as dishes range from goats'-cheese and asparagus soufflé, via lasagne of aubergine, caviare and Parmesan croustillant, to lamb cutlet couscous. There is a supplement for foie gras, which has appeared pot-au-feu style in a clear broth infused with truffle oil, but judging by reporters' enthusiasms the starter of choice seems to be a 'brilliantly done' puff pastry tarte Tatin of sweet shallots with a dark balsamic drizzle. Fish, given equal billing among main courses, aims for the top end of the market, typically featuring sea bass, scallops, or perhaps red mullet with ratatouille, tagliatelle and crab sauce. Finish with passion fruit crème brûlée, or apple tart with calvados ice cream. Both food and wine are ambitiously priced – house French is £15, but there is relatively little to drink under £20 a bottle – but Bistro Daniel in the basement is 'more rustic' in terms of both design and food, and less expensive.

CHEF: Daniel Gobet PROPRIETORS: Daniel Gobet and Aziz Ahmed OPEN: Mon to Fri L 12 to 2.30, Mon to Sat D 7 to 10.45 CLOSED: Christmas, bank hols MEALS: Set L £15 (2 courses) to £18.50, Set D £25.50 (2 courses) to £37 SERVICE: 12.5% (optional) CARDS: Amex, Delta, MasterCard, Switch, Visa DETAILS: 25 seats. 10 seats outside. Private parties: 8 main room. Children's helpings. Wheelchair access (not WC). Music ● Lancaster Gate £5

Anglesea Arms £   map 12

35 Wingate Road, W6 0UR
TEL: (0181) 749 1291   COOKING 4
FAX: (0181) 749 1254 and 8591   COST £22–£37

'Uncommonly good food' is what's on offer at this large, four-square neighbourhood pub in a leafy part of West London. The décor is no-frills bare boards and brick walls, a single bright modern painting taking up one wall, the hatch into the kitchen another; or you can sit outside at ordinary pub trestles. Dan Evans eschews frills too in his rustic, seasonal meals. 'Great-value' dishes that have delighted this year include a 'gooey, sweet and creamy' onion and

Emmental tart served just warm, and a huge plateful of gamey pigeon pieces, slices of chorizo, black grapes and French beans in a piquant dressing. Other magpie ideas – some simple, some less so – include courgette flowers stuffed with goats' curd and purple basil then deep-fried in beer batter, and baby leeks and sprouting broccoli with a blood orange hollandaise. Main courses, meanwhile, run to boiled Gloucester Old Spot bacon with pineapple and a poached egg, and whole roast John Dory with Jersey Royals, spinach and cep butter sauce. Desserts seem to undergo fewer changes, so you are likely to hit upon a creamy lemon tart with a blob of vanilla ice cream, or Yankee chocolate truffle cake. Service has come under fire from reporters for being slow, though one visitor found staff 'bright and friendly'. Wines are a fun, modern slate with plenty by the glass. House Italian or Vin de Pays d'Oc is £8.95.

CHEF: Dan Evans   PROPRIETORS: Dan and Fiona Evans   OPEN: all week 12.30 to 2.45 (1 to 3.45 Sun), 7.30 to 10.45 (10 Sun)   CLOSED: 1 week from 24 Dec   MEALS: alc (main courses £7 to £10)   SERVICE: not inc   CARDS: Delta, MasterCard, Switch, Visa   DETAILS: 73 seats. 16 seats outside. Private parties: 12 main room. Vegetarian meals. Children's helpings. Wheelchair access (not WC). No music   ⊖ Ravenscourt Park, Shepherd's Bush

Arancia £   [NEW ENTRY] map 12

52 Southwark Park Road, SE16 3RS   COOKING 1
TEL: (0171) 394 1751   FAX: (0171) 394 1044   COST £14–£32

This former corner shop in south London is now a small, intimate local restaurant offering a stylish and restrained Italianate menu. Friendly and enthusiastic staff weave their way between tightly packed tables delivering smoked beef salad, potato and Provolone gnocchi, and spaghetti with seafood. An inspection meal yielded generously piled bruschetta with roasted vegetables, and a boldly dressed rocket salad with a slice of grilled Provolone, while main courses have included red peppers (stuffed with rice, salt-cod, raisins and aubergines) and chicken, served on a salad of potato, goats' cheese and salsa verde. Puddings get the thumbs up: ice cream cake layered with sponge, or a good slice of melting chocolate goo, here called semi-freddo. The wine list contains fewer than twenty bottles, all under £20 and all Italian. House wines are £8.

CHEF: C. O'Sullivan   PROPRIETORS: A. Rossi and C. O'Sullivan   OPEN: Tue to Sat 12 to 3, 7 to 11   CLOSED: 25 and 26 Dec   MEALS: alc (main courses £8.50 to £9). Set L and D £7.50 SERVICE: not inc, card slips closed   CARDS: Delta, MasterCard, Switch, Visa   DETAILS: 36 seats. 15 seats outside. Vegetarian meals. Music   (£5)

Aroma II £   [NEW ENTRY] map 15

118–120 Shaftesbury Avenue, W1V 7DJ
TEL: (0171) 437 0377 and 0370   COOKING 3
FAX: (0171) 437 0377   COST £24–£69

Eat on the ground floor with a view of busy Shaftesbury Avenue, or in the rather dark basement. The former is painted yellow and has two fish tanks – one dominating a whole wall – to keep you company. Menus are long, taking in Cantonese, Szechuan and Peking-style dishes, while specials of the day concentrate on whole braised pork knuckle, deep-fried marinated chitterling, and braised clams with black-bean sauce. An inspection meal started with a fine assortment of cold meats – beef infused with five-spice, succulent pork knuckle with jellyfish, smoked white fish, and pork terrine – and proceeded to slightly disappointing vegetarian 'duck': bean curd deep-fried to resemble the skin and steamed to remind you of the flesh. Main courses generally, however, are well reported, for example casserole of goulash (beef brisket), and Dover sole cooked two ways: sautéed with five-spice, or stir-fried with asparagus and served on deep-fried bones for those who enjoy a good crunch. Desserts major on more familiar fritters, ice cream and pancakes. Service is efficient and mostly friendly. The wine list, by Saccone & Speed, provides ample food-matching opportunities. House vins de table are £8.20.

CHEF: David Tam   PROPRIETORS: Ken and Kitty Lee   OPEN: all week noon to 11.30 (10.30 Sun)   MEALS: alc (main courses £6 to £24). Set L from £9 (min 2), Set D before 7 and after 10 £9 (min 2), and Set D all evening £16.50 to £22   SERVICE: 12.5% (optional), card slips closed   CARDS: Amex, Delta, Diners, MasterCard, Switch, Visa   DETAILS: 120 seats. Private parties: 80 main room, 40 private room. Vegetarian meals. Children's helpings. Wheelchair access (also WC). Occasional music. Air-conditioned   ⊖ Leicester Square, Piccadilly Circus (£5)

Asakusa £ | NEW ENTRY | map 13

265 Eversholt Street, NW1 1BA
TEL: (0171) 388 8399 and 8533
FAX: (0171) 388 7589

COOKING 1
COST £19–£39

This Japanese café may be unsophisticated, but it's the feeling of being warmly welcomed into a family that makes this corner of Mornington Crescent so popular. 'Wildly idiosyncratic' clientele choose from menus ranging over most of the Japanese repertoire, and from the 'wallpaper' of handwritten notices listing special and seasonal dishes. Sushi are less notable than, for example, the starter/side dish of maguro nuta (tuna with special soybean paste); or fresh, flavourful, well-seared gyoza (Japanese-style Peking dumplings). Reports say tempura ranges from 'competent' prawns and vegetables to 'perfect' and certainly unusual cuttlefish. Seekers after other unknown trifles might consider kazunoku – herring roe diced into a thin broth – or mysterious, succulent tori-o, described as yakitori of chicken tails. House wine is £7.80, or drink Kirin beer, saké or Japanese plum wine.

CHEF: Mr Ishida   PROPRIETOR: Mr Hirayama   OPEN: Mon to Sat D only 6 to 11.30 (11 Sat)   CLOSED: Christmas, New Year, bank hols   MEALS: alc (main courses £4.30 to £12). Set D £15 to £18   SERVICE: 12%   CARDS: Amex, Delta, Diners, MasterCard, Switch,Visa   DETAILS: 40 seats. Private parties: 40 main room, 30 private room. Vegetarian meals. Music.   ⊖ Mornington Crescent (£5)

'Staff were extremely dutiful, but I had to tell them to go and find out what brand the mineral water was, and the people at the next table had to tell them to go and find out what the cheeses were: Stilton and Cheddar, what a feat of memory that must have required.'
(On eating in Wiltshire)

Assaggi

map 13

The Chepstow, 39 Chepstow Place, W2 4TS
TEL: (0171) 792 5501

COOKING 3
COST £39–£59

In a terrace of large white houses in a wide leafy street, the first-floor dining room is simply and boldly decorated with blocks of colour on canvas, wooden tables and chairs, and a dramatic display of exotic flowers. It is not a place to stand on ceremony, rather somewhere 'to enjoy a natter and some good food', and specialises in starters or 'sample' portions, although with enough main courses to compose a square meal too. The style is 'rustic rather than refined', using mostly humble ingredients to produce a veal and vegetable terrine with onion mash and roast yellow pepper; and thin pliable bread 'like a Chinese pancake' for wrapping cured ham, grilled Pecorino and rocket leaves. First-rate materials have included well-timed red mullet fillets draped over a pile of varied leaves and quartered artichoke hearts, and golden yellow bottarga (dried grey mullet roe) shaved over young fennel. Finish with rice pudding and caramel sauce, or a wedge of moist Amaretto tart with a scoop of creamy vanilla ice cream. Service is 'matter of fact' and 'keen to ensure we understood what was in things when we asked about them'. Around twenty Italian wines start with house Sardinian red and white at £10.95.

CHEF: Nino Sassu   PROPRIETORS: Pietro Fraccari and Nino Sassu   OPEN: Mon to Sat 12.30 to 2.30, 7.30 to 11   CLOSED: 2 weeks Christmas   MEALS: alc (main courses £14 to £18)   SERVICE: not inc, card slips closed   CARDS: Amex, Delta, Diners, MasterCard, Switch, Visa   DETAILS: 35 seats. Vegetarian meals. Children's helpings. No music   ⊖ Notting Hill Gate

Atlantic Bar and Grill ♥

map 15

20 Glasshouse Street, W1R 5RQ
TEL: (0171) 734 4888   FAX: (0171) 734 3609

COOKING 2
COST £26–£85

With a reservation, you should be able to get past the security cordon guarding the roped-off doorway easily enough, beyond which the vast, pillared, mirrored underground space and its occupants provide their own entertainment. The menu, too, is diverting in Californian fashion, hiding ingredients in a thicket of information about origins and cooking: wok-seared Sri Lankan-spiced yellow-fin tuna loin served with wild parsley and aubergine relish with roasted bell pepper pesto, for instance, or paillarde of Hebridean salmon with creamed champagne, lobster torpedo mash and crisp pancetta. The glory is that the cooking always seems to stay on an even keel, however busy and frenetic (and noisy) it gets, and the kitchen's heart is in the right place: it uses some free-range and organic items, the chicken in the Caesar salad is oak-smoked on the premises, and upmarket fish get equal main-course billing alongside meats. Finish with an Atlantic chocolate box, perhaps, and drink a cocktail or two from the legendary bar. As to wines, some fine bottles from both sides of the Atlantic are there for those who can afford them, but there is also a fair selection under £20. Thirteen are offered by the large or very large glass from £2.50/£6.50, and house wine is £12.50.

CHEF: Richard Sawyer   PROPRIETOR: Oliver Peyton   OPEN: Mon to Fri L 12 to 3, all week D 6 to 12 (10.30 Sun)   CLOSED: 25 and 26 Dec, 1 Jan, Easter Sun and Mon   MEALS: alc (main courses £7 to £22). Set L £14.50, Set D 6 to 7 £14.50 (2 courses) to £16.50. Cover £1   SERVICE: 12.5% (optional), card slips closed   CARDS: Amex, Delta, Diners, MasterCard, Switch, Visa   DETAILS: 180 seats. Private parties: 10 main room, 70 private room. Music. Air-conditioned ⊖ Piccadilly Circus

Aubergine ❦

NEW ENTRY   map 14

11 Park Walk, SW10 0AJ   COOKING 6
TEL: (0171) 352 3449   FAX: (0171) 351 1770   COST £35–£95

On the surface, it seems that nothing has changed. The dark purple awning is still in place, as are dramatic flower displays, and colourful contemporary landscapes on distressed yellow walls. But all this hides a seismic shift that will have escaped the attention of few in the solar system. After five years (just as the last edition of the *Guide* went to press), Gordon Ramsay left Aubergine and A to Z Restaurants, amid much acrimony, to open his own place. Anybody would find it difficult to follow in Ramsay's footsteps, but comparisons are pointless, and in any case William Drabble is a worthy chef in his own right, having cooked at Pied-à-Terre (see entry, London) and Michael's Nook (see entry, Grasmere) among others.

Shellfish and foie gras figure prominently among first courses in typically high-French fashion, the repertoire ranging from wintery daubes to summery bouillons and emulsions. At inspection it was, perhaps predictably, the simpler dishes that showed best: queen scallops with purées of pea and artichoke; and a mound of cold salad leaves and warm vegetables dressed with truffled balsamic vinaigrette, dotted with blobs of velvety asparagus purée. Attempts at more complex dishes (boudin of pigeon with foie gras) may not be in the same league, and timing may depart slightly from ideal, but desserts are high-powered, judging by mango tarte Tatin with crisp flaky pastry, and an 'architectural splendour' of dense but moist chocolate Negus under an arch of bitter chocolate, with a ball of dark, pungent chocolate sorbet. The bulk of the extensive wine list is given over to Bordeaux, Burgundy and the Rhône, with many bottles from star châteaux or producers commanding some fairly astronomical prices (those hoping to find some cheap bins will soon be brought down to earth). House Chardonnay is £15.

CHEF: William Drabble   PROPRIETOR: A To Z Restaurants   OPEN: Mon to Fri L 12 to 2.30, Mon to Sat D 6.45 to 10.30   CLOSED: Christmas to New Year, 2 weeks Aug, bank hols   MEALS: Set L £15 (2 courses) to £50, Set D £39.50 to £50   SERVICE: 12.5% (optional), card slips closed CARDS: Amex, Delta, Diners, MasterCard, Switch, Visa   DETAILS: 50 seats. Private parties: 44 main room. Vegetarian meals. Children's helpings. No cigars/pipes in dining room. Wheelchair access (not WC). No music. Air-conditioned   ⊖ Gloucester Road

The Guide *relies on feedback from its readers. Especially welcome are reports on new restaurants appearing in the book for the first time. All letters to the* Guide *are acknowledged.*

Avenue
map 15

7–9 St James's Street, SW1A 1EE
TEL: (0171) 321 2111   FAX: (0171) 321 2500
EMAIL: chefs@egami.co.uk

COOKING 5
COST £33–£64

Avenue's stark glass frontage brings the twenty-first century to a street that remains a fragment of old London, within a stone's throw of St James's Palace. Inside, it is spacious and spotless, with a fashionably long bar and stylish table settings. The bare white décor is softened by low-level lighting to provide a relaxing ambience, helped along by 'adroit and capable' service.

The minimalism extends to menu descriptions, which can be as cryptic as 'Italian delicacies' or 'tomato tagliatelle'. In any case, nothing makes too many demands on the palate: what is delivered are mainly light, fresh, Mediterranean flavours based around fish, pasta and salads, plus some more robust offerings such as pork daube with fondant potato and tapénade. Upmarket nursery fare usually makes an appearance, in the form of fish cakes and fish fingers.

The kitchen's performance is never less than competent and frequently impresses: Gorgonzola tart has a fondant texture and sweet, crumbly pastry, while veal escalope with roast red onions and mustard mash is 'thoughtfully composed and perfectly appetising'. Puddings range from satisfying warm chocolate tart and crème brûlée, to a judiciously balanced champagne jelly with a passion fruit syrup and citrus salad. The wine list astutely juggles Old and New Worlds, and sixteen wines are under £20. House wine is £14.50.

CHEF: Dean Carr   PROPRIETOR: Chris Bodker   OPEN: Mon to Sat 12 to 3, 5.45 to 12 (12.30 Fri and Sat), Sun 12 to 3.30, 6.30 to 10   CLOSED: D 24 Dec, 25 to 28 Dec, L 31 Dec, 1 Jan   MEALS: alc (main courses £12 to £17). Set L Mon to Sat £17.50 (2 courses) to £19.50, Set D 5.45 to 7.30 and 10.15 to closing £14.50 (2 courses) to £16.50   SERVICE: 12.5% (optional), card slips closed   CARDS: Amex, Delta, Diners, MasterCard, Switch, Visa   DETAILS: 180 seats. Vegetarian meals. Wheelchair access (also WC). Occasional music. Air-conditioned   ⊖ Green Park

Babur Brasserie
[NEW ENTRY]   map 12

119 Brockley Rise, SE23 1JP
TEL: (0181) 291 2400   FAX: (0181) 291 4881

COOKING 2
COST £14–£44

It is impossible to miss this Indian restaurant in a Forest Hill shopping parade: the bright frontage with white arches would stand out even if it weren't surmounted by a life-sized prowling tiger. If the food lived up to its billing, this would be the world's best Indian restaurant. As things stand, it is certainly well above the curry-house average, offering some fairly unusual dishes: try, for example, cold mango soup to start, then duck Darjeeling in a spicy sauce with orange zest, with a side order of oonbhariu, a cheery assembly of bananas, sweet potato, aubergine and shallots. Service from waiters smartly dressed in tapestry waistcoats is efficient, sympathetic and smiling. House French on a short, interesting wine list is £7.95, or try a Royal Bengal Tiger cocktail – 'it does the roaring, you do the flying'.

CHEF: Enam Rahman   PROPRIETOR: Babur 1998 Ltd   OPEN: Sat to Thur L 12.15 to 2.15, all
week D 6 to 11.15   CLOSED: 25 and 26 Dec   MEALS: alc (main courses £7 to £12). Buffet L Sun
£8.95   SERVICE: not inc   CARDS: Amex, Delta, Diners, MasterCard, Switch, Visa   DETAILS: 56
seats. Private parties: 20 main room. Vegetarian meals. Children's helpings. Music. Air-
conditioned (£5)

Back to Basics £   map 15

21A Foley Street, W1P 7LA   COOKING 2
TEL: (0171) 436 2181   FAX: (0171) 436 2180   COST £21–£50

An informal, bustly seafood restaurant to the north of Oxford Street, Back to
Basics uses a daily delivery of fresh fish and shellfish to inventive and popular
effect. Preparations are not necessarily mainstream, so you may find mahi mahi
with rocket, red onions, new potatoes and mustard butter among the smoked
fish platters and lobster salads. Enjoyed by one diner was a generous serving of
fisherman's soup, followed by king scallops steamed in a paper case with a
white wine sauce. Meals might end with bread-and-butter pudding with
whisky sauce, or bananas baked in rum. Service, 'by pleasing young Polish
ladies', is 'brisk and smiling'. One complaint from reporters, however, has been
the restaurant's practice of leaving credit card slips open even though an
'optional' 10 per cent service charge has been added. The 'alternative cellar' of
French classic wines backs up a rather perfunctory main list. Prices start at £9.95.

CHEF/PROPRIETOR: Stefan Pflaumer   OPEN: Mon to Fri 12 to 3, 6 to 10   CLOSED: 3 weeks
Christmas, 3 weeks summer, bank hols   MEALS: alc (main courses £7.50 to £16.50)   SERVICE:
10% (optional)   CARDS: Amex, Delta, Diners, MasterCard, Switch, Visa   DETAILS: 40 seats. 55
seats outside. Private parties: 40 main room. Vegetarian meals. Children's helpings. No
cigars/pipes in dining room. Occasional music   ✈ Oxford Circus (£5)

Bali Sugar ✸✶   NEW ENTRY   map 13

33A All Saints Road, W11 1HE   COOKING 4
TEL: (0171) 221 4477   FAX: (0171) 221 9955   COST £25–£65

When the partnership that owns the renowned Sugar Club moved its flagship to
Soho (see entry), they relaunched the old Notting Hill premises as Bali Sugar.
Stripped-wood flooring, pine chairs and mustard coloured walls are visible
during the daytime, although 'lighting' is a misnomer for the evening's
low-wattage illumination. Still, all eyes are on the food, and Claudio Aprile
continues the white-hot fusion style that Peter Gordon forged: full of Far Eastern
gleanings and diverting sweet-savoury juxtapositions.

Menus might offer seared tuna with peanut-chyote salsa, purple potatoes and
coriander mojo; and adobo-marinated chicken breast with chorizo mash,
avocado and guajillo chilli sauce. Not even *Larousse Gastronomique* can help you
out with these references, so ask the staff. Given such a larder, it would be
surprising if the food were not vibrantly flavoured, and indeed it is. Even better,
components can work well together, for example grilled king prawns with
chillied black-bean sauce, and simple tuna on a niçoise salad with tapénade.
Desserts also cross boundaries, with varying degrees of success: rich chocolate
tart with an improvable basil and honey cream, for instance. The bill soon adds

up (vegetables are charged extra), so maybe try just two starters to keep it under control. Wines are a resourceful collection from around the world, but prices jump quickly above £20; they start at £10.50, however, and a few are offered by the glass.

CHEF: Claudio Aprile   PROPRIETORS: Ashley Sumner and Vivienne Hayman   OPEN: all week 12.30 to 3, 6.30 to 11   MEALS: alc (main courses £7.50 to £17)   SERVICE: not inc, card slips closed   CARDS: Amex, Delta, Diners, MasterCard, Switch, Visa   DETAILS: 65 seats. 20 seats outside. Private parties: 45 main room. Vegetarian meals. No children under 7. No smoking in 1 dining room. No music   ⊖ Westbourne Park

Balzac Bistro   map 12

4 Wood Lane, W12 7DT
TEL: (0181) 743 6787 and 5370   COOKING 2
FAX: (0181) 997 1378   COST £23–£41

Not far from the BBC's West London nerve centre, Balzac is the kind of bistro that has come to seem more and more like the distilled elixir of Frenchness. Here be escargots with garlic butter, crêpes aux fruits de mer, and veal escalope in mushroom and brandy cream sauce. A pair of regulars write that the quality of ingredients seems never less than A1, and care is taken in presentation too. One proceeded from fine sardines to salmon with beurre blanc and noted that even the red cabbage (not everybody's favourite vegetable) was 'mysteriously enjoyable'. A sweet pancake doused in orange liqueur and served with good ice cream makes a fitting way to conclude. Service is commended for being 'friendly and welcoming without being over-attentive'. The overwhelmingly French wine list manages to find a corner for the odd novelty such as a Uruguayan Chardonnay-Viognier. House wines by Georges Duboeuf are £9.40.

CHEF: Frank Vera   PROPRIETOR: Paulo Tarelli   OPEN: Mon to Fri L 12 to 2.30, Mon to Sat D 6.30 to 10.45   CLOSED: 2 weeks Christmas, bank hols   MEALS: alc (main courses £8 to £14.50). Set L £13.90, Set D £13.90 to £15.90. Cover £1   SERVICE: 10%   CARDS: Amex, Delta, Diners, MasterCard, Switch, Visa   DETAILS: 80 seats. Private parties: 60 main room, 40 private room. Vegetarian meals. No-smoking area. Wheelchair access (not WC). Music. Air-conditioned ⊖ Shepherd's Bush   (£5)

Bank ♥   map 13

1 Kingsway, WC2B 6XF   COOKING 5
TEL: (0171) 379 9797   FAX: (0171) 379 9014   COST £28–£84

With so many former temples of Mammon converted into large, swanky restaurants, Bank has a certain amount of competition to contend with, yet it manages to pull in the crowds. First-time visitors report that they enjoyed looking into the long kitchen, and at the big splashy murals and heavy glass panels hanging from the ceiling, despite the noisy atmosphere. The menu runs around busily taking in 'crisp, spicy' chicken and shrimp nam rolls with 'fiery' mango salsa, Baltic herring with Swedish mustard and new potatoes, and even fish and chips with mushy peas. Seafood features strongly, appropriately enough for a group that also owns Fish! in Borough Market (see entry): simply grilled whole lemon sole at one end of the spectrum, grilled tuna, aubergine, courgettes and Thai dressing at the other; in between, seared scallops with red wine and bacon is 'comfort food at its best'.

Meat dishes encompass a similar range, including glazed belly pork with Chinese cabbage, and salt beef with braised lentils, while desserts return home for bread-and-butter pudding, or spotted dick with crème anglaise. Service is welcoming and helpful – 'clearly on the ball despite laid-back appearances' – and breakfast is a treat not to be missed. Wines are a blend of Old World and New arranged simply by style: 'Juicy Aromatic' or 'Full Firm', for example. While there are plenty of bottles under £20, starting with house French at £12.50, City types boasting a healthy bank balance will no doubt be heading for the cellar of finer French fare.

CHEF: Christian Delteil   PROPRIETORS: Christian Delteil and Tony Allen   OPEN: all week 12 to 3, 5.30 to 11.30 (10 Sun)   CLOSED: 25 Dec, bank hols   MEALS: alc (main courses £9.50 to £26). Set L Mon to Fri and D all week before 7pm £13.90 (2 courses) to £17.50   SERVICE: 12.5% (optional), card slips closed   CARDS: Amex, Delta, Diners, MasterCard, Switch, Visa   DETAILS: 200 seats. Vegetarian meals. Children's helpings. Wheelchair access (also WC). No music. Air-conditioned   ⊖ Holborn

Belair House

map 12

Gallery Road, Dulwich Village, SE21 7AB
TEL: (0181) 299 9788   FAX: (0181) 299 6793

COOKING 4
COST £36–£59

The listed Georgian building, set in parkland, is considered an asset for Dulwich, an area otherwise deprived of good eating places. Discreet original paintings – 'nothing abstract, hardly bold, never garish' – relieve the predominantly white interior, where Colin Barnett's modern food retains an element of comfort. Seared foie gras accompanies a cappuccino of white bean and bacon soup, and Dover sole comes with langoustine fritter and risotto. Novelty is not allowed to get the upper hand, yet interest is maintained with brawn of pike, beetroot polenta (to accompany pancetta-wrapped monkfish), and scrambled duck egg on brioche with anchovy, a savoury that vies for attention with banana vol-au-vent and a dark chocolate and mint fondant. Set lunch is good value, but 'look out for extras', advises one reporter, specifying vegetables, coffee and the 'optional' charge for smooth, professional service. A bright, up-to-date list of some sixty wines includes a dozen-strong house selection that starts at £14 and takes in Guigal's Côtes du Rhône (£19) and Palliser Estate Sauvignon Blanc (£23.50).

CHEF: Colin Barnett   PROPRIETOR: Gary Cady   OPEN: Mon to Sat 12 to 2.30, 7 to 10.30, Sun 12 to 3, 7 to 10   CLOSED: bank hols   MEALS: alc Mon to Sat (main courses £15.50 to £17.50). Set L £12.50 (2 courses) to £15.50, Set D £24.95   SERVICE: 12.5% (optional), card slips closed CARDS: Amex, Delta, Diners, MasterCard, Switch, Visa   DETAILS: 100 seats. 60 seats outside. Private parties: 85 main room, 40 private room. Car park. Vegetarian meals. Children's helpings. No cigars/pipes in dining room. Wheelchair access (also WC). Music (£5)

Card slips closed *in the details at the end of an entry indicates that the total on the slips of credit cards is closed when handed over for signature.*

Belgo Noord   map 13

72 Chalk Farm Road, NW1 8AN
TEL: (0171) 267 0718   FAX: (0171) 284 4842   COOKING 3
EMAIL: mynam.mavros@belgo-restaurants.co.uk   COST £25–£52

While the Belgo name may be more familiar to some for its takeover of the Ivy and Le Caprice (see entries, London), the original continues to serve its way through mountains of mussels and chips, accompanied by lakes of beer. Indeed, apart from the noise, the feeling of eating in a monastic brewing hall is strong, thanks to long refectory tables, waiters dressed as Trappist monks, the absence of comfortable seating, and a whole series of no-nonsense menus. It is possible to pay £35 for a three-course 'gourmand' meal (the centrepiece may be wild rabbit, cod, or beef fillet, each cooked in a different beer), but by no means necessary. Prices start at £5 for a one-course lunch, and a beat-the-clock system operates on weekday evenings before 7.30 (order at 6.30 to pay £6.30, for example).

It may be going a trifle far to claim, as Belgo does, that Belgian food is 'Europe's last undiscovered culinary secret', but the style is sufficiently distinctive to survive such oddities as mussels in Congo sauce, and offers a glimpse into the world of salade liégeoise, wild boar sausages, meatless choucroute, and waterzooi chicken. Waffles, pancakes and ice creams bring up the rear. Tables are rented out for two hours at a time, and the range of Belgian beers (it claims to have the widest in the UK) includes Pilsners, weissbiers, Kriek, Gueuze, regional specialities, Trappist and other monastic ales.

CHEF: Johnny Johnson   PROPRIETOR: Belgo Group plc   OPEN: all week 12 to 3, 6 to 11.30 (12 to 11.30 Sat and Sun)   CLOSED: 25 and 31 Dec   MEALS: alc (main courses £8 to £17). Set L £5 (1 course) to £35, Set D £19.50 to £35   SERVICE: 15% (optional), card slips closed   CARDS: Amex, Delta, Diners, MasterCard, Switch, Visa   DETAILS: 140 seats. Private parties: 25 main room, 15 private room. Vegetarian meals. Children's helpings. No pipes /cigars in dining room. No music. Air-conditioned   ⊖ Chalk Farm (£5)

Bertorelli's ♥ ⅓✷   map 15

44A Floral Street, WC2E 9DA   COOKING 1
TEL: (0171) 836 3969   FAX: (0171) 836 1868   COST £26–£51

Part of Groupe Chez Gérard, which incorporates Livebait, Café Fish, Soho Soho and Brasserie St Quentin (see entries, London), Bertorelli's has another outlet at 19–23 Charlotte Street. Lengthy, traditional Italian menus offer a run of antipasti and pasta dishes – tagliatelle carbonara, spaghetti with clams – in both the restaurant and slightly cheaper café. Where the latter serves pizza half a dozen ways, the former goes in for grills and roasts of fish and meat: scallops in lemon butter sauce, calf's liver with cotechino sausage, or breadcrumbed veal cutlet with salsa verde. Service keeps up a swift pace, while wines (champagnes excepted) all hail from Italy, and many stay usefully under £20 despite the presence of some of the best growers. Veronese house white and red are £9.95, or you could stay in Verona and try the Arcadia rosé instead for £12.75.

CHEF: Maddalena Bonino   PROPRIETOR: Groupe Chez Gérard   OPEN: Mon to Sat 12 to 3, 5.30 to 11.30   CLOSED: 25 and 26 Dec   MEALS: alc (main courses £7.50 to £14). Café Set L and D 5.30 to 7 and 10 to 11.30 £9.95. Cover £1.50   SERVICE: 12.5% (optional), card slips closed CARDS: Amex, Delta, Diners, MasterCard, Switch, Visa   DETAILS: 125 seats. Private parties: 60 main room. Free parking at D. Vegetarian meals. No smoking in 1 dining room. Wheelchair access (not WC). No music in restaurant. Air-conditioned   ⊖ Covent Garden

Bibendum 🍾

map 14

Michelin House, 81 Fulham Road, SW3 6RD
TEL: (0171) 581 5817   FAX: (0171) 823 7925
EMAIL: manager@bibendum.co.uk

COOKING 5
COST £41–£80

Stylishly converted from an Edwardian garage, and widely regarded as one of London's most attractive dining rooms, Bibendum appeals in all moods and seasons. Its integrated Michelin-contoured design makes it a compelling and gratifying space, well suited to the food's reassuring foundation of approachable British, French and Italian standards. Old favourites – Burgundy snails, Baltic herrings, Bresse chicken with tarragon, and deep-fried fillet of plaice with chips and tartare sauce – are joined by newer dishes from a slowly but continually changing repertoire: perhaps rabbit fricassee, or calves' brains 'en persillade' with red wine sauce.

Materials and treatments are impressively varied, ranging from lightly smoked eel on a thin pancake, to pink roast veal with Gorgonzola polenta, although output has varied, chips alone running the gamut from crisp to soggy. Desserts, though less well reported, have included intense mango sorbet, and chocolate marquise, dark and rich 'as it should be'. Staff are generally discreet, attentive and professional, but have also been described as 'intrusive'. Those who prefer simple seafood might consider the Oyster Bar: for at least four kinds of oyster, fresh crab with well-dressed salad, or a seafood platter. The huge wine list covers the vinous globe in terms of grapes and styles, while the compass of vintages within France alone is astounding. House wines open with Vin de Pays des Côtes du Tarn at £12, but for something out of the ordinary try the 1995 Seña from Chile (£65).

CHEFS: Matthew Harris and Jamie Younger   PROPRIETORS: Sir Terence Conran, Lord Hamlyn, Simon Hopkinson and Graham Will   OPEN: all week 12 to 2.30 (3 Sat and Sun), 7 to 11.30 (10.30 Sun)   CLOSED: 24 Dec D, 25 and 26 Dec   MEALS: alc (main courses £14.50 to £22; after 9.30pm main courses £8 to £12.50). Set L £23 (2 courses) to £27.50   SERVICE: 12.5% (optional), card slips closed   CARDS: Amex, Delta, Diners, MasterCard, Switch, Visa   DETAILS: 72 seats. Children's helpings. Wheelchair access (not WC). No music. Air-conditioned   ⊖ South Kensington   (£5)

Big Chef

map 12

Second Floor, Cabot Place East,
Canary Wharf, E14 4QT
TEL: (0171) 513 0513   FAX: (0171) 513 0551

COOKING 3
COST £29–£67

The restaurant's change of name from MPW may or may not be a light-hearted reference to a certain national fast-food chain, but the menu at the Canary Wharf outpost of the Marco Pierre White empire certainly offers grown-up food, even if it starts from some everyday favourites: fillet steak with chips and béarnaise, Cumberland sausage with potato purée, or calf's liver with bacon. Fish, for example, comes with exemplary chips that 'stayed crisp to the very last' plus a dark green quenelle of minted pea purée with 'serious pea flavour', while two crisp spring rolls of tiger prawns and spring onion, sitting on a piquant ginger chutney, are 'a far cry from the Chinese takeaway standard'. Desserts that draw praise include a luxuriously rich chocolate tart, described as 'a ravishing treat'. If some items on the carte seem a little pricey, the reasonable menu du jour might lure trade in the evening when the shopping mall setting is otherwise deserted. Wines are arranged in order of price from £12 per bottle.

CHEF: Robert Arnott   PROPRIETORS: Jimmy Lahoud and Marco Pierre White   OPEN: Mon to Fri 12 to 2.30, 5.30 to 9   CLOSED: 25 Dec, bank hols   MEALS: alc (main courses £11.50 to £17). Set L £14.95 (2 courses) to £17.95, Set D £12.95 (2 courses) to £16.95   SERVICE: 12.5% (optional), card slips closed   CARDS: Amex, Delta, Diners, MasterCard, Switch, Visa   DETAILS: 150 seats. 40 seats outside. Private parties: 200 main room, 15 private room. Vegetarian meals. Wheelchair access (also WC). No music. Air-conditioned   ● Canary Wharf

---

Birdcage
map 15

110 Whitfield Street, W1P 5RU   COOKING 4
TEL: (0171) 323 9655   FAX: (0171) 323 9616   COST £43–£69

Considered witty rather than gimmicky, Birdcage is nevertheless 'pure theatre from start to finish'. Space is limited, not least because the room is filled with weird artefacts and decorative objects, while barely legible menus (pasted into old books) are perversely handwritten in a bizarre microscopic script. The self-confessed fusion food may have something of a 'backpacking' feel to it, cheerily picking up ideas from all over, but it pursues an idiosyncratic rather than fashion-conscious line, taking in pickled mackerel with Peruvian mash, and Indian risotto with plantain and lotus root.

Materials have included first-class poached skate wing on penne in a rich and flavourful fish broth, and curries are well rendered: Thai-spiced coconut chicken with couscous, or Tibetan lamb curry with pesto rice. Herbs and spices often come to the fore, as in a Patagonian shepherd's pie (strips of lamb in a powerful 'coriander soup' with okra), and dishes typically arrive in several parts, in small containers on a slate tile. Finish, perhaps with a trio of sorbets: passion fruit with mango, bitter chocolate with whisky, and raspberry with chilli. Drinks include dramatic toy-like cocktails with moving parts, and an origami-style wine list is presented in a wire cage; 'but by this time nothing would have surprised us'. The short list flies around the world picking up some fine and rare bottles along the way. Most are perched above £20; house wines are £19.50.

CHEF: Michael von Hruschka   PROPRIETORS: Caroline Faulkner and Michael von Hruschka OPEN: Mon to Fri L 12 to 2.30, Mon to Sat D 6 to 11.15   MEALS: Set L £19.75 (2 courses) to £26.50, Set D £28 (2 courses) to £36.50   SERVICE: not inc   CARDS: Amex, Delta, Diners, MasterCard, Switch, Visa   DETAILS: 35 seats. 6 seats outside. Private parties: 30 main room. Vegetarian meals. No-smoking area. Wheelchair access (not WC). Music   ● Goodge St   (£5)

Bistrorganic

map 13

46 Golborne Road, W10 5PR COOKING 3
TEL: (0181) 968 2200   FAX: (0181) 968 1441 COST £26–£42

What was Woz has now gone 80 per cent organic: not just for the sake of it, menus announce, but because organic food should taste better. The kitchen has the knack of 'making something you take for granted taste really great', remarks one visitor to these two floors, the upstairs soft yellow and grey with ornate candelabra and sentimental Edwardian pictures, the downstairs red and sumptuous. The 'simple Mediterranean feasts' that Matthew Barnett conjures up to the Worrall Thompson blueprint start with good bread, then you dip into what you fancy from the menu (there's no obligation to have a formal meal). A five-dish antipasti provides samples of salmon fish cake, tomato and butter bean paste, rocket and Parmesan salad, a dab of liver with caramelised onions, and red pepper and mozzarella salad. Or you might stay traditional with Cumberland sausages or cottage pie, classic with Caesar salad or eggs Benedict, or stumble on tender calf's liver with colcannon and 'superb' home-cured bacon. Honey and walnut meringue cake, pannacotta with grappa, or rich and smooth crème brûlée might be among the handful of puddings, or there's Staffordshire cheese with quince marmalade. Just under half the wines on the short, cosmopolitan list are organic, although the four Chilean house wines (£13 a bottle, £3.75 a glass) are not.

CHEF: Matthew Barnett   PROPRIETORS: Antony and Jacinta Worrall Thompson   OPEN: Tue to Sun L 12 to 4, Mon to Sat D 7 to 11   CLOSED: 1 week Christmas, bank hols   MEALS: alc (main courses £7 to £11)   SERVICE: 12.5% (optional), card slips closed   CARDS: Amex, Delta, MasterCard, Switch, Visa   DETAILS: 70 seats. Private parties: 35 private room. Vegetarian meals. Children's helpings. Music. Air-conditioned   ⊖ Ladbroke Grove, Westbourne Park
£5

Blakes Dining Room

map 13

31 Jamestown Road, NW1 7DB
TEL: (0171) 482 2959   FAX: (0171) 284 3066 COOKING 3
EMAIL: blake-s@rocketmail.com COST £26–£47

Deep colours, giant candle-lights and substantial plasterwork are the fashion-defying decorative keynotes in the first-floor dining room of this Victorian pub, and the building's solidity keeps out the noise from the bar downstairs. Sympathetic staff are happy to explain any of the less familiar items on the fusion menu. The cooking covers not just European and Asian territory but also North African, with occasional American interventions. Even if Caribbean lamb steak gigot sounds more like confusion than fusion, results are generally successful. There are simple classics too, such as terrine of foie gras or grilled poussin with ratatouille and roast potatoes. Chicken and lamb tagine, couscous royal, and sweet-and-sour vegetable pastilla are North African dishes which appear in set menus for at least eight people. To finish, Keskul Turkish rice pudding adds another exotic element. The bar menu offers an equally wide range, from sweet-and-sour chicken wings to grilled tiger prawns, or a mini-steak baguette. Most of the forty wines on the list are priced under £20; house wines are £10.80.

CHEF: L. Belaidi   PROPRIETORS: Robert Carmen and Irvin Blake   OPEN: Mon to Sat 12 to 3, 6.30 to 11, Sun 12 to 4.30, 6.30 to 10.30   CLOSED: 25 and 26 Dec, 1 Jan   MEALS: alc (main courses L £6.50 to £9, D £8 to £14). Set L £15 (min 8, Set D £20 to £25 (both min 8). Bar menu available all week 12 to 10   SERVICE: 12.5% (optional), 15% for parties of 8 or more; card slips closed   CARDS: Amex, Delta, MasterCard, Switch, Visa   DETAILS: 140 seats. 40 seats outside. Private parties: 54 main room, 90 private room. Vegetarian meals. Children's helpings. No cigars in dining room. Wheelchair access (not WC). Music. Air-conditioned   ⊖ Camden Town

Bluebird ⬭   map 14

350 King's Road, SW3 5UU	COOKING 3
TEL: (0171) 559 1000 FAX: (0171) 559 1111	COST £27–£88

With its 'trademark Conran' brushed steel, designer chairs and blue sail-like objects suspended from the ceiling, Bluebird strikes some visitors as akin to 'an avant-garde kite shop', while others praise its 'marvellous feeling of light'. Cool and clinical it may be, but it is comfortable enough, and service continues to please with its friendly professionalism. A minimalist menu pushes all the right modish buttons – seared this, wood-roasted that – while also seeming to parody a few outdated classics: prawn cocktail with Melba toast is stylishly presented in a Martini glass, and chicken Kiev comes with roast tomatoes. In the main, however, the food aims to impress with fashionable ingredients, from linguine with mussels and chilli jam, through rabbit with butter beans, to mango jelly with sesame biscuit. Although output can be inconsistent (not unusual in large restaurants) praise comes in for 'impeccable' calzone (from the wood-fired oven) stuffed with roasted vegetables and mozzarella. Eating from the carte will soon boost costs, but fixed-price lunch and pre-theatre menus are thought 'reasonably priced'. Brunch is popular at weekends. Six house wines start at £12.75 the bottle or £3.75 the glass.

CHEF: Andrew Sargent   PROPRIETOR: Conran Restaurants   OPEN: Mon to Fri 12 to 3.30, 6 to 11, Sat and Sun 11 to 4, 6 to 11.30 (10.30 Sun)   CLOSED: 25 Dec   MEALS: alc (main courses £9.50 to £29). Set L Mon to Fri £12.75 (2 courses) to £15.75, Set L Sat and Sun £17.50, Set D 6 to 7 £12.75 (2 courses) to £15.75   SERVICE: 12.5%, card slips closed   CARDS: Amex, Delta, Diners, MasterCard, Switch, Visa   DETAILS: 240 seats. Private parties: 12 main room, 24 private room. Vegetarian meals. Children's helpings. Wheelchair access (also WC). Music. Air-conditioned   ⊖ Sloane Square

Blue Elephant   map 12

4–6 Fulham Broadway, SW6 1AA ●	
TEL: (0171) 385 6595 FAX: (0171) 386 7665	COOKING 1
EMAIL: blueelephantlondon@msn.com	COST £38–£71

'Completely OTT' was one visitor's verdict after surveying this well-known Thai restaurant's interior jungle, complete with carp pool, 'stunning' flower displays, cascades and bridges. Silk costumes worn by able waitresses add to the display. The long menu of Thai classics ranges from 'fab' fish cake starters, via red and green curries, to marine life such as ouan talay (seafood salad with lemon grass and chilli), and a separate vegetarian menu also offers plenty of choice. Many opt for the set meal, which provides tasters of six starters and six main dishes, plus dessert. An inspector found the food competently rendered, if a little sweet, and enjoyed his prawn curry, while 'seriously hot' tom yam koong – a clear broth with spicy prawns – impressed another. As with the menu, the wine list is varied but pricey, with bottles picked to match the food. House wines open at £10.50.

CHEF: Rungsan Mulijan   PROPRIETOR: Blue Elephant International plc   OPEN: Sun to Fri L 12 to 2.30, all week D 7 to 12.30 (10.30 Sun)   CLOSED: 24 Dec to 3 Jan   MEALS: alc (main courses £7.50 to £19.50). Set L and D £30 to £35 (min 2). Cover £1.50   SERVICE: not inc   CARDS: Amex, Delta, Diners, MasterCard, Switch, Visa   DETAILS: 240 seats. Private parties: 260 main room. Vegetarian meals. Children's helpings. Wheelchair access (also WC). Music. Air-conditioned
⊖ Fulham Broadway

Blue Print Café

map 13

| Design Museum, Butlers Wharf, SE1 2YD | COOKING 5 |
| TEL: (0171) 378 7031   FAX: (0171) 357 8810 | COST £34–£60 |

Sharing a white concrete box of a building with the Design Museum, this stark but undeniably stylish restaurant offers spectacular views over the Thames. Bare white Formica tables – set with black rubber table mats and elegant glasses – might suggest a café, but everything else, including the prices, tells you that this is a serious modern restaurant.

Jeremy Lee's cooking is imbued with good taste. Everything makes culinary sense, ingredients are exemplary and dishes are well conceived and executed. The broadly classical menu probably owes more to Elizabeth David than to current trends yet still appeals to contemporary palates. An inspection meal started with a 'fresh-tasting and robustly wholesome' salad of Jersey Royals with peas and broad beans and went on to impress with main courses of bold simplicity: pan-fried turbot accompanied by a smooth and strongly flavoured fennel purée, and rump of Hereford beef with roast potatoes and a 'sublime' gravy flavoured with rosemary and garlic. Puddings might include petit pot au chocolat, or a cake such as lemon and polenta, or orange and almond. Service is efficient and particularly obliging. The wine list is enticing and up to date, but mark-ups are high, with prices starting around £14.

CHEF: Jeremy Lee   PROPRIETOR: Conran Restaurants   OPEN: all week L 12 to 3, Mon to Sat D 6 to 11   MEALS: alc (main courses £11 to £18.50)   SERVICE: 12.5% (optional), card slips closed   CARDS: Amex, Delta, Diners, MasterCard, Switch, Visa   DETAILS: 66 seats. 55 seats outside. Vegetarian meals. Wheelchair access (also WC). No music   ⊖ Tower Hill, London Bridge
£5

Brackenbury £

map 12

| 129–131 Brackenbury Road, W6 0BQ | COOKING 4 |
| TEL: (0181) 748 0107   FAX: (0181) 741 0905 | COST £20–£41 |

Reporters continue to sing the praises of the Brackenbury, which, despite changes of ownership, has maintained enviable consistency over the years it has been serving this part of West London. Green and yellow décor, 'thrown together' pictures and ornaments, and a mantelshelf of books all add up to 'a relaxed, cool and bohemian feel', yet menus have always mined a productive seam of fashion-conscious urban cooking. Service can be relaxed to the point of needing the occasional prod, but mostly runs smoothly, and the carefully sourced food keeps people returning. Layered presentations are much in favour: roast cod, for example, comes cushioned on a stratum of spinach, itself resting on pea purée, the whole thing topped with crisp-fried onion rings. It can be robust food (or 'heavy handed' in one case), with seasonings ranging from piccalilli (with smoked mackerel) via salsa verde (with grilled sardines) to a soy, chilli and ginger dressing with duck breast and lentils. Light but 'powerfully chocolatey' bocca negra with crème fraîche is a good way to finish, or there is the option of a single, impeccable cheese such as Wigmore or Roquefort. Wines are a sound international selection, the vast majority coming in under £20, with house French £9.50.

CHEF: Marcia Chang Hong   PROPRIETORS: David Watson   OPEN: Sun to Fri L12.30 to 2.45, Mon to Sat D 7 to 10.45   CLOSED: 25 Dec, Easter, bank hols   MEALS: alc (main courses £7 to £13). Set L £9.50 (2 courses) to £12   SERVICE: not inc   CARDS: Amex, Delta, Diners, MasterCard, Switch, Visa   DETAILS: 50 seats. 20 seats outside. Private parties: 25 main room. Vegetarian meals. Children's helpings. No cigars/pipes in dining room. No music
● Hammersmith

Bradleys

map 13

25 Winchester Road, NW3 3NR

COOKING 4

TEL: (0171) 722 3457   FAX: (0171) 431 4776

COST £19–£49

There is a garden to look at (but not to sit in) with bushes dotted here and there, all very typical of this leafy road behind Swiss Cottage. The dining room is intimate and minimally decorated, with honey-coloured rag-rolled walls, parquet floor and closely packed tables; combined with reasonably efficient service from black-clad staff, it makes for a relaxed and friendly atmosphere. Simon Bradley's menu shows particular strength and confidence with Mediterranean-influenced dishes, sardines escabèche or terrine of duck rillettes and foie gras being typical. A 'star' at main course has been fillet steak with a goats'-cheese crust and a red onion hash brown, but the emphasis appears to be on fish, perhaps whole baked sea bass with fennel and tomato, or grilled tuna with niçoise vegetables, crispy capers and aïoli. More exotic dishes include an inspector's starter of tender chargrilled squid with tabbouleh and harissa, while desserts have a French flavour: lemon and raspberry soufflé, tarte Tatin or crème brûlée. An almost exclusively New World wine list has a fair range, both of bottles and prices. House Chilean is £10.50.

CHEF: Simon Bradley   PROPRIETORS: Simon and Jolanta Bradley   OPEN: Sun to Fri L 12 to 3, Sat to Thur D 6 to 11   CLOSED: 25 and 26 Dec   MEALS: alc (main courses £9.50 to £15.50). Set L Mon to Fri £10, Set L Sun £14 (2 courses) to £17   SERVICE: not inc, 12.5% for parties of 5 or more   CARDS: Amex, Delta, MasterCard, Switch, Visa   DETAILS: 65 seats. Private parties: 65 main room. Vegetarian meals. Children's helpings. No cigars/pipes in dining room. Wheelchair access (not WC). Music. Air-conditioned   ● Swiss Cottage   (£5)

Restaurateurs justifiably resent no-shows. If you quote a credit card number when booking, you may be liable for the restaurant's lost profit margin if you don't turn up. Always phone to cancel.

Brady's £

513 Old York Road, SW18 1TF
TEL: (0181) 877 9599
COST £17–£25

A small room with wooden tables and chairs, weatherboarding, and fishy friezes provides the backdrop to Luke Brady's ten-year-old fish 'n' chip shop. Regular and daily items are written up on boards, typically listing salmon fish cakes, rollmop herrings, and potted shrimps with brown toast and a gesture of salad. Fish is either battered or grilled: typically cod, haddock or plaice, but there may also be lemon or Dover sole, sea bream and tuna. Prices vary according to size, supplies are fresh, and everything comes with chips and a tray of sauces, including aïoli and ketchup. Finish with either treacle tart or apple crumble. They also do take-aways. Five white wines cost around £10, but house vin de pays is £7.95.

CHEF: Luke Brady   PROPRIETORS: Luke and Amelia Brady   OPEN: Mon to Sat D only 6.30 to 10.30 (10.45 Thur and Fri)   CLOSED: Christmas, Easter, bank hols   MEALS: alc (main courses £4.50 to £8)   SERVICE: 10% (optional)   CARDS: none   DETAILS: 36 seats. Children's helpings. No music

---

Brasserie St Quentin
map 14

243 Brompton Road, SW3 2EP
COOKING 3
TEL: (0171) 589 8005   FAX: (0171) 584 6064
COST £27–£59

With the exception of pan-fried tuna with stir-fried vegetables and chilli oil sauce, few of the kitchen's ingredients would have caused a stir in a nineteenth-century Paris restaurant. One reader began with prosciutto con melone, and continued with poached salmon and hollandaise, finishing with lemon tart. The carte offers such classics as stuffed artichoke with a poached egg and mushrooms, chicken and leek terrine, and seared scallops with fennel and orange salsa – oh! the twentieth century has arrived after all, perhaps coinciding with the new chef. Tables are as close as in many Parisian brasseries, and the ambience derives from tinted mirrors, sparkling chandeliers, and traditional red and gold. Service, too, is mainly French and friendly. The wine list is defiantly Gallic too: Churchill's 1983 is listed under 'Portos'. Other wines rise gently from vin de pays at £10, taking in some highly respected growers along the way.

CHEF: Sharon Pengelley   PROPRIETOR: Groupe Chez Gérard   OPEN: all week L 12 to 3 (3.30 Sun), 6.30 to 11 (10.30 Sun)   MEALS: alc (main courses £9 to £18). Set L and D 6.30 to 7.30 £11.50 (2 courses)   SERVICE: 12.5% (optional), card slips closed   CARDS: Amex, Diners, MasterCard, Switch, Visa   DETAILS: 73 seats. Private parties: 55 main room, 18 private room. Vegetarian meals. Children's helpings. No cigars/pipes in dining room. No music. Air-conditioned   ⊖ Knightsbridge, South Kensington   (£5)

The 2001 Guide will be published before Christmas 2000. Reports on meals are most welcome at any time of the year, but are particularly valuable in the spring (no later than June). Send them to The Good Food Guide, FREEPOST, 2 Marylebone Road, London NW1 4DF. Or email your report to guidereports@which.co.uk.

Butlers Wharf Chop House ♥

map 13

36E Shad Thames, Butlers Wharf, SE1 2YE
TEL: (0171) 403 3403

COOKING 2
COST £37–£78

It may sound like a cheap and cheerful place selling chops and ale to the working class, but a glance at the prices will soon knock that idea on the head. More realistically, it represents an escape from the City, just across Tower Bridge. The style conjures up a certain kind of laddish Englishness, taking in classics of fish and chips with mushy peas, steak and kidney pudding with or without oysters, and roast beef with Yorkshire pudding. Desserts are in like vein – Cambridge burnt cream, bread-and-butter pudding – while separate seafood and weekend menus offer jellied eels, sandwiches, and crab mayonnaise. Wines may not be exactly cheap, but the selection around £20 should raise a smile, as should the fine French wines for those with more money to throw about.

CHEF: David Hollins   PROPRIETOR: Conran Restaurants   OPEN: Sun to Fri L 12 to 3, Mon to Sat D 6 to 11   MEALS: alc D (main courses £13.50 to £29.50). Set L £19.75 (2 courses) to £23.75. Bar food available   SERVICE: 12.5% (optional), card slips closed   CARDS: Amex, Delta, Diners, MasterCard, Switch, Visa   DETAILS: 120 seats. 48 seats outside. Private parties: 40 main room. Vegetarian meals. Wheelchair access (also WC). Music   ⊖ Tower Hill, London Bridge

Cactus Blue

NEW ENTRY   map 14

86 Fulham Road, SW3 6HR
TEL: (0171) 823 7858   FAX: (0171) 823 8577

COOKING 2
COST £28–£49

'Architecturally a little chaotic,' thought one: after navigating the glassed-in staircase, make your way past the bar to the split-level dining area under a large, steeply sloping skylight. Walls are hung with various 'Mexican cultural signifiers', as if to set the scene for the Cal-Mex cooking. An inspection meal started with a simple but appealing quesadilla with ground beef, jalapeño and Jack cheese, and even better red peppers stuffed with crab then battered and deep fried. Complex assemblies are not unknown, for example full-flavoured yellowfin tuna rubbed with spices, sitting on spicy couscous, accompanied by blobs of tomato salsa and guacamole, plus a drizzle of herb oil. Ambitious-sounding desserts have included Yucatan coconut pie ('a thin-crusted tart with masses of fresh coconut') with mango and ginger jam. Brunch on weekends includes a wide selection, from main dishes to 'benedicts', 'skillets', 'sandwiches' and 'sides', accompanied on Sunday by live jazz. Service is 'friendly and helpful', and the wine list includes some Mexican names, as well as over forty tequilas; house wines are £11.50.

CHEF: Andrew Barber   PROPRIETOR: Maxwell's Restaurants Ltd   OPEN: Sat and Sun brunch 12 to 4, all week D 5.30 to 11.45 (11 Sun)   CLOSED: 25 and 26 Dec   MEALS: alc (main courses £7 to £14)   SERVICE: 12.5% (optional), card slips closed   CARDS: Amex, Diners, MasterCard, Switch, Visa   DETAILS: 120 seats. Private parties: 30 main room, 50 private room. Vegetarian meals. Children's helpings. No cigars/pipes in dining room. Wheelchair access (not WC). Occasional music   ⊖ South Kensington (£5)

New main entries and restaurant closures are listed near the front of the book.

Café dell' Ugo

map 13

56–58 Tooley Street, SE1 2SZ
TEL: (0171) 407 6001   FAX: (0171) 357 8806

COOKING 1
COST £26–£57

It sounds Italian, and although this buzzing lower bar and upper restaurant, all in one cavernous room formed by a railway arch near London Bridge Station, gives the occasional nod to Italy, it also scampers wherever its polyglot chefs fancy. In an eye-catching setting that includes pretty tiles, gilt-plaster mirrors, ochre brick walls and a bicycle, the mostly obliging waiters provide 'unambiguous steers' through the menu and wines. If you don't fancy wild boar, ostrich, shark or kangaroo, choose perhaps a 'mille-feuille' of grilled aubergine, mozzarella and sun-dried pepper to start, followed by chargrilled mackerel marinated in lime, chilli and coriander, or maybe Italian (yes) braised lamb. Sauces are good, and coffee punchy. For pudding, try cloutie dumplings or settle for a fruity brûlée. Of the thirty or so wines, ten are sold by the glass and little is over £20. Prices start at £10.

CHEF: Nick Lang   PROPRIETOR: Simpsons of Cornhill plc   OPEN: Mon to Fri L 12 to 3, Mon to Sat D 6 to 11   CLOSED: Christmas to New Year, Easter Sat, bank hols   MEALS: alc (main courses £9.50 to £21). Set L and D £13 (2 courses) to £16   SERVICE: 12.5% (optional), card slips closed   CARDS: Amex, Delta, Diners, MasterCard, Switch, Visa   DETAILS: 70 seats. Private parties: 85 main room. Vegetarian meals. Children's helpings. No cigars/pipes in dining room. Music ⊖ London Bridge (£5)

Café du Jardin ▼

map 15

28 Wellington Street, WC2E 7BD
TEL: (0171) 836 8769 and 8760
FAX: (0171) 836 4123

COOKING 3
COST £21–£50

With good views of busy Covent Garden from its large street-level windows, and closely packed tables smartened up by starched linen, this bistro is well placed for pre- and post-theatre eating. It revels in Mediterranean materials from pesto to mozzarella, from olive crostini to bresaola with Parmesan shavings, and serves up dishes of potato and sage dumplings with mascarpone, and pasta with grated Sardinian bottarga.

Tony Howorth embraces lots of other styles too, though, producing anything from smoked salmon and scrambled eggs, to braised shank of lamb, by way of grilled ostrich fillet. He makes liberal use of oils – truffled for pasta, chillied for deep-fried crab cake, and curried with creamed smoked haddock – and is not averse to a few Eastern ideas, such as sautéed shrimps and chicken in green Thai coconut sauce with lime-scented basmati. Desserts tend to be weighty, as in apple tart with caramel sauce, or sticky toffee pudding with fudge sauce. Service is not a strong point. The wine list covers the world, and careful scrutiny repays the adventurous. House white and red are £9.50.

CHEF: Tony Howorth   PROPRIETORS: Robert Seigler and Tony Howorth   OPEN: Mon to Sat 12 to 3, 5.30 to 12, Sun 12 to 11   CLOSED: 24 and 25 Dec   MEALS: alc (main courses £8.50 to £14). Set L and D 5.30 to 7.30 and 10 to 12 £9.95 (2 courses) to £13.50   SERVICE: 15% (optional), card slips closed   CARDS: Amex, Delta, Diners, MasterCard, Switch, Visa   DETAILS: 110 seats. 20 seats outside. Private parties: 70 main room, 70 private room. Vegetarian meals. Wheelchair access (not WC). Music. Air-conditioned   ⊖ Covent Garden

Café Fish

map 15

36–40 Rupert Street, W1V 7FR	COOKING 2
TEL: (0171) 287 8989 FAX: (0171) 287 8400	COST £27–£58

Could the shellfish plates and platters be too generous for *Guide* readers? Few reporters mention them, although oysters, scallops, and mussels as well as simple grilled prawns, tuna, sardines, swordfish and sole are widely approved. So are more complex dishes such as lobster thermidor, and baked monkfish: served either with chorizo, or with smoked bacon, mushrooms and spinach on a potato galette. Few report on desserts either, although tarte Tatin, and crème brûlée have been commended. The cover charge includes fish pâté and the varied breads. Service is 'cheerful, well informed, friendly and professional', and although some find it noisy, the bustling ambience is generally appreciated. The Canteen downstairs offers an express menu of one, two or three courses as well as bar snacks, shellfish and grills. Wines are helpfully arranged by style and sensibly priced, with thirteen available by the standard or large glass from £3.25/£4.

CHEF: Andrew Magson PROPRIETOR: Groupe Chez Gérard OPEN: all week 12 to 3, 5.30 to 11.30 (10.30 Sun) CLOSED: 4 to 5 days Christmas MEALS: alc (main courses £9 to £20). Set D 7 to 11.30 £18.50. Cover £1.50 SERVICE: 12.5% (optional), card slips closed CARDS: Amex, Delta, Diners, MasterCard, Switch, Visa DETAILS: 195 seats. Private parties: 12 main room. Vegetarian meals. No-smoking area. Wheelchair access (also WC). No music. Air-conditioned ⊖ Piccadilly Circus, Leicester Square

Café Japan £

map 13

626 Finchley Road, NW11 7RR	COOKING 5
TEL: (0181) 455 6854	COST £19–£50

Yes, Café Japan is inexpensive, unfussy and unpretentious, but this doesn't stop it producing some of the best Japanese food – imaginative, skilfully executed and attractively presented – to be found in London. It is a clean, bright, spacious and relaxed place attracting a casually dressed bunch of diners, about half of whom are Japanese. The furnishings are predominantly wooden: parquet floors, beams, chairs and bare tables. On the menu, brought by young, pleasant waitresses dressed in blue 'happi' coats, 'today's assortment' augments a varied choice of set meals based around sukiyaki, shabu-shabu (thinly sliced beef and vegetables boiled at table), and dishes such as salt-grilled mackerel accompanied by miso soup, rice and pickles. Sushi is outstanding and available in assortments or individually priced. Salmon and avocado inside-out roll has been highly praised, 'the roll freshly made, the nori still crisp, all exactly as it should be'. An inspector also vouched for deep-fried tofu yakitori and anago eel tempura. Ice cream made with chunks of candied chestnut provides a 'creamy, sweet' end to a meal. To drink, there's a choice of three Japanese beers, plus saké, house wine (£8.50) or Japanese plum wine.

CHEF: Masaru Okayama PROPRIETOR: Koichi Konnai OPEN: Wed to Sun L 12 to 2.30, all week D 5.30 to 10.30 MEALS: alc (main courses £6.50 to £14). Set D £12 to £19.50 SERVICE: not inc CARDS: Delta, MasterCard, Switch, Visa DETAILS: 36 seats. Private parties: 6 main room. Vegetarian meals. No smoking on sushi counter. Music. Air-conditioned ⊖ Golders Green

Café Spice Namaste

maps 12 and 13

16 Prescot Street, E1 8AZ
TEL: (0171) 488 9242   FAX: (0171) 481 0508
247 Lavender Hill, SW11 1JW
TEL: (0171) 738 1717   FAX: (0171) 738 1666

COOKING 3
COST £30–£52

There may exist an edible quadruped, or biped, which has escaped Cyrus Todiwala's menu – and someone from a remote village in the Subcontinent might complain that his regional cuisine is therefore not represented – but it is unlikely. The bright South Indian technicolour décor is similar at both the original and the new Clapham address, and is as striking as the menu. Here, the unconventional is normal. Reports praise crab and fish won tons with a chilli relish 'not so hot or strong as to mask the crab flavour'; a warm chaat of chickpeas, crushed pooris, coriander and tamarind sauce; and 'sensational' home-made pickles with poppadums. There have been contradictory reports on kozhi vartha kari (a Tamil-style chicken curry), and Goanese bebinca (layers of pancake compressed with nutmeg and saffron), but desserts are generally approved, especially carrot halva. At Prescot Street Mrs Todiwala leads the 'tremendously friendly and helpful' staff, but service at Lavender Hill could be better organised. Wines, listed by style, and mostly well described, are fairly priced with house wines at £10.50.

CHEFS: Cyrus Todiwala and Angelo Collaco (Prescot Street), Briston D'Souza (Lavender Hill) PROPRIETORS: Cyrus Todiwala and Michael Gottlieb   OPEN: Prescot Street Mon to Fri L 12 to 3, Mon to Sat D 6.15 to 10.30; Lavender Hill Sun L 12 to 3, all week D 6 to 11.30 (10.30 Sun) CLOSED: 25 Dec to 1 Jan, bank hol Mons   MEALS: alc (main courses £6 to £15)   SERVICE: 12.5% (optional), card slips closed   CARDS: Amex, Delta, Diners, MasterCard, Switch, Visa   DETAILS: 120 seats. Private parties: 80 main room. Vegetarian meals. Children's helpings. Music. Air-conditioned   ⊖ Aldgate (Prescot Street)   £5

Cambio de Tercio ♟

map 14

163 Old Brompton Road, SW5 0LJ
TEL: (0171) 244 8970   FAX: (0171) 373 8817

NEW CHEF
COST £27–£50

Spanish food has not had such a good press as Italian over recent years, although the country is richly endowed with prime materials. Cambio de Tercio has had a good track record in dealing with them, and although there was a change of chef as the *Guide* went to press, newest menus promise Andalucian oxtail in red wine sauce with poached apples, Segoviana-style suckling pig, and then perhaps crème Catalan, or Spaniish cheese with quince marmalade. Spanish wine producers have had to cope with increased competition from the New World, but the all-Spanish list (champagne excepted) proves that the old country still has plenty to offer, whether the preference is for fresh and fruity new-style whites or classic red Riojas. Nine attractive wines by the glass are good value from £2.60, as are the seven William & Humbert sherries at £3.

CHEF: Diego Ferrer   PROPRIETORS: Abel Lusa and David Rivero   OPEN: all week 12.15 to 2.30, 7 to 11   CLOSED: 26 Dec to 2 Jan   MEALS: alc (main courses £9 to £15)   SERVICE: not inc; 12.5% for parties of 6 or more   CARDS: Amex, Delta, MasterCard, Switch, Visa   DETAILS: 45 seats. 10 seats outside. Private parties: 60 main room, 17 and 28 private rooms. Wheelchair access (not WC). Music   ⊖ Gloucester Road

Canteen
map 12

Unit G4, Harbour Yard, Chelsea Harbour, SW10 0XD COOKING 6
TEL: (0171) 351 7330   FAX: (0171) 351 6189 COST £31–£54

Check first before turning up, since there is a chance the restaurant could move during the currency of the *Guide*. Chelsea Harbour may not have proved quite the buzzing, thriving honey pot its planners had in mind, but the Canteen has held its head up well considering how far it is from the West End centre of gravity. The food, certainly, is mainstream, its French and Italian thrust given occasional impetus from other sources: a dish of lobster tempura, for example, with Asian greens, Chinese noodles and ginger dressing. For the most part, however, the repertoire stays in Mediterranean mode, as meals begin with a risotto (perhaps of red wine, or of smoked salmon with fromage frais and spring onions), a salad (of artichokes and poached egg with rocket), or maybe tarte Tatin of plum tomatoes and red onions.

Similar sunny treatment works well with fish – sea bream with provençale vegetables, or hake and langoustine with lobster vinaigrette and crushed new potatoes – while meats characteristically adopt an earthier approach, producing pigeon breasts with creamed cauliflower and game sauce, or calf's liver with black pudding and 'sauté mash'. The menu seldom changes, and the kitchen is well drilled to produce a high level of consistency throughout, desserts included: expect crêpes Suzette soufflé, a délice of cassis and apple, or iced banana parfait. Italian, Spanish and New World wines add interest and variety to a predominantly French list that starts with house Chardonnay and Merlot at £14.

CHEF: Ray Brown   PROPRIETORS: Michael Caine and Claudio Pulze   OPEN: Mon to Fri L 12 to 2.30, Mon to Sat D 6.30 to 11   CLOSED: Christmas, Easter, bank hols   MEALS: alc (main courses £11 to £14.50). Set L £15.50 (2 courses) to £19.50   SERVICE: Mon to Fri not inc, Sat 12.5% (optional)   CARDS: Amex, Delta, MasterCard, Switch, Visa   DETAILS: 120 seats. Private parties: 70 main room. Vegetarian meals. Wheelchair access (also WC). No music. Air-conditioned   ⊖ Fulham Broadway

Cantaloupe
| NEW ENTRY | map 13

35–42 Charlotte Road, EC2A 3PD COOKING 2
TEL: (0171) 729 5566   FAX: (0171) 613 4111 COST £25–£44

Hoxton's regeneration is nicely epitomised in this 'cavernous shed' of a restaurant, which wears its industrial origins on its sleeve in the form of exposed ventilation ducts, bare wooden tables and minimalist chairs, some sporting parts of packaging materials stamped 'This Way Up'. A modern British menu is underpinned by traditional Middle Eastern and Spanish ideas, such as pigeon breast in filo pastry with raisins and cinnamon, or chargrilled chermoula grey mullet served with saffron rice, harissa and yoghurt. Not everything has been successful, but roast confit duck leg with spiced sweet potato and grilled greens has been hailed 'a visual delight' and 'very bistro, with its gutsy flavours'. Desserts might be spiced up with cumin shortbread, but otherwise stick to traditional terrain of lemon tart, chocolate torte and crème brûlée in various guises. In the bar, a tapas menu is offered from noon (later on weekends) to midnight. Music suits the venue, being loud and popular. House wines cost £8.90.

CHEFS: Henry Brereton and Dave Cook   PROPRIETORS: Richard Bigg and Nigel Foster   OPEN: Mon to Fri L 12 to 3, Mon to Sat D 6 (7 Sat) to 11.30   CLOSED: 25 to 30 Dec, L bank hols   MEALS: alc (main courses £8 to £13.50). All-day tapas menu in bar   SERVICE: 12.5% (optional), card slips closed   CARDS: Delta, MasterCard, Switch, Visa   DETAILS: 50 seats. Private parties: 12 main room. Vegetarian meals. Children's helpings. Music. Air-conditioned   ⊖ Old Street
(£5)

▲ The Capital ☺
map 14

22–24 Basil Street, SW3 1AT
TEL: (0171) 589 5171   FAX: (0171) 225 0011

COOKING 7
COST £36–£91

The place and procedure remain as before: weave your way from hotel reception through the bar to restaurant reception, and contact the maître d' at the earliest opportunity to ensure that 'the well-oiled machine purrs into life'. The dining room is not large, but tables are well spaced, and the surreal air engendered by wooden sculptures attached to mirrors is soon forgotten in the face of a generous carte (seven choices per course), and a five-course tasting menu. Eric Chavot moved from his own restaurant in Fulham Road to take over the Capital's kitchen in March 1999, when Philip Britten left, after a distinguished decade, to pursue other interests.

Chavot offers a rich and occasionally inventive version of French haute cuisine. Starters tend to major on foie gras and shellfish: five plump, sweet, seared scallops, for example, tasting 'just as they should', with a 'nearly perfect' spring onion risotto. Prime cuts and materials (pot roast lobster, beef fillet with horseradish topping), still allow room for saddle of rabbit with veal sweetbread, and a whimsical 'shepherd's pie' with lamb fillet. Pasta has been worked successfully into more than one dish: for example a 'magical' raviolo filled with truffled foie gras, accompanying two small legs and two enormous breasts of 'pink and rested' pigeon; a classic combination maybe, but one done with a degree of 'individuality, great skill and a sense of balance'.

Desserts are equally captivating: thinly sliced strawberries on a biscuit pastry base, topped with a disc of lime-flavoured Chiboust, or a tall cyllinder of thin chocolate biscuit containing layers of coffee flavoured cream, toffee mousse, and coffee ice cream, all nonchalantly resting on crunchy praline made with puffed wheat. This was a dish that impressed visually, technically, and in terms of pure enjoyment. If classy food deserves classy wine, then the predominantly French list happily obliges, but bottles under £25 (apart from Levin house wines at £14.50) are scarce.

CHEF: Eric Crouillère-Chavot   PROPRIETOR: David Levin   OPEN: all week 12.30 to 2.15, 7 to 11.15   MEALS: alc (main courses £22). Set L £24.50, Set D £60   SERVICE: 12.5% (optional), card slips closed   CARDS: Amex, Delta, Diners, MasterCard, Switch, Visa   DETAILS: 36 seats. Private parties: 8 main room, 10 and 24 private rooms. Jacket and tie preferred. No cigars/pipes in dining room. Wheelchair access (not WC). No music. Air-conditioned   ACCOMMODATION: 48 rooms, all with bath/shower. TV. Phone. Room only £180 to £350 plus VAT. Baby facilities ⊖ Knightsbridge

Le Caprice

map 15

Arlington House, Arlington Street, SW1A 1RT
TEL: (0171) 629 2239   FAX: (0171) 493 9040

COOKING 4
COST £37–£78

As the last edition of the *Guide* went to press, the Belgo Group bought not only this restaurant, but its sisters Ivy and Sheekey's (see entries). Mark Hix remains in executive charge of the cooking, and the modern brasserie idiom continues pretty much as before. This is the place to come for comforting eggs Benedict, sautéed foie gras with apple, and deep fried haddock with chips and minted pea purée. The range extends to Thai-baked sea bass, and Mexican chicken salad, followed by retro baked Alaska, seasonal rhubarb tart, and long-standing Scandinavian iced berries with white chocolate sauce. Although a sense of indulgence is never far away, the cooking seems to be less thrilling than it was, and service has lost its polish. The well-chosen, sharply focused wine list offers choice for low as well as high spenders. House wines start at £11.25.

CHEFS: Mark Hix and Elliot Ketley   PROPRIETORS: Belgo Group, Christopher Corbin and Jeremy King   OPEN: Mon to Sat 12 to 3, 5.30 to 12, Sun 12 to 3.30, 6 to 12   CLOSED: 25 and 26 Dec, 1 Jan, Aug bank hol   MEALS: alc (main courses £10 to £22). Sun brunch menu. Cover £1.50   SERVICE: not inc   CARDS: Amex, Delta, Diners, MasterCard, Switch, Visa   DETAILS: 80 seats. Private parties: 8 main room. Vegetarian meals. Wheelchair access (not WC). Music. Air-conditioned

Chapter Two

NEW ENTRY   map 12

43–45 Montpelier Vale, SE3 0TJ
TEL: (0181) 333 2666   FAX: (0181) 355 8399

COOKING 2
COST £31–£48

Set on the edge of Blackheath village, this sister establishment to Chapter One (see entry, Farnborough) is decorated in similar style with ochre paint, palest yellow linen cloths and modern stripy paintings, all giving a 'very cool, classy' impression and a relaxed atmosphere. The menu follows the same trend too: 'modern European with portions on the generous side', as one reporter described it. Starters range from soft-boiled egg with grilled asparagus and rocket leaves, to a wild mushroom and ox cheek salad – 'all warm and meaty, dark and caramelised' – with piccalilli. Presentation sometimes seems to take priority over flavour in main courses (timid seasoning for example at inspection), but pork knuckle ravioli with wild mushrooms and a truffle jus has impressed, as have roast veal on saffron mash, and salmon on pea risotto. Desserts are hardly adventurous, but none the worse for that: roasted plums with vanilla and fudge ice cream, or strawberry shortbread with lemon curd ice cream. The short wine list is centred in France with a brief trot round the 'rest of the world'. French house wines are £13.50.

CHEF: Adrian Jones   PROPRIETOR: Selective Restaurants Ltd   OPEN: Mon to Sat 12 to 2.30, 6.30 to 10.30, Sun 12 to 3.30, 7 to 9.30   MEALS: Set L Mon to Sat £14.50 (2 courses), Set D Mon to Thur £19.50, Set D Fri and Sat £22.50, Set L Sun £16   SERVICE: 12.5% (optional), card slips closed   CARDS: Amex, Delta, Diners, MasterCard, Switch, Visa   DETAILS: 70 seats. Private parties: 50 main room. Vegetarian meals. Children's helpings. Wheelchair access (also WC). Occasional music. Air-conditioned

Charco's

map 14

1 Bray Place, SW3 3LL
TEL: (0171) 584 0765   FAX: (0171) 838 0134

COOKING 2
COST £27–£44

Smoked emu salad with asparagus and water chestnuts is quite typical of Chris
Wellington's penchant for surprising combinations of ingredients, many of
which work well. He juggles Spanish influences – chilli-hot gazpacho elegantly
served in a lidded mini-tureen – with more far-flung ideas: monkfish with rice
and red Thai curry, or French beans with chilli and ginger. Desserts are equally
imaginative, producing some subtle contrasts of flavour and texture in, for
example, caramelised pear with candied walnuts and Roquefort. Chelsea
wine-bar habitués enjoy this eclectic cooking in the cheerfully decorated, blue
and white basement with lively modern art on the white walls. The wine list,
arranged by grape variety, rarely strays above £20, and an impressive number
are sold by the glass, starting at £2.20, £10 the bottle.

CHEF: Chris Wellington   PROPRIETOR: Pillarcrest Ltd   OPEN: Mon to Sat 12 to 2.30 (3 Sat), 6 to
10.30   MEALS: alc (main courses £10 to £12.50). Set L and D 6 to 7.30 £9.50 (2 courses)
SERVICE: not inc, 12.5% for parties of 5 or more   CARDS: Amex, Delta, MasterCard, Switch,
Visa   DETAILS: 59 seats. 8 seats outside. Private parties: 40 main room. Vegetarian meals.
Occasional music. Air-conditioned   ● Sloane Square (£5)

Le Chardon £

| NEW ENTRY | map 12

65 Lordship Lane, SE22 8EP
TEL: (0181) 299 1921

COOKING 3
COST £20–£49

Floor-to-ceiling tiles, surrounded by a border of Scottish thistles, date from the
time this was a grocer's shop. The theme – later perpetuated as Thistell's wine
bar – continues under new French ownership. Other Victorian features to
survive include old shop shelves and weighing scales, now Frenchified by
oilcloths, Parisian street signs, Edith Piaf and far from prickly service. Classic
and well-executed neighbourhood bistro favourites, with leanings to the South
of France (panaché de poissons on fennel for example) appear on the printed
menu or blackboard. Prices, particularly for the set-price lunch, are reasonable,
and helpings are generous: 'chunky, robust and garlicky' pork terrine, or tender
calf's liver topped with a fan of ripe mango. First courses are weighted towards
seafood, supplemented perhaps by gazpacho or onion soup, vegetarians are
given some choice, and authentic bistro puddings have included 'irreproachable' crème brûlée. The compact wine list (all French, bar three bottles) is
divided into categories such as 'fruity and aromatic whites' and 'light and fruity
reds – can be served chilled'. House wine is £9.30.

CHEF: Patrick Thomas   PROPRIETOR: Robert Benayer   OPEN: all week noon to 11   CLOSED:
bank hols   MEALS: alc (main courses £9 to £10). Set L Mon to Sat £5.95 to £8.95 (2 courses), Set
L Sun £12.50   SERVICE: 10% (optional)   CARDS: Amex, Delta, Diners, MasterCard, Switch,
Visa   DETAILS: 50 seats. 25 seats outside. Private parties: 100 main room. Vegetarian meals.
Children's helpings. Wheelchair access (not WC). Occasional music (£5)

London restaurants by cuisine are listed near the front of the book.

Cheng-Du

map 13

9 Parkway, NW1 7PG	COOKING 1
TEL: (0171) 485 8058	COST £26–£52

Reports on this civilised and attractive restaurant in Camden Town emphasise the restful décor and well-spaced tables. Most also mention pleasant and skilful service, even extending to the handling of wine from the well-chosen short list. The menu, not as long as most Chinese encyclopedias, offers just two set meals, taking in sautéed Ganshow scallops and prawns, and sizzling lamb slices in the Yin version, and Hunanese chicken fillets, and double-cooked pork in the Yang. The carte encompasses Peking and Szechuan as well as the Cantonese repertoires, and among curiously 'modern Chinese' special selections are salmon in egg fu-yung, and sesame steak with teriyaki sauce. Although flavours are a mite muted for authenticists, ingredients are excellent, generally well presented and carefully cooked. Wines on the succinct list stay mostly under £20; Italian house wine is £9.60. Note that card slips are left open although service is included on the bill.

CHEF: Mr Soon   PROPRIETOR: Gingerflower Ltd   OPEN: all week 12 to 2.30, 6.30 to 11.30
MEALS: alc (main courses £4 to £16). Set L and D £20.50 (min 2)   SERVICE: 12.5%   CARDS:
Delta, MasterCard, Switch, Visa   DETAILS: 75 seats. Private parties: 24 main room. Vegetarian
meals. Wheelchair access (not WC). Occasional music   ⊖ Camden Town

Chez Bruce 🍾

map 12

2 Bellevue Road, SW17 7EG	COOKING 5
TEL: (0181) 672 0114 FAX: (0181) 767 6648	COST £34–£59

Bruce Poole's five-year-old restaurant facing Wandsworth Common is a relaxed place: somewhere to enjoy rather than worship the food, and very popular, which means it can get noisy. His modern Anglo-French food has wide appeal, from a spicy squid salad to roast rump of lamb with courgette fritter, and displays a degree of comfort in, for example, a smooth brandade of smoked haddock topped with pearly chunks of the undyed fish, 'a perfectly timed poached egg' and a swirl of hollandaise. Flavours, textures and timing have been notably good: in thick steaks of roast halibut 'cut from an enormous fish', served with a neat ball of noodles, in a garlic- and thyme-infused jus containing wild mushrooms.

The cheeseboard is recommended, along with a whole range of desserts: crème brûlée, lemon tart 'made with fine pastry', chocolate pudding with praline parfait, and tarte Tatin. Friendly and helpful staff are a bonus, and Bruce Poole flings down a challenge: 'Which other London restaurant offers what we do for £25?' He is similarly bullish about the cost of his wines. Some 225 quality bins are presented without pretension, simply split by colour then arranged in ascending order of price. While the consequent flitting about from grape to grape and top grower to grower may confuse some, it certainly helps those with a target figure in mind. The starting point is £11.95.

The nearest underground station is indicated at the end of London entries.

CHEF: Bruce Poole PROPRIETORS: Bruce Poole and Nigel Platts Martin OPEN: all week L 12 (12.30 Sat and Sun) to 2, Mon to Sat D 7 to 10.30 CLOSED: 1 week Christmas, bank hol Mons MEALS: Set L Mon to Sat £21.50, Set L Sun £23.50, Set D £25 SERVICE: 12.5% (optional), card slips closed CARDS: Amex, Delta, Diners, MasterCard, Switch, Visa DETAILS: 75 seats. Private parties: 80 main room, 18 private room. Children's helpings No young children at D. Wheelchair access (not WC). No music. Air-conditioned ➔ Clapham South, Balham

Chez Liline
map 12

101 Stroud Green Road, N4 3PX COOKING 4
TEL: (0171) 263 6550 FAX: (0171) 272 9719 COST £26–£50

The warm family feeling makes it hard to believe that the room seats as many as forty-six. Its simple décor is enlivened by tiling 'pictures', and a swordfish head juts out of the wall. The wide range of fish and shellfish is prepared in various styles, from classical French to the gallicised Indian of Mauritius. Assiette de crustaces consists of just three items: quite enough when they are ultra-fresh tiger prawns, tiny, tender squid with a fine dressing, and half a lobster. Dishes of the day might include accurately cooked scallops and asparagus in a cream sauce. Small, well-flavoured, tender French mussels and clams mauriciènne come in a broth with herbs, tomato and chilli, all discreetly used. Such cooking cannot be rushed, concluded an inspector, who was happy to accept that delays can happen at busy times. To finish, there might be refreshing mango sorbet garnished with kiwi fruit, physalis and raspberry coulis. Modestly priced wines, mostly French, cost from £10.25.

CHEFS: Mario Ho Wing Cheong and Pascal Doudrich PROPRIETOR: Mario Ho Wing Cheong OPEN: Mon to Sat 12.30 to 2, 6.30 to 10 CLOSED: bank hols MEALS: alc (main courses £9.50 to £17). Set L and D £12.75 (2 courses) SERVICE: not inc CARDS: Amex, Delta, MasterCard, Switch, Visa DETAILS: 46 seats. Private parties: 20 main room. Children's helpings. No cigars/pipes in dining room. Music ➔ Finsbury Park £5

Chezmax
map 13

168 Ifield Road, SW10 9AF NEW CHEF
TEL: (0171) 835 0874 FAX: (0171) 244 0620 COST £29–£53

As the Guide went to press, chef Zak El Hamdou left to cook at Stepping Stone (see entry, London), and a new chef was yet to be appointed.

PROPRIETORS: Graham Thomson and Steven Smith OPEN: Tue to Fri L 12 to 2.30, Tue to Sat D 7 to 11 CLOSED: Christmas, Aug, bank hols MEALS: Set L £14.50 (2 courses) to £17.50, Set D £23.50 (2 courses) to £27.50 SERVICE: 12.5% (optional), card slips closed CARDS: Amex, Delta, Diners, MasterCard, Switch, Visa DETAILS: 50 seats. Private parties: 16 main room. Children's helpings. No pipes/cigars in dining room. No music ➔ West Brompton

Chez Moi

map 12

1 Addison Avenue, W11 4QS	COOKING 5
TEL: (0171) 603 8267 FAX: (0171) 603 3898	COST £25–£56

'Another reliable meal,' summed up an off-duty inspector, confirming that, for some at least, the appeal of this long-distance runner (it opened its doors in 1967) on the edge of Holland Park remains undimmed. Whether attempts to bring itself up to date with chicken dhosa, a 'Japanese' interpretation of seared scallops, and Moroccan lamb tagine are successful is open to question, although a starter of 'oursins' appears to have triumphed: scampi, scallop and prawn are transformed into a porcupine-like shape by angel-hair pasta, then deep-fried and accompanied by spicy Italian mostarda di frutta. 'Sounds weird but it works well.'

Since 'the cooking is so good when it is simple and classic', it is probably wise to explore those parts of the repertoire first, taking in quail's eggs and smoked salmon in a pastry case, sole goujons with tartare sauce, or pan-fried venison with ginger rösti and red wine sauce. Pastrywork and ice creams (coffee with praline, for example) are singled out for praise, and cheeses are kept in good condition. A largely French and predominantly mainstream wine list nevertheless manages to find room for a robust Uruguayan red made from the Tannat grape, and puts up an Australian red and South African white house wine at £10.75.

CHEF: Richard Walton   PROPRIETORS: Colin Smith and Richard Walton   OPEN: Mon to Fri L 12.30 to 2, Mon to Sat D 7 to 11   CLOSED: bank hols   MEALS: alc (main courses £12.50 to £17). Set L £15   SERVICE: not inc   CARDS: Amex, Delta, Diners, MasterCard, Switch, Visa   DETAILS: 45 seats. Private parties: 16 main room. Vegetarian meals. Children's helpings. No young babies. No cigars/pipes in dining room. Wheelchair access (not WC). No music. Air-conditioned ⊖ Holland Park

Chez Nico at Ninety Park Lane

map 15

Grosvenor House, 90 Park Lane, W1A 3AA	COOKING 10
TEL: (0171) 409 1290 FAX: (0171) 355 4877	COST £44–£120

The setting fails to arouse much comment, beyond the fact that it is an expansive yet rather conservative hotel dining room (with no lounge or bar for pre-meal drinks) in which mirrors are perhaps the most noteworthy decorative feature. Nevertheless, what comes out of it is 'one of the best meals we've ever had' for one couple, 'flawless' for another. The food is not ground-breaking or inventive, rather it develops slowly over time. One of its strengths is that it can appear remarkably straightforward – asparagus risotto, grilled Dover sole with tartare sauce, lobster ravioli, braised knuckle of veal – and yet be unsurpassed.

Soothing textures (lamb you can cut with a fork) are also characteristic, pointing to a cuisine that does not aim to excite or challenge, but one that is meant to satisfy and reward. Among examples are a 'comforting' ballottine of quail – the boned bird stuffed with foie gras and a few other things, tasting gamey, earthy and rich – on a pile of lamb's lettuce, with a superior potato crisp on top, all in a 'dark and shimmering' sauce. Likewise veal sweetbread: rolled into a sausage shape, bound with pancetta then sliced, served with fresh morels tossed in cream, and a small pile of cabbage with the crunchy texture of bean sprouts.

Timing, freshness and quality can all be taken for granted, and the sense of picking just the right flavour combinations is helped by a penchant for tried-and-tested ideas: an evocative Mediterranean terrine of saffroned red mullet, for example, combined with dark-skinned aubergine and soft potato, all in a well-judged basil oil dressing. More impressively still, dishes are stripped to their essentials, so they have a clear focus and a sense that nothing could improve them, either by addition or subtraction. Such is the case particularly with desserts: lemon tart, thin apple tart, crème brûlée, and chocolate cake hardly sound as if they will set the pulse racing, but when the plates arrive they do.

There is a welcome restraint with incidentals: no waves of appetisers (apart from a taste of soup), and no pre-dessert. While there have been a few disappointments (always amplified by the prices), the overwhelming majority find it good value; the 'gastronomic menu' at £75 (per person for at least two) finding particular favour. Service, although less than sharp at inspection, generally manages the right mix of attention, knowledge, assistance and friendliness. Wines are high quality, but at prices that put many of them out of reach for ordinary drinkers. There are no house wines and (by the time service charge has been added) nothing under £20.

CHEFS: Nico Ladenis and Paul Rhodes   PROPRIETORS: Nico and Dinah Jane Ladenis   OPEN: Mon to Fri L 12 to 2, Mon to Sat D 7 to 11   CLOSED: 10 days Christmas, 4 days Easter, 2 weeks Aug   MEALS: Set L £25 (2 courses) to £65, Set D £53 (2 courses) to £75 (min 2)   SERVICE: 12.5% (optional), card slips closed   CARDS: Amex, Diners, MasterCard, Visa   DETAILS: 65 seats. Private parties: 80 main room, 20 private room. No children under 6. No pipes in dining room. No music. Air-conditioned   ⊖ Marble Arch

---

Chinon

map 12

| 23 Richmond Way, W14 0AS | COOKING 5 |
| TEL: (0171) 602 5968   FAX: (0171) 602 4082 | COST £39–£59 |

Chinon has a lot going for it. It may be 'odd,' 'strange', 'eccentric', but it looks inviting, there is a patio-garden view at the back, 'some of the décor is nice,' and close-together tables accommodate a mixed crowd who look very much at home. At inspection, moreover, the food was 'consistently good'. An ambitious carte weaves together French and oriental threads with fresh ingredients at the heart of things, showing to good effect in a long skewer of fat grilled prawns served with a mound of chillied couscous, and steamed sea bass with scallops, each in a gingery dressing.

Portions are 'enormous', but presentation is impressive, typically a centrepiece surrounded by 'little samples of tasty tit-bits': an artichoke, for example, has been fashioned to look like a mushroom – its heart the base, its stalk the stem, and its purple frill of leaves parked on top 'like an atom bomb exploding' – circled by peeled broad beans and lots of Parma ham. Likewise at dessert, a ramekin of pale pink, thin crusted crème brûlée, with a little fruit pulp worked into it, might be girdled with fresh summer berries. Service can be 'bossy'. Around thirty wines, roughly split between France, the rest of Europe and the

New World start with house red and white at £14. Note that not all the information below can be confirmed, since the restaurant has not returned the *Guide*'s questionnaire.

CHEF: Jonathon Hayes   PROPRIETORS: Barbara Deane and Jonathon Hayes   OPEN: Mon to Sat D only 7 to 10.45   MEALS: alc (main courses £12 to £18)   SERVICE: 12.5% (optional)   CARDS: Amex, Delta, MasterCard, Switch, Visa   DETAILS: 60 seats. 6 seats outside. Private parties: 30 main room, 30 private room. No children. Music. Air-conditioned   ⊖ Shepherd's Bush

Chiswick   map 12

131 Chiswick High Road, W4 2ED   COOKING 3
TEL: (0181) 994 6887   FAX: (0181) 994 5504   COST £20–£48

The outside of this friendly neighbourhood restaurant has been repainted to 'show a brighter face', although inside is much as before. Owner Adam Robinson is now in the kitchen, producing a menu that changes twice daily, which allows the inclusion of rarely available treats such as scrambled goose egg with salmon caviare, in an appetite-awakening Sunday brunch. His interpretation of modern British cooking avoids the usual Asian ingredients, but still allows some lively ideas, such as salsa verde with skate and mash, and lamb's sweetbread with pappardelle, broad beans, mustard and bacon. Sea trout is Welsh, asparagus English, and lobster native. Desserts might include hot raspberry zabaglione, or a refreshing combination of summer berries, Beaujolais soup, jelly and sorbet. Service is friendly, although not always as efficient as it might be. Wines on the fairly priced list offer a good spread of styles from around the world; house wines from France and Sardinia are £10.50. The Salt House (see entry) in St John's Wood is under the same ownership.

CHEF: Adam Robinson   PROPRIETORS: Adam and Kate Robinson   OPEN: Sun to Fri L 12.30 to 2.45 (12 to 3 Sun), Mon to Sat D 7 to 11   CLOSED: bank hols   MEALS: alc (main courses £6.50 to £14.50). Set L and D before 8pm £9.50 (2 courses) to £12.95   SERVICE: not inc, 12.5% for parties of 6 or more, not inc   CARDS: Amex, Delta, MasterCard, Switch, Visa   DETAILS: 75 seats. 10 seats outside. Private parties: 10 main room. Vegetarian meals. No-smoking area, no cigars/pipes in dining room. No music   ⊖ Turnham Green

---

indicates that there has been a change of chef since last year's Guide, *and the Editor has judged that the change is of sufficient interest to merit the reader's attention.*

The text of entries is based on unsolicited reports sent in by readers, backed up by inspections conducted anonymously. The factual details under the text are from questionnaires the Guide *sends to all restaurants that feature in the book.*

Prices quoted in the Guide *are based on information supplied by restaurateurs. The prices quoted at the top of each entry represent a range, from the lowest meal price to the highest; the latter is inflated by 20 per cent to take account of likely price rises during the year of the* Guide.

Chor Bizarre

map 15

16 Albemarle Street, W1X 3HA
TEL: (0171) 629 9802 and 8542
FAX: (0171) 493 7756
EMAIL: cblondon@aol.com

COOKING 1
COST £29–£69

A glorious hotchpotch of Indian artefacts and furniture greets customers to Chor Bizarre: named, like its New Delhi parent, after chor bazaar, the thieves' market. Choose a table (some are marble topped, some are of dark wood covered in silver; one even has a canopy over it), sit at a comfy chair and relish the display of carvings, mirrors, old weapons and what-not. Young, disconcertingly casual staff take the order. Food is not quite as spectacular, yet features a few dishes rare to Britain: bater ka achaar (pickled quail); tak-a-tak tawa (griddle-cooked mounds of mince, chicken liver and fish). There's also a choice of thali set meals, interesting vegetarian dishes (including cauliflower with cashew nuts), and achaar gosht (lamb with pickled spices), recommended for its 'sour, slightly chillied, slightly salty flavour'. The drinks list, chosen to match the food, includes several wines by the glass. House wines start at £13.75.

CHEF: Deepinder Singh Sondhi   PROPRIETOR: Mahendra Kaul   OPEN: all week 12 to 3, 6 to 11.30 (10.30 Sun)   CLOSED: 25 and 26 Dec, 1 Jan   MEALS: alc (main courses £12 to £17). Buffet L Mon to Fri £12.95 (2 courses), Set pre-theatre D £11 (2 courses) to £21   SERVICE: 12.5% (optional), card slips closed   CARDS: Amex, Delta, Diners, MasterCard, Switch, Visa   DETAILS: 50 seats. Private parties: 50 main room, 35 private room. Vegetarian meals. Children's helpings. Music. Air-conditioned   ● Green Park

Christopher's

map 15

18 Wellington Street, WC2E 7DD
TEL: (0171) 240 4222   FAX: (0171) 836 3506

COOKING 2
COST £27–£75

A sweeping stone staircase leads to the theatrical main dining room in this Victorian building near Covent Garden. Comfortable, with a lively atmosphere and lots of elbowroom, it is modelled on the steak and lobster houses of America's eastern seaboard, serving up crab cake with red pepper mayo, and pan-fried Louisiana oysters with rice cake and BBQ sauce. Tender ribeye steak comes with red cabbage and thin chips, burger is served without the traditional bun, and there are plenty of other options beyond the surf 'n' turf routine, including 'spicy and stimulating' smoked tomato soup, breast of corn-fed chicken with Parmesan mash and red wine glaze, and baked New York cheesecake. Service is easy-going, and the 50p cover charge is donated to charity. As well as classics from the Old World and some interesting ones from the New, the list offers over fifty wines by the glass. Bottle prices start at £12.

CHEF: Adrian Searing   PROPRIETOR: Christopher Gilmour   OPEN: all week L 12 to 2.45, Mon to Sat D 6 to 11.45   CLOSED: 25 and 26 Dec, 1 Jan, Good Fri, Easter Mon   MEALS: alc (main courses £11.50 to £22). Set D 6 to 7 and 10 to 11.45 £14.50 (2 courses) to £17.50. Cover 50p SERVICE: 12.5% (optional), card slips closed   CARDS: Amex, Delta, Diners, MasterCard, Switch, Visa   DETAILS: 160 seats. Children's helpings. No music. Air-conditioned   ● Covent Garden

Chutney Mary

map 12

535 King's Road, SW10 0SZ
TEL: (0171) 351 3113   FAX: (0171) 351 7694
EMAIL: 100540.1020@compuserve.com

COOKING 2
COST £38–£62

There is more space to eat now that most of the upstairs reception area has been converted into a second dining room. These are 'upmarket environs' with prices to match, where the cooking embraces three main principles. First, dishes are based on the food eaten in Indian homes, not restaurants. Second, they are regionally based and might include Goan crab cake, or Malabar chicken curry (with coconut milk) from Kerala. Third, spices are freshly stone-ground; results are mixed, but an inspector's gosht ki Nihari, a complex, balanced lamb curry from Lucknow, convinced with its 'bright and aromatic' spicing.

Dinner offers a four-course tasting menu as well as plates of starter selections that might include foie gras samosa, a 'subtly spiced' skewer of vegetables, and a light but earthy lentil dumpling (papri chat) with beaten yoghurt. Chutney Mary's chutneys vary, the best one at inspection (coriander and coconut) accompanying a light moong dumpling starter. Lovers of Indian sweets are advised to head for the rasmalai: scant in sugar but 'delicate and well balanced'. Multinational staff are generally (but not always) knowledgeable and courteous, and wines are grouped by style, the better to match the food. House French is £11.50.

CHEF: Hardev Singh Bhatty   PROPRIETORS: Namita Panjabi and Ranjit Mathrani   OPEN: all week 12.30 to 2.30 (3 Sun), 7 to 11.30 (10.30 Sun)   CLOSED: D 25 Dec   MEALS: alc (main courses £9.50 to £16). Set L Mon to Sat £12.50 (2 courses) to £15, Set L Sun £15, Set D 10 to 11.30 £12.50 (2 courses) to £15, Set D £31.50. Cover £1.50   SERVICE: 12.5% (optional), card slips closed   CARDS: Amex, Delta, Diners, MasterCard, Switch, Visa   DETAILS: 150 seats. Private parties: 50 main room, 32 private room. Vegetarian meals. Children's helpings. Wheelchair access (not WC). Music. Air-conditioned   ⊖ Fulham Broadway

Cicoria £

map 13

280 West End Lane, NW6 1LJ
TEL: (0171) 431 4188

COOKING 1
COST £21–£41

Appearing in last year's *Guide* as Billboard Café, this humble, airy, festive, contemporary Italian neighbourhood venue off the Finchley Road changed its name in January 1999 after a long-running dispute with the owners of America's *Billboard* magazine. A generous carte deals in salady starters, pasta with a choice of eight sauces, and grills of chicken, beef, lamb or fish. These are supplemented by a simple, short-choice set menu, and a few daily dishes from soups to baked cheesecake or fresh figs with fromage frais. Weekend brunch brings eggs (scrambled), eggs (fried) and more eggs (choice of omelette), along with filled baguettes and ciabatta. A handful each of Italian and New World wines share the honours on a mostly under-£20 list, starting with house Trebbiano and Sangiovese at £9.75.

Use the lists towards the front of the book to find suitable restaurants for special occasions.

CHEF: A. Piludu   PROPRIETORS: M.T. Nateghi and L. Smith   OPEN: Sat noon to 11.30, Sun noon to 10.30, Mon to Fri D 6.30 to 11 (11.30 Fri)   CLOSED: 25 and 26 Dec, 1 Jan, Easter Sun   MEALS: alc (main courses L £4.50 to £6.50, D £6.50 to £13.50). Set D £9.95 (2 courses) to £12.95   SERVICE: 10%, card slips closed   CARDS: Amex, Delta, MasterCard, Switch, Visa   DETAILS: 50 seats. 6 seats outside. Private parties: 60 main room. Vegetarian meals. Children's helpings. Wheelchair access (not WC). Music. Air-conditioned   ⊖ West Hampstead ⑤

Circus   map 15

1 Upper James Street, W1R 4BP	COOKING 4
TEL: (0171) 534 4000 FAX: (0171) 534 4010	COST £27–£64

A lively corner venue with a reception committee guarding the entrance, this large, expansively windowed room with black-tiled floor, white walls, taupe seating and subdued lighting struck an older visitor as 'stark, dim and noisy'. Soho may be for the young, but Richard Lee's brasserie-style menu has universal appeal, taking in crab raviolo with roast artichokes to start, and generally light main courses: brill with enoki mushrooms, leek and Parmesan tart, or rabbit with herb butter. 'Comfort food done well' is one assessment of the style, occasioned by a crisp smoked haddock risotto cake topped with spinach and a poached egg that 'Delia would have been proud of', all surrounded by runny hollandaise. Output is variable but, at its best, sound judgement is evident: in, for example, accurately timed, crisp-skinned cod on a bed of haricot and young broad beans. Baked Alsaka appears among desserts, alongside white chocolate torte with blueberries. Service could be more astute for its 12.5%, and the sharply chosen, family-grouped wines could be more sympathetically priced; house French is £14.50.

CHEF: Richard Lee   PROPRIETOR: Chris Bodker   OPEN: Mon to Sat 12 to 3, 6 to 12; bar Mon to Sat noon to 1.30am (3am Fri and Sat)   CLOSED: 24 Dec D, 25 to 28 Dec, 31 Dec L, 1 Jan   MEALS: alc (main courses £10.50 to £17.50). Set L and D before 7.30 and after 10.15 £14.75 (2 courses) to £16.75 (always available in bar)   SERVICE: 12.5% (optional), card slips closed   CARDS: Amex, Delta, Diners, MasterCard, Switch, Visa   DETAILS: 130 seats. Private parties: 12 main room, 16 private room. Vegetarian meals. Wheelchair access (not WC). No music. Air-conditioned   ⊖ Piccadilly Circus

City Rhodes   map 13

1 New Street Square, EC4A 3BF	COOKING 6
TEL: (0171) 583 1313 FAX: (0171) 353 1662	COST £43–£88

Tricky to find it may be, but this first-floor restaurant is a striking oasis amid the drab Holborn and City architecture. Gaze at photographs of the great showman in the entrance lobby, and climb the stairs to a dramatically modern blue dining room of light wood and metallic surfaces, where a generous and confident carte awaits. Despite a characteristic reworking of some traditional British ideas – perhaps 'boldly flavoured' duck and ham faggot on roast potato with creamy parsnip, or a deconstructed lemon meringue dessert (the highlight of an inspection meal) – the kitchen takes a more broadly European line with pressed tomato cake and peppered goats' cheese, or roast black-leg chicken with truffled cabbage.

It is not always easy to tell who does the cooking at Gary Rhodes's restaurants – he lists himself both here and at Rhodes in the Square (see entry, London) – but whoever it is impresses with fresh ingredients, spot-on timing and generally well-defined flavours: poached loin of lamb on a crunchy shallot and foie gras tartlet for example. Vegetables – including 'exemplary' buttered spinach and mashed potato – are charged extra. After sticky cranberry and walnut tart with vanilla ice cream, or baked egg custard with nutmeg ice cream, first-rate Jaffa cakes come with disappointing coffee. Service from formally dressed male staff is 'agreeable, upbeat, friendly and smilingly confident', while an 'eye-wateringly expensive' wine list (with only half a dozen bottles below £20) starts at £16.

CHEF: Gary Rhodes and Michael Bedford   PROPRIETOR: Gardner Merchant   OPEN: Mon to Fri 12 to 2.30, 6 to 9   CLOSED: bank hols   MEALS: alc (main courses £16 to £25.50)   SERVICE: 12.5% (optional), card slips closed   CARDS: Amex, Delta, Diners, MasterCard, Switch, Visa   DETAILS: 100 seats. Private parties: 12 main room, 12 private room. Vegetarian meals. Wheelchair access (also WC). Music. Air-conditioned   ● Chancery Lane, Blackfriars

▲ Claridge's
map 15

Brook Street, W1A 2JQ
TEL: (0171) 629 8860   FAX: (0171) 499 2210
EMAIL: info@claridges.co.uk

COOKING 6
COST £39–£106

The dining room at Claridge's is a listed example of art deco interior design, immaculately preserved and ready to weather the times ahead as the hotel enters its second century. Although the ratio of staff to customers is thrillingly large, there is surprisingly little of the front-of-house hauteur that such venerable shrines are often prey to. Unusually, also, various fixed-price menus turn out to be as imaginative as the carte. Seared foie gras with mango, ginger and a hazelnut tuile is from the gastronomic 'Menu Sonata', while red mullet with lemon couscous and sauce antiboise is available to those who come for the 'Dinner-Dance' option.

The kitchen obviously moves with the times, whether dealing with 'saddle' of monkfish wrapped in pancetta with sauce gribiche and gremolata, or guinea fowl, given the confit treatment for breast and leg, and served with girolles in a truffle bouillon. Simpler things are done well too: a starter salad of artichokes and asparagus one lunchtime for example. More artistry is lavished on desserts of bitter chocolate 'chalice' with praline cream, and caramelised apple mille-feuille with star anise ice cream. Petits fours are as good as they should be, and if that lottery windfall is burning a hole in your pocket you will be able to make a serious dent in it with the wine list. Non-vintage Moët & Chandon is £53 for a start. For those on a budget, house French is £18.50.

CHEF: John Williams   PROPRIETOR: Savoy Group   OPEN: all week 12.30 to 3, 7 to 11   MEALS: alc (main courses £16 to £39). Set L £29.50 to £38, Set D £39 to £58   SERVICE: net prices, card slips closed   CARDS: Amex, Delta, Diners, MasterCard, Switch, Visa   DETAILS: 100 seats. Private parties: 20 main room, 14 private room. Vegetarian meals. Children's helpings. Jacket and tie (exc Sat and Sun L). No-smoking area. Wheelchair access (also WC). Music Fri and Sat. Air-conditioned   ACCOMMODATION: 200 rooms, all with bath/shower. TV. Phone. Room only £265 to £320. Rooms for disabled   ● Bond Street

Clarke's 🍷 ✸

map 13

124 Kensington Church Street, W8 4BH
TEL: (0171) 221 9225   FAX: (0171) 229 4564

COOKING 6
COST £34–£56

Sally Clarke is one 'celebrity' chef who hardly bothers with the business of being famous, save to maintain the excellence of her restaurant's output. Over the course of a decade and a half she has stayed with her tried and tested formula: using impeccable ingredients to produce 'simple but perfectly executed dishes that hide the considerable skill required in delivery'. For most visitors, there is hardly any question of admiring the décor – a restrained combination of cream-coloured walls, white napery, plain glasses and fresh flowers – because the food is the draw.

At lunch, each course (with three or four options) is given a single price – £8, £14, and £7 respectively – while dinner, by contrast, is four courses with no choice. One of the kitchen's strengths is the equal concern it gives to both detail and the bigger picture: wild rocket 'of outstanding quality', for example, accompanies warm smoked eel and green olive crostini; and a deep-fried artichoke 'with no residual oiliness' partners organic Glenarm salmon with a chive and white wine sauce. Sound materials give dishes their impetus, whether a girolle mushroom tart, or a salad of crisp pancetta, marinated Wiltshire beetroot (both red and yellow varieties) and peashoots.

Desserts too garner high praise: Yorkshire rhubarb and blood orange trifle, or rum baba with poached quince and prunes. Given that wines hail only from California, France and Italy, choosing a bottle might seem a simple task, but the various possibilities are so enticing and of such good pedigree that it is actually quite difficult to decide which to plump for. Prices begin in France at £9.

CHEFS: Sally Clarke and Elizabeth Payne   PROPRIETOR: Sally Clarke   OPEN: Mon to Sat 12.30 to 2, 7 to 10   CLOSED: 10 days Christmas, Easter, 2 weeks Aug   MEALS: alc L (main courses £14), Set D £42   SERVICE: net prices, card slips closed   CARDS: Amex, Diners, MasterCard, Switch, Visa   DETAILS: 90 seats. Private parties: 14 main room. Vegetarian meals. No smoking in dining room. Wheelchair access (not WC). No music. Air-conditioned   ⊖ Notting Hill Gate

Club Gascon

NEW ENTRY map 13

57 West Smithfield, EC1A 9DS
TEL: (0171) 796 0600
FAX: (0171) 796 0601

COOKING 4
COST £40–£92

First, it is not a club. Sited between Smithfield Market and St Bartholomew's Hospital, it evokes an informal feel with marble-effect walls, wooden floorboards, a silvery ceiling and inexpensive fixtures and fittings; and with not a lot of spare space, its popularity ensures a permanent buzz. Portions are deliberately small: 'French tapas', as several have christened them. Some thirty savoury dishes are divided into sections covering charcuterie (first-rate saucisson sec and andouille), vegetables (pipérade with stewed beans), seafood (grilled scallops), duck (confit or cassoulet), the market (braised ox cheek in orange sauce) and at least nine ways with foie gras.

The food has genuine roots in south-west France (from where many of the high-class ingredients are sourced) yet is not boringly traditional. Results have been variable, but praise has been heaped on fine rillettes, chargrilled foie gras with grapes and sweet onion marmalade, and thick-cut chips cooked in duck fat. What saucing there is works well, timing is good, textures are carefully considered – two crisp filo pastry rolls enclosing smoked eel fillet with a frothy horseradish cream, for example – and there is an appealing simplicity to much of it, including, at inspection, a skewer of rare grilled duck hearts with dressed frizzy leaves. Sharp-eyed service is resolutely French ('friendly, helpful and efficient', one called it), although the telephone booking system has provoked a few niggles. Given so much foie gras, more sweet whites by the glass might be expected, but enthusiasm for regional wines (including Irouléguy) cannot be faulted. Prices start at £10.50.

CHEF: Pascal Aussignac   PROPRIETORS: Vincent Labeyrie and Pascal Aussignac   OPEN: Mon to Fri L 12 to 2, Mon to Sat D 7 to 10 (10.30 Sat)   CLOSED: 1 week after Christmas, bank hols   MEALS: alc (main courses £3 to £13.50). Set L and D £30   SERVICE: 12.5% (optional)   CARDS: Delta, MasterCard, Switch, Visa   DETAILS: 60 seats. Private parties: 60 main room. Vegetarian meals. Wheelchair access (not WC). Occasional music. Air-conditioned   ⊖ Barbican, St Paul's

Coast ♥

map 15

26B Albemarle Street, W1X 3FE   COOKING 4
TEL: (0171) 495 5999   FAX: (0171) 495 2999   COST £38–£72

Some dining rooms seem to be ageless: just as fashionable after five years (a long time in London restaurant circles) as when they opened. Coast, however, does not appear to be one of them. Beyond the big plate glass windows of the former Volvo showroom, goggle-eyed lights bulge out of a green background, while shiny brown tables and squirrelly ashtrays seem 'mannered rather than functional'. A typically '90s menu, meanwhile, deals in a familiar range of global flavours, from tuna carpaccio with roast beetroot and wasabi mayonnaise, to pan-fried cod with trevise and white bean salad.

A northern connection (Oliver Peyton also owns Mash & Air in Manchester; see entry) doubtless accounts for grilled Goosnargh chicken, and this is one of the rare cosmopolitan restaurants to use that undervalued country staple, lovage, in this case to make pesto for a spring vegetable broth. The range from relatively light (lobster sausage on minted pea purée) to more substantial (roast pork with nutmeg gnocchi) is echoed in desserts: citrus and champagne jellied terrine, or warm chocolate tartlet with coffee ice cream. At two choices per course the fixed price lunch doesn't give much away, but the carte is well endowed and weekend brunch is generous to a fault. Fine wines from France and Italy are balanced by impressive offerings from North America and Australasia on a list that still finds room for some drinkable bottles under £20. The house selection of fifteen wines by the large glass starts at £4.40.

CHEF: Adam Gray   PROPRIETOR: Oliver Peyton   OPEN: all week L 12 to 3 (3.30 Sat and Sun), Mon to Sat D 6 to 11.30   CLOSED: 25 and 26 Dec, 1 Jan, Easter Sun and Mon   MEALS: alc (main courses £13.50 to £22). Set L £19.50 (2 courses) to £25, Set D £35   SERVICE: 12.5% (optional), card slips closed   CARDS: Amex, Delta, Diners, MasterCard, Switch, Visa   DETAILS: 120 seats. Private parties: 15 main room, 30 private room. Vegetarian meals. Wheelchair access (not WC). Occasional music. Air-conditioned   ⊖ Green Park

The Collection

map 14

264 Brompton Road, SW3 2AS	COOKING 1
TEL: (0171) 225 1212 FAX: (0171) 225 1050	COST £31–£68

The 1999 edition of the *Guide* suggested that the converted warehouse on two levels, with its exposed brickwork, metal columns and designer-clad staff, is good for trendy twenty-somethings. We are informed by one couple this time that it is also fun for the over-sixties; they appreciated the 'delightful, attentive young staff' and were not in the least fazed by duck noodle spring roll with plum chilli sauce, nor by corn-fed chicken with chorizo, lentils and greens. Lunches and brunches are supplemented by an extensive evening menu that shows plenty of imagination, coming up with typically modern combinations of crab and mascarpone tartlet, or marinated lamb with sweet potato, red onion and pickled chillies. Vegetables are charged extra, and filling desserts include highly commended almond waffles with caramelised bananas and vanilla ice cream. A tempting cocktail list offers aperitif options, and a well-chosen set of international wines is arranged by style. Prices start at £11.95.

CHEF: Cass Titcombe   PROPRIETOR: Signature Restaurants Ltd (Belgo plc)   OPEN: all week 12 to 3 (4 Sat and Sun), 6.30 to 11.15 (10.30 Sun)   CLOSED: 3 days Christmas, 1 Jan   MEALS: alc (main courses £10.50 to £16). Bar food available   SERVICE: 15% (optional), card slips closed   CARDS: Amex, Delta, Diners, MasterCard, Switch, Visa   DETAILS: 150 seats. Private parties: 150 main room. Vegetarian meals. Children's helpings. Wheelchair access (also WC). Music. Air-conditioned   ⊖ South Kensington

Como Lario

map 14

22 Holbein Place, SW1W 8NL	COOKING 2
TEL: (0171) 730 9046 FAX: (0171) 244 8387	COST £26–£55

A tiled floor, Venetian blinds, young customers and 'masses of squeezed-in tables' keep the decibels up and the atmosphere animated at this smart northern Italian restaurant; motor-racing fanatics will find themselves especially welcome since the proprietor is one too. Lombardy cuisine, 'not overly rustic', is the preoccupation, producing starters of wind-dried boar with rocket salad, and charcoal-roasted ham and artichokes. 'It is very Italian in that it knows that some of the traditional elements are often the best cornerstones,' reckoned one visitor, a view borne out by the range of fairly conventional pasta dishes, chargrilled Dover sole, and a reliance on chicken and veal main courses, some of it cooked 'a piacere', or as you like it. The forty-strong wine list is equally Italian, lacking vintages. House Sicilian is £10.

CHEF: Giancarlo Moeri   PROPRIETOR: Guido Campigotto   OPEN: Mon to Sat 12.30 to 2.45, 6.30 to 11.30   CLOSED: Christmas, Easter, bank hols   MEALS: alc (main courses £8 to £18). Cover £1.25   SERVICE: not inc   CARDS: Amex, Delta, Diners, MasterCard, Switch, Visa   DETAILS: 80 seats. Private parties: 55 main room, 30 and 55 private rooms. Vegetarian meals. Children's helpings. No pipes. Wheelchair access (not WC). No music. Air-conditioned   ⊖ Sloane Square

The Guide*'s top-rated restaurants are listed near the front of the book.*

▲ The Connaught

map 15

16 Carlos Place, W1Y 6AL
TEL: (0171) 499 7070   FAX: (0171) 495 3262
EMAIL: info@the-connaught.co.uk

COOKING 6
COST £49–£163

In 2000 Michel Bourdin clocks up twenty-five years at this formal clubby address in the heart of Mayfair, although very little has changed in that time: it feels 'preserved rather than evolving'. For example, the 'workmanlike' turbot and lobster pâté with 'blush-making' sauce pudeur that was on the menu in Bourdin's first year (as recorded in the 1976 *Guide*) is still there, though it now costs £22. Hallowed portals still offer a 'stately welcome', the dining room still greets with a whiff of butane from chafing dish burners, and the wood panelling and crimson plush are as comforting as ever, 'as is the menu if you're not paying'.

This reads like *Larousse Gastronomique* come to life, with croustade d'oeufs de caille Maintenon, and trio de saucisses maison pomme purée 'Cadurcienne'. The range is enormous, from a starter of sherry-drenched summer fruits ('the sort of thing a dinner party hostess might have done twenty or thirty years ago') to a chartreuse of gamey partridge looking 'exactly like an Escoffier illustration', its inverted bowl shape immaculately decorated with haricots verts and carrot julienne in herringbone formation. This classic dish 'tasted as good as it looked': and who would go to all that trouble for a dinner party?

There are, of course, luxuries – 'unctuous', truffle-studded foie gras terrine, or fifty precious grammes of beluga caviare at £2.40 per gramme – as well as daily menus and the weekly round of lunch dishes: on Tuesday, for example, braised gammon carved from a big joint, served with peach sauce, caramelised onion and a pineapple ring. A trolley (one of many) delivers blanc mange, or 'nicely eggy' bread-and-butter pudding, and well-trained staff deliver 'smooth, non-intrusive' service. To offer no wine under £20 takes real effort nowadays, but the Connaught has succeeded admirably. House Graves and Chardonnay are £22.

CHEF: Michel Bourdin   PROPRIETOR: The Blackstone Group   OPEN: all week 12.30 to 2.30, 6 to 10.45   MEALS: alc (main courses £13.50 to £39.50). Set L £27.50, Set D £45   SERVICE: 15% CARDS: Amex, Delta, Diners, MasterCard, Switch, Visa   DETAILS: 100 seats. Private parties: 10 main room, 12 and 22 private rooms. Vegetarian meals. Children's helpings. Jacket and tie at D. Wheelchair access (also WC). No music. Air-conditioned   ACCOMMODATION: 90 rooms, all with bath/shower. TV. Phone. Room only £280 to £360. Rooms for disabled. Baby facilities (*The Which? Hotel Guide*)   ⊖ Bond Street, Green Park

Cookhouse

map 12

56 Lower Richmond Road, SW15 1JT
TEL: (0181) 785 2300

COOKING 3
COST £30–£39

Bright, friendly, open and informal, with the air of 'an up-market café', the Cookhouse delivers food that aspires to be 'better than a good cook would make at home', according to one visitor, and serves that purpose well to a predominantly young constituency. Menus are short, but the appeal lies in a combination of bright flavours – red mullet and fennel brochette with shallot and ginger dressing, or chargrilled squid with coriander and ginger pesto – and sensible use of less usual meats and cuts. These might include shin of pork, pot-roast rabbit, or lambs' sweetbreads, the latter providing one reporter with 'the sort of helping your grandmother would give you if you'd been away for a year'. Honesty and lack of pretence show themselves in straightforward yet gently innovative dishes from skate wing with paprika aïoli, to tea-smoked pigeon with lentils, while yet more grandmotherly input produces desserts such as lemon-curd tart with blackcurrant jam. This a BYO restaurant, and the token £2.50 corkage charge also covers bread and nibbles.

CHEF: Tim Jefferson   PROPRIETORS: Tim Jefferson and Amanda Griffiths   OPEN: Tue to Sat D only 7 to 11   CLOSED: Christmas   MEALS: alc (main courses £13 to £14). Cover £2.50, inc corkage   SERVICE: not inc   CARDS: Delta, MasterCard, Switch, Visa   DETAILS: 28 seats. Private parties: 30 main room. Children's helpings. No cigars/pipes. Wheelchair access (not WC). Occasional music. Air-conditioned   ⊖ Putney Bridge ⓔ5

Le Coq d'Argent ▼

NEW ENTRY   map 13

1 Poultry, EC2R 8EJ

COOKING 4

TEL: (0171) 395 5000   FAX: (0171) 395 5050

COST £34–£106

Take a lift up through the 'space-age building' in the heart of moneyland and emerge on the roof to the 'surreal' sight of a garden, with tables and chairs for fine-weather eating. Stroll around, admire the cityscape below, and walk through heavy glass doors into the curved and dark-wooded dining room. Sir Terence has done it again, design-wise: provided a smart venue for suits to lunch off a bar menu of caviare, shellfish mayonnaise, or fish and chips, or extend the choice with Francophile restaurant options of sole meunière, or rich coq au vin on a mound of buttery mashed potato. Soft-poached hen's egg in a tarragon-flavoured jelly was an early starter that doesn't appear to have stood the test of time, but classic leanings are echoed in a flavourful lobster bisque, 'beautifully timed' giant scallops with tomatoes, and a feuilleté of veal kidney and sweetbreads. Desserts adopt an equally reassuring stance with almond parfait, or poached apple with cinnamon and calvados ice cream. Service is polite, cheerful, willing and well paced. The wine list is a veritable treasure trove where France is concerned, with quite a few gems also sparkling among the Vins Etrangers. A few bottles can be discovered below the £20 mark, beginning with house vin de pays at £13.50.

CHEF: Stephen Goodlad   PROPRIETOR: Conran Holdings Ltd   OPEN: Sun to Fri L 11.30 to 2.30, Mon to Sat D 6 to 9.30   CLOSED: D 24 Dec, 25 to 28 Dec, 1 to 3 Jan   MEALS: alc (main courses £10.50 to £21). Set L Sun £17.50 (2 courses)   SERVICE: 12.5% (optional), card slips closed   CARDS: Amex, Diners, MasterCard, Switch, Visa   DETAILS: 146 seats. 50 seats outside. Private parties: 130 main room. Vegetarian meals. Wheelchair access (also WC). No music. Air-conditioned   ⊖ Bank

▲ *County Hall Restaurant*

map 13

County Hall, SE1 7PB

COOKING 4

TEL: (0171) 902 8000   FAX: (0171) 928 5300

COST £32–£71

It seems hard to get away from the fact that this was once the headquarters of the Greater London Council, but its conversion to a hotel, among other things, is generally well received. David Ali's menus reach far and wide for inspiration:

fillet of sea bream and cod brandade with pesto and sauce antiboise, for example, or braised pork en crépinette with polenta cake. Dishes can be colourful – a pale green pea and pine nut risotto scattered with Gorgonzola and surrounded by bright orange oil, for example – and flavour combinations are well handled, as one reporter found with a starter of cracked wheat flavoured with mint and apricots, topped with warm sardines and small salad leaves. Desserts, meanwhile, run to an unusual papillotte of aubergine and apple with Greek yoghurt, or crêpe suzette soufflé. Kitchen service can be slow, though front-of-house staff are 'excellent and very helpful'. Nearly a hundred wines are divided by style, varied in origin, and stay mostly under £30. Prices open at £13.95 for Chardonnay and Syrah from Dom. Chancel in Vaucluse.

CHEF: David Ali   PROPRIETOR: Whitbread plc   OPEN: all week noon to 11 (10.30 Sun)   MEALS: alc (main courses £9.50 to £19.50). Set L and D noon to 7 £12.50 (1 course) to £19.50, Set D 7 to 11 £19.50   SERVICE: not inc   CARDS: Amex, Delta, Diners, MasterCard, Switch, Visa   DETAILS: 100 seats. Private parties: 500 main room, 40 to 200 private rooms. Vegetarian meals. Children's helpings. Wheelchair access (also WC). Music. Air-conditioned   ACCOMMODATION: 200 rooms, all with bath/shower. TV. Phone. Prices on application. Rooms for disabled. Swimming pool (*The Which? Hotel Guide*)   ⊖ Westminster £5

Criterion Brasserie

map 15

224 Piccadilly, W1V 9LB   COOKING 5
TEL: (0171) 930 0488   FAX: (0171) 930 8380   COST £28–£55

Conjuring up the Ottoman Empire in the middle of Piccadilly, Criterion inhabits a rococo-style Grade II-listed building, its marbled walls studded with semi-precious stones, its gold mosaic ceiling stretching back an impressive 45 metres. Chefs may come and go – Darren Bunn started at the beginning of 1999, and Tim Payne, executive chef for the MPW group, was listed last year at Quo Vadis – but the cooking remains focused on the kind of modern brasserie dishes thrown up by Italian, French and British traditions. Expect clam chowder with shellfish ravioli, foie gras terrine, and wild mushroom tartlet with poached egg and hollandaise.

A generous carte (some thirty savoury items) delivers an appealing mix ranging from summery red mullet salad to wintery braised pork cheeks with ginger, and the cooking produces generally well-defined flavours. One visitor began with ballottine of salmon rolled in herbs, on a gently sharp fromage blanc, and finished with a mould of champagne jelly alongside raspberries, black-berries and blueberries, surrounded by a ring of passion fruit sauce. Reception is efficient rather than personal, and service is anxious to get going: 'within five minutes of ordering I was sitting in front of a glass of champagne, my glass of wine, my water and my first course'. Wines are pricey for the context, but start with house vin de pays at £13.

CHEFS: Tim Payne and Darren Bunn   PROPRIETORS: Jimmy Lahoud and Marco Pierre White   OPEN: Mon to Sat L 12 to 2.30, all week D 6 to 12 (10.30 Sun)   CLOSED: Christmas   MEALS: alc (main courses £13 to £16). Set L and D before 7pm £14.95 (2 courses) to £17.95   SERVICE: 12.5% (optional), card slips closed   CARDS: Amex, Delta, MasterCard, Switch, Visa   DETAILS: 180 seats. Private parties: 250 main room. Vegetarian meals. Wheelchair access (also WC). No music   ⊖ Piccadilly Circus

Crowthers
map 12

481 Upper Richmond Road West, SW14 7PU   COOKING 4
TEL/FAX: (0181) 876 6372   COST £28–£40

Here is a simple recipe for enjoyment. Take one small plum-coloured room, then pour a glass of sherry, or a Kir or Myr, to take with feta-stuffed spring roll nibbles. Then add a 'subtle, well-balanced' tart of red onion and asparagus, or scallops with spicy rice and a light curry sauce. Wait a little before cutting into a tender piece of lamb through a cumin and coriander crust, and add a few mouthfuls of 'pungent, gutsy' Puy lentil sauce and rösti. If lamb is not your thing, try duck breast with lime and ginger instead. From time to time dip into simple, well-cooked vegetables, and add sips of wine chosen from a short list which is geared to France (including house wines at £9.85) but with enough New World interest, and which succeeds in being thoroughly in tune with the food. Finish the whole with hazelnut vacherin, indulgent caramel ice cream, or dark chocolate almond torte with orange crème anglaise. Good coffee with chocolate truffles and shortbread would be an optional addition. Stir throughout with owners who care about detail, cook with assurance and run the place like clockwork.

CHEF: Philip Crowther   PROPRIETORS: Philip and Shirley Crowther   OPEN: Tue to Fri L 12 to 2, Tue to Sat D 7 to 10   CLOSED: 1 week Christmas, 2 weeks Aug   MEALS: Set L £16 (2 courses) to £18.50, Set D £18.75 (2 courses) to £23.75   SERVICE: not inc   CARDS: Delta, MasterCard, Switch, Visa   DETAILS: 32 seats. Private parties: 32 main room. Children's helpings. Wheelchair access (not WC). No music. Air-conditioned £5

Cucina
map 13

45A South End Road, NW3 2QB   COOKING 3
TEL: (0171) 435 7814   FAX: (0171) 435 7815   COST £27–£48

Cheerful, efficient staff, a big, bright yellow room decorated with vivid artworks, and an ambition to serve the denizens of South End Green with fashionable fusion cuisine are what characterise this local restaurant close to the Heath. The food is so exotic and inventive that it takes some dexterity to handle all the different cooking styles. These run from starters of hot-and-sour tiger prawn laksa with a coconut and lime gremolata, or black truffle potatoes with asparagus and Taleggio sauce, to main courses of chargrilled mahi mahi with Cajun-spiced sweetcorn and pepper 'succotash', or tandoori guinea fowl with cauliflower and caraway curry and grilled cheese naan. Given such busy food, some dishes may only be partially successful (as at inspection). 'Stick to the less whacky dishes,' advised one reporter, while another singled out main courses as the most successful. Desserts, meanwhile, have included pineapple hot cakes with rum and raisin ice cream, and a dense, truffley chocolate mousse. The wine list majors on bottles from the New World and prices are modest. Six house wines start at around £11.

London Round-ups listing additional restaurants that may be worth a visit can be found after the main London section.

CHEFS: Stephen Baker and Andrew Poole   PROPRIETORS: Vernon Mascarenhas, Stephen Baker and Andrew Poole   OPEN: all week L 12 to 2.30 (3 Sun), Mon to Sat D 7 to 10.30 (11 Fri and Sat) CLOSED: Christmas, Easter Sun, bank hol Mons   MEALS: alc exc Sun L (main courses £8.50 to £14.50). Set L Mon to Sat £10 (2 courses), Set L Sun £12.95 (2 courses) to £15.95, Set D £16.95   SERVICE: not inc   CARDS: Amex, Delta, MasterCard, Switch, Visa   DETAILS: 85 seats. Private parties: 30 main room. No cigars/pipes in dining room. Music. Air-conditioned ⊖ Belsize Park

Dakota ♀ map 13

127 Ledbury Road, W11 2AQ	COOKING 2
TEL: (0171) 792 9191 FAX: (0171) 792 9090	COST £30–£55

Dakota's corner site, large windows, deep blue banquettes and brown and orange walls make for a bright, open dining room, but any simplicity this might suggest in the food is soon dispelled. The aim is contemporary south-west American dining with a focus on vibrant flavours and unusual ingredients. A sister establishment to Montana, Idaho and Canyon (see entries, London and Richmond), it shares a similar style. Chillies appear with regularity but always with restraint: in a hot-sweet jam to accompany coriander-crusted lamb sweetbreads, for example, or adding a kick to jalapeño and spring onion bread. Results can be uneven, but among successes have been lightly spiced marinated kingfish, baked in banana leaves and accompanied by chipotle bean stew and plantain crisps. Pumpkin and pecan pie with butterscotch sauce gets good marks for its light filling, or there might be caramelised quince and sweet cheese chimichanga with stem ginger ice cream. Service is willing and pleasant. The wine list is arranged by style, and although the focus is on the USA it does not ignore the rest of the world. Prices kick off in France at £11.

CHEF: Daniel McDowell   PROPRIETOR: Montana plc   OPEN: all week 12 to 3.30, 7 to 11 (10.30 Sun)   CLOSED: 25 Dec   MEALS: alc (main courses £8.50 to £14.50). Set L Mon to Fri £11.95 (2 courses)   SERVICE: 12.5% (optional)   CARDS: Amex, Delta, MasterCard, Switch, Visa DETAILS: 70 seats. 30 seats outside. Private parties: 110 main room, 25 private room. Vegetarian meals. Children's helpings. Music. Air-conditioned   ⊖ Ladbroke Grove

Daphne £ map 13

83 Bayham Street, NW1 0AG	COOKING 1
TEL: (0171) 267 7322 FAX: (0171) 482 3964	COST £21–£37

The aim, apparently, is to transport you to Cyprus with the aid of, among other things, plenty of black and white photographs of this sun-drenched island on the walls. Closely packed tables make for a friendly atmosphere, reinforced by welcoming and enthusiastic staff. The usual array of starters, hot and cold, as well as main courses of moussaka, afelia and plenty of grills keep customers happy, but there is also much to be gained from the specialities, which range from cuttlefish, cooked in its own ink with white wine and olive oil, and served with feta cheese and spinach, to simple chargrilled sea bass. Reasonably priced bottles from Greece and Cyprus are the staples of the wine list, with around half a dozen from France. House French is £10.75 a litre.

CHEFS: Lambros Georgiou and Myltos Tsaroullas PROPRIETORS: Pani
Lymbouris OPEN: Mon to Sat 12 to 2.30, 6 to 11.30 CLOSED: 25 and 26 Dec,
alc (main courses £6.50 to £12.50). Set L £5.75 (2 courses) SERVICE: no
MasterCard, Switch, Visa DETAILS: 85 seats. 30 seats outside. Private parties:
Vegetarian meals. Children's helpings. Wheelchair access (also women's
⊖ Camden Town £5

Daphne's

map 14

112 Draycott Avenue, SW3 3AE

TEL: (0171) 589 4257 FAX: (0171) 581 2232

COOKING 4

COST £31–£77

With its polished flagstone floor and earth-coloured walls, this seems like a little piece of Italy transferred to Chelsea. On bright summer days the garden room roof rolls back, and large white parasols come out: just what the well-groomed customers appear to want, as they tuck into beef carpaccio with rocket and Parmesan, or marinated octopus with new potatoes. Lee Purcell sticks to the tried and tested Italian-influenced formula with undoubted success, according to a couple whose Sunday lunch started with strips of battered and deep-fried courgettes, followed by pink lamb, and roast salmon. Salads get their own section – artichoke, black olive and pecorino, perhaps, or Caesar with chicken – as do risotto and pasta: spaghetti with cherry tomatoes and basil, maybe, or linguine with clams. Roasts and grills move from simple swordfish with tomato and pistachio, to calf's liver with fennel gratin. Desserts have brought forth 'intense' chocolate mille-feuille, and a 'perfect combination' of pannacotta with stewed rhubarb. Staff are 'charming and not nearly as cool as reputed'. The wine list starts in Italy, moves on to France and ends up with a section on other countries, with only a sprinkling in each section below £20. Prices start at £13.

CHEF: Lee Purcell PROPRIETOR: Belgo plc OPEN: all week 12 to 2.45 (12.30 to 3.45 Sun), 7 to
11.15 (10.30 Sun) MEALS: alc (main courses £8.50 to £21.50) SERVICE: 15% (optional), card
slips closed CARDS: Amex, Delta, Diners, MasterCard, Switch, Visa DETAILS: 120 seats.
Private parties: 100 main room, 40 to 80 private rooms. Vegetarian meals. Children's helpings.
No music. Air-conditioned ⊖ South Kensington

Del Buongustaio 🍷

map 12

283 Putney Bridge Road, SW15 2PT

TEL: (0181) 780 9361

COOKING 2

COST £28–£45

Described by one happy customer as 'a restaurant for those who like their Italian food bold', Putney's popular osteria serves a complex and copious menu, with a dozen each first and main courses. Many of the traditional Italian meat dishes have been historically researched by Aurelio Spagnuolo, former chef and co-owner until early 1999, who is succeeded by his second chef. Dating from the Renaissance period, these dishes are not so much exciting as 'solid, wholesome and satisfying'. Calf's liver might be cooked with butter, sage and marsala, for instance, and served with figs gratiné with prosciutto, while boned guinea fowl has come stuffed with artichoke and speck and served with spinach. Smoothly textured ice creams make fine accompaniments to puddings of chocolate torta, or espresso pannacotta. The bipartite wine list offers a good range of styles and flavours from Italy and Australia, with many bottles costing less than £20. House wines start at £8.80.

CHEF: Gianni Saidù   PROPRIETOR: D. Patel   OPEN: Sun to Fri L 12.30 to 3 (3.30 Sun), all week D 6.30 to 11.30 (10.30 Sun)   CLOSED: Christmas and New Year   MEALS: alc (main courses £9 to £12). Set L £9.50 (2 courses), Set D £24.50. Cover 90p   SERVICE: not inc; 10% for groups   CARDS: Amex, Delta, MasterCard, Switch, Visa   DETAILS: 60 seats. Vegetarian meals. Children's helpings. No cigars/pipes in dining room. Wheelchair access (not WC). Music. Air-conditioned   ⊖ East Putney £5

Delfina Studio Café   map 13

50 Bermondsey Street, SE1 3UD
TEL: (0171) 357 0244   FAX: (0171) 357 0250   COOKING 4
EMAIL: book@delfina.org.uk   COST £28–£50

Acres of pale floorboards and white walls lead, eventually, into the exhibition space of this delightfully laid-back studio. The restaurant itself is light and airy, with paintings and metal-legged lime-coloured tables adding to the pleasant, 'relaxed but classy' atmosphere. Maria Elia's cooking draws inspiration from the Levant, much of the Orient and most of the Americas, producing dishes rich in flavour and strong in presentation. Sometimes they are downright inventive, as in aromatic venison with sour cherry shiitake tartlet and sherry infused vegetables. Typically they come in several parts, and spices crop up all over the place: in a starter of bok choy parcels of seared marinated tuna and gingered chilli crab, with Thai tabbouleh and a dipping sauce, and in a main course of roast monkfish with chilli, chickpeas, chorizo and baba ghanoush. Things calm down towards dessert, but only a bit, taking in quince and Amaretto tart with mascarpone, or lychees with lemon grass and ginger syrup and coconut ice cream. Service is relaxed, the atmosphere unpretentious but still classy. The wine list dips into all the right places, and prices stay mostly below £20. House wines, from Delfina's own Spanish vineyards, are £10.95.

CHEF: Maria Elia   PROPRIETORS: Digby Squires/Delfina Entrecanales   OPEN: Mon to Fri L only 12 to 3.30   CLOSED: 23 Dec to 2 Jan   MEALS: alc (main courses £10 to £16)   SERVICE: 12.5% (optional), card slips closed   CARDS: Amex, Delta, Diners, MasterCard, Switch, Visa   DETAILS: 70 seats. Private parties: 500 main room, 40 to 270 private rooms. Vegetarian meals. Children's helpings. Wheelchair access (also WC). No music   ⊖ London Bridge £5

La Dordogne   map 12

5 Devonshire Road, W4 2EU   COOKING 5
TEL: (0181) 747 1836   FAX: (0181) 762 7925   COST £27–£48

Just off Chiswick High Street is this homage to a part of south-west France that has always been held in great affection by the British. A double-fronted restaurant, with an optimistic little terrace of outside tables, it bears a Gallic stamp all the way through, from prints of châteaux, and smartly turned-out staff in monochrome attire, to bilingual menus on which, as ever, dishes tend to lose something in translation.

Richard Hondier arrived in June 1999 and on the evidence of an early inspection appears set to uphold the standards set here over the years, even to raise them. Salade gourmande delivers all one would expect to see in its native region: hot and cold smoked duck breast, thinly sliced French saucisse and a piece of foie gras on a heap of impeccably dressed leaves. Scallops are given a lightly toasted surface, sliced and fanned on a croûton topped with tomato concasse, in a featherlight ginger sauce. Other classic sauce accompaniments include saffron cream with turbot, and cassis with duck magret. Lobster and oysters in season remain a speciality. Desserts are equally French – a rich mousse au chocolat blanc with parfait glacé pistache and sauce à l'orange – as are the 'A1 condition' cheeses: Fourme d'Ambert, Livarot, Pont l'Evêque, Reblochon and an unpasteurised Brie. 'Impeccable' service is provided by 'smart young Frenchmen', and the reasonably priced wine list majors on guess where, offering a good choice of half-bottles and wines by the glass. House wines start at £9.50.

CHEF: Richard Hondier   PROPRIETOR: La Dordogne Ltd   OPEN: Mon to Fri L 12 to 2, all week D 7 to 10   CLOSED: 4 days at Easter, 5 days at Christmas, bank hols   MEALS: alc (main courses £9.50 to £12.50). Set L £18 (2 courses). Cover £1   SERVICE: 10%   CARDS: Amex, Delta, Diners, MasterCard, Switch, Visa   DETAILS: 80 seats. 20 seats outside. Private parties: 30 main room, 20 to 30 private rooms. Vegetarian meals. Occasional music   ⊖ Turnham Green (£5)

Eagle £   map 13

159 Farringdon Road, EC1R 3AL   COOKING 2
TEL: (0171) 837 1353   COST £18–£35

What was once a long Victorian bar at the back of this corner pub is now divided roughly in half, a kitchen majoring on chargrilled food to the right, a bar serving sensibly priced and sourced wines along with real ales and good bottled beers to the left. The experience, reporters find, is lively and fun, as long as you don't mind noise and crowds. Order drinks and food at the bar, pay, and grab one of the not-terribly-comfortable chairs scattered around the tables of varying height. The food is robust, gutsy even, the focus somewhere to the south of Spain. First courses are hardly necessary and the format encourages one-course dining: bruschetta piled with mozzarella, trevisse, punterella, pine nuts, mint, oregano and balsamico; Portuguese belly pork and beans casseroled with chorizo and pancetta; or grilled halibut steak with salsa romesco. If you are still hungry, there is Manchego cheese, or Portuguese custard tarts. Italian house wine is £9.50.

CHEF: Tom Norrington-Davies   PROPRIETOR: Michael Belben   OPEN: all week L 12.30 to 2.30 (3.30 Sat and Sun), Mon to Sat D 6.30 to 10.30   MEALS: alc (main courses £6 to £11)   SERVICE: not inc   CARDS: none   DETAILS: 60 seats. 24 seats outside. Children's helpings. Music   ⊖ Farringdon

L'Escargot 🗍   map 15

48 Greek Street, W1V 5LQ   COOKING 5
TEL: (0171) 439 7474   FAX: (0171) 437 0790   COST £30–£72

This old Soho address is awash with art, from Hockney and Matisse to Miró and Chagall, with a 'cool and relaxing' first-floor dining room devoted to Picasso: not just pictures but a showcase full of his large jugs. The cooking has a broadly

89

European focus, in the shape of duck magret accompanied by gratin dauphinoise, root vegetables and spring greens; or saddle of rabbit with boudin noir served with sautéed girolles and grain mustard beurre blanc. The chef knows what he is doing', commented an inspector who, despite some disappointing fish and enthusiastic salting, enjoyed a starter of pink, tender quail topped with foie gras, surrounded by morels and truffles in a first-rate winey sauce.

Presentation is good, and desserts confirm the kitchen's soundly based skills in a well-judged five-part assiette of chocolate, and prune and armagnac soufflé with scoops of prune ice cream. Although the rather expensive set-price meal consists of only three courses, it does include an appetiser and pre-dessert. The ground-floor dining room, meanwhile, offers a generous range of dishes from lamb's tongue salad to snail tart with poached egg, from Bresse pigeon to braised pork cheek. A grand selection of aristocratic wines favours those with bottomless pockets: there is precious little under £20, although house wine is £13.

CHEFS: Andrew Thompson and Brendan Fyldes PROPRIETOR: Jimmy Lahoud OPEN: Mon to Fri L 12.15 to 2.15, Mon to Sat D 6 to 11.30 CLOSED: 25 and 26 Dec, 1 Jan MEALS: ground floor alc (main courses £13 to £16). Ground floor Set L £14.95 (2 courses) to £17.95, Picasso Room Set L £27.50 to £42, ground floor Set D 6 to 7.30 £14.95 (2 courses) to £17.95, Picasso Room Set D £42 SERVICE: Ground floor 12.5%, Picasso Room 15% (optional), card slips closed CARDS: Amex, Delta, Diners, MasterCard, Switch, Visa DETAILS: 120 seats. Private parties: 20 main room, 26 and 60 private rooms. Vegetarian meals. No cigars/pipes in dining room. Wheelchair access to ground floor only (also men's WC). Occasional music. Air-conditioned ⊖ Leicester Square, Tottenham Court Road

L'Estaminet

map 15

14 Garrick Street, WC2E 9BJ
TEL: (0171) 379 1432 FAX: (0171) 379 1530

COOKING 1
COST £20–£52

In the heart of theatreland, this useful French eatery has been praised for its good-value pre-theatre meals, which offer the simplest combinations – soup, fish with frites, chicken stew, tarts and fruit salads – from a bourgeois repertoire at a fraction of the carte prices. Otherwise, the smart surroundings alert diners to a largely conservative culinary approach – French onion soup, perhaps, or snails provençale style – although it is 'not all rich cooking and heavy sauces'. Even though vegetarians are unlikely to find anything substantial on the menu, a goats' cheese omelette especially prepared for one was 'technically perfect'. Trolleys may defy modernity but exhibit a 'stupendous selection' of French cheeses on the one hand and, on the other, endless fruit tarts made with good, buttery pastry and eggy cream. Staff are genuinely welcoming, and the wine list shows restraint in its pricing, with French house wines at £9.90.

CHEF: Philippe Tamet PROPRIETOR: Christian Bellone OPEN: Mon to Sat 12 to 2.30, 5.45 to 11 CLOSED: 25 Dec, bank hols MEALS: alc (main courses £10 to £15.50). Set D 5.45 to 7.30 £10.99 (£14.50 Sat) SERVICE: 12.5%, card slips closed CARDS: Amex, Delta, MasterCard, Switch, Visa DETAILS: 60 seats. Private parties: 20 private room. No pipes in dining room. Wheelchair access (not WC). Music ⊖ Leicester Square, Covent Garden

The Good Food Guide *is a registered trade mark of Which? Ltd.*

Euphorium

map 13

203 Upper Street, N1 1RQ	COOKING 2
TEL: (0171) 704 6909 FAX: (0171) 704 6089	COST £30–£55

Stark, minimalist, and very designed, Euphorium is popular with locals who crowd in at weekends, buy bread from the bakery next door, and while away the hours over Sunday brunch. The restaurant menu has a distinctly 'café' feel to it, with some dishes – fish cakes, chicken Caesar salad, or scallops with spicy sausage and sesame dressing – coming in two sizes. The output has been judged 'simple, seasonal and well done' by those who have eaten grilled asparagus with Parmesan and truffle oil, crevettes in garlic butter, and aubergine 'cannelloni'. Chicken on creamy mash is also a 'winner'. Desserts might include fresh fruit pavlova, or bitter chocolate tart. Service is charming and welcoming, and the broad wine list largely stays below £25. House wines are £10.50.

CHEF: Peter Arrowsmith   PROPRIETOR: Marwan Badran   OPEN: Sun to Fri L 12 to 2.30 (3.30 Sun), Mon to Sat D 6 to 10.30   CLOSED: 10 days Christmas, 3 days Easter, bank hols   MEALS: alc (main courses £8 to £14.50)   SERVICE: 12.5% (optional), card slips closed   CARDS: Amex, Delta, MasterCard, Switch, Visa   DETAILS: 80 seats. 45 seats outside. Private parties: 80 main room, 40 private room. Vegetarian meals. Children's helpings. No cigars/pipes in dining room. Wheelchair access (not WC). Occasional music. Air-conditioned   ⊖ Highbury & Islington, Angel (£5)

Fifth Floor 🍾

map 14

Harvey Nichols, 109–125 Knightsbridge, SW1X 7RJ	COOKING 4
TEL: (0171) 235 5250 FAX: (0171) 823 2207	COST £36–£99

Once through the crowd thronging the bar, visitors are greeted by *faux-naif* Caribbean paintings in primary colours, smartly dressed tables, and ergonomically challenged chairs that seem designed specifically to deter custom. The inviting menu does the opposite. Some dishes are as straightforward as a plate of Iberian black pig ham, but many more are 'multifaceted': for example, a thick tortilla-like pancake containing a wealth of white crabmeat and a sliver of well-timed red mullet, all surrounded by a glossy, mahogany-coloured ribbon of hyper-reduced red wine sauce.

The food is usually arranged in stacks: pink Barbary duck breast slices, for instance, on a livid green underlay of spinach and foie gras purée, topped with stanchions of crunchy Jerusalem artichoke, whose bitterness helped offset the 'sweet as toffee' gelatinous sauce. It says something about the pace of change in London that this kind of food, so evocative of the 1990s, can now seem rather weighty and rich, but at its best the kitchen impresses with well-balanced dishes, such as the 'sour, appetising' flavours of a pair of fleshy, generously cured Bismarck herrings sitting on pickled beetroot, topped with quenelles of whipped cream and horseradish, around them a trail of shredded cooked egg.

Desserts come with a recommended wine by the glass: Quady's Elysium with a light, buttery, baked cherry sponge pudding, for example, and similar helpful advice may well prove welcome when it comes to selecting a bottle from the huge main list. Whether your preference is for old claret and Burgundy, or fruity wines in the modern style, and whatever the state of your bank balance, you will be spoiled for choice. Harvey Nichols' own-label French house wines start at

£12.50. Another restaurant, Foundation, serves up mostly Mediterranean dishes in the dramatic, cavernous basement.

CHEF: Henry Harris   PROPRIETOR: Harvey Nichols   OPEN: all week L 12 to 3 (3.30 Sat and Sun), Mon to Sat D 6.30 to 11.30   CLOSED: D 24 Dec, 25 and 26 Dec, D bank hol Mons   MEALS: alc (main courses £11 to £35). Set L £23.50   SERVICE: 12.5% (optional), card slips closed   CARDS: Amex, Delta, Diners, MasterCard, Switch, Visa   DETAILS: 120 seats. Private parties: 110 main room. Children's helpings. No pipes in dining room. Wheelchair access (also WC). No music. Air-conditioned   ⊖ Knightsbridge

Fina Estampa

map 13

150–152 Tooley Street, SE1 2TU   COOKING 4
TEL/FAX: (0171) 403 1342   COST £27–£49

Bianca Jones hails from Lima and first gained recognition for her Peruvian cooking at a café above a pub. Together with her English husband Richard (who manages front-of-house), she moved in 1994 to this homely space that's pleasantly cluttered with Peruvian ornaments. Welcoming, informative waiters will show you past the bar and grand piano to a seat. Potatoes are a prominent feature of Bianca's 'brilliant' home cooking, whether in the classic starter of papa à la huancaina (new potatoes covered in a tangy, cheesy sauce using mild yellow chillies) or the main course of carapulcra: potatoes dried Inca-style, in a spicy sauce, cooked with pork and chicken and served with fried cassava and parsley rice. Seafood and fish are also highlights: try the highly rated ceviche. There's a choice of more familiar options for dessert, including baked apple and toffee cheesecake. Asking for a 10 per cent cover charge in addition to stating 'service charge is not included' is one of Fina Estampa's few drawbacks. The wine list features several South American labels – Chilean house wine is £9 – but the pisco sour is reason in itself to visit: 'a perfect cocktail'.

CHEF: Bianca Jones   PROPRIETORS: Richard and Bianca Jones   OPEN: Mon to Sat 12 to 2.30, 6.30 to 10.30   MEALS: alc (main courses £8 to £15). Set L £9.50 (2 courses). Cover 10% SERVICE: not inc, card slips closed   CARDS: Amex, Delta, Diners, MasterCard, Switch, Visa DETAILS: 100 seats. Private parties: 60 main room, 20 to 50 private rooms. Vegetarian meals. Children's helpings. Music   ⊖ London Bridge

First Floor

map 13

186 Portobello Road, W11 1LA   COOKING 5
TEL: (0171) 243 0072   FAX: (0171) 221 9440   COST £35–£54

Above a pub on the famous market street, and under new ownership, First Floor is still busy serving modern British food in a setting aptly described by one correspondent as epitomising 'a sort of upmarket Gothic, Bohemian elegance'. The décor is certainly fussier than the food, with faux-ancient pillars, gilt-framed mirrors, outsized candles, statues, busts and 'languid' blue curtains lending atmosphere to the dining room. Adam Abbott's menu promotes favourite proteins within a framework of modern accompaniments – tender chump of lamb, for instance, with confit potatoes, minted jus and pea purée – and despite minor lapses there is no doubting the seriousness of the kitchen's efforts. Chocoholics should not miss the 'astonishing' chocolate plate for dessert, an

artistically presented collection, incorporating white chocolate mousse top.
with raisin ice cream, powerfully flavoured dark chocolate ice cream, and a disk
of dark chocolate with orange segments. Service has been described as
'consistently friendly, knowledgeable and attentive'. A short and reasonably
varied wine list should keep most drinkers happy, and mark-ups are not too
high, with house wines from £10.50.

CHEF: Adam Abbott   PROPRIETOR: Anthony Harris   OPEN: all week 12 to 3.30, 7.30 to 11 (11.15
Sat, 10 Sun)   CLOSED: 25, 26 and 31 Dec, during Notting Hill Carnival, bank hols   MEALS: alc
(main courses £10 to £15)   SERVICE: 12.5%, card slips closed   CARDS: Amex, Delta, Diners,
MasterCard, Switch, Visa   DETAILS: 54 seats. 20 seats outside. Private parties: 60 main room,
30 and 40 private rooms. Vegetarian meals. Music   ⊖ Ladbroke Grove

---

Fish!

| NEW ENTRY | map 13

Cathedral Street, SE1 9AL   COOKING 3
TEL: (0171) 836 3236   FAX: (0171) 379 9014   COST £26–£58

The idea is as simple as it is laudable: to source impeccably fresh fish, in
accordance with the UN Food and Agriculture Organisation's code of conduct for
responsible fisheries, to either steam or grill it, and serve it as plain as can be
with only minimal saucing and accompaniments. Such an up-to-date aim gets a
setting to match: a trendy, stylish conversion of a Victorian pavilion hard by
Southwark Cathedral. The 'greenhouse effect' from its glass sides and roof can
make it noisy when busy, as it tends to be when the Food Lovers' Borough
Market is in full swing, and its 'diner' design means condiment and cruet sets,
hand wipes, paper serviettes, and furniture that ensures you won't linger.

Ticks on the menu, which doubles as a placemat, indicate the selection
available – perhaps mullet, monk, lemon sole, sea bass, cod and organic salmon –
and if the sauce doesn't match the fish, that is your problem, since you choose
between salsa, hollandaise, herb butter, olive oil dressing, and red wine gravy.
Starters take the form of prawn cocktail, potted shrimps, first-rate dressed crab,
or a dish of mussels (perhaps with chilli, lemon grass and coconut milk), and
there is also fish cake, fish sausage, and fish and chips with mushy peas;
everything, indeed, except fish fingers. Naturally it stands or falls by freshness
and accuracy of timing, both of which have varied: at inspection, second-rate
halibut, decent tuna, and excellent black sea bream. Nobody seems to bother
with dessert, service is impressive, and wines are a short, unfussy selection with
nine by the glass. House Touraine is £9.90. A raw fish counter, with nationwide
delivery, is attached.

CHEF: Claire Rankin   PROPRIETOR: BGR plc   OPEN: Mon to Sat 11.30 to 3, 5.30 to 11
CLOSED: 25 Dec, bank hols   MEALS: alc (main courses £8 to £17)   SERVICE: 12.5% (optional),
card slips closed   CARDS: Amex, Delta, Diners, MasterCard, Switch, Visa   DETAILS: 100 seats.
50 seats outside. Children's helpings. No music. Air-conditioned   ⊖ London Bridge

---

*'The veg lady rushed up to offer me cauliflower, oily fried aubergine, and three kinds of
potato, including one type of mash to go with the mash that already came with my main
course.'* (On eating in Essex)

NEW ENTRY map 14

...e, SW3 1NQ   COOKING 5
1500 FAX: (0171) 584 1464   COST £37–£98

...xtravagant use of space, in an awfully expensive street, points to
...tion at this modern Italian newcomer. The front is a bar, and its smart
di... ..oom is done out in creams and browns, with grey stone sculptures, and a
glass ceiling to lighten the feel at lunchtime. Lunch is relatively affordable,
while the carte's prices are geared to the area, and a five-course Grand Menu
(taking in lobster salad with cold tomato soup and summer truffle risotto)
weighs in at £50.

Materials tend to be chosen from the posher end of the food chain: wild
salmon, for instance, and sea bass, either roasted with porcini and sea urchins, or
grilled with ratte potatoes. There are simple roasts and grills of tuna, poussin,
and veal chop, but the carte's imaginative ideas are well worth a look: prawns
with crispy pig's trotter, red mullet with veal marrow, or a pairing of pan-fried
scallops with steamed foie gras. This is not traditional Italian cooking, rather a
contemporary fusion incorporating a few foreign ingredients and techniques.

Meals might begin with a salad – of spring vegetables with cucumber sorbet,
or of asparagus with Parmesan, quail's egg and truffle – and end with
caramelised fruit skewers accompanied by lavender sorbet. The wine list covers
Italy before taking a look at the classic regions of France, then ends with a token
glance at the rest of the world. There is little under £20, although house
Chardonnay is £16, Cabernet £19.

CHEF: Fabio Trabocchi   PROPRIETORS: Riccardo Mazzucchelli and Sami Hawa   OPEN: Tue to
Sat L 12.30 to 3, Mon to Sat D 7 to 11   CLOSED: 24 Dec to 4 Jan, 15 to 31 Aug, bank hols
MEALS: alc (main courses £12.50 to £27). Set L £10 (1 course) to £19.50, Set D £50. Bar menu 12
to 11. Cover £2   SERVICE: 12.5% (optional), card slips closed   CARDS: Amex, Delta, Diners,
MasterCard, Switch, Visa   DETAILS: 98 seats. Private parties: 70 main room. Vegetarian meals.
Children's helpings. Music. Air-conditioned   ⊖ Knightsbridge (£5)

Four Seasons £   map 13

84 Queensway, W2 3RL   COOKING 2
TEL: (0171) 229 4320   COST £22–£57

Even early-evening bookings may mean queuing in the doorway for twenty
minutes or so, such is the popularity of this long-standing Chinese restaurant in
bustling Queensway. The basic décor evokes little admiration except perhaps
for mirrors that make the place look double its real size. It is food that matters
here. Popular roast meats are on show at the front of the room and also appear on
the menu's 130 numbered dishes. Hidden in that throng are such rare delicacies
as stewed duck with mandarin peel, and steamed chicken with Chinese
mushrooms and green vegetables. Another thirty-eight 'chef's special recommended' dishes include more rarities: stir-fried fillet of Dover sole in
scrambled egg, and steamed egg with dried scallop and diced prawn. For £20
you may explore the mysterious secret recipe for curried sea bass. Service once
again has come under fire for being brusque and rushed, and for the fact that
credit card slips are left open even though 12.5 per cent service is added to the
bill. House wines are £8.50.

CHEF: Norman Lo   PROPRIETOR: Bill Chin   OPEN: all week noon to 11.15   MEALS: alc (main courses £5 to £20). Set D £11 to £17 (min 2)   SERVICE: 12.5%   CARDS: Amex, Delta, MasterCard, Switch, Visa   DETAILS: 80 seats. Private parties: 100 main room. Vegetarian meals. Music   ⊖ Bayswater, Queensway

French House Dining Room   map 15

49 Dean Street, W1V 5HL   COOKING 4
TEL: (0171) 437 2477   FAX: (0171) 287 9109   COST £28–£46

Occupying a small first-floor room above a well-known Soho pub (named for its role as a meeting place for the free French during World War II), this has 'a slightly old-fashioned feel' thanks to wood panelling and bare floorboards. The daily-changing carte can accommodate casual snackers as well as serious diners and, like its sibling St John (see entry, London), it makes a virtue of some less usual ingredients: battered skate nobs with tartare sauce, for example, or grilled ox heart and chicory salad. The simple, down-to-earth approach – epitomised by braised duck with carrots, or roast lamb with barley – extends to vegetarian items such as buckwheat pancake with beetroot and mint, and homely desserts of rhubarb custard tart or lemon curd ice cream. Some three dozen mostly French wines start with vin de table at £10.

CHEF: Margot Henderson   PROPRIETORS: Melanie Arnold and Margot Henderson   OPEN: Mon to Sat 12 to 3.15, 6 to 11.15   CLOSED: 25 Dec to 1 Jan, bank hols   MEALS: alc (main courses £8.50 to £16)   SERVICE: not inc   CARDS: Amex, Delta, Diners, MasterCard, Switch, Visa   DETAILS: 30 seats. Private parties: 30 main room. Vegetarian meals. Children's helpings. No music   ⊖ Leicester Square

Frith Street Restaurant   NEW ENTRY   map 15

63–64 Frith Street, W1V 5TA   COOKING 6
TEL: (0171) 734 4545   FAX: (0171) 287 8624   COST £33–£57

Claudio Pulze and Stephen Terry caused quite a stir when they opened this joint venture in October 1998. Six months later Terry left, and Jason Atherton (formerly head chef at Manchester's Mash and Air, see entry) took over. His tenure, however, is likely to be short-lived too, since he is scheduled to move to Vinum when it opens (part of Vinopolis, the grand new museum of wine on Bankside) during the currency of the *Guide*. In the meantime, however, there are treats in store from a confident kitchen. The food is 'contemporary without being too fashionable', its clearly focused Mediterranean perspective evident in a salad of red mullet escabèche with tapénade, and potato and goats'-cheese gnocchi with basil and roast tomato.

Among highlights have been a dish so 'sensational' that an inspector, who could barely believe it the first time, returned a few days later to make sure it was still as good. Although in essence no more than a piece of fish on a spring vegetable broth, it displayed deft cooking of sparkling fresh, crisp-skinned sea bream, the broth enlivened with a spoonful of well-judged pistou. Standards have wobbled a little, but at its best the kitchen's simple approach and light touch has produced a salad of leaves and asparagus with a sweet-and-sour dressing of honey and lemon (including zest) that 'evoked the freshness and colours of summer'.

Value is considered good, whether on the lunch and early evening menu (two choices per course) or at dinner (eight choices), and service is helpful and efficient. A wide-ranging, high-quality wine list is not greedily priced. House French Chardonnay and Pinot Noir are £13 and £14, and eight wines are available by the glass.

CHEF: Jason Atherton   PROPRIETOR: Cuisine's Collection   OPEN: Mon to Fri L 12 to 2.45, Mon to Sat D 6 to 11   CLOSED: 25 Dec, 1 Jan, bank hols   MEALS: Set L and D before 7pm £15 (2 courses) to £19.50, Set D £19.50 (2 courses) to £23.50   SERVICE: 12.5% (optional), card slips closed   CARDS: Amex, Delta, Diners, MasterCard, Switch, Visa   DETAILS: 60 seats. Occasional music. Air-conditioned   ⊖ Tottenham Court Road

Fung Shing 🍴

map 15

15 Lisle Street, WC2H 7BE

COOKING 4

TEL: (0171) 437 1539   FAX: (0171) 734 0284

COST £29–£63

Light wood panelling, canary yellow walls and aquamarine tablecloths bring elegance beyond Chinatown norms. 'Chef's specials' on the Cantonese menu are praised as really special. In an inspector's stewed duck with yam in hotpot, the richness of the bird happily contrasted with the sweetness of yam, and extra savour came from a bed of coriander. Simple roasted crispy pigeon with dips of rough salt and dark vinegar has also been approved, while a small crab with ginger and spring onion was wonderfully sweet and fresh despite being slightly overcooked. Stuffed squid with seafood, and ostrich with yellow bean sauce, or ginger and spring onion, remain in the short list of chef recommendations (as distinct from his specials) and fearless menu explorers may do better than those treading familiar paths. Service is adequate. Accurate vintages and producers' names inspire confidence in the wide-ranging list of fifty wines; French house wine is £12.

CHEF: Mr Chung   PROPRIETOR: Forum Restaurant Ltd   OPEN: all week 12 to 11.15   CLOSED: 24 to 26 Dec, L bank hols   MEALS: alc (main courses £7.50 to £26). Set L £16, Set D £16 to £30   SERVICE: 10%, card slips closed   CARDS: Amex, Delta, Diners, MasterCard, Switch, Visa   DETAILS: 120 seats. Private parties: 50 main room, 25 and 50 private rooms. Vegetarian meals. Music. Air-conditioned   ⊖ Leicester Square

Gaudí

NEW ENTRY   map 13

63 Clerkenwell Road, EC1M 5PT

COOKING 3

TEL: (0171) 608 3220   FAX: (0171) 250 1046

COST £23–£56

Gaudí pays homage to Barcelona's great architect in more than name: its décor is also enjoyably gaudy, with groups of towering church candles adding atmosphere and light to that from back-lit brass salamanders on the yellow brick walls. There are also coloured tiles inspired by Gaudí mosaics. Opening hours are not authentically Spanish but the food mostly is (with some French influences). Appetisers, such as a version of sausage roll made with chorizo in filo pastry, get things off to a good start, and the pace is maintained through 'very moreish' halved baby artichokes tossed with smoked ham and dressed with truffle oil, perhaps followed by 'tender, velvety' baby squid stuffed with spinach and pine nuts and served swimming in their ink, which is flavoured with orange. Andalusian-influenced meat dishes include subtle rabbit confit, and guinea fowl with almond and saffron sauce. To finish, poached pear comes with delicate Rioja and cinnamon ice-cream. The compact, all-Spanish wine list offers a mix of distinguished bottles and bright new styles, at prices that are not unreasonable; house wines are £11.50.

CHEF: Nacho Martinez   PROPRIETOR: John Newman   OPEN: Mon to Fri 12 to 2.30, 7 to 10.30   MEALS: alc (main courses £12.50 to £16). Set L £12.50 (2 courses) to £15   SERVICE: 12.5% (optional), card slips closed   CARDS: Amex, Delta, Diners, MasterCard, Switch, Visa   DETAILS: 100 seats. 4 seats outside. Private parties: 150 main room, 50 private room. Vegetarian meals. Children's helpings. Wheelchair access (not WC). No music. Air-conditioned   ⊖ Farringdon

Le Gavroche ♟

43 Upper Brook Street, W1Y 1PF
TEL: (0171) 408 0881 and 499 1826
FAX: (0171) 491 4387

map 15

COOKING 7
COST £42–£142

Those taking a millennial opportunity to reflect on our culinary history may note that Le Gavroche, which opened in 1967, introduced top-class gastronomy to the UK. Its alumni (including Marco Pierre White, Pierre Koffmann, Gordon Ramsay and Rowley Leigh) point to the wider debt we owe the Roux brothers. The restaurant itself is an institution – ask any American with an expense account – that has triumphed over the low ceiling, dark green walls, and less-than-comfortable banquette seating of its 'austere' basement dining room, where large displays of flowers afford the only relief from a male-dominated clubby feel. A couple of dishes remain from Albert Roux's time, notably soufflé suissesse, but son Michel, while loyal to classic French cooking, has simplified and updated the food, producing, for example, hot foie gras with a crispy pancake of cinnamon-flavoured duck, and sweetbread rissoles with a sweet-and-sour jus.

Prices can reach as high as £30 for a starter of smooth lobster mousseline, served with caviare and a champagne sauce, a tag that reflects expensive raw materials rather than convincing with its flavour. Indeed, while technique and flavours are generally good, their combinations tend not to arouse much in the way of passion. It is 'ordinary' food, albeit at a high level of execution: a generous helping of fresh langoustines in a creamy gingery bouillon, or saddle of rabbit on a potato galette with a Parmesan crisp. The best course at inspection was dessert, which included that old Gavroche favourite, omelette Rothschild, a fluffy pan-fried omelette soufflé of apricot and Cointreau ('it is difficult to make this any better'), and the assiette du chef which, for £24, delivers a 'perfect' rum baba with a slice of fresh pineapple, chocolate fondant, toffee ice cream, and sablé of raspberries that 'takes the world of biscuits to another dimension'. This 'sheer artistry' outshines everything else.

Staff cope well with limitations imposed by large serving trays in a confined space, and the set three-course lunch (which includes a half-bottle of wine) remains a jewel in the crown. If it's French and famed for its high quality, chances are it will be on the massive wine list, usually in several different vintages, which may be one reason why bottles attracting four-figure price tags

97

outnumber those under £20 by a ratio of five to one. The knowledgeable sommeliers, however are far from condescending when it comes to dispensing helpful advice.

CHEF: Michel Roux   PROPRIETOR: Le Gavroche Ltd   OPEN: Mon to Fri 12 to 2, 7 to 11   CLOSED: Christmas to New Year, bank hols   MEALS: alc (main courses £28 to £37). Set L £37 (inc wine) to £78, Set D £78   SERVICE: 12.5% (optional), card slips closed   CARDS: Amex, Delta, Diners, MasterCard, Switch, Visa   DETAILS: 60 seats. Private parties: 80 main room, 20 private room. Jacket and tie. No cigars/pipes in dining room. Occasional music. Air-conditioned   ⊖ Marble Arch

Gay Hussar

map 15

2 Greek Street, W1V 6NB
TEL: (0171) 437 0973   FAX: (0171) 437 4631

COOKING 1
COST £28–£51

Opened in 1952, the Gay Hussar has 'old-timer' written all over it, from the dark wood-panelled walls and shelves of books (with a biography of Denis Healey at one end, von Ribbentrop at the other), to its loyal customers, to the unchanging Magyar food. Expect slices of brawn (pressed boar's head) with horseradish and a spicy chutney, and white fish terrine to start, followed by duck livers with onions and paprika, or wiener schnitzel. Standards may be variable, but a regular recommends chilled wild cherry soup, minced veal with Savoy cabbage and caraway seeds, and cream cheese pancakes. The 'sheer calorific might' of large portions means that desserts are less commonly reported on, and wine prices may seem high for the quality. House Hungarian is £10.50.

CHEF: Laszlo Holecz   PROPRIETOR: The Restaurant Partnership   OPEN: Mon to Sat 12.15 to 2.30, 5.30 to 10.45   CLOSED: Christmas, Easter, bank hols   MEALS: alc (main courses £11.50 to £16). Set L £15 (2 courses) to £18   SERVICE: 12.5% (optional), card slips closed   CARDS: Amex, Delta, Diners, MasterCard, Switch, Visa   DETAILS: 70 seats. Private parties: 40 main room, 12 and 22 private rooms. Vegetarian meals. Children's helpings. Wheelchair access (not WC). No music. Air-conditioned   ⊖ Tottenham Court Road   £5

Globe

map 13

100 Avenue Road, NW3 3HF
TEL: (0171) 722 7200   FAX: (0171) 722 7227
EMAIL: globerella@aol.com

COOKING 3
COST £24–£41

Decorated in Swedish colours of blue and yellow, but with enough glass to generate a Mediterranean glare, Globe feels a 'good-hearted' place to eat: the weekday lunchtime deal is worth noting, including as it does a glass of house wine, mineral water, and tea or coffee. Otherwise, one or two weekly specials – Thai beef salad, and seared scallops on a salt cod fish cake – join the already roving carte of spicy corn chowder, chargrilled squid and chorizo, and beef fillet with bubble and squeak. Salsas tend to feature – perhaps a bright tomato and olive version beside seared swordfish and warm potato salad – and portions are generous, although desserts such as dark chocolate brownie with maple syrup ice cream are ready and waiting for those with the appetite. Service is attentive and speedy, and wines are mostly under £20, with house Chardonnay and Barbera from nothern Italy at £9.95.

CHEF: Terry Williamson   PROPRIETOR: Neil Armisan   OPEN: Mon to Fri L 12 to 2.30, Mon to Sat D 6 to 11, Sun 11.30 to 3, 7 to 10   MEALS: alc Sun brunch and all week D (main courses £11 to £13.50). Set L Mon to Fri £12.50 (2 courses) to £14.50   SERVICE: not inc, 12.5% for parties of 6 or more   CARDS: Amex, Delta, MasterCard, Switch, Visa   DETAILS: 80 seats. Private parties: 80 main room, 20 private room. Vegetarian meals. Children's helpings. No cigars/pipes in dining room. Wheelchair access (not WC). Music. Air-conditioned   ⊖ Swiss Cottage

The Globe   `NEW ENTRY`   map 13

Shakespeare's Globe, New Globe Walk, SE1 9DR
TEL: (0171) 928 9444   FAX: (0171) 902 1574   COOKING 1
EMAIL: globe@milburn.co.uk   COST £30–£47

Views over the river to St Paul's are enjoyed from every table in this airy, white-walled space, where useful pre- and post-theatre dining is provided, as well as meals for bankside strollers in between; in season there are three full sittings, which may account for the hectic pace of service. A menu mercifully free of Shakespearean allusions might offer artichoke hearts with minted cracked wheat, or bream with grilled endive and anchovy butter. For such an operation, advance preparation is sensible – perhaps a starter of chicken and asparagus terrine with a 'frothy, creamy' lemon and chervil dressing – while main courses favour quick cooking methods, as in briefly seared scallops with crunchy stir-fried leeks. A wobbly tower of passion fruit jelly with toasted coconut, or blackcurrant brûlée tart, might be contenders for dessert. A limited but adequate wine list starts at £11.50, but there are plenty of soft drinks if you want to keep your head clear for the Elizabethan dialogue.

CHEF: Eddie Grimes   PROPRIETOR: Millburns Restaurants Ltd   OPEN: all week 12 to 2.30, 5.30 (6 Oct to Apr) to 10.30   CLOSED: Sun D Oct to Apr, 24 and 25 Dec   MEALS: alc (main courses £11 to £16.50). Set L and D May to Sept £16 (2 courses) to £20   SERVICE: not inc   CARDS: Amex, Delta, Diners, MasterCard, Switch, Visa   DETAILS: 90 seats. Private parties: 90 main room, 75 to 500 private rooms. Vegetarian meals. Wheelchair access (also WC). Music   ⊖ London Bridge/Mansion House

Golden Dragon   map 15

28–29 Gerrard Street, W1V 7LP   COOKING 2
TEL: (0171) 734 1073/2763   FAX: (0171) 734 1073   COST £17–£48

This bright, bustling Chinese restaurant in the heart of Soho's Chinatown offers a long, long carte, plus, for those bewildered by choice, a number of set meals (minimum two to five people), as well as a wide-ranging selection of dim sum that pulls in the lunchtime crowds. Besides familiar Cantonese offerings of won ton soup, roast duck, sweet-and-sour pork, stir-fried beef with black bean sauce and so on, there are some interesting dishes for authenticists: perhaps hotpot-cooked sea slug with duck web. Also on the carte is crab prepared in four styles, lobster in six, not forgetting steamed, stewed or baked eel. The menu has its oddities: 'Peking set meal' is anything but, including as it does aromatic crispy duck, spicy prawns and crispy shredded beef with chilli (all from Szechuan), plus satay chicken and Singapore noodles. However, the 'special banquet' for five or more offers an unchallenging but varied assortment for £20 per person. Service has veered from competent to muddled. The respectable, fully detailed wine list has house wines at £8.50.

CHEF: Y.C. Man   PROPRIETOR: Evernell Ltd   OPEN: Mon to Sat 12 to 11.45 (12 Fri and Sat), Sun 11 to 11   CLOSED: 25 Dec   MEALS: alc (main courses £6 to £20). Set L and D £10.50 to £20 (all min 2)   SERVICE: 10%   CARDS: Amex, Delta, Diners, MasterCard, Switch, Visa   DETAILS: 250 seats. Private parties: 350 main room, 15 and 40 private rooms. Vegetarian meals. Wheelchair access (not WC). Music. Air-conditioned   ⊖ Leicester Square

Gordon Ramsay ♟   [NEW ENTRY] map 14

68 Royal Hospital Road, SW3 4HP   COOKING 9
TEL: (0171) 352 4441 FAX: (0171) 352 3334   COST £39–£102

Absent from last year's *Guide* after he left Aubergine (as we went to press), Gordon Ramsay is now established in the premises vacated by Pierre Koffmann, who has relocated La Tante Claire to the Berkeley Hotel (see entry). The space, as before, consists of a long entrance corridor and small drinks area, but the square room now feels a mite sharper, with a penchant for glass in various forms: frosted, mirrored, sculpted into ornaments and placed in alcoves. 'If there is a better restaurant in the British Isles (for lunch) please will you let me know,' pleaded one visitor, while another concluded that 'without doubt, Ramsay's cooking is the most exciting in London', attributing his edge to a well-documented 'hunger to be the best'.

The best is exactly what this kitchen can turn out on a good day: for example a 'startling' dish of diced raw scallop assembled into a cylindrical block (lined with caviare, resting on cucumber) and served cold so that it melts like ice cream on the tongue, and yet remains 'fat and juicy, sweet and buttery', the whole bathed in a chilled basil consommé. Such 'fanatical attention to detail and tremendous flair' is also applied to stalwarts of foie gras – crisp outside, wobbly and melting within, relying on braised endive for a balancing bitterness – and to plump, pink Bresse pigeon with a delicate texture yet 'intense farmyard flavour'. Fish, meanwhile, has produced incomparably fresh sea bass, its skin scored like pork crackling, served with langoustine beignets in a coating of the lightest batter.

Pasta is well rendered, typically thin, evenly rolled and shaped, perhaps into five ravioli filled with white crab meat, the absence of brown meat compensated for by a shellfishy bisque freshened up with lemon grass. This bright and clasically simple style works particularly well with seafood. By contrast, slow-cooked dishes (not known for being picturesque) sometimes have to be squeezed into the demanding restaurant format: for example a deconstructed shin of beef reassembled into a cylinder, its multi-stage handling requiring a slice of foie gras to restore some character. In this stellar context, some dishes may appear 'ordinary' by comparison, while others are not as consistent as they might be: pistachio soufflé, for example, has ranged from 'wooden' to one that was 'executed as perfectly as you could hope for'.

Cheerful, highly trained and attentive French staff are ably overseen by Jean-Claude Breton, although the restaurant's claim that there is no time limit on tables does not accord with reality. Head sommelier Thierry Berson 'always manages to direct us to exceptional bottles', of which there are many on the Francophile list, and they carry the sorts of price tags that such fine wines inevitably command. House wines change regularly, but as the *Guide* went to press they were from Bergerac and cost £15.

CHEF/PROPRIETOR: Gordon Ramsay   OPEN: Mon to Fri 12 to 2.30, 6.45 to 10.45   CLOSED: bank hols   MEALS: Set L £28, Set D £50   SERVICE: not inc   CARDS: Amex, Delta, Diners, MasterCard, Switch, Visa   DETAILS: 40 seats. No music. Air-conditioned   ⊖ Sloane Square

Gourmet Garden £ map 12

59 Watford Way, NW4 3AX   COOKING 1
TEL: (0181) 202 9639   FAX: (0181) 203 5229   COST £17–£51

A fairly basic décor doesn't deter a mixed crowd from coming to this bustling restaurant. Thailand, represented by tom yum soups, has joined Malaysia, Singapore and several Chinese regions on the main menu. Ayam percik (baked chicken), nonya chicken curry and sambal king prawns are among delicacies from the 'Malaysian and Singaporean Food Corner', and many more are listed in the fifty 'chef's recommendations'. The highly flavoured shrimp relish, balachaung, enlivens crab, Dover sole and various vegetables. Another tiny fish, ikan bilis, Malaysia's crisp retort to the anchovy, appears with braised aubergine and minced chicken in claypot. A separate vegetarian menu offers many beancurd dishes, a good assortment of 'garden vegetables', and meatless versions of spring rolls, won tons and goose lettuce wraps. And lest we forget, the standard Chinese menu is there too. House wine is £7.50.

CHEF: Kia Lian Tan   PROPRIETORS: Annie and Kia Lian Tan   OPEN: Wed to Mon 12 to 2.15 (2.45 Sun), 6 to 11.15 (10.45 Sun)   CLOSED: 25 and 26 Dec, 2 weeks from end July to mid-Aug   MEALS: alc (main courses £4 to £16). Set L and D £10.80 to £14.80   SERVICE: not inc   CARDS: Amex, Delta, Diners, MasterCard, Switch, Visa   DETAILS: 70 seats. Private parties: 70 main room. Vegetarian meals. Children's helpings. Music. Air-conditioned   ⊖ Hendon Central

Granita map 13

127 Upper Street, N1 1QP   COOKING 4
TEL: (0171) 226 3222   FAX: (0171) 226 4833   COST £23–£43

One large plate-glass window, one long, thin room, each wall painted a vivid and different colour, the floor pale wood, and tables wooden too: Islington doesn't get more minimalist than this. A pot of beurre échiré sits on each table, and customers are welcomed with 'good designer bread'. Atmosphere is provided by welcoming and informal staff, and usually a full house. Ahmed Kharshoum's menus show a distinctly Mediterranean feel, as opposed to an overtly Italian theme. While grilled English asparagus is served with Taleggio, tomato and toast, rump of beef comes with oregano, nutmeg, cumin, patatas ala pobre, and spring peas. Chargrilling is a favourite cooking medium, producing pink chump of lamb with mujadarrah, yoghurt, cucumber and rocket, or rare tuna with chickpeas, carrots, tomatoes and potatoes. Salads are consistently interesting: cos with feta, black beans and cumin vinaigrette, or red oak lettuce with Manchego, grapes and crunchy garlic chips. Desserts have included orange and cardamom ice cream with Middle Eastern fruit salad, semifreddo tasting 'like a Christmas pudding ice cream', and almond, lemon and orange cake with

vanilla ice cream. The wine list is concise, global and well priced, opening at
£10.50.

CHEF: Ahmed Kharshoum   PROPRIETORS: Vikki Leffman and Ahmed Kharshoum   OPEN: Wed
to Sun L 12.30 to 2.30 (3 Sun), Tue to Sun D 6.30 to 10.30 (10 Sun)   CLOSED: 12 days Christmas,
5 days Easter, 2 weeks Aug   MEALS: alc D (main courses £9.50 to £13). Set L Wed to Sat £11.95
(2 courses) to £13.95, Set L Sun £12.50 (2 courses) to £14.50   SERVICE: not inc   CARDS:
MasterCard, Switch, Visa   DETAILS: 72 seats. Private parties: 65 main room. Vegetarian meals.
Children's helpings. No small children after 8pm. No cigars/pipes in dining room. Wheelchair
access (not WC). No music. Air-conditioned   ⊖ Angel, Highbury & Islington

Grano
NEW ENTRY map 12

162 Thames Road, W4 3QS
TEL/FAX: (0181) 995 0120

COOKING 4
COST £30–£64

Grano occupies a corner site near the Thames, although it has no view of the
water. Brick walls and wooden floors lend a bistroesque character, while
starched white linen tablecloths and good cutlery suggest something rather
more. Dishes can be elaborate but are firmly rooted in Italian peasant cooking;
colours are bright, and flavours are robust and fresh. Starters major on fish and
vegetarian dishes, with perhaps a meat offering in the form of guinea fowl
ravioli, well balanced by cream of potatoes and truffle oil; other pasta successes
have included calamari tortelloni with a 'rich and subtle' ragoût of scallops and
asparagus. Waxy potatoes have also featured in a supporting role: in a salad with
warm langoustines and a wild rice cake, and (in a special of the day) topped with
turbot fillets and sautéed baby globe artichokes in a fruity olive oil dressing, a
dish that was 'simple, fresh, vibrant and packed with flavour'. Desserts run to
rich marsala mousse with chocolate meringue, and pear mousse and strawberry
coulis. Service is efficient and professional, and the entirely Italian (except for
champagne) wine list features some serious bottles; house Chardonnay and
Montepulciano are £12.50.

CHEFS: Alessio Brusadin and Roberto Neri   PROPRIETORS: Mauro Santoliquido and Maurizio
Remerici   OPEN: Tue to Fri and Sun L 12 to 2.30, Mon to Sat D 7 to 10.30   CLOSED: 23 Dec to 4
Jan, last week Aug, bank hols   MEALS: alc D (main courses £14.50 to £20). Set L £15 (2 courses)
to £24, Set D £35   SERVICE: 12.5%, card slips closed   CARDS: Amex, Delta, Diners,
MasterCard, Switch, Visa   DETAILS: 55 seats. Private parties: 30 main room, 30 private room.
Children's helpings. Wheelchair access (not WC). Music   ⊖ Gunnersbury £5

Great Eastern Dining Room
NEW ENTRY map 13

54–56 Great Eastern Street, EC2A 3QR
TEL: (0171) 613 4545   FAX: (0171) 613 4137

COOKING 4
COST £25–£43

A black exterior, black Venetian blinds and a discreet sign in neon red suggest a
studied attempt not to be noticed. Inside, City suits gather at the large bar,
replaced as the evening wears on by less formally clad locals. The dining room,
somewhat smaller in size, is part of the same space even though it has a separate
entrance; dark wooden panelling and subtle lighting contribute to a relaxed,
informal, stylish atmosphere. The menu is essentially Italian, both in format and
content: antipasti, primi, secondi, contorni and dolci. It may not look wildly
exciting on paper, reckoned one visitor, but 'it's all in the execution'. Beef

carpaccio with rocket and Parmesan, for example, comes with a potent lime vinaigrette, and 'perfectly' seared tuna is accompanied by a well-balanced salad of roasted mixed peppers and red onion in chilli oil. Chilli might also be used to liven up seafood casserole with white beans and garlic – 'a wonderfully honest, wholesome dish' containing clams, mussels, chunks of squid and sea bream – while balsamic vinegar is made into a jus to accompany calf's liver with wilted spinach. Contorni – in the shape of rocket salad, or olive oil mash –are 'very pleasant'. Desserts maintain the Italian theme, and the fine sense of judgement, with grilled plums with Amaretto mascarpone, and a more globally influenced iced white chocolate mousse with raspberry compote. A reasonably priced wine list has its heart in Italy, though it takes something of a wander around the rest of the world too. Six house wines are £9.50 to £14, and are available by the large and small glass.

CHEF: John Coxon   PROPRIETOR: Will Ricker   OPEN: Mon to Fri L 12.30 to 3, Mon to Sat D 6.30 to 10.45   CLOSED: Christmas, bank hols   MEALS: alc (main courses £7.50 to £10)   SERVICE: 12.5% (optional), card slips closed   CARDS: Amex, Delta, Diners, MasterCard, Switch, Visa DETAILS: 72 seats. Private parties: 100 main room. Vegetarian meals. Wheelchair access (not WC). No music   ⊖ Old Street

Greenhouse 🍴   map 15

27A Hays Mews, W1X 7RJ   COOKING 5
TEL: (0171) 499 3331   FAX: (0171) 499 5368   COST £31–£70

The Greenhouse is set back from the street, its canopied entrance rather incongruous in the locale. 'Little of the décor seems to have changed for years,' mused an inspector, casting an eye over the large ceiling fans and still-life prints of flowers, fruit and vegetables. The menu, too, retains its English-with-attitude theme: chicken consommé, rillettes of salmon with caviare, or Cornish crab with a 'fresh sea taste' in tomato vinaigrette. A few luxury ingredients are perhaps to be expected – foie gras in the parfait, champagne in the sauce for poached halibut – but success does not depend on them. Reporters have enjoyed, for example, corn-fed breast of chicken with baby leeks and wild mushroom risotto, and accurately timed pan-fried cod in a herb crust surrounded by a glazed sabayon. Desserts have included poached Yorkshire rhubarb ('strongly cinnamon-flavoured') with vanilla ice cream and roasted coconut, and light bread-and-butter pudding with apricot compote. Service is professional if a little impersonal. The short wine list is good on half-bottles; a fine-wine list is available on request. Own-label house wines are £12.

CHEF: Jeff Galvin   PROPRIETORS: David and Margaret Levin   OPEN: Sun to Fri L 12 to 2.30 (12.30 to 3 Sun), all week D 6.30 to 11 (10 Sun)   CLOSED: 25 and 26 Dec, 1 Jan, bank hols MEALS: alc (main courses £14.50 to £22.50). Set L £14.50 (2 courses) to £19.50. Cover £1 SERVICE: not inc; 12.5% for parties of 10 or more   CARDS: Amex, Delta, Diners, MasterCard, Switch, Visa   DETAILS: 90 seats. Private parties: 10 main room. Children's helpings. No pipes in dining room. Wheelchair access (not WC). No music. Air-conditioned   ⊖ Green Park

Report forms are at the back of the book; write a letter if you prefer; or email us at guidereports@which.co.uk.

Green Olive

map 13

5 Warwick Place, W9 2PX
TEL: (0171) 289 2469   FAX: (0171) 289 4178

COOKING 2
COST £27–£51

Wooden floors and orange or brick walls give a 'country' feel to this Italian sibling of the Purple Sage, Red Pepper and White Onion (see entries, all London). There are no frills, and space is at a premium, but a seasonally changing set-price menu of two to four courses (vegetables are charged extra) is supplemented by a blackboard of daily dishes that generally include pasta, risotto, fish, and anything else of interest that Stefano Savio has been able to lay his hands on. Bottarga, boar prosciutto, and cheeses are among speciality items that travel a long way to get here: boar's head has even appeared as dish of the day. Otherwise there might be calf's liver, ravioli filled with beetroot and Taleggio, or braised leg of rabbit, followed by conventional desserts of warm chocolate brownie or citrus cheesecake. Service is brisk but agreeable, and the place is considered good value for money, although the balance of wine prices is tilted significantly over £20. House Italian is £12.50.

CHEF: Stefano Savio   PROPRIETOR: Bijan Behzadi   OPEN: Sat and Sun L 12.30 to 2.30, all week D 7 to 10.45 (10.30 Sun)   CLOSED: Christmas, Easter, bank hols   MEALS: alc L (main courses £7.50 to £12.50). Set D £20.50 (2 courses) to £26.50   SERVICE: not inc   CARDS: Amex, Delta, MasterCard, Switch, Visa   DETAILS: 52 seats. Private parties: 15 main room. Vegetarian meals. Children's helpings. No cigars. Wheelchair access (not WC). Music. Air-conditioned ⊖ Warwick Avenue

Gresslin's

map 13

13 Heath Street, NW3 6TP
TEL: (0171) 794 8386   FAX: (0171) 433 3282

COOKING 5
COST £21–£52

A cheerful colour scheme of pumpkin and pale yellow sets the tone for Michael Gresslin's bright and breezy approach to food in his clean-lined Hampstead restaurant. The dining room may be narrow, but his style certainly isn't. East meets West in most of London's fashionable restaurants nowadays, but rarely are the encounters so successful and unexpected as here. Mr Gresslin has a knack for balancing flavours that really resonate. These might include sauté lambs' kidneys on couscous salad with teriyaki sauce, or duck confit with chilli and lime marmalade glaze, roasted cassava and Puy lentils.

Despite the kaleidoscopic menu, cooking techniques are unfussy, allowing the flavours their due. Occasionally the boldness backfires, but mostly the results are pleasing: a risotto of sweet potatoes, trompettes-de-mort and truffle oil at inspection was a 'commendable combination of delicate flavours', while calf's liver with caramelised apples, potatoes and sage jus was judged 'top notch'. Puddings are infused with the same spirit of adventure: curried chocolate fritters with caramelised bananas, honey and pecan nuts have been 'surprising, stunning', the zingy curry flavour neatly emphasising the chocolate. Service is friendly and willing, although it may sometimes buckle under pressure. The short wine list features some big-flavoured bottles to match the food, with house wine at £10.50.

CHEF: Michael Gresslin   PROPRIETORS: Mr and Mrs Michael Gresslin, and Sir Harold and Mr Gervase Hood   OPEN: Tue to Sun L 12.30 to 2.30, Mon to Sat D 7 to 10.30   CLOSED: bank hols, exc 25 Dec   MEALS: alc (main courses £8.50 to £13.50). Set L Tue to Sat £8.95 (2 courses) to £11.95, Set L Sun £14.95 (2 courses) to £17.95, Set D Mon to Thur £14.95 (2 courses) to £17.95   SERVICE: 12.5% (optional), card slips closed   CARDS: MasterCard, Switch, Visa DETAILS: 56 seats. Private parties: 18 main room, 18 private room. Vegetarian meals. Children's helpings. No-smoking area. Music. Air-conditioned   ⊖ Hampstead

▲ Halkin Hotel
map 14

5 Halkin Street, SW1X 7DJ
TEL: (0171) 333 1234   FAX: (0171) 333 1100   COOKING 4
EMAIL: res@halkin.co.uk   COST £40–£92

Milan springs to mind as you click or shuffle your way across the restaurant's acres of marble, the lack of view made up for with copious mirrors, light relief coming from the odd vase of white flowers: it's all very chic, a feeling reinforced by Armani-clad waiting staff. The menu covers a good range of appealing-sounding dishes, and luxury ingredients are liberally mingled with more interesting ones. Alongside scrambled eggs with black truffle, there may be hare terrine, or sole served with a sauce of bottarga and orange. Unusual combinations have included a dish of lobster tail and pink pigeon breast served with intensely flavoured pea raviolis, although the hoped-for 'amazing fusion of flavours' failed to materialise. Cheeses, however, are kept in cracking condition, served with figs, grapes and toasted breads. Ambitious desserts have included panettone soufflé, and a warm mango tart in an elaborate spun sugar cage with nutty ice cream. Prices continue to elicit complaints from reporters, although there is value to be had from the set lunch and menu degustazione. The wine list naturally majors on Italy with some older vintages, although prices here are high too. Italian house wines are £17.50 (£3.50 per glass).

CHEF: Stefano Cavallini   PROPRIETOR: Como Holdings   OPEN: Mon to Fri L 12.30 to 2.30, all week D 7.30 to 11 (7 to 10 Sun)   CLOSED: 25 and 26 Dec, some bank hols   MEALS: alc (main courses £23 to £28). Set L £25, Set D (menu degustazione) £55   SERVICE: 10% (optional), card slips closed   CARDS: Amex, Delta, Diners, MasterCard, Switch, Visa   DETAILS: 50 seats. Private parties: 50 main room, 30 private room. Vegetarian meals. No cigars/pipes in dining room. Wheelchair access (also WC). Music. Air-conditioned   ACCOMMODATION: 41 rooms, all with bath/shower. TV. Phone. Room only £255 to £525. Rooms for disabled. Baby facilities (The Which? Hotel Guide)   ⊖ Hyde Park Corner

Helter Skelter
map 12

50 Atlantic Road, SW9 8JN   COOKING 2
TEL/FAX: (0171) 274 8600   COST £23–£45

Bare plaster and plain wooden flooring maintain a relaxed air in this informal neighbourhood restaurant opposite Brixton Market. 'Colourful and appealing' modern international cooking is delivered by young, smart staff with 'particular charm'. Specials are chalked on a blackboard, which supplements the main menu. Invention is everywhere, from a ricotta, spinach and Gorgonzola tart served with herb salad and red pepper ketchup, to brochette of venison with spinach, polenta, liquorice jus and parsnip chips. Sometimes it seems as if several dishes are combined into one, for example artichoke heart stuffed with tabbouleh, served with small crisp falafel and spicy harissa yogurt. In this context, crispy Thai fish cakes with a racy salsa of mango, lime and coriander, seem mainstream. Desserts are slightly calmer but still come with a twist, as in lime sorbet with a shot of Tequila, or strawberry tarte Tatin with thyme garnished with vanilla ice cream. The wine list makes much of the New World without forgetting the Old. Four house wines are £9.50 or £12.

CHEFS: John Swerdlow and Martin Hart   PROPRIETORS: John and Natasha Swerdlow   OPEN: Sun 12.30 to 10.30, Mon to Sat D 7 to 11 (11.30 Fri and Sat)   MEALS: alc (main courses £9.50 to £13). Set Sun L and D £14.80   SERVICE: 10% (optional)   CARDS: Amex, Delta, MasterCard, Switch, Visa   DETAILS: 60 seats. Private parties: 20 main room. Vegetarian meals. Wheelchair access (not WC). Music   ⊖ Brixton   £5

Hilaire ♥

map 14

68 Old Brompton Road, SW7 3LQ   COOKING 7
TEL: (0171) 584 8993   FAX: (0171) 581 2949   COST £37–£63

Redecorated since the last edition of the *Guide*, but in almost exactly the same style, with yellow clapboard walls and shoehorned tables, it is clear that Hilaire thrives on continuity, which is just how the regulars like it. There is no hiding the fact that reporters are divided in their assessment of the cooking, but the appeal for a supporter is 'Bryan Webb's flair and imagination, enterprising combinations of ingredients, and intended collisions of flavours and textures'.

The long, ambitious, attractive menus are adjusted daily around the produce available, but since Bryan Webb has an established network of suppliers, built up over a dozen years, it should not be surprising if the same materials, and thus dishes, recur. He does observe the seasons, however, to the extent of serving prime cuts of lamb from April to November, and offering grouse, partridge and pheasant in succession between August and January. Fish is a strength, producing 'terrific' sea bass and 'a great piece' of turbot at one meal, both distinguished by their ultra-freshness, and 'difficult to beat for simple excellence'. The same might be said of first-course salads of dressed crab, or 'light and tasty' smoked eel. Offal is also treated well, perhaps calf's kidney with a pile of spinach topped with crunchy rösti, or sauté foie gras on a potato pancake.

Perhaps because of the generous portions, most reporters seem to go without dessert, but options have included cappuccino crème brûlée, chocolate cheese-cake, and almond and apricot tart. Service is friendly and efficient, and 'Sue Webb makes a first-class hostess'. Wines are a worldly bunch, arranged helpfully by style, and if some are unfamiliar, the server's advice has proved reliable: an inspector was grateful for the recommendation of Prince Albert Pinot Noir 1996 from Geelong, Australia. House wines start at £14 and keep under £20.

Several sharp operators have tried to extort money from restaurateurs on the promise of an entry in a guidebook that has never appeared. The Good Food Guide *makes no charge for inclusion.*

CHEF/PROPRIETOR: Bryan Webb OPEN: Mon to Fri L 12.15 to 2.30, Mon to Sat D 6.30 to 11.30 CLOSED: 10 days Christmas, 2 weeks Aug, bank hols MEALS: Set L £18.50 (2 courses) to £23.50, Set D 6.30 to 7.30 and 10 to 11.30 £18.50 (2 courses) to £25.25, Set D £30 to £33 SERVICE: 12.5% (optional), card slips closed CARDS: Amex, Delta, Diners, MasterCard, Switch, Visa DETAILS: 50 seats. Private parties: 40 main room, 20 private room. Children's helpings. No cigars/pipes in dining room. Wheelchair access (not WC). No music. Air-conditioned ⊖ South Kensington (£5)

Ibla
map 15

89 Marylebone High Street, W1M 3DE
TEL: (0171) 224 3799 FAX: (0171) 486 1370

COOKING 4
COST £30–£49

Charming all-Italian staff add to the relaxed atmosphere of this former high-street shop, done out in strong shiny green at the front and a dark and equally shiny red in the room at the back. Food arrives from the basement and is served from a portable trestle. Maurizio Morelli demonstrates a sureness of touch by delivering well-balanced food that often shows a sense of adventure: 'ravishingly light' white onion tartlet with pumpkin sauce, for example, 'fresh-tasting' salmon galantine with aubergine sauce, or first-rate monkfish and sweetbreads in balsamic jus: and those are just for starters. Mains draw equal praise, particularly 'light and delicate' turkey roulade with bacon and sautéed potato, and duck breast with a citrus and stock-based sauce. Desserts run from the unusual – sweet aubergine, fried then coated with chocolate and served with orange sauce ('very tasty and better than I expected') – to a more standard light and tangy cold lime soufflé. Despite its charm, service for one was 'inattentive', and wines on the mostly Italian 100-plus-bottle list edge towards the pricey end of the scale: only seven are under £20. Reds start at £16, whites £14.

CHEF: Maurizio Morelli PROPRIETOR: Aimpoint Ltd OPEN: Mon to Sat 12 to 2.30, 7 to 10.30 CLOSED: 2 weeks Christmas, 2 weeks end Aug MEALS: Set L £15 (2 courses) to £18, Set D £22 (2 courses) to £25 SERVICE: not inc CARDS: Amex, Delta, MasterCard, Switch, Visa DETAILS: 45 seats. Private parties: 22 main room. Vegetarian meals. Children's helpings. No music. Air-conditioned ⊖ Baker Street, Bond Street

Idaho
NEW ENTRY map 12

13 North Hill, N6 4AB
TEL: (0181) 341 6633 FAX: (0181) 341 5533
EMAIL: idaho@montana.plc.uk

COOKING 3
COST £21–£54

South-western USA cuisine is the style in this latest branch of a fast-growing chain (see Montana) named after north-western states of the Union, suggesting that someone doesn't know their Oregon from their Arizona. But they do know their onions, or at least their zucchini blossoms stuffed with Picos blue cheese, which come with high praise, and chargrilled marinated squid with basil aïoli, charred jalapeño and tomatillo salsa. Successful main dishes have included grilled mahi-mahi, and Aberdeen Angus ribeye with all the trimmings, which here include black-eye pea compote and buttermilk red chilli onion rings. Reports of peach and sweet cheese chimichanga ('like a square doughnut') are mixed. The decorative style is late-'90s cool, with stone floors, stainless steel, and lots of wood. Tables have linen cloths and 'curiously attractive' brown paper over-cloths, but tubular framed chairs have plywood seats 'of numbing discomfort'. The terrace outside is covered and heated. A medium length wine list opens with house wines at £11, and includes five red and five white by the glass, and a knock-out list of cocktails.

CHEF: Allison Sewell   PROPRIETOR: Montana plc   OPEN: all week 12 to 3.30 (11.30 to 4 Sat and Sun), 6.30 to 11   MEALS: alc (main courses L £6 to £9, D £10 to £16). Set L Mon to Fri £10 (2 courses) to £12   SERVICE: 12.5% (optional), card slips closed   CARDS: Amex, Delta, MasterCard, Switch, Visa   DETAILS: 120 seats. 45 seats outside. Private parties: 65 main room, 16 private room. Car park. Vegetarian meals. Children's helpings. Wheelchair access (also WC). Music. Air-conditioned   ⊖ Highgate

Inaho £
map 13

4 Hereford Road, W2 4AA
TEL: (0171) 221 8495

COOKING 3
COST £15–£39

Bigger than a garden shed, though not by much, this neighbourhood restaurant soon makes visitors forget they are in London, transporting them to Tokyo, with its authentic Japanese décor and mix of Japanese and local clientele. The wide-ranging menu is a miniature version of that in smarter places, and prices are miniaturised too. Beef, pork and chicken are there, but fish and vegetables are more important. Set meals look good value, offering an appetiser (perhaps deep-fried bean curd, or aubergine topped with miso and sesame paste), soup, salad, yakitori, sashimi and a main dish of either tempura or teriyaki with rice. Sushi – the real thing, made to order with the freshest fish – are limited in variety but do include such unusual items as salmon skin, the strangely named ebi-q (prawn and cucumber), and ume-shiso, which exquisitely combines pickled plum and beefsteak plant. Drink house wine at £7.50, or warm saké; or better still the dry saké served chilled, another bargain at £6.50 for 375ml.

CHEF: Mr S. Otsuka   PROPRIETOR: Mr H. Nakamura   OPEN: Mon to Fri L 12.30 to 2.30, Mon to Sat D 7 to 11   CLOSED: 2 weeks Christmas/New Year, 4 days Easter, 1 week summer, bank hols   MEALS: alc (main courses £6.50 to £12). Set L £8 to £10, Set D £20 to £22   SERVICE: 10%   CARDS: Delta, MasterCard, Visa   DETAILS: 20 seats. Private parties: 6 main room. Vegetarian meals. No children under 10. No cigars in dining room. Music. Air-conditioned ⊖ Notting Hill Gate

L'Incontro
map 14

87 Pimlico Road, SW1W 8PH
TEL: (0171) 730 3663 and 6327
FAX: (0171) 730 5062

COOKING 2
COST £35–£80

Due to undergo refurbishment as the *Guide* went to press – with plans for open fireplaces, and a party room designed by David Linley – L'Incontro keeps its style as before: 'refined Venetian', although with so much borrowing of ideas these days we may be forgiven for thinking of it as more generally Italian. A wide-ranging carte takes in variously linguine with clams, radicchio risotto, and baccala mantecato (salt cod mousse served with polenta) to start, followed by cuttlefish in ink sauce, or grilled veal chop with rosemary. Ricotta and spinach gnocchi appears among the specialities, the set-price lunch looks relatively good value, and desserts tend to be homespun tiramisù or perhaps almond tart. Wines

– mostly top-notch Italians – are proudly marked up, although Antinori house wine is £15.75.

CHEF: Simone Rettore   PROPRIETOR: Gino Santin   OPEN: Mon to Fri L 12.30 to 2.30, all week D 7 to 11.30 (10.30 Sun)   CLOSED: 25 and 26 Dec, Easter Sun, some bank hols   MEALS: alc (main courses £16 to £27.50). Set L £16.50 (2 courses) to £20.50. Cover £1.50   SERVICE: not inc CARDS: Amex, Delta, Diners, MasterCard, Switch, Visa   DETAILS: 65 seats. Private parties: 70 main room, 35 private room. Vegetarian meals. Children's helpings. No pipes in dining room. Wheelchair access (not WC). Occasional music. Air-conditioned   ⊖ Sloane Square

---

▲ Inter-Continental, Le Soufflé ♥    map 14

1 Hamilton Place, W1V 0QY
TEL: (0171) 409 3131 and 318 8577
FAX: (0171) 491 0926
EMAIL: london@interconti.com

COOKING 5
COST £41–£96

Pause in the clubby bar off the main lobby, before entering 'one of the most successful restaurant spaces we've encountered in a large, international hotel', replete with subdued lighting, lavish flower arrangements, and well-spaced tables. The spotlight tends to ignore big hotel kitchens unless the chef is in his 30s, so it misses Peter Kromberg, who has been here for a quarter of a century. His carte is full of luxury items – truffles, shellfish, wild mushrooms and foie gras – but he is not afraid to offer crispy pig's trotter salad as a contrast. In any case, the repertoire keeps up with developments, enlivened with all sorts of other materials from Italian to oriental, such as warm carpaccio of sea bass with lemon and coriander dressing.

Two-course business lunches ('one-hour service guaranteed') may be plainer sailing but are no less indulgent, offering truffle risotto, mousseline of Arbroath smokies, and spiced duck breast with artichokes, roast peppers and foie gras. Soufflés range from lobster with caviare to Grand Marnier with chocolate. Service 'from the telephone call to make the reservation to the final farewell, from every member of the team, is outstanding': what should be industry-standard is rare enough in London to be noteworthy. Wines are concentrated on the classic regions of France, although the sommelier's selection opens in England and the list finishes with a selection of fine wines from the New World. House French is £16.

CHEF: Peter Kromberg   PROPRIETOR: Bass Hotels and Resorts   OPEN: Tue to Fri and Sun L 12.30 to 3, Tue to Sat D 7 to 10.30 (11 Sat)   CLOSED: 2 weeks Christmas, L during Aug, bank hols   MEALS: alc D (main courses £19.50 to £28). Set L £19.50 (2 courses) to £33.50, Set D £39 to £65   SERVICE: not inc   CARDS: Amex, Delta, Diners, MasterCard, Switch, Visa   DETAILS: 80 seats. Vegetarian meals. Children's helpings. No pipes in dining room. No-smoking area. Music. Air-conditioned   ACCOMMODATION: 460 rooms, all with bath/shower. TV. Phone. Room only £280 to £295. Rooms for disabled   ⊖ Hyde Park Corner   £5

The Guide *office can quickly spot when a restaurateur is encouraging customers to write recommending inclusion. Such reports do not further a restaurant's cause. Please tell us if a restaurateur invites you to write to the* Guide.

Istanbul Iskembecisi £ map 12

9 Stoke Newington Road, N16 8BH   COOKING 3
TEL: (0171) 254 7291   COST £17–£27

Many restaurants have sprung forth from Dalston's Turkish community since Istanbul Iskembecisi first opened in the early 1990s, yet few can compete with the seemly furnishings (chandeliers included), the good-natured waiters ('courteous, with appropriate pride in their success') and hearty cooking to be found here. One regular enjoyed the 'wonderfully smoky' aubergine salad from the long meze list that has many meat-free choices. Vegetarian main courses have also won plaudits, notably falafel. Meat eaters have a large number of kebabs to choose from, plus 'traditional Turkish dishes' that include green peppers stuffed with minced lamb and fresh herbs. Space should be left for desserts, among which is a highly rated coconut milk pudding sprinkled with pistachio nuts. The restaurant is popular late into the night with local Turks and others attracted by the 'amazing value'. The short, multinational wine list includes five Turkish labels, all at £7.50.

CHEFS: Hasan Karadag and Ahmet Kurultan   PROPRIETORS: Ali Demir and Ahmet Poyraz   OPEN: all week noon to 5am   MEALS: alc (main courses £5.50 to £8.50)   SERVICE: not inc   CARDS: Amex, Delta, Diners, MasterCard, Switch, Visa   DETAILS: 80 seats. Private parties: 80 main room. Vegetarian meals. Children's helpings. Wheelchair access (not WC). Music. Air-conditioned   ● Highbury & Islington (£5)

Itsu ⑤ NEW ENTRY map 14

118 Draycott Avenue, SW3 2HP   COOKING 3
TEL: (0171) 584 5522   FAX: (0171) 581 8716   COST £27–£41

Glass wraps itself all the way round this corner site; some people sit inside and gaze out, others stand outside and peer in. An unusual partnership – owner Julian Metcalfe founded the Pret-à-Manger chain, Clive Fretwell used to cook at Le Manoir aux Quat' Saisons (see entry, Great Milton) – has produced 'the premier conveyor belt restaurant in London', where fish and vegetarian items understandably predominate, although this is not Japanese food. Every available space is used for dining, and it represents the ultimate in casual eating: walk in any time, eat (and spend) as much or as little as you like. Individual dishes are inexpensive – from £2.50 to £3.50, priced according to plate colour – but our inspector got carried away and spent over £100 for two: easy to do when the quality of ingredients is so high. Enjoy salmon sashimi, spinach with sesame sauce, skilfully assembled smoked salmon with avocado and flying fish eggs, seared tuna with ginger mustard sauce, well-balanced beetroot-cured salmon with dill sauce, and – 'one of the highlights' – grilled eel roll. Avoid the coconut rice pudding. Since you help yourself, there isn't any service to speak of, and not much wine either, just seventeen bottles starting at £11.75.

CHEF: Clive Fretwell   PROPRIETOR: Julian Metcalfe   OPEN: all week 12 to 11 (10 Sun)   CLOSED: Christmas   MEALS: alc (plate prices £2.50 to £3.50)   SERVICE: not inc, card slips closed   CARDS: Amex, Delta, MasterCard, Switch, Visa   DETAILS: 75 seats. Vegetarian meals. Children's helpings. No smoking in dining room. Music. Air-conditioned   ● South Kensington

Ivy

map 15

1 West Street, WC2N 9NE
TEL: (0171) 836 4751   FAX: (0171) 240 9333

COOKING 5
COST £27–£82

In 1999 this much-loved old stager at the heart of theatreland, together with its sister restaurants Le Caprice and Sheekey's (see entries, both London), were acquired by the Belgo Group. Since there is no need to change a winning formula, the Ivy's chapel-like ambience of dark wood panelling and stained glass, criss-crossed by myriad staff and overlaid with happy chatter, continues undisturbed.

The sectioned menu reflects an approach to catering from bygone days, moving as it does from hors d'oeuvres and salads, through eggs, pasta and rice, to arrive at desserts, puddings and savouries. While there are dishes that our forebears would readily have recognised – potted shrimps, spotted dick, braised beef cooked in stout, and deep-fried haddock with chips and mushy peas (sorry, minted pea purée) – the Ivy is too canny not to seduce more contemporary tastes as well. Reports have praised Jerusalem artichoke and rosemary soup with a Parmesan wafer, Thai-spiced sea bass with fragrant rice and a soy dip, and pork tenderloin on lemon polenta. Desserts were, for one party, the highlights, with elderflower jelly with summer fruits and thick Jersey cream particularly outstanding, or you might prefer a cheese course that comprises Spanish Cabrales and Manchego served with a fig tart and quince jelly. A list of a dozen wines by the glass provides price relief from the energetically marked-up offerings on the main list. Bottle prices open at £11.25.

CHEFS: Alan Bird and Des McDonald   PROPRIETORS: Belgo Group   OPEN: all week 12 to 3 (3.30 Sun), 5.30 to 12   CLOSED: 25 and 26 Dec, 1 Jan, Aug bank hol   MEALS: alc (main courses £9 to £23.50). Set L Sat and Sun £15.50. Cover £1.50   SERVICE: not inc   CARDS: Amex, Delta, Diners, MasterCard, Switch, Visa   DETAILS: 100 seats. Private parties: 6 main room, 60 private room. Vegetarian meals. Wheelchair access (not WC). No music. Air-conditioned   ⊖ Leicester Square

Iznik £

map 13

19 Highbury Park, N5 1QJ
TEL: (0171) 354 5697 and 704 8099
FAX: (0171) 354 5697

COOKING 3
COST £17–£30

'The clutter of Turkish bric-à-brac gives a friendly feel,' reckoned one reporter – although as the *Guide* went to press a few 'cosmetic improvements' were under way – and Adem Oner and his staff provide most cordial service in this family-run place. Starters, best shared as meze, are mostly vegetarian: borek (little pastry parcels), fava (puréed broad bean salad), and falafel have been praised. Spinach with yoghurt and garlic, leeks with carrots, and courgettes with feta cheese are other possibilities. Strict carnivores will find little for them in this part of the menu, but main dishes are more meaty with chicken and lamb in various grilled kebabs and baked dishes. Generous portions ensure that few people get to dessert – a pity, because as well as the usual pastries there are pears, quince or blackberries combined with rice, semolina or bread. Turkish house wine is £8.95, and the rest of the list is mostly New World and intelligently chosen.

CHEF: Saim Berik   PROPRIETORS: Adem and Pirlanta Oner   OPEN: all week 10 to 3, 6 to 11
CLOSED: Christmas   MEALS: alc (main courses L £5.50 to £7, D £7.50 to £9.50)   SERVICE:
10%   CARDS: Delta, MasterCard, Switch, Visa   DETAILS: 76 seats. Private parties: 76 main
room. Vegetarian meals. Music   ⊖ Highbury & Islington

Jenny Lo's Teahouse £   map 13

| 14 Eccleston Street, SW1W 9LT | COOKING 2 |
| TEL: (0171) 259 0399   FAX: (0171) 823 6331 | COST £18–£28 |

'Oriental fast-food restaurant' is Jenny Lo's own description, but it's more like
an Eastern street-food stall than a Western burger bar. In a stark but warm-
coloured room, diners sit at shared tables for eight. The paper place mats double
as menus and orders are taken by young, friendly waiters, just as in a full-blown
restaurant. Meals are based on a bowl of noodles – fried or in soup – or on rice
with various meats and vegetables on top, and variety is impressive on the short
menu. Side dishes (familiar as starters elsewhere) include spring rolls, spare
ribs, 'seaweed' and won ton soup. Less usual but welcomed by many are onion
cakes (thick pancakes stuffed with pork fat and spring onion) to keep out the
Peking winter. Stir-fried bok choy adds a healthy touch to the carnivore options.
Drink 'therapeutic tea', or house wine at £9.50 – there is no other.

CHEF: Jenny Lo   PROPRIETORS: Jenny and Vivienne Lo   OPEN: Mon to Sat 11.30 (12 Sat) to 3, 6
to 10   CLOSED: bank hols   MEALS: alc (main courses £5 to £7)   SERVICE: not inc   CARDS:
none   DETAILS: 30 seats. 6 seats outside. Private parties: 20 private room. Vegetarian meals.
Occasional music   ⊖ Victoria

Kastoori £   map 12

| 188 Upper Tooting Road, SW17 7EJ | COOKING 1 |
| TEL/FAX: (0181) 767 7027 | COST £19–£30 |

Decked out in blue and yellow after a bout of redecorating, Kastoori is a bright,
cheerful venue in which to sample Indian vegetarian cooking. The Thanki
family have Ugandan-Gujarati roots, and ingredients from both regions feature
on the varied menu. There's an 'exotic' menu too, although the dishes on it are
not always available. One reporter was pleased to find that the samosas which
started his meal were 'dark and smoky', with cloves to the fore. To follow, there
might be fresh-tasting tomato curry, along with well-flavoured and -textured
bhatura bread. Gooey, nougat-like shrikand topped with chopped nuts is a good
way to finish. The modest prices are appreciated by reporters, though one felt
that small portions 'make it more expensive than it might be'. Helpful service has
long been an attraction, and wines, from £7.50, are a notch above the norm.

CHEF: Manoj Thanki   PROPRIETOR: Dinash Thanki   OPEN: Wed to Sun L 12.30 to 2.30, all week
D 6 to 10.30   CLOSED: 25 Dec, 1 week mid-Jan   MEALS: alc (main courses £3.50 to £5.50). Set
L and D £7.75 to £15.50   SERVICE: not inc, card slips closed   CARDS: MasterCard, Visa
DETAILS: 82 seats. Private parties: 20 main room. Vegetarian meals. Children's helpings.
Wheelchair access (not WC). No music. Air-conditioned   ⊖ Tooting Broadway (£5)

All entries, including Round-ups, are fully indexed at the back of the Guide.

Kensington Place ♥

201–209 Kensington Church Street, W8 7LX   COOKING 6
TEL: (0171) 727 3184   FAX: (0171) 229 2025   COST £25–£63

With 'enough good-natured clamour and noise for two restaurants', Rowley
Leigh's glass-fronted, hard-edged Kensington landmark is a popular venue for
conspicuously amiable eating. A long menu mixes old favourites – fish soup,
herb omelette, Toulouse sausages, or roast cod with champ and anchovy gravy –
with handwritten additions of whatever else comes along: wild sea trout with
Swiss chard, or braised haunch of hare. Some might cherish this as an
institution, but it stands by the quality of the output: accurate timing is applied
to griddled scallops (served with pea purée and mint vinaigrette), producing a
'simple but well-executed dish'. A sense of balance characterises such all-time
classics as chicken and goats'- cheese mousse with black olives and 'balsamic
jam', and the cooking typically has an appealing straightforwardness, expressed
for example in nuggets of veal kidneys on leek and potato cake in a
tarragon-flecked cream sauce.

The upbeat style continues into desserts of grilled pineapple with chilli syrup
and coconut ice cream, despite more homely lemon tart or steamed chocolate
pudding. Although bustle is part of the appeal, service can be hard-pressed at
times. One reporter, in desperation, used his mobile phone to call from table to
reception desk, eliciting profuse apologies but only slightly better results. Wines
are a cosmopolitan collection of old and new styles, presented without
pretension and at some pocket-friendly prices. Twenty-odd wines by the glass
begin at £3.25.

CHEF/PROPRIETOR: Rowley Leigh   OPEN: all week 12 to 3 (3.30 Sat and Sun), 6.30 to 11.45
(10.15 Sun)   CLOSED: 24 Dec to 26 Dec, 1 Jan   MEALS: alc (main courses £10 to £16.50). Set L
Sun to Fri £14.50   SERVICE: not inc, card slips closed   CARDS: Amex, MasterCard, Switch,
Visa   DETAILS: 150 seats. Private parties: 150 main room. Vegetarian meals. Children's
helpings. Wheelchair access (also WC). No music. Air-conditioned ⊖ Notting Hill Gate

Kulu Kulu Sushi £
NEW ENTRY map 15

76 Brewer Street, W1R 3PH   COOKING 1
TEL: (0171) 734 7316   FAX: (0171) 734 6507   COST £15–£24

This basic café offers little in the way of décor or service, the latter being mostly
provided by the kaiten (conveyor belt), which brings an endless stream of sushi
priced from £1.20 a plate. Salmon, tuna, squid, mackerel and horse mackerel are
modestly priced favourites, and the sashimi plate is good value too. Most are of a
quality equalled only in the better traditional sushi bars. For recherché
delicacies such as tobiko (flying fish roe) ask the chef and in due time it appears.
Everything is prepared by hand: sushi behind the counter, the rest, including
noodles, fried chicken, and tofu, in the kitchen behind the scenes. Serve yourself
green tea (free), or order beer, saké, or house wine at £12 a bottle.

CHEF/PROPRIETOR: Mr K. Toyama   OPEN: Mon to Sat 12 to 2.30 (3.45 Sat), 5 to 10   CLOSED: 25
and 26 Dec, bank hols   MEALS: alc (sushi £1.20 to £3, main courses £9 to £10)   SERVICE: not
inc   CARDS: Delta, MasterCard, Switch, Visa   DETAILS: 30 seats. Vegetarian meals. No-
smoking area. Music. Air-conditioned ⊖ Piccadilly Circus

▲ Landmark London, The Dining Room

map 13

222 Marylebone Road, NW1 6JQ
TEL: (0171) 631 8230   FAX: (0171) 631 8080

COOKING 5
COST £39–£80

This high-ceilinged, elegant room, with acres of carpet and a great deal of pink, cream and grey is rather more drawing room than dining room. Luxury is apparent, the surroundings rich and opulent. Andrew McLeish continues to treat first-class ingredients skilfully, and brings a light touch to classic dishes: ragoût of sea bass and turbot with fennel jus, for example, or scallops with sauce vierge. One reporter started with a flavourful espresso cup of asparagus soup, before moving on to a thick slice of salmon ballottine with caviare in the centre, a purée of mint leaves and roasted scallops; another enjoyed a cep and mushroom tart served with truffle jus and smooth mashed potato. More robust main courses have included braised oxtail with pancetta and celeriac purée, and braised cheek and pan-fried fillet of Aberdeen Angus in port sauce. Desserts come in for considerable praise both for content and presentation: lime mousse surrounded by pineapple rings, blackberries and raspberries, for example, or Grand Marnier soufflé with a compote of blood oranges. Professional service is 'courteous and attentive', and 'interested in the way the food was received', according to another. The wine list is extensive and expensive. House wines are £18.50.

CHEF: Andrew McLeish   PROPRIETOR: The Landmark London   OPEN: Sun to Fri L 12.30 to 2.30, Mon to Sat D 7 to 10.30   MEALS: alc (main courses £17.50 to £22.50). Set L £26, Set D £36.95 to £42   SERVICE: not inc   CARDS: Amex, Delta, Diners, MasterCard, Switch, Visa   DETAILS: 80 seats. Vegetarian meals. Children's helpings. Wheelchair access (also WC). Music. Air-conditioned   ACCOMMODATION: 298 rooms, all with bath/shower. TV. Phone. Room only £270 to £1,440. Rooms for disabled. Baby facilities. Swimming pool (*The Which? Hotel Guide*)
◉ Marylebone, Baker Street

▲ Lanesborough, The Conservatory

map 14

1 Lanesborough Place, SW1X 7TA
TEL: (0171) 259 5599   FAX: (0171) 259 5606
EMAIL: info@lanesborough.co.uk

COOKING 4
COST £34–£79

A curved glass ceiling, palms, chandeliers on heavy chains, Chinese carpets and the sound of water all contribute to an oasis atmosphere of some sophistication and expense. Paul Gayler's menu cheerfully plunders from various cuisines, with perhaps Eastern and North African flavourings to the fore: lamb shank, for instance, with chickpea polenta, and cumin-spiced roasted root vegetables, considered 'a big machismo dish, moist, unctuous, rich, but balanced'. Vegetarians are well catered for, having an impressive menu of their own to choose from. Dishes can be quite busy, as an inspection meal indicated, starting with sautéed scallops, wrapped in heavily smoked salmon, on a pool of caviare swirled into crème fraîche. Technique is not always as skilful as it might be, given the generally fine materials, but the kitchen has produced some creditable dishes: for example crisp-skinned roast sea bass, set on a velvety purée of celeriac and potato, with caramelised vegetables and coriander jus. Desserts at inspection were 'a *tour de force*': cappuccino brûlée with an edible brandy-snap teaspoon, or plum pizzete with rhubarb cardamom jam and coconut and saffron ice cream. Service has come in for praise too: 'staff are some of the nicest in

London'. The wine list aims for the top and is priced accordingly, although with a little ferreting and help from the sommelier you can still drink around the £20 mark.

CHEF: Paul Gayler   PROPRIETOR: Rosewood Hotels   OPEN: all week 12 to 2.30, 6.30 to 12
MEALS: alc (main courses £14.50 to £27). Set L £20.50 (2 courses) to £25.50, Set D £30.50
SERVICE: net prices, card slips closed   CARDS: Amex, Delta, Diners, MasterCard, Switch, Visa
DETAILS: 106 seats. Private parties: 80 main room, 14 to 100 private rooms. Vegetarian meals.
Children's helpings. Wheelchair access (also WC). Music. Air-conditioned   ACCOMMODATION:
95 rooms, all with bath/shower. TV. Phone. Room only £235 to £410. Rooms for disabled. Baby
facilities   ● Hyde Park Corner

Langan's Brasserie
map 15

Stratton Street, W1X 5FD   COOKING 1
TEL: (0171) 491 8822   FAX: (0171) 493 8309   COST £31–£60

The mother of all London brasseries seems to have been here for ever, quietly having its ups and downs, pleasing the crowds if not all reporters. Nobody pretends that food is the main draw, when there are celebrities to watch, a glitzy atmosphere to absorb, and a slick operation to admire, at least on the ground floor: upstairs, the Venetian Room is quieter. But it does deliver decent renditions of many staples, all day long, from a Franglais carte that begins with soufflé au épinard (ground floor only), and cheerily calls in on oeufs pochés au haddock fumé, hot potted shrimps on toast, Langan's bangers, and cod and chips. Desserts are equally traditional, whichever side of the Channel they hail from: vacherin Montmorency, English raspberries with clotted cream, or rhubarb fool. Around three dozen wines at ungrasping prices start with house French at £11.50.

CHEF: Ken Whitehead   PROPRIETORS: Richard Shepherd and Michael Caine   OPEN: Mon to Fri
12.15 to 11.45, Sat 7 to 12   CLOSED: Christmas, Easter, bank hols   MEALS: alc (main courses
£10.50 to £15). Cover £1.50   SERVICE: 12.5% (optional)   CARDS: Amex, Delta, Diners,
MasterCard, Switch, Visa   DETAILS: 220 seats. Vegetarian meals. Music. Air-conditioned
● Green Park

Lansdowne £
map 13

90 Gloucester Avenue, NW1 8HX   COOKING 2
TEL: (0171) 483 0409   FAX: (0171) 722 5424   COST £20–£34

In this honest, unpretentious 'godsend of a local pub', food is ordered at the bar and tables are available on a first-come, first-served basis. A short blackboard menu changes twice daily, and dishes that sound like starters can stand alone as lunch or supper: perhaps a 'refreshing summery combination' of Serrano ham, broad beans, new potatoes and mint. 'Equally generous and satisfying' main dishes might include grilled squid with couscous, rocket and tomato salsa, and tender and flavoursome grilled lamb chops with spinach, lentils, and tapénade. 'Organic produce is used where possible', and Neal's Yard cheeses may include Mrs Appleby's Cheshire, Waterloo and Stilton. The short wine list lacks vintages, but prices are modest. House French is £9. Plans are afoot to convert the upstairs into another dining room.

CHEFS: Amanda Pritchett and Mark Watkins   PROPRIETOR: Amanda Pritchett   OPEN: Tue to Sun L 12.30 (1 Sun) to 2.30, all week D 7 to 10   CLOSED: 25 to 30 Dec, 1 Jan   MEALS: alc (main courses £6.50 to £10.50). Set L Tue to Sat £5 (1 course, inc wine), Set L Sun £15   SERVICE: not inc   CARDS: Delta, MasterCard, Switch, Visa   DETAILS: 90 seats. 30 seats outside. Private parties: 24 private room. Vegetarian meals. No music   ⊖ Chalk Farm

Launceston Place ♟   map 14

1A Launceston Place, W8 5RL   COOKING 3
TEL: (0171) 937 6912   FAX: (0171) 938 2412   COST £28–£57

Located in a quiet backwater of ever-so-smart Kensington, this corner building is a series of interconnecting rooms with comfortable, homely furnishings, and walls hung with attractive prints and watercolours. The menu draws inspiration largely from the Mediterranean – twice-baked cheese soufflé, or piedmontese peppers with rocket salad illustrate the style – with occasional flurries further afield in the shape of spiced Malaysian noodles with roasted pumpkin, or Szechuan peppered duck with sweet-and-sour sauce. Main courses have embraced 'tender and pink' spiced lamb with apricots and couscous, and sea bass with white beans, black olives, peppers and gremolata. Desserts include a brace of brûlées served with Brazil-nut biscotti, and winter fruit salad with ginger and cinnamon syrup. A favourably priced wine list begins with house Chardonnay at £10.75 (claret is £12.50), then darts from one major region to another, collecting an appealing array of bottles as it goes.

CHEF: Phillip Reed   PROPRIETOR: Simon Slater   OPEN: Sun to Fri L 12.30 to 2.30 (3 Sun), Mon to Sat D 7 to 11.30   CLOSED: 25 Dec, 1 Jan, bank hols   MEALS: alc (main courses £15 to £16.50). Set L and D Mon to Fri before 8pm £14.50 to £17.50   SERVICE: not inc   CARDS: Amex, Delta, MasterCard, Switch, Visa   DETAILS: 80 seats. Private parties: 12 and 25 private rooms. Vegetarian meals. No pipes in dining room. Wheelchair access (not WC). No music. Air-conditioned   ⊖ Gloucester Road

Laurent £   map 13

428 Finchley Road, NW2 2HY   COOKING 1
TEL: (0171) 794 3603   COST £21–£32

Good, but basic with a rather restricted menu is the overall impression of this north London stalwart. The starter, for there is only one, is brik à l'oeuf, gooey on the inside, crisp on the outside. Proceed to couscous, the choice being whether to have fish, vegetarian, complet (lamb and merguez) or royal (essentially lamb with a mixed grill of more lamb). Crêpe suzette is the only dessert apart from sorbet, ice cream and crème caramel. Portions are enormous, so sharing is advised. The room has functionality written all over it, with the odd plant and posters of Tunisia. Plastic-clothed tables are close together, and service is 'pleasant and friendly'. House wines are £9.

CHEF/PROPRIETOR: Laurent Farrugia   OPEN: Mon to Sat 12 to 2, 6 to 11   CLOSED: first 3 weeks Aug, bank hols   MEALS: alc (main courses £7 to £11.50)   SERVICE: not inc   CARDS: Amex, Delta, MasterCard, Visa   DETAILS: 36 seats. Private parties: 18 main room. Vegetarian meals. Children's helpings. Wheelchair access (not WC). No music   ⊖ Golders Green

Lawn 🥄

map 12

1 Lawn Terrace, SE3 9LJ
TEL: (0171) 379 0724   FAX: (0171) 379 9014

COOKING 3
COST £27–£64

No sooner had Nick Hall opened One Lawn Terrace than the owners of Bank (see entry, London) swept in and bought it up, renaming it Lawn along the way. The two-level dining area with a 'great high ceiling' is bright and airy, with a 'cool and functional' feel, and the food keeps south-east Londoners up to date with restaurant trends, without them having to trek into town. Salt cod mash topped with a neatly trimmed poached egg and slivers of bacon is a 'comforting' way to start a meal, and Thai-spiced fish and crab cakes come with a refreshing salad of cucumber and red onion shavings. Food is well presented, often stacked high, with sauces drizzled underneath and around, and seasoning can be enthusiastic. Accurate timing helped to make pink duck breast (served with rösti, spring greens and diced vegetables) a success at inspection. Chips are 'good and fat', while 'sweet and fresh-tasting' mushy peas also get the thumbs up. Adventurous desserts run to lemon grass and lime leaf rice pudding, and pear maple crème brûlée with crispy pear. Service is friendly, and wines are grouped by style, starting at £13.50.

CHEFS: Christian Delteil and Eddie Grappy   PROPRIETORS: BGR plc   OPEN: Tue to Sun L 12 (11.30 Sun) to 6, Mon to Sat D 6 to 11   CLOSED: 25 Dec, some bank hols   MEALS: alc (main courses £11 to £15.50). Set L Tue to Fri £11.95 (2 courses) to £15.50, Set D 6 to 10.30 Tue and Weds, 6 to 7.30 Thur to Sat £11.95 (2 courses) to £15.50   SERVICE: 12.5% (optional), card slips closed   CARDS: Amex, Delta, Diners, MasterCard, Switch, Visa   DETAILS: 150 seats. Private parties: 12 main room, 22 private room. Vegetarian meals. Children's helpings. Wheelchair access (also WC). Music. Air-conditioned

Lee Fook

map 13

98 Westbourne Grove, W2 5RU
TEL: (0171) 727 0099   FAX: (0171) 727 8773

COOKING 1
COST £27–£60

Décor is above local standards, and the mainly Cantonese cooking is good enough to make the place a regular haunt of chefs from top Chinatown restaurants. As an example to the rest of us they often choose from the daily specials or, better still, leave the decision to the chef. Seafood is a major feature, and Dover sole, sea bass, lobster and crab are prepared in several ways. Carnivores can enjoy braised belly pork with preserved vegetables, and could consider a half or whole Szechuan spicy chicken with sweet basil. Fine teas include pu-erh, a soft mellow brew, and ti kwan yin, a premium variety of oolong. House wines are £12.

CHEF: Ringo Lo   PROPRIETORS: Ringo Lo and John Hau   OPEN: all week noon to 11.30 (11 Sun)   CLOSED: 24 to 26 Dec   MEALS: alc (main courses £6.50 to £28). Set D (min 2) £16 to £28   SERVICE: not inc   CARDS: Delta, Diners, MasterCard, Switch, Visa   DETAILS: 80 seats. Private parties: 90 main room. Vegetarian meals. Occasional music. Air-conditioned   ⊖ Bayswater, Notting Hill Gate (£5)

The Guide's longest-serving restaurants are listed near the front of the book.

Leith's 🍷

map 13

92 Kensington Park Road, W11 2PN
TEL: (0171) 229 4481   FAX: (0171) 221 1246

COOKING 6
COST £39–£91

Enter down a cobbled alleyway next to an old church, through a token bar, into a series of living rooms in this large Victorian house. Its 'genteel' atmosphere derives as much from the comfortable middle-class domestic surroundings and affluent clientele as from the maturity that comes with thirtieth birthday celebrations. The vegetarian strand retains its strong appeal – mozzarella and basil tart, or casserole of wild mushrooms and sweet potato with a pea and garlic risotto – and the seasonally changing carte is balanced by a weekly set-price menu that allows mixing between the two.

Materials are fresh and well handled, 'sympathetic treatment' generally makes the most of them, and technical accomplishment is evident: in, for example, accurately timed crisp-skinned sea bass (served on heavily saffroned polenta in a squid and bacon minestrone); and in two cylinders of pink rabbit accompanied by a thin raviolo of diced wild mushrooms. Some interesting, even imaginative, combinations work well on the plate, among them a simple-sounding jellied pork terrine, incorporating ham, foie gras, garlicky pork sausage and tongue, all held together in a light jelly, and well partnered by a characterful apricot chutney. Pistachio soufflé has proved 'a good example of the soufflé maker's art', or there may be chocolate and passion fruit meringue pie to finish. Wines are chosen with quality as the prime consideration, and prices follow where that leads, occasionally below £20, but mostly above. Famous names, and rare and exclusive bins, are drawn from both hemispheres, and if some are unfamiliar, then the man behind the list, Nick Tarayan, or one of his team will be happy to advise. An octet of house wines starts at £17.50.

CHEF: Alastair Ross   PROPRIETORS: Sir Christopher Bland, Caroline Waldegrave, Nick Tarayan and Alex Floyd   OPEN: Tue to Fri L 12.15 to 2.15, Mon to Sat D 7 to 11.30   CLOSED: 2 weeks Christmas to New Year, bank hols exc Good Fri, L and Mon D in Aug   MEALS: alc (main courses £21.50 to £32.50). Set L £19.50 (2 courses) to £24.25, Set D £29.50 (2 courses) to £37   SERVICE: 12.5% (optional), card slips closed   CARDS: Amex, Delta, Diners, MasterCard, Switch, Visa
DETAILS: 70 seats. Private parties: 45 main room, 4 to 36 private rooms. Vegetarian meals. No children under 7. Wheelchair access (not WC). No music. Air-conditioned   ⊖ Notting Hill Gate

Leith's Soho 🍷

map 15

41 Beak Street, W1R 3LE
TEL: (0171) 287 2057   FAX: (0171) 287 1767

COOKING 2
COST £31–£66

Handy for pre- and post-theatre eating, this offshoot of the original Leith's (see above) is a long, narrow, low-ceilinged room with movable dividers to break up the minimalist space. Aiming for a broad contemporary target, it offers soups and salady starters alongside ungreasy shiitake spring rolls, a 'worthy' wholemeal tomato and mozzarella tart, and prawn cocktail, which apparently outsells all other starters by two to one. Accurate timing is the norm – for roast scallop halves around a pile of couscous topped with a thin 'biscuit' tasting of curry – and lightness is balanced by a degree of comfort and richness: in a risotto of spinach, pea and black trumpet mushrooms, or in a steamed chocolate pudding with pistachio ice cream. Slicks of sauce are splashed across plates of 'workmanlike' food, but flavours in quite a number of dishes have simply failed to excite, and at these prices reporters are not forgiving. At least the wine list offers a good range of palate-pleasing flavours and, with twenty-two available by the glass, sampling is encouraged. Prices begin at £11.75 in the Vin de Pays d'Oc.

CHEF: Alex Floyd   PROPRIETORS: Sir Christopher Bland, Caroline Waldegrave, Nick Tarayan and Alex Floyd   OPEN: Mon to Fri L 12 to 2.30, Mon to Sat D 6 to 11.15   CLOSED: 2 weeks Christmas to New Year, bank hols   MEALS: alc (main courses £10.50 to £17.50). Set L and pre-theatre Set D 6 to 7 £16.50 (2 courses) to £19.50   SERVICE: 12.5% (optional), card slips closed   CARDS: Amex, Delta, Diners, MasterCard, Switch, Visa   DETAILS: 45 seats. Private parties: 45 main room, 20 private room. Children's helpings. Wheelchair access (not WC). No music. Air-conditioned   ● Piccadilly Circus, Oxford Circus

Lindsay House ▼

map 15

21 Romilly Street, W1V 5TG
TEL: (0171) 439 0450   FAX: (0171) 437 7349

COOKING 7
COST £40–£69

It may at first seem like a club (you have to ring the bell to get in) but this eighteenth-century house in the heart of Soho feels less intimidating inside, indeed very much understated, with ancient floorboards, small tables, and chairs swathed in white petticoats. Similarly with the food, Richard Corrigan's preoccupation is with flavour, not decoration: 'no fuss, no gimmicks, just straightforward honest cooking based on excellent ingredients.' The style tends towards highly savoury, robust dishes. Strong flavours (often convincing, occasionally discordant) are typical, as in a 'cuisine grand-mère classic' of braised shin of veal with creamy-textured wild mushroom risotto.

Given his speciality, the cooking is considered 'offally good' by one reporter (sweetbreads come with a properly crisp crust), and a well-balanced menu incorporates plenty of fish to counteract the richness, perhaps even a combination of both: monkfish has been paired with ham hock, savoury-salty split peas and shallot vinaigrette. While the cooking can produce a 'roller-coaster ride from sheer perfection to sheer perversity', when it is on form it is hard to beat for 'flair, originality and sheer joyousness', for example in a light, wobbly Jerusalem artichoke mousse, served with finely shredded but still slightly crunchy apple.

So sturdy is the food that few reporters make it to dessert, even when it is included in the price. 'Friendly but not familiar' staff, in long pinnies over dark trousers, deliver well-paced service. The lengthy wine list is helpfully divided into grape variety and/or style, which means that a Californian Marsanne finds itself rubbing shoulders with a Cassis in the Rhône-style white section, for example. Those finding it hard to choose from the plethora of fascinating bins should consult the sommelier's selection (from £15.50), which includes several wines by the glass (from £3.50).

CHEF: Richard Corrigan   PROPRIETOR: Corrigan Restaurants Ltd   OPEN: Mon to Fri L 12 to 2.30, Mon to Sat D 6 to 11   CLOSED: 1 week at Christmas, 1 week in August, bank hols   MEALS: alc L (main courses £17 to £20). Set L £23, Set D £38   SERVICE: 12.5% (optional), card slips closed CARDS: Amex, Delta, Diners, MasterCard, Switch, Visa   DETAILS: 60 seats. Private parties: 40 main room, 8 and 20 private rooms. Vegetarian meals. Children's helpings. No music. Air-conditioned   ● Leicester Square

Livebait 🍽

maps 13 and 15

43 The Cut, SE1 8LF
TEL: (0171) 928 7211   FAX: (0171) 928 2279
21 Wellington Street, WC2E 7DN
TEL: (0171) 836 7161   FAX: (0171) 836 7141

COOKING 2
COST £30–£90

Black and white tiled walls lend both establishments a certain pie-and-mash
atmosphere. Noise levels tend to reverberate, and not everyone takes to the
Formica tables and plastic padded seats, but overall the busy and relaxed
atmosphere works well. 'The kitchen mixes styles with panache and good
humour,' wrote one reporter about the Waterloo branch, enthusiastic about his
starter of tempura squid with truffle mash and salad, 'a mini-meal in itself';
another praised carpaccio of scallops with tomato vinaigrette and deep-fried
crisp shallots. Covent Garden has a bar area, where seafood can be taken with a
glass of wine or beer. Half a skate wing with warm tomato salsa impressed one
reporter, who followed it with a 'tastier-than-it-looked' main-course bouillabaisse. Sea bass with chips and taramasalata 'slid down rather well' for
another. Portions are generous, but those who make it to dessert might choose
treacle and coconut tart with vanilla ice cream, or steamed hazelnut pudding
with chocolate anglaise. Service is keen but can fail to deliver, and waiting times
come in for criticism. The wine list, grouped by style, offers good and varied
drinking, with Muscadet heading the whites at £11.95.

CHEFS: M. Feildel (The Cut), Bridget Chick (Wellington Street)   PROPRIETOR: Groupe Chez
Gérard   OPEN: Mon to Sat 12 to 3 (3.30 Wellington Street), 5.30 to 11.30   CLOSED: 25 and 26
Dec, 1 Jan   MEALS: alc (main courses £13 to £41). Set L Mon to Fri £15.50 (2 courses) to £19.50,
Set L Sat £10 (2 courses), Set D 5.30 to 7 and 10 to 11.30 £15.50 (2 courses) to £19.50, Set D 7 to
10 £19.50 (2 courses) to £24.50   SERVICE: 12.5% (optional), card slips closed   CARDS: Amex,
Delta, Diners, MasterCard, Switch, Visa   DETAILS: 100 seats (The Cut), 120 seats (Wellington
Street). 10 seats outside (The Cut). Private parties: 30 main room (The Cut), 200 main room
(Wellington Street). Children's helpings. No cigars/pipes in dining room. Wheelchair access
(also WC) (The Cut). Occasional music   ⊖ Waterloo (The Cut), Covent Garden (Wellington
Street)

Lobster Pot

map 13

3 Kennington Lane, SE11 4RG
TEL: (0171) 582 5556

COOKING 2
COST £23–£56

'This is a great place to go for straightforward fish cookery of a high standard,'
summed up one visitor. Quirky it may be, and tiny, but the owners' charm,
enthusiasm, 'delightfully personal' service and evident cooking skills transcend
the seagull noises, Breton shirts, portholes, and the sight of fellow diners 'sitting
with bibs, tearing sea creatures apart'. Among the specialities are a seafood
platter, bouillabaisse Bretonne, cayenne-spiked mussels in tomato sauce, and of
course lobster 'the way you want it', on one occasion poached with a dash of
Pernod in the stock. Timing is accurate, materials fresh (sea bass and crab
steamed 'en papillotte' for one reporter), and there are meat options as well,
followed by familiar desserts such as chocolate profiteroles and tarte Tatin.
House Muscadet is £10.50.

CHEF: Hervé Régent   PROPRIETORS: Hervé and Nathalie Régent   OPEN: Tue to Sat 12 to 2, 7 to 10.45   CLOSED: 24 Dec to first week Jan   MEALS: alc (main courses £14.50 to £22.50). Set L £15.50, Set L and D £22.50   SERVICE: not inc, card slips closed   CARDS: Amex, Delta, Diners, MasterCard, Switch, Visa   DETAILS: 30 seats. Private parties: 28 main room, 28 private room. No cigars/pipes in dining room. Wheelchair access (not WC). Music. Air-conditioned ⊖ Kennington £5

Lola's
map 13

The Mall Building, 359 Upper Street, N1 0PD   COOKING 4
TEL: (0171) 359 1932   FAX: (0171) 359 2209   COST £24–£45

Natural daylight and a civilised, good-humoured atmosphere pervade this first-floor dining room in Islington, where the tempo swings easily from peaceful to bustling. The style is generally light, with plenty of fish and vegetable dishes, quite a few 'assemblies' among starters, and what a regular calls 'many old friends'. Although flavours do not always convince, vivid spicing can produce some upbeat dishes: tataki of beef comes with spinach, hot mustard, and a soy and ginger dressing ('a great flavour combination'), while chicken harira consists of shredded breast in a broth with chilli, saffron, cumin, ginger and lemon juice, plus chickpeas, new potatoes and flat bread: 'perfect winter comfort food'.

Desserts triumphed at inspection: Greek yoghurt and poppy seed ice creams with crisp filo wafers and poached dried apricots; and a bitter chocolate tart, with the 'densest, darkest' filling and dabs of crème fraîche. Lunchers should note the 'bargain' set-price deal, which usually includes items from the carte. Although not universally praised, service is generally efficient and correct, and the unstuffy wine list is full of genuine interest, not least in Italy. House Sicilian white is £9.75, Coteau Varois red £10.50.

CHEF: Juliet Peston   PROPRIETORS: Morfudd Richards and Carol George   OPEN: all week 12 to 2.30 (3 Sat and Sun), 6.30 to 11 (7 to 10 Sun)   CLOSED: some bank hols   MEALS: alc (main courses £10 to £15). Set L Mon to Fri £10 (2 courses)   SERVICE: not inc, 12.5% for parties of 5 or more   CARDS: Amex, Delta, Diners, MasterCard, Switch, Visa   DETAILS: 80 seats. Vegetarian meals. Children's helpings. Music. Air-conditioned   ⊖ Angel

Lomo £
NEW ENTRY map 14

222 Fulham Road, SW10 9NB   COOKING 2
TEL/FAX: (0171) 349 8848   COST £23–£34

This all-day grazing operation is brought to us by the owners of Lola's (see entry above). Call it tapas and it sounds old hat, call them raciones and it all seems as bang up to date as the cosmopolitan curves, hard edges, bright colours and bar stools at high round tables. The food's success is due to a combination of dramatically improved Spanish produce, and generally intelligent handling. Lomo itself (cured pork loin) is served with a small fluffy-crispy pancake, plus some creamy goats' cheese and a grainy olive paste, while firm-textured sizzling prawns are spiced with chilli and garlic. A degree of anglicisation may temper some of the character, but for the most part the rule is 'good ingredients simply prepared'. The traditional Spanish accompaniment, sherry, is well represented by Lustau and Valdespiño, while lovers of Pedro Ximenez should try it with pan perdido or poured over vanilla ice cream. Other Spanish wines (and the occasional foreign interloper) are up to date and sensibly priced, and most are also available by the large glass or quarter litre. Prices start at £9.75 a bottle.

CHEF: Sue Lewis   PROPRIETORS: Carol George, Morfudd Richard and Julian Richer   OPEN: all week 8.30am to midnight (11pm Sun)   CLOSED: 25 and 26 Dec, 1 Jan   MEALS: alc (main courses £2.50 to £7)   SERVICE: not inc   CARDS: Amex, Delta, Diners, MasterCard, Switch, Visa   DETAILS: 55 seats. Vegetarian meals. Music   ⊖ South Kensington

Lou Pescadou   map 13

| 241 Old Brompton Road, SW5 9HP | COOKING 2 |
| TEL: (0171) 370 1057   FAX: (0171) 244 7545 | COST £21–£61 |

With the emphasis very much on the sea, the dining space (divided into four areas) goes in for cliché nautical cloths, pictures of fishing boats, and a porthole for a front window. This is the place for old-style French dishes, whether cheesy amuse-gueules with delicate pastry, great bread, juicy escargots in a buttery parsley sauce, the sweetest of scallops in a provençale fricassee, or the remarkable mayonnaise that comes with an overflowing seafood platter. Moules marinière, poulet grillé à l'estragon, and endives braisées are also dishes to stir old memories, many of them on the weekday lunchtime and weekend evening set meals. Sweets are very much in nostalgic vein too: charlotte aux poires, mousse au chocolat, and intense fruit sorbets. The friendly all-French waiters aim to please, while the short all-French wine list helpfully goes to the trouble of describing many of the less expensive bottles. House wine is £10.50.

CHEF: Laurent David   PROPRIETORS: Daniel Chobert and Laurent David   OPEN: all week 12 to 3, 6.30 to 12   CLOSED: 2 weeks Christmas   MEALS: alc (main courses £7.50 to £14). Set L weekdays £9.90, Set D weekends £13.50. Cover £1.50   SERVICE: 15% (optional), card slips closed   CARDS: Amex, Delta, Diners, MasterCard, Switch, Visa   DETAILS: 65 seats. 24 seats outside. Private parties: 18 main room. Vegetarian meals. Children's helpings. Wheelchair access (not WC). No music. Air-conditioned   ⊖ Earls Court £5

Love ⅝✱ £   NEW ENTRY   map 15

| 62/64 Weymouth Street, W1N 3LL | COOKING 1 |
| TEL: (0171) 487 5683   FAX: (0171) 935 9506 | COST £12–£23 |

Done out in 'minimalist, New Age' style, with massive refectory tables, wooden benches and distempered walls, the café – like the floristry business at the front of the store and the central tank full of soothing exotic fish – is part of the Aveda cosmetics shop and its carefully calculated body-and-soul-in-harmony ethos. Its menu is brief but interesting, a vegetarian emphasis evident in tagliatelle with mixed herbs and organic mushrooms, and flatbread with Middle Eastern dips. But it also goes in for Californian-style dishes of chargrilled salmon with niçoise salad, incorporating (along with the usual marinated olives, tomatoes, new potatoes, red onions, and hardboiled eggs) 'bouncily fresh greens – like an instant infusion of vitamins'. Service is laid back, and enjoyment extends to the wholesome, non-alcoholic drinks.

CHEF: Risto Vidakovic   PROPRIETOR: Kevin Gould   OPEN: Mon to Sat L only 12 to 6.45
CLOSED: Christmas, New Year, bank hols   MEALS: alc (main courses £5 to £7)   SERVICE: not inc   CARDS: Amex, Delta, Diners, MasterCard, Switch, Visa   DETAILS: 40 seats. Vegetarian meals. Children's helpings. No smoking in dining room. Music   ⊖ Regents Park

Lundum's   c 20 7373 7774   NEW ENTRY   map 14

119 Old Brompton Road, SW7 3RN   COOKING 3
TEL: (0171) 373 7774   FAX: (0171) 373 4472   COST £22–£51

The only Danish restaurant in London? It claims to be, and at lunchtimes smørrebrød (warm and cold open sandwiches), herrings and other traditional Danish specialities are the mainstays on offer in a split-level cream-coloured dining room with large gilt mirrors. In the evening, a more modern and serious menu swings into action with wider European influences. Frisée salad with Rosenborg (Danish Blue), pine kernels and balsamic vinaigrette, for example, might be followed by roast lamb with roast shredded potato and an intriguing vanilla and chilli sauce. The house speciality is duck – cured for 52 hours then roasted and served with horseradish sauce – and a section of the menu is devoted to various ways with salmon: gravad lax, smoked, tartare, or grilled and served with cucumber and red onion. To finish, consider an 'open pancake parcel' containing orange mousse, accompanied by preserved kumquats. Service is 'keen to please'. The wine list offers little from the New World, concentrating on France, and opens with house wines at £11.50.

CHEFS: Frank Dietrich and Tanja Jensen   PROPRIETORS: the Lundum family and partners   OPEN: all week L 12 to 3, Mon to Sat D 6 to 10.30   CLOSED: Christmas   MEALS: alc (main courses £4.50 to £15.50). Set L Mon to Sat £12.50 (2 courses) to £15.50, Set D £15.50 (2 courses) to £19.50   SERVICE: 12.5%, card slips closed   CARDS: Amex, Delta, MasterCard, Switch, Visa   DETAILS: 40 seats. 15 seats outside. Private parties: 40 main room. Vegetarian meals. Children's helpings. No cigars before 3pm. Music. Air-conditioned   ⊖ Gloucester Road

Magno's   map 15

65A Long Acre, WC2E 9JH   COOKING 1
TEL: (0171) 836 6077   FAX: (0171) 379 6184   COST £27–£57

'The feel is comfortable, French and reliable,' summed up one couple. Given its Covent Garden location, with a score of playhouses within ten minutes' walk, it should be no surprise that pre- and post-theatre suppers are a draw: one reporter enjoyed a meal of spinach and cheese quiche, turkey strips with Chinese spices, and white chocolate and raspberry tart, all 'competently produced and served quickly'. Staples of snails in garlic butter, or coq au vin, share the pricier carte with braised shank of lamb, and roast kid with cherry sauce, followed by crème brûlée. House French is £10.95 a litre.

If a restaurant is new to the **Guide** *this year (did not appear as a main entry in the last edition),* **NEW ENTRY** *appears opposite its name.*

CHEF: David Bourg   PROPRIETOR: Salvatore Caltagirone   OPEN: Mon to Fri L 12 to 2.30, Mon to Sat D 5.30 to 11.30   MEALS: alc (main courses £11 to £16). Set L and D £13.95 (2 courses) to £16.95, Set D 5.30 to 7.15 and 10 to 11.30 £10.95 (2 courses)   SERVICE: 12.5%   CARDS: Amex, Delta, Diners, MasterCard, Switch, Visa   DETAILS: 66 seats. Private parties: 75 main room. Vegetarian meals. Children's helpings. No cigars/pipes in dining room. Music. Air-conditioned ⊖ Covent Garden

Maison Novelli 🍞 map 13

29 Clerkenwell Green, EC1R 0DU   COOKING 4
TEL: (0171) 251 6606   FAX: (0171) 490 1083   COST £46–£78

The Novelli trademarks are still here – purply blue walls, mint-green paintwork, squiggles all over the menu – but Jean-Christophe Novelli's relationship with his namesake restaurant seems increasingly tenuous. He it was who gave the place character in its early days, not least by cooking northern French dishes that reflected his roots. In place of offal (no more pigs' trotters) and fondly remembered dishes such as beer and endive soup, the current menu is cast in more global mode. Brochette of salmon and scallop comes on citrus couscous; a thin slice of tuna is poked inside a hot and crispy blini; and an 'Andalusian' dish assembles Dover sole and powerful chorizo into a tower with the help of oven-dried tomatoes and aubergine.

The menu doesn't appear to change much: Mike Bird, who was at Novelli W8 (see entry, London), inherited this one from his predecessor. The carte's prices are not tempered by a set-lunch option, but the kitchen has produced notable successes, all the better for being simple: lavender-roast duck breast, for example, with acacia honey sauce. Desserts, also a strong point, have included flavoured crème brûlée accompanied by 'inspired' chocolate brandy-snaps, and another brochette, this time of fruits on a Grand Marnier sabayon. Service at lunch is geared to those in a hurry. The wine list leans towards France and, except for a quartet of house vins de pays (£15.50 a bottle), is tilted towards the quality end of the market with prices to match. Next door, Novelli EC1 offers a less expensive alternative on a carte that might take in skate and whelk salad, grilled ribeye steak, and banana tarte Tatin.

CHEF: Michael Bird   PROPRIETOR: Jean-Christophe Novelli   OPEN: Mon to Fri 12 to 2.30, 6.30 to 11.15   MEALS: alc (main courses £15 to £21.50)   SERVICE: 15% (optional), card slips closed   CARDS: Amex, Delta, Diners, MasterCard, Switch, Visa   DETAILS: 60 seats. 12 seats outside. Private parties: 35 main room, 35 private room. Vegetarian meals. Children's helpings. No music. Air-conditioned   ⊖ Farringdon

Mandarin Kitchen £ map 13

14–16 Queensway, W2 3RX   COOKING 4
TEL: (0171) 727 9012   FAX: (0171) 727 9468   COST £17–£60

Renowned for its fish and seafood dishes, this long-established Chinese restaurant occupies large premises on busy Queensway. Even so, by nine o'clock there's often a queue. Despite resembling a tunnel at the rear, the interior is fairly bright, with pictures lending cheer. A lengthy menu takes in the breadth of Cantonese cuisine, excepting offal dishes but including robust flavours like salted fish and chicken fried rice, and texture foods such as jellyfish with cucumber. Shellfish is the highlight, though, especially the 'live' crabs and lobsters. Pot of crab with bean noodle and dry shrimps in chilli sauce is one diner's favourite: 'this time it was better than ever – masses of dried shrimps and a good amount of bamboo shoot'. Praise has come too for an appetiser of 'fat and juicy' razor clams instead of the usual prawn crackers, but complaints are not unknown, and usually concern service, which can veer towards disdainful. However, staff were helpful and prompt during inspection. Wines include some heavyweight Bordeaux and Burgundies, with the New World hardly getting a look in. House wine costs from £10.50.

CHEF: K.W. Man   PROPRIETOR: Helen Cheung   OPEN: all week 12 to 11.30   CLOSED: 26 to 27 Dec   MEALS: alc (main courses £6 to £25). Set L £9.90, Set D £9.90 to £30   SERVICE: not inc   CARDS: Amex, Delta, Diners, MasterCard, Switch, Visa   DETAILS: 120 seats. Private parties: 100 main room. Vegetarian meals. No music. Air-conditioned   ⊖ Queensway

Mantanah £

map 12

2 Orton Buildings, Portland Road, SE25 4UD
TEL: (0181) 771 1148   FAX: (0181) 771 2341

COOKING 4
COST £21–£43

The décor in this unassuming family restaurant shows 'utter disregard for fashion', its pale pink walls and apricot linen napkins contrasting with royal blue tablecloths. Friendly service and good Thai cooking are appreciated by local residents and even a visitor from the motherland, who noted 'authenticity, good taste and superb presentation', making him 'feel at home, or even better'. The long menu covers all regions of Thailand and nearly a third of it is devoted to vegetarians. Conventional ideas mix with fancifully named dishes such as 'Pink Lady' (deep-fried aubergine with chilli sauce), or 'New Adventure', which includes sataw, a type of bean native to southern Thailand and an acquired taste. A vegetarian version of classic pad Thai noodles with fried bean curd has been endorsed, while moo pad king (sliced pork lightly cooked with oyster mushrooms) comes in a finely balanced sauce with spring onions, garlic and ginger. More than one reporter has praised tom yum goong (prawn soup), comprising tender crustaceans in a chilli-hot broth with well-handled, complex spice combinations. Occasional uncharacteristic lapses and ordinary desserts and coffee fail to take the shine off the experience. House wine is £7.95.

CHEF: Tym Srisawatt   PROPRIETORS: Mr and Mrs K.S. Yeoh   OPEN: Tue to Sun D only 6.30 to 11   CLOSED: 25 and 26 Dec, 1 Jan   MEALS: alc (main courses £5.50 to £7.50). Set D £15 to £20   SERVICE: not inc, card slips closed   CARDS: Amex, Delta, Diners, MasterCard, Switch, Visa   DETAILS: 40 seats. Private parties: 40 main room. Vegetarian meals. No cigars in dining room. Wheelchair access (not WC). Music. Air-conditioned   £5

Mash ♥ 🍞

map 15

19–21 Great Portland Street, W1N 5AB
TEL: (0171) 637 5555   FAX: (0171) 637 7333

COOKING 3
COST £30–£51

Described as 'cool' by our younger correspondents and 'noisy as a canteen' by older ones, Mash continues to surprise and delight with its pale surfaces, huge stainless steel brewing vessels, and witty '70s-style photo murals in the bar. The first-floor restaurant's well-used wood-fired oven is one of the principal attractions, turning out freshly baked ciabatta, exotic pizzas, and wood-roasted Goosnargh chicken with artichokes, almonds and preserved lemons. Not all dishes live up to their interesting menu descriptions, but desserts such as summer pudding, and chocolate and Rice Krispies fondant, benefit from careful cooking and incongruously old-fashioned but attractive presentation. Praise has been garnered for breakfasts and weekend brunch, which can be as varied as pizza with duck confit and bok choy, and vanilla French toast with crispy bacon and quince syrup. The micro-brewery sells kegs of beer to take away, and trendy office workers email their orders for lunchtime bento boxes. Wines are arranged by grape or regional varietals and offer a good choice of styles from both hemispheres. While the likes of Ch. Lafite, Stag's Leap and Jim Barry make some stellar contributions, more ordinary fare can be had from £12.50 upwards.

CHEF: Matthew Fanthorpe   PROPRIETOR: Oliver Peyton   OPEN: Mon to Sat 12 to 3, 6 to 11.30, Sun 11 to 5   CLOSED: 25 and 26 Dec, 1 Jan, Easter Sun and Mon   MEALS: alc (main courses £6.50 to £13.50). Set L £16.50   SERVICE: 12.5% (optional), card slips closed   CARDS: Amex, Delta, Diners, MasterCard, Switch, Visa   DETAILS: 140 seats. Private parties: 30 main room. Vegetarian meals. Music. Air-conditioned   ⊖ Oxford Circus

Matsuri

map 15

15 Bury Street, SW1Y 6AL   COOKING 4
TEL: (0171) 839 1101   FAX: (0171) 930 7010   COST £21–£89

Although known for its teppanyaki hotplates – around which you sit in this L-shaped dining room decorated with Japanese fans and lanterns – Matsuri also majors on sushi, a good way to start a meal here. Choose on a piece-by-piece basis, or from one of the variety of set-menu options. One reporter sampled a variety, including highly rated sea urchin and 'stunningly' fresh eel, flying fish roe and yellowtail. Sashimi of tuna, yellow fish and salmon have also come in for praise, along with the advice not to skip on the peppery, spicy mizuna leaves. Steamed scallops with a butter sauce has an uncharacteristically 'East meets West' air about it, but sirloin teppanyaki ('raw as requested', with a caramelised soy crust), has been well received. Bento boxes appear at lunchtime, staff are enthusiastic and helpful, and the wine list is wide-ranging; prices open at £18. Alternatively, there are sixteen bottles of saké to choose from.

CHEF: Kanehiro Takase   PROPRIETOR: Shigemi Matsuda   OPEN: Mon to Sat 12 to 2.30, 6 to 10.30   CLOSED: bank hols   MEALS: alc (main courses £6.50 to £30). Set L £10 to £25, Set D £20 (6 to 7pm) to £55   SERVICE: 12.5% (optional), card slips closed   CARDS: Amex, Delta, Diners, MasterCard, Visa   DETAILS: 130 seats. Private parties: 18 main room, 8 private room. Vegetarian meals. Children's helpings. Wheelchair access (also WC). Music. Air-conditioned ⊖ Green Park, Piccadilly Circus

All details are as accurate as possible at the time of going to press, but chefs and owners often change, and it is wise to check by telephone before making a special journey. Many readers have been disappointed when set-price bargain meals are no longer available. Ask when booking.

Melati

map 15

21 Great Windmill Street, W1V 7PH
TEL: (0171) 437 2745

COOKING 1
COST £25–£60

Ranged over three plain wooden floors in the heart of Soho, with beige walls and closely packed tables, this is something of an institution, having served genuine-ish Malay/Indonesian food since 1981. The menu is long, with starters followed by rice and noodle dishes, then the principal meats, fish and seafood. Fresh sotong goreng (squid fritters) come in a light batter, chicken satay is given an 'OK' peanut sauce, and nasi lemak (coconut rice garnished with fish, prawns and egg) was 'the star of the evening' for one reporter. Desserts have included 'well-balanced and well-flavoured' quay dada (a good-sized pancake with coconut filling) and es chin chow (grass jelly with ice and syrup). Service is somewhat chaotic but willing, and the short wine list features house French and Italian for around £9; or drink Tiger beer.

CHEF: Sjamsir Alamsjah   PROPRIETORS: Margaret Ong and Sjamsir Alamsjah   OPEN: all week noon to 11.30 (12.30 Fri and Sat)   CLOSED: 25 Dec   MEALS: alc (main courses £6 to £7.50). Set D £45 (inc wine)   SERVICE: not inc; 10% for parties of 5 or more   CARDS: Amex, Delta, MasterCard, Switch, Visa   DETAILS: 100 seats. Private parties: 40 main room. Vegetarian meals. No cigars in dining room. Music   ✈ Piccadilly Circus £5

Mem Saheb ✱ £

map 15

65 Amsterdam Road, E14 3UU
TEL: (0171) 538 3008   FAX: (0181) 984 0655
EMAIL: memsaheb@memsaheb.demon.co.uk

COOKING 2
COST £17–£38

Docklanders should 'appreciate what a gem they have on their doorstep', enthused a reporter after a trip to this classy Indian restaurant with its view of the Thames and the Millennium Dome. Mem Saheb's lacklustre, modern exterior hides a comfortable, spacious bar and dining room furnished in burnt sienna colours with bare wooden flooring. 'Impressively enthusiastic' staff add to the appeal. Though the menu has a few commonplace curries, there are plenty of enticing regional specials: lamb xacuti from Goa, 'richly flavoured, with well-balanced spicing', and sag paneer bora, a 'cake' of spinach filled with paneer cheese in a mild tomato sauce. Bangladeshi cooking is to the fore – try boal dopiaza (fillets of a freshwater fish with onions in a spicy gravy) – though occasional food festivals feature the cuisine of other Indian regions. Imported Sunny beer is a highlight of the drinks list. House wine is £6.95.

CHEF: Anwar Hussain   PROPRIETORS: Mridul Kanti Das, Rabiul Hoque and Iuliana Kadir   OPEN: Mon to Fri L 12 to 2.30, all week D 6 to 11.30   CLOSED: 25 and 26 Dec   MEALS: alc (main courses £6 to £10). Set L £10.95. Cover £1   SERVICE: not inc   CARDS: Amex, Delta, Diners, MasterCard, Switch, Visa   DETAILS: 70 seats. 25 seats outside. Private parties: 45 main room, 45 private room. Car park. Vegetarian meals. Children's helpings. No smoking in 1 dining room. Wheelchair access (not WC). Music. Air-conditioned £5

£5 indicates that the restaurant has elected to participate in the Good Food Guide voucher scheme. For full details, see page 6.

Mesclun £   map 12

24 Stoke Newington Church Street, N16 0LU	COOKING 3
TEL: (0171) 249 5029 FAX: (0171) 275 8448	COST £21–£39

This unassuming blue-fronted neighbourhood restaurant competes in a street sporting eateries of every kind of cuisine and décor. Refurbishment has brought air-conditioning and smoke purifiers, while the food is praised for both its value and quality. Broadly European in style, dishes also stray Eastwards for roast duck with spring onions, soy and coriander. Among starters, mussels come in a mouclade, and pan-fried chicken livers with balsamic reduction and baby-spinach salad. Main courses are largely straightforward: pork with prunes, smoked bacon and pickling onions, for example, or chump of lamb with a basil-infused stock reduction. Fish is offered as a choice of two, 'fresh from the market each day'. Salad comes four ways, including the restaurant's namesake, and side dishes of vegetables arrive automatically with main courses. Desserts stand above the norm: mixed fruit compote with muscat custard, or zabaglione and amaretti semifreddo with butterscotch sauce. Service is informed and on the ball, and wines are keenly priced, with almost all bottles under £20; house wines are £9.95.

CHEFS: Dirceu Pozzebon and Ozan Çiçek   PROPRIETORS: Salih Çiçek and Dirceu Pozzebon OPEN: all week D only 6 to 11   CLOSED: 25 Dec to 2 Jan   MEALS: alc (main courses £7.50 to £12), Set D before 7.30 £10.95 (2 courses) to £12.95   SERVICE: 10% (optional), card slips closed   CARDS: Delta, MasterCard, Switch, Visa   DETAILS: 36 seats. Private parties: 40 main room. Vegetarian meals. Children's helpings. Wheelchair access (also women's WC). Music. Air-conditioned (£5)

Mezzo   map 15

100 Wardour Street, W1 3LE	[NEW CHEF]
TEL: (0171) 314 4000 FAX: (0171) 314 4040	COST £28–£66

Restaurants of this size (and they don't come much bigger) rely on an army of kitchen staff. Since most of them will probably just carry on as before, a change of executive chef may not make all that much difference to standards. In any case, Guy Bossom and Tony Moyse remain as head chefs in Mezzo and Mezzonine respectively, although as the *Guide* went to press a new executive had yet to be appointed, and we understand the menus will continue more or less in their present form. With live music every night, plus a dance floor (hence the cover charge), it is clear that food is not the only draw at Mezzo, but it aims for a broadly European style that takes in hummus ravioli, saddle of rabbit with black pudding, a few grills, and lots of shellfish. Mezzonine's net, meanwhile, spreads from fish and chips with aïoli to Vietnamese spring roll by way of Thai red pork curry. Both have time limits on tables. Vin de Pays d'Oc house wines are £12.75.

CHEF: Guy Bossom (Mezzo) and Tony Moyse (Mezzanine)   PROPRIETOR: Conran Restaurants OPEN: Mezzo Sun to Fri L 12 to 3, all week D 6 to 12 (1 Fri and Sat, 11 Sun); Mezzonine Mon to Sat 12 to 3 (4 Sat), 5.30 to 1 (3 Fri and Sat)   CLOSED: 25 Dec, 1 Jan   MEALS: Mezzo alc (main courses £9.50 to £17.50). Set L Mon to Fri £12.50 (2 courses) to £15.50, Set L Sun £15.50, Set D before 7pm £14. Mezzonine alc (main courses £6 to £12.50). Set L and D before 7pm £8.50 (2 courses) to £11.50. Cover £5   SERVICE: 12.5% (optional), card slips closed   CARDS: Amex, Delta, Diners, MasterCard, Switch, Visa   DETAILS: Mezzo 350 seats, Mezzonine 190 seats. Private parties: 1000 main room, 44 private room. Vegetarian meals. Wheelchair access (also WC). Music. Air-conditioned   ⊖ Piccadilly Circus £5

Mirabelle ♥

CLASSIC 2000 COOKING

map 15

56 Curzon Street, W1Y 8DL
TEL: (0171) 499 4636   FAX: (0171) 499 5449

COOKING 6
COST £26–£79

There is much to observe on the way downstairs from pavement level, past green leather sofas, over the dark parquet floor, through the long bar, and into an airy dining room. But detail does not obscure the sense of grand design; rather, the sympathetic re-creation of a historical site induces a feeling of wellbeing. MPW trade marks range from dramatic flower arrangements to a generous and comforting menu that takes in endive tarte Tatin with scallops, and braised pork cheek with ginger. 'Classics' of one sort or another are a much-appreciated strength, from omelette Arnold Bennett, via Caesar salad, to snails bourguignon.

Mirabelle scores in its capacity to prepare such familiar dishes with care and sound judgement, most notably a rich, sweet, smooth rendering of foie gras parfait on a lake of jellied and acidulated stock. And it makes a good job of poached, undyed smoked haddock on sliced Jersey potatoes, surmounted by a 'perfectly timed poached egg', with a drizzle of beurre blanc. Reporters find desserts equally impressive – a light and creamy iced nougat parfait with a red fruit coulis, for instance – and have heaped praise on the sour-dough rolls. Service from 'masses of staff', many of them French, is attentive and responsive (but note that credit card slips are left open even though 12.5 per cent 'optional' service is included on the bill). Peripherals concerning comfort (seating, smoking, draughts, etc.) have taken the shine off things for some reporters. Set-price lunches (including Sunday) are a comparative bargain.

Although drinkers on a budget will find their choice somewhat restricted, there is no denying the quality and appeal of wines on the large main list, and an extensive collection of fine wines is also available on request. Prices start at £14.50 in the Côtes du Rhône and end at £30,000 in Bordeaux with 1847 d'Yquem (no takers yet then . . .).

CHEF: Charlie Rushton   PROPRIETOR: Marco Pierre White   OPEN: all week 12 to 2.30 (3 Sun), 6 to 11.30 (10.30 Sun)   CLOSED: 1 Jan   MEALS: alc (main courses £13 to £25). Set L Mon to Sat £14.95 (2 courses) to £17.95, Set L Sun £14.50   SERVICE: 12.5% (optional)   CARDS: Amex, Delta, Diners, MasterCard, Switch, Visa   DETAILS: 120 seats. Private parties: 120 main room, 36 and 48 private rooms. Music. Air-conditioned   ⊖ Green Park

£ means that it is possible to have a three-course meal, including coffee, half a bottle of house wine and service for £25 or less per person, at any time the restaurant is open, i.e. at dinner as well as lunch. It may be possible to spend considerably more than this, but by choosing carefully you should find £25 or less achievable.

If you have access to the Internet, you can find The Good Food Guide online at the Which? Online web site (http://www.which.net).

Mirch Masala £

map 12

1416 London Road, SW16 4BZ
TEL: (0181) 679 1828

COOKING 2
COST £11–£29

Norbury might be a suburb of Lahore, not London, if this basic eating house is anything to go by. Its plastic-topped tables are always fully occupied, many with family parties. Cutlery, paper napkins and glasses for BYO wine or beer (no corkage) are brought to the table by members of the family who also cook and own the place. They claim everything is prepared to order, with more or less ginger, garlic or what you will, as required, but they don't always seem to believe that some native Londoners like a really hot curry. Lamb, in karahi or their 'new authentic deigi dishes' (curries), is often on the bone for extra flavour, and tandoori grills are probably the best choices.

CHEF: Raza Ali   PROPRIETORS: Raza Ali, Mrs Azra Ali and Raiz Ali   OPEN: Tue to Sun 12 to 12, also open bank hol Mon   MEALS: alc (main courses £3.50 to £8). BYO (no corkage)   SERVICE: not inc, card slips closed   CARDS: Delta, Diners, MasterCard, Switch, Visa   DETAILS: 70 seats. Private parties: 100 main room. Vegetarian meals. Children's helpings. No-smoking area. Wheelchair access (also WC). Music. Air-conditioned (£5)

Mr Kong £

map 15

21 Lisle Street, WC2H 7BA
TEL: (0171) 437 7341

COOKING 3
COST £21–£44

A highly reputed Chinatown restaurant, Mr Kong attracts varying reports about its service, veering from 'detached, rather brusque' to 'very pleasant and efficient'. Similarly, its furnishings please some ('clean and bright') and perturb others ('basic and spartan'). However, the culinary skill of chef/owner Mr Kong is widely acknowledged. Dining takes place in two rooms, the ground floor (with its green carpets and pink tablecloths) having the edge over the basement. The wide-ranging Cantonese menu takes in scores of stir-fries, hotpots, barbecued meats and adventurous combinations of flavour and texture, such as stewed oysters with roasted pork and mushrooms, and stuffed fish maw with baby clams, prawn paste and steamed vegetables. The chef's specials are worth exploring, including a starter of deep-fried prawn rolls with coriander, and an inspector relished the 'robust flavours' of braised belly pork with yam hotpot. Another diner commended the 'crisp skin and excellent flesh' of Peking duck. The short wine list rarely strays outside France, although it offers Tsing Tao Chardonnay for £13.50.

CHEF/PROPRIETOR: Mr Kong   OPEN: all week noon to 2.45am   CLOSED: Christmas   MEALS: alc (main courses £6 to £12). Set L and D (min 2 to 8) £9.30 to £22   SERVICE: not inc   CARDS: Amex, Delta, Diners, MasterCard, Switch, Visa   DETAILS: 110 seats. Private parties: 50 main room. Vegetarian meals. Music. Air-conditioned   ⊖ Leicester Square

Not inc *in the details at the end of an entry indicates that no service charge is made and any tipping is at the discretion of the customer.*

Mitsukoshi

map 15

Dorland House, 14–20 Regent Street, SW1Y 4PH
TEL: (0171) 930 0317 FAX: (0171) 839 1167

COOKING 4
COST £34–£82

Mitsukoshi now follows the usual Japanese practice of lower prices at lunchtime, though at dinner 15 per cent service is still added (note that card slips are left open). Staff are pleasant and helpful, although the décor does not match the distinction of the food. Chawan mushi, a garnished savoury egg custard, features in many of the wide range of set menus along with sashimi, tempura, grilled eel or beef, and even modest pork cutlet. At dinner the carte is longer, with a variety of rice and noodles in soup. Among many delicacies is grilled shishamo – the finest of small fish – and hirame, thinly sliced turbot sashimi. Unusual sushi include hand-rolled yellowtail or toro with leek, and flying fish roe.The mainly French wine list lacks details. House wines are £15, or drink saké.

CHEFS: Mr Y. Motohashi and Mr Kitano PROPRIETOR: Mitsukoshi (UK) Ltd OPEN: Mon to Sat 12 to 2.30, 6 to 9.30 CLOSED: Christmas, Easter MEALS: alc (main courses £4.50 to £23). Set L £12 to £40, Set D £20 to £50 SERVICE: not inc L, 15% D CARDS: Amex, Diners, Switch, Visa DETAILS: 90 seats. Private parties: 55 main room, 12 and 22 private rooms. Vegetarian meals. Children's helpings. Music. Air-conditioned ⊖ Piccadilly Circus

Miyama

map 15

38 Clarges Street, W1Y 7PJ
TEL: (0171) 499 2443 FAX: (0171) 493 1573

COOKING 4
COST £24–£79

Consistency is a watchword of this eighteen-year-old Japanese restaurant on a quiet Mayfair street. Regulars – mostly Japanese, many on business – have come to expect well-prepared, attractively presented food from a menu covering most of Japan's main cooking styles: sushi, sashimi, grilled or fried fish, tempura and teppanyaki. Novices have a series of set meals for guidance. Ingredients are of a high quality – witness ultra-fresh tuna sashimi – and the kitchen's skills are amply demonstrated by 'extremely delicate' deep-fried bean curd in soya broth. Main courses maintain the standard; teppanyaki beef is fine tender fillet steak 'cooked with a light touch', while salmon teriyaki produces two fillets grilled just so and served with 'richly flavoured' sauce. Service, too, is laudable, from courteous waitresses dressed in simple kimonos. The bright dining room is furnished with black and chrome chairs, with white walls and geometric-patterned prints. Downstairs is a teppanyaki hot-plate bar area, together with more private rooms. House wines on the otherwise staid and limited wine list are £10; instead, drink saké or try Japan's top-selling beer, Asahi Super Dry.

CHEF/PROPRIETOR: Mr F. Miyama OPEN: Mon to Fri L 12 to 2.30, all week D 6 to 10.30 CLOSED: 25 Dec, 1 Jan MEALS: alc (main courses £10.50 to £24). Set L £12 to £18, Set D £34 to £42 SERVICE: 15%, card slips closed CARDS: Amex, Delta, Diners, MasterCard, Switch, Visa DETAILS: 64 seats. Private parties: 4 and 8 private rooms. Wheelchair access (not WC). Music. Air-conditioned ⊖ Green Park

To find a restaurant in a particular area use the maps at the centre of the book.

Mon Plaisir

map 15

21 Monmouth Street, WC2H 9DD
TEL: (0171) 836 7243 and 240 3757   COOKING 3
FAX: (0171) 240 4774   COST £25–£52

This busy French bistro dates from the 1940s and its main dining room has been convincingly restored to the period, its walls covered with pictures, posters, mirrors and a large blackboard for daily specials. It can be 'cramped and noisy' at peak times, but diners admire the cheerful 'no-nonsense atmosphere' in which food can be ordered, served and paid for within a two-hour time span. Despite the restaurant's longevity, the menu has moved far beyond classics of onion soup, steak frites with béarnaise sauce and tarte Tatin, yet there is no doubting the popularity of such dishes, which win plaudits for their 'good, robust flavours'. Those who yearn for more modern and ambitious food can choose from quail confit with ravioli of pea purée and pearl barley; spring onion and Roquefort risotto; or loin of rabbit served with sweetcorn, ham and leek mousse and Puy lentils. Early-evening set menus delight theatre-goers with their good value. French house wines cost £8.95 for red and £9.50 for white.

CHEF: Patrick Smith   PROPRIETOR: Alain Lhermitte   OPEN: Mon to Fri L 12 to 3, Mon to Sat D 5.50 to 11.30   CLOSED: bank hols   MEALS: alc (main courses £9.50 to £16). Set L £14.95, Set D before 7.15pm £11.95 (2 courses) to £14.95   SERVICE: 12.5% (optional), card slips closed CARDS: Amex, Delta, Diners, MasterCard, Switch, Visa   DETAILS: 90 seats. Private parties: 30 main room. Vegetarian meals. Children's helpings. No cigars/pipes in dining room. Wheelchair access (not WC). Air-conditioned   ✤ Covent Garden

Montana

map 12

125–129 Dawes Road, SW6 7EA   COOKING 2
TEL: (0171) 385 9500   FAX: (0171) 386 0337   COST £22–£52

Montana is part of a contemporary American-style mini-chain that is sprouting up around London (see also Dakota and Idaho, London, and Canyon, Richmond). In an American Indian setting of spears, feathers and old photographs of Big Chiefs, and under an indigo sky of a ceiling, you will almost certainly need help from the staff to sort out your ancho jams from your serrano salsas. The seasonally changing menu spans more than just the Midwest, whether a Rhode Island chowder of smoked scallop, mussel and fennel, or wild boar and butternut squash quesadilla. For pudding there might be caramelised banana chimichanga with Brazil nut praline ice cream. Not only are breads 'simply wonderful', but they are offered more than once, and free: try the mint and garlic one. Briefly described wines – more over £20 than under – are by no means exclusively American but do reflect the West Coast obsession with all things healthy in that organic ones are highlighted. House wine (not organic) is £11.

CHEF: Daniel McDowell   PROPRIETOR: Montana Restaurants Ltd   OPEN: Fri to Sun L 12 to 3.30, all week D 7 to 11 (11.30 Fri and Sat, 10.30 Sun)   MEALS: alc D (main courses £11 to £15). Set L £10 (2 courses) to £12.50. Brunch menu Sat and Sun 12 to 3.30   SERVICE: 12.5% (optional) CARDS: Amex, Delta, MasterCard, Switch, Visa   DETAILS: 70 seats. Private parties: 70 main room. Vegetarian meals. Children's helpings. Music. Air-conditioned   ✤ Fulham Broadway

▲ *Montcalm Hotel, Crescent* map 13

Great Cumberland Place, W1A 2LF	COOKING 4
TEL: (0171) 402 4288 FAX: (0171) 724 9180	COST £26–£44

For luxurious comfort, first-rate service, bargain prices and an intoxicating menu, the Montcalm Hotel's restaurant in a Georgian crescent behind Marble Arch would be hard to beat. 'Do stress what a delightful experience it is,' urges one visitor. Stephen Whitney (ex-Mosimann's and the Savoy; see entry, London) has the skill and experience to take a 'whole mad assortment of ingredients and work them into an elegant and original whole'. Towers are a typical way of presenting them: artichoke heart filled with white crabmeat (turned green with guacamole), topped by a pastry case containing cumin-spiced potato, the whole given a frilly edge of pink grapefruit and sweet chilli sauce.

The range extends from an offaly dish of pink calf's liver, bacon, sweetbreads and black pudding, combined with cinnamon-glazed apple balls and delicately sweet quince purée, to tender rolls of chicken breast on saffron potatoes in a sea of richly saffroned fish broth containing squid, prawn, mussels, white fish and clam in the shell. Puddings are also highly decorative, taking in a dramatic long triangle of sharp lemon tart with caramel on top. The shortish wine list is big in France, but unless you wish to pay West End prices keep to the half-bottle of easy-drinking Californian red, or Vin de Pays d'Oc Chardonnay, that is included in the price of set meals. House wines are £15.

CHEF: Steve Whitney   PROPRIETOR: Montcalm Hotel Nikko   OPEN: Mon to Fri L 12.30 to 2.30, all week D 6.30 to 10.30   CLOSED: some bank hols   MEALS: Set L and D £19 (2 courses) to £24 (inc wine)   SERVICE: not inc   CARDS: Amex, Diners, MasterCard, Switch, Visa   DETAILS: 60 seats. Private parties: 80 main room, 20 to 60 private rooms. Vegetarian meals. Children's helpings. Music. Air-conditioned   ACCOMMODATION: 120 rooms, all with bath/shower. TV. Phone. Room only £205 to £395. Rooms for disabled. Baby facilities   ⊖ Marble Arch (£5)

Moro map 13

34–36 Exmouth Market, EC1R 4QE	COOKING 6
TEL: (0171) 833 8336 FAX: (0171) 833 9338	COST £25–£39

This is a 'gem of a place' that is 'still jumping' after three years. A dimly lit, low-ceilinged room with bare floorboards and a long bar culminates in a small open-to-view kitchen at the far end, where meat sears on the chargrill, and 'great steaming bowlfuls' of rustic Spanish fare emerge from a wood-fired oven. Full of lively invention, it draws inspiration from all over the southern Mediterranean, including North Africa and the Middle East, and aims for bold, direct flavours: a starter of loosely scrambled egg and broad beans comes with shaved flakes of pungent botarga (dried, salted tuna roe), while a small filo pastry brik, filled with chicken and dusted with icing sugar, is variously spiked with coriander, cinnamon, orange blossom water and 'hot, hot harissa'.

Pink, juicy, wood-roasted breast of duck with okra and chickpeas is an object lesson in how to serve duck with sweet fruity accompaniments (a reduction of pomegranate juice and molasses) and do it with 'grace and savour'. Accompaniments to a charcoal-grilled leg of lamb – cinnamoned loquats, and home-made yoghurt scattered with tiny black pungent seeds – likewise produced 'a triumphant match' for our inspector. Desserts appeal for their simplicity, as in scoops of 'deeply alluring' rosewater and cardamom ice cream sprinkled with powdered cinnamon. Even when busy there is no great sense of hurry, just unflappable and workmanlike service. Chunks of salty, crusty ciabatta or rough wholemeal bread arrive at the start with olive oil for dipping, and the whole thing is 'astonishingly good value', helped by fairly priced wines from just three countries – France, Italy and, of course, Spain – with a token bottle from Portugal. House French is £9.50.

CHEFS: Mr and Mrs Sam Clark   PROPRIETORS: Mr and Mrs Sam Clark, and Mark Sainsbury
OPEN: Mon to Fri 12.30 to 2.30, 7 to 10.30   CLOSED: 1 week Christmas, bank hols   MEALS: alc
(main courses £9.50 to £13.50)   SERVICE: not inc, 12.5% for parties of 7 or more   CARDS:
Amex, Delta, MasterCard, Switch, Visa   DETAILS: 80 seats. 15 seats outside. Private parties:
100 main room. Vegetarian meals. Wheelchair access (also WC). No music. Air-conditioned
⊖ Farringdon

Moshi Moshi Sushi £

maps 12 and 13

Unit 24, Liverpool Street Station, EC2M 7QH
TEL/FAX: (0171) 247 3227
7–8 Limeburner Lane, EC4M 7HY
TEL: (0171) 248 1808   FAX: (0171) 248 1807
Level 2, Cabot Place East, Canary Wharf, E14 4QT
TEL: (0171) 512 9911   FAX: (0171) 512 9201

COOKING 1
COST £12–£23

A third branch of London's original purveyor of conveyor-belt sushi opened at Canary Wharf late in 1998. Each version has a slightly different atmosphere but an identical format: sit at the bar, watching the various nori rolls and nigiri sushi rattle round on colour-coded plates, grabbing whatever takes your fancy (an illustrated card aids identification) as it whizzes past, and order specials from one of the chefs: watching the flashing blades at work behind the bar is equally entertaining. 'Geta' (wooden 'slippers' bearing a selection of sushi) are also available, but aren't as much fun. It is not everyone's cup of tea, but for those prepared to put up with uncomfortable bar stools and rubbing elbows with their neighbours, it is an enjoyable experience, and value for money is unquestionable. Miso soup, free green tea and Japanese beers are supplied by roaming waiters. Details below are based on Liverpool Street and may be slightly different for other branches (note that Limeburner Lane is open only for lunch).

CHEF: Hong Suli   PROPRIETOR: Caroline Bennet   OPEN: Mon to Fri 11.30 to 9   CLOSED: 24 Dec
to 1 Jan   MEALS: alc (plate prices £1.20 to £2.90). Set L and D £4.90 to £11.50 (all 1 course).
Cover 50p   SERVICE: none, card slips closed   CARDS: Delta, MasterCard, Switch, Visa
DETAILS: 75 seats. Vegetarian meals. No smoking in dining room (Liverpool Street only).
Wheelchair access (not WC). Music. Air-conditioned   ⊖ Liverpool Street

The 2001 Guide *will be published before Christmas 2000. Reports on meals are most welcome at any time of the year, but are particularly valuable in the spring (no later than June). Send them to* The Good Food Guide, *FREEPOST, 2 Marylebone Road, London NW1 4DF. Or email your report to guidereports@which.co.uk.*

Museum Street Café 🍴 £

map 15

47 Museum Street, WC1A 1LY
TEL/FAX: (0171) 405 3211   COOKING 5
EMAIL: bookings@museumstreetcafe.demon.co.uk   COST £24–£38

It is now more a restaurant than a café, so the owners tell us, as it no longer opens for breakfast, afternoon teas or weekend brunches, but does for dinner on Tuesday to Friday. Menus are totally vegetarian, and draw their inspiration from all over, showing off immaculate ingredients to best advantage. There is always a soup, maybe Jerusalem artichoke, or watermelon gazpacho, and a pasta option such as mushroom tortelloni with baby spinach, slow-cooked courgettes and chipotle oil. Tarts, meanwhile, might be topped with caramelised onions, lentils and purple sprouting broccoli, or something cheesier like Wensleydale, dried tomatoes, leeks and saffron. For those with room, the Valrhona chocolate cake is a consistent winner; otherwise, home-made caramel or espresso ice creams might tempt. An invigorating glass of fresh carrot and ginger juice makes a good aperitif, and the tiny wine list offers genuine variety at friendly prices. Languedoc varietals are £10.50.

CHEFS/PROPRIETORS: Mark Nathan and Gail Koerber   OPEN: Mon to Fri 12 to 3, Tue to Fri D 6 to 9.30   CLOSED: 2 weeks Christmas, 1 week Easter, bank hols   MEALS: alc (main courses £8 to £9.50)   SERVICE: not inc   CARDS: Amex, Delta, MasterCard, Switch, Visa   DETAILS: 40 seats. 6 seats outside. Private parties: 30 main room. Vegetarian meals. No smoking in dining room. Wheelchair access (also WC). Occasional music   ⊖ Holborn, Tottenham Court Road

Neal Street Restaurant

map 15

26 Neal Street, WC2H 9PS   COOKING 5
TEL: (0171) 836 8368   FAX: (0171) 240 3964   COST £44–£75

'Will all Conran dining rooms look this good after [almost] thirty years?' pondered one visitor to this early example. High ceilings, sharp spotlights, and cream-painted brick walls give the place a bright yet relaxed feel, while jars of preserved vegetables and baskets of mushrooms point to the owner's 'passions'. Antonio Carluccio seems like a man with an enjoyable hobby rather than a job, so it seems perfectly natural that he should come round to greet customers after meals. It also seems right that he should lay his hands on some fine ingredients, and that Kirk Vincent should do very little to them. Mushrooms (some wild, some less so) come simply sautéed, or in a well-constructed salad with rocket and crispy bacon; or there might be a simple plate of prosciutto to start.

Beyond that the food combines rustic and cosmopolitan strands in foie gras with balsamic sauce, sweetbreads with sweet-and-sour onions, and fried calamari. Pasta has included a vegetable-stuffed raviolo with a poached egg on top, surrounded by a delicately truffle-flavoured juice, and fish is well handled, judging by an agreeable dish of sea bream with samphire and seaweed. To finish, fried Sardinian raviolo with orange honey sounds the one to go for, although the bitter chocolate pot is highly rated. Service is sharp and responsive, and deserves a 10 per cent charge, thought one visitor; shame they add 15 per cent then. Wines are mostly Italian, bolstered by a few bins from France and a sole Californian Chardonnay, with only the two house wines (£11 each) costing less than £20 once the service charge has been applied.

CHEF: Kirk Vincent   PROPRIETOR: Antonio Carluccio   OPEN: Mon to Sat 12.30 to 2.30, 6 to 11
CLOSED: Christmas, bank hols   MEALS: alc (main courses £14 to £20)   SERVICE: 15% (optional),
card slips closed   CARDS: Amex, Delta, Diners, MasterCard, Switch, Visa   DETAILS: 65 seats.
Private parties: 12 main room, 24 private room. Vegetarian meals. No pipes in dining room.
Wheelchair access (not WC). No music. Air-conditioned   ● Covent Garden

New Hoo Wah £   map 15

37 Gerrard Street, W1V 7LJ	COOKING 1
TEL: (0171) 434 0540 FAX: (0171) 434 0521	COST £18–£56

For dim sum at lunchtime this eating hall packs in Chinese families, business
parties and others. Those prepared in the kitchen such as spring rolls, roast pork
buns and paper prawns are ordered by ticking boxes on the paper menu. Stuffed
tofu, aubergine and peppers are cooked at the 'street stall' by the window. The
special lunch menu offers dishes that may only appeal to seekers after
authenticity, ranging from pan-fried scrambled egg with silver fish and chive, to
snake soup with noodle in a wooden barrel. Dinner is a more conventional,
mainly Cantonese menu. Fried smoked chicken with red chilli, chopped green
onions and salt is 'simple but very good'. Every sort of seafood is listed
separately, and care is needed to avoid ordering similarly prepared dishes.
House wine is £8.50, or drink tea: oolong or po-li rather than jasmine.

CHEF: Mr Man   PROPRIETOR: Michael Yeung   OPEN: all week 12 to 11.15   CLOSED: 25 and 26
Dec   MEALS: alc (main courses £6 to £16). Set D £9.50 to £20 (all min 2)   SERVICE: 10%
CARDS: Amex, Delta, Diners, MasterCard, Switch, Visa   DETAILS: 200 seats. Private parties: 200
main room, 50 private room. Vegetarian meals. Music. Air-conditioned   ● Leicester Square

New Tayyab £   **NEW ENTRY** map 12

83 Fieldgate, E1 1JU	
TEL/FAX: (0171) 247 9543	COOKING 2
EMAIL: tayyabs@lineone.net	COST £11–£25

The fresh aroma of spicy cooking greets visitors to this basic Pakistani eating
house, with even more basic prices. It is simply furnished with an L-shaped
counter, and elegant brass water pitchers on glass-topped tables. Shish kebabs
and tender mutton tikka are grilled on revolving bars, while the fierce tandoor
behind is mainly for bread, including soft naan. Curries – though that word is
not on the menu – come in steel karahis. Intriguing daily specials take in paya
(lambs' trotters), while vegetables include dhal karela (whole lentils with bitter
gourd). This Islamic establishment is closed for the month of Ramadan and is, of
course, unlicensed but they willingly provide corkscrew and glasses (at no
charge) for your own wine or beer. Alternatively, drink delicately salted and
spiced lassi from engraved metal tumblers. It is open only in the evening, but the
even more basic original Tayyabs a few doors along does lunch.

CHEFS: M. Tayyab and S. Tayyab   PROPRIETOR: M. Tayyab   OPEN: all week D only 5 to 12
MEALS: alc (main courses £3.50 to £9)   CLOSED: Ramadan   CARDS: none   DETAILS: 80 seats.
Vegetarian meals. Music   ● Whitechapel, Aldgate

Nico Central

map 15

35 Great Portland Street, W1N 5DD	COOKING 3
TEL: (0171) 436 8846 FAX: (0171) 436 3455	COST £37–£65

Nico Ladenis has long since moved on to more exalted surroundings, but his name lingers on at this slightly cramped art deco restaurant, which offers a spare, short menu of classic brasserie staples. Hearty dishes such as goats' cheese and red pepper terrine, best end of lamb with couscous, and guinea fowl with red cabbage and plum sauce continue to please for their 'good, clean flavours'. Fish is a strong point, sometimes coupled with robust partners: baked fillet of sea bream with garlic mash, for example, or deep-fried halibut with mushy peas and crispy potatoes. Boldly flavoured desserts, from a pastry chef on good form, might include a 'tangy' caramelised lemon tart with an intense Cassis sauce. Service is generally swift and efficient, although perhaps not always as solicitous as it might be. House red wine is £13.50, white £13, from a list that does a decent job of representing the New World as well as France.

CHEF: J.P. Patrunot   PROPRIETOR: Restaurant Partnership   OPEN: Mon to Fri L 12 to 2, Mon to Sat D 7 to 11 (6.30 to 11.30 Sat)   CLOSED: Christmas, bank hols   MEALS: Set L £20.50 (2 courses) to £23.50, Set D £25.50   SERVICE: 12.5% (optional), card slips closed   CARDS: Amex, Delta, Diners, MasterCard, Switch, Visa   DETAILS: 50 seats. Private parties: 50 main room, 12 private room. Vegetarian meals. No children under 8. No cigars/pipes in dining room. Wheelchair access (not WC). Music. Air-conditioned   ⊖ Oxford Circus

Nicole's

map 15

158 New Bond Street, W1Y 9PA	COOKING 4
TEL: (0171) 499 8408 FAX: (0171) 409 0381	COST £40–£73

The minimalist interior of this impressive basement space is somewhat disarming given the no-holds-barred approach to the cooking, which is firmly Italian with Californian influences. Wood and pale colours predominate, with a brown leather banquette along one wall and a rather clever use of mirrors. Those on serious shopping expeditions can lunch on a separate, less time-consuming menu at the bar, but for those whose attention is firmly on the food, a crostini collection might tempt to start, or a salad of watercress, red chicory, fennel and blood orange. A combination of fine materials and accurate timing showed at inspection in 'sweet, fresh, plump' skewered scallops, served with potato pancake and spring vegetables; and in a dish of crisp duck leg confit, accompanied by a rich, meaty roasted duck sausage, on a light and minty couscous, set off by an impressive date and almond chutney. Desserts offer a 'luscious and sexy' hot chocolate soufflé with dark chocolate sauce, and an elegant fruit salad of blood orange, pineapple, melon, mango and grapes. Service is discreet, cool and professional, and wines are mostly French with the odd nod to other countries. A fair number are offered by the glass, starting in France at £3.25 (£11.50 a bottle).

CHEF: Annie Wayte   PROPRIETOR: Stephen Marks   OPEN: Mon to Sat L 11.30 to 5.30, Mon to Fri D 6.30 to 10.45   CLOSED: bank hols   MEALS: alc (main courses £15.50 to £22). Cover £1. Bar L available   SERVICE: 12.5% (optional), card slips closed   CARDS: Amex, Delta, Diners, MasterCard, Switch, Visa   DETAILS: 90 seats. Private parties: 100 main room. No-smoking area. Music. Air-conditioned   ⊖ Green Park, Bond Street

Nobu

map 15

19 Old Park Lane, W1Y 4LB	COOKING 5
TEL: (0171) 447 4747 FAX: (0171) 447 4749	COST £30–£93

After three years, Nobu is as happening as ever. A first- floor restaurant with bars for drinks and sushi, it has a large eating space broken up by pillars and tinted glass partitions, with much animated activity from customers, and constant motion from an army of staff dressed in Issey Miyake black. They are well informed, friendly, and give sound advice, which is just as well, since it is not immediately clear how best to select dishes to make up a meal. Some 145 of them are grouped into special appetisers, new-style sashimi, soup and rice, salads, special dishes, sushi and sashimi, sushi roll, main dishes, kushiyaki and tempura. One way out is the omakase (chef's choice) of several courses (for £60).

This is not straightforward Japanese food: a South American influence shows up in a couple of items, and in liberal use of lime juice and jalapeño peppers. 'Generally the simplest dishes were best,' summed up an inspector predictably, among them yellowtail tuna sashimi, topped with slices of jalapeño, in a soy and lime sauce. Stick with raw seafood and there are lots of rewarding dishes – scallop with plum sauce and caviare, for example – although permutations of soy, miso and lime can make for some repetitive saucing.

Cooked dishes tend to be fancier: for example a piece of darkly caramelised, sweet-tasting cod with miso, or a dessert of tropical sorbet to dip into a warm pineapple soup, accompanied by 'gyozas' (spoonfuls of chocolate, nut, pine-apple and apricot wrapped in dough and deep-fried). Plates arrive 'fast and furiously', bills can soon mount up, and the wine list divides its allegiances between Europe and the New World, with South African house wines £14.50; there's also a decent choice of sakés.

CHEF: Mark Edwards   PROPRIETORS: Nobu Matsuhisa, Mr and Mrs Ong and Myriad Group OPEN: Mon to Fri L 12 to 2.15, all week D 6 to 10.15 (11.15 Sat, 9.45 Sun)   MEALS: alc (main courses £7.50 to £22.50). Set L £20 to £40, Set D £60   SERVICE: 12.5% (optional), card slips closed   CARDS: Amex, Delta, Diners, MasterCard, Switch, Visa   DETAILS: 150 seats. Private parties: 250 main room, 12 to 40 private room. Vegetarian meals. No cigars/pipes in dining room. Wheelchair access (also WC). No music. Air-conditioned   ⊖ Hyde Park Corner

Novelli W8

map 13

122 Palace Gardens, W8 4RT	COOKING 3
TEL: (0171) 229 4024 FAX: (0171) 243 1826	COST £26–£56

Swags of linen cover the windows, tiny spotlights dangle from rails and, thanks to mirrors at either end, the long, narrow, purple dining room looks as if it goes on forever. Jason Ward has taken over the kitchen from Mike Bird, who has moved to Maison Novelli (see entry). In the process the menu has changed its identity (no cassoulet terrine any more, no pig's trotter) in favour of an all-purpose Mediterranean approach, easily interchangeable with many others. In among richly textured fish soup, or aubergine and yoghurt tian, is a less usual warm terrine made from pumpkin, ratte potatoes and Beaufort cheese, on a slick of chocolatey balsamic sauce. Good materials are evident – in 'a terrific piece' of pearly white cod in a strongly saffroned white bean ragoût – and accurate timing has produced beef fillet ('first-class in all respects apart from flavour') cooked blue as requested, in a stock-based sauce. Finish with strawberry sablé, or summer fruit terrine with champagne jelly, and drink from a serviceable list with a dozen or more wines by the glass, starting with house Dom. Virginie at £14.

CHEF: Jason Ward   PROPRIETOR: Jean-Christophe Novelli   OPEN: all week 12 to 3, 6 to 11
MEALS: alc (main courses £10.50 to £16.50). Set L £12.50 (2 courses) to £15   SERVICE: 12.5%
(optional)   CARDS: Amex, Delta, Diners, MasterCard, Switch, Visa   DETAILS: 60 seats. 12 seats
outside. Private parties: 55 main room. Vegetarian meals. Children's helpings. No pipes in dining
room. Wheelchair access (not WC). Music. Air-conditioned   ⊖ Notting Hill Gate (£5)

Oak Room Marco Pierre White   map 15

21 Piccadilly, W1V 0BH   COOKING **8**
TEL: (0171) 437 0202   FAX: (0171) 437 3574   COST £49–£188

Designed by Norman Shaw on the scale of an ocean liner, the Oak Room (though now smaller than originally) still recalls the baroque grandeur of the Edwardian era; to its acres of limed oak panelling and Murano glass chandeliers, Marco Pierre White has added oil paintings and his trade-mark flower displays of fifty red roses or white lilies 'resembling frozen fireworks'. With his hands no doubt full looking after a growing restaurant empire, he is missed by those who have followed his progress over the years, many nostalgic for the magic days in Battersea and at the Hyde Park Hotel.

His dishes, however, live on. Even readers who have never eaten here may be familiar with some of them – tarte Tatin of endives with seared scallops, oysters in champagne gelée, and foie gras parfait among them – which may appear on the menus of other Marco Pierre White restaurants such as Criterion Brasserie and Mirabelle (see entries, both London). Those in a position to compare the renderings are more prone to go into raptures about the Oak Room's versions, judged a 'tour de force', 'spectacular', and 'exquisite'.

The cooking has been 'on brilliant form', producing 'dazzlingly fresh' red mullet fillets, and just-cooked saddle of rabbit with herb risotto. What reporters expect of this operation, though, is ruthless consistency, and while the food offers tantalising 'glimpses of excitement, of brilliant technique, and of clever combinations', it seems to lack the defining passion, direction and control of Marco at his best; at worst it has shown simply poor technique, timing and judgement. Yet when it sets to, the kitchen can produce some unbeatable dishes, for example a 'sensational' starter of baby leeks bound in aspic, topped with a dollop of salty caviare and dressed with a light, summery vinaigrette to emphasise their sweetness.

Likewise, not all desserts have hit the bull's-eye, but classics such as lemon tart, and the dramatic caramel and ice cream Pyramid, have been up to scratch, and the kitchen's take on floating islands (marbled with pink praline) is impressive. Service, with the exception of the maitre d', has failed to impress any of our reporters. Those who compare this (favourably) with some of Europe's top restaurants are 'mildly shocked' by the much higher prices here, an effect to which the wines contribute. Premium growers and grands crus are the stars of the France-focused list, where even the house wines are £30 each.

CHEF: Robert Reid   PROPRIETOR: Marco Pierre White   OPEN: Mon to Fri L 12 to 2.30, Mon to Sat D 7 to 11.15   CLOSED: 2 weeks Christmas, 2 weeks Aug   MEALS: Set L £29.50, Set D £55 to £90   SERVICE: not inc   CARDS: Amex, Delta, MasterCard, Switch, Visa   DETAILS: 70 seats. Private parties: 90 main room. Jacket and tie. No cigars in dining room. Wheelchair access (also WC). No music. Air-conditioned   ⊖ Piccadilly Circus

L'Odéon ♀ 🍴

map 15

65 Regent Street, W1R 7HH
TEL: (0171) 287 1400   FAX: (0171) 287 1300

COOKING 5
COST £32–£71

Colin Layfield's menu at this smart West End eatery offers 'something for everyone'. Observe the trendy ingredients, worked up into 'some straight-up dishes' as well as 'inventive and unusual combinations', from crab cakes with parsley sauce to foie gras with piccalilli, from baked cod or lamb shank (both served with risotto) to pigeon with wild mushroom ravioli. Techniques are varied, and work effectively, producing a 'subtle and delicate' cappuccino-style globe artichoke and orange soup, for example, or crab and saffron tart on seaweed salad with gazpacho sauce. Presentation is attractive, and timing accurate: an inspector's roast skate was 'cooked to a T', fanned into an arch, and served with garlic mash, artichokes and parsley sauce.

Desserts tend to pile on the sweetness, judging by one that combined smooth, custardy banana tart with a large blob of vanilla cheesecake and a fudgy butterscotch sauce. Service is agreeable, and it is worth asking for a seat by the windows which look out over the hubbub of Regent Street; otherwise most visitors are happy to enjoy the art deco theme, with wall lamps 'like giant inedible ice cream cones' and frosted-glass partitions. A fine-wine list is available on request; the main one offers an appealing selection of flavours and styles, with France and Australia making the most significant contributions. The house selection of fifteen wines is available by the bottle or glass from £12 and £3.20 respectively.

CHEF: Colin Layfield   PROPRIETORS: Pierre and Kathy Condou   OPEN: Mon to Sat 12 to 2.45, 5.30 to 11.30   CLOSED: last 2 weeks Aug, bank hols   MEALS: alc (main courses £14.50 to £21). Set L and D 5.30 to 7 £15.50 (2 courses) to £19.50. Cover £1.50   SERVICE: not inc; 12.5% for parties of 6 or more   CARDS: Amex, Delta, Diners, MasterCard, Switch, Visa   DETAILS: 250 seats. Private parties: 250 main room, 20 private room. Vegetarian meals. Children's helpings. No-smoking area. Wheelchair access (also WC). Music. Air-conditioned   ⊖ Piccadilly Circus

Odette's ⬤

map 13

130 Regents Park Road, NW1 8XL
TEL: (0171) 586 5486 and 8766
FAX: (0171) 586 2575

COOKING 5
COST £20–£60

A reporter familiar with Odette's over the years still finds it hard to pinpoint its appeal. On the one hand, it seems an old smoothie, 'romantic and intimate' on a sultry summer's evening, the open frontage allowing a breeze to cool the dining room. Then again, it has never been stuck in a culinary timewarp, but has continued to develop through changes of kitchen personnel and the rollercoaster of London restaurant fashion. At bottom, it is a highly successful, and largely consistent local restaurant with a conservatory room and basement wine bar in the agreeable environs of Primrose Hill village.

Simon Bradley has moved up from sous-chef to impress his own style on the menus, introducing pickled mackerel and smoked eel with a celeriac and radish 'coleslaw', and corn-fed chicken with Indian spices, khoubiz bread and pineapple chutney. At its best the food delivers decisive flavours: for example in an inspection dinner that began with a salad ('more like a thick, soupy stew') of fruits de mer in a buttery juice with Spanish white beans and a dressing of chilli, lemon and parsley. Following it was a robust rump of spring lamb marinated in lemon, thyme and rosemary, served with new season's garlic and young courgettes, a dish that 'pulled no fancy tricks'. Desserts mostly keep the side up with warm, rich, 'oozingly soft' chocolate mousse with nougat ice, and service is 'slick, efficient, unobtrusive'. There is something for everyone on the drinks list, with its judicious blend of food friendly wines from around the world, simply arranged by style. Attention is paid to quality both above and below the £20 mark, while thirty wines by the glass (including some excellent dessert wines) assist those who like to mix and match. House French and Italian are £10.95.

CHEF: Simon Bradley   PROPRIETOR: Simone Green   OPEN: Mon to Fri L 12.30 to 2.30, Mon to Sat D 7 to 11   CLOSED: 1 week Christmas, bank hols   MEALS: alc (main courses £9.50 to £17.50). Set L £10   SERVICE: not inc   CARDS: Amex, Delta, Diners, MasterCard, Switch, Visa   DETAILS: 60 seats. 10 seats outside. Private parties: 30 main room, 8 and 30 private rooms. Vegetarian meals. Children's helpings. No music   ⊖ Chalk Farm

Offshore   NEW ENTRY   map 13

148 Holland Park Avenue, W11 4UE
TEL: (0171) 221 6090   COOKING 2
FAX: (0171) 313 9700 and 603 0779   COST £27–£74

Proving something about the eye of the beholder is a decorative feature mentioned in all reports: the giant model blue marlin/swordfish/shark. Vivid paintings on white walls contribute to a breezy atmosphere, as does the clientele, local, international or both. Service usually 'tries to please' but is far from brisk, perhaps thinking, as an inspector noted, 'that the Mauritian theme includes the pace of the resort island life'. Certainly chef Sylvain Ho Wing Cheong's cooking with exotic ingredients demonstrates the Indian/French/South East Asian influences on that island. Lobster doesn't just nestle on a cushion but is 'sleeping on its bed of spicy Chinese noodles'. Carefully cooked dry tiger prawn curry rouge is strongly spiced, and the flavours of three exotic fish in assiette créole 'speak out individually'. Cod baked with fennel shows that the kitchen can deliver restrained dishes too. Few of the bottles on the interesting wine list are less than £20, although house red is £13.50, white £12.50.

CHEF: Sylvain Ho Wing Cheong   PROPRIETOR: Papela Ltd   OPEN: all week 12 to 3, 6 to 11 CLOSED: 25 and 26 Dec, bank hols (inc Sun)   MEALS: alc (main courses £11.50 to £26.50). Set L £14.50 (2 courses) to £18, Set D £18.75 (2 courses) to £33   SERVICE: not inc   CARDS: Amex, Delta, MasterCard, Switch, Visa   DETAILS: 65 seats. 12 seats outside. Private parties: 80 main room, 22 and 24 private rooms. Vegetarian meals. Children's helpings. Wheelchair access (not WC). Occasional music. Air-conditioned   ⊖ Holland Park, Shepherd's Bush £5

Old Delhi

NEW ENTRY | map 13

48 Kendal Street, W2 2BP
TEL: (0171) 723 3335

COOKING 2
COST £36–£84

The décor is 'a suave and sophisticated version of Arab/Indian', the menu fairly evenly split between Iranian and Indian dishes. Start perhaps with 100 grammes of caviare, or choose poppadoms with mint chutney, mixed pickle and hot mango chutney. To follow might be 'rich and savoury' mirza-ghasemi (a mash of spiced aubergine and egg with fried, diced garlic on top), along with olivieh salad (a combination of chicken, egg, potato and pickled baby cucumber). The usual samosas and bhajias are also listed, along with dhal, a variety of tikkas and Indian main courses, but an inspection meal took the Iranian route with faisinjan: charcoal-roasted duck which is then simmered in a sauce of ground walnuts and pomegranate. Saffron rice is cooked just right, and a request for tadigh (crispy-bottomed rice fried with butter), though not on the menu, was gladly met and equally gladly consumed. Mint tea has lacked mintiness, and at £5 for a pot for two seems a little expensive. Service is good, but note that credit card slips are left open even though 15 per cent is added to the bill. Most bottles on the short wine list are over £20, although house red and white are £11.50.

CHEFS: Mr Bhatti and Mr H. Jalalrand   PROPRIETOR: Oldelms Ltd   OPEN: all week 12.30 to 3.30 (1 to 4 Sat and Sun), 6.30 to 11   MEALS: alc (main courses £8 to £25)   SERVICE: 15% (optional) CARDS: Amex, Delta, Diners, MasterCard, Switch, Visa   DETAILS: 54 seats. Private parties: 14 main room. Vegetarian meals. No children under 10 after 8pm. Wheelchair access (not WC). Occasional music (£2 cover). Air-conditioned   ⊖ Marble Arch

Olivo

map 13

21 Eccleston Street, SW1W 9LX
TEL: (0171) 730 2505

COOKING 2
COST £28–£53

If the Sardinian sun is not actually shining, it is certainly evoked by the bright yellow and blue modern interior, a cheerful, bustling atmosphere helped along by 'brisk and efficient' service, and of course the food. Starters emphasise salads (yellow pepper and caper), and pasta (fine tagliarini in a 'seafood pesto'), along with chargrilled vegetables, marinated fish and beef carpaccio. Chargrilling is indeed the favoured technique, applied across the board to rolled pork fillet, marinated lamb, and tuna or swordfish, although duck has been roasted, sea bream baked, and sweetbreads served with cannellini beans and artichoke heart. Main courses tend to be meaty, while desserts combine some familiar ideas (vanilla pannacotta) with sebada, a traditional Sardinian deep-fried pastry shell filled with cheese and dressed with honey. Cheeses are Italian, as is the short, reasonably priced wine list. House Sardinian is £10.50. A sister restaurant, Oliveto, is around the corner at 49 Elizabeth Street (tel: (0171) 730 0074).

CHEFS: Marco Melis and Giuseppe Sanna   PROPRIETORS: Mauro Sanna and Jean-Louis Journade   OPEN: Mon to Fri L 12 to 2.30, all week D 7 to 11   CLOSED: Christmas, bank hols MEALS: alc D (main courses £12 to £13.50). Set L £15 (2 courses) to £17. Cover £1.50   SERVICE: not inc   CARDS: Amex, Delta, MasterCard, Switch, Visa   DETAILS: 45 seats. Vegetarian meals. No cigars/pipes in dining room. No music. Air-conditioned   ⊖ Victoria

1 Lombard Street

| NEW ENTRY | map 13

1 Lombard Street, EC3 9AA
TEL: (0171) 929 6611   FAX: (0171) 929 6622

COOKING 4
COST £38–£91

Formerly the Bank of Kuwait, in a seriously financial part of town close to the Bank of England and Mansion House, 1 Lombard Street comes in two parts. At the front is a large noisy brasserie, where 'City types come for a six o'clock swill with a bottle of bubbly and something to soak it up,' and a small, quiet dining room behind, with mushroom-coloured fabrics, comfortable chairs and elegant table settings. The food's European theme (fancifully connected to an 'interpretation' of Titian's *Rape of Europa* on the wall) takes in an impressive starter of wood pigeon breast – cut into small chunks and laid on braised endive, with a beetroot and juniper vinaigrette – and poached lamb fillet with summer vegetables in a mint broth.

This may be 'conservative food, conservatively cooked,' but an inspection meal turned up a perfectly decent smoked haddock and pastry 'sandwich' with hard-boiled quails eggs, surrounded by a creamy froth, and a dish of chicken breast (skin on) and thigh (boned and stuffed) with dried morels (not all the food is seasonal) in a vin jaune sauce. Finish, as one pair did, with iced prune and armagnac soufflé, and bitter Ecuadorian chocolate pyramid.

If restaurant prices are pitched at luxury level, the brasserie offers some relief plus a wide range of items from pasta, via pig's trotter galette and a dozen seafood dishes, to coq au vin and lemon tart. Sharply chosen wines on the restaurant's list are arranged by style (although 'medium subtle' sounds an odd category), with little under £20; house French white is £13, Australian red £14.75.

CHEF: Herbert Berger   PROPRIETOR: Soren Jessen   OPEN: Mon to Fri 11.30 to 3, 6 to 10
CLOSED: bank hols   MEALS: alc (main courses restaurant £23 to £26.50, brasserie £10 to £10.50). Set L and D restaurant £32 (2 courses) to £36. Bar tapas menu available Mon to Fri
SERVICE: 12.5% (optional)   CARDS: Amex, Delta, Diners, MasterCard, Switch, Visa   DETAILS:
40 seats (restaurant), 150 seats (brasserie). Private parties: 400 main room, 40 private room.
Vegetarian meals. Music. Air-conditioned   ⊖ Bank

192 ▼

map 13

192 Kensington Park Road, W11 2ES
TEL: (0171) 229 0482   FAX: (0171) 229 3300

COOKING 1
COST £24–£47

If membership of the Groucho Club is not a realistic option, the next best thing might be to hie to Kensington Park Road, where its restaurant outpost, the perennially fashionable 192, still draws the crowds. Redecoration and refurbishment have introduced more booths and corner tables, but the daily-changing menus still speak a recognisably contemporary patois. Black pudding with bubble and squeak and a poached egg, and baked sea bass with mushroom confit and polenta are the kinds of changes London expects to see rung these days. More robust appetites might opt for roast chump of lamb with red cabbage. Vegetables and salads (including *de rigueur* rocket and Parmesan) are charged separately. Wines change with the seasons, but quality producers are a constant, and there is a broad sweep of flavours from around the world. House vin de pays is £10.50, and around thirty wines are offered by the glass.

LONDON

CHEF: Michael Knowlson   PROPRIETOR: The Groucho Club plc   OPEN: all week 12.30 to 3 (3.30 Sat and Sun), 6.30 (7 Sun) to 11.30 (11 Sun)   CLOSED: 25 and 26 Dec, 1 Jan   MEALS: alc (main courses £7.50 to £12.50). Set L Mon to Fri £11.50 (2 courses), Set L Sun £12.50   SERVICE: not inc, 12.5% for parties of 6 or more   CARDS: Amex, Diners, MasterCard, Switch, Visa   DETAILS: 96 seats. 16 seats outside. Private parties: 12 main room. Vegetarian meals. No-smoking area. Wheelchair access (not WC). Occasional music. Air-conditioned   ⊖ Ladbroke Grove, Notting Hill Gate

▲ One-O-One

NEW ENTRY   map 14

101 Knightsbridge, SW1X 7RN
TEL: (0171) 290 7101   FAX: (0171) 235 6196

COOKING 5
COST £43–£87

Occupying a smart address, and a big chunk of expensive pavement, this glossy and appropriately 'goldfish bowl' of a dining room is tacked on to the Sheraton Park Tower Hotel. Its relaunch has brought a well-stocked shiny bar, expansive tables, big square pillars with foodie pictures, and a menu that (boldly for a hotel) majors in fish. Pascal Proyart hails from Brittany, which may explain the preoccupation. He generally deals in top-of-the-range items such as turbot, red mullet, lobster and, his favourite, sea bass, which is served four ways: among them poached (with caviare and shallot cream sauce), baked in a salt crust (for two), and roasted (set on a pile of asparagus spears and crushed potatoes with girolles).

As ever in these circumstances, the simplest dishes seem to work best; his fondness for invention sometimes plays to the gallery – he is strong on visual appeal and artifice – but also comes up with some interesting partnerships. One starter, for example, consisted of thinly sliced scallops covered in a rich, glazed, eggy-creamy, truffle-flecked sabayon, topped with wild mushrooms and small shaved curls of smoked foie gras. There are a few meat dishes too, including beef fillet and 'Pascal's chicken Kiev'. The Brittany background may help to account for a crêpe covered by 'ultra-thin' slices of mango and banana, although most desserts are in more international mode: chocolate tart with orange custard, or strawberry Tatin. Only one wine (a rosé) comes in under £20, but there are plenty in three figures. House Chilean red and French white are £20 and £25.

CHEF: Pascal Proyart   PROPRIETOR: Starwood Hotels and Resorts   OPEN: all week 12 to 2.30, 7 to 10.30   MEALS: alc (main courses £14.50 to £28). Set L £21 (2 courses) to £25, Set D £42 to £49 (whole tables only)   SERVICE: not inc, card slips closed   CARDS: Amex, Delta, Diners, MasterCard, Switch, Visa   DETAILS: 86 seats. Private parties: 20 main room. Vegetarian meals. Wheelchair access (not WC). No music. Air-conditioned   ACCOMMODATION: 295 rooms, all with bath/shower. TV. Phone. Room only £335 to £359. Rooms for disabled. Baby facilities   ⊖ Knightsbridge (£5)

L'Oranger

NEW ENTRY   map 15

5 St James's Street, SW1A 1EF
TEL: (0171) 839 3774   FAX: (0171) 839 4330

COOKING 6
COST £37–£71

Following the hoo-ha within the A To Z Restaurant Group just as last year's *Guide* went to press, when Gordon Ramsay walked out of Aubergine (see entry) and Marcus Wareing simultaneously left L'Oranger, a neat re-shuffle has promoted Wareing's former colleague, Kamel Benamar, to the position of

Terms and Conditions

- The vouchers in *The Good Food Guide 2000* are valid from 1 October 1999 until 30 September 2000. Only one £5 voucher can be used per table booked (for a minimum of two people). No photocopies or any other kind of reproduction of vouchers will be accepted. The vouchers may not be used in conjunction with any other promotion scheme.

- The vouchers are redeemable against a pre-booked meal for a minimum of two people. For a voucher to be redeemable, the customer must mention at the time of booking his or her intent to use a voucher. The £5 is to be deducted from the final bill inclusive of VAT (and, if applicable, service), with the participating restaurant bearing the cost of the £5 discount.

- Participating establishments, which are highlighted in the pages of *The Good Food Guide 2000* by a symbol (£5) at the end of entries, may exclude certain times of day, certain days of the week, or specific menus from the scheme, as long as they (a) advise customers of the restrictions at the time of booking, and (b) accept the vouchers at a minimum of 70% of sessions when the restaurant is open.

Terms and Conditions

- The vouchers in *The Good Food Guide 2000* are valid from 1 October 1999 until 30 September 2000. Only one £5 voucher can be used per table booked (for a minimum of two people). No photocopies or any other kind of reproduction of vouchers will be accepted. The vouchers may not be used in conjunction with any other promotion scheme.

- The vouchers are redeemable against a pre-booked meal for a minimum of two people. For a voucher to be redeemable, the customer must mention at the time of booking his or her intent to use a voucher. The £5 is to be deducted from the final bill inclusive of VAT (and, if applicable, service), with the participating restaurant bearing the cost of the £5 discount.

- Participating establishments, which are highlighted in the pages of *The Good Food Guide 2000* by a symbol (£5) at the end of entries, may exclude certain times of day, certain days of the week, or specific menus from the scheme, as long as they (a) advise customers of the restrictions at the time of booking, and (b) accept the vouchers at a minimum of 70% of sessions when the restaurant is open.

Terms and Conditions

- The vouchers in *The Good Food Guide 2000* are valid from 1 October 1999 until 30 September 2000. Only one £5 voucher can be used per table booked (for a minimum of two people). No photocopies or any other kind of reproduction of vouchers will be accepted. The vouchers may not be used in conjunction with any other promotion scheme.

- The vouchers are redeemable against a pre-booked meal for a minimum of two people. For a voucher to be redeemable, the customer must mention at the time of booking his or her intent to use a voucher. The £5 is to be deducted from the final bill inclusive of VAT (and, if applicable, service), with the participating restaurant bearing the cost of the £5 discount.

- Participating establishments, which are highlighted in the pages of *The Good Food Guide 2000* by a symbol (£5) at the end of entries, may exclude certain times of day, certain days of the week, or specific menus from the scheme, as long as they (a) advise customers of the restrictions at the time of booking, and (b) accept the vouchers at a minimum of 70% of sessions when the restaurant is open.

kitchen supremo. Fish remains dominant, and the fixed-price formula (with supplements) is still in place. The cooking, though a lot simpler now, is no less effective. An inspection meal turned up a starter of braised Swiss chard and soft bone marrow in a clear veal broth, and a dish of pink lamb combining well with fennel, artichoke, and confit tomato. Ingredients are sound, and timing is impressive, producing scallops 'so rare they were almost sashimi', and a 'simply delivered' tranche of turbot with broad beans and asparagus tips.

Finish with a summery roast white peach scented with basil and lemon, accompanied by a flaky tuile, or Caraib chocolate fondant. When the weather is fine, sit under a parasol in the courtyard; the rest of the time enjoy the genteel atmosphere of the dining room with its wood panelling, tall vases filled with flowers, banquette seating and luminous atrium. Service – all French and all male – can be slow, linguistically challenged, or filled with Gallic charm, depending on your point of view. France provides the backbone of the wine list, with judicious selections from other major wine countries adding interest. Those searching for bottles under £20 will find just three to choose between.

CHEF: Kamel Benamar PROPRIETOR: A To Z Restaurants OPEN: Mon to Fri L 12 to 2.30, Mon to Sat D 6 to 11 CLOSED: 24 to 30 Dec, bank hols MEALS: Set L £19.50 (2 courses) to £23.50, Set D £33.50 SERVICE: not inc, 12.5% for parties of 7 or more CARDS: Amex, Delta, Diners, MasterCard, Switch, Visa DETAILS: 60 seats. 12 seats outside. Private parties: 50 main room, 20 private room. Vegetarian meals. No children under 10. Wheelchair access (not WC). No music. Air-conditioned ⊖ Green Park

Orrery
map 15

55 Marylebone High Street, W1M 3AE
TEL: (0171) 616 8000 FAX: (0171) 616 8080
COOKING 6
COST £35–£101

'Stylish' is a common description of what more than one reporter considers 'my favourite Conran restaurant'. Long and narrow, on the small side, quiet, with professional and attentive service from charming and efficient staff, it seems the only link it has with other Conrans is the quality of design. Part of the appeal lies in a menu that, despite such standards as foie gras terrine with Sauternes jelly, or Bresse pigeon with Savoy cabbage, makes room for less usual calves' sweetbreads, roast saddle of rabbit with sage and thyme jus, or slices of lambs' tongue piled on mash with a sticky, shiny brown sauce.

'Correctly made' pasta is a feature (perhaps crab cannelloni with a lemon and balsamic sauce), while accurate timing shows in anything from steaks, via 'expertly cooked' sea bass, to risottos that stand out for both flavour and texture. 'Hard to fault technically' – applied specifically to crème brûlée with rhubarb compote – seems to be a fair summing up generally. Alternatively, for dessert there might be raspberry mille-feuille, or 'light and creamy' prune and armagnac parfait, as well as a serious and well-presented Anglo-French cheeseboard. Incidentals, from an intensely flavoured pre-starter soup to bread and coffee, are also impressive. The only real drawback is the cost; those with £20 to spend on wine will find little to excite them, although there are many heavenly bottles from France, Italy and the New World above that. House wines from France are £12 for Chardonnay, £13 for Corbières.

CHEF: Chris Galvin   PROPRIETOR: Conran Restaurants Ltd   OPEN: all week 12 to 3, 7 to 11 (10.30 Sun)   CLOSED: Good Fri   MEALS: alc (main courses £14.50 to £22.50). Set L £23.50, Set D Mon to Sat £45 to £75 (inc wine), Set D Sun £28.50 to £75 (inc wine)   SERVICE: 12.5% (optional), card slips closed   CARDS: Amex, Delta, Diners, MasterCard, Switch, Visa   DETAILS: 80 seats. Private parties: 80 main room. Vegetarian meals. No pipes in dining room. Wheelchair access (also WC). No music   ⊖ Baker Street, Regent's Park

Orsino ♟

map 12

119 Portland Road, W11 4LN   COOKING 2
TEL: (0171) 221 3299   FAX: (0171) 229 9414   COST £23–£53

This buzzy, stylish Holland Park outpost of regional Italian cooking delivers certainly competent, sometimes 'inspired', food, which at its best allows intense flavours to complement each other well. You might kick off with a salad of arugula, dandelion, artichoke and Parmesan, or pappardelle with hare, red wine and pine nuts, before heading for Dover sole with anchovies and capers, or perhaps a pizza topped with spinach, red onion, roast peppers and goats' cheese. For dolci there's lemon tart or cappuccino mousse, or a sweet-savoury combination of pecorino with pear, or a glass of dessert wine with biscuits. The all-Italian (champagne excepted) wine list is alluring; Umbrian house wines are £11.50 a litre. A sister restaurant, Orso, is at 27 Wellington Street, WC2 (tel. (0171) 240 5269).

CHEF: Anne Kettle   PROPRIETOR: Orsino Restaurants Ltd   OPEN: all week noon to 11.30 (11 Sun)   CLOSED: 24 and 25 Dec   MEALS: alc (main courses £7.50 to £15). Set L and D exc 7.30 to 10 £11.50 (2 courses) to £15.50   SERVICE: not inc   CARDS: Amex, MasterCard, Switch, Visa   DETAILS: 100 seats. Private parties: 36 private room. Vegetarian meals. No music. Air-conditioned   ⊖ Holland Park

Osteria Antica Bologna ♟ £

map 12

23 Northcote Road, SW11 1NG   COOKING 3
TEL/FAX: (0171) 978 4771   COST £21–£46

Aurelio Spagnuolo has carved out a singular style of Italian cooking, served in a rustic but intimate setting of heavy timber tables near Clapham Junction. He starts with interesting materials – goat, rabbit, smoked tuna – and produces some rich and vibrant flavours: organic lamb, for instance, sautéed with garlic, egg, asparagus and pecorino. Ancient Roman dishes (his forte) combine savoury with sweet: hypotrimma is not a recipe for fitness but grilled chicory with ricotta, honey, mint, dates, sultanas and toasted pine nuts. There are masses of vegetarian choices, and plenty of room for manoeuvring between starters, pasta and main courses. Indeed, a selection of assaggi (each in two sizes) is a sensible option, perhaps taking in a warm salad of Napoli sausage with lentils and grilled fennel, or stuffed artichoke with a nut, honey and coriander sauce. Alternatives to familiar tiramisù include 'dulcias domesticas cum tiropatinam': dates stuffed with nuts, fried with honey and served with 'roman custard'. Good names abound on the all-Italian wine list, and descriptions are straightforward and enthusiastic. Most bottles are under £20, with 'earthy Sicilian' house wine £7.90 for a 75cl jug.

CHEF: Aurelio Spagnuolo PROPRIETORS: Rochelle Porteous and Aurelio Spagnuolo OPEN: Mon to Fri 12 to 3, 3 to 11 (11.30 Fri), Sat 12 to 11.30, Sun 12 to 10.30 CLOSED: 10 days Christmas MEALS: alc (main courses £6 to £14). Set L £8.50 (2 courses). Cover 70p SERVICE: 10% (optional), card slips closed CARDS: Amex, Delta, MasterCard, Switch, Visa DETAILS: 75 seats. 12 seats outside. Private parties: 40 main room. Vegetarian meals. Children's helpings. No cigars/pipes in dining room. Wheelchair access (not WC). Music. Air-conditioned £5

Oxo Tower Restaurant 🍾

map 13

Oxo Tower Wharf, Barge House Street, SE1 9PH COOKING 5
TEL: (0171) 803 3888 FAX: (0171) 803 3838 COST £37–£81

If the supposed secret of a successful restaurant is 'location, location, location', then the Oxo Tower – 'one of the most spectacular dining spots in London' – is a textbook example: 'one can almost touch St Paul's', reckoned a night-time visitor. Both bar and brasserie share the view, but this entry refers specifically to the restaurant (step out of the lift on the eighth floor and turn east). Not everyone gets a table by the window, of course, but the food also commands attention with its sharp interpretations of classic ideas, from poached spinach and ricotta dumplings (served with pan-fried chicken livers) to smoked haddock and leek tortelloni with a properly poached egg.

Main courses tend to major on fresh and well-timed fish: red mullet on baby leeks with a frothy saffron emulsion, or Dover sole served with a lime, ginger and coriander butter and stir-fried egg noodles. The food can be quite rich, as one might expect if ordering pan-fried beef fillet with foie gras and Madeira sauce, but is also seasonally aware. A November dinner included grey-legged partridge served with chestnuts, sprouts and bread sauce: 'real, traditional stuff.' Desserts span the range from poire Belle Hélène, via hot chocolate fondant, to pineapple tarte fine with yoghurt and black pepper ice cream. Service has see-sawed from 'flawed' to 'surprisingly good'.

Head sommelier Robert Giorgione's wine list has been on a body-building course over the past year and now boasts a massive range from France, Italy and the New World, but lovers of fine wine can rest assured that quality hasn't been sacrificed in the pursuit of quantity. A sizeable number of appealing bottles cost less than £20, and a forty-strong house selection helps to simplify selection.

CHEF: Simon Arkless PROPRIETOR: Harvey Nichols OPEN: all week 12 to 3 (3.30 Sun), 6 to 11.30 (6.30 to 10.30 Sun) CLOSED: 25 Dec MEALS: alc (main courses £12 to £26). Set L £26.50 SERVICE: 12.5% CARDS: Amex, Delta, Diners, MasterCard, Switch, Visa DETAILS: 135 seats. 75 seats outside. Wheelchair access (also WC). Occasional music ⊖ Blackfriars

Palais du Jardin

map 15

136 Long Acre, WC2E 9AD COOKING 2
TEL: (0171) 379 5353 FAX: (0171) 379 1846 COST £29–£62

The 'Jardin' is, of course, Covent Garden, and if you hit early-evening drinks time at this trendy, noisy, brasserie and oyster/seafood bar, you may have difficulty squeezing past the throng to the mirrored restaurant area: it is not a place for an intimate conversation. A large all-French menu deals in simple starters: an assembly of smoked chicken and prawns on a chicory and walnut salad, perhaps, or a crab cake with sweetcorn relish. Main dishes have an attractive ring to them, whether approached in French or English – fricassée d'homard et volaille au riz noir, crème de coriandre, or fillet of beef in a herb crust with a celeriac mousse – although flavours may not always match presentation. Vegetables are charged extra. Desserts are something of an afterthought: 'we tried the only two available,' and banana tarte Tatin just beat a trio of chocolate mousses. Wines are pretty well all French and offer plenty of choice under £25. House wine is £9.50.

CHEF: Winston Matthews   PROPRIETOR: Le Palais du Jardin Ltd   OPEN: restaurant all week 12 to 3.30, 5.30 to 12; oyster bar all week noon to midnight   CLOSED: 25 and 26 Dec, half-day 1 Jan   MEALS: alc (main courses £9.50 to £19.50)   SERVICE: 12.5% (optional), card slips closed   CARDS: Amex, Delta, Diners, MasterCard, Switch, Visa   DETAILS: 350 seats. 20 seats outside. Vegetarian meals. Wheelchair access (also WC). Music. Air-conditioned   ⊖ Covent Garden, Leicester Square

Passione   NEW ENTRY map 15

10 Charlotte Street, W1P 1HE   COOKING 4
TEL: (0171) 636 2833   FAX: (0171) 636 2889   COST £27–£42

Small and unassuming, this 'light, pleasant and informal' newcomer has outside tables, apparently obligatory in this increasingly thriving street, although the frontage is so narrow that the two together seat just five. Wherever they are, tables are booked for the evening, service is 'perfectly competent', and reactions to the cooking justify the name. All the modern Italian touchstones are here, from 'rich, creamy, subtly flavoured' sorrel risotto, via chargrilled vegetables and salady starters (an immaculately dressed one of baby cuttlefish, octopus and squid for our inspector) to lamb cutlets with artichokes and potatoes. Polenta makes its presence felt too: as a crust for sea bass, or chargrilled (which makes it 'as exciting as it can be') to accompany calf's liver with onions in gravy. Limoncello (a lemon liqueur) and wild strawberries combined to provide one visitor with the 'best ice cream I've ever had'. Two other desserts are fruit (perhaps strawberries with orange and mint), or maybe a deep-fried Sicilian pastry filled with ricotta and candied fruit. The short, well-chosen Italian wine list stays largely below £20, with house wines at £9.50.

CHEF: Gennaro Contaldo   PROPRIETORS: Gennaro Contaldo, Gennaro D'Urso and Liz Przybylski   OPEN: Mon to Fri L 12.30 to 2.30, Mon to Sat D 7 to 10.30   CLOSED: Christmas to New Year, bank hols   MEALS: alc (main courses £8.50 to £14)   SERVICE: 10% (optional), card slips closed   CARDS: Amex, Delta, Diners, MasterCard, Switch, Visa   DETAILS: 40 seats. 5 seats outside. Private parties: 30 main room, 12 private room. Vegetarian meals. Wheelchair access (not WC). No music   ⊖ Goodge Street, Tottenham Court Road

Pétrus   NEW ENTRY map 14

33 St James's Street, SW1 1HD   COOKING 7
TEL: (0171) 930 4272   COST £32–£50

Marcus Wareing, it will be remembered, left L'Oranger (at the other end of the street, see entry) just as the last edition of the *Guide* went to press. His new premises (previously called 33 St James's) look as though they mean business, with a big glass frontage, and sharply lit tables down either side of a long room that manages to feel simultaneously 'smart, formal and intimate'. The menu's fair and simple pricing (there are no supplements) is an object lesson to many, given the consistently high standard of cooking. The only choice at lunch is between cheese and dessert, while dinner offers seven or eight options per course.

The appeal is simple, direct, unfussy food that is easy to understand. High-quality materials are handled well, from ravioli of quail topped with a slice of white truffle, to venison on rösti with spinach and cabbage. Dishes have a classic air about them – pressed terrine of rabbit, or properly seared foie gras with caramelised endive and a small potato crisp – and the food's refreshing lack of artifice (apart, perhaps, from the decorative squiggles that stand in for sauces in starters and desserts) is readily apparent: in well-timed skinless halibut, with braised cos lettuce and grapefruit segments in a lightly acidulated sauce, for example.

'I get the impression of a chef who has tailored his food to the needs of customers, rather than aiming to show off how clever he is,' volunteered one visitor, after eating a dessert of poached apple halves sandwiched between jumbled flakes of browned filo pastry, served with a scoop of crème fraîche ice cream. Delays between arrival and eating have been registered, and while junior service may lack a little polish there is enough authority from the top to overcome any problems. The restaurant's claim not to impose time limits on tables, however, did not accord with our inspector's experience. Wines are predominantly French (including house white at £15 and red at £16) and feature many prestigious names, not least that of the restaurant's namesake. Eighteen vintages of Pétrus are offered (some also in magnum) to those who wish (and can afford) to drink the real 'house wine': prices start at £370 for the 1992 and reach £12,300 for a bottle of the 1947.

CHEF: Marcus Wareing   PROPRIETOR: Gordon Ramsay Restaurants Ltd   OPEN: Mon to Fri L 12 to 2.45, Mon to Sat D 6.45 to 11   CLOSED: 25 Dec, 1 Jan, bank hols   MEALS: Set L £19.50, Set D £28   SERVICE: not inc   CARDS: Amex, Delta, Diners, MasterCard, Switch, Visa   DETAILS: 55 seats. No cigars in dining room. Wheelchair access (not WC). No music. Air-conditioned ⊖ Green Park

Pharmacy Restaurant & Bar   🍴   map 13

150 Notting Hill Gate, W11 3QG   COOKING 4
TEL: (0171) 221 2442   FAX: (0171) 243 2345   COST £26–£63

Pharmacy's set-up, for those who haven't heard, is a Damien Hirst art joke, from medicine bottles in the bar to metallic silver wallpaper, adorned with images of tablets and pills, in the upstairs restaurant. Michael McEnearney, who began his tenure in March 1999, cooks in a reasonably adventurous style, although his ideas may not be as way out as the concept leads one to anticipate. Cockles cooked with chorizo and small white beans in a Heinzy-looking sauce of tomatoes and piquillo pepper was an outstanding first course at inspection, the strong flavours combining sympathetically into something sharp and memorable. At the same meal, halibut was lightly fried and accompanied by a mixture of wild mushrooms and celeriac purée, the sort of meaty treatment that can often suit this fish. Meat preparations have included duck breast with caramelised endive and clove-scented apricots, as well as more mainstream grilled sirloin with Jersey Royals and red wine butter sauce. To finish, there's fashionable orange and almond cake with Greek yoghurt ice cream, 'nicely tart' passion fruit gratin, or crème catalan with quince. Cheerful service helps the Pharmacy's medicine go down smoothly. Wines are exceptional in range and quality, but prices are a touch forbidding, even for plutocratic Notting Hill. Fourteen house choices are available by the glass; bottle prices open at £11.50.

CHEF: Michael McEnearney   PROPRIETOR: Hartford plc   OPEN: all week 12 to 2.45, 6.45 to 10.45   CLOSED: 25 and 26 Dec, 1 Jan, L bank hols   MEALS: alc (main courses £8.50 to £18.50). Set L £15.50 (2 courses) to £17.50   SERVICE: 12.5% (optional), card slips closed   CARDS: Amex, Delta, Diners, MasterCard, Switch, Visa   DETAILS: 200 seats. Private parties: 120 main room. Vegetarian meals. Children's helpings. No music. Air-conditioned   ⊖ Notting Hill Gate

Phoenix ⌂   map 12

162 Lower Richmond Road, SW15 1LY   COOKING 3
TEL: (0181) 780 3131   FAX: (0181) 780 1114   COST £24–£48

On a corner site with bright walls, mirrors, paintings and old black and white photographs, Phoenix has a pleasant and airy atmosphere. As at its sister restaurant Sonny's (with branches in London and Nottingham, see entries), the food draws on a wide range of influences, but Carol Craddock seems to prefer well-tried combinations to out-and-out innovation: chilled curried apple soup perhaps, or calves' kidneys with bacon and rösti. At their most basic, results are 'absolutely satisfactory' – wild mushroom and spinach ravioli for instance – but some dishes achieve greater synthesis of flavours: at inspection, deep-fried avocado and artichoke with tomato salsa and crème fraîche; and a brace of pink quail, marinated in juniper, then grilled, and served with Muscat raisin sauce and some 'nice, sloppy' polenta. Desserts, sorry, puds take in just as much variety in their way: pannacotta comes with cherry compote, and 'admirable' passion fruit parfait is paired with mango salad. Service from 'white-apron-clad waiters sporting pagers' is solicitous, even if delivery is not without error. The wine list's brief annotations take on a Goolden-esque quality – 'honey and cream,' 'blueberries and ginger' – but they refer to well-chosen bottles from around the world. House vin de pays is £9.50.

CHEF: Carol Craddock   PROPRIETORS: Rebecca Mascarenhas and James Harris   OPEN: Sun to Fri L 12.30 to 2.30 (12 to 3 Sun), all week D 7 to 11.30 (10 Sun)   CLOSED: bank hols   MEALS: alc (main courses £9.50 to £13.50). Set L £12 (2 courses) to £17.50   SERVICE: not inc   CARDS: Amex, Delta, Diners, MasterCard, Switch, Visa   DETAILS: 85 seats. 35 seats outside. Private parties: 30 main room. Vegetarian meals. Children's helpings. No cigars/pipes in dining room. Wheelchair access (also WC). Music. Air-conditioned   ⊖ Putney Bridge   (£5)

Pied-à-Terre ▼   map 15

34 Charlotte Street, W1P 1HJ
TEL: (0171) 636 1178   FAX: (0171) 916 1171   COOKING 8
EMAIL: p-a-t@dircon.co.uk   COST £41–£111

Chairman Mao and President Johnson, in 1960s pop art incarnation, stare down from the far wall of one of the least intimidating of London's top restaurants. The red-upholstered chairs may be of the 'Torquemada' design school, but tables are generous in size and fairly spaced, there is no obligation to whisper in hushed tones, and in prospect is 'a smooth operation firing on all cylinders'. Choice is generous, with the option of an eight-course tasting menu for the whole table, and, while the food is ambitious and sometimes complex, the kitchen brigade is now large enough to ensure that standards remain consistently high: 'what in the past seemed at times like artifice has now become simply art.'

At this level properly sourced materials and a high degree of skill can be taken for granted, a combination that has produced roast langoustines on leek purée, alternating with delicate langoustine ravioli, and a Catalonian dish pairing slivers of tender pork belly with scallop and earthy celeriac purée. But it is the ability to make partnerships work effectively that puts the food in top gear, as in an intensely flavoured quail consommé of great clarity, enlivened with fresh herbs, with a single piece of quail meat in the centre; or a 'dazzling' little casserole of white beans and diced bacon, which offset the richness of its accompanying lobe of foie gras. This is 'cooking of the highest calibre'.

Vertical arrangements are a favoured way of presenting food: for example, pink Bresse pigeon on a Savoy cabbage leaf wrapped around first-rate sauerkraut, topped with a bush of deep-fried carrot slivers; or a dessert version layering caramelised apple between sheets of almond filo pastry, served with a winning apple sorbet of 'faultless texture'. Cheeses (all French) are of a quality and condition rarely encountered in London restaurants. Extras would make a very fine meal in themselves, culminating in trays of petits fours, one devoted entirely to chocolate.

The casually dressed maître d' is 'all charm', fluent in the ways of the menu, 'attentive without being pushy', and the 'friendly and impressive' sommelier advises expertly on the wine list if given half the chance. His domain is an enviable array of the great and the good, priced for expense accounts, plus a few unusually interesting bottles from Spain, and a positively gargantuan selection from Burgundy. House Vin de Pays des Coteaux de Murviel is £17 (red), £18 (white).

CHEF: Tom Aikens   PROPRIETORS: David Moore and Tom Aikens   OPEN: Mon to Fri L 12.15 to 2.15, Mon to Sat D 7 to 10.45   CLOSED: 1 week Christmas, 1 week New Year, last week Aug   MEALS: Set L £19.50 (2 courses) to £49, Set D £35.50 to £60 (whole table)   SERVICE: 12.5% (optional), card slips closed   CARDS: Amex, Delta, Diners, MasterCard, Switch, Visa   DETAILS: 36 seats. Private parties: 7 main room, 16 private room. Wheelchair access (not WC). No music. Air-conditioned   ⊖ Goodge Street

Le Pont de la Tour ♈   map 13

| 36D Shad Thames, Butlers Wharf, SE1 2YE | COOKING 4 |
| TEL: (0171) 403 8403   FAX: (0171) 403 0267 | COST £41–£84 |

Conran's riverine gastrodrome, with its fine food shops, sleek young professionals, towering displays of fruits de mer and spectacular views of the City skyline over the Thames certainly has its polished charms. It is a 'handsome, swaggering' restaurant, reached though a hectic bar with live piano music, that deals in conservative yet often luxurious Anglo-French food: grilled Dover sole, chateaubriand with bearnaise, or crêpe Parmentier with smoked salmon and caviare.

Decent materials and accurate timing have produced creditable sea bass fillet, and pink wood-pigeon breast with lentils and foie gras, as well as an appealing starter of cannelloni stuffed with pumpkin and ricotta, although our correspondence also reveals many disappointments. Nobody has a good word to say about desserts, for example, and time limits on closely packed tables, plus an extra charge for vegetables on the carte, are among the niggles that have taken the shine off things for some reporters. Plentiful though it is, there is little to recommend the service either, apart from the sommeliers, who are praised for being 'knowledgeable and helpful'. Although the quality of wines throughout the lengthy list is not open to question – whether looking at the many mature clarets and Burgundies or the classy array of New World bins – some of the prices may raise an eyebrow. Wines under £20 can be found, however, starting with house Vin de Pays d'Oc at £11.95.

CHEF: David Burke   PROPRIETOR: Conran Restaurants   OPEN: Sun to Fri L 12 to 3, all week D 6 to 11.30 (10.30 Sun)   CLOSED: 25 Dec, Good Fri   MEALS: alc D (main courses £17.50 to £22) and Sun L (main courses £11 to £14.50). Set L Mon to Fri £28.50, Set D 6 to 6.45 and 10.30 to 11.30 £19.50   SERVICE: 12.5% (optional), card slips closed   CARDS: Amex, Delta, Diners, MasterCard, Switch, Visa   DETAILS: 160 seats. 102 seats outside. Private parties: 8 main room, 20 private room. Vegetarian meals. Wheelchair access (also WC). No music   ⊖ Tower Hill, London Bridge

Prism 🍷

NEW ENTRY map 13

147 Leadenhall Street, EC3V 4QT   COOKING 4
TEL: (0171) 256 3888   FAX: (0171) 256 3883   COST £37–£59

Harvey Nichols' latest offshoot is this super-chic City restaurant, located in the old Bank of America building and making the most of its majestic ceilings, marble floors and proud neo-classical columns. Modern furnishings and towering flower arrangements help to make it 'a glorious place to impress clients', and the business community certainly appears to be its target market. Simon Shaw, previously at Fourth Floor in Leeds (see entry), has produced a long menu that mostly follows a tried-and-tested European route, though oriental influences appear, perhaps in the form of seared scallops with Chinese-style duck dumpling, chilli and soy. Starters range from generally straightforward assemblies – a refreshing salad of Asian pear, Roquefort and pine kernels – to Moroccan spiced chicken livers with lemon couscous and lightly tangy chilli sauce.

'A light touch and understanding of flavours' characterise the cooking, producing successful dishes of pancetta-wrapped monkfish with potato hash and red wine sauce, and roast corn-fed chicken with soft polenta and wild mushrooms. Desserts run from 'classic' lemon tart, through apple strudel and rum baba to citrus fruit salad. Cheeses are served in prime condition and service is well-oiled. The wine list covers the whole spectrum of styles and prices, including some fine wines from Italy and the New World, but no doubt big-name clarets and Burgundies will be called to table most often. House French is £12.50, and there is a very good choice of wines by the glass starting at £3.50.

CHEF: Simon Shaw   PROPRIETOR: Harvey Nichols   OPEN: Mon to Fri 11.30 to 3.30, 6.30 to 10.30   CLOSED: 25 Dec   MEALS: alc (main courses £9.50 to £14.50)   SERVICE: 12.5%, card slips closed   CARDS: Amex, Delta, Diners, MasterCard, Switch, Visa   DETAILS: 120 seats. Private parties: 30 and 40 private rooms. Wheelchair access (not WC). No music   ⊖ Bank

Purple Sage £ | NEW ENTRY | map 15

92 Wigmore Street, W1H 9DR · COOKING 3
TEL: (0171) 486 1912   FAX: (0171) 486 1913 · COST £22–£50

The fourth addition to Bijan Behzadi's colourful basket, alongside Red Pepper, Green Olive and White Onion (see entries, London), Purple Sage occupies a smart-fronted cavernously high room with big pillars, wooden tables and chairs, and a relaxed, informal atmosphere. It possesses that essential bit of kit for making a really successful pizza, a wood-burning oven (visible in the open-plan kitchen) that turns out thin, crisp bases topped with various combinations of mozzarella, chopped fresh tomatoes, ham, anchovies and so on. Ask for some bread (garlic, or oil-drizzled ciabatta), and start with a salad, or perhaps a more ambitious skewer of smoky chargrilled squid and sweet scallop (materials are manifestly fresh) served with lemon-dressed fennel, celery and sun-dried tomatoes. Pasta options might include rocchetti with chicken livers or linguine with clams, and chargrilled main courses are split between fish and meat: perhaps tuna with asparagus, or corn-fed chicken with courgettes. Finish with mascarpone and lemon cheesecake, or a crumbly meringue dish incorporating chewy dates, creamy chocolate ice cream and crunchy coffee granita. A short Italian wine list combines interest and value. House Montepulciano d'Abruzzo red and Locorotondo white are £9.50.

CHEF: Paolo Zanca   PROPRIETOR: Bijan Behzadi   OPEN: Mon to Fri L 12 to 2.30, Mon to Sat D 6 to 10.30   MEALS: alc (main courses £6 to £14.50)   SERVICE: 12.5% (optional), card slips closed   CARDS: Amex, Delta, MasterCard, Switch, Visa   DETAILS: 120 seats. Private parties: 35 main room. Vegetarian meals. No cigars/pipes in dining room. Wheelchair access (not WC). Music. Air-conditioned   ⊖ Bond Street

Putney Bridge ✎ · map 12

Embankment, SW15 1LB · COOKING 4
TEL: (0181) 780 1811   FAX: (0181) 780 1211 · COST £30–£82

With the arrival of ex-L'Odéon chef Anthony Demetre at this 'sleek, clean and serene' riverside eatery, the level of culinary ambition remains high. Out of the kitchen come some fairly demanding dishes with sophisticated-sounding garnishes: a salad of scallops, courgette beignets and tomato confit with pesto; or highly rated carpaccio of beef with truffle oil and a turret of aubergines, for example. Accurate timing shines through a main course of plainly grilled fillet of beef, and a restrained hand is behind a delicate sauce of coffee and cardamom with tender, gamey roast breast of Anjou pigeon on polenta. Although a few wish portions were bigger, everybody agrees that the pastry chef is a whizz. An intense soup of berries is served with a frothy cream tasting of lemon grass and ginger, and an assiette au chocolat comes in three parts: a wedge of glossy bitter tart, a tall cone concealing white mousse, and a ball of sorbet on a tuile, with dabs of 'inspiring' apricot purée in between. The kitchen may tend to over-reach itself at times, but most customers commend the 'visual drama' of dishes, not to mention the specially commissioned crockery, the surroundings, eager and authoritative service, and the Thames views from every table. Also adding value are appetisers presented before starters and desserts, and good-quality petits fours. The wine list matches the menu, being largely French and pricey. House Argentinian is £13.50.

CHEF: Anthony Demetre   PROPRIETOR: Gerald Davidson   OPEN: all week L 12 to 2.30, Mon to Sat D 7 to 11   CLOSED: 25 and 26 Dec   MEALS: Set L £13.50 (2 courses) to £17, Set D £30 (2 courses) to £50   SERVICE: 12.5% (optional), card slips closed   CARDS: Amex, Delta, Diners, MasterCard, Switch, Visa   DETAILS: 120 seats. Private parties: 100 main room. Vegetarian meals. Children's helpings. Wheelchair access (also WC). No music. Air-conditioned ⊖ Putney Bridge

Quaglino's

map 15

16 Bury Street, SW1Y 6AL   COOKING 4
TEL: (0171) 930 6767   FAX: (0171) 839 2866   COST £26–£73

Perhaps the glamorous model of every big, clattery, modern restaurant in the capital, Quaglino's remains unsurpassed for many as a place to see and be seen, its very design, reminiscent of a '30s cruise ship, lending itself to people watching. As they hang over the balcony of the mezzanine, bar flies will enjoy the long list of cocktails; others will find the rows of banquette seating comfortable enough as a setting for a classic meal of, say, calves' liver and bacon, roast pork with crackling, or lobster mayonnaise. Seafood is plentiful, with a range from caviare to oysters, to clams, to scallops with chorizo. The kitchen's ouput, and hence reports, are mixed, however, results ranging from under-par fish and chips to 'unpretentious and well-presented' Caesar salad. Some individual dishes have been highly rated: penne in a spicy, creamy mushroom sauce with pine nuts; and chicken and snail bourguignon, which formed part of 'the best meal in the last twelve months' for one reporter. But others find themselves wondering 'what all the fuss is about'. Perhaps the Quaglino's experience also depends on when you go; those who prefer a less frenetic atmosphere might try a weekend lunch. Active and passive smoking are both encouraged. The wine list is as neat as an accounts book and anyone drinking on a budget would do well to stick with the Vin de Pays d'Oc at £12.75; more pleasing tipples begin at £20 and over.

CHEF: Henrik Iverson   PROPRIETOR: Conran Restaurants   OPEN: all week 12 to 3, 5.30 to 12 (1am Fri and Sat, 11 Sun)   MEALS: alc (main courses £11 to £24). Set L £12.50 (2 courses) to £15, Set D Mon to Sun 5.30 to 6.30 and Mon to Thur 11 to 12 £12.50 (2 courses) to £15 SERVICE: 12.5% (optional), card slips closed   CARDS: Amex, Delta, Diners, MasterCard, Switch, Visa   DETAILS: 267 seats. Private parties: 500 main room, 40 private room. Vegetarian meals. Children's helpings. Wheelchair access (also WC). Music. Air-conditioned   ⊖ Green Park, Piccadilly

The Guide *is totally independent, accepts no free hospitality, and survives on the number of copies sold each year.*

Quality Chop House

map 13

92–94 Farringdon Road, EC1R 3EA   COOKING 3
TEL: (0171) 837 5093   FAX: (0171) 833 8748   COST £24–£76

It is a decade since Charles Fontaine revitalised this Victorian diner in what, at the time, seemed an out-of-the-way spot. Since then other restaurateurs have moved into EC1, the Chop House has expanded and fallen in love with seafood, but the basic seating, no-nonsense approach and reasonable pricing remain at the heart of the enterprise. After a meal of rich fish soup, 'meaty and flavoursome' Toulouse sausage with onion gravy, and rice pudding 'as it should be' with apricot jam, all with change from £20, one reporter felt he had received 'full value for money'. The gamut of dishes runs from jellied eels to grilled lobster, from eggs, bacon and chips to beluga caviare, from potted shrimps to grilled rump steak, all straightforward ideas that don't go in for frills. It is likewise with puddings of chocolate cake and apple crumble, and a compact but serviceable wine list that starts at £11.

CHEF/PROPRIETOR: Charles Fontaine   OPEN: Sun to Fri L 12 to 3.30 (4 Sun), all week D 6.30 (7 Sun) to 11.30   CLOSED: 10 days Christmas to New Year   MEALS: alc (main courses £7 to £22)   SERVICE: not inc; 10% for parties of 5 or more   CARDS: Delta, MasterCard, Switch, Visa   DETAILS: 60 seats. Private parties: 6 main room. Vegetarian meals. Children's helpings. No-smoking area. No music. Air-conditioned   ⊖ Farringdon

Quincy's

map 13

675 Finchley Road, NW2 2JP   COOKING 4
TEL: (0171) 794 8499   COST £33–£40

Dark green walls and sepia photographs are a far cry from cosmopolitan glitter, but Quincy's exudes a much appreciated warm and friendly atmosphere, and close-together tables can make it feel romantic. A monthly-changing menu (five choices per course) explores a largely European repertoire. Although it appears to exclude pork, bacon and shellfish (perhaps in deference to the local Jewish community), it has no trouble finding materials to play with: ballottine of rabbit with sweetcorn polenta, or warm smoked haddock paired oddly but happily with cold potato salad. 'This is not a place for those who don't like rich food in gigantic portions,' advised one visitor. Meat and poultry tend to be well cooked and flavours interestingly combined: perhaps in 'well-conceived' chicken boudin with crushed peas and tarragon jus, or a plate of roast lamb fillet and meatballs, with chickpeas, preserved lemon and cumin. Finish with apple crumble tart, or a more ambitious apricot Linzertörte with peach anglaise and pistachio syrup, crowned by strawberry sorbet. Staff are both good-humoured and efficient. Around thirty wines with impeccable credentials are offered at extremely fair prices. House Duboeuf is £10 a bottle, but start with a glass of Joseph Perrier champagne for a mere £3.50.

CHEF: David Philpott   PROPRIETOR: David Wardle   OPEN: all week D only 7 to 10.30 (11 Sat)   MEALS: Set D £25   SERVICE: not inc   CARDS: Amex, Delta, MasterCard, Switch, Visa   DETAILS: 30 seats. Private parties: 8 main room. Vegetarian meals. Children's helpings. No cigars/pipes in dining room. Wheelchair access (not WC). Music. Air-conditioned   ⊖ Golders Green

Quo Vadis

map 15

26–29 Dean Street, W1A 6LL	COOKING 6
TEL: (0171) 437 9585 FAX: (0171) 439 1933	COST £34–£57

This old theatreland address, still with its stained-glass windows, was thoroughly refurbished just as the *Guide* went to press, and is now adorned with paintings by Marco Pierre White himself, which will perhaps add some of the 'zest and atmosphere' that one reporter thought was previously lacking. In common with his other ventures, the menu includes a few luxuries, but the cooking is never more ambitious or fancier than the kitchen can handle. Now working largely within a European brasserie context, it offers reassurance in the form of simple classics from different repertoires: omelette Arnold Bennett, Caesar salad, English asparagus with hollandaise, and truffled foie gras parfait.

Indeed, its feeling for comfort is what seems to drive it. Poached eggs come several ways (Benedict, or on smoked haddock with Jersey Royals), and chips and béarnaise accompany grilled lobster and ribeye steak. Perhaps it is also this strand that unites a range of items running from moules marinières done 'by the book', via roast pheasant with bread sauce, to desserts of chocolate and chestnut torte, or pineapple tarte Tatin. Service is efficient and attentive; but then co-owner Fernando Peire was maitre d' at the Ivy for a number of years. The wine list's change of emphasis mirrors the food's, as it now deals in rather more approachable bottles of generally sound pedigree from around the world. House Italian Pinot Grigio and French Merlot are £14 and £14.50.

CHEF: Phil Cooper   PROPRIETORS: Marco Pierre White, Fernando Peire and Jimmy Lahoud OPEN: all week 12 to 2.45, 5.30 to 11.45 (10.45 Sun)   CLOSED: 25 Dec   MEALS: alc (main courses £9.50 to £16.50)   SERVICE: 12.5% (optional), card slips closed   CARDS: Amex, Delta, Diners, MasterCard, Switch, Visa   DETAILS: 100 seats. Private parties: 16 and 40 private rooms. Vegetarian meals. Wheelchair access (not WC). No music. Air-conditioned   ⊖ Leicester Square

Rani £

map 12

7 Long Lane, N3 2PR	COOKING 1
TEL/FAX: (0181) 349 4386	COST £23–£38

The vegetarian Gujarati cooking at this Finchley stalwart is 'as excellent as ever', says a reader who enjoyed vall papri chat (beans and onions on crisp, flat puris), and undhia (a slow-cooked dish of Kenyan aubergines, peas, guvar, valour, tindora, pigeon peas, potatoes and fried fenugreek balls). His highest praise was for more familiar bhel puri and aakha ringal (more aubergine, this time paired with ground peanuts). Specials of the day might include tindoora sak (slow-cooked Chinese cucumbers), or semi-exotic Brussels sprouts with cassava cream. Thalis are interesting, and there's a children's menu. The real surprise, though, is Italian dough pizzas (all vegetarian), produced in a separate kitchen. A fusion of the two cultures if ever there was, they include a banana methi version: ripe bananas, mozzarella, tomatoes and fenugreek. Service is 'friendly and efficient'. House wines change monthly, and are around £10. The branch in Richmond has now closed.

CHEF: Sheila Pattni PROPRIETOR: Jyotindra Pattni OPEN: Sun 12.15 to 10.30, Mon to Sat D only 6 to 10.30 CLOSED: 25 and 31 Dec MEALS: alc (main courses £6 to £8.50). Set L and D £12.45 (2 courses) SERVICE: 10% (optional), card slips closed CARDS: Amex, Delta, MasterCard, Switch, Visa DETAILS: 70 seats. Private parties: 50 main room. Vegetarian meals. Children's helpings. Wheelchair access (not WC). Music ⊖ Finchley Central £5

Ransome's Dock 🍾

map 12

35–37 Parkgate Road, SW11 4NP
TEL: (0171) 223 1611 and 924 2462
FAX: (0171) 924 2614

COOKING 5
COST £30–£58

Canal barges provide an obligingly picturesque backdrop to the bright blue walls, Matisse posters and strings of dried red chillies in Martin Lam's Battersea dining room. He takes supplies seriously, using free-range eggs (scrambled with smoked salmon or bacon for brunch at weekends), fish from sustainable sources, and 'as much organically reared meat and poultry as possible'. Despite an hors d'oeuvre plate featuring Spanish charcuterie, and some Cal/Ital flourishes, it is regional British items that stand out, from Morecambe Bay potted shrimps and Norfolk smoked eel to Guernsey veal (though Dutch calf's liver) and 'Shorthorn' sirloin steak, served with mustard and tarragon sauce and big chips.

Accurate timing makes the most of these materials, as do the generally simple treatments: house-smoked pigeon breasts with apricot chutney, noisette of English lamb with Savoy cabbage and roast root vegetables, or Greek yoghurt with honey to finish. Ice cream is from Rocombe Farm in Devon, and among dinner 'specials' might be warm chocolate tart with crème fraîche and blueberries. The two-course lunch – oxtail soup, perhaps, followed by cod and chips with tartare sauce – sounds a steal. The wine list combines quality with imagination, offering an eclectic range of bottles (and halves and magnums) at prices that are fair. And if the tour of the world's lesser-known producers serves to whet the appetite for adventure, a glass of one of the excellent Almacenista sherries from Lustau (£3.85) might be a good way to top and tail a meal.

CHEF: Martin Lam PROPRIETORS: Martin and Vanessa Lam OPEN: all week 12 to 11 (3.30 Sun) CLOSED: Christmas, Aug bank hol MEALS: alc (main courses £9.50 to £17.50). Set L Mon to Fri £11.50 (2 courses) SERVICE: 12.5% (optional), card slips closed CARDS: Amex, Delta, Diners, MasterCard, Switch, Visa DETAILS: 55 seats. 25 seats outside. Private parties: 14 main room. Car park D and weekends only. Vegetarian meals. Children's helpings. No pipes in dining room. Music. Air-conditioned ⊖ Sloane Square

Rasa/Rasa W1 🌶✱

maps 12 and 15

55 Stoke Newington Church Street, N16 0AR
TEL: (0171) 249 0344 FAX: (0171) 249 8748
6 Dering Street, W1R 9AB
TEL: (0171) 629 1346

COOKING 3
COST £22–£47

Both the Stoke Newington original and the more upmarket Soho offshoot have bright, modern interiors, with pink walls and tiled stone floors, a far cry from the flock wallpaper and artefacts once associated with Indian restaurants. The cooking, too, is out of the ordinary: entirely vegetarian and focused on the traditional cuisine of Kerala. Menus are more or less identical at each (though prices are significantly higher at Rasa W1: some dishes are more than double the price of their counterparts at Rasa) and are helpfully annotated to aid those unfamiliar with anything more exotic than chicken tikka.

The poppadom pre-starter selection is 'a must', yielding a tray not only of poppadoms but also achappam, pappadavadai (poppadoms with extra crunch and crackle) and chena upperi (spiced potato chips). These are best accompanied by the selection of chutneys. Starters are typically snacky things such as vadai (deep-fried patties of mixed lentil batter laced with spices) or boli (deep-fried slices of spiced plantain), while main courses focus on dhosas – rice pancakes with various fillings – or curries, which range from beet cheera pachadi (beetroot and spinach blended with yoghurt, roasted coconut, mustard seeds and curry leaves) to rasa kayi (mixed vegetables cooked with ginger, garlic and fennel). Desserts include pal payasam, a rice pudding with cashew nuts and raisins. The wine list is wide-ranging, with house wines at £9.50. A third restaurant, Rasa Samudra, has opened at 5 Charlotte Street, W1P 1HD, (tel: (0171) 637 0222). Like its siblings, it offers traditional Keralan cooking, but those who know that samudra means sea will not be surprised that the emphasis at the new branch is on fish and shellfish.

CHEFS: Rajan Karattil (Rasa), R.S. Binuraj (Rasa W1)   PROPRIETOR: Sivadas Sreedharan   OPEN: Rasa Sun L 12 to 2.30, all week D 6 to 10.45; Rasa W1 Mon to Sat L 12 to 2.30, all week D 6 to 10.30 (11 Fri and Sat)   CLOSED: 24 Dec to 31 Dec (Rasa W1)   MEALS: Rasa alc (main courses £5 to £5.50). Set L and D £15. Rasa W1 alc (main courses £10 to £11). Set L and D £22.50   SERVICE: 12.5% (optional), card slips closed   CARDS: Amex, Delta, Diners, MasterCard, Switch, Visa   DETAILS: 40 seats (Rasa), 90 seats (Rasa W1). Private parties: 40 main room (Rasa) 50 main room (Rasa W1). Vegetarian meals. No smoking in dining rooms. Wheelchair access (not WC). Music. Air-conditioned   ➋ Oxford Circus (Rasa W1)

Redmond's

map 12

170 Upper Richmond Road West, SW14 8AW   COOKING 5
TEL: (0181) 878 1922   FAX: (0181) 878 1133   COST £32–£43

Redmond and Pippa Hayward strike just the right balance between the familiar and the novel in their exemplary neighbourhood restaurant, which is why they have built up a core of loyal regulars. Pippa's warm and hospitable style ensures that everything runs smoothly in the bright, contemporary-looking yellow and blue dining room, while Redmond's cooking matches the vibrancy of the surroundings. The menu is certainly eclectic, spanning highly rated curried mussel and coconut soup; a dish of sea bass with fennel, mint, tabbouleh and curry oil; and well-timed roast pigeon with butternut squash polenta, accompanied by seared foie gras and balsamic jus. Yet novelty is never allowed to triumph over good taste, and flavours are well balanced. On busy nights, thanks to a small kitchen, it can be a victim of its own success, but despite a spot of inconsistent timing, reporters generally agree that Redmond's is 'a cut above'.

First-rate puddings include classic indulgences such as pear and chocolate tart, tarte Tatin, or an extraordinarily effective pairing of strawberries, balsamic vinegar and 'spicy' black pepper ice cream. Wines are well chosen to match the food and include some house wines of real character from £11.50.

CHEF: Redmond Hayward   PROPRIETORS: Redmond and Pippa Hayward   OPEN: Sun to Fri L
12 to 2.30, Mon to Sat D 7 to 10.30   CLOSED: 4 days Christmas, bank hols exc Good Fri
MEALS: Set L £12.50 (1 course) to £21.50, Set D £20 (2 courses, exc Sat) to £24.50   SERVICE: not
inc; 10% for parties of 6 or more   CARDS: Delta, MasterCard, Switch, Visa   DETAILS: 54 seats.
Private parties: 54 main room. Vegetarian meals. Children's helpings. No cigars/pipes in dining
room. Wheelchair access (not WC). No music. Air-conditioned

Red Pepper £

map 13

| 8 Formosa Street, W9 1EE | COOKING 2 |
| TEL: (0171) 266 2708 | COST £22–£47 |

Space is limited, decoration minimal and the menu basic, but still the locals pile
into this small Little Venice sibling of the Green Olive, Purple Sage and White
Onion (see entries, all London). For your trouble choose from pastas, well-
reported pizzas, or something from the blackboard – finely timed chargrilled
tuna with rocket, red pepper and black olive paste, say ? for your main course.
Starters are distinctly Italian and slightly unusual: smoked swordfish carpaccio,
perhaps, or 'a generous helping of first-rate' Parma ham, with blanched
courgettes, sun-dried tomato paste and Sardinian bread. 'Intensely lemony' torta
limone and tiramisù are characteristic puddings. Service could be more
customer-friendly. The all-Italian wine list offers good mid-range drinking,
with house wine starting at £9.

CHEFS: Paolo Zanca, Franco Parisi and Pasquale Manni   PROPRIETORS: Mr and Mrs B.
Behzadi   OPEN: Sat and Sun L 12.30 to 2.30 (3.30 Sun), all week D 6.30 to 10.45 (10.30 Sun)
CLOSED: 25 and 26 Dec, Easter Sun   MEALS: alc (main courses £6 to £13)   SERVICE: not inc,
12.5% for parties of 5 or more   CARDS: Delta, MasterCard, Switch, Visa   DETAILS: 50 seats. 26
seats outside. Private parties: 25 main room, 25 private room. Vegetarian meals. Children's
helpings. No cigars in dining room. Wheelchair access (not WC). Music. Air-conditioned
◉ Warwick Avenue

Rhodes in the Square

map 13

| Dolphin Square, Chichester Street, SW1 | COOKING 6 |
| TEL: (0171) 798 6767   FAX: (0171) 798 5685 | COST £34–£70 |

With its smart, cool, stylish décor in lush blue with lots of mirrors, this is in a
'brave' out-of-the-way location, thought one reporter. The burst of fiery
enthusiasm that characterised its early output seems to have settled down to a
gentle simmer, but it still delivers modern dishes with varying degrees of input
from the British repertoire: omelette Arnold Bennett at one end, warm Thai salad
at the other, and a faggot of spiced minced pigeon somewhere in between.

Although red-blooded dishes are never far away – calf's liver steak with blue
cheese and bacon gnocchi, for example – seafood has figured more prominently
in reports, including 'carefully cooked' scallops with red onion compote, and
'sublimely fresh' grilled herb-crusted cod. Vegetarian options, meanwhile, run
to a wild mushroom pancake gâteau. For dessert, milky rice pudding (served
'rather formally' in a saucepan with a side dish of rhubarb jam) is awarded high
marks for its 'unaffected execution and flavour'. Obliging service ensures that
everything runs smoothly, and one appealing feature of the wine list is a range of

around twenty available by the glass, although prices generally remain unsympathetically high for ordinary drinkers. House wines are around £16.

CHEF: Gary Rhodes PROPRIETOR: Gardner Merchant OPEN: Mon to Fri and Sun L 12 to 2.30, Mon to Sat D 7 to 10 CLOSED: Christmas, bank hols MEALS: alc D (main courses £15 to £22.50). Set L Mon to Fri £16.50 (2 courses) to £19.50, Set L Sun £24.50 SERVICE: 12.5% (optional) CARDS: Amex, Delta, Diners, MasterCard, Switch, Visa DETAILS: 80 seats. Private parties: 110 main room. Vegetarian meals. No cigars in dining room. Wheelchair access (not WC). Music. Air-conditioned ● Pimlico

Riva
map 12

169 Church Road, SW13 9HR COOKING 5
TEL/FAX: (0181) 748 0434 COST £27–£53

'Seasonal northern Italian cooking' is the draw at Andrea Riva's modest restaurant in a row of shops in Barnes. The unshowy style extends from a small, mirrored dining room to a menu that deals in straightforward assemblies of grilled vegetables brushed with herbed oil, San Daniele ham with pears, or a plate of mozzarella, spinach, cherry tomatoes and mushrooms. 'Simple but good' is how one visitor summed up the approach, and in this respect the food honestly reflects its roots. Farinaceous dishes might include gnocchi with wild mushrooms, or spaghetti with mussels, clams and bottarga, while main courses have turned up grilled squid with herbs, and sturgeon fillets with black truffle and juniper berries.

Despite its generally humble stance, this is 'not food for the faint-hearted', judging by calf's liver with garlic-flavoured polenta, and braised shin of pork with mashed potatoes in a honey and balsamic sauce. Alongside familiar desserts of pannacotta and tiramisù, expect to find sweet milk gnocchi, and crêpes of prunes and blueberries stewed in grappa, with nutmeg ice cream. Around thirty wines are well chosen and fairly priced. House wine is £9.95.

CHEF: Francesco Zanchetta PROPRIETOR: Andrea Riva OPEN: Sun to Fri L 12 to 2.30, all week D 7 to 11 (11.30 Sat, 9.30 Sun) CLOSED: 25 Dec, last 2 weeks Aug, bank hols MEALS: alc (main courses £8.50 to £14.50) SERVICE: 10%, card slips closed CARDS: Amex, MasterCard, Switch, Visa DETAILS: 45 seats. 8 seats outside. Private parties: 40 main room. Vegetarian meals. Children's helpings. No cigars/pipes in dining room. Wheelchair access (not WC). Occasional music. Air-conditioned ● Hammersmith

River Café ▼
map 12

Thames Wharf Studios, Rainville Road, W6 9HA COOKING 6
TEL: (0171) 381 8824 FAX: (0171) 381 6217 COST £42–£71

No doubt most people who have watched Rose Gray and Ruth Rogers cooking on TV want to experience it first hand. The food looks fresh and exciting, and appears to be produced effortlessly in seconds. Who can resist? And therein lies a problem. 'If ever a place has become too popular for its own good, this one is as good an example as you will find.' Given its popularity, there is understandably pressure on its close-together tables; hence there is a time limit, we are told, on 20 per cent of them. This and its attendant booking problems, plus service that can be 'rushed and forgetful', and dishes that run out, can make it all seem 'more like a military operation than eating out'. This highly processed feel is at odds with the informal style of food, and with what Italians consider normal.

The saving grace is that, when it comes, the food is all but universally praised, by first-timers for its quality, by regulars for its consistency: 'particularly fine' sardines, 'the best squid I have ever had', 'exceptional' turbot, and pork 'with real flavour' served with spinach and balsamic sauce. Simplicity is a keynote – in tagliatelle with nettles, butter and Parmesan, for example – and one reporter with a late lunch slot, who found little beyond a green salad with 'lots of herby flavours', a plate of 'pretty good' cheese, and a tasty caramel ice cream, certainly enjoyed the lot. Wood roasting, too, is a particularly successful technique: perhaps spatchcocked Bresse pigeon with spinach and porcini gratin. To finish, chocolate nemesis provided one reporter with a 'moment of brilliance'. Except for champagnes, the wine list is all Italian and offers a wide array of styles and flavours from historical to ultra-modern. House wines are £9.50, but do take a look at the seasonal selection of reserve wines for older vintages from the likes of Aldo Conterno, Angelo Gaja and Monte Vertine.

CHEFS: Rose Gray, Ruth Rogers and Theo Randall   PROPRIETORS: Rose Gray, Ruth Rogers and Richard Rogers   OPEN: all week L 12.30 to 3, Mon to Sat D 7 to 9.30   CLOSED: 10 days Christmas, Easter, bank hols   MEALS: alc (main courses £17 to £26)   SERVICE: 12.5% (optional), card slips closed   CARDS: Amex, Delta, Diners, MasterCard, Switch, Visa   DETAILS: 100 seats. 40 seats outside. Children's helpings. No cigars/pipes in dining room. Wheelchair access (also WC). No music   ⊖ Hammersmith

R.K. Stanleys

map 15

6 Little Portland Street, W1N 5AG
TEL: (0171) 462 0099   FAX: (0171) 462 0088
EMAIL: manager@rkstanleys.co.uk

COOKING 3
COST £26–£43

The Great British Banger has found a sympathetic home in this spacious room not far from Oxford Street. The meat comes from an organic farm in Wales, all sausages are made on the premises (viewing is welcomed), and the 'magnificent seven' range includes 'succulent' Simple Stanley (made from pork), a game version, a vegetarian Glamorgan, and a chillied Caribbean-style jerk sausage. There are starters of black pudding salad, or steamed mussels, but note that portions are substantial: Bratwurst comes with sauerkraut, grilled bacon, caramelised pears and champ. Those who make it through to dessert have enjoyed sweet fig pudding with a 'terrific' toffee sauce, and a champion lavender rice pudding with vanilla ice cream and mint syrup. Service is enthusiastic yet relaxed, and drinks include organic cider, interesting bottled beers and real ales. House wine is £10.75.

CHEF: Vincent Riakporhe   PROPRIETOR: Fred Taylor   OPEN: Mon to Sat 12 to 3.30, 6 to 11.30; bar area 12 to 11   CLOSED: 24 Dec to 3 Jan, bank hols   MEALS: alc (main courses £7.50 to £13; all sausage dishes £6.50 3.30 to 7 and 10.30 to 11.30)   SERVICE: 12.5% (optional), card slips closed   CARDS: Amex, Delta, MasterCard, Switch, Visa   DETAILS: 140 seats. Private parties: 20 main room. Vegetarian meals. Children's helpings. No-smoking area. Wheelchair access (also WC). No music. Air-conditioned   ⊖ Oxford Circus

The Guide *always appreciates hearing about changes of chef or owner.*

Roussillon

NEW ENTRY map 14

16 St Barnabas Street, SW1W 8PB
TEL: (0171) 730 5550   FAX: (0171) 824 8617   COOKING 3
EMAIL: galexis505@aol.com   COST £28–£62

Renamed (it used to be Marabel's) and refurbished, Roussillon combines rather formal French décor and service with modern, innovative food. 'Garden' and 'summer' menus (both five courses) contribute to the 'slightly veggie drift' of the place – Charentais melon with Indonesian pepper jelly on the former, lobster salad on the latter – while a main menu (with a few supplements) happily indulges in grilled pigeon, and lamb fillet with 'crunchy organic lemon'. Alexis Gauthier is committed to seasonality and clearly cares about provenance, and although his cooking may not have quite the impact reporters are expecting, ideas can be intriguing. The last item on one menu, for instance, was a 'spicy à la coque organic Red House Farm goose egg' served with gingerbread fingers and a maple infusion. At other times, simplicity is taken to extremes – a starter of sautéed English peas was 'literally a bowl of fresh peas' – although our inspector concluded that the such treatment was to be applauded in an age when so many other chefs cannot resist tinkering. Reporters are divided on the issue of value for money. Staff are all French, as are most of the wines, with half a dozen by the glass and a minuscule choice of halves. Two from Roussillon open proceedings at £14.50 for white, £15 for red.

CHEF: Alexis Gauthier   PROPRIETORS: James and Andrew Palmer, and Alexis Gauthier   OPEN: Mon to Fri L 12 to 2.30, Mon to Sat D 7 to 10.30   CLOSED: Christmas, 16 to 29 Aug, bank hols   MEALS: Set L £13.50 (2 courses) to £16, Set D £22 (2 courses) to £35   SERVICE: 12.5% (optional), card slips closed   CARDS: Amex, Delta, Diners, MasterCard, Switch, Visa   DETAILS: 55 seats. Private parties: 59 main room, 28 private rooms. Vegetarian meals. Children's helpings. No music. Air-conditioned   ✪ Sloane Square £5

Royal China

maps 13 and 15

13 Queensway, W2 4QJ
TEL: (0171) 221 2535   FAX: (0171) 792 5752
40 Baker Street, W1M 1DA
TEL: (0171) 487 4688 and 3123   COOKING 4
FAX: (0171) 487 4688   COST £26–£78

The décor – walls panelled with black and gold lacquered waves, reeds and flying birds – is virtually the same at both the Baker Street and Bayswater branches. The latter is more cavernous, and the semi-partition with glazed apertures is a great visual trick: you are not sure if you are looking at fellow diners or your own reflection. Menus are basically similar too, but there are enough differences to indicate that the chefs' individuality is respected. Dim sum are recommended at lunchtime, and although their names and content are the same, they display far greater delicacy compared with many of their Chinatown equivalents. Also praised are soft-shell crab with a lively but well-judged coating of diced peppers, chilli and soy, and 'carefully cooked, nicely spicy' Szechuan prawns. 'Unbelievably tender' belly pork with vegetables is the favourite main course of one regular, Singapore noodles 'are as good as one could hope for', and 'stunning' bok choy is timed to perfection. House wines, from

France and Chile, are £9.50 and £12. Note that, although a service charge is included, credit card slips may be left open. A third branch is at 68 Queens Grove, NW8, (tel: (0171) 586 4280).

CHEFS: (Queensway) Yuk Cheung Man and Wai Hung Law; (Baker Street) David Peng PROPRIETOR: Royal China Group OPEN: all week noon to 11 (11.30 Fri and Sat, 10 Sun) MEALS: alc (main courses £5.50 to £18). Set L (Baker Street) £8 (2 courses) to £23, Set D £23 to £29 (set meals min 2) SERVICE: 12.5% CARDS: Amex, Delta, Diners (exc Baker Street), MasterCard, Switch, Visa DETAILS: 200 seats (Queensway), 100 seats (Baker Street). Private parties: 240 main room, 6 to 40 private rooms (Queensway); 80 main room, 10 to 12 private rooms (Baker Street). Vegetarian meals. Music. Air-conditioned ⊖ Queensway, Baker Street

RSJ ▮   map 13

13A Coin Street, SE1 8YQ	COOKING 3
TEL: (0171) 928 4554 FAX: (0171) 401 2455	COST £25–£49

This corner site on the South Bank has seen its immediate environs smartened up over the couple of decades that RSJ has been here. Its own décor is 'chic' but in a minimal sort of way, with metal-backed chairs and vases of long twigs. Under the direction of executive head chef Ian Stabler, former senior sous-chef Frédéric Ducros cooks in a more or less contemporary French style, although the risottos are still in evidence and fried cod is Cajun-spiced: a 'well-conceived and well-cooked' dish, according to our inspector. Duck foie gras terrine with port jelly and toasted brioche is a crowd-pleasing starter, and while fish is very much the focus of main courses, red-meat eaters will find roast beef fillet served with wild mushrooms, sage polenta and a truffled sauce. Warm spiced apple and sultana cake comes with 'good-quality' vanilla ice cream and a restrained butterscotch sauce, and passion fruit crème brûlée is 'properly crunchy'. Service is generally efficient.

Nigel Wilkinson's legendary Loire wine list opens with a three-page guide to the grapes and vintages of this often overlooked region; in addition, most are annotated, so novices needn't feel nervous. Instead, take advantage of the great value for money afforded by the comparative unpopularity of these great wines, and it is well worthwhile to try one of the sweet whites. House Saumur is £10.75.

CHEFS: Ian Stabler and Frédéric Ducros PROPRIETOR: Nigel Wilkinson OPEN: Mon to Fri L 12 to 2.30, Mon to Sat D 5.30 to 11 CLOSED: 4 days from 24 Dec MEALS: alc (main course £10 to £16). Set L and D £14.95 (2 courses) to £16.95 SERVICE: 12.5% (optional), card slips closed CARDS: Amex, Delta, Diners, MasterCard, Switch, Visa DETAILS: 90 seats. 12 seats outside. Private parties: 8 main room, 22 and 30 private rooms. Vegetarian meals. Children's helpings. No cigars/pipes in dining room. Music. Air-conditioned ⊖ Waterloo £5

Rules   map 15

35 Maiden Lane, WC2E 7LB	COOKING 4
TEL: (0171) 836 5314 FAX: (0171) 497 1081	COST £37–£51

People make pilgrimages to Rules, and desire to eat ptarmigan within its picture-clad walls in their closing years. Many are intoxicated by the notion that literary London has been nourished here for more than 200 years. More mundanely, many readers say how useful these atmospheric rooms are after shopping or an exhibition, or before the opera or theatre, and how charming and efficient the service. The reality is not so different from the reputation, and the place continues to deliver teal, wild duck, hare, venison and crayfish from its own Pennine estate, served with nostalgic British accompaniments of quince marmalade, crab apple jelly, pease pudding and bubble and squeak. First courses of Cornish crab meat layered in pasta with diced tomato give way to main courses of game pie with root vegetable purée. Finish with plum crumble with sloe gin, or a savoury, such as grilled mushrooms on walnut and raisin toast. House claret and Alsace white are £11.95, but the list offers fifty or so other sharp choices from classic areas.

CHEF: David Chambers   PROPRIETOR: John Mayhew   OPEN: all week 12 to 11.30 (10.30 Sun)
CLOSED: 4 days Christmas   MEALS: alc (main courses £14 to £18). Set pre-theatre D (3 to 6pm)
£16.95 (2 courses)   SERVICE: not inc   CARDS: Amex, Delta, Diners, MasterCard, Switch, Visa
DETAILS: 132 seats. Private parties: 6 main room, 10 to 22 private rooms. Vegetarian meals.
Children's helpings. Wheelchair access (not WC). No music. Air-conditioned   ⊖ Charing
Cross, Covent Garden (£5)

Sabras

map 12

263 Willesden High Road, NW10 2RX   COOKING 4
TEL: (0181) 459 0340   COST £27–£38

For over quarter of a century, the Desai family have been treating Willesdenites, and many from further afield, to some of London's best Indian vegetarian cooking. Both the setting and the premises (a small predominantly white room behind plate-glass windows) are unassuming, but reporters continue to applaud the 'serious cooking'. Start with street-style snacks such as de luxe sev puri: crisp puris filled with spicy potato, yoghurt and the Desais' 'wonderful' chutneys. Main courses are an appetising and unusual collection of regional dishes, ranging from Mysore masala dosai (a crisp rolled pancake, its potato and onion filling enlivened by spices and chutneys) to East African Asian makkai-kaju (sweetcorn and cashew nuts in a mild tomato sauce) and Gujerati-style bataka-nu-shak (potatoes cooked in freshly ground spices). Desserts, too, are made in-house and include a choice of four kulfis. Service is unfailingly courteous. Organic juices, a variety of lassi drinks (try the smooth-textured sweet version), or a choice of three Indian beers are alternatives to the succinct wine list. House wines are £10.95.

CHEFS/PROPRIETORS: Hemant and Nalinee Desai   OPEN: Tue to Sat D only 6.30 to 10.30
CLOSED: Dec 25, bank hol Mons   MEALS: alc (main courses £6 to £7). Set D £6.50 to £15.50
SERVICE: 12.5%, card slips closed   CARDS: Amex, Delta, Diners, MasterCard, Switch, Visa
DETAILS: 32 seats. Private parties: 32 main room. Vegetarian meals. Wheelchair access (not
WC). Music   ⊖ Dollis Hill (£5)

Saigon Thuy £

NEW ENTRY   map 12

189 Garratt Lane, SW18 4DR   COOKING 1
TEL: (0181) 871 9464   COST £21–£35

Lacquered pictures on white-painted walls and subtle lighting lend something of a soft note to this long, narrow Vietnamese restaurant with its pine furniture and polished wood floor. This corner of South East Asia has not been particularly well represented in London in recent years, so a serious newcomer is welcome. 'Service is charming, the food authentic,' summed up one visitor who found traditional spring rolls 'very good indeed', and then went on to enjoy stir-fried prawns with cashew nuts. Also finding favour has been a fresh prawn salad spiced with coriander, chilli and honey, or you might try a sizzling plate of scallops with a rich tomato-based sauce. Desserts follow the sugared route of banana in coconut 'soup' with tapioca, and crisp apple fritters. The wine list is adequate and reasonably priced, with house wines £8.75.

CHEF/PROPRIETOR: Mrs T. Nguyen   OPEN: all week D only 6 to 11   CLOSED: 25 Dec, 1 Jan   MEALS: alc (main courses £3.50 to £6.50)   SERVICE: not inc   CARDS: Delta, MasterCard, Switch, Visa   DETAILS: 50 seats. 8 seats outside. Private parties: 30 main room, 20 private room. Vegetarian meals. Children's helpings. Wheelchair access (not WC). Music

St John

MAN WITH 2000 A MISSION

map 13

26 St John Street, EC1M 4AY
TEL: (0171) 251 0848   FAX: (0171) 251 4090

COOKING 5
COST £31–£50

Doubling as a bar and restaurant in still-trendy Clerkenwell, this barely converted smokehouse in concrete and white stone harbours a kitchen with attitude. If supermarkets (and, sadly, most butchers) had their way, carnivores would exist on a monotonous diet of pork chops, leg of lamb and fillet steak, while all the interesting bits get mushed up, tinned and sold to the nation's pets. Fergus Henderson's one-man (not his fault) campaign to reverse this would be worth supporting even if the cooking were not as good as it is. He makes a virtue of pig kidneys, chitterlings, veal marrow bones, ox tongue and blood cakes, typically serving up a skewer of dark, rich, grilled venison heart with a texture halfway between meat and liver. 'It is a place to sit, chew the fat and swallow it,' suggested one visitor.

Appropriately described as 'gutsy', this is essentially 'simple food, simply served', and comes in generous portions. But Henderson is not a suicidal restaurateur: only one or two internal organs appear on any given menu, the rest being taken up with crab mayonnaise, grilled razor clams, Manx kippers, pigeon with lentils and peas, or Gloucester Old Spot chop. Savouries – Eccles cake with Lancashire cheese was 'a triumph' for one visitor, a disappointment for another – provide a viable alternative to desserts of Dorset apple cake, baked custard with rhubarb, or prune suet pudding. Service is 'friendly and efficient', and non-smokers will be pleased to learn that air-conditioning has been installed. Around a dozen wines are available by the glass on the French wine list, where bottle prices start at £11.

CHEF: Fergus Henderson   PROPRIETORS: Fergus Henderson and Trevor Gulliver   OPEN: restaurant Mon to Fri L 12 to 3, Mon to Sat D 6 to 11.30; bar Mon to Sat 11 to 11   CLOSED: Christmas and Easter   MEALS: alc (main courses £8.50 to £14)   SERVICE: not inc   CARDS: Amex, Delta, Diners, MasterCard, Switch, Visa   DETAILS: 100 seats. Private parties: 150 main room, 20 private room. Vegetarian meals. No music. Air-conditioned   ⊖ Farringdon

'I was relieved to discover that "escalope of chicken Holstein" is not chicken cooked in lager.' (On eating in London)

Loos

map 14

2–64 Kinnerton Street, SW1X 8ER	COOKING 4
TEL: (0171) 235 4444 FAX: (0171) 259 5703	COST £27–£62

Fashion is transcended by the red plush Indian-style décor, while plain cream walls are relieved by paintings and elaborate displays of dried flowers. In the cooking, too, fashion is not the keynote, rather delivery of traditional, serious Indian/Pakistani cuisine (at serious prices) that caters to the locals in this secluded part of affluent Knightsbridge. Meat dishes are the strong point, while vegetarians get a modest look-in with a vegetable kebab and some chickpea and lentil options in the 'Vegetables etc.' section of the menu. All tandoori grills and some other dishes are marked on the menu as 'cooked to order', entailing up to twenty-five minutes' wait before they arrive. The result is tender meat and firm prawns, suffused with complex spicy flavours. Chicken karahi comes with a balanced sauce of ginger, chillies and tomatoes, while curries – here called saalan – include gurda masala (chopped lambs' kidneys in hot spices), and murgh korma (chicken with spices, yoghurt and kewra). Naan is remarkably light and fluffy, while rice, both plain and pilau, is carefully cooked. Warm carrot halva is a fine example of its kind, and home-made kulfi is first-rate too. Drinks prices have raised hackles; non-vintage champagne is £42.50, and only rather indifferent bottles exist below £20. House wine is £12.50.

CHEF: Abdul Aziz   PROPRIETOR: Mr M. Salahuddin   OPEN: Mon to Sat 12 to 2.30, 7 to 11.15   CLOSED: 25 Dec, bank hols   MEALS: alc (main courses £11 to £16). Set L £16. Cover £1.50   SERVICE: 12.5% (optional), card slips closed   CARDS: Amex, Delta, Diners, MasterCard, Switch, Visa   DETAILS: 70 seats. Private parties: 70 main room. Vegetarian meals. No children under 6 at D. No music. Air-conditioned   ⊖ Hyde Park Corner, Knightsbridge   £5

Salt House

NEW ENTRY   map 13

63 Abbey Road, NW8 0AE	COOKING 1
TEL: (0171) 328 6626 FAX: (0171) 625 9168	COST £21–£40

Sunlight shines through huge stained glass windows into the light, airy, comfortably civilised square dining room. This is a pub with a restaurant, where banquettes are more comfortable than wooden chairs, and generously sized, well-spaced tables bear smart flowers. Good-humoured staff competently serve from a frequently changing menu with six choices at each course, and salads are a strong point: Tuscan, with tomatoes, onions, olives, peppers and chunks of toast in a punchy dressing; or slices of tasty pigeon with French beans and pancetta. Onion and thyme soup has been declared a 'triumph', and main courses have included well- rendered cod with chips and aïoli, a vine tomato tarte Tatin with rocket and pesto, and grilled calf's liver with polenta and 'lots of rich boozy gravy to have with it'. The short, modestly priced wine list features a dozen by the glass in two sizes. Vin de pays is £9 for white, £9.50 for red.

CHEF: Andrew Green   PROPRIETOR: Robinson Restaurants Ltd   OPEN: Tue to Sun L 12 to 3 (4 Sat and Sun), all week D 6 (7 Sat and Sun) to 10   MEALS: alc (main courses £6.50 to £13). Set L £9.50 (2 courses) to £12.50   SERVICE: 12.5% (optional), card slips closed   CARDS: Amex, Delta, MasterCard, Switch, Visa   DETAILS: 40 seats. 40 seats outside. Private parties: 30 private room. Vegetarian meals. Children's helpings. No music. Air-conditioned   ⊖ St John's Wood   £5

Sarkhel's

map 12

199 Replingham Road, SW18 5LY

TEL: (0181) 870 1483   FAX: (0181) 874 6603

COOKING 2

COST £19–£42

Since opening this small, unassuming Indian restaurant at the end of 1997, Udit Sarkhel, former executive chef at the Bombay Brasserie (see London Round-ups), has gained much attention for his cooking. The menu is refreshingly different from the high-street norm, and dishes from the Indian regions include a few from Sarkhel's native Goa. Mundane poppadoms give no indication of the treats to come. One reporter admired a starter of ragara pattice: mashed potato cake 'zinging with fresh spices'. Goan prawn masala has also gained plaudits, as has baigan bhurta (chargrilled mashed aubergine) and 'ultra-light' gulab jamun. Service has been described as 'slick and friendly' and 'totally charming', though you might need to ask to see the specials list, where enticements such as salli boti (lamb with apricots) await. Several wines from the concise, varied list are available by the glass. House wine is £9.90. As the *Guide* went to press, plans were afoot to extend the seating area and install a spice shop.

CHEF: Udit Sarkhel   PROPRIETORS: Udit and Veronica Sarkhel   OPEN: Sun L 12 to 2.30, Tue to Sun D 6 to 10.30 (11 Fri and Sat)   CLOSED: 25 and 26 Dec   MEALS: alc (main courses £5 to £10). Set L Sun £9.95, Set D (min 6) £12.95 to £14.95   SERVICE: not inc   CARDS: Delta, MasterCard, Switch, Visa   DETAILS: 38 seats. Private parties: 43 main room. Vegetarian meals. Music. Air-conditioned   ⊖ Southfields   £5

Sartoria ♥

map 15

20 Savile Row, W1X 1AE

TEL: (0171) 534 7000   FAX: (0171) 534 7070

COOKING 5

COST £32–£71

One reporter visited Sartoria for a second time because it (and Conran Restaurants in general) had been given such a hard time by the press. He couldn't believe that his own first judgement was so wide of the mark; and, as he discovered, Sartoria wasn't as black as it had been painted. True, it is heavily themed, distractingly so for some, with most tailoring references squeezed somewhere on to crockery (button motif), upholstery (needle and thread), and stationery (the bill arrives on a pin cushion). But behind all this lies a good stab at contemporary, lively and essentially simple Italian food, served in a sharply lit, clean-lined dining room.

Meat (osso buco, grilled pork loin) comes a long way down the daily-changing list of dishes, preceded by a herby, lemony Salcombe crab starter, a crisp-based pizzetta topped with potatoes, artichokes and rosemary, or a dish of organic beets with horseradish and crème fraîche. Farinaceous dishes have included semolina gnocchi with chicken and pumpkin, and, among fish options, well-timed turbot has come with braised vegetables, celery and red chard among them. Chocolate Nemesis River Café betrays Darren Simpson's indebtedness to a previous job, while rhubarb – poached with zabaglione, or stewed with pannacotta – is a welcome nod to seasonal abundance. An all-Italian wine list will excite followers of fashionable producers, although prices are such that they may have to dip into their clothing allowance, particularly if they have a fancy for a Super-Tuscan. But, if threadbare pockets are a problem, trendy Arcadia house wines at £14 supply the answer.

CHEF: Darren Simpson   PROPRIETOR: Conran Restaurants   OPEN: Mon to Sat L 12 to 3, all week D 6.30 to 11.30 (6 to 10.30 Sun)   CLOSED: 25 and 26 Dec   MEALS: alc (main courses £10 to £20). Set L Sat £16.50 (2 courses) to £19.50   SERVICE: 12.5% (optional)   CARDS: Amex, Delta, Diners, MasterCard, Switch, Visa   DETAILS: 120 seats. Private parties: 14 main room, 16 and 32 private rooms. Vegetarian meals. Wheelchair access (also WC). No music. Air-conditioned   ⊖ Oxford Circus, Piccadilly Circus   £5

▲ The Savoy, Grill Room   map 15

The Strand, WC2R 0EU
TEL: (0171) 420 2065 and 2066
FAX: (0171) 240 6040   COOKING 5
EMAIL: info@the-savoy.co.uk   COST £51–£136

Shiny and gleaming, the Savoy is one of London's classics, capable of creating 'a certain excitement about going aboard a great ocean liner of a hotel'. The Grill Room is a discreet and predominantly male preserve, as if designed 'for the man who'd rather be in a club', and tries to cover all bases with a menu that mixes classic, old-fashioned and modern dishes: veal sweetbreads with Sauternes jus, omelette Arnold Bennett, and ricotta cannelloni with grilled peppers, anchovies and capers. What this committee approach may lack in thrills it makes up for with solid cooking skills: there may be 'nothing to astonish', but there is 'nothing to embarrass either'.

Trolleys are the institutional lifeblood, delivering their regular cargo of items to a soothing sidereal rhythm: roast rib of beef with Yorkshire pudding for Thursday lunch, best end of pork with gooseberries and apple on Tuesday evening, and so on. Another trolley brings dessert, unless you prefer the equally antiquated drama of flaming crêpes suzette. Service may suffer from a lack of organisation. A very traditional cellar provides little scope for those expecting change from £20, although house French red and white manage to limbo dance under the barrier at £18.50 and £19 respectively.

CHEF: Simon Scott   PROPRIETOR: Blackstone Real Estate   OPEN: Mon to Fri L 12.30 to 2.30, Mon to Sat D 6 to 11.15   CLOSED: Aug, bank hols   MEALS: alc (main courses £25 to £48). Set L £27.95, Set pre-theatre D £29.75, Set D Sun to Thur £39.50 to £70, Set D Fri and Sat £43.50 to £70   SERVICE: not inc, card slips closed   CARDS: Amex, Delta, Diners, MasterCard, Switch, Visa   DETAILS: 85 seats. Private parties: 20 main room, 12 to 100 private rooms. Vegetarian meals. Jacket and tie. No pipes in dining room. Wheelchair access (also WC). No music. Air-conditioned   ACCOMMODATION: 207 rooms, all with bath/shower. TV. Phone. B&B £314 to £365. Rooms for disabled. Baby facilities. Swimming pool (*The Which? Hotel Guide*)   ⊖ Charing Cross   £5

Searcy's ✥   map 13

Level 2, Barbican Centre, Silk Street, EC2Y 8DS   COOKING 2
TEL: (0171) 588 3008   FAX: (0171) 382 7247   COST £32–£62

If there are decent views from the Barbican, this has one of them: a long narrow second-floor room done in primary colours overlooking the fountains and St Giles Cripplegate Church. Pascal Deroubaix stepped into Tom Ilic's shoes after the last edition of the *Guide* appeared, and continues to produce modish food along the lines of veal sweetbreads with onion marmalade and sage cream, and carpaccio of scallops with red pepper purée and wild leaves. First courses can seem like smaller versions of mains, which may explain why the latter shone more brightly at inspection: rare cannon of lamb with a 'sweet vernal flavour'; and a thick, fresh, 'majestically firm' halibut fillet on cherry tomatoes with spinach and a vinaigrette-style paprika sauce. Finish maybe with a nutty pistachio crème brûlée with walnut sauce, or a cold wedge of glazed Alsatian apple tart with buttery shortcrust pastry. The food deserves more assured service. Around fifty wines combine old and new styles, starting with house French at £10.95.

CHEF: Pascal Deroubaix   PROPRIETOR: Searcy Tansley & Co   OPEN: Sun to Fri L 12 to 2.30, all week D 5 to 10.45 (6.30 Sun, and 9 in July)   CLOSED: 24 and 25 Dec, weekends and D in Aug   MEALS: alc (main courses £17.50 to £21.50). Set L and D £18.50 (2 courses) to £21.50   SERVICE: not inc   CARDS: Amex, Delta, Diners, MasterCard, Switch, Visa   DETAILS: 130 seats. Private parties: 30 main room. Vegetarian meals. Children's helpings. No-smoking area. Wheelchair access (also WC). No music. Air-conditioned   ⊖ Barbican, Moorgate £5

755 Fulham Road

map 12

755 Fulham Road, SW6 5UU
TEL: (0171) 371 0755   FAX: (0171) 371 0695

COOKING 6
COST £27–£69

Well down the Fulham Road, this smart, minimalist, yellow and blue restaurant rates highly for comfort in both surroundings and food. A long and varied carte indicates a busy kitchen that serves starters of crab and smoked haddock cannelloni, or seared mackerel with cauliflower brandade, aubergine caviare and red pepper dressing. It also balances a good showing of fashionable fish (red mullet and sea bass for example) against earthier dishes of braised oxtail and pig's trotter, all done in contemporary Anglo-French style, even down to griddled foie gras with Yorkshire pudding and Madeira gravy.

Set dinner was considered 'remarkable value' by one who started with a Thai seafood soup appetiser followed by raw salmon with ginger and soy dressing, then lambs' tongue with caper jus and truffled mash, finishing with a plate of poached pear, raspberries, strawberries and ice cream. Service is 'a mixture of efficiency and low-key friendliness', and wines play off the Old World against the New, starting with a quartet of French house wines at £12.50.

CHEF: Alan Thompson   PROPRIETORS: Alan and Georgina Thompson   OPEN: Tue to Sun L 12.30 to 2.30 (12 to 4 Sun), Tue to Sat D 7 to 11   CLOSED: 1 week Christmas, 4 days Easter, 2 weeks summer   MEALS: alc Tue to Sat L and D (main courses £12.50 to £20). Set L £12.50 (2 courses) to £16, Set D Tue to Sat £18 (2 courses) to £22   SERVICE: not inc   CARDS: Amex, Delta, MasterCard, Switch, Visa   DETAILS: 50 seats. Private parties: 50 main room, 35 private room. Children's helpings. Wheelchair access (not WC). No music. Air-conditioned   ⊖ Parsons Green £5

Sheekey's

NEW ENTRY   map 15

28-32 St Martin's Court, WC2N 4AL
TEL: (0171) 240 2565   FAX: (0171) 240 8114

COOKING 5
COST £31–£87

Handy for theatreland, in a short walkway linking Leicester Square and St Martin's Lane, J. Sheekey has been revived by the team that made the reputations of the Ivy and Caprice. Some reporters' memories go back a long way: if not to the 1890s, when it was founded, then at least to the 1950s, 'when they served steamed fish only' and it was famous for its discomfort. As a reporter observed in a late-1960s edition of the *Guide*, you had to 'squeeze into part-ownership' of a shared table. Nowadays, increased space is divided up into 'semi-compartments', their panelled walls hung with celebrity photographs, but the emphasis on 'fresh and carefully cooked' seafood remains: jellied eels, well-timed scallops with strips of bacon, grilled baby squid looking like 'tiny white rugby balls', on creamy polenta.

Supplies tend to favour native rather than exotic varieties – Cornish crab, or Dover sole with buttery hollandaise – and the menu balances traditional and modern treatments without being sidetracked by excessive flights of fancy. Combinations are straightforward yet attractively varied, incorporating poached egg (with smoked cod), chips and peas (with haddock) and seaweed risotto (with sea bass). Four dishes typically change by the day, and a comforting nursery theme runs through desserts, taking in spotted dick, treacle tart, and a 'fine, light, fluffy' chocolate soufflé. Service has varied from 'ordinary', through 'smooth and welcoming', to 'speedy without being pushy'. A compact wine list features a good range of sharply chosen bottles including sensible red varietals for the context: Pinot Noir, Gamay, Merlot. Half-bottles are in good supply, and over a dozen wines are available by the glass. Prices start at £11.25 for Trebbiano di Puglia from Pasqua.

CHEF: Tim Hughes PROPRIETORS: Jeremy King and Chris Corbin OPEN: all week 12 to 3 (3.30 Sun), 5.30 to 12 CLOSED: 25 and 26 Dec, 1 Jan, bank hols MEALS: alc (main courses £9.50 to £27). Set L Sat and Sun £9.75 (2 courses) to £13.50. Cover £1.50 SERVICE: not inc CARDS: Amex, Delta, Diners, MasterCard, Switch, Visa DETAILS: 105 seats. Vegetarian meals. Children's helpings. No cigars in dining room. Wheelchair access (not WC). No music. Air-conditioned ✪ Leicester Square

Simply Nico map 13

48A Rochester Row, SW1P 1JU	COOKING 4
TEL: (0171) 630 8061 FAX: (0171) 828 8541	COST £36–£63

With its polished wooden floor and strategically placed mirrors to help with the illusion of space, this yellow dining room that once housed Nico Ladenis's premier restaurant serves an appealing selection of familiar dishes. There are no bizarre ingredients or way-out combinations, no wild ambition, just a comforting range of staples from fish soup, via chicken liver and foie gras parfait, to sole with tartare sauce, and cassoulet. Properly cooked risottos have included a cep version, and one with Parma ham and Parmesan, and mushroom and artichoke tartlet with hollandaise has met with wide approval.

Fish generally impresses, perhaps in the form of salmon fillet on Puy lentils surrounded by a ring of creamy mustard sauce, or two fillets of sea bass, in a pool of bright red pepper coulis, stuffed with well-flavoured, creamy-textured basil mousse. One or two items (beef and veal, for example) carry a supplement, and potatoes (purée or chips) are charged extra. Expect raspberry crème brûlée, chocolate mousse, or perhaps a cherry sponge with alcohol-soaked fruit to finish. Tables are turned over quickly (so don't dawdle if you want coffee) and service bustles along to keep pace. Some sixty varied wines, with only a handful under

£20, aim for reliability. House wines are a red Tannat from Uruguay (£21) and Boschendal Sauvignon Blanc from South Africa (£19.50).

CHEF: Richard Hugill   PROPRIETOR: The Restaurant Partnership   OPEN: Mon to Fri L 12 to 2, Mon to Sat D 7 to 11   CLOSED: Christmas, Easter, bank hols   MEALS: Set L £20.50 (2 courses) to £23, Set D £25.50   SERVICE: 12.5% (optional), card slips closed   CARDS: Amex, Delta, Diners, MasterCard, Switch, Visa   DETAILS: 45 seats. Private parties: 12 main room. No children under 10. No cigars/pipes in dining room. No music. Air-conditioned   ⊖ Victoria

Singapore Garden

map 13

83–83A Fairfax Road, NW6 4DY
TEL: (0171) 328 5314   FAX: (0171) 624 0656

COOKING 2
COST £17–£69

The Garden has lost some of its verdancy following refurbishment and now has an uncluttered, brighter feel, with cream walls, dark wood parquet flooring and frosted-glass partitions between the two rooms. Food remains of a high standard, making the restaurant very popular. The menu leans towards the Chinese style of Singaporean cooking, with plenty of stir-fries, and an 'absolutely first-class' braised bean curd with shredded pork and Chinese mushrooms. 'Mixed three greens' – crunchy mange-tout, sprouting broccoli and spring greens – also have their fans. Look to the Singaporean and Malaysian specialities for extra spice, including daging curry (with beef) and Singapore laksa seafood soup. Staff are pleasant, and the entire operation is well organised. The wine list, informatively annotated, contains an alluring blend of Old and New World flavours. House wines cost from £10.95.

CHEF: Mrs S.K. Lim   PROPRIETORS: the Lim family   OPEN: all week 12 to 2.45, 6 to 10.45 (11.15 Fri and Sat)   CLOSED: 1 week Christmas   MEALS: alc (main courses £5.50 to £25). Set L £6.25 (2 courses) to £8, Set D £17.50 to £30   SERVICE: 12.5% (optional), card slips closed   CARDS: Amex, Delta, Diners, MasterCard, Switch, Visa   DETAILS: 100 seats. 10 seats outside. Private parties: 50 main room, 50 private room. Vegetarian meals. No cigars in dining room. Music. Air-conditioned   ⊖ Swiss Cottage

Snows on the Green

map 12

166 Shepherd's Bush Road, W6 7PB
TEL: (0171) 603 2142   FAX: (0171) 602 7553
EMAIL: sebastian@snowsonthegreen.freeserve.co.uk

COOKING 2
COST £26–£47

Despite its location on one of West London's busiest roads, this 'relaxed and sunny' restaurant has an airy Mediterranean feel, thanks to warm pastel colours, prints of lavender fields, and olive oil on the tables. The menu follows suit, with dishes such as chargrilled focaccia with sweet peppers and mozzarella, red onion and anchovy tart, and veal carpaccio with tonnato dressing. Modern bistro classics get a look-in too: cured salmon with potatoes, pickled cucumber and beetroot relish, perhaps, or chargrilled calf's liver with bacon and spinach. Robust combinations have been undermined by timid seasoning on occasion, but decent raw materials are usually correctly cooked. 'Exemplary' puddings tend to steal the show: try stewed pear in a berry sauce with cold rice pudding, or strawberry pavlova. Efficient staff make you feel welcome, and a short wine list squeezes in plenty of good value from France, Italy and the New World, with French house wine at £10.95.

CHEF/PROPRIETOR: Sebastian Snow OPEN: Mon to Fri L 12 to 3, Mon to Sat D 6 to 11 CLOSED: 4 days Christmas, bank hol Mons MEALS: alc (main courses £9 to £14). Set L £13.50 (2 courses) to £16.50 SERVICE: not inc, card slips closed CARDS: Amex, Delta, Diners, MasterCard, Switch, Visa DETAILS: 80 seats. 12 seats outside. Private parties: 30 main room, 20 private room. Vegetarian meals. Children's helpings. Wheelchair access (not WC). Occasional music. Air-conditioned ⊖ Hammersmith

Soho Soho

map 15

11–13 Frith Street, W1V 5TS
TEL: (0171) 494 3491 FAX: (0171) 437 3091

COOKING 2
COST £26–£58

'Diners tend to look around them to see if anyone famous is there,' noted a reporter, glad to be in the cool, calm, mushroom-coloured upstairs room of this popular venue. Andrew Parkinson has taken over as chef, and continues the broadly Mediterranean style of his predecessor, turning out steamed sea bream on linguine, and French 'black leg chicken' on a wild mushroom risotto cake. To start, vegetable terrine with roasted peppers and aubergines is arranged on the plate as a smiling face, while asparagus comes with a light vinaigrette, crisp Parmesan tuile and roasted tomatoes. Main courses featuring lamb and salmon disappointed slightly at inspection, but a taster dish of puddings delighted with its samples of 'creamy, tangy' passion fruit brûlée; lemon tart with poached apple; a baby pavlova; and chocolate mousse. Pleasant staff are clad in garçon mode. Twenty wines of each colour are mostly French and scantily described. Red and white Vin de Pays d'Oc are £9.95. Downstairs is the rôtisserie, where the format is all-day roasts, grills, salads and omelettes.

CHEF: Andrew Parkinson PROPRIETOR: Groupe Chez Gérard OPEN: Mon to Fri L 12 to 2.30, Mon to Sat D 5.30 to 11.30 CLOSED: Easter Mon MEALS: alc (main courses £11 to £15). Set D 5.30 to 7.15 and 10.15 to 11.30 £12.50 (2 courses) to £15.50. Cover £1.50 SERVICE: 12.5% (optional), card slips closed CARDS: Amex, Delta, Diners, MasterCard, Switch, Visa DETAILS: 70 seats. Private parties: 70 main room, 60 to 80 private rooms. Car park at D. Vegetarian meals. No cigars in dining room. Music. Air-conditioned ⊖ Leicester Square, Tottenham Court Road

Soho Spice

NEW ENTRY map 15

124–126 Wardour Street, W1V 3LA
TEL: (0171) 434 0808 FAX: (0171) 434 0799
EMAIL: info@sohospice.co.uk

COOKING 1
COST £24–£42

Soho buzzes with new vigour in this 'bar-café-tandoor', with its ground-floor restaurant and downstairs bar. Few customers are over thirty years old, and the noise level is not soothing. Vibrant colours – purple, orange, green, maroon – make a striking backdrop, and care for design extends to waiters' kurta jackets and to paper tablemats illustrating spices, which are also seen in glass jars around the room. The menu offers just three lamb and three chicken out of eighteen main courses, which range from tandoori quails with chillies and fennel, to curried tilapia. Designed for Westerners, they come with rice, naan, dhal and vegetables of the day. Portions are generous, and those who prefer sharing Indian-style should order starter and main-course 'selections': one of each makes a meal for two. Pre-theatre and lunch menus are good value and come even more quickly. Service is friendly, attentive, and skilled even in serving wine from the short, annotated list, where house wine is £11.95.

CHEFS: Kuldeep Singh and Sunder Singh Rana   PROPRIETOR: Amin Ali   OPEN: all week noon to 12 (3am Fri and Sat, 10pm Sun)   CLOSED: 25 Dec   MEALS: alc (main courses £8 to £15). Set L and D 5 to 7 £7.50 (2 courses), Set D £15.95   SERVICE: not inc   CARDS: Amex, Diners, MasterCard, Switch, Visa   DETAILS: 140 seats. Private parties: 200 main room, 40 private room. Vegetarian meals. No smoking in 1 dining room. Wheelchair access (also WC). Music. Air-conditioned   ✪ Tottenham Court Road, Leicester Square   £5

Sonny's

map 12

94 Church Road, SW13 0DQ   COOKING 5
TEL: (0181) 748 0393   FAX: (0181) 748 2698   COST £24–£48

Located on the high street of one of London's quaintest 'villages', this 'ideal neighbourhood restaurant' boasts only discreet changes to its appearance after a major refit that led to a temporary closure in autumn 1998. It seems lighter and brighter, has a new fireplace and glass frontage, so yet more passers-by can admire the collection of noteworthy paintings and photography, and spy on diners enjoying the modern British food. Leigh Diggins continues to produce what one reporter acclaims as 'thoughtful cooking at reasonable prices'.

His creations range from pan-fried John Dory with pea and mint risotto, through roasted pig's trotter with chorizo, to Barbary duck breast with red onion tarte Tatin with peas and morels. Combinations can be daring – sweetbreads with a liquorice glaze – and presentation errs towards a 'preference for vertical edifices and dribbled patterns of sauce in contrasting colours'. Puddings take in tarts – pear Tatin, or rhubarb and almond – as well as buttermilk bavarois served with poached plums and a light almond biscuit. Service is 'young, trendy, male and casual'. The wine list details a faddish selection and is wittily annotated, with prices opening at £9.50. Sonny's shop next door sells 'gourmet pantry essentials' such as organic tea and orange curd, and, with Sonny's in Nottingham and Phoenix in Putney under the same ownership, gives the impression of a burgeoning foodie empire.

CHEF: Leigh Diggins   PROPRIETORS: Rebecca Mascarenhas and James Harris   OPEN: all week L 12.30 to 3.30 (12 to 4 Sun), Mon to Sat D 7.30 to 11   MEALS: alc (main courses £10.50 to £14). Set L Mon to Sat £12 (2 courses), Set L Sun £17.50   SERVICE: not inc   CARDS: Amex, Delta, Diners, MasterCard, Switch, Visa   DETAILS: 100 seats. Private parties: 8 main room, 20 private room. Vegetarian meals. Children's helpings. No cigars/pipes in dining room. Music. Air-conditioned   ✪ Hammersmith   £5

Sotheby's Café ✿✗

map 15

34–35 New Bond Street, W1A 2AA   COOKING 2
TEL: (0171) 293 5077   FAX: (0171) 293 5920   COST £26–£42

The auction house café serves its purpose well. As a weekday lunchtime bolt-hole in a posh part of London, where shopping can get very serious, it serves regenerative upmarket snacks such as lobster club sandwich alongside risotto (perhaps of roast butternut squash with broad beans, peas, spinach and goats' cheese) and chargrilled tuna with fennel mash. Ideas and techniques are admirably simple – follow cream of Jerusalem artichoke soup with duck breast salad and marbled fudge brownie – service is prompt, and a short wine list offers fair choice by the large glass. House Italian is £11.50 a bottle.

CHEF: Caroline Crumby   PROPRIETOR: Sotheby's   OPEN: Mon to Fri 12 to 3 (also breakfast 9.30 to 11.30, afternoon tea 3 to 4.45)   CLOSED: Christmas and New Year, last 2 weeks Aug, bank hols   MEALS: alc (main courses £10 to £15)   SERVICE: net prices, card slips closed   CARDS: Amex, Delta, Diners, MasterCard, Switch, Visa   DETAILS: 46 seats. Private parties: 10 main room. Vegetarian meals. No smoking in dining room. Wheelchair access (not WC). No music. Air- conditioned   ⊖ Green Park

Spiga ✎   map 15

| 84–86 Wardour Street, W1V 3LF | COOKING 2 |
| TEL: (0171) 734 3444   FAX: (0171) 734 33332 | COST £28–£49 |

Part of the A To Z restaurant group (along with London main entries Aubergine, L'Oranger and Zafferano, and London Round-up La Spighetta), Spiga's décor is 'trendy minimalist retro' in variations on brown, tan and beige. Efficient Italian waiters in olive jackets ('smart Gucci-styled prison wear') usually cope with monolingual Brits. Possibly they are advised by chef Nick Melmoth-Coombs (formerly of Neal Street Restaurant, see entry) whose translations on the monthly-changing menu are entirely accurate. Pizzas from a wood-fired oven are the highlight, with such original toppings as suckling pig and rocket; prosciutto with wild mushrooms; Gorgonzola and speck; and ortolana (mozzarella, aubergines, zucchini and much more). The bases are notable not only for their galactic circumference, but also their thickness, or lack of it. Pasta, and old-fashioned meat and fish main courses, don't quite reach the same heights, but lemon and mascarpone tart, or 'boozy' tiramisù , have made happy endings. There is a short Italian wine list; house wines are £10.50.

CHEF: Nick Melmoth-Coombs   PROPRIETOR: A–Z Restaurants   OPEN: all week 12 to 3, 6 to 12 (11 Sun to Tue)   MEALS: alc (main courses £7 to £13.50)   SERVICE: 12.5% (optional), card slips closed   CARDS: Amex, Delta, MasterCard, Switch, Visa   DETAILS: 110 seats. Private parties: 30 main room. Vegetarian meals. Children's helpings. Wheelchair access (also WC). Music. Air-conditioned   ⊖ Piccadilly Circus

Spread Eagle   [NEW ENTRY]   map 12

| 1–2 Stockwell Street, SE10 9JL | COOKING 3 |
| TEL: (0181) 853 2333   FAX: (0181) 305 1666 | COST £22–£51 |

The Spread Eagle, a Greenwich coaching inn dating from the seventeenth century, has been a stalwart of the *Guide* London Round-ups for a number of years. Sitting opposite Greenwich Theatre, its prime position for the millennium celebrations is given impetus by the arrival of Bernard Brique, whose bilingual menus indicate the centre of culinary gravity. Start perhaps with terrine d'aubergine et poivrons rouges, before proceeding to médaillons de lotte à la moutarde. An inspector who decided to buck the trend and try out the Danish sweet pickled herrings with a soft-boiled egg, curried mayonnaise, rye bread and a glass of schnapps was impressed by everything from the delicate cure of the fish to the timing of the egg, and the roar of alcohol in the little glass. Main courses run to tender veal sirloin, served in a lemon and thyme stock sauce on a freshly made risotto full of ceps; desserts include a nutty, chewy iced nougat with raspberry coulis; and a plethora of petits fours is served with coffee. Service is smilingly attentive and efficient with it. Like the food, the wine list majors in France. There are plenty of half-bottles, and prices are not too steep; house Réserve du Patron is £9.75.

CHEF: Bernard Brique   PROPRIETOR: Richard Moy   OPEN: all week L 12 to 3, Mon to Sat D 6.30 to 10.30, Sun 12 to 6.45   CLOSED: 25 to 30 Dec   MEALS: alc (main courses £9 to £14). Set L £10.75 (2 courses) to £13.75, Set L Sun £9.75 (2 courses), Set D £13.75   SERVICE: 12.5% (optional), card slips closed   CARDS: Amex, Diners, MasterCard, Switch, Visa   DETAILS: 80 seats. 30 seats outside. Private parties: 45 main room, 12 to 45 private rooms. Vegetarian meals. Children's helpings. Wheelchair access (not WC). Occasional music. Air-conditioned (£5)

The Square 🍾

map 15

6–10 Bruton Street, W1X 7AG

COOKING **8**

TEL: (0171) 495 7100   FAX: (0171) 495 7150

COST £50–£101

The appeal, in a nutshell, is immaculate food in a cosseting environment. Parquet flooring, abstract paintings on lightly washed walls, and tables 'in full dress' present a rather formal face, but this is not a stuffy dining room. Philip Howard has been at The Square for a decade, developing from very good (at the King Street address) into a 'must-do for anybody on the serious gastronomic circuit'. His menus, offering 'masses of choice', are cast in contemporary European mould, and, among the themes to emerge, pasta seems a favoured device, turning up as a bulging roll of cannelloni filled with shredded trout and green leek, accompanied by plump crayfish tails, or as wafer-thin sheets alternating with crab and basil, in a creamy, frothy, crustacean sauce.

Another attraction is 'stunningly fresh fish timed exquisitely', from transparently white fillet of turbot on buttered chopped leeks to wild salmon with a smooth green purée of potatoes and watercress. Dishes may sound simple, but descriptions hide a wealth of effort and skill, not to mention richness. Bresse pigeon, for example, is separated into its constituent parts: rare, crisp-skinned breasts on an underlay of diced cabbage and bacon; a gamey mixture of liver and 'other offaly bits' under another cabbage leaf; and criss-crossed legs, all in a sticky reduction. Then a copper pan of truffled mash arrives to complete the ensemble.

The food stands out for its balancing of flavours, sound construction, and accuracy of seasoning: for example, in a stuffed rabbit leg wrapped in thin pancetta, laid on buttery puff pastry containing caramelised onion, and given a light, well-integrated, mustard-enriched sauce. Desserts can be 'seriously rich', but, like everything else, are well judged: a bitter and 'extremely fine' chocolate fondant with a scoop of orange and vanilla ice cream, for example, or a passion fruit and orange tart with crisp pastry and a smooth sweet-sharp custard. Cheeses are carefully presented in increasing order of strength, and incidentals, including 'very fine' bread, are well up to standard. Formal staff are 'everywhere but nowhere' and work hard to justify the 12.5 per cent service charge.

Wine service in particular is exemplary, from the sommelier's helpful advice, to the correct glasses and the decanting of wine at table, which is no less than the many high-calibre bottles on the lengthy list deserve. Burgundy takes pride of place, closely followed by Bordeaux, although Australia fights hard for attention with fifteen vintages of Penfolds Grange. More dry wines by the glass would be helpful; for bottles under £20, regional France is a good place to start.

CHEF: Philip Howard PROPRIETORS: Philip Howard and Nigel Platts-Martin OPEN: Mon to Fri 12 to 2.45, 7 to 11 CLOSED: 25 and 26 Dec, 1 Jan MEALS: alc L (main courses £16.50 to £20). Set D £45 to £65 SERVICE: 12.5% (optional), card slips closed CARDS: Amex, Delta, Diners, MasterCard, Switch, Visa DETAILS: 70 seats. Private parties: 85 main room, 18 private room. Children's helpings. No cigars/pipes in dining room. Wheelchair access (also WC). No music. Air-conditioned ⊖ Green Park

Sree Krishna £

map 12

192–194 Tooting High Street, SW17 0SF
TEL: (0181) 672 4250

COOKING 1
COST £17–£34

South Indian vegetarian specialities are the main draw at this long-established Tooting address, many based on rice and lentil flours, such as variously garnished dosai pancakes, uthappam (a version of pizza), and vadai (savoury 'doughnuts'). Iddly (steamed cakes) are based on rice and black gram, while uppuma is semolina fried in ghee with onions. The range also takes in more varied dishes from Kerala and from Cochin, among them cheemeen poriyal (stir-fried king prawns), more familiar chilli chicken, and something called meat-fry. An unusual southern curry is chicken kozhi varutha. House wines are £7.50. Two new branches are Pallavi in Twickenham and Kerala Bhavan in Croydon.

CHEF: M. Kutti PROPRIETORS: Mr T. Haridas and family OPEN: all week 12 to 3, 6 to 11 (12 Fri and Sat) CLOSED: 25 and 26 Dec MEALS: alc (main courses £4 to £7) SERVICE: 10%, card slips closed CARDS: Amex, Diners, MasterCard, Visa DETAILS: 60 seats. Private parties: 60 main room, 70 private room. Vegetarian meals. Children's helpings. Wheelchair access (also WC). Music. Air-conditioned ⊖ Tooting Broadway (£5)

Sri Siam Soho £

map 15

16 Old Compton Street, W1V 5PE
TEL: (0171) 434 3544 FAX: (0171) 287 1311

COOKING 2
COST £23–£48

Behind an 'understated, grey exterior' is a tastefully modern dining room with a pleasingly relaxed ambience, which has over the years been consistently the best place for Thai food in Soho. The menu offers few surprises to those familiar with the cuisine, but those not fully au fait will appreciate the helpful notes. As well as the carte of around sixty items – the usual range of soups, salads, seafood, curries and noodle dishes – there is a vegetarian menu which, it is claimed, is approved by the Vegetarian Society, and a selection of useful set menus. The repertoire extends from stir-fried mussels with lemon grass and chilli, via papaya salad with carrot, cabbage, lime juice and peanuts, to thinly sliced beef with mint, coriander and a lime and chilli dressing. Over thirty well-chosen wines are mostly priced under £20, with house French £9.50.

All entries in the Guide *are re-researched and rewritten every year, not least because restaurant standards fluctuate. Don't rely on an out-of-date* Guide.

CHEF: W. Rodpradith   PROPRIETOR: Oriental Restaurant Group plc   OPEN: Mon to Sat L 12 to 3,
all week D 6 to 11.15 (10.30 Sun)   MEALS: alc (main courses £7 to £10.50). Set L and D £13.99 to
£19.99   SERVICE: 12.5% (optional), card slips closed   CARDS: Amex, Diners, MasterCard,
Switch, Visa   DETAILS: 140 seats. Private parties: 40 main room, 26 and 30 private rooms.
Vegetarian meals. Children's helpings. Wheelchair access (not WC). Music. Air-conditioned
⊖ Leicester Square (£5)

Stephen Bull ▮   map 15

5–7 Blandford Street, W1H 3AA   COOKING **6**
TEL: (0171) 486 9696   FAX: (0171) 224 0324   COST £34–£52

With its low-key décor, pale-coloured modern paintings and close-set tables, the
original of Stephen Bull's trio (see entries below) presents a cool, mature setting
for some attractively understated cooking. Here is a kitchen that deals in 'often
simple, straightforward ideas, yet with an intelligent streak of novelty': perhaps
garlic soup with sage and Gruyère fritters, or tartare of mackerel with oriental
accompaniments. Much of the food, however, runs along familiar lines, taking in
twice-baked goats' cheese soufflé with beetroot salad, or grilled leg of lamb
steak with roasted chips and sauce paloise. Its everyman appeal also strikes a
balance between the richness of foie gras terrine, the comfort of smoked haddock
brandade with poached egg and hollandaise, and some less exalted but equally
appealing ideas, from alsacienne cabbage broth to potato gnocchi. Vegetarian
options (there are usually a couple) are as enticing as anything else on the menu:
for example, sautéed ceps and Jerusalem artichokes with a crisp onion tart. If
there is a 'classical' element to the style, then it figures is desserts too, as a parfait,
an apple and plum jalousie, or meringue with bananas and butterscotch sauce.
Service is 'attentive and quick-reacting'. Around a hundred flavourful wines are
helpfully arranged by style, 'light & fruity' whites or 'silky & refined' reds, for
example. Prices are very reasonable considering the postcode, starting at £11.50
with house vin de pays.

CHEF: Rob Jones   PROPRIETOR: Stephen Bull   OPEN: Mon to Fri L 12 to 2.30, Mon to Sat D 6 to
10.30   CLOSED: 1 week Christmas, bank hols   MEALS: Set L £22 (2 courses) to £26, Set D
£27.50   SERVICE: not inc, card slips closed   CARDS: Amex, Delta, Diners, MasterCard, Switch,
Visa   DETAILS: 55 seats. Private parties: 55 main room. Vegetarian meals. Children's helpings.
No cigars/pipes in dining room. Wheelchair access (not WC). No music. Air-conditioned
⊖ Bond Street, Baker Street

Stephen Bull St Martin's Lane ▮   map 15

12 Upper St Martin's Lane, WC2H 9DL   COOKING **4**
TEL: (0171) 379 7811   FAX: (0171) 836 3855   COST £29–£53

The décor is studiedly minimal. A long bar of polished pine and a grey-tiled floor
stretch away as far the eye can see, while the tall tan leather banquettes reminded
one reporter of 'an osteopath's surgery'. John Hardwick, an associate of Stephen
Bull from early days, took over the kitchen in May 1999, but the Bull signature
style is preserved, indicated perhaps by a starter of 'perfectly textured'
goats'-cheese soufflé with soused tomatoes. Other classical renderings might
include a rich and well-balanced parfait of foie gras and chicken livers with pear
chutney. While main-course materials and timing did not show up well at

177

inspection, reporters otherwise have praised braised shoulder of lamb with neeps, and roast crisp-skinned breast of corn-fed chicken in a truffle-flavoured wild mushroom sauce: 'no-nonsense cooking done with panache' is how it appeared. Good ideas abound at dessert stage too: geranium cream with mango and sablé biscuits, or prune and armagnac tart with rum and raisin ice cream. Irish cheeses are well kept and come with good oatmeal biscuits. Service elicits no complaints. A cosmopolitan wine list follows the Stephen Bull practice of categorising bottles by style and offering plenty of good drinking above and below £20. French house white is £10.75, red £11.95.

CHEF: John Hardwick   PROPRIETOR: Stephen Bull   OPEN: Tue to Fri L 12 to 2.30, Tue to Sat D 5.45 to 11.30   CLOSED: 1 week Christmas, bank hols   MEALS: Set L £15 (2 courses) to £19, Set D £28.50   SERVICE: not inc, card slips closed   CARDS: Amex, Delta, Diners, MasterCard, Switch, Visa   DETAILS: 60 seats. Private parties: 60 main room. Vegetarian meals. Children's helpings. No cigars/pipes in dining room. Wheelchair access (not WC). No music. Air-conditioned   ⊖ Leicester Square

Stephen Bull Smithfield ♥
map 13

71 St John Street, EC1M 4AN
TEL: (0171) 490 1750   FAX: (0171) 490 3128

COOKING 3
COST £30–£51

After eight years, Stephen Bull's brightly coloured St John Street branch is wearing well. Built for large numbers, with small close-together tables, it operates a compact but varied menu typically listing three fish and three meat main courses, a quartet or more of vegetarian items, and a generous raft of starters including cold ones such as scallop ceviche with avocado salsa, and a plate of Spanish delicacies. Given a handful of items that can be eaten as either a starter or main course, it all adds up to a welcome adaptability that casual eaters are free to exploit. Risotto-making skills are persuasive, and 'admirable soups' have included beetroot and apple, and leek and potato, while a lobster, coconut and noodle laksa has impressed for its powerful 'freshly pulverised' spices.

Steaks ('usually ribeye') are correctly cooked, and fish, according to a regular who has eaten mackerel, skate, cod and salmon, is 'always beautifully fresh and carefully cooked'. 'They have a better selection of desserts than anywhere I know,' according to an enthusiast who cites coffee mousse with almond wafers, and bread-and-butter pudding with toffee sauce. The stylistically arranged wine list explores some interesting corners without compromising on quality, and makes a serious attempt to feature exciting wines at affordable prices (plus a few prestigious bins for the City suits). The house selection starts at £11.50.

CHEF: Danny Lewis   PROPRIETOR: Stephen Bull   OPEN: Mon to Fri L 12 to 2.30, Mon to Sat D 6 to 10.30   CLOSED: 1 week Christmas, bank hols   SERVICE: not inc, card slips closed   CARDS: Amex, Delta, Diners, MasterCard, Switch, Visa   DETAILS: 120 seats. Private parties: 80 main room. Vegetarian meals. Children's helpings. No cigars/pipes in dining room. Wheelchair access (not WC). Occasional music. Air-conditioned   ⊖ Farringdon

The Guide *relies on feedback from its readers. Especially welcome are reports on new restaurants appearing in the book for the first time. All letters to the* Guide *are acknowledged.*

Stepping Stone 🍴✶

123 Queenstown Road, SW8 3RH   NEW CHEF
TEL: (0171) 622 0555   FAX: (0171) 622 4230   COST £24–£48

Visitors to this 'exceedingly smart', boldly coloured and fairly minimally decorated restaurant and bar have typically emerged feeling upbeat about the place, pleased not least with 'waitresses ablaze with well-mannered informality', as well as with the classy, modern food. As the *Guide* went to press, however, Zak El Hamdou, who has worked at Chezmax, was due to take charge of the kitchen. Since we had no menus, we could not confirm whether the cooking style (twice-baked soufflé, roast belly of Gloucester Old Spot pork, and chocolate tart with passion fruit sorbet) was set to change, so reports are especially welcome. A wide-ranging wine list is constantly in flux, starting at £11 for whatever the house wine happens to be, and barely rising above £20 to encourage customers to be adventurous.

CHEF: Zak El Hamdou   PROPRIETORS: Gary and Emer Levy   OPEN: Sun to Fri L 12.30 to 2.30 (3 Sun), Mon to Sat D 7 to 11 (10.30 Mon)   CLOSED: 25 to 28 Dec, bank hol Mons   MEALS: alc (main courses £9 to £16). Set L £11.75 (2 courses), Set L Sun £16.50, Set D 7 to 8.45 £11.75 (2 courses) to £15, Set D £23.50   SERVICE: not inc;10% for parties of 6 or more   CARDS: Amex, Delta, Diners, MasterCard, Switch, Visa   DETAILS: 70 seats. Private parties: 80 main room. Vegetarian meals. Children's helpings. No smoking in 1 dining room. Wheelchair access (not WC). No music. Air-conditioned

Sugar Club 🍴✶

21 Warwick Street, W1R 5RB   COOKING 5
TEL: (0171) 437 7776   FAX: (0171) 437 7778   COST £36–£63

Now settled into its 'cavernous' new premises, the 'fun and funky' Sugar Club seems to have gained a new lease of life. It can veer from stark when empty to noisy when full but feels 'like a grown-up restaurant', with acid-etched glass, a stunning mural, and some 'enormously comfortable' timber chairs. Ideas are brash and showy, some demand a leap of faith, and the kaleidoscope of ingredients and flavours can sound bewildering: tea-smoked organic sea trout with mango, papaya, chilli and coriander salad; or lemon grass, ginger and Parmesan risotto cake, with a dollop of fiery coconut chutney.

The generous carte's enticing dishes stretch fusion food to its limits, and the approach, it seems, can be applied to almost anything, including Perigord pigeon, served with ginger-chilli lentils, roast sweet potatoes and rocket salsa. More ordinary-sounding items are no less successful – for example, breast of corn-fed chicken with wok-fried spinach ('as good as I've had') – although the 'signature dish' of seared scallops with sweet chilli sauce and crème fraîche may not always live up to its reputation. Imaginative treatment extends to desserts too: perhaps one of black sticky rice, banana and coconut pudding with pandan syrup and lime. Sourdough bread is highly rated. At its best, service is 'among the friendliest in London', although it is not always at its best. An intelligent selection of wines comes at a price – most are significantly over £20 – although moderate drinkers can choose from around twenty by the glass. House Merlot is £12.50, Trebbiano £10.50. It is advisable to pre-book, particularly for seating in the non-smoking dining room.

CHEF: Peter Gordon   PROPRIETORS: Ashley Sumner and Vivienne Hayman   OPEN: all week 12 to 3, 6 to 11   MEALS: alc (main courses £12.50 to £18.50)   SERVICE: not inc, card slips closed   CARDS: Amex, Delta, Diners, MasterCard, Visa   DETAILS: 130 seats. Private parties: 80 main room. Vegetarian meals. No smoking in 1 dining room. Wheelchair access (not WC). No music   ⊖ Oxford Circus, Piccadilly Circus

Le Suquet

map 14

104 Draycott Avenue, SW3 3AE
TEL: (0171) 581 1785   FAX: (0171) 225 0838

COOKING 3
COST £22–£76

Pierre Martin's long-standing fish restaurant is testimony to the British love affair with France. It recalls rosy seaside holidays, where a mixture of jollity and relaxation accompanies large plates of seafood and copious jugs of local wine. And the other thing is, as with some of the best holidays, whenever you go back it is always the same. Freshness is the key to success, treatments appropriately simple: oysters as they come (claires, belons, natives), roast langoustines, mussels marinière, scallops provençale, and main-course grills of sea bass, bream or lobster. Other elementary ideas – bouillabaisse, skate with capers – take their place alongside non-fishy items such as foie gras, snails, and coq au vin. There is nothing here to frighten traditionalists. Prices are geared to the neighbourhood, and a short wine list opens with house red and white from the Var at £11.

CHEFS: Philippe Moron and Jean-Yves Darcel   PROPRIETOR: Pierre Martin   OPEN: all week 12 to 3, 7 to 11.30 (all day Sat and Sun)   MEALS: alc (main courses £10 to £30). Set L £13. Cover £1   SERVICE: 15% (optional), card slips closed   CARDS: Amex, Delta, Diners, MasterCard, Switch, Visa   DETAILS: 70 seats. Private parties: 16 to 25 private rooms. Music. Air-conditioned ⊖ South Kensington

Sushi-Say

map 12

33B Walm Lane, NW2 5SH
TEL: (0181) 459 7512   FAX: (0181) 459 2971

COOKING 3
COST £26–£77

'A railway carriage crossed with a garret' is how one reader sees this long, thin room. With bare, close-set wooden tables and simple décor, the ambience is informal. But even in this corner of Willesden, that doesn't imply budget catering. A long carte covers most of the Japanese repertoire except for table-cooked sukiyaki and nabe dishes. The nine-dish set menu includes a 'fabulous' chawan-mushi (savoury egg custard) with a large prawn and spring onions; and yakitori, 'better than at speciality restaurants in Japan' because a little fat is left in the skewered chicken pieces to give them tenderness and flavour. Tempura, teriyaki salmon, and miso soup have all been very good, and the centrepiece of an inspection meal was a generous plate of fish sushi, including halibut, mackerel, tuna and salmon. Service is pleasant but can be slow. House wine is £9.50, but note the list of chilled sakés, the most expensive made with organic rice.

Report forms are at the back of the book; write a letter if you prefer; or email us at guidereports@which.co.uk.

CHEF: Mr K. Shimizu PROPRIETORS: Mr K. and Mrs Y. Shimizu OPEN: Tue to Sun D only 6 to 10.30 CLOSED: 25 and 26 Dec, 1 Jan, 1 week Aug MEALS: alc (main courses £6 to £19). Set D £17.50 to £27.50 SERVICE: not inc CARDS: Amex, Delta, MasterCard, Switch, Visa DETAILS: 36 seats. Private parties: 20 main room, 6 private room. Vegetarian meals. No-smoking area. Wheelchair access (not WC). No music. Air-conditioned ⊖ Willesden Green

Tajine

NEW ENTRY map 15

7A Dorset Street, W1H 3FE
TEL/FAX: (0171) 935 1545

COOKING 1
COST £25–£37

It's Moroccan all right, but not quite as we know it. Modern prints on terracotta walls, garden lanterns and blue tablecloths add a definite London feel to this popular local. Most of the menu, however, is firmly North African, with the usual hummus, tabbouleh and merguez supplemented by fried kidneys, liver with herbs, and various b'stilla and briouats. At inspection, couscous royale – hefty chunks of lamb, a whole assortment of vegetables and a fiery harissa sauce – as well as spicy, fruit-laden chicken tajine kedara, proved their native rustic credentials. Desserts, curiously, head to Europe for caramelised pear in brandy, and chocolate mousse, but Morocco is also represented by a selection of sticky, nutty pastries. Service is confident and bustling. The wine list has a few Moroccan bottles, with other bins garnered from around the world. Prices start at £10.50.

CHEF: Gonul Ozturk PROPRIETOR: Mehdi Barradi OPEN: Mon to Fri L 12 to 3, Mon to Sat D 6 to 11 MEALS: alc (main courses £8.50 to £10). Set L £7.95 (2 courses) SERVICE: not inc CARDS: Delta, Diners, MasterCard, Switch, Visa DETAILS: 42 seats. 8 seats outside. Private parties: 53 main room. Vegetarian meals. Children's helpings. No cigars/pipes in dining room. Wheelchair access (not WC). Music. Air-conditioned ⊖ Baker Street £5

Tamarind

map 15

20 Queen Street, W1X 7PJ
TEL: (0171) 629 3561 FAX: (0171) 499 5034

COOKING 2
COST £28–£64

One can eat lunch for £10 at this warm and luxurious Indian restaurant in the heart of Mayfair, the 'express' menu offering poppadom and chutneys, and a main course with vegetables, naan and rice. The set-price lunch adds three starters, a choice of tandoori or curry main dish, and dessert, while the pre-theatre menu includes the cost of a taxi to theatreland. The short carte is well varied, with four vegetarian starters and others featuring prawns, scallops, squid, and chicken livers. Kebabs from the tandoori oven include monkfish marinated in saffron and yoghurt, and ground lamb with green peppers and coriander. Curries comprise such old friends as sag gosht, together with less familiar John Dory with crispy spinach, or prawns in light onion sauce with carom seeds. They also cook game in season. The respectable wine list features a house selection of six interesting bottles between £13.50 and £17.00

NEW CHEF *is shown instead of a cooking mark where a change of chef occurred too late for a new assessment of the cooking.*

CHEF: Atul Kochhar   PROPRIETOR: Halcyon Hotel   OPEN: Sun to Fri L 12 to 3, all week D 6 to 11.30 (10.30 Sun)   CLOSED: 25 Dec, 1 Jan   MEALS: alc (main courses £10.50 to £17.75). Set L £10 (2 courses) to £16.50, Set D 6 to 7 £22.50, Set D £28.50   SERVICE: not inc L, 12.5% D CARDS: Amex, Delta, Diners, MasterCard, Switch, Visa   DETAILS: 95 seats. Private parties: 110 main room. Vegetarian meals. Music. Air-conditioned   ⊖ Green Park £5

La Tante Claire ♥ ⅚✳   NEW ENTRY   map 14

Wilton Place, SW1X 7RL
TEL: (0171) 823 2003   FAX: (0171) 823 2001   COOKING 8
EMAIL: tanteclaire@relaischateau.fr   COST £42–£115

Whatever Pierre Koffmann's reasons were for moving last year from the premises now occupied by Gordon Ramsay (see entry) to the Berkeley Hotel, reporters were naturally keen to observe any changes in style or standards. The first thing they notice is a spacious, 'assured and elegant' dining room done in shades of mint green and pinky purple, with theatrical flower displays, a wine rack occupying one entire wall, and painted wooden fruit for table decoration. The next is a menu that begins in classic French vein with foie gras and shellfish in various forms: perhaps scallops with squid ink sauce, or a warm slice of foie gras on a potato galette with a sweet caramelised sauce tasting like butterscotch. Meat and seafood are given roughly equal billing among main courses, which range from roast lobster to venison with bitter chocolate.

Broadly speaking, while a few reporters see little difference in the new kitchen's food, the majority conclude that this has not been a move for the better. Opinions seem to reflect a variability in standards that was not characteristic of the old Tante Claire. Even at one meal, the food can see-saw from an impressive Jerusalem artichoke mousse in a creamy soup pungent with black truffle, and an 'exemplary' pig's trotter, to some quite disappointing dishes. This indeed was the conclusion of an inspection meal that began well with an appetiser of bouncy lobster mousse in a well-judged shellfish sauce. Its highlight was an innovative starter of scallop, formed into a sausage shape with a slice of black truffle at the centre, rolled in Parma ham and steamed; the combination of technique, judgement, flavours and textures (leaves of briefly blanched Savoy cabbage adding a light crunch) made for a memorable dish. To finish, a blackberry-filled croustade (a speciality of Koffmann's native south-west France), was completely unworthy; indeed desserts in general do not seem to have shone brightly.

Service has impressed very few, having taken the shine off several meals, but appears to have improved with time. The three-course lunch, however, has been dubbed 'best value in town'. Wines are entirely French (with the exception of the fortifieds and one English Müller-Thurgau), and, unsurprisingly, the renowned châteaux and producers of Bordeaux, Burgundy and the Rhône hold sway. Those unwilling to pay for such finery should look to the regional wines, helpfully arranged by major grape variety, for bottles under £20.

CHEF/PROPRIETOR: Pierre Koffmann   OPEN: Mon to Fri L 12.30 to 2, Mon to Sat D 7 to 11 CLOSED: 25 to 31 Dec, bank hols   MEALS: alc (main courses £22 to £35). Set L £28   SERVICE: 12.5% (optional), card slips closed   CARDS: Amex, Delta, Diners, MasterCard, Switch, Visa DETAILS: 45 seats. Private parties: 70 main room, 14 private room. Car park. Vegetarian meals. No children under 8. Jacket and tie. No smoking in 1 dining room. Wheelchair access (also WC). No music. Air-conditioned   ⊖ Hyde Park Corner

Tate Gallery Restaurant 🍷

map 13

Millbank, SW1P 4RG
TEL: (0171) 887 8825   FAX: (0171) 887 8902

COOKING 3
COST £30–£57

The wine list has long been the heady focus of a visit to this bustling space, with tables squeezed in and the famous Rex Whistler mural providing an unparalleled background. The room can get noisy, but has a 'very pleasant atmosphere despite that'. Richard Zuber concentrates on first-rate ingredients for his one-page menus, and what he delivers, according to an inspector, is 'not a creative tour de force, but good eating'. Quality shines through particularly in starters that are simple assemblies – lobster and mango salad, or smoked salmon blinis, for example – and in fish and meat: roast rack of lamb, or impeccably timed sea bass. Those for whom dessert is the highlight of a meal may enjoy date brûlée tart, 'really quite special' hazelnut parfait, or 'first-rate' bitter chocolate tart. Service is cheerfully informal and unobtrusive, and when it comes to selecting a wine from the legendary list the advice, whether from sommelier Hamish Anderson on the wine list, or the waitresses, has been universally praised. Although there is much that catches the eye below £20, prices – particularly for the French old masters – are so generous that this is one venue where paying that bit extra brings rewards.

CHEF: Richard Zuber   PROPRIETOR: Trustees of the Tate Gallery   OPEN: all week L only 12 to 2.45 (4 Sun)   CLOSED: 24 to 26 Dec   MEALS: alc (main courses £9.50 to £15.50). Set L £15.75 (2 courses) to £18.50. Min £15.75   SERVICE: not inc, card slips closed   CARDS: Amex, MasterCard, Switch, Visa   DETAILS: 80 seats. Vegetarian meals. No-smoking area. Wheelchair access (also WC). No music. Air-conditioned   ⊖ Pimlico

Teatro

map 15

93–107 Shaftesbury Avenue, W1V 7AE
TEL: (0171) 494 3040   FAX: (0171) 494 3050
EMAIL: teatroclub@m.j.n.com

COOKING 5
COST £31–£60

Climb the stairs, scurry along the corridor, past the long, elegant bar into a cool, light, stylish dining room where a few dark red paintings relieve plain white walls. 'It doesn't feel like Soho', but this mecca of football (Lee Chapman) and media (Leslie Ash) is a relaxed and enjoyable place. The menu shows a penchant for fish (cod with crushed potatoes and garlic broth), pasta (langoustine linguine) and salads (a 'modern, professional' niçoise) and lists a 'foie gras du jour'. Risottos are well reported, whether lobster or cep, and there is substance to the food, be it a rich and velvety velouté of artichoke and walnuts, or crisp, breadcrumbed discs of moist, chopped pig's trotter with ravigote sauce.

Chocolate cake with mandarin sorbet, and chocolate tart with milk ice cream come recommended, or there may be apricot clafoutis or treacle tart. Predominantly French staff are 'brisk and efficient'. The three-course fixed-price menu is good value, but with some main courses on the carte nearing £20, the bill can mount quickly, helped along by some high wine prices (Cloudy Bay Chardonnay at £40, for example) on an otherwise intelligent list. Consolingly, French house wine – 'everything a house wine should be' – is £12.

CHEF: Stuart Gillies   PROPRIETORS: Lee Chapman and Leslie Ash   OPEN: Mon to Fri L 12 to 2.45, Mon to Sat D 6 to 11.45   CLOSED: 25 to 31 Dec, L bank hols   MEALS: alc (main courses £15.50 to £20). Set L and D before 7.30 £15 (2 courses) to £18. Cover £1.50   SERVICE: 12.5% (optional), card slips closed   CARDS: Amex, Delta, Diners, MasterCard, Switch, Visa   DETAILS: 100 seats. Private parties: 80 main room. Vegetarian meals. Children's helpings. No pipes in dining room. Wheelchair access (also WC). No music. Air-conditioned   ⊖ Leicester Square

Teca ❦ ⁵⁄★

NEW ENTRY   map 15

54 Brooks Mews, W1Y 2NY   COOKING 4
TEL: (0171) 495 4774   FAX: (0171) 491 3545   COST £31–£65

Occupying a corner site just behind Claridge's, this is a bright, modern Italian restaurant, whose hard reflective surfaces (padded banquette seating excepted) include a wall of glass fronting a temperature-controlled cabinet (the 'teca') stocked with Italian wines. An agreeably short carte, bolstered by a couple of announced extras, takes in three or four pasta and rice dishes, and splits main courses evenly between fish and meat: perhaps John Dory with a silky chickpea sauce, or boned, stuffed saddle of rabbit wrapped in pancetta. It makes use of Swiss chard, Castelluccio lentils and braised radicchio, but also brings soy sauce (with grilled scallops) and apple tart to the party, as if to confirm that it's a London Italian after all.

This is 'deceptively simple' food with a welcome clarity of expression, based on sound ingredients: thin scallop slices and wild mushrooms on fresh leaves, or just-pink venison on crusty, soft-centred polenta. Pasta itself is first-rate, judging by delicate ravioli containing a blend of skate and artichoke in a rich buttery sauce. Predictable tiramisù might share the pudding list with dates stuffed with white chocolate mousse, accompanied by a mint sauce. Wines reflect the diversity that excites Italian oenophiles, though there is very little under £20. Half a dozen house wines range from £14 to £26.

CHEF: Marco Torri   PROPRIETOR: Marco Bacchetta   OPEN: Mon to Sat 12 to 2.30 (3 Sat), 7 to 10.30   CLOSED: bank hols   MEALS: alc (main courses £15 to £20). Set L £16 (2 courses) to £19   SERVICE: 12.5% (optional), card slips closed   CARDS: Amex, Delta, MasterCard, Switch, Visa   DETAILS: 90 seats. 20 seats outside. Private parties: 90 main room. Children's helpings. No smoking in 1 dining room. Wheelchair access (not WC). Music. Air-conditioned   ⊖ Bond Street £5

10

map 13

10 Cutlers Garden Arcade, Devonshire
Square, EC2M 4YA   COOKING 4
TEL: (0171) 283 7888   FAX: (0171) 626 4859   COST £26–£66

The advantage of eating in a windowless basement, according to one visitor, is that you don't have to sit and watch the surrounding City being dug up by pneumatic drills. A spiral staircase leads down to a wide, bright room decorated in 'phosphorescent aquamarine', with murals, mirrors, and a menu in brasserie format. It is not quite the 'Italian starters, Chinese mains and Olde English puddings' that one reporter suggested, but it is certainly a free and easy, mix and match style of cooking, with a few dishes – pasta or risotto, for example – offered as either a starter or main course. A lively kitchen turns up chicken tagine, two fried eggs on bubble and squeak ('double egg and bubble', as the menu has it), roast ham knuckle with chilli jam, and as much seafood as most of us can handle: crab mayonnaise, salmon fish cakes, pepper-crusted tuna, and tempura lobster with chips. Plain puddings might include lemon tart or apple and blackberry crumble. Sixty young but sharply chosen wines are usefully arranged by style. House Vin de Pays d'Oc is £11.50.

CHEF: Richard Ross   PROPRIETOR: Terry Pullen   OPEN: Mon to Fri 12 to 2.30, 5.30 to 9.30
CLOSED: 24 Dec to 4 Jan, bank hols   MEALS: alc (main courses £7 to £22.50). Set D £15.95
SERVICE: 12.5% (optional), card slips closed   CARDS: Amex, Delta, Diners, MasterCard, Switch,
Visa   DETAILS: 120 seats. Private parties: 120 main room. Vegetarian meals. Wheelchair access
(also WC). Music. Air-conditioned   ⊖ Liverpool Street

Tentazioni
map 13

2 Mill Street, Lloyd's Wharf, SE1 2BD   COOKING 4
TEL: (0171) 237 1100   COST £30–£58

With only a little effort, those visiting the Millennium Dome or working in the City should be able to find their way to this former dock warehouse on the South Bank, which concentrates on food rather than décor. Since 1998 Alessio Brusadin, who used to work at the Halkin Hotel (see entry, London), has altered the menu format slightly: his four-course options with wine have been replaced by a five-course dinner (in addition to the carte) and more realistic set prices at lunchtime. The style is modern Italian, which is to say essentially simple, colourful, and modestly inventive with occasionally humble materials: buckwheat pasta is combined with cabbage and melted cheese, red mullet comes with turnip tops and Sicilian cherry tomatoes. The range extends from a salad of strips of sole laid over a heap of fresh leaves with a good dressing, via venison navarin with polenta gnocchi, to chocolate mousse served with prunes in armagnac. Service is keen and responsive, and the short, mostly central and northern Italian wine list aims for quality. House wines are £11.50.

CHEFS: Alessio Brusadin and Nicola Ducceschi   PROPRIETORS: Mauro Santoliquido and Alessio
Brusadin   OPEN: Tue to Fri L 12 to 2.30, Mon to Sat D 7 to 10.30   CLOSED: 25 Dec to 4 Jan, last
week Aug, bank hols   MEALS: alc D (main courses £14 to £16.50). Set L £15 (2 courses) to £19,
Set D £35   SERVICE: 12.5% (optional), card slips closed   CARDS: Amex, Delta, Diners,
MasterCard, Switch, Visa   DETAILS: 50 seats. Private parties: 35 main room. Children's
helpings. Music   ⊖ London Bridge (£5)

Terrace
NEW ENTRY   map 13

33C Holland Street, W8 4LX   COOKING 4
TEL: (0171) 937 3224   FAX: (0171) 937 3323   COST £24–£69

Light and airy, rather noisy when full, and simply decorated with wood and cane seats at close-set tables (with the added luxury of a heated outdoor terrace) this could be a typical late-1990s place. But reporters praise its more timeless virtues, including charming, relaxed service, and Sam Metcalfe's interesting but not outlandish ideas. Well, not generally, although fillet steak with seared foie gras and red wine jus on macaroni cheese may come close. His Anglo-European menu also takes in pork fillet with apple and ginger purée, and a rich and creamy wild mushroom risotto with truffle oil. Dishes please the eye and palate equally: for example, pan-fried skate wing on bright green spring cabbage with a golden-coloured sauce of lemon and capers.

The two-course early-evening menu, devised for patrons of the Royal Albert Hall or opera in Holland Park, might include smoked haddock fish cake with quail's eggs and sorrel butter sauce, or an excursion Eastwards in the form of crispy duck confit with bok choy, shiitake mushrooms and soy. To finish, hot cherry pudding is a typical comforter, along with chocolate mousse trifle, or brioche with raisins and apricots. Wines on the mostly French list carry a maximum mark-up of £15, adding to the appeal of the finer fare. House French is £11.

CHEF: Sam Metcalfe   PROPRIETOR: Steven Loveridge   OPEN: all week L 12 to 2.30, Mon to Sat D 5.45 in summer, 7 in winter to 10.30   MEALS: alc (main courses £10.50 to £22.50). Set L £12.50 (2 courses) to £14.50, Set D 5.45 to 7 £14.50 (2 courses)   SERVICE: 12.5% (optional), card slips closed   CARDS: Amex, Delta, Diners, MasterCard, Switch, Visa   DETAILS: 27 seats. 14 seats outside. Private parties: 26 main room. Vegetarian meals. No music. Air-conditioned
⊖ High Street Kensington (£5)

Thai Garden ⅚✶ £

map 12

249 Globe Road, E2 0JD

COOKING 2

TEL: (0181) 981 5748

COST £24–£34

Although basically furnished, the Garden is more stylish than the exterior suggests. Seafood (centring on prawns and pomfret) and vegetarian dishes (often featuring mushrooms, aubergines or bean curd) are the main focus here. King prawn satay comes with sauce 'unlike the usual peanut butter-type stodge' but 'quite thin, with finely chopped peanuts and a really fresh flavour' enlivened by 'a good dose of chilli'. Mixed seafood salad is a big plate piled with large, green-lipped mussels, crab claws, chunks of squid, and prawns in a 'zingy, tasty lime and basil dressing'. Salad kak comprises mixed leaves, grated cabbage and carrot, boiled eggs and potato crisps out of a packet: 'it worked much better than I imagined it would,' writes a reporter. The decent, short wine list starts at £7.50 for house red and white and rises ever so gently to no more than £15.

CHEF: Naphaphorn Duff   PROPRIETORS: Jack and Suthinee Hufton   OPEN: Mon to Fri L 12 to 2.45, all week D 6 to 10.45   CLOSED: bank hols   MEALS: alc (main courses £4.50 to £7). Set L and D 6 to 7.30 £7.50 (2 courses), Set D £16 to £21   SERVICE: 10%, card slips closed   CARDS: Delta, Diners, MasterCard, Visa   DETAILS: 32 seats. Private parties: 20 main room, 14 private room. Vegetarian meals. No smoking in 1 dining room. Wheelchair access (not WC). Music
⊖ Bethnal Green (£5)

Thailand ⅚✶

map 12

15 Lewisham Way, SE14 6PP

COOKING 4

TEL/FAX: (0181) 691 4040

COST £29–£51

It was wise to make this tiny restaurant a no-smoking area, for one wouldn't want the ceiling obscured by blue haze: it is the major feature of the décor, a back-lit map of South East Asia. The menu, in English, lists main ingredients of the many stir-fries, curries, noodle dishes and six sorts of fried rice. Spiced rice balls or steamed Lao sticky rice are suggested to accompany Laotian dishes, including really hot salads with papaya, and a hot-and-sour 'lap' dish of pork, beef or chicken. Another Lao speciality is cold rice noodles with beef or chicken cooked in coconut milk, galangal, chilli paste and herbs. Chicken and pork satay, chicken wings, prawns, spare ribs, and steak are chargrilled. House wines at £9.50 head a short, modestly priced list with some interesting bottles, and there's a good collection of malt whiskies.

CHEF/PROPRIETOR: Mrs G. Herman   OPEN: Tue to Sat D only 6 to 10.30   MEALS: alc (main courses £6 to £11). Set D £20   SERVICE: not inc, card slips closed   CARDS: MasterCard, Delta, Switch, Visa   DETAILS: 25 seats. Private parties: 25 main room. Vegetarian meals. No small children. No smoking in dining room. Music. Air-conditioned   ⊖ New Cross, New Cross Gate   (£5)

Titanic   [NEW ENTRY]   map 15

81 Brewer Street, W1R 3FH   COOKING 3
TEL: (0171) 437 1912   FAX: (0171) 439 4747   COST £25–£54

Launched at the end of 1998, Titanic immediately proved a gift for headline writers, although Marco himself had already mischievously set the tone: it is directly above Atlantic (see entry), and menus are headed White Star Line. Given a prominent central bar and lots of room to drink, an avowed aim to provide 'disco glamour', and the availability of breakfast in the wee small hours, it is clear that its tilt is towards more general entertainment than simply eating. But give the food its due: it does not try too hard and succeeds admirably at the level at which it is pitched, which is unashamedly modern British. Fish comes in a light batter with fine chips, pea purée and tartare sauce, and minced tuna burger arrives in a standard sesame seed bun with the usual trimmings.

From a generously endowed list the kitchen has turned out 'decent' saffron risotto, 'competent' onion tart, and a slab of crisp pork on bok choy with soy-enriched cooking juices. Finish maybe with fluffy lemon meringue pie, or an 'admirably light' bread-and-butter pudding in vanilla-flavoured custard. Service has varied from poorly organised and 'lacklustre' to 'faultless'. A 100-strong, sensibly arranged, cosmopolitan wine list starts with house vin de pays at £13.

CHEF: Peter Reffell   PROPRIETORS: Marco Pierre White and Jimmy Lahoud   OPEN: Mon to Sat L 12 to 2.30, all week D 5.30 to 11.30 (10.30 Sun); all week breakfast 12 to 2am   CLOSED: 25 and 26 Dec, 1 Jan, Sun in Aug   MEALS: alc (main courses £9 to £17). Set L £10.50 (2 courses) to £13.50   SERVICE: 12.5% (optional), card slips closed in restaurant, open in bar   CARDS: Amex, Delta, Diners, MasterCard, Switch, Visa   DETAILS: 250 seats. Private parties: 350 main room. Wheelchair access (not WC). Music. Air-conditioned   ⊖ Piccadilly Circus

Tokyo Diner ⅝✳ £   map 15

2 Newport Place, WC2H 7JJ   COOKING 2
TEL: (0171) 287 8777   FAX: (0171) 434 1415   COST £9–£20

A lively, jolly setting for budget Japanese food, Tokyo Diner provides a varied choice of quick meals together with a menu giving useful guidance for novices. Sit on cushioned stools at tiny tables and decide between donburi (meal-in-one) dishes with rice, bowls of soup noodles, mild Japanese curries, sushi, or bento box set meals. Polite, young Japanese staff (tips not accepted) take the orders. A seafood fry bento box consists of three substantial slices of salmon sashimi, a glass noodle salad topped by crab sticks, and fine chunks of fresh salmon, mackerel and a prawn, 'well fried in breadcrumbs'. Adding to the appeal are crisp little savoury biscuits served with the wine, and decent rice. 'Very acceptable' house wine is £6.90.

CHEFS: Harue Ito, Ilsong Lee and Hiroko Hasegawa   PROPRIETOR: Richard Hills   OPEN: all week 12 to 12   MEALS: Set L and D £4 (1 course) to £13   SERVICE: none, card slips closed   CARDS: Delta, MasterCard, Switch, Visa   DETAILS: 86 seats. Vegetarian meals. No smoking in 1 dining room. Wheelchair access (not WC). Music. Air-conditioned   ⊖ Leicester Square

▲ *Townhouse Brasserie* £   [NEW ENTRY]   map 15

24 Coptic Street, WC1A 1NT
TEL: (0171) 636 2731   FAX: (0171) 580 1028   COOKING 3
EMAIL: townhousebrasserie@btinternet.com   COST £21–£46

Occupying the ground floor of a seventeenth-century building (with a first-floor Georgian dining room for private parties), this is nevertheless a modern operation, with much blond and dark wood set off by a mural and colourful prints. Candles and well-spaced tables give it an intimate air, and it feels more like a café than brasseries normally do. The cooking goes in for generous portions of attractively presented food, calling on France, Italy, South East Asia and the Americas for ideas, and explores a range of hot, sweet-and-sour flavours: battered and deep-fried avocado, aubergine, peppers and courgette are served with a sweet chilli dressing, for example.

There is clear talent in the kitchen, ingredients are put to sound use, and accurate timing has made a success of chargrilled kingfish fillet, served with a chilli and garlic aïoli, while roast chicken (or Cornish hen, as the menu has it) has come with tasty skin, and shiitake mushrooms in a sweet-sour sauce. Desserts generally take a simple route, with banoffi pie, or a 'very creamy' white chocolate ice cream. Careful choosing can mean an inexpensive meal, although extras (canapés, bread and vegetables) mount up. A short, bright, well-judged list makes good use of non-classic wine regions; prices are fair, with house wines starting at around £11.

CHEF: Lloyd Lewars   PROPRIETORS: Joanna and Lloyd Lewars   OPEN: Mon to Fri noon to 11, Sat 3 to 11, Sun noon to 8   CLOSED: 25 and 26 Dec, 1 Jan, bank hols   MEALS: alc (main courses £6.50 to £14). Set L and D £9.95 (2 courses) to £12.45   SERVICE: not inc; 10% for parties of 4 or more   CARDS: Amex, Delta, Diners, MasterCard, Switch, Visa   DETAILS: 75 seats. 6 seats outside. Private parties: 40 main room, 40 private room. Vegetarian meals. Children's helpings. Wheelchair access (not WC). Music   ACCOMMODATION: 4 rooms. TV. Phone. B&B £25 to £45 ⊖ Tottenham Court Road

Prices quoted in the Guide *are based on information supplied by restaurateurs. The prices quoted at the top of each entry represent a range, from the lowest meal price to the highest; the latter is inflated by 20 per cent to take account of likely price rises during the year of the* Guide.

Turner's ♨

map 14

87–89 Walton Street, SW3 2HP   COOKING 4
TEL: (0171)584 6711   FAX: (0171)584 4441   COST £31–£37

Brian Turner's blue and yellow restaurant in smart Walton Street looks much as it always has, with net curtains, banquette seats and linen cloths, and although the Great Yorkshireman himself no longer cooks these days, the style retains its European leanings. The generous carte, for example, offers seafood and liver starters – crab cervelas with spiced cucumber salsa, or a rich version of chicken liver and foie gras pâté – alongside butter bean and garlic soup. Main courses offer a good balance of fish and meat options, including roast monkfish with pepper and coriander compote, and pink roast rack of English lamb which, at inspection, required 'a certain amount of sawing and chewing'. A savoury, perhaps a variation on deep-fried goats' cheese, offers an alternative to iced lemon Chiboust, or apple and almond cake, and the set-price lunch is considered good value: one couple enjoyed calf's liver with caramelised onions followed by chocolate terrine. Sharper service would be welcomed. Champagne, white Burgundy and claret are the wine list's strongest suits (helped along by a good range of spirits), at suitably upmarket prices. Ten house wines range from £14 to £23.50.

CHEF: J. Lucas   PROPRIETOR: Brian Turner   OPEN: Mon to Sat 12.30 to 2.15, 7.30 to 11   CLOSED: Christmas, bank hols   MEALS: Set L and D £14.50 (2 courses) to £17   SERVICE: not inc   CARDS: Amex, Delta, Diners, MasterCard, Switch, Visa   DETAILS: 56 seats. Private parties: 56 main room, 6 private room. Children's helpings. Wheelchair access (not WC). Music. Air-conditioned   ⊖ South Kensington

Two Brothers £

map 12

297–303 Regents Park Road, N3 1DP   COOKING 2
TEL: (0181) 346 0469   FAX: (0181) 343 1978   COST £18–£44

The 'smart, snazzy' exterior gives the first clue that this is no ordinary fish and chip shop. Inside, the spacious room has a 1950s feel, with mirrored pillars and pictures of whales and sharks. Lack of pretension extends to the down-to-earth service that's enjoyed by a multicultural mix of customers. Blackboard specials augment a menu that runs from battered cod, haddock and plaice fillets (with steaming, grilling or frying in matzo meal as options), to halibut steak, and prawns with garlic butter. An inspector found starters of gazpacho (a special) and fish soup to be outshone by main courses, including a 'juicy, sweet' special of pan-fried salmon with soy sauce and ginger. Big portions mean only the ravenous order desserts of perhaps apple pie, or fresh fruit salad. Wines (mostly whites) include a house Côtes de Duras (£9.50) from the proprietors' own vines.

CHEFS/PROPRIETORS: Leon and Tony Manzi   OPEN: Tue to Sat 12 to 2.30, 5.30 to 10.15   CLOSED: Christmas, last 2 weeks Aug, bank hols and the Tue following   MEALS: alc (main courses £7.50 to £17)   SERVICE: not inc, card slips closed   CARDS: Amex, MasterCard, Switch, Visa   DETAILS: 90 seats. Children's helpings. No-smoking area. Music. Air-conditioned ⊖ Finchley Central

Upper Street Fish Shop £ map 13

324 Upper Street, N1 2XQ	COOKING 1
TEL/FAX: (0171) 359 1401	COST £16–£30

Tradition survives in Islington. The owners say they fry their fish the same way the family has done for three generations, although it can be grilled or poached on request. Modernity has crept in to the extent that you can precede fish and chips – from skate, through calamari, to halibut – with Irish oysters or moules marinière. House specials include smoked haddock with a cream sauce, lemon sole rolls stuffed with scallops and crabmeat, and home-made fish lasagne. Puddings and ice creams are listed on a blackboard. It's unlicensed, so bring your own wine. Even if you don't, you'll find the atmosphere 'cheery'.

CHEF: Stuart Gamble   PROPRIETORS: Alan and Olga Conway   OPEN: Tue to Sat L 12 to 2.15 (3 Sat), Mon to Sat D 5.30 to 10.15   CLOSED: Christmas, New Year, 7 days Easter, 7 days Aug bank hol   MEALS: alc (main courses £7.50 to £12.50). Unlicensed; BYO (no corkage)   SERVICE: not inc   CARDS: none   DETAILS: 50 seats. Children's helpings. Wheelchair access (not WC). No music. Air-conditioned   ⊖ Angel

The Vale ⅝✱ £ NEW ENTRY map 13

99 Chippenham Road, W9 2AB	COOKING 3
TEL: (0171) 266 0990 FAX: (0171) 286 7224	COST £19–£44

What was a pub on this corner site has, over the years, had various conservatories added, giving a light and airy feel and a view of the busy road outside. All the 'entrances, rooms and levels' prompted one reporter to wish for a ball of string to help relocate her table. The cooking is billed as 'traditional English and Mediterranean with some modern influences', and at inspection successfully turned out 'delicately flavoured' deep-fried skate fish cakes with tartare sauce, and a large, creamy aubergine and goats' cheese filo roll with a sauce of black olives, capers and tomatoes. Crisp-skinned, 'ultra-fresh' fillet of grey mullet has come with a winning fennel purée and red wine sauce, and chump of slightly pink lamb is served with a ragoût of properly cooked sweetbreads in a rich brown mint-flavoured gravy. Desserts that have pleased include chocolate and brandy fondant, served hot with ice cream and a 'Jackson Pollock-like splash of chocolate', and grilled plums with honey and ice cream. Service is enthusiastic and knowledgeable, and most of the bottles on the short wine list are below £20; house French is £10.

CHEF: Robin Tarver   PROPRIETORS: Francesca Melman and Robin Tarver   OPEN: Sun to Fri L 12.30 to 3 (4 Sun), all week D 7 to 11 (10.30 Sun)   CLOSED: Christmas, New Year   MEALS: alc (main courses £7 to £14). Set L £7.50 (2 courses) to £10, Set D £10.50 (2 courses) to £13.50   SERVICE: 12.5% (optional), card slips closed   CARDS: Delta, Diners, MasterCard, Switch, Visa   DETAILS: 70 seats. 25 seats outside. Private parties: 15 main room, 40 private room. Vegetarian meals. Children's helpings. No smoking in 1 dining room. Occasional music. Air-conditioned   ⊖ Maida Vale, Westbourne Grove

Card slips closed *in the details at the end of an entry indicates that the total on the slips of credit cards is closed when handed over for signature.*

Veeraswamy

map 15

101 Regent Street, W1R 8RS
TEL: (0171) 734 1401   FAX: (0171) 439 8434

COOKING 1
COST £26–£48

The view over Regent Street is 'continuously interesting' from this bright, modern, first-floor room cleanly decorated in vivid colours. Although the menu plays on the regionality of Indian food, it is structured along conventional lines of starters, main courses (vegetarian and non-vegetarian listed separately in each case) and puddings. Diversity and complexity come across in the spicing, its heat signalled on the menu with chilli symbols (one for medium hot, two for hotter). Start perhaps with pani puri (puffed wheat biscuits with a chilled lentil, potato and tamarind 'cocktail'), and go on to Malabar prawn curry with turmeric and mango. Main courses are meant to be complete, so check carefully before ordering side dishes. Desserts major on refreshing sorbets and ice creams, with gulab jamun and kulfi among the offerings. Service is efficient, and the wine list is a model of compatibility with the food. House Vin de Pays d'Oc is £11.50.

CHEF: Gowtham Kumar   PROPRIETORS: Namita Panjabi and Ranjit Mathrani   OPEN: Mon to Sat 12 to 2.30, 5.30 to 11.30, Sun 12.30 to 3, 6 to 10   CLOSED: 26 Dec   MEALS: alc (main courses £9.50 to £13.50). Set L and D 5.30 to 6.30 £11 (2 courses) to £14. Cover £1.50   SERVICE: 12.5% (optional), card slips closed   CARDS: Amex, Diners, MasterCard, Switch, Visa   DETAILS: 135 seats. Private parties: 150 main room, 36 private room. Vegetarian meals. Children's helpings. Wheelchair access (not WC). Music. Air-conditioned   ⊖ Piccadilly Circus

Villandry 🍴

map 15

170 Great Portland Street, W1N 5TB
TEL: (0171) 631 3131   FAX: (0171) 631 3030

COOKING 3
COST £29–£58

Reached through the well-stocked grocery shop (worth allowing extra time for) Villandry calls itself a 'foodstore restaurant', and it has no shortage of interesting ingredients to call on. Wooden floors induce clatter, noise tends to bounce off the white walls and high ceiling, and tables are close together, so this is no place for a quiet head to head during busy mealtimes. It deals in light dishes – a choice of salads among starters, pasta for main course, perhaps – and its contemporary approach is evident in, for example, tuna with grilled aubergine and preserved lemon.

Recommended soups have included sweet potato with coconut milk, and pumpkin with pancetta, and main-course tarts seem popular: 'slithery' mushroom and Parmesan for one reporter, a 'beautifully tremblant' artichoke and broccoli version for another, served with a mountain of frisée salad. Simple desserts might run to provençale yoghurt with honey and fresh fruit, or baked rhubarb with custard. Service (for which there is a 12.5 per cent charge) can be 'a little chaotic' at times, but is friendly enough for the most part. French and Italian wines dominate the sixty-strong wine list, where house wine is £11.50.

CHEFS: Steve Evernett-Watts and Rosalind Carrarini   PROPRIETORS: J.C. and R. Carrarini   OPEN: all week L 12.30 to 3, Mon to Sat D 7 to 10   CLOSED: 25 and 26 Dec, Easter Mon   MEALS: alc (main courses £9.50 to £15)   SERVICE: 12.5% (optional), card slips closed   CARDS: Amex, Delta, MasterCard, Switch, Visa   DETAILS: 100 seats. Private parties: 100 main room, 10 and 20 private rooms. Vegetarian meals. Children's helpings. No smoking in dining room. Wheelchair access (not WC). No music. Air-conditioned   ⊖ Great Portland Street

Vong

map 14

Berkeley Hotel, Wilton Place, SW1X 7RL	COOKING 5
TEL: (0171) 235 1010 FAX: (0171) 235 1011	COST £34–£82

A glossy, marble-floored bar area stands at the head of the grand staircase down to the restaurant, which has bags of life and glamour, yet more marble, and mirrored walls allowing good views of the activity. Cheerful, informative and relaxed French waiters contribute to the enjoyment and sense of occasion. The fusion of French and Thai cooking may have become a cliché, but it generally succeeds. Crisp, ungreasy spring rolls with fresh-tasting crab come with a sweetly nutty tamarind sauce, and on the table are five more seasonings: sea salt, Chinese five-spice, chilli sauce, crisp-fried shallot and nam prik. Chopped raw queen scallops marinated in lime juice, served with coriander leaves and water chestnuts 'exploded' with fresh, sharp flavours for one visitor. Invention also runs to satay sweetbreads (each piece run through by a stick of liquorice) accompanied by a baked lemon and pieces of poached pear. There are dissenters, with one reader finding Thai spices used in a 'tentative, prissy manner', but the consensus is that the cooking is a 'refreshing alternative' to the usual repertoire.

The fusion calms down a little at dessert stage, producing crispy rice crêpes, figs baked in port, and a 'pretty sensational' combination of roasted banana, chocolate-stuffed filo parcels, and ice cream. Lunchtime and early-evening set-price 'black plate' menus are considered excellent value. A hundred wines on a mostly high-priced list are well chosen to match the food. The least expensive red is £16, white £18.

CHEFS: Jean-Georges Vongerichten and Shaun Gilmore   PROPRIETOR: Savoy Group plc
OPEN: all week 12 to 2.30, 6 to 11.30 (10 Sun)   CLOSED: 25 Dec, 1 Jan   MEALS: alc (main courses £13 to £29.50). Set L £15 (2 courses) to £20, Set D 6 to 7 £17.50, Set D £45   SERVICE: 12.5% (optional), card slips closed   CARDS: Amex, Delta, Diners, MasterCard, Switch, Visa
DETAILS: 130 seats. Private parties: 250 main room. Vegetarian meals. Wheelchair access (not WC). No music. Air-conditioned   ⊖ Hyde Park Corner

Wagamama ⁵✳ £

map 15

4 Streatham Street, WC1A 1JB	
TEL: (0171) 323 9223 FAX: (0171) 323 9224	
10a Lexington Street, W1R 3HS	
TEL: (0171) 292 0990 FAX: (0171) 734 1815	COOKING 1
EMAIL: mail@wagamama.com	COST £16–£30

Noodles in nearly infinite variety are the basis of the menus in these popular health-focused restaurants modelled on traditional Japanese ramen shops: indeed one found it 'cleansing' to consume an enormous bowl of fresh, crisp vegetables in a light broth with a few noodles. Besides a large variety of soupy noodle dishes with chicken, seafood, beef, pork or vegetables, there are fried ones (for example, amai udon: 'fat white noodles' with egg, tofu, prawns and peanuts), as well as rice dishes (chicken tama: chargrilled chicken with egg, ginger and wine sauce), and curries (yasai katsu: sweet potato, aubergine and pumpkin). Side dishes of chicken dumplings, or chargrilled vegetables dipped in yakitori sauce, add to the appeal. Popularity means that the hubbub at communal tables makes private conversation difficult, though not impossible, and the computer-aided service can be 'a bit chaotic', although the menu stresses that dishes arrive in whatever order they are ready. Green tea is free (on request), and there are Japanese beers, saké and wines from £9.25. It seems that healthy eating can cause rapid expansion, for there are new branches in Camden Town and Wigmore Street, with more promised.

CHEFS: Soon Sin (Streatham Street), Brian McEwan (Lexington Street)   PROPRIETOR: Wagamama Ltd   OPEN: all week noon to 11 (12.30 to 10.30 Sun)   CLOSED: 25 and 26 Dec   MEALS: alc (main courses £5 to £7.50)   SERVICE: not inc   CARDS: Amex, Delta, MasterCard, Switch, Visa   DETAILS: Vegetarian meals. No smoking in dining rooms. No music. Air-conditioned   ⊖ Tottenham Court Road, Piccadilly Circus

White Onion
map 13

297 Upper Street, N1 2TU
TEL/FAX: (0171) 359 3533

COOKING 4
COST £23–£52

This 'modern, chic and uncluttered' Islington restaurant, with its purple and blue matt walls and contemporary black furniture, is not far from the Almeida Theatre, and only a fifteen-minute brisk walk from Sadlers Wells ('well worth the exercise'). It comes from the same stable as the Red Pepper, Green Olive and Purple Sage (see entries, all London), and offers pan-European cooking with a focus on the Mediterranean. Presentation is a strong point, and most reporters find that it 'tastes as good as it looks': a salad of roasted aubergine and courgette with crispy sweet potatoes, for example, or piccata of guinea fowl with streaky bacon and vinaigrette.

Main-course meats and fish are equally successful, whether fillet of beef à la ficelle, or steamed fillets of sole on a bed of gratin dauphinoise in a light, creamy, white wine sauce. Desserts have included a chestnut mousse that comes sandwiched between layers of 'ultra-fine' biscuits, served with chestnut ice cream and orange confit; and a chocolate soufflé that was 'as good as everything else'. Service is 'warm' as well as 'highly professional and efficient'. The wine list favours the Old World over the New but achieves a wide-ranging selection. Three house wines start at £9.50.

CHEF: Eric Guignard   PROPRIETOR: Bijan Behzadi   OPEN: Sat and Sun L 12 to 2.30, all week D 6.30 to 11 (7 to 10.30 Sun)   CLOSED: 25 and 26 Dec, 1 Jan   MEALS: alc Mon to Sat D (main courses £8 to £14.50). Set L Sat £10 (2 courses) to £14.50, Set L and D Sun £15 (2 courses) to £19.50   SERVICE: not inc   CARDS: Amex, Delta, MasterCard, Switch, Visa   DETAILS: 63 seats. Private parties: 30 main room. Vegetarian meals. Children's helpings. No cigars/pipes in dining room. Wheelchair access (also WC). Music. Air-conditioned   ⊖ Angel, Highbury & Islington

Wilsons
map 12

236 Blythe Road, W14 0HJ
TEL: (0171) 603 7267   FAX: (0171) 602 9018

COOKING 1
COST £28–£43

An old joke asks why bagpipers walk when they play. Answers vary from 'to try to get away from the sound' to 'it's harder to hit a moving target'. At his proudly Scottish restaurant, Robert Wilson – 'a pleasant middle-aged chap' who combines a relaxed approach with 'a certain dignity as befits his years' – is likely to sound a skirl late in the evening for the benefit of those who take the instrument more seriously. Before that, the appeal is generous servings of plain food at prices to satisfy locals and regulars: cock-a-leekie soup, salmon fish cakes, Finnan haddock 'pudding' (like kedgeree), and calf's liver with bacon, followed perhaps by well-balanced raspberry queen of puddings. Beef is Glenbervie Aberdeen Angus, while haggis, served with mashed potato and highly rated swede, comes with a tot of whisky, of which there is no shortage on the premises. A short wine list hovers around £20, but house red and white are £10.50.

CHEFS/PROPRIETORS: R. Wilson and R. Hilton   OPEN: Mon to Sat D only 7 to 10   CLOSED: Christmas, Easter, bank hols   MEALS: alc (main courses £9.50 to £15). Set L £6.50 (2 courses)   SERVICE: 12.5% (optional), card slips closed   CARDS: Delta, MasterCard, Switch, Visa   DETAILS: 44 seats. Private parties: 44 main room. Vegetarian meals. Children's helpings. Wheelchair access (not WC). Music. Air-conditioned   ⊖ Hammersmith, Shepherd's Bush

Wiltons
map 15

55 Jermyn Street, SW1Y 6LX
TEL: (0171) 629 9955   FAX: (0171) 495 6233

COOKING 3
COST £36–£108

Wilton's is a cross between the Connaught and Rules (see entries, London). It shares their historical perspective, tracing its origins back 250 years, takes an Edwardian view of matters culinary, and specialises in fish and game. Simple seafood dishes include old-fashioned lobster cocktail, potted shrimps, and crab in various guises: plainly dressed, paired with avocado, or sharing a caper-rich mousse with smoked salmon. Nostalgia extends to whitebait, hot or cold consommé, sole Colbert, and kedgeree, while unchanging grills of steak or lamb cutlets are supplemented by seasonal game such as 'plump, tender' roast grouse, not hung for very long in one reporter's view, but cooked exactly as requested, and served with bread sauce and liver pâté on toast. And talking of toast, it takes savouries seriously, serving anchovies and mushrooms that way as an alternative to rhubarb and strawberry pie, or firm-textured summer pudding. 'Totally discreet service' is administered by waitresses in long jackets, and anybody looking for change from £20 on the French-dominated wine list can choose between red or white house wine, both £17.50.

CHEF: Ross Hayden   PROPRIETORS: Rupert Hambro and partners   OPEN: Sun to Fri 12 to 2.30, 6 to 10.30   CLOSED: bank hols   MEALS: alc (main courses £15 to £29). Set L Sun £19.75. Cover £1.50   SERVICE: not inc   CARDS: Amex, Diners, MasterCard, Switch, Visa   DETAILS: 100 seats. Private parties: 20 main room, 18 private room. Jacket and tie. Wheelchair access (not WC). No music. Air-conditioned   ⊖ Green Park

Zafferano
map 14

15 Lowndes Street, SW1X 9EY
TEL: (0171) 235 5800   FAX: (0171) 235 1971

COOKING 7
COST £30–£69

'Another stunning meal here,' began a regular visitor to London's best Italian restaurant. Another finds it hard to think of anywhere that is 'more enjoyable or better value (particularly at lunchtime)'. Small tables are immaculately set (this is quite a smart neighbourhood) and it feels 'expensive but laid back'. What it offers are impeccable and devoutly seasonal ingredients, carefully and confidently handled: 'like the best kind of home-cooked food', according to one, although travellers to Italy find that it compares favourably with some of the top restaurants there. Generosity of choice is, like much else, hard to fault, and the range extends from a sweet-and-sour skate salad, via gnocchi with smoked cheese, to rabbit with Parma ham and polenta.

The cooking, as so often, is at its best when simplest: in summer, for example, a mound of tiny, tender carrots, peas, broad beans, green beans, sugar-snap peas, turnips and roast plum tomatoes topped with salad leaves, all in a restrained dressing. That may sound ridiculously easy, but most readers can surely think of a chef who would make a mess of it. Out of the kitchen, too, come textbook risottos – of saffron topped with foie gras, or of quail ('dazzling, the grains tender and suffused with a remarkably intense chicken stock') – and pasta in various forms: perhaps ravioli filled with osso buco. Rolled stuffed pork, meanwhile, is not the usual lump of meat but three neat sausages enclosing herbs and soft cheese, accompanied by a pile of first-rate courgette 'frites'.

Equal enthusiasm attends desserts of plum and almond tart with grappa ice cream, and pineapple sorbet sandwiched between chunks of fresh, and crisp circles of, pineapple. Good breads come with pungent olive oil for dipping, and espresso and cappuccino are the real thing. Staff are smart, friendly and discreet, and render service that is attentive without being fussy, while the exclusively Italian wines (apart from champagne) combine intriguing variety with classic denominations and top producers. There are even some under £20, including house Verdicchio and Rosso Piceno at £11.

CHEF: Giorgio Locatelli   PROPRIETOR: A To Z Restaurants   OPEN: Mon to Sat 12 to 2.30, 7 to 11   MEALS: Set L £17.50 (2 courses) to £20.50, Set D £26.50 (2 courses) to £36.50   SERVICE: not inc   CARDS: Amex, Delta, Diners, MasterCard, Switch, Visa   DETAILS: 55 seats. Private parties: 6 private room. Vegetarian meals. Children's helpings. Wheelchair access (not WC). Music. Air-conditioned   ⊖ Knightsbridge

Zaika

NEW WAVE 2000 INDIAN

NEW ENTRY   map 14

257–259 Fulham Road, SW3 6HY
TEL: (0171) 351 7823
FAX: (0171) 376 4971

COOKING 5
COST £23–£47

Restaurants have come and gone in the last few years on this Fulham Road site, the latest makeover introducing swaths of multicoloured muslin around the window and artefacts in niches in a wall. These small differences, however, signal substantial changes in the kitchen. Vineet Bhatia brings a unique style to Indian cooking, marrying techniques and ingredients in an inspired manner. The multiple-dish approach of so much Indian food has been dropped in favour of a more European three-course formula, plus a five-course jugalbandi menu for a minimum of two people.

Among starters, tandoori home-smoked salmon with mustard and dill looks to be a pretty unbeatable 'signature dish': the skin 'beautifully crispy and the flesh just a touch rare in the middle'. Those who collect crossover ideas might want to stick one or two of these in their album: perhaps an Indian risotto with red onions and coriander, topped with crispy prawns, or grilled honey-mustard chicken on smoked aubergine. Recommended main courses have included conventional but 'refined' rogan josh, and pastry-crusted lamb biryani cooked in a sealed pot, accompanied by a vegetable stir-fry. Light paratha comes flavoured with mint leaves, and chutneys are praised too. Desserts run to chocolate samosas, and tricoloured bread pudding (with three sauces: saffron, almond and cardamom, and pistachio and basil). The wine list is small, but well focused, with bottles from around the world. Chardonnay and Montepulciano are each £12.50.

CHEF: Vineet Bhatia PROPRIETORS: Claudio Pulze, Raj Sharma and Vineet Bhatia OPEN: Mon to Fri L 12 to 2.30, Mon to Sat D 6 to 10.45 CLOSED: 24 Dec to 2 Jan MEALS: alc (main courses £8.50 to £12). Set L £9.95 (2 courses) to £11.95, Set D £20 (min 2) SERVICE: 12.5% (optional), card slips closed CARDS: Amex, Delta, MasterCard, Switch, Visa DETAILS: 68 seats. Private parties: 75 main room, 16 private room. Vegetarian meals. No cigars/pipes in dining room. Wheelchair access (not WC). No music. Air-conditioned ⊖ South Kensington

Zen Central   map 15

20 Queen Street, W1X 7PJ
TEL: (0171) 629 8089 and 8103   COOKING 4
FAX: (0171) 493 6181   COST £39–£79

Flash, but no flash in the pan, Zen Central has been serving luxurious pan-Chinese food since the late 1980s. Its interior is very much of that decade – lots of glass, black, grey and steel, with mirrors along one wall – yet comfortable despite the minimalism. There's a buzz to the place in the evenings, when tapes of Chinese pop music play and 'courteous and professional' staff take the orders. The menu is peppered with luxury ingredients, so a meal might begin with steamed scallops with black-bean sauce and continue with pan-fried fillet of prawn in champagne and orange sauce. More luxury (at luxury prices) comes in the guise of shark's fin ('braised fluffy' or 'clear'), whole suckling pig, and whole Szechuan duck, although staples such as Singapore noodles, and sweet-and-sour pork are available too. Red bean paste pancake (it must be ordered for two) is a good way to end a meal. There's a fair choice of white Burgundies among the wines, though prices on the list can be high. House Chardonnay is £16.

CHEF: Chris Kwan PROPRIETOR: Tealeaf Ltd OPEN: all week 12.15 to 2.30, 6.30 to 11.15 (10.45 Sun) CLOSED: 24 and 25 Dec MEALS: alc (main courses £10.50 to £16). Set L £15 (2 courses) to £30, Set D £25 to £38. Cover £1 SERVICE: 15% (optional), card slips closed CARDS: Delta, Diners, MasterCard, Switch, Visa DETAILS: 90 seats. Private parties: 90 main room, 20 private room. Vegetarian meals. Children's helpings. Wheelchair access (not WC). Music. Air-conditioned ⊖ Green Park £5

London round-ups

With so many venues vying for attention, finding a place to eat out in London that offers the right blend of food, location, style and price to suit the occasion can often be very much down to pot luck. This section aims to make choosing easier by providing details of a broad range of restaurants, bistros, cafés, hotel dining rooms, and so on, that are deserving of attention, though they do not merit a full entry. There are also one or two rising stars, well worth keeping an eye on, and in some cases establishments have been included here rather than in the main entries because of significant late changes or a lack of positive feedback. Reports on these places are particularly welcome. Brief details of opening times are given in each entry where available. Note that on 22 April 2000 London telephone codes and numbers will change, as follows: the code (0171) will become (020) followed by a 7, and the code (0181) will become (020) followed by an 8. For example: (0171) 222 1234 will change to (020) 7222 1234, and the number (0181) 333 1234 will change to (020) 8333 1234.

Andrew Edmunds   W1
46 Lexington Street   map 15
(0171) 437 5708
In the restaurant's own words 'the loyal clientèle understand the vagaries of Andrew Edmunds and are more than willing to put up with sitting elbow to elbow with the next table'. A new chef was taking over as the *Guide* went to press, but cooking is expected to continue as before, using good ingredients in a mainly modern European eclectic repertoire with occasional oriental excursions. Bookings are taken no more than a week ahead. Most of the wine list is priced below £20, and only one Burgundy goes over £30. Open all week.

Anna's Place   N1
90 Mildmay Park   map 13
(0171) 249 9379
A friendly neighbourhood restaurant with a small weather-resistant garden at the rear. The mainly Swedish menu opens with traditional starters such as sill tallrik (marinated herrings) or gravadlax, and includes a vegetarian choice, plus main courses such as fillet of reindeer with leek and potato cake, shank of pork, or pan-fried cod with beetroot sauce. Open Sat L and Mon to Sat D.

Apprentice   SE1
Butlers Wharf Chef School,   map 13
31 Shad Thames
(0171) 234 0254
The restaurant of the Butler's Wharf Chef School provides a set menu and a carte prepared by the budding Marcos of tomorrow. Real money is spent eating here and standards are accordingly high. Typical dishes might be a pressed cod and salmon terrine, or poached chicken dumpling with coriander cream sauce, followed by roast saddle of rabbit with penny-bun noodles, finishing with rich chocolate ganache, or blueberry and mint muffin with balsamic ice cream. Waiting staff are students too. Closed Sat and Sun.

Aurora   W1
49 Lexington Street   map 15
(0171) 494 0514
Dark wooden boards, rustic tables and ochre walls set the scene at this bustling and lively Soho eaterie. Start with good bread and olives or antipasto and move on to fresh anchovy fillets, chump of lamb with chickpea and mint salad or grilled sardines. Finish with 'very intense' lemon tart or cheesecake. Service is laid back. Closed Sun.

Bam-Bou
W1
1 Percy Street · map 15
(0171) 323 9130

Set over four floors of a Georgian town house, this latest branch of the Mogens Tholstrup empire (see The Collection and Daphne's, London main entries) has taken the cooking of colonial French Vietnam as its theme, though some invention has embellished the style. Enticing options on the menu of around a dozen choices per course may include grilled chicken brochette with lemon grass and peanuts; spicy raw beef with aromatic basil, lime and chilli; and crab cakes with galangal sauce. Closed Sun.

Belgo Centraal
WC2
50 Earlham Street · map 15
(0171) 813 2233

Covent Garden sibling of Belgo Noord (see main entry) that follows the same formula of mussels, frites and beer. For a change, try other more or less authentically Belgian dishes, ranging from carbonnade to shark confit with green mustard and purple chard, all served by waiters dressed as Trappist monks. Lunch and early evening deals are a good-value way to sample the fun. Another branch is at 124 Ladbroke Grove, W10, (0181) 982 8400, and Bierodrome, a more basic version with the emphasis on guess what, is at 173 Upper Street, N1, (0171) 226 5835. The chain has also expanded to Bristol, Dublin and New York. Open all week.

La Belle Epoque
SW3
151 Draycott Avenue · map 14
(0171) 460 5000

Open-fronted brasserie in a food complex, specialising in fish. Choose from fruits de mer platters, lobster every which way or hot crustacea. Otherwise start with Parma ham and melon, or fish cake with a rocket salad; main courses might be baked red snapper on sweet fennel mash or breast of duck on a grapefruit and pineapple compote. Closed Sun D.

Beotys
WC2
79 St Martin's Lane · map 15
(0171) 836 8768/8548

Long-standing family-run restaurant serving classic and Greek-Cypriot dishes from the past. French menu with English subtitles offers good kalamari, moules, and potted shrimps as starters, and 'les entrées' might run to deep-fried breast of chicken with garlic butter, or veal escalope with capers, anchovies and fried egg. Portions are generous and sauces can be rich. Daily plats de jour might take in crêpe fruits de mer, game in season, and fresh Scottish wild salmon or Cornish lobster; lemon meringue pie for afters has been recommended. Closed Sun.

Boisdale
SW1
15 Eccleston Street · map 13
(0171) 730 6922

The Belgravia location, oak floors, oak bar and panelled walls give Boisdale a clubby feel, but the long list of malt whiskies confirms that its heart lies in Scotland. Hands-on owner Ranald Macdonald Younger of Clanranald has an unimpeachable pedigree, as does the menu: Rannoch Moor supplies smoked venison and duck, salmon comes from Dunkeld and Orkney, and scallops are hand-dived from the Hebrides. Vegetables are often organic. Closed Sat L and Sun.

Bombay Brasserie
SW7
Courtfield Road · map 14
(0171) 370 4040/373 0971

Other jungles may be shrinking but the brasserie's luxuriously verdant conservatory has almost doubled in size to accommodate about 160. The menu reflects the cosmopolitan nature of Bombay itself, spanning India's culinary styles: as well as dishes from the northwest, there are specialities from Mangalore, south India, and Goa, the latter including lobster, prawns and Dover sole. Thalis provide a balanced, varied meal on one plate. There is also a daily changing lunch buffet. The Brasserie is one of the pioneers of matching fine wine with Indian food. Open all week.

Books for Cooks   W11
4 Blenheim Crescent   map 13
(0171) 221 1992
There is nowhere else quite like this. The
only way to tell if a cookery book is any
good is to try the recipes, but we can't do
that until we have bought the book, by
which time it may be too late. Eric
Treuille and Ursula Ferrigno, themselves
authors of a book on bread, do the hard
work and test recipes from the thousands
of books, old and new, on sale in this
long-established browsers' shop off
Ladbroke Grove. Pay £10 for three
courses: anything from Italian meze to
duck leg curry; vegetarian option always
available. Two sittings Mon to Sat, noon
and 1.45pm. Booking essential.

Brown's Hotel, 1837 Restaurant   W1
Albemarle Street   map 15
(0171) 408 1837
Chef Gregory Nicholson was due to leave
this 'haven of civilisation' just as the
Guide was going to press and a
replacement was being sought. A
tendency towards luxury ingredients has
been a feature, as has a 'degree of artistry'
in the food, and a successor would
presumably be expected to follow suit.
Sommelier John Gilchrist's superb wine
list is not to be missed and the real fun is
to be had with wines by the glass: some
200 are served impeccably, with prices
ranging from £4 to £180. Reports please.
Closed Sat L and Sun.

Bu-San   N7
43 Holloway Road   map 13
(0171) 607 8264
This family-run restaurant at the
Highbury Corner end of the busy
Holloway Road serves authentic Korean
food in un-fussy surroundings. The
extensive menu takes in appetisers such
as oe muchim (pickled cucumber), ho bak
bokum (fried marrow) and jo ge sal
bokum (fried scallops with spicy sauce).
Meat (pork, chicken and beef) features
strongly in main courses, and seafood
might appear as dam chy tang (mussels
with white radish and carrots) or gul

tuigim (deep-fried oysters). Set meals
include one-pot lunches. Closed L Sat and
Sun.

Le Cadre   N8
10 Priory Road   map 12
(0181) 348 0606
David Misselbrook has been producing
staunchly French food at his
neighbourhood restaurant for over a
decade now. The welcome is warm and
the service friendly. Begin with foie gras
and duck liver parfait, or mille-feuille of
Devon crab, then move on to confit of
chicken with vermouth tarragon sauce,
or breast of duck with bitter red cherries.
Finish with bread-and-butter pudding or
praline crème brûlée glazed with almond
and nougat. Closed Sat L and Sun.

Café du Marché   EC1
22 Charterhouse Square   map 13
(0171) 608 1609
Hidden away down an alley off
Charterhouse Square, this restaurant
offers a real taste of France that can make
visitors forget they are really in the heart
of the City. Aside from the décor, this
atmosphere is created by a menu of fish
soup, pipérade with Bayonne ham,
bouillabaisse, suprême of chicken with
sauce Choron, and fruit tart or crème
caramel to finish. Closed Sat L and Sun.

Café Portugal   SW8
5A and 6A Victoria House   map 13
(0171) 587 1962
'It isn't a posh place but it has long been
treasured by us south Londoners,' wrote
one fan of this authentic Portuguese
restaurant, run by a husband and wife
team. It has two parts: a tapas bar and
shop in one half, and a restaurant next
door, offering a good range of traditional
dishes from a stew of beans with smoked
meat and chorizo, or rabbit casserole with
fries, to fried sardines with grilled
peppers, or sautéed salt cod with potatoes
and hard-boiled egg. Closed Mon.

Casablanca   W6
264 King Street   map 12
(0181) 741 1177
North Africa and the eastern
Mediterranean provide much of the
menu's inspiration, producing a wide
range of hot and cold meze and charcoal
grills, as well as some more familiar
options that seem odd in the context:
prawn cocktail, for example. It is set on
two floors, on one a 'formal eating room',
on the other an atmospheric wine bar
with traditional low seating and tables,
and North African music. Closed Mon L.

Chapel   NW1
48 Chapel Street   map 13
(0171) 402 9220
This pub/restaurant just off the Edgware
Road is a pleasant place with (usually)
welcoming staff. It's a local oasis of
Western food (even if the bread is Arab)
offering a daily-changing menu.
Generous portions of homely dishes
might include fish croquettes with
roasted vegetables, chilled watercress
soup, gnocchi with artichoke hearts, and
stuffed chicken breasts with rocket and
Brie. More exotic than homely are seared
marlin steak with anchovy chive dressing,
and bison steak with parsnips and
mustard. Open all week.

Che   SW1
23 St James's Street   map 14
(0171) 747 9380
This former bank claims to have the
largest collection of Cuban cigars in
London, which can be enjoyed in the bar
over an expertly mixed cocktail. The
first-floor dining room, its décor
dominated by concrete and glass, shot to
fame when James Kirby opened in late
1998, but he left as the *Guide* went to
press. On offer is a menu ranging from
fish and chips or house burger to more
sophisticated veal cutlet with Jerusalem
artichoke purée, or pan-fried native
lobster with asparagus and white beans.
Vegetables, cover charge and 12.5%
service bump up the bill. Reports please.
Closed Sat L and Sun.

Chez Gérard   W1
8 Charlotte Street   map 15
(0171) 636 4975
The Chez Gérard brand has expanded and
currently boasts eight restaurants in the
capital, all offering unashamedly French
cooking. Onglet and frites have been 'as
good as ever', and steak in one form or
another is definitely the focus. The menu
extends to onion tart or fish soup to start,
and main course alternatives to red meat
such as grilled salmon with lemon and
watercress, or corn-fed French chicken.
Vegetarians also have a couple of starters
and main courses to choose from. A
three-course set-price menu is good value
at £15.95. Closed Sat L. Branches at 14
Trinity Square, EC3, (0171) 480 5500; 64
Bishopsgate, EC2, (0171) 588 1200; 31
Dover Street, W1, (0171) 499 8171; 119–
120 Chancery Lane, WC2, (0171) 405
0290; 3 Yeoman's Row, SW3, (0171) 581
8377; Opera Terrace, First Floor, Covent
Garden Central Market, WC2, (0171) 379
0666; 84–86 Roseberry Avenue, EC1,
(0171) 833 1515.

Chuen Cheng Ku   W1
17 Wardour Street   map 15
(0171) 734 3281
'The parade of trolleys bearing freshly
steamed dim sum is a winning formula,'
according to a confirmed fan of this long-
established Chinatown favourite. It is a
family-friendly place and a regular notes
that there is even a smile on the face of
waiters these days, perhaps because they
now sport fetching green dragon
costumes. As well as dim sum (available
all week 11 to 5.30), Chinese-style
afternoon tea is reckoned to be excellent
value. There is also a long, standard
Cantonese menu. Open all week.

Clerkenwell Restaurant & Bar   EC1
73 Clerkenwell Road   map 13
(0171) 831 7595
Open only for lunch (and dinner in
December until Christmas), this friendly
Italian restaurant offers a varied carte
which might turn out a salad of spider
crab and mixed shellfish or grilled Roman

artichokes to start, then main courses of poached salmon fillet on a warm salad of summer vegetables, or pumpkin gnocchi with oyster mushrooms. Desserts might include warm date loaf with mascarpone and brandy, or lemon tart with vodka-marinated Cape gooseberries. A moderately priced wine list naturally majors on Italy.

Le Colombier   SW3
145 Dovehouse Street   map 14
(0171) 351 1155
French-owned converted pub with a buzzy atmosphere and an open-air terrace under an awning for summer eating. The carte features traditional starters of fish soup, snails in puff pastry and warm goats' cheese salad, plus various oysters, while main courses offer a choice of fish such as baked sea bass with thyme, or scallops with wild mushrooms. Meat might be breast of duckling in lime sauce, or rabbit with a cider sauce and fresh pasta. Desserts include crêpes Suzette, cheese or baked Alaska for two.

Corney & Barrow   WC2
116 St Martin's Lane   map 15
(0171) 655 9800
West End outpost for a chain of City wine bars. It is full of bustle, with a ground-floor wine bar and mezzanine brasserie with spare modern décor. Modern European cooking with a fishy accent might take in yellow-fin tuna tartare, or grilled halloumi with roast aubergine and basil to start, followed by Moroccan-spiced fish kebab with aromatic rice and muhummra purée, or Bulgarian spinach and feta pie with roast tomato salsa. The wine list is lengthy, diverse and fairly priced. Closed Sun D.

Daquise   SW7
20 Thurloe Street   map 14
(0171) 589 6117
This Polish restaurant not far from the V&A offers Eastern European food at reasonable prices. Reporters struggle to describe the décor, but 'dated' and

'informal' seem to be the consensus. The potato pancake (a house speciality) has been a 'revelation'. Otherwise, the menu ranges from starters of barszcz with uska (beetroot soup with wild mushroom ravioli) to smoked salmon blinis, followed by Russian Zrazy (minced pork and veal rolled and stuffed with mushrooms) or Bavarian pork knuckle. Finish on pancakes with ice cream and orange caramel sauce. Drink Polish vodka. Open all week.

Depot   SW14
Tideway Yard   map 12
(0181) 878 9462
Waterfront brasserie in a renovated Victorian stableyard overlooking the Thames. Recommended dishes have been salmon rillettes, cod fish cakes with tomato sauce, and cherry crêpes. More unusual offerings might be a chilled soup of beetroot, ginger and coconut, followed by mackerel tandoori with kumera mash, finishing with chilled lemon posset; excellent pudding wines are only £3 a glass. Open all week.

Diwana Bhel Poori   NW1
121 Drummond Street   map 13
(0171) 387 5556
The star of Drummond Street. Be warned that décor, service and menu are fairly basic, and that even the heartiest appetites will have trouble managing the enormous portions, and appreciate some of the best value Indian snacks in London: pooris, samosas and dhosas (a meal in themselves) are the things to go for. Wash them down with good salt lassi. Handy for Euston station. Open all week.

Ebury Wine Bar   SW1
139 Ebury Street   map 13
(0171) 730 5447
Lively wine bar offering snacks downstairs, and a panelled dining room upstairs with a full menu delivering

contemporary flavours. Start with a warm salad of mussels, roasted peppers and balsamic onions, then move on to baked cod with kaffir lime sauce and noodles, or perhaps seared kangaroo with Thai spices. Finish with pear and almond tart or Mars bar spring roll; twenty wines by the glass. Open all week.

Efes Kebab House   W1
80 Great Titchfield Street   map 15
(0171) 636 1953
Not much has changed at Efes over its twenty-five years. Meze are still the best way for newcomers to explore the menu of Turkish stalwarts, starting with cold dips and moving on to hot dishes such as deep-fried diced lambs' liver and a selection of grills. The quality of the meat is second to none, the Kofte 'as good as ever'. Drink Turkish wine or beer and finish with 'excellent' coffee and Turkish delight. Service is 'cheerful'. Closed Sun. A second branch is nearby at 175–177 Great Portland Street, W1, (0171) 436 0600.

English Garden   SW3
10 Lincoln Street   map 14
(0171) 584 7272
Just off the King's Road, with a pleasant conservatory ambience, this restaurant has had a refurbishment and a change of chef since the last edition of the *Guide*. An attractively presented terrine of cod brandade wrapped in cured salmon has been described as 'very good, carefully made and well flavoured', while loin of pork with sage and onion stuffing on grain mustard sauce has come with 'tasty' seasonal vegetables. Desserts might include a bitter chocolate confection, or summer pudding with crème fraîche; attentive and friendly service.

Enoteca Turi   SW15
28 Putney High Street   map 12
(0181) 785 4449
This small Italian restaurant close to Putney Bridge produces dishes such as Mediterranean fish cakes with spicy salsa rossa, parmigiana of aubergine, saddle of wild boar, and halibut with savoury zabaglioni. To finish: tartufo, or pannacotta with nectarines. An extensive Italian wine list offers eleven by the glass. Closed Sat L and all day Sun.

Fire Station   SE1
150 Waterloo Road   map 13
(0171) 620 2226
An open-plan kitchen contributes to the informal, lively atmosphere pervading this Grade II listed building that retains much of the feel of its former incarnation. The menu reveals an 'all too vivid imagination' but while some experiments with the global flavour palette may not quite manage the balancing act, success has come in the form of steamed scallops with black beans, coriander and chilli; roast lamb and chickpea tagine; and potato and spinach gnocchi with spicy tomato salsa.

Fish Central   EC1
149–151 King's Square   map 13
(0171) 253 4970
The City of London may not be renowned for fish & chips, but it has a real gem in this 'superior chippie'. Take-away or sit down in the restaurant next door and expect first-class fish. Stalwarts like cod, haddock, plaice, skate and huss are deep-fried in batter or matzo meal, or simply grilled. The menu extends to fish soup and grilled sardines to start, and more ambitious main courses of fish casserole and Dover sole meunière. Licensed. Closed Sun.

Formula Veneta   SW10
14 Hollywood Road   map 14
(0171) 352 7612
Open-air eating in summer in the courtyard at the rear is a plus at this trendy Italian restaurant just off the Fulham Road. Recommended dishes have included smoked mozzarella and artichokes in filo pastry with a tomato salsa, grilled lemon sole, and escalope of veal in an Emmental sauce. Friendly and competent service. Closed Sun.

Four Regions SE1
County Hall map 13
(0171) 928 0988
Chinese food in a sumptuous setting with a unique view over the Thames to Big Ben and the Houses of Parliament. Fresh abalone, crispy chicken, sizzling seafood platter, and double-cooked pork are among dishes on the latest menu. Various set-price meals for two and four people are also available. The function room is a great wedding venue.

Frederick's N1
Camden Passage map 13
(0171) 359 2888
Useful Islington restaurant offering good-value two-course set lunches and pre-theatre dinners. Start with classic gazpacho, or pineapple-cured salmon, and go on to rabbit, prune and potato pie, or pork chop with apple sauce. Desserts include tarte Tatin, nougat glacé, and ice creams, or opt for cheese. Frederick's is licensed for marriages. Closed Sun.

Gate W6
51 Queen Caroline Street map 12
(0181) 748 6932
Handy for Hammersmith shoppers, Gate offers vegetarian food with an international dimension. Starters of green banana fritters or Caesar salad are suitable for vegans, or go for goats' cheese, artichoke and grilled fig salad, and follow with pasta of the day or baked stuffed pepper. The Japanese platter includes buckwheat noodles in dashi stock, served with sushi rolls and pickled vegetable salad. Sweet lovers might try chocolate and apricot tart or papaya pancakes. Wines on the brief list continue the vegetarian/vegan theme. Closed Sat L and Sun.

Gilbey's W5
77 The Grove map 12
(0181) 840 7568
Like its sibling establishments in Amersham (see entry, England round-ups) and Eton, this is one for wine buffs: a wide range of good French wines are available at retail prices. To accompany the drink is an appealing mix-and-match menu that might offer green herb risotto, ballottine of salmon with salmon roe, Indian-spiced blanquette of lamb, and cod fillet croustade with poached egg and sorrel sabayon. Open all week.

Goolies W8
21 Abingdon Road map 13
(0171) 938 1122
This friendly and informal neighbourhood restaurant offers a bar and casual dining on its lower level and more formal meals upstairs. The cooking is in a familiar modern European vein that ranges from roast pigeon on red cabbage to goats' cheese and grilled vegetable risotto with rocket pesto, via quickly grilled tuna served simply with French beans. Finish on a contemporary note with lime and ginger crème brûlée. Open all week.

Great Nepalese NW1
48 Eversholt Street map 13
(0171) 388 6737
Redecoration has worked well and the display of newspaper and guide reviews remains to reflect the Manandhars' pride in the family's Nepalese cooking. Start with mamocha (Nepalese ravioli) or subtly spiced chicken livers with mushroom and onions. Mutton features in several main dishes including thick dumba curry, while intriguing vegetarian options include kalo dal (black lentils) and gundruk ko tarkari (pickled vegetables). Good Kathmandu Nepalese beer comes in large bottles. Open all week.

Greek Valley NW8
130 Boundary Road map 13
(0171) 624 3217
Friendly helpful service makes this north-west London taverna a sympathetic place. Sample much of the menu by making your choice the meze supreme (£15 per head for two or more), which include dips of cod's roe, chickpeas, yoghurt and cucumber, and aubergine paste; it

continues with grilled halloumi cheese and other hot starters; then lamb on the bone, skewered chicken and lamb, salad and rice. House wines include retsina. Open Mon to Sat D only.

Halcyon, The Room   W11
129 Holland Park   map 13
(0171) 221 5411

The pleasant basement dining room in this elegant, intimate hotel looks out to an ornamental garden and patio. Tables are well-spaced, the atmosphere relaxed, and service attentive. Into this milieu arrived new chef Toby Hill, formerly at Gordleton Mill, Lymington (see main entry), as we went to press. Earlier recommended dishes have included scallops in crisp pastry with a light lobster sauce, whole leg of duck confit with oriental sauce, and 'irresistible' desserts such as a rich gooey chocolate cake. Reports on the new regime, please. Closed Sat L.

Holly   SE15
38 Holly Grove   map 12
(0171) 277 2928

Peckham arrives on the culinary map of London with the opening of this new venture from a Dutch chef and his German wife. The cooking is a blend of European styles and shows an inventive streak. Start, for example, with a salad combining lemon sole, brill and grey mullet with beetroot in a mild mustard dressing, perhaps followed by poached rabbit with pear sauce and thyme baked potatoes, or pan-fried monkfish with potato and spinach mash. Vegetarians might be offered a casserole of pine nuts, tomatoes, artichoke, potatoes and onions. Open Tue to Sat D only.

ICA Café   SW1
12 Carlton House Terrace   map 15
(0171) 930 0493

I is for Institute, not International, but the menu of this fashionably contemporary café suggests otherwise. The short day menu is mainly Italian, perhaps offering sautéed pork with peppers and polenta,

or pasta with mushroom, cabbage and potato. From 5.30 there are 'bar eats' such as healthy-sounding deep-fried skewers of tofu, or free-range organic beef burger. The alternative is 'street foods' from two countries changed monthly. The Thai version could include sweet-sour mango salad, or grilled sweet chilli chicken wings. Italian might include Sicilian fish kebabs, or suppli (fried rice balls stuffed with mozzarella). Short, well chosen wine list, cocktails a speciality. Open all week.

Jen   W1
7 Gerrard Street   map 15
(0171) 287 8193

An interesting and unusual menu, self-styled as 'Hong Kong cuisine', sets this place apart from many of its Chinatown rivals. A dish of various duck parts – wings, gizzards and tongues included – with soya cuttlefish may appeal to none but the most hardened seekers of authenticity, though there are plenty of less challenging options to accommodate Western palates, such as a hotpot of braised aubergine with diced pork and salted fish, crabmeat and noodle casserole, or beef brisket in soup with Chinese celery. Open all week.

Jindivick   N1
201 Liverpool Road   map 13
(0171) 607 7710

Baked spangled emperor bream glazed with chilli-spiced Thai jam is typical of the highly individual style of this informal corner venue in Islington. Seared sugar-cured salmon wrapped in nori is another enticingly out-of-the-ordinary possibility, while at the more familiar end of the scale might be steak with fries and béarnaise, or pan-fried calf's liver with Parma ham and sage. Weekend brunches are famously good, and children are well catered for. Closed Mon L and Sun D.

Konditor & Cook   SE1
Young Vic Theatre, 66 The Cut   map 13
(0171) 620 2700

There is more to Konditor & Cook than

their excellent cakes and pastries, but
don't forget to leave room for them.
Expect friendly and helpful service in this
unpretentious theatre restaurant open
from noon to 8pm. Pan-fried red mullet
with couscous and red pepper sauce has
been recommended. Other dishes might
include a galette of goats' cheese or an
antipasti platter, and then there are the
cakes. Another branch at 22 Cornwall
Road, SE1 offers a take-away service
only. Closed Sun.

Lahore Kebab House   E1
2 Umberston Street   map 13
(0171) 488 2551
Authentic Pakistani café that continues to
turn out some of the best-value kebabs,
curries, dhal and biryani in London,
though there are signs that standards
have slipped a little as the décor has
improved: one reporter felt that the place
'looks more like a restaurant' these days
but that the cooking had 'lost the zing
that I remember'. Unlicensed, but they
will provide a corkscrew free of charge if
you BYO.

Lavender   SW11
171 Lavender Hill   map 12
(0171) 652 7502
A 'jolly place', good for families, with
very basic décor and a blackboard menu
offering straightforward dishes of
chargrilled chicken breast; liver with Puy
lentils, red onion and spinach; and
mozzarella salad with Toulouse sausage.
Pleasant and willing staff complete the
picture. Other branches at 24 Clapham
Road, SW9, 112 Vauxhall Walk, SE11,
and 61 The Cut, SE1, with another
planned for Putney. Open all week.

Leith's at Dartmouth House   W1
English-Speaking Union,   map 15
37 Charles Street
(0171) 499 4005
Delightful neo-classical house with lots of
marble, home to the English-Speaking
Union, and offering lunch from Monday
to Friday in the members' dining room.
Start with gorgonzola and mascarpone

cheesecake or smoked haddock tart, then
grilled breast of mustard chicken,
finishing with chestnut and whisky
mousse or chocolate tart. The staff are
friendly. Open Mon to Fri L.

Lemonia   NW1
89 Regents Park Road   map 13
(0171) 586 7454
Artichokes with broad beans, octopus
salad, and hare stifado are just some of
the daily specials that have appeared on
the blackboard at this popular Greek
restaurant in Primrose Hill. Meze are the
speciality, and meals can be based around
a selection of these or something from the
charcoal grill (marinated lamb, chicken,
quails) or traditional dishes such as
kleftiko or moussaka. Closed Sat L and
Sun D.

**London Hilton, Windows Rooftop
Restaurant**   W1
22 Park Lane   map 15
(0171) 493 8000
Fabulous views of London on a fine day
from this posh, expensive restaurant.
Cooking is classy and essentially
traditional, as demonstrated by the
Business Lunch menu, which offers a
selection of cold hors d'oeuvres followed
by a roast carved from the trolley. From
the carte, start perhaps with pan-fried
langoustines and courgettes with thyme
and wild mushrooms, followed by pan-
fried fillet of beef with polenta, and a
mustard and horseradish sauce. Closed
Sat L and Sun D.

Mandalay   W2
444 Edgware Road   map 13
(0171) 258 3696
Many readers may not consider
themselves familiar with authentic
Burmese cuisine, but they will none the
less recognise many of the dishes on the
lengthy menu at this bright, cheerful and
moderately priced café: it is a style that
bears recognisable similarities to Indian,
Chinese and Thai cooking, taking in
shrimps and beansprouts with three
sauces (tamarind, chilli and soya), lamb

curry, crisp and light spinach fritters, fermented tea leaf salad, and 'twice-fried' fish. Closed Sun.

Manzi's   WC2
1–2 Leicester Street   map 15
(0171) 734 0224

'Famous for fish since 1928,' declares the menu, and there's no arguing with that. Simpler treatments show off the excellent fish and seafood to their best: oysters *au naturel*, a platter of smoked fish, deep-fried skate in good batter, or plaice or Dover sole grilled on the bone, all accompanied by fine chips.

Recommended as a good place for pre-theatre meals and lunches. Closed Sun L.

Marquis   W1
121A Mount Street   map 15
(0171) 499 1256

Stylish, modern décor belies the fact that this is something of a Mayfair institution, owned by the same Italian family for over forty years. Seasonal game is a speciality, and while some items on the menu are distinctly old-fashioned, others show modern sensibilities: salmon carpaccio with rocket sauce, or seared scallops with salsa verde and cracked wheat, for example. Prompt and attentive service is much appreciated. Closed Sat and Sun L and Sun D.

Mezzanine   SE1
National Theatre, South Bank map 13
(0171) 452 3600

On the mezzanine floor, predictably, of the National Theatre with great views of the river only visible from a few tables. Choose from no-choice set meals, or a carte offering 'excellent' fish soup, confit of duck with ceps and a Madeira jus, or 'flavoursome and tender' stuffed chicken breast. Puddings such as chocolate trellis with praline sauce have been described as 'spectacular'. Closed Sun.

Momo   W1
25 Heddon Street   map 15
(0171) 434 4040

Foodie London's attachment to North African cooking continues unabated, which partly explains the difficulty reporters find in booking a table at this still fashionable address, now in its third year. The atmosphere, created by 'over-the-top' Moroccan décor, music and belly dancers, has as much to do with its continuing popularity as the selection of authentic tagines, pastries and grills. But a 'pungent and refreshing' version of brandade made with skate and coriander, and a tagine of duck confit sweetened with pear, carrots and figs, have been among dishes to impress. Open all week.

Moxon's   SW4
14 Clapham Park Road   map 12
(0171) 627 2468

Fish is the business at this modern, bright and lively restaurant on a side road off Clapham Common opened by a former fishmonger. Wooden floors and tables, church chairs, and fishy paintings and designs on Roman blinds set the scene for oysters with spinach, garlic and Parmesan; crab ravioli with seared scallops and a butter sauce; grilled whole bream with ratatouille; or fillet of brill on a potato cake with a tomato and herb sauce. Amaretti crème brûlée has been 'delicious', and a Toblerone parfait 'clever'. Open all week D and Sun L.

New World   W1
1 Gerrard Place   map 15
(0171) 434 2508

'This place is majestic,' enthused one fan of this popular Chinatown venue, who also reckoned that set meals are 'amazing value' and that it is a good place for pre-theatre meals. The long menu is gentle on those not too familiar with Cantonese cooking – a novice praised dim sum despite being perplexed at the format – as it never deviates very far from the standard repertoire, though more esoteric options for the adventurous include shredded jellyfish.

Osteria Basilico   W11
29 Kensington Park Road   map 13
(0171) 727 9957/9372
Busy café-style trattoria with wooden
tables, useful for visitors to Portobello.
Lots of pizzas, pastas and some more
modern dishes such as bruschetta con
pomodoro e rucola, chargrilled swordfish,
or pan-fried strips of beef with spinach
and wild mushrooms in balsamic vinegar
with Parmesan flakes. Takeaway pizzas
also available. Open all week.

Patisserie Valerie   W1
R.I.B.A., 66 Portland Place   map 15
(0171) 580 5533
You would expect a café on the first floor
of the Royal Institute of British
Architects' offices to be well designed,
and Patisserie Valerie does not disappoint.
It is a large room, making good use of
light and with a terrace for warm days. 'A
cut above the usual coffee bar', lunches
might see seared tuna fillet with rocket,
roasted cherry tomatoes, basil and pesto
sauce alongside a confit of duck, plus a
pasta of the day, but cakes and pastries
are particularly recommended. Open
Mon to Sat 8 to 6.

Pizzeria Castello   SE1
20 Walworth Road   map 13
(0171) 703 2556
In this independent pizzeria near the
Elephant and Castle, pasta and pizza in
near infinite variety are the mainstays.
But 'house specials' might include fillet
steak, and some gems from the seafood
treasury: halibut, squid, king prawns and
scampi. Involtini affumicati is an original
starter or main dish, of prawns and
carrots in cocktail sauce, wrapped in
smoked salmon. Service is quick, but they
don't rush you out. Italian wines match
the food in interest, flavour and low
prices. Closed Sat L and all day Sun.

The Poet   EC3
20 Creechurch Lane   map 13
(0171) 623 3999
'City dining for the millennium' is the
aim at this bar/restaurant on a corner site,
with large windows, blue and yellow
walls, overhead TVs showing sport, and
lots of 'buzz and atmosphere'. Expect
oysters served with soda bread; warm
potato salad with sardines and
romanesco, which was a 'visual delight';
and blackened swordfish steak with a
'good' salsa. Finish with coconut and
chocolate parfait which, unusually for a
chocolate dessert, was 'refreshing'. A
change of chef as we went to press, so
more reports please. Open Mon to Fri L.

Poons   WC2
4 Leicester Street   map 15
(0171) 437 1528
'Simple, unassuming, excellent value for
money' is the general consensus on this
Chinatown standard. Rapid turnover and
large capacity mean that queues are
never very long, even at busy periods
(which is most of the time). From a long
menu that never strays too far off the
beaten track, fish cake and turnip
casserole served in an earthenware pot,
and slices of deep-fried chicken with
orange sauce were appealing discoveries
for one couple. Open all week.

Poons   WC2
27 Lisle Street   map 15
(0171) 437 4549
This Chinatown stalwart is still the place
to go for the famous wind-dried meats:
duck, pork, liver and sausages. Plain
pastel walls and a grey tiled floor make
for a pleasant environment, and plastic
table cloths demonstrate that the beauty
is not in the incidentals. This is a noisy,
bustling place and great fun. The menu
ranges from lamb and tofu hotpot to fried
eels with chilli. Drink tea or something
from the short wine list. Open all week.

Poons   W2
Unit 205, Whiteleys,   map 13
151 Queensway
(0171) 792 2884
'A convenient and relaxing stop after a
heavy day's shopping,' was one reporter's
verdict on this branch of Poons, located
upstairs in Whiteleys shopping centre.

Décor is stylish and comfortable and service is notably good. The long carte runs through the standard Cantonese repertoire; reporters have rated aubergine and shredded pork in red bean sauce, quick-fried shredded eels and prawns with chilli anise pepper.

Porte des Indes   W1
32 Bryanston Street   map 13
(0171) 224 0055

Rivalling nearby Marble Arch is the marble waterfall inside this spectacular eating palace. The menu covers the Subcontinent from Parsee sole steamed in banana leaves, to crab Malabar, and Goanese pork vindaloo. It also embraces the tastes of the French Indian colonies with cassoulet de fruits de mer, policha meen (marinated fish), and cheese and herb stuffed aubergine beignets. For an overview of the food take the 'grand menu maison' or a more modest thali (there is a seafood version as well as the usual vegetarian and non-vegetarian options); or try the lunch or Sunday brunch buffet. Closed Sat L.

Randall & Aubin   W1
16 Brewer Street   map 15
(0171) 287 4447

Split personality is no problem for this mini-brasserie specialising in seafood platters and meat from the rotisserie. Grills and roasts sit comfortably with fruits de mer; or choose from the list of hot baguettes. Roast salmon with bok choy, Japanese fish cakes, and caviare are listed as hors d'oeuvres. It is not inexpensive, but what was once Soho's most distinguished butcher-cum-delicatessen is always busy and has kept much of its charm and character.

Saga   W1
43–44 South Molton Street   map 15
(0171) 629 3931

The owners claim that this is the longest-standing Japanese restaurant in the UK. With its old-fashioned décor it certainly looks the part, and the long menu covers all areas of traditional Japanese cooking, from sushi to sukiyaki. The daily specials are reckoned to be a good bet, though since they are often listed without English translations, non-Japanese may have to take pot luck. Drink one of the impressive range of sakés. Closed Sun L.

Selasih   W1
114 Seymour Place   map 13
(0171) 724 4454

Authentic Malaysian food at very reasonable prices (buffet lunch is a bargain £4.95) is served here in a relaxed and cheerful atmosphere set by batik prints, Malay pop music and an animated crowd of cheerful diners. At the time of going to press the restaurant was planning to expand both menus and dining room, and to install an ice machine so that authentic Malaysian desserts could be added to the repertoire. Reports please.

62 Restaurant & Theatre Bar   SE1
62 Southwark Bridge Road   map 13
(0171) 633 0831

Next to Southwark Playhouse, this bright, relaxing place has modern art on the walls for sale, and a view into the kitchen. Getting the thumbs up from reporters have been lightly grilled Serrano ham with cherry tomatoes, rocket and walnut oil; gazpacho with noodles and tiger prawns; and crostini of pigeon breast. Desserts – 'a high point' – have included fragrant poached pear with mango sorbet, and 'exemplary' lemon and rasberry tart. Pre-theatre set dinners available. Closed Sat L and all day Sun.

Sofra   WC2
36 Tavistock Street   map 15
(0171) 240 3773

This is part of an above-average chain of Turkish restaurants that has scaled down recently, though menus remain unchanged. A wide carte lists meze, salads, grills, pastries and seafood; special deals include an excellent-value 'healthy' option, offering a good variety of hot and cold meze for two people. A small cover charge pays for bread fresh from the oven, good olives and – if you are lucky – live guitar music. Branches at 18 Shepherd Street, W1, (0171) 493 3320, and 1 St Christopher's Place, W1, (0171) 224 4080. Open all week.

Sonata   W1
36 Wigmore Street   map 15
(0171) 487 4874

Change of name and ownership for this basement restaurant just beside the main entrance to the concert hall. A short menu is enhanced by a dish of the day and competent, friendly service. A party of five recommended terrine of salmon with sweet mustard sauce, pan-fried calf's liver, and corn-fed breast of chicken with red onion dauphinoise. Almond and apricot tart, apple and cinnamon crème brûlée, and wild berry and praline tiramisù made satisfactory endings. Closed Sun.

La Spighetta   W1
43 Blandford Street   map 15
(0171) 486 7340

A sister to Spiga and under the watchful eye of Giorgio Locatelli of Zafferano (see main entries), this basement restaurant has the *sine qua non* of pizza cookery: a wood-fired oven. Try the version with shrimps, palm hearts and rocket, or the 'Gastone' with beetroot, cherry tomatoes and olives. Alternatively, go for pasta or main courses that may include calf's liver or pan-fried cod with lentils. The tiramisù is worth saving room for. Service has been friendly and efficient. Closed Sun L.

Stafford Hotel   SW1
16–18 St James's Place   map 15
(0171) 493 0111

Opulent but compact hotel in the heart of St James's with prices that suit the area, though set-price menus offer a reasonable alternative to the carte. Chris Oakes's cooking is essentially traditional by nature, dealing in such classics as steak, kidney and real ale pie with black pudding bubble and squeak; duck with orange sauce and Anna potatoes; and

sticky toffee pudding, though occasional nods to fashion turn up in the shape of, for example, poached bream fillet on vegetable couscous with a tomato, olive oil and balsamic dressing. Closed Sat L.

Tatsuso   EC2
32 Broadgate Circle   map 13
(0171) 638 5863

On the ground floor is a teppanyaki bar, while downstairs is a smart dining room with a sushi bar along one wall and well-spaced tables divided by slatted wooden screens. The menu covers all bases: sashimi, soups, braised dishes, grills and tempura, and bento boxes provide a useful lunch option. Prices, particularly of wines, are pitched at expense accounts. Attentive service is from waitresses in kimonos and men in suits. Closed Sat and Sun.

Thai Bistro   W4
99 Chiswick High Road   map 12
(0181) 995 5774

Congregate at long shared tables in this clean-cut, brightly-lit modern noodle shop. There are standard, regional and vegetarian menus, also some encouragement to order Thai-style, sharing dishes to go with rice. Starters include satay, fish cakes, spring rolls and laab (chopped chicken with lemon grass and chilli). Chicken fried with garlic, coriander, galangal and chillies is recommended along with 'reliable' pad Thai noodles with bean curd, dried prawns, ground peanuts and bean sprouts. The vegetarian menu is as long as the carnivore. Closed Tue and Thur L.

3 Monkeys   SE24
136–140 Herne Hill   map 12
(0171) 738 5500

A dramatic conversion has turned this former bank into the latest of the new breed of stylish, upmarket Indian restaurants. The involvement of chef Udit Sarkhel (see Sarkhel's main entry) is cause for optimism, and although much of the menu may sound familiar, early signs are that the cooking is well above curry house average. At the heart of the dining room is the 'theatre kitchen' where, in full view of diners on the floor above, chefs show off their traditional skills, including use of the tandoor, tawa and sigri grill. Closed Mon.

Toffs   NW10
38 Muswell Hill Broadway   map 12
(0181) 883 8656
'Haddock and chips are always excellent,' according to a regular at this Muswell Hill chippie. Fish is fried to order, batter is crisp and grease-free, and extras include 'very good' home-made tartare sauce, and 'the best gherkins I have come across'. Those who insist on three courses can start with prawn cocktail, and round off a truly English meal with spotted dick and custard. Closed Sun and Mon.

Vama – The Indian Room   SW10
438 Kings Road   map 14
(0171) 351 4118
Classy, expensive Chelsea Indian specialising in the cooking of the northwest, much of which involves the tandoor. Crab, lobster, quail, venison, duck and partridge are among the more esoteric items to be given the clay oven treatment, as well as the usual chicken and lamb. Half of the menu is given over to interesting vegetarian dishes such as field mushrooms stuffed with paneer cheese and pomegranate, or spiced okra deep-fried in chickpea batter. Open all week.

Vasco & Piero's Pavilion   W1
15 Poland Street   map 15
(0171) 437 8774
The Pavilion provides a simple but elegant environment with warm apricot walls, modern pictures and flower arrangements. An excellent-value fixed-price Italian menu might offer fresh pappardelle with strips of marinated salmon, followed by triangles of grilled polenta with asparagus and Parmesan, or grilled breast of 'gamey' guinea fowl with juniper berries and mixed julienne

vegetables. Good strong coffee to finish. Closed Sat L and Sun.

Village Bistro   N6
38 Highgate High Street   map 12
(0181) 340 5165/0257
Neighbourhood French bistro with relaxed atmosphere and friendly service. Lunch is a set menu, dinner à la carte, both with similar offerings along the lines of baked field mushrooms with Stilton, or brandade of smoked haddock to start, followed by escalope of veal with blue cheese mash, fried egg and capers, or halibut steak with dill. Desserts range from white chocolate and cappuccino parfait to orange mousse with two chocolate sauces; a short wine list includes nine half-bottles. Open all week.

Vrisaki   N22
73 Myddleton Road   map 12
(0181) 889 8760
Although quite unprepossessing from the outside, once past the take-away counter a vast dining room is revealed, serving what one reporter called 'the best Greek food in London'. The special meze meal for two has been praised, but it is not for the faint-hearted, opening with over a dozen cold starters, including good home-made taramasalata and hummus, plus various dips and salads, moving on to smoked mackerel and salmon, and finally the grilled meats: sheftalia, lamb chops and lamb shish kebab. Service goes at a pace. Closed Sun.

Willie Gunn's   SW18
422 Garrett Lane   map 12
(0181) 946 7773
Modern British cuisine is delivered at this wine bar and large-windowed restaurant on a corner of a busy road in Earlsfield. Crab spring rolls, or eggs Benedict with a toasted muffin, might be a good way to begin, before lemon sole with roasted fennel, or roast pheasant with beetroot mash. Soda bread is recommended. Finish with a selection of cheeses, ice creams or sorbets. Open all week.

Wodka W8

12 St Albans Grove map 14
(0171) 937 6513
Here you can be relaxed or stimulated by the eponymous vodkas and the feng shui-ed décor. It's a heady mix and so is the menu, firmly based in Poland with a few 'modern eclectic' additions. Crayfish, herrings, warm smoked eel, barscz (borscht), or kazanka (black sausage) might be followed by rabbit with spinach and boczek, roast duck with apricot and spring onion, or poached salt beef with coleslaw and hot pepper relish. Finish with cheesecake, apple strudel or, to clear the head, vodka marinated berries. Closed Sat and Sun L.

Yo! Sushi W1

52 Poland Street map 15
(0171) 287 0443
A bright, noisy conveyor-belt sushi bar where nori rolls and nigiri sushi are produced by machines, and robot drinks trolleys trundle round dispensing drinks. There are also human chefs and waiters (attracted by pressing a help button) who take orders for specials, warm saké and cooked items (miso soup, teriyaki, tempura). The Soho original has been cloned in new branches at Harvey Nichols Food Hall, SW1, (0171) 235 6114; Oz Complex, Finchley Road, NW6, (0171) 431 4494; Selfridges, W1, (0171) 318 3944 and Bluewater Shopping Centre, Kent, (01322) 383555. Open all week.

Yoshino W1

3 Piccadilly Place map 15
(0171) 287 6622
Good-value authentic Japanese restaurant hidden down an alley off Piccadilly. Some English has crept into the long menu, but it probably still helps to take a Japanese friend, since some of the translations are not terribly informative. In any case, you will need a second person to be able to order the speciality, oden, comprising various ingredients of your choice from a long list (perhaps scallops, tofu and mooli) cooked in a light broth. Closed Sun.

England

ALDEBURGH Suffolk   map 6

Lighthouse 🍴✻ £

77 High Street, Aldeburgh IP15 5AU	COOKING **4**
TEL/FAX: (01728) 453377	COST £20–£37

Eager reporters testify to the ongoing popularity of the Lighthouse, which traditionally has jostled for culinary prominence with Regatta (see entry below). It resembles a shop from the outside (a former incarnation), but makes good, bistroesque use of its ground-floor dining room, patio and first-floor no-smoking area. There are no frills to the décor, which takes in bare pine tables, linen napkins, colourful pictures and posters advertising local events, and 'no silly extras' to pay for on the menu. The ever evolving repertoire allows for informal lunches of Peasenhall ham with two free-range fried eggs and a handful of thick chips, followed by 'dark and crispy' walnut flan with toffee ice cream; at dinner, perhaps six Loch Fyne oysters with shallot vinegar, then irresistible variations on the local seafood trail, such as grilled Aldeburgh cod with scallops on spinach. Diners' small caveats – calf's liver could have been better trimmed – are balanced by an appreciation of the warm and cheerful service and of most dishes' overall success in terms of flavour and imagination. Anything that isn't made on the premises (such as ice cream) is bought in from an enviable network of local suppliers. The seventy-strong wine list meanders the world, with most bottles under £20 and a sprinkling of half-bottles; seven house wines are £10.95 or less.

CHEFS: Sara E. Fox and Guy Welsh   PROPRIETORS: Sara E. Fox and Peter G.R. Hill   OPEN: all week 12 to 2.30, 7 to 10 (earlier and later by arrangement)   CLOSED: 2 weeks Jan, 1 week Oct   MEALS: alc L (main courses £6 to £10). Set D £13.50 (2 courses) to £15.75   SERVICE: not inc, card slips closed   CARDS: Delta, MasterCard, Switch, Visa   DETAILS: 95 seats. 25 seats outside. Private parties: 45 main room, 20 and 25 private rooms. Vegetarian meals. No smoking in 1 dining room. Wheelchair access (also WC). No music. Air-conditioned (£5)

Regatta 🍴✻ £

171 High Street, Aldeburgh IP15 5AN	COOKING **4**
TEL/FAX: (01728) 452011	COST £18–£45

It's all hands on deck at this brisk and shipshape seafood restaurant: a busy night found the proprietor out the back smoking sprats, a 'jolly local lady' waiting on tables, and kitchen staff coming out to help towards the end of the evening. The blackboard menu has become more focused of late, offering immaculately fresh local fish, 'perfectly and simply cooked' and served with bright-tasting sauces such as watercress tartare or black olive dressing. Home-smoked fish is a speciality; mussels with saffron dipping sauce, or a risotto of 'succulent' smoked squid, peas and broad beans. Meat dishes attract as much praise, with one reporter singling out an 'intensely gamey' pithiviers of pheasant and 'perfectly roasted' partridge. Puddings range from the classic (crème brûlée, lemon tart) to the playful (pussyfoot piña colada sorbet). A children's menu offers real cooking rather than junk-food equivalents, and Regatta will even pack up a beach picnic for you. The short wine list adds to the impression of all-round good value, with house wine at £9.50.

CHEF: R.E. Mabey   PROPRIETORS: Mr and Mrs R.E. Mabey   OPEN: all week 12 to 2 (2.30 Sat and Sun), 6 to 10 (later during concerts)   CLOSED: Wed and Thur Nov to end Mar   MEALS: alc (main courses £7 to £18). Set L and D 6 to 7 £8 (2 courses) to £10   SERVICE: not inc   CARDS: Amex, Delta, Diners, MasterCard, Switch, Visa   DETAILS: 100 seats. 6 seats outside. Private parties: 40 main room, 30 private room. Vegetarian meals. Children's menu (exc Sat D). No smoking in 1 dining room. Occasional music   £5

ALTRINCHAM   Greater Manchester   map 8

Juniper

21 The Downs, Altrincham WA14 2QD   COOKING 7
TEL: (0161) 929 4008   FAX: (0161) 929 4009   COST £34–£63

It is four years since the citizens of Altrincham woke to find Paul Kitching and his refined cooking on their doorstep. The kitchen of the terraced suburban dining room is a source of skilfully prepared food, typically presented as an appealing carte, although some Fridays bring themed, set-price, multi-course dinners: perhaps of fish, lamb, or an unusual white poultry and egg meal, offering a centrepiece of grilled corn-fed chicken breast with poached egg and dill butter sauce. Fish is a strength – perhaps two moist fillets of braised codling in a red wine sauce – and timing and seasoning are spot on. The challenge to serve offal in Altrincham – albeit foie gras or veal sweetbreads – continues, producing for one reporter a contrasting study in sweetness: a lobe of rich foie gras hidden in a light creamy, frothy parsnip soup.

Saucing tends towards slicks of this and that: sweet, nutty, chargrilled scallops on a thin herb pancake, with dabs of balsamic glaze and oil-based emulsion, or a layered terrine of 'juicy, gamey' quail meat, alternating with carrot and leek, bound in a jellied stock, surrounded by dots of oil and sauce verte. Presentation is impressive, the elements in a dish attractively arranged without help from unnecessary garnishes: indeed those looking to Juniper for their daily intake of five portions of vegetables will not be swallowing the government's recommended amount.

Ideas and combinations all seem to work effectively, whether a savoury pink pigeon breast, arranged on a disc of black pudding, or a signature rice pudding soufflé served with rosemary ice cream. Bread, usually a choice of two or three, is 'exemplary' and coffee comes with 'impeccable' petits fours from an accomplished pastry chef. There may be a lot of effort behind the scenes, but all is calm, unhurried yet well-drilled out front. Prices on the annotated, French-dominated wine list have raised a few eyebrows. House vin de pays is £17 (£4 a glass).

CHEF: Paul Kitching   PROPRIETORS: Nora and Peter Miles   OPEN: Tue to Fri L 12 to 2, Mon to Sat D 7 to 10   CLOSED: 1 week summer, bank hols   MEALS: alc (main courses L £11 to £16, D £15 to £20)   SERVICE: not inc, card slips closed   CARDS: Amex, Delta, MasterCard, Switch, Visa   DETAILS: 45 seats. Private parties: 28 main room, 12 private room. No children. Music. Air-conditioned (£5)

ALVECHURCH Worcestershire   map 5

Mill ♥

Radford Road, Alvechurch B48 7LD   COOKING 3
TEL: (0121) 447 7005   FAX: (0121) 447 8001   COST £24–£44

Especially pretty when lit up at night, the tall, red-brick old mill stands back from the busy main road, attracting many Birmingham residents to the 'solid, comfy, safe' restaurant within. White walls, dark beams and cane furniture typify the interior, where a 'friendly, chatty welcome' is provided by members of the McKernon family, whose 'down-to-earth Brumminess' is found refreshing. Supplementing the carte are 'excellent-value' set dinner menus that change monthly. The food tends to veer away from adventure towards 'good, fresh flavours' based on quality ingredients treated with technical adeptness. Reporters have enjoyed 'a generous plateful' of duck breast with caramelised banana and black pepper, and warmed goats' cheese served with thin char-grilled slices of aubergine, red pepper and courgette. Smoked haddock and potato soup with crispy leeks gets the thumbs up, as do roast rack of lamb with a herb crust and rosemary sauce, and lemon tart with 'zesty' lime sorbet. Stylish wines on the main list (supplied by Tanners of Shrewsbury) are attractively priced, but do take a look at the fine wine section for mature French and Spanish classics and vintage ports, also priced favourably. House wine is £9.25.

CHEF: Carl Timms   PROPRIETORS: Geoffrey, Vivienne and Stefan McKernon   OPEN: Tue to Sat D only 7 to 8.30 (9.15 Fri and Sat)   CLOSED: first week Jan, first two weeks Aug   MEALS: alc (main courses £12.50 to £17). Set D Tue to Thur £15 (2 courses) to £17.50   SERVICE: not inc CARDS: Amex, Delta, MasterCard, Switch, Visa   DETAILS: 30 seats. Private parties: 30 main room. Car park. Vegetarian meals. No children under 5. No smoking in dining room. Music (£5)

AMBERLEY West Sussex   map 3

▲ *Amberley Castle, Queen's Room* 🛏 ✳

Amberley BN18 9ND
TEL: (01798) 831992   FAX: (01798) 831998   COOKING 5
on B2139, between Storrington and Bury Hill   COST £32–£57

White peacocks and peahens patrol the grounds of this ancient pile of stone, while someone with 'remarkable taste' has given the suits of armour soft toy monkeys to hold. The east wing went up in 1103, but the main body of the castle dates from the late fourteenth century. Much is now a picturesque ruin but the barrel-vaulted dining room lays claim to a section of the older part. The most recent addition is Billy Butcher, former sous-chef at Gravetye Manor, (see entry, East Grinstead), who arrived in May 1999 to put his stamp on the cooking.

A degree of indulgence is perhaps warranted in these surroundings – duck confit and foie gras terrine, for example, or pithiviers of globe artichoke with truffled new potatoes – but luxuries are not overdone. An industrious kitchen partners main courses with light mousses, mousselines and the like: a lemony, frothy 'cappuccino' in the case of first-class, accurately roasted Rye Bay scallops on a mound of tomato risotto. Dinner is six courses, including an appetiser, an intermediate soup or salad, and tiny 'slivers' of cheese, after a dessert of maybe dark cherry soufflé with pecan ice cream and thick, creamy, vanilla-speckled custard. Service can be rather 'stiff and formal', and wines are mostly French and expensive, although southern France offers a good selection under £20, and half a dozen house wines start at £13.95 (£4.50 a glass).

CHEF: Billy Butcher   PROPRIETORS: Martin and Joy Cummings   OPEN: all week 12 to 2, 7 to 9   MEALS: Set L £12.50 (2 courses) to £17.50, Set D £35   SERVICE: not inc, card slips closed   CARDS: Amex, Delta, Diners, MasterCard, Switch, Visa   DETAILS: 60 seats. 20 seats outside. Private parties: 48 main room, 12 private room. Car park. Vegetarian meals. No children under 12 in dining room. Jacket and tie. No smoking in dining room. Occasional music   ACCOMMODATION: 20 rooms, all with bath/shower. TV. Phone. B&B £145 to £300. No children under 12 in accommodation

---

AMBLESIDE Cumbria   map 8

Glass House ⅚✶

Rydal Road, Ambleside LA22 9AN	COOKING 3
TEL: (01539) 432137 FAX: (01539) 431139	COST £19–£42

Next to a glass factory under the same ownership, this converted mill occupies several open-plan floors. The space is full of character (local oak and other traditional materials went into its reconstruction), and the format is flexibly geared to the variety of needs that visitors bring. There is a children's menu, a one- or two-course lunch for a fiver, and an 'early doors' price concession before 8pm, as well as a carte offering as many vegetable and fish options as meat ones. Starter assemblies of vegetables and salads (broad bean, feta and pickled tomato on olive flat bread, for example) are followed by chargrilled tuna with tapénade fritter, pot roast lamb shank with Moroccan spices, or deep-fried courgette and spinach risotto cakes. Desserts keep up the interest with rhubarb and ginger Alaska, and warm chocolate fondant with peanut butter ice cream. An Italian red and white at £8.95 kick off the nearly thirty-strong wine list – with almost all bottles under £20 – or opt for one of the bottled beers.

CHEF: Stuart Birkett   PROPRIETOR: Adrian Sankey   OPEN: all week 12 (11 weekends) to 10   CLOSED: 25 Dec   MEALS: alc (main courses L £4.50 to £7, D £8 to £15). Set L Mon to Fri £5 (1 or 2 courses), Set D 6 to 8 £9.95 (2 courses)   SERVICE: not inc, card slips closed   CARDS: Amex, MasterCard, Switch, Visa   DETAILS: 80 seats. 30 seats outside. Private parties: 100 main room. Car park. Vegetarian meals. Children's helpings. No smoking in dining room. Wheelchair access (not WC). Music   (£5)

All entries, including Round-ups, are fully indexed at the back of the Guide.

▲ *Rothay Manor* ♟ ⚞✗

Rothay Bridge, Ambleside LA22 0EH
TEL: (015394) 33605   FAX: (015394) 33607
EMAIL: hotel@rothaymanor.co.uk
off A593 to Coniston, ¼m W of Ambleside

COOKING 3
COST £21–£48

An elegant white building fronted by an immaculate lawn, Rothay is comfortably furnished with armchairs and settees, an open fire, and plenty of flowers. It 'puts you in a good frame of mind' for what is to come: anything from two to five courses at dinner, with three choices at the main stages. Its traditional predilection produces a thick slice of rough pork terrine with a pool of Cumberland sauce to begin, broccoli and chervil soup to follow, and maybe a satisfyingly plump leg and breast of 'strong-flavoured, moist, dark' mallard in rosemary sauce for main course. Finish perhaps with a charlotte filled with strawberry mousse, or a hot apple and mixed-fruit pie in a creamy custard. All is delivered by efficient but unhurried service. Wines range from old-fashioned (Mateus Rosé, anyone?) to bang-up-to-date: d'Arenberg in South Australia's McLaren Vale, for example. Prices start at a lowly £12 for house wines and remain fair even when the giddy heights of first-growth clarets are reached. Halves and their equivalents (half a whole bottle at three-fifths of the full price) are generous too.

CHEFS: Jane Binns and Colette Nixon   PROPRIETORS: Nigel and Stephen Nixon   OPEN: all week 12.30 (12.45 Sun) to 2 (1.30 Sun), 7.45 to 9   CLOSED: 3 Jan to 3 Feb   MEALS: Set L £13.50, Set D £24 (2 courses) to £30. Light L available Mon to Sat   SERVICE: not inc, card slips closed CARDS: Amex, Delta, Diners, MasterCard, Switch, Visa   DETAILS: 70 seats. Private parties: 36 main room, 34 private room. Car park. Vegetarian meals. Children's helpings. No children under 10 at D. No smoking in dining room. Wheelchair access (also WC). No music. Air-conditioned ACCOMMODATION: 18 rooms, all with bath/shower. TV. Phone. B&B £70 to £170. Rooms for disabled. Baby facilities (*The Which? Hotel Guide*) £5

AMERSHAM Buckinghamshire   map 3

Kings Arms

30 High Street, Old Amersham HP7 0DJ
TEL: (01494) 726333   FAX: (01494) 433480

COOKING 2
COST £22–£45

This black and white pub-restaurant in the antique-shopped old part of town is a 'long, straggly' building that shows its fourteenth-century origins in beams and creaking floorboards. Food is much more up-to-date, presented smartly on large white plates set against white tablecloths with fresh flowers and candles. Reporters have found that some dishes promised more than they delivered, but one enjoyed 'tender, moist' marinated beef on a bed of cold fennel, dotted round with tiny chunks of beetroot and tomato, followed by 'flaky, melt-in-the-mouth' salmon, with mustard and dill sauce and 'spaghetti' of vegetables, and a dark chocolate gâteau surrounded by a pretty patterned coulis of raspberry and sugar. House Chilean red and South African white are £10, and plenty of distinguished wines are to be had for under £20.

CHEF: Gary Munday PROPRIETOR: John Jennison OPEN: Tue to Sun L 12 to 2, Tue to Sat D 7 to 9.30 CLOSED: 4 days Christmas MEALS: alc Tue to Sat (main courses £13 to £16.50). Set L Tue to Sat £10.50 (2 courses) to £13.50, Set L Sun £16, Set D Tue to Fri £17, Set D Sat £25 SERVICE: not inc CARDS: Amex, Delta, Diners, MasterCard, Switch, Visa DETAILS: 30 seats. Private parties: 50 main room, 12 to 50 private rooms. Car park. Vegetarian meals. Children's helpings. No cigars/pipes in dining room. Wheelchair access (not WC). No music (£5)

APPLETHWAITE Cumbria   map 10

▲ *Underscar Manor* ⁵✳

Applethwaite CA12 4PH
TEL: (017687) 75000   FAX: (017687) 74904   COOKING 6
off A66, ½m N of Keswick   COST £36–£78

This 'not to be missed' Italianate villa is well sited in 40 acres, with Skiddaw behind and Derwentwater out front. It appears to be at the centre of a wildlife theme park, with a lawn full of red squirrels and an ever increasing display of toy bears and squirrels decorating the lounge, but the major achievement is a reliable ten-year partnership between owners and chef. It is one of few places round about to take lunch as seriously as dinner, both offering a full carte in which Robert Thornton makes good use of modish partnerships, particularly among first courses: spicy couscous with seared scallops, for example.

Quality and freshness of materials are not in question, their handling typically expert: in a simple starter of herb-crusted halibut, maybe, or seared foie gras with brandied grapes and Sauternes sauce. Main courses tread more traditional ground, perhaps roast saddle of local venison with half a dozen vegetables, or a well-balanced ragoût of lobster in its own broth with pasta and quenelles. A mini-selection of seven desserts of 'breathtaking quality' shows the kitchen's skills to good effect, and the cheeseboard comes in for praise too. On the downside, some dishes may appear rather involved, to the extent that accompaniments can take over, and one who ate the 'surprise' menu of six courses (the first more of an appetiser, the last coffee) felt it did not meet the expected standard. Aside from that, staff are knowledgeable, and 'impeccable in presentation and manner', and the largely French wine list does not ignore those of modest means. House French is £15.

CHEF: Robert Thornton PROPRIETORS: Pauline and Derek Harrison, and Gordon Evans OPEN: all week 12 to 1, 7 to 8.30 (9 Sat) MEALS: alc (main courses £19 to £28). Set L £25, Set D £30 SERVICE: not inc, card slips closed CARDS: Amex, MasterCard, Switch, Visa DETAILS: 50 seats. 16 seats outside. Private parties: 30 main room. Car park. Vegetarian meals. No children under 12 in dining room. Jacket and tie. No smoking in dining room. No music ACCOMMODATION: 11 rooms, all with bath/shower. TV. Phone. D,B&B £95 to £250. No children under 12 in accommodation (*The Which? Hotel Guide*)

'[The restaurant's] "famous" fish cake was obviously famous for having little fish in it, although we made out bits of salmon and a coddy white fish. "Famous potato cake" would have been nearer the mark.' (On eating in Hampshire)

ARNCLIFFE North Yorkshire   map 8

▲ *Amerdale House* ✱

Arncliffe, Littondale BD23 5QE   COOKING 4
TEL: (01756) 770250 FAX: (01756) 770266   COST £39–£47

Whether viewed as a remote corner of the Yorkshire Dales, or as slap bang in the middle of good walking country, Amerdale is a quiet, spacious country house with an appealingly informal approach. Nigel Crapper is a hands-on proprietor, who 'clearly loves to cook', as he does seven days a week during the season, although this year he has an assistant, enabling him to extend the repertoire a little. Dinner is four courses, the first offering a salad, something fruity, or maybe mushroom tart, followed by pasta, fish, or a flavourful tomato and basil soup. The style is simple, not too rich, using first-rate materials, including notably fresh fish: deep-fried halibut with salsa verde, perhaps.

Main courses typically offer a straight choice between meat and fish – crisp-skinned chargrilled breast of barbary duck has impressed – before one of two desserts such as chocolate tart or blackberry and apple crumble with custard; the alternative is a plate of local cheeses that might take in Coverdale, Blue Wensleydale or Swaledale goats'. Bread is highly rated, and service is friendly, 'graceful and professional'. A good selection under £20 is a feature of the compact yet interestingly varied round-the-world wine list, which does well for half-bottles and starts with house wine around £13 (£2.95 a glass).

CHEFS: Nigel Crapper and Anthony Chamley PROPRIETORS: Paula and Nigel Crapper OPEN: all week D only 7.30 to 8.30 CLOSED: mid-Nov to mid-Mar MEALS: Set D £29 SERVICE: not inc, card slips closed CARDS: MasterCard, Switch, Visa DETAILS: 24 seats. Car park. Children's helpings. No children under 7 in dining room. No smoking in dining room. No music ACCOMMODATION: 11 rooms, all with bath/shower. TV. Phone. D,B&B £77 to £137. Baby facilities (*The Which? Hotel Guide*)

ASENBY North Yorkshire   map 9

▲ *Crab & Lobster* ✱

Dishforth Road, Asenby YO7 3QL
TEL: (01845) 577286 FAX: (01845) 577109   COOKING 2
off A168, between A19 and A1   COST £25–£53

Not surprisingly, fish is the main attraction at this exuberantly themed pub, with thatched crabs crawling across a thatched roof, lobster pots festooning the walls, and every available inch crammed with bric-à-brac (including a six-foot wooden alligator). The menu, too, is pretty crowded, causing an obviously talented kitchen staff to slip up occasionally. The restaurant offers classically inclined dishes (lobster thermidor, grilled Dover sole), while the brasserie – stand at the bar to order – goes for a more global approach (halibut and blue lobster Thai curry, Cajun whitebait). Carnivores are not neglected, and the chips are great. Puddings seem to have been inspired by a raid on a sweet shop – Milky Bar truffle cake, Malteser ice cream – but also include crème brúlée and lemon tart. Waiting staff do a sterling job weaving between packed tables. The wine list is

219

divided by style, so you can choose between ripe and plummy or gentle and soft. House wine is £10.95.

CHEFS: Steve Dean and David Barnard   PROPRIETORS: David and Jackie Barnard   OPEN: all week 12 to 2.30, 6.30 to 10 (12 to 10 Sun Easter to Sept)   MEALS: alc (main courses £11.50 to £19.50). Set L £14.95, Set D Sun to Fri £19.95. 'Garden jazz barbecue' Sun in summer £12.50 SERVICE: not inc, card slips closed   CARDS: Amex, Delta, MasterCard, Switch, Visa   DETAILS: 140 seats. 80 seats outside. Private parties: 70 main room, 8 to 70 private rooms. Car park. Vegetarian meals. Children's helpings. No smoking in dining room. Occasional music ACCOMMODATION: 10 rooms, all with bath/shower. TV. Phone. B&B £65 to £85. Rooms for disabled

---

ASHBOURNE Derbyshire   map 8

▲ *Callow Hall* ♟ ⁵⅟⁄✳

Mappleton Road, Ashbourne DE6 2AA
TEL: (01335) 343403   FAX: (01335) 343624
¾m NW of Ashbourne, turn left off A515 at crossroads
with Bowling Green pub on left; Mappleton Road first   COOKING 4
on right   COST £28–£59

Callow Hall is very much a do-everything family concern: bacon is cured, sausages made, marmalades stirred, fish chosen from the early-morning slab. Catering is in the Spencer blood, with sixth-generation Anthony alongside his father David in the kitchen, and Emma together with her mother Dorothy providing good-natured and professional service. A meal here is an elegant and well-paced country-house experience. Swags, tassels and chandeliers abound. Sip your drink in one of the squashy sofas in the bar before removing to the dramatic red or the elegant greeny-yellow dining room. For a Cook's tour of the kitchen's capabilities, consider grilled red mullet with tapénade dressing; roast guinea fowl laid on a mound of tangy onion marmalade, its leg stuffed with sausage meat and pistachio nuts, poured round with a rich wine sauce; or a creamy-textured peach sorbet. Potatoes come three ways, along with crisp turnips and mange-tout. Helpings are not for the faint-hearted, and it would be a shame to miss out on the glorious concoction of almonds, apples, apricots and mincemeat that goes into Callow flan, or a warm raspberry and blackberry frangipane tart with custard. Sunday lunch is a more straightforward affair. Wines – just names, no annotations – come from around the world, and drinkers have no need to leap over the £30 hurdle unless they wish to try some of the finer French offerings. House wines start at £11.20.

CHEFS: David and Anthony Spencer   PROPRIETORS: David, Dorothy and Anthony Spencer OPEN: Sun L 12 to 1.30, Mon to Sat D 7.15 to 9 (Sun D residents only)   CLOSED: 25 and 26 Dec, 1 Jan   MEALS: alc D (main courses £19 to £20). Set L Sun £19.50, Set D £37   SERVICE: not inc CARDS: Amex, Diners, MasterCard, Switch, Visa   DETAILS: 60 seats. Private parties: 35 main room, 20 and 25 private rooms. Car park. Vegetarian meals. Children's helpings. No smoking in dining room. Wheelchair access (also WC). No music   ACCOMMODATION: 16 rooms, all with bath/shower. TV. Phone. B&B £80 to £150. Rooms for disabled. Baby facilities. Fishing (*The Which? Hotel Guide*)

AYLESBURY Buckinghamshire   map 3

▲ *Hartwell House* ⁵⅍

Oxford Road, Aylesbury HP17 8NL
TEL: (01296) 747444   FAX: (01296) 747450
EMAIL: info@hartwell-house.com   COOKING 4
on A418, 2m from Aylesbury towards Oxford   COST £34–£64

For 'luxurious surroundings and attention to detail', one couple reckoned this history-steeped country-house hotel hard to beat. Standing in 90 acres of parkland, with a trout lake and ruined church, it comes with impeccable historical credentials – it was once home to exiled King Louis XVIII of France – and a grandiose feel to match. If the food seems pricey, therefore, it shouldn't take a rocket scientist to work out that we are paying for the surroundings as well as a degree of luxury and refinement in the cooking. Roger Barstow wheels out champagne, oysters and caviare to make a sauce for salmon, and knocks up a truffle dressing to accompany a starter trio of wood pigeon, venison and quail. In addition, he rings the seasonal changes – red mullet on a potato and fennel purée with spinach and asparagus in early summer, for example – and takes puddings seriously, turning out a banana trio that has included a tiny banoffi pie, a parfait, and 'light and crisp' banana fritters. 'Service, from the moment the massive oak door swung open, was knowledgeable and attentive.' Wines are clearly aimed at the well heeled – if you wish to pay £55 for a bottle of Cloudy Bay Sauvignon Blanc 1997, you may – but tread carefully through the rather grand list, and some affordable bins will reveal themselves. Half a dozen French house wines cost £13.90 or more.

CHEF: Roger Barstow   PROPRIETOR: Historic House Hotels Ltd   OPEN: all week 12.30 to 1.45, 7.30 to 9.30   CLOSED: dining-room closed to non-residents Christmas to New Year   MEALS: Set L £20.50 (2 courses) to £27.50, Set D £44   SERVICE: net prices, card slips closed   CARDS: Delta, MasterCard, Switch, Visa   DETAILS: 60 seats. 20 seats outside. Private parties: 60 main room, 18 to 60 private rooms. Car park. Vegetarian meals. No children under 8 in dining-room. Jacket and tie at D. No smoking in dining room. Wheelchair access (2 steps; also WC). Occasional music   ACCOMMODATION: 46 rooms, all with bath/shower. TV. Phone. Room only £130 to £365. Rooms for disabled. No children under 8 in accommodation. Swimming pool. Fishing (*The Which? Hotel Guide*) £5

AYMESTREY Herefordshire   map 5

▲ *Riverside Inn* ⁵⅍ £   [NEW ENTRY]

Aymestrey HR6 9ST
TEL: (01568) 708440   FAX: (01568) 709058   COOKING 1
on A4110, 6m NW of Leominster   COST £19–£41

Occupying two floors of a long, well-preserved half-timbered sixteenth-century inn on the banks of the River Lugg, this is 'very much the local pub'. Lawns and trestle tables beckon in fine weather, and a convivial atmosphere prevails; indeed its complete lack of pretence is an undoubted plus, from the dining room's rough stone walls and well-spaced bare wooden tables, to André Cluzeau's 'dead simple' food. He cooks a longish menu, supplemented by a

ENGLAND

blackboard of daily Cornish seafood that might include seared scallops of 'pristine freshness' with a dressed salad.

Free-range and locally reared meat features among materials – three cutlets of Marches lamb on a mound of ratatouille-like vegetables for an inspector – the garden supplies some herbs and saladings, and game (perhaps well-hung venison with red cabbage) comes from local shoots. Improveable vegetables are served separately, and puddings, which don't appear to vary much, might include ice creams, lemon tart, and fruit crumbles. A basic laminated wine list starts with house Australian at £9.95.

CHEFS: André Cluzeau, Marcel Hilhorst and Simon Lewis   PROPRIETORS: Steve and Val Bowen   OPEN: all week 12 to 2.30, 7 to 9.45   CLOSED: 25 Dec   MEALS: alc (main courses £5 to £15). Light L available Mon to Fri   SERVICE: not inc, card slips closed   CARDS: Delta, MasterCard, Switch, Visa   DETAILS: 80 seats. 40 seats outside. Private parties: 40 main room, 12 to 40 private rooms. Car park. Vegetarian meals. Children's helpings. No children under 7 in dining room. No smoking in 1 dining room. No music   ACCOMMODATION: 5 rooms, all with bath/shower. TV. B&B £25 to £60. Rooms for disabled. Fishing (£5)

BAKEWELL Derbyshire   map 8

Renaissance ⅝✳

Bath Street, Bakewell DE45 1BX   COOKING 3
TEL: (01629) 812687   COST £29–£47

After the small but comfortable bar, the spacious dining room comes as quite a surprise, with its pitched ceiling, beams, stone walls and a view through French windows on to a garden. Service is 'attentive and relaxed', and food decidedly French, a reflection of Eric Piedaniel's origins. Cream, butter and eggs frequently feature, as in a starter of lobster and chicken cervelas: a rich sausage filled with a smooth mousseline of chicken, eggs and cream, studded with lobster and served on a sauce of cream and spring onions. Other choices might be grilled sardines with new potatoes and a parsley noisette butter, or a terrine of pheasant and foie gras of 'good flavour'. A complimentary sorbet – say, white Burgundy and cinnamon – arrives inter-course, to be followed by perhaps spinach and Parmesan soufflé with a white wine and mustard sauce; or 'pink, quite tender and well-flavoured' medallions of venison, complete with a whole poached pear, Cassis sauce and broccoli purée. Ice cream makes a good choice from the extensive dessert menu. The wine list kicks off in France before venturing into the New World, with a representative each from Spain and Italy. House wines are £9.99.

CHEF: E. Piedaniel   PROPRIETORS: E. and C. Piedaniel, and D. Béraud   OPEN: Tue to Sun L 12 to 2, Tue to Sat D 7 to 9.30   CLOSED: first 2 weeks Jan, first 2 weeks Aug   MEALS: Set L and D £19.95 plus supplements. Bar L available   SERVICE: not inc   CARDS: Delta, MasterCard, Switch, Visa   DETAILS: 70 seats. Private parties: 50 main room, 25 private room. Vegetarian meals. Children's helpings. No smoking in dining room. Wheelchair access (also WC). Music

'Service was professional, helpful, highly trained, except for not knowing which dish was for who, or what was in things.' (On eating in Somerset)

BARNET Hertfordshire   map 3

Mims

63 East Barnet Road, Barnet EN4 8RN	COOKING 6
TEL/FAX: (0181) 449 2974, changing to (020) 8449 2974	COST £24–£34

If this low-key, understated restaurant is 'slightly eccentric', then most reporters count that as a plus. Don't expect luxury. Sitting in a suburban row of shops, it wastes no effort on carpets or tablecloths, although investment in mirrors and a tiled floor has given it a feeling of 'warm minimalism', and it does splash out on paper napkins for dinner. Typically described as 'imaginative', Ali Al-Sersy's food might take in an unlikely-sounding but successful aubergine and cheese pancake, turn crab into a sausage or pack it into ravioli, and use smoked flavours: in soups (smoked tomato with basil froth) or in the shape of smoked chicken with pasta and mushrooms.

Fresh ingredients and accurate timing can be taken for granted, presentation is a colourful delight (grilled mackerel served with grilled asparagus wrapped in red pepper), and materials are layered and towers built, all without recourse to extraneous materials. In the meantime, the simple-sounding handwritten menu does not give much away. 'Banana ice cream', for example, has produced a slice of pineapple surmounted by two banana-shaped lengths of dense, creamy, intensely flavoured banana ice cream, the plate decorated with caramelised banana. There may be longueurs in service ('just settle in and don't rush them,' advises one) although it is polite, courteous and generally efficient. Not all reporters are equally thrilled with the food, and it would not be the first choice for vegetarians, but supporters consider it 'the best food for miles around' (the words 'oasis' and 'desert' have been pressed into service) and 'superb value' with it. Thirty wines stay mostly below £20, starting with house French at £9.50.

CHEF/PROPRIETOR: A. Al-Sersy   OPEN: Tue to Fri 12 to 2.30, 6.30 to 10.30, Sat 12.30 to 11, Sun 12.30 to 10.30   MEALS: Set L £10.50 (2 courses), Set D £14 (2 courses) to £18.50   SERVICE: not inc   CARDS: Delta, MasterCard, Visa   DETAILS: 45 seats. Private parties: 60 main room. Wheelchair access (also WC). Music £5

BARNSLEY South Yorkshire   map 9

Armstrongs ♟

102 Dodworth Road, Barnsley S70 6HL	COOKING 4
TEL: (01226) 240113	COST £37–£50

At a time when many restaurants think of tempting in customers with early-evening deals, two-course options and the like, Nick Pound is heading in the opposite direction. 'We have dropped lunches, vegetarian menus and cheap deals,' he writes, 'to concentrate on what we feel we do best,' namely three-course dinners. Reporters are enthusiastic, and the rather spartan décor is soon eclipsed by cooking that 'seems to get even more imaginative and assured'. The range is wide and choice generous: there is certainly no question of the kitchen taking things easy.

The style is broadly European, with occasional Far Eastern input, starting perhaps with twice-baked cheese soufflé (with tomato confit and tapénade), or seared squid (with butternut squash and salsa verde). The quality of materials shows through in seafood – 'immaculate' scallops, and 'wonderful' gurnard – and in 'superb' lamb: maybe noisettes with minted broad bean purée. Despite Italian bread-and-butter or hot chocolate puddings, desserts include some lively numbers such as warm pineapple with coconut milk and coriander, and rhubarb partnered with won tons and a rhubarb and liquorice mousse. Service has been 'understanding and efficient', and wines on the interestingly varied list are helpfully grouped by region and/or varietal. For a fresh look at Sauvignon Blanc, try the Poggio alle Gazze 1997 from acclaimed Italian producer Tenuta dell'Ornellaia (£19.50). Otherwise, house wines from France, Chile and Germany are £12.50 a bottle, £3.50 a glass.

CHEF: Nick Pound   PROPRIETORS: Nick Pound and Deborah Swift   OPEN: Tue to Sat D only 7 to 9.30   MEALS: Set D Tue to Thur £25, Set D Fri and Sat £30   SERVICE: not inc   CARDS: Amex, Diners, MasterCard, Switch, Visa   DETAILS: 50 seats. Private parties: 36 main room. Car park. Vegetarian meals. No cigars/pipes in dining room. Wheelchair access (not WC). Music

---

BARWICK Somerset   map 2

▲ *Little Barwick House* ✦

Barwick BA22 9TD
TEL: (01935) 423902   FAX: (01935) 420908
take first exit off A37 roundabout 1m S of Yeovil; Little   COOKING 5
Barwick House ¼m on left   COST £33–£42

Daughter Emma has joined the kitchen team in this unpretentious family-run restaurant – the Colleys have been here for twenty years – which explains the jars of 'Emma's jam' and other comestibles in the entrance hall. Aperitifs are served at comfortable armchairs and sofas in the lounge, while dinner is taken in the dark, high-ceilinged dining room decorated with red walls, heavy curtains and Indian carpets. Vegetarians are well catered for with leek and tarragon tartlet, or goats' cheese and chive pancakes, while the main menu (with a generous seven or eight options per course) deals in up-to-date ideas of pork brochette Thai-style, or roast poussin with harissa, alongside more traditional Sussex pie.

Game is a feature in season, while fish main courses might offer a choice between a pan-fried selection served with pastis mayonnaise, and a stew of prawns, salmon, sole, mussels and sea bass with a powerful rouille. Dinner for one couple began with a ramekin of moist, flaked Finnan haddock with a cheesy cream sauce, and a well-turned-out salad incorporating roast cherry tomatoes, grilled shallots, Italian dried ham and a light Parmesan fritter. Finish perhaps with a lemony crème brûlée or a light Amaretto cheesecake. Wines are well chosen, offering good-value drinking from around the world. Eight house wines, red, white and rosé, are all £10.90 a bottle.

'When I asked if the filling of the tart was "a sort of frangipane", I might as well have been speaking a little-known variant of Matabele.' (On eating in London)

CHEF: Veronica Colley   PROPRIETORS: Christopher and Veronica Colley   OPEN: Mon to Sat D only 7 to 9 (9.30 Sat); Sun D residents only   CLOSED: Christmas and New Year   MEALS: Set D £20.90 (2 courses) to £25.90   SERVICE: net prices, card slips closed   CARDS: Amex, Delta, Diners, MasterCard, Switch, Visa   DETAILS: 40 seats. Private parties: 40 main room, 20 private room. Car park. Vegetarian meals. Children's helpings. No smoking in dining room. No music. Air-conditioned   ACCOMMODATION: 6 rooms, all with bath/shower. TV. Phone. D,B&B £76.50 to £133 (*The Which? Hotel Guide*)   (£5)

BASLOW Derbyshire   map 9

▲ *Fischer's Baslow Hall* ♟ ⁵✳

Calver Road, Baslow DE45 1RR   COOKING 8
TEL: (01246) 583259   FAX: (01246) 583818   COST £37–£73

Weathered Derbyshire stone and mullioned windows make this Edwardian house, up a short, steeply curving drive, appear much older than it is. The reassuring feel – meals begin with a drink in the atmospheric sitting room with its assortment of sofas, chairs and 'fragrant' log fire – is reinforced by a kitchen that doesn't seek to break new ground or experiment with exotic combinations. Pink lamb slices, for example, arranged on rösti over spinach, with roast garlic cloves in a tomato and tarragon reduction, may be the kind of dish that crops up all over the place, but here it stands out for both careful sourcing and meticulous, confident treatment.

The menu offers the usual choice of luxury ingredients, yet dishes are often quite straightforward: for example, pink, well-flavoured pigeon breasts, in a strong stock reduction with Puy lentils, served with a minced pie-sized puff pastry pithiviers of foie gras. What sets the food apart from most of the competition is the dedication to prime-quality materials, allied to concern for accurate timing and seasoning that together guarantee maximum flavour. Three roast scallops with brown butter vinaigrette, for example, were partnered at one meal by a small conventionally dressed bundle of dill and chives (there is a well-stocked kitchen garden) providing a 'brilliant herbal contrast' to the sweet scallops. Saucing is accomplished too, a strongly crustacean one giving depth to a starter of crab raviolo.

Desserts deal elegantly with matters of unity and contrast, whether exploring the potential of a single item – different ways with apple or rhubarb, perhaps – or producing a well-balanced chocolate and raspberry soufflé, served with a small jug of chocolate pouring sauce and a sorbet tasting of 'the essence of raspberries'. A high-quality selection of British and French cheeses arrives on a trolley, incidentals (appetisers, bread and petits fours) are up to scratch, and generally professional service under the supervision of Susan Fischer is friendly, 'leisurely but not slack'. The wine list concentrates on quality, which isn't to say that the bottles under £20 aren't worth drinking: an inspector was very happy with the Montgras Chilean Merlot (£17.50) that was recommended to accompany pigeon and lamb. House wines from France and Italy are £13. Café Max, although less ambitious and less expensive, also delivers the goods.

♦ *denotes an outstanding wine cellar;* ♟ *denotes a good wine list, worth travelling for.*

CHEF: Max Fischer PROPRIETORS: Max and Susan Fischer
to Sat D 7 to 9.30 (Sun D residents only) CLOSED: 25 and 2
(2 courses) to £24, Set L Sun £24, Set D £45 SERVICE: no
MasterCard, Switch, Visa DETAILS: 76 seats. 16 seats out
12 and 24 private rooms. Car park. No children under 12 in di
dining room. Wheelchair access (not WC). No music AC
bath/shower. TV. Phone. B&B £80 to £130. Baby facilities (Ti

BATH Bath & N.E. Somerset

▲ *Bath Priory* ⁙✴

Weston Road, Bath BA1 2XT
TEL: **(01225) 331922** FAX: **(01225) 448276**

With a wide, low, Georgian stone frontage adorned
smart wooden boxes, the prettily manicured Priory
cards magnate Andrew Brownsword, has been 'c
Brocade-draped French windows lead from the d
garden (vegetables and fruit are grown in the grou
furnished with big, squashy sofa-banquettes and 'su chairs. The menu
offers a simple three-way choice at both savoury stages, followed by four
desserts or cheese, with a good line in comfort food: even the lunch menu goes in
for foie gras, lobster risotto and ribeye steak.

Robert Clayton's strength is to show off prime ingredients well, 'without too
much messing about': at inspection, for example, three fat, stickily caramelised
scallops, with crisp salad leaves in a benign dressing. Careful cooking has also
produced creamy textured seared foie gras with caramelised grapefruit
segments. There is 'nothing too intense' about flavours; and if they err on the
mild side, that is to the benefit of the principal materials, which have included
first-rate calf's liver, and moist, perfectly timed lemon sole with little to distract
attention from its 'ultra high quality' beyond crushed potatoes, spinach and basil
leaves.

The classically inclined style culminates in desserts of praline crème brûlée, or
a densely chocolatey but not too sweet fondant, with a dribble of intense orange
custard; or there is a trolley of some twenty cheeses 'all in good nick'. In its brief
trip around the world the wine list picks up eight house recommendations
between £15 and £20, including South African Chardonnay and Italian
Primitivo.

CHEF: Robert Clayton PROPRIETOR: Andrew Brownsword OPEN: all week 12 to 1.45, 7 to 9.45
(10 Sat) MEALS: Set L £15 (2 courses) to £20, Set D £37.50 SERVICE: not inc, card slips
closed CARDS: Amex, Delta, Diners, MasterCard, Switch, Visa DETAILS: 50 seats. Private
parties: 60 main room, 20 private room. Car park. Vegetarian meals. Children's helpings. No
children under 7 in dining room. No smoking in dining room. Wheelchair access (also WC).
Occasional music ACCOMMODATION: 28 rooms, all with bath/shower. TV. Phone. B&B £140 to
£270. Rooms for disabled. Swimming pool

---

*'A human hair found in sea bass was greeted [by the proprietor] with, "Well, I wonder
whose it was?"* (On eating in Norfolk)

Clos du Roy

1 Seven Dials, Saw Close, Bath BA1 1EN	COOKING 1
TEL: (01225) 444450 FAX: (01225) 404044	COST £21–£50

The musical theme is hard to miss, given a bar with a piano key design, a whole orchestra of instruments festooning the pale yellow walls, and giant staves draped around windows overlooking the square below. A range of menus goes in for hearty bistro food – a well-judged medium-rare steak béarnaise – as well as some unusual combinations, such as grenadine dressing and red onion marmalade with a starter of black pudding. The kitchen has a penchant for fruit with savoury dishes – turbot and crab ballottine with a creamed blackcurrant sauce, or chicken with glazed figs – although reporters (and an inspector) have found some materials and their treatment unconvincing. Finish perhaps with a coconut and mango variation on crème brûlée, or iced nougat terrine. Expect a warm welcome and attentive and courteous service from French staff, and drink from a list of wines arranged by style, with a good selection under £20. House wine is £9.95.

CHEF: Simon King PROPRIETORS: Philippe and Emma Roy OPEN: all week 12 to 2, 6 to 10.30 MEALS: alc (main courses £13 to £18.50). Set L Mon to Sat £9.95 (2 courses) to £13.95, Set L Sun £11.95, Set D £16.50 (2 courses) to £19.50 SERVICE: not inc, card slips closed CARDS: Amex, Diners, MasterCard, Visa DETAILS: 80 seats. 10 seats outside. Private parties: 90 main room. Vegetarian meals. Children's helpings. No smoking in dining room. Wheelchair access (not WC). Occasional music £5

01225 - 426000

Green Street Seafood Café

WEST COUNTRY 2000 FISH

NEW ENTRY

6 Green Street, Bath BA1 2JY	COOKING 3
TEL: (01225) 448707 FAX: (01225) 447794	COST £26–£43

In a city with something of a reputation for grandeur when it comes to eating out, one reporter was gratified to find a place fittingly sited above an award-winning fish market, where the best of the catch can be enjoyed in bright, casual surroundings. Blackboard specials supplement printed menus, and choice – both of raw materials and culinary styles – is enticingly broad, taking in proper brandade with a soft-poached egg; lobster in a spaghetti dish with toasted pine nuts, basil and garlic; and seared scallops with broad beans and thyme. At inspection, a boiled Newlyn crab with tarragon mayonnaise was 'incredibly fresh', while a main-course special of grilled brill with lemon and spring onion mash was generous and carefully seasoned, appealingly garnished with cooked red pepper in a slick of olive oil. Impeccably seasonal vegetables are charged extra: buttery Jersey Royals, asparagus, and deep-fried courgettes with pesto at a June dinner. To finish, there may be chocolate tart or quietly impressive vanilla bavarois with raspberries. Promptly efficient service is commended for finding the time to chat. The short, predominantly white wine list brings plenty of sharply etched flavours to bear on the food. Prices open at £8.75.

CHEFS: Andy Bird and Mitchell Tonks PROPRIETOR: Mitchell Tonks OPEN: Tue to Sat 12 to 3, 6 to 11 MEALS: alc (main courses £7.50 to £13) SERVICE: not inc CARDS: Amex, Delta, Diners, MasterCard, Switch, Visa DETAILS: 30 seats. Private parties: 18 main room. Vegetarian meals. Children's helpings. Music £5

▲ *Lettonie* ♥ ⚒

35 Kelston Road, Bath BA1 3QH	COOKING 7
TEL: (01225) 446676 FAX: (01225) 447541	COST £41–£84

Large rooms, high ceilings and antique furniture give this Georgian house the feel of a stately home. The dining room, with decorative bunches of glass grapes on its white linen cloths, is less ornate, appropriately so since the food is quite capable of making its own impression. 'It is not just a meal, but a display of fine cooking', reckoned an inspector, using 'display' to indicate the spectacle, showmanship, visual puns, and (literally) pyrotechnics in the case of the famous flaming duck egg starter. Stuffed with its own soft, creamy, scrambled contents, and topped with caviare, it comes with a shot of iced vodka, reminding us that the food is 'as much a feast for the eye as for the stomach'. It is certainly the latter: portions can seem generous in this day and age, with waves of appetisers (including a stuffed frog's leg at table), and a flamboyant pre-dessert chocolate cream egg contributing to the bulk.

This is 'grand dining in old-fashioned style' as Latvia meets French haute cuisine, producing kipper tortelloni with scallops and tomato in a Sauternes cream sauce, or bortsch terrine with shredded beef pirogi and soured cream. There are some lighter dishes, for example an inverted flowerpot of delicate, airy, pale pike and crayfish mousse 'with a gently fishy flavour', but they tend to be outnumbered by weightier ones such as loin of venison on a bed of creamy sauerkraut with a dark game sauce, or pork fillet with crisp honey-glazed belly, successfully combining richness and sweetness. Dinner is the showcase, but lunch has produced a well-prepared terrine of pressed pork and ham, marinated beef skirt with a grain mustard sauce, and strawberry compote with matching ice cream.

Desserts tend to be relatively straightforward. 'You get exactly what it says on the menu': for example, a dark brown blob of bitter chocolate mousse with prune and armagnac ice cream, or an assiette of satsuma featuring crème brûlée, mousse and ice cream. Service has had its ups and downs, but Siân Blunos is gracious, unobtrusive and quietly efficient, gliding about in 'long black drapey clothes' to make sure everything runs as smoothly as possible. The wine list rushes through Spain, Italy and the New World then heads back to France for a more leisurely tour of Bordeaux and Burgundy. Half a dozen house wines under £20 include the spicy, dry Douro red from Quinta de la Rosa at £17.55.

CHEF: Martin Blunos PROPRIETORS: Siân and Martin Blunos OPEN: Tue to Sat 12 to 2, 7 to 9.30 CLOSED: 2 weeks from New Year, 2 weeks Aug MEALS: Set L £15 (2 courses) to £25, Set D £44.50 SERVICE: not inc CARDS: Amex, Delta, Diners, MasterCard, Switch, Visa DETAILS: 38 seats. Private parties: 38 main room, 8 private room. Car park. Children's helpings. No smoking in dining room. Wheelchair access (also WC). Music ACCOMMODATION: 4 rooms, all, with bath/shower. TV. Phone. B&B £95 to £150 (*The Which? Hotel Guide*) £5

'By all means continue them in their current rating [in The Good Food Guide*]. The technical skills and raw materials are worth it. But if you could give just the slightest hint in the entry that this is the place to go if you're a pretentious gourmet nincompoop, that would be nice.'* (On eating in Wales)

Moody Goose ✱

7A Kingsmead Square, Bath BA1 2AB	COOKING 5
TEL/FAX: (01225) 466688	COST £31–£51

Decidedly larger than life, the eponymous pottery bird keeps a rather peevish eye on things, providing an unexpectedly light touch at this somewhat solemn and formal basement restaurant. The décor in the three small interconnecting rooms is cool and subdued, with cream walls, French watercolours and comfortable wicker chairs. Stephen Shore's 'technically brilliant' cooking matches the formality of the surroundings but it's certainly not subdued. Bold but refined flavours are the key. Dishes are carefully composed so that each element comes into its own. At inspection, a terrine of Cornish fish was a chunky slab of firm, jellied 'extraordinarily fresh' fish layered with spinach and wrapped in 'tissue-paper-thin ham'; the accompanying oyster fritter in its 'crisp, light-as-air batter' provided a considered contrast of texture and temperature. 'Exemplary' sea bass comes with a smooth horseradish cream that hit 'exactly the right piquant note'. Occasional glitches, such as a mushroom ravioli served with braised red cabbage that 'seemed to belong to another dish', don't detract from the overall impression of excellence.

Desserts, such as warm caramelised rice pudding with glazed pears, give an elegant edge to nursery food, while 'rich and dense' bitter chocolate torte is 'light and uncloying'. Service is efficient and well paced but, while one reporter felt there was a pleasant atmosphere, others have found it 'clinical' and tense: 'food of this standard should be something to celebrate but the whole place needs to relax a bit.' The wine list is carefully selected to match the food's clean, direct flavours. Eight house wine start at £11.

CHEF: Stephen Shore   PROPRIETORS: Stephen and Victoria Shore   OPEN: Mon to Sat 12 to 2, 6 to 9.30 (10 Sat)   CLOSED: 2 weeks Jan, bank hols (exc 25 Dec)   MEALS: alc (main courses £15 to £17.50). Set L and D 6 to 7 £10, Set D £20   SERVICE: not inc   CARDS: Amex, Delta, Diners, MasterCard, Switch, Visa   DETAILS: 30 seats. Private parties: 22 main room, 8 private room. Vegetarian meals. Children's helpings. No children under 7. No smoking in dining room. Music

No. 5 Bistro £ ✱

5 Argyle Street, Bath BA2 4BA	
TEL: (01225) 444499 FAX: (01225) 318668	COOKING 3
EMAIL: chome@globalnet.co.uk	COST £22–£45

Bistro by name and nature, its bare floorboards, poster-covered walls, paper cloths and napkins, and wax encrusted bottles with candles set the tone, pop music adding a backdrop. The atmosphere is 'relaxed', the menu 'appealing'. Start with stalwarts of provençale fish soup, or smoked chicken salad with chicory, tomato and orange, or something a little more exploratory, like grilled sardines served with sweet pepper butter sauce. Fishy main courses range from fillet of cod with a herb crust and citrus butter, to pan-fried monkfish with lemon grass, ginger, coriander and chilli, while fillet steak comes with mixed peppers, red wine and garlic, and duck with pineapple and black pepper. For dessert, try an 'excellent' meringue with ice cream and chocolate sauce, or blackcurrant and cinnamon tart with fromage frais. The wine list is keenly priced, opening with

229

house French at £8.95, and there is a good list of bottled beers and non-alcoholic drinks (Fentiman's ginger beer, elderflower pressé).

CHEFS: Stephen Smith, Paul Hearne and Sarah Grantins   PROPRIETORS: Stephen Smith and Charles Home   OPEN: Tue to Sat L 12 to 2.30, Mon to Sat D 6.30 to 10 (10.30 Fri, 11 Sat) CLOSED: 1 week Christmas   MEALS: alc (main courses L £6 to £10, D £12 to £16)   SERVICE: not inc   CARDS: Amex, Delta, Diners, MasterCard, Switch, Visa   DETAILS: 35 seats. Private parties: 8 main room. Vegetarian meals. Children's helpings. No smoking in dining room. Wheelchair access (not WC). Music

▲ *Queensberry Hotel, Olive Tree* 🍷 ⁵⋇

Russel Street, Bath BA1 2QF
TEL: (01225) 447928   FAX: (01225) 446065
EMAIL: queensbury@dial.pipex.com

COOKING 6
COST £24–£53

The serene, stylish Queensberry, just minutes from the crowded town centre, inspires a loyal, enthusiastic following for its 'little gem' of a restaurant: a bright contemporary basement dining room, whose Mediterranean colours coexist happily with the Georgian elegance of the hotel. Matthew Prowse shows confidence, lightness of touch and lots of good modern ideas in his cooking, as well as a grasp of all the right priorities – 'good sourcing, sensitive timing and seasoning, and freshness of flavour' – to produce a generous carte that ranges from salad of veal sweetbreads and bresaola with asparagus and red wine dressing, to baked halibut with warm oyster, shellfish and orange sauce. 'Perfectly timed, sweet' scallops with 'intense' roasted tomato and fennel had a 'great crossfire of flavours' for one reporter, who was further impressed by a salad of marinated stir-fried strips of duck breast, 'full of warm, deep duck flavour'. Menus change frequently but regulars like to see their favourites reappearing: provençale fish soup with 'good, strong fish and saffron flavours', for example, and a 'divinely rich' gratin dauphinois.

Puddings tempt the greedy and the virtuous in equal measure: 'gooey' soft meringue with fruit and mascarpone cream, or chocolate and coffee tart, perhaps, for the former, and lemon jelly with marinated cherries for the latter. 'Excellent' home-made fudge with coffee is difficult to resist, and service is provided by friendly, authoritative, informative staff. An impressive but unintimidating wine list favours France in the main, but there are some decidedly useful contributions from Italy and the New World. House wines from the Côte de Tarn and Gascogny are £11.50; six wines by the glass from four countries are all £3.

CHEF: Matthew Prowse   PROPRIETORS: Stephen and Penny Ross   OPEN: Mon to Sat L 12 to 2, all week D 7 to 10   CLOSED: 1 week Christmas and New year   MEALS: alc (main courses £12.50 to £18). Set L £12.50 (2 courses) to £14.50, Set D £24   SERVICE: not inc, card slips closed CARDS: Delta, MasterCard, Switch, Visa   DETAILS: 70 seats. Private parties: 40 main room, 35 private room. Vegetarian meals. Children's helpings. No smoking in dining room. Wheelchair access (also WC). Music. Air-conditioned   ACCOMMODATION: 29 rooms, all with bath/shower. TV. Phone. B&B £90 to £210. Rooms for disabled. Baby facilities (*The Which? Hotel Guide*)

'When questioned on the choice of puddings, "How full are you?" is not the ideal reaction.' (On eating in Oxfordshire)

Richmond Arms

7 Richmond Place, Lansdown, Bath BA1 5PZ   COOKING 2
TEL: (01225) 316725   COST £19–£31

Set in an unexpectedly rural enclave of Bath, about a mile from the centre, the Richmond Arms is a prime example of that encouraging recent phenomenon, the gastro-pub. It looks traditional from the outside, but the interior has been impressively converted, and minimally adorned with Asian artefacts. Light lunches mix oriental and Mediterranean modes, and the evening menu expands on the theme. A May dinner began inspiringly with a bowl of 'sweet, firm and slightly chewy' chargrilled squid tossed in fettuccine with lemon, garlic and capers, and 'authentic' South East Asian flavours were apparent in a generous prawn and chicken laksa. Steaks are reportedly well-handled, and vegetarian dishes receive equal imaginative effort: witness a main course of layered celeriac, potatoes and blue cheese with chickpeas, chilli, garlic and coriander. A fashionable Sephardic boiled orange and almond cake was well rendered, served with an Amaretto sabayon, or there may be cinnamon-scented chocolate pots. Well-kept seasonal Usher's beers provide an alternative to a small but flavourful collection of wines that stays usefully under £11.

CHEFS: Marney Cunningham and Gary Lewis   PROPRIETORS: John and Marney Cunningham
OPEN: Tue to Sun L 12 to 2, Tue to Sat D 6 to 8.30 (9 Fri and Sat)   MEALS: alc (main courses L £3.50 to £5.50, D £7 to £9)   SERVICE: not inc   CARDS: none   DETAILS: 30 seats. 20 seats outside. Private parties: 20 main room. Vegetarian meals. No children under 14. No music

▲ Royal Crescent, Brasserie/Pimpernel's £✳

16 Royal Crescent, Bath BA1 2LS   COOKING 5
TEL: (01225) 823333   FAX: (01225) 339401   COST £25–£83

Although under the same overall control, by Steven Blake, the two restaurants on this site aim in different culinary directions. Pimpernel's occupies a small, intimate and comfortable room in the basement of the main house, whose décor does nothing to prepare visitors for the Eastern-influenced Anglo-French cooking. The degree of crossover varies dish by dish, some as Eastern as bluefin tuna with wakame and orange miso, others as Western as baked turbot with crab cannelloni, the rest somewhere in between: seared lamb with rice dumplings, for example, or squab pigeon with lime sauce and ginger dressing. One who opted for the six-course tasting menu at £55 enjoyed a 'nicely balanced and generally harmonious' meal that included venison consommé, steamed sea bass with seared scallops, and a centrepiece of 'accomplished' roast pigeon; goats' cheese and two desserts followed, one a banana soufflé with caramel ice cream, the other a pyramid of lime jelly on Malibu mousse. 'Extras' are well done, everything runs smoothly, staff are 'alert and friendly', and the sommelier 'is to be praised for his guidance'.

Despite its name, the Brasserie – in the Dower House, overlooking an acre of garden – felt more like 'a posh restaurant' to one visitor, given its brocade-covered sofas, 'serious wing chairs' and wood carvings, not to mention its starched tablecloths, and the evening prices. Here the style is more mainstream, producing braised lamb shank, and Bresse chicken with wilted greens and mushrooms. Fish options have ranged from baked fillet of codling with mussel liquor, to roast salmon with Swiss chard and red wine risotto, and desserts from strawberry soufflé to spiced plum tart with cardamom ice cream. Lunchtime brings good value. The wine list in both restaurants was under review as the *Guide* went to press.

CHEF: Steven Blake   PROPRIETOR: Cliveden Ltd   OPEN: Brasserie all week 12.30 to 2, 7 to 9.30; Pimpernel's Tue to Sat D only 7 to 10   CLOSED: Christmas exc residents   MEALS: Brasserie alc D (main courses £14 to £22). Set L £12 (2 courses) to £15, Set D £28 (2 courses) to £36; Pimpernel's alc D (main courses £19.50 to £25). Set D £44 to £55   SERVICE: not inc   CARDS: Amex, Delta, Diners, MasterCard, Switch, Visa   DETAILS: Brasserie 50 seats, 20 seats outside. Pimpernel's 22 seats. Private parties: 76 main room (Brasserie), 32 main room (Pimpernel's), 30 to 100 private rooms. Car park. Vegetarian meals. No smoking in dining room. Music. Air-conditioned   ACCOMMODATION: 45 rooms, all with bath/shower. TV. Phone. Room only £190 to £695. Rooms for disabled. Baby facilities. Swimming pool (*The Which? Hotel Guide*)

Woods

9–13 Alfred Street, Bath BA1 2QX	COOKING 2
TEL: (01225) 314812 FAX: (01225) 443146	COST £27–£48

'Pricey' by name, but far from pricey in what he cooks up, David Price runs what is in effect a good neighbourhood brasserie in a terraced house opposite the Assembly Rooms high above Bath. Everyone comments on the value for money, particularly of the set-price menus, eaten in the L-shaped, high-ceilinged room abuzz with conversation. Simple at lunchtime, lengthier in the evenings, these always include a soup, perhaps roasted red pepper and garlic, while the carte might run to salady starters, such as roasted pigeon breast with smoked chicken, or prawns, Chinese noodles and vegetables. Similarly, you can more or less count on a seasonal casserole – perhaps beef with shiitake mushrooms and shallots – among other dinner dishes of salmon with a herby Parmesan top, lambs' kidneys with a mustardy sauce, or a filo parcel concealing mushroom, celery and onion pâté. Puddings might be Bakewell tart, or lemon and ginger sponge with orange caramel sauce. Other than a dozen or so wines under £14 available by the glass, all bottles are from France or New Zealand and come helpfully and enthusiastically described. House wine is £10.

CHEFS: David Price and Kevin Barrett   PROPRIETORS: Mr and Mrs David Price   OPEN: Mon to Sat 12 to 3, 6 to 11   CLOSED: 25 and 26 Dec, 1 Jan   MEALS: alc (main courses £9.50 to £15.50). Set L £7 (2 courses), Set D £12.25 (2 courses) to £22.50   SERVICE: not inc   CARDS: MasterCard, Visa   DETAILS: 140 seats. 12 seats outside. Private parties: 100 main room, 40 private room. Vegetarian meals. Children's helpings. No cigars/pipes in dining room. Wheelchair access (also WC). Music

'We have never eaten there . . . because it used to have things like deep-fried breadcrumbed Camembert with a fruit coulis on the menu and I always suspected I could live without that. And as I have never eaten it anywhere and as I am still alive, I must have been right.' (On eating in Hampshire)

Not inc *in the details at the end of an entry indicates that no service charge is made and any tipping is at the discretion of the customer.*

BEAMINSTER Dorset   map 2

▲ *Bridge House* ⁵⁄✳

3 Prout Bridge, Beaminster DT8 3AY
TEL: (01308) 862200   FAX: (01308) 863700   COOKING 2
EMAIL: enquiries@bridge-house.co.uk   COST £22–£40

'Intimate, secluded and personal' is how thirteenth-century Bridge House struck
one visitor, thanks partly to its thick walls and log fire in the giant hearth in the
lounge. The restful pink and green dining room is a 'pale, pretty, small room'
where Simon Clewlow's short lunch and extended dinner menus offer many
dishes with a familiar ring: a filo parcel of goats' cheese with tomato and basil, or
medallions of pork tenderloin with apricot stuffing. 'We now use even more
local products than in previous years', writes Peter Pinkster, pointing to roast
rack of lamb, fillet of beef with sauté mushrooms, seafood such as mussels or
grilled scallops, breakfast eggs, and Denhay bacon and cheese. Puddings
confirm the Anglo-French thrust of the cooking, offering crêpes suzette and
Dorset apple cake with clotted cream. A fairly priced wine list starts with a dozen
house recommendations at around £10.

CHEF: Simon Clewlow   PROPRIETOR: Peter Pinkster   OPEN: all week 12 to 2, 7 to 9   CLOSED: 29
Dec to 3 Jan   MEALS: Set L £8.75 (2 courses) to £12.50, Set D Sun to Fri £21.50, Set D Sat
£25.50   SERVICE: not inc, card slips closed   CARDS: Amex, Delta, Diners, MasterCard, Switch,
Visa   DETAILS: 36 seats. 16 seats outside. Private parties: 40 main room, 16 private room. Car
park. Vegetarian meals. Children's helpings. No smoking in dining room. Wheelchair access (not
WC). No music   ACCOMMODATION: 14 rooms, all with bath/shower. TV. Phone. B&B £50 to
£112. Rooms for disabled (*The Which? Hotel Guide*)

BEVERLEY East Riding of Yorkshire   map 9

Wednesdays ♟ £

8 Wednesday Market, Beverley HU17 0DG   COOKING 2
TEL/FAX: (01482) 869727   COST £24–£43

Wendy and Matthew Rowley's plans to convert the upper floor to a private
dining room may ease the rather cramped conditions downstairs at their popular
banana-yellow place at the minster end of town. Helped by Tim Durrance,
Wendy picks up on Mediterranean and Eastern influences but also injects
oomph into traditional favourites for her 'excellent-value' food. Sea bass with
lime-laden Thai rice, and seafood gratin in a creamy, fruity sauce have been
singled out for praise, while pork and marjoram sausages with a red onion mash
have won compliments for both chef and butcher. Vegetarians are well provided
for, with three-cheese tagliolini, or a risotto of peas, roasted garlic and Taleggio
with leeks. Go for something with pastry for pudding, perhaps orange and
cardamom cream tart, or you might find a steamed pudding, a crumble or a fruity
crème brûlée. Wines are grouped by style, such as 'weightier, oaked whites' and
'lighter reds', with many bottles under £20, and there are some tempting
digestifs. Four house wines are all £9.75.

CHEFS: Wendy Rowley and Tim Durrance   PROPRIETORS: Matthew and Wendy Rowley, and Robert Griffin   OPEN: Mon to Sat 12 to 2, 7 to 9.30   CLOSED: 31 Dec   MEALS: alc (main courses £7.50 to £15). Set L £7.50 (2 courses)   SERVICE: not inc   CARDS: Delta, MasterCard, Switch, Visa   DETAILS: 65 seats. 15 seats outside. Private parties: 40 main room, 20 and 40 private rooms. Vegetarian meals. Children's helpings. Wheelchair access (not WC). Music (£5)

BIDDENDEN Kent

West House

NEW ENTRY

28 High Street, Biddenden TN27 8AH   COOKING 4
TEL: (01580) 291341   FAX: (01580) 291341   COST £34–£41

Susan and David Cunningham have swapped the vagaries of the London futures market for the equally risky business of running a restaurant but, judging by numerous enthusiastic reports, this investment should pay off. 'A real find,' wrote one reporter; 'an absolute bargain,' confirmed another. Not least of the attractions is West House itself, a red-roofed, heavily beamed building with a 'fabulously, genuinely ancient' interior and stylishly restrained décor that includes beautiful wooden tables, huge still-life paintings, and fat candles on spiral holders.

Susan works alone in the kitchen and, with just six tables to look after, David is sole waiter. The short menu gives local produce a Conranesque treatment (a reflection of Susan's training at the Butler's Wharf chef school), producing 'melt in the mouth' blue cheese and pear galette; crab, tomato and saffron tart; and pork tenderloin with creamed cabbage and rösti potato. An inspector was impressed at the exceptional amount of care taken – from 'very professional' bread to 'fresh, attractive' petits fours – even if the style may sometimes seem 'effortful' at the expense of flavour balance. But good materials provide a firm foundation, whether seafood (four scallops on a herb risotto) or meat (slices of lamb rolled like a sausage round a nut and apricot stuffing). Rhubarb compote with ginger ice cream has been judged 'perfect in its direct simplicity and clear flavours'. Service is 'friendly, helpful and not at all stuffy', and the predominantly French wine list is 'ungrasping', with six by the glass and house wine £10.50.

CHEF: Susan Cunningham   PROPRIETORS: Susan and David Cunningham   OPEN: Wed to Sat D only 7 to 9   CLOSED: 1 week autumn, 25 and 26 Dec, 1 Jan, 3 weeks Jan   MEALS: Set D £22.50   SERVICE: not inc, card slips closed   CARDS: Delta, MasterCard, Switch, Visa   DETAILS: 20 seats. Private parties: 20 main room. Car park. Vegetarian meals. No pipes/cigars in dining room. Music (£5)

'Bread was presented in a basket by the waiter without a word. I asked, "What have we got here?" No reply. "Brown or white?" I suggested. "They're a mixture of the same," he said.' (On eating in Hampshire)

Prices quoted in the Guide *are based on information supplied by restaurateurs. The prices quoted at the top of each entry represent a range, from the lowest meal price to the highest; the latter is inflated by 20 per cent to take account of likely price rises during the year of the* Guide.

BIRCH VALE   Derbyshire   map 8

▲ *Waltzing Weasel*

New Mills Road, Birch Vale SK22 1BT
TEL/FAX: (01663) 743402
EMAIL: waltzing.weasel@zen.co.uk   COOKING 3
on A6015, ½m W of Hayfield   COST £27–£40

A venerable 200-year-old inn serving 'high-quality pub-style meals' sums up
the Weasel. Bar food runs to hot buttered shrimps on toast, egg mayonnaise, and
salt beef, while across the dining room's polished oak tables might come
'esoteric casseroles' such as stifado, Spanish pollo al chilindron, or lamb tagine.
Much of the time, however, it adopts the more familiar mode of cheese soufflé, or
a 'rich and very good' seafood tart made with salmon, prawns, lobster and crab.
Lemony-tasting treacle tart and chocolate mousse have been highly rated, and
service has been 'cheerful and helpful', although the ship has not been as tightly
run as a couple of reporters would have wished. Four French house wines under
£10 head up a serviceable list.

CHEF: George Benham   PROPRIETORS: Michael and Linda Atkinson   OPEN: all week 12 to 2, 7
to 9   MEALS: alc L (main courses £7 to £12.50). Set D £22.50 (2 courses) to £25.50. Bar menu L
and D   SERVICE: net prices, card slips closed   CARDS: Amex, Delta, MasterCard, Switch,
Visa   DETAILS: 36 seats. Private parties: 40 main room. Car park. Vegetarian meals. Children's
helpings. No children under 5 in dining room. Wheelchair access (not WC). Occasional music.
Air-conditioned   ACCOMMODATION: 8 rooms, all with bath/shower. TV. Phone. B&B £38 to £98.
Rooms for disabled (*The Which? Hotel Guide*)

BIRDLIP   Gloucestershire   map 2

▲ *Kingshead House* ▼

Birdlip GL4 8JH
TEL: (01452) 862299   COOKING 2
¼m off A417 between Gloucester and Cirencester   COST £25–£46

The scale is small in this semi-detached building of old grey Cotswold stone. A
flag-floored lounge is linked by an open door to the dining room, where bare
boards and a rug hint at the lack of artifice. Good raw materials (including herbs
from the garden) provide a firm foundation for Judy Knock's gentle style of
country cooking. Lunch is a carte typically featuring salads, pasta and rice dishes
followed by spiced fish cakes or cheese tart, while dinner is priced according to
the main course: home-made spinach gnocchi, perhaps, steamed brill with
broad beans, or roast saddle of rabbit with cabbage and bacon. These might
follow saumon persillé, or an upbeat terrine of crab with chilli salsa, before
Pompadour's ribbons: layers of apricot purée and fromage frais with a sorbet of
the latter. Wines are mostly Old World and from some highly respected growers
– Albert Mann and Henri Pellé among them – and many fall comfortably below
the £20 mark. House wines from Germany and France start at £11.

235

CHEF: Judy Knock   PROPRIETORS: Mr and Mrs W.W. Knock   OPEN: Tue to Fri and Sun L 12.30 to 2, Tue to Sat D 7.30 to 9.45   CLOSED: 25 to 27 Dec, 1 to 4 Jan   MEALS: alc Tue to Fri L (main courses £8 to £13.50). Set L Sun £17.50, Set D £25 to £27.50   SERVICE: not inc; 10% for parties of 6 or more   CARDS: Amex, MasterCard, Visa   DETAILS: 34 seats. 8 seats outside. Private parties: 34 main room. Car park. Vegetarian meals. Children's helpings. Wheelchair access (not WC). Music   ACCOMMODATION: 1 room, with bath/shower. TV. B&B £40 to £70   (£5)

BIRKENHEAD   Merseyside   map 8

Beadles

15 Rosemount, Oxton, Birkenhead L43 5SG   COOKING 3
TEL: (0151) 653 9010   COST £23–£41

Shortly before last year's *Guide* hit the shelves, Beadles' previous owners upped sticks and Mellanie Dixon-Peel, once of Ciboure in London, took over the stoves. The restaurant, in one of Birkenhead's leafier suburbs, is done in a gastonomically aware colour scheme of 'sage green and lemon', and cheeringly adorned with prints and original paintings, while the cooking emphasises simple, strong flavours, and combinations that make sense. Warm mousse of leeks and mushrooms with beurre blanc is a gentle way to start, smoked goose breast with raspberry vinaigrette a slightly more exotic one. Fish is thoughtfully treated, a piece of cod fillet given a warm dressing of tomatoes, olive oil, parsley and thyme, and a June meal turned up fine rack of lamb presented on a powerfully flavoured spinach and mushroom underlay. Puddings are sticky crowd-pleasers along the lines of praline floating islands or treacle tart with custard, and the carefully selected cheeseboard has been highly recommended. A weekly-changing fixed-price menu with a good range of choice supplements the carte. The wine list is short and sensible, and won't add too much to the final bill. House French is £8.75.

CHEF: Mellanie Dixon-Peel   PROPRIETORS: Mellanie Dixon-Peel and Richard Peel   OPEN: Tue to Fri and Sun L 12 to 2 (2.30 Sun), Tue to Sat D 7 to 9.30   CLOSED: 1 week Nov, 1 week Feb, 2 weeks Aug   MEALS: alc D (main courses £12.50 to £16). Set L and D (exc Sat D) £11.75 (2 courses) to £14.95   SERVICE: not inc, 10% for parties of 8 or more   CARDS: Delta, MasterCard, Switch, Visa   DETAILS: 32 seats. Private parties: 35 main room. Vegetarian meals. No children under 7 exc at Sun L. No smoking before coffee. Wheelchair access (not WC). Music   (£5)

BIRMINGHAM   West Midlands   map 5

Chung Ying   £

16–18 Wrottesley Street, Birmingham B5 4RT   COOKING 1
TEL: (0121) 622 5669   FAX: (0121) 666 7051   COST £22–£50

Still considered the pick of the city's Chinese restaurants, this old stager does things on a typically big scale, seating 250 and serving even more dishes. The redoubtable dim sum listing produced for one lunchtime couple a varied and satisfying meal of five dishes (including vegetable spring rolls, char siu, and chicken with green pepper in black bean sauce) for less than £15. Specials might run to steamed fish head, and steamed pork pie with dried squid or salted egg, while the rest covers much familiar Cantonese territory in the shape of soups (bean curd), casseroles (goose webs with mushroom), offal (ox tripe with pickled cabbage) and sizzling dishes (beef with black pepper). Rice and noodle dishes are plentiful, and fish ranges from fried shredded eel to stewed oyster with roast belly pork. House wine is £11.

CHEF: T.C. Tsang   PROPRIETOR: Siu Chung Wong   OPEN: all week 12 to 11.30 (10.30 Sun) CLOSED: 25 Dec   MEALS: alc (main courses £6 to £12). Set D £13 to £20 (all min 2 or more) SERVICE: 10% (optional)   CARDS: Amex, Delta, Diners, MasterCard, Switch, Visa   DETAILS: 250 seats. Private parties: 130 main room, 130 private room. Vegetarian meals. Wheelchair access (not WC). Music. Air-conditioned

▲ Hyatt Regency, Number 282   NEW ENTRY

2 Bridge Street, Birmingham B1 2JZ
TEL: (0121) 643 1234   FAX: (0121) 616 2323   COOKING 5
EMAIL: hrbirm@hrb.co.uk   COST £25–£63

Linked to Birmingham's International Convention Centre, this giant glass tower attracts its fair share of delegates. Chef Roger Narbett has been lured in from the Lygon Arms (see entry, Broadway) and is aiming as high as the building itself. His dishes are labour-intensive in both technique and presentation, but his disciplined approach, and knack for combining the classic and the contemporary, augur well. An inspector appreciated the twist given to Cornish crab and 'wonderfully seared' scallops by a curry sauce that owed more to the Empire than trendy Thai combinations: 'a bold stroke and well worth the effort'. An appealing spin was also given to a mini-rack of 'perfectly cooked' Cotswold lamb with a 'nicely creamy' pea and mint risotto. For dessert a parcel of white chocolate with kir-marinated griottine cherries was 'a decadent joy from the first to the last spoonful'. It's a shame that the 'soulless' dining room doesn't rise to the occasion, but a major revamp is promised and, in the meantime, diners can entertain themselves with a view of the busy kitchen through a large window. A compact, well-chosen wine list has plenty around the £20 mark, with house wine at £12.95.

CHEF: Roger Narbett   PROPRIETOR: NEC Group   OPEN: Mon to Fri L 12 to 2, Mon to Sat D 7 to 9.45   CLOSED: bank hols   MEALS: alc (main courses £13 to £18). Set L £14.50 (2 courses) to £16.50, Set D £19.50   SERVICE: not inc   CARDS: Amex, Delta, Diners, MasterCard, Switch, Visa   DETAILS: 80 seats. Private parties: 80 main room, 20 to 200 private rooms. Car park. Vegetarian meals. Children's helpings. Wheelchair access (also WC). Music. Air-conditioned ACCOMMODATION: 319 rooms, all with bath/shower. TV. Phone. Room only £85 to £170. Rooms for disabled. Baby facilities. Swimming pool

Leftbank

79 Broad Street, Birmingham B15 1AH   COOKING 2
TEL: (0121) 643 4464   FAX: (0121) 643 5793   COST £23–£58

A stylish and even opulent conversion of an old banking hall, with lots of gold and silver in the décor and jazz standards on the sound system, this determinedly modern purveyor of eclectic British cuisine scores points not least for its presentation of food. Combinations can be ambitious, as in monkfish with a galette of aubergine and tomato topped by silver sprats and with anchovy purée, while a starter of tuna steak with linguini, coconut and Thai herbs has 'plenty of powerful flavour'. Desserts often impress, with their jagged shards of chocolate and spun sugar doodles: 'beautifully creamy' coffee truffle torte, for example, or perhaps choose a lemon assiette consisting of parfait terrine, cheesecake and sorbet in a tuille basket. Service is young and willing, if not always know-ledgeable, and wines on the world-trotting list stay mostly below £20; house wines, from France, are £9.90.

CHEF: Bill Marmion   PROPRIETORS: Caroline and Chris Benbrook   OPEN: Mon to Fri L 12 to 2, Mon to Sat D 7 to 10   CLOSED: 25 Dec to 2 Jan   MEALS: alc (main courses £11.50 to £20.50). Set L £12 (2 courses) to £14.50   SERVICE: not inc   CARDS: Amex, Delta, Diners, MasterCard, Switch, Visa   DETAILS: 70 seats. Private parties: 54 main room, 16 private room. Vegetarian meals. Children's helpings. No cigars in dining-room. Wheelchair access (also WC). Music. Air-conditioned

Maharaja £

23–25 Hurst Street, Birmingham B5 4AS	COOKING 2
TEL: (0121) 622 2641 FAX: (0121) 622 4021	COST £18–£34

Lamb bara, chicken Samarkand, chicken badami or tandoori mackerel are among the daily specials in this unpretentious, long-established restaurant a stone's throw from the Birmingham Hippodrome. Further proof that it is a far from standard curry house is the omission from the menu of vindaloo, and other curries dubiously named after places that have never heard of them. The North Indian cooking maintains its high standards, as confirmed by a reader who noted that 'the food always has been and remains of an extremely high calibre'. Another regular visitor pronounced 'rogan josh as good as ever'. A score of wines are very fairly priced, from French house wine at £7.50 to Chablis at £16.85.

CHEFS: Gurmaj Kumar and Jaskarn Dhillon   PROPRIETOR: Mr N.S. Batt   OPEN: Mon to Sat 12 to 2, 6 to 11   CLOSED: bank hols   MEALS: alc (main courses £6.50 to £8). Set L and D £12.70 SERVICE: 10%, card slips closed   CARDS: Amex, Diners, MasterCard, Switch, Visa   DETAILS: 62 seats. Private parties: 26 main room, 30 private room. Vegetarian meals. Wheelchair access (also WC). Music. Air-conditioned

Restaurant Gilmore

27 Warstone Lane, Hockley, Birmingham B18 6JQ	COOKING 2
TEL: (0121) 233 3655 FAX: (01543) 415511	COST £24–£49

The hotchpotch of modern, interwar and 'sternly Victorian factory buildings' of Birmingham's Jewellery Quarter are a reminder of the city's varied industrial heritage, but 'jovial and jolly' Paul Gilmore's conversion manages a 'small and intimate' feel. The more expensive set menu offers greater choice, further extended by a blackboard of dishes at supplementary prices: seared tuna and foie gras with charred red onions, or Scottish beef fillet with black pudding and oyster mushrooms. The main thrust of the cooking takes in a richly flavoured pâté or terrine to start (perhaps a game version served with red onion marmalade), followed by braised John Dory on ratatouille, or a vegetarian option such as vanilla risotto with shiitake and scallions. Desserts generally take a comforting turn in the form of coffee and Tia Maria mousse, or bread-

and-butter pudding. Three Vin de Pays d'Oc house wines at £10.50 head up a serviceable and reasonably varied list.

CHEF: Paul Gilmore   PROPRIETORS: Paul and Dee Gilmore   OPEN: Tue to Fri L 12 to 2, Tue to Sat D 7 to 9.30   CLOSED: 25 Dec to second week Jan, 1 week Easter, first 2 weeks Aug, Tue after bank hols   MEALS: Set L £12.50 (2 courses) to £21.50, Set D £21.50   SERVICE: not inc   CARDS: Amex, Delta, Diners, MasterCard, Switch, Visa   DETAILS: 36 seats. Private parties: 42 main room. Vegetarian meals. Children's helpings. No-smoking area. Wheelchair access (also WC). Music. Air-conditioned £5

BIRTLE   Greater Manchester   map 8

▲ *Normandie* ♥ £

Elbut Lane, Birtle BL9 6UT
TEL: (0161) 764 3869 and 1170
FAX: (0161) 764 4866   COOKING 4
off B6222, 3m NE of Bury   COST £19–£42

Perched on a hill overlooking the Manchester plain, this old stone pub with its modern extension looks and feels much as it has always done: a vaguely Spanish atmosphere emanates from the dining room's rough plaster walls, pillars and archways. Paul Bellingham aims largely for tried and tested ideas with a strong French accent – provençale-style fish soup, or tarragon-stuffed chicken breast in a creamy morel sauce – and while the cooking may not be strong on passion, it does deliver workmanlike results: 'superbly fresh' steamed brill fillets on a less successful prawn raviolo, or 'moist and tender' duck leg confit with cannellini beans and diced beetroot. Well-flavoured terrines – of pork, or spring vegetables, or ham and foie gras – are recommended, as is a 'satisfyingly creamy' banana crème brûlée with an intense dark chocolate sorbet. Bread is highly rated, and efficient service is 'careful rather than confident'. Set meals are reasonably priced, there are light bar lunches and sandwiches, and no service charge is made or expected, all plus-points for those with an eye on value. Indeed, good value appears to be the guiding principle of the wine list, both within France and beyond her borders. House Vin de Pays des Côtes du Tarn is £9.95 a bottle, £2.25 a glass.

CHEF: Paul Bellingham   PROPRIETORS: Mr and Mrs M. Moussa   OPEN: Mon to Fri L 12 to 2, Mon to Sat D 7 to 9.30   CLOSED: 2 weeks from 26 Dec, 1 week Easter, bank hols exc 25 Dec   MEALS: alc (main courses £10 to £17). Set L £12.50, Set D £15. Light L available   SERVICE: none, card slips closed   CARDS: Amex, Delta, Diners, MasterCard, Switch, Visa   DETAILS: 60 seats. Private parties: 65 main room. Car park. Vegetarian meals. No cigars/pipes in restaurant. No-smoking area. Wheelchair access (also WC). Music   ACCOMMODATION: 23 rooms, all with bath/shower. TV. Phone. B&B £59 to £79. Rooms for disabled (*The Which? Hotel Guide*) £5

'[The waitress] did provide some fine entertainment when, on refusing to allow a table of four Germans to move to a larger table in a deserted restaurant, she helpfully told them, "It's too complicated to explain why, but you can't move."' (On eating in London)

▲ *means accommodation is available.*

239

BISHOP'S WALTHAM Hampshire   map 2

Wine Bar £   NEW ENTRY

8 High Street, Bishop's Waltham SO32 1AA   COOKING 2
TEL: (01489) 894476   COST £21–£38

Oenophiles should set a course through the main thoroughfare of this small town near Southampton to find the Hugheses' basement restaurant beneath the wine shop. Wooden cases, labels and wine maps form the décor, and the plank flooring, low lighting and wheelback chairs set an appropriate tone. Blackboard menus offer the likes of goats' cheese crostini, roasted peppers and coriander pesto, or roast cod with champ, crisp leeks and grain mustard sauce. Quickly seared strips of calf's liver showed skill in handling at inspection, and were accompanied by a 'bouncy mound' of saladings in a light mustard vinaigrette. Crème brûlée seems spot-on for textural contrast, and the chocolate mousse with a distinct tang of orange has been given the thumbs-up. Service is totally informal, yet well-drilled. One or two wines represent each region in each colour, and choices are sound. House wines start at £8.95.

CHEFS: Jamie Darby and Paul Waite   PROPRIETORS: Mr and Mrs P.J. Hughes   OPEN: Mon to Sat 12 to 2.30, 7 to 9.30   CLOSED: 25 Dec to 1 Jan, bank hols   MEALS: alc (main courses £7 to £13)   SERVICE: not inc   CARDS: Delta, MasterCard, Switch, Visa   DETAILS: 90 seats. Private parties: 60 main room. Vegetarian meals. No children under 14. No-smoking area. Music. Air-conditioned (£5)

BLACKPOOL Lancashire   map 8

September Brasserie

15–17 Queen Street, Blackpool FY1 1PU   COOKING 3
TEL: (01253) 623282   FAX: (01253) 299455   COST £22–£43

Described by one visitor as 'a fine oasis' in otherwise gastronomically deserted Blackpool, this is a brasserie that takes its modern credentials seriously, from the first-floor open-plan dining room with bare tables, to a repertoire that includes crab and coriander dumplings, and comforting frisée salad with black pudding and poached egg. Materials range from proudly local – pheasant and teal served with creamed mushrooms and mash – to distinctly exotic, as in Canadian bison, braised in organic ale and accompanied by spätzli. Terrines might feature in either savoury or sweet form: Stilton, pear and spinach to start, or white chocolate to finish. A concise but enterprising wine list includes South African Hárslevelü and Argentinian Barbera, as well as a vegetarian organic Saumur Champigny. Portuguese red and South African white house wines are under £13.

CHEF/PROPRIETOR: Michael Golowicz   OPEN: Tue to Sat 12 to 2, 7 to 10; pre- and post-theatre D by arrangement   CLOSED: 1 Jan   MEALS: alc (main courses L £6 to £10.50, D £8.50 to £14.50). Set D £15.80 (2 courses) to £18.50   SERVICE: not inc   CARDS: Amex, Delta, Diners, MasterCard, Switch, Visa   DETAILS: 45 seats. Private parties: 40 main room. Children's helpings. Music (£5)

BLAKENEY Norfolk   map 6

▲ *White Horse Hotel*

4 High Street, Blakeney NR25 7AL
TEL: (01263) 740574   FAX: (01263) 741303   COOKING 2
off A149 between Cley and Morston   COST £25–£42

Given the diversity of people who come through Blakeney – walking the coastal
path, bird-watching, or seal-spotting at Blakeney Point – it is no surprise that the
White Horse, a few yards from the quay, caters for them on several levels, with a
lamp-lit bar 'tastefully done' in cream and dark wood, a pine-tabled bistro, and a
restaurant dining room overlooking the courtyard of the old coaching inn. The
latter offers a monthly-changing carte, with blackboard additions, of 'robust and
strongly flavoured' food that might major on roast Norfolk partridge with
braised cabbage, grills of Dover sole or sirloin steak, and goats'-cheese risotto.
Start with bruschetta, or smoked eel and horseradish, consult the blackboard for
a pudding, and drink from a list of around forty reliable wines, the majority
under £15. House Australian is £9.95.

CHEF: Christopher Hyde   PROPRIETOR: Daniel Rees   OPEN: Tue to Sat (and bank hol Sun) D
only 7 to 9   MEALS: alc (main courses £9 to £16.50). Bar menu available all week L and D
SERVICE: not inc   CARDS: Amex, Delta, MasterCard, Switch, Visa   DETAILS: 35 seats. 100 seats
outside. Private parties: 36 main room. Car park. Vegetarian meals. No children under 14.
Occasional music   ACCOMMODATION: 10 rooms, all with bath/shower. TV. Phone. B&B £25 to
£80. Garden (*The Which? Hotel Guide*)

BOLTON ABBEY North Yorkshire   map 9

▲ *Devonshire Arms, Burlington Restaurant* 🍴✶

Bolton Abbey BD23 6AJ
TEL: (01756) 710441   FAX: (01756) 710564   COOKING 5
at junction of A59 and B6160, 5m NW of Ilkley   COST £29–£58

Set in picturesque Wharfedale, this property has been in the Devonshire family
since 1753, but it still manages to move with the times. Leisure facilities are a
feature – although a free riverside walk in the fresh air, past the twelfth-century
Augustinian priory up to The Strid, may blow away just as many cobwebs – and
the food sets out to appeal to a cross-section of visitors. The Burlington
Restaurant represents the posher end, with a simple deal of three courses (plus
sorbet and coffee at dinner), in which Andrew Nicholson aims for a refined
cooking style. He fashions a terrine from ham hock and foie gras, makes a
sausage of duck, and a soufflé from Stilton, which he serves with a plum sauce.

The cosmopolitan approach uses familiar devices, such as cep risotto to partner
breast of guinea fowl, as well as an occasional exotic excursion for variety:
anise-marinated salmon, for example, has been served with lemon grass,
Japanese rice and a ginger beurre blanc. In essence, the kitchen's industry
translates into a pleasingly indulgent result, not least in desserts of iced
pistachio parfait with pear ravioli, or caramelised fig Tatin with a white
chocolate and armagnac ice cream. Service remains a weak link, while sixty
wines by the glass are supplemented by a traditional 'fine and rare' collection by

the bottle. Lee Canning meanwhile presides over an approachable menu in the bold modern brasserie, offering fish cakes, sausage and mash, grilled cod with crab sauce, and pressed goats' cheese with plum tomatoes in both starter and main-course sizes (£5 and £8.75).

CHEF: Andrew Nicholson   PROPRIETORS: The Duke and Duchess of Devonshire   OPEN: Sun L 12 to 2, all week D 7 to 10   CLOSED: Christmas   MEALS: Set L Sun £18.95, Set D £37   SERVICE: not inc, card slips closed   CARDS: Amex, Delta, Diners, MasterCard, Switch, Visa   DETAILS: 65 seats. Private parties: 12 main room, 12 to 100 private rooms. Car park. Vegetarian meals. Children's helpings. Jacket and tie. No smoking in dining room. Wheelchair access (also WC). No music   ACCOMMODATION: 41 rooms, all with bath/shower. TV. Phone. B&B £110 to £325. Rooms for disabled. Baby facilities. Swimming pool. Fishing (*The Which? Hotel Guide*)

BOUGHTON LEES   Kent   map 3

▲ *Eastwell Manor* 🍞 ⚡✗

Eastwell Park, Boughton Lees TN25 4HR
TEL: (01233) 213000   FAX: (01233) 635530   COOKING 5
on A251, 3m N of Ashford   COST £27–£74

The old grey-stone house, with gables, battlements and mullioned windows, seems to be 'expanding like mad' with extra bedrooms, apartments, a health spa and leisure complex. By contrast, the ancient, chandeliered, dark wood-ceilinged dining room remains as before, with a pianist tucked against the wall behind the cheese trolley. The kitchen, meanwhile, is now under the supervision of Steven Black, who appeared in the last edition of the *Guide* at Thornbury Castle (see entry, Thornbury). Ingredients are seriously well sourced and, although luxuries abound, there is a good balance in the menu between seafood starters and more earthy main courses.

The food is certainly technically accomplished, and dishes are well thought out: for example, a tripartite dish of lamb in May, each component resting on its own individual cake of vegetables, the loin on gratin dauphinoise, sweetbreads on layered Mediterranean vegetables, and the kidney on silky spinach, all in a pool of glossy brown stock-based sauce. Timing (along with some of the ideas) tends to be 'conservative', so dishes may appear to lack sparkle, although an inspector's simply presented starter of green asparagus ribbons laid across two peeled langoustines and four scallops, in a light, frothy butter sauce, was 'very fresh, very restrained'.

Trios are also likely to occur at dessert stage: for example, a dish of pear consisting of a soufflé, a sorbet, and a 'subtly and clearly flavoured' whole skinned pear marinated and cooked in red wine and spices. Formal hierarchical service (main courses are domed, bottles placed out of reach, and dishes wheeled around on trolleys) is overseen by a helpful and well-informed manager. The annotated, predominantly French wine list dips only occasionally below £20. House vin de pays Chardonnay is £13, Dom. Chancel Syrah £14.

'Unfortunately, the food is really quite ordinary even for its extraordinarily ordinary ambitions.' (On eating in Essex)

CHEF: Steven Black   PROPRIETOR: Mr T. Parrett   OPEN: all week 12 to 2.30, 7 to 10   MEALS: alc (main courses £18.50 to £25). Set L £15, Set D £30   SERVICE: not inc, card slips closed   CARDS: Amex, MasterCard, Visa   DETAILS: 70 seats. Private parties: 110 main room, 12 to 70 private rooms. Car park. Vegetarian meals. Children's helpings. No smoking in dining room. Wheelchair access (also WC). Music   ACCOMMODATION: 60 rooms, all with bath/shower. TV. Phone. B&B £150 to £350. Rooms for disabled. Baby facilities. Swimming pool (*The Which? Hotel Guide*)
£5

BOWNESS-ON-WINDERMERE Cumbria   map 8

▲ *Linthwaite House* ✠✳

Crook Road, Bowness-on-Windermere LA23 3JA
TEL: (01539) 488600   FAX: (01539) 488601   COOKING 4
EMAIL: admin@linthwaite.com   COST £22–£51

This is the Lake District style in full cry: a comfortable hotel surrounded by rambling gardens and wooded hillside, with views over Lake Windermere, a 'sumptuous, spacious' dining room, and well-drilled staff serving three-course dinners topped and tailed by canapés, a chef's 'bonne bouche', and petits fours with coffee. A balanced menu generally incorporates a red meat (perhaps rack of lamb), a white meat (roast saddle of rabbit), salmon plus one other fish (lemon sole on truffle butter sauce, say), and a vegetarian option (such as ragoût of oyster mushrooms with cream and cognac). Other country-house favourites include starters of asparagus with hollandaise, or courgette and cucumber soup, and it is worth considering British cheese (a small portion each of ten different ones) as an alternative to desserts of crème brûlée (a fixture), lemon syllabub, or warm poached strawberries spiked with green peppercorns. Cru classé clarets from the 1980s add gravitas to a list that is otherwise simply arranged by varietal/style for ease of selection. House claret is £18.75, house white, a Chardonnay from New Zealand's Hawkes Bay region, is £16.95.

CHEF: Ian Bravey   PROPRIETORS: Mike Bevans, Handmade Hotels   OPEN: Sun L 12.30 to 1.30, all week D 7 to 9   MEALS: Set L £15, Set D £35. Bar L available Mon to Sat   SERVICE: net prices, card slips closed   CARDS: Amex, Delta, MasterCard, Switch, Visa   DETAILS: 40 seats. 20 seats outside. Private parties: 40 main room, 20 private room. Car park. Vegetarian meals. Children's helpings. No children under 7 at D. No smoking in dining-room. Wheelchair access (1 step; also WC). Occasional music   ACCOMMODATION: 26 rooms, all with bath/shower. TV. Phone. D,B&B £81 to £288. Rooms for disabled. Baby facilities. Fishing (*The Which? Hotel Guide*) £5

Porthole Eating House 🍾

3 Ash Street, Bowness-on-Windermere LA23 3EB
TEL: (015394) 42793   FAX: (015394) 88675   COOKING 4
EMAIL: gianni.berton@which.net   COST £18–£51

The Italian input at this white-fronted seventeenth-century cottage, in one of Bowness's oldest (now pedestrianised) streets, owes a lot to Gianni Berton's family back home, although the food is a real mix of ideas, ranging from prawn cocktail and snails to grilled Dover sole, from charcoal grilled steaks to Thai chicken stir-fry. A weekly-changing 'speciality' menu of seasonal dishes and recommended wines is the repository of 'new' items along the lines of baby halibut fillet with Savoy cabbage, and veal kidney with black pudding in a sherry vinegar reduction, as well as a vegetarian option such as tomato and rosemary risotto. Puddings incorporate standard tiramisù or orange Positano alongside vanilla ice cream with rumtopf. Judy Berton is considered 'one of the best front-of-house performers in the Lake District'. Highly prized wines from Europe and Australia are liberally scattered through the pages of the Porthole's impressive list. Mark-ups are certainly fair at the lower end of the spectrum, with plenty of good drinking to be had under £20, but wine buffs should be aware that many of the finer, rarer wines are listed as 'p.o.a.', which might be tiresome when it comes to making your selection. House Italian is £11 for a litre.

CHEF: Andrew Fairchild PROPRIETORS: Judy and Gianni Berton OPEN: Mon, Wed to Fri and Sun L 12 to 2.30, Wed to Mon D 6.30 to 10.30 MEALS: alc (main courses L £5 to £9, D £9.50 to £15) SERVICE: not inc, card slips closed CARDS: Amex, Delta, Diners, MasterCard, Switch, Visa DETAILS: 40 seats. 24 seats outside. Private parties: 40 main room, 40 private room. Vegetarian meals. Children's helpings. Music

---

BRAITHWAITE Cumbria   map 10

▲ Ivy House ▼ ⅝✸

Braithwaite CA12 5SY
TEL: (017687) 78338 FAX: (017687) 78113   COOKING 3
just off B5292 Keswick to Braithwaite road   COST £30–£39

Everybody starts the evening with drinks in the red ground-floor lounge, then climbs the stairs to a green dining room with candlelit tables, where regimen dictates an early, good-value four-course dinner. A roving chef's eye produces Thai pork satay with peanut sauce and cucumber relish, Brie pancakes with redcurrant jelly, and perhaps roasted aubergine with pesto and local goats' cheese. Soups (the second course) may be as traditional as curried parsnip or carrot and coriander, while main courses tend towards meat, offering leg of Mansergh Hall lamb with mint sauce, or sirloin steak with Cajun spices. Menus are varied enough – one couple who stayed a few days 'ate well and differently each night' – and desserts are recited (some diners hear the spiel many times in one evening), for example a plum variant on bread-and-butter pudding, or lemon tart with lemon curd ice cream. Quasi-formal service is considered 'northern' on the grounds that 'waiters do not whisper', and wines are a cosmopolitan bunch, showing some seasonal variation. The short but imaginative list draws from good producers yet keeps prices mostly under £20; eight vins de pays are £10.95 each.

CHEFS: Wendy Shill and Peter Holten PROPRIETORS: Nick and Wendy Shill OPEN: all week D only 7 to 7.45 CLOSED: 30 Dec to 30 Jan MEALS: Set D £21.95 SERVICE: not inc CARDS: Amex, Delta, Diners, MasterCard, Switch, Visa DETAILS: 30 seats. Private parties: 12 main room. Car park. Vegetarian meals. Children's helpings. No children under 6. No smoking in dining room. Music ACCOMMODATION: 12 rooms, all with bath/shower. TV. Phone. D,B&B £50 to £120. Baby facilities

---

The Guide *always appreciates hearing about changes of chef or owner.*

BRAMPTON Cumbria   map 10

▲ *Farlam Hall*

Brampton CA8 2NG
TEL: (016977) 46234   FAX: (016977) 46683
EMAIL: farlamhall@dial.pipex.com   COOKING 3
on A689, 2½m SE of Brampton (not at Farlam village)   COST £40–£50

Dinner is an event at this comfortable, out-of-the-way Victorian country house,
which welcomes guests warmly and treats them to 'immaculate' service.
Everybody sits down between eight o'clock and half-past for four courses plus
coffee (and a sorbet on Saturdays), with a choice of three items at each stage
(more for puddings). Barry Quinion, who has been at the stoves now for a
quarter of a century, cooks in gentle Anglo-French style, changing the menu
daily and producing main courses of seafood roulade, calf's liver with mash, and
pork with wild mushrooms. A goats'-cheese soufflé might start the ball rolling,
or green bean and smoked bacon soup, and a cheeseboard appears before
desserts such as peach parfait with shortbread and peach compote, or chocolate
nut fudge pie with crème fraîche. Wine prices are rather more affordable outside
the classic French regions – look at the reliable antipodeans, for example –
starting with house red and white at £13.50.

CHEF: Barry Quinion   PROPRIETORS: the Quinion and the Stevenson families   OPEN: all week D
only 8 to 8.30   CLOSED: 26 to 30 Dec   MEALS: Set D Sun to Fri £30, Set D Sat £31   SERVICE: not
inc   CARDS: Delta, MasterCard, Switch, Visa   DETAILS: 45 seats. Private parties: 45 main room.
Car park. No children under 5 in dining room. Wheelchair access (not WC). No music
ACCOMMODATION: 12 rooms, all with bath/shower. TV. Phone. D,B&B £120 to £250. No children
under 5 in accommodation (*The Which? Hotel Guide*)

BRAY Berkshire   map 3

Fat Duck ♟

1 High Street, Bray SL6 2AQ   COOKING 8
TEL: (01628) 580333   FAX: (01628) 776188   COST £39–£98

Reporters who have been astonished by the incongruity between food and
surroundings, and suffered hard wooden chairs in what has seemed like 'a
makeshift wine bar', will be pleased to learn that changes in décor and layout are
on the way. The Blumenthals are aiming for greater comfort (a lounge area for
pre- and post-dinner drinks is planned) and a better-equipped kitchen. Heston
Blumenthal insists that it will not result in a more formal or expensive set-up,
nor a change of culinary direction. That will be a relief to many: 'the three best
meals I ate last year were all at the Fat Duck,' noted an off-duty inspector.
  The cooking is exciting because Blumenthal is a one-off. He does not do Grand
Cuisine, and is not an imitator. He dissects modern cooking, and reshuffles the
components in a highly personal way. 'There are no simple dishes,' reckoned
one observer; 'everything undergoes an odyssey.' This might begin with an
inch-thick slab of foie gras sitting on slices of marinated salmon, on a handful of
crystallised seaweed, the plate drizzled with an oyster-flavoured vinaigrette, or
with a 'brilliantly conceived and executed' cuttlefish cannelloni, which one

reporter voted his dish of the year: sections of the body are filled with a farce of duck confit, duck ham, foie gras, cuttlefish and maple syrup, then presented on parsley purée.

Main courses veer towards offal, duck, plus perhaps game, fish and a vegetarian option. Combinations of taste and texture readily reveal themselves, although occasional voices ask if there is perhaps one ingredient too many in a dish, as if the cooking may at times be too inventive for its own good. Others, however, maintain the food is greater than the sum of its parts. Significantly, the highlight of an inspection meal was a 'simple, classic' variant on tarte Tatin, served with pungent ice cream flavoured with Tahitian vanilla. But it is difficult to resist a millefeuille of pain d'epices ice cream with pineapple and chilli jelly, which requires A-level chemistry to set the pineapple juice: a reporter who described Blumenthal as 'almost obsessive' was correct, apart from the 'almost'.

'I do like the unstuffy atmosphere and informal approach,' wrote one visitor, although the casual air disguises knowledgeable, helpful staff. The food may not be cheap, but reporters feel they have received good value for money, exceptionally so on the set-price lunch. Sommelier John Walden has joined the Fat Duck team and his influence on the wine list is already apparent, although further changes are promised (including, we would hope, a less confusing layout). Some particularly fine wines have been introduced to the Burgundy, Bordeaux and American pages, but not at the expense of lower-priced bottles, as there is still good drinking to be had under £20. There are no half-bottles, but thirty wines are offered by the glass, as are several fine sherries.

CHEF: Heston Blumenthal   PROPRIETORS: Heston and Susanna Blumenthal   OPEN: Tue to Sun L 12 to 2 (2.30 Sun), Tue to Sat D 7 to 9.30 (10 Fri and Sat)   CLOSED: 2 weeks Christmas MEALS: alc (main courses £18.50 to £27.50). Set L Tue to Sat £23.50   SERVICE: not inc, card slips closed   CARDS: Amex, MasterCard, Switch, Visa   DETAILS: 45 seats. 20 seats outside. Private parties: 55 main room. Children's helpings. Wheelchair access (1 step; also WC). Occasional music

---

▲ Waterside Inn

Ferry Road, Bray SL6 2AT
TEL: (01628) 620691   FAX: (01628) 784710   COOKING 9
EMAIL: waterinn@aol.com   COST £48–£176

Despite an element of chinoiserie in the dining room, and in the mini pagodas on the terrace overlooking the Thames, this is essentially a small corner of England that will be forever France. One who had not visited for ten years was heartened that 'its original standards and principles are unchanged'. The Waterside exists to show just how good refined French cooking can be. Although 'technically almost faultless', this is not food to make the earth move, rather it is 'a highly efficient demonstration of the culinary arts'. At its best it achieves 'true simplicity' using first-rate ingredients, as well as a rare harmony that stems from sound culinary judgement and a respect for the classics.

One of the highlights has to be pan-fried medallions of lobster with a 'simply breathtaking' sauce of white port with hints of ginger and honey. Indeed, saucing is a strength: for example, a cep-flavoured 'jus' to accompany pink, crisp-skinned pigeon, served with fondant potato 'cooked in duck fat for added flavour' and foie gras wrapped in leek. Foie gras, of course, appears regularly, pan-fried with rhubarb and pear to start, or perhaps as a stuffing for monkfish served with an 'outstanding red wine sauce'. Fish and shellfish are used lavishly among first courses, rabbit is likely to show up among mains, alongside Bresse chicken, Challandais duck, and perhaps lamb in the form of poached fillet and confit in a horseradish-flavoured bouillon.

French cheeses are kept in prime condition, and dessert samples come round on a 'dim sum' trolley. The real things exude 'sheer artistry and they alone are worth the trip here': an alcoholic hot plum soufflé 'of supreme texture', a 'sublime' pear tarte Tatin, or the plate of six desserts that includes raspberry gratin, pistachio crème brûlée, rum baba, chocolate délice, vanilla ice cream, and a 'perfect example of what a pear sablé should be'. The whole package is wrapped in benchmark 'smooth as silk' professional service. Domes are lifted with perfect timing, napkins are changed if you leave the table, and returned on a silver platter, although the practice of giving unpriced menus to ladies, even when they are paying, seems faintly ridiculous in this day and age. It is best not to eat here if counting the pennies. One hardened gourmet, who choked on £34.50 for a lobster starter, found the prices 'simply terrifying . . . and that's before the wine list lands on your table'. Its contents are as resolutely French as the rest of the operation and there's no disputing their quality; but any restaurant should be able to offer at least a reasonable selection of decent wines at affordable prices these days, and the Waterside can manage only three under £20. House white is £19, house claret £26. At least Evian water is free.

CHEFS: Michel Roux and Mark Dodson   PROPRIETOR: Michel Roux   OPEN: Wed to Sun L 12 to 2 (2.30 Sat and Sun), Tue to Sun D 7 to 10   CLOSED: 26 Dec to 27 Jan, 4 days from Easter Mon, Sun D 1 Oct to 30 April   MEALS: alc (main courses £30.50 to £49.50). Set L all week £29.50 and £68, Set L Sat and Sun £44.50, Set D £68   SERVICE: 12.5% (optional), card slips closed   CARDS: Amex, Diners, MasterCard, Switch, Visa   DETAILS: 75 seats. Private parties: 80 main room, 8 private room. Car park. Vegetarian meals. Children's helpings. No children under 12 in dining room. No cigars in dining-room. Wheelchair access (not WC). Occasional music   ACCOMMODATION: 9 rooms, all with bath/shower. TV. Phone. Room only £145 to £260. No children under 12 in accommodation

---

BRIGHTON East Sussex   map 3

Black Chapati

12 Circus Parade, New England Road,
Brighton BN1 4GW   COOKING 4
TEL: (01273) 699011   COST £28–£43

In a parade of shops near a junction on the London road into the town, the Chapati may be 'entirely missable by those who haven't been before', although it seems so popular that most people probably have been before. It is a 'modest beacon of quality' delivering a solid, consistent performance, where Eastern flavourings predominate, at least in savoury dishes, and where Stephen Funnell's level of innovation continues to hold sway. India may be represented by skewered chicken with leavened bread, aloo ghobi and lentils, but the net extends much wider, taking in a starter of grilled mackerel with Thai salad and egg noodles, and a main-course roast rack of lamb with couscous, spiced pumpkin broth and harissa.

The kitchen avoids the extremes wrought in the name of fusion food and allows enough room for fish and vegetable dishes: roast cod with shrimp and lime leaf sauce, or braised bean curd with pickled bean sprouts and steamed rice. To finish, tropical fruit salad takes its place alongside vin santo with almond and chocolate biscotti, or sesame doughnuts with honey ice cream. Two ciders and a trio of beers complement the micro-list of eleven wines, which start at £9.95.

CHEFS/PROPRIETORS: Stephen Funnell and Lauren Alker   OPEN: Tue to Sat D only 7 (6.30 Sat) to 10   CLOSED: 2 weeks Christmas, 2 weeks July   MEALS: alc (main courses £10 to £12.50)   SERVICE: 10%, card slips closed   CARDS: Amex, Delta, MasterCard, Switch, Visa   DETAILS: 32 seats. Private parties: 8 main room. Vegetarian meals. Wheelchair access (not WC). Music

Gingerman | NEW ENTRY |

| 21A Norfolk Square, Brighton BN1 2PD | COOKING 2 |
| TEL/FAX: (01273) 326688 | COST £25–£34 |

This narrow restaurant in a quiet street, just off a pretty square between Western Road and the sea, pleases reporters for its congenial atmosphere, light, modern décor, and a good-value set-price menu that scores highly for trendy ingredients: bok choy, truffle oil, chorizo, sea bass. Ben McKellar – the eponymous redhead – handles them deftly. Diners have enjoyed roasted tiger prawns in gazpacho – 'great colour and flavour' – and 'punchy' gingered duck spring roll. Calf's liver with shallot mash in winter, and 'lovely, gooey' roast sweet potato in summer, or grilled tuna with lentils, further show the style. Roasting is a favoured technique, applied to rabbit, belly pork, salmon and vegetables, while ceps and fried quails' eggs on toast could provide a savoury alternative to 'warm and unctuous' apricot feuilleté. Service 'jollies along nicely'. The short wine list covers the globe, with plenty under £15; French house wine is £9.25.

CHEF: Ben McKellar   PROPRIETORS: Ben and Neil McKellar, and Pamela Abbott   OPEN: Wed to Sun L 12.30 to 2, Tue to Sat D 7.30 to 10   CLOSED: 2 weeks winter, 2 weeks summer   MEALS: Set L Mon to Sat £9.95 (1 course) to £14.95, Set L Sun and Set D £17.95 (2 courses) to £21.50   SERVICE: not inc   CARDS: Amex, Delta, Diners, MasterCard, Switch, Visa   DETAILS: 32 seats. Private parties: 32 main room. Children's helpings. No-smoking area. Music

One Paston Place

| 1 Paston Place, Brighton BN2 1HA | COOKING 6 |
| TEL: (01273) 606933   FAX: (01273) 675686 | COST £27–£60 |

Up a gently sloping hill, 50 yards from the seafront, east of the Palace Pier, a large glass door leads into the single dining room, where a stripped wooden floor, trompe l'oeil country scene, and assorted mirrors and watercolours create a relaxed yet 'light and pleasantly formal' impresssion. Mark Emmerson's contemporary French-based food takes in squab pigeon with ceps, and an unusual starter of scallops paired with a ragoût of pig's trotter and lentils, topped with langoustine beignet. The cooking is skilful, and flavours work well together, as in a comforting dish of chargrilled asparagus and artichoke with a creamy morel sabayon, or neatly trimmed rabbit served with a 'post-modernist ratatouille' incorporating crispy ratte potatoes.

The kitchen keeps its eye on the seasons – a light, creamy sauce full of peas and broad beans in late May, to accompany fillets of sea bass and red mullet – but is not averse to ideas from further afield, as in a crab soup with Thai spices. Modest invention, meanwhile, extends to 'wonderfully cooked' foie gras accompanied by slices of contrastingly sharp green rhubarb and thin crisps of Szechuan pepper. 'Assiettes' range from a duck-based Landaise version to start, to a plate of five desserts: tart rhubarb tart with good pastry, fennel crème brûlée, top-notch coffee ice cream, raspberry shortcake, and chocolate mousse made from half white, half milk. Service from Nicole Emmerson and helpers has been generally professional, and the wine list takes a predominantly French and traditional stand. House Tannat red and Gros Manseng white from Alain Brumont are £11.

CHEF: Mark Emmerson   PROPRIETORS: Mark and Nicole Emmerson   OPEN: Tue to Sat 12.30 to 2, 7 to 10   CLOSED: first 2 weeks Jan, first 2 weeks Aug   MEALS: alc (main courses £16.50 to £17.50). Set L £14.50 (2 courses) to £16.50, Set D £38   SERVICE: 10%, card slips closed   CARDS: Amex, Delta, Diners, MasterCard, Switch, Visa   DETAILS: 45 seats. No cigars/pipes in dining-room. Wheelchair access (not WC). Music. Air-conditioned

Terre à Terre ⅰ✷ £

71 East Street, Brighton BN1 3HQ   COOKING 4
TEL: (01273) 729051   FAX: (01273) 327561   COST £23–£38

Any lingering doubts over whether vegetarian food has cast off its lentils and sandals image should be instantly dispelled by a visit to Terre à Terre. Bright orange walls, a large, blue central bar and vibrant oil paintings give an impression of 'immense vigour'. And while 'a vicious acoustic' makes it best suited to the young at heart, those who don't mind the aural onslaught can expect 'an evening of nothing but delight'.

So wildly inventive is the menu that it is quite possible to find nothing immediately recognisable: poke mole, scorched rice paper lumpia potsticker, and walnut ravioli frisbee, for example, take a bit of explaining. Yet it is a tribute to the kitchen's keen understanding of flavour and technique that even the wackiest-sounding dishes turn out to be triumphs of good taste. Focaccia breads are one speciality, rösti another: try it with traditional Swiss raclette or with griddled aubergine and sweet potato plus burned tomato and red onion salsa. Portions are huge, but the curious can taste their way around the menu in small bites with tapas. Desserts continue in the same innovative vein: pancakes come with pistachio ice cream, smashed strawberries and craggy honeycomb bites; roast rhubarb and raspberry sabayon trifle with a snap-crackle demerara top. Service is friendly but not always quite up to speed. The wine list has garnered organic bottles from all over the world, starting with French house wine at £9.50.

CHEFS: Paul Morgan, Lawrence Glass and Ricky Hodgson   PROPRIETORS: Amanda Powley and Philip Taylor   OPEN: Mon 6 to 10.30, Tue to Sun 12 to 10.30   CLOSED: 25 and 26 Dec, 1 Jan   MEALS: alc (main courses £5 to £9)   SERVICE: not inc, 10% for parties of 6 or more   CARDS: Amex, Delta, Diners, MasterCard, Switch, Visa   DETAILS: 80 seats. Private parties: 8 main room. Vegetarian meals. Children's helpings. No smoking in 1 dining room. No cigars/pipes in dining room. Wheelchair access (also WC). Music. Air-conditioned

Whytes

33 Western Street, Brighton BN1 2PG   COOKING 3
TEL/FAX: (01273) 776618   COST £30–£36

The Whytes packed their bags and left this compact, homely restaurant just off Brighton's western seafront early in 1999 but new owner John Anthony kept on the name, and Paul Gunn has picked up the baton of Ian Whyte's culinary style with impressive composure. The expansive range takes in warm potato salad with chorizo and salsa verde, Moroccan-spiced braised lamb shank with dried apricot and pine nut couscous, and rhubarb crème brûlée, and the touch is assured. The chunky consistency of a game and pickled walnut terrine was well served by its accompanying sharp chutney of grape and fig at an early meal under the new regime. Sea bass with asparagus and a creamy saffron sauce was a richly sustaining fish special, and a breast and leg of guinea fowl sauced with wild mushrooms and Madeira made similar impact. Puddings are still recited at table: a baked half-apple topped with rhubarb crumble and banana ice-cream, or maybe a tart such as pear and almond with mascarpone. The wine list was being overhauled at the time of going to press; house vins de pays are £9.65.

CHEF: Paul Gunn   PROPRIETOR: John Anthony   OPEN: Tue to Sat D only 7 to 9.30   CLOSED: 26 Dec to 1 Jan, bank hols   MEALS: Set D £17.50 (2 courses) to £21   SERVICE: not inc   CARDS: Amex, Delta, MasterCard, Switch, Visa   DETAILS: 36 seats. Private parties: 30 main room, 12 private room. Vegetarian meals. No cigars/pipes in dining room. No-smoking area. Music

---

BRIMFIELD Herefordshire   map 5

▲ Roebuck 🌟 £

Brimfield SY8 4NE
TEL: (01584) 711230   FAX: (01584) 711654
EMAIL: roebuckinn@demon.co.uk
just off A49 Leominster to Ludlow road, 4m W of   COOKING 3
Tenbury Wells   COST £23–£46

Chefs of the light, contemporary school, David Willson-Lloyd and Jonnie Waters supplement the monthly-changing menu at this 'country dining pub' in the village centre with blackboard specials according to their fancy and whatever local produce is available. Among a selection of English classics – steak and mushroom pudding, griddled calf's liver, roast chicken breast and 'our famous fish pie' – appear several more modern choices along the lines of boudin of chicken and wild mushrooms, tiger prawns wrapped in bacon on couscous, or pumpkin, rocket and pine nut ravioli. For one diner, a special of monkfish stuffed with lobster mousse, followed by an 'exceptionally good' lemon tart, made a fine spring meal. Vegetables are served separately and in quantity. Service is 'not posh, not familiar, not by robots'. Wines are enthusiastically presented, and are arranged by style, including reds for 'traditional British fayre'; most are under £20, with a handful of finer bottles, and house French and South African are £9.95.

CHEFS: Jonathan Waters and David Willson-Lloyd PROPRIETORS: David and Susan Willson-Lloyd OPEN: all week 12 to 2.30, 7 to 9.30 CLOSED: 25 Dec MEALS: alc (main courses £8 to £20) SERVICE: not inc, card slips closed CARDS: Delta, MasterCard, Switch, Visa DETAILS: 100 seats. 25 seats outside. Private parties: 44 main room. Car park. Vegetarian meals. Children's helpings. No smoking in dining room. Wheelchair access (not WC). No music ACCOMMODATION: 3 rooms, all with bath/shower. TV. Phone. B&B £45 to £60. Baby facilities (*The Which? Hotel Guide*) £5

BRISTOL Bristol   map 2

Bell's Diner ✸ £

1–3 York Street, Montpelier, Bristol BS6 5QB
TEL: (0117) 924 0357 FAX: (0117) 924 4280
take Picton Street off Cheltenham Road (A38) – runs   COOKING 5
into York Road   COST £23–£46

A converted grocer's shop in the heart of Montpelier provides an informal setting for Christopher Wicks's sharp, contemporary cooking. In winter a real fire burns in the snug front room, which retains the original shop fittings. The back room is brighter and more modern, with views over a small courtyard garden.

The daily-changing menu reflects influences from a variety of cuisines – Indian bean stew with coriander-creamed onions; roast pumpkin gnocchi; Spanish sardine casserole with almonds – but really the style is all the chef's own. It owes a lot to his clever sourcing and imaginative treatment of unusual produce. 'We are still using wild ingredients from local pickers,' he writes, adding that he snaps up local zander and pike, pairing them with choucroute and wood sorrel respectively. Freshwater eel presents more of a challenge, but roasted and served with pancetta it should persuade any doubters. Classic dishes often find favour, such as provençale fish soup and a 'very good' tomato tarte Tatin. Puddings of cherry and almond tart, and chocolate St-Emilion might be served with 'farm cream'. Service is courteous and efficient, and a well-balanced international wine list offers good value, with house wine at £9.95.

CHEFS: Christopher Wicks and Steven Plaister PROPRIETOR: Christopher Wicks OPEN: Tue to Fri and Sun L 12 to 2.30, Mon to Sat D 7 to 10.30 (11 Sat) CLOSED: 24 to 30 Dec, Sun L April to Sept MEALS: alc (main courses £7.50 to £16) SERVICE: not inc, 10% for parties of 8 or more CARDS: Amex, Delta, MasterCard, Switch, Visa DETAILS: 60 seats. Private parties: 35 main room. Vegetarian meals. Children's helpings. No smoking in dining room. Music £5

Glass Boat

Welsh Back, Bristol BS1 4SB   COOKING 5
TEL: (0117) 929 0704 FAX: (0117) 929 7338   COST £26–£47

The setting, a converted barge moored on Bristol's waterfront, is superb, with copious windows allowing views from every table in the bright, elegant and airy dining room. New chef Jason Deason scans the world for inspiration, a reporter commenting, 'he has a light hand with strong flavours, a degree of flair and his own style.' Thus roasted vine tomato soup is flavoured with smoked garlic, while salmon tartare is layered with white crab meat and served with pickled cucumber and black keta. An inspector appreciated the interesting combination of flavours and textures in starters of three small, crisp pork and date rissoles flavoured with herbs and spices, and served with a cauliflower mash; and arancini goats'-cheese risotto, presented as a crisp croquette, the cheese melting inside. At the same meal, intensely flavoured seared salmon escalopes came on a bed of couscous with a thick, spicy saffron and tomato jus, and 'plump and tender' roast saddle of lamb stuffed with buttered spinach was successfully accompanied by a white wine and thyme sauce. Desserts also get high marks, particularly a 'soft, light and moist' espresso pound cake with Turkish coffee ice-cream. Service is 'polite and friendly', and the wine list leans towards France, but not at the expense of other countries. House wines are £9.95.

CHEF: Jason Deason   PROPRIETOR: Arne Ringner   OPEN: Mon to Fri L 11.45 to 2, Mon to Sat D 6.30 to 11   CLOSED: 24 to 26 Dec   MEALS: alc (main courses L £7 to £11, D £13 to £15.50). Set L £10.95 (2 courses), Set D £17.50   SERVICE: 10%, card slips closed   CARDS: Amex, Delta, MasterCard, Switch, Visa   DETAILS: 130 seats. Private parties: 40 main room, 60 private room. Vegetarian meals. Children's helpings. No cigars/pipes in dining room. Wheelchair access (not WC). Occasional music. Air-conditioned   (£5)

Harveys

12 Denmark Street, Bristol BS1 5DQ   COOKING 3
TEL: (0117) 927 5034   FAX: (0117) 927 5001   COST £28–£72

Sherry casks and Bristol blue glass bottles symbolise the historical role of these converted medieval wine cellars. 'Everything feels expensive,' noted one visitor, eyeing the elegant glassware, boldly coloured artwork, and jazzy modern crockery. The cheaper lunch option offers a choice of two items per course: perhaps sweet-tasting pea soup with slices of chicken and bacon roulade, before fresh, crisp-skinned sea bass served with an unusual combination of couscous and spring cabbage, followed by apple turnovers dredged in cinnamon sugar. Most effort seems to be directed at the more elaborate and luxury-strewn alternatives – duck and foie gras terrine, loin of lamb on herb risotto – with price supplements for langoustine rissoles in truffle marinade, or beef with truffle mash. While the kitchen appears well versed in the classical repertoire, it doesn't always pull out all the stops: passion, referred to in the brochure, was 'exactly what was lacking' at inspection. Service is young, formal and French, and fine French wines are certainly not lacking from a list which is so thick that bookmarks are provided. Prices are very fair at all levels, from fully mature top-class clarets to below-£20 bins, of which there is a good selection. House French is £14, but don't neglect to try the sherries and ports.

CHEF: Daniel Galmiche   PROPRIETOR: John Harvey & Sons   OPEN: Mon to Fri L 12 to 2, Mon to Sat D 7 to 10.45   CLOSED: bank hols   MEALS: Set L £14.95 (2 courses) to £39.95, Set D £33.95 (2 courses) to £39.95   SERVICE: net prices   CARDS: Amex, Delta, Diners, MasterCard, Switch, Visa   DETAILS: 120 seats. Private parties: 120 main room, 50 private room. Music. Air-conditioned

The Good Food Guide *is a registered trade mark of Which? Ltd.*

Hunt's

26 Broad Street, Bristol BS1 2HG
TEL/FAX: (0117) 926 5580

'Everything he produces is a little masterpiece,' reckoned one ~~~ and Anne Hunt's forty-seater, which in 2000 celebrates its first ~~~~~ in the old commercial part of the city. The cooking inhabits such reassuringly familiar territory as leek and potato soup, crab gratin, and baked goats' cheese with sweet onion marmalade, variously available on the main carte and on the list of light one-plate lunchtime dishes: 'these are not bar snacks,' insists Andrew Hunt of home-made tagliatelle, salmon with watercress sauce, and chicken basquaise. While it might offer the 'best fish in central Bristol', according to one reporter – perhaps baked Cornish hake with mushrooms and garlic – the kitchen still leans heavily towards meat: maize-fed guinea fowl comes with apples and calvados, venison medallions arrive with sweet dill gherkins, sour cream and tarragon. Desserts may eschew the fruity end of the spectrum in favour of crème brûlée, chocolate marquise and walnut and treacle tart. Around forty wines, mostly French, explore some lesser-known producers and are helpfully annotated. Half a dozen house wines start at £9.95.

CHEF: Andrew Hunt   PROPRIETORS: Mr and Mrs A.J. Hunt   OPEN: Tue to Fri L 12 to 2, Tue to Sat D 7 to 10   CLOSED: 2 weeks Christmas, 1 week Easter, last 2 weeks Aug   MEALS: alc (main courses L £6 to £15.50, D £11.50 to £15.50)   SERVICE: not inc, card slips closed   CARDS: Amex, Delta, MasterCard, Switch, Visa   DETAILS: 40 seats. Private parties: 26 main room. Children's helpings. Wheelchair access (not WC). Occasional music

Markwicks ▮

43 Corn Street, Bristol BS1 1HT   COOKING 6
TEL/FAX: (0117) 926 2658   COST £27–£54

'A star place' reckons one visitor who makes a beeline for this oak-panelled former bank vault whenever he is in Bristol. The atmosphere is 'refined', the tablecloths are starched but the staff are not; indeed, it is a welcoming, unstuffy environment in which to enjoy a classically based style of cooking: confit of duck with potato pancake and onion marmalade, roast squab pigeon with Madeira sauce, or calves' sweetbreads with morel mushrooms. Seafood is dictated by the market: perhaps Cornish crab and langoustine salad, hake fillet with fennel and red pepper sauce, or plump scallops 'bursting with flavour'.

'If we have made any changes in recent years,' writes Stephen Markwick, 'it is towards our sourcing of food supplies.' Together with Barry Haughton of Rocinantes (see entry below) and Martin Lam of Ransome's Dock (see entry, London), he is in the process of setting up a pilot organic market garden scheme to grow vegetables specifically for a group of restaurants. Is there any reason why this should not set a pattern for co-operative restaurants in other parts of the country? Chocolate typically figures in at least one dessert, perhaps in pancakes with roasted banana and coconut sorbet, and there is usually a hot soufflé, maybe pecan and butterscotch. Stellar producers from the Rhône, Alsace and California – Guigal, Trimbach and Joseph Phelps, to name but three – feature in a globe-trotting wine list that prides itself on keeping prices as low as possible to

…rage experimentation. At the front is an attractive collection of house …nes starting at £11.50, but don't forget to take a look at the bin-ends at the back.

CHEF: Stephen Markwick   PROPRIETORS: Stephen and Judy Markwick   OPEN: Mon to Fri L 12 to 2, Mon to Sat D 7 to 10   CLOSED: 1 week Christmas, 1 week Easter, last 2 weeks Aug, bank hols   MEALS: alc (main courses £15.50 to £17.50). Set L £14.50 (2 courses) to £17.50, Set D £25.50   SERVICE: not inc, card slips closed   CARDS: Amex, Delta, Diners, MasterCard, Switch, Visa   DETAILS: 45 seats. Private parties: 10 main room, 6 and 20 private rooms. Children's helpings. No music

River Station

The Grove, Bristol BS1 4RB   COOKING 4
TEL: (0117) 914 4434   FAX: (0117) 934 9990   COST £21–£49

An espresso bar and delicatessen occupy the ground floor of this stark, modern glass and steel building; fine views of the docks from the bright, spacious upstairs dining room, with its wooden tables and open kitchen, can make it seem like eating on a large boat. A mix of West Country and Continental materials generates a regularly changing menu full of ideas. Locally sourced eggs and poultry, Glenarm organic salmon, line-caught bass and dived scallops all play a part, and dishes are kept pleasingly straightforward, starters tending towards simple compilations: vine tomato salad with buffalo mozzarella and broad beans, or air-dried ham with apples and cornichons.

Although not everything hits the mark, a dish of crab cakes with chilli sauce and pickled papaya was made 'exciting' by the freshness of materials and balance of flavours, and grilled slip sole has come with 'wonderful fat chips' and tartare sauce. The 'simple but nice' assessment extends to desserts of grilled peaches with mascarpone, or Cheddar strawberries with rosemary-flavoured pannacotta. Poor service has occasionally let the side down: 'could do much better' sums up the majority feeling. A sharply chosen wine list, arranged by style and fairly priced, includes a dozen house wines by the glass, starting with Italian varietals at £9.50 (£2.75).

CHEFS: Peter Taylor, Byron Wheeler and Simon Green   PROPRIETORS: Shirley-Anne Bell, Mark Hall, John Payne and Peter Taylor   OPEN: all week 12 to 2.30, 6 to 10.30 (11 Fri and Sat, 9 Sun) CLOSED: 26 and 27 Dec   MEALS: alc (main courses £7.50 to £15). Set L Mon to Fri £10.50 (2 courses) to £12.75, Set L Sun £12.75 (2 courses) to £15   SERVICE: not inc   CARDS: Delta, Diners, MasterCard, Switch, Visa   DETAILS: 120 seats. 30 seats outside. Private parties: 120 main room. Vegetarian meals. No-smoking area. No music

Rocinantes ♚

85 Whiteladies Road, Bristol BS8 2NT   COOKING 4
TEL: (0117) 973 4482   FAX: (0117) 974 3913   COST £23–£47

'The food gets better and better,' wrote one reporter of this hive of conviviality in well-heeled Clifton. Rocinantes provides lively Bristolians with multinational bottled beers, loud music and Spanish and Mediterranean cooking from 'a kitchen with a sure touch' that uses mostly (70 per cent) organic produce. Whether you sit outside, in the noisy bar at the front, or in the quiet restaurant at the back and on the first floor, the same tapas and full menu are served throughout. Careful sourcing of ingredients pays off: tapas (from patatas bravas to salt cod brandade) are 'exquisite', the paella 'outstanding', and bread (baked on the premises) is considered by one reporter 'the best in Bristol'. Full meals could start with seared scallops with a pea, mint and olive oil purée (a combination that 'worked really well'), followed by pork fillet with smoked bacon en croûte, and finishing on a dessert of pine nut and ricotta tart. Service, too, is commendable: 'all seemed keen we were enjoying ourselves.' The organic theme extends to an appealingly varied wine list, with eleven bins falling into that category (five of them are also available by the glass). Prices are fair, starting at £9.95 for house Spanish or French.

CHEF/PROPRIETOR: Barnabas Haughton   OPEN: all week L 12 to 3, Mon to Sat D 6 to 11 (and Sun 6 to 10.30 in summer)   CLOSED: 24 Dec D, 25 and 26 Dec, 1 Jan   MEALS: alc (main courses £9.50 to £17.50). Set L £10.95 (2 courses)   SERVICE: not inc, 10% for parties of 5 or more   CARDS: Amex, Delta, Diners, MasterCard, Switch, Visa   DETAILS: 85 seats. 35 seats outside. Private parties: 50 main room, 30 private room. Vegetarian meals. Children's helpings. Wheelchair access (not WC). Occasional music

---

BRITWELL SALOME   Oxfordshire   map 2

The Goose ✼✖

Britwell Salome OX9 5LG   COOKING 5
TEL: (01491) 612304   FAX: (01491) 614822   COST £31–£48

Perch at one of the high stools in the pink bar or sit at one of the plain wooden tables in the more dramatic bottle-green dining room. Either way, 'one can be guaranteed an interesting and satisfying meal' at this village pub. Chris Barber's modest venture catches the spirit of the times: choice is sensibly limited to three items per course on a daily-changing menu that takes pride in local and seasonal produce, some of it organic, some of it wild. Attention thus concentrated, he has turned out 'rustic' gnocchi with pesto sauce, and a crisp langoustine risotto cake 'a bit like a fish cake', on a small pool of 'correctly made' chive beurre blanc.

Main courses use prime cuts, whether fish – grilled sea bass with leeks, or 'a thick slab of tuna' with roast vegetables – or meat, such as a pork chop with kidney in a grain mustard sauce with tiny whole sweet beetroot. Dessert might offer a choice between creamy-textured mulberry sorbet, crème brûlée with 'a super custard base', or cheese. 'Really good' service from 'local lads and lasses' adds to the appeal, and the compact wine list offers fair choice under £20, including nine house wines around £11 to £13.

CHEF/PROPRIETOR: Chris Barber   OPEN: Tue to Sun L 12 to 2, Tue to Sat D 7 to 9.30   MEALS: alc (main courses £12 to £16). Set D £20 (2 courses) to £25   SERVICE: not inc   CARDS: Delta, MasterCard, Switch, Visa   DETAILS: 50 seats. 16 seats outside. Private parties: 32 main room. Car park. Children's helpings. No smoking in dining room. No music

---

'It is a measure of the sheer scale and grandeur of the dining room that I completely missed a grand piano lurking in one corner until a pianist started playing.'
(On eating in London)

BROADHEMBURY Devon	map 2

Drewe Arms

Broadhembury EX14 0NF	
TEL/FAX: (01404) 841267	COOKING 3
off A373, between Cullompton and Honiton	COST £26–£46

The Drewe Arms is that rare bird, 'an unspoiled pub' next to the church, in an equally unspoiled village of thatched houses. Menus are chalked on boards – a set price for three courses, or individually priced dishes – and items can be interchanged and eaten anywhere there's a seat. Fish, often simply done, is the attraction, whether in the form of an open brown-bread sandwich (crab with mayo, perhaps) and salad, half a lobster, turbot with hollandaise, or steamed sea bass with pesto. 'Mixed seafood starter' doesn't appear to give much away, but one reporter found it a 'delightful and interesting' assembly of mussels, prawns, herring, gravad lax, langoustine and more besides. There is meat too (venison with wild mushroom sauce), while desserts tend towards straightforward crème brûlée, or steamed apricot pudding with marmalade sauce. Chardonnay and Sauvignon Blanc are the main white varietals on a sensibly priced wine list, which starts with house red and white at £10.

CHEFS/PROPRIETORS: Nigel and Kerstin Burge   OPEN: all week L 12 to 2, Mon to Sat D 7 to 10
MEALS: alc (main courses £9.50 to £15). Set L and D £22.50   SERVICE: not inc   CARDS: none
DETAILS: 40 seats. 50 seats outside. Private parties: 24 main room. Car park. Children's helpings. Wheelchair access (also WC). No music

BROADWAY Worcestershire	map 5

▲ Dormy House ♥ ⁵✳

Willersey Hill, Broadway WR12 7LF	
TEL: (01386) 852711 FAX: (01386) 858636	
EMAIL: reservations@dormyhouse.co.uk	COOKING 5
just off A44, 1m NW of Broadway	COST £28–£64

Although it dates from the seventeenth century, Dormy House has been extensively remodelled and, according to one visitor, 'has more the air of a modern conference hotel nowadays'. Still, from its position on the steep, wooded escarpment above Broadway, it has fine views of the extensive Vale of Evesham. The Tapestry dining room is located in a conservatory, which feels modern despite large tapestries depicting medieval scenes. Drawing strongly, but not slavishly, on the country-house tradition, Alan Cutler offers a carte, table d'hôte and six-course gourmet menu.

Raw ingredients are 'carefully chosen' and used in dishes that are praised for being 'intricate' but not unduly complex. A highly accomplished starter of quenelles of Cornish turbot and Scottish salmon comes with a textbook shellfish risotto and chervil butter sauce, for example, while loin of Welsh farmed venison is served with a pithiviers of spinach and red cabbage, with an 'impeccable' peppered port sauce. Finish with a 'technically perfect' roasted plum soufflé or a selection of British cheeses. Attention is focused on the main event (among peripherals, only petits fours are of a standard), but service has garnered considerable praise, both in terms of knowledge and enthusiasm. Classical French wines are in the majority on the well-annotated list, though a coalition of countries from both hemispheres makes some minor yet worthy contributions. The voting stays with France for the house wines, with prices beginning at £10.75.

CHEF: Alan Cutler   PROPRIETOR: Jorgen Phillip-Sorensen   OPEN: Sun to Fri L 12.30 to 2, all week D 7 to 9.30   CLOSED: 24 to 26 Dec   MEALS: alc (main courses L £7.50 to £11, D £15.50 to £21). Set L £19.50, Set D £30.50   SERVICE: not inc   CARDS: Amex, Delta, Diners, MasterCard, Switch, Visa   DETAILS: 80 seats. Private parties: 40 main room, 8 and 14 private rooms. Car park. Vegetarian meals. Children's helpings. No children under 6. No smoking in 1 dining room. Occasional music. Air-conditioned   ACCOMMODATION: 48 rooms, all with bath/shower. TV. Phone. B&B £73 to £174. Rooms for disabled. Baby facilities (*The Which? Hotel Guide*)

▲ *Lygon Arms* ✹✸

Broadway WR12 7DU
TEL: (01386) 852255   FAX: (01386) 858611   COOKING 5
EMAIL: info@the-lygon-arms.co.uk   COST £40–£82

One reporter came all the way from Saudi Arabia to celebrate his fiftieth birthday, indicating something of the debt the British Tourist Board owes to this picturesque sixteenth-century hotel as an icon of our heritage industry. Equally engaging inside, with barrel-vaulted ceiling, minstrels' gallery and assorted baronial trappings, it lays on a lavish menu in which foie gras makes a few appearances: in a starter with wood pigeon, or mixed with truffle and stuffed into a breast of maize-fed chicken. This is, by any yardstick, a busy kitchen. Veal tournedos, for example, has been served with an apple tarte Tatin, a mushroom and Madeira risotto, parsnips, and a grain mustard sauce: like a Cornish miner's pasty it seems to combine starter, main course, vegetables and pudding all in one dish. Whether this is seen as inventive or merely 'ingredient overload' seems to depend on personal predilection.

Despite the presence of plain grilled Dover sole or English lamb cutlets, the kitchen appears happiest when it is innovating, perhaps partnering a vanilla, honey and apricot ravioli with a yoghurt and black pepper sorbet. Timing is accurate, and technical accomplishment evident, even if extras (nibbles, bread, coffee and petits fours) have been disappointing, and service may not be as sharp as this outpost of the Savoy Group warrants. An old-fashioned, classically oriented wine list delivers high quality at prices that allow little under £20. House French is £15.

CHEF: Graeme Nesbitt   PROPRIETOR: Savoy Group   OPEN: all week 12.30 to 2.15, 7.30 (7 Fri and Sat) to 9.15 (9.30 Fri and Sat)   MEALS: alc (main courses £17.50 to £27.50). Set L £25.50, Set D £39.50   SERVICE: not inc, card slips closed   CARDS: Amex, Delta, Diners, MasterCard, Switch, Visa   DETAILS: 90 seats. 40 seats outside. Private parties: 90 main room, 12 to 70 private rooms. Car park. Vegetarian meals. Children's helpings. No children under 8. No smoking in dining room. Wheelchair access (also WC). No music   ACCOMMODATION: 65 rooms, all with bath/shower. TV. Phone. B&B £112 to £255. Rooms for disabled. Baby facilities. Swimming pool (*The Which? Hotel Guide*)

BROCKENHURST Hampshire map 2

Le Poussin ♥ ⅚✗

The Courtyard, Brookley Road,
Brockenhurst SO42 7RB COOKING 7
TEL: (01590) 623063 FAX: (01590) 623144 COST £35–£52

Take the alleyway next to the bookshop and walk through a conservatory into
the calm of a small, cream and deep-green dining room that is 'demure, discreet,
smart, restrained, intimate'. Alex Aitken's cooking has an appealing simplicity
and clarity about it – one visitor praised the lack of 'theatrical mixtures' – and is
distinguished by a high degree of skill and technical accomplishment. Another
much-appreciated aspect is the lightness of such first courses as a 'runny and
very tasty' cheese soufflé, or a trio of salmon (herb-coated, smoked and mousse)
served with a mixed-leaf salad. New Forest mushrooms are a bonus in these
parts, appearing in a number of dishes: tagliatelle with ceps, red mullet with
chanterelles, or a small skinless boudin blanc on a strewing of trompettes,
chanterelles and cauliflower fungus.

Other seasonal items have included a couple of winter specialities – roast
game set in Madeira jelly with foie gras, and boned, stuffed saddle of rabbit –
while fish is deftly treated, perhaps cod with a light 'bouffant-style' topping of
herbs and brown and white crabmeat, with split green peas and a light butter
sauce. Hot passion-fruit soufflé is an all-year-round winner, bread is an 'integral
part of the enjoyment', and the two-course lunch deal is considered particularly
good value. Meals are well paced, and service is 'friendly, hospitable and
discreet'.

Bordeaux buffs (of both red and sweet) will be particularly attracted to the
decidedly Francophile wine list, while Francophobes will find good drinking in
the 'Other Countries' section. Prices quickly leap over £20, but this simply
reflects the quality of what's on offer. House wines change regularly and might
include St-Aubin 1993, Roland Dagneau (£16; £4 a glass) and Montgras Merlot
1997, Colchagua Valley (£14.50; £3.50 a glass).

CHEF: Alex Aitken   PROPRIETORS: Alex and Caroline Aitken   OPEN: Wed to Sun 12 to 1.30, 7 to
9   MEALS: Set L £15 (2 courses) to £22.50, Set D £22.50 (2 courses) to £30   SERVICE: not inc
CARDS: Delta, MasterCard, Switch, Visa   DETAILS: 25 seats. 12 seats outside. Private parties:
30 main room. Car park. No smoking in dining room. Wheelchair access (not WC). No music

BROMSGROVE Worcestershire map 5

▲ Grafton Manor ⅚✗

Grafton Lane, Bromsgrove B61 7HA
TEL: (01527) 579007 FAX: (01527) 575221
EMAIL: steven@grafman.u-net.com
off B4091, 1½m SW of Bromsgrove COOKING 4
COST £30–£54

The Morris family have lately refurbished the dining-room of their ancient
red-brick, mullion-windowed manor house, bringing in new chairs, oil
paintings and, of course, William Morris wallpaper. In the kitchen, Simon
Morris, long a devotee and exponent of Indian cookery, now has a cookery book

under his belt, and even when not in the throes of his February Indian food festival includes one or two Indian dishes on the set menus. Chilli prawn fry and Goan coconut chicken curry with Goan hash browns are typical examples, the spices from the Birmingham food markets, and the integral vegetables from the manor's considerable gardens. It is still possible to steer a modern and broadly Mediterranean course through the menu, choosing perhaps a tomato and basil tart with grilled sardines, and confit duck with a garlic crust and flageolet beans, finishing with crème brûlée, or apricot and Amaretto mousse, rather than Punjabi rabdi with cumin shortbread. Reporters have commented on long waits for service. Given the manor's photogenic appeal and its fifteenth-century chapel, it is not surprising that wedding parties often close the dining room on Saturdays. Wines hail from all over, and the local flag is flown by Three Choirs. House French is £11.75.

CHEFS: Simon Morris and William Henderson   PROPRIETORS: the Morris family   OPEN: Sun to Fri L 12.30 to 1.30, all week D 7.30 to 9.30   MEALS: Set L mon to Fri £20.50, Set L Sun £18.50, Set D £27.85 to £32.75   SERVICE: not inc, card slips closed   CARDS: Amex, Delta, Diners, MasterCard, Switch, Visa   DETAILS: 60 seats. Private parties: 50 main room, 50 private room. Car park. Vegetarian meals. Children's helpings. No smoking in dining room. Wheelchair access (also men's WC). No music   ACCOMMODATION: 9 rooms, all with bath/shower. TV. Phone. B&B £85 to £150. Rooms for disabled (*The Which? Hotel Guide*)

BRUTON Somerset   map 2

Truffles

95 The High Street, Bruton BA10 0AR   COOKING 4
TEL/FAX: (01749) 812255   COST £23–£40

Step down off the high street into this comfortable room with its dark green walls, exposed beams and well-spaced tables where for over a decade Martin Bottrill has been cooking classically inspired but globally influenced food. Reduced-price midweek suppers are a feature, as are Thai themed evenings, Mr Bottrill taking time out to head as far afield as the Oriental Hotel in Bangkok for inspiration. Front-of-house, overseen by Denise Bottrill, is professional and relaxed.

'Tasty' appetisers of perhaps warm shortcrust cases containing poached salmon and white cheese sauce, or pineapple and Stilton, set the ball rolling. To start might be a 'quite simple but very good' field mushroom topped with marinated peppers, grilled goats' cheese and pesto, or squid deep-fried in tempura with oriental salad and shellfish dressing. Main courses continue the classical-global theme: fillets of pan-fried monkfish with warm tomato salsa, olives and capers, or medallions of pork with caramelised apples and a calvados sauce. Breast of duck with peppery pineapple and hoisin sauce comes perfectly pink and crispy-skinned, while lamb cutlets are topped with duxelles, wrapped in filo and served with a tarragon and sherry sauce. Desserts are praised for a lightness of touch, as in ginger pudding with cinnamon ice cream, or banana and coconut mousse with a hint of rum served with gingered banana. The wine list is strong on half-bottles, scans the world and interestingly features the second wines of some well-known châteaux in the claret section. Chilean house wines start at £11.50.

CHEF: Martin Bottrill   PROPRIETORS: Denise and Martin Bottrill   OPEN: Sun L 12 to 2, Tue to Sat D 7 to 10   CLOSED: 2 weeks Feb   MEALS: Set L Sun £13.95, Set D Tue to Thur £12.95, Set D Tue to Sat £22.50   SERVICE: not inc, card slips closed   CARDS: Delta, MasterCard, Switch, Visa   DETAILS: 22 seats. Private parties: 24 main room. Vegetarian meals. No children under 8. No smoking while others eat. Wheelchair access (not WC). No music £5

BUCKLAND Gloucestershire   map 5

▲ *Buckland Manor* 🍷 ⁵⁄✳

Buckland WR12 7LY
TEL: (01386) 852626   FAX: (01386) 853557
EMAIL: buckland-manor-uk@msn.com   COOKING 4
off B4632, 2m SW of Broadway   COST £34–£86

Electronic gates glide open for guests to approach the grand, ancient, honey-coloured stone manor, through acres of grounds past magnificent mature trees, perfect lawns, superb flowerbeds. Inside all is sedate and luxurious. Pale painted oak panelling hung with oil portraits, a huge fireplace and blue velvet curtains form the setting for elegant meals. Taking some of its supplies from the Vale of Evesham, plus some more far-flung exotica, the kitchen under Kenneth Wilson aims to produce classic English and French dishes 'with a lighter touch'. Much of it fits into the luxury class, from a paupiette of smoked and marinated salmon with keta caviare, via fillet of Angus beef with truffled lentils, asparagus and foie gras hollandaise, to chocolate tart with macadamia nut ice cream and poached kumquats. The carte is supplemented at lunch by a fixed-price menu, while Sunday lunch is more of a traditional but still luxurious occasion. Consider at the outset what you might like for dessert, as some, such as the Manor's trademark soufflés (a pecan, raisin and whisky version served with maple and pecan ice cream, for example), require twenty minutes. Of course, any spare moments could be spent perusing the hefty wine list of 593 bins. Bordeaux and Burgundy are so well represented that it is easy to overlook Australia, let alone the fine California section. Fabulous wines are there for those who can afford them, but a reasonable attempt has also been made to provide good drinking under £20, with house wines starting at £14.70.

CHEF: Kenneth Wilson   PROPRIETORS: Roy and Daphne Vaughan   OPEN: all week 12.30 to 1.45, 7.30 to 9   MEALS: alc (main courses £24 to £29). Set L Mon to Sat £23.50, Set L Sun £28.50. Light snacks available Mon to Sat   SERVICE: not inc   CARDS: Amex, Delta, Diners, MasterCard, Switch, Visa   DETAILS: 36 seats. 20 seats outside. Private parties: 36 main room. Car park. No children under 8 in dining room. Jacket and tie. No smoking in dining room. No music   ACCOMMODATION: 13 rooms, all with bath/shower. TV. Phone. B&B £185 to £335. Rooms for disabled. No children under 12 in accommodation. Swimming pool (*The Which? Hotel Guide*)

'The quail had been boned by a trained chimp using a road drill.'
(On eating in London)

See inside the front cover for an explanation of the symbols used at the tops of entries.

BUCKLAND Oxfordshire   map 2

▲ *Lamb Inn* ⁙✳ £

Lamb Lane, Buckland SN7 8QN	COOKING 2
TEL: (01367) 870484 FAX: (01367) 870675	COST £20–£52

Made of honey-coloured Cotswold stone, this well-kept country pub serves the same traditionally oriented food in its beamed bar and dining room extension, from a regularly changing blackboard menu. Despite occasional forays into more exotic realms (perhaps green Thai chicken curry), Paul Barnard's cooking covers a broad swath of European territory, starting with peperonata soufflé, grilled halloumi, and Cullen skink. Game is a feature in season – roast grouse, or saddle of hare – beef is Scottish grass-fed, and fish might run to sea bass with Pernod sauce, monkfish ragoût, or salmon fish cakes, followed by junket, Bakewell tart or a savoury. 'Good-sized portions served by a friendly team' is the style, although one reporter was surprised to be charged for extra bread. The fifty-strong wine list leans heavily towards France but is balanced by some choice selections from beyond her borders. Half a dozen house wines are good value, from £9.95 a bottle, £1.75 a glass.

CHEF: Paul Barnard PROPRIETORS: Paul and Peta Barnard OPEN: all week 12 to 2 (2.45 Sun), 6.30 to 9.30 CLOSED: D 24 Dec to 26 Dec MEALS: alc (main courses £5.50 to £19.50). Set L Sun £19.95 SERVICE: not inc, card slips closed CARDS: Amex, Delta, MasterCard, Switch, Visa DETAILS: 65 seats. 45 seats outside. Private parties: 80 main room, 18 private room. Car park. Vegetarian meals. Children's helpings. No smoking in dining room. Music ACCOMMODATION: 4 rooms. TV. Phone. B&B £37.50 to £57.50 (£5)

BURNHAM MARKET Norfolk   map 6

Fishes' ⁙✳ £

Market Place, Burnham Market PE31 8HE	COOKING 3
TEL: (01328) 738588 FAX: (01328) 730534	COST £20–£46

Even in winter, visitors' cars and green wellies are much in evidence in this north Norfolk village. Easily recognisable on the wide main street that sandwiches the green, Gillian Cape's simple, light, airy, blue and white restaurant has remained 'reassuringly unchanged' over the twenty-seven years she has been here. Choice is generous, even for the set-price lunch, which covers much the same ground as the evening carte, beginning with thick, rich, 'honest' crab soup with a chunk of brown bread, Brancaster mussels with garlic, or their own potted shrimps. Main courses revolve around plainly presented fish – skate wing, Dover sole, grilled whole plaice with fresh herbs and melted butter, halibut with hollandaise – and come with salad or a jacket potato that is 'crisp without and evenly cooked within'. Homely desserts include rhubarb meringue pie, and bramble and plum crumble spiced with cloves and cinnamon. Staff are quiet, casual and efficient, and wines from the Chablisienne Cooperative are highlighted on the good-value white-dominated list. House French is £8.50.

CHEFS: Gillian Cape and Paula Ayres PROPRIETOR: Gillian Cape OPEN: Tue to Sun and bank hol Mon L 12 to 2, Tue to Sat D 6.45 to 9.30 (9 weekdays out of season) CLOSED: 24 to 27 Dec, 3 weeks Jan MEALS: alc D (main courses £8 to £15). Set L Tue to Fri £12.75, Set L Sat, Sun and bank hol Mon £14.75 SERVICE: not inc, card slips closed CARDS: Amex, Delta, Diners, MasterCard, Switch, Visa DETAILS: 42 seats. Private parties: 14 main room. Children's helpings. No children under 5 after 8.30. No smoking in dining room. Wheelchair access (not WC). No music (£5)

BURRINGTON Devon   map 1

▲ *Northcote Manor* ✸✖ | NEW ENTRY |

Burrington EX37 9LZ
TEL: (01769) 560501 FAX: (01769) 560770
EMAIL: rest@northcotemanor.demon.co.uk   COOKING 3
off A377, 4m NW of Chulmleigh   COST £35–£50

This secluded early-eighteenth-century manor house, reached by half a mile of single-track road, has a long and varied history, most recently taking in extensive refurbishment by new owners David and Marian Boddy and the arrival of Chris Dawson, previously in the *Guide* at Ynyshir Hall in Wales (see entry, Eglwysfach). The medieval-themed dining room, with wrought iron wall lamps and interesting murals, is a 'calm and relaxing' place to enjoy an elaborate style of cooking that might produce a starter of 'perfectly cooked' fillets of Dover sole and dorade topped with two small spring rolls containing moist pieces of lobster meat, and sauced with a chive and truffle velouté. Equally involved main courses run to 'extremely tender' leg and breast of duck on a potato galette with stir-fried vegetables and black bean sauce, also with a spring roll, this time of duck and spring onion. Poached chicken breast, meanwhile, comes with a pithiviers of black pudding, leeks and wild mushrooms. The kitchen's industry is maintained at dessert stage to produce an assiette of strawberries: in batter, a brûlée and with chocolate. Service is relaxed, attentive and personal, and the global wine list is confident and fairly priced, starting with house Chilean at £12.30.

CHEF: Chris Dawson PROPRIETORS: David and Marian Boddy OPEN: all week 12.30 to 1.30 (booking essential L), 7 to 9 CLOSED: Jan MEALS: Set L £18.50 (2 courses) to £25.50, Set D £29.50. Light L available SERVICE: not inc, card slips closed CARDS: Amex, Delta, Diners, MasterCard, Switch, Visa DETAILS: 30 seats. 20 seats outside. Private parties: 35 main room. Car park. Vegetarian meals. Children's helpings. No smoking in dining room. Occasional music ACCOMMODATION: 11 rooms, all with bath/shower. TV. Phone. D,B&B £98 to £275. Baby facilities (£5)

'Around it was the "salsa", which would have been more accurately described as fruit salad.' (On eating in London)

£ *means that it is possible to have a three-course meal, including coffee, half a bottle of house wine and service for £25 or less per person, at any time the restaurant is open, i.e. at dinner as well as lunch. It may be possible to spend considerably more than this, but by choosing carefully you should find £25 or less achievable.*

BURTON ON THE WOLDS Leicestershire

map 5

Langs ✣

Horse Leys Farm, 147 Melton Road, Burton on the Wolds LE12 5TQ	COOKING 3
TEL/FAX: (01509) 880980	COST £20–£43

Beyond the small flag-floored bar – in a low brick building set back from the road, a mile or so out of the village – is a cream-painted L-shaped dining room with wicker chairs, where Gordon Lang's carte is supplemented by a two-course lunch deal. Main courses are centred around corn-fed chicken, beef fillet, or roast rack of lamb, the last perhaps served with a halved kidney, on a bed of celeriac 'tagliatelle' and spinach. Seafood seems a good way to begin – perhaps a Mediterranean-flavoured terrine with chunks of salmon, or a rich, creamy lobster bisque – and daily fish additions to the menu have included sea bass with olive mash, and John Dory in champagne sauce. Flavours may not always be as convincing as they should, but meats are cooked as requested, and desserts run to a coffee-flavoured chocolate pot, and a light frothy-textured crème brûlée with a crisp topping. A rather cautious wine list starts with house Côtes du Rhône and Jurançon sec at £10.95.

CHEF: Gordon Lang   PROPRIETORS: Gordon Lang and Paul Simms   OPEN: Tue to Fri and Sun L 12 to 2.15, Tue to Sat D 7.15 to 9.45   MEALS: alc Tue to Fri (main courses £10.50 to £15). Set L Tue to Fri £10.50 (2 courses), Set L Sun £12.75   SERVICE: not inc, card slips closed   CARDS: Delta, MasterCard, Switch, Visa   DETAILS: 40 seats. 8 seats outside. Private parties: 48 main room. Car park. Vegetarian meals. Children's helpings. No smoking in dining room. Wheelchair access (also WC). Music

BURY ST EDMUNDS Suffolk

map 6

Maison Bleue at Mortimer's ✣

30/31 Churchgate Street, Bury St Edmunds IP33 1RG	COOKING 2
TEL: (01284) 760623 FAX: (01284) 761611	COST £24–£43

Although not actually on the coast, Maison Bleue does its best to simulate a seaside atmosphere with assorted nautical paraphernalia, old pine floorboards, a 'duck-egg blue and Suffolk pink' colour scheme, and a huge mural of a beach and lighthouses. Paper tablecloths point to an informal approach, and the menu deals in generous servings of fresh fish cooked *à point*, some as traditionally French as poached salmon with hollandaise, or grilled turbot béarnaise, some as modern as smoked haddock and coriander fish cake with tomato salsa. The seafood platter, which needs 24 hours' notice, comes in three versions: regular, with spider crab, or with lobster. Token meat dishes and desserts might include coq au vin and crème brûlée. Service is attentive and French, and wines understandably major on whites, packing in a fair range of styles for less than £20. A trio of house wines starts at £8.95.

'According to the till receipt, our waitress was called Matthew.' (On eating in London)

CHEF: Pascal Canevet   PROPRIETOR: Régis Crepy   OPEN: Mon to Sat 12 to 2.30, 6.30 to 9.30 (10 Fri and Sat)   CLOSED: bank hol Mons   MEALS: alc (main courses £9 to £14.50). Set L £6.95 (1 course) to £14.95, Set D £17.95   SERVICE: not inc   CARDS: Amex, Delta, MasterCard, Switch, Visa   DETAILS: 80 seats. Private parties: 40 main room, 12 and 40 private rooms. Children's helpings. No smoking in dining room. Wheelchair access (not WC). Music

---

CAMBRIDGE Cambridgeshire   map 6

Midsummer House

Midsummer Common, Cambridge CB4 1HA	COOKING **5**
TEL: (01223) 369299 FAX: (01223) 302672	COST £33–£75

With its lemon-coloured conservatory, and comfortable dining room with well-spaced tables, Midsummer House exudes an atmosphere that is 'pleasantly garden house', helped by views across to a pedestrian bridge over the Cam. Plans are afoot to refurbish, following the appointment of Daniel Clifford as head chef. His food shows consistent invention and good taste within a solid repertoire: 'high marks', wrote one reporter, 'outstanding', said another. An inspection meal started with an appetiser of creamy, foamy, light vichyssoise and then moved on to seared scallops with truffle vinaigrette, 'a neat, minimal presentation'. What the menu describes as a mosaic of provençale vegetables is a colourful terrine sitting on a mousseline of goats' cheese, surrounded by tapénade and sun-dried tomatoes, making a 'clean and refreshing' impact, while foie gras terrine comes interestingly on top of crushed haricots blancs surrounded by a 'cappuccino' of peas and pancetta.

Contrasting flavours and textures are continually highlighted: fillet of cod on a bed of aubergine caviare with oyster beignets and tapénade butter, for instance, or pink roast squab, on top of endive with the tiniest morels. For dessert, there might be a trio of apples – mille-feuille, mini-Tatin and sorbet – or 'well-judged' cardamom ice cream accompanying dark chocolate fondant. Service has been called 'superb', although one found it 'uneven', and long waits between courses also occasion comment. The wine list focuses on France, but there is also good hunting in the New World. The house selection opens at £12.95.

CHEF: Daniel Clifford   PROPRIETOR: Russell Morgan   OPEN: Sun and Tue to Fri L 12 to 2, Tue to Sat D 7 to 10   MEALS: Set L Sun £25, Set L Tue to Fri £19.50, Set D £35 (2 courses) to £39.50 SERVICE: not inc   CARDS: Amex, Delta, MasterCard, Switch, Visa   DETAILS: 50 seats. 10 seats outside. Private parties: 50 main room, 6 to 16 private rooms. Vegetarian meals. No smoking while others eat. Wheelchair access (not WC). No music   (£5)

22 Chesterton Road ♥

22 Chesterton Road, Cambridge CB4 3AX	COOKING **3**
TEL: (01223) 351880 FAX: (01223) 323814	COST £33–£49

Seascapes, mirrors and candles are the form at this town house near the river, creating something of a domestic impression. Despite opening Brasserie 22 in Newmarket, the kitchen has not been deflected off its course, still offering an Anglo-European framework of pork and duck rillettes, lambs' liver and bacon, and 'exceptional' seafood risotto, interspersed with a few Asian flavours for variety: monkfish with green curry and coconut sauce, for example. Ideas are lively but sensibly contained, menus short but attractively balanced and varied, with game, offal and fish playing an integral role, and desserts tend to be soothing: warm chocolate and walnut sponge, or mascarpone and custard tart. Perceptions of service have varied from stiff and 'technically correct' to relaxed and unstuffy. The wine list opens with some stylish bottles from France then flies around the world, pausing to pick up a couple of interesting bins from here and there. Good-value drinking remains a priority, with house wines from France, Australia and Chile costing £9.25 or £11.25 a bottle.

CHEFS: Ian Reinhardt and Martin Cullum   PROPRIETOR: David Carter   OPEN: Tue to Sat D only 7 to 9.45; L by arrangement for parties of 10 or more   CLOSED: 1 week Christmas   MEALS: Set D £23.50   SERVICE: not inc   CARDS: Amex, Delta, Diners, MasterCard, Switch, Visa   DETAILS: 38 seats. Private parties: 26 main room, 12 private room. Vegetarian meals. No children under 10. No smoking while others eat; no cigars/pipes in dining room. Occasional music. Air-conditioned

---

CARLTON-IN-COVERDALE North Yorkshire   map 9

▲ Foresters Arms ¾✳

Carlton-in-Coverdale DL8 4BB
TEL/FAX: (01969) 640272
off A684, 5m SW of Leyburn

DALES 2000 INN

COOKING 4
COST £18–£51

'I cannot speak too highly of the standards of reception, accommodation, food and drink provided,' began one enthusiastic reporter, also citing the appeal of the Foresters' 'delightful' out-of-the-way location. A characterful old inn, with beams and flagged floors, it takes an informal approach to eating, a serious view of cooking, and a particular pride in fish: perhaps soup with rouille and bruschetta, or crab spring rolls to start, followed by whiting with lobster sauce, or sea bream with onion marmalade and tarragon cream. A balance is struck between lighter dishes (scrambled egg with smoked salmon at lunch, for example) and heartier ones, such as roast ox kidney with venison loin, or cassoulet of Toulouse sausage and black pudding. Desserts lean towards the chocolate and toffee end of the spectrum, and the annotated cheese menu includes local Richard III Wensleydale and Stinking Bishop. For those who stay, breakfast is a bonus. Around fifty fairly priced wines play off the Old World against the New, starting with house Chardonnay and Merlot from France at £9.60.

CHEF/PROPRIETOR: B.K. Higginbotham   OPEN: Wed to Sun L 12 to 2, Tue to Sat D 7 to 9.30 CLOSED: bank hol Mons   MEALS: alc (main courses £8 to £19). Light L menu Tue to Sat. SERVICE: not inc, card slips closed   CARDS: Delta, MasterCard, Switch, Visa   DETAILS: 60 seats. 24 seats outside. Private parties: 36 main room, 15 private room. Car park. Vegetarian meals. Children's helpings. No smoking in 1 dining room. Wheelchair access (not WC). Music ACCOMMODATION: 3 rooms, all with bath/shower. TV. B&B £40 to £70. Baby facilities (*The Which? Hotel Guide*)

'It's no wonder they "suggest" gratuity; otherwise it might not enter any diner's head.' (On eating in Oxfordshire)

CARNKIE Cornwall   map 1

Basset Count House 🦶✷

Lower Carnkie TR16 8SP
TEL: (01209) 215181   COOKING 5
just outside Redruth on B3297 to Helston   COST £21–£39

No expense has been spared in restoring this Georgian count house, where a
large gravel sweep leads to a low granite façade. The sitting rooms with their
open fires, lots of polished woodwork, sponged walls and comfortable sofas are
'most welcoming on a chilly day'. Ann Long, who has been cooking in this part
of the country for many years, provides a concise, focused menu that allows her
to maintain control and manage all the cooking herself. One reporter described
the style as 'pleasant rather than exciting', though starters may include inventive
soups such as tomato, parsnip and apple, and an unusual but enjoyable dish of
duck and chicken in orange jelly. Main courses can also sound intriguing:
chicken breast stuffed with rabbit and venison, or salmon and asparagus
wrapped in poppy seed puff pastry, served with broad bean cream sauce. A
small selection of desserts might include a 'cloudlike' raspberry oatmeal
meringue. Sunday lunch looks to be very good value. Service has been described
as 'cheery and mostly competent'. Some fifty wines roam the world, but might be
more enterprisingly chosen. House French is £9.50.

CHEF: Ann Long   PROPRIETOR: R.J. Milan   OPEN: Sun L 12 to 2, Wed to Sat D 7 to 9   MEALS:
Set L £14.50, Set D £20 (2 courses) to £25   SERVICE: not inc, card slips closed   CARDS: Delta,
MasterCard, Switch, Visa   DETAILS: 36 seats. Private parties: 12 main room, 12 private room.
Car park. No children under 10. No smoking in dining room. Wheelchair access (also WC). No
music

CARTERWAY HEADS Northumberland   map 10

▲ *Manor House Inn* 🦶✷ £

Carterway Heads, Shotley Bridge DH8 9LX
TEL/FAX: (01207) 255268   COOKING 3
on A68, 3m W of Consett   COST £16–£30

'Not too cutesy or trendy', and now given a coat of yellow wash and proper
tablecloths, this welcoming moorland pub goes in for hand-pulled beers, sixty
or so malt whiskies, a lovingly put-together wine list starting at £7.95 for house
French, and a blackboard full of surprises and not-such-surprises. Pretty well all
the starters can be portioned up to main courses and may include local kippers,
or baked tomatoes with spinach and aubergine. Stir-fried Szechuan wild
mushrooms in filo pastry, roast red snapper, and sea bass stuffed with Italian
vegetables are clearly not run-of-the-mill pub fare, although the arrival of three
types of potato – mashed, boiled and roast – as well as a choice of other
vegetables reminds you that this is a generous kitchen at heart. Moira Brown
makes the puddings, including chocolate caramel ice-cream and almond cake
with white chocolate sauce. Service is welcoming and considerate. Even if you
don't eat here, visit the inn for its fast-increasing collection of jugs hanging from
the ceiling.

CHEF: Peter Tiplady PROPRIETORS: Chris and Moira Brown OPEN: all week 12 to 2.30, 7 to 9.30 (9 Sun) CLOSED: 25 Dec eve MEALS: alc (main courses £4.50 to £11) SERVICE: not inc, card slips closed CARDS: Amex, MasterCard, Switch, Visa DETAILS: 58 seats. 24 seats outside. Private parties: 50 main room. Car park. Vegetarian meals. Children's helpings. No smoking in main restaurant. Wheelchair access (not WC). No music ACCOMMODATION: 4 rooms. TV. B&B £24.50 to £43 (£5)

CARTMEL Cumbria   map 8

▲ Aynsome Manor ⁵✸

Cartmel LA11 6HH
TEL: (015395) 36653   FAX: (015395) 36016   COOKING 2
off A590, ½m N of village   COST £19–£35

The dining room at this pastoral Georgian hotel has been redecorated, the panelled walls painted white and the magnificent ceiling shown off to best advantage. The menu, too, has had a makeover, so that it now includes more salad starters and lighter saucing, but presentation is as traditional as ever: the soup tureen is left on the table, potatoes are cooked two ways (such as Anna and parisienne), and sweets arriving on a trolley are 'doused with cream'. From the five-course set dinner (reduced in price if courses are omitted), 'tasty, moist' smoked trout mousse has found favour, as have a 'good, thick, creamy' leek and watercress soup, and plaice fillet grilled 'just long enough', served with a sharp and tangy caper, gherkin and lime butter. Meat is a forte, from 'perfectly cooked' rack of lamb with a mint jelly tartlet to pork medallions with a 'good, rich, dark' red wine sauce. Service is friendly and the wine list good value, with house wines at £10.50 per litre and a new selection of New World choices.

CHEFS: Victor Sharratt and Chris Miller PROPRIETORS: Tony, Margaret, Chris and Andrea Varley OPEN: Sun L 1 (1 sitting), Mon to Sat D 7 to 8.30 (residents only Sun D) CLOSED: 2 to 30 Jan MEALS: Set L Sun £12.25, Set D £16.50 to £19.50 SERVICE: not inc, card slips closed CARDS: Amex, Delta, MasterCard, Switch, Visa DETAILS: 30 seats. Private parties: 30 main room. Car park. Vegetarian meals. No children under 5 at D. Jacket and tie. No smoking in dining room. No music ACCOMMODATION: 12 rooms, all with bath/shower. TV. Phone. D,B&B £56 to £115. Baby facilities (The Which? Hotel Guide) (£5)

▲ Uplands ⁵✸

Haggs Lane, Cartmel LA11 6HD
TEL: (015395) 36248   FAX: (015395) 36848
EMAIL: uplands@kencomp.net
2½m SW of A590, 1m up road opposite   COOKING 5
Pig and Whistle   COST £23–£43

Halfway between Cartmel and Grange-over-Sands, this quiet, soothing house, with Morecambe Bay visible from the dining room window, reaches its fifteenth anniversary in 2000. The food makes no attempt to raise eyebrows or adopt a challenging pose with exotic ideas; this is a very English style of cooking which appeals for its 'practice makes perfect' consistency: 'this is the only restaurant we go to fairly regularly where we come away every time feeling satisfied with everything we have eaten,' writes a supporter. Tom Peter tends to ring changes in the economical way that good cooks do. To start, refreshing mango and melon might provide a background for crab on one occasion, for Morecambe Bay shrimps in lightly curried mayonnaise on another, while a mustard and honey sauce has partnered loin of veal, and pan-fried pork with paprika and onion, both to good effect.

The tureen of soup, left on the table for second helpings, is 'an institution': perhaps pea, pear and watercress, which comes with its customary whole small loaf of cut-it-yourself warm dark bread. Straightforward fish dishes rely on prime materials and accurate timing – sea bass with fennel sauce, or firm halibut with cucumber, dill and lemon sauce – and vegetables might include anything from plain green beans to beetroot with lime. As an alternative to simple strawberry shortbread, or raspberry and apple pie, there may be something more alcoholic to finish: prune and armagnac ice cream in a brandy-snap basket, or fresh figs with 'enough Pernod to fail a breathalyser'. The balanced list of French and New World wines is fairly priced, starting with house Chilean red, Australian Chardonnay and Côtes de Gascogne white at £10.75.

CHEF: Tom Peter   PROPRIETORS: Tom and Diana Peter   OPEN: Thur to Sun L 12.30 for 1 (1 sitting), 7.30 for 8 (1 sitting)   CLOSED: Jan and Feb   MEALS: Set L £15, Set D £27   SERVICE: not inc, card slips closed   CARDS: Amex, Delta, MasterCard, Switch, Visa   DETAILS: 28 seats. Private parties: 32 main room. Car park. Vegetarian meals. No children under 8 in dining room. No smoking in dining room. Wheelchair access (not WC). No music   ACCOMMODATION: 5 rooms, all with bath/shower. TV. D,B&B £71 to £142. No children under 8 in accommodation (*The Which? Hotel Guide*) £5

CASTLE COMBE Wiltshire   map 2

▲ *Manor House* ⁵⨉

Castle Combe SN14 7HR
TEL: (01249) 782206   FAX: (01249) 782159
EMAIL: enquiries@manor-house.co.uk   COOKING 4
on B4039, 3M NW of junction with A420   COST £31–£87

This is the place to come for a quintessential English country-house experience. Electronic gates swish open to reveal a splendid, impeccably maintained manor house, parts of which date from the sixteenth century, set in acres of manicured lawns, with fountains, massive trees and its own trout stream. Inside, it's 'a real rabbit warren' of small rooms, including wood-panelled bars and comfortable lounges. The dining room, by contrast, is huge, with tables so well spaced that you may need a telescope to see your nearest neighbours.

If the setting is lavish, then meals are designed to match: dinner is preceded by 'a huge cake-stand full of nibbles', and the food can be positively baroque in style, with various garnishes, fritters, sauces and flavoured oils. Expensive ingredients are given a formal treatment: warm mousse of foie gras, for example, comes with pear chutney and Sauternes gelée, fillet of turbot with lobster mousse, tagliolini and crustacean oil. While the main element of each dish is usually handled with care – 'crisp, tasty' duck confit, and 'succulent' fillet steak – the tendency to over-egg the omelette may mean that not everything lives up to expectations. A 'classical section' of the carte features retro dishes of Dover sole, rack of lamb and crêpes suzette. One lunchtime visitor who enjoyed the set menu thought that all the extras added up to great value for money; evenings, though, are more inclined to put a strain on purses. Staff are 'charming', but service is 'slightly over-flunkied' for some. A 'big, butch and expensive' wine list starts with house wine at £18.50.

CHEF: Mark Taylor   PROPRIETOR: Manor House Hotel (Castle Combe) Ltd   OPEN: all week 12 to 2, 7 to 9.30   MEALS: alc D (main courses £22.50 to £26). Set L £16.95 (2 courses) to £18.95, Set D £35   SERVICE: not inc, card slips closed   CARDS: Amex, Delta, Diners, MasterCard, Switch, Visa   DETAILS: 105 seats. 20 seats outside. Private parties: 105 main room, 12 to 30 private rooms. Car park. Vegetarian meals. Children's helpings. Jacket and tie. No smoking in dining room. Wheelchair access (also WC). No music   ACCOMMODATION: 45 rooms, all with bath/shower. TV. Phone. Room only £120 to £350. Rooms for disabled. Baby facilities. Swimming pool. Fishing (*The Which? Hotel Guide*)

CAUNTON Nottinghamshire	map 5

Caunton Beck £

Main Street, Caunton NG23 6AB	COOKING 2
TEL: (01636) 636793 FAX: (01636) 636828	COST £15–£45

This converted pub is run along the same lines as its sister establishment Welford Place (see entry, Leicester), although natually it has a more rural feel. The principle of 'eat what you like, when you like' is expressed in a breakfast menu (also available in the afternoons), an all-day sandwich menu (toasted ham and cheese with pickle, or bacon and curried egg), a seasonal menu, and a daily menu that might produce steak and kidney pie, or salmon fish cakes with a chive and lemon butter sauce. From September to just before Easter there is also a three-course deal for two people, with half a bottle of wine thrown in. Portions can be substantial, but those who make it to dessert have enjoyed a 'beautifully presented' brandy-snap basket filled with fresh fruit and vanilla ice cream; or there may be homely jam sponge. Check the blackboards for up-to-the-minute additions to the forty-strong wine list, which is arranged by style and starts with four house wines at £10.45.

CHEFS: Paul Vidic, Jamie Matts and Adrian Graves   PROPRIETORS: Michael and Valerie Hope, and Paul Vidic   OPEN: all week 8am to 11pm   MEALS: alc (main courses £5.50 to £16.50). Set L and D £25 for 2 people, inc wine (Sept to Easter only)   CARDS: Amex, Delta, Diners, MasterCard, Switch, Visa   DETAILS: 120 seats. 40 seats outside. Private parties: 55 main room, 30 private room. Car park. Vegetarian meals. Children's helpings. Wheelchair access (also WC). No music   £5

'Marion had a chocolate roly-poly pudding, which was odd as she'd ordered something else completely, but since the wine glasses are the size of baptismal fonts she didn't notice until it was almost all gone.' (On eating in Glasgow)

The 2001 Guide *will be published before Christmas 2000. Reports on meals are most welcome at any time of the year, but are particularly valuable in the spring (no later than June). Send them to* The Good Food Guide, *FREEPOST, 2 Marylebone Road, London NW1 4DF. Or email your report to guidereports@which.co.uk.*

CHADDESLEY CORBETT Worcestershire   map 5

▲ *Brockencote Hall* ⁵⁄✱

Chaddesley Corbett DY10 4PY
TEL: (01562) 777876   FAX: (01562) 777872
on A448, Kidderminster to Bromsgrove road, just   COOKING 3
outside village   COST £33–£75

A large lake at the front reflects the slightly austere lines of this 'serenely elegant' house of many dining rooms, and a seriousness of purpose characterises the enterprise. Foie gras, goats' cheese and mushrooms are delivered fresh from Périgord every week, pork (cooked with haricot beans) is from Norfolk, while the snails (with potato, bacon, onion and garlic) come from Hereford. The kitchen weaves dishes around a contemporary French core, producing a mussel flan with sea vegetable and frothy lentil cream, and squab pigeon with stuffed cabbage and ceps. Even the more exotic flavours – candied lemon spiked with saffron and cumin to accompany sea bass – do not disturb the feel of 'posh country-house' cooking. Fruity desserts might include a 'minestrone', or a terrine served with basil and lemon sorbet, while bitter chocolate blinis come with peanut brittle ice cream. A page of New World offerings is grafted on to a classically inclined French wine list where prices do not go out of their way to be user-friendly, although a handful of house wines come in under £20.

CHEF: Didier Philipot PROPRIETORS: Joseph and Alison Petitjean OPEN: Sun to Fri L 12 to 1.30, Mon to Sat D 7 to 9.30 CLOSED: 1 Jan MEALS: alc (main courses £22.50). Set L £21.50, Set D £26.50 SERVICE: not inc, card slips closed CARDS: Amex, Delta, Diners, MasterCard, Switch, Visa DETAILS: 50 seats. Private parties: 40 main room, 10 and 20 private rooms. Car park. Children's helpings. No smoking in dining room. Wheelchair access (also WC). No music ACCOMMODATION: 17 rooms, all with bath/shower. TV. Phone. B&B £97 to £150. Rooms for disabled. Baby facilities (*The Which? Hotel Guide*) (£5)

CHAGFORD Devon   map 1

▲ *Gidleigh Park* 🍾 ⁵⁄✱

Chagford TQ13 8HH
TEL: (01647) 432367   FAX: (01647) 432574
EMAIL: gidleighpark@gidleigh.co.uk
from Chagford Square turn right at Lloyds Bank into
Mill Street, take right fork after 150 yards, follow lane   COOKING 8
for 1½m   COST £44–£97

At the end of a long and winding Devon lane, Gidleigh emerges like a secret hideaway: a calm and orderly place with woodland gardens, a small river rushing past the front, and a gentle smell of woodsmoke. Oak panelling, linenfold doors and chintzy sofas give it an old-fashioned air, and 'magnificent' views extend over open countryside. A weekly-changing 'tasting' menu has replaced the old 'speciality' one, but the £60 four-course version retains its bedrock role, offering generous choice.

The kitchen is not averse to indulgences. Indeed, the truffle bill must be huge, but they are properly used: a white haricot bean soup with grated white truffle was 'just like drinking silk', while a truffley aroma pervaded a 'deeply sensuous' tartlet of quail and quails' eggs. Fish and shellfish 'in peak condition' are among the many delights, taking in scallops that are crisp outside, 'like mother of pearl' inside, and a thin pasta pouch bursting with fresh, sweet, firm langoustines. Innovation and pyrotechnics are not the kitchen's strongest suit, but at least most dishes work; those that didn't at inspection were described as 'confused', lacking focus. Accurate timing, however, has made the best of materials, from an 'ace' piece of turbot with morels and spring vegetables in beurre blanc, to a neatly jointed 'pleasantly gamey' roast partridge on a scattering of winter vegetables in a Gewurztraminer sauce. Another game dish – saddle of venison with braised pork belly, lettuce, roast figs and chestnut purée – provided one off-duty inspector with her best dish of the year.

Desserts mostly focus on fruit and ice cream, rather than chocolate. A plate of four orange desserts – peel 'confit' enclosing a parfait, a light mousse with candied orange, a sorbet between slices of crystallised orange, and a tartlet filled with crème patissière – impressed for exploring the full potential of the fruit: 'a triumph, to do so much with one flavour'. Extras include very fine bread, and the usual country house array of nibbles and petits fours. As for service, Catherine Endacott's front-of-house skills have been singled out for praise. The wine list has been justly lauded for its mark-up policy (£30 is the maximum profit) but its contents also deserve praise. At first glance, France might seem to have claimed all of Paul Henderson's attention, with its display of mature Alsaces, venerable Burgundies, old Bordeaux and ancient Loires. However, a closer look reveals plenty of fine wines from Germany, Italy and California. Eight wines by the glass start at £4.

CHEF: Michael Caines PROPRIETORS: Kay and Paul Henderson OPEN: all week 12.30 to 2, 7 to 9 MEALS: Set L Mon to Thur £22 to £30, Set L Fri to Sun £27.35, Set L all week £60, Set D £60 to £65 SERVICE: net prices, card slips closed CARDS: Delta, Diners, MasterCard, Switch, Visa DETAILS: 35 seats. Private parties: 30 main room. Car park. Children's helpings. No children under 7 in dining room. No smoking in dining room. Wheelchair access (not WC). No music ACCOMMODATION: 14 rooms, all with bath/shower. TV. Phone. D,B&B £235 to £435. Baby facilities. Fishing

---

▲ 22 Mill Street ⚹✳

22 Mill Street, Chagford TQ13 8AW	COOKING 7
TEL: (01647) 432244 FAX: (01647) 433101	COST £28–£46

Given the tiny reception area with a single small settee, loud Muzak, and a large golden retriever asleep by the fire – 'we spent two days clambering over him' – most people go straight to their table: either in the front dining room, with large plate windows and the air of a converted shop, or in the back room next to the wine store. The owners are friendly, straightforward and committed, the service capably handled by Amanda Leaman, while Duncan Walker's food is generally simple and unfussy, yet for the most part intensely flavoured.

Dinner starts with an appetiser soup, considered a wise move since 'this man can do soup', according to one who chose a deep-flavoured smoked haddock version with poached quails' eggs from the three-course menu. Fish has also produced accurately timed, 'juicy and firm' red mullet, served with 'silky and delectable' leeks in a saffron broth, while risotto, a dish that typically sorts the men from the boys, has been 'brilliant' according to one who ate a saffron version with rabbit.

Presentation is not laboured, 'just simple'; and the style is not so much innovative as well-practised without seeming contrived or over-refined. Everything 'hung together well' for one reporter in a dish that combined a 'sensuous' chunk of calf's sweetbread and kidney with a pile of 'terrific' finely shredded Savoy cabbage flecked with smoky bacon, in a properly reduced stock sauce. The balance achieved is also expressed in an inspector's roast squab pigeon (including two meaty thighs and a couple of fried livers) served with a port reduction, plus a light amalgam of lemon zest, crème fraîche, olive oil and sage dribbled over, which contrasted well with the meat's richness.

Desserts display a penchant for classical simplicity, from highly rated hot soufflés (raspberry, or prune and armagnac), via chocolate and almond pithiviers, to a cinnamon-poached pear with lemon grass crème brûlée, the crackly topping served separately as a disc of caramel. Value is considered good, and 'copious' breakfasts await those who stay. Around fifty well-chosen wines start with house Italian white at £12.50 and Californian red at £14.25.

CHEF: Duncan Walker PROPRIETORS: Amanda Leaman and Duncan Walker OPEN: Tue to Sat L 12 to 1.45, Mon to Sat D 7.15 to 9 CLOSED: 2 weeks Jan MEALS: Set L £14.95 (2 courses) to £15.95, Set D £24.50 (2 courses) to £27 SERVICE: net prices, card slips closed CARDS: Delta, MasterCard, Switch, Visa DETAILS: 30 seats. Private parties: 14 main room, 12 private room. No children under 12 in dining room. No smoking in dining room. Wheelchair access (not WC). Music ACCOMMODATION: 2 rooms, both with bath/shower. TV. B&B £45

CHEESDEN Greater Manchester   map 8

NORTH-WEST 2000 STAR

Nutters ⅝✳

Edenfield Road, Cheesden OL12 7TY   COOKING 6
TEL/FAX: (01706) 650167   COST £28–£47

'This is an exciting place to eat, a bit of an adventure,' writes one visitor to the Nutter family's moorland ex-pub with its peachy-hued dining-room. Jean Nutter (admin) and Rodney (wine) are right behind their son Andrew in his various enterprises (set out in framed newspaper cuttings dotted on walls), and he continues to demonstrate the 'talent, passion and flair' in the kitchen that can deliver cutting-edge results. This is cooking that achieves what it sets out to do, be it a comforting dish of properly cooked, juicy pork medallions in a chunky plum sauce, or a soup of yellow pepper and sweetcorn with Roquefort ravioli. But ambition is high, and old themes are re-invented, reconstructed, seen from a novel angle: for example a starter of thin beef fillet, cooked one side only so it was still completely rare on top, served on a bed of horseradish and celeriac, their fieriness tempered by boiling in beef stock.

Main courses maintain the creative momentum, as it becomes clear that, if he were not upon the cooking stage, Mr Nutter might be an architect, so keen is he on building towers. One consisted of a ground floor of mashed potato and roast garlic, leading to a first floor of sweet red onion, climbing up to a duck confit capped with a roof of deep-fried shredded leek; around this, guard soldiers on sentry duty, were half a dozen pieces of duck breast, and paddling in the moat was more duck, each piece supporting piles of steamed blueberries. A busy dish, certainly, but also 'a winning combination of colours, textures and flavours'. Cheeses are many and varied, and savouries such as melting goat's cheese with a bacon and chive dressing are compelling competitors for hot mango, apple and raisin fritters, or a crème brûlée successfully combining the tartness of lime with the creaminess of the custard. If the staff smiled a bit more, it might help. Wines are mostly French with a sprinkling from Spain and the New World. Nutters Oakwood White and Red (£10.80) are from Australia.

CHEF: Andrew Nutter PROPRIETORS: Rodney, Jean and Andrew Nutter OPEN: Wed to Mon 12 to 2, 7 (6.30 Sat) to 9.30 CLOSED: first 2 weeks Aug MEALS: alc (main courses £10 to £16.50). Set L £19.95, Set D £29.95 SERVICE: not inc CARDS: Amex, Delta, MasterCard, Switch, Visa DETAILS: 48 seats. Private parties: 82 main room, 30 private room. Car park. Children's helpings. No smoking in dining room. Wheelchair access (also WC). Music

---

CHELTENHAM Gloucestershire map 5

Le Champignon Sauvage ▼

24–26 Suffolk Road, Cheltenham GL50 2AQ COOKING 7
TEL/FAX: (01242) 573449 COST £28–£69

A few minutes' walk from the town centre, this looks like an old pub from outside, with a sign saying 'restaurant Français' as if it were a snails and frogs' legs outfit. Inside, however, all is cool and calm, smart and comfortable. A bright yellow and blue colour scheme, and some modern paintings, make it feel 'very Provençal'. The ambitious cooking aims for a refined style involving a lot of skill and workmanship, both of which are liberally evident, and which allow the kitchen to offer some complex dishes: for example, a raviolo of rabbit topped with tiny slices of fillet and sweet onion, surrounded by wild mushrooms and skinned broad beans in a reduced sticky sauce. And this was just a lunchtime starter.

Even simple-sounding dishes benefit from the painstaking approach: a bowl of sandy-coloured, creamy-textured crab soup with well-balanced flavours of coriander, lemon grass and chilli. Presentation is effective because components are arranged attractively on a plate, without the help of superfluous decorative flourishes: a filleted wing of skate on a bed of creamy mash, for example, combined with the 'spring green colours' of capers, green peppercorns, asparagus, spring onion, and watercress sauce. A separate plate of vegetables seemed slightly out of place, according to an inspector, given the integrity of main courses.

Cheeses are generous in scope, and desserts are as busy as the rest of the meal, perhaps involving an oriental flavouring – mango with a Thai-spiced cream and red wine syrup – or a roasted fruit: maybe strawberries on a smear of caramel surrounding an iced peach parfait. Portions are well judged throughout, and service from Helen Everitt-Mathias, who is 'given to smiling, and just the right amount of conversation,' is first class. The restaurant does not always appear to receive the popular support which the food deserves; hard to believe especially considering the exceptional lunchtime and evening 'menu du jour' deals. The wine list is an added attraction, particularly for its fair prices that even extend to mature first-growth clarets. Mostly French, as befits the setting, it none the less finds room for some choice New World bins. House wines from France and South Africa start at £9.95.

CHEF: David Everitt-Matthias   PROPRIETORS: David and Helen Everitt-Matthias   OPEN: Tue to Sat 12.30 to 1.30, 7.30 to 9   CLOSED: 10 days Christmas, 4 days Easter, 2 weeks summer, bank hols   MEALS: Set L £14.50 (2 courses) to £18.50, Set D Tue to Fri £15.50 (2 courses) to £19.95, Set D Tue to Sat £29.50 (2 courses) to £40   SERVICE: not inc   CARDS: Amex, Diners, MasterCard, Switch, Visa   DETAILS: 28 seats. Private parties: 22 main room. No smoking before 10pm. Wheelchair access (not WC). No music   £5

Mayflower

32–34 Clarence Street, Cheltenham GL50 3NX	COOKING 1
TEL: (01242) 522426 FAX: (01242) 251667	COST £15–£54

A 'lively restaurant' with 'sensible prices and generous portions' is how one described this long-running, popular Chinese restaurant. The long carte is supplemented by a range of set meals that offer wide variety without delving into highly exotic ingredients, and include a seafood feast for four. There are special events too, including a frivolous wine-tasting followed by a light buffet, and a possibly more serious Wok 'n' Roll '60s evening. Vegetarians have a page of the menu to choose from, with interesting and unusual dishes such as double mushroom soup, mock duck with pancakes, and mock duck egg foo yung. House wines are £9.50 and sixty more at fair prices are well balanced between the Old and New Worlds. Sparkling wine, good with Chinese food, is well represented with excellent, not overpriced champagnes, and others from Australia, Spain and Italy.

CHEFS: Mr C.F. Kong and Mrs M.M. Kong   PROPRIETORS: the Kong family   OPEN: Mon to Sat L 12 to 1.45, all week D 6 to 10 (10.30 Fri and Sat)   CLOSED: 24 to 26 Dec   MEALS: alc (main courses £5 to £12). Set L £6.75, Set D £18 (2 courses) to £19.75   SERVICE: not inc   CARDS: Amex, Delta, Diners, MasterCard, Switch, Visa   DETAILS: 120 seats. Private parties: 80 main room, 40 private room. Vegetarian meals. Music. Air-conditioned   £5

Le Petit Blanc ⁺✳ £

Queen's Hotel, The Promenade, Cheltenham GL50 1NN	NEW CHEF
TEL: (01242) 266800 FAX: (01242) 266801	COST £23–£50

Occupying the ground floor of, but quite separate from, the Queen's Hotel, Petit Blanc has a feel that is 'masculine and plain'. It ministers to all-day grazers, children, lunchtime snackers, shoppers in need of a break, hungry diners, and anyone who fancies a bite of French provincial cooking, enlisting the aid of a few British and Asian ideas along the way. Sausage and mash with onion gravy thus finds itself alongside deep-fried crab cake with green onion risotto and chilli oil, while pig's cheek, and braised rabbit with mustard reflect the owner's roots. Philip Alcock replaced Stephen Nash, who has gone to a new branch in Birmingham, scheduled to open after the *Guide* has gone to press, but we understand that the cooking is likely to continue in the same vein as before. Staff are young, dapper, informal, welcoming and generally efficient, and around thirty attractively varied wines stay mostly under £25, starting with house red and white at £9.95.

CHEF: Philip Alcock   PROPRIETOR: Raymond Blanc   OPEN: all week 12 to 3.30, 6 to 11
CLOSED: 25 Dec   MEALS: alc (main courses £7 to £16.50). Set L and D before 7 £12.50 to £15.
Bar-brasserie menu served all day   SERVICE: not inc, card slips closed   CARDS: Amex, Delta,
Diners, MasterCard, Switch, Visa   DETAILS: 150 seats. 25 seats outside. Vegetarian meals.
Children's helpings. No smoking in dining room. Wheelchair access (not WC). Music.
Air-conditioned

CHESTER Cheshire   map 7

▲ *Chester Grosvenor Hotel, Arkle* ♥ ⅝✻

Eastgate, Chester CH1 1LT   COOKING 6
TEL: (01244) 324024   FAX: (01244) 313246   COST £39–£89

This is a place where people come to get 'the works' and, for those who can afford it, every kind of gastronomic luxury is here. It's not exactly racy, for a restaurant named after a racehorse: the windowless dining room, with its huge skylight, stone pillars and heavy silverware, has a genteel, slightly dated atmosphere. Waiters in DJs and tails provide 'dutiful, very observant' service and wheel white-clothed trolleys around bearing everything from bread to cheese.

Simon Radley's accomplished, intricate cooking takes its cue from France and Italy, with dishes such as pressed Bresse chicken and foie gras, and langoustine ravioli with sauce vierge. 'Compositions' are one way the kitchen shows off its skills: a veal version with sweetbreads and kidney pudding, osso bucco and roast fillet; or one of pork with stuffed trotter, crisp honey-roast belly and crackling. Technique is everything, and at best this produces 'nicely wobbly' hot scallop fondant, topped with an 'amazingly crisp' potato wafer, 'a big lump' of Beluga caviare and a whole scallop 'in absolutely perfect condition'. At times, though, dishes can seem too clever for their own good – an intricate garnish of mushroom stalk, its cap replaced by a blob of wild mushroom mousse – although many of the basic combinations are well tried, for example roast pigeon with cep tagliatelle and 'utterly decadent' foie gras.

Puddings continue the multifaceted approach, with 'a trio' of chocolate pyramids, or 'a collection' of caramel desserts incorporating steamed butterscotch pudding, crème caramel, and iced praline parfait. Classic wines from classic vintages are the hallmark of the hefty wine list, although fans of the New World will also find much to excite them (including seventeen vintages of Opus One). Those celebrating a win at the Derby will find plenty to splash out on, but there is lots of good drinking for ordinary punters as well. House French is £12 for the white, £12.75 the red. A separate brasserie offers a more informal menu along the lines of garlic chicken with roast tomatoes and mozzarella, and Cumberland sausages with onion sauce.

'My dessert looked like Jackson Pollock had fallen into a Jacuzzi. The raspberry coulis was a lurid vortex of red, yellow and brown; we never realised that raspberries came in all these colours.' (On eating in Yorkshire)

CHEF: Simon Radley PROPRIETOR: Grosvenor Estate Holdings Ltd OPEN: Tue to Sat 12 to 2.30, 7 to 9.30 (10 Sat) CLOSED: 24 Dec D to 30 Dec, bank hols MEALS: Set L £25 to £48, Set D £40 to £48 SERVICE: not inc CARDS: Amex, Diners, MasterCard, Switch, Visa DETAILS: 40 seats. 40 seats outside. Private parties: 22 main room. Car park. Children's helpings. No smoking in dining room. Wheelchair access (also WC). Music. Air-conditioned ACCOMMODATION: 85 rooms, all with bath/shower. TV. Phone. Room only £130 to £225. Rooms for disabled. Baby facilities

CHINNOR Oxfordshire map 2

Sir Charles Napier

Sprigg's Alley, nr Chinnor OX9 4BX
TEL: (01494) 483011 FAX: (01494) 485311
exit 6 from M40; at Chinnor roundabout turn right, continue straight up hill; Sprigg's Alley signposted after 1m

COOKING **4**
COST **£34–£55**

In 2000 Julie Griffiths celebrates twenty-five years at this stand-alone house in the Oxfordshire countryside. The theme is rustic, with low beams, nooks, crannies, an idiosyncratic mix of take-it-or-leave-it furniture – if things don't match, that's the way it's meant to be – and 'sculpture everywhere you turn'. The kitchen puts out an 'enticing' menu that leans towards fish and fowl with the occasional rabbit or veal dish adding variety, and while the set-price lunch is a simple affair (provençale torte, linguine with clams) the carte weighs in with sea bream and saffron mash, partridge and lentils, and saddle of lamb with couscous. Herbs and spices have sometimes met with a raised eyebrow – cardamom in a pea risotto to accompany scallops, for example – but if you are shown a basket of freshly gathered mushrooms in autumn, the advice is to go for them.

Hot chocolate pot was the pick of desserts for one party, and there is a choice of blues, goats' and others on the English cheeseboard. The welcome is warm, service friendly and informal, and wines are a joy to behold. That the wine buyers know their business is clearly demonstrated by the wide range of quality bins, featuring famous names and new discoveries at pocket-friendly prices. Those who don't have time to peruse the main list (or to enjoy the informative section introductions), will be well served by the house selection of eight stylish wines priced between £15.50 and £24.

CHEFS: David Jones and José Cau PROPRIETOR: Julie Griffiths OPEN: Tue to Sun L 12 to 2.30 (3.30 Sun), Tue to Sat D 7 to 10 CLOSED: 25 and 26 Dec MEALS: alc (main courses £11.50 to £16.50). Set L Tue to Sat £15.50 (2 courses), Set D Tue to Fri £15.50 (2 courses) SERVICE: 12.5% (optional), card slips closed CARDS: Amex, Delta, Diners, MasterCard, Switch, Visa DETAILS: 70 seats. 70 seats outside. Private parties: 45 main room, 25 to 45 private rooms. Car park. Vegetarian meals. Children's helpings. No children under 7 at D. No smoking in 1 dining room. Wheelchair access (not WC). Occasional music

'Diners sat at dark wooden tables, close together, constantly disturbed by the numerous waiters who noisily jostled trolleys up and down, wobbled the floorboards, and generally made us feel as though we were eating on the M6.' (On eating in Wales)

CHIPPING NORTON Oxfordshire   map 2

Chavignol ♥ ⅚✳

7 Horsefair, Chipping Norton OX7 5AL	COOKING 6
TEL/FAX: (01608) 644490	COST £35–£64

Occupying an old building on the elevated side of the market square is a small domestic-scale dining room 'unflashily' decorated with decent pictures. The menu, on the other hand, looks like something from a jazzy Islington hotspot, not the demure Cotswolds. This is not wildly experimental have-a-go fusion food, however. Rather it puts a modestly inventive spin on some classical ideas: from a straightforward poached duck egg in puff pastry with hollandaise and asparagus, to breast and confit leg of local duck with caramelised pears and cinnamon sauce. Although dishes can be quite involved – 'this is food one simply would not cook at home' – they still appear well focused. Fillet of beef, for example, comes with an oxtail and tarragon ravioli, on a horseradish and celeriac purée.

Fish is subject to varied and sometimes busy treatments, including monkfish medallions stuffed with pesto mousse on a basil and pasta galette, and red mullet on tapénade mash with haricots verts fried in cider batter. Desserts are out of the same mould, producing for example a galette of caramelised bananas on a shortbread biscuit, served with vanilla ice cream and balsamic-marinated strawberries. Regulars are impressed by the 'uniformly excellent' food, and its reliability from one occasion to another. The wine list is brimming with fine, classical bottles from France, and quality remains high when it spills into other regions. Plenty of good drinking is to be had for around £20 (house French is £13) and half-bottles, or their equivalent, are readily available.

CHEF: Marcus Ashenford   PROPRIETORS: Mark and Donna Maguire   OPEN: Tue to Sat 12.15 to 2, 7 to 9.45   CLOSED: 3 weeks Jan   MEALS: Set L £19 (2 courses) to £25 (limited menu Tue L), Set D £38 to £42   SERVICE: not inc   CARDS: Amex, Delta, Diners, MasterCard, Switch, Visa DETAILS: 26 seats. Private parties: 22 main room, 8 private room. Vegetarian meals. No smoking in dining room. No music £5

CHOBHAM Surrey   map 3

Quails

1 Bagshot Road, Chobham GU24 8BP	COOKING 3
TEL/FAX: (01276) 858491	COST £25–£47

Liver red and bottle green wallpaper contrasts with turquoise and yellow padded chairs at this horseshoe-shaped room on a busy street corner, where an appealing strain of up-to-date Anglo-French cooking delivers 'neat and sharp' results. Roe deer, red mullet, rack of lamb and pork tenderloin are among main-course materials the kitchen likes to use, and accurate timing and careful seasoning have made a success of, for example, pale pink partridge breast with a cardamom-scented jus, and an enormous 'macho' dish of well-hung, full-flavoured beef fillet served rare on a tiny raft of black pudding.

Meatless dishes fare well too, judging by sweet, firm, opalescent halibut, and creamy, spinach-speckled risotto with silky oyster mushrooms, while salad dressings (orange and coriander for a smoked chicken and avocado salad in one case) are appreciated. Enterprising desserts have included chocolate crème brûlée served with cumin shortbread. Staff are efficient and friendly, while 'Mrs Wale is charming, helpful, and knowledgeable about her wines'. Made from a fair number of grape varieties, these are arranged by style and provide decent choice under £20. House vin de pays is £9.95.

CHEF: Christopher Wale   PROPRIETORS: the Wale family   OPEN: Tue to Fri L 12 to 2, Tue to Sat D 7 to 9.30   CLOSED: 26 Dec, 1 Jan   MEALS: alc (main courses L £8.50 to £15.50, D £14 to £15.50). Set L £11.95 (2 courses) to £14.95, Set D Tue to Fri £15.95 (2 courses) to £18.95   SERVICE: not inc   CARDS: Amex, Delta, Diners, MasterCard, Switch, Visa   DETAILS: 50 seats. Private parties: 50 main room. Car park. Vegetarian meals. No cigars/pipes in dining room. Wheelchair access (not WC). Occasional music. Air-conditioned   £5

CHRISTCHURCH Dorset

map 2

Splinters

12 Church Street, Christchurch BH23 1BW	COOKING 3
TEL: (01202) 483454 FAX: (01202) 480180	COST £30–£54

'We are very fortunate to have this on our doorstep,' writes a local. Set in a cobbled street that leads to the magnificent Priory Church, Splinters offers a warm welcome in the agreeable surroundings of a bar, a first-floor drawing room, and a series of small dining rooms with bare floorboards, wicker chairs, shiny pews, white linen and elegant glasses. Described as 'unpretentious', it nevertheless piles on the ingredients in earnestly modern fashion, producing, for example, a dish of salmon fillet with crab and coriander ravioli, chilli and tomato jam, spring onion salsa, and more homely new potatoes. 'We got very excited at the sight of the menu,' wrote one reporter, who went on to enjoy an 'elegant' mousse of avocado and tomato, and crisp-skinned guinea fowl. Finish with caramelised lemon tart or a platter of chocolate desserts. Service is a strong point, and there is a fair choice of wines under £20 outside the classic regions. House Roussillon red is £11.90, Languedoc white £12.45.

CHEF: Jason Davenport   PROPRIETORS: Robert Wilson and Timothy Lloyd   OPEN: Tue to Sat 12 to 2, 7 to 10 (10.30 Sat)   CLOSED: 26 to 29 Dec   MEALS: alc L (main courses £9.50 to £16). Set D £27 (2 courses) to £32   SERVICE: not inc   CARDS: Amex, Delta, Diners, MasterCard, Switch, Visa   DETAILS: 42 seats. 6 seats outside. Private parties: 24 main room, 8 to 24 private rooms. Vegetarian meals. No smoking in dining-room. Music   £5

CLAYGATE Surrey

map 3

Le Petit Pierrot

4 The Parade, Claygate KT10 0NU	COOKING 2
TEL: (01372) 465105 FAX: (01372) 467642	COST £27–£49

For ten years the Brichots have been installed in this intimate (some say cramped) and deservedly popular French restaurant, in a parade of shops in suburban Surrey. Bright pink cloths cover the small tables, little pierrots and masks adorn the place, and Madame oversees. Decently cooked cod, rack of lamb and Gressingham duck come in for commendation, as do side plates of vegetables, and an impressive pear tarte Tatin. For further glimpses of the modern/classical style, consider Jerusalem artichoke soup with chervil, potted rabbit, or noodles with crab and chilli as a starter, then méli-mélo de poissons et crustaces, calf's liver sauté with sage and lime, or a vegetable and ginger crêpe. The same menu obtains at lunch and dinner, with lunchtime prices thought to offer particularly good value. Wines are reasonably priced, inevitably French, and include plenty of half-bottles. House Bouches-du-Rhône is £10.25. Ask if you want guidance as there are no notes.

CHEF: Jean-Pierre Brichot   PROPRIETORS: Jean-Pierre and Annie Brichot   OPEN: Mon to Fri L 12.15 to 2.15, Mon to Sat D 7.15 to 9.30   CLOSED: 25 Dec to 30 Dec, bank hols   MEALS: Set L £11.25 (2 courses) to £19.25, Set D £22.50   SERVICE: not inc   CARDS: Amex, Delta, Diners, MasterCard, Switch, Visa   DETAILS: 32 seats. Private parties: 32 main room. Vegetarian meals. No children under 9. Music. Air-conditioned

CLITHEROE Lancashire   map 8

Auctioneer 🍴✳

New Market Street, Clitheroe BB7 2JW   COOKING 3
TEL: (01200) 427153   FAX: (01200) 444518   COST £19–£52

The restaurant is just by the market, and the Van Heumens also run a delicatessen in town, so sourcing ingredients cannot be a problem. Henk Van Heumen maintains a shortish carte, periodically adding dishes from a particular country or region, such as Sicily, Sardinia or Andalusia. Thus fine-weather visitors, who might prefer the terrace with its moorland views to the rather dark and heavily furnished main room, could opt for South African Hoopenburg onion and cheese tart, as well as bresaola rolled round warm goats' cheese and served with raspberries: 'original and creative, the fruit an inspired complement'. When the menu isn't being 'themed', you can find starters of provençale fish soup, and farmhouse terrine, followed by medallions of venison with liver pâté, or 'good, moist' pork fillet in a herby crust. The 'rendez-vous of desserts' permits a taste across the range (perhaps pecan ice cream, apple pie, lemon cheesecake, bread-and-butter pudding and chocolate parfait), all competently produced. Service could be spruced up. Ten house wines at £11 head up a list that includes some interesting bottles from most areas.

CHEF: Henk Van Heumen   PROPRIETORS: Henk and Frances Van Heumen   OPEN: Fri to Sun L 12 to 1.30, Wed to Sun D 7 to 8.30 (9.30 Sat)   MEALS: alc (main courses £10.50 to £17.50). Set L £8.95 (2 courses) to £10.95, Set D £19.75   SERVICE: not inc   CARDS: Amex, Delta, MasterCard, Switch, Visa   DETAILS: 48 seats. Private parties: 24 main room, 24 private room. Vegetarian meals. Children's helpings. No smoking in 1 dining room. Music. Air-conditioned (£5)

'The table next to us were accident prone. First the waitress spilled wine over them, then they set fire to themselves.' (On eating in Berkshire)

The Guide *always appreciates hearing about changes of chef or owner.*

COCKERMOUTH Cumbria
map 10

Quince & Medlar 🍴✳ £

13 Castlegate, Cockermouth CA13 9EU
TEL: (01900) 823579

COOKING 2
COST £23–£29

Centrally placed, with 'homely period décor' and a cheerful welcome, this family-run vegetarian restaurant has successfully passed the ten-year landmark. 'We are not vegetarians, but both my wife and I really enjoyed the carefully cooked and well-presented food,' wrote one satisfied customer, confirming the appeal to more than doctrinaire supporters. After buckwheat blinis with roasted beetroot, or an asparagus and creamed horseradish tart, main courses tend to pile on the ingredients – perhaps baked sweet potato with green lentils, leeks and grated spiced carrot, topped with cheese and served with mustard sauce, all accompanied by extra vegetables – but that does not prevent the kitchen from turning out 'light as a feather' cheese pie, and 'fresh as a daisy' salad. Finish with a fruity dessert (compote, or fruit and nut meringue) and drink from a short but inexpensive collection of bottles – 'all wines listed are organic' – starting with house French at £7.80.

CHEFS/PROPRIETORS: Colin and Louisa Le Voi   OPEN: Tue to Sat D only 7 to 9.30   CLOSED: 1 week mid-Nov, 24 to 26 Dec, 2 weeks mid-Jan   MEALS: alc (main courses £9)   SERVICE: not inc, card slips closed   CARDS: MasterCard, Visa   DETAILS: 26 seats. Private parties: 14 main room. Vegetarian meals. No children under 6. No smoking in dining room. Music

---

COLERNE Wiltshire
map 2

▲ *Lucknam Park* 🍷 🍴✳

Colerne SN14 8AZ
TEL: (01225) 742777   FAX: (01225) 743536
EMAIL: reservations@lucknampark.co.uk
off A420 at Ford, 6m W of Chippenham

COOKING 5
COST £41–£98

Set in 500 acres, this restored Palladian mansion dating from 1720 is geared towards the corporate end of the market, with conference and leisure facilities, and an equestrian centre, among its attractions. Chandeliers and heavily swagged curtains feature in the pink and green dining room, and the food is appropriately comforting ('safe' one called it), in the sense that it stays within fairly traditional confines, tossing in a few luxuries here (risotto of ceps and truffle) and flirting with a few bright Eastern flavourings there, usually in seafood: tian of crab with a lime-dressed rocket and mango salad, for example, or brill in a langoustine and coriander bouillon.

The main menu is a carte of around five choices per course, items from which can be substituted for dishes on the set-price menu at a supplement: for foie gras terrine with Muscat jelly, or roast sea bass with noodles and oyster tempura. Aside from that, expect to find lamb served with roasted aubergine and tomato confit, or venison with bacon and stuffed cabbage, followed by chocolate fondant with pistachio ice cream, or apple tart with rum and raisin ice cream. Service is 'half-French, half-English', and the jacket and tie rule for men can make them feel 'hot and uncomfortable'. Wines are predominantly French and feature plenty of grand bins (at some rather grand prices). Those without the benefit of a corporate expense account should look to 'Les Provinces Françaises', Spain, Chile or even England for a variety of bottles under £20; house French is £16.

CHEF: Paul Collins   PROPRIETOR: Lucknam Park Hotels Ltd   OPEN: Sun L 12.30 to 2.30, all week D 7.30 to 9 (7 to 10 Fri and Sat)   MEALS: alc D (main courses £25 to £29). Set L Sun £25, Set D £40   SERVICE: not inc, card slips closed   CARDS: Amex, Delta, Diners, MasterCard, Switch, Visa   DETAILS: 80 seats. Private parties: 80 main room, 36 private room. Car park. Vegetarian meals. Children's helpings. No children under 12 at D. Jacket and tie. No smoking in dining room. Wheelchair access (also WC). Occasional music   ACCOMMODATION: 41 rooms, all with bath/shower. TV. Phone. Room only £135 to £625. Rooms for disabled. Baby facilities. Swimming pool (*The Which? Hotel Guide*)

COLN ST ALDWYNS   Gloucestershire   map 2

▲ *New Inn* ╡✸ | NEW ENTRY |

Coln St Aldwyns GL7 5AN
TEL: (01285) 750651   FAX: (01285) 750657
EMAIL: stay@new-inn.co.uk
off B4425, Cirencester to Burford road, 2m SW of   COOKING 1
Bibury   COST £33–£46

At this substantial and ancient Cotswold stone inn, all covered with ivy, Stephen Morey caters for a well-heeled crowd, taking local produce and creating British-plus-Mediterranean dishes. Choose from the three-course menu in the rustic hop-decorated bar (which has its own generous carte of slightly simpler offerings) or comfortable lounge, before moving into the light, pine-chaired restaurant, where obliging young staff serve. Start perhaps with a good creamy risotto with plenty of haddock and plump prawns, or a salad of smoked duck. To follow, roast cod fillet has come with a well-judged velouté containing gherkins and capers, or you could go for roast lamb with a black olive sauce. At dessert stage, one diner was particularly taken with a caramelised lemon tart. This is a fine real ale establishment, and wines too – many under £20 – offer the prospect of good drinking. House French is £10.75.

CHEF: Stephen Morey   PROPRIETORS: Brian and Sandra-Anne Evans   OPEN: all week 12 to 2 (2.30 Sun), 7 to 9 (9.30 Fri and Sat)   CLOSED: 1 Jan   MEALS: Set L £17.50 (2 courses) to £21.50, Set D £22.50 (2 courses) to £26.50. Bar menu available   SERVICE: not inc   CARDS: Amex, Delta, MasterCard, Switch, Visa   DETAILS: 32 seats. 50 seats outside. Private parties: 20 main room. Car park. Vegetarian meals. No children under 10 in dining room. No smoking in dining room. Wheelchair access (also WC). No music   ACCOMMODATION: 14 rooms, all with bath/shower. TV. Phone. B&B £68 to £115. No children under 10 in accommodation (*The Which? Hotel Guide*)

Occasional music *in the details at the end of an entry means live or recorded music is played in the dining room only rarely or for special events.* No music *means it is never played.*

If a restaurant is new to the Guide *this year (did not appear as a main entry in the last edition),* NEW ENTRY *appears opposite its name.*

COOKHAM Berkshire   map 3

Alfonso's

19–21 Station Hill Parade, Cookham SL6 9BR   COOKING **4**
TEL: (01628) 525775   COST £30–£45

Alfonso's is very much a 'local – the sort we all wish we had nearby', writes an inspector. The somewhat unlikely location is a small parade of shops next to the station, but, inside, a green and white colour scheme, dark wood and lighted candles create a pretty setting. Maria and Alfonso Baena make 'a perfect front-of-house couple', providing deft and cheerful service. The predominant style is English produce paired with Mediterranean flavourings (wild local mushrooms with oven-dried tomatoes and a provençale dressing) and served with well-crafted sauces. Local rabbit, for example, comes with plenty of dark, cinnamon-scented gravy, while 'juicy' braised salmon steak topped with mozzarella is brought to table in its own terracotta pot with 'lots of rich tomato gravy pungent with oregano'. Meat cookery is a strength, producing pink roast rack of English lamb, and much-applauded loin of Berkshire pork, marinated Argentinian-style and cooked on wood embers. Puddings include a light crème caramel, and a chocolate marjolaine with Grand Marnier cream. An interesting range of Spanish wines is the highlight of the fifty-strong list, although house wine, at £9.25, is French.

CHEFS: Mr and Mrs Richard Manzano   PROPRIETORS: Mr and Mrs Alfonso Baena   OPEN: Mon to Fri L 12.30 to 2, Mon to Sat D 7 to 10 (10.30 Sat)   CLOSED: 2 weeks Aug, bank hols   MEALS: Set L £7.50 (2 courses), Set D £18.50 (2 courses) to £21.50   SERVICE: not inc   CARDS: Amex, Delta, Diners, MasterCard, Visa   DETAILS: 34 seats. Private parties: 34 main room. Car park. Children's helpings. No pipes in dining room. Wheelchair access (not WC). Occasional music

CORSCOMBE Dorset   map 2

▲ *Fox Inn* 🍴✳ £

Corscombe DT2 0NS
TEL/FAX: (01935) 891330
off A356, 6m SE of Crewkerne   COOKING **2**
                                                              COST £20–£38

The Fox encapsulates many people's idea of what a country pub should be like. Thatched, white-fronted, with roses round the door, flag and tile floors, stone and plaster walls, and big wood-burning fireplaces, it treats food seriously yet without pretension: 'plain, hearty and decent' is how it appeared to one visitor. Among the resources Martyn Lee is able to call on are local venison, bison and wild boar, fish from Cornish day boats, rabbit from the postman, scallops from the baker who occasionally goes diving, wild garlic and nettles from behind the pub, and herbs from the garden. Menu and blackboard between them typically offer fourteen starters, around twenty fish and meat main courses, half a dozen vegetarian items, and ten puddings. Few culinary stones are left unturned, as dishes range from chicken tom yum soup to kedgeree, and from a 'gutsy, honest' gratin of crab and brill to a rustic, dark green Castilian soup. Puddings, on the other hand, are very British: apple crumble, sticky toffee. A compact but interesting wine list increases the sense of value by remaining mostly below £20. Six house wines (starting at £9.50) are also available by the glass.

CHEF: Will Longman   PROPRIETORS: Martyn and Susie Lee   OPEN: all week 12 to 2, 7 to 9 (9.30 Fri and Sat)   CLOSED: 25 Dec (exc for drinks)   MEALS: alc (main courses £5.50 to £13.50) SERVICE: not inc, card slips closed   CARDS: Delta, MasterCard, Switch, Visa   DETAILS: 60 seats. 34 seats outside. Private parties: 34 main room, 20 and 34 private rooms. Car park. Vegetarian meals. Children's helpings. No smoking in 1 dining room. Wheelchair access (1 step; not WC). No music   ACCOMMODATION: 3 rooms, all with bath/shower. B&B £45 to £80 (*The Which? Hotel Guide*)

CORSE LAWN Gloucestershire   map 2

▲ *Corse Lawn House* 🍷 ⚡

Corse Lawn GL19 4LZ
TEL: (01452) 780771   FAX: (01452) 780840   COOKING 3
on B4211, 5m SW of Tewkesbury   COST £27–£59

As a restaurant location a car wash does not sound particularly inviting, yet its predecessor – a big pond designed as an eighteenth-century drive-in coach wash – provides an attractive setting for this clutch of red-brick buildings where the Hines have plied their trade since 1978. The format is generous to a fault, offering a carte and set-price options at lunch and dinner, plus a long bistro menu, so the kitchen has its work cut out. It delivers a range of Anglo-French dishes along the lines of hare terrine with prune and cherry relish, crab sausage in a seafood sauce, and roast partridge with game chips, and is obviously as happy with venison, pigeon and guinea fowl as with loin of pork and fillet of beef. Chocolate mille-feuille has been recommended, or there may be hot orange sponge or raspberry soufflé. Staff, we are told, 'could not have been more helpful'.

Happily for those seeking modest drinking, ten house wines are sourced mostly from the 'little' regions of France, with prices starting at £9.95. Mr Hine Snr's Francophilia is further evidenced by a long line of classics including some excellent older vintages, while a growing number of New Zealand bins reflects Mrs Hine Jnr's continuing loyalty to her home country: if your wallet doesn't stretch to Cloudy Bay prices, wander up the road to Wairau River and try their Sauvignon Blanc 1996, £19.80.

CHEFS: Baba Hine and Andrew Poole   PROPRIETORS: the Hine family   OPEN: all week 12 to 2, 7 to 9.30   CLOSED: 25 and 26 Dec   MEALS: alc (main courses £16 to £20). Set L Mon to Sat £14.95 (2 courses) to £16.95, Set L Sun £17.95, Set D £25   SERVICE: not inc, card slips closed CARDS: Amex, Delta, Diners, MasterCard, Switch, Visa   DETAILS: 80 seats. 40 seats outside. Private parties: 80 main room, 18 and 30 private rooms. Car park. Vegetarian meals. Children's helpings. No smoking in dining room. Wheelchair access (also WC). No music ACCOMMODATION: 19 rooms, all with bath/shower. TV. Phone. B&B £65 to £120. Rooms for disabled. Baby facilities. Swimming pool

---

⚡ *indicates that smoking is either banned altogether or that a dining-room is maintained for non-smokers. The symbol does not apply to restaurants that simply have no-smoking areas.*

COTTESMORE Rutland   map 6

Sun Inn ⭐ £ | NEW ENTRY |

25 Main Street, Cottesmore LE15 7DH   COOKING 2
TEL: (01572) 812321 FAX: (01572) 812861   COST £17–£40

'I wish this was my local,' mused one reporter, taken by the 'archetypal
picture-postcard pub'. Inside is all beams, nooks and crannies, with stencilled
sunflowers blossoming on yellow walls. The same menu is available in bar and
smart dining room, offering a range of sandwiches and panini (toasted ciabatta
with various toppings) plus light meals/starters of warm crottin de Chavignol on
Caesar salad; Thai-style king prawns and scallops; or artichoke and fennel soup
'packed with flavour'. Main courses, supplemented by a specials board, might
take in fish and shellfish 'symphonie' with pistou, veal sauté with courgette and
roasted pepper, or a skewer of monkfish and scallops with 'wonderfully soft
corals'. For dessert crème brûlée is 'beautifully presented' with strawberries and
blueberries. Service is French in style: 'no fuss, no bother and child-friendly.'
The equally French wine list is reasonably priced. 'Les Vins du Soleil' start at
£8.95.

CHEF/PROPRIETOR: Franck Garbez OPEN: all week L 12 to 2, Mon to Sat D 6.30 to 10 CLOSED:
25 Dec MEALS: alc (main courses £6 to £15) SERVICE: not inc, card slips closed CARDS:
Delta, MasterCard, Switch, Visa DETAILS: 70 seats. 30 seats outside. Private parties: 80 main
room, 100 private room. Car park. Vegetarian meals. Children's helpings. No smoking in 1 dining
room. Wheelchair access (not WC). Music

CRANBROOK Kent   map 3

▲ Kennel Holt Hotel 🍴 ⭐

Goudhurst Road, Cranbrook TN17 2PT   COOKING 3
TEL: (01580) 712032 FAX: (01580) 715495   COST £39–£54

Everything about this secluded Elizabethan manor house betokens loving care.
Five immaculate acres of garden feature neatly clipped yew hedges with topiary
birds, smart rose beds and a pretty white-fenced pond. Inside, the oak-panelled
lounge has deep sofas by the fire and a choice of art books and opera scores to
browse through, while the dining room sports stiff white linen, unusual table
posies, and prints of Victorian actors striking theatrical poses in spangly
costumes. Since chef Valentine Rodriguez's departure, proprietor Neil Chalmers
has taken up position at the stoves again, although the well-structured menu
continues in much the same vein: light, modern dishes using carefully sourced
materials, and firmly rooted in the seasons. In spring, this might mean starting
with wild mushroom lasagne or a 'decent, freshly made' risotto of spinach and
Swiss chard with fried Parma ham, followed by lamb with a mint jus, or
blanquette of veal with asparagus risotto. Vegetables are 'excellent', and
home-made bread 'outstanding'. Desserts have included berry crème brûlée,
exotic fruit kebabs, and a 'nicely balanced' iced armagnac and prune soufflé.
Service 'couldn't have been better' for one reporter, although perhaps the wine
list could, as a number of bottles are no longer available. House wine is £12.50.

CHEF: Neil Chalmers PROPRIETORS: Neil and Sally Chalmers OPEN: Tue to Sat D only 7.30 to 8.45 (L by arrangement, Sun D residents only) CLOSED: 3 weeks Jan MEALS: Set D £27.50 to £32.50 SERVICE: 10% (optional), card slips closed CARDS: Delta, MasterCard, Switch, Visa DETAILS: 25 seats. 6 seats outside. Private parties: 8 main room, 18 private room. Car park. Vegetarian meals. No children under 10 in dining room. No smoking in dining room. Occasional music ACCOMMODATION: 10 rooms, all with bath/shower. TV. Phone. B&B £85 to £165. Baby facilities (*The Which? Hotel Guide*)

CRONDALL Hampshire   map 2

Chesa

Bowling Alley, Crondall GU10 5RJ   COOKING 3
TEL/FAX: (01252) 850328   COST £41–£54

Despite the address there are no signs of skittles: just a front room in a modern house, adapted to seat twenty people at most, many of whom appear to be 'well-heeled regulars'. Mr Clark serves, Mr Hughes cooks using a wide variety of ingredients, with an emphasis on crafting and interesting presentations: a red bream and zander mousse, for example, filled with squid ink fettuccine and shellfish, in a gewurztraminer sauce. The kitchen's enterprising way with seafood (which predominates among starters) might also take in red mullet fillets on herb noodles with a red pepper sauce, or Dover sole fillet wrapped around a lobster mousse, although an inspection meal indicated that materials may not always be at their peak. Provençale-style fish soup, however, is a 'classic': deep ochre with a rich chunky texture and deep seafood savour, served with spicy rouille, croûtons and Gruyère. Meat main courses – locally reared beef fillet, or 'fine-quality' pink loin of English lamb – are generally served traditionally, while desserts have included a more exotic lime and pistachio soufflé with mango sauce. Meals are taken at a leisurely pace, prices are 'not inconsiderable for a small country restaurant', and the predominantly French wine list starts around £12.

CHEF: P.H.O. Hughes PROPRIETORS: P.H.O Hughes and E.J. Clark OPEN: Wed to Fri and Sun L 12.30 to 1, Wed to Sat d 7.30 to 8.30 CLOSED: 3 weeks Jan, 3 weeks Aug MEALS: Set L £24 (2 courses) to £29, Set D £27 (2 courses) to £32.50 SERVICE: 10% (optional), card slips closed CARDS: Amex, MasterCard, Switch, Visa DETAILS: 20 seats. Private parties: 16 main room. Car park. No pipes/cigars in dining room. Wheelchair access (also WC). No music

---

CROSTHWAITE Cumbria   map 8

▲ *Punch Bowl Inn* ⅚✳

Crosthwaite LA8 8HR
TEL: (015395) 68237 FAX: (015395) 68875   COOKING 4
EMAIL: info@punchbowl.freeserve.co.uk   COST £18–£37

After dividing his time for a period between here and his other venture, the Spread Eagle at Sawley (see entry), Steven Doherty is once more immersed full-time in this inn next to the church in a sprawling little village. Framed gourmet menus on the walls may seem to set a formal tone, but the cooking is reassuringly unpretentious, provoking 'an inward yippee!' in one reporter. A plate of charcuterie seems to leave nothing out, incorporating duck and pork rillettes, bresaola, air-dried ham, and chicken liver and foie gras parfait, with a slug of white truffle oil for good measure. Chargrilled peppers with tomatoes, olives and anchovies may be a lighter way to start. An inspector was impressed by the careful balancing of flavours in roast cod fillet with fennel purée, cherry tomatoes and crisped sage leaves, while specials have included confit duck legs with sauté potatoes and garlic butter. Sticky Tunisian orange cake with lemon curd and crème anglaise is one of the more unusual puddings offered. Even without the early-evening weekday 'beat-the-clock' system, readers agree it all represents exemplary value. So too does the wine list, which is broad-minded in its mingling of French and New World bottles, although its service may not always be commensurate with the quality. Look out for the blackboard selection of wines by the glass. House French is £12 a litre.

CHEF: Steven Doherty   PROPRIETORS: Steven and Marjorie Doherty   OPEN: all week 12 to 2, 6 to 9 (6.30 to 9.30 Sat)   CLOSED: 2 weeks Nov, 25 Dec   MEALS: alc (main courses £8 to £10.50). Set L Mon to Fri £7.95 (2 courses) to £9.50, Set L Sun £9.95 (2 courses) to £11.95   SERVICE: not inc, card slips closed   CARDS: Amex, MasterCard, Switch, Visa   DETAILS: 60 seats. 18 seats outside. Private parties: 30 main room. Car park. Vegetarian meals. Children's helpings. No smoking in dining room. No music   ACCOMMODATION: 3 rooms, all with bath/shower. TV. B&B £38 to £55 (*The Which? Hotel Guide*)

CRUDWELL Wiltshire   map 2

▲ *Crudwell Court* ❦ ✸

Crudwell, nr Malmesbury SN16 9EP
TEL: (01666) 577194   FAX: (01666) 577853
EMAIL: crudwellcrt@compuserve.com   COOKING 2
on A429, 3m N of Malmesbury   COST £19–£54

The wood-panelled dining room and conservatory extension of this grey Cotswold-stone hotel overlook the fish pond and walled garden, while a strong old-fashioned streak runs through the Anglo-French operation. A terrine (guinea fowl and quail) and mousse (perhaps asparagus) are usually among the starters, along with a plate of smoked salmon for a £6 supplement. Occasional contemporary notes – monkfish in coriander batter – do little to ruffle the traditional spread of roast rabbit saddle with bacon, grilled duck breast with pear sauce, or coffee and hazelnut roulade. The introduction to the wine list makes a strong case for venturing into the New World, but the canny collection of French bins makes a much stronger one for staying closer to home. Four French house wines are between £9.75 and £11.50 a bottle, £2.75 to £3 a glass.

CHEF: Chris Amor   PROPRIETOR: Nick Bristow   OPEN: all week 12.30 to 2, 7.30 to 9.30   MEALS: Set L £7.50 (2 courses), Set D £19.50 to £25.95   SERVICE: not inc, card slips closed   CARDS: Amex, Delta, Diners, MasterCard, Switch, Visa   DETAILS: 90 seats. Private parties: 40 main room. Car park. Vegetarian meals. Children's helpings. No smoking in dining room. Occasional music   ACCOMMODATION: 15 rooms, all with bath/shower. TV. Phone. B&B £50 to £114. Baby facilities. Swimming pool (*The Which? Hotel Guide*) (£5)

DARGATE Kent	map 3

Dove

NEW ENTRY

Plum Pudding Lane, Dargate ME13 9HB	COOKING 3
TEL: (01227) 751360	COST £25–£41

'The smell of lilac blossom greeted us,' wrote a reporter after a late-spring visit to this pretty pub, clad in masses of climbing plants. Who could resist the chance to eat in Plum Pudding Lane? It conjures up visions of comforting, hearty, essentially English sustenance and this, despite a few modern frills and Mediterranean furbelows, is what the Dove provides. Bare floorboards, scrubbed wooden tables and pictures of the pub in former days make a relaxed, unpretentious setting for both drinkers and diners. In winter you can warm your toes at a well-stoked log fire; in summer, sit in the flower-filled garden.

The culinary rule of thumb is local produce prepared simply but imaginatively. Thus saddle of new-season lamb is roasted and paired with tomato and basil jus; scallops are fried and dished up with chargrilled vegetables. Fish is often cooked whole, with simple accompaniments (lemon sole with asparagus; plaice with capers and shallots), although one reporter enjoyed a 'superb' thick fillet of halibut with 'lovely, crunchy' brown shrimps. Puddings such as 'well-cooked' apple and almond tart, and passion fruit and orange crème brûlée, are made with care. The modestly priced wine list offers some bargains, starting at £10 for Côtes du Rhone.

CHEF: Nigel Morris PROPRIETORS: Nigel and Bridget Morris OPEN: Tue to Sun L 12 to 2, Tue to Fri D 7 to 9 MEALS: alc (main courses £10 to £15). Bar menu available SERVICE: not inc, card slips closed CARDS: Amex, Delta, MasterCard, Switch, Visa DETAILS: 20 seats. 20 seats outside. Car park. Children's helpings. Music

DARTMOUTH Devon	map 1

Aragua ♥

St Saviours Square, Dartmouth TQ6 9DH	COOKING 3
TEL/FAX: (01803) 832224	COST £24–£64

Given the exotic pitch of at least some of the food, the surroundings are surprisingly spartan. Wooden floor and white walls are relieved only by a small selection of wooden sculptures and a few Hispanic pots. What it may lack in jungle atmosphere, it goes some way toward making up with South American stews: one of fish in coconut millk with rice and banana fritters, another of chicken with sweetcorn fritters. But this rather individual approach to fusion food also takes in simple asparagus with hollandaise, Tuscan chickpea passata with crispy calamari, and eight large, locally caught, sweet-salty scallops with wild rice. Expect also a few luxuries in the shape of Iranian sevruga caviare – an optional extra to cornmeal pancake with smoked salmon and crème fraîche – and 'splendid' poached oysters with scrambled egg. Apart from a single substantial dish such as chicken breast with saffron risotto, light meals are the form at lunch, from huevos rancheros to ewes'-milk cheese with quince jelly. Standards appear to vary, and puddings have not drawn much enthusiasm. Wines from South America priced between £13.50 and £30 head up a lively list, with France and the 'rest of the world' making some useful contributions. Six wines of the week are offered by the glass, or perhaps try the Aragua rum punch (£3).

CHEFS: Franz and Elizabeth Conde   PROPRIETORS: Franz and Elizabeth Conde, and Patricia Thomas   OPEN: Fri to Sun L 12 to 2, Wed to Sat D 7 to 9 (9.30 Sat and summer; open bank hols and all week D in summer)   CLOSED: Christmas week   MEALS: alc (main courses L £4.50 to £11, D £12.50 to £21). Set L Sun £16.50   SERVICE: not inc, card slips closed   CARDS: Delta, MasterCard, Switch, Visa   DETAILS: 40 seats. Private parties: 40 main room. Car park. Children's helpings. No smoking while others eat. Music (£5)

Carved Angel 🍷 🥖 ✳

2 South Embankment, Dartmouth TQ6 9BH   COOKING 5
TEL: (01803) 832465   FAX: (01803) 835141   COST £41–£73

'You need to be prepared for this,' noted a visitor, looking out of the window watching passers-by watching her. And there is something else to be aware of. Nick Colley left in May 1999, and David Jones arrived from Lewtrenchard Manor (see entry, Lewdown) to take charge of the open-to-view kitchen. Joyce Molyneux retains an advisory role, good materials continue to be sourced locally, but the repertoire has undergone a few changes. Provençale fish soup, seemingly as long running as *The Mousetrap*, has taken a back seat, and in place of grilled razor clams with garlic butter to start, or a puff pastry of kidneys and sweetbreads, we now get saddle of rabbit with fennel and olive ravioli, or roast quail with oregano polenta. In other words, the approach is equally enterprising, but has broadened a little, embracing Italy with a will.

Not for nothing was Joyce Molyneux celebrated as a leading chef, and while the cooking may not now be in the same class, it has produced creditable dishes of grilled cod with a sharp-tasting tarragon-imbued hollandaise, and best end of lamb with a timbale of ratatouille and a well-flavoured rosemary sauce. At inspection, some vegetables were better than others, and a few other items could have been improved – 'at these prices I would have expected more consistency' – but the day ended on a high note of richly flavoured passion fruit crème brûlée with a crisp, caramelised top. Cheese comes 'in perfect condition', extras (appetisers, breads, coffee) are good, and wines continue to impress with their value for money and variety. The list is by no means the most extensive in the *Guide*, but wine buffs will find much to excite their interest, particularly if they have a penchant for digestifs. Six house wines are all £15 a bottle, £3 a glass.

CHEF: David Jones   PROPRIETORS: Joyce Molyneux, Meriel Matthews and Zoë Wynne   OPEN: Tue to Sun L 12.30 to 2.30, Tue to Sat D 7 to 9.30   CLOSED: 1 week Christmas, 6 weeks from 1 Jan   MEALS: alc L (main courses £16 to £25). Set L Tue to Sat £15 and £25 (both 2 courses) to £30, Set L Sun £38, Set D £28 (1 course) to £48   SERVICE: net prices, card slips closed   CARDS: Delta, MasterCard, Switch, Visa   DETAILS: 50 seats. Private parties: 40 main room, 16 and 18 private rooms. Vegetarian meals. Children's helpings. No smoking in dining room. No music (£5)

'There's Muzak: all sorts and everywhere. The classical bits included "Ride of the Valkyries", which does not aid the digestive processses. [The proprietress] sings along to some of it.' (On eating in Wales)

Carved Angel Café ✠ £

7 Foss Street, Dartmouth TQ6 9DW
TEL: (01803) 834842

COOKING 2
COST £22–£26

More of a cherub than a fully fledged angel, this offshoot of the original (see above) shares the same owners, philosophy (including an open-to-view kitchen) and suppliers. It occupies the cheerful surroundings of what was Billy Budd's, its pine tables and chairs making for an 'unpretentious and agreeable' setting for morning coffee, afternoon teas with scones, cakes and biscuits (plus a champagne version with smoked salmon sandwich), simple lunches and a blackboard of daily dishes and evening meals (on Friday and Saturday).

It does exactly what it sets out to do, according to an inspector, producing 'imaginatively conceived and skilfully prepared' light meals of soup (thick lentil and thyme with a blob of soured cream), or crisp sweetcorn fritters with a bright orange pimento sauce and an 'exceptionally good' salad to balance it. Expect also lamb's liver, roast skate wing, and puffy profiteroles bulging with cream, served with butterscotch sauce. Service is amiable and efficient, and all six wines (at £11) come in two glass sizes.

CHEF: Lindsay Wakeman   PROPRIETORS: Meriel Matthews, Joyce Molyneux and Zoë Wynne   OPEN: Mon to Sat L 12 to 3, Fri and Sat D 6.30 to 9.30   CLOSED: 5 days Christmas, 3 weeks from 1 Jan   MEALS: alc (main courses £8). Light lunches available   SERVICE: net prices, card slips closed   CARDS: Delta, MasterCard, Switch, Visa   DETAILS: 34 seats. Private parties: 34 main room. Vegetarian meals. No smoking in dining room. No music

Cutter's Bunch

33 Lower Street, Dartmouth TQ6 9AN
TEL/FAX: (01803) 832882

COOKING 2
COST £32–£39

Fish and game tend to predominate on the regularly changing blackboard menu at this lively bistro near the Yacht Club, where Nick Crosley aims for largely local, and thus seasonal, produce. Legs of game birds are typically made into a confit, the breasts briefly braised with wild mushrooms (in the case of pheasant) or cherry and port (partridge). Rack of local lamb gets a conventional mint béarnaise, but the kitchen also dabbles in far-flung ideas such as home-made merguez with couscous, or a mix of sautéed tiger prawns, monkfish, squid and scallops, with lime, ginger, nam pla and coriander. A short but varied wine list features half a dozen by the glass, and prices start around £10.50.

CHEF: Nick Crosley   PROPRIETORS: Nick and Jo Crosley   OPEN: Thu to Tue D only 7 to 10   CLOSED: 2 weeks Nov, 2 weeks May   MEALS: alc (main courses £14)   SERVICE: not inc, card slips closed   CARDS: Delta, MasterCard, Switch, Visa   DETAILS: 32 seats. Private parties: 32 main room. Children's helpings. No cigars/pipes in dining room. Music £5

'Your inspector's pigeon breast was tender; ours was dry, a bit curled up, and tough and difficult to chew. The piece we brought home was rejected by our cat.'
(On eating in Cumbria)

DEDDINGTON Oxfordshire   map 5

Dexter's ⁵⭑

Market Place, Deddington OX15 0SA
TEL/FAX: (01869) 338813   COOKING 3
EMAIL: dexteruk@globalnet.co.uk   COST £28–£65

Since last year Dexter's has moved across Market Place to occupy two floors of
this old building. Vibrant colours, still in evidence amid the exposed beams and
varnished plank flooring, combine with a twisted metal 'tree' and two fish
sculptures – a marlin on the ground floor, a tarpon upstairs – to produce what one
observer described as a 'Florida ambience'. The menu is as lively as the
surroundings, revelling in contemporary flavourings of beetroot jus, black
olives, red salsa, or pieces of crisply frazzled duck accompanied by a ball of salad
dressed with hoi sin.

Good-quality materials such as Angus beef and organic chicken establish a
firm foundation, and generally simple cooking techniques – searing, grilling,
roasting – are applied: to fish, for example, producing well-seared but 'nicely
underdone' sea trout with thick kettle chips, and wild sea bass fillet with fine
linguini, stem ginger and soy. Some assemblies and flavour combinations
seemed arbitrary at inspection, but among desserts cheesecakes have impressed:
one of white chocolate with maple syrup, another a 'rich and firm' armagnac
version with a trail of prune compote. Some thirty roving wines start with house
French at £11.50.

CHEFS: Jamie Dexter Harrison, Brad Morris and Stuart Cox   PROPRIETORS: Jamie Dexter
Harrison and Roger Blackburn   OPEN: Tue to Sun L 12 to 2.15, Tue to Sat D 7 to 9.30   MEALS:
alc (main courses £11.50 to £20). Set L Tue to Sun and D Tue to Fri £14.50 (2 courses) to £18
SERVICE: 10% (optional), card slips closed   CARDS: Amex, Delta, MasterCard, Switch, Visa
DETAILS: 70 seats. Private parties: 70 main room. Vegetarian meals. Children's helpings. No
smoking in 1 dining room. Wheelchair access (not WC). Occasional music

DEDHAM Essex   map 6

▲ Le Talbooth ▮

Gun Hill, Dedham CO7 6HP
TEL: (01206) 323150   FAX: (01206) 322309   COOKING 4
EMAIL: ltreception@talbooth.co.uk   COST £31–£68

The thatched and beamed restaurant, a short (complimentary) car ride from the
comfortable hotel, is picturesque enough to feel 'like stepping into a calendar'.
Indeed, the surroundings – gardens, floodlights, river – are such an integral part
of things that eating here had an element of 'British theme-park dining
experience' about it for one reporter. Given lunchtime roasts (Tuesday leg of
lamb, Wednesday pork), along with Barnsley chop, salmon steak, and loin of
venison, it is easy to see why it struck one visitor as 'British cooking and no
nonsense', although there is rather more to it than that.

Starters have included foie gras terrine, and lemon-grass and basil soup, while
desserts – 'we have been consistently impressed with the quality,' writes a
regular – run to orange sachertorte, fig and marsala trifle, and hot red cherry tart.

Service might be a little sharper, but the wine list cuts no corners when it comes to quality. An impressive South African presence reveals the Milsom family's long association with that country, and all the wines are now shipped direct from the vineyards; the Vergelegen Sauvignon Blanc 1998 and Warwick Trilogy 1995 are specially recommended (both £18.95 a bottle). The influence of Colchester-based merchants Lay & Wheeler can still be seen – particularly in the fine claret and Burgundy sections. House South African is £12.50.

CHEF: Terry Barber   PROPRIETORS: Gerald and Paul Milsom   OPEN: Mon to Sat 12 to 2, 7 to 9.30, Sun Sept to May 2 to 4 only, Sun June to Sept 12 to 2, 7 for 7.30 (1 sitting, for barbecue) MEALS: alc (main courses £15.50 to £22). Set L Mon to Fri £19, Set L Sat and Sun and Set D all week £24   SERVICE: 10%, card slips closed   CARDS: Amex, Delta, Diners, MasterCard, Switch, Visa   DETAILS: 75 seats. 50 seats outside. Private parties: 80 main room, 34 private room. Car park. Vegetarian meals. Children's helpings. No smoking while others eat. No music ACCOMMODATION: 10 rooms, all with bath/shower. TV. Phone. B&B £95 to £175. Rooms for disabled. Baby facilities (*The Which? Hotel Guide*)

DENMEAD Hampshire   map 2

Barnards ⁵✳

Hambledon Road, Denmead PO7 6NU
TEL/FAX: (01705) 257788, changing to
(023) 9225 7788   COOKING 2
on B2150, 2m NW of Waterlooville   COST £21–£49

In a row of shops, with exposed brick walls, where much of the décor is provided by the tables and chairs themselves, this family-run business ploughs a familiar Anglo-French furrow. The food may hold few surprises, but it uses fresh, local produce to turn out a starter of crab with marie-rose sauce, a layered terrine of leeks and skate with mustard mayonnaise, and a mushroom vol-au-vent with Madeira sauce. Meats range from simple grilled fillet steak, to turkey rolled in bacon and wrapped in pastry with a sage and onion sauce, while sea bass, monkfish and scallops have made up the seafood side of the equation. Nostalgic desserts might include rhubarb fool, or a fruit-filled choux pastry ring with raspberry ice cream and sauce. A cleverly chosen globe-trotting wine list is fairly priced, starting with house French at £10.

CHEF: David Barnard   PROPRIETORS: David and Sandie Barnard   OPEN: Tue to Fri L 12 to 1.45, Tue to Sat D 7 to 9.45   CLOSED: 2 weeks Christmas, 2 weeks Aug   MEALS: alc (main courses £10.50 to £17). Set L £10 (2 courses) to £12.50   SERVICE: not inc, card slips closed   CARDS: Amex, Delta, MasterCard, Switch, Visa   DETAILS: 45 seats. 12 seats outside. Private parties: 34 main room, 22 and 34 private rooms. Car park. Vegetarian meals. Children's helpings. No smoking in dining room. Wheelchair access (not WC). Music   £5

Card slips closed *in the details at the end of an entry indicates that the total on the slips of credit cards is closed when handed over for signature.*

£5 *indicates that the restaurant has elected to participate in the* Good Food Guide *voucher scheme. For full details, see page 6.*

DERBY Derbyshire	map 5

Darleys 🍷 ✗

Darley Abbey Mill, Darley Abbey, Derby DE22 1DZ
TEL: (01332) 364987 FAX: (01332) 541356   COOKING 4
of A6, 2m N of city centre   COST £25–£57

Beside a fast-flowing river, just over a rickety toll bridge (nobody collects) with 'more potholes than tarmac', this smartly converted mill is stylishly decorated but 'not overdone'. Shortly after the *Guide* went to press last year, Ian Wilson came up through the ranks to take charge of the kitchen, maintaining a similar style and format. This is modern cooking with its feet on the ground, executed to a degree that inspires confidence, for example in a deeply flavoured leek and Cheddar risotto with 'perfectly (and I mean perfectly) cooked rice . . . served in a teacup'. Other Mediterranean input has taken the form of chargrilled chicken breast with a mould of ratatouille, and a roast sea bass version of salade niçoise.

Many combinations retain traditional partnerships, some re-invented with a modest flourish: honey roast Barbary duck breast comes with a mini glazed apple tart and aniseed reduction, while beef tournedos is accompanied by Stilton rarebit and cauliflower cappuccino. In similar fashion, desserts have included iced tiramisù parfait encased in dark chocolate; alternatively, first-rate cheeses come with home-made chutney and biscuits. Lunch is reasonably priced, service is 'efficient and knowledgeable', and wines on the annotated list occasionally wander off well-trodden paths (try Italy). House French varietals are £13.

CHEF: Ian Wilson PROPRIETOR: David Pinchbeck OPEN: all week L 12 to 2.30 (3 Sun), Mon to Sat D 7 to 10 (6.30 to 10 Fri and Sat) CLOSED: bank hols MEALS: alc (main courses £12.50 to £18.50). Set L £12.50 (2 courses) to £14.50, Set D £22 SERVICE: not inc CARDS: Amex, Delta, Diners, MasterCard, Switch, Visa DETAILS: 70 seats. Private parties: 70 main room. Car park. Vegetarian meals. Children's helpings. No smoking in dining room. Wheelchair access (not WC). Music. Air-conditioned £5

DINTON Buckinghamshire	map 3

La Chouette 🍷

Westlington Green, Dinton HP17 8UW
TEL/FAX: (01296) 747422   COOKING 5
off A418, 4m SW of Aylesbury   COST £20–£57

Next to the green in a village of thatched cottages, 'The Owl' is reminiscent of small country restaurants throughout Europe in its concentration on good materials, and in its 'idiosyncratic' chef/patron, who chalks up a decade here in 2000. Since he is Belgian, it is only reasonable to expect a menu listing salmon cooked in wheat beer, and farm rabbit 'as we do it in Brussels'. Seafood figures prominently – in salads of skate wing, or crab with avocado – or perhaps as a large tuna steak with a creamy shellfish sauce, and the approach is generally straightforward. Monkfish is paired with chicory, lamb chops come with beans, and portions seemed 'exactly right' to one visitor. Crêpes suzette is a typical dessert.

The £11 lunch (three courses in under an hour for busy folk) is considered 'tremendously good value', and although effort may be focused more on the food than on the niceties of service ('one could cavil at the service charge,' noted a reporter who felt that 'one doesn't tip the patron'), Frédéric Desmette seems happy enough to chat to those who are interested. Bottled beers (from Belgium, of course) are offered to those immune to the Gallic charms of the wine list. M. Desmette chooses his producers wisely from outside the classic regions as well as within – witness the presence of Dom. de Trévallon's Coteaux d'Aix-en-Provence reds and Alain Brumont's Madirans. House French is £10.50.

CHEF/PROPRIETOR: Frédéric Desmette   OPEN: Mon to Fri L 12 to 2, Mon to Sat D 7 to 9   MEALS: alc (main courses £10.50 to £16). Set L £11 to £36, Set D £27.50 to £36   SERVICE: 12.5% (optional), card slips closed   CARDS: Amex, Delta, MasterCard, Visa   DETAILS: 35 seats. 12 seats outside. Private parties: 40 main room. Car park. Children's helpings. No cigars/pipes in dining room. Music

---

DISS Norfolk   map 6

▲ *Salisbury House* 🔆

Victoria Road, Diss IP22 3JG	COOKING 1
TEL/FAX: (01379) 644738	COST £23–£49

Surrounded by an acre of gardens, Salisbury House offers two eating options: a small lemon-yellow bistro at the back, or a more formal chandeliered dining room. There is a fair degree of overlap between the two menus, except the bistro has more choice and is cheaper. An old-fashioned provincial approach to the food produces deep-fried Camembert, pork and herb terrine with Cumberland sauce, and pheasant casserole Normandy-style. A main course of red fish in dill sauce has come with an impressively crispy deep-fried julienne of leeks, and one couple finished happily enough with a marbled coffee and chestnut ice cream, and a plate of cheese that included Gubbeen and Shropshire Blue. Well-spread and varied wines at fair prices are a feature of both the short bistro and longer restaurant list (bistro-goers can also order from the full list). House vin de pays Chardonnay and Syrah are both under £10.

CHEF/PROPRIETOR: Barry Davies   OPEN: Tue to Sat D only 7.30 (7.15 bistro) to 8.45   CLOSED: Christmas   MEALS: bistro alc (main courses £7 to £8.50); restaurant Set D £24.95 to £32   SERVICE: not inc   CARDS: MasterCard, Visa   DETAILS: 36 seats. 10 seats outside. Private parties: 22 main room, 14 private room. Car park. Vegetarian meals. Children's helpings. No smoking in dining room. Music   ACCOMMODATION: 3 rooms, all with bath/shower. TV. B&B £40 to £82 (*The Which? Hotel Guide*)

Weavers £

Market Hill, Diss IP22 3JZ	COOKING 2
TEL: (01379) 642411	COST £24–£39

The name comes from the building's origins as a chapel for one of the weavers' guilds that were big in these parts in the Middle Ages. It has played many other roles but these days is a welcoming restaurant on two floors, tables made pretty with flowers or flower lamps. William Bavin offers plenty of choice, with a lengthy fixed-price and a separate vegetarian menu, plus a carte at dinner. Neat contemporary ideas share the limelight with some fanciable old-fashioned ones: at one end of the scale, fried cabbage with garlic, tomato and haricot bean broth, or poached pigeon-breast with fruity risotto and spicy apricot sauce; at the other, steak, kidney and mushroom pie, and trifle. A couple of dozen wines around the £10 mark are designed to appeal to all tastes; otherwise pick from the broad international list.

CHEF/PROPRIETOR: William Bavin   OPEN: 12 to 1.30, 7 to 9 (9.30 Sat)   CLOSED: 2 weeks Christmas   MEALS: alc (main courses £10 to £14). Set L £7.95 (2 courses) to £10.75, Set D £14.95   SERVICE: not inc, card slips closed   CARDS: Amex, Delta, Diners, MasterCard, Switch, Visa   DETAILS: 80 seats. Private parties: 40 main room, 50 private room. Vegetarian meals. Children's helpings. No smoking before 2 L, 9.30 D. Music

---

DONCASTER South Yorkshire   map 9

▲ Hamilton's ⅝✕ | NEW ENTRY |

Carr House Road, Doncaster DN4 5HP
TEL: (01302) 760770   FAX: (01302) 768101   COOKING 5
EMAIL: ham760770@aol.com   COST £32–£64

Built in 1856, some time before the bypass on which it stands, this formerly aristocratic residence has been done up, seemingly at great expense, and with 'exaggerated opulence'. Sweep through the glass door, across polished wooden floors, past dinner jacketed staff, and come to rest in the dining room beside a white grand piano. 'Is this really Doncaster?' enquired one puzzled reporter. The monthly-changing menu (as lavishly turned out as everything else) at first seems 'OTT', but the range of materials and treatments is impressive, from confit duck leg with piccalilli to pea and ham fritter, from crab dumplings in herb broth to calf's liver and bacon.

Seafood (sourced from Cornwall) has included 'brilliantly prepared' crisply seared, flavourful scallops with bacon, on a bed of Savoy cabbage with a tangy but sweet cider sauce-cum-dressing. Lack of fussiness and adornment give the food a welcome simplicity, and an inspection meal was distinguished by its consistency: prime ingredients, careful preparation and fine saucing came together in a main course of pink lamb served with rösti, whole garlic cloves, a small tian of ratatouille vegetables, and a first-class stock and red wine reduction. The centrepiece and highlight of a five-course surprise menu was a Bresse pigeon ravioli, served in a red wine sauce made from 'gallons of veal stock reduced to a tablespoon'.

Desserts are just as impressive, judging by a toffee and banana spin on bread-and-butter pudding, and an intensely flavoured summer fruit jelly in a pool of strawberry syrup. The wine list was in a state of flux as the *Guide* went to press, but half a dozen house wines (also available by the glass) start around £12.

The text of entries is based on unsolicited reports sent in by readers, backed up by inspections conducted anonymously. The factual details under the text are from questionnaires the Guide *sends to all restaurants that feature in the book.*

CHEF: Christopher Randle-Bissell   PROPRIETOR: Hamilton's Ltd   OPEN: Sun to Fri (and Sat on race days) L 12 to 3, all week D 6 (5 on race days) to 10   CLOSED: 26 Dec, 1 Jan   MEALS: alc (main courses £14.50 to £18.50). Set L and Mon to Thur D £14.95 (2 courses) to £19.95   SERVICE: not inc   CARDS: Amex, Delta, MasterCard, Switch, Visa   DETAILS: 56 seats. Private parties: 65 main room, 24 to 150 private rooms. Car park. Vegetarian meals. Children's helpings. No smoking in 1 dining room. Wheelchair access (not WC). Music. Air-conditioned   ACCOMMODATION: 5 rooms, all with bath/shower. TV. Phone. B&B £70 to £110   (£5)

DORRINGTON Shropshire   map 5

▲ Country Friends ⁵⭑

Dorrington SY5 7JD
TEL: (01743) 718707
EMAIL: whittaker@countryfriends.demon.co.uk   COOKING 6
on A49, 5m S of Shrewsbury   COST £39–£52

Traffic on the busy A49 roars past this black and white half-timbered building but inside there's an air of self-assured calm: 'it's very sure of what it's about and wants to do it properly.' Once a manor house, it has been added to in a rather hotchpotch style, and the warren-like interior is 'a bit old-fashioned and staid', with down-to-earth and capable staff. Yet despite the archetypally English atmosphere, the food goes beyond any roast-beef stereotype. Charles Whittaker's cooking is confident and flavourful, based on excellent ingredients creatively combined without any pyrotechnics or fuss.

Ideas are deceptively simple and properly executed: a well-integrated starter of calf's liver with a sweet potato purée and mustard and caper dressing, for example, or 'superb' halibut balanced by a subtle asparagus sauce. A soufflé of tomato, red pepper and pesto 'releases a lovely waft of pepper as it is cut', revealing a small pool of pesto that 'really boosts the taste'. Desserts – 'light' pear mousse or 'weighty' chocolate tart – are equally well crafted. The wine list is intelligently sourced, with plenty of half-bottles. House wines are £11.95.

CHEF: Charles Whittaker   PROPRIETORS: Charles and Pauline Whittaker   OPEN: Tue to Sat 12 to 2, 7 to 9 (9.30 Sat)   CLOSED: 2 weeks early July   MEALS: Set L and D £27 (2 courses) to £33.50. Light L available   SERVICE: not inc   CARDS: MasterCard, Switch, Visa   DETAILS: 45 seats. Private parties: 40 main room. Car park. Vegetarian meals. No smoking in dining room. Wheelchair access (not WC). No music   ACCOMMODATION: 3 rooms, 1 with bath/shower. D,B&B £75 to £115   (£5)

DREWSTEIGNTON Devon   map 1

▲ Hunts Tor ⁵⭑

Drewsteignton EX6 6QW   COOKING 3
TEL/FAX: (01647) 281228   COST £30–£40

Small and compact this restaurant may be, but reports are full of praise for Sue Harrison's assured cooking and the generous welcome from Chris Harrison. The setting is pure English village, with thatched cottages, a couple of pubs and a post office. Three or four courses (the fourth a selection of local cheeses in excellent condition) with no choice is the format, though preferences can be discussed when booking, which needs to be at least 24 hours in advance. Typically straightforward starters have included crab soup, and red mullet with pesto and tomato coulis. Imaginative main courses might turn up a pairing of guinea fowl with a Thai-style sauce of coconut, coriander and lime; roast cod on a bed of spinach with a spicy sesame oil dressing; or duck with lentils and a ginger and coriander sauce. Among desserts could be crème brûlée, lemon tart, or steamed golden syrup sponge with vanilla custard. The wine list is short and to the point, with a bias towards France. House wine is £12.

CHEF: Sue Harrison   PROPRIETORS: Sue and Chris Harrison   OPEN: all week D only 7.30 (1 sitting; 24 hours' notice required)   CLOSED: end Oct to Mar   MEALS: Set D £20 to £23 SERVICE: not inc   CARDS: none   DETAILS: 8 seats. Private parties: 8 main room. Car park. Vegetarian meals. No children under 10 at D. No smoking in dining room. Music ACCOMMODATION: 3 rooms, all with bath/shower. TV. B&B £35 to £65. No children under 10 in accommodation (*The Which? Hotel Guide*)

DRYBROOK Gloucestershire   map 5

Cider Press ⁵⁄ₓ

The Cross, Drybrook GL17 9EB
TEL/FAX: (01594) 544472   COOKING 4
EMAIL: cider.press@virgin.net   COST £27–£41

This unassuming corner-shop conversion manages to be homely and smart at the same time. The peach and terracotta walls are hung with bright posters and apple-themed pictures, the tables set with green and yellow cloths and sparkling cutlery. Subdued lighting and big vases of flowers create a relaxing atmosphere, aided by a warm and solicitous welcome. 'Fish is a speciality and rightly so,' commented a reporter. What's available depends on the daily delivery from Cornwall but might include 'flavoursome' John Dory served on the bone with a shallot and mushroom compote, or red mullet fillets, cooked 'crisp on the outside, flaky inside', with anchovy and onion stuffing. Free-range meat is prepared with a light touch and some original flavour combinations: fillet of beef with Chinese radish, or roast duck with walnut sauce and Umbrian lentils. Steamed organic vegetables make a simple but effective accompaniment. Home-made ice creams, such as banana and caramel, have been well received; alternatively, choose from the 'interesting and varied' cheeseboard. Long waits between courses irritated one reporter, another found service 'excellent'. The affordable wine list includes something for all tastes, starting with French house wine at £8.95.

CHEF: Christopher Challener   PROPRIETOR: Bernadette Elizabeth Fitzpatrick   OPEN: Tue to Sat D only 7 to 11 (D Sun and Mon and L by arrangement)   CLOSED: first 2 weeks Jan   MEALS: alc (main courses £12.50 to £15)   SERVICE: not inc   CARDS: Delta, MasterCard, Visa   DETAILS: 24 seats. 8 seats outside. Private parties: 28 main room. No smoking in dining room. Wheelchair access (not WC)

'*The extra mineral water needed to take away the taste at the end of the meal was not charged.*' (On eating in London)

Bistro 21 ⚡✗

Aykley Heads House, Aykley Heads,
Durham DH1 5TS   COOKING 4
TEL: (0191) 384 4354   COST £23–£45

Part of a group run by Terence Laybourne from his Newcastle flagship (see entry; also Café 21, Ponteland, and Brasserie 21, Sunderland), this former farmhouse near the police headquarters to the north of the city is not the most obvious location for a restaurant, but the place has been sympathetically restored. Rustic chic is the style, enhanced by dried flowers, clay pots, farming implements and other 'olde worlde' paraphernalia. Craig Edmund executes some clever ideas, confidently mixing old-fashioned and Mediterranean strands, as typified by starters ranging from moist ham knuckle terrine with roast vegetables and a rich tartare-like sauce, to Middle Eastern antipasto, including couscous salad and falafel. The carte might offer fritto misto with tapénade, hummus and aïoli, or salmon with asparagus and hollandaise, while a blackboard of daily specials provided one luncher with tender monkfish topped with deep-fried spinach over large wedges of garlicky potatoes. A blackberry vodka sorbet had 'just the right boozy tang shining through the fruitiness', while baked Alaska and spotted dick, rarely sighted these days, are other possibilities. Service is polite but sometimes haphazard. Wines are a lively bunch, offering plenty of good drinking from around the world. House Duboeuf is £10.50.

CHEF: Craig Edmund   PROPRIETORS: Terence and Susan Laybourne   OPEN: Mon to Sat 12 to 2.30, 6 to 10.30   CLOSED: bank hols   MEALS: alc (main courses £9 to £13.50). Set L £12 (2 courses) to £14.50   SERVICE: not inc   CARDS: Amex, Delta, Diners, MasterCard, Switch, Visa
DETAILS: 90 seats. 24 seats outside. Private parties: 60 main room, 12 to 20 private rooms. Car park. Vegetarian meals. Children's helpings. No smoking in dining room. Wheelchair access (also WC)

Forsters ⚡✗

2 St Bedes, Station Road, East Boldon NE36 0LE
TEL: (0191) 519 0929
just off A184 Newcastle to Sunderland road,   COOKING 3
3m NW of Sutherland   COST £24–£44

The Forsters are approaching the end of their first decade in this simple neat suburban dining room, where they serve dinner only but go to the trouble of offering two menus. The three-course set-price version (not available Saturdays) aims for good value, starting with mussels marinière, or toasted muffin with smoked salmon, poached egg and hollandaise, followed by chicken 'schnitzel-style', or sirloin steak, and finishing with tiramisù, or sticky toffee pudding. Although the carte overlaps to a degree, it is the repository of slightly more ambitious ideas, such as grilled king prawns with a Thai-style dipping sauce, or guinea fowl in a calvados cream sauce. Vegetarians need to order 48 hours in advance but can avail themselves of a variety of soups, pasta dishes, risotto, soufflés or omelettes, and those who opt to finish with cheese will find that it comes with a glass of LBV port. A short and sympathetically priced wine list starts with house Duboeuf at £8.50.

CHEF: Barry Forster   PROPRIETORS: Barry and Sue Forster   OPEN: Tue to Sat D only 7 to 9.30 CLOSED: 1 week May, 2 weeks Aug, bank hols   MEALS: alc (main courses £13.50 to £16). Set D Tue to Fri £17.50   SERVICE: not inc   CARDS: Amex, Delta, Diners, MasterCard, Visa   DETAILS: 30 seats. Private parties: 30 main room. Car park. Children's helpings. No children under 8. No smoking in dining room. Music   (£5)

EASTBOURNE East Sussex   map 3

▲ *Mirabelle* ⁵✳

Grand Hotel, Jevington Gardens,
Eastbourne BN21 4EQ   NEW CHEF
TEL: (01323) 435066   FAX: (01323) 412233   COST £29–£61

After a lengthy closure for extensive refurbishment, the restaurant re-opened just as the *Guide* went to press. Keith Mitchell remains as executive chef, but we have no feedback on either the new décor or Mark Wilkinson, who is to be head chef. Having spent some time cooking at, among others, the Arkle in Chester, Winteringham Fields in Winteringham, and Le Poussin in Brockenhurst (see entries), it should come as no surprise that he sets out a modern European stall, complete with oriental flourishes and a few luxuries, and that his approach demands advanced technical skills. Among dishes visitors are likely to encounter on the carte might be a salad of pigeon and walnut with game jus and chorizo, pan-fried halibut on prawn and fennel risotto with vanilla butter, and Malibu roasted pineapple with mango ice cream and passion fruit sauce. A posh wine list includes a few regional French and other wines under £20. Ten house wines start at £12.95.

CHEFS: Keith Mitchell and Mark Wilkinson   PROPRIETOR: Elite Hotels   OPEN: Tue to Sat 12.30 to 2, 7 to 10   MEALS: alc D (main courses £18.50 to £23). Set L £19.50, Set D £28.50 to £32.50 SERVICE: 10%, card slips closed   CARDS: Amex, Delta, Diners, MasterCard, Switch, Visa DETAILS: 50 seats. Private parties: 60 main room. Car park. Vegetarian meals. Children's helpings. Jacket and tie. No smoking in dining room. Wheelchair access (also WC). Music. Air-conditioned   ACCOMMODATION: 152 rooms, all with bath/shower. TV. Phone. B&B £115 to £305. Rooms for disabled. Baby facilities. Swimming pool   (£5)

EAST CHILTINGTON East Sussex   map 3

Jolly Sportsman   NEW ENTRY

Chapel Lane, East Chiltington BN7 3BA
TEL: (01273) 890400
off Novington Lane between B2116 and   COOKING 1
Plumpton Green   COST £26–£41

Bruce Wass's reason for buying a pub (he already runs Thackeray's House; see entry, Tunbridge Wells) was because 'it is the only kind of place where the average person is truly relaxed'. That feeling is further encouraged by the 'down-to-earth feel' of both bar and dining room extension, the latter painted creamy yellow with wooden floors, bright pictures, and dramatically warped tables. Blackboards supplement a printed menu, and the cooking, though variable, is enterprising for the circumstances. A degree of heartiness is to be expected – an 'authentic'-tasting Alsatian choucroute with ham, duck leg confit, and three kinds of sausage – although the kitchen has also produced homely leek, ham and lentil soup, and chicken liver parfait with a discreetly sweet red onion marmalade. Materials include undyed smoked haddock (in puff pastry), and fine Aberdeen Angus ribeye steak. Desserts are not a strength, service has been 'cheery but a bit dippy', and beers and wines both offer good drinking, the latter assembled into a kindly priced list starting with house French at £8.75.

CHEF: Richard Willis PROPRIETORS: Bruce and Gwyneth Wass OPEN: Tue to Sun and bank hol Mon L 12.30 to 2 (12 to 4 Sun and bank hol Mon), Tue to Sat D 7 to 10 CLOSED: 25 and 26 Dec, 1 Jan MEALS: alc (main courses £8.90 to £13.50). Bar meals available SERVICE: 10% at D CARDS: Delta, MasterCard, Switch, Visa DETAILS: 45 seats. 80 seats outside. Private parties: 40 main room, 18 private room. Car park. Vegetarian meals. Children's helpings. Wheelchair access (also WC). No music £5

EAST END Hampshire   map 2

East End Arms £   NEW ENTRY

East End SO41 5SY
TEL/FAX: 01590 626223
EMAIL: jennie@eastendarms.co.uk
off B3054, 2m E of Lymington; follow signs for Isle of   COOKING 4
Wight ferry and continue 2m   COST £21–£38

The East End Arms may sound like a sibling of the Queen Vic but is in fact in a sleepy little village near Lymington. John Illsley, he of the George at Yarmouth (see entry), has been running this place for a decade or so, but recently acquired in Paul Sykes a chef to put East End on the map. The décor may be pretty basic, but the menu is full of enticements. Black pudding with apple cake and cinnamon dressing quite wrong-footed a Lancastrian who, in Hampshire, had not expected such an impeccably sourced pudding: full of 'the requisite chewy bits' and cleverly counterpointed with supporting flavours. The local catch supplies ever-changing seafood that may include freshly dressed crab, sardines with parsley butter, or main-course halibut fillet in a lavender-scented cream sauce with potato purée and pea fritters. A reporter who thought chicken casserole with smoked haddock and baby leeks sounded so preposterous she had to try it found it excellent: 'a terrific invention'. Coffee parfait reveals hidden depths of flavour, or perhaps choose gooseberry tart with gooseberry toffee and clotted cream. An admirably concise wine list offers a fair spread of styles, opening with house Australian at £10.

CHEF: Paul Sykes PROPRIETOR: J.E. Illsley OPEN: Tue to Sun L 12 to 2, Tue to Sat D 7 to 9 (9.30 Fri and Sat) CLOSED: 25 and 26 Dec, 1 Jan MEALS: alc (main courses £6 to £12). Light L menu available SERVICE: not inc CARDS: MasterCard, Switch, Visa DETAILS: 34 seats. 60 seats outside. Private parties: 25 main room. Car park. Children's helpings. Wheelchair access (not WC). Music £5

EAST GRINSTEAD   West Sussex   map 3

▲ *Gravetye Manor* 🍷 ✻

Vowels Lane, East Grinstead RH19 4LJ
TEL: (01342) 810567   FAX: (01342) 810080
EMAIL: gravetye@relaischateaux.fr   COOKING 7
off B2110, 2m SW of East Grinstead   COST £39–£101

Gabled and chimneyed, with William Robinson's 'natural' garden to stroll
round, and much oak panelling inside, Gravetye has a feeling of permanence
about it: an 'anachronistic paradise', one called it, sensing that the house had
achieved perfection. The kitchen's ambition, likewise, is pitched at the highest
level, and on the whole is not misplaced. Intelligently structured menus balance
fish and meat main courses, preceded perhaps by game terrine, a foie gras dish,
or intensely flavoured tomato consommé poured over lightly poached quails'
eggs and chopped tomato. Seafood is the other strong suit: at inspection, moist,
well-flavoured crab risotto garnished with 'difficult to imagine better' scallops.

There is no faulting the technical expertise, selection of ingredients is
impeccable, and the cooking maintains a reassuring confidence and integrity, for
example in small rolls of chervil-stuffed lemon sole partnered with braised
frogs' legs and shelled langoustines. Individual dishes are carefully thought
through with little needless embellishment, and even complex ones are
coherent: a moist, ham-wrapped saddle of rabbit, for instance, featuring 'a
tremendous collection of shapes, colours and textures' among its components of
offal, leg meat, pasta, and a polenta and wild mushroom 'sausage'. Occasionally,
and perhaps more so in desserts than elsewhere, 'the kitchen feels obliged to
exert its influence over every ingredient', but the skill level never falters: an
assiette of chocolate desserts incorporates a thick, creamy 'milk shake' with a
hint of coffee, while a mille-feuille (three thin biscuits) on the nougatine theme
is spiked with crystallised lime peel.

Gravetye offers a 'proper' three-course lunch, instead of the apology for one
that many country restaurants do, although a couple who ate on Sunday were
considerably underwhelmed by theirs. Attentive but personable service is 'one
of the best features', and given net prices and careful choice the value can be
good. Classical and venerable bottles (and magnums and half-bottles) from
France dominate the wine list, which none the less finds plenty of room for some
grand bins from Germany and the New World. Prices swiftly hurdle the £20
barrier but this merely reflects the quality on offer, and there is a good choice
under £30. House Burgundy is £18 for white, £19.50 for red.

CHEF: Mark Raffan   PROPRIETORS: Peter Herbert and family   OPEN: all week 12.30 to 1.45, 7.30
to 9.30 (9.45 Sat, 8.45 Sun)   CLOSED: D 25 Dec exc for residents   MEALS: alc (main courses £20
to £34). Set L £29, Set D £38   SERVICE: net prices, card slips closed   CARDS: MasterCard,
Switch, Visa   DETAILS: 55 seats. Private parties: 8 main room, 16 private room. Car park.
Vegetarian meals. No children under 7 in dining room. Jacket and tie at D. No smoking in dining
room. Wheelchair access (not WC). No music   ACCOMMODATION: 18 rooms, all with
bath/shower. TV. Phone. Room only £135 to £260. No children under 7 exc babies in
accommodation. Baby facilities. Fishing (*The Which? Hotel Guide*)

EAST WITTON North Yorkshire   map 8

▲ *Blue Lion*

East Witton DL8 4SN
TEL: (01969) 624273 FAX: (01969) 624189   COOKING 3
on A6108 between Masham and Leyburn   COST £21–£49

Once a coaching inn, the Blue Lion – which has been 'restored and not spoiled' –
continues to discharge its twin roles as a pub with bar meals and (in the
evenings) a restaurant. 'Dark wood, log fires and friendly staff' provide the
setting for a blackboard of sophisticated bar food from Thai crab cake with chilli
jam, via smoked wild boar sausage with bubble and squeak, to steak and kidney
suet pudding. The restaurant's carte is in the same mould, taking an upbeat
approach to a wide range of materials – onion and blue Wensleydale tart, cep
risotto, and smoked pork fillet with a honey and clove sauce – while still finding
room for traditional chargrills of steak, chicken and salmon. Vegetarians are not
neglected, and innovative desserts have included iced liquorice terrine with
poached pears, and prune tart with Guinness ice cream and caramel sauce. A
fairly priced, carefully sourced, wide-ranging wine list starts with twenty house
recommendations from £9.50 to £16.

CHEF: John Dalby   PROPRIETOR: Paul Klein   OPEN: Sun L 12 to 2.15, all week D 6.45 to 9.30. Bar
meals available L and D all week. No food served 25 Dec   MEALS: alc (bar main courses £7 to
£14, restaurant main courses £11 to £16.50). Set L Sun £14.70   SERVICE: not inc   CARDS:
Delta, MasterCard, Switch, Visa   DETAILS: 90 seats. 20 seats outside. Private parties: 45 main
room, 18 private room. Car park. Vegetarian meals. Children's helpings. Wheelchair access
(also WC). No music   ACCOMMODATION: 12 rooms, all with bath/shower. TV. Phone. B&B £55 to
£95. Rooms for disabled. Baby facilities (*The Which? Hotel Guide*)

EDENBRIDGE Kent   map 3

Honours Mill

87 High Street, Edenbridge TN8 5AU   COOKING 4
TEL: (01732) 866757   COST £23–£50

The Mill seems to come into its own in fine weather, when visitors can sit with
an aperitif by the millstream or take advantage of a table on the balcony (new
since last year). The first-floor dining room, meanwhile, remains 'immaculate',
with its starched white linen, rather formal service, and menus that offer a choice
in two price bands, the more expensive one running to half a dozen items per
course, plus fish and daily specials. The style struck one reporter as more
bistro-like than he expected from the surroundings, and indeed the repertoire
takes in starters of smoked haddock timbale with poached egg, wild mushroom
risotto, and roasted Mediterranean vegetables.

   Main courses, on the other hand, have included cassoulet, pork with
watercress sauce, and roast best end of Hever lamb stuffed with black pudding.
While there may be few innovative surprises, 'each dish is carefully prepared',
according to one who lunched on warm duck salad on spinach leaves, black
bream fillets with courgette and mange-tout, and butterscotch and raspberry
pavé. The Anglo-French approach has also produced desserts of crème brûlée,

301

bread-and-butter pudding with vanilla custard, and prune and armagnac ice cream. France dominates the wine list (look to regional varietals for decent drinking under £15), although there is still room for bottles from Chile, Uruguay and the antipodes. House French is £10.15.

CHEF: Martin Radmall   PROPRIETORS: Neville, Duncan and Giles Goodhew   OPEN: Tue to Fri and Sun L 12.15 to 2, Tue to Sat D 7.15 to 10   MEALS: Set L Tue to Fri £12.50 (2 courses) to £32.75, Set L Sun £23.50, Set D Tue to Fri £19.95 to £32.75, Set D Sat £32.75   SERVICE: not inc   CARDS: Delta, MasterCard, Switch, Visa   DETAILS: 38 seats. 16 seats outside. Children's helpings. No music   (£5)

ELLAND West Yorkshire map 8

La Cachette 🍷 £

7–10 Town Hall Buildings, Elland HX5 0EU   COOKING 2
TEL: (01422) 378833   FAX: (01422) 377899   COST £21–£41

Rated highly for service and informality as well as the food, this 'pleasantly light and airy' restaurant operates a flexible system that includes bar meals, sandwiches and tapas in addition to the main business: 'everybody should find something they fancy,' predicted one reporter. Among the options might be squid with chilli and garlic, or sausages (lamb and mint, or wild boar and apple) with red cabbage, followed by apple and sultana sponge. Old favourites, from deep-fried Brie, to pepper steaks, to grilled haddock with spinach in a cheese sauce, show no sign of waning in popularity, while a list of daily specials incorporates a couple of fish dishes, with perhaps Thai chicken salad or stuffed roast pepper to start. High-quality wines walk hand in hand with low mark-ups on a list that impresses with its round-the-world range of styles and flavours. Plenty of good bottles are to be had at under £15, but if you are in the mood for a celebration – and feeling patriotic – try the excellent English sparkler, Nyetimber Première Cuvée Chardonnay Brut 1992, £23.50.

CHEF: Sean Walker   PROPRIETOR: C&O Partnership   OPEN: Mon to Sat 12 to 2.30, 6 to 10 (11 Fri and Sat)   MEALS: alc (main courses £7.50 to £14). Set D £10.95 to £13.95 (inc wine); Set D not available after 7 Sat   SERVICE: not inc   CARDS: Amex, Delta, MasterCard, Switch, Visa   DETAILS: 200 seats. Private parties: 80 main room, 14 to 28 private rooms. Vegetarian meals. Children's helpings. Wheelchair access (1 step; not WC). Music. Air-conditioned   (£5)

ELSTREE Hertfordshire map 3

▲ *Edgwarebury Hotel* 🍷✕   NEW ENTRY

Beaufort Restaurant, Barnet Lane, Elstree WD6 3RE
TEL: (0181) 953 8227, changing to (020) 8953 8227   COOKING 3
FAX: (0181) 207 3668, changing to (020) 8207 3668   COST £34–£57

This model of repro Tudor splendour, not far off the A1, enjoys hilltop views of London. It is close to where *EastEnders* is filmed, and viewers may recognise the dining room when the script calls for a posh dinner out. Chris Fisher offers – in the fixed-price menu that appears alongside a 'Plain and Simple' carte – a style of cooking that may surprise and excite with, for example, a 'minestrone' of frogs' legs and smoked bacon, or a pithiviers of snails with creamed nettles and slow-roasted garlic. An inspector commended the generosity and freshness of a ragoût of Cornish seafood garnished with tapénade croûtons and fennel as a first course. Fishy main courses may involve monkfish, cod or skate in the summer, while meaty options run to saddle of rabbit with wild mushrooms, a cake of parsnip and potato, and well-seasoned shredded green cabbage. The full dessert menu looks a better bet than the cakes trolley, with offerings like warm savarin of Agen prunes with crème fraîche ice cream and armagnac. Service is pleasant. The wine list offers just enough choice, and mark-ups are fairly light. House French is £11.50.

CHEF: Chris Fisher   PROPRIETOR: Corus and Regal Hotels   OPEN: Sun to Fri L 12.30 to 2.15 (2.30 Sun), all week D 7 to 9.45 (9.30 Sun)   MEALS: alc L Mon to Fri, D Mon to Sat (main courses £14 to £19). Set L and D £24.95 (2 courses) to £29.50   SERVICE: not inc   CARDS: Amex, Delta, Diners, MasterCard, Switch, Visa   DETAILS: 50 seats. Private parties: 20 main room, 18 and 40 private rooms. Car park. Children's helpings. No smoking in dining room. Wheelchair access (not WC). Music   ACCOMMODATION: 47 rooms, all with bath/shower. TV. Phone. Room only £110 to £180. Baby facilities   (£5)

ELY Cambridgeshire   map 6

Old Fire Engine House ⅙✷

25 St Mary's Street, Ely CB7 4ER   COOKING 2
TEL: (01353) 662582   COST £29–£44

More than three decades on, Ann Ford and Michael Jarman's enthusiasm for simple, locally sourced food remains undimmed: they take fish (pike or zander) from Fen rivers, game (pigeon or hare) from local shoots, and use Norfolk asparagus and samphire when they can. Rickety floors and bare wooden tables are indicative of the relaxed and informal approach, honesty of intent is apparent, and the food takes priority: 'at one point we overheard someone in the kitchen call for chives, so a body went out to cut some; they couldn't be fresher'. It is a family-run enterprise and homeliness is the style, marked by tomato and onion soup, egg mayonnaise, game pie, and cold ham with baked potato. Puddings echo the theme, taking in syllabub, meringues, apple pie, sherry trifle and lots of cream. Service can be both 'full of fun and efficient'. Reporters have criticised the small wine glasses, although they were pleased with the wines that were poured into them. France is the mainstay of the well-priced list, so New World fans will find few outlets for their enthusiasm. However, house Chardonnay and Cabernet Sauvignon from Chile's Concha y Toro offer good drinking at £8.

CHEF: Terri Baker   PROPRIETORS: Ann Ford and Michael Jarman   OPEN: all week L 12.15 to 2, Mon to Sat D 7.15 to 9   CLOSED: 2 weeks from 24 Dec, bank hols   MEALS: alc (main courses £13 to £15.50)   SERVICE: not inc   CARDS: Delta, MasterCard, Switch, Visa   DETAILS: 56 seats. 16 seats outside. Private parties: 36 main room, 22 private room. Car park. Vegetarian meals. Children's helpings. No smoking in 1 dining room. No music

---

The Guide *is totally independent, accepts no free hospitality, and survives on the number of copies sold each year.*

map 2

Spencers £

| 36 North Street, Emsworth PO10 7DG | COOKING 3 |
| TEL/FAX: (01243) 372744 | COST £19–£39 |

The ground floor is a brasserie – 'no trimmings, but good value for money' – while the book-lined restaurant, with a fire in winter, is up a short flight of steep stairs. After 12 years, seafood remains Denis Spencer's priority. A separate list of around a dozen main-course options might run from plain grilled Dover sole, via deep-fried skate wing with paprika aïoli, to an oriental treatment such as scallops in oyster sauce with Chinese leaves. The rest of the carte is generous with main courses too – braised lamb shank, or roast pork steak among them – while starters take in soup, chicken liver pâté, and more fish. Half a dozen salads and a few pasta dishes make up the rest, and meals typically end with familiar baked Alaska or bread-and-butter pudding. A short, functional wine list starts with house wines from France (£8.95) and Australia (£9.75).

CHEF: Denis Spencer   PROPRIETORS: Denis and Lesley Spencer   OPEN: Mon to Sat 12 to 2, 6 to 10.30   CLOSED: 24 to 26 Dec, Easter Mon   MEALS: alc (main courses £7 to £12.50)   SERVICE: not inc   CARDS: Amex, Delta, Diners, MasterCard, Switch, Visa   DETAILS: 65 seats. Private parties: 30 main room, 10 private room. Vegetarian meals. No smoking in 1 dining room. Music. Air-conditioned   (£5)

36 on the Quay

| 47 South Street, Emsworth PO10 7EG | COOKING 7 |
| TEL: (01243) 375592   FAX: (01243) 375593 | COST £32–£65 |

The rustic whitewashed exterior of this eighteenth-century building down by the quayside gives little indication of the sophistication within. Swagged curtains, thick carpets, and stencilled yellow walls add up to 'cheerful décor', and Ramon Farthing, who clearly enjoys experimenting, is skilled enough 'successfully to combine the classic with the adventurous'. The menu says, quite rightly, that freshly prepared food can involve waiting time, although, even allowing for this, patience was stretched at inspection, indicating perhaps just how ambitious the food can be. For example, crisp caramelised ravioli of wild rabbit and chicken, with spinach, on creamed haricots with truffle oil, was 'a most accomplished original dish which only an extremely talented chef could have achieved'.

Dishes are presented with artistic flair, and, while they may be complicated, it is with good reason: 'accessories complement the main ingredient and add an important dimension to the end result.' Layers of red mullet and fennel, for example, achieve their 'assorted taste thrills' with the help of spicy paprika potatoes and courgette twists, while a 'juicy, gutsy, definitive' Scotch beef fillet was served with Madeira sauce, creamed shallots and garlic confit. The spinach forming part of each dish was treated differently, a 'sure test of how much effort the chef is prepared to make' in the quest for balance.

Workmanship is evident at every turn, not least in desserts of 'faultless' chocolate and coffee parfait with crème anglaise, and a lemon quartet that included ('forgive the ecstasies') tart, ice cream, fluffy soufflé, and crème brûlée that was 'everything a crème brûlée should be'. The Quay's wine list has a good catch of classy French bins, while a trawl through the New World sections proves equally rewarding. The quality is reflected in the prices, though the 'perfectly good' French house white is £13.50, as is the red.

CHEF: Ramon Farthing   PROPRIETORS: Ramon and Karen Farthing   OPEN: Tue to Fri L 12 to 1.45, Mon to Sat D 7 to 9.45   CLOSED: 2 weeks early Jan, 1 week early Oct, bank hols   MEALS: Set L £16.50 (2 courses) to £19.50, Set D £31.95 to £40   SERVICE: not inc   CARDS: Amex, Delta, Diners, MasterCard, Switch, Visa   DETAILS: 35 seats. Private parties: 30 main room, 10 private room. Car park. Vegetarian meals. Children's helpings. No smoking in 1 dining room. Music

---

EPWORTH   North Lincolnshire   map 9

Epworth Tap ▮ ⁵✗

9–11 Market Place, Epworth DN9 1EU
TEL: (01427) 873333   FAX: (01427) 875020   COOKING 4
3m S of M180 junction 2   COST £24–£42

One visitor to Helen Wynne's homely flagstoned old pub was amazed and delighted to find the place virtually the same after a dozen years: 'like slipping on a favourite old jacket which still makes you feel good.' The cooking is exemplified by accurate timing and a generosity of spirit: one diner's intense asparagus soup, for instance, was made from the whole stem, not just the trimmings, and perfectly sautéed hake in a saffron and lemon sauce came strewn with unannounced juicy queenies. The range extends from pâtés, or spiced duck breast with a raspberry dressing, to casseroles – perhaps venison, successfully involving lovage in its sauce – or rack of Lincolnshire lamb with a herb and mustard crust. In pub style, vegetables come already plated, and if you order cheese it will be a no-choice variety, but all in good condition. Alternatively, go for a fruity meringue, or bread-and-butter pudding. 'Laidback jazz and service are the order of the day.' The remarkably low prices, particularly for mature fine wines, mean that although there is a generous array of good-quality bottles under £20, this is one place where it makes financial sense to move upmarket. Whatever the preference – top claret, venerable burgundies, old Rhônes, Spanish classics or New World stars – you won't be disappointed. French house red is £10.50, white £11.50.

CHEF/PROPRIETOR: Helen Wynne   OPEN: Wed to Sat D only 7.30 to 9.15   CLOSED: 2 weeks from 26 Dec   MEALS: alc (main courses £9.50 to £13.50). Set D Sat £22   SERVICE: not inc, card slips closed   CARDS: Delta, MasterCard, Switch, Visa   DETAILS: 60 seats. Private parties: 40 main room, 26 private room. No smoking in 1 dining room. Music   (£5)

Restaurateurs justifiably resent no-shows. If you quote a credit card number when booking, you may be liable for the restaurant's lost profit margin if you don't turn up. Always phone to cancel.

ERPINGHAM Norfolk   map 6

▲ Ark ⅚✳

The Street, Erpingham NR11 7QB
TEL/FAX: (01263) 761535   COOKING 4
3m off A140 Cromer road, 4m N of Aylsham   COST £23–£44

This flint and brick building on a quiet country road is unassuming outside and
in, with pine woodwork, rag-rolled walls in subdued colours, and a log fire. But
what the Ark may lack in cosmopolitan polish it more than makes up for in
simple honesty of intent. The Kidds are doing 'a serious and caring job' serving
up country cooking without frills and flounces. Materials include organic
poultry, rare breeds of meat (loin of Gloucester Old Spot pork with a stuffing of
apple, orange and ginger), mushrooms (a good selection under a puff pastry hat
for one autumn visitor), and game in season: impressively timed pheasant
breast, complete with thigh and drumstick, served with 'unbeatable' lentils.

Vegetables – pink fir apple potatoes, tasty carrots and waxy yellow beans –
come from local growers or the garden. Homely puddings might take in
blackcurrant and apple crunch crumble, or almond and apricot meringue, and
'terrific bread' is a bonus. Wines are mostly French, keenly priced and
enthusiastically introduced. House wines from France, Chile and Australia are
£10 or £10.50.

CHEF: Sheila Kidd   PROPRIETORS: Mike and Sheila Kidd   OPEN: Sun L 12.30 to 2, Tue to Sat D
7.30 to 9.30   CLOSED: 25 and 26 Dec, possibly early Jan, some of Oct   MEALS: Set L Sun
£15.25, Set D £21.25 (2 courses) to £25   SERVICE: not inc   CARDS: none   DETAILS: 26 seats. 12
seats outside. Private parties: 30 main room, 8 private room. Car park. Vegetarian meals.
Children's helpings. No smoking in dining room. Wheelchair access (also WC). No music
ACCOMMODATION: 3 rooms, 2 with bath/shower. TV. D,B&B £65 to £135. Rooms for disabled.
Baby facilities

EVERSHOT Dorset   map 2

▲ Summer Lodge 🍾

Summer Lane, Evershot DT2 0JR
TEL: (01935) 83424   FAX: (01935) 83005   COOKING 6
EMAIL: sumlodge@sumlodge.demon.co.uk   COST £24–£79

'I always feel that I am living in the style to which I would like to become
accustomed when I relax in this beautiful old country house,' wrote one regular
visitor. Summer Lodge manages to be luxurious yet homely at the same time,
which is perhaps why so many people return for regular fixes of the Corbetts'
hospitality. Drinks and canapés are taken in the comfortable drawing room
before moving on to the immaculate dining room, which 'gleams and glitters in
the nicest possible way'.

Tim Ford is a practised exponent of country-house cooking, so although you
won't find anything here to frighten the horses, you will find quietly confident
techniques applied to sophisticated but unshowy dishes. Local produce is used
wherever possible and many reporters comment on the sheer quality of the
ingredients, well illustrated by a starter of sweetbreads with 'bold and zesty'

rocket pesto, and sweetly fresh brill with basil crushed potatoes. Another diner enjoyed ravioli of languoustine, followed by tournedos of beef served with onion marmalade, wild mushrooms and a rich, deeply flavoured sauce. Recommended puddings have included tarte Tatin and a milk chocolate cheesecake with dark chocolate sauce, while a top-class cheeseboard is usually on offer, too.

Some have felt that, next to the temptations of the more expensive carte, the evening set menu is disappointingly restrictive. Set lunches, however, provide 'exceptional value'. Service is from 'attentive but not intrusive' French staff. The 'charming and very good' wine waiter presides over a list that impresses with its breadth of coverage, in terms of both geography and pricing. Mature Burgundies, Rhônes and cru classé clarets abound, while the variety of bottles from both hemispheres under £20 is to be applauded. Half-bottles are numerous too. The house selection of fifteen wines starts in France at £12.50.

CHEF: Timothy Ford   PROPRIETORS: Nigel and Margaret Corbett   OPEN: all week 12 to 2, 7.30 to 9 (9.30 Fri)   MEALS: alc (main courses L £9 to £17, D £22 to £26). Set L £13.75 to £18.50, Set D £37.50   SERVICE: not inc, card slips closed   CARDS: Amex, Delta, Diners, MasterCard, Switch, Visa   DETAILS: 40 seats. 16 seats outside. Private parties: 20 main room, 24 private room. Car park. Vegetarian meals. Children's helpings. No children under 7 at D. No smoking while others eat. Wheelchair access (also WC). Occasional music   ACCOMMODATION: 17 rooms, all with bath/shower. TV. Phone. B&B £125 to £245. Rooms for disabled. Baby facilities. Swimming pool (*The Which? Hotel Guide*)

EXETER Devon   map 1

Lamb's ✳

| 15 Lower North Street, Exeter EX4 3ET | COOKING 2 |
| TEL: (01392) 254269   FAX: (01392) 431145 | COST £29–£48 |

Flying the flag for Exeter, in a listed five-storey terraced house under the iron bridge, Lamb's makes good use of local produce in a seasonally changing round-the-world carte and on a couple of set-price menus. Typifying the bolder, brighter end of the flavour spectrum might be vegetable tempura with sweet chilli dip, or chicken satay with a lime, coriander and yoghurt sauce, while home-smoked trout fish cakes have come more traditionally with parsley sauce, and free-range pork chop with a grain mustard and cider sauce. There is usually a vegetarian option on all menus, and a fish of the day on the carte, while the 'wonderful selection' of local cheeses might include a Devon version of Emmental. Alternatively, finish with steamed Exeter pudding and clotted cream, or rhubarb crème brûlée with Cornish ginger fairings (a type of biscuit originally bought at fairs). Staff are young and friendly, wines balance interest with good value, half-bottles are generous, and half a dozen house wines are £10.

CHEF: Alison Aldridge   PROPRIETORS: Ian and Alison Aldridge   OPEN: Tue to Fri L 12 to 2, Tue to Sat D 7 to 10   MEALS: alc L and Tue to Thur D (main courses £11 to £17). Set L £15 (2 courses) to £19, Set D Tue to Thur £15 (2 courses) to £19, Set D Fri and Sat £23   SERVICE: not inc   CARDS: Amex, Delta, MasterCard, Switch, Visa   DETAILS: 46 seats. 10 seats outside. Private parties: 26 main room, 26 private room. Vegetarian meals. Children's helpings. No smoking in 1 dining room. Wheelchair access (not WC). No music   £5

EYNSHAM Oxfordshire   map 2

▲ *Baker's* ¾✳

---

4 Lombard Street, Eynsham OX8 1HT   COOKING 4
TEL: (01865) 881888   FAX: (01865) 883537   COST £24–£61

Philip Baker's restaurant induces a calming effect, partly owing to the generous
supply of flickering candles amid the dining room's foliage, pot plants and
starched white napery, and partly because of the 'relaxed, caring and correct'
service from 'helpful, professional and polite' staff. He operates a set-price menu
designed for broad appeal, a newly introduced 'lunch rapide', and a more
expensive and ambitious carte that has included properly seared scallops topped
with parsley purée, surrounded by a creamy textured cod brandade sauce; and a
meaty, moist guinea fowl sausage generously endowed with pistachio nuts,
served with braised chicory in a correctly reduced sauce.

An indication of the cooking's complexity can be gained from a generous fillet
of impressively fresh, crisp-skinned roast sea bass sitting on extremely al dente
leeks, with a sandcastle-shaped tian of aubergine and tomato, plus strips of
fennel and diced red pepper, plus a garnish of tomato skin and deep-fried basil
leaves, all in a well-reduced salty sauce dotted with pools of green olive oil. A
separate dish of vegetables is also provided. At inspection, the accompanying ice
creams (gingerbread with rhubarb soufflé, honeycomb with glazed apple tart)
proved a hit. Around forty widely sourced wines are fairly priced, starting with
house vin de pays at £10.95.

CHEF: Philip Baker   PROPRIETORS: Philip Baker, Amanda Hill and Donald Baker   OPEN: all week
L 12 (12.30 Sun) to 2.30, Tue to Sat D 7 to 10.30   CLOSED: bank hols exc 25 Dec   MEALS: alc
(main courses £17.50 to £19.50). Set L Mon to Sat £12.50 (2 courses) to £16.50, 'lunch rapide'
Mon to Sat £7.50 (2 courses) to £9.50, Set L Sun £12 (2 courses) to £14.50, Set D £15.50 (2
courses) to £19.50   SERVICE: not inc   CARDS: Delta, MasterCard, Switch, Visa   DETAILS: 50
seats. Private parties: 60 main room, 15 private room. Car park. Vegetarian meals. Children's
helpings. No smoking in 1 dining room. Wheelchair access (not WC). Music   ACCOMMODATION:
2 rooms, both with bath/shower. TV. Phone. B&B £55 to £60 (*The Which? Hotel Guide*)

FARNBOROUGH Kent   map 3

Chapter One

Farnborough Common, Locksbottom,
Farnborough BR6 8NF   ┌─────────┐
                                                     │ NEW CHEF │
TEL: (01689) 854848   FAX: (01689) 858439   └─────────┘
                                                      COST £29–£55

The half-timbered, neon-lit exterior belies a cool, modern dining room, all cream
and ochre walls, with navy-blue cloth covers on chairs, around well-spaced
tables. Staff sport collarless shirts with black waistcoats and provide friendly
and helpful service. As the *Guide* went to press Paul Dunstane, who has worked
at the Orrery and the Bluebird in London and at Harveys in Bristol (see entries),
was due to take charge of the kitchen. Menus, we were told, are unlikely to
change much in the short term, and may offer dishes along the lines of assiette of
pork with caramelised apple, pot-roast lamb on a potato and celeriac dauphinoise, and seafood risotto with salmon, with perhaps chocolate sponge

soufflé to finish. The wine list is divided between France and the rest of the world, with pricing fair but hardly generous. Ten house wines, listed by country only, start at £11 a bottle, £3 per glass.

CHEF: Paul Dunstane PROPRIETOR: Selective Restaurants Group OPEN: all week 12 to 2.30 (3.30 Sun), 6.30 (7 Sun) to 11 (11.30 Fri and Sat, 9.30 Sun) MEALS: alc (main courses £13.50 to £18.50). Set L Mon to Sat £16 (2 courses) to £19.50, Set L Sun £16. Bar L available Mon to Sat SERVICE: 10% (optional), card slips closed CARDS: Amex, Delta, Diners, MasterCard, Switch, Visa DETAILS: 120 seats. Private parties: 120 main room, 55 private room. Car park. Vegetarian meals. Children's helpings. No cigars/pipes in dining room. Music. Air-conditioned (£5)

FAVERSHAM Kent   map 3

Read's ▮

Painter's Forstal, Faversham ME13 0EE
TEL: (01795) 535344   FAX: (01795) 591200   COOKING 7
on Eastling road, 2m S of Faversham   COST £30–£62

Accolades continue to pour in for this deceptively modest-looking restaurant, and if the surroundings aren't quite as stylish as the cooking they are at least 'comforting and welcoming', with deep sofas in the bar and attractive views of the garden and Kentish downs. The menu features foodie quotations spanning Gandhi to Winnie the Pooh, which left one couple unsure 'whether this was ghastly or quite fun'. The food is serious stuff, though.

David Pitchford's cooking demonstrates an impressive range of skills, applied to impeccable raw materials. Efforts are made to use local suppliers and the menu often spells out the provenance of ingredients: Kentish lamb, Whitstable turbot, Owen Court asparagus. Well-composed dishes feature clever if conservative combinations: a 'grand' dish of veal escalope in brioche crumbs, complemented by the saltiness of anchovies and capers, and the richness of a runny fried egg; or sesame roast duck with ginger stir-fried vegetables and a spiced plum sauce. Puddings are as technically demanding as the rest of the menu, yet a 'well-risen' hot passion fruit soufflé served with an intensely flavoured coconut ice cream 'passed the test with flying colours', as did the 'chocoholics anonymous' plate.

Expectations are so high that small imperfections can niggle, from rather cautious flavouring in some dishes to 'unimpressive' bread rolls, but 'friendly and forthcoming' staff provide attentive service under Rona Pitchford's watchful eye. A mixed assortment of some sixty 'best buys', most of them under £20, is thoughtfully provided as a preface to the main wine list. However, those prepared to peruse the following forty-odd pages will be rewarded with some particularly fine wines from France, Italy, Spain, Australia and California at not unreasonable prices. House wines are £14.

CHEF: David Pitchford PROPRIETORS: David and Rona Pitchford OPEN: Tue to Sat 12 to 2, 7 to 9.30 MEALS: Set L £18.50, Set D £22 to £38 SERVICE: not inc, card slips closed CARDS: Amex, Delta, Diners, MasterCard, Switch, Visa DETAILS: 40 seats. 12 seats outside. Private parties: 40 main room, 20 private room. Car park. Vegetarian meals. Children's helpings. No pipes/cigars in dining room. Wheelchair access (not WC). No music (£5)

FERNHURST Surrey   map 3

Kings Arms ![symbol]

Midhurst Road, Fernhurst GU27 3HA   COOKING 2
TEL: (01428) 652005   COST £21–£42

With regulation beams, low ceilings and an inglenook fireplace, this L-shaped
pub (originally seventeenth century) combines a bar and restaurant, the latter
offering a free-ranging list of dishes toted round on a blackboard. The food is a
'cut above pub grub', from ploughman's and sandwiches at one end, through
corned beef hash with fried egg, or cod in beer batter, to chicken Kiev wrapped
in filo on a bed of spinach. The cooking has its ups and downs but is rarely too
ambitious, preferring instead traditional French onion soup or daube of beef,
alongside provençale tart with pesto dressing, or chicken liver risotto. The
selection of dishes changes every month or so, although quite a few of the
puddings are less dependent on season: baked chocolate mousse cake with
coffee cream, or steamed orange pudding with Grand Marnier sauce and
marmalade ice cream. Most of the wines are under £20, and house French (one of
a handful available by the glass) is £9.25.

CHEF: Michael Hirst   PROPRIETORS: Michael and Annabel Hirst   OPEN: all week L 12 to 2.30,
Mon to Sat D 7 to 10   CLOSED: some days Christmas, bank hols   MEALS: alc (main courses L
£5.50 to £14, D £8.50 to £14)   SERVICE: not inc   CARDS: Delta, MasterCard, Switch, Visa
DETAILS: 45 seats. 40 seats outside. Private parties: 28 main room, 12 private room. Car park.
Vegetarian meals. Children's helpings. No children under 14 after 7pm. No smoking in 1 dining
room. No music

FERRENSBY North Yorkshire   map 9

▲ General Tarleton ![symbol]

Harrogate Road, Ferrensby HG5 0QB   COOKING 5
TEL: (01423) 340284   FAX: (01423) 340288   COST £25–£48

This is Denis Watkins's 'other' Yorkshire enterprise (see Angel Inn, Hetton): a
historic pub in a pretty village with brick cottages and a duck pond. The formula
is thoroughly modern and flexible. Full of alcoves, oak beams and a big old
fireplace in the bar, it can still be used either as a pub (note the draught beers) or
as a brasserie where you order as much or as little as you like. The slightly more
formal, stone-walled restaurant is a tranquil place serving food with rather more
ambition: for example a fine tart of Finnan haddock with poached egg and
smoked salmon, or terrine of rabbit, foie gras, truffle and pencil leeks.

   Well-sourced raw materials include sweet grilled scallops (with aubergine
and Parmesan crisps in a sauce vierge), and, while John Topham has an eye for
presentation, flavour is given priority, not least in lamb dishes: three pink cutlets
with a peppery potato and mushroom galette, or slowly roasted shoulder with
crisp, salty, fatty skin. Among desserts – including lemon tart, and melting
chocolate pudding – rhubarb and custard is 'a good deal more interesting than its
description': sharp sorbet and tart compote are topped with crisp, deep-fried
custard 'reminiscent of pancakes'. Mixed reports indicate that the food appears
to vary in quality, and, while a degree of patience is to be expected, 'slow service'

has marred some experiences; an inspector, however, appreciated the calm pace of things as well as the 'relaxed, friendly and thoroughly professional staff'. Half a dozen house wines under £16 head up a French-dominated list that nevertheless manages to include bottles from Chile and Israel.

CHEF: John Topham   PROPRIETORS: Denis and Juliet Watkins, and John Topham   OPEN: Sun L 12 to 2, Mon to Sat D 6 to 9.30. Bar food available   CLOSED: 25 Dec   MEALS: Set L Sun £17.50, Set D 6 to 7.15 £13.50 (2 courses) to £16.50, Set D £25   SERVICE: not inc   CARDS: Amex, Delta, MasterCard, Switch, Visa   DETAILS: 145 seats. 45 seats outside. Private parties: 45 main room. Car park. Vegetarian meals. Children's helpings. No smoking in dining room. Wheelchair access (not WC). No music   ACCOMMODATION: 14 rooms, all with bath/shower. TV. Phone. Room only £57.50 to £65. Rooms for disabled. Baby facilities   (£5)

FLETCHING East Sussex   map 3

▲ *Griffin Inn* | NEW ENTRY |

Fletching TN22 3SS
TEL: (01825) 722890   FAX: (01825) 722810
off A272, between Maresfield and Newick, 3m NW of   COOKING 2
Uckfield   COST £24–£44

While still very much a pub – country prints on the walls, dark patterned carpet and pool table in the public bar – the Griffin reveals a modern approach to food. Start perhaps with grilled polenta with roasted peppers, marinated black olives, anchovies and Parmesan, or jellied terrine of monkfish, capsicum scallion and skate with salsa verde, and move on to loin of lamb with borlotti beans, or local veal with celeriac and potato mash. Thursday is fish night, which might start with a 'definitive combination' of pan-fried marinated squid with a sweet chilli and tomato sauce, and proceed to correctly cooked paella Valenciana (with tiger prawns, clams, mussels and salmon), or chargrilled marinated swordfish with guacamole ('moist and full of real flavour'). Puddings run to rich and nutty treacle tart, or pannacotta with rhubarb compote. Service is efficient and enthusiastic, and the fairly priced wine list favours Europe, but not to the exclusion of the New World. House wines start at £9.80.

CHEF: Jason Williams   PROPRIETORS: Nigel and Bridget Pullan   OPEN: all week 12 to 2.30, 7 to 9.30   CLOSED: Sun D in winter, 25 Dec   MEALS: alc (main courses £8.50 to £15.50). Set L Sun £17.50. Bar menu available L and D   SERVICE: not inc   CARDS: Amex, Delta, Diners, MasterCard, Switch, Visa   DETAILS: 60 seats. 30 seats outside. Private parties: 45 main room, 20 private room. Car park. Vegetarian meals. Children's helpings. Wheelchair access (not WC). No music   ACCOMMODATION: 8 rooms, all with bath/shower. TV. B&B £55 to £85. Rooms for disabled (*The Which? Hotel Guide*)   (£5)

'It was very expensive, but it did include a half-bottle of Pichon Lalande 1983, a glass of Coutet, a glass of champagne and a bottle of water. I knew I should not have ordered the water.' (On eating in London)

New main entries and restaurant closures are listed near the front of the book.

FOLKESTONE Kent

map 3

Pauls

2A Bouverie Road West, Folkestone CT20 2RX   COOKING 1
TEL: (01303) 259697   FAX: (01303) 226647   COST £17–£31

Although this is a handy stopping-off point for Channel hoppers, it seems to be mostly locals who make use of the easy-going bistro, now a venerable quarter of a century old. Inexpensive buffet lunches have their appeal, but the long menu offers a more varied range of items, from venison sausage, via gnocchi in a creamy spinach sauce, to sirloin steak with Stilton butter. Much of the fish comes from Hythe – perhaps brill in a wild mushroom sauce – and cream plays a vital role in both savoury sauces and desserts from the trolley. Wines take their £20 ceiling seriously, starting with house French at £8.65.

CHEFS: Paul Hagger and Chris Bradford: PROPRIETORS: Paul and Penny Hagger   OPEN: all week 12 to 2.30, 7 to 9.30   CLOSED: 1 week Christmas   MEALS: alc (main courses £11). Set L Mon to Sat £4.95 (1 course), Set L Sun £9.95, Set D Sun to Fri £9.95   SERVICE: not inc   CARDS: Delta, MasterCard, Switch, Visa   DETAILS: 120 seats. 40 seats outside. Private parties: 100 main room, 20 to 100 private rooms. Car park. Vegetarian meals. Wheelchair access (also WC). No music

FOSS CROSS Gloucestershire

map 2

Hare & Hounds £ |NEW ENTRY|

Foss Cross GL54 4NN   COOKING 3
TEL: (01285) 720288   COST £20–£37

Like its sister operation the Churchill Arms (see entry, Paxford), this is intended to be 'a pub with food, rather than a restaurant with beer'. The partnership, which includes Sonya Kidney and Leo Brooke-Little (of Marsh Goose, see entry, Moreton-in-Marsh) have kept the bare stone walls, flagstones and solid oak floors and beams, and have installed rustic wooden tables and old chairs. The log fires are working again, and a certain smokiness goes with the territory. A blackboard menu changes daily, the half-dozen starters and main courses based on whatever Richard Burkert has found at its peak. Meat and fish are expertly cooked: calf's liver with confit of onions, for example, and sea bass with spinach and a powerful creamy grain mustard sauce. Reports are enthusiastic about lively-sounding starters of smoked pigeon salad with pools of gently spicy pineapple and red pepper salsa, and crisp, moist fish cakes hinting of chilli. Desserts range from lightly textured sticky toffee pudding with notable butterscotch sauce, to glazed bananas with a brandy-snap of chocolate ice cream. If real ales are in short supply, remember the short wine list starts at £9.95.

CHEF: Richard Burkert   PROPRIETORS: Sonya Kidney, Leo Brooke-Little, Shaun Davis and Emma Copley   OPEN: all week 12 to 2.15, 7 to 9.15   MEALS: alc (main courses £7 to £12) SERVICE: not inc   CARDS: Delta, MasterCard, Switch, Visa   DETAILS: 85 seats. 30 seats outside. Private parties: 15 main room. Car park. Wheelchair access (also WC). No music

The Gamp £ ⚡✳

Claypit Lane, Foulsham NR20 5RW   COOKING 2
TEL: (01362) 684114   COST £17–£36

Hanging baskets and Virginia creeper decorate the outside of this spacious, well-maintained, 200-year-old building in a secluded village. Its 'cottagey' style and 'tea room' feel – pink décor, copper table tops in the bar, and a garden room overlooking the herb patch – is emphasised by homely dishes and good baking, although the cooking extends beyond that to a generous tuna kebab with garlic sauce and crispy seaweed, and a handful of simple dishes from the grill: chicken breast, Dover sole and rump steak among them.

One reporter chose 'the most strange-sounding starter (lamb and apricot crumble) out of curiosity and regretted it'; much better was a main course of thinly sliced grilled calf's liver with matchstick potatoes and a red wine sauce. A lack of seasoning characterised an inspection meal, but pudding turned up trumps: a 'gâteau' of shortbread rounds with summer berries and lots of cream. A wine list entirely bereft of vintages stays mostly below £20 and starts with house French at £7.95.

CHEF: Simon Nobbs   PROPRIETORS: Daphne and Andy Bush   OPEN: Wed to Sat and first and third Sun in month L 12 to 1.30, Tue to Sat D 7 to 9.30   CLOSED: first 2 weeks Jan   MEALS: alc Wed to Sat L and Tue to Sat D (main courses £9 to £16.50). Set L and D £11.95   SERVICE: net prices, card slips closed   CARDS: Delta, MasterCard, Switch, Visa   DETAILS: 40 seats. 6 seats outside. Private parties: 42 main room. Car park. Vegetarian meals. Children's helpings. No smoking in dining room. Wheelchair access (also WC). No music

FOWEY Cornwall   map 1

Food for Thought

The Quay, Fowey PL23 1AT   COOKING 4
TEL: (01726) 832221   FAX: (01726) 832077   COST £29–£58

The Billingsleys have spent over two decades at this old customs house down by the quay, where 'you don't see much of the harbour, but you can occasionally see big ships coming in past the window'. Seafood is naturally a strong suit, although there is plenty of meat too; and plenty of choice, given three separate fixed-price menus. Options, interest and workmanship increase with price, moving perhaps from gravad lax on the cheapest menu, through a smoked haddock and leek chowder, to scallop risotto on the most expensive. This latter also brings half a grilled lobster with garlic butter, and local sea bass with hollandaise.

Elsewhere there might be provençale salad, braised lamb shank, or Barbary duck breast with Puy lentils, ending up with tangy lemon tart, pannacotta, or bread-and-butter pudding with clotted cream. A couple of reporters have been miffed at arrangements: one was told that bookings for fewer than four people were not taken on Saturday evenings, while another wondered whether restaurants should let pre-booked customers know if they would be sharing the restaurant with a large party. House wine is £8.75.

CHEF: Martin Billingsley   PROPRIETORS: Martin and Caroline Billingsley   OPEN: Mon to Sat D only 7 to 9.30   CLOSED: Jan and Feb   MEALS: Set D Mon to Fri £19.95 to £29.95, Set D Sat £24.95 to £29.95   SERVICE: not inc, card slips closed   CARDS: MasterCard, Visa   DETAILS: 42 seats. Private parties: 20 main room. Children's helpings. Wheelchair access. Occasional music

---

FRESSINGFIELD Suffolk   map 6

Fox and Goose ♥ ⁵⁺✕

Fressingfield IP21 5PB
TEL: (01379) 586247   FAX: (01379) 586688
EMAIL: paoleary@compuserve.com   COOKING 1
on B1116, 3½m S of Harleston   COST £24–£51

This white-painted brick and timber building opposite the church has a well-worn, lived-in feel. Old beams, yellow walls and a tiled floor point to its unchanging ways, as indeed do the menus. A carte offers a choice of raw (marinated salmon), cold (Caesar salad) and hot starters – maybe eggs served Benedict-style, or filled with a mix of spiced prawns and crab and then deep-fried – followed by poached chicken breast with a cassoulet of butter beans and chorizo. Bar snacks, a vegetarian menu and set-price menus increase the options, and Sunday lunch brings roast sirloin with Yorkshire pudding. Poor fish and less-than-expert handling of lambs' liver took the shine off an inspection meal, but the kitchen is also capable of producing perfectly good vanilla-flecked crème brûlée with a light, crisp topping, and lightly textured sticky toffee pudding with a sauce tasting 'like old-fashioned treacle toffee'. A gander at the wine list reveals some top producers from France and beyond. House wines are £13.50.

CHEF: Maxwell Dougal   PROPRIETORS: Tim and Pauline O'Leary   OPEN: all week 12 to 2, 7 to 9 (9.30 Sat)   CLOSED: 25 and 26 Dec   MEALS: alc (main courses £9.50 to £15). Set L Mon to Sat £9.50 (2 courses) to £12.50, Set L Sun £13.50, Set D Mon to Fri £17.50   SERVICE: not inc   CARDS: Delta, MasterCard, Switch, Visa   DETAILS: 50 seats. 16 seats outside. Private parties: 32 main room, 20 private room. Car park. Vegetarian meals. Children's helpings. No smoking in dining room. No music

---

GATESHEAD Tyne & Wear   map 10

▲ Eslington Villa ⁵⁺✕

8 Station Road, Low Fell, Gateshead NE9 6DR
TEL: (0191) 487 6017   FAX: (0191) 420 0667
leave A1 (M) at Team Valley Retail World exit, enter
Eastern Avenue at a roundabout and at top turn left   [NEW CHEF]
into Station Road   COST £24–£50

After five years this quiet, traditional, suburban hotel with a leafy garden has a new chef, who arrived just as the *Guide* was going to press. The style continues along similar lines – a broadly European tilt with some some exotic flourishes – and the kind of dishes to expect might include Thai crab salad, or Cheddar and basil fritters with sauce vierge to start, followed by salmon with red onion confit, or lamb chump with olive oil mash, finishing with Black Forest chocolate trifle.

Most of the thirty or so wines on the list stay comfortably under £20, starting with house French at £10.50. Reports please.

CHEF: Alan O'Neil   PROPRIETORS: Nick and Melanie Tulip   OPEN: Sun to Fri L 11.45 to 1.45, Mon to Sat D 6.45 to 9.45 (10 Sat)   CLOSED: Christmas, bank hols   MEALS: alc (main courses £16 to £18). Set L Mon to Fri £9.95 (2 courses), Set L Sun £16.95, Set D Mon to Fri £18.45 (2 courses) to £22.45   SERVICE: not inc   CARDS: Amex, Delta, Diners, MasterCard, Switch, Visa DETAILS: 55 seats. 12 seats outside. Private parties: 55 main room, 18 private room. Car park. Vegetarian meals. Children's helpings. No smoking in dining room. Wheelchair access (also WC). Music   ACCOMMODATION: 12 rooms, all with bath/shower. TV. Phone. B&B £30 to £69.50 (*The Which? Hotel Guide*)

GILLINGHAM Dorset   map 2

▲ *Stock Hill House* ⁵✹

Stock Hill, Gillingham SP8 5NR
TEL: (01747) 823626   FAX: (01747) 825628
EMAIL: reception@stockhill.net   COOKING 5
off B3081, 1m W of Gillingham   COST £32–£52

Extensive grounds surround this large, grey-stone Victorian house where the Hausers have been plying their trade for the past fifteen years. Drapes, mirrors, busy wallpaper and lush fabrics in the lounge are all in good taste, the dining room is slightly more sedate, and the whole place is patently well cared for down to the last detail. A sensibly sized menu might include salad of black pudding and bacon with a poached egg, followed by partridge on red cabbage, or more experimental sea witch stuffed with banana. Prime ingredients are generally handled with care, dishes are well focused, and a reporter who stayed three nights found 'not one dish that did not delight'.

A characteristic device seems to be a 'dumpling' to accompany some main courses: made of highly seasoned leg meat encased in pasta, for example, to partner duck breast in thyme sauce. Enthusiastic use of herbs is also a feature, helped by a well-stocked kitchen garden: a dribble of strong pesto lends vibrancy to moist seared scallops, while a herb dressing adds intensity to an otherwise simple tomato and mozzarella timbale. Likewise among desserts, a slice of Alsatian apple flan is innovatively spiced with coriander syrup to good effect. Service has been professional, knowledgeable, charming, indeed 'exemplary', while the wine list relies on classical French offerings for impact, a handful of Austrians for interest, and a few from elsewhere. House wines (there are four, not counting fizz) start at £14.95.

CHEF: Peter Hauser   PROPRIETORS: Peter and Nita Hauser   OPEN: Tue to Fri and Sun L 12.30 to 1.30, all week D 7.30 to 8.45   MEALS: Set L £22, Set D £32   SERVICE: not inc, card slips closed CARDS: MasterCard, Switch, Visa   DETAILS: 34 seats. Private parties: 24 main room. Car park. Children's helpings. Jacket and tie. No smoking in dining room   ACCOMMODATION: 9 rooms, all with bath/shower. TV. Phone. D,B&B £105 to £300. No children under 7 in accommodation (*The Which? Hotel Guide*)   (£5)

London restaurants by cuisine are listed near the front of the book.

GOLCAR West Yorkshire	map 8

▲ *The Weavers Shed*

Knowl Road, Golcar HD7 4AN
TEL: (01484) 654284   FAX: (01484) 650980
EMAIL: info@weavers-shed.demon.co.uk
on B6111, 2m W of Huddersfield from A62

COOKING 5
COST £24–£51

'There is a real determination here to seek out and nurture quality sources of supply,' noted one visitor to this convivial restaurant-with-rooms, converted from a former cloth-finishing mill. And indeed, chef-owner Stephen Jackson's passion for good ingredients underpins the whole enterprise. Besides using local suppliers – a leaflet in the bedrooms acknowledges everyone from the cheesemonger to the gardener – he has established a kitchen garden that has made the restaurant largely self-sufficient in vegetables, herbs and fruit (no mean feat in the North).

The kitchen pays its dues to 'modern British' – potato-crusted tiger prawns with roast tomato and coriander dressing, for example – but there is also a strong comfort factor, evinced by a fondness for hearty vegetable accompaniments such as mashed roots with braised lamb shank. Both modern and traditional strands are handled deftly. A starter of crab dumplings with truffle oil has been 'simply sensational', while calf's liver with mash has been described as 'well balanced, full flavoured and beautifully presented'. Vegetables, as you might expect, come in for plenty of praise, as do breads, such as treacle, or cheese and onion. Puddings might include 'gooey' hot chocolate fondant, or a 'brilliant' banana tarte Tatin with rum and raisin ice cream. Coffee is served with an interesting posset, such as kirsch or elderflower. 'Competent, friendly' service ensures that everything runs smoothly. The well-chosen wine list has plenty under £20, with house wine at £10.95.

CHEFS: Stephen Jackson, Ian McGunnigle and Robert Jones   PROPRIETORS: Stephen and Tracy Jackson   OPEN: Tue to Fri L 12 to 2, Tue to Sat D 7 to 10   CLOSED: 25, 26 and 31 Dec, 1 Jan, bank hols   MEALS: alc (main courses £12.50 to £16.50). Set L £9.95 (2 courses) to £13.95   SERVICE: not inc   CARDS: Amex, Diners, MasterCard, Switch, Visa   DETAILS: 65 seats. Private parties: 40 main room, 35 private room. Car park. Vegetarian meals. Children's helpings. No cigars/pipes in dining room. Music   ACCOMMODATION: 5 rooms, all with bath/shower. TV. Phone. B&B £30 to £65. Rooms for disabled. Baby facilities (*The Which? Hotel Guide*)   £5

GORING Oxfordshire	map 2

Leatherne Bottel

Goring RG8 0HS
TEL: (01491) 872667   FAX: (01491) 875308
on B4009 out of Goring, 5m S of Wallingford

COOKING 3
COST £30–£61

Unseen from the road, this converted pub comforts with a fire in winter, but arguably comes into its own in summer, when you can sit inches from the river and enjoy a peaceful view with not another building in sight. Rag-rolled orange décor, reminiscent of a Tuscan villa, and a few 'decadent touches' – cigars, exotic photographs, caviare – combine to produce a generally relaxed atmosphere. The cooking relies less on complicated cooking for impact, than on unusual combinations and treatments: for example, hot smoked salmon with dandelion leaves, roasted jumping rice, 'Bloody Mary' ice cream and basil olive oil.

The repertoire rings the changes, with seafood predominating in summer, game and offal in winter, but standards of food and service appear to have seesawed markedly over the year, with quite a few reporters registering disappointment, and prices have raised more than one eyebrow. An inspection meal, however, showed up predominantly good materials and dishes, including fresh-tasting roast baby squid, neatly packed with minted couscous and served with a racy, sweet-and-sour tamarind sauce; and successful nougat glacé with a creamy Amaretto sauce. Prices escalate pretty fast on a short but varied wine list that starts with Italian house red and white at £14.50.

CHEFS: Keith Read and Julia Storey   PROPRIETOR: Keith Read   OPEN: all week L 12.15 to 2.30, Mon to Sat D 7.15 to 9.30   CLOSED: 24 and 25 Dec   MEALS: alc (main courses £16 to £20). Set D Mon to Fri £19.50   SERVICE: 12.5%, card slips closed   CARDS: Amex, Delta, MasterCard, Switch, Visa   DETAILS: 60 seats. 75 seats outside. Private parties: 20 main room, 12 private room. Car park. Vegetarian meals. No children. No pipes. No music. Air-conditioned   £5

GRANGE IN BORROWDALE   Cumbria   map 10

▲ *Borrowdale Gates Hotel* ❦ ✳

Grange in Borrowdale CA12 5UQ
TEL: (017687) 77204   FAX: (017687) 77254   NEW CHEF
off B5289, 4m S of Keswick, ½m N of village   COST £22–£43

The situation is sublime, with phenomenal views from the newly refurbished restaurant over wooded gardens to the fells and crags beyond. Terry and Christine Parkinson run their comfortable Victorian whitewashed-stone hotel with friendliness, professionalism and vigour, and the kitchen has made good use of local supply lines for its daily-changing five-course dinner menus. As the *Guide* went to press Michael Heathcote returned to the stoves (he was listed here in the 1998 edition) and intends to maintain a similar style. Before the change, this included ravioli of scallops; wild venison with creamed celeriac, roasted onions and a port and thyme sauce; and Victoria plum frangipane flan. Cheeses might include Mrs Kirkham's Lancashire, or Nantbwla Caerphilly. Weekday lunches are a lighter affair, while Sunday lunch is very traditional. Wines on the moderately Francophile list are accompanied by snippets of useful information, and half-bottles are liberally scattered throughout. House French from Georges Blanc is £11.75.

CHEF: Michael Heathcote   PROPRIETORS: Terry and Christine Parkinson   OPEN: all week 12.15 to 1.30, 7 to 8.45   CLOSED: Jan   MEALS: Set L Sun £14.50, Set D £27. Light L available Mon to Sat   SERVICE: not inc   CARDS: Amex, Delta, MasterCard, Switch, Visa   DETAILS: 60 seats. 20 seats outside. Car park. No children under 7 in dining room. Children's helpings Sun L. No smoking in dining room. Wheelchair access (also WC). No music   ACCOMMODATION: 29 rooms, all with bath/shower. TV. Phone. B&B £40 to £140. Rooms for disabled. Baby facilities (*The Which? Hotel Guide*)

GRASMERE Cumbria   map 8

▲ *Michael's Nook* 🍷 🥪 ⚡

Grasmere LA22 9RP
TEL: (015394) 35496   FAX: (015394) 35645   COOKING 6
EMAIL: m-nook@wordsworth-grasmere.co.uk   COST £49–£82

'An idiosyncratic hotel with cooking to match,' summed up one visitor. The substantial Victorian house of Lakeland stone stands above the hubbub of Grasmere on the slopes of Greenbank Fell. White-painted cast-iron tables and wooden benches provide opportunity for admiring the view over pre-prandial drinks when weather permits, and the comfortable if slightly worn interior – a floral bar, a main dining room in deep red, and a smaller 'oak room' – goes in for antiques and polished tables in a big way. The place seems to be strong on rules and procedures, noted an inspector, 'but is relaxed about breaking them'. In particular, it is possible to dip in and out of the various menus: set-price five-course dinner, daily 'chef's recommendation', and several alternative dishes.

Michael Wignall, who took over just as the last edition of the *Guide* went to press, goes beyond the usual prime cuts and luxury ingredients found in many country-house hotels. Although he seems happy enough with, for example, moist, crisp-skinned red mullet accompanied by a sandwich of tomato slices and turbot brandade, there is also a preoccupation with powerful, earthy flavours. Much use is made of innards and extremities, be it foie gras to partner loin of venison, or an 'assiette' of pork consisting of a boudin in Madeira sauce, the fillet topped with deep-fried strips of crunchy ear, and a small trotter with a creamy filling. Despite modish gestures, such as vegetable and fruit crisps, the cooking has its own personality, pairing a thin, moist, goats'-cheese-filled raviolo with roast scallop slices, for example, and getting the best out of rhubarb by partnering a fromage blanc mousse with green dice in a pink syrup, plus some spears of the dried fruit. Service is competent, pleasant and informative.

The wine list is lovingly compiled, with page after page of serious bottles – particularly from Bordeaux, Burgundy and the Rhône – and, naturally, they command some serious prices. But a real effort has also been made to provide an excellent choice of wines under £20, and half-bottles seem to go on for ever. House wines from France and Australia start at £11.75.

CHEF: Michael Wignall   PROPRIETORS: Mr and Mrs R.S.E. Gifford   OPEN: all week 12.30 to 1, 7.30 to 8.30   MEALS: Set L from £37.50, Set D from £48   SERVICE: not inc   CARDS: Amex, Delta, Diners, MasterCard, Switch, Visa   DETAILS: 50 seats. Private parties: 40 main room, 40 private room. Car park. No children under 7 in dining room. Jacket and tie. No smoking in dining room. Wheelchair access (also WC). No music   ACCOMMODATION: 14 rooms, all with bath/shower. TV. Phone. D,B&B £138 to £275. No children under 7 in accommodation (*The Which? Hotel Guide*) (£5)

Dining rooms where music, either live or recorded, is never played are signalled by No music *in the details at the end of an entry.*

▲ *White Moss House* ▮

Rydal Water, Grasmere LA22 9SE
TEL: (015394) 35295 FAX: (015394) 35516
EMAIL: dixon@whitemoss.demon.co.uk
on A591, at N end of Rydal Water

COOKING 6
COST £37–£44

A single sitting is the format in this unaffected house (once owned by Wordsworth) in the heart of the Lakes. Five-course dinners served at bare wooden tables in the small dining room offer no choice before dessert, and follow a well-rehearsed pattern. The first course is a combination soup (fennel, asparagus and apple perhaps, or celeriac and cauliflower with Stilton croûtons), the second a fish duo or trio, typically either a soufflé – perhaps of Coniston char and River Eden smoked salmon with Westmoreland smoked cheese – or a pairing of salmons (Shetland and Eden) with mustard sauce and salad leaves.

The Dixons have fair claim to being at the forefront of the movement towards wild and organic food, sourcing a fair amount from Lakeland: Mansergh Hall lamb for example, roast mallard with Lyth Valley damsons, or thick slices of 'juicy' roast Cumbrian venison fillet marinated in juniper and red wine, served with a rich blackberry and blueberry sauce. The cooking is well executed, with an enviable consistency of delivery. It may not be particularly adventurous with flavours, but it does achieve what it sets out to do, with none of the common faults over timing or balance.

Vegetables are served separately, cheeses arrive at the correct temperature, and puddings are in the traditional mould of bread-and-butter, sticky toffee, or Eton Mess. 'Don't forget the breakfast,' advised one who started the day with a 'Barnsley' kipper split into two fat halves. Standards are well maintained on the wine list, which harks back to mature vintages (1928 for the clarets) and looks forward to new discoveries. The eminently sensible practice of following each classic region with a selection of similarly styled New World offerings means that red Burgundies, for example, precede Pinot Noirs from Australia, California and New Zealand. Prices are very fair throughout, and the mostly French house selection starts at £10.50.

CHEFS: Peter Dixon and Robert Simpson PROPRIETORS: Sue and Peter Dixon OPEN: Mon to Sat D only 8pm (1 sitting) CLOSED: Dec to Feb MEALS: Set D £28 SERVICE: not inc, card slips closed CARDS: MasterCard, Switch, Visa DETAILS: 18 seats. Car park. Children's helpings. No smoking in dining room. Wheelchair access (not WC). No music ACCOMMODATION: 8 rooms, all with bath/shower. TV. Phone. D,B&B £69 to £180. Fishing (*The Which? Hotel Guide*)
£5

GREAT GONERBY Lincolnshire map 6

Harry's Place

17 High Street, Great Gonerby NG31 8JS
TEL: (01476) 561780
on B1174, 1m N of Grantham

COOKING 7
COST £53–£81

'Utterly delightful' was the opinion of one visitor to this 'deeply eccentric' family-run operation. The scale is domestic: only three sizeable pine tables laid with old-fashioned cutlery in the dusty-pink front room of a Georgian house, and 'an absurdly limited menu' of two items per course to choose from. But it has none of the false bonhomie of the country-house hotel, thanks to Caroline Hallam, who welcomes 'as if you were coming to stay for the weekend' and brings out a plate of puff pastry tartlets and a basket of freshly baked granary bread. Harry Hallam then single-handedly produces 'a virtuoso expression of modern British cooking'.

Sourcing is impeccable, taking in free-range French poultry, young Scottish roe deer, and wild fish: perhaps brill from Filey with pistou and tapénade, or a seared Scottish salmon fillet with an intensely citrus beurre blanc. Fresh herbs are used in profusion without swamping the flavour of other ingredients: for example, a scattering of parsley, basil and chives on seared Orkney scallops, which also came with red pepper and precisely blanched orange peel. Dishes are intricate and look attractive, yet the food is not overworked. Sliced loin of lamb with mushrooms, for example, was considered a 'simple' success, despite an artfully constructed accompanying pile of courgettes, aubergines and tomatoes, and another of finely shredded leeks, red onion and wild rice.

Balance is an important component of both dishes and meals. 'Colour, taste and texture – everything was right,' summed up an inspector, who ended with the hybrid but 'feather-light' caramel mousse brûlée, its sweet caramel flavour counterbalanced by three or four ripe raspberries and strawberries. Water is free, and coffee is refilled, but the cost can still be high, especially given a twelve-strong wine list with nothing under £20. Red and white house wines cost £4.50 a glass.

CHEF: Harry Hallam   PROPRIETORS: Harry and Caroline Hallam   OPEN: Tue to Sat 12.30 to 2, 7 to 9.30   CLOSED: 25 and 26 Dec, bank hols   MEALS: alc (main courses £22.50 to £27.50) SERVICE: not inc   CARDS: MasterCard, Visa   DETAILS: 10 seats. Private parties: 10 main room. Car park. Children's helpings. No children under 5. No smoking in dining room. Wheelchair access (not WC). No music   £5

GREAT MILTON Oxfordshire   map 2

▲ Le Manoir aux Quat' Saisons 🍷 ⍟

Church Road, Great Milton OX44 7PD
TEL: (01844) 278881   FAX: (01844) 278847
EMAIL: lemanoir@blanc.co.uk   COOKING 9
off A329, 1m from M40 junction 7   COST £48–£129

As building work is completed, the Manoir returns to the calming environment that Raymond Blanc originally envisaged. No visit is complete without a tour of the gardens, to watch vegetables grow, smell the herbs, or compare statues of birds with real ones. Eating takes place at generously spaced tables in the discreetly lit conservatory, or in the more conventional but brightly coloured dining room. Since last year there has been an increasing sense of confidence and reliability in the cooking, capped by the appointment of Gary Jones – the high-flying former head chef at Cliveden (see entry Taplow) – as the *Guide* went to press. Whether the style of cooking will alter as a result remains to be seen.

Although workmanship is typically applied unstintingly – for example, to a rabbit dish of dark brown shoulder and leg confit, surrounded by minuscule chops – the kitchen is 'unafraid to do some things simply', such as suckling pig in rosemary jus with plain steamed vegetables, or a large meaty veal chop, cooked pink, served with green beans, penne and wild mushrooms. Seafood dishes, meanwhile, have produced a starter of fat shelled langoustines, mixed with pasta and black truffle (luxuries are taken for granted in this kitchen), and a characteristic tripartite dish of red mullet, John Dory and scallop, served escabèche-style with marinated carrot and onion, unified by an 'unbeatable' herb and lime vinaigrette.

Offal is happily given a proper role, and treated as well as anywhere. Foie gras might feature in a terrine, and accurate slow cooking has produced a 'perfect example' of sticky oxtail – braised, boned and reassembled – in a well-reduced sauce, and pig's trotter filled with a moist eggy mix, partnered by tongue, kidney and sweetbread: 'a classic of its kind'. There has always been an element of whimsy, an artistic leg-pull, to some of the more visually stunning desserts, evidenced by a palette of sorbets and ice creams consisting of a trompe l'oeil artist's palette, looking like real wood but made from biscuit, with scoops of passion fruit, cassis, apple, vanilla and pistachio 'paint', and an edible sugar paintbrush with a dark handle and white bristles.

Prices are serious, of course (at least, £30 for a small portion of 'outstanding' lemon verbena risotto was considered so), but they do include service, a rare enough event to warrant favourable comment, and the set-price lunch is considered 'superb' value. 'Intelligent service' has raised itself a notch since last year, and M. Blanc's tours of the dining room are appreciated. The hefty wine list shows more pedigree and good breeding than a Crufts champion, and while you certainly won't be sold a pup, you won't be offered any real bargains either. These are serious wines – outstanding claret, wonderful Burgundy, superb super-Tuscans – at serious prices, but bottles under £30, even some under £20, can be found, with the south of France or South America being good places to begin the search.

CHEFS: Raymond Blanc and Gary Jones   PROPRIETOR: Raymond Blanc   OPEN: all week 12.15 to 2.45, 7.15 to 9.45   MEALS: alc (main courses £30 to £42). Set L Mon to Sat (exc bank hols) £32, Set L and D £72   SERVICE: not inc   CARDS: Amex, Delta, Diners, MasterCard, Switch, Visa   DETAILS: 110 seats. Private parties: 8 main room, 55 private room. Car park. Vegetarian meals. Children's helpings. No smoking in dining room. Wheelchair access (also WC). No music. Air-conditioned   ACCOMMODATION: 32 rooms, all with bath/shower. TV. Phone. B&B £230 to £550. Baby facilities (*The Which? Hotel Guide*)   £5

GREAT MISSENDEN Buckinghamshire   map 3

La Petite Auberge

107 High Street, Great Missenden HP16 0BB   COOKING 4
TEL: (01494) 865370   COST £34–£52

Pictures of the Eiffel Tower and other French landmarks confirm where La Petite Auberge is coming from. Occupying the long front room of a terraced house, it feels domestic in scale, and the fact that you can see into the kitchen 'adds to the atmosphere'. The Martels are 'a genuinely caring and friendly couple', he cooking to order, she keeping everyone happy in the interim. Choice of materials is interesting. On the one hand they include such luxuries as foie gras (in a terrine) and caviare (served with freshwater prawns wrapped in cabbage leaves), and on the other roe deer, guinea fowl, calf's liver, and grey-legged partridge with chestnuts, all welcome additions to the more traditional British diet of chicken, pork, beef and lamb. 'A good-value dinner' was the conclusion of one who ate asparagus with herb sauce, scallops with green mustard sauce, and lemon tart. There are no house wines on the short French list, but prices start at £10.50 for Muscadet, £13.20 for Brouilly.

CHEF: Hubert Martel   PROPRIETORS: Mr and Mrs Hubert Martel   OPEN: Mon to Sat D only 7.30 to 10   CLOSED: 2 weeks Christmas, 2 weeks Easter, bank hols   MEALS: alc (main courses £14.50 to £17)   SERVICE: not inc   CARDS: MasterCard, Visa   DETAILS: 30 seats. Private parties: 30 main room. Wheelchair access (also WC). No music

---

GREAT YELDHAM Essex   map 3

White Hart 🍷 ✳ £

Poole Street, Great Yeldham CO9 4HJ
TEL: (01787) 237250   FAX: (01787) 238044
on A604, between Haverhill and Halstead,   COOKING 4
6m NW of Halstead   COST £20–£51

A 500-year-old building in a large garden, with stone-flagged terrace, large bar, oak-panelled dining room and lots of beams is the setting for some attractive-sounding modern food. Members of the Huntsbridge group, of which this is one (see also Three Horseshoes, Madingley, and Pheasant Inn, Keyston), are largely autonomous chef-run operations, though all share a policy of informal eating from a free-ranging carte, here taking in tiger prawn and noodle soup, red pepper and mozzarella tart, and heftier rack of lamb with potato and aubergine moussaka. Fish is a strong suit. At its best this is an 'extremely capable kitchen', but performance is uneven, disappointing some reporters, while providing others with 'comforting' lambs' liver with cabbage, mash and onion gravy, and 'inspiring' chickpea tart with potato curry. Finish, perhaps, with one of the many ice creams, or plum and almond tart.

Another feature shared by Huntsbridge members is an appealing range of around a hundred wines skilfully put together by Master of Wine John Hoskins and helpfully presented by style. Good drinking can be had at all price levels (house wines start at £9.75 a bottle, £1.85 a glass), but diners looking for a treat should note that mark-ups become lower as the wines get more expensive.

CHEF: Roger Jones   PROPRIETOR: Huntsbridge Ltd   OPEN: all week 12 to 2, 6.30 to 9.30 (7 to 9 Sun)   CLOSED: D 25 and 26 Dec, D 1 Jan   MEALS: alc (main courses £5 to £16.50). Set L £8.50 (2 courses) to £12.25   SERVICE: not inc, card slips closed   CARDS: Amex, Delta, Diners, MasterCard, Switch, Visa   DETAILS: 120 seats. 40 seats outside. Private parties: 80 main room, 30 private room. Car park. Vegetarian meals. Children's helpings. No smoking in dining room. Wheelchair access (not WC). Occasional music

---

If you have access to the Internet, you can find The Good Food Guide *online at the* Which? *Online web site (http://www.which.net).*

HAMBLETON

HALIFAX West Yorkshire   map 9

Design House 🍴

Dean Clough Mills, Halifax HX3 5AX   COOKING 3
TEL: (01422) 383242 FAX: (01422) 322732   COST £23–£45

While the rest of this Victorian carpet mill has been given over to offices, one ground-floor corner contains a café, delicatessen and restaurant, under new ownership since the last edition of the *Guide*. The restaurant majors on functionality, with pale-coloured walls, spotlights and blue Formica table tops. Stark this may be, but it provides a fitting contrast to the food. Michael Ricci, who has taken over from his previous boss David Watson, continues in similar vein, with well-constructed and well-executed dishes delivered, on the whole, with aplomb. Start perhaps with richly flavoured asparagus and truffle risotto in May, or 'superb' squid with chilli dressing and rocket. Main courses have included a trio of fish (lemon sole, red snapper and tuna) all perfectly cooked, and served on an aubergine and caviare cake with a delicate red wine jus. Alternatives might be braised ham hock with star anise, or saddle of lamb with Anna potatoes and spinach. For dessert, poached pear comes with Muscat pannacotta, and a jug of custard arrives with a large portion of caramelised apple crumble. Service is friendly and willing, and the wine list, mostly under £20, is globally sourced with a good selection of half-bottles. House wines are £9.50.

CHEF: Michael Ricci PROPRIETOR: Christian Rooney OPEN: Mon to Fri L 12 to 2, Tue to Sat D 6.30 to 10 CLOSED: 25 Dec, 1 Jan MEALS: alc (main courses £9 to £15). Set L £10.95 (2 courses) to £14.95, Set D Tue to Thur £10.95 (2 courses) to £14.95 SERVICE: not inc CARDS: Amex, Delta, MasterCard, Switch, Visa DETAILS: 70 seats. 12 seats outside. Private parties: 70 main room. Vegetarian meals. Music. Air-conditioned

---

HAMBLETON Rutland   map 6

▲ *Hambleton Hall* 🍴 ✿

Hambleton LE15 8TH
TEL: (01572) 756991 FAX: (01572) 724721
EMAIL: hotel@hambletonhall.com   COOKING 8
off A606, 3m SE of Oakham   COST £31–£101

With views over its well-maintained gardens towards Rutland Water (the village sits on a peninsula jutting into the lake), this is about as tranquil a setting as one could wish for: enjoy it with a drink on the terrace in fine weather. The house is a welcoming place with grand flower arrangements, comfortable furnishings, and courteous international staff who engender a mood of 'relaxed conviviality'. All this inspires confidence, a feeling bolstered by a bountiful menu overflowing with gratifying dishes, and confirmed by the first arrivals: tiny but 'exciting' morsels with drinks, then perhaps a coffee cup of clear, chilled 'essence of tomato', alongside first-rate bread.

The profusion of dishes, on a carte that is changed twice a year, is awash with intricate gestures, including pasta accompaniments to main courses, such as foie gras ravioli with pigeon pot-au-feu, or mushroom tortellini with roast veal sweetbreads. But the food does not lose sight of its purpose, and is equally capable of offering simply prepared pan-fried foie gras on a bed of marinated aubergine, or crabmeat quenelles with salad. Materials veer towards prime species and cuts – lobster and turbot, fillet of beef, loins of venison, rabbit, hare and lamb – and, although luxuries abound, they don't actually take over.

Prices may seem high but most reporters do not mind paying for quality and consistency. 'We couldn't have done better for balance or for sheer pleasure,' reckoned one couple who opted for the no-choice set menu and ate earthy mushroom ravioli; roast rump of lamb with a tian of Mediterranean vegetables in an 'intense lamb-y sauce'; and caramelised lemon tart with fresh raspberries. Other appealing desserts have included a tart of blackberry and wafer-thin slices of apple on filo pastry with vanilla ice cream: 'I am still trying to get this right in my own kitchen.'

The food 'really does deserve fine wine,' opined one reporter, and there are certainly many to choose from on the massive list. Classical French regions are given the full treatment, while elsewhere the Swiss and Californian collections stand out for interest and quality, as do dessert wines. Thirty 'wines of the moment', set in price bands from around £16 and upwards, simplify selection; otherwise the 'helpful and knowledgeable' wine waiter will oblige.

CHEF: Aaron Patterson   PROPRIETORS: Tim and Stefa Hart   OPEN: all week 12 to 1.30, 7 to 9.30   MEALS: alc (main courses £20 to £35). Set L Mon to Fri £19.50, Set D £35   SERVICE: net prices, card slips closed   CARDS: Delta, Diners, MasterCard, Switch, Visa   DETAILS: 60 seats. Private parties: 40 main room, 14 and 20 private rooms. Car park. Vegetarian meals. Children's helpings. No babies in dining room. No smoking in dining room. Wheelchair access (also WC). No music   ACCOMMODATION: 15 rooms, all with bath/shower. TV. Phone. B&B £125 to £295. Rooms for disabled. Baby facilities. Swimming pool (*The Which? Hotel Guide*)

HAMPTON HILL   Greater London   map 3

Monsieur Max

133 High Street, Hampton Hill TW12 1NJ
TEL/FAX: (0181) 979 5546, changing to   COOKING 6
(020) 8979 5546   COST £27–£58

Never mind the anonymous suburban street. Once inside, this is more like a Lyonnais brasserie, with bare wooden floors and art deco mirrors, although further planned refurbishment is intended to create a more 'cosseting' atmosphere, and add a new kitchen. In all this the robust, substantial French bourgeois cooking style remains. Stuffed breast of Bresse chicken comes in a rich vin jaune sauce with morels, dauphinoise and two kinds of cabbage, for example, while a 'benchmark' dish of 'moist, flavourful' Burgundian snails sharing a puff pastry pithiviers with pancetta, vegetables and 'lots of garlic' was the most accomplished dish at an inspection meal.

Max Renzland has many fans, most of whom are willing to forgive a few inconsistencies and technical shortcomings, or the enthusiasm that sometimes gets the better of sauces, because of the sheer generosity of the cooking. The carte lists around twenty savoury dishes, and portions can be large, incorporating several diverse elements, including pasta: loin of Anjou rabbit with sweetbread, black pudding, and pesto-stuffed cannelloni is a dish 'packed with flavours'. Good materials provide a firm foundation, from accurately timed sea bass to 'sweet, tender' roast squab pigeon, cheeses are kept in good condition, and rice pudding with an infusion of cognac caramel is a popularly endorsed dessert. Service is good-natured, courteous and plentiful, and prices are considered reasonable, although a few supplements lie in wait. Wine prices, however, leave little room for manoeuvre under £20, although there are some very classy bottles on the improved list. House wine is £9.50.

CHEFS: Max Renzland, Alex Bentley and Morgan Meunier   PROPRIETOR: Max Renzland   OPEN: Sun to Fri L 12 to 2.30, all week D 7 to 10.30   CLOSED: 24 Dec to 2 Jan   MEALS: Set L Mon to Fri £13 (2 courses) to £17, Set L Sun £23.50, Set D £23.50   SERVICE: 12.5% (optional), card slips closed   CARDS: Amex, Delta, Diners, MasterCard, Switch, Visa   DETAILS: 75 seats. Private parties: 8 main room. Vegetarian meals. Children's helpings. No children under 8. No cigars/pipes in dining room. Wheelchair access (not WC). No music. Air-conditioned (£5)

HAROME North Yorkshire   map 9

Star Inn 🍴✷

Harome YO6 5JE
TEL: (01439) 770397   FAX: (01439) 771833   COOKING 4
off A170, 3m SE of Helmsley   COST £22–£46

'This is a pub that really isn't,' as one reader commented, for though the building is traditional, complete with thatch, wonky walls, beams and old-fashioned heavy furniture, the food stretches far beyond the usual pub standard. Chef/proprietor Andrew Pern shops locally where he can, and brings precision, deftness and style to his cooking while remaining true to Yorkshire roots – portions are generous – and Jacquie Pern handles front-of-house with warmth and efficiency. Reporters have enjoyed lobster risotto 'with huge chunks of lobster', and 'moist, flaky, sweet-tasting' fillet of turbot on buttery mash and spinach, served with a white wine sauce laced with 'just the right amount' of cream. Praise has also been lavished on crab salad – 'I could taste the sea' – which might come with Bloody Mary dressing. 'Lovely lemony' lemon tart gets high marks, banana bread-and-butter pudding too; or, for ditherers, there is the 'miniature selection' of desserts. Vegetarians have their own short menu, offering perhaps plum tomato tarte Tatin with basil salad, and lunchtime sandwiches might include seared tuna niçoise. Black Sheep Ale has been recommended, while the sixty-odd-bottle wine list roams the world, and is helpfully grouped by suitability for different types of food. House wine is £11.

CHEF: Andrew Pern   PROPRIETORS: Andrew and Jacquie Pern   OPEN: Tue to Sat 11.45 to 2, 6.45 to 9.30, Sun 12 to 6   CLOSED: 1 week Nov, 25 Dec, 2 weeks Jan   MEALS: alc (main courses £7 to £15)   SERVICE: not inc, card slips closed   CARDS: Amex, Delta, MasterCard, Switch, Visa   DETAILS: 60 seats. 30 seats outside. Private parties: 35 main room, 10 private room. Car park. Vegetarian meals. Children's helpings. No smoking in 1 dining room. Occasional music

---

'It has to be said that service was erratic. When our starters arrived they were described as "chickpeas and, er, the other stuff", while coffee was unconventionally served before dessert.' (On eating in London)

HARROGATE   North Yorkshire   map 8

Drum and Monkey £

5 Montpellier Gardens, Harrogate HG1 2TF	COOKING 4
TEL: (01423) 502650 FAX: (01423) 522469	COST £18–£40

This long-established seafood restaurant is such an institution that some people arrive up to an hour before the doors open for lunch in order to guarantee a place in the downstairs bar; alternatively, book well ahead for the slightly quieter upstairs dining room. The draw is top-quality ingredients, made into simple dishes prepared with the confidence of many years' experience: a mix of mussels, white fish and prawns in a savoury roulade, with a light and well-balanced sweet-and-sour dressing, for example, or 'perfectly cooked' sea trout with asparagus hollandaise.

Garlic butter must be made by the bucket load, and is used to anoint anything from big Mediterranean prawns (choose shell-on or -off) to lobster (not always A1) or lemon sole fillet. Desserts are hardly the point, though ice cream might be 'just the ticket'. 'Coffee is excellent and plentiful. For £1.50 you could carry on being topped up if it weren't for the fact that the whole of Harrogate is queuing up for your table.' Service is orderly, and as for value, 'I don't know how they do it for the price.' Wines, mostly young and white, are also fairly priced, starting with house Duboeuf at £7.85.

CHEFS: Keith Penny and Tina Nuttall   PROPRIETOR: William Fuller   OPEN: Mon to Sat 12 to 2.30, 6.30 to 10.15   CLOSED: 24 Dec D to 2 Jan   MEALS: alc (main courses £5 to £14.50)   SERVICE: not inc   CARDS: Delta, MasterCard, Switch, Visa   DETAILS: 50 seats. Private parties: 8 main room. Children's helpings. No music

---

HARWICH   Essex   map 6

▲ The Pier at Harwich ▼

The Quay, Harwich CO12 3HH	COOKING 2
TEL: (01255) 241212 FAX: (01255) 551922	COST £28–£68

This year the more straightforward, family-oriented Ha'penny Pier has scored better for both food and 'efficient and friendly service' than the first-floor dining room with its ambitious menu of scallops in balsamic vinegar, monkfish with ratatouille, and halibut Cordon Rouge, all of which proved disappointing for one party. The Ha'penny is a simply but cheerfully decorated room with bright fishy murals, paper tablecloths and a blackboard listing daily variations to the printed menu. One visitor enjoyed a half-pint glass-tankard of 'the freshest prawns' with home-made mayonnaise, and 'very fresh' haddock in crisp batter, served with a mountain of thick-cut, ungreasy chips, tartare sauce and malt vinegar. Whether you dine upstairs or down you will be presented with a seafood-friendly wine list where good-value drinking at all levels reveals the hand of local merchants Lay & Wheeler. Pier Hotel partner Richard Wheeler highlights the Lay & Wheeler Champagne (£28.50 a bottle) as 'a delicious aperitif or a wonderful accompaniment to fish dishes,' but then, he would say that, wouldn't he? House wines begin at £8.95.

CHEF: Chris Oakley   PROPRIETOR: Mr G. Milsom   OPEN: all week 12 to 2, 6 to 9.30   CLOSED: D 25 Dec   MEALS: alc Mon to Sat L, all week D (main courses £8.50 to £30). Set L Mon to Sat £17.50, Set L Sun £15 (2 courses) to £16.50, Set D £19.50   SERVICE: 10%, card slips closed CARDS: Amex, Delta, Diners, MasterCard, Switch, Visa   DETAILS: 80 seats. Private parties: 100 main room, 40 private room. Car park. Vegetarian meals. Children's helpings. No cigars/pipes in dining room. Wheelchair access (not WC). Music   ACCOMMODATION: 6 rooms, all with bath/shower. TV. Phone. B&B £53 to £85. Baby facilities (*The Which? Hotel Guide*)

HASTINGS   East Sussex   map 3

Röser's ▮

64 Eversfield Place, St Leonards on Sea,
Hastings TN37 6DB   COOKING 7
TEL/FAX: (01424) 712218   COST £28–£66

You could easily drive past here without knowing it was a restaurant, as an inspector did. Twice. Only a garish sign and a faintly curved bow window with a few bottle-glass panes give it away. Inside, two rows of partly curtained cubicles are hardly the last word in restaurant design, but nobody comes here for the décor. It is the simple and direct appeal of Gerald Röser's honest cooking that is the draw. His core repertoire may seem a little static – pike soufflé with a smoked salmon and dill sauce, and port-marinated wild boar ham are among the regulars – but the carte is fleshed out by more frequently changing set-price meals, along with specials of foie gras salad with avocado and smoked salmon, or local red mullet with artichoke, tomato and olives.

Technical skills are not in question, timing is impeccable, and flavours are intense: for example, a generous chargrilled beef tournedos 'exceptional in taste and texture', sitting on 'unsurpassed' rösti, with a pool of concentrated Madeira and stock sauce scattered with morels. Dishes are characterised by 'a total lack of anything superfluous', and as such remain an object lesson to many chefs. The food may not be formally arranged, but dishes are 'sparely presented' and appeal to the senses: a heap of small scallops, for example, corals and all, piled in the centre of a large plate, deriving intrinsic visual impact from asparagus tips, diced tomato, and a creamy, deeply flavoured saffron sauce.

Caramelised lime cream with bitter orange sauce remains triumphant among desserts, but there may also be chocolate mousse with coffee cream sauce, or rhubarb and ginger terrine served with blobs of translucent coulis and a creamy vanilla sauce. Among first-rate extras, bread stands out, and service by Jenny Röser could not be bettered. A hefty wine list gives Burgundy and Bordeaux the full treatment before turning its attention to other major regions and countries. Quality is high throughout, whether in the upper echelons or around the £20 mark. A greater choice of wines by the glass would be appreciated by some, but that is the only quibble. French house wines start at £11.50.

CHEF: Gerald Röser   PROPRIETORS: Gerald and Jenny Röser   OPEN: Tue to Fri L 12 to 2, Tue to Sat D 7 to 10   CLOSED: first 2 weeks Jan, last 2 weeks June   MEALS: alc (main courses £16 to £25). Set L £19.95, Set D Tue to Fri £22.95   SERVICE: net prices, card slips closed   CARDS: Amex, Delta, Diners, MasterCard, Switch, Visa   DETAILS: 30 seats. Private parties: 16 main room, 30 private room. Vegetarian meals. No music   (£5)

HAWORTH West Yorkshire	map 8

▲ *Weavers* ✦ £

13–17 West Lane, Haworth BD22 8DU	COOKING 3
TEL: (01535) 643822 FAX: (01535) 644832	COST £22–£45

It may back on to the Brontë Parsonage Museum, but Weavers is much more than a tourist restaurant, attracting locals as well as visitors with 'consistently high-standard' food. The 'warm and inviting' first-floor dining room – once part of a barn attached to weavers' cottages – is decorated in soft ochre colours, with bobbins hanging from the windows. Downstairs, a bar has relaxing old tub chairs and sofas. The Rushworths ensure their cooking keeps up with food trends without compromising the homely approach. An inspector praised the excellent ingredients (many locally sourced) in a meal that began with a light aubergine soufflé with roasted vegetable salad and 'dramatic' lemon oil dressing, and continued with seared fillet of sea bass served with herbed potato cake and a red wine and shallot gravy. Roast confit of duck, and beef fillet with a wild mushroom sauce also receive acclaim. A light brown-bread ice cream with apricot sauce makes a fine finale, while well-paced service adds to the appeal. Wines, too, attract praise; the good-value list is arranged by style and is well balanced between Old and New World. House wine is £9.95.

CHEFS/PROPRIETORS: Colin and Jane Rushworth   OPEN: Tue to Sat D only 6.30 to 9   CLOSED: 2 weeks Christmas, 1 week late June   MEALS: alc (main courses £7.50 to £16.50). Set D Tue to Fri 6.30 to 7.30 £10.95 (2 courses) to £13.50   SERVICE: not inc, card slips closed   CARDS: Amex, Delta, Diners, MasterCard, Switch, Visa   DETAILS: 62 seats. Private parties: 45 main room, 16 private room. Vegetarian meals. Children's helpings. No smoking in dining room. Music. Air-conditioned   ACCOMMODATION: 3 rooms, all with bath/shower. TV. Phone. B&B £50 to £75 (*The Which? Hotel Guide*) (£5)

HAYDON BRIDGE Northumberland	map 10

General Havelock Inn ✦

Ratcliffe Road, Haydon Bridge NE47 6ER	
TEL: (01434) 684376	COOKING 1
on A69, 100yds from junction with B6319	COST £20–£38

Angela Clyde's handwritten menus promise simple, appetising and good-value dishes. You can eat in either the bar of this friendly, dark green pub or the restaurant, a lofty stone room overlooking the river, comfortable with cushions, long pink banquettes, and flowery curtains and chair seats. Soup is sure to feature, and almost certainly a terrine – chicken, gammon and duck liver, say – or lightly devilled prawns or crab. Pork fillet and chicken breast in some guise usually find their way on to the menu, as does cod, baked simply with lemon and parsley, or jazzed up with mozzarella, mushrooms and prawns. Poached pear with butterscotch sauce, and raspberry meringue get singled out among puddings. The beer is Tetley Bitter, the wines a score or so of modestly priced bottles starting at £9.90.

CHEF: Angela Clyde   PROPRIETORS: Ian and Angela Clyde   OPEN: Wed to Sun L 12 to 1.15, Wed to Sat D 7 to 8.45   MEALS: alc Wed to Sat L (main courses £6 to £6.50). Set L Sun £12.25, Set D £19.50   SERVICE: not inc   CARDS: none   DETAILS: 28 seats. 8 seats outside. Private parties: 28 main room. Children's helpings. No smoking in dining room. Wheelchair access (also WC). Occasional music

---

HAYWARDS HEATH   West Sussex   map 3

Jeremy's at Borde Hill ⚞✳

Balcombe Road, Haywards Heath RH16 1XP
TEL: (01444) 441102   FAX: (01444) 417928   COOKING 5
EMAIL: jeremys.bordehill@btinternet.com   COST £28–£48

The entrance to Borde Hill Gardens is just out of Haywards Heath on the Balcombe road, where the single-storey restaurant leads off a small courtyard into a bright world of Mediterranean colours – purple bar, yellow, ochre and terracotta dining room – with cooking to match. Borde Hill's food may be in generally more European mould than the Crabtree's (see entry, Lower Beeding), but it is still gently inventive and appealing, with no sense of either straitjacket or trial and error. It goes in for starters of duck liver pâté with rhubarb relish, freshly made Parmesan and ratatouille tart, and lightly cooked red bream fillet with a well-judged lemon grass and coconut vinaigrette.

Main courses are served in deep bowls, and although results may be a bit 'unfocused', they have an appealing heart-on-sleeve air about them: 'really enjoyable food that is not tarted up for show'. Pink calf's liver has come with rashers of smoky, salty bacon, sweet potato and caramelised red onions, while two separate kinds of Mediterranean vegetables have accompanied flavourful grilled chump of lamb, an occasional flash of coriander or hint of rosemary enlivening the whole dish. Supplies include organic vegetables from nearby villages, and local cheeses, while desserts run to poached pear with ginger ice cream, and accomplished crème brûlée. Service is clued up, and wines are a worldly bunch, offering interest and variety at pocket-friendly prices, starting in Italy at £10.50.

CHEF: Jeremy Ashpool   PROPRIETORS: Jeremy and Vera Ashpool   OPEN: Tue to Sun L 11.30 to 2.30, Tue to Sat D 7.30 to 10.30   CLOSED: 25 Dec and D on 26 Dec and 1 Jan   MEALS: alc (main courses £11 to £16.50). Set L Tue to Sat £13.50 (2 courses) to £17.50, Set L Sun £15.50 (2 courses) to £19.50, Set D £15 (2 courses) to £19.50   SERVICE: 10%, card slips closed   CARDS: Amex, Delta, Diners, MasterCard, Switch, Visa   DETAILS: 45 seats. 25 seats outside. Private parties: 50 main room. Car park. Vegetarian meals. Children's helpings. No smoking in dining room. Wheelchair access (not WC). Occasional music   (£5)

⚞✳ *indicates that smoking is either banned altogether or that a dining-room is maintained for non-smokers. The symbol does not apply to restaurants that simply have no-smoking areas.*

Occasional music *in the details at the end of an entry means live or recorded music is played in the dining room only rarely or for special events.* No music *means it is never played.*

Sundial ⁵⨯

| Gardner Street, Herstmonceux BN27 4LA | COOKING 4 |
| TEL: (01323) 832217 | COST £32–£76 |

You have to admire the single-minded confidence of Giuseppe and Laure Bertoli. Proprietors of the Sundial for more than three decades, this charming couple have never faltered in their dedication to a style of cooking that could be described as French bourgeois. Monsieur pops in and out of the kitchen to negotiate an ingredient substitution, or minister to the cardiac-conscious (although vegetarian meals are available only with notice), while Madame presides over the old-fashioned dining room, with its harvest-festival-style central display table and gilt-framed landscapes. The restaurant's culinary reputation still rests on great fresh fish, typically fillets of Dover sole rolled with salmon and served with lobster sauce, or feuilleté of lobster, crab and prawns, but there are excellent meat dishes too. A pair of 'just seared' ostrich fillets marinated in port, each wearing a flattened mushroom cap, have arrived on salty brown rösti in a tomatoey sauce. Puddings are the weak link, but may include crème brûlée, French apple tart, and chocolate mousse. The wine list is mainly a tour de France, picking up some classic bottles along the way. House vin de pays is £14.25.

CHEF: G. Bertoli PROPRIETORS: Mr G. and Mrs L. Bertoli OPEN: Tue to Sun L 12.30 to 2 (2.30 Sun), Tue to Sat D 7 to 9.30 (10 Sat) CLOSED: Christmas to 20 Jan, 9 Aug to early Sept MEALS: alc (main courses £17.50 to £27.50). Set L £15.50 (2 courses) to £19.50, Set D £27.50 to £39.50 (min 2) SERVICE: 10%, card slips closed CARDS: Amex, Delta, Diners, MasterCard, Switch, Visa DETAILS: 50 seats. 20 seats outside. Private parties: 60 main room, 23 private room. Car park. Children's helpings. No smoking in dining room. Wheelchair access (not WC). Music £5

Angel Inn ▮ ⁵⨯

Hetton BD23 6LT	
TEL: (01756) 730263 FAX: (01756) 730363	COOKING 6
off B6265, 5m N of Skipton	COST £28–£46

Anybody aiming to eat in the bar of this old stone pub should remember to turn up on time: one Sunday luncher observed the doors open 'as the pips went on the car radio', followed by a rush 'reminiscent of the January sales'. How the Angel achieves consistency in the face of such a busy operation (the dining room is a little calmer) is a source of wonder to reporters. The food's 'comfort' rating runs high throughout – smoked cod with poached egg, black pudding, grain mustard sauce and mash, for example – and is often given a racy southern European twist, in the form of braised salt beef brisket with zampone and herb dumplings, or confit shoulder of Yorkshire lamb with pesto and olive mash.

 Denis Watkins has found one solution to meat supplies which could be a blueprint for the future. Lothersdale lamb, raised to the Angel's specifications, comes direct from the farm (June to February), enabling the kitchen to use the whole carcass without waste, and allowing both restaurant and farmer to benefit financially. Seafood recommendations, meanwhile, range from 'jolly good fish soup with all the accoutrements' to a huge slab of roast salmon (portions are generous) with horseradish mash. A 'major innovation' is that vegetables are now served on the plate. Finish, perhaps, with baked queen of puddings, or prune and armagnac rice condé, served by 'helpful and friendly young staff'.

The wine list is such good value that one reporter was tempted to 'take up residence for a week and work [his] way through it', although with around 170 bottles to try, we'd recommend a longer stay. 'How many pubs can produce Riedel glasses to match the wine?' mused another satisfied customer, and certainly, the twenty-two wines by the glass (from £1.95) present a more realistic seven-day challenge. Burgundy lovers, in particular, will think they have died and gone to heaven.

CHEFS: Denis Watkins, John Topham and Bruce Elsworth   PROPRIETORS: Denis and Juliet Watkins, and John Topham   OPEN: restaurant Sun L 12 to 2, Mon to Sat D 6 to 9.30; bar 12 to 2.15 (2.30 Sun), 6 to 10 (9 Sun)   CLOSED: 1 Jan, 2 weeks mid-Jan   MEALS: Set L £19.75, Set D before 7pm £16.50, Set D £29.95   SERVICE: not inc, card slips closed   CARDS: Amex, MasterCard, Switch, Visa   DETAILS: 170 seats. 60 seats outside. Private parties: 40 main room. Car park. Vegetarian meals. Children's helpings Sun L. No smoking in 1 dining room. Wheelchair access (not WC). No music. Air-conditioned   £5

HEXHAM Northumberland   map 10

▲ *Hexham Royal Hotel* ✳ £   NEW ENTRY

Priestpopple, Hexham NE46 1PQ
TEL: (01434) 602270   FAX: (01434) 604084   COOKING 2
EMAIL: service@hexham-royal-hotel.co.uk   COST £15–£36

This Georgian coaching-inn, opposite the bus station, has been gentrified both in purpose and name (it was once called the Low Grey Bull). A golden dome is the most striking external feature, but the Pellys, owners since 1998, have made a trim job of the interior. The Priestpopple Brasserie occupies the ground floor, while a more formal restaurant with swagged curtains and draped dining chairs is one floor up. Philip Mason reflects a similar diversity in his menus. Three fried quails' eggs adorn a whole quail on a bed of curly endive dressed with walnut oil and sherry vinegar; coarsely chunky salmon fish cakes come with a correctly made parsley sauce; and pheasant sausages are served on wild garlic and herb risotto with red wine sauce. This is straightforward cooking that knows its constituency, offering roast beef with Yorkshire pudding on Sundays, and treacle tart or meringues with raspberries and cream to finish. Service could do with a prod, but it is all exemplary value, and a selection from the jumbled-up wine list won't weigh too heavily on the bill either. Prices start at a bargain £7.50.

CHEF: Philip Mason   PROPRIETOR: Anthony Pelly   OPEN: Tue to Sat 12 to 2.30, 5.30 to 9.30 CLOSED: 25 Dec   MEALS: alc (main courses £7 to £12.50). Set L £6.99 (2 courses) to £8.99, Set D before 7.30 £7.99 (2 courses) to £9.99. Bar meals available all week   SERVICE: not inc, card slips closed   CARDS: Amex, Delta, MasterCard, Switch, Visa   DETAILS: 70 seats. Private parties: 100 main room, 40 and 100 private rooms. Car park. Vegetarian meals. Children's helpings. No smoking in 1 dining room. Wheelchair access (not WC). Music   ACCOMMODATION: 10 rooms, all with bath/shower. TV. Phone. B&B £35 to £60   £5

HINDON Wiltshire	map 2

▲ *Grosvenor Arms* ⁵⋇

Hindon SP3 6DJ	COOKING 4
TEL: (01747) 820696 FAX: (01747) 820869	COST £27–£44

A Georgian inn with impressive cooking in stylish surroundings, Grosvenor Arms still functions as a pub, but with a dining room that offers a 'theatre-style' view into the glass-fronted kitchen. Here Paul Suter's 'skill in timing, in sauce making, and in sourcing of materials' is applied to a slew of modern dishes, some of which – fish cakes with tomato sauce, or grilled goats'-cheese salad – are offered in either 'adequate' or 'ample' portions. Prime cuts of meat and fish are the norm, including rack of lamb, turbot fillet and saddle of local rabbit, all put to good use by a kitchen that achieves 'spot-on balance of flavours'. Among desserts, caramelised chocolate and honey brûlée is perhaps the most individual. Manager Rachel Hanlon is a 'charming, natural hostess'. Wines from France dominate a pro-European list (even the half-bottles are all French), although Australia brings its special brand of charm to the short New World selection. Six house wines are all £9.95 a bottle, £2.50 a glass.

CHEF: Paul Suter   PROPRIETOR: West Country Village Inns   OPEN: all week 12 to 2, 7 to 9 (9.30 Sat)   MEALS: alc (main courses £9 to £13.50). Bar menu Mon to Sat L, Mon to Fri D   SERVICE: not inc   CARDS: Delta, MasterCard, Switch, Visa   DETAILS: 60 seats. 40 seats outside. Private parties: 40 main room. Car park. Vegetarian meals. Children's helpings. No children under 5. No smoking in dining room. No music   ACCOMMODATION: 7 rooms, all with bath/shower. TV. Phone. B&B £45 to £85 (*The Which? Hotel Guide*) (£5)

HINTON CHARTERHOUSE Bath & N.E. Somerset	map 2

▲ *Homewood Park* ⁵⋇

Hinton Charterhouse BA3 6BB	
TEL: (01225) 723731 FAX: (01225) 723820	COOKING 7
off A36, 6m SE of Bath	COST £35–£82

A long curving drive leads to this large, attractive, Georgian stone house, where bright rooms look out over well-kept gardens and lawns. It is peaceful, elegant, 'genteel, but not stuffy', and puts on an impressive display of culinary and waiting skills: experienced, confident service is immaculate; 'we wanted for nothing'. Lunch looks appealing, but the seasonally changing evening carte is where the kitchen's energy seems to be concentrated. We can take for granted freshness, accurate timing, technical accomplishment (in 'filigree-thin' spinach ravioli, for instance) and luxurious concentrated sauces. This is powerful cooking, but there is also a deftness about it that prevents it coming across as heavy, even in a dish of ruby-red roast squab pigeon, 'fabulously rich and tender, almost like liver', with a complement of soft celeriac cream and reduced port sauce.

Dishes are presented imaginatively and artistically, but despite trails of nuts and specks of berry colour, this is not so much garnish as the meal itself that has been thoughtfully arranged on the plate, as in a 'visually striking' column of boneless oxtail meat, cut into slices and arranged in a spiral, accompanied by cone-shaped roast parsnips and other vegetables. First courses may sometimes skirt the acceptable limits of complexity, but vegetables are lightly and evenly cooked and served fairly plain, and desserts have impressed: for example, a fluffy chocolate soufflé with a blob of rich-tasting vanilla ice cream ('more grown-up than it sounds'), and a cone of dark chocolate filled with thick, fruity raspberry purée, with a dark chocolate sorbet to the side. Other than a few classics, the predominantly European wine list appears to delight in lesser-known producers, but country-house prices narrow the options for ordinary drinkers. House French is £16.

CHEF: Andrew Hamer   PROPRIETOR: A. Moxon   OPEN: all week 12 to 2, 7 to 9.30   MEALS: alc (main courses £18 to £26). Set L £19.50 to £22.50   SERVICE: not inc   CARDS: Amex, Diners, MasterCard, Switch, Visa   DETAILS: 50 seats. 20 seats outside. Private parties: 80 main room. Car park. Children's helpings. No smoking in dining room. Wheelchair access (also WC). No music   ACCOMMODATION: 19 rooms, all with bath/shower. TV. Phone. B&B £109 to £249. Rooms for disabled. Baby facilities. Swimming pool (*The Which? Hotel Guide*)

HOLT Norfolk   map 6

Yetman's ♥ ✖

37 Norwich Road, Holt NR25 6SA   COOKING 4
TEL: (01263) 713320   COST £41–£56

These two converted cottages – bright yellow outside, a 'restful avocado' in the tiny cocooning lounge, pale primrose in the dining room – have been the Yetmans' preserve for a dozen years. The set-up is informal, and Peter Yetman does a good impression of being laid back, for example bringing 'floaty things' (croûtons spread with rouille) to add to a deeply fishy soup. The daily-changing menu offers an appealing range of dishes, from four chargrilled skewered king prawns with red chilli jam, via wild mushroom risotto (a 'sad disappointment' at inspection), to an accurately poached egg and good ham on fine brioche with excellent hollandaise: 'a comforting dish well rendered.'

Materials show up well – untrimmed noisettes 'tasting properly of lamb' – and seafood has come in for praise, from three sizeable crab cakes served with red pepper mayonnaise, to a 'fresh and perfectly timed' tail piece of cod on a bed of sweet potato mash. Among the fruits used in desserts might be pear (with mincemeat in strudel pastry) and quince, perhaps toasted with apple in a pancake, or roasted and served chilled in maple syrup. Peter's enthusiasm for wine leaps off the pages of his favourably priced list as it tours the New World before dropping into Italy, France and Spain. Wines by the glass change regularly, but the Yetmans' allegiance to Sauvignon Blanc is a constant; try the 1998 Seresin Marlborough version for £17.95.

CHEF: Alison Yetman   PROPRIETORS: Alison and Peter Yetman   OPEN: Sun L 12.30 to 2, Wed to Sun D and Mon D in summer and bank hols 7.30 to 9.30   CLOSED: 25, 26 and 31 Dec   MEALS: Set L and D £23.75 (2 courses) to £32.50   SERVICE: not inc   CARDS: Amex, Delta, MasterCard, Switch, Visa   DETAILS: 30 seats. Private parties: 20 main room, 10 and 20 private rooms. Vegetarian meals. No smoking in dining room. No music

HONLEY West Yorkshire map 8

Mustard and Punch

6 Westgate, Honley HD7 2AA COOKING **4**
TEL: (01484) 662066 COST £26–£41

At Dorota Pencak's and Anna Young's individual upstairs-downstairs bistro the mustard jars and all sorts of *Punch* paraphernalia – cartoons, hats – were inherited from a previous incumbent and have become something of an institution. The owners describe their food as 'European with Asiatic influences', and Christopher Dunn is clearly thoroughly at home with the style, producing, for instance, a warm salad of duck livers with celeriac rémoulade and redcurrant dressing; other appealing starters might be crispy king prawn won tons with mango and coriander salsa, and smoked sea trout on blinis. One diner's grilled fillet of beef with roasted root vegetables was accompanied by an intense mushroom croustade, while gâteau of roasted provençale vegetables with goats' cheese and a Moroccan dressing sounds more than promising. Chocolate brownies, and tarts of coconut or treacle are satisfying ways to finish. Two-course set meals (Tuesday to Thursday only) are good value, dinner including half a bottle of house wine (Chilean, otherwise priced at £9.50 per bottle). The other bottles on a wide-ranging list are mostly under £20.

CHEF: Christopher Dunn PROPRIETORS: D. Pencak and A. Young OPEN: Tue to Fri L 12 to 2, Tue to Sat D 7 to 10 CLOSED: 25 Dec, 1 Jan MEALS: alc (main courses £10 to £15). Set L £5.95 (2 courses), Set D Tue to Thur £14.95 (2 courses, inc wine) SERVICE: not inc CARDS: Delta, MasterCard, Switch, Visa DETAILS: 60 seats. Private parties: 36 main room. Car park. Vegetarian meals. No cigars/pipes in dining room. Music

HORNCASTLE Lincolnshire map 9

Magpies

71–75 East Street, Horncastle LN9 6AA
TEL: (01507) 527004 FAX: (01507) 524064 COOKING **4**
EMAIL: magpies@FSBDial.co.uk COST £19–£25

The cottage-style setting of this old-established family-run restaurant remains the same, save for a pair of smart tartan sofas in the bar; the only other change to this rare Lincolnshire gem is the introduction of a lower-priced set menu, deservedly picked up with alacrity by locals. 'Gone are the sea bass and pigs' trotter sausage,' as one remarked, yet the fare is still adventurous, even if the menu is not always explicit about every ingredient. A 'hearty, wholesome dish of superbly timed sweetbreads and asparagus' comes with unadvertised mushrooms, and chorizo-crusted cod, though 'fragrant and moist', was served with pan juices rather than a promised velouté; yet, given the results and low prices, most customers are happy to accept the chefs' spontaneity. Recurring favourites are a salad of Toulouse sausage and potato, Scottish salmon with tarragon velouté, and fillet of Lincoln Red beef. Even vegetables are hailed as 'a triumph of timing', and judged to be an important element of the cuisine. Despite mixed standards in some dishes – chocolate marquise, 'a triumph of its type', comes with under-par ice cream – desserts such as lemon brûlée, and a pyramid of nougat glacé with raspberry coulis, mostly garner praise. Wines are a classy collection and include some rare stars, such as Sean Thackrey's Pleiades from California's Marin County (£23). House French is £10.

CHEFS: Matthew and Simon Lee   PROPRIETORS: the Lee family   OPEN: Sun L 12.30 to 2.30, Tue to Sat D 7.15 to 10   CLOSED: 2 weeks Aug   MEALS: Set L Sun £12.50, Set D £14   SERVICE: not inc   CARDS: MasterCard, Visa   DETAILS: 40 seats. 25 seats outside. Private parties: 40 main room, 10 private room. Children's helpings. No smoking in dining room. Wheelchair access (not WC). Music £5

HORNDON ON THE HILL Essex   map 3

▲ Bell Inn ✏️ ⁵✱

High Road, Horndon on the Hill SS17 8LD
TEL: (01375) 642463   FAX: (01375) 361611
EMAIL: bell-inn@thefree.net
from M25 junction 30/31 take A13, then B1007 to   COOKING 2
Horndon   COST £26–£43

After fourteen years Sean Kelly has left for France, and his sous-chef Finlay Logan has taken over in the Bell's kitchens. In contrast to the age of the building (500-odd years), the menu is super-modern, calling on chic ingredients of shiitake mushrooms, roasted pineapple and black pudding. Mackerel and anchovy terrine with beetroot jelly as a starter gives some indication of the style, as does one luncher's 'stunningly fresh' plaice, with tiny flecks of chorizo sausage in its creamy sauce. Although sometimes dishes sound more exciting than they prove to be, incidentals such as bread and plainly cooked vegetables are good, and for pudding there may be the richest of chocolate tarts, or a sandwich of Scotch pancake and banana parfait. This is not a place for a quiet meal, but service in the central courtyard or the three bars, one with a lofty beamed ceiling, is attentive and well paced. Plenty of bottles on the wine list or the bar's 'Fast List' are worth a try. House Australian is £9.75.

CHEF: Finlay Logan   PROPRIETORS: J.S.B. and C.M. Vereker   OPEN: all week 12 to 1.45, 7 to 9.45   CLOSED: 25 Dec to 6 Jan   MEALS: alc (main courses £10 to £13.50)   SERVICE: not inc, card slips closed   CARDS: Amex, Delta, MasterCard, Switch, Visa   DETAILS: 80 seats. 36 seats outside. Private parties: 10 main room, 26 and 36 private rooms. Car park. Vegetarian meals. Children's helpings. No smoking in dining room. No music   ACCOMMODATION: 15 rooms, all with bath/shower. TV. Phone. Room only £45 to £75. Rooms for disabled. Baby facilities (*The Which? Hotel Guide*)

HORTON Northamptonshire   map 5

French Partridge 🍾 ⁵✱

35 YEARS 2000 IN THE GUIDE

Horton NN7 2AP
TEL: (01604) 870033   FAX: (01604) 870032   COOKING 6
on B526, 6m SE of Northampton   COST £33–£40

What reporters seem to enjoy about the French Partridge is that, although it moves gently with the times, it is still recognisably the same as it has always been. 'My wife and I were their first ever customers thirty-odd years ago and have been going regularly ever since.' With this edition, the Partridges celebrate an unbroken thirty-five years in the *Guide* – 'Mrs P is as welcoming as ever, and never seems to change or age' – and although another generation has come on board, the format remains a good-value, well-balanced, four-course, Anglo-French menu that alters every couple of months and delivers food with 'a strong culinary intelligence behind it'.

Menus are designed to build up towards the main event. Start in low gear with red pepper soup, or gravad lax, shift up to baked cod with a herb crust, or soft-boiled egg and mushrooms in a pastry case, and by the time you get to boned rabbit leg stuffed with pork, wrapped in filo pastry and served with a wild mushroom sauce, you are really motoring. Or there might be slow-roast belly of pork, or steamed suet pudding of lamb and kidneys. 'Everything is cooked or prepared without corner-cutting,' reckoned one visitor, not least desserts: classic Paris-Brest perhaps, or mango pannacotta.

Low prices are combined with high quality on the cleverly constructed wine list both to encourage and to reward the adventurous: 'I have found it quite safe to order wines that I have never heard of,' reports one regular. The eight-bottle French house selection is a good case in point, offering a Chénas from Trenel at £13, for example. Half-bottles are generous too.

CHEFS: David and Justin Partridge   PROPRIETORS: David and Mary Partridge   OPEN: Tue to Sat D only 7.30 to 9   CLOSED: 2 weeks Christmas, 2 weeks Easter, 3 weeks July to Aug   MEALS: Set D £28   SERVICE: net prices   CARDS: none   DETAILS: 45 seats. Private parties: 24 main room. Car park. Vegetarian meals. No smoking in dining room. Wheelchair access (not WC). No music

---

HOVE East Sussex   map 3

Quentin's

42 Western Road, Hove BN3 1JD   COOKING 2
TEL/FAX: (01273) 822734   COST £29–£35

At his small and friendly 'gem of a restaurant' – quirkily furnished and dimly lit – Quentin Fitch cooks with a light touch, mostly letting ingredients do the work. A local fisherman, for example, is called on for daily supplies, which might turn up as simply grilled fillet of bass with mustard potatoes. Other local contributions include meat, game and vegetables, which might be turned into pink-cooked lamb on couscous, wood pigeon stuffed with cumin, rice and raisins, or baked onion stuffed with ricotta and wild mushrooms. While ideas span the globe – from kedgeree fish cakes with masala dressing, to duck breast with noodles and bean sprouts – flavour combinations are well considered, for example a puffy goats'-cheese soufflé with an 'inspired' fig and walnut chutney. Among desserts of 'knickerbocker glory' cheesecake, and an apricot and Madeira version of crème brûlée, the 'signature' pudding – an individual apple pie with an oat and nut topping, served with lavender ice cream – is highly rated. Service is not fast, but Quentin supplies regular bulletins on the progress of your order. Well-chosen house wine is £9.95 on a concise and largely French list.

The Guide*'s longest-serving restaurants are listed near the front of the book.*

CHEF: Quentin Fitch   PROPRIETORS: Quentin and Candy Fitch   OPEN: Tue to Fri L 12 to 2, Tue to Sat D 7 to 9.30   CLOSED: 2 weeks Aug   MEALS: Set L £7.95 (1 course) to £19.95, Set D £17.95 (2 courses) to £19.95   SERVICE: not inc, 12% for parties of 6 or more   CARDS: Amex, Delta, Diners, MasterCard, Switch, Visa   DETAILS: 28 seats. Private parties: 10 main room, 20 private room. Vegetarian meals. No cigars/pipes in dining room. Wheelchair access (not WC). No music. Air-conditioned

---

HOVINGHAM North Yorkshire   map 9

▲ *Worsley Arms* ⚡✕

| Hovingham YO62 4LA | COOKING 2 |
| TEL: (01653) 628234   FAX: (01653) 628130 | COST £23–£45 |

Confident in its role of gently old-fashioned country hotel, popular with shooting parties and wedding guests, the well-heeled honey-stone Worsley Arms offers visitors two dining possibilities. The restaurant, quite dark and formal, is the place for simple starters and 'beautifully presented ' honey-roast Goosnargh duck, or pan-fried sea bass with caviare cream. Yorkshire appetites have been known to moan about the minuscule portions of vegetables, but one couple were delighted with their 'minimal and marvellous' mashed chive potatoes and roast shallots. The Cricketer's Bistro at the back, playing up its name to the full in décor and menu, has pleased with haunch and sausage of venison served with celeriac mash, and also presents some alluring vegetarian choices, and a lunchtime sandwich. 'The Last Wicket' may be sticky toffee pudding, or blackcurrant ice, while in the restaurant pistachio brûlée with an apple sorbet comes highly recommended. Presentation of dishes throughout the hotel is commented on favourably. The restaurant wine list – a handful of good bottles from each main country or area – gets pared down to fourteen of each colour, all under £13, in the bistro. House wines are £11.50 in the restaurant, £8.95 in the bistro.

CHEF: Andrew Jones   PROPRIETOR: A.E. Rodger   OPEN: bistro all week 12 to 2, 7 to 9.30, restaurant Sun L 12 to 2, all week D 7 to 9.30   MEALS: bistro alc (main courses £8.50 to £15); restaurant Set L Sun £16, Set D £25   SERVICE: not inc, card slips closed   CARDS: Amex, Delta, Diners, MasterCard, Switch, Visa   DETAILS: bistro 28 seats, restaurant 60 seats. 150 seats outside. Private parties: 60 main room, 10 and 30 private rooms. Car park. Vegetarian meals. Children's helpings. No smoking in dining room. Wheelchair access (also WC). Music   ACCOMMODATION: 18 rooms, all with bath/shower. TV. Phone. B&B £60 to £90. Rooms for disabled. Baby facilities   (£5)

HUDDERSFIELD West Yorkshire   map 9

Bradley's ⚡✕ £

| 84 Fitzwilliam Street, Huddersfield HD1 5BB | COOKING 1 |
| TEL: (01484) 516773   FAX: (01484) 538386 | COST £13–£46 |

Fitzwilliam Street has been chopped up by various urban developments; the bit you want is the one that bridges the ring road and then slopes down to town. The split-level bistro's popularity is such that many more covers have lately been added, presumably to cope with the lunchers and evening early-birders who know a bargain when they see one. The unfussily described menu, boosted by a few blackboard suggestions, contains neat ideas aplenty, such as pan-fried chicken livers with a sweet-and-sour onion tartlet, and 'excellent' asparagus won ton. Main-course attractions come pell-mell too: game cobbler, duck breast with a caramelised onion and fig tart, and monkfish tail with a sweet pepper sauce, perhaps accompanied by extras of carrot, swede and ginger purée, and skin-on chips. The dessert choice 'was recited in an automaton singsong, as if we had touch-tone phones and should press our choice now'. Poached pear in a rhubarb and orange syrup sweetened by a layer of spun sugar was one outcome, while another option might be date and walnut pudding with maple syrup. The wine list (from £9.50 a bottle) includes ten by the glass.

CHEFS: Jonathan Nichols and Glenn Varley   PROPRIETORS: Jonathan Nichols and Andrew Bradley   OPEN: Mon to Fri L 12 to 2, Mon to Sat D 6 to 10 (10.30 Fri and Sat)   CLOSED: bank hols, exc 25 and 26 Dec   MEALS: alc (main courses £7.50 to £15). Set L £6.25, Set D Mon 6 to 9, Tue to Fri 6 to 7.30, Sat 6 to 7 £13.95 (inc wine)   SERVICE: not inc   CARDS: MasterCard, Switch, Visa   DETAILS: 130 seats. Private parties: 130 main room, 55 and 75 private rooms. Car park (D only). Vegetarian meals. Children's helpings. No smoking in 1 dining room. Wheelchair access (also WC). Music. Air-conditioned

▲ Lodge Hotel ♥ ⁵✳

48 Birkby Lodge Road, Birkby,	
Huddersfield HD2 2BG	COOKING 3
TEL: (01484) 431001 FAX: (01484) 421590	COST £21–£45

Service is friendly and 'the Birleys care about their guests' at this well-kept, stone-built, wood-beamed, family-run house in a suburb of Huddersfield. Start in the lounge, busy with chintzy sofas and lots of lamps, and move to a dining room with a fleur-de-lys motif and a brace of unusual chandeliers, where the quality and freshness of ingredients is appreciated: in accurately grilled plaice, or first-class fillet steak with both béarnaise and a dark Madeira sauce. Set-price menus are the form, the most expensive consisting of 'three proper courses' plus a mid-meal sorbet or soup, and dishes are generally well conceived. A chunky galantine of duck, for example, comes with a dollop of sweetly spicy apricot chutney to cut through the richness; and six scallops together with their corals and smoked bacon arrive in a sweet chilli sauce, sprinkled with Gruyère and lightly grilled. Desserts also get high marks, judging by a dark chocolate tart with a puddle of mango sauce, and a baked Granny Smith apple generously stuffed with cranberries and sultanas, served with a blob of cinnamon ice cream. The 130-strong wine list features prime examples from around the world, and mark-ups are far from greedy. Nine house wines are either £10.95 or £11.25.

CHEFS: Kevin and Garry Birley, and Richard Hanson   PROPRIETORS: Kevin and Garry Birley   OPEN: Sun to Fri L 12 to 1.45, Mon to Sat D 7.30 to 9.30   CLOSED: 26 to 28 Dec, 30 Dec, 1 Jan   MEALS: Set L £10.95 (2 courses) to £13.95, Set D £16.95 (2 courses) to £23.95   SERVICE: not inc, card slips closed   CARDS: Amex, Delta, Diners, MasterCard, Switch, Visa   DETAILS: 80 seats. Private parties: 62 main room, 8 to 22 private rooms. Car park. Vegetarian meals. Children's helpings. No children under 5. No smoking in dining room. Wheelchair access (also WC). Music   ACCOMMODATION: 12 rooms, all with bath/shower. TV. Phone. B&B £60 to £80. Rooms for disabled. Baby facilities (The Which? Hotel Guide)

Thorpe Grange Manor

Thorpe Lane, Almondbury, Huddersfield HD5 8TA
TEL: (01484) 425115 FAX: (01484) 311798   COOKING 5
off A629, 2m E of Huddersfield   COST £22–£49

Fledging this may be – in its third year during 2000 – but it aims high, starting
with the advantage of a stone-built eighteenth-century manor house set in two
and a half acres, and a sense of space and comfort within. It is an industrious
kitchen, offering a generous carte, vegetarian and 'gourmet' options, an
early-evening deal, and set-price menus. Modern French and traditional British
ideas (Sunday lunch brings roast beef and Yorkshire pudding) combine to
produce much of interest, not least Dover sole topped with lobster soufflé, or
suckling pig with pithiviers of black pudding. Dishes are 'well thought out, well
executed', yet with a degree of playfulness in presentation that recalls Jason
Neilson's mentor Raymond Blanc: a starter of aubergine 'caviar', for example,
comes as a bird's nest of shredded vegetables containing aubergine 'eggs'.

Desserts echo the Anglo-French approach – witness sticky toffee soufflé –
while generally ploughing a classic furrow with chocolate fondant and pistachio
ice cream, or a light and skilfully done blackberry mille-feuille. Meals begin and
end with small plates of goodies, and the highly rated bread may be flavoured
with olive and shallot or walnut and sultana. Service combines young helpers
with an upper echelon of experienced and capable staff. The wine list has
enough choice to provide interest and variety without being confusing, and
mark-ups are kind. Six house wines start at £9.95 a bottle, £2.50 a glass.

CHEF: Jason Neilson   PROPRIETORS: Ronald, Gillian and Jason Neilson, and Ruth Woods
OPEN: Tue to Fri and Sun L 12 to 2, Tue to Thur D 6 to 9.30, Fri and Sat D 7 to 9.30   CLOSED: 1 to
18 April   MEALS: alc Tue to Fri L, Tue to Sat D (main courses £13.50 to £17). Set L Tue to Fri
£12.50 (2 courses) to £14.95, Set L Sun £14.95, Set D £19.95, Set D Tue to Thu before 7pm
£12.95 (2 courses)   SERVICE: not inc   CARDS: Delta, MasterCard, Switch, Visa   DETAILS: 60
seats. 20 seats outside. Private parties: 80 main room, 40 private room. Car park. Vegetarian
meals. No children after 7.30. No cigars/pipes in dining room. Wheelchair access (also WC).
Music. Air-conditioned (£5)

HUNSTRETE Bath & N.E. Somerset   map 2

▲ Hunstrete House ⁙✸

Hunstrete BS39 4NS
TEL: (01761) 490490 FAX: (01761) 490732   COOKING 4
off A368, 4m S of Keynsham   COST £30–£82

Comfortable rather than grand, Hunstrete is a calm, relaxing, 'pampering' place.
The long, low building in weathered Cotswold stone contains a maze of rooms
and corridors, its décor 'just worn enough around the edges to feel lived in'.
Menu options include one each for vegetarians and children, and a six-course
tasting version. High-quality ingredients provide a solid foundation: two thick
bricks of 'skilfully cooked' Glenarm salmon with sweet, crisp skin, stacked at a
rakish angle and accompanied by concentrated semi-dried cherry tomatoes; or
moist garlic-scented guinea fowl with fondant potato and a scattering of lentils.

Technique is sound, and bold flavours do emerge, although greater attention to balance and proportion would have made more impact on our inspector. The food is rather more cream-laden than the menu might suggest, whether in savoury courses, or a wedge of light, milky chocolate mousse with a ball of ice cream and a luminous orange sauce. Cheese 'for enthusiasts' is treated with the respect it deserves: an informative annotated menu lists a dozen, mostly unpasteurised, which are 'at their peak of maturity', from oozing, spoon-ripe Bath, via stinking Epoisses and rich Blue Vinney, to complex nutty Cheddar and crumbly Swaledale. French staff, who seem rather exotic in such a quintessentially English setting, 'materialise when you need them'. Ninety per cent of the wines are over £20, but there is relief in the south of France, Italy, and parts of the New World. Four house wines are £14.95.

CHEF: Stewart Eddy PROPRIETOR: Hunstrete House Ltd OPEN: all week 12 to 2, 7 to 9.30
MEALS: alc Mon to Sat L, all week D (main courses £23 to £25). Set L £14.95 (2 courses) to
£19.95, Set D Sun to Thur £29.95, Set D all week £55 SERVICE: not inc CARDS: Amex, Delta,
Diners, MasterCard, Switch, Visa DETAILS: 50 seats. 12 seats outside. Private parties: 50 main
room, 14 and 30 private rooms. Car park. Vegetarian meals. Children's helpings. No smoking in
dining room. Wheelchair access (also women's WC). Occasional music ACCOMMODATION: 23
rooms, all with bath/shower. TV. Phone. Room only £98 to £130. Swimming pool (*The Which?*
Hotel Guide)

HURSTBOURNE TARRANT Hampshire   map 2

▲ *Esseborne Manor* ♟ ⁵⅄⚹

Hurstbourne Tarrant SP11 0ER
TEL: (01264) 736444 FAX: (01264) 736725
EMAIL: esseborne_manor@compuserve.com   COOKING 3
on A343, 1½m N of Hurstbourne Tarrant   COST £24–£53

From being a rural retreat, this small manor house has recently become an 'executive retreat', attracting a business clientele and losing its 'very English' look along the way. The transition involves major building work, unfinished as the *Guide* went to press. Ben Tunnicliffe's style is modern European with an occasional nod towards the Far East, taking in seared red bream with ginger, cucumber and Thai fragrant rice, and fillet of beef with roasted beetroot and garlic confit. At inspection, a simple main course (would there were more) of peppered lamb chump was a success, the 'really good, generous rough meat' nicely timed, and harmoniously paired with a 'big pile of skinned broad beans'. A degree of 'tarting up with non-essentials' marred other dishes, despite some good-quality raw materials. Substantial puddings might include Derby pie with bourbon ice cream, while chilled lemon sabayon with blueberries should fit the bill for lighter appetites. Service has been inconsistently 'bright and cheerful' for some, lacklustre for others, and wine service has also failed to come up to scratch on occasion. Fortunately, the wines themselves are an appealing collection, drawn mainly from classical French regions with added attractions from the New World. House Australian is £13.50.

▐ *denotes an outstanding wine cellar;* ♟ *denotes a good wine list, worth travelling for.*

CHEF: Ben Tunnicliffe   PROPRIETOR: I. Hamilton   OPEN: all week 12 to 2, 7 to 9.30   MEALS: alc (main courses £11.50 to £19.50). Set L £10 (2 courses) to £13, Set L Sun £12 (2 courses) to £15, Set D £14 (2 courses) to £18   SERVICE: not inc, card slips closed   CARDS: Amex, Delta, Diners, MasterCard, Switch, Visa   DETAILS: 50 seats. 30 seats outside. Private parties: 30 main room, 50 private room. Car park. Vegetarian meals. Children's helpings. No smoking in dining room. Wheelchair access (also WC). Occasional music   ACCOMMODATION: 15 rooms, all with bath/shower. TV. Phone. B&B £88 to £160. Rooms for disabled   (£5)

HUXHAM Devon   map 1

▲ *Barton Cross* ᵍ✳

Huxham, Stoke Canon EX5 4EJ
TEL: (01392) 841245   FAX: (01392) 841942   COOKING 2
on A396 to Tiverton, 4m N of Exeter   COST £25–£42

Occupying three converted, thatched, beamed cottages, this hotel restaurant draws on its regional roots, serving a range of seafood from grilled local scallops, via crab risotto with deep-fried squid, to poached turbot minestrone. It also enrols the help of Somerset goats' cheese (served croustade-style with a sweet potato and chilli salad), wild mushrooms (in a tart topped with foie gras), and spring lamb (assembled into a 'platter' of lamb pasty, liver, kidney, sweetbreads, cutlet and sausage). If anything seems too elaborate, the kitchen offers to cook food more plainly on request. Finish with banana parfait, raspberry crêpe soufflé, or lemon crème brûlée, and drink from a varied, fairly priced, hundred-strong wine list that starts with ten house recommendations between £9.25 and £12.75.

CHEF: Paul George Bending   PROPRIETOR: B.A. Hamilton   OPEN: Mon to Sat 12.30 to 2, 6.30 to 9.30   MEALS: Set L £18.50, Set D £25   SERVICE: not inc, card slips closed   CARDS: Amex, Delta, MasterCard, Switch, Visa   DETAILS: 50 seats. 15 seats outside. Private parties: 35 main room, 12 private room. Car park. Vegetarian meals. Children's helpings. No smoking in dining room. Wheelchair access (also WC). Occasional music   ACCOMMODATION: 9 rooms, all with bath/shower. TV. Phone. B&B £59.50 to £90. Rooms for disabled. Baby facilities   (£5)

ILKLEY West Yorkshire   map 8

Box Tree 🍾 ᵍ✳

37 Church Street, Ilkley LS29 9DR   COOKING 8
TEL: (01943) 608484   FAX: (01943) 607186   COST £39–£65

The Box Tree's 'quirky appeal' is a distinct plus. 'It's a mixture of country cottage and camp antique shop, with a touch of sophisticated gloss', according to one visitor. Walls are thickly hung with framed paintings, porcelain cats monopolise a couple of chairs by the entrance, and tables are set with crisp linen, flowers and a decorative glass tree. Thierry LePrêtre-Granet's combination of classical French cooking techniques with occasional exotic touches is a winning one. What gives the food its vitality, indeed its identity and character, is the use of sharp flavours to point up the main item: for example, 'an inspired combination' of nutty, sweet Cornish scallops served with a sweet-sour fruit chutney enlivened by lemon grass and coriander seed.

Materials are well sourced, and seasoning and timing are spot on: deep red gamey-flavoured wood pigeon breasts, for example, wrapped in cabbage leaf and capped by thin slices of crisp potato rösti, all in a rich brown stock flavoured with juniper; or a 'scrupulously trimmed, pink and juicy' lamb cutlet, coated in a sweetbread mousse, in a rich stock reduction subtly but decisively spiked with garlic. Portions are well judged, and luxuries are properly handled, as in a silky-smooth terrine of duck foie gras sparsely layered with pieces of deep-flavoured prune, served with toasted walnut and raisin bread.

Desserts may elicit less excitement, but they have included a workmanlike tuile sandwich of chocolate mousse with a creamy coffee sauce, and baked pears in custard with vanilla ice cream and chocolate sorbet. Prices – the same at lunch and dinner – are considered reasonable given the quality. Cheeses may not be up to the same standard, and service problems, not for the first time, have taken the shine off otherwise enjoyable experiences. But extras are tiptop, from a plate of 'impeccable' canapés, through a small cup of creamy, piquant red pepper soup, to a plateful of petits fours from 'an expert pastry chef'. The wine list is dominated by a classic, no-expense-spared French section, but also finds room for some fine offerings from Spain, Italy and the New World. Mark-ups are reasonable, and there are numerous bottles below £20 from France and elsewhere. House Burgundy is £14.

CHEF: Thierry LePrêtre-Granet   PROPRIETOR: The Box Tree Restaurant (Ilkley) Ltd   OPEN: Tue to Sun L 12 to 2.30, Tue to Sat D 7 to 9.30   CLOSED: Christmas to New Year, last two weeks Jan   MEALS: Set L and D £19.50 (2 courses) to £40   SERVICE: not inc, card slips closed   CARDS: Amex, MasterCard, Switch, Visa   DETAILS: 50 seats. Private parties: 30 main room, 12 and 16 private rooms. Car park. Vegetarian meals. Children's helpings. No smoking in dining room. Wheelchair access (not WC). Occasional music

Farsyde £   NEW ENTRY

38A The Back Grove, Ilkley LS29 9EE
TEL: (01943) 602030   FAX: (01943) 435334   COOKING 4
EMAIL: farsyde@btinternet.com   COST £18–£36

This 'hidden-away gem' is modestly located behind the famous Bettys tea rooms (see Round-ups, Ilkley), but there's nothing diffident about it. Green and orange signs announce its presence, and the airy split-level dining room feels bright and contemporary, with yellow walls and wooden floor. Chef/owner Gavin Beedham spent five years in the rather grander setting of the Devonshire Arms (see entry, Bolton Abbey), but Farsyde signals a back-to-basics approach: imaginative modern cooking at keen prices in a bistro setting. Mediterranean flavours and fashionable ingredients predominate, but a backbone of classic techniques and sensible partnerships gives the cooking an edge over many who flirt with the style. Thus, wild mushroom risotto is garnished with a poached egg and sherry vinaigrette; rump of lamb with aubergine caviare and mushroom and port sauce. Accurate timing has been applied to salmon fillet served with a beurre blanc of just the right consistency, and adroit combinations continue with desserts: apple brûlée with chocolate and mint ice cream, perhaps, or pear Tatin with almond parfait. Staff are 'knowledgeable, obliging and polite' and don't hurry diners. Simpler dishes feature at lunchtime, and Wednesday night is fish night. The irreverently annotated wine list kicks off with French house wine at £7.75.

CHEF/PROPRIETOR: Gavin Beedham   OPEN: Tue to Sun L 11.30 to 2.30 (12 to 3.30 Sun), Tue to Sat D 6 to 10   MEALS: alc (main courses L £3 to £6.50, D £9 to £13.50). Set L £10.50, Set D Tue to Thur 6 to 7.30 £10.50 (2 courses)   SERVICE: not inc   CARDS: Delta, MasterCard, Switch, Visa   DETAILS: 50 seats. Vegetarian meals. Wheelchair access (not WC). Music

IPSWICH Suffolk   map 6

Mortimer's Seafood Restaurant

Wherry Quay, Ipswich IP4 1AS   COOKING 2
TEL: (01473) 230225   COST £23–£49

Overlooking the marina, this light, airy seafood restaurant offers a generous choice (over forty items, not counting desserts), starting with potted shrimps, marinated herrings, and oysters three ways: natural, topped with cheese sauce, or grilled with garlic butter. Quality and range of fish are impressive, as is that other vital attribute, freshness, while sauces tend to be rich: turbot comes with saffron and shrimp hollandaise, lemon sole with a creamy white wine sauce containing mushrooms, prawns and mussels. Daily blackboard specials respond to deliveries from Grimsby market, and might include chargrilled sea bream, or cod au gratin. Dessert choice runs to lemon chiffon, chocolate pot and tiramisù. Service could be more enthusiastic. Alsace features prominently among white wines on a sound, ninety-strong list; house French is £9.75.

CHEFS: Kenneth Ambler and Eric Kerfa   PROPRIETOR: Kenneth Ambler   OPEN: Mon to Fri L 12 to 2, Mon to Sat D 6.30 to 9 (8.30 Mon)   CLOSED: 24 Dec to 5 Jan   MEALS: alc (main courses £6.50 to £18)   SERVICE: not inc   CARDS: Amex, Delta, Diners, MasterCard, Switch, Visa   DETAILS: 85 seats. Private parties: 15 main room, 25 private room. Children's helpings. No smoking in 1 dining room. Wheelchair access (not WC). Occasional music (£5)

Scott's Brasserie

4A Orwell Place, Ipswich IP4 1BB   COOKING 3
TEL: (01473) 230254   FAX: (01473) 218851   COST £21–£36

It would be perfectly possible to dine at this leafy first-floor brasserie on prawn cocktail, chargrilled steak with shoestring fries, and vanilla ice-cream: and why not, if they are of good quality? But Scott Davidson roams more widely in his quarterly-changing set menus, boosted by weekly specials. Lunchers report on the good value of Bermuda fish chowder with black rum and sherry peppers, and filo-wrapped king prawns – both 'excellent' – while Cromer crab cakes, braised Norfolk lamb shank and Suffolk pork escalope fly the flag for East Anglia. Puddings are largely conventional and rich, with ginger and lemon steamed pudding, and triple chocolate torte. Young staff serve attentively. Three dozen serviceable wines are sensibly priced under £20, with house wine £9.95.

All entries, including Round-ups, are fully indexed at the back of the Guide.

CHEF: Scott Davidson PROPRIETORS: Scott Davidson and Charles Lewis OPEN: Mon to Fri L 12 to 2.30, Mon to Sat D 6.30 to 9.30 (10 Sat) CLOSED: Christmas, 1 Jan, bank hols MEALS: Set L £9.95 (2 courses) to £12.95, Set D £16.95 (2 courses) to £19.95 SERVICE: not inc, 10% for parties of 8 or more CARDS: Amex, Delta, MasterCard, Switch, Visa DETAILS: 70 seats. Private parties: 35 main room, 35 private room. Vegetarian meals. Children's helpings. Music

---

IXWORTH Suffolk   map 6

Theobalds ♥ ✻

68 High Street, Ixworth IP31 2HJ   COOKING 4
TEL/FAX: (01359) 231707   COST £30–£58

The year 2000 marks the 350th birthday of this sympathetically restored house (now joined with next door), where Geraldine and Simon Theobald produce meals remarkable for their light approach, variety and calmly attentive service. Old favourites and new ideas may involve scallops, mussels, calf's liver, guinea fowl, gravlax or hare. Take, for example, typical starters of grilled sardines with basil and olive oil dressing, globe artichokes with toasted walnuts and hollandaise, or clear winter vegetable soup with cheese and herb dumplings. Main courses usually come deftly (and alcoholicly) sauced, such as roast lobster on tagliatelle with a saffron and Noilly-Prat sauce, though one customer forswore any accompaniment for his best end of lamb and revelled in the quality of the meat alone. Vegetables may include 'ace' sauté potatoes.

Simon sees plenty of possibilities for caramelisation, so if you have missed out on roast quail with caramelised apples and grapes, or lamb noisettes on candied aubergines with a sherry and rosemary sauce, you can later home in on caramelised lemon and lime tart with matching sorbet, or chocolate and caramelised walnut mousse with caraway crème anglaise. Amuse-gueules (perhaps a crab tartlet or two), and petits fours are as good as the breads. Wines are straightforwardly listed by colour and price. Some very respected if less familiar names adorn the higher echelons in both full bottles and halves, but 'trying the unusual has rarely been a mistake here,' says one contented regular. House French is £14.60.

CHEF: Simon Theobald PROPRIETORS: Simon and Geraldine Theobald OPEN: Sun and Tue to Fri L 12.15 to 1.30, Tue to Sat D 7.15 to 9.15 CLOSED: 2 weeks Aug, bank hols MEALS: alc (main courses L £9, D £11.50 to £19.50). Set L Sun £17.95 SERVICE: not inc CARDS: Delta, MasterCard, Switch, Visa DETAILS: 50 seats. 8 seats outside. Private parties: 50 main room, 20 private room. Vegetarian meals. Children's helpings. No children under 8 at D. No smoking in dining room. No music

---

'Then there are the ice skaters: two tall lads who permanently walk about in white shirts and black trousers with one hand cupped behind their back, like a Dutch speed-skating silver medallist.' (On eating in Scotland)

The Good Food Guide *is a registered trade mark of Which? Ltd.*

JEVINGTON East Sussex   map 3

Hungry Monk ⅄✕

Jevington BN26 5QF
TEL/FAX: (01323) 482178   COOKING 3
off A22 between Polegate and Friston   COST £37–£58

The Monk aims for a private-house atmosphere, with a series of little log-fired
sitting rooms and private dining rooms, and has a balancing act to perform. On
the one hand it must appear unchanging, so that folk who have been eating here
for over thirty years – since its first appearance in the *Guide* – won't notice any
difference: hence banoffi pie, and the glass of port included in the price. On the
other, it must try to keep up with the world around it, hence prawn fish cake
with Thai sauce, or roast rabbit with couscous. Menus change every couple of
months, using fish from Newhaven (tuna tartare, perhaps), locally shot game
(pheasant consommé), and meat and vegetables that are 'increasingly organic'. A
strong sense of comfort also pervades the food, from bacon and potato cake
Benedict, via baked sugared ham with bubble and squeak, to lemon syrup
roulade. The wine list is strongest in France, particularly Bordeaux, or the
patriotic might like to try one of the characterful English wines. House wines
start at £11 per bottle, £2.50 per glass.

CHEFS: Claire Burgess and Sharon Poulton PROPRIETORS: Nigel and Susan Mackenzie OPEN:
Sun L 12 to 2.30, all week D 7.15 to 10 CLOSED: 24 to 26 Dec, bank hols MEALS: Set L and D
£24.95 SERVICE: not inc, 12.5% for parties of 8 or more, card slips closed CARDS: Amex
DETAILS: 38 seats. Private parties: 16 main room, 6 to 16 private rooms. Car park. Vegetarian
meals. Children's helpings. No children under 3. No smoking in dining room. Occasional music.
Air-conditioned (£5)

KENILWORTH Warwickshire   map 5

Restaurant Bosquet ▼

97A Warwick Road, Kenilworth CV8 1HP   COOKING 5
TEL: (01926) 852463   COST £37–£53

Little changes at this welcoming and unpretentious house where the Ligniers
continue their double act, Jane conducting business out front, Bernard inter-
preting the cooking of south-west France in a typically confident, controlled and
down-to-earth way. Given its origins, there is no shortage of duck in its various
forms: stuffed neck, for example, or magret with lentils, or a partnership of confit
and foie gras in a starter salad. Truffle crops up, too, in a dressing for asparagus,
or giving a boost to the polenta that comes with saddle of venison.

   Dishes are on the substantial side, their rich and powerful flavours
emphasising the traditional nature of this distinctive cuisine, which simply aims
to get the best out of good materials without too many distractions. Yet this is not
formula cooking, since it also produces a cream of duck soup served with
profiteroles stuffed with foie gras, and seafood dishes along the lines of spaghetti
with lobster and herb sauce, or scallops with saffron and squid ink sauce.
Desserts might include chocolate and orange gâteau, or a strawberries and cream
biscuit cup with lime ice cream. Wines are entirely French and include some
classy bottles from the south-west alongside more expected but none the less

welcome clarets, Burgundies, Rhônes, et al. Prices are reasonable, with house wines starting at £12.50.

CHEF: Bernard Lignier   PROPRIETORS: Bernard and Jane Lignier   OPEN: Tue to Sat D only 7 to 9.15 (L by appointment)   CLOSED: 1 week Christmas, 3 weeks Aug   MEALS: alc (main courses £16). Set D Tue to Fri £25   SERVICE: not inc   CARDS: Amex, Delta, MasterCard, Switch, Visa   DETAILS: 26 seats. Private parties: 30 main room. Children's helpings. Wheelchair access (not WC). No music

Simpson's 😋✳

101–103 Warwick Road, Kenilworth CV8 1HL	COOKING 5
TEL: (01926) 864567 FAX: (01926) 864510	COST £28–£60

A double shop conversion on Kenilworth's main street, Simpson's takes the business of serving food seriously, to the extent that the walls are decorated with framed menus from establishments all across Europe. The dining room is in two halves, on either side of an entrance corridor that leads towards the bar. Clearly, the influence of some of those international menus has rubbed off on the kitchen, as the range is trendily hard to characterise, but strikes the right sorts of chords. A terrine of corn-fed chicken, foie gras, bacon and trompette mushrooms, with accompanying toasted brioche swaddled in a serviette, made one reader 'feel glad to be alive'. Portions err on the small side, but what there is is impressive, as shown by a main course of monkfish that sported two tiny bulbs of steamed fennel, and a linear heap of basil risotto overlaid with alternating slices of chorizo and carrot, a dish that was 'spot on' for timing, presentation and conception. Calf's liver is more classically partnered with creamed potato, bacon and sauce diable, but is brought off with no less aplomb, while vegetarians might opt for, say, cannelloni of mushrooms and spinach with tarragon sauce. A good selection of pudding wines is offered to go with such temptations as roast pear feuilleté with caramel sauce and walnuts or, more diverting to the palate, hot lemon soufflé with thyme ice cream. The cosmopolitan wine list, arranged simply in ascending order of price, offers good value across a broad range of varieties and styles, starting with house French at £11.50.

CHEFS: Andreas Antona and Luke Tipping   PROPRIETOR: Andreas Antona   OPEN: Mon to Fri L 12.30 to 2, Mon to Sat D 7 to 10   MEALS: Set L £10 (2 courses) to £17.50, Set D £21.95 (2 courses) to £32.50   SERVICE: 10% (optional), card slips closed   CARDS: Amex, Delta, Diners, MasterCard, Switch, Visa   DETAILS: 70 seats. Private parties: 8 main room, 50 private room. Car park. Vegetarian meals. Children's helpings. No smoking in 1 dining room. No music. Air-conditioned

'We never saw any of the staff again, apart from a back view of one of the waiters who came into the bar area, climbed up on a stool, grabbed a very large bottle of Armagnac from the top shelf and disappeared back into the kitchen, giggling.'
(On eating in the West Country)

The Guide *always appreciates hearing about changes of chef or owner.*

▲ Swinside Lodge 🍴

Grange Road, Newlands, Keswick CA12 5UE
TEL/FAX: (017687) 72948
off A66 Penrith to Cockermouth road; turn left at   COOKING 4
Portinscale and follow Grange road for 2m   COST £28–£41

In a peaceful setting above Derwent Water, this small Lakeland hotel is the
essence of rural simplicity. So relaxing is a visit here that guests do not even face
the dilemma of what to have for dinner. A no-choice (except for dessert) menu
takes care of that, although alternative dishes can be provided if requested in
advance. Some advance planning might also be necessary if you want to drink:
unlicensed premises mean it's bring your own.

It is a simple formula that works, as regulars will testify. After complimentary
sherry, everyone sits down together to enjoy wholesome, straightforward but
accomplished cooking: perhaps a tart of red onion and caraway to start, followed
by a soup. Main courses vary with the season – lamb with couscous and
rosemary has appeared in April, pork with gooseberry tartlet in summer – and
vegetable accompaniments are generous. A choice of puddings might include an
ice cream such as lemon curd, or prune and brandy, and something more
substantial like apple streusel cake, with cheese an optional fifth course. Extras
are all home-made, from a 'wonderful' selection of breads to cheese biscuits and
chocolates.

CHEF: Christopher Astley   PROPRIETOR: Graham Taylor   OPEN: all week D only 7.30 to 8 (1
sitting)   CLOSED: Dec and Jan   MEALS: Set D £25 to £28. Unlicensed: BYO (no corkage)
SERVICE: not inc, card slips closed   CARDS: Delta, MasterCard, Switch, Visa   DETAILS: 18
seats. Private parties: 18 main room. Car park. No smoking in dining room. No music
ACCOMMODATION: 7 rooms, all with bath/shower. TV. D,B&B £77 to £170. No children under 10 in
accommodation (*The Which? Hotel Guide*)

The Glasshouse   [NEW ENTRY]

14 Station Parade, Kew TW9 3PZ
TEL: (0181) 940 6777, changing to (020) 8940 6777   COOKING 6
FAX: (0181) 940 3833, changing to (020) 8940 3833   COST £30–£46

Opened in the spring of 1999, this joint venture by Nigel Platts-Martin of The
Square and Bruce Poole of Chez Bruce (see entries, London) does indeed have
floor-to-ceiling windows, front and side, along with a stripped wood floor, and
modern art on its remaining white walls. Anthony Boyd, who has worked in
both parent kitchens, oversees a simply and clearly expressed modern British
menu that might take in an oyster and salmon ragoût with asparagus and Jersey
Royals, braised leg of rabbit with Parmesan gnocchi, and brochette of lambs'
kidneys and merguez sausage, served with both couscous and celeriac mash.

The result is 'a triumph', according to one visitor. Careful preparation, precise
timing and good materials have combined to produce steamed halibut on a bed
of spring vegetables, with a fluffy shrimp omelette, surrounded by a classic

beurre blanc; and a well-balanced shoulder of pork with sweet apple, fondant potato and crispy Savoy cabbage. Although sounding like a variant on kedgeree, a well-executed curried smoked haddock and coriander risotto has proved a 'harmonious and original' first course. Desserts were the least successful part of an inspection meal – 'I later discovered that the regular pastry chef was having a night off, which was of little comfort to diners eating here this evening' – but cheese is a sensibly limited selection, 'all in fine fettle'. One might say the same about the wine list, although prices soon disappear over the £20 horizon. House French is £13.50.

CHEF: Anthony Boyd   PROPRIETOR: Larkbrace Ltd   OPEN: all week L 12 to 2.30, Mon to Sat D 7 to 10.30   CLOSED: 3 days Christmas, bank hols   MEALS: Set L £17.50, Set D £25   SERVICE: 12.5% (optional), card slips closed   CARDS: Amex, Delta, MasterCard, Switch, Visa   DETAILS: 65 seats. Private parties: 50 main room. Children's helpings. No babies at D. No music. Air-conditioned

---

KEYSTON Cambridgeshire   map 6

Pheasant Inn ▮ ⁵⅟✳ £

Keyston PE18 0RE
TEL: (01832) 710241   FAX: (01832) 710464   COOKING 4
on B663, 1m S of junction with A14   COST £24–£47

'This is a clever operation designed to appeal to all comers, all ages and all pockets,' summed up one visitor. The transition from thatched village pub to a successful 'food pub', with beams and a big fireplace still intact, shows what can be done with a little ingenuity and common sense. As with other establishments in the Huntsbridge group (see the White Hart, Great Yeldham; and Three Horseshoes, Madingley), the Pheasant is chef-run, which tends to put the emphasis where it matters from our readers' point of view. A wide-ranging menu runs from spinach and ricotta ravioli, via pan-fried scallops with a bittersweet courgette chutney flavoured with thyme and orange, to pink lamb cutlets with a rich gratin dauphinoise. 'You can eat anything, anywhere you like,' one reporter was pleased to find. Portions are 'generous but manageable', the kitchen is adaptable, not least where children are concerned, and service is 'prompt, polite and efficient'.

As at its sister establishments, the wine list is an appealing range of around 100 international bins skilfully put together by Master of Wine John Hoskins and helpfully presented by style. Good drinking can be had at all price levels (house wines start at £9.75 a bottle, £1.85 a glass), but mark-ups sensibly decrease as the quality rises.

CHEF: Martin Lee   PROPRIETOR: Huntsbridge Ltd   OPEN: all week 12 to 2, 6.30 (6 Sat, 7 Sun) to 10 (9.30 Sun)   MEALS: alc (main courses £9 to £16)   SERVICE: not inc   CARDS: Amex, Delta, Diners, MasterCard, Switch, Visa   DETAILS: 120 seats. 28 seats outside. Private parties: 30 main room. Car park. Vegetarian meals. Children's helpings. No smoking in dining room. Occasional music

---

See inside the front cover for an explanation of the symbols used at the tops of entries.

KING'S CLIFFE   Northamptonshire   map 6

King's Cliffe House ♈ ⅙✹

31 West Street, King's Cliffe PE8 6XB
TEL/FAX: (01780) 470172   COOKING 4
EMAIL: ahkwil@kingshouse.freeserve.co.uk   COST £25–£43

The house, in a 'quaint, isolated' village, yet not far from the A1, dates variously from Georgian to Victorian times. Drinks and home-marinated olives are served in a small cottagey lounge, the dining room is 'neatly set out with a homely feel', and the food's broadly English character derives in large part from carefully sourced materials: many are local and therefore seasonal (look out for mushrooms), some organic, others free-range or additive-free. A starter plate of mixed fish, for example, might include home-smoked eel from the River Nene. The cooking generally avoids exotic and spectacular ideas in favour of, for example, a tartlet of spinach with soft quail's egg and hollandaise, or steamed sea bass on mixed mushroom sauce.

One summer visitor enjoyed a full-flavoured plate of 'gooseberry goodies', including crème brûlée, ice cream, and 'plain stewed' with elderflower, while a winter one finished with a variation on sticky toffee pudding with apricots. The entire waiting staff consists of one person: Andrew Wilshaw (for it is he) is 'courteous and helpful throughout', and answers questions 'with knowledgeable enthusiasm'. Wines are chosen with intelligence and a sense of adventure, offering good choice from all over the globe and prices geared to encourage experimentation: for example, Ca' del Solo Malvasia Bianca 1996 from California's Bonny Doon Vineyard is a modest £14.50, and six house wines begin in France at £9.95.

CHEFS/PROPRIETORS: Emma Jessop and Andrew Wilshaw   OPEN: Wed to Sat D only 7 to 9.30   CLOSED: 25 and 26 Dec, 1 Jan, bank hols   MEALS: alc (main courses £11 to £15)   SERVICE: net prices   CARDS: none   DETAILS: 20 seats. Private parties: 20 main room. Car park. Vegetarian meals. Children's helpings. No smoking in dining room. No music

KING'S LYNN   Norfolk   map 6

Rococo ♈

11 Saturday Market Place, King's Lynn PE30 5DQ
TEL/FAX: (01553) 771483   COOKING 5
EMAIL: rococorest@aol.com   COST £26–£57

The pulsating colour scheme at Rococo seems designed to stick in the memory, for all that the tone of the place is comfortingly domestic rather than voguishly frantic. Inviting sofas with magazines to hand may tempt you to rest awhile before dining, and Nick Anderson's approach is one of good cheer and civility. He proudly announces that his kitchen is using more in the way of local supplies than ever before, as the numbers of independent quality food producers continue to grow, and his cooking style echoes that diversity.

High-class comfort food may be one view of it. Sautéed wild mushrooms on brioche toast with a poached duck egg, or roast loin of Norfolk lamb with swede fondant and mustard spätzli won't lack for supporters. Performance, however, has varied during the course of a meal, from a garnish of shrimp tortellini that added little to a dish of roast monkfish, to well-balanced duck magret and confit with 'smokie' vegetables and gratin dauphinois. Puddings are reckoned to be a strong suit, with both lemon tart on a citrus caramel sauce, and caramelised rice pudding with a duo of fruit sauces showing up well. Service might be sharpened up a bit, particularly with regard to the archaic practice of confiscating the wine bottle once the first glasses have been poured, and then not noticing when refills are needed. A pity this, for the wines on offer are eminently quaffable, drawn from a cosmopolitan collection of producers renowned for their high standards. Four pages of 'personal choice' wines begin with a southern French Chardonnay for £12.95; Merlot is £11.95.

CHEFS: Nick Anderson and Alex Howard   PROPRIETORS: Anne and Nick Anderson   OPEN: Tue to Sat L 12 to 1.30, Mon to Sat D 7 to 10   CLOSED: 24 to 31 Dec, 1 to 2 May   MEALS: Set L £9.50 (1 course) to £14.50, Set D £24.50 (2 courses) to £34.50   SERVICE: not inc, card slips closed   CARDS: Amex, Delta, Diners, MasterCard, Switch, Visa   DETAILS: 40 seats. Private parties: 40 main room. Vegetarian meals. Children's helpings. No smoking while others eat. Wheelchair access (also WC). Music   (£5)

KINGTON Herefordshire   map 5

▲ *Penrhos Court* ✸✱

Kington HR5 3LH
TEL: (01544) 230720   FAX: (01544) 230754
EMAIL: martin@penrhos.co.uk
on A44, ½m E of Kington

COOKING 4
COST £40–£51

There may be a sudden vogue for organic restaurants, but Daphne Lambert and Martin Griffiths claim to have got there first and have the Soil Association certificate to prove it. At Penrhos Court, going organic isn't a lifestyle choice; it simply ensures continuity for this extraordinarily tranquil thirteenth-century smallholding that has always had close ties to the land. Daphne's cooking has embodied the principles of good eating and sound nutrition for twenty years. But an inspector noted that it has acquired a new sophistication of late, so that these principles 'seemed in harmony as never before'. Dinner is served in the magnificent medieval hall, all 'wonky' flagstones and enormous wooden beams. A simple four-course menu, with no choice before main, is the format. Impeccably fresh ingredients, 'clear and subtle' flavours and good timing ensure that it is a successful one. A summer meal started with well-balanced potato and lovage soup, then vegetable sushi filled with good red rice that 'a lesser cook would have been afraid wasn't interesting enough'. Sea bass was perfectly judged, as was the accompanying ginger and chive cream sauce. Bread is 'brilliant', and desserts such as lemon geranium cake, or papaya with ginger syllabub pretty good as well. The organic commitment extends to the wine list, with house wine at £13.50.

Use the lists towards the front of the book to find suitable restaurants for special occasions.

CHEF: Daphne Lambert   PROPRIETORS: Daphne Lambert and Martin Griffiths   OPEN: all week D only 7.15 to 9.30   MEALS: Set D £29.50 to £31.50   SERVICE: not inc, card slips closed   CARDS: Amex, Delta, MasterCard, Switch, Visa   DETAILS: 70 seats. 200 seats outside. Private parties: 80 main room, 20 and 50 private rooms. Car park. Vegetarian meals. Children's helpings. No smoking in dining room. Wheelchair access (not WC). Occasional music   ACCOMMODATION: 15 rooms, all with bath/shower. TV. Phone. B&B £50 to £110 (surcharge on credit card payments). Rooms for disabled. Baby facilities (*The Which? Hotel Guide*)

KIRKHAM Lancashire   map 8

Cromwellian

16 Poulton Street, Kirkham PR4 2AB   COOKING 4
TEL: (01772) 685680   FAX: (01772) 684381   COST £26–£40

'Homely' furnishings, knick-knacks that include family photographs, and 'good, honest home cooking' have combined to produce a successful formula for the Fawcetts. Peter Fawcett provides 'very good' service while Josie Fawcett's cooking elicits praise for its down-to-earth no-nonsense approach. A few pre-meal hors d'oeuvres – quiche and 'a little liver mixture', say – arrive before starters of broccoli, pea and mint soup, or 'nicely presented' white Stilton and filo parcels with roasted peppers. Main courses stick to the chicken or salmon or steak route, the last attracting a £5 supplement, although an inspector observed 'the Fawcetts know what they want to provide to the local restaurant-going community'. The beef might come with a spicy tomato salsa; chicken with Puy lentils, bacon and Madeira sauce; and salmon with a niçoise-style salad. Vegetables are plainly cooked, with the exception of the house speciality, a variation of dauphinoise that was enjoyed by two reporters who together 'managed to devour quite a large dish'. Finish with chocolate and pear upside-down sponge, or apricot and almond crumble. Ice cream is bought in from Cheshire Farms. There is a good showing of halves on the global wine list, which is decisive, some countries limited to one choice. House wines are £10.50.

CHEF: Josie Fawcett   PROPRIETORS: Peter and Josie Fawcett   OPEN: Tue to Sat D only 7 to 9 CLOSED: 1 week Feb, 2 weeks Sept   MEALS: Set D £16   SERVICE: not inc, card slips closed CARDS: Amex, Delta, Diners, MasterCard, Switch, Visa   DETAILS: 28 seats. Private parties: 10 main room, 10 private room. Vegetarian meals. Wheelchair access (not WC). No music   (£5)

LANGAR Nottinghamshire   map 5

▲ *Langar Hall* ⚡✳

Langar NG13 9HG
TEL: (01949) 860559   FAX: (01949) 861045
EMAIL: langarhall-hotel@ndirect.co.uk   COOKING 3
between A46 and A52, 4m S of Bingham   COST £24–£59

Langar Hall is, by the owner's admission, an 'unusual restaurant in the country', in fact on the edge of a village, with a pillared hall, statues of nude ladies, and marbled Adam columns. It is a place that owes much of its considerable character to Imogen Skirving, who 'keeps things on track'. A generous carte departs only rarely from traditional ideas: lambs' sweetbreads are served with caper sauce, roast cod comes with parsley sauce, and venison with port sauce.

Twice-baked cheese soufflé, a regular fixture and a warmly recommended way to start, uses local Colston Bassett Stilton; other quality materials include naturally reared meats (some from rare breeds) from nearby Northfield Farm. Vegetables are 'hearty' and well cooked, and the two-course set-price lunch might offer leek and potato soup followed by shark steak with aïoli relish. The seasons may occasionally stretch a little, producing raspberry shortbread in April, and strawberry sabayon in November, but results are sound, the shortbread proving the highlight of one reporter's meal. Although France provides most of the wines, the range is encouragingly wide, quality is high, and the house selection points to some of the more interesting bottles under £20. Prices start at £10.

CHEF: Toby Garratt   PROPRIETOR: Imogen Skirving   OPEN: all week 12 to 2, 7 to 9.30 (10 Fri and Sat, 8.30 Sun)   MEALS: alc (main courses £10 to £22). Set L £10 (2 courses), Set D £17.50   SERVICE: 5% (optional), card slips closed   CARDS: Amex, Diners, MasterCard, Switch, Visa   DETAILS: 60 seats. 12 seats outside. Private parties: 46 main room, 10 and 22 private rooms. Car park. Vegetarian meals. Children's helpings. No smoking in 1 dining room. Wheelchair access (also WC). Occasional music   ACCOMMODATION: 10 rooms, all with bath/shower. TV. Phone. B&B £65 to £150. Baby facilities. Fishing (*The Which? Hotel Guide*) (£5)

LANGFORD BUDVILLE Somerset   map 2

▲ *Bindon Country House, Wellesley Restaurant* ⁵⁄★

Langford Budville TA21 0RU
TEL: (01823) 400070   FAX: (01823) 400071   COOKING 2
EMAIL: bindonhouse@msn.co.uk   COST £26–£69

When they renovated this exotically gabled seventeenth-century house, Mark and Lynn Jaffa took as their theme Arthur Wellesley, Duke of Wellington, even giving the peacocks which strut in the gardens the names of Arthur, Kitty (his wife) and Mrs Arbuthnot (the other woman). Visitors to these sumptuous surrounds in the serenest of settings must expect luxury and adornment in spades, particularly of Patrick Robert's haute cuisine. He works through various cappuccinos and nages before arriving at the climax of his decorative powers, the desserts: adventures in biscuitry and spun sugar 'like something out of a Miró painting'. Start with poached egg draped over grilled smoked salmon, graduate to roast guinea fowl with wild mushroom ravioli, and end with a trilogy of chocolate, or citrus tart with raspberry ice cream. Welcome and service are appreciated for their warmth and promptness. The wine list is stuffed with classic names from classic areas at prices you might expect; there are also four house wines of each colour for less than £16.50.

'When taking the order for the main course we were asked, "Beef or lamb?" I asked, "How are they done?" and the waiter said, "Cooked." I am not sure if he was being funny or not.'
(On eating in Hampshire)

CHEF: Patrick Robert   PROPRIETORS: Mark and Lynn Jaffa   OPEN: all week 12 to 2, 7.30 to 9.30   MEALS: alc L (main courses £16 to £18.50). Set L Mon to Sat £12.95 (2 courses) to £16.95, Set L Sun £18.95, Set D £29.50   SERVICE: not inc, card slips closed   CARDS: Amex, Delta, Diners, MasterCard, Switch, Visa   DETAILS: 50 seats. 30 seats outside. Private parties: 50 main room, 25 private room. Car park. Vegetarian meals. Children's helpings. Jacket and tie. No smoking in dining room. Wheelchair access (also WC). Music   ACCOMMODATION: 12 rooms, all with bath/shower. TV. Phone. B&B £85 to £155. Baby facilities. Swimming pool (*The Which? Hotel Guide*) £5

LANGHO Lancashire   map 8

▲ *Northcote Manor* ♟ ⚹

Northcote Road, Langho BB6 8BE
TEL: (01254) 240555   FAX: (01254) 246568
EMAIL: reservations@ncotemanor.demon.co.uk   COOKING 7
on A59, 8½m E of M6 exit 31   COST £26–£74

Since the last edition of the *Guide* the dining room has undergone a complete transformation, and the face-lift has worked a treat: it now feels 'fresher, brighter and modern', helped by some attractively colourful fabrics. The food's focus remains as before, with local produce imparting a regional feel to some of the dishes: black pudding appears in a starter with buttered trout on a mustard and watercress sauce, and potted shrimps come with a broad bean, asparagus and tomato salsa. Nigel Haworth's cooking runs mostly along classical lines – breast of wood pigeon comes with foie gras, black pea purée, bacon and cabbage – but it keeps up interest with its modestly enterprising partnerings, such as the coriander samosas that come with lobster bisque, for instance.

A couple of seafood dishes can be taken as a starter, intermediate or main course: for example lightly browned, soft-textured, fresh-tasting scallops with a truffled chive purée. Generally first-class materials, spot-on timing and skilful saucing characterised an inspection meal, whose centrepiece was pink loin of lamb on creamy dauphinois potatoes in a deep brown, well-reduced sauce incorporating Madeira and foie gras. An ice cream or sorbet is typically slotted into desserts: a rose petal version on top of hot chocolate pudding, for example, and a Lancashire cheese ice cream with apple crumble soufflé. Dinner is leisurely, and Craig Bancroft leads a team of knowledgeable and obliging staff who are 'correct but not stuffy', a description that could equally be applied to the wine list. Drawing as much inspiration from the New World as from the Old, it offers a fair spread under £20 while also providing plenty of opportunities to splash out. House Spanish and Italian are both £14.50.

CHEF: Nigel Haworth   PROPRIETORS: Craig Bancroft and Nigel Haworth   OPEN: all week 12 to 1.30 (2 Sun), 7 to 9.30 (10 Sat)   CLOSED: 25 Dec, 1 Jan   MEALS: alc (main courses £17 to £23.50). Set L £16, Set D £37   SERVICE: 10% (optional)   CARDS: Amex, Delta, Diners, MasterCard, Switch, Visa   DETAILS: 90 seats. Private parties: 90 main room, 30 private room. Car park. Vegetarian meals. Children's helpings. Jacket and tie. No smoking in dining room. Wheelchair access (not WC). Music   ACCOMMODATION: 14 rooms, all with bath/shower. TV. Phone. B&B £80 to £130. Rooms for disabled. Baby facilities (*The Which? Hotel Guide*)

▲ *Langley House Hotel* ♥ ⅝✕

Langley Marsh, Wiveliscombe TA4 2UF
TEL: (01984) 623318   FAX: (01984) 624573
EMAIL: user@langley.in2home.co.uk   COOKING 5
½m N of Wiveliscombe   COST £40–£54

Look out for the large gold cricket hanging like a guild's trademark from the side
of this cream-painted building; otherwise it's easy to miss. A curved drive leads
through 'quintessentially English' gardens to a house so unlike a hotel that one
couple had difficulty locating the front door. Inside, it feels like a family home,
and Anne Wilson's 'polite and welcoming manner adds to the sense that you
have escaped to a posh friend's country home rather than a hotel'.

Most visitors come for old-fashioned hospitality and sound cooking rather
than excitement and novelty: Peter Wilson's daily-changing menu (no choice
until dessert) is light and fresh in style. A regular starter is pear marinated in
walnut oil with mild, herby cream cheese, which might be followed by roast sea
bass with a herb crust, or 'fabulously fresh' halibut, 'expertly grilled' and served
with two 'light, naturally sweet' pepper sauces. Meat cookery doesn't quite
reach the highs, but dishes such as honey-roasted duck with a well-flavoured
apple, calvados and thyme sauce please none the less. Icky sticky pudding comes
with 'a rich pool' of toffee sauce, or there might be strawberry galette or a
syllabub. Cheeses in 'tiptop condition' included Capricorn and Somerset
Camembert. The largely classical French wine list affords rich pickings for those
who like mature wines, while some choice selections from the New World help
to ring the changes. House vin de pays is £12.50, but prices swiftly climb above
£20 in almost every region, Chile being the notable exception.

CHEF: Peter Wilson   PROPRIETORS: Peter and Anne Wilson   OPEN: all week D only 7.30 to
8.30   MEALS: Set D £27.50 to £32.50   SERVICE: not inc, card slips closed   CARDS: Amex,
MasterCard, Visa   DETAILS: 20 seats. 8 seats outside. Private parties: 18 main room, 18 private
room. Car park. Vegetarian meals. Children's helpings. No children under 7 at D. No smoking in
dining room. Wheelchair access (not WC). No music   ACCOMMODATION: 8 rooms, all with
bath/shower. TV. Phone. B&B £75 to £127.50. Baby facilities (*The Which? Hotel Guide*) (£5)

▲ *Angel* ⅝✕ £

Market Place, Lavenham CO10 9QZ
TEL: (01787) 247388   FAX: (01787) 248344
EMAIL: angellav@aol.com   COOKING 2
on A1141, 6m NE of Sudbury   COST £18–£32

Situated in one of England's prettiest marketplaces, this ancient inn offers 'good
pub food, above the local average' at fair prices. A deceptively simple-sounding
and homely menu is served at plain wooden tables around an enormous
fireplace in a beamed dining area. Game (terrine with Cumberland sauce, roast
venison) and fish (grilled plaice, turbot fillet with crayfish tails) appear
alongside braised rabbit, and steak and ale pie. Some fish is home-smoked. In

summer, finish with strawberry meringue roulade, at other times chocolate fudge cake or steamed syrup sponge. Service has been 'excellent' but is not universally deemed a strength. Very few wines reach above £20 – indeed, the ten house wines stay mostly below £10 and can be taken on a part-bottle basis.

CHEFS: Mike Pursell and Chris Boyle   PROPRIETORS: Roy and Anne Whitworth, John and Val Barry   OPEN: all week 12 to 2.15, 6.45 to 9.15   CLOSED: 25 and 26 Dec   MEALS: alc (main courses £5 to £11)   SERVICE: not inc, card slips closed   CARDS: Amex, Delta, MasterCard, Switch, Visa   DETAILS: 100 seats. 60 seats outside. Private parties: 50 main room, 12 and 50 private rooms. Car park. Vegetarian meals. Children's helpings. No smoking in 1 dining room. Wheelchair access (not WC). Occasional music   ACCOMMODATION: 8 rooms, all with bath/shower. TV. Phone. B&B £43 to £85. Rooms for disabled. Baby facilities (*The Which? Hotel Guide*)   (£5)

▲ Great House 🐟✳

Market Place, Lavenham CO10 9QZ
TEL: (01787) 247431   FAX: (01787) 248007   COOKING 2
EMAIL: greathouse@clara.co.uk   COST £24–£54

The dining room of this exceptionally handsome house on the corner of the square is smart yet surprisingly cottagey: all-French staff have to take care not to nudge diners as they pass. Outside, gas heaters in the courtyard are one solution to capricious temperatures. The Crépys have been running their restaurant-with-rooms for fifteen years now, relying on trusted local suppliers for everything but cheese, which comes straight from Rungis. Lunch can be a full meal, or a single dish such as omelette or lamb navarin. Dinner offers an equally wide but more elaborate choice – gâteau of marinated foie gras with pistachios and prunes, maybe, or ballottine of smoked salmon with aubergines and anchovy butter – followed by something roast or pan-fried such as duck with ceps, or halibut on scrambled eggs. Dishes from the carte require separate vegetables. Pain perdu aux poires, or a Pernod version of crème brûlée indicate the style of desserts. The wine list majors on France but with plenty more besides, including half-bottles. House wines start at £10.20.

CHEF: Régis Crépy   PROPRIETORS: Mr and Mrs R. Crépy   OPEN: Tue to Sun L 12 to 2.30, Tue to Sat and occasional Sun and Mon D 7 to 9.30 (10 Sat)   CLOSED: last 3 weeks Jan   MEALS: alc (main courses L £7.50 to £9, D £14 to £19). Set L £9.95 (2 courses) to £14.95, Set D £18.95   SERVICE: not inc   CARDS: Amex, Delta, MasterCard, Switch, Visa   DETAILS: 45 seats. 30 seats outside. Private parties: 60 main room. Children's helpings. No smoking in dining room   ACCOMMODATION: 5 rooms, all with bath/shower. TV. Phone. B&B £55 to £112. Baby facilities (*The Which? Hotel Guide*)

LEEDS West Yorkshire   map 8

Brasserie Forty Four

44 The Calls, Leeds LS2 7EW   COOKING 5
TEL: (0113) 234 3232   FAX: (0113) 234 3332   COST £21–£47

Like its sister and neighbour Pool Court (see entry), Brasserie Forty Four has had a makeover, edging away from brown minimalism with the help of a black floor, silver furniture, and chair backs in 'a natty colourful tapestry effect'. The format and style of food have hardly changed, though. There are still good-value deals at lunchtime and early evening, as well as familiar Turkish spiced aubergine, or salt-cod 'fish cakes' with a Jackson Pollock of piquillo pepper sauce and olive oil coating the plate. The cosmopolitan menu runs the gamut from a terrine of herbed pork and Bury black pudding to deep-fried duck won tons, by way of pizza, paella, and 'The Posh Pastie': a moist filling of potted duck, foie gras, prunes and truffled Madeira sauce in a light pastry.

Plainer steaks or calf's liver, with a side order of skin-on fries, might suit some of the 'hearty noisy Yorkshire businessmen' who choose this as a base from which to set the world to rights. Desserts are truly assorted, taking in brioche and milk chocolate pudding with hazelnut cream, and Sambuca and blackcurrant parfait. Wines are equally mixed in terms of origin, cannily chosen, and fairly priced across a range from £10 to £40. House Côtes de Duras white is £9.90, Rowlands Brook Shiraz-Cabernet £10.50.

CHEF: Jeff Baker   PROPRIETOR: Michael Gill   OPEN: Mon to Fri L 12 to 2, Mon to Sat D 6.30 to 10.30 (11 Fri and Sat)   CLOSED: bank hols   MEALS: alc (main courses £8 to £13.50). Set L £9.75 (2 courses) to £12.95, Set D 6.30 to 7.15 £9.75 (2 courses) to £12.95   SERVICE: 10% (optional), card slips closed   CARDS: Amex, Delta, Diners, MasterCard, Switch, Visa   DETAILS: 90 seats. Private parties: 90 main room, 50 private room. Vegetarian meals. Children's helpings. No cigars/pipes in dining room. Music. Air-conditioned   (£5)

Fourth Floor 🦐

| Harvey Nichols, 107–111 Briggate, Leeds LS1 6AZ | COOKING 4 |
| TEL: (0113) 204 8000   FAX: (0113) 204 8080 | COST £27–£52 |

Often crowded at lunchtime, and never really intimate, the wide open dining room occupies part of the food department, with rooftop views from the huge windows in winter, and from an open terrace in summer. Wood, chrome, and a stainless steel kitchen give it a modern look, largely untouched by colour or fabrics. Former sous-chef Richard Allen spent a year in Australia before returning in January 1999 to take over an appealing, cosmopolitan menu that ranges from a bowl of Thai chicken noodles, via a 'moist, sweet, rich' parfait of chicken livers and foie gras (with a 'brilliant foil' of tomato and mint chutney), to an impressive langoustine risotto with scallops and mussels.

Good ingredients, fine accompaniments, and articulate presentation are the order of the day. Main courses may involve a lot of chargrilling and roasting, but they are done to good effect, typically accompanied by 'fabulous gravy': sizzling pink beef fillet with truffle polenta and an intense Madeira jus, for instance, and a similarly accomplished rump of tender young lamb, with aubergines to soak up the rich red wine and rosemary sauce. Desserts – exotic fruit ravioli, or banoffi tart with butterscotch sauce – do not elicit quite the same excitement, but service is both friendly and professional. Note limited evening openings, which also bring valet parking and live music. The sharply chosen varied wines (many also available retail) start at £11.95 and include fair choice by the glass.

New main entries and restaurant closures are listed near the front of the book.

CHEF: Richard Allen   PROPRIETOR: Harvey Nichols plc   OPEN: Mon to Sat L 12 to 3, Thur to Sat D 6 (7 Sat) to 10   CLOSED: 25 and 26 Dec, 1 Jan   MEALS: alc (main courses £10 to £16). Set L £15 (2 courses) to £17.50, Set D £14 (2 courses) to £16.50   SERVICE: 10% (optional), card slips closed   CARDS: Amex, Delta, Diners, MasterCard, Switch, Visa   DETAILS: 85 seats. 12 seats outside. Private parties: 200 main room. Vegetarian meals. Children's helpings. No-smoking area. Wheelchair access (also WC). Music. Air-conditioned

Leodis 🍶

Victoria Mill, Sovereign Street, Leeds LS1 4BJ	COOKING 4
TEL: (0113) 242 1010 FAX: (0113) 243 0432	COST £25–£51

This converted riverside warehouse, one of the first modern-style brasseries in Leeds, still maintains a lively, vibrant atmosphere and puts up a generous and appealing menu. If brasserie food is meant to offer a degree of comfort, then starters alone will do the job, in the form of pearl barley risotto with peas, Toulouse sausage with leek purée, or poached egg and mushroom croustade. Come to that, so will desserts of Yorkshire curd tart and 'wonderful, very thick, strongly dark' chocolate marquise. Reports suggest that the cooking has been variable, but for the most part the kitchen is able to turn out successful dishes of, for example, moist risotto with tender scallops and deep-fried squid, and a shellfish terrine 'bursting with flavour and freshness'. While meat dishes tend to be hearty, along the lines of calf's liver with rösti and bacon, or steak and Guinness pudding, a trio of vegetarian options might include tomato and basil tart.

Phil Richardson arranges his international collection of wines by price, with those over £25 labelled with refreshing honesty as 'expensive'. Wines from South Africa and Spain are highlighted, while fine-wine connoisseurs are invited to gaze at the 'odd bottles from their cellars in Paris' which, along with the expected *cru classé* clarets, include a couple from California's stellar Merryvale winery. Six house wines are £11.95 a bottle, £2.80 a glass.

CHEF: Steven Kendell   PROPRIETORS: Steven Kendell, Martin Spalding and Phil Richardson   OPEN: Mon to Fri L 12 to 2, Mon to Sat D 6 to 10 (11 Fri and Sat)   CLOSED: 25 and 26 Dec, 1 Jan, L bank hols   MEALS: alc (main courses £7 to £15). Set L £14.95, Set D (not after 7.15 Sat) £14.95   SERVICE: not inc   CARDS: Amex, Delta, Diners, MasterCard, Switch, Visa   DETAILS: 180 seats. 60 seats outside. Private parties: 180 main room. Vegetarian meals. Children's helpings. Wheelchair access (also WC). Music

Pool Court at 42

44 The Calls, Leeds LS2 7EW	COOKING 6
TEL: (0113) 244 4242 FAX: (0113) 234 3332	COST £33–£58

A nautical air pervades this restaurant down by the water ('the theme from *Titanic* was playing tonight'), with its smart cool grey and deep blue colour scheme. The food has never shied away from luxuries and takes a thoroughly modern approach in the form of corn-fed chicken 'pot-au-feu' with foie gras dumpling and truffle, or native oysters in a champagne velouté; even vegetarians do well out of this, with a 'pithiviers' of truffle and Parmesan potatoes on creamed parsley. The style ranges from devoutly French salade landaise to a very

Yorkshire chunk of Whitby cod, by way of Piedmont ravioli. While first courses at a meal in May tended to major on very cold pre-prepared dishes, some starters have been 'outstanding': for example, a well-balanced bavarois of piquillo peppers with creamed salt-cod and tapénade.

A foundation of good materials has produced crusted fillet of lamb, not pink as requested but served with a white bean purée and 'wonderful, deep, rich' thyme-flavoured roasting juices; and a crisp-skinned, lean roast breast and well-cooked leg of Lincolnshire duckling, served with orange-tinted natural juices. There is a feeling that some gestures – from appetisers, bread and pre-dessert to the garnishing of certain dishes – are beginning to overshadow the real goal of showing off quality produce at its best, which is one of the principles that this restaurant has long espoused. Service, although professional, could do with chivvying up a bit: the formal atmosphere is in marked contrast to the lively, relaxed brasserie next door. Wines are arranged by grape variety and aim for quality, which comes at a price. House Chilean Cabernet is £17.25, Australian Sauvignon £18.75. For those (and there are some) who forget what they have ordered, a printed card listing your dishes is now presented, and the bill comes with a sample menu and a recipe.

CHEF: Jeff Baker   PROPRIETORS: Michael and Hanni Gill   OPEN: Mon to Fri L 12 to 2, Mon to Sat D 7 to 10 (10.30 Fri and Sat)   CLOSED: bank hols   MEALS: Set L £14 (2 courses) to £29.50, Set D £29.50 (2 courses) to £35   SERVICE: 10%, card slips closed   CARDS: Amex, Diners, MasterCard, Switch, Visa   DETAILS: 38 seats. 20 seats outside. Private parties: 38 main room. Vegetarian meals. Children's helpings. No cigars/pipes in dining room. Wheelchair access (also WC). Music. Air-conditioned (£5)

Rascasse ▼

| Canal Wharf, Water Lane, Leeds LS11 5BB | COOKING 7 |
| TEL: (0113) 244 6611   FAX: (0113) 244 0736 | COST £25–£59 |

Big windows make the most of canal-side views at this large renovated warehouse, where old stone and new wood combine to make an effective setting for some sharp modern brasserie cooking. French is the orientation, and familiar ingredients are treated to a degree of invention without losing sight of the reasoning behind classic combinations. Mediterranean fish soup with all the trimmings is 'hard to beat', with a deep flavour of roasted shellfish and fennel, and just the right consistency, while a luxurious dish of pigeon breast, topped with foie gras and wrapped in cabbage leaf, was 'easily up there with the best' for an inspector. Likewise an enviable crisply topped crème brûlée 'makes you appreciate why this is a classic dish in the first place'.

Accurate timing has a lot to do with success: of calf's liver (served on creamy pomme purée and wilted spinach leaves with a well-reduced red wine sauce), and of 'splendidly moist' chunks of roast monkfish surrounded by a fricassee of wild mushrooms. Risotto-making skills are 'spot on' too, producing an enjoyable version from humble button mushrooms and a drizzle of truffle oil. Salads are impressive, whether simply green or with herbs, although dishes are generally self-contained enough not to need extra vegetables. The Fastrack menu continues to offer good value. Gaps in service have given rise to a few niggles, but staff (French and Yorkshire) are generally well versed in what's on the menu.

LEEDS

Wines are presented without pretension, with easily affordable bottles sitting side by side with classy bins. A trio of varietals from Canada and Mexico give added interest to a list that gains much of its substance from the Old World. Nine wines by the glass cost between £3.20 and £4.40.

CHEF: Simon Gueller PROPRIETORS: Simon Gueller and Nigel Jolliffe OPEN: Mon to Fri L 12 to 2, Mon to Sat D 6.30 to 10 (10.30 Fri and Sat) CLOSED: 1 week after Christmas, bank hol Mons MEALS: alc (main courses £10.50 to £17.50). Set L £13.50 (2 courses) to £17, Set D Mon to Fri 6.30 to 7.30 £13.50 (2 courses) to £17 SERVICE: not inc CARDS: Amex, Delta, Diners, MasterCard, Switch, Visa DETAILS: 100 seats. 25 seats outside. Private parties: 50 main room. Car park. Vegetarian meals. No pipes; cigars only after coffee. Wheelchair access (also WC). Music. Air-conditioned

Salvo's £

115 Otley Road, Headingley, Leeds LS6 3PX COOKING 2
TEL: (0113) 275 5017 FAX: (0113) 278 9452 COST £20–£38

Smartly kitted out, with a bar to one side, this long-running Italian's appeal is based on food that is 'fresh, not too expensive, and decently served'. It deals in hearty portions ('no wonder students love it'), whose mainstays are pizza – from simple mozzarella and tomato to a 'carnevale' version combining spicy sausage, meatball, chicken, ham, pepperoni, garlic butter and lots of cheese – and pasta: traditional spaghetti bolognese, or tagliatelle with smoked salmon. Some of the materials are sourced from Italy – the man who supplies fresh seafood also brings in sun-dried tomatoes, marinated anchovies, and olive oil from his cousin's farm in Puglia – and some of the ideas are not: for example, duck breast on oriental stir-fried vegetables with ginger and oyster sauce. Desserts might run to lemon polenta cake with citrus crème fraîche, or sticky toffee pudding. A modest wine list featuring mainly Italy and the New World is sympathetically priced, starting with house Italian at £9.75.

CHEFS: Michael Leggiero and Pam Nelson PROPRIETORS: the Dammone family OPEN: Mon to Sat 12 to 2, 6 to 10.45 (5.30 to 11 Fri and Sat) CLOSED: 24 to 26 Dec, 31 Dec, 1 Jan, some bank hols MEALS: alc (main courses £6 to £13) SERVICE: not inc CARDS: Amex, Delta, Diners, MasterCard, Switch, Visa DETAILS: 65 seats. Private parties: 15 main room. Vegetarian meals. Children's helpings. No-smoking area. No cigars/pipes in dining room. Wheelchair access (not WC). Music. Air-conditioned

Sous le Nez en Ville

The Basement, Quebec House, Quebec Street,
Leeds LS1 2HA COOKING 4
TEL: (0113) 244 0108 FAX: (0113) 245 0240 COST £19–£49

Handy for the station, but also in a Jekyll and Hyde part of the city (populated by office workers during the day, night clubbers after dark) the bare-boarded wood-panelled basement maintains a steady course. Its broadly European style takes in starters of goats'-cheese bruschetta with tomato and chilli jam, chicken and mushroom risotto, and roast French black pudding with champ mash. Red-blooded main-course grills and roasts – of ribeye steak or loin of venison – share the billing with chicken and wild mushrooms steamed 'en papillotte', and maybe an unusual partnership of braised rabbit with sun-dried tomtaoes and haggis. Seafood remains a highlight, however, delivering bright sounding plates of grilled sardines with coriander tapénade, roast salt cod with pickled samphire, and monkfish with Thai leaves and bean sprouts. Desserts tend to be more traditional, along the lines of raspberry cheesecake or sticky toffee pudding. The early-evening set-price menu is varied, interesting, and makes economic sense compared with the carte, not least because it includes a half-bottle of house wine (normally £9.50 a bottle). The wine list is designed to appeal both to mature drinkers and young palates, and pays as much attention to those on a limited budget as it does to the well-heeled. Claret buffs with an eye for a bargain need look no further than page 12, while others will delight in the spread of wines from some of the world's finest producers.

CHEF: Andrew Carter   PROPRIETOR: C.R.C.R. Partnership   OPEN: Mon to Sat 12 to 2.30, 6 to 10 (11 Fri and Sat)   CLOSED: bank hols   MEALS: alc (main courses £8 to £14.50). Set D before 7.30 (7 Sat) £15.95 inc wine   SERVICE: not inc   CARDS: Amex, Delta, Diners, MasterCard, Switch, Visa DETAILS: 86 seats. Private parties: 100 main room, 20 private room. Vegetarian meals. Occasional music (£5)

LEICESTER Leicestershire   map 5

Welford Place £

9 Welford Place, Leicester LE1 6ZH   COOKING 3
TEL: (0116) 247 0758   FAX: (0116) 247 1843   COST £19–£41

Opened as a Victorian gentlemen's club in 1877, Welford Place now operates as a flexible city centre meeting place and reading room, open for fifteen hours of eating and drinking six days a week throughout the year. Such an approach, edging towards the 24-hour society, is about as user-friendly as an eating house can get. Cooked English breakfast runs until noon, while sandwiches (BLT, smoked salmon) and light dishes of baked cheese soufflé with wild mushrooms, or potato and sausage salad with grain mustard dressing, are available all the time. Main meals stretch from roast guinea fowl with cabbage and bacon, via a vegetarian plate of couscous and ratatouille in filo pastry, to lemon cream tart or chocolate parfait. Around forty reasonably priced wines start with house French at £10.25.

CHEF: Paul Vidic   PROPRIETORS: Michael and Valerie Hope, and Paul Vidic   OPEN: Mon to Sat 8am to 11pm   MEALS: alc (main courses £6 to £17). Set L and D £12.50, Set D before 6 £25 for 2 people, inc wine. Breakfast and snack menus available   CARDS: Amex, Delta, Diners, MasterCard, Switch, Visa   DETAILS: 216 seats. Private parties: 80 main room, 16 to 70 private rooms. Vegetarian meals. Children's helpings. No music (£5)

'The rule here seems to be, if an ingredient can be seen under the microscope and you can attribute it to a trendy source, then list it on the menu.' (On eating in London)

Dining rooms where music, either live or recorded, is never played are signalled by No music *in the details at the end of an entry.*

LIDGATE

LEWDOWN Devon   map 1

▲ *Lewtrenchard Manor* 🍔 ⋇

Lewdown EX20 4PN
TEL: (01566) 783256   FAX: (01566) 783332
EMAIL: s&j@lewtrenchard.co.uk
off A30 Okehampton to Launceston road,   COOKING 5
turn left at Lewdown   COST £27–£49

Although it attracts an international crowd, this comfortable Jacobean pile (its
gardens are a feature) has a timeless quality about it. Heavy, dark-wood
furniture and panelling are lightened by great vases of flowers and chintz
upholstery, tables are large, well-spaced and candlelit, and warmth comes
equally from log fires and 'bright and hostessy' Sue Murray. As David Jones
departed for the Carved Angel (see entry, Dartmouth), Kevin Barron arrived to
take charge of the kitchen. His plainly worded menus, glued into a big leather
wallet, are well designed, varied, and indicate a busy kitchen, yet results on the
plate are clear and simple.

Quality ingredients and accurate timing have come together in, for example, a
piece of monkfish 'so fresh it was a revelation', served with tortellini filled with
spinach and ricotta, on a small pool of velvety fish sauce. Textures add to the
appeal, in a creamy crab pâté on a crisp croûton, and materials include roast local
pork fillet and hog's pudding (a pork and cereal sausage) served with potatoes
cooked in cider. Underlying all this is a classical eye that pairs pigeon with foie
gras, and binds together cubes of parsley-speckled ham hock into a terrine that is
not a million miles from jambon persillé.

Ice creams are good, judging by a Malteser version and a rum and raisin
version, and caramelised fluffy-grained rice pudding is 'like the very best
home-made'. A strong South African section on the wine list may reflect the
owners' nostalgia, but also offers high quality, good variety and fair pricing, and
delivers house wines at £10 each.

CHEF: Kevin Barron   PROPRIETORS: James and Sue Murray   OPEN: Sun L 12 to 1.30, all week D
7 to 9   MEALS: Set L £19.50, Set D £32   SERVICE: not inc, card slips closed   CARDS: Amex,
Delta, Diners, MasterCard, Switch, Visa   DETAILS: 35 seats. Private parties: 8 main room, 16
private room. Car park. No children under 8 at D. No smoking in dining room. Music
ACCOMMODATION: 9 rooms, all with bath/shower. TV. Phone. B&B £85 to £165. No children
under 8. Fishing (The Which? Hotel Guide) £5

LIDGATE Suffolk   map 6

Star Inn

Lidgate CB8 9PP
TEL: (01638) 500275   COOKING 1
on B1063, 6m SE of Newmarket   COST £20–£38

Pinkwashed in the East Anglian manner, this traditional English pub is formed
from two Elizabethan cottages, with pretty gardens front and back. Log fires are a
draw, as well as heavy oak tables, candles, friendly service, and 'a great
atmosphere'. And, of course, the food: garlicky Mediterranean aromas waft

361

around, telling of fish soup, paella, scampi provençale, lamb roasted with garlic and wine, monkfish marinière, and lambs' kidneys in sherry. The lady behind these surprises, in the middle of the small village in racehorse land, is an energetic and charming Catalan, who can also magic up a 'rich and brilliant' bread-and-butter pudding. Greene King IPA and Abbot are on handpump, and the wine list has been considerably boosted in the Rioja department, including a house Rioja at £11.

CHEF/PROPRIETOR: Maria Teresa Axon   OPEN: all week L 12.15 to 2 (2.30 Sun), Mon to Sat D 7.15 to 9.45   CLOSED: No food on 25 and 26 Dec, 1 Jan   MEALS: alc (main courses £9.50 to £12.50). Set L Mon to Sat £8.50 (2 courses), Set L Sun £12.50   SERVICE: not inc, card slips closed; 10% for parties of 10 or more   CARDS: Amex, Delta, MasterCard, Switch, Visa DETAILS: 55 seats. 25 seats outside. Private parties: 26 main room. Car park. Vegetarian meals. Children's helpings. Occasional music (£5)

LIFTON Devon   map 1

▲ *Arundell Arms* ⚞✳

Lifton PL16 0AA
TEL: (01566) 784666   FAX: (01566) 784494
EMAIL: arundellarms@btinternet.com   COOKING 4
just off A30, 3m E of Launceston   COST £28–£53

Made of dark grey stone, and creeper-clad, this comfortable old coaching inn is more than just a centre for the hunting, shooting and fishing fraternity. They have, admittedly, much to keep them occupied (including a 20-mile stretch of the River Tamar), but it is not necessary to know one end of a rod from the other to eat here. Standards remain 'predictably good', according to one visitor, in what amounts to a 'small ballroom' of a dining room, complete with ornate cornicing and dangling chandelier. The reasons are not hard to find. Materials are well sourced, mostly from the south-west – meat from Launceston, fish from Looe, cheese from Tavistock – and Philip Burgess has been at the helm for nigh on a decade; his daily-changing five-course set dinner (which replaces the old three-course version) runs in tandem with a menu priced according to the number of courses taken.

The style rarely strays far from its classical roots, taking in smoked haddock with poached egg; skate wing with scallops, St Enodoc asparagus and herb butter; and duck with pan-fried chicken livers and peppercorn sauce. Finish perhaps with chocolate soufflé or a prune and saffron cream tart. Staff are attentive, wines predominantly French but with dependable contributions from elsewhere, and the selection of half-bottles is welcomed. Half a dozen house wines start at £10. A newly opened second operation is the Dartmoor Inn in Lydford (see entry).

CHEFS: Philip Burgess and Nick Shopland   PROPRIETOR: Anne Voss-Bark   OPEN: all week 12.30 to 2, 7.30 to 9.30   CLOSED: 24 and 25 Dec, 26 Dec D, 31 Dec   MEALS: Set L £15.50 (2 courses) to £19, Set D £28.50 to £35.50. Light L available   SERVICE: not inc   CARDS: Amex, Diners, MasterCard, Switch, Visa   DETAILS: 70 seats. Private parties: 80 main room, 50 private room. Car park. Vegetarian meals. Children's helpings. No young children at D. No smoking in dining room. Music   ACCOMMODATION: 28 rooms, all with bath/shower. TV. Phone. B&B £44 to £110. Baby facilities. Fishing (*The Which? Hotel Guide*) (£5)

LINCOLN Lincolnshire   map 9

Jew's House ✦

15 The Strait, Lincoln LN2 1JD	COOKING 3
TEL: (01522) 524851 FAX: (01522) 520084	COST £16–£52

This Wold-stone double-fronted former shop is accessed down a passageway at the rear of the building as ancient as the house itself, which dates from around the twelfth century. That the internal space is as small as it is comes as no surprise, but this in no way detracts from a busy, comfortable, relaxed atmosphere, helped along by subdued traditional jazz. The menu is short on description, and remains predominantly Anglo-French, with significant nods towards the Mediterranean: tagliatelle with wild mushrooms, perhaps, or grilled goats' cheese salad with smoked bacon. The terse descriptions, however, translate on the plate as well-executed and balanced flavours and textures. Start with wild mushrooms in puff pastry, or fish soup with rouille and croûtons, and move on to noisette of lamb, or magret of duck with beetroot. Desserts come in for praise: lemon tart with crème fraîche, and tarte Tatin with calvados. Service is polite and efficient. The well-chosen wine list is keenly priced, with house wines starting at £10.25.

CHEF: Richard Gibbs PROPRIETORS: Richard and Sally Gibbs OPEN: Tue to Sat 12 to 1.30, 7 to 9 CLOSED: 25 and 26 Dec, 1 Jan MEALS: alc (main courses £13 to £16). Set L £5 (2 courses) to £7.50, Set D £25 SERVICE: not inc CARDS: Amex, Delta, Diners, MasterCard, Switch, Visa DETAILS: 26 seats. Private parties: 30 main room. Vegetarian meals. No smoking in dining room. Music

Wig & Mitre £

30 Steep Hill, Lincoln LN2 1TL	COOKING 4
TEL: (01522) 535190 FAX: (01522) 532402	COST £21–£47

Breakfast, daily and seasonal menus, and another for sandwiches and snacks, are the eating options at this 'splendid old pub' near the castle and cathedral; all are available throughout and all except breakfast can be taken from early in the morning until late at night. The informal tone is enhanced by the owners' invitation to 'use it as a meeting place, eating house, reading room or watering hole'. Décor of greens and reds 'looks like a *Changing Rooms* medieval conversion', thought one, while the cooking style is a mix of traditional and modern: from smoked haddock rarebit, Stilton mousse, or steak, kidney and ale pie, to seared smoked salmon with couscous, bream on Parmesan mash, or warm salad of chorizo with marinated potatoes. Desserts aim towards traditional custard tart or chocolate roulade with coffee bean sauce. Service is 'friendly, if not polished', and one reporter felt more could be done to provide for non-smokers. The main wine list, grouped by style, offers plenty under £20, including house French at £10.45. It is also worth looking at the blackboard list for bin-ends and seasonal offers, or drink Sam Smith's beer.

CHEFS: Paul Vidic, Peter Dodd and Mark Cheseldine PROPRIETORS: Valerie and Michael Hope, and Paul Vidic OPEN: all week 8am to 11pm MEALS: alc (main courses £6 to £17) SERVICE: not inc CARDS: Amex, Delta, Diners, MasterCard, Switch, Visa DETAILS: 120 seats. Private parties: 60 main room, 20 private room. Vegetarian meals. Children's helpings. No music £5

LINTON   West Yorkshire   map 8

▲ *Wood Hall* ⁵⚹

Trip Lane, Linton LS22 4JA
TEL: (01937) 587271   FAX: (01937) 584353
from Wetherby take A661 N for ½m, turn left to
Sicklinghall and Linton, then left to Linton and Wood   COOKING 3
Hall, and turn right in Linton opposite Windmill pub   COST £22–£55

Surrounded by 100 acres of woodland and manicured lawns at the end of a long,
dramatic drive, Wood Hall goes in for regular country-house hotel pursuits with
conference facilities, a health club and beauty salon. Dark wooden panelling and
a fleur-de-lys motif run through the house, and green- and crimson-embossed
velvet sets the tone in the dining room. Despite Thai crab cake, and seared
scallops with ginger and vanilla couscous, the kitchen tends not to go
adventuring much, preferring to stay in the realms of an impressively flavoured
duck confit, or a moist terrine of chicken and forest mushrooms wrapped in York
ham and served with onion chutney.

Dishes are well conceived and executed, timing is accurate, and ingredients
are sound, producing for example salmon fillet on a bed of spinach on a citrus
butter sauce, with coriander-flecked new potatoes. Vegetables are served
separately as well as being part of the main course, which might seem excessive
anywhere but Yorkshire. Vegetarian and low fat 'healthy options' are marked on
the menu, but if you see 'turkey dinosaurs', you have the children's version.
Desserts are a strong point, and the miniature selection samples lavender parfait,
mascarpone sorbet, a crisp, tangy lemon tart and 'small, dry brown cake'
supposedly derived from a recipe by Grandma Pomfret. Service is friendly,
despite the formal surroundings, and the wine list offers a fair range of prices and
tastes, starting at £11.95 for house wine and climbing steeply to expense-account
regions.

CHEF: Philip Pomfret   PROPRIETOR: Arcadian International   OPEN: Sun to Fri L 12 to 2, all week
D 7 to 9   MEALS: alc (main courses £18 to £20). Set L Sun £13.50, Set L Mon to Fri £15.95, Set D
£24.95. Bar food available   SERVICE: not inc, card slips closed   CARDS: Amex, Delta,
MasterCard, Switch, Visa   DETAILS: 80 seats. 35 seats outside. Private parties: 130 main room,
20 to 130 private rooms. Car park. Vegetarian meals. Children's helpings. No smoking in dining
room. Wheelchair access (also WC). Music   ACCOMMODATION: 42 rooms, all with bath/shower.
TV. Phone. B&B £95 to £170. Swimming pool. Fishing

LITTLE SHELFORD   Cambridgeshire   map 6

Sycamore House ♥ ⁵⚹

1 Church Street, Little Shelford CB2 5HG   COOKING 4
TEL: (01223) 843396   COST £31–£38

Ancient woodwork, low ceilings, and a cream-painted dining room characterise
this friendly, former pub on the edge of a straggling village. Tables are
generously spaced, service by Susan is considerate, and value is undoubted.
Michael's menus change daily, and balance meat, fish and vegetarian dishes
well, perhaps incorporating crisp red mullet with tapénade, roast rack of lamb

with creamed onions, or stuffed red pepper with herby couscous. The pattern is a simple three-course dinner, plus a carefully dressed mid-meal salad, that typically offers a soup (spinach and Stilton, or white bean and lentil) among the four starters.

'Genuine skill applied intelligently' is the kitchen's forte, and assured technique combines with tried and tested, but none the less appealing, ideas to produce Lancashire cheese sausage with chutney, Huntingdon fidget pie, and roast loin of pork with prunes. Five puddings still allow plenty of scope for variety: perhaps something chocolatey, a sorbet, and a brandy-snap basket filled with an inventive ice-cream such as lemon curd, or mincemeat and Grand Marnier. The wine list goes in for lots of exclamation marks and some splendid names at good prices: Sauzet's Puligny-Montrachet premier cru 1994 for £34.95, and Rockford's Basket Press Shiraz 1996, Barossa Valley, South Australia, for £22, to name but two. The house white Bordeaux is £9.95, the red Côtes du Rhône from Guigal £10.95.

CHEF: Michael Sharpe   PROPRIETORS: Michael and Susan Sharpe   OPEN: Tue to Sat D only 7.30 to 9   CLOSED: 25 Dec   MEALS: Set D £22.50   SERVICE: not inc, card slips closed   CARDS: Delta, MasterCard, Switch, Visa   DETAILS: 24 seats. Private parties: 24 main room. Car park. Vegetarian meals. No children under 12. No smoking in dining room. No music (£5)

LIVERPOOL Merseyside   map 8

Becher's Brook 🍴✳

| 29A Hope Street, Liverpool L1 9BQ | COOKING 5 |
| TEL: (0151) 707 0005   FAX: (0151) 708 7011 | COST £27–£82 |

This end-of-terrace Georgian house has been refurbished to give whitewashed brick walls, bare pine floorboards and green-painted woodwork. Tables and chairs are 1950s-style, the overall effect is 'clean and functional', and the décor's simplicity is quite a contrast to David Cooke's food. Although it is classically based, Japanese influences and modern ideas give direction to his eclectic menu. Bread and hors d'oeuvres come in for praise, as does a first course mille-feuille of foie gras and sautéed potatoes, with apple to cut through the richness. An assiette of terrines – pork and apricot, foie gras, chicken liver parfait, and mixed fish wrapped in leek – along with various chutneys and sauces is 'a real feast of a starter'. Others are no less accomplished: pigs' trotters stuffed with duck confit, or fillet of haddock en papillote with mussels, coconut and lemon grass.

Main courses, too, are complex and elaborate, for example roast lobster, served cold, on a smoked haddock and crab brandade, with Japanese salad in a dressing of coriander, orange and ginger. The Mediterranean flag is flown by poached halibut on braised provençale-style vegetables with sorrel butter sauce, and cannon of lamb with a sun-dried tomato crust, but the Japanese theme creeps in again later. Banana is coated in tempura batter and served on a banana biscuit, with butterscotch and rum-spiced caramel sauces and passion fruit ice cream. Otherwise consider rhubarb tarte Tatin, or an assiette of white and dark chocolate. Service has veered from 'poor' to 'delightful, bright and cheerful', and some criticism is levelled at the prices. The wine list scans the world, with plenty of choice at most price levels. The Proprietors' Selection starts at £13.90.

CHEFS: David Cooke and Gerard Hogan PROPRIETORS: Mr and Mrs David Cooke OPEN: Mon to Fri L 12 to 4, Mon to Sat D 5 to 10 CLOSED: 25 and 31 Dec, bank hols MEALS: alc (main courses £12.50 to £28). Set L and D 5 to 6.30 £17.75 SERVICE: not inc, 10% for parties of 8 or more CARDS: Amex, Delta, Diners, MasterCard, Switch, Visa DETAILS: 38 seats. Private parties: 40 main room. Vegetarian meals. Children's helpings. No children under 7. No smoking in dining room. Music

Far East £

27–35 Berry Street, Liverpool L1 9DF
TEL: (0151) 709 3141 and 6072
FAX: (0151) 708 9798

COOKING 2
COST £21–£48

The Far East seems just about all that is left of Liverpool's old Chinatown, according to one who considers it a mature restaurant where food has always come first; 'cleanliness is respected but interior decorators are not'. Standards vary, even during the course of a meal, with a strong suggestion that dishes most popular with Westerners may be the least successful. However, an inspector found a dish of lightly battered cod fillets with stir-fried vegetables to be a good example of the new wave, just as an 'authentically fatty and bony' roast duck, with crisp skin and 'voluptuously moist' rich meat, was of the old school. Dim sum have included a 'rare treat' of bat col sui mai (Chinese mushrooms and pork balls); accurately cooked if 'blandly spiced' salt and chilli spare ribs; flavourful fried crabmeat ball; and beef cheung fun made with good-quality meat and just enough ginger to give it lift, served with an 'excellent' rice pancake. Tea is free and liberally topped up. House French wine is £9.10.

CHEF: Chi-Keung Cheung PROPRIETOR: Ma-Sang Ho OPEN: all week noon to 11 (1am Fri and Sat) CLOSED: 25 and 26 Dec, Good Fri MEALS: alc (main courses £5.50 to £10.50). Set L £6 (2 courses) to £6.80, Set D £15 to £19.80 (all min 2 to 6 people) SERVICE: not inc CARDS: Amex, Diners, MasterCard, Switch, Visa DETAILS: 200 seats. Private parties: 250 main room, 60 private room. Car park. Vegetarian meals. Children's helpings. Wheelchair access (not WC). Music. Air-conditioned

Tai Pan £

W.H. Lung Building, Great Howard Street,
Liverpool L5 9TZ
TEL: (0151) 207 3888 FAX: (0151) 207 0100

COOKING 1
COST £21–£42

Less than two years into its life, Tai Pan has become a popular choice for Chinese cuisine in the locality, with 'a real buzz to the atmosphere'. Like its Manchester parent (see entry) it is sited above an oriental supermarket and occupies a capacious room featuring a dragon motif on green walls. The large menu incorporates popular crossover dishes, such as aromatic crispy duck, together with authentic Cantonese food – roast crunchy belly pork, say – and banquet dishes, such as steamed sea bass with ginger and spring onions (part of the most elaborate of the set meals, for two or more diners). 'Impressive' dim sum are served in the traditional manner, on trolleys, every Sunday. House wine is £8.50.

CHEF: Mr Khan   PROPRIETOR: Mr Chan   OPEN: all week 12 to 11 (9.30 Sun)   MEALS: alc (main courses £6 to £10.50). Set L £5.45 (2 courses) to £8.45, Set D £14 to £25 (min 2 people) SERVICE: not inc, card slips closed   CARDS: Amex, Delta, Diners, MasterCard, Switch, Visa DETAILS: 320 seats. Private parties: 250 main room, 70 private room. Car park. Vegetarian meals. Wheelchair access (also WC). Music. Air-conditioned

Ziba ♟ ꙮ   NEW ENTRY

15–19 Berry Street, Liverpool L1 9DF	COOKING 4
TEL: (0151) 708 8870 FAX: (0151) 707 1930	COST £21–£50

Berry Street is on the edge of Chinatown, and this relative newcomer to a city gastronomy that is developing late but fast is a few doors up from Far East (see entry). It was once a car showroom – Ziba's four-square logo is discreetly etched into the windows – and space has been used well to create an airy, relaxed, split-level dining room in the best modern tradition. Neil McKevitt is a refugee from the world of hotel catering, and the move here has enabled him to spread his wings in style.

Ideas are bold and trendy, incorporating crab and saffron soup with spinach gnocchi, and roast suckling pig served with champ and parsleyed butter beans. A slice of guinea fowl terrine, with foie gras running through it, is cleverly partnered with a layered cylinder of beetroot and orange, while a thick piece of beef fillet has been well served by its garnish of black truffle and an underlay of mixed mushrooms. Classical ideas are confidently brought off too, for example a pear and almond tart with pear sorbet, although fruits are not that plentiful among desserts. There is genuine imagination here, made all the more enjoyable by the obliging ministrations of staff. Ziba's cheerfully cosmopolitan wine list opens with four fruity examples under £10 each, and ends with a small selection of finer fare. In between, agreeably priced bottles are helpfully grouped by style, ranging from 'full-flavoured oaky whites' to 'big, chunky, powerful brutes'.

CHEF: Neil McKevitt   PROPRIETOR: Bispham Green Brewery Company Limited   OPEN: all week L 12 to 2.30 (3 Sun), Mon to Sat D 6 to 10 (10.30 Sat)   CLOSED: 25 and 26 Dec, most bank hols MEALS: alc (main courses £9.50 to £15.50). Set L and D 6 to 7 £10.50 (2 courses) to £13.50 SERVICE: not inc; 10% for parties of 8 or more   CARDS: Amex, Delta, MasterCard, Switch, Visa DETAILS: 120 seats. 30 seats outside. Private parties: 120 main room, 8 private room. Car park. Vegetarian meals. Children's helpings. No smoking in 1 dining room. Wheelchair access (also WC). Music (£5)

LOCKINGTON   East Riding of Yorkshire   map 9

▲ Rockingham Arms

52 Front Street, Lockington YO25 9SH	COOKING 3
TEL: (01430) 810607 FAX: (01430) 810734	COST £40–£49

Son Matthew has joined Sue Barker in the kitchen of this country restaurant-with-rooms (once a pub) to produce the two- or three-course set dinners. The half-dozen or so choices at each stage, 'all very appealing', are boosted by blackboard offerings of dill-crusted halibut, or pan-fried beef with a Madeira jus. Every kitchen has its favourite ingredients; here they include chicken livers – sautéed with fenugreek and chilli, and in a flavourful parfait with a fruitily sweet dressing – and belly pork, either done as a moist confit, or served with spring greens and a spiced plum sauce. There is a fondness for oriental ingredients, and for rösti and roast vegetables, which accompany all main courses. Saucing is 'gutsy', judging by a creamy dill version that enhanced a trio of fish on olive oil mash. Interest is maintained at pudding stage in the shape of orange and pecan sponge with toffee sauce, and a 'better-than-sex' bread-and-butter pudding. From sixty-plus wines it will not be difficult to find suitable partners for the food, given plenty of good names under £20, especially in the New World groups. Prices start at £12.95 for Chilean Merlot and Sauvignon Blanc.

CHEFS: Sue Barker and Matthew Barker   PROPRIETORS: David and Sue Barker   OPEN: Tue to Sat D only 7 to 10   CLOSED: Christmas and New Year, 2 weeks in summer, bank hols   MEALS: Set D £23.95 (2 courses) to £27.95   SERVICE: not inc   CARDS: Delta, MasterCard, Switch, Visa   DETAILS: 60 seats. Private parties: 14 main room. Car park. Vegetarian meals. No children under 10. Occasional music   ACCOMMODATION: 3 rooms, all with bath/shower. TV. B&B £85 to £110   (£5)

LONG CRENDON Buckinghamshire   map 2

▲ Angel Inn ♥ 🍴

47 Bicester Road, Long Crendon HP18 9EE
TEL: (01844) 208268   FAX: (01844) 202497   COOKING 2
on B4011, 2m NW of Thame   COST £25–£53

Steve and Angie Good's seafood-plus restaurant, located at one end of the village's main street, reels in diners with fish delivered daily from Billingsgate and Cornwall. The ten or so blackboard choices are all in a different modern key: bream fillet lies on black noodles with a lobster cream sauce, while crispy sea bass comes on chargrilled vegetables with a Thai green coconut and lime curry sauce. Non-fish dishes may be based on local game, black pudding or wild mushrooms. Typical starters are spicy moules, or chargrilled squid and merguez salad, with the promise of a warm marmalade and chocolate bread-and-butter pudding with vanilla custard, or iced Toblerone parfait, later. Sunday lunch is a traditional roast, while lunches on other days bring cod and chips, chicken and veg stir-fry, or filled baguettes. Service is by cheerful ladies in plum-coloured aprons. The shoal of fish-friendly white wines is to be expected, but those who are resolutely red in their drinking tastes will also find plenty of decent catches, particularly if they cast their lines in the Australian and Californian direction. House wines are £11.95 or £12.95 a bottle; all seven are £2.70 a glass.

CHEFS: Trevor Bosch and Donald Joyce   PROPRIETORS: Steve and Angie Good   OPEN: all week L 12 to 2.30, Mon to Sat D 7 to 10   MEALS: alc Mon to Sat (main courses L £7 to £11.50, D £10.50 to £17.50). Set L Sun £12.95 (2 courses) to £14.95   SERVICE: not inc   CARDS: Delta, MasterCard, Switch, Visa   DETAILS: 75 seats. 30 seats outside. Private parties: 35 main room, 8 to 35, 70 private rooms. Car park. Vegetarian meals. Children's helpings. No smoking in 1 dining room. Wheelchair access (not WC). Music   ACCOMMODATION: 3 rooms, all with bath/shower. TV. Phone. B&B £55 to £65. Baby facilities (*The Which? Hotel Guide*)   (£5)

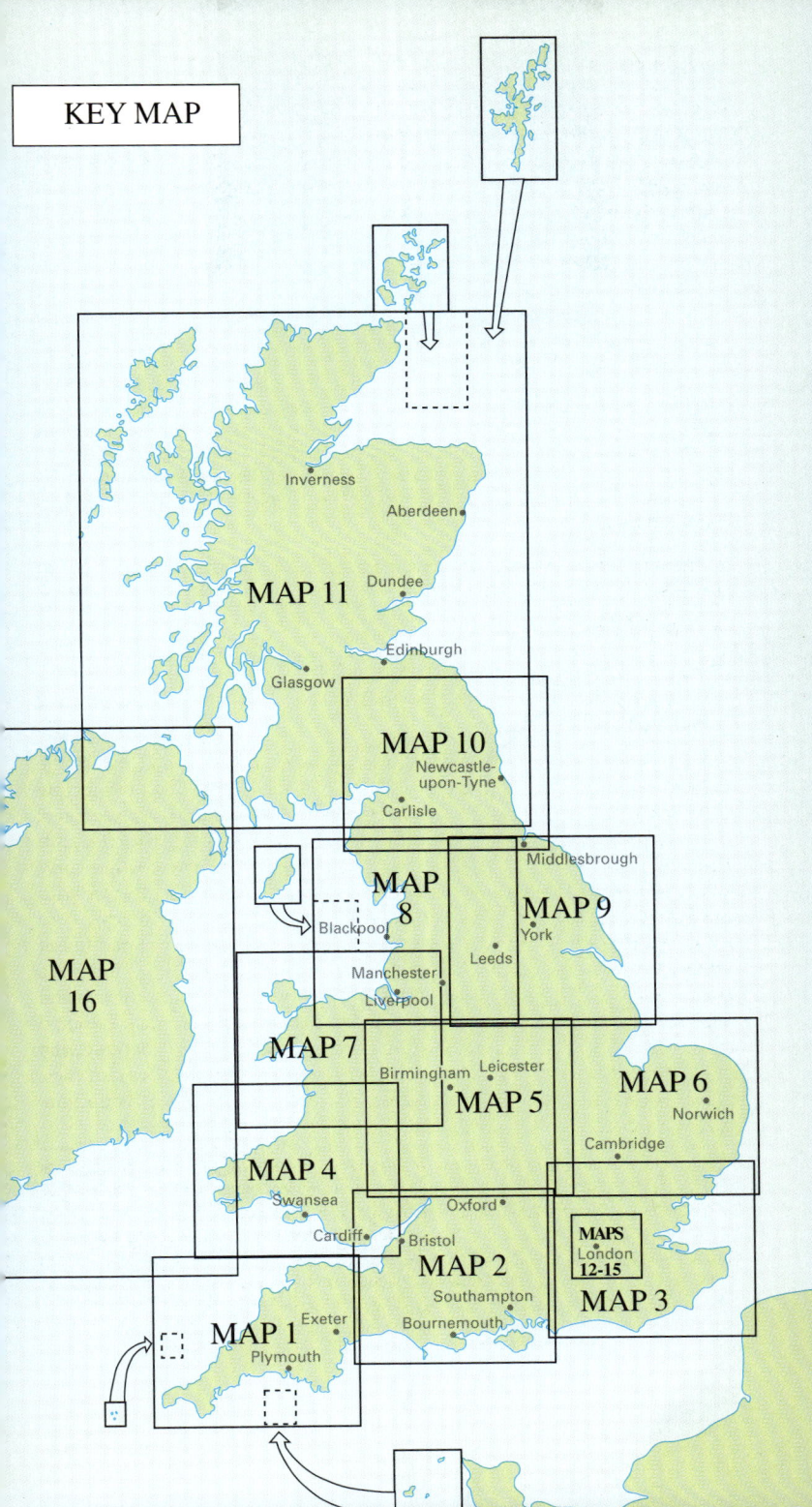

KEY MAP

MAP 11

Inverness
Aberdeen
Dundee
Edinburgh
Glasgow

MAP 10

Newcastle-
upon-Tyne
Carlisle
Middlesbrough

MAP 16

MAP 8

Blackpool
Manchester
Liverpool

MAP 9

York
Leeds

MAP 7

MAP 5

Birmingham
Leicester

MAP 6

Norwich
Cambridge

MAP 4

Swansea
Cardiff
Bristol

MAP 2

Oxford
Southampton
Bournemouth

MAPS
London
12-15

MAP 3

MAP 1

Exeter
Plymouth

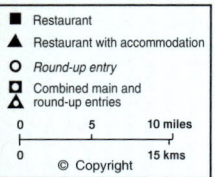

MAP 1

- ■ Restaurant
- ▲ Restaurant with accommodation
- ○ *Round-up entry*
- ▣ Combined main and
- △ round-up entries

0   5   10 miles

0   15 kms

© Copyright

4

Isles of Scilly
28 miles WSW of Land's End

New Grimsby

▲ **St Martin's**

○ *Tresco*

Hugh Town

Lundy Island

*B u d e
B a y*

*Port Isaac
Bay*

New Polzeath ○

B o d m i

▲ **Padstow**

Wadebridge

A39

R. Camel

Colliford
Re

Watergate Bay

• Bodmin

A30

C O R N W A L L

Newquay •

Ligger Bay

A392

A30

St Austell •

○ **Fowey**

A390

○ *Grampound*

St Austell Bay

A30B

Fal

Portreath ■

A390

○ **Truro**

A39

*St Ives
Bay*

A30

St Ives ▣

▲ **Portloe**

*Veryan
Bay*

Carnkie ■

A394

A30

A39

▲ **St Mawes**

St Just •

Penzance ■

A394

R. Hayle

Constantine

Falmouth

Maenporth

*Falmouth
Bay*

○ *Mousehole*

Porthleven ■

Mawnan Smith ▲

Mawgan ○

Gillan ○

*Lands
End*

*M o u n t ' s
B a y*

Lizard Point

MAP 2

MAP 3

Restaurant
Restaurant with accommodation
Round-up entry
Combined main and
round-up entries

0   5   10 miles
0   15 kms
© Copyright

Great Yeldham
Nayland
Dedham
Manningtree
6
Felixstowe
Harwich
Gosfield
Coggeshall
Colchester
Dunmow
Braintree
Felsted
ESSEX
Clacton-on-Sea
Imsford
Horndon on the Hill
Southend-on-Sea
R. Thames
Gravesend
Chatham
Maidstone
Whitstable
Faversham
Dargate
Canterbury
Margate
Pegwell
Bay
R. Stour
Deal
KENT
Boughton Lees
Barham
St Margaret's at Cliffe
Wye
Ashford
Dover
Sissinghurst
Biddenden
Folkestone
Sandgate
Cranbrook
STRAIT OF DOVER
Rye
Westfield
Dungeness
stmonceux
Hastings

MAP 4

- ■ Restaurant
- ▲ Restaurant with accommodation
- ○ *Round-up entry*
- ▣ Combined main and
- △ round-up entries

```
0          5        10 miles
0                   15 kms
        © Copyright
```

C A R D I G A N

B A Y

○ Newquay

A487

Fishguard Bay   *Newport Bay*   ○ Cardigan

R. Teifi

▲ Newport
A487

Porthgain   Mathry   ▲ Fishguard
■   ■   *A40*

St. David's
Head   ▲ Pontfaen

Ramsey   Welsh Hook   Rosebush
Island   ▲ ■
■ St David's ○   Wolf's Castle
          Solva   **P E M B R O K E S H I R E**   **C A R M A**

S t . B r i d e s   ○ Carmarthen
B a y   *A40*
                    Broad   *A40*
Skomer Island   Haven ▲ ○ Haverfordwest   *A40*

Broad Sound   *A477*   ○ Laugharne

Skokholm Island   Milford   *A478*
                    Haven ●
                              A477
                    ■ Pembroke   ○ Tenby
                                          Carmarthen
                                          Bay
                          Caldey
                          Island
                                                   ○ Reynoldsto

B R I S T O L

MAP 7

Restaurant ■
Restaurant with accommodation ▲
Round-up entry ○
Combined main and round-up entries ▣
Combined main and round-up entries ◬

0   5   10 miles
0   15 kms
© Copyright

I R I S H

S E A

Holyhead Bay

Anglesey

○ Church Bay

Llyn Alaw

Red Wharf Bay

Conwy Bay

Llandudno ▲

Glanwydden ○

Colwyn ◉

Holyhead ●

ISLE OF ANGLESEY

Holy Island

Menai Strait

▲ Beaumaris

● Bangor

A55

Lla Gi

A470

▲ Llanddeiniolen

Caernarfon ●

Foel Fras 942

Carnedd Dafydd 1044

A5

CONW

■ Llanberis

Glyder Fawr 999

▲ Capel Garmon

▲ *1085 Snowdon*

872 Carnedd Moel-siabod

C a e r n a r f o n

B a y

GWYNEDD

A487

Llyn Peninsula

Criccieth ■

Portmeirion ■

▲ Talsarnau

● Pwllheli

Tremadog Bay

▲ Harlech

◬ Abersoch

Bardsey Sound

Ganllwyd ▲

Aran Be 884

Aran Faw 905

○ Llanaber

A494

A470

Bardsey Island

Barmouth ●

Penmaenpool

Dolgellau ■

Cader Idris 893 ▲

○ Talyllyn

C A R D I G A N

B A Y

Aberdovey ▲

▲ Eglwysfach

A487

C a m b r i a n M o u n t a i n s

A489

Aberystwyth ●

A44

CEREDIGION

A487

◁ 4 ▷

MAP 9

- ■ Restaurant
- ▲ Restaurant with accommodation
- ○ *Round-up entry*
- ▣ Combined main and
- △ round-up entries

```
0           5          10 miles
0                      15 kms
```
© Copyright

△ 10

Whitby

A171

■ Scarborough

A170

A64

A65

Flamborough Head

Langtoft

A166

● Bridlington

B r i d l i n g t o n
B a y

66

A168

Yorkshire Wolds

A163

ST RIDING

A1035 A165

■ Lund ■ Lockington

YORKSHIRE

A1079

A1035

▣ Beverley

Walkington ▲

Hull

KINGSTON
UPON HULL

A63

● Kingston
upon Hull

ringham ▲ ○ Barton-upon-Humber

R. Humber

A15

Spurn Head

A166

TH
LNSHIRE

● Grimsby

Scunthorpe ● ● Cleethorpes

A18

A173 N.E.
LINCOLNSHIRE

M180

A15

A18

A46

A15

A1103

A631

A18

Louth ●

A46

A15

T h e   W o l d s

A158

A158

A16

A57 L I N C O L N S H I R E

■ Lincoln

A158

● Horncastle

Burgh
le Marsh
A158 ○

▽ 6

Skegness ●

11

A702

A721

A702

A703

A72 Peebles

A72

A697

A68

A697

Biggar

Into '07

A702

Culter Fell 755

M74

Hart Fell 808

Daer Res.

Moffat

Queensberry 697

A74(M)

A74

A701

e Nith

Dumfries

A75

A74(M)

R. Esk

A7

Galashiels

Gattonside

Melrose

Selkirk

B O R D E R S

Hawick

A7

A68

Ednam

Caldcleugh 608

The Chev

Kielder Water

DUMFRIES & GALLOWAY

A7

Canonbie

Brampton

A69

A689

A689

A74

R. Eden

A7

A689

Carlisle

A44

A69

A42

Melmerby

Cross Fell 893

A596

M6

A596

Cockermouth

A66

Skiddaw 931

Applethwaite

Penrith

A6

Workington

Bassenthwaite Lake

Braithwaite

A66

Watermillock

Tirril

Keswick

Ullswater

Ullswater

Cov Gre Res.

A6

Whitehaven

Derwent Water

Grange in Borrowdale

Haweswater

Appleby

Ennerdale Water

Krummock Water

C U M B R I A

A595

Wast Water

Scafell Pike 977

Grasmere

A66

A591

8

MAP 10

- ■ Restaurant
- ▲ Restaurant with accommodation
- ○ Round-up entry
- ▣ Combined main and round-up entries
- △

0 — 5 — 10 miles
0 — 15 kms
© Copyright

11

Berwick-upon-Tweed

Swinton

Holy Island

Farne Is.

Wark

The Cheviot
815

H I L L S

R. Aln

Alnwick

Alnmouth

A697

A1

A697

A68

A696

NORTHUMBERLAND

A1068

R. Blyth

Haydon
Bridge

Corbridge

Hexham

A69

R. Tyne

A68

Great
Whittington

R. Pont

Ponteland

Seaton Burn

Newcastle
upon Tyne

Gateshead

Tynemouth

East Boldon

TYNE
&
WEAR

A1

A194(M)

Sunderland

Derwent Res.

Carterway
Heads

A692

Consett

Stanley

Chester-le-
Street

A19

A1(M)

DURHAM

A68

Willington

Durham

A167

A688

HARTLEPOOL

A179

Hartlepool

Tees Bay

A689

Redcar

Romaldkirk

A688

Barnard Castle

A66

A68

A689

STOCKTON-
ON-TEES

Middlesbrough

REDCAR

A171

MIDDLES
BROUGH

A66

Yarm

R. Tees

A19

A172

Stokesley

9

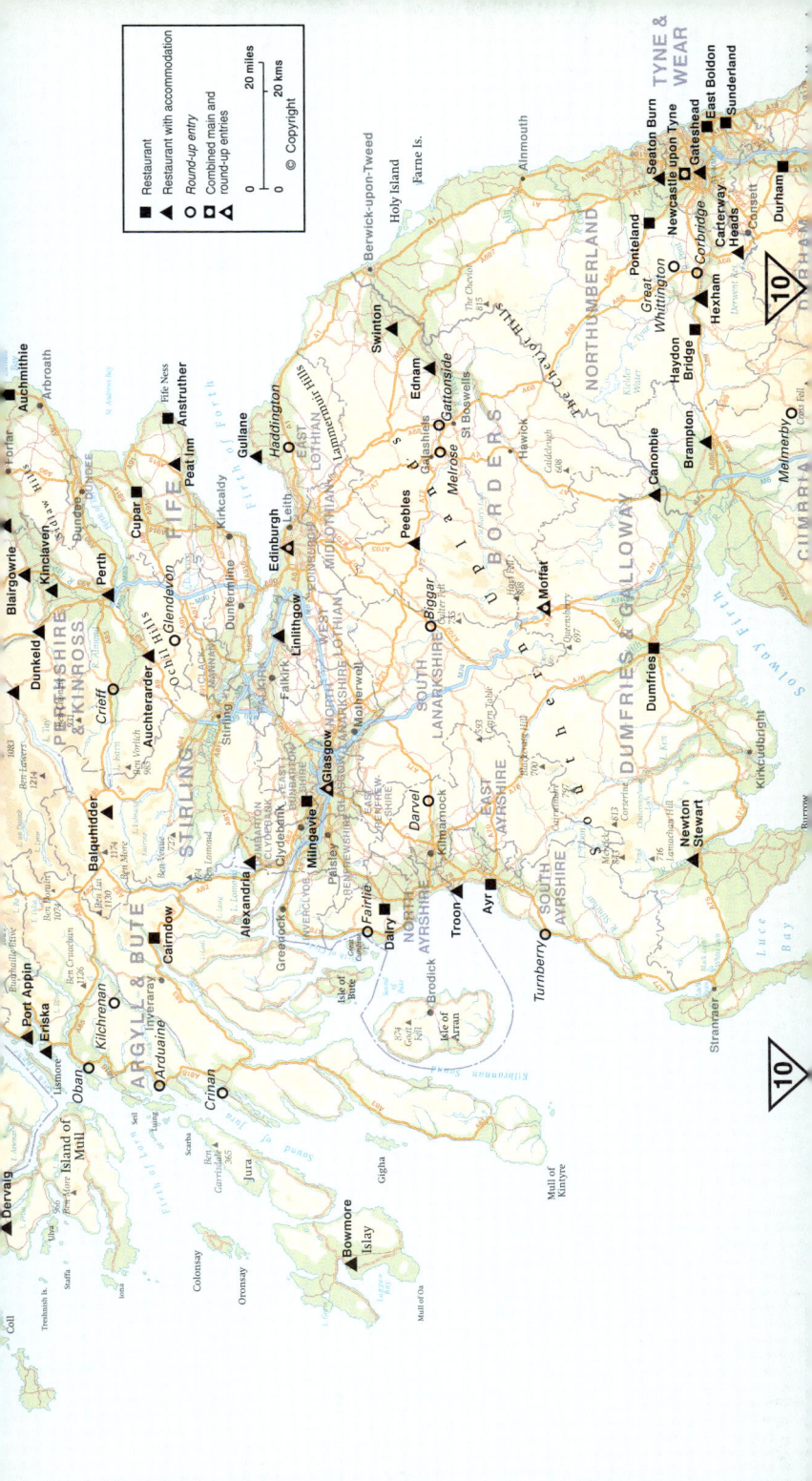

Legend

- ■ Restaurant
- ◣ Restaurant with accommodation
- ○ *Round-up entry*
- ◁ Combined main and round-up entries

20 miles

20 kms

© Copyright

10

TYNE & WEAR

Seaton Burn
Newcastle upon Tyne
Gateshead
East Boldon
Sunderland
Ponteland
Corbridge
Carterway Heads
Consett
Durham

NORTHUMBERLAND

Great Whittington
Hexham
Haydon Bridge
Brampton

CUMBRIA
Melmerby

Berwick-upon-Tweed
Holy Island
Farne Is.
Alnmouth

Swinton
Ednam
Gattonside
St Boswells
Galashiels
Melrose
Hawick

The Cheviot Hills
The Cheviot

Auchmithie
Arbroath
Forfar

Fife Ness
Anstruther
Peat Inn

Gullane
Haddington
EAST LOTHIAN

Firth of Forth

Kirkcaldy
Leith
Edinburgh
Dunfermline
Linlithgow
WEST LOTHIAN
MIDLOTHIAN
Falkirk

Peebles

BORDERS

Moffat

Canonbie
Dumfries
Newton Stewart

DUMFRIES & GALLOWAY
Kirkcudbright

Solway Firth

Blairgowrie
Kinclaven
Perth
Dunkeld
Cupar
Dundee
Glendevon
FIFE

PERTHSHIRE & KINROSS
Crieff
Auchterarder
Ochil Hills

Balquhidder
STIRLING
Stirling

Alexandria
Milngavie
Glasgow
Paisley
Clydebank
EAST RENFREWSHIRE
NORTH LANARKSHIRE
Motherwell

Biggar
SOUTH LANARKSHIRE

Port Appin
Eriska
Lismore
Oban
Cairndow
Inveraray
ARGYLL & BUTE
Kilchrenan
Arduaine
Crinan

Balquhidder

Darvel
Kilmarnock
EAST AYRSHIRE
Fairlie
Dalry
NORTH AYRSHIRE
Troon
Ayr
SOUTH AYRSHIRE
Turnberry

Brodick
Isle of Arran
Isle of Bute

Stranraer
Luce Bay

Dervaig
Island of Mull
Coll
Tiree
Staffa
Iona

Bowmore
Islay
Colonsay
Oronsay
Jura
Gigha
Mull of Kintyre
Mull of Oa

10

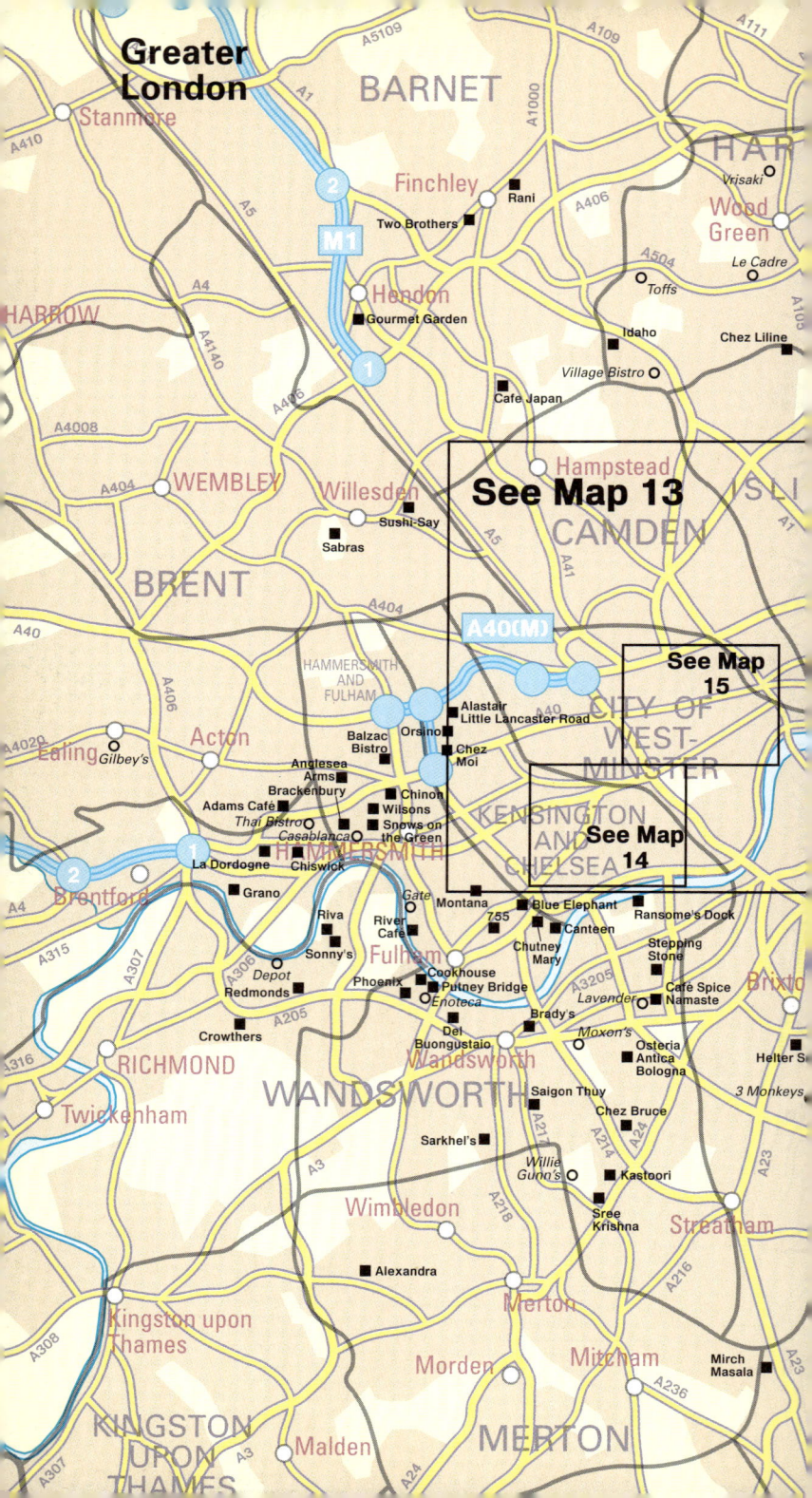

Greater London

BARNET

A5109 · A109 · A111 · A1000 · A406 · A5 · M1 · A1

HAR

Stanmore

Vrisaki

Finchley

Rani ■

Wood Green

Two Brothers ■

A504

Le Cadre ○

Hendon

Toffs ○

Gourmet Garden ■

Idaho ■

Chez Liline ■

Village Bistro ○

Cafe Japan ■

A406 · A105 · A4 · A4140 · A406 · A4008

WEMBLEY

Hampstead

See Map 13

ISLI

CAMDEN

Willesden

Sushi-Say ■

Sabras ■

BRENT

A404 · A404 · A41 · A5 · A1

A40(M)

See Map 15

CITY OF WEST- MINSTER

Alastair ■
Little Lancaster Road

Orsino ○

Balzac Bistro ■

Chez Moi ■

HAMMERSMITH AND FULHAM

Anglesea Arms

Brackenbury

Chinon ■

Adams Café ■

Wilsons ■

Thai Bistro ○

Snows on the Green ■

Casablanca

La Dordogne ■

Chiswick

HAMMERSMITH

See Map 14

KENSINGTON AND CHELSEA

Grano ■

Brentford

Montana ■

Blue Elephant ■

Ransome's Dock ■

Gate ○

755 ■

Riva ■

River Café ○

Canteen ■

Stepping Stone ■

Sonny's ■

Chutney Mary ■

Fulham

Depot

Phoenix ■

Cookhouse ■

Café Spice Namaste ■

Redmonds ■

Putney Bridge ■

Lavender ○

Enoteca ○

Brady's ■

Brixto

Crowthers ■

Del Buongustaio ■

Moxen's ○

Osteria Antica Bologna ■

RICHMOND

WANDSWORTH

Saigon Thuy ■

Chez Bruce ■

Helter S

3 Monkeys

Twickenham

Sarkhel's ■

Kastoori ■

Willie Gunn's ○

Wimbledon

Sree Krishna ■

Streatham

A3 · A216 · A23

Alexandra ■

Merton

Kingston upon Thames

Morden

Mitcham

Mirch Masala ■

KINGSTON UPON THAMES

Malden

MERTON

A308 · A307 · A3 · A24 · A236 · A23

EDMONTON

CHIGWELL

A1010

A10

A112

Woodford

A123

Hainault

A1112

4

REDBRIDGE

A12

A503

Walthamstow

A124

WALTHAM
FOREST

A104

A10

sclun
sa

nbul
ecisi

HACKNEY

ILFORD

A123

A406

A11

A118

NEWHAM

Barking

A13

Thai Garden

A102(M)

A114

BARKING &
DAGENHAM

HACKNEY

A11

East Ham

A13

New
Tayyab

TOWER
HAMLETS

A13

CITY

Poplar

R. Thames

Thamesmead

Moshi Moshi
Sushi

Big Chef

Mem Saheb

Woolwich

A206

OUTHWARK

A2

Greenwich

A102(M)

A205

A209

A202

Spread
Eagle

GREENWICH

A2

Holly

Thailand

Lawn

Chapter Two

A2

AMBETH

Lewisham

A20

Eltham

A210

Le Chardon

Babur Brasserie

A205

A20

ir
e

Dulwich

Catford

A205

A222

LEWISHAM

A211

Sidcup

Crystal Palace

A2212

A208

MAP 12

BROMLEY

A21

Beckenham

A208

A224

Mantanah

A21

■ Restaurant
▲ Restaurant with accommodation
○ Round-up entry

0   5km

0   4 miles

© Copyright

BROMLEY

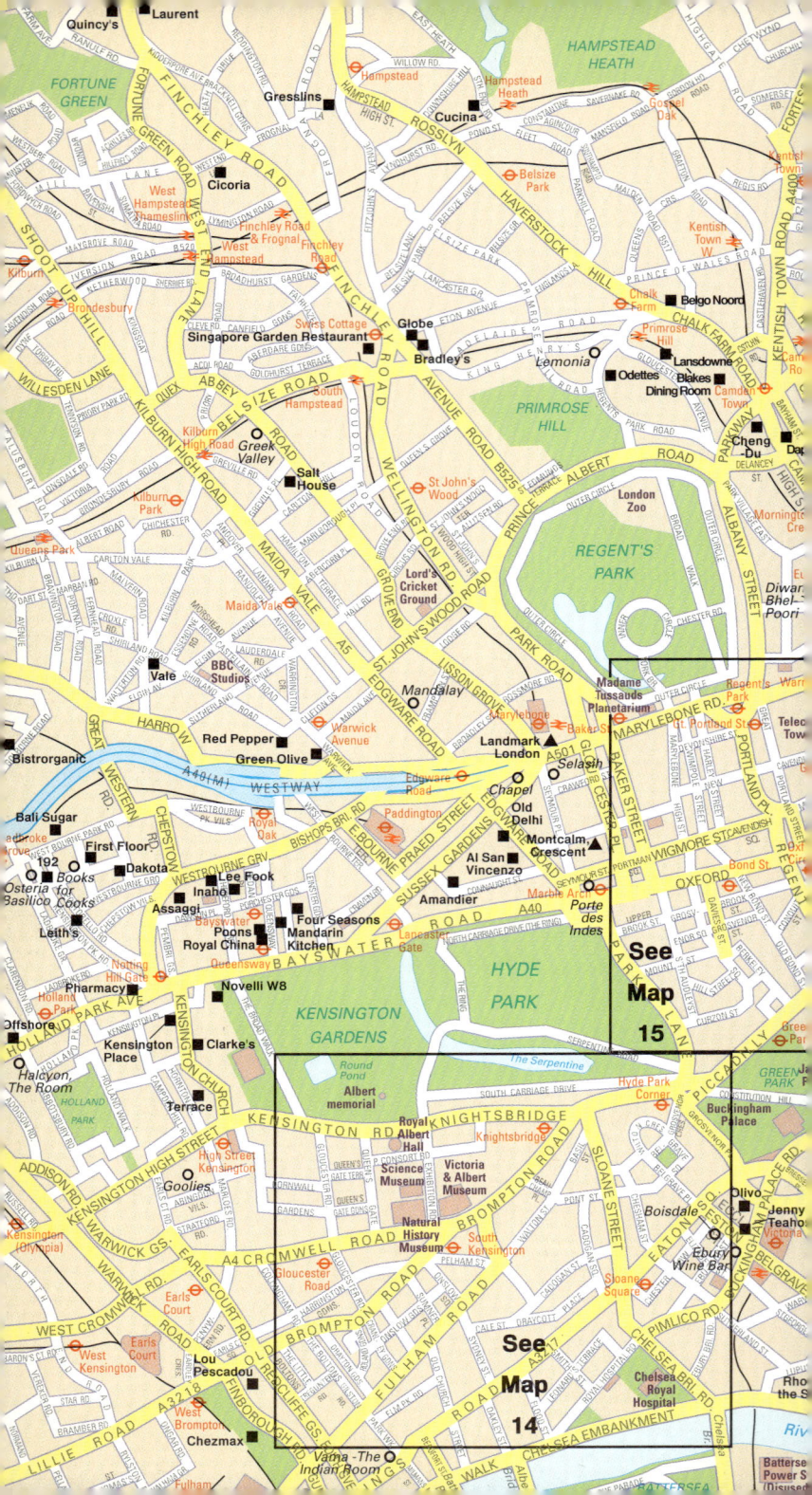

Central
London

MAP 13

■ Restaurant
▲ Restaurant with accommodation
○ Round-up entry

0   440   880 yds
0   800m

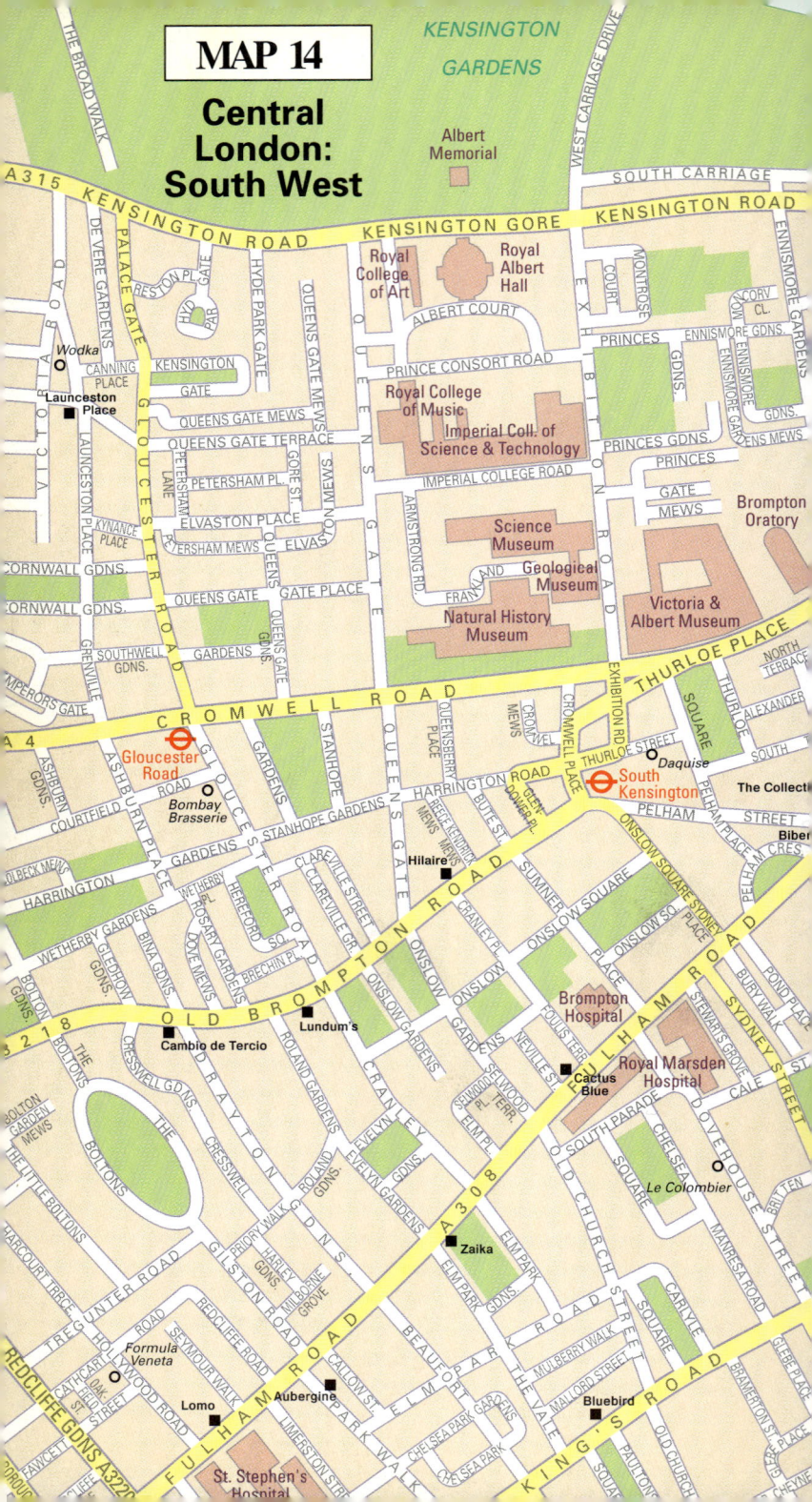

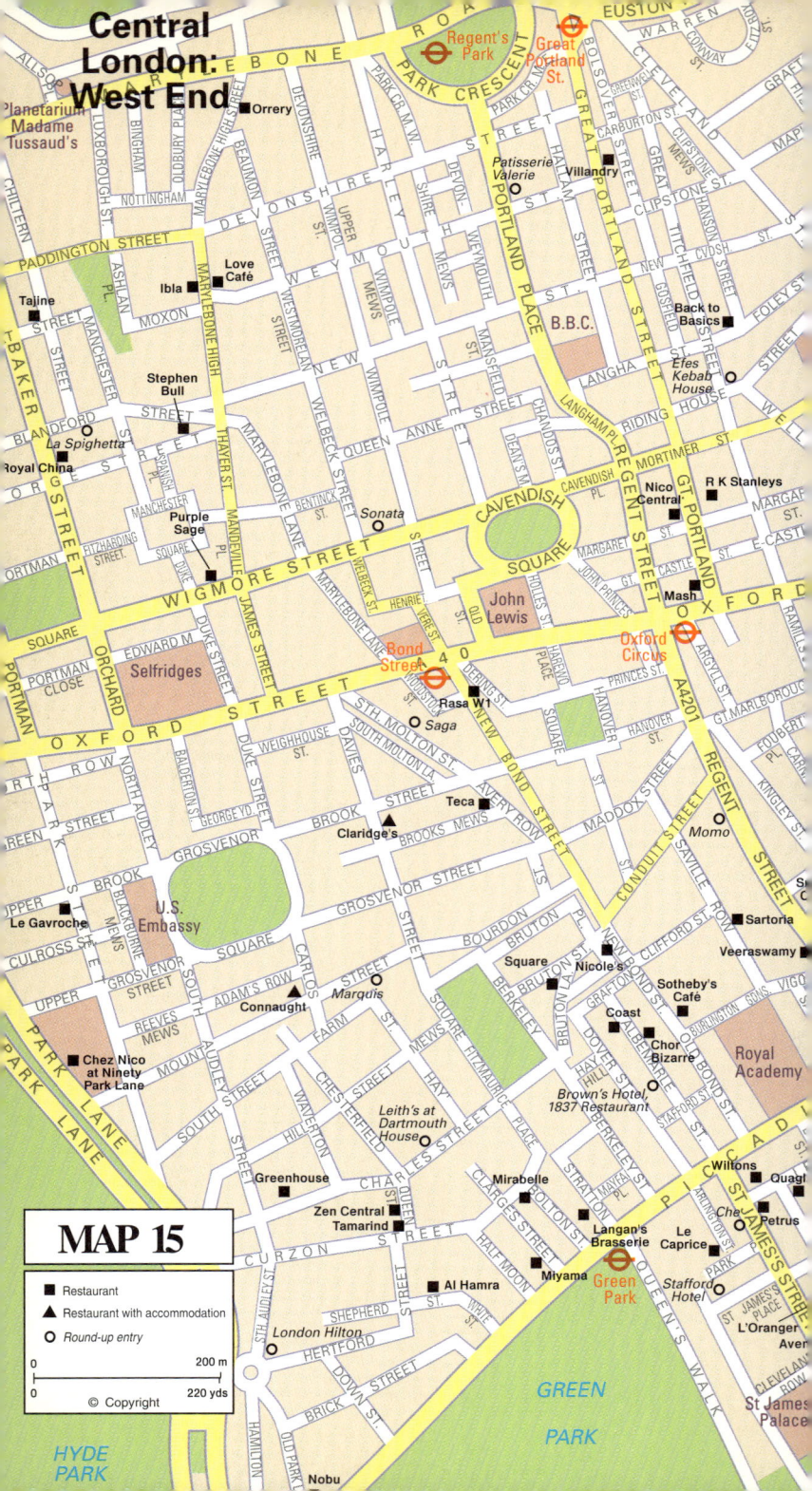

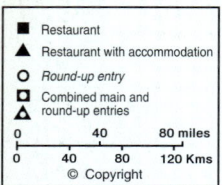

MAP 16

■ Restaurant
▲ Restaurant with accommodation
○ *Round-up entry*
◻ Combined main and
△ round-up entries

0   40   80 miles
0   40   80   120 Kms
© Copyright

A T L A N T I C

O C E A N

Inishtrahull Sound

Rathlin I.

Rosapenna

Portrush
Coleraine

Londonderry ▲ **LONDONDERRY** ■ **Limavady**

DONEGAL
Strabane

▲ **Donegal**

T Y R O N E

ANTRIM

Ballyclare ■
Carrickfer
Bangor ■

Antrim
■ **Belfast** ◻ **Holywood**

Lurgan

Donegal Bay

FERMANAGH

Portadown

DOWN

Sligo
■ **Blacklion**

Enniskillen

ARMAGH
Armagh ■

Monaghan
MONAGHAN

Downpa

St. John's

Ballina ▲
Crossmolina

S L I G O

▲ **Castlebaldwin**
Carrick-
on-Shannon

Fenagh

LEITRIM

Cavan

C A V A N

I R I S H

SEA

Newport ▲

M A Y O

ROSCOMMON

Longford

LOUTH

Drogheda

M E A T H

Letterfrack ▲

▲ **Oughterard**

Moycullen ▲

G A L W A Y

Galway

Athlone
WESTMEATH

Dunshaughlin

Howth ■
▲ **Dublin**

DUBLIN

Grand Canal

OFFALY

KILDARE

Ballyvaughan ▲ ▲ **Kinvara**
Lisdoonvarna ▲

Birr

Portlaoise

Kildare

M7

Wicklow ▲

C L A R E

L A O I S

WICKLOW

Shannon

LIMERICK

TIPPERARY

KILKENNY

Arklow

Gorey ▲

Adare ▲

Tipperary

Kilkenny ▲

CARLOW

Listowel

L I M E R I C K
Kilmallock

■ **Cashel**

Kilmaganny

WEXFORD

Tralee

Kanturk ▲

Clonmel

ATLANTIC OCEAN

Dingle ▲

K E R R Y

Killorglin

▲ **Mallow**

C O R K

Midleton ■

Waterford ■

WATERFORD

ST. GEORGE'S CHANNEL

Kenmare ▲

Ballylickey ▲

Durrus ▲ ▲ **Bantry**

Ahakista ■
Schull ■ ■ **Ballydehob**

Cork ■ ▲ **Shanagarry**
Douglas ▲ ○ **Cobh**

LONG MELFORD Suffolk   map 6

Scutchers Bistro

Westgate Street, Long Melford CO10 9DP   COOKING **2**
TEL: (07000) 728824   FAX: (07000) 785443   COST £23–£44

Brightly coloured fabrics, pine tables and modern lighting combine seamlessly
with old beams in this ancient house, which dates from the fifteenth century. The
carte's simple luxuries might include roast lobster, or grilled Dover sole, and for
such a small menu there are several daring combinations – perhaps goats'-cheese
terrine with pear and red wine compote – alongside old favourites of tournedos
Rossini, steak chasseur and knickerbocker glory. Meals might begin with
'decent' smoked haddock and leek chowder, and end with blueberry and
almond tart served with a good lemon-curd ice cream. Bread and olives need
ordering separately to start, and service at inspection rather lacked warmth.
Wines are full of perennials from Lay & Wheeler, with a commendable number
of half-bottles, although most are listed without a vintage. Ten house wines
range between £9.20 and £13.

CHEF: Nicholas Barrett   PROPRIETORS: Nicholas and Diane Barrett   OPEN: Tue to Sat 12 to 2, 7
to 9.30   CLOSED: 4 days Christmas, first week Jan, last week Aug   MEALS: alc (main courses
£7.50 to £14.50)   SERVICE: not inc   CARDS: Amex, Delta, MasterCard, Switch, Visa   DETAILS:
75 seats. 45 seats outside. Private parties: 75 main room. Car park. Vegetarian meals.
Children's helpings. No cigars/pipes in dining room. Wheelchair access (also WC). No music

---

LONGRIDGE Lancashire   map 8

Paul Heathcote's

104–106 Higher Road, Longridge PR3 3SY
TEL: (01772) 784969   FAX: (01772) 785713
EMAIL: longridge@Heathcotes.co.uk
from Preston, follow Town Centre signs, drive uphill
though centre of Longridge, then turn left, following   COOKING **6**
signs for Jeffery Hill   COST £32–£82

At the crest of a small hill on the edge of town, the collection of stone cottages
looks an unlikely spot for a fine restaurant. Chintz-covered sofas in the
split-level lounge, and seriously dressed tables in three interconnected dining
spaces, are described as 'comfortable but not opulent'. New head chef Steven
Forgie's menus continue to run the gamut of set-price options, a carte, and a
lengthy 'gourmet' dinner. The change has struck visitors differently, one finding
that 'everything has gone up a gear' while an inspector was rather less
convinced. But high-quality locally sourced materials – Goosnargh duck breast,
perhaps served with a pithiviers of the leg – remain at the heart of the operation.

Wide-ranging skills are a strength, too, as the kitchen has turned out
well-timed broad bean risotto with a juicy seared scallop on top, all infused with
the salty tang of Parmesan, and a 'stunning' terrine combining poultry with a
central nugget of sweetbread that was so 'unctuous it could have been foie gras',

all surrounded by pickled vegetables to cut the richness. Foie gras itself has been successfully pan-fried and served on sticks of roasted honey-glazed parsnip, while humbler ingredients provide a satisfying contrast: bortsch terrine in a light jellied beetroot stock, for example, or a lozenge-shaped confit of nicely fatty pork shoulder, topped with a square of crisp crackling. Hot pistachio soufflé that 'actually tasted of pistachios', served with a rich bitter chocolate sorbet, suitably impressed one visitor. The pace of meals tends to be sedate, with formal yet 'pleasant and relaxed' service, and even if the food seems expensive, it still 'warrants the price tag'. The lengthy wine list boasts some extremely fine bottles from France and the New World, but unfortunately those with a limited drinks budget will find little to shout about. House French is £13.50.

CHEFS: Steven Forgie and Paul Heathcote PROPRIETOR: Paul Heathcote OPEN: Fri and Sun L 12 to 2, Tue to Sun D 7 to 9.30 CLOSED: 1 Jan MEALS: alc D Tue to Sat (main courses £16 to £26). Set L £22.50, Set D Tue to Sat £38 to £55, Set D Sun £25 SERVICE: 10% (optional), card slips closed CARDS: Amex, Delta, Diners, MasterCard, Switch, Visa DETAILS: 60 seats. Private parties: 65 main room, 16 private room. Car park. Vegetarian meals. Children's helpings. No smoking in dining room. Wheelchair access (not WC). Music

LOWER BEEDING West Sussex map 3

Jeremy's at the Crabtree

Brighton Road, Lower Beeding RH13 6PT
TEL: (01403) 891257 FAX: (01403) 891606
EMAIL: jeremys.crabtree@btinternet.com COOKING 3
on A281, just S of village COST £21–£42

Jeremy Ashpool's original venture (see Haywards Heath for his other) is a custard-coloured roadside pub with a bright, relaxed and cheerful dining room, and a short, interesting menu that changes daily to accommodate fresh supplies. Fish gets fair billing both as a starter – a variation on mackerel escabèche using peppers and courgette – and for mains: halibut with asparagus and braised cabbage, or skate with chive hollandaise. In terms of ambition, the kitchen 'doesn't overreach itself', but its 'world on your plate' ideas one evening included tabouleh, hummus and rosemary mash with an inspector's well-flavoured rack of lamb, which might easily have shed half its accompaniments (they included roast garlic sauce and deep-fried vegetables as well) to good advantage. Extra vegetables are served separately.

After such busy main courses, puddings appear unusually simple: pear and plum crumble perhaps, or a translucent, pink, 'children's birthday party' raspberry jelly in a champagne glass. Extras (apart from coffee) are well up to standard – 'I'd be happy to go there again just for the springy, yeasty, crisp-crusted bread' – while junior service, though led by a capable and efficient Italian manager, is the least successful part of the operation. A wide-ranging list of dependable names starts with a handful of house wines at £11.

'We passed on the sweets and couldn't face the cheese, having seen one of the waiters at a nearby table try to distinguish between "hard" and "soft" by prodding his fingers into each piece.' (On eating in Cornwall)

CHEFS: Vera Ashpool and Fredi Djuric PROPRIETORS: Jeremy and Vera Ashpool OPEN: all week L 12.30 to 2, Mon to Sat D 7.30 to 10 CLOSED: 25 Dec, D bank hols MEALS: alc Mon to Sat L (main courses £9.50 to £11.50). Set L Mon to Sat £6.50 (1 course) to £10.50 (2 courses), Set L Sun £16.50, Set D £12.50 (Mon to Thur only) to £25 SERVICE: not inc Mon to Sat L, 10% Sun L and D, card slips closed CARDS: Amex, Delta, Diners, MasterCard, Switch, Visa DETAILS: 45 seats. 35 seats outside. Private parties: 26 and 30 private rooms. Car park. Vegetarian meals. Children's helpings. No smoking in 1 dining room. Wheelchair access (not WC). No music (£5)

LOWER SLAUGHTER Gloucestershire   map 5

▲ *Lower Slaughter Manor*

Lower Slaughter GL54 2HP
TEL: (01451) 820456 FAX: (01451) 822150
EMAIL: lowsmanor@aol.com   COOKING 5
off A429, at sign 'The Slaughters'   COST £37–£85

'Idyllic' applies to both the village, especially out of season, and the well-appointed seventeenth-century house of mellow stone, with well-manicured lawns front and back, each with a small formal garden. It is no stranger to luxury, judging by the fabrics and carved ceiling in the dining room, and by a menu (the set dinner has been replaced by a carte) that takes in foie gras terrine, roast lobster, and accurately sautéed scallops and asparagus dotted with finely chopped black truffle. Foie gras, ceps, morels and caviare find their way into sometimes powerful sauces, perhaps roast fillet of veal, served with a pea and ham risotto and foie gras sauce.

Good raw materials feature: for example, roast rack of lamb at inspection, its decorative garnish including spinach, a halved kidney, semi-dried tomatoes and black olives, which was followed by a 'technically excellent' apple soufflé with less convincing cinnamon ice cream. Cheeses appear less tempting than desserts, which might also take in warm chocolate fondant with blueberries and mascarpone ice cream. 'Supernumerous incidentals' seem to increase with every change of chef: bowls of crisps, nuts and olives, four other nibbles with drinks, three appetisers at table, a pre-dessert, and a whole cake stand of petits fours. Plentiful heavily accented service is 'formal but friendly'. High prices present a problem, which the French-dominated wine list (a 'gigantic book') compounds, although it contains lots of classy bottles. Ten house wines range from £19.50 to £34.

CHEF: Dominic Blake PROPRIETORS: Roy and Daphne Vaughan OPEN: all week 12 to 2, 7 to 10 MEALS: alc (main courses £22 to £29). Set L £19.95 to £24.95 SERVICE: not inc CARDS: Amex, Delta, Diners, MasterCard, Switch, Visa DETAILS: 45 seats. Private parties: 30 main room, 20 private room. Car park. Vegetarian meals. Children's helpings. No children under 8 in dining room. No smoking in dining room. Occasional music ACCOMMODATION: 16 rooms, all with bath/shower. TV. Phone. B&B £135 to £350. No children under 8 in accommodation. Swimming pool (*The Which? Hotel Guide*) (£5)

---

 indicates that there has been a change of chef since last year's Guide, *and the Editor has judged that the change is of sufficient interest to merit the reader's attention.*

LOW LAITHE   North Yorkshire   map 9

Dusty Miller

Low Laithe, Summerbridge HG3 4BU
TEL: (01423) 780837   COOKING 6
on B6165, 2m SE of Pateley Bridge   COST £17–£58

It pays to know the reputation of this modest-seeming restaurant, set in a cottage on the main road through the small village, and staffed almost exclusively by the quietly assured Dennisons. Regulars travel for miles to enjoy the welcoming atmosphere and Anglo-French cooking, to the extent that the proprietors have B&B recommendations to hand and frequently give out-of-town guests a lift back to their lodgings. The menu is handwritten, and its contents also give the impression of a resolutely old-fashioned establishment.

From roasted asparagus with Parmesan, or Whitby crab salad, through saddle of venison with port gravy, or crisp roast duckling with apples and calvados, the secret lies in the outstanding quality of ingredients and Brian Dennison's culinary flair. A main course of baked turbot, halibut and scallops, sprinkled with sea salt and sitting on a bed of baby spinach, was described as 'heaven' by one correspondent, and sauce boats with refills are clearly appreciated as a thoughtful gesture. Desserts tend towards variations on old favourites, such as de luxe bread-and-butter pudding, in which the middle is soft, the top crisp and the raisins drunk with Grand Marnier. Extras might include an appetiser of tiny blinis with cream cheese and smoked salmon, or a brochette of large, warm prawns, not to mention free mineral water. The wine list is brief and specialises in French bottles, spanning a price range from £9.90 to £385.

CHEF: Brian Dennison   PROPRIETORS: Brian and Elizabeth Dennison   OPEN: Tue to Sat D only 7 to 11   CLOSED: 24 to 27 Dec, 2 weeks Aug or Sept, bank hols   MEALS: alc (main courses £17 to £20). Set D £24, Set D Tue to Sat after 9 £9.90   SERVICE: not inc   CARDS: Amex, MasterCard, Visa   DETAILS: 48 seats. Private parties: 30 main room, 18 private room. Car park. No children under 9. Wheelchair access (not WC). Music

---

LUDLOW   Shropshire   map 5

Courtyard ⁵⁄* £

Quality Square, Ludlow SY8 1AR   COOKING 2
TEL: (01584) 878080   COST £18–£26

A large counter with cakes on display confirms that this is as much a café as a restaurant. It is warm and welcoming, and 'if you sit at the right table you can watch the chef at work', although Jane Lloyd was due to have a baby as the *Guide* was published, and has adjusted the opening times to suit – lunchtimes only now – although she may revert to dinners at a later date. Simple but lively sounding dishes on a frequently changing blackboard menu (some are marked for vegetarians, some for coeliacs) might include baked crab with lime and ginger, spinach and Stilton risotto cakes, or smooth textured salmon and smoked salmon sausages with a 'very proficient' chive sauce. Portions are generous: a 'rich and satisfying' sticky toffee pudding proved enough for two, although a lemon balm ewes'-milk ice cream sounds a more refreshing way to finish.

Service is 'spot on', and a short, serviceable, fairly priced wine list starts with house Australian at £9.50.

CHEF/PROPRIETOR: Jane Lloyd   OPEN: Mon to Sat L only 12 to 2 (also open D from 6pm during Ludlow festival)   CLOSED: 25 and 26 Dec, 1 Jan, May bank hol   MEALS: alc (main courses £5 to £6.50)   SERVICE: not inc   CARDS: none   DETAILS: 30 seats. 8 seats outside. Private parties: 12 main room. Vegetarian meals. No smoking in 1 dining room. Occasional music. Air-conditioned

Merchant House ⁵✗

Lower Corve Street, Ludlow SY8 1DU
TEL: (01584) 875438   FAX: (01584) 876927

COOKING 8
COST £35–£42

'When rival restaurateurs in Ludlow speak reverentially of "Shaun" you sense that the man is a force to be reckoned with.' His small black-and-white timbered terraced house draws no attention to itself and wastes no time or effort on frills. 'We usually spend the first ten minutes in an unfamiliar restaurant redesigning the décor,' admitted one reporter, but not here, where curtains, pictures, furniture and settings all suggested 'discreetly exquisite taste and made us feel very optimistic about the food'.

The overriding impression is of simplicity, which exposes the quality of materials. Knowledgeable buying from good suppliers provides a firm foundation, and 'spot-on' timing certainly sends the dazzlingly fresh fish into orbit: 'sumptuous' red mullet, or 'firm, sweet, fleshy sea bass', with a gently savoury basil and crème fraîche sauce. Fish may be the strongest suit, but no matter what he turns his hand to, Shaun Hill ensures that every component on a plate is there for a purpose: 'just pink', flavourful squab pigeon, moist yet firm and slightly gamey, with a spring vegetable risotto, for example, or 'still just bloody' venison, distinctly but not too powerfully flavoured, with goats'-cheese 'gnocchi' and a reduced stock sauce. The simple conception and construction of dishes gives them a welcome clarity and focus.

When it comes to dessert, there are no spun-sugar baskets or other affected tricks. Instead he makes wonderful pastry in all its incarnations, creamy custards, parfaits and ice cream. Intense fruit sauces figure in clean-tasting lychee and mango sorbet with fruit salad, or poached pear with a delicately lemon-flavoured but 'deeply satisfying' crème caramel, 'just as you hope this dish will be'. 'Unfussy' service from Anja Hill and a helper is gentle and relaxed, and the absence of gesture is welcomed. Pricing is an example to the trade: not only is the food great value, but service is included. The fifty-strong wine list is an exciting collection of bottles at fair prices; makeweights don't get a look in. House Aquileia del Friuli and Le Volte are £13.50.

CHEF: Shaun Hill   PROPRIETORS: Shaun and Anja Hill   OPEN: Sat L 12.30 to 2, Tue to Sat D 7 to 9   CLOSED: 1 week Christmas, 1 week spring   MEALS: Set L and D £28.50   SERVICE: net prices, card slips closed   CARDS: Delta, MasterCard, Switch, Visa   DETAILS: 24 seats. Private parties: 10 main room. No smoking in dining room. Wheelchair access (not WC). No music

All entries in the Guide *are re-researched and rewritten every year, not least because restaurant standards fluctuate. Don't rely on an out-of-date* Guide.

▲ *Mr Underhill's* ♀ ⅚✳

Dinham Weir, Ludlow SY8 1EH	COOKING 7
TEL: (01584) 874431	COST £34–£46

Backed by the ramparts of Ludlow Castle, Mr Underhill's is a restaurant-with-rooms. One end of the long, narrow, warmly decorated dining room overlooks a weir, and tables are well spaced and well dressed. Dinner follows a set three-course format with no choice until pudding, unless arranged before-hand. The style may not always excite, but ingredients of the highest quality are handled with skill. A fat chunk of salmon to start, for example, crisply seared outside, yet perfectly underdone, sits on a bed of chopped, creamed leeks in a thin but flavourful tomato 'soup'. On another occasion an impeccably timed thick slice of fresh cod was rolled in a herb crust and set on a similarly light tomato coulis flecked with olive oil.

The menu appears to ring the changes on a relatively small but seasonally changing repertoire – salmon or cod followed by beef is an oft-reported arrangement – but the cooking is done with care. Good-quality beef, for example, is served rare, sliced, and topped with roasted carrot and parsnip, surrounded by a stock reduction 'with lashings of chopped parsley in it', or alternatively with a tarragon-flavoured jus and dauphinois potatoes. Game and poultry have also made an appearance: pheasant wrapped in Savoy cabbage, with truffle-oiled mashed potato, and duck with provençale herbs.

A sound technical grasp underpins the cooking, not least in desserts, where a shortcrust pastry tart filled with a first-rate lemon-curd mix has been endorsed, along with a 'rich and eggy' Italian-style bread-and-butter pudding. Cheeses have arrived in variable condition, and assessments of booking arrangements, welcome and general warmth vary, but service mostly by local young women is able and willing. High-quality wines from France form the centrepiece of a cleverly composed wine list, with intelligent selections from the New World providing agreeable side attractions. Fans of Arizona's Callaghan Vineyards will be disappointed to learn that supplies are drying up, but Judy Bradley is working on a new Italian section that may console some. Prices are more than fair, with house wines starting at £12.

CHEF: Chris Bradley   PROPRIETORS: Chris and Judy Bradley   OPEN: Wed to Mon D only 7.15 to 8.30 (L by arrangement)   MEALS: Set D £25 to £28.50   SERVICE: not inc   CARDS: MasterCard, Visa   DETAILS: 30 seats. 40 seats outside. Private parties: 30 main room. Car park. Children's helpings. No smoking in dining room. No music   ACCOMMODATION: 6 rooms, all with bath/shower. TV. Phone. B&B £60 to £100. Fishing (£5)

Oaks ♀ ⅚✳

17 Corve Street, Ludlow SY8 1DA	
TEL: (01584) 872325 FAX: (01584) 874024	COOKING 4
EMAIL: koak@globalnet.co.uk	COST £35–£42

Oaks is 'a comforting kind of place', with mismatched chairs in the bar, and oak panelling and well-spaced tables in a dining room that is 'reminiscent of posh, old-fashioned English hotels'. A degree of elaboration and ambition show up in presentation and cooking, and some starters might sound like main courses –

breast of partridge, for example, with celeriac and Puy lentils in a Madeira jus – although quantities are sensibly judged and the balance is generally good. Sourcing is taken seriously, and materials veer towards the luxury end of the spectrum, from Dover sole and scallops to veal cutlet stuffed with foie gras. Vegetarians need to make themselves known when booking, but fish may appear on the menu in the form of sea bass with tomato and fennel confit, or a 'wonderfully rich' crayfish soup with a cheese-laden crust and 'sub-aquatic' asparagus and morels.

Cheeses are unpasteurised, and desserts might include dark chocolate marquise with banana sorbet, or a tangy lemon mousse. The background music is not appreciated by all, though praise has come in for bread, knowledgeable service and the wine list. The last is a catholic collection from the world's major wine regions, more or less guaranteed to provide something that will appeal. House wines from Portugal, France and England are priced between £9.95 and £12.90.

CHEF/PROPRIETOR: K.H. Adams OPEN: Wed to Sat L 12 to 1.30, Tue to Sat and bank hol Sun D 7 to 9 (9.30 Fri and Sat) CLOSED: 1 week spring, 1 to 2 weeks autumn MEALS: Set L £19 (2 courses) to £24, Set D £19 (2 courses; Tue to Thur only) to £24 SERVICE: not inc, card slips closed CARDS: Delta, MasterCard, Switch, Visa DETAILS: 30 seats. Private parties: 20 main room, 14 private room. Car park. Children's helpings. No children under 8. No smoking in dining room. Occasional music. Air-conditioned

---

▲ *Overton Grange* ¦✳ `NEW ENTRY`

Hereford Road, Ludlow SY8 4AD COOKING 7
TEL: (01584) 873500 FAX: (01584) 873524 COST £38–£60

There is no sign yet that Ludlow has reached full capacity as far as good restaurants are concerned. This one, small and intimate, inhabits a house 'of no particular style or age', its green paint and wood panelling hardly a match for the kitchen's cosmopolitan output. It is a place that confounded a pet theory for one visitor, concerning the relation between a chef's ability to cook and the menu's ability to communicate, or even spell, in either French or English. Cornish lobster with peas becomes homard de Corniche et petits poids, and 'Granit Smith' apples sound as if they might damage your teeth.

Claude Bosi's French background brings a penchant for native produce. Chicken from Bresse is served in two parts, breast with asparagus confit followed by leg with salad; three fresh, giant, well-timed langoustines from Brittany are served on a smear of smooth celeriac and apple purée, surrounded by a moat of creamy, curry-flavoured sauce, producing impressive combinations of flavour and texture. Indeed, 'impeccably top-class' ingredients and sensitive treatment (often with minimal intervention) are what give the cooking its power, even in such conventional dishes as roast lamb fillet in a parsley crust, served with similarly treated potatoes, plus a blob of aïoli-like garlic purée and a trickle of well-reduced stock-based sauce. Other main-course vegetable components tend to be conspicuous by their absence.

Desserts generally come in two parts, one of them an ice cream: roast pineapple with coconut ice, or an unusual avocado soufflé with a silky and intense chocolate ice cream. Bread is 'the best', and 'brilliant' appetisers include poached quail's egg on a ratatouille mixture, and a lobster and lentil tart.

'Friendly, unassuming, funny' Igi Gonzalez oversees the service and provides tasting notes for a wide-ranging and appealing wine list. There are few bottles under £20, although four house wines cost £12 (£2.50 a glass).

CHEF: Claude Bosi   PROPRIETOR: Grange Hotel Ltd   OPEN: Sun to Fri L 12.30 to 1.45, all week D 7.30 to 9.45 (10 Fri and Sat)   CLOSED: second and third week Jan   MEALS: alc (main courses £12 to £18.50). Set L £25 (2 courses) to £28, Set D £22.50 to £38   SERVICE: not inc, card slips closed   CARDS: Delta, MasterCard, Switch, Visa   DETAILS: 35 seats. 15 seats outside. Private parties: 60 main room, 6 to 20 private rooms. Car park. Children's helpings. No smoking in dining room. Wheelchair access (also WC). Music   ACCOMMODATION: 14 rooms, all with bath/shower. TV. Phone. B&B £57 to £120. Fishing

---

LUND   East Riding of Yorkshire   map 9

Wellington Inn | NEW ENTRY |

19 The Green, Lund YO25 9TE
TEL: (01377) 217294   FAX: (01377) 217192
take B1284 out of Beverley toward Driffield   COOKING 3
and Malton   COST £27–£40

The tiny Wold village of Lund can take some finding on a dark night but when you get there the recently revitalised Wellington Inn is warm and welcoming, with a large log fire and friendly, knowledgeable staff. The new owners have opened a small, smart restaurant, but the rest of the pub remains very much a local in character: flagstone floors, old beams and cask ales. Lunchtime dishes are chalked up on a blackboard and eaten in the bar. In the evenings an à la carte menu in the more formal restaurant offers down-to-earth cooking based on good ingredients and quality saucing. Smoked haddock fish cakes with curried apple sauce are a big hit, blue Wensleydale cheese and onion tart scores highly for its 'excellent pastry and creamy contents', while 'pink, crisp-skinned' duck breast comes with a sage and onion jus and bubble and squeak. Accompanying vegetables are 'just right', and old-fashioned puddings might include jam sponge and custard, and a 'sweet, plain, simple' orange bread-and-butter pudding. The fairly priced wine list majors on the New World, with Chilean house wine at £9.75.

CHEFS: Sarah Warburton and Toby Greensides   PROPRIETORS: Russell Jeffery and Sarah Warburton   OPEN: Tue to Sat D only 7 to 9.30. Bar L available   CLOSED: 25 Dec, 1 Jan   MEALS: alc (main courses £12 to £14.50)   SERVICE: not inc, card slips closed   CARDS: Delta, MasterCard, Switch, Visa   DETAILS: 42 seats. 12 seats outside. Private parties: 30 main room, 12 private room. Car park. Music. Air-conditioned

---

'We arrived in the middle of nowhere to find the chef and sous-chef lounging listlessly on the wisteria-covered porch, a toothpick dangling out of the chef's mouth. It looked like the opening scene from a spaghetti Western. I half expected to hear, "So you wanhh some steenking feeshcakes with Thai salsa, gringo? Whatta you think thees ees – Quagleenos?" All this perhaps followed by riotous laughter, gunshots and that music that follows Clint Eastwood everywhere.' (On eating in Essex)

LYDFORD Devon   map 1

Dartmoor Inn ¾ £ | NEW ENTRY |

Lydford EX20 4AY
TEL: (01822) 820221   FAX: (01822) 820494   COOKING 4
off A386 Okehampton to Tavistock road   COST £20–£45

This new venture by Philip Burgess from the Arundell Arms (see entry, Lifton) is
'the best news for this part of Devon for a long time', says a local. Philip oversees
both operations and Ian Brown has transferred from Arundell to the Dartmoor.
Refurbishment hasn't masked the essential character of the place: dark wood,
log fires, ships' lanterns and oak barrels mark this out as a country pub where
locals can pop in for a drink at the bar, even if dining is now the main business.
The Burgesses aim to serve 'real food', and farmhouse sausages with onion
gravy, and chargrilled chicken with summer herbs certainly fit the bill. Results
are simple but 'flavours are good,' according to a couple who enjoyed turnip
soup, then deep-fried cod with herb mayonnaise and 'an enormous bowl of good
chips'. Saffron crops up frequently: in a casserole of scallops with 'firm and
moist' Cornish red mullet; in a dressing for crab; and in a cream to accompany
strawberries and polenta cake. Chocolate pudding has proved irresistible, while
crème brûlée comes with clotted cream and crumbly biscuits. Karen Burgess
greets arrivals and is 'a joy to talk to'. A short, interesting wine list stays mainly
below £20, with house wine at £9.50.

CHEFS: Philip Burgess and Ian Brown   PROPRIETORS: Karen and Philip Burgess, and Anne
Voss-Bark   OPEN: Tue to Sun L 12 to 2.30, Tue to Sat D 6.30 to 10   CLOSED: 1 week after New
Year, bank hol Mons   MEALS: alc (main courses £5.50 to £17.50). Set D £14 (2 courses) to
£17.50   SERVICE: not inc, card slips closed   CARDS: Delta, MasterCard, Switch, Visa
DETAILS: 75 seats. Private parties: 20 main room, 10 and 20 private rooms. Car park. Vegetarian
meals. No children in bar. No smoking in 1 dining room. Occasional music (£5)

LYDGATE Greater Manchester   map 8

▲ White Hart ¾

51 Stockport Road, Lydgate OL4 4JJ
TEL: (01457) 872566   FAX: (01457) 875190   COOKING 5
on A6050, 3m E of Oldham   COST £20–£45

'Another place in north Manchester which provides very proficient, modern
cooking in unpretentious surroundings,' summed up one visitor. The 200-
year-old stone building – variously a brewery, police station, school house, and
Home Guard look-out point in its time – now functions as both restaurant and
brasserie. It is also home of the Saddleworth Sausage Company, one of whose
exemplars appears on the attractive brasserie menu with mash and onion gravy,
alongside pork pie with chutney (both home-made), wild mushroom spring
roll, and cod tempura.
   Meat tends to dominate – lamb shank, or beef suet pudding in the brasserie,
loin of venison or calf's liver in the restaurant – but options are otherwise
balanced, and luxuries are not unknown on the restaurant's set-price menu,
which might include terrine of duck breast with foie gras, or roast asparagus

ENGLAND

with truffled linguine pasta. Pithiviers of rhubarb indicates an unhackneyed approach to desserts, while bread has been 'magnificent'. There are two wine lists, the longer one combining several interesting bottles below £20 with some classic ones above; ten house wines (most available by the glass on the shorter list) start at £10.

CHEF: John Rudden PROPRIETORS: Charles Brierley and John Rudden OPEN: restaurant Sun L 12 to 2.30, Tue to Sat D 7 to 10; brasserie all week 12 to 2.30, 6 to 9.30 (10 Sat) MEALS: restaurant Set L £16, Set D £25.75. Brasserie alc (main courses £8 to £14). Set L Mon to Fri £11.50. BYO £10 SERVICE: not inc, card slips closed CARDS: Amex, Delta, MasterCard, Switch, Visa DETAILS: 120 seats. 20 seats outside. Private parties: 70 main room. Car park. Vegetarian meals. Children's helpings. No smoking in restaurant. Wheelchair access (also WC). Music ACCOMMODATION: 5 rooms, all with bath/shower. TV. Phone. B&B £55 to £70 (£5)

LYMINGTON Hampshire   map 2

▲ *Gordleton Mill, Provence* 🍴 ❊

Silver Street, Hordle, Lymington SO41 6DJ
TEL: (01590) 682219 FAX: (01590) 683073   COOKING 4
EMAIL: bookings@gordleton-mill.co.uk   COST £24–£69

Patrons sitting on the terrace overlooking the sumptuous gardens, and listening to the sussurations of the stream that flows by the dining room windows, may have been unaware of a spot of turbulence behind the scenes in the spring of 1999, when it seemed that Jean-Christophe Novelli was about to buy Gordleton Mill. The deal came to nothing and Alan Dann has now taken up the reins in the kitchen, bringing more of a Provençal style to the fixed-price menus. Invention is evident in first courses of marinated monkfish with fennel cream on blinis with tomato and basil, and crab and scallop salad with crisp leeks and a spinach sauce. Presentation is elegant and ambitious, as shown by a main course of lamb loin, boned and propped up against a potato tuile, or a pavé of halibut studded with shards of truffle. A wobbling, slightly warm caramel mousseline with subtle rosemary ice cream and red berry fruits impressed at inspection, though one or two other items didn't quite pass muster. The wine list betrays a distinct partiality towards France, but lets in some quality bottles from other countries. House Sauvignon Blanc from Vanel is £13.80, Merlot £14.

CHEF: Alan Dann PROPRIETOR: William Stone OPEN: Tue to Sun 12 to 2, Tue to Sat D 7 to 9.30 CLOSED: Jan MEALS: Set L and D £21.50 (2 courses) to £24.50, Set L Tue to Fri £9.50 (2 courses) to £14.50, Set D £45 SERVICE: not inc CARDS: Amex, Delta, Diners, MasterCard, Switch, Visa DETAILS: 36 seats. 12 seats outside. Private parties: 50 main room. Car park. No children under 3 in dining room. No smoking in dining room. Wheelchair access (also WC). Music. Air-conditioned ACCOMMODATION: 8 rooms, all with bath/shower. TV. Phone. B&B £76 to £180

The 2001 Guide will be published before Christmas 2000. Reports on meals are most welcome at any time of the year, but are particularly valuable in the spring (no later than June). Send them to The Good Food Guide, FREEPOST, 2 Marylebone Road, London NW1 4DF. Or email your report to guidereports@which.co.uk.

LYMPSTONE Devon   map 1

▲ *River House* ✦✶

The Strand, Lympstone EX8 5EY   COOKING 1
TEL: (01395) 265147   COST £29–£57

As well as the restaurant overlooking the River Exe, Shirley and Michael Wilkes
run cookery classes, a catering service, offer accommodation, and manage an
allotment that provides most of the kitchen's vegetable needs. Monthly-
changing two- or three-course dinner-party-style menus show a Mediterranean
influence. Starters such as red onion and pepper tart with melted Brie, or
provençale fish soup, may be followed by 'pink, tasty and tender' rack of lamb
with rosemary, oregano and a Madeira sauce, or simple skate with black caper
butter. Desserts, many served with home-made ice-creams, include the modest
'best bread-and-butter pudding in the world', and breads come in interesting
varieties like orange and cardamom. Plenty of half-bottles and wines by the
glass are useful features of the carefully chosen but slightly pricey list; house
wine is £10.75/£11.25.

CHEF: Shirley Wilkes PROPRIETOR: Michael Wilkes OPEN: Tue to Sat 12 to 1.30, 7 to 9 (9.30
Sat) CLOSED: 25 to 27 Dec, 1 Jan, bank hols MEALS: alc L (main courses £7.50 to £10.50). Set
L £12 (2 courses) to £35.50, Set D £31 (2 courses) to £35.50 SERVICE: not inc CARDS: Amex,
Delta, MasterCard, Visa DETAILS: 40 seats. Private parties: 40 main room, 14 private room.
Vegetarian meals. Children's helpings. No children under 6 in dining room. No smoking in dining
room. Wheelchair access (not WC). No music ACCOMMODATION: 3 rooms, all with
bath/shower. TV. B&B £62 to £108. No children under 6 in accommodation (£5)

MADINGLEY Cambridgeshire   map 6

Three Horseshoes ▮ ✦✶

High Street, Madingley CB3 8AB   COOKING 3
TEL: (01954) 210221 FAX: (01954) 212043   COST £26–£50

This pretty thatched pub – in reality, more of an informal and 'affable' restaurant
– follows the Huntsbridge formula of serving food to casual callers in the bar, to
those who book in the conservatory dining room, and at tables outside if weather
permits. The food adopts a 'best bits from everywhere' approach, taking in
curried dhal soup, deep-fried tuna and nori roll, and chargrilled rump of lamb
with preserved lemon and herb couscous. If the identity of the place confuses
some reporters, so, too, does the quality of the cooking: one of the few consistent
points to emerge is that reporters disagree about it. Roasting and chargrilling are
the main cooking methods, applied to salmon and sea bass, chicken and beef,
which are then given a bright-sounding accompaniment: for chicken breast, for
example, it might be creamed leeks and peas, mint-flavoured dauphinois, mint
and caper dressing, and a red wine sauce.

Puddings, which not everybody gets round to, have included pineapple tarte
Tatin with rum ice cream, and caramelised lemon tart, while service has been
'attentive and fairly prompt, with smiles'. As with other members of the
Huntsbridge group, the wine list has been skilfully put together by John
Hoskins MW, and features around one hundred attractive bins helpfully

presented by style. Good drinking can be had at all price levels (house wines start at £9.75 a bottle, £1.85 a glass), with mark-ups proportionately less at the higher end of the list.

CHEF: Richard Stokes   PROPRIETOR: Huntsbridge Ltd   OPEN: all week L 12 to 2, Mon to Sat D 6.30 to 9.30 (10 Sat)   MEALS: alc (main courses £9 to £17)   SERVICE: not inc   CARDS: Amex, Delta, Diners, MasterCard, Switch, Visa   DETAILS: 110 seats. 45 seats outside. Private parties: 60 main room. Car park. Vegetarian meals. No smoking in dining room. Wheelchair access (not WC). No music

---

MAENPORTH Cornwall   map 1

Pennypots

Maenporth TR11 5HN   COOKING 6
TEL: (01326) 250251   FAX: (01326) 251040   COST £44–£53

Part of the Maenporth Estate of luxury holiday lets, this bright, airy first-floor room looks out over a bay framed by lush green headlands: a scene to rival any in Cornwall. Dried flowers and artificial plants may not match the seascape, but fine weather opens up the balcony for drinks, and a glass wall offers protection from the elements the rest of the year. Kevin Viner is a keen advocate of locally available ingredients, of which perhaps the most obvious is seafood: steamed sea bass fillets, for example, with a velouté of Helford oysters flavoured with saffron and Noilly Prat. He also makes effective use of combinations, perhaps ravioli of crab with 'fat and just seared' scallops, in a creamy sauce flecked with coriander, chives and lemon grass; or precisely roasted turbot steak, with tiger prawns and squid, in a 'satisfyingly fishy' lemon and thyme sauce.

Game, vegetables and herbs are also sourced from nearby, but most ideas seem to originate in Europe: loin of spring lamb may be roasted in olive oil, garlic and parsley with a thyme tomato jus, while duck has come as grilled breast and crisply skinned confit of leg, served with red cabbage, roughly mashed olive oil potatoes, and a red wine sauce. Chocolate temptation beckons at dessert stage – a 'quite complicated' tower of white and dark chocolate in a lake of black cherry coulis – as may vanilla crème brûlée, served with strawberries and peaches in caramel syrup. Service is 'willing and friendly', and the wine list is wide-ranging and accessible, starting with house offerings at £9.50. Downstairs, Oceans Bar and Grill has a menu that is more family orientated.

CHEFS: Kevin Viner, Peter McGregor and David Gingell   PROPRIETOR: Kevin Viner   OPEN: Tue to Sat D only 7 to 9.30   CLOSED: Christmas, 1 Jan, 4 weeks in winter   MEALS: Set D £28 to £33.50   SERVICE: not inc, card slips closed   CARDS: Amex, Delta, Diners, MasterCard, Switch, Visa   DETAILS: 40 seats. 12 seats outside. Private parties: 50 main room. Car park. Children's helpings. No smoking before 10pm. Wheelchair access (also WC). Music. Air-conditioned

---

'At [a nearby] table an animated, voluble young woman "offered" her companion bits of her dishes by more or less throwing them at him, not always with an entirely accurate aim.' (On eating in Cambridgeshire)

MAIDENCOMBE Devon	map 1

▲ *Orestone Manor* ᵉ✳

Rockhouse Lane, Maidencombe TQ1 4SX
TEL: (01803) 328098   FAX: (01803) 328336
EMAIL: manor@orestone.co.uk   NEW CHEF
on A379 between Torquay and Teignmouth   COST £24–£57

Impressive sea views and a fine weather terrace make this once-Georgian house
('Gothicised' by its mid-Victorian owner) an agreeable spot. Stephen Sanders
took over from Wayne Pearson too late for us to receive any feedback on the
cooking, but his menus seem to favour the Mediterranean for starters –
provençale onion tart, or roasted red pepper soup with basil – more traditional
guinea fowl with wild mushrooms and a mustard sauce for mains, and perhaps
rhubarb crumble with clotted cream for dessert. The reasonably priced wine list
is sufficiently multinational to include an English choice. House wines from
Australia and France start at £11.95.

CHEF: Stephen Sanders   PROPRIETORS: Bill and Gill Dagworthy   OPEN: Sun L 12 to 1.30, all
week D 7 to 9   CLOSED: first 2 weeks Jan   MEALS: Set L third Sun of month £11.25 (2 courses)
to £12.95, Set L Sun £21, Set D £24.50 (2 courses) to £34.50   SERVICE: not inc, card slips
closed   CARDS: Amex (3.5% surcharge), Delta, MasterCard, Switch, Visa   DETAILS: 40 seats.
Private parties: 80 main room, 14 private room. Car park. Children's helpings. No babies. No
smoking in dining room. Music   ACCOMMODATION: 18 rooms, all with bath/shower. TV. Phone.
B&B £55 to £110. Baby facilities. Swimming pool (£5)

MALMESBURY Wiltshire	map 2

▲ *Old Bell* 🍷 ᵉ✳

Abbey Row, Malmesbury SN16 0AG   COOKING 4
TEL: (01666) 822344   FAX: (01666) 825145   COST £24–£44

'Reputedly the oldest inn in Britain' manages to be both grand yet approachable.
Bar snacks, sandwiches and light dishes (tomato tart and chunky chips) are
served in the Great Hall, while the candlelit dining room, with chandeliers, an
antique dresser, and crisp table linen, offers fixed-price menus that deal in more
serious food. Meals revolve around meaty centrepieces, some slow cooked –
braised beef sirloin, or a thick pork chop, served beside a fanned pear with
spring cabbage and asparagus – others are served 'slightly pink', such as roast
rack of lamb with creamy mash and garlic cloves.

Strong traditional leanings are balanced by minestrone soup with aïoli, or
salmon with a couscous crust, but even first courses can be as red-blooded as
gamey tasting roast loin and braised leg of hare in a reduced sauce, or sautéed
chicken livers with a shallot tarte Tatin topped by melting Brie. Desserts
sometimes come in two parts – moist chocolate fondant with pistachio ice cream
– and good shortcrust pastry has helped to make a success of tangy caramelised
lemon tart with raspberry sorbet. Service is obliging, wines include some classy
bottles, but there is little relief under £20 outside four house varietals at £14.

CHEF: Michael Benjamin   PROPRIETORS: Nigel Chapman and Nicholas Dickinson   OPEN: all week 12 to 2.30 (12.30 to 2 Sun), 7 to 9.30   MEALS: Set L £11.75 (2 courses) to £15, Set D £19.75 to £26. Bar meals available   SERVICE: not inc, card slips closed   CARDS: Amex, Delta, Diners, MasterCard, Switch, Visa   DETAILS: 80 seats. 30 seats outside. Private parties: 80 main room, 14 to 40 private rooms. Car park. Vegetarian meals. Children's helpings. No children at D. No smoking in dining room. Wheelchair access (not WC). Music   ACCOMMODATION: 31 rooms, all with bath/shower. TV. Phone. B&B £75 to £180. Baby facilities. Swimming pool. Fishing (*The Which? Hotel Guide*)

MALVERN WELLS Worcestershire   map 5

Croque-en-Bouche ▮ ✁✗

221 Wells Road, Malvern Wells WR14 4HF
TEL: (01684) 565612
EMAIL: croque@globalnet.co.uk   COOKING 8
on A449, 2m S of Great Malvern   COST £33–£56

The house, as far as diners are concerned, consists of little more than a small sitting room for pre-dinner drinks and a front room that recalls the shop it once was, furnished in apricotty colours with warm wood and large displays of flowers. It is an unshowy setting for a well-rehearsed routine that begins in earnest with the arrival of a whole tureen of help-yourself soup, perhaps thick smoked haddock with tomato and celery, of enough character and depth of flavour to warrant a second helping. Thereafter there is a choice of three intermediate dishes – typically either fish, such as crab and lobster croustade, or vegetable, maybe artichoke heart filled with asparagus – and three mains, usually based on meat.

Marion Jones's cooking does not follow fashion. It stands for more timeless values of simple but careful treatment, at its best when using combinations with a track record. Materials include Orkney beef fillet, or perhaps salt marsh lamb 'beyond rare but still tender' stuffed with vegetables and infused with garlic, in a thyme-flavoured gravy: a dish of 'honest, positive flavours'. A creamy, nutmeg-flavoured potato gratin accompanies, and an 'intriguing' salad of leaves from the garden follows, with enough components to make each mouthful taste different.

Desserts often come in two parts, sometimes with an unusual ice cream: Jaffa cake with geranium ice cream, plum and almond tart with a rose pelargonium version, or a thin glazed pineapple tart with a scoop each of banana and coconut ice creams. Service from Robin Jones doesn't please those looking for lots of warm smiles, or vegetarians who have not made their wishes known in advance, or late arrivals, although one couple, careful to arrive precisely on time, received a 'comparatively jovial welcome'. In truth, his is a simple matter-of-fact approach, free of bluster; ask if you want to know anything, otherwise he assumes you can ladle out soup and pour wine without fuss.

A word to the wise: even the condensed version of the restaurant wine list runs to eighteen pages, and we are talking small print here, so do request a preview copy by post (for a charge of £3) or e-mail (free) if you wish to make your selection at leisure. However, if over a thousand attractively priced bottles from all over the world is a daunting prospect, then look to the evening's mini-list or seek Robin Jones's advice. House white is £12.50, red £11.50.

CHEF: Marion Jones PROPRIETORS: Marion and Robin Jones OPEN: Thur to Sat D only 7 to 9.30 CLOSED: Christmas to New Year, 1 week May, 1 week Sept MEALS: Set D Thur £25 to £29, Set D Fri and Sat £35 to £38 SERVICE: net prices, card slips closed CARDS: Delta, MasterCard, Switch, Visa DETAILS: 22 seats. Private parties: 6 main room, 6 private room. No smoking in dining room. Wheelchair access (not WC). No music

Planters

191–193 Wells Road, Malvern Wells WR14 4HE
TEL: (01684) 575065   COOKING 3
on A449, 3m S of Great Malvern   COST £29–£43

Planters is converted from several shops, making the interior somewhat 'higgledy-piggledy', but all 'spick and span, very cared for'. It is overseen by Sandra Pegg, whose Liverpudlian background explains the Beatles collage on one wall, and serves deftly prepared food, mostly inspired by South East Asia, with impressive spicing and attention to detail. There is a gourmet menu for two, a rijsttafel (a group of side dishes served with rice), and a carte which might start with vaday (Sri Lankan lentil rissoles served with coconut and yoghurt), or chicken and lamb satay; perhaps the best opening option is a mini-selection of satays together with deep-fried king prawns. Main-courses of pickled lamb stir-fried with onions, or deep-fried fish in a sweet red ginger sauce, are accompanied by generous stir-fried vegetables and coconut rice. For dessert, the mood swings West: oranges in caramel sauce with ginger ice cream and shortbread, or crème brûlée with a cashew crunch topping. The relatively large wine list globe-hops in search of suitable partners for the food, in the main succeeding well and offering reasonable prices. House wine is £8.50.

CHEF: Chandra de Alwis PROPRIETOR: Sandra Pegg OPEN: Tue to Sat D only 7 to 9 (9.30 Fri and Sat) CLOSED: Tue Jan to Easter MEALS: alc (main courses £8.50 to £9). Set D £16.95 to £24.95 SERVICE: not inc, card slips closed CARDS: MasterCard, Switch, Visa DETAILS: 32 seats. Private parties: 30 main room. Vegetarian meals. No cigars/pipes in dining room. Wheelchair access (not WC). No music £5

MANCHESTER Greater Manchester   map 8

Bridgewater Hall ⅝✸   NEW ENTRY

Lower Mosley Street, Manchester M2 3WS   COOKING 3
TEL/FAX: (0161) 950 0000   COST £26–£32

Manchester's new concert hall, home to the Hallé, is an impressive modern structure beside the Rochdale Canal. A Stalls Café Bar serves sandwiches and light meals, while the Charles Hallé restaurant will come as a pleasant surprise for those expecting the usual cafeteria style. Deep blues and pale greys are the backdrop, and, apart from potage Yehudi Menuhin, a fixed-price menu offers standard-sounding dishes along the lines of feta cheese salad, and salmon in watercress sauce.

Among good raw materials have been well-flavoured chicken breast with wild mushrooms, served in a well-reduced stock sauce, and expert presentation has produced a visually arresting dish of perfectly timed asparagus risotto spilling out of a pancake tuile (shaped to look like a knocked-over plant pot) with deep-fried leeks. Accurate seasoning and careful balancing were also a feature of an inspection meal, evident in a 'winning combination' of salty smoked halibut with slicks of sweet red pepper coulis, and in a powerfully flavoured, garlic-infused venison terrine, served with lentils in a robust vinaigrette. Desserts and cheeses appear to be of less interest. A tiny wine list starts with Chilean red and Spanish white at £11.95.

CHEF: Robert Kisby   PROPRIETOR: Hallgen Ltd   OPEN: all week L 12 to 2, D 5 to 7.30 and 9.30 to 11 (D times may vary, depending on concert evenings – phone to check)   CLOSED: Christmas, bank hols   MEALS: Set D £14.50 (2 courses) to £17.50   SERVICE: not inc, card slips closed CARDS: Delta, MasterCard, Switch, Visa   DETAILS: 210 seats. Private parties: 150 main room, 20 to 150 private rooms. Vegetarian meals. No smoking in dining room. Wheelchair access (also WC). Occasional music. Air-conditioned   £5

Chiang Rai

1st Floor, 762–766 Wilmslow Road,
Manchester M20 2DR   COOKING 2
TEL: (0161) 448 2277   FAX: (0161) 438 0695   COST £17–£43

This is now the only Chiang Rai, the Princess Street place having been sold. Its somewhat austere look of white walls and metal chairs is relieved by typically large numbers of customers, and service which, while charming, is sometimes rather laid back. Seafood features strongly in the Thai menu, with a welcome guest appearance from prawn tempura 'cooked with a light touch so the flavours of the prawns and accompanying vegetables shine through'. Pla jian (deep-fried fish with 'dry fluffy-textured' shredded pork and mushrooms) stands out for flavour, and as one of the few dishes which are not stir-fries or curries. The vegetarian menu includes mushroom satay, vegetable tempura, and a rarity in the form of black fungus salad. A short, interesting wine list starts with house wine at £9.50, and only *premier cru* Chablis over £18.

CHEF: Sunnaporn Klintaworn   PROPRIETORS: Mr and Mrs Parkhouse   OPEN: Tue to Fri L 12 to 2, Tue to Sat D 6 to 10.30   CLOSED: bank hols   MEALS: alc (main courses £7 to £10). Set L £5 to £9, Set D £21.30 to £22.20 (all min 2)   SERVICE: not inc, 10% for parties of 7 or more; card slips closed   CARDS: Amex, Delta, Diners, MasterCard, Switch, Visa   DETAILS: 90 seats. Private parties: 100 main room, 80 private room. Vegetarian meals. Children's helpings. Music   £5

▲ Crowne Plaza Midland, French Restaurant

Peter Street, Manchester M60 2DS
TEL: (0161) 236 3333   FAX: (0161) 932 4100   COOKING 4
EMAIL: sales@mnccl.demon.co.uk   COST £49–£80

A pianist plays in the lobby, and much else continues to reflect the grand-hotel style of this city landmark. Although windowless, and not flattered by its lighting, the oval dining room impresses with its high ceiling, mirrored panels and ornate plasterwork. A year or so on, Paul Reed's cooking has settled into a workmanlike treatment of the classical repertoire, updated with a few flourishes, producing marinated salmon and crab with confit potato salad, followed perhaps by 'tender and moist' Bresse pigeon on a salad of Kenya beans with hazelnuts. A degree of invention is evident in tea-smoked fillet of beef, and in an oyster dish featuring three warm ones with a caper butter sauce, and three cold with cucumber gazpacho. Although a few luxuries and accompaniments may be repeated on the carte, variety extends from scallop minestrone to a range of offal that might take in stuffed pig's trotter, sweetbreads on mushroom risotto, and of course duck liver: either pressed and served with Sauternes jelly, or in a 'well-conceived' dish of roast codling with foie gras sauce. Desserts do not appear to be a strong point, nor is the wine list, but service is headed by a maître d' 'of the old school' for whom nothing is too much trouble. House Vin de Pays d'Oc is £13.50.

CHEF: Paul Reed   PROPRIETOR: Bass Hotels and Resorts   OPEN: Mon to Sat D only 6.30 to 10.30 (11 Fri and Sat)   CLOSED: bank hols   MEALS: alc (main courses £13.50 to £26.50). Set D £38   SERVICE: not inc, card slips closed   CARDS: Amex, Delta, Diners, MasterCard, Switch, Visa   DETAILS: 45 seats. Private parties: 450 main room, 1 to 450 private rooms. Vegetarian meals. Children's helpings. No cigars in dining room. Wheelchair access (also WC). Music. Air-conditioned   ACCOMMODATION: 303 rooms, all with bath/shower. TV. Phone. Room only £99 to £175. Rooms for disabled. Baby facilities. Swimming pool (*The Which? Hotel Guide*)
(£5)

Koreana £

Kings House, 40A King Street West,
Manchester M3 2WY
TEL: (0161) 832 4330   FAX: (0161) 832 2293   COOKING 2
EMAIL: 113036.1764@compuserve.com   COST £12–£39

'Absolutely charming' service wins firm friends for this long-established Korean restaurant, whose other attractions include a pleasant wood-panelled basement setting, and remarkable value. Pricing can be confusing – 'probably the model that the privatised rail companies use,' according to one reporter – but for £13.50, diners can construct their own three-course meal. There are also set banquets (handy for novices), a vegetarian section and a sizeable carte. Competent renditions of Korean classics are delivered, including soups, stir-fries, hotpots and that Seoul-food staple, bulgogi (marinated meat grilled at table). Starters include sushi: two pieces each of salmon, prawn, squid, vegetable and 'terrific' tuna thrilled one reporter. A main course of baked cod with 'robust flavour' also elicited praise, as has the 'sticky' Korean rice-cake dessert. House wine costs £7.95; a bottle of Hite Korean beer is £2.25.

CHEFS: Mrs H. Kim and Cheung Hong   PROPRIETOR: Koreana Ltd   OPEN: Mon to Fri L 12 to 2.30, Mon to Sat D 6.30 to 10.30   CLOSED: 1 week Christmas, 1 Jan, D bank hols   MEALS: alc (main courses £6.50 to £16). Set L £5.50 to £8, Set D £13.50 to £19.50 (parties only)   SERVICE: card slips closed   CARDS: Amex, Delta, Diners, MasterCard, Switch, Visa   DETAILS: 60 seats. Private parties: 60 main room. Vegetarian meals. Music (£5)

'It was the juice that was so interesting: clear, very salty water containing pieces of chopped-up tomato, made further attractive with blobs of olive oil floating about. It looked like a naval disaster. [My husband] tasted the fluid and remarked that it must have made the fish feel at home.' (On eating in Devon)

ENGLAND

Kosmos Taverna £

248 Wilmslow Road, Manchester M14 6LD   COOKING 2
TEL: (0161) 225 9106   FAX: (0161) 256 4442   COST £14–£38

An 'enjoyable rustic' meal in generous portions can be expected at this popular
taverna. Kosmos occupies a simple, long room, decorated with Greek memorabilia, that is just about ready for its next lick of paint. No-frills presentation
extends to the food ('of a sound standard'), and staff are efficient. The expansive
menu includes a host of hot and cold starters (many of them vegetarian), Greek
casseroles, chargrilled meats and several fish dishes. A large starter of chicken
livers fried with garlic and scrambled eggs won support, while to follow,
chargrilled sea bass with a gratin of potatoes and asparagus (a special) was
pronounced 'very fresh and perfectly cooked'. Kosmos' kleftiko (using lean
lamb steak rather than the usual knuckle) also has its fans. Charlotta – trifle with
rosewater flavoured custard – makes a light, interesting end to a meal. Nearly all
wines come from Greece or Cyprus; prices start at £7.50.

CHEF: Loulla Astin   PROPRIETORS: Stewart and Loulla Astin   OPEN: Sun L 1 to 5, all week D 6 to
11.30 (12.30 Fri and Sat)   CLOSED: 25 and 26 Dec, 1 Jan   MEALS: alc (main courses £6 to
£12.50). Set L £5 (2 courses), Set D before 7.30 £7.95   SERVICE: not inc   CARDS: Amex, Delta,
MasterCard, Switch, Visa   DETAILS: 90 seats. Private parties: 40 main room. Vegetarian meals.
Children's helpings. No pipes in dining room. Music. Air-conditioned (£5)

Lime Tree ▼ ✦

8 Lapwing Lane, West Didsbury,
Manchester M20 2WS   COOKING 2
TEL: (0161) 445 1217   FAX: (0161) 445 5039   COST £21–£45

Seasonal French/Mediterranean food with a traditional English backbone and
dollops of the Orient could sum up the cooking at this neighbourhood restaurant
in one of Manchester's leafy suburbs. The inside is leafy too, with a new glass
roof on the conservatory, and a new bar. Starting at home, toad-in-the-hole and
potted crab sit confidently beside salmon and asparagus lasagne and red Thai
mussel ragoût. Similarly for main courses, fish and chips and praiseworthy fish
cakes share the billing with Cajun-spiced monkfish, vegetable baklava, and
fillet of beef with Stilton butter and rösti, while desserts range from hot and
sticky or cold and creamy. Giving in to recommendations of aperitifs, and dessert
wines to accompany individual puddings, may upset the reasonable pricing,
particularly of the set-lunch and early-evening meals. Wines from France, Italy,
Iberia and the New World offer quality at manageable prices, with enthusiastic
and informed tasting notes aiding selection. Half a dozen house wines are all
£9.75 a bottle, £2.75 a glass.

CHEFS: Damian Kay and Jason Dickinson   PROPRIETOR: Patrick Hannity   OPEN: Tue to Fri and
Sun L 12 to 2.30, all week D 6 to 10.30   CLOSED: 25, 26 and 31 Dec, 1 Jan, bank hols   MEALS:
alc (main courses L £6.50 to £11, D £9.50 to £14). Set L Tue to Fri £9.95 (2 courses), Set L Sun
£12.95, Set D 6 to 7 £9.95 (2 courses)   SERVICE: not inc   CARDS: Amex, Delta, MasterCard,
Switch, Visa   DETAILS: 80 seats. 25 seats outside. Private parties: 40 main room. Vegetarian
meals. Children's helpings. No smoking in 1 dining room. Music

Lincoln

NEW ENTRY

1 Lincoln Square, Manchester M2 5LN   COOKING 2
TEL: (0161) 834 9000   FAX: (0161) 834 9555   COST £22–£58

Just off the Victorian Gothic Albert Square, Lincoln Square is a relatively peaceful backwater in the city centre. Floor-to-ceiling windows run the length of a large, ground-floor dining room, and the 'impressive modern-design job' features a smart bar, blond wood, pools of blue light on white walls, and well-set tables. A generous carte combines a range of European and oriental ideas, from asparagus and pea risotto with mint butter, to Szechuan spiced duck breast with noodles, won tons and a honey and soy sauce. Despite this, a strongly traditional vein runs through the repertoire – chunks of avocado with crab meat, fat prawns and marie rose sauce ('the real thing, though') – while Sunday lunch has brought pink roast loin of pork with sage and onion stuffing. Finish maybe with pannacotta or treacle tart. The operation is 'managed charmingly by the daughter of the family'. House wines are £11 on a short list, about evenly spread between Europe and the New World.

CHEF: Jem O'Sullivan   PROPRIETOR: Fred Done   OPEN: Sun to Fri L 12 to 2.30, Mon to Sat D 6 to 10.30 (11 Fri and Sat)   CLOSED: 25, 26 and 31 Dec, 1 Jan, bank hols   MEALS: alc (main courses £12.50 to £19.50). Set L Mon to Fri £12.50 to £14.95, Set D Mon to Fri before 7pm £12.50 to £14.95   SERVICE: 10% (optional)   CARDS: Amex, Delta, MasterCard, Switch, Visa   DETAILS: 90 seats. Private parties: 100 main room. Vegetarian meals. Wheelchair access (also WC). Music. Air-conditioned

Little Yang Sing

17 George Street, Manchester M1 4HE   COOKING 2
TEL: (0161) 228 7722   FAX: (0161) 237 9257   COST £17–£52

Sterling efforts have been made with Little Yang Sing's little basement, which now looks smart with its blue carpet, office-type chairs and mirrored panels. This Chinatown fixture offers a long menu of expected Cantonese stir-fries, but also lamb dishes and an impressive vegetarian section, including a few pairings (such as stir-fried yam with vegetables) that provide a textural alternative to the general crunchiness. Unusually, dim sum are now served into the evening, and the selection is tempered to European tastes, but deep-fried prawn dumplings (served with sweetened mayonnaise) have won plaudits: 'the prawns inside juicy and full of flavour'. An inspector also approved fillet of monkfish with spicy garlic sauce, served with strips of leek: 'an interesting variation on the spring onion theme'. Service is amiable, and the wine list offers a fair selection; house French is £9.95.

CHEF: K.K. Yeung   PROPRIETOR: L.Y.S. Ltd   OPEN: all week 12 to 11.30   CLOSED: 25 Dec   MEALS: alc (main courses £7.50 to £12.50). Set L £9, Set D £16 (min 2)   SERVICE: 10%   CARDS: Amex, Delta, MasterCard, Switch, Visa   DETAILS: 90 seats. Private parties: 90 main room. Vegetarian meals. Children's helpings. Occasional music. Air-conditioned

'My bread-and-butter pudding was good . . . but it was French, and I can't expect it to be as good as one from Hartlepool.' (On eating in Oxford)

Mash and Air ☕

40 Chorlton Street, Manchester M1 3HW | NEW CHEF
TEL: (0161) 661 6161   FAX: (0161) 661 6060   COST £22–£61

On the ground floor is Mash bar; above it is Mash brasserie, whose Cal/Ital style includes thin-based pizzas from a wood-fired oven; and on the top floor is Air, the smarter, shiny and 'scrupulously maintained' restaurant, now offering just a set-price menu, at dinner only. Having cooked in two of its sister establishments (Coast, and Atlantic Bar & Grill: see entries, London), Paul Wadham arrived too late for us to receive any feedback on the changes, but his menus at Air promise a continuation of the vitality that characterised his predecessor's style – seared tuna with wasabislaw and anchovy beignets – while taking a predominantly European bias in the shape of free-range Goosnargh chicken with vegetable risotto, and chocolate mousse with coffee ice cream. The wine list is simply arranged by varietal/blend and offers enough choice without becoming confusing. House wines in both Mash and Air are £13 a bottle and beers from the in-house microbrewery (ask for a tour) are £2.40 a pint.

CHEF: Paul Wadham   PROPRIETOR: Oliver Peyton   OPEN: Air Tue to Sat D only 6.30 to 11 (11.30 Sat); Mash Mon to Sat 12 to 3, 5 to 11 (12.30 Sat)   CLOSED: 25 and 26 Dec, 1 Jan, Easter Sun and Mon   MEALS: Air alc (main courses £14 to £19.50); Mash alc (main courses £6.50 to £12.50). Set L and D before 7pm £11 (2 courses) to £13.50   SERVICE: 10% (optional), card slips closed   CARDS: Amex, Delta, Diners, MasterCard, Switch, Visa   DETAILS: Air 120 seats, Mash 106 seats. Private parties: 175 main room (Air), 100 main room (Mash), 15 private room. Car park. Vegetarian meals. Wheelchair access (also WC). Music. Air-conditioned

Moss Nook

Ringway Road, Manchester M22 5WD
TEL: (0161) 437 4778   FAX: (0161) 498 8089   COOKING 6
on B5166, 1m from Manchester Airport   COST £26–£66

Heavy drapes, art deco lights, dark red upholstery and flock wallpaper combine to produce an ambience that feels a long way from the nearby airport. It is a serious place with a 'small but interesting menu', where staff announce extra daily dishes, and perform other ceremonial duties such as lifting silver domes, topping up glasses assiduously, and presenting the bill in an engraved wooden box. Kevin Lofthouse aims high, and his upmarket materials – sauté foie gras with morels on a rösti potato cake, or glazed lobster and scallops to start, for example – doubtless help to account for some of the highish prices. He adopts a generally classical approach, serving tournedos Rossini, grilled Dover sole meunière, and honey-glazed duckling with a plum sauce. Dishes are 'beautifully presented' and flavours kept in focus by a sense of balance. The highlight of the meal for one visitor was an 'outstanding' apple pie with vanilla sauce, and chocolate lovers get a fair deal. The £20 barrier is soon breached on a French-dominated wine list that includes some good bottles quite apart from the 'fine wine' section. House French is £9.95.

CHEF: Kevin Lofthouse   PROPRIETORS: Pauline and Derek Harrison   OPEN: Tue to Fri L 12 to
1.30, Tue to Sat D 7 to 9.30   CLOSED: 2 weeks Christmas   MEALS: alc (main courses £18 to
£25). Set L £18.50, Set D £31.50   SERVICE: net prices, card slips closed   CARDS: Amex, Delta,
MasterCard, Switch, Visa   DETAILS: 65 seats. 20 seats outside. Private parties: 55 main room.
Car park. Vegetarian meals. No children under 12. Jacket and tie. No pipes in dining room. No
music

New Emperor £ | NEW ENTRY |

52–56 George Street, Manchester M1 4FH
TEL: (0161) 228 2883   FAX: (0161) 228 6620   COOKING 2
EMAIL: newemperor@cwcom.net   COST £23–£48

Despite pictures and artefacts, the décor of this large restaurant may seem 'a trifle
bleak', according to a regular, who appreciated that efforts are being rightly
concentrated on producing consistently fine cooking, using high-quality ingredients. Results have included tender, sweet, full-flavoured and robustly
spiced spareribs with chilli and salt; and light, crisp, deep-fried battered squid.
Available in the evening as starters are high-quality dim sum, including siu mai,
steamed beef dumplings and paper-wrapped prawns. Dishes change with the
seasons, and some surprises in the long, otherwise standard Cantonese list
include 'pak far' (bean curd soup), king prawn with sliced ham, and Spanish
fried rice. Service may be pressed but responds to genuine interest in the food. A
caring attitude is suggested by the availability of a vegetarian menu and full
facilities for disabled people. House wine is £9.50.

CHEF: Tommy Chan   PROPRIETOR: K.L Lee   OPEN: all week 12 to 11.45 (1am Sat)   MEALS: alc
(main courses £5.50 to £10). Set L £3.80 (1 course) to £12 (2 courses, min 2), Set D £15.50 to
£29.50 (all min 2)   SERVICE: 10%   CARDS: Amex, Delta, Diners, MasterCard, Switch, Visa
DETAILS: 270 seats. Private parties: 200 main room, 20 private room. Vegetarian meals.
Wheelchair access (also WC). Music. Air-conditioned

Nico Central

Mount Street, Manchester M60 2DS   COOKING 3
TEL: (0161) 236 6488   FAX: (0161) 236 8897   COST £24–£50

Primrose yellow adorns the walls, and the tall ceilings, square mirrored pillars
and art deco interior are reminiscent of a Parisian bistro. Enter via the Midland
Hotel, of which it is physically a part, or from the street. The restaurant is one of a
fast-expanding group (see also Simply Nico and Nico Central, both London) run
by Roy Ackerman's Restaurant Partnership that use Nico Ladenis's name,
though he is only a consultant. The menu criss-crosses between France and Italy,
opening perhaps with a soufflé of Roquefort and pears, cep risotto, or a firm slice
of mixed charcuterie terrine with a predominant flavour of liver, on a powerfully
vinegar-dressed celeriac and apple rémoulade. Main courses are in similar vein,
producing a 'tender and full-flavoured' duck leg confit with 'creamy, smooth'
garlic mash, and a 'satisfying' shank of lamb with root vegetables and potato
purée. Desserts – crème caramel, summer pudding, prune and Armagnac
clafoutis – are generally regarded as good, and several reporters have used the
words 'friendly' and 'efficient' to describe service from a mainly French team.

The sixty-bottle wine list leans towards France, but not exclusively, and should you wish to push the boat out – prices are a little steep – there is a fine wine section.

CHEF: Steven Dray   PROPRIETOR: The Restaurant Partnership   OPEN: all week 12 to 2.30, 5.30 to 11 (10 Sun)   CLOSED: 25 Dec, bank hols   MEALS: Set L £13.50, Set D £24   SERVICE: 10%, card slips closed   CARDS: Amex, Delta, Diners, MasterCard, Switch, Visa   DETAILS: 100 seats. Private parties: 100 main room. Vegetarian meals. Children's helpings. No cigars in dining room. Wheelchair access (not WC). Music. Air-conditioned   £5

Rhodes & Co   NEW ENTRY

| Waters Reach, Trafford Park, Manchester M17 1WS | COOKING 4 |
| TEL: (0161) 868 1900   FAX: (0161) 868 1901 | COST £24–£50 |

This joint venture, their first outside London (another may have opened by the time the *Guide* appears), confirms Gary Rhodes as a brand name. The restaurant sits in a new hotel on the edge of Salford Quays, or the 'threshold of heaven' for United fans, since it faces the North Stand. Black and grey seating, bare blond-wood tables, and booths arranged either side of a central spine of tables make it look like 'a classy diner', while the menu lists a familiar string of British brasserie perennials such as cod and chips, egg Benedict with Cheshire ham, tuna niçoise, and braised lamb shank, served with a small jug of sauce to pour over.

A kitchen working within its capacity 'gets all its priorities right': materials, timing and seasoning are all 'spot on'. At inspection a simple Caesar salad skilfully assembled 'all the correct ingredients in the right proportions' and avoided any temptation to gild the lily, while a 'surprisingly successful' boneless chicken breast, scattered with grated cheese and grilled, came with a creamy tomato sauce. Desserts run to steamed chocolate pudding, banana brûlée, and smooth-textured, sharp-tasting lemon parfait, while cheeses are kept in good condition, and served at room temperature. Service is friendly, informative and efficient, and a short wine list starts with house Argentinian at £12.

CHEF: Ian Morgan   PROPRIETOR: Gardner Merchant   OPEN: Mon to Fri L 12 to 2.30, all week D 6.30 to 9.45   CLOSED: 25 and 31 Dec, 1 Jan   MEALS: alc D (main courses £7.50 to £15). Set L £11.50 (2 courses). Bar meals available   SERVICE: 10% (optional), card slips closed   CARDS: Amex, Delta, Diners, MasterCard, Switch, Visa   DETAILS: 100 seats. Private parties: 60 main room, 60 private room. Car park. Vegetarian meals. Children's helpings. Wheelchair access (also WC). Music. Air-conditioned

Simply Heathcotes

Jacksons Row, Manchester M2 5WD	
TEL: (0161) 835 3536 FAX: (0161) 835 3534	COOKING 4
EMAIL: simply@heathcotes.co.uk	COST £22–£50

Big, brash, and brightly lit, this city centre conversion, occupying two spacious floors of a building that once housed a registry office, is a colourful, contemporary urban restaurant where noise ('and there is plenty of it') bounces off hard surfaces. A welcome vitality about the food stems from a playfulness with classic ideas: piccalilli and ham hock soup, 'precisely timed' thin fillet steak on an ale sauce with horseradish risotto, or hotpot of mussels, a sort of moules marinière enlivened with background chilli heat, chickpeas and couscous. Resources local to the Heathcote empire (see entries, Preston and Longridge) include chicken and duckling from Goosnargh, and a chowder of Morecambe Bay shrimps to accompany roast lobster. First courses may outshine mains, but an element of comfort runs through from a starter of black pudding, via hash browns with poached egg and baked-beans, to a 'finisher' of bread and butter pudding. Food is 'efficiently delivered' by young staff, and while bowls of olives are charged extra, the pre-theatre option looks fair value. The forty-strong, well-chosen wine list covers a wide price range (house French is £11.50), with around a dozen available by the glass.

CHEF: James Gingell   PROPRIETOR: Paul Heathcote   OPEN: all week 11.45 to 2.30, 5.30 (6 Sun) to 11 (9.30 Sun)   CLOSED: bank hols exc Good Friday   MEALS: alc (main courses £11.50 to £30). Set L and D before 7 £10.50 (2 courses) to £12.50   SERVICE: 10% (optional), card slips closed   CARDS: Amex, Delta, Diners, MasterCard, Switch, Visa   DETAILS: 210 seats. Private parties: 180 main room, 50 to 120 private rooms. Vegetarian meals. No cigars/pipes in dining room. Wheelchair access (also WC). Music. Air-conditioned

Tai Pan £

81–97 Upper Brook Street, Manchester M13 9TX	COOKING 2
TEL: (0161) 273 2798 FAX: (0161) 273 1578	COST £21–£46

Refurbishment since last year has produced a long bar and more tables in this 'solid example of a Hong Kong-style eating house' overlooking Upper Brook Street. 'My opinion of the cooking remains unchanged,' writes a regular, who doesn't come here for cutting-edge invention or flair, nor for 'cheap and cheerful' Chinese food, but more for consistent output of mainly repertoire standards: fried sliced beef in oyster sauce, sweet-and-sour chicken, egg-fried rice. Dim sum plates stand out for variety and quality (especially on Sunday): among highlights are steamed whelks with satay sauce, beef dumpling with ginger and spring onion, and 'one we called The Alien': a quail's egg on seafood stuffing wrapped in pastry that was 'beginning to dissolve into [its] sauce'. Two- and three-course lunchtime options under a tenner add to the appeal, and around forty wines start at £8.20 for house French red and white.

CHEF: H.S. Woo   PROPRIETOR: G.H. Chan   OPEN: all week 12 to 11.30 (9.30 Sun)   MEALS: alc (main courses £6.50 to £11.50). Set L £5.45 (min 2), Set L and D £14 to £28 (all min 2)   SERVICE: 10%, card slips closed   CARDS: Amex, Delta, Diners, MasterCard, Switch, Visa   DETAILS: 300 seats. Private parties: 300 main room, 100 private room. Car park. Vegetarian meals. Wheelchair access (also WC). Music. Air-conditioned

Yang Sing   NEW ENTRY

3 Charlotte Street, Manchester M1 4HB	COOKING 6
TEL: (0161) 236 2200 FAX: (0161) 236 5934	COST £25–£45

Yang Sing planned to move back to its premises at 34 Princess Street in autumn 1999 after fire forced a move. Reports refer of course to the temporary Charlotte Street address from which they will carry the entire staff (and the telephone number). Those reports indicate that 'consummate reliability and high standards' have been maintained. Gerry Yeung, the link between his brother's cooking and the customers, has encouraged waiting staff to advise 'without steering them towards the most expensive, or most anglicised dishes'. One of the few reservations concerns the tolerance of smoking throughout the restaurant.

A full range of dim sum is offered until 4.30 (some are available later, but only as starters). A reader who admitted a prejudice against coconut and steamed dim sum was surprised to find that steamed seafood (queenies and king prawns) and yam tarts with coconut sauce 'worked marvellously'. Feather-light, ultra-short pasties filled with wind-dried oyster and char siu were successful too, as were more conventional woo kok and char siu cheung fun. Pork chops Shanghai style, and casserole of aubergine with prawns and squid, were high points of one meal, stir-fried fish with asparagus spears enjoyed at another. One brave group finished with deep-fried hedgehog buns, while a fruit platter of melon, pineapple, mango, Sharon fruit and tangerine segments has made 'a brilliant end' for others. There are special menus for vegetarians and children. The mostly French wine list includes fine clarets and Burgundies, but also offers some choice New World bins. Prices are fair throughout, and four house wines in three colours are all £9.95 a bottle.

CHEF: Harry Yeung   PROPRIETOR: Yang Sing Ltd   OPEN: all week 12 to 11   CLOSED: 25 Dec
MEALS: alc (main courses £7 to £10.50). Set L and D £15 (min 2) to £22 (min 6). Dim sum menu
available L   SERVICE: 10%, card slips closed   CARDS: Amex, Delta, Diners, MasterCard,
Switch, Visa   DETAILS: 220 seats. Private parties: 220 main room, 30 to 240 private rooms.
Vegetarian meals. Music. Air-conditioned

MANNINGTREE Essex   map 6

Stour Bay Café   NEW ENTRY

39–43 High Street, Manningtree CO11 1AH   COOKING 3
TEL: (01206) 396687   FAX: (01206) 395462   COST £18–£43

Manningtree claims to be the smallest town in the UK, so it should be no problem finding this Grade II-listed late-sixteenth-century building, painted a pretty shade of green. Inside is a mix of beams, exposed brickwork and bright orangey-pink walls adorned with works for sale by local artists. Stas Anastasiades' cooking style aims to reflect 'modern British themes with a Pacific flavour', producing starters of gravad lax with a mustard, lime and dill sauce, or a 'plump, light, airy' faggot of fish and shellfish with spicy tomato coulis. To follow, chicken breast roasted with lemon and tamarind is served with yam confit and thyme jus, while pink-roasted harissa-marinated rump of lamb comes with couscous and 'excellent' tzatziki to offset the spiciness. Successful desserts have included roast rocha pear with maple syrup and ice cream, the pear 'perfect, with a slightly charred taste'. An inspector found the food 'enjoyable and imaginative', adding the caveat that 'the chef is rather enthusiastic about spicing'. Service from Mark Bright is 'welcoming and most attentive'. The wine list is organised by grape then price, mixing the Old World in with the New, and gives a helpful introduction to each section. Prices are fair, house selections starting at £9.25.

CHEF: Stas Anastasiades PROPRIETORS: Mark and Emma Bright OPEN: Tue to Fri L 12 to 2, Tue to Sat D 7 to 9.30 CLOSED: after L 26 Dec for 3 weeks MEALS: alc D (main courses £7 to £15). Set L £8.50 (2 courses) to £10 SERVICE: not inc CARDS: Amex, Delta, MasterCard, Switch, Visa DETAILS: 50 seats. Private parties: 50 main room. Vegetarian meals. Wheelchair access (not WC). Music

---

MARSDEN West Yorkshire   map 8

▲ Olive Branch

Manchester Road, Marsden HD7 6LU
TEL: (01484) 844487   COOKING 2
on A62, between Slaithwaite and Marsden   COST £22–£51

A bistro atmosphere has been carefully created at this converted pub, where basic décor, an informal style, and 'friendly staff who know what they are about' put on a convincing show. Cards and blackboards take the place of a written menu, and orders are taken at the bar. Fresh raw materials, particularly seafood, are commendable, and the cooking touches on most current preoccupations, from leek risotto to lambs' sweetbreads with couscous. Fish might be given an oriental treatment – roast monkfish fillet with Tabasco and chilli oil, or sea bass with Chinese noodle cake and yellow pepper cream – while meats have included braised lamb shank with tomato, flageolet beans and cumin. Desserts, somewhat unusually, do not revert to British staples but continue the restless search for excitement with aniseed parfait and blackberry coulis, or an intensely flavoured warm Belgian chocolate tart with orange custard. A wide-ranging annotated wine list offers plenty of interest under £20. House French is £9.90.

CHEFS: John Lister and Paul Kewley PROPRIETORS: John and Ann Lister OPEN: Wed to Fri and Sun L 12 to 1.45, all week D 6.30 to 9.30 (4.30 to 8.30 Sun) CLOSED: first 2 weeks Jan, last week June MEALS: alc (main courses £10.50 to £17.50). Set L £13.90 SERVICE: not inc, card slips closed CARDS: Amex, Delta, MasterCard, Switch, Visa DETAILS: 68 seats. Private parties: 36 main room. Car park. Vegetarian meals. Wheelchair access (not WC). Music ACCOMMODATION: 3 rooms, all with bath/shower. TV. Phone. Room only £50 to £55 (£5)

MARSH BENHAM Berkshire   map 2

Water Rat ¾ £   BERKS 2000 TREAT   NEW ENTRY

Marsh Benham RG20 8LY
TEL: (01635) 582017 FAX: (01635) 37338   COOKING 5
off A4 between Newbury and Hungerford   COST £20–£34

Carole Evans is no stranger to the *Guide*, having been listed for some years at the Roebuck in Brimfield (see entry), followed by a brief spell at the Three Horseshoes, Batcombe. She has now arrived in this picture-postcard Berkshire village, cooking uncomplicated modern food in a thatched country pub covered in clematis. The tried-and-true mix of earlier Evans menus is preserved here, taking in Mediterranean modes (sun-dried tomato and vegetable soup with basil and olive oil), French classicism (crisped duck confit with orange cider sauce and fondant potatoes), and true-Brit steak-and-kidney pie with green beans, carrots and mash. That confit was a whole leg from a bird that 'had really strutted its stuff in the farmyard', its accompaniments supporting the intensely flavourful meat without confusing the issue. Fish is equally intelligently handled, as attested by a reader who enjoyed a thick fillet of skate garnished with crunchy capers and rosemary. Cream from a local herd of Jerseys anoints the sticky toffee pudding, and a reporter who has followed Carole Evans's progress was delighted to find the poppyseed parfait of olden days restored to the repertoire. Freshly baked breads should not be missed. Care and attention in compiling each short geographical section is evident throughout the wine list, which opens with half a dozen house selections at £9.50 a bottle, or £2.50 for a 175ml glass.

CHEF: Carole Evans PROPRIETOR: Tricrane Ltd OPEN: all week L 12 to 2, Tue to Sat 7 to 9 CLOSED: 25 and 31 Dec MEALS: alc (main courses £5 to £14.50). Set L Sun £8.95 (1 course) to £15.95 SERVICE: not inc CARDS: Delta, MasterCard, Switch, Visa DETAILS: 60 seats. Private parties: 30 main room, 25 private room. Car park. Vegetarian meals. Children's helpings. No smoking in 1 dining room. Wheelchair access (also WC). Occasional music

---

MASHAM North Yorkshire   map 9

Floodlite £

7 Silver Street, Masham HG4 4DX
TEL: (01765) 689000   COOKING 5
off A6108, 9m NW of Ripon   COST £18–£44

It is some fourteen years since the Floods opened their simple, unadorned shop conversion in the main street close to the market square, yet first-time visitors continue to be surprised by the quality of the cooking. Plainly fitted out 'without being stark', it is an unassuming place offering both a fixed-price menu and more generous carte. A terrine of 'meaty salmon and moussey pike' seems to be a fixture, and game appears in various guises, from hare pâté (with blackcurrant sauce) to roast saddle of roe deer with wild mushrooms. But one of the striking things about the cooking is its ability to impress with ordinary-sounding dishes: mushrooms with garlic and cream in filo pastry, or ripe avocado pear with prawns to start, followed by grilled chicken breast with ratatouille, or two large slices of lamb's liver with onions and crisp bacon in a strong dark gravy. Meals might finish with a sharp-tasting gooseberry and apple pie, or a highly rated version of old-fashioned bread-and-butter pudding with blackberry and apple. A modest pricing policy applies equally to food and to the wide-ranging wine list, which starts with half a dozen house wines under £10.

CHEF: Charles Flood PROPRIETORS: Charles and Christine Flood OPEN: Fri to Sun L 12 to 2, Tue to Sat D 7 to 9 CLOSED: 2 weeks Jan, 1 week Oct MEALS: alc (main courses £9 to £16.50). Set L £12.50, Set D £12.50 (2 courses) to £15 SERVICE: not inc, card slips closed CARDS: Amex, MasterCard, Visa DETAILS: 36 seats. Private parties: 28 main room. Children's helpings. No music £5

'[The head waiter] performed as if he was an American cheerleader trapped within the body of Basil Fawlty.' (On eating in Cambridgeshire)

MAWNAN SMITH Cornwall   map 1

▲ Nansidwell 🍴✖

Mawnan Smith TR11 5HU
TEL: (01326) 250340   FAX: (01326) 250440
EMAIL: bomrerob@aol.com
off A494 Helston road, take left fork at Red Lion   COOKING 3
in village   COST £25–£69

The advice is to roll up the curved drive in early-evening sunlight to get the best
view of this attractive stone house and its gardens. Inside, it is 'gracious' with
deep chintz sofas, swagged curtains, huge flower arrangements, lots of books,
log fires and antique furniture. The Robertsons and Tony Allcott have 'gone
organic' over pretty well everything: meats, breads, dry goods, vegetables and
wines ('we can even tell you the name of one of the organic Cheddar cows'). The
five-course set-price dinner menu (additional choices carry a supplement) has
no particular weak spots, from nibbles of home-made crisps, tiny seafood
vol-au-vents and vegetable kebabs through to house chocolates and almond
paste confections. In between, guests have been impressed by pastrywork: a
'masterpiece' of a tartlet, for example, containing mushrooms 'bursting with
flavour'. Presentation is attractive without being fussy, from pink lamb cutlets
on a mound of buttery leeks spiked with walnuts, to a pretty garnish of mango
and melon slices for rich duck terrine. Puddings are often fruit-based and served
with ice cream or clotted cream. Wines are a well-balanced collection, starting
with house Spanish at £12.

CHEF: Anthony Allcott   PROPRIETORS: Jamie and Felicity Robertson   OPEN: all week 12.30 to
1.30, 7 to 9   CLOSED: Jan   MEALS: Set L £12.75 (2 courses) to £16.75, Set D £30   SERVICE: not
inc   CARDS: Delta, MasterCard, Switch, Visa   DETAILS: 40 seats. 20 seats outside. Private
parties: 40 main room. Car park. Vegetarian meals. Children's helpings. No children under 7 at
D. No smoking in dining room. Wheelchair access (not WC). No music   ACCOMMODATION: 12
rooms, all with bath/shower. TV. Phone. B&B £47 to £180. Rooms for disabled. Baby facilities
(£5)

MELBOURN Cambridgeshire   map 6

Pink Geranium 🍴✖

25 Station Road, Melbourn SG8 6DX
TEL: (01763) 260215   FAX: (01763) 262110   COOKING 5
just off A10, 2m N of Royston   COST £32–£84

Both the colour and the flower (in real and fake form) dominate this sixteenth-
century thatched cottage, with its oak beams and log fire, from the pink-washed
outside walls to the drawing room decked out in pink chintz sofas and
armchairs. Steven Saunders is a busy man, dividing his time between here and
nearby Sheene Mill (see below), as well as writing cookery books and appearing
on television, while Mark Jordan's cooking is as sumptuous and luxurious as
the setting, both in presentation (towers are a recurring theme) and ingredients.
It is also fond of bright flavours, serving up foie gras with a 'piquant, subtly
fruity' apricot, grape and mango salsa, and an inspector's 'outstanding' monkfish

and aubergine brochette with jalapeño couscous and coconut and coriander 'froth'. Tournedos of Black beef has come more straightforwardly with 'a nice selection of vegetable nibbles', including minute turnips with their tops, whole roast garlic cloves, and plenty of rich red wine gravy. Desserts also score highly for presentation: pear crème brûlée, for example, with an elaborate caramel lattice, or a trio of sorbets arranged on a biscuit 'hand'. Variable standards, long delays and staff shortages have taken the shine off the occasion for some reporters; others have found service 'caring, intelligent, attentive and on the ball'. The confident wine list kicks off with twenty-two bottles under £15 and then makes its way around the world.

CHEF: Mark Jordan PROPRIETORS: Steven and Sally Saunders OPEN: Tue to Sat 12 to 2, 7 to 10 MEALS: alc (main courses £18 to £28). Set L £14, Set D £30 to £50 SERVICE: not inc CARDS: Amex, Delta, MasterCard, Switch, Visa DETAILS: 60 seats. 20 seats outside. Private parties: 18 main room, 18 private room. Car park. Vegetarian meals. Children's helpings. No children under 10 at D. No smoking in dining room. Wheelchair access (not WC). No music (£5)

▲ Sheene Mill   [NEW ENTRY]

Melbourn SG8 6DX
TEL: (01763) 261393   COOKING 2
EMAIL: steven@stevensaunders.co.uk   COST £23–£60

Set in its own grounds overlooking the River Mell, this black and white timbered, seventeenth-century former water mill may look from the outside like a large tea room, but the interior is fashionably painted in bright colours. It calls itself a brasserie, but foodwise has been likened to a gastropub, 'though it clearly sets out to be more glamorous than that'. It was acquired in late 1997 by Steven Saunders of Pink Geranium (see above), and delivers dishes such as smoked haddock and watercress soup with a 'true flavour', and a panaché of langoustines and salmon with basil oil which gets top marks for presentation. These might be followed by roast chump of lamb with redcurrant and mint; a vegetarian 'tower' of mushrooms sandwiched with pesto, tomatoes and red peppers and topped with cheese; or chargrilled ribeye steak with 'first-class' chips. Desserts come in for particular praise: an apple strudel flavoured with cinnamon, and a 'light and moussey' mixed berry cheesecake. Service is prompt and friendly, and the wine list offers some good bottles at fair prices. Eleven house wines start at £10.

CHEFS: Alex Williams and Steven Saunders PROPRIETORS: Steven and Sally Saunders OPEN: all week L 12 to 2.30, Mon to Sat D 6.30 to 10.30 MEALS: alc (main courses £9 to £21). Set L Mon to Sat £10 (2 courses) to £14, Set L Sun £18.50 SERVICE: not inc, card slips closed CARDS: Amex, Delta, MasterCard, Switch, Visa DETAILS: 120 seats. 50 seats outside. Private parties: 120 main room. Car park. Vegetarian meals. Children's helpings. No smoking before coffee. Wheelchair access (not WC). Music ACCOMMODATION: 9 rooms, all with bath/shower. TV. Phone. B&B £40 to £100 (The Which? Hotel Guide) (£5)

The Guide relies on feedback from its readers. Especially welcome are reports on new restaurants appearing in the book for the first time. All letters to the Guide are acknowledged.

MELKSHAM Wiltshire   map 2

▲ *Toxique* 🍴✳

187 Woodrow Road, Melksham SN12 7AY   COOKING 4
TEL: (01225) 702129   FAX: (01225) 742773   COST £31–£49

'The whole Toxique experience is mildly eccentric, bohemian, great fun,' wrote
one overnight guest at this restaurant-with-rooms set in a Georgian farmhouse
just outside town. The interior design – achieved inexpensively with deep,
striking paints, bright, modern paintings by Peter Jewkes and exotic touches
with drapes and cushions – signals a creative streak that is also at work in the
kitchen. Dishes may sound simple, but their execution impresses: five 'juicy and
plump' seared scallops with their corals, for example, in a fruity, mouth-
cleansing salad of chicory and orange. Indeed, flavour matching is approached
with a degree of skill and imagination, be it a dash of horseradish in the
dauphinois potatoes that accompany seared fillet steak, or grilled red mullet on a
bed of fluffy couscous with a sauce of preserved lemons and rosemary.

Despite conservative timing, and the odd disappointing dessert, reporters are
enthusiastic, not least for plum and almond tart with Amaretto crème fraîche, or
the house speciality, a rich layered chocolate torte. Hotel guests benefit from a
fine breakfast, and the wine list combines appealing global choices with
unfrightening prices. French house wines are £11 to £13.50.

CHEF: Helen Bartlett   PROPRIETORS: Helen Bartlett and Peter Jewkes   OPEN: Sun L 12.30 to 2,
Wed to Sat D 7.30 to 10   MEALS: Set L Sun £18.50 (2 courses) to £21.50, Set D £31   SERVICE:
not inc, card slips closed   CARDS: Amex, Delta, Diners, MasterCard, Switch, Visa   DETAILS: 40
seats. Private parties: 24 main room. Car park. Vegetarian meals. No smoking in dining room.
Music   ACCOMMODATION: 5 rooms, all with bath/shower. D,B&B £95 to £160 (*The Which? Hotel
Guide*)

MIDDLEHAM North Yorkshire   map 8

▲ *Waterford House* 🍷 🍴✳

Kirkgate, Middleham DL8 4PG   COOKING 2
TEL: (01969) 622090   FAX: (01969) 624020   COST £30–£52

The stone-built hotel just off the cobbled village square is filled with books,
quality antiques and Victoriana. It is a friendly, homely place with a self-styled
'dinner-party atmosphere', where Brian Madell (a 'remarkable' host) talks
diners through the menu and wine list. Game is a regular feature, local supplies
include meat, cheese and organic vegetables, and seafood dishes tend to
incorporate two or three species: perhaps a starter of prawns, salmon and firm
white fish in a creamy sauce topped with cheese and breadcrumbs, or a main
course of wild Irish salmon, brill, halibut and sea bass with beurre blanc.

Although many dishes are turned out well – a salad of crisp duck livers, bacon
and black pudding, or a rich broccoli and Brie soup – standards and timing do
slip from time to time as the kitchen, enthusiastic as it is, struggles to meet all its
commitments. Oenophiles should do themselves a favour and stay overnight, for
it would be a shame to miss what is surely a unique opportunity to sample
glasses of wine from over 900 bins, including many venerable and rare classics.

Brian will open virtually any bottle and serve a glass (equal to a quarter-bottle) for a quarter of the price. Failing that, house wines start at £9.50.

CHEF: Everyl Madell PROPRIETORS: Everyl and Brian Madell OPEN: all week D only 7 to 10 (L by arrangement) MEALS: alc (main courses £14 to £19). Set L £19.50, Set D £22.50 to £29.50 SERVICE: not inc, card slips closed CARDS: Delta, MasterCard, Switch, Visa DETAILS: 20 seats. Private parties: 24 main room. Car park. Children's helpings. No smoking in dining room. No music ACCOMMODATION: 5 rooms, all with bath/shower. TV. Phone. B&B £50 to £95. Baby facilities (The Which? Hotel Guide) £5

MIDDLESBROUGH Middlesbrough

map 10

Purple Onion

80 Corporation Road, Middlesbrough TS1 2RF COOKING 3
TEL: (01642) 222250 FAX: (01642) 248088 COST £20–£55

Given that Claes Oldenburg's giant painted metal 'bottle', made up of strings of words, stands not far away in a small park, a sense of visual fun obviously comes in handy in Middlesbrough. It would certainly help to make customers feel at home in this cavernous and entertaining ground-floor 'Victorian fantasia', where plants, lamps, mirrors, giant candles, flock wallpaper and music – 'the sort John Peel plays' – vie for attention. An equally arresting menu stars a busy San Franciscan fish stew with toasted sourdough bread (at dinner only), alongside crab and salmon fish cakes on a Thai sauce, smoked haddock and spring onion risotto, and, inevitably perhaps, purple onion soup. Look to the boards for the day's fish, and to the laminated plastic menu for steaks, calf's liver and rack of lamb, and finish with a homely dessert of chocolate and cherry sponge, sticky toffee, or a summer berry fool. The forty-strong wine list crams in a variety of styles, and house Vin de Pays d'Oc is £10.95.

CHEFS: Graham Ben and Tony Chapman PROPRIETORS: John and Bruno McCoy OPEN: all week L 12 to 2.30, Mon to Sat D 5 to 10.30 (11 Fri and Sat) CLOSED: 25 Dec, 1 Jan MEALS: alc (main courses L £5 to to £10, D £15 to £18) SERVICE: not inc CARDS: Delta, Diners, MasterCard, Switch, Visa DETAILS: 80 seats. Private parties: 20 main room, 26 private room. Vegetarian meals. Children's helpings. Wheelchair access (also WC). Music. Air-conditioned

MIDHURST West Sussex

map 3

Maxine's ⅜✕

Elizabeth House, Red Lion Street,
Midhurst GU29 9PB COOKING 1
TEL: (01730) 816271 COST £26–£45

Looking like a contender for the title of 'oldest house in Britain', this half-timbered, one-roomed restaurant derives its 'tea room' image from a low, beamed ceiling, dark wood panelling and lace curtains. It ploughs a largely familiar furrow with salmon in sorrel sauce, and rack of lamb 'seriously crusted' with rosemary, served with a sauceboat of garlic and rosemary gravy. A few modern-sounding dishes provide contrast in the shape of crab cakes with coriander sauce, or a squat tower of simply grilled aubergine and goats' cheese with a salad of crisp leaves. Main courses come with vegetables on the plate, and a cheesy potato gratin served separately. Dutch apple tart ('on the menu forever') recalls the owners' origins, or there might be a marzipan-filled flaky pastry pie with a glazed fanned pear to the side. An inspector felt that some raw materials might be improved; service has varied from 'casual but unsmiling,' to 'efficient and charming'; and forty-plus wines start with house French at £9.95.

CHEF: Robert de Jager   PROPRIETORS: Robert and Marti de Jager   OPEN: Wed to Sun L 12 to 1.30, Wed to Sat D 7 to 9   CLOSED: 26 Dec   MEALS: alc (main courses £11 to £16.50). Set L Wed to Sun and D Wed to Fri £16.95   SERVICE: net prices, card slips closed   CARDS: Amex, Delta, MasterCard, Switch, Visa   DETAILS: 24 seats. Private parties: 30 main room. Children's helpings. No smoking in dining room. No music

---

MILTON ERNEST Bedfordshire   map 6

Strawberry Tree 🍴✹   **NEW ENTRY**

Radwell Road, Milton Ernest MK44 1RY   COOKING 5
TEL: (01234) 823633   COST £28–£51

The primose-washed walls and neatly manicured thatch of what was once a tea room lend a distinctly cottagey theme to this family enterprise, confirmed by comfortable sofas, toby jugs and porcelain figures inside. 'Strawberry Twee were the words that sprang to to mind' for one visitor, though the cooking inhabits an entirely different world. Two brothers, Jason and Andrew Bona, are in charge of the kitchen, while their parents manage front-of-house in 'exemplary' fashion. Bread is home-made, vegetables and herbs home-grown, ingredients sourced locally and organically where possible. The food embraces many fashionable ideas and handles them successfully, from a fine, creamy-textured cappuccino soup of haricot beans and truffle, to a dish of crisp, golden crusted spiced cod with a warm salad of roast fennel, green beans, Jersey Royals and a slick of basil oil.

One of the things the kitchen does well is to put a refined spin on some traditional ideas. A gratin of potato gnocchi, macaroni, spinach and ceps, for example, is 'like a glorified macaroni cheese' with a luxuriant dash of truffle oil to smarten it up. Likewise a Kiev-style chicken breast (stuffed with parsley butter and roasted) proved 'simple but effective', accompanied by noodles in a creamy sauce with grapes (Veronique style) flavoured with tarragon. Desserts score highly too: a parfait combining rich white chocolate with fresh lime, for example, and crème brûlée like a 'feather-light parfait,' topped with a tiny scoop of intensely flavoured apple sorbet. A short wine list is not in the same league, but starts with a pair of house wines at £12.50.

CHEFS: Jason and Andrew Bona   PROPRIETORS: John and Wendy Bona   OPEN: Wed to Fri and Sun L 12 to 1.45, Tue to Sat D 7.30 to 8.30   CLOSED: 2 weeks Jan   MEALS: Set L Wed to Fri £17, Set L Sun £18.50, Set D £29   SERVICE: not inc, card slips closed   CARDS: Delta, MasterCard, Switch, Visa   DETAILS: 22 seats. Private parties: 18 main room, 8 private room. Car park. Children's helpings. No smoking in dining room. Wheelchair access (not WC). No music £5

Dining rooms where music, either live or recorded, is never played are signalled by No music *in the details at the end of an entry.*

Annie's

3 Oxford Street, Moreton-in-Marsh GL56 0LA	COOKING 2
TEL/FAX: (01608) 651981	COST £32–£50

Flagged floors, a beamed ceiling and family photographs give this single room a cottagey feel. A note on the window – 'English and French Country Cooking' – dispels any doubt about the kitchen's orientation, and a handwritten menu confirms the thrust with spinach roulade, and herb crusted lamb in Madeira sauce. Salads (a lightly dressed duck confit version at one meal) might set the ball rolling, and spicy flavours are deployed in, for example, lamb sweetbreads with a hot, sweet, sharp chilli jam. Daily specials, embracing fish, game and offal, are announced: monkfish fillet in a chunky tomato sauce, or high-quality venison fillet in brandy and peppercorn sauce with dauphinoise potatoes. Desserts have included a light sticky toffee sponge in a rich butterscotch sauce scattered with freshly roasted pecans. Annie welcomes and oversees 'anxious to please' service. Three courses may not come cheap, but wines include a fair number of bottles under £20: four French house wines are £12.50.

CHEF: David Ellis   PROPRIETORS: David and Anne Ellis   OPEN: Mon to Sat D only 7 to 9.30 (L by arrangement)   CLOSED: late Jan to early Feb   MEALS: alc (main courses £15.50 to £20) SERVICE: net prices, card slips closed   CARDS: Amex, Diners, MasterCard, Visa   DETAILS: 30 seats. Private parties: 30 main room. Children's helpings. No smoking while others eat. Music
£5

Marsh Goose ♥ ✳

High Street, Moreton-in-Marsh GL56 0AX	COOKING 6
TEL: (01608) 653500 FAX: (01608) 653510	COST £29–£49

If you hear the sustained thrum of a thriving economy in Gloucestershire these days, it is owing in no small measure to the indefatigable efforts of the Brooke-Little/Kidney partnership. A third venture has been added to their catering empire (see Churchill Arms, Paxton, and Hare & Hounds, Foss Cross), cookery courses are running, and there is a delicatessen next door. The Goose is near the end of a honey-coloured terrace on Moreton's broad main thoroughfare, its warm Cotswold stone walls and fireplace given a decorative splash with some local contemporary art.

Matthew Laughton works with confidence in the house style, which is often about making something bold out of surprisingly modest raw materials: a large baked field mushroom as a starter, stuffed with black olives, roasted peppers and feta; or equally simple fried herring roe with bacon and capers in browned butter, which excited a reporter for its immaculate ingredients. Roast loin of Gloucester Old Spot pork accompanied by apple sauce, balsamic vinegar and fat raisins has also impressed, while an inspector commended the inclusion of the liver and kidneys in a sauté of rabbit with ceps and green peppercorns. Puddings show the same care and attention in balancing flavours: coconut and Malibu parfait with banana fritters, and poached peach with raspberry coulis and pear purée have been particular triumphs. Some reporters have felt that service seems a trifle inexperienced, if willing enough. Quality is high on the stylistically grouped wine list, with the emphasis on youthful and lively rather than venerable stock. House wines from Australia, France and Spain are £12.50 a bottle, £3.25 a glass.

CHEFS: Matthew Laughton   PROPRIETORS: Sonya Kidney and Leo Brooke-Little   OPEN: Tue to Sun L 12.30 to 2.30, Tue to Sat D 7.30 to 9.30   MEALS: alc L Tue to Sat (main courses £9 to £14.50). Set L Sun £20, Set D £29.50   SERVICE: not inc   CARDS: Amex, Delta, Diners, MasterCard, Switch, Visa   DETAILS: 52 seats. Private parties: 20 main room. Vegetarian meals. No smoking in dining room. Wheelchair access (also WC). No music

---

MORSTON Norfolk   map 6

▲ *Morston Hall* ♟

Morston NR25 7AA
TEL: (01263) 741041   FAX: (01263) 740419
EMAIL: reception@morstonhall.demon.co.uk   COOKING 6
on A149, 2m W of Blakeney   COST £27–£49

This flint and brick house on the north Norfolk coast is comfortable, relaxed and unpretentious. Start with drinks by the fire in the stone-flagged hall or in the conservatory, before a set (no-choice) meal of four courses (the second usually fish) that is well judged for quantity, with accurate timing applied to fresh ingredients, and careful saucing. Perhaps it is easier to cook such a meal than one with lots of choice, but that takes nothing away from the 'sense of balance and good judgement that marks out the cooking as a fine example of its style'.

A typical meal might begin with a nugget of 'perfectly seared' foie gras on brioche with a spot-on Sauternes sauce, followed by two fillets of 'springy fresh' Dover sole on tagliatelle vegetables with beurre blanc; then rack of pink lamb served with cabbage and a 'textbook' sauce. The food may not surprise with exotic flavours, but impresses for the care taken: 'no fireworks here, just fine cooking', backed up by an increasing list of organic supplies. Meals end with either a generous serving of 'perfectly ripe' cheese with home-made biscuits, or a classically inclined dessert such as pear bourdaloue tart with nougatine ice cream. Good bread and olives contribute to the appeal, as does 'friendly, helpful and discreet' service. The stylistically arranged wine list might not be the longest on record but it still allows some flexibility: one reporter who requested a Sauternes was informed that 'the kitchen had used it all up in the cooking', but was more than happy with the Aussie botrytis Semillon offered in its place. Eleven wines by the glass priced between £2.50 and £3.50 assist those who like to mix and match; house French is £9.90.

CHEFS: Galton Blackiston and Danny Smith   PROPRIETORS: Galton and Tracy Blackiston, and Justin Fraser   OPEN: Sun L 12.30 for 1 (1 sitting), all week D 7.30 for 8 (1 sitting)   CLOSED: 3 weeks Jan   MEALS: Set L Sun £20, Set D £32   SERVICE: not inc, card slips closed   CARDS: Amex, Delta, Diners, MasterCard, Switch, Visa   DETAILS: 40 seats. Private parties: 40 main room. Car park. Children's helpings. No smoking while others eat. Wheelchair access (also WC). No music   ACCOMMODATION: 6 rooms, all with bath/shower. TV. Phone. D,B&B £95 to £190. Baby facilities (*The Which? Hotel Guide*)

MOULSFORD Oxfordshire   map 2

▲ *Beetle & Wedge* ♉ ⅗✳

Ferry Lane, Moulsford OX10 9JF
TEL: (01491) 651381   FAX: (01491) 651376   COOKING **5**
off A329, down Ferry Lane to river   COST £31–£56

Making the most of its prime riverside location – understandably popular for business meetings and seminars – the Beetle & Wedge has a pretty garden for al fresco summer drinks, and a choice for eating of either boathouse or restaurant in the main house. While there is some overlap between the two, the former tends to adopt a brasserie approach, with charcoal grills and a range of simple starters from salads to moules marinière. The dining room, with its terracotta tiles, ragged paintwork walls and good view, is rather more traditional in outlook: alcohol, cream and butter combine to produce some rich sauces.

Dishes may be 'multifaceted', but they are technically well executed and not fussily presented: young, tender, flavourful artichoke hearts have come with a pile of wild mushrooms and hollandaise sauce of the right creamy consistency. Materials are well sourced – some locally grown and organic – which shows to good effect in, for example, a large, well-hung fillet of properly textured rare beef, served with a rich wild mushroom sauce, and yet more accurate timing has produced fresh plump scallops, crisped on the surface, pearly inside, on a huge pool of sweet tomato salsa. 'Beautifully cooked' vegetables, including broccoli with hollandaise and dauphinois potatoes, are served separately, and 'dinner-party' desserts might include a well-made raspberry and strawberry pavlova with a creamy champagne sorbet.

The restaurant wine list draws heavily on classical French regions, with just one page devoted to Italy and another to 'wines from other areas'. The quality of some of the bins is reflected in their prices, but perfectly palatable bottles can be had for under £20, including six French house wines at £13.50 each. The boathouse offers a small selection from the main cellar.

CHEFS: Richard Smith and Olivier Bouet   PROPRIETORS: Kate and Richard Smith   OPEN: boathouse all week 12.30 to 2, 7.30 to 10, dining room Tue to Sun L 12.30 to 2, Tue to Sat D 7.30 to 10   CLOSED: 28 Dec to 2 Jan   MEALS: boathouse alc (main courses £10 to £17.50). Dining room Set L £27.50, Set D £35   SERVICE: not inc   CARDS: Amex, Delta, Diners, MasterCard, Switch, Visa   DETAILS: 95 seats. Private parties: 64 main room, 64 private room. Car park. Vegetarian meals. No smoking in dining room. Wheelchair access (also WC). Occasional music   ACCOMMODATION: 10 rooms, all with bath/shower. TV. Phone. B&B £95 to £150. Rooms for disabled. Baby facilities (*The Which? Hotel Guide*)

'There was an extended family at a nearby table which punctuated its eating with the loud crack of breaking chopsticks and ritual cries of "Yer little sod, give up messing."'
(On eating in Merseyside)

⅗✳ indicates that smoking is either banned altogether or that a dining-room is maintained for non-smokers. The symbol does not apply to restaurants that simply have no-smoking areas.

MOULTON North Yorkshire   map 9

Black Bull Inn ♀

Moulton DL10 6QJ
TEL: (01325) 377289   FAX: (01325) 377422
EMAIL: sarah@blackbullinn.demon.co.uk   COOKING 4
1m SE of Scotch Corner   COST £23–£51

'Consistency is everything,' proclaimed one reader, who after thirty visits to the Black Bull still found the fish 'some of the best I've ever tasted'. After thirty-seven years under the same ownership, this grand old pub/restaurant – 'almost in the middle of nowhere', yet just a detour from the A1 – runs 'like clockwork', serving up an elegant repertoire based on fish and Aberdeen Angus beef that is pretty much untouched by fads and fashions. There is a buzzing, lively bar – oak beams, log fire and brass-topped tables – but those here for the food can choose to sit in the conservatory, the fish bar, or in the more hushed and genteel atmosphere of an immaculately restored 1932 Pullman railway carriage. An inspector couldn't wait to return after his meal: confit leg of duck with a deeply flavoured "applemint" and ginger sauce; perfectly poached halibut with a champagne butter sauce; and apple and cinnamon crumble served on an 'excellent' crisp shortcrust base.

Efficient, knowledgeable staff ensure that the atmosphere remains easy and relaxed, despite the phenomenal turnover. Fine Burgundies and vintage champagnes at very good prices are the dual attractions of a wine list that also has plenty of appeal in the claret and Rhône departments. A trio of French house wines at £8.50 each provides a cheerful start, while a page of wines from the southern hemisphere draws things to a satisfactory conclusion.

CHEF: Paul Grundy   PROPRIETORS: G.H. and A.M.C. Pagendam   OPEN: Mon to Fri L 12 to 2, Mon to Sat D 6.45 to 10.15   CLOSED: 24 to 26 Dec   MEALS: alc (main courses £15 to £20). Set L £14.95. Bar meals available Mon to Sat L   SERVICE: not inc   CARDS: Amex, Delta, Diners, MasterCard, Switch, Visa   DETAILS: 100 seats. 16 seats outside. Private parties: 30 main room, 10 and 30 private rooms. Vegetarian meals. No children under 7. No music

---

'At the end of the meal we felt a yen for some chocolate and asked if there was any to be had in the kitchen. There wasn't, but in an act of supreme self-sacrifice the waiter, who seemed to understand these things, offered us the last half bar of Cadbury's Dairy Milk from his own personal supply. He even broke it into pieces of four square and placed them on a saucer to improve presentation. Now that's what I call good service.'
(On eating in London)

£ *means that it is possible to have a three-course meal, including coffee, half a bottle of house wine and service for £25 or less per person, at any time the restaurant is open, i.e. at dinner as well as lunch. It may be possible to spend considerably more than this, but by choosing carefully you should find £25 or less achievable.*

Not inc *in the details at the end of an entry indicates that no service charge is made and any tipping is at the discretion of the customer.*

ENGLAND

NEAR SAWREY Cumbria   map 8

▲ *Ees Wyke* ⁵⨉

Near Sawrey LA22 0JZ
TEL/FAX: (015394) 36393   COOKING 2
on B5286 from Hawkshead   COST £29–£35

Guests are asked to present themselves downstairs at 7pm for pre-dinner drinks, in what was once Beatrix Potter's holiday home, overlooking Esthwaite. Margaret Williams delivers front-of-house with 'enthusiasm, good humour and professionalism', while John Williams cooks a well-judged five-course menu. To start, there might be crispy duck with barbecue sauce, or tomato, pear and tarragon soup. A no-choice intermediate course follows: poached eggs florentine, for example, or an asparagus and goats'-cheese tartlet. Main courses tend to be restrained and classic, as in noisettes of pork Normandie, or an 'impressive' ballottine of chicken with a light, creamy mushroom sauce. Cheeses are in good condition, and desserts might include a 'smooth and creamy' soufflé of orange and Cointreau. The wine list, at just over forty bottles, is well chosen and fairly priced, with three house wines starting at £9.50.

CHEF: John Williams   PROPRIETORS: Margaret and John Williams   OPEN: all week D only 7 for 7.30 (1 sitting)   CLOSED: Jan and Feb   MEALS: Set D £22   SERVICE: not inc, card slips closed   CARD: Amex   DETAILS: 20 seats. Private parties: 20 main room. Car park. No children under 8 in dining room. No smoking in dining room. No music   ACCOMMODATION: 8 rooms, all with bath/shower. TV. D,B&B £58 to £120. No children under 8 in accommodation (*The Which? Hotel Guide*)

NEW ALRESFORD Hampshire   map 2

▲ *Hunters* ⁵⨉   **NEW ENTRY**

32 Broad Street, New Alresford SO24 9AQ   COOKING 2
TEL/FAX: (01962) 732468   COST £24–£47

Hunters looks like an antique shop, thought one visitor, an impression reinforced by the Royal Doulton china for sale. Like its siblings – Hunters in Winchester (see entry), and Berties in Romsey – it is a small, welcoming place with a garden eating-area at the back. Inside, the idyllic tone is echoed in wallpaper depicting eighteenth-century French aristocratic life. Nicholas Wentworth's carte is supplemented by blackboard specials and a fixed-price dinner menu. 'Fresh and creamy' watercress soup is a simple way to start a meal, though trend-setters might prefer seared king scallops with fennel and dill risotto and a trickle of lobster oil. Presentation is inventive, as in a version of pommes Anna made with celeriac that accompanied a piece of Aberdeen Angus fillet. Desserts are often caramelised: a pear tarte Tatin with praline ice-cream, or blowtorched lemon curd tartlet with lime sorbet. Service is eager and cheery. Wines supplied by Eldridge Pope are a mixed bag, nearly all between £10 and £20. Nine house selections start at £10.25 a bottle, £2.65 a glass.

CHEF: Nicholas Wentworth   PROPRIETOR: Martin Birmingham   OPEN: Mon to Sat (and Sun L June to Aug) 12 to 2, 7 to 9.30   CLOSED: 24 to 31 Dec, some bank hols   MEALS: alc (main courses L £7, D £11 to £17). Set L £5 (1 course), Set D £12 (2 courses) to £15   SERVICE: not inc, 10% for parties of 6 or more   CARDS: Amex, Delta, Diners, MasterCard, Switch, Visa   DETAILS: 32 seats. 20 seats outside. Private parties: 80 main room. Vegetarian meals. Children's helpings. No smoking in dining room. Wheelchair access (not WC). Music   ACCOMMODATION: 3 rooms, all with bath/shower. TV. B&B £45 to £55   (£5)

NEWCASTLE UPON TYNE   Tyne & Wear   map 10

Courtney's ✻

| | NEW ENTRY |

5–7 The Side, Newcastle upon Tyne NE1 3JE   COOKING 2
TEL: (0191) 232 5537   COST £25–£66

Located in one of Newcastle's oldest streets, Courtney's has come under new ownership since it last appeared in the *Guide*. Swathes of curtains, dark carpets, white tablecloths, sculpted napkins and low lighting set the scene for a fairly conservative cooking style that occasionally allows more exotic touches such as wok-fried carrots and bean sprouts, or roasted halloumi cheese. Tomato soup has proved a 'surprisingly complex' starter, incorporating a drizzle of pesto and garlic-flavoured olive oil, while other endorsements have included poached halibut with cockles, scallops and fennel on tagliatelle, and 'slightly pink' roast duck breast with apples, thyme and cherries. Local varieties might feature among the assorted cheeses, while desserts have offered 'light and fluffy' chocolate and amaretto parfait. House wines are £12.95 on a short list with not much under £20.

CHEF: Iain Hunter   PROPRIETOR: Diane Miller   OPEN: Mon to Fri L 12 to 2, Mon to Sat D 6 (6.30 Sat) to 10.30   CLOSED: 1 week Christmas   MEALS: alc D (main courses £12 to £24.50). Set L £10.95 (2 courses) to £12.95   SERVICE: not inc   CARDS: Amex, Delta, Diners, MasterCard, Switch, Visa   DETAILS: 36 seats. Private parties: 36 main room. Vegetarian meals. Children's helpings. No smoking in 1 dining room. Wheelchair access (not WC). Music. Air-conditioned   (£5)

Fisherman's Lodge ✻

Jesmond Dene, Newcastle upon Tyne NE7 7BQ   COOKING 5
TEL: (0191) 281 3281   FAX: (0191) 281 6410   COST £27–£74

Even when forewarned of the unusual setting, one couple were surprised to leave a city street, two miles from the centre, and drive along a tree-lined track beside a river in search of this grey-stone lodge. It is plushly decorated, with a Chinese-inspired dining room whose black woodwork and upholstery are set off by generous displays of fresh flowers. As a fish restaurant, this is not the brassy, wave-crashing, scent-of-seaweed kind, more a traditional sort of place taking an 'old-fashioned' view of things, from moules marinière, via deep-fried monkfish with mayonnaise, to halibut with herb butter: scoring highest at inspection was a dish of six accurately timed scallops on a well-flavoured, creamy mushroom risotto. Despite the name, it is not exclusively devoted to fish and finds plenty of room for cheese soufflé, roast lamb shank, and Kielder venison pudding with port sauce. Apple and sultana crumble in a hazelnut pastry basket was 'a reminder of how good traditional puds can be' for one reporter, who found the service 'unobtrusive' despite the waiter's 'large and vivid Mickey Mouse tie'. The extensive, well-balanced wine list makes a serious effort under £20; house Languedoc is £12.50.

CHEFS: Steven Jobson and Paul Amer PROPRIETORS: Franco and Pamela Cetoloni OPEN: Mon to Fri L 12 to 2, Mon to Sat D 7 to 11 CLOSED: bank hols MEALS: alc (main courses £18.50 to £28). Set L £17.80, Set D Mon to Fri £29.50 SERVICE: not inc CARDS: Amex, Delta, MasterCard, Switch, Visa DETAILS: 65 seats. 40 seats outside. Private parties: 20 main room, 14 and 43 private rooms. Car park. Vegetarian meals. Children's helpings. No children under 9 at D. No smoking in dining room. Wheelchair access (also WC). No music

Metropolitan ✹ £

35 Grey Street, Newcastle upon Tyne NE1 6EE
TEL: (0191) 230 2306 FAX: (0191) 230 2307 COOKING 3
EMAIL: info@metropolitanbrasseries.co.uk COST £19–£41

Business is carried out all day, but no longer does this former site of the Bank of England deal in finance. Early-morning coffees to late-evening suppers are served in the tall elegant room, now kitted out with art deco-style mirrors and brightly painted walls. The atmosphere is 'full of bustle', the food 'well presented and generally of a high standard'. Set lunches and early-bird suppers are offered, while the carte focuses, both in content and price, on a bistro style, with starters such as seared tuna niçoise, or chicken and pork confit terrine with pear chutney. Combinations tend to be simple and effective, for example pot-roasted beef with bubble and squeak, or honey-roasted ham with mash, savoy cabbage and red wine jus. Desserts pay homage to the location in the shape of chocolate nemesis with Newcastle Brown Ale ice cream, while more exotic choices might include pineapple tarte Tatin with coconut ice cream. The wine list from Lay & Wheeler has a good selection by the glass and opens with house French at £8.95; there is a wide range of cocktails for the more adventurous.

CHEFS: Nick Gardiner and Andrew Weatherill PROPRIETORS: Sean Parkinson and Nick Gardiner OPEN: Mon to Sat 12 to 3, 6 to 10.45 CLOSED: 25 and 26 Dec MEALS: alc (main courses £3 to £14). Set L £8.95 (2 courses) to £11.95. Light L menu available all day until 6pm; early-supper menu Mon to Fri 5 to 7 SERVICE: 10% (optional), card slips closed CARDS: Amex, Delta, Diners, MasterCard, Switch, Visa DETAILS: 170 seats. Private parties: 170 main room, 32 private room. Vegetarian meals. Children's helpings. No smoking in 1 dining room. Wheelchair access (also WC). Music. Air-conditioned (£5)

The 2001 Guide will be published before Christmas 2000. Reports on meals are most welcome at any time of the year, but are particularly valuable in the spring (no later than June). Send them to The Good Food Guide, FREEPOST, 2 Marylebone Road, London NW1 4DF. Or email your report to guidereports@which.co.uk.

All entries in the Guide are re-researched and rewritten every year, not least because restaurant standards fluctuate. Don't rely on an out-of-date Guide.

Card slips closed in the details at the end of an entry indicates that the total on the slips of credit cards is closed when handed over for signature.

21 Queen Street ▼

19–21 Queen Street, Princes Wharf, Quayside,
Newcastle upon Tyne NE1 3UG
TEL: (0191) 222 0755   FAX: (0191) 221 0761

COOKING 8
COST £28–£63

The quayside and waterfront continue to develop around this eloquent pioneer of good eating, unrivalled in the region. Clean cut, a bit understated, it relies on splashes of colour rather than fabrics to make an impact, plus a few abstract paintings, and 'big flowers in shiny tin buckets', all done with class. 'Rarely have we visited a restaurant with so friendly, knowledgeable yet unpretentious an atmosphere,' approved one visitor.

The kitchen's strength is an intelligent interpretation of ideas, some French, some Italian; some fashionable, some not; some from the North East, some from the Far East. The result is 'sometimes dazzling' food that extends from Laybourne favourites such as ham knuckle and flavoured mash, through gutsy French fare – a warm salad of salt pork, griddled foie gras and Puy lentils with 'lots of happy blends of rich and light, sweet and savoury' – to tempura of prawns with crisp, grated, lemon-grass-infused cabbage 'like hot coleslaw'. Top-notch ingredients and eye-catching presentation are a feature: garnishes are 'not just there as window dressing'. At one meal a fillet steak 'full of meaty flavours that could only have come from aged beef', was served with oil-rich meat juices, a pair of dramatic ten-inch long antennae of dry-roasted parsnip, and two kinds of potato: a crisp wafer-thin round on top, gentle goats'-cheese mash underneath.

Multiple and themed dishes include duck five ways. 'Worth every penny' of its supplement, it delivers variety without confusion: a chunk on the bone, slow-cooked with wine and herbs ('like kleftiko'); a fat, smoky-tasting sausage; slices of rare breast; grilled liver topped with a fried quail's egg; plus a crisply battered 'confit' on a separate plate. Echoing the idea, there might be three crème brûlées to follow – rhubarb, vanilla, and ginger – or else a rich chocolate tart with a ball of espresso ice cream, or fromage frais soufflé with strawberry compote. Nicholas Shottel orchestrates front-of-house, overseeing expert, good-natured, attentive and 'absolutely professional' service. Wines have been selected with an unerring eye for quality, be they French (the majority) or any other nationality. Half-bottles are refreshingly varied, and house French is £12.50. The *Guide* was informed as it went to press that the restaurant had been put on the market; if sold, the business, including the current team, would move to new premises in the area.

CHEF: Terence Laybourne   PROPRIETOR: Terence and Susan Laybourne   OPEN: Mon to Fri L 12 to 2, Mon to Sat D 7 to 10.30   CLOSED: bank hols   MEALS: alc (main courses £18.50 to £23.50). Set L £14.50 (2 courses) to £17.50   SERVICE: not inc   CARDS: Amex, Delta, Diners, MasterCard, Switch, Visa   DETAILS: 70 seats. Private parties: 60 main room. Children's helpings. No pipes in dining room. Wheelchair access (not WC). Music

'We asked the sommelier about the 1957 Chateau Latour, and he gave us the clear impression that it would not be worth bothering with. If it was not worth bothering with, I wonder why anybody would want to pay £230 for a bottle.' (On eating in London)

NEW MILTON Hampshire   map 2

▲ *Chewton Glen, Marryat Restaurant* ▮ ✳✕

Christchurch Road, New Milton BH25 6QS
TEL: (01425) 275341 FAX: (01425) 272310
EMAIL: reservations@chewtonglen.com
from A35 follow signs to Walkford and Highcliffe;
take second turning on left after Walkford down   COOKING 6
Chewton Farm road   COST £42–£86

Luxuriously decorated, in immaculate grounds, Chewton Glen manages to
retain the atmosphere of the private house it once was, despite growing from
eight bedrooms when the Skans bought it in 1966 to its present fifty-three,
including suites. It is also a 'purringly professional operation', with 130 staff on
hand to cater for most whims. Against this background Pierre Chevillard's menu
flags up vegetarian items, 'chef's signature dishes' (braised pork cheeks and
lobster with baby root vegetables), plus something called 'wellness choice' (San
Daniele ham with figs and spinach, for example) presumably for those puffing
between the health club, golf course, croquet lawn and swimming pool.
'Expensive but cosseting' was one summing up of the style.

Fish is given prominent billing, in the form of simple, well-timed grilled
lemon sole, or aromatic braised sea bass fillet with shiitake mushrooms and bean
sprouts; other dishes benefit from a modicum of invention, for example a
well-composed salad of beans with foie gras and celeriac chips. One or two items
(foie gras terrine, Dover sole) attract a price supplement, main courses come with
vegetables whether or not they seem to be required, and bread (half a dozen
varieties) is replenished as fast as you eat it. Endorsements for desserts (each of
which comes with a recommended wine by the glass) range from a 'refreshing
and light' summer pudding served with clotted cream, to a rich dark chocolate
mousse in a thin, light pastry case with julienne of caramelised orange.

Vines grow over the restaurant and some of the world's greatest wines are
found within it. Mark Walter's 500-plus list doesn't just rely on famous clarets,
grand cru Burgundies and top champagne houses to gain its cachet: Italy,
Australia, California, and even the Ukraine all make impressive contributions.
Many bottles under £20 can be found, including the house claret and New
Zealand Chardonnay at £16.25 and £17.25 respectively.

CHEF: Pierre Chevillard PROPRIETORS: Martin and Brigitte Skan OPEN: Tue to Sun L 12.30 to
1.45, all week D 7.30 to 9.45 MEALS: Set L Sun £13.50 (2 courses), Set L Tue to Sat £30, Set D
£45 SERVICE: not inc CARDS: Amex, Delta, Diners, MasterCard, Switch, Visa DETAILS: 120
seats. 60 seats outside. Private parties: 130 main room. Car park. Vegetarian meals. No children
under 7 in dining room; high teas for children. Jacket and tie at D. No smoking in dining room. No
music. Air-conditioned ACCOMMODATION: 53 rooms, all with bath/shower. TV. Phone. D,B&B
£289 to £620. Rooms for disabled. No children under 7 in accommodation. Swimming pool (*The
Which? Hotel Guide*)

If you have access to the Internet, you can find The Good Food Guide *online at the
Which? Online web site (http://www.which.net).*

NORTHLEACH Gloucestershire

map 2

Old Woolhouse

Market Place, Northleach GL54 3EE
TEL: (01451) 860366

COOKING 5
COST £58–£69

Sharing the market square with a bakery, newsagent and wine merchant, this discreet building of Cotswold stone (there is no obvious sign to indicate a restaurant) has the air of a French auberge, a feeling underscored by its French owners, who have been here nigh on three decades and do everything themselves. Against a background of net curtains, an oak dresser, log fires and wooden beams, Mrs Astic recites a dinner menu that offers a choice between two starters, three mains – followed by salad and cheese – and three desserts. What stands out is the quality and freshness of ingredients, in a repertoire that errs towards classical French cooking, typically starting with crab and scallops in a spicy sauce, or hot foie gras mousse with wild mushrooms. Seasonal game – partridge, venison or hare – shares the billing with chicken in vinegar sauce, or calf's liver and kidney in cassis. Main courses come with potato gratin, and desserts might run to strawberry shortcake or almond tart. There is no house wine, nothing by the glass, and the Astics have not supplied the *Guide* with a wine list.

CHEF: Jacques Astic   PROPRIETORS: Jacques and Jenny Astic   OPEN: Tue to Sat D only from 8; L and D other days by arrangement   CLOSED: 25 Dec   MEALS: Set D £40   SERVICE: not inc   CARDS: none   DETAILS: 18 seats. Private parties: 18 main room. Wheelchair access (not WC). No music

---

NORTON Shropshire

map 5

▲ Hundred House Hotel 🍴✳

NEW ENTRY

Norton TF11 9EE
TEL: (01952) 730353   FAX: (01952) 730355
EMAIL: hphundred-house@compuserve.com
on A442 midway between Telford and Bridgnorth

COOKING 3
COST £29–£55

The hotel – a long, narrow, red-brick building with a garden – is on the main road through Norton, which amounts to little more than a watering hole in itself. An old red-tiled floor, and glossily varnished wood panelling, lend warmth to the dining room, as do the front-of-house efforts of various members of the Phillips family. The style is fresh and modern, fusing ideas from different traditions: smoked haddock is served, for example, with curried tomatoes, deep-fried leeks and tsatsiki, while more traditional poached salmon and king prawns came together in a June salad, garnished with oily grilled asparagus and a delicate fennel mayonnaise.

Local supply lines furnish the menus with Bobbington boar (robustly flavoured with mustard, horseradish and spring onion), farmed venison from Ludlow, and meats from the Welsh borders such as spring lamb, served with battered aubergine slices sandwiching whole chickpeas. Extra vegetables are charged for but may not be necessary. Finish with caramel rice pudding, or well-made ice creams from a wide selection. The mainly French wine list opens with no fewer than eleven house wines, all at £12 and all sold by the glass.

CHEF: Stuart Phillips PROPRIETORS: Henry, Sylvia, David and Stuart Phillips OPEN: all week 12 to 2.30, 6 to 9.45 CLOSED: 31 Dec MEALS: alc exc Sun L (main courses £10.50 to £18). Set L Sun £12.95 (2 courses) to £15.95 SERVICE: not inc CARDS: Amex, Delta, MasterCard, Switch, Visa DETAILS: 70 seats. 40 seats outside. Private parties: 30 main room. Car park. Vegetarian meals. Children's helpings. No smoking in 1 dining room. Occasional music ACCOMMODATION: 10 rooms, all with bath/shower. TV. Phone. B&B £69 to £120. Baby facilities (*The Which? Hotel Guide*) (£5)

NORWICH Norfolk

map 6

Adlard's 🍾

79 Upper St Giles, Norwich NR2 1AB
TEL: (01603) 633522 FAX: (01603) 617733
EMAIL: adlards@netcom.co.uk

COOKING 6
COST £30–£59

As the *Guide* went to press, major refurbishment was due at this streetside restaurant, where gently paced service from a 'charming, helpful lady' delivers generally fine cooking. It seems at home with indulgent ingredients – roast foie gras with caramelised onions, poached oysters in watercress soup – but there is a welcome simplicity in the final result. At one meal, for example, a layered starter of crisp potato discs and sweetbreads, sitting on a slick of onion purée in a stock-based sauce, was done with confident restraint, and 'no piling on of extras to impress'.

Ingredients are prime (turbot, scallops and red mullet among seafood, for example), textures carefully considered, and dishes well crafted yet not contrived, as in a herb-crusted braised neck fillet of lamb cooked with olives in a dark rich sauce. Of main courses, duck seems to meet with least approval. Other niggles have focused on small portions, high prices, and uneven quality, but a contrary view says that 'Adlard's goes from strength to strength in its own inimitable style', producing well-composed meals of accurately timed dishes in which flavour is paramount. And few would grumble at the lunchtime value on a short-choice set-price menu (which can be mixed and matched) that offers artichoke risotto, spiced monkfish with sesame pancake, and pear and almond tart.

The wine list should certainly generate some contented murmurs. Old World traditional styles are balanced by New World charmers, many offered at attractive prices. Quality is the watchword (and a few wise words helpfully introduce each wine). Both the house red (Australian) and white (Spanish) are good value at £12.50 a bottle, £3.50 a glass; indeed, the 1997 Basa was praised by one reporter as the best Rueda he had tasted.

CHEF: Roger Hickman PROPRIETOR: David Adlard OPEN: Tue to Sat L 12.30 to 1.45, Mon to Sat D 7.30 to 10.30 CLOSED: Christmas to 4 Jan MEALS: Set L £19, Set D £33 to £36 SERVICE: not inc CARDS: Amex, Delta, Diners, MasterCard, Switch, Visa DETAILS: 40 seats. Private parties: 36 main room. Vegetarian meals. No smoking until after main course. No music. Air-conditioned (£5)

Marco's ✸✖

17 Pottergate, Norwich NR2 1DS	COOKING 2
TEL: (01603) 624044	COST £25–£48

Ring the bell and a waitress comes to open the door. 'No, I have no idea why either,' confessed a reporter, but after thirty years, Marco Vessalio has his customers pretty well weighed up, serving a good-value three-course lunch alongside a generous carte in a smartly appointed pale-yellow box of a dining room. The Italian input is occasionally limited to the red wine used to sauce local barley-fed beef, though at other times it extends to 'soft and voluptuous' home-made gnocchi with creamy tomato sauce. Neither old wave nor new, the style is simple, taking in saffron pancakes stuffed with crab; chicken breast with lemon sauce; and zabaglione. An exclusively Italian wine list offers interest and quality; house Soave and Valpolicella are £12.50.

CHEF/PROPRIETOR: Marco Vessalio OPEN: Tue to Sat 12 to 2, 7 to 10 CLOSED: Christmas, bank hols MEALS: alc (main courses £15.50 to £17). Set L £15 SERVICE: not inc, card slips closed CARDS: Amex, Delta, Diners, MasterCard, Switch, Visa DETAILS: 22 seats. Private parties: 20 main room. Vegetarian meals. Children's helpings. No smoking in dining room. Wheelchair access (not WC)

NOTTINGHAM Nottinghamshire	map 5

Hart's

Standard Court, Park Row, Nottingham NG1 6GN	COOKING 6
TEL: (0115) 911 0666 FAX: (0115) 911 0611	COST £21–£47

Considered 'a big boost for Nottingham', Hart's has attracted a trail of well-deserved support. Shiny woodwork and glass, splashes of bright colour, and abstract art on its white walls produce a distinctly modern feel, but 'impeccable' service from smartly clad, attentive, polite and friendly staff also plays a part in achieving a 'relaxed yet professional' atmosphere. A contemporary, cosmopolitan menu rises to the occasion, offering a mix of lightly prepared, Mediterranean-influenced dishes (red mullet with fennel purée, or tomato tart with mozzarella and pesto) alongside beef sirloin with béarnaise, or moist, crisply glazed duck breast with onion marmalade and turnip gratin.

The lightness of touch shows itself time after time, in strikingly fresh crab risotto, 'brilliant' grilled squid with a salad dressed in lemon oil, and well-seared, firm-textured, flavourful scallops, just raw in the middle, served with truffled mash and sauce vierge. Of the vegetarian options, an impressive array of wild mushrooms, in a lightly creamy gravy dotted with peas and broad beans, has been singled out. Dessert combinations are enthusiastically endorsed too: a tart of chocolate and banana, for example, and a fine, tangy lemon tart with deeply flavoured raspberry sorbet. Lunch is good value, and a compact wine list combines interest, variety and reasonable prices. House French is £9.50.

The Good Food Guide *is a registered trade mark of Which? Ltd.*

CHEF: Mark Gough PROPRIETOR: Tim Hart OPEN: all week 12 to 2, 7 (pre-theatre menu from 6.30) to 10.30 (9.30 Sun) CLOSED: D 25 Dec, 26 Dec, L 31 Dec, 1 Jan MEALS: alc (main courses £7.50 to £21). Set L £10 (2 courses) to £13.50. Pre-theatre menu available SERVICE: 10%, card slips closed CARDS: Amex, Delta, MasterCard, Switch, Visa DETAILS: 85 seats. 40 seats outside. Private parties: 20 main room, 12 private room. Vegetarian meals. Children's helpings. No-smoking area. Wheelchair access (also WC). No music

Merchants

|NEW ENTRY|

29–31 High Pavement, Nottingham NG1 1HE COOKING 4
TEL: (0115) 958 9898 FAX: (0115) 941 4322 COST £22–£57

Clive Dixon, no stranger to the *Guide*, did a long stint at the Lords of the Manor (see entry, Upper Slaughter), before opening this place in the trendily rejuvenated heart of Nottingham in 1998. Next to St Mary's Church, opposite the Galleries of Justice, it is a part of the city that comes alive in the evening. The beamed interior has been modernised with tiled floors, mirrors, chrome and strategically placed greenery, and all the right buttons are pushed on an equally up-to-date menu that is voguish both for its ingredients and techniques.

Flavour combinations are, on the whole, impressively worked out, be they grilled crottin de Chavignol with spiced couscous, marinated aubergine and peppers, or a less conventional pairing of scallops with slow-cooked belly pork, the whole invigorated with Thai spices. Even more complex ideas have proved successful, including a main dish of honey-glazed Barbary duck breast served on vanilla-scented quinoa with a confit of the leg, a potato tian, swede cooked in duck fat, and a sauce of spiced port.

Desserts likewise range from a straightforward lemon tart with rhubarb purée, to a more inventive pineapple roasted with chilli, vanilla and caramel, served with coconut ice cream. 'Very friendly and accommodating' service keeps everybody happy, and, talking of accommodation, twenty-nine rooms are being planned as the *Guide* went to press. Wines, a fairly typical mix from France and the New World, are arranged by style, and there is a useful opening slate of halves. House French is £10.95.

CHEF: Clive Dixon PROPRIETORS: Robert Beacham and John Whitehead OPEN: Sun to Fri L 12 to 3, Mon to Sat D 7 to 10.30 MEALS: alc D (main courses £9 to £16.50). Set L Mon to Fri £8 (1 course) to £13.50, Set L Sun £8 (1 course) to £16 SERVICE: not inc, 10% (optional) for parties of 8 or more CARDS: Amex, Delta, MasterCard, Switch, Visa DETAILS: 65 seats. Private parties: 80 main room, 16 private room. Vegetarian meals. Children's helpings. Wheelchair access (also WC). Occasional music. Air-conditioned

---

OCKHAM Surrey map 3

▲ *The Chapel at The Hautboy* 🍸✷

Ockham Lane, Ockham GU23 6NP COOKING 5
TEL: (01483) 225355 FAX: (01483) 211176 COST £49–£69

With its vaulted ceiling, stained-glass window, wood panelling and Italian-style biblical frescoes, this Victorian Gothic dining room understandably has 'bags of character'. Since last year the Chapel's opening hours have been pared down to dinner only, four nights a week, when the offer is either three or four courses (plus an appetiser and mid-meal sorbet). The kitchen is no stranger to luxuries, and puts a lot of effort into dishes, adding basil ravioli and sliced truffles to a tomato soup, or a 'cannelloni' of sweetbreads and mushrooms to a main course of lamb.

Ideas may lean towards familiar partnerships – duck with apples and braised red cabbage – but are lively enough. Terrine of smoked chicken and ham hock, for example, comes with a sweet pepper and radish salsa, and pheasant is served on a bed of curried leeks. Expect to finish with a parfait in a spun-sugar cage, a red berry soup, or a mango tarte Tatin with vanilla ice cream and passion fruit coulis. A traditionally oriented wine list puts France in the driving seat and includes a few bottles under £20. House red and white are £14.

CHEF: Darren Tidd   PROPRIETORS: Richard and Mags Watney   OPEN: Wed to Sat D only 7 to 9.30   CLOSED: first 2 weeks Jan   MEALS: Set D £35 to £42   SERVICE: not inc   CARDS: Amex, Delta, Diners, MasterCard, Switch, Visa   DETAILS: 45 seats. 40 seats outside. Private parties: 60 main room, 60 and 115 private rooms. Car park. Vegetarian meals. No smoking in dining room. Music. Air-conditioned   ACCOMMODATION: 5 rooms, all with bath/shower. TV. Phone. B&B £98 to £125. Baby facilities (£5)

OLD BURGHCLERE Hampshire   map 2

Dew Pond ♥ ⁵⁄✗

Old Burghclere RG20 9LH
TEL: (01635) 278408   FAX: (01635) 278580   COOKING 6
off old A34, 3m W of Kingsclere   COST £37–£60

'I didn't catch a glimpse of the rural views,' confided one winter visitor ruefully, settling into one of the lived-in armchairs in these sixteenth-century combined drovers' cottages and appreciating the log fire instead. Keith Marshall's food has an appealing modern tilt, starting off perhaps with a warm salad of scallops and crispy squid in a chillied coriander dressing, or chicken mousseline sausage with foie gras and lemon beurre blanc. If there is more of an Eastern input than previously, it may be because 'we have in our employment a fully qualified Japanese chef'. The food appeals because it is unshowy yet attractively presented and well judged. An inspection meal, for example, turned up a juicy, honey-burnished, boned quail wrapped around a light, springy, tarragon-imbued mousse, sitting on crisp rösti and strewn with wild mushrooms: 'a technical triumph that was spot-on for flavour and texture'.

A well-balanced menu mixes prime cuts such as roast lamb, offal in the form of calf's liver (with red onion marmalade), and game, maybe saddle of roe deer with root vegetables. Fish, which varies according to the market, has included 'springy fresh brill' with vegetables and crème fraîche. Seasoning tends to be light, while desserts confirm the kitchen's serious credentials, as in roast pear covered with a thin layer of caramel, with a dribble of bitter chocolate sauce. The wine list seeks out good growers from around the world and displays their wares by style: the Clare Valley's Jeffrey Grosset supplies an 'aromatic white' Polish Hill Dry Riesling 1997 (£15.75), a 'weightier red' Gaia 1996 (£21) and a 'notably fine' Chardonnay 1996 (£24.50), for example. Four house wines are £11.95 a bottle, £3 a glass.

ENGLAND

CHEF: Keith Marshall   PROPRIETORS: Keith and Julie Marshall   OPEN: Tue to Sat D only 7 to 10
CLOSED: last week Dec, first week Jan, 2 weeks Aug   MEALS: Set D £25   SERVICE: not inc
CARDS: Amex, Delta, Diners, MasterCard, Switch, Visa   DETAILS: 50 seats. Private parties: 50
main room, 25 private room. Car park. No children under 5. No smoking in dining room.
Wheelchair access (not WC). No music £5

OMBERSLEY Worcestershire
map 5

Venture In ⚡✕
NEW ENTRY

Main Road, Ombersley WR9 0EW   COOKING 2
TEL: (01905) 620552   COST £21–£42

Toby Fletcher took over this 'visibly ancient' half-timbered building, one of a
trio of pubs on a slip road off the A449, at the beginning of 1998, leaving much of
the décor as it was. 'It hasn't been spoilt by having money thrown at it,' reckoned
one visitor, observing the wood-burning inglenook fire in the pubby bar lounge,
and the single stone wall and busy carpet in the two-part dining room. The food
may appear somewhat dated, and 'rather fancy for the circumstances', but
better-than-average raw materials have included two seared scallops, each on
half a sun-dried tomato, on a mound of correctly made risotto. While cooking
and saucing have been variable, the kitchen has turned out a 'boneless chop' of
first-class pink veal, with nuggets of sweetbread and a strewing of mushrooms,
in a dark, glossy well-reduced sauce. Vegetables (some deep-fried) are served
separately, and desserts have included a wedge of glazed lemon tart with
blackcurrant coulis and scoops of mascarpone. More informed service would be
appreciated, as would better-quality incidentals. Around thirty varied wines
start with a house trio at £9.

CHEF/PROPRIETOR: Toby William Fletcher   OPEN: Tue to Sun L 12 to 2, Tue to Sat D 7 to 9.45
CLOSED: 2 weeks winter, 2 weeks summer, 26 Dec   MEALS: Set L Tue to Sat £13.95 (2 courses)
to £15.95, Set L Sun £13.95, Set D £25.95 to £26.95   SERVICE: not inc, card slips closed
CARDS: Delta, MasterCard, Switch, Visa   DETAILS: 32 seats. Private parties: 32 main room. Car
park. Vegetarian meals. No children under 10 at D. No smoking in dining room. Music.
Air-conditioned

OSWESTRY Shropshire
map 7

▲ Sebastians ⚡✕

45 Willow Street, Oswestry SY11 1AQ
TEL: (01691) 655444   FAX: (01691) 653452   COOKING 3
EMAIL: sebastians.rest@virgin.net   COST £30–£40

'The price was reasonable, the service charming, and the atmosphere friendly,'
volunteered one visitor to this beamed and panelled French provincial-style
restaurant. Since last year the à la carte menu has gone, leaving a two- or
three-course option (plus appetiser) with the odd supplement: perhaps for a
nage of Dover sole with Dublin Bay prawns. Dishes may not be straight out of
Elizabeth David, but many have a familiar ring: starters of fish soup with rouille,
or smoked salmon parcel with avocado and prawns, followed perhaps by roast
breast of duck with an apple and potato pancake in red wine sauce. Otherwise,

414

ham dumplings and a mead sauce have added interest to honey-roast breast of duck, and Roquefort cheese (a kitchen staple) has contributed 'an agreeable edge' to chicken breast served with asparagus sauce. Everyday desserts include strawberry vacherin, banana pancakes, and lemon tart, and France is the strongest suit on a fifty-strong wine list that starts with house red (Côtes du Ventoux) and white (Picpoul de Pinet) at £10.95.

CHEF: Mark Sebastian Fisher   PROPRIETORS: Michelle and Mark Sebastian Fisher   OPEN: Tue to Sat D only 6.30 to 10   CLOSED: 25 and 26 Dec, 1 Jan   MEALS: Set D £18.50 (2 courses) to £22.50   SERVICE: not inc, card slips closed   CARDS: Amex, Delta, MasterCard, Switch, Visa DETAILS: 40 seats. 30 seats outside. Private parties: 60 main room. Vegetarian meals. Children's helpings. No smoking in dining room. Wheelchair access (not WC). Music   ACCOMMODATION: 4 rooms, all with bath/shower. TV. Phone. Room only £35 to £45. Baby facilities   (£5)

OXFORD   Oxfordshire   map 2

▲ Al-Shami £

| 25 Walton Crescent, Oxford OX1 2JG | COOKING 2 |
| TEL: (01865) 310066   FAX: (01865) 311241 | COST £21–£38 |

Oxford has taken to Lebanese dining, and on most nights Al-Shami is filled with university types and others. Located on a quiet crescent, the restaurant has a light interior with potted plants aplenty. The cover charge provides a bountiful platter of raw vegetables: a foil for the varied meze that range from 'creamy, citric' hummus to fried lambs' brains. Sojuk (spicy Armenian sausages) were relished by one diner, who also enjoyed the 'nutty flavour and slight chilli kick' of mohammara bil-jawz (a paste of nuts and red peppers). Main courses are mostly grilled meats, with some vegetarian and fish dishes. One reporter found kibbeh bil-siniyeh (a disc of ground lamb and bulgur stuffed with pine kernels) 'dry as a bone', while others have recommended grilled garlic chicken and mixed grill. Desserts include 'interesting' Lebanese pastries. Service is capable and generally congenial. Arak, Almaza beer and several vintages of Ch. Musar are on the drinks list. House Lebanese is £9.99.

CHEF: Mimo Mahfouz   PROPRIETOR: Al-Shami Cuisine Oxford   OPEN: all week noon to midnight   MEALS: alc (main courses £6 to £12). Cover £1   SERVICE: not inc, card slips closed; 10% for parties of 6 or more   CARDS: MasterCard, Switch, Visa   DETAILS: 90 seats. Private parties: 90 main room, 45 private room. Vegetarian meals. Wheelchair access (also WC). Music   ACCOMMODATION: 12 rooms, all with bath/shower. TV. Phone. B&B £35 to £45   (£5)

Cherwell Boathouse 🍷 ⅝✳

| 50 Bardwell Road, Oxford OX2 6ST | COOKING 3 |
| TEL/FAX: (01865) 552746 | COST £25–£33 |

'In many ways just the sort of place I like,' wrote one reporter: 'simple, unpretentious, serving good food at reasonable prices with no frills but excellent service.' Starters have come in for particular praise: fish and shellfish terrine with lobster sauce pleased one party of winter lunchers, while another enjoyed black pudding salad with strips of crisp bacon and a honey-based dressing. Main courses don't let the side down either, whether fillets of sea bass (at a £5 supplement) with black linguine in a tomatoey dressing, or flavourful roast meats from shank of lamb to chicken that 'really tasted like a free-range chicken' with mushroom sauce . Cheeses tend to be English, in good condition and served with fruit, salad and biscuits. Honey seems to be a kitchen favourite, appearing in an ice cream with brandy, and in an almond bread-and-butter pudding.

Being owned by one half of London merchants Morris & Verdin does help when it comes to putting together a high-quality wine list at generous prices. Bordeaux and Burgundy make the biggest splashes, house wines start at a lowly £8.50 a bottle, £2.50 a glass, and there is plenty of opportunity to push the boat out: Ch. Mouton-Rothschild 1970 is a snip at £140, for example.

CHEFS: Gerard Crowley and Wayne Cullen   PROPRIETOR: Anthony Verdin   OPEN: Tue to Sun L 12 to 2, Tue to Sat D 6 to 10.30   CLOSED: 24 to 31 Dec   MEALS: Set L Tue to Fri in summer £12.50 to £18.50, Set L Sat and Sun £19.50, Set D £20.50   SERVICE: not inc, 10% for parties of 6 or more   CARDS: Amex, Delta, Diners, MasterCard, Switch, Visa   DETAILS: 60 seats. 16 seats outside. Private parties: 50 main room, 100 private room. Car park. Vegetarian meals. Children's helpings. No smoking in dining room. Wheelchair access (also WC). No music £5

Lemon Tree

268 Woodstock Road, Oxford OX2 7NW	COOKING 4
TEL/FAX: (01865) 311936	COST £26–£57

Doing its best to look like a Mediterranean villa, this airy, spacious orangey-yellow building overlooking a walled garden is simply decorated, with chequered floor, plants and a greenhouse-style glass roof. It has a 'real zing' about it, and a modern-sounding menu to match. Coatings, confits, and fruit and vegetable crisps are indicators of the style: chargrilled loin of tuna coated in chermoula, for example, or scallops dusted with dried scallop roe and served with apple crisps and sweet chilli dressing. A note on the menu sets out the stall with regard to free-range French chickens, Scottish beef, and Cornish lamb, the last perhaps offered as the knuckle end of a shoulder, with a borlotti bean and chorizo stew. The carte also lists Perigord squab pigeon served in two parts – as a rare breast and confit leg – on a slice of black pudding: and that's just a starter. Lemon tart, only to be expected, shares dessert billing with other tarts (perhaps chocolate) and pies (pecan). Service is 'fast and affable', and a sensibly short wine list starts with house French white and Chilean red at £9.95.

CHEF: Robert Inglestone   PROPRIETOR: Clinton Pugh   OPEN: all week noon to 11   CLOSED: 1 week from 24 Dec   MEALS: alc (main courses £10 to £16). Set L Mon to Fri £12.50 (2 courses) to £17   SERVICE: not inc, card slips closed; 10% for parties of 5 or more   CARDS: Amex, Delta, MasterCard, Switch, Visa   DETAILS: 100 seats. 30 seats outside. Private parties: 100 main room. Car park. Vegetarian meals. Wheelchair access (also WC). Music £5

indicates that there has been a change of chef since last year's Guide, *and the Editor has judged that the change is of sufficient interest to merit the reader's attention.*

The text of entries is based on unsolicited reports sent in by readers, backed up by inspections conducted anonymously. The factual details under the text are from questionnaires the Guide *sends to all restaurants that feature in the book.*

OXFORD

▲ Old Parsonage Hotel, Parsonage Bar

1 Banbury Road, Oxford OX2 6NN
TEL: **(01865) 310210**   FAX: **(01865) 311262**   COOKING 2
EMAIL: oldparsonage@dial.pipex.com   COST £30–£48

Close to the junction of Woodstock and Banbury Roads, the Parsonage is indeed a venerable site. A brochure lists previous owners and tenants back to 1308, although since 1320 the sole owner has been University College; the front door is three centuries old, and Oscar Wilde roomed here for a while when he was a student. The interior, however, is quite modern: start in the stylish tile-floored bar, climb three steps to the lounge-dining room, and choose from a menu of salady starters – maybe stir-fried prawns with chilli, pesto and coriander on a bed of couscous – or perhaps a moist twice-baked spinach and Parmesan soufflé. Good-quality fresh materials underpin the cooking, and a long list of varied mains might include breast of guinea fowl, poached smoked haddock with spinach in a chive butter sauce, or a rich, buttery pastry tart of trumpet and oyster mushrooms. Finish with baked Alaska, or a 'huge, enjoyable' pear tarte Tatin, and drink from a sharply chosen, fair-value wine list which starts around £13.

CHEF: Alison Watkins   PROPRIETOR: Jeremy Mogford   OPEN: all week 12 to 3, 6 to 11   CLOSED: 25 and 26 Dec   MEALS: alc (main courses £10 to £13)   SERVICE: not inc   CARDS: Amex, Diners, MasterCard, Switch, Visa   DETAILS: 37 seats. 30 seats outside. Private parties: 12 main room. Car park. Vegetarian meals. No pipes in dining room. Wheelchair access (not WC). Occasional music. Air-conditioned   ACCOMMODATION: 30 rooms, all with bath/shower. TV. Phone. B&B £125 to £170. Rooms for disabled (*The Which? Hotel Guide*)

Le Petit Blanc ⅚✳

71–72 Walton Street, Oxford OX2 6AG   NEW CHEF
TEL: **(01865) 510999**   FAX: **(01865) 510700**   COST £22–£46

Popular, and at times noisy, Raymond Blanc's original offshoot (another may have opened in Birmingham by now) carries the flag for mainly French food served up in a flexible format: a carte, plus a day-long rotation of supplementary menus for breakfast, lunch, afternoon tea and a 'bargain' early-evening menu, plus a children's menu that might include pasta with tomato sauce, grilled chicken and fries, and chocolate cake. Martin White arrived just as the *Guide* went to press, but the style looks like continuing unchanged (Raymond Blanc, we are told, still oversees the cooking), taking in a generous spread from Caesar salad to foie gras and chicken liver parfait, from terrine de porc persillé with sauce gribiche, to lemon tart. A cannily chosen list of three dozen wines starts with house Blanc blanc and Blanc rouge at £9.95, and includes a handful by the glass.

CHEFS: Raymond Blanc and Martin White   PROPRIETOR: Blanc Restaurants Ltd   OPEN: all week breakfast 11 to 12, L 12 to 2.45 (3.15 Sat and Sun), afternoon tea 3.30 to 6, D 6 to 10.45 (6.30 to 9.45 Sun)   CLOSED: 25 Dec   MEALS: alc (main courses £7 to £15). Set L 12 to 3pm and D 6 to 7pm £12.50 (2 courses) to £15. Children's menu £5.95 (2 courses) to £7.50   SERVICE: not inc; 10% for parties of 8 or more   CARDS: Amex, Delta, Diners, MasterCard, Switch, Visa   DETAILS: 145 seats. Private parties: 145 main room, 18 private room. Vegetarian meals. Children's helpings. No smoking in 1 dining room. Wheelchair access (also WC). Music. Air-conditioned £5

417

ENGLAND

White House

2 Botley Road, Oxford OX2 0AB
TEL: (01865) 242823   FAX: (01865) 793331

COOKING 1
COST £25–£42

Near the railway station, with a garden at the back for fine-weather eating, this is a pub with a friendly welcome, a café-style setting and 'above-average' food. A large laminated menu offers a wide variety of styles and plenty of choice, starting with tuna fish cake in a pesto-like coriander and coconut dressing, or two wooden skewers of plump pieces of chicken breast with 'juicy' prawns, served satay-style with a strong peanut-flavoured sauce. The food does not aim for finesse, opting instead for lots of oil and butter, and hearty student-friendly portions of duck breast with fried black pudding, or two roast cod fillets, both served on copious amounts of flavoured mash. Alternatively, there may be 'well-cooked chips'. Some starters can be big enough for a main course – 'you won't leave hungry' – which may explain why reports on desserts are few and far between. Service is efficient, and nearly forty wines are reasonably priced, starting with house Vin de Pays du Gers at £9.95.

CHEF: Christopher Bland   PROPRIETOR: Whites Restaurants Oxford Ltd   OPEN: all week 12.30 to 2.30, 6.30 to 9.30   MEALS: alc (main courses £8.50 to £11). Bar food available 12.30 to 2.30, 6.30 to 7.30   SERVICE: not inc   CARDS: Amex, Delta, Diners, MasterCard, Switch, Visa DETAILS: 60 seats. 40 seats outside. Private parties: 40 main room. Car park. Vegetarian meals. Children's helpings. Wheelchair access (also WC). Occasional music £5

PADSTOW Cornwall   map 1

Brock's ✦   NEW ENTRY

The Strand, Padstow PL28 8AJ
TEL: (01841) 532565   FAX: (01841) 533199
EMAIL: brockx@compuserve.com

COOKING 3
COST £26–£51

Here is a surprise: a corner of the Padstow restaurant scene that isn't owned by Rick Stein. The Brocklebanks opened in 1997, and acquired a French chef in February 1999, since when the place has hit top gear. Perched above an estate agent's, looking down on the cheery bustle of Middle Street, it has a bright Mediterranean feel, enhanced by the cooking style and, naturally, the freshness of local seafood.

Seared scallops in a beurre blanc of spring onion and rosemary typifies the confident tone that pervades many dishes, while fish soup, although retaining its accompaniments of 'garlicky and glossy' aïoli and Parmesan croûtons, is given an Indian twist with aromatic cumin and turmeric. Meat is not neglected, indeed has produced an accurately timed lamb steak with red cabbage, dauphinoise and a port sauce. Sensuous desserts have included poached apricots and pears in Drambuie sabayon, and calvados parfait with cinnamon beignets and black-currant coulis. 'Cheerful, helpful' service generally obliges. A smallish wine list gives equal prominence to Europe and the New World, with most bins under £20. House Chilean is £11.25 a bottle, or £5 for a large glass.

CHEF: Sylvain Lesenne   PROPRIETORS: Tim and Hazel Brocklebank   OPEN: Tue to Sat L 12.15
to 2, Mon to Sat D 7 to 9.30 (10 Fri and Sat)   CLOSED: 25 and 26 Dec, 11 Jan to 11 Feb, Mon D in
winter   MEALS: alc (main courses L £8 to £11, D £15 to £16). Set D £18 (2 courses) to £21.50
SERVICE: not inc   CARDS: Delta, MasterCard, Switch, Visa   DETAILS: 45 seats. Private parties:
35 main room, 20 private room. Children's helpings. No smoking in dining room. Wheelchair
access (not WC). Music

Margot's 🍴✱

11 Duke Street, Padstow PL28 8AB	COOKING 1
TEL: (01841) 533441	COST £18–£38

Adrian Oliver was head chef under the previous owner, and he and his wife
Julie took over Margot's at the beginning of 1999. They continue to offer
'well-presented, tasty home cooking', serving up light lunches of leek and
potato soup, squid stir-fry, and grilled goats' cheese with tapénade, plus dinners
with around four choices per course. The menu is adapted to the daily
availability of materials, including seafood: warm salad of scallops with
pistachio dressing, or skate wing with garlic, anchovy, and olive oil mash. Main
courses incorporate potatoes – sautéed with calf's liver, new with baked cod in
chive butter sauce – but also come with a bamboo steamer of praiseworthy
vegetables. Popular desserts have included saffron poached pears with
Sauternes jelly, and bread-and-butter pudding. Service is relaxed, informed and
'non-fussy', and a brief wine list stays comfortably under £20, starting with a
quintet of interesting house wines around £10.

CHEF: Adrian Oliver   PROPRIETORS: Adrian and Julie Oliver   OPEN: Wed to Sun 12 to 2, 7 to 9.30
(reduced opening in winter)   CLOSED: Jan   MEALS: alc L (main courses £4 to £5). Set D £18.95
(2 courses) to £22.95   SERVICE: not inc   CARDS: Delta, MasterCard, Switch, Visa   DETAILS: 30
seats. Private parties: 30 main room. Children's helpings. No smoking in dining room. Music
(£5)

▲ *Rick Stein's Café* 🍴✱   [NEW ENTRY]

Middle Street, Padstow PL28 8AP	COOKING 2
TEL: (01841) 532700 FAX: (01841) 532942	COST £21–£30

'Concentrate on the word café, rather than on Rick Stein,' advised one visitor.
Next door to the delicatessen (formerly Middle Street Café), it aims for brisk
turnover and good value, and sets a cheerful, informal tone with terracotta floor
tiles, big bold posters, and French-style marble-topped tables. Cutlery is
brought in a napkin, so forget frills. A short and to-the-point menu is
supplemented by a blackboard of specials propped on the mantelpiece, and
simple, modern, mostly seafood dishes are the stock in trade. Thai fish cakes,
mussels and chips, and grilled kipper are the sorts of things to expect, alongside
expertly made, creamy rocket risotto, a well-dressed salad of chicken livers
('How would you like them cooked?'), and glistening field mushrooms on
toasted ciabatta with generous shavings of Parmesan. Salt-cod with chickpeas,
'the masterpiece of the evening' for one party, came in a rich fishy broth with
chopped parsley and lots of olive oil. Desserts appear to be less successful, and
the tiny wine list (five whites, four reds) starts with Vin de Pays d'Oc at £9.90.

CHEF: Karen Crawford   PROPRIETORS: Rick and Jill Stein   OPEN: Mon to Sat 12 to 2.30, 6.30 to 9.30   CLOSED: 25 and 26 Dec, 10 to 30 Jan   MEALS: alc (main courses L £5.50 to £7.50, D £9.50). Set D £15.95   SERVICE: not inc   CARDS: Delta, MasterCard, Switch, Visa   DETAILS: 40 seats. 12 seats outside. Private parties: 8 main room. Vegetarian meals. Children's helpings. No smoking in dining room. Music   ACCOMMODATION: 3 rooms, all with bath/shower. TV. Phone. B&B £45 to £80. Baby facilities

▲ St Petroc's   NEW ENTRY

4 New Street, Padstow PL28 8EA   COOKING 4
TEL: (01841) 532700   FAX: (01841) 532942   COST £33–£40

Despite the merchandising and paraphernalia that attends celebrity cheffery, making Padstow a place of pilgrimage for many, at least Rick Stein does it tastefully. This light, bright room, with chrome yellow walls, modern paintings and pubby tables with bentwood chairs, has an air of confidence that is unusual outside large cities. It offers a relatively affordable way to experience the Rick Stein approach, with a kitchen under the control of David Pope, whom some readers may remember from Crahan in Trevenen (in the 1999 *Guide*).

He oversees a straightforward-sounding menu of five or six items per course that deals in lemon sole with lemon-grass butter, and grilled salmon with basil pesto, but also includes meaty dishes of roast Barbary duck breast, or chargrilled sirloin steak with salsa verde and chips. Among fishy successes have been delicately flavoured grilled plaice 'nicely offset by sweet peppers', and light, crispy, miniature, fresh-tasting salmon fish cakes, served with tartare sauce. A meal might start with a hefty portion of sweet chargrilled mackerel in a well-judged Thai dressing, and finish with classic crème brûlée. The atmosphere is helped by informal and friendly service that sets a busy pace without making people feel rushed. Some thirty round-the-world wines start with vins de pays red and white at £10.75 and £12.95.

CHEF: David Pope   PROPRIETORS: Rick and Jill Stein   OPEN: Tue to Sun 12 to 2, 7 to 9.30   CLOSED: 20 to 27 Dec   MEALS: alc (main courses £11.50 to £12). Set L and D £21   SERVICE: not inc   CARDS: Delta, MasterCard, Switch, Visa   DETAILS: 45 seats. Private parties: 12 main room, 12 private room. Children's helpings. Music. Air-conditioned   ACCOMMODATION: 13 rooms, all with bath/shower. TV. Phone. B&B £40 to £130. Baby facilities (£5)

▲ Seafood Restaurant 🍷

Riverside, Padstow PL28 8BY   COOKING 6
TEL: (01841) 532700   FAX: (01841) 532942   COST £38–£91

Some, apparently, come on coach trips just to photograph the restaurants in Rick Stein's Padstow portfolio (see entries), never mind eat at them, which gives an indication of his cult status; others make sure they go in winter, when things are quieter. Although the bright, airy dining room is often packed, it still gives out a cheery, welcoming feel. Expectations are naturally high – partly on account of Rick Stein's fame and evident commitment to high quality, partly because of the prices – so the food has a lot to live up to. In practice, sometimes it does, sometimes it doesn't. Stein is a man who garners much personal support and enthusiasm, and reporters obviously wish he did all the cooking; but he doesn't, which may go some way towards accounting for the variability in standards.

At its best the food can be 'outstanding, a sheer delight', especially when it is not 'overdressed': perhaps simple, crisp brill goujons with a classic tartare sauce, or well-timed turbot with hollandaise. Despite showcasing some of Rick Stein's 'greatest hits', such as Goan fish curry, the cooking doesn't always flatter the amazing produce available: spicing can be strong for its context, and roasting and chargrilling do not always produce the desired effect. First courses generally please, however, including deep-fried sand eels sprinkled with parsley and garlic, fish and shellfish soup, and spicy mussels with black beans, coriander and spring onions.

Puddings seem to be on a roll, judging by recent reports of 'perfect' pannacotta with baked plums, and squishy meringue with summer fruits. Grilled pineapple with peanut butter ice cream 'sounds weird, but it worked'. Service is professional, but warm and friendly. The selection of current enthusiasms is an obvious place to start on the wine list, but do take a look at the array of high-quality and intriguing wines (in both colours) that follows. Such is the spread of varieties and styles that practically any seafood match can be catered for, including less obvious combinations such as Manzanilla sherry with grilled fish, for example. French house white is £12.95.

CHEF: Rick Stein   PROPRIETORS: Rick and Jill Stein   OPEN: Mon to Sat 12 to 1.30, 7 to 10 (possibly 9.30 out of season)   CLOSED: 19 to 26 Dec   MEALS: alc (main courses £14.50 to £38). Set L £28, Set D £34   SERVICE: not inc   CARDS: Delta, MasterCard, Switch, Visa   DETAILS: 100 seats. Private parties: 12 main room. Vegetarian meals. Children's helpings. No children under 3 in dining room. Wheelchair access (not WC). Music. Air-conditioned   ACCOMMODATION: 13 rooms, all with bath/shower. TV. Phone. B&B £50 to £140. Baby facilities (The Which? Hotel Guide)

PAINSWICK   Gloucestershire   map 2

▲ Country Elephant ⅝✳

New Street, Painswick GL6 6XH
TEL/FAX: (01452) 813564   COOKING 3
on A46 Cheltenham to Stroud road   COST £28–£49

Just up the main road from the church, this tiny Cotswold stone restaurant, dimly candlelit at dinner, offers a warm reception (booking is essential), and a 'personal, almost domestic' atmosphere. This may be because Robert Rees's approach is framed by some strongly held views, among them that smoking (active or passive) is not a good idea, that pouring wine can safely be left to customers, and that organic produce is best. Set meals are just that (with no choice), while the carte offers a sensibly limited three or four items per course, and dishes turn up some appealing combinations: snails and scallops with Pernod herb butter, or smoked eel with crisp pancetta and creamed potato. Main courses typically include a couple of fish dishes too, maybe skate with bulgur and carrot butter, while trademark onion confit accompanies beef medallion. Vegetables are 'a bit standard', and puddings appear to be less successful than savoury courses. Ten wines by the glass feature on the thirty-plus round-the-world list, with about half under £20. House South African white is £10.80, Australian red £12.

421

CHEF/PROPRIETOR: Robert Rees   OPEN: Tue to Sun L 12 to 2, Tue to Sat D 7 to 10   CLOSED: 1 week Christmas   MEALS: alc (main courses £14 to £15). Set L Tue to Sat £13 (2 courses) to £18, Set L Sun £15 (2 courses) to £18, Set D £18 (2 courses) to £20   SERVICE: not inc   CARDS: Amex, Delta, Diners, MasterCard, Switch, Visa   DETAILS: 28 seats. 20 seats outside. Vegetarian meals. Children's helpings. No smoking in dining room. Wheelchair access (not WC). Music ACCOMMODATION: 1 room, with bath/shower. TV. Room only £28 to £34 (£5)

PAULERSPURY Northamptonshire   map 5

▲ *Vine House* ⅗✱

100 High Street, Paulerspury NN12 7NA
TEL: (01327) 811267   FAX: (01327) 811309   COOKING 4
off A5, 2m SE of Towcester   COST £32–£44

Considered a 'gem of a place', with a small herb garden that may be used for drinks in fine weather, this 300-year-old converted house and cottage is not on the grand scale that its self-styled 'country-house hotel' description conjures up. Rather it has a 'homely atmosphere', and a gently updated provincial style of cooking to match. Dinner offers four choices per course, perhaps starting with chicken and oyster mushroom pâté, followed by roast home-cured Cornish cod with lentils, then apple terrine with whipped cream.

Marcus Springett strikes a few contemporary notes, maybe serving salmon with a caper and lemon jelly and watercress sauce, but generally keeps his feet on the ground: saddle of wild rabbit, for example, comes with a smoked bacon and sage suet roll in a mustard sauce. Meals start with a small cup of soup (pea was highly rated at a June dinner), and might finish with a champagne rhubarb mousse. Julie Springett is variously described as 'welcoming' and 'somewhat assertive' in her approach, but is also, as the menu makes clear, 'allergy aware', inviting enquiries from sufferers about ingredients. A serviceable wine list starts with house Dalwood blends from Australia at £11.95.

CHEF: Marcus Springett   PROPRIETORS: Julie and Marcus Springett   OPEN: Thur and Fri L 12.30 to 1.30, Mon to Sat D 7.15 to 8.45 (9.15 Sat)   CLOSED: 2 weeks Christmas   MEALS: Set L £21, Set D £24.95   SERVICE: not inc   CARDS: MasterCard, Visa   DETAILS: 45 seats. Private parties: 30 main room, 10 private room. Car park. No smoking in dining room. No music ACCOMMODATION: 6 rooms, all with bath/shower. TV. Phone. B&B £49 to £69 (£5)

PAXFORD Gloucestershire   map 5

▲ *Churchill Arms* £

Paxford GL55 6XH   COOKING 4
TEL: (01386) 594000   FAX: (01386) 594005   COST £21–£42

Churchill Arms poses many questions. Is it a pub, a restaurant, a brasserie? Why does Sonya Kidney have so many thrilling ideas? Why do some consider the cooking under-rated, others over-rated? As to identity, its pitch is a 'food pub' in a quiet, unspoilt village, and perhaps we are so unused to finding 'a pub lunch streets ahead of the usual' that the effect can be confusing. Dishes are chalked on a board: hot goats'-cheese soufflé with coriander and walnut pesto; stuffed quail with beetroot, sultanas and ginger; apple pie with clotted cream.

On the plus side is fresh seasonal food, simply but imaginatively cooked: from 'splendid' leek soup and fish cakes, via 'plaice at its very best' drizzled with soy sauce, to notable thin chips. Grumbles include smoke, lack of parking, service veering from 'amicable and efficient' to 'lacklustre', and the fact that bookings aren't taken. Some also complain that it gets very full very quickly, which jolly well serves the restaurant right for giving people what they want. Beer is £1.60 a pint, water £1.63 a pint. Two dozen sensibly chosen wines are mostly under £20, including eight house wines at £9.50.

CHEF: Sonya Kidney PROPRIETORS: Sonya Kidney and Leo Brooke-Little OPEN: all week 12 to 2.15, 7 to 9.15 MEALS: alc (main courses £7 to £12) SERVICE: not inc CARDS: Delta, MasterCard, Switch, Visa DETAILS: 60 seats. 40 seats outside. Private parties: 12 main room. Vegetarian meals. Children's helpings. No music ACCOMMODATION: 4 rooms, all with bath/shower. TV. Phone. B&B £40 to £70 (*The Which? Hotel Guide*)

PENZANCE Cornwall map 1

Harris's ✱

46 New Street, Penzance TR18 2LZ COOKING 2
TEL: (01736) 364408 FAX: (01736) 333273 COST £37–£56

'If you are in the area, it is worth knowing about,' concluded one visitor to this long-established, very pink restaurant in a narrow side street. 'There is no place at Harris's for pseudo Thai/Indian/Pacific Rim cooking,' writes Roger Harris, who concentrates instead on Western ways with fish: goujons of sole, salmon pancakes with cheese sauce, and scallops with salad leaves and a herb dressing. There is plenty for meat eaters too, though, from Cumberland sausages with onion and mash, to venison with beetroot and caraway seed. To finish, chocolate torte comes with blackcurrant sorbet, and treacle tart with clotted cream. Prices are considered rather high, although the wine list offers fair choice under £20, starting with house French at £11.50.

CHEF: Roger Harris PROPRIETORS: Roger and Anne Harris OPEN: Tue to Sat L 12 to 2, Tue to Sun D 7 to 9.30 MEALS: alc (main courses £15 to £21.50) SERVICE: 10%, card slips closed CARDS: Amex, Delta, MasterCard, Switch, Visa DETAILS: 40 seats. Private parties: 20 main room. No smoking in 1 dining room. Music

---

PETER TAVY Devon map 1

Peter Tavy Inn ✱ | NEW ENTRY |

Peter Tavy PL19 9NN
TEL: (01822) 810348 FAX: (01822) 810835 COOKING 2
off A386, 3m NE of Tavistock COST £16–£33

This early-seventeenth-century grey-stone inn, through the village at the end of a rough lane, is 'a fun place' and tends to be packed even on 'quiet' nights. At lunch the blackboard menu offers pub standards, plus some more interesting options such as minted lamb and orange casserole, or spicy vegetables en croûte. In the evening the kitchen steps up a gear to produce, for example, a 'dim sum' starter: two spicy prawn balls, a vegetable samosa, and a chilli-spiced prawn mixture wrapped in filo. Main courses might include tender rack of lamb with a

423

well-suited sauce of gooseberry and mint, or fillet of beef with a dark, crusty exterior and moist, pink interior, served with creamy garlic-flavoured mash and proper gravy. Cheeses are local, and desserts such as chocolate truffle torte, or crispy-topped strawberry and rhubarb crumble, come with 'an immense dollop' of clotted cream. Wines, supplied by Saccone and Speed, are a short selection with nothing over £13.

CHEF: Stephen Byrne   PROPRIETORS: Graeme and Karen Sim   OPEN: all week 12 to 2, 7 (6.30 July and Aug) to 9   CLOSED: 25 Dec   MEALS: alc (main courses L £4.50 to £7, D £7 to £13) SERVICE: not inc, card slips closed   CARDS: Delta, MasterCard, Switch, Visa   DETAILS: 80 seats. 100 seats outside. Private parties: 40 main room. Car park. Vegetarian meals. Children's helpings. No smoking in 1 dining room. Music   £5

PLUMTREE Nottinghamshire   map 5

Perkins ⁵✳

Old Railway Station, Plumtree NG12 5NA
TEL: (0115) 937 3695   FAX: (0115) 937 6405   COOKING 2
off A606, 2m S of Nottingham   COST £22–£39

People mill round the bar amid the good-natured, relaxed staff who typically play to a house of satisfied regulars. Beyond is a conservatory overlooking the old railway line, and there are even tables outside for the hardy. Cooking can be impressive, taking in 'topnotch' partridge with game chips; light fish cakes of smoked haddock and salmon with creamy tartare sauce; chargrilled sea bream; and just-pink roast lamb. The fixed-price lunch is especially good value: perhaps chicken and celery soup followed by smoked haddock with leeks and potato gratin. Puddings run to tarts (including an intense lemon version), pavlovas, perhaps a crumble and a chocolate pot. A short but decent choice of fairly priced bottles opens with a quartet of house wines under £10.

CHEFS: Tony Perkins and Hugh Cocker   PROPRIETORS: Tony and Wendy Perkins   OPEN: Tue to Sun L 12 to 2 (2.30 Sun), Tue to Sat D 6.30 to 9.45   CLOSED: 1 week Christmas, bank hols exc Good Friday   MEALS: alc Tue to Sat (main courses £8 to £11.50). Set L Tue to Sat £9.75 (2 courses), Set L Sun £11.50 (2 courses) to £14.95   SERVICE: not inc   CARDS: Amex, Delta, Diners, MasterCard, Switch, Visa   DETAILS: 73 seats. 24 seats outside. Private parties: 30 main room, 30 private room. Car park. Vegetarian meals. No smoking in 1 dining room. Wheelchair access (not WC). Occasional music. Air-conditioned

---

PLYMOUTH Devon   map 1

Chez Nous ♟

13 Frankfort Gate, Plymouth PL1 1QA   COOKING 5
TEL/FAX: (01752) 266793   COST £46–£55

Being part of a concrete shopping centre can't be easy for a serious restaurant, but at least it brings customers within range. Neither the small shop front with white-slatted shutters, nor the rectangular half-panelled room inside, seems to change much. Red and white cloths cover the tables, Gallic posters and 'gastronomic memorabilia' decorate the walls and, for anybody still in doubt about where it's coming from, French *chansons* claim the airwaves. The blackboard menu – three courses for a fixed price – is written in French too, and aims for simple modern classics.

Well placed for fresh supplies of seafood, the kitchen has turned out scallops with an understated ginger-flavoured cream sauce, and 'simple and good' grilled cod with pistou. Meat is equally well chosen, competently cooked, and generously served: a sauté of chicken livers in gravy on green beans, or a combination of fillets of pork and beef in a creamy mustard sauce. To finish, clove-flavoured pears in red wine come with a prune and armagnac ice cream, and nougat glacé is served, oddly, with sliced star fruit, a Chinese gooseberry, chocolate sauce and raspberry coulis. A few *vins d'autres pays* are provided, but given the range of fine French bottles offered at very fair prices it would seem a little unnecessary to break away from the Gallic theme. Six *vins de la maison* are £10.50 *la bouteille*.

CHEF: Jacques Marchal   PROPRIETORS: Suzanne and Jacques Marchal   OPEN: Tue to Fri L 12.30 to 2, Tue to Sat D 7 to 10.30   CLOSED: 3 weeks Feb, 3 weeks Sept, bank hols   MEALS: Set L and D £34   SERVICE: not inc   CARDS: Amex, Diners, MasterCard, Switch, Visa   DETAILS: 28 seats. Private parties: 28 main room. Wheelchair access (not WC). Music. Air-conditioned

---

PONTELAND Northumberland   map 10

Café 21

35 The Broadway, Darras Hall, Ponteland NE20 9PW   COOKING 4
TEL/FAX: (01661) 820357   COST £20–£42

Occupying two shop fronts, on a commuter estate north-west of Newcastle, this is a 'light and spacious' bistro-style operation, one of four outlets run by Terence and Susan Laybourne (see 21 Queen Street, Newcastle). Its informal style takes in wooden chairs, tablecloths, a few prints and a daily-changing blackboard menu of largely French-influenced food, from game terrine to spinach and Cheddar soufflé, from a strongly flavoured, creamy wild mushroom risotto with shaved Parmesan, to sirloin steak with garlic butter and chips. Dishes are attractively presented – red mullet has been surrounded by red and yellow peppers and cherry tomatoes alternating with aubergine, and topped with a first-rate tapénade cream – and desserts might include crème brûlée, pavlova, or a light pastry tart of passion fruit purée. Service from 'young waiters in 'garçon'-like aprons is charmingly 'upmarket Geordie' and generally attentive. Given the early-evening deal, it is worth rolling up before 7pm if possible. A short, roving and fairly priced wine list leads off with house Duboeuf at £10.

CHEF: Adrian Watson   PROPRIETORS: Terence and Susan Laybourne   OPEN: Sat L 12 to 2.30, Mon to Sat D 5.30 to 10.30   CLOSED: bank hols   MEALS: alc (main courses £9 to £13.50). Set L Sat £10.50 (2 courses) to £12.50, Set D 5.30 to 7 £10.50 (2 courses) to £12.50   SERVICE: not inc   CARDS: Amex, Delta, Diners, MasterCard, Switch, Visa   DETAILS: 65 seats. Private parties: 30 main room. Vegetarian meals. Children's helpings. Wheelchair access (also WC). Music

---

'I must say in all honesty that the results on the plate were not quite as appalling as I had expected them to be on the basis of the menu.' (On eating in Wales)

POOLE Dorset   map 2

▲ *Mansion House* ▼ ⁵⭑

Thames Street, Poole BH15 1JN   COOKING 2
TEL: (01202) 685666   FAX: (01202) 665709   COST £26–£45

Historic, handsome, comfortable and luxurious, this is 'the poshest restaurant in South Dorset by far'. Given golden-wood panelling, grand paintings and fine table settings, it is no wonder that many customers dress up to the nines for it; nor, given the location, should a penchant for seafood surprise. This takes many forms, from 'properly cooked' salmon in white wine sauce, via red mullet with black olive and tomato couscous, to a deep-fried crab parcel with mango and avocado salsa. Flavours may not always live up to expectation, but generous set menus run the gamut from two large ravioli filled with Gorgonzola, to breast of duck with shiitake and beansprouts, and main courses come with a side dish of 'every vegetable under the sun'. Bread-and-butter pudding has long been a Mansion House favourite, or there may be peach and raspberry clafoutis. Staff are friendly, and service is smooth without being stuffy. Wines fall into two main categories: good-value bins from the major wine regions (most under £30, many under £15), and classy clarets and Burgundies with no upper limit (which isn't to say that they are overpriced). Halves are generous too. House recommendations, running to more than twenty bottles, start at around £13.

CHEF: Gerry Godden   PROPRIETORS: Robert Leonard, and Jackie and Gerry Godden   OPEN: Sun to Fri L 12 to 2, Mon to Sat and Sun preceding bank hols D 7 to 9.30   CLOSED: 31 Dec, bank hol Mon L   MEALS: Set L £16.50, Set D £19.85 (2 courses) to £24.45   SERVICE: not inc   CARDS: Amex, Delta, Diners, MasterCard, Switch, Visa   DETAILS: 85 seats. Private parties: 100 main room, 14 to 36 private rooms. Car park. Vegetarian meals. Children's helpings. No children under 5 exc Sun L. No smoking in 1 dining room. Occasional music. Air-conditioned ACCOMMODATION: 32 rooms, all with bath/shower. TV. Phone. B&B £60 to £125. Baby facilities (*The Which? Hotel Guide*) £5

PORTHLEVEN Cornwall   map 1

▲ *Critchards* ⁵⭑

The Harbourside, Porthleven TR13 9JA   COOKING 2
TEL: (01326) 562407   FAX: (01326) 564444   COST £26–£63

It would perhaps be surprising if this harbourside restaurant did not specialise in seafood. After ten years the Critchards have got the measure of their suppliers – Newlyn is the source – and offer a wide range of shellfishy starters and fish main courses. Like any good specialist they deal in more than just the usual restaurant varieties of red mullet, sea bass or monk, turning out pan-fried strips of gurnard with garlic and olives, oriental-style grey mullet, and lemon hake with a coriander and yoghurt sauce. Despite a few Eastern flavourings – Bangkok mussels or Cantonese scallops – some dishes come as plain as oysters with tarragon vinegar, or simply grilled lobster. Long delays are the main problem to surface among reports, suggesting that better organisation in the kitchen would not go amiss; and it might also encourage reporters to stay for desserts of coconut bavarois, lemon tart or chocolate and coffee mousse. Some

forty wines make a good effort to keep prices within reason. House French is
£10.95.

CHEF: Jo Critchard   PROPRIETORS: Steve and Jo Critchard   OPEN: Mon to Sat D only 6.30 to
9.30 (10 summer)   CLOSED: Jan   MEALS: alc (main courses £9 to £28)   SERVICE: not inc, card
slips closed   CARDS: MasterCard, Switch, Visa   DETAILS: 44 seats. Private parties: 30 main
room. Vegetarian meals. Children's helpings. No children under 6 in dining room. No smoking in
dining room. Occasional music   ACCOMMODATION: 2 rooms, both with bath/shower. TV. B&B
£48 to £58 (£5)

PORTLOE Cornwall   map 1

▲ *Tregain* ⸙✳

Portloe TR2 5QU   COOKING 2
TEL/FAX: (01872) 501252   COST £17–£47

Clare Holdsworth hardly lets up. In a small, unspoiled fishing village, with a
beach and coastal footpath nearby, she runs the village shop and post office,
along with a daytime café serving coffee, home-made cakes and light lunches
(Sunday is omelette day), and opens it as a fully fledged restaurant in the
evening. Local ingredients are the mainstay, especially seafood, which might
show up as crab soup, scallops with ginger and cashew nuts, or turbot with
sorrel sauce. 'We use saffron and clotted cream regularly,' she writes, 'because
they are particularly Cornish', alongside seasonal asparagus and new potatoes.
Outside seafood, dinner might offer spiced lamb with apricots and honey,
treacle pudding, and a West Country cheeseboard. A short, fairly priced wine list
starts with house wines at £8.75.

CHEF/PROPRIETOR: Clare Holdsworth   OPEN: all week L 11.30 to 3.30, Mon to Sat and Sun bank
hol D 7 to 8.30   CLOSED: Nov to Mar   MEALS: alc (main courses L £3.50 to £10.50, D £8.50 to
£18)   SERVICE: not inc, card slips closed   CARDS: Delta, MasterCard, Switch, Visa   DETAILS:
22 seats. 12 seats outside. Private parties: 24 main room. Vegetarian meals. Children's
helpings. No smoking in dining room. Occasional music   ACCOMMODATION: 2 rooms. B&B £20
to £40

PORTREATH Cornwall   map 1

Tabb's £

Tregea Terrace, Portreath TR16 4LD   COOKING 2
TEL/FAX: (01209) 842488   COST £18–£41

Swing left at the pleasure-crafted harbour, look back, and the discreetly signed
restaurant is there under the viaduct. The low stone building, once a forge, is run
by Nigel and Melanie Tabb, both Cornish born and bred, and decorated with
hopeful artists' paintings. 'We Do It All' could be their borrowed motto, right
from selecting all the produce rather than having it delivered, through to the
creation of luxury chocolates and ice creams. Menu descriptions show Nigel's
enthusiastic intentions to let ingredients speak for themselves, maybe chicken
livers (a favourite ingredient) baked with ginger, chilli, spring onion and garlic,
or duck breast braised with bacon and tarragon. Further indications of the style
that tends to make regulars out of first-timers are a lemony salad of pan-fried

427

chicken fillets with coriander and cucumber chutney, monkfish with oyster mushrooms and tomato tapénade, and baked vegetables with apples and toasted pine nuts. The wine list is short but adequate, house wine a modest £8.95.

CHEF: Nigel Tabb   PROPRIETORS: Nigel and Melanie Tabb   OPEN: Sun L 12.15 to 1.45, Wed to Mon D 7 to 9   CLOSED: 2 weeks Nov, 2 weeks Jan, 26 Dec, 1 Jan   MEALS: alc D (main courses £10.50 to £15). Set L Sun £12, Set D £12 (2 courses) to £15   SERVICE: not inc, card slips closed   CARDS: Delta, MasterCard, Visa   DETAILS: 30 seats. Private parties: 30 main room. Vegetarian meals. Children's helpings. No cigars/pipes in dining room. Wheelchair access (not WC). Music (£5)

POULTON-LE-FYLDE Lancashire   map 8

▲ River House

Skippool Creek, Thornton-le-Fylde,
Poulton-le-Fylde FY5 5LF
TEL: (01253) 883497   FAX: (01253) 892083
from roundabout junction of A585 and B5412 follow   COOKING 3
signs to Skippool Creek   COST £34–£64

The lack of change is a source of comfort at this 1830s gentleman-farmer's house that overlooks the hills, water and mud of the creek. Take drinks in the canine-free conservatory or in the 'we like dogs' bar, before moving to well-spaced bare tables in the dining room, Linda Scott's domain. Bill Scott, enthusiast and eccentric, sticks to his formula consolidated over nearly thirty years of serving local fish, meat and game with classic sauces: mallard or venison with cranberry sauce, pheasant with game sauce, chateaubriand with béarnaise. 'Food is expensive,' thought an inspector, 'but excellent ingredients with no shortcuts are guaranteed.' Reporters have commended home-made walnut and dried apricot bread, soufflé suissesse (a River House hallmark), and quick-roasted eye fillet of lamb in a herby crust with a garlicky rosemary cream sauce. Crisp orange shortbread accompanying 'ever so creamy' ice cream has also delighted. From the 150 or so wines listed by country, it should not be hard to find a good match for the food. House wine is £12.50.

CHEF/PROPRIETOR: Bill Scott   OPEN: Mon to Sat 12 to 2, 7.30 to 9.30   MEALS: alc (main courses £16 to £23). Set L and D £25 (for whole party only)   SERVICE: not inc   CARDS: Delta, MasterCard, Switch, Visa   DETAILS: 40 seats. Private parties: 40 main room, 14 private room. Car park. Vegetarian meals. No children under 7. Music   ACCOMMODATION: 4 rooms, all with bath/shower. TV. Phone. B&B £65 to £80 (The Which? Hotel Guide) (£5)

POWERSTOCK Dorset   map 2

▲ Three Horseshoes 🍴✗

Powerstock DT6 3TF
TEL: (01308) 485328   FAX: (01308) 485328   COOKING 1
off A3066 at Gore Cross, 4m NE of Bridport   COST £25–£43

'We are a country pub and don't pretend to be anything else,' writes Mark Johnson, from a tiny unspoilt village where there are 'no shops, no streetlights, just us'. With the coast only six miles away, seafood naturally plays a starring role, appearing in dishes as straightforward as hake with provençale sauce, tuna with salsa verde, or squid stir-fried with garlic, chilli and ginger. Game, also local, might turn up as pigeon terrine or wild boar sausages, while nearby Denhay Farm supplies gammon and air-dried ham. Finish with homely bread-and-butter pudding or pears poached in red wine, and drink real ale or a modest bottle from the predominantly under-£15 wine list.

CHEF: Mark Johnson   PROPRIETORS: Mark and Sue Johnson   OPEN: all week 12 to 2, 7 to 9.30   CLOSED: no food 25 Dec   MEALS: alc (main courses £8.50 to £16). Bar menu available L and D   SERVICE: not inc   CARDS: Delta, MasterCard, Switch, Visa   DETAILS: 60 seats. 30 seats outside. Private parties: 55 main room, 20 private room. Car park. Vegetarian meals. Children's helpings. No children under 8 after 8.30 in dining room. No smoking in dining room. Wheelchair access (also WC). No music   ACCOMMODATION: 3 rooms, 2 with bath. TV. No children under 8 in accommodation. B&B £35 to £50 (£5)

PRESTBURY Cheshire   map 8

▲ *White House*

New Road, Prestbury SK10 4DG
TEL: (01625) 829376   FAX: (01625) 828627   COOKING 2
on A538, 4m N of Macclesfield   COST £23–£62

Right in the centre of the village, whitewashed of course, with lots of flowers, and serving a 'largely well-heeled clientele', this long-established restaurant welcomes with a spacious bar, a light, calm, low-ceilinged dining room, and efficient and friendly service. Its ambitious and wide-ranging menu reflects an enthusiastic kitchen, offering up-to-date ingredients and ideas. Seafood is given characteristically bright treatment – seared scallops with sweet chilli relish, or brill on a potato cake with beetroot dressing – and local materials include braised lamb shank with green olives, and peppered loin of Tatton Park venison with braised red cabbage. Among highlights have been an inspector's well-timed calf's liver on a savoury leek and pancetta risotto, and desserts, which are considered worthy 'of particular note': maybe tropical fruit pudding with custard, or light-textured tiramisù ice cream decorated with summer fruits. Set menus deliver good value, bread has impressed, cheeses (including organic) are served cold, and fifty-plus wines are attractively varied and sensibly priced. House Vieille Ferme is £12.95.

CHEFS: Ryland Wakeham and Mark Cunniffe   PROPRIETORS: Ryland and Judith Wakeham   OPEN: Tue to Sun L 12 to 2, Mon to Sat D 7 to 10   CLOSED: 25 Dec, 1 Jan   MEALS: alc (main courses £11 to £17). Set L £12.95, Set D Tue to Fri £14.95 (2 courses) to £17.95. Bar food available   SERVICE: not inc, card slips closed   CARDS: Amex, Delta, Diners, MasterCard, Switch, Visa   DETAILS: 75 seats. 12 seats outside. Private parties: 60 main room, 28 and 40 private rooms. Car park. Vegetarian meals. Children's helpings. No smoking in dining room before 10pm. Wheelchair access (not WC). Music   ACCOMMODATION: 11 rooms, all with bath/shower. TV. Phone. Room only £40 to £120. No children under 10 in accommodation (*The Which? Hotel Guide*)

Report forms are at the back of the book; write a letter if you prefer; or email us at guidereports@which.co.uk.

PRESTON Lancashire map 8

Heathcote's Brasserie

23 Winckley Square, Preston PR1 3JJ
TEL: (01772) 252732   FAX: (01772) 203433
EMAIL: brasserie@heathcotes.co.uk

COOKING 4
COST £22–£44}

Mostly white, with ceiling-high radiators and brightly coloured artwork on the walls, Paul Heathcote's Preston outlet provides stylish surroundings in which to eat brasserie food 'of considerable refinement'. A generous carte benefits from a degree of invention, producing smoked chicken and coconut milk soup, and elderflower-marinated salmon, but locally sourced materials (Goosnargh chicken and duckling) play an important role, as does the straightforward approach: a starter of baby artichokes simply baked with thyme, followed by Lancashire hotpot, made with diced lamb and beef in a 'rich, thick gravy', with traditional sliced potatoes on top.

Standards vary, but at its best the kitchen has turned out pink chicken livers with a simple leaf garnish, 'accurately cooked' tempura of three or four fish with a bean salad, and 'fine, tender' braised venison, its sauce enlivened with raisins and cinnamon sticks. Desserts appear to excite less interest, but service is praised for being both relaxed and attentive. Those looking for a good deal might try the two- or three-course lunch, also served early evenings, or the downstairs room that goes in for light dishes, snacks, fish and chips, and spit-roast meat of the day (perhaps good-quality rare beef) made into a sandwich. A change of wine policy means there are now 'only' ten available by the glass, on an appealing forty-strong list that starts with house French at £11.50.

CHEF: Jamie Holland   PROPRIETOR: Paul Heathcote   OPEN: all week 12 (12.30 Sun) to 2.30, 7 to 10.30   MEALS: alc (main courses £10.50 to £13). Set L and D 7 to 8 £10.50 (2 courses) to £12.50. Bar menu available Mon to Thur 11 to 6.45, Fri and Sat 11 to 10   SERVICE: 10% (optional), card slips closed   CARDS: Amex, Diners, MasterCard, Switch, Visa   DETAILS: 160 seats. Private parties: 90 main room, 80 private room. Vegetarian meals. Children's helpings. No cigars/pipes in dining room. Wheelchair access (not WC). Music. Air-conditioned

RAMSBOTTOM Greater Manchester map 8

Village Restaurant ▮ ⅝ £

16–18 Market Place, Ramsbottom BL0 9HT
TEL: (01706) 825070   FAX: (01706) 822005
off A56/M66, 4m N of Bury

COOKING 4
COST £22–£36

In an age when many restaurants appear cloned and expensive it is refreshing to mark the continued success (all fifteen years) of Ros Hunter's and Chris Johnson's individual, if somewhat uncompromising, approach. Sourcing of organic food, always a strength, has reached new heights with the opening of Ramsbottom Organics at 76 Bridge Street, some 50 yards away. As the *Guide* went to press, Ramsons (on the Market Place site) was due to blossom into an enoteca, aiming to combine the virtues of an Italian wine bar, simple café, and off-licence under one roof, reflecting an increasing in-house enthusiasm for Italian produce.

The Village Restaurant, meanwhile, continues to offer its simple two-course weekday lunches and four-course Saturday dinners, plus a new free-ranging carte (not available Saturday dinner) that covers most of the kitchen's repertoire from Caesar salad via potted Morecambe Bay shrimps to rare rump of lamb or entrecôte steak. Cooking without salt is pursued with missionary zeal, and since there are no frills – indeed many dishes may not appear to involve much 'cooking' at all – it tends to have a straightforward feel to it: Cumbrian ham salad, cold roast beef, or a smooth, fine-textured chicken liver pâté on pecan and sultana toast. Sticky toffee pudding served with yogurt is a regular dessert, although blackcurrant cheesecake and Lancashire cheese make viable alternatives. If you have a few minutes to spare before your meal, it would be well worth perusing the shelves of the wine cellar, as any of the bottles can be bought and then drunk in the restaurant for a corkage charge of £5 for 'ordinary' wines, rising to £9 for 'fine' wines (shop price of £15 or more). Otherwise choose from the short list of two dozen, or try one of the many beers or ciders. Organic house French is £9.50.

CHEF: Ros Hunter   PROPRIETORS: Ros Hunter and Chris Johnson   OPEN: Wed to Sun L 12.30 (12 Sat, 1 Sun) to 2.30 (3.30 Sun), Wed to Sat D 7 (8 Sat) to 9.30   MEALS: alc Wed to Sun L, Wed to Fri D (main courses £6.50 to £11.50). Set L Wed to Sat £6.50 (2 courses), Set D Sat £25   SERVICE: not inc, card slips closed   CARDS: Delta, MasterCard, Switch, Visa   DETAILS: 42 seats. Private parties: 30 main room, 12 private room. Vegetarian meals. No smoking in dining room. No music   (£5)

RAMSGILL North Yorkshire   map 8

▲ *Yorke Arms* ⸙✳ £

Ramsgill, nr Pateley Bridge HG3 5RL
TEL: (01423) 755243   FAX: (01423) 755330   COOKING 6
EMAIL: enquiries@yorke-arms.co.uk   COST £24–£49

Beside the village green, a few miles north of Pateley Bridge near Gouthwaite reservoir, this eighteenth-century creeper-covered inn – once a shooting lodge – feels unspoiled. Amid flag floors, stone fireplaces, dark pews, an old dresser and bare wooden tables, the Atkinses 'manage to create an enthusiastic but sincere, friendly and calm atmosphere'. The moorland round about is not just used for walking but also as a source of grouse, pheasant, woodcock, partridge and venison (perhaps served with wild mushrooms and port sauce). Local meats (Nidderdale lamb shank, Yorkshire ham and eggs) and cheeses add to the sense of a cook who is in touch with her roots and takes inspiration from her materials.

If the food has a 'rustic' feel, it is a compliment to that integrity and purpose, and if it has a cosmopolitan feel, it is thanks to Frances Atkins's wide experience. Warm salad of black pudding sits beside Thai-spiced fish cakes, followed by anything from halibut with cheesy mash to braised pig's cheek. Steamed syrup pudding, and Yorkshire curd tart with rum custard cannot fail to appeal in these parts. Good value seems to be a priority, not least on the sixty-strong wine list, where eight house wines start at £11.

CHEF: Frances Atkins   PROPRIETORS: Gerald and Frances Atkins   OPEN: all week L 12 to 1.45, Mon to Sat D (Sun D residents only) 7 to 8.45   MEALS: alc (main courses £8 to £16)   SERVICE: not inc   CARDS: Amex, Delta, Diners, MasterCard, Switch, Visa   DETAILS: 80 seats. 60 seats outside. Private parties: 40 main room, 40 private room. Car park. Vegetarian meals. No smoking in dining room. Wheelchair access (not WC). Music   ACCOMMODATION: 13 rooms, all with bath/shower. TV. Phone. D,B&B £70 to £140 (*The Which? Hotel Guide*)   £5

REIGATE Surrey   map 3

Dining Room 🍴✳

59A High Street, Reigate RH2 9AE	COOKING 5
TEL/FAX: (01737) 226650	COST £23–£55

Occupying a creamy-yellow first-floor dining room, with heavily curtained windows overlooking the street, this popular restaurant (there are sometimes two sittings at dinner) plants its feet firmly in the modern camp. In the search for excitement, menus deploy a range of varied accompaniments – preserved lemon, beetroot chutney, coriander and lime pesto – and first courses have turned up crab and chilli cakes with coconut rice, Roquefort beignets with sweet-and-sour sauce, and baked rock oysters with wasabi butter. Likewise with main courses: pink loin of lamb has come with integral vegetables and a 'powerful pesto', while chicken breast rubbed with Moroccan spices and served with a tagine of courgettes and squash is recommended for 'succulence and flavour'. Vegetables ('excellent olive oil mash' for one party) are charged extra, even on the set menus. Flavours, however, were disappointingly muted at inspection, the highlight of which was a caramel ice cream paired with thin, crispy sheets of chocolate; or there may be mango tartlet, or a meringue tower with sour cherries and clotted cream. Service could be more attentive. Around twenty fine wines supplement the short, regular list, which stays mostly under £20. House Vin de Pays de l'Aude is £9.50.

CHEF: Tony Tobin   PROPRIETOR: Elite Restaurants Ltd   OPEN: Sun to Fri L 12 to 2 (12.30 to 2.30 Sun), Mon to Sat D 7 to 10.30   CLOSED: Christmas, Easter   MEALS: alc exc Sun L (main courses £16.50). Set L Mon to Fri £10 (2 courses) to £13.50, Set L Sun £25, Set D £16.95 (2 courses)   SERVICE: 10% (optional), card slips closed   CARDS: Amex, Diners, MasterCard, Switch, Visa   DETAILS: 50 seats. Private parties: 50 main room. Children's helpings. No smoking in dining room. Music. Air-conditioned   £5

RICHMOND Surrey   map 3

Burnt Chair 🍷

5 Duke Street, Richmond TW9 1HP	
TEL: (0181) 940 9488, changing to (020) 8940 9488	COOKING 3
FAX: (0181) 940 7879, changing to (020) 8940 7879	COST £25–£50

The menu changes once a month at the 'neat, clean and unaffectedly stylish' Burnt Chair, which regulars consider to be 'the best place in the area'. Reporters are almost uniformly delighted with the ambitious cuisine and the characterful front-of-house presence of Mr Oo. The restaurant's staple, Devon 'wild beef' (farmed, but free to roam over Dartmoor), has been upgraded to rump, served in a myriad ways throughout the year but always in typically generous portions. Meals might begin with an appealing soup – smoked haddock vichyssoise, or a spicy one of red lentil, coriander and coconut – and progress to well-timed rare duck on apple purée. Saucing, meanwhile, has ranged from a dark, strongly flavoured reduction with braised fillet of lamb, to a 'wonderfully tasty, clear ginger and spring onion broth' with a giant raviolo of scallops.

Burnt Chair is also a pudding-lover's dream, serving a hefty but high-quality trio of banana desserts consisting of parfait, cake and mousse, not to mention an 'assiette of desserts', which 'virtually feeds two'. Weenson Oo's passion for wine is evident, both in the collection of rarely seen North American bottles and the intelligent tasting notes that accompany everything on his list. Burgundy is another old favourite, while the appearance of a Swiss duo reveals a new attraction. Such wines do not come cheap, but house vin de pays is £9.75.

CHEFS: Weenson Oo, Colin Gibbons and Richard West PROPRIETOR: Weenson Oo OPEN: Mon to Sat D only 6 to 11 CLOSED: 1 week Christmas, 10 days Aug, bank hols MEALS: alc (main courses £10.50 to £15). Set D 6 to 7.30 Mon to Fri, 6 to 7 Sat £15 (2 courses). Cover £1 SERVICE: not inc; 12.5% for parties of 4 or more CARDS: Delta, MasterCard, Switch, Visa DETAILS: 36 seats. Private parties: 36 main room. Vegetarian meals. Children's helpings. No smoking until 11pm. Wheelchair access (not WC). Music (£5)

Canyon
NEW ENTRY

Riverside, Richmond TW10 6UJ
TEL: (0181) 948 2944, changing to (020) 8948 2944
FAX: (0181) 948 2945, changing to (020) 8948 2945

COOKING 4
COST £25–£56

Anyone still under the impression that salsa is a dance craze should hurry along the towpath to this new Richmond riverside eatery. A sister of Montana, Dakota and Idaho (see entries, London), it offers contemporary south-west American cuisine in a building resembling an L-shaped ranch set around a desert garden of rocks and cacti. Even diners with reservations about Mexican-influenced food have been impressed by complex combinations such as flavourful rare tuna, topped with an 'intense' garlic, coriander and lime sauce, accompanied by a wild rice and couscous salad, with an aubergine and smoked jalapeño salsa. Rump of lamb presents another typically involved possibility: crusted with chestnut and molasses, it is served with green onion and chipotle gratin and Cascabel marmalade. Though the cooking features 'lots of chillies of different sorts', dishes are not swamped with strong flavours. Corn tortillas and barbecued chicken burrito come into their own on the weekend brunch menu, and well-received desserts include Michigan cherry and chocolate cake with coconut ice cream, and berry chimichanga with honey crunch chocolate ice cream. Wines hail in the main from California and offer a fair selection under £20.

CHEFS: Daniel Mcdowell and Justin Walker PROPRIETOR: Montana Plc OPEN: all week 12 to 3.30 (11 to 4 Sat and Sun), 7 (5.30 Sun) to 11 MEALS: alc (main courses £9 to £15.50). Set L £10.95 (2 courses) to £14. SERVICE: 12.5% (optional) CARDS: Amex, Delta, MasterCard, Switch, Visa DETAILS: 95 seats. 95 seats outside. Private parties: 95 main room. Vegetarian meals. Children's helpings. No-smoking area. Wheelchair access (also WC). Music. Air-conditioned

Chez Lindsay £

11 Hill Rise, Richmond TW10 6UQ
TEL: (0181) 948 7473, changing to (020) 8948 7473   COOKING 1
FAX: (0181) 332 0129, changing to (020) 8332 0129   COST £19–£53

Lindsay Wotton proudly flies the flag for Breton cooking in her yellow-brick former shop by Richmond Bridge. This means wild salmon, artichokes, and white asparagus in season. The rest of the time there are galettes galore: griddled buckwheat pancakes appearing in either 'classic' form (filled with combinations of eggs, cheese, ham and onions) or as 'specialities', with andouille and mustard, or smoked salmon and cream. Seafood is the other main strand – clams with garlic and parsley butter, cotriade, or cold seafood platter – backed up by braised lamb shank, or grilled sirloin steak. Desserts are firmly back in pancake territory, with iced versions, flambé versions, or a simple 'jam of your choice'. Cider is the recommended accompaniment, or try a wine from the Loire such as Cheverny. House vin de pays is £9.75.

CHEFS: Lindsay Wotton, Moise Diabate and Sylvain Regent   PROPRIETOR: Lindsay Wotton
OPEN: all week 11 (12 Sun) to 3, 6 to 11 (10 Sun)   CLOSED: 25 Dec   MEALS: alc (main courses £4.50 to £17.50). Set L Mon to Sat (exc bank hols) £5.99 (2 courses) to £9.99, Set L Sun and bank hols £9.99, Set D Sun to Fri £9.99   SERVICE: not inc   CARDS: Delta, MasterCard, Switch, Visa
DETAILS: 48 seats. Private parties: 50 main room, 36 private room. Vegetarian meals. Children's helpings. No cigars/pipes while others eat. Wheelchair access (not WC). Music (£5)

RIDGEWAY Derbyshire   map 9

Old Vicarage ₹✳

Ridgeway Moor, Ridgeway S12 3XW
TEL: (0114) 247 5814   FAX: (0114) 247 7079
EMAIL: eat@theoldvicarage.co.uk   COOKING 6
off A616, on B6054 nearly opposite Village Church   COST £45–£69

Although not far from Sheffield and the motorways, this old-fashioned country house exudes a sense of calm. Drinks arrive at comfortable settees in the lounge, and there are two dining rooms, one slightly formal, the other a plant-strewn, candlelit conservatory. Relatively few restaurants stick to a set-price format only, but here the deal is an uncompromising £30 for three courses, £42 for four, the same at lunch and dinner. Choice extends to five or six items per course, and the kitchen is at home with a wide range of materials, culinary styles and techniques.

This produces a diversity of dishes, some as far-flung as scallop sashimi and aubergine with pickled ginger and lime dressing, others as European as Gressingham duck breast with lentils and a sausage made from the leg meat. In between come fusion dishes of, perhaps, brill with a coriander and cumin crust in a sherry vinegar sauce. Sourcing is careful to pick prime produce – fillet of new season lamb, roast squab pigeon with an apple and forcemeat stuffing, or Aberdeen Angus fillet with tapénade crust – and a vegetarian main course is always provided: perhaps a risotto of wild mushrooms and butternut squash, served with a morel soup. A few unusual flavours find their way into desserts – woodruff ice cream to accompany mango and cardamom in peach schnapps –

although caramelised rice pudding comes more conventionally with mulled fruits. As the *Guide* went to press the wine list was in a state of flux.

CHEFS: Tessa Bramley, Nathan Smith and Andrew Gilbert PROPRIETOR: Tessa Bramley
OPEN: Tue to Fri and Sun L 12.30 to 2.30, Tue to Sat D 7 to 10.30 CLOSED: 26 and 31 Dec, 1 Jan MEALS: Set L and D £30 to £42 SERVICE: not inc, card slips closed CARDS: Amex, Delta, Diners, MasterCard, Switch, Visa DETAILS: 50 seats. 16 seats outside. Private parties: 46 main room, 24 private room. Car park. Vegetarian meals. Children's helpings. No smoking in dining room. Wheelchair access (not WC). Occasional music (£5)

RIPLEY North Yorkshire   map 9

▲ *Boar's Head* ♟

Ripley HG3 3AY
TEL: (01423) 771888 FAX: (01423) 771509   COOKING 4
EMAIL: boarshead@ripleycastle.co.uk   COST £23–£54

Not only the Boar's Head but the entire estate village of Ripley, small as it is, seems imbued with the feudal presence of the Ingilbys. Formerly a coaching stop called the Star Inn, but renamed to commemorate a fourteenth-century incident in the family's history, this is now an 'elegant, welcoming, country-house-style hotel' with a restaurant and informal bistro. The posher end of the spectrum is represented by spinach and walnut gnocchi, potted duck in sweet port jelly, and 'a presentation of very individual soups on one plate'. Prime materials are given sometimes unusual treatment – medallions of Yorkshire lamb with a haggis hollandaise – and main courses combine the lightness of poached fish in a lemon-scented court-bouillon with the heartiness of oak-smoked fillet of pork with flageolet beans and braised artichokes. Niggles include vegetables on the raw side of al dente, a plea that menus might be more flexible, and a mix-up over a booking, but service has been 'excellent', and wines are both reassuring and appealing. Sir Thomas has kept prices at reasonable levels on his 200-strong list and is able to recommend many personal favourites – noblesse oblige indeed. Ripley Castle 'Joanis' Vin de Pays de Vaucluse 1997, rouge et blanc, is £12.

CHEF: Steve Chesnutt PROPRIETORS: Sir Thomas and Lady Ingilby OPEN: all week 12 to 2, 7 to 9.30 MEALS: Set L £15, Set D £27.50 to £35. Bar/bistro menu available SERVICE: not inc, card slips closed CARDS: Amex, Delta, Diners, MasterCard, Switch, Visa DETAILS: 40 seats. 60 seats outside. Private parties: 40 main room, 25 to 65 private rooms. Car park. Vegetarian meals. Children's helpings. Wheelchair access (also WC). Occasional music ACCOMMODATION: 25 rooms, all with bath/shower. TV. Phone. B&B £95 to £135. Rooms for disabled. Fishing (*The Which? Hotel Guide*) (£5)

'The dress code said jacket and tie for men. Apparently, women can turn up in thongs, thigh-length rubber waders and snorkels and show any amount of bosom and will still be served, but men must be seen to be sweating and uncomfortable in jackets and ties.'
(On eating in London)

(£5) *indicates that the restaurant has elected to participate in the* Good Food Guide *voucher scheme. For full details, see page 6.*

435

RIPLEY Surrey   map 3

Michels

13 High Street, Ripley GU23 6AQ
TEL: (01483) 224777   FAX: (01483) 222940   COOKING 5
off A3, 4m SW of Cobham   COST £27–£74

This large detached house has a stylish open-plan layout, its atmosphere created
by a mix of muted colours, stripped wood, antiques, and some of Erik Michel's
accomplished paintings. His European approach to food takes in ravioli of green
asparagus with truffle dressing to start, or thin slices of scallop and a whole coral
baked in the shell, while mains might include organic free-range duck breast, or
steamed sea bass and red mullet with lobster sauce.

The monthly-changing no-choice set dinner is for whole tables only but comes
with three different wines, while the fixed-price lunch on weekdays has come
down in price and offers a choice of three items per course. As far as the carte is
concerned, it may be worth asking Karen Michel's advice, since her suggestion
of boned and accurately roast quail breasts with dried morel mushrooms proved
to be one of the better dishes at inspection.

To finish, a neat, chunky, lightly spiced apple tarte Tatin typically comes with
a scoop of cinnamon ice cream, and pre-selected British and Irish cheeses are
served in good condition. Home-made items include milk bread and slices of
coarse-crusted wholemeal with raisins. Prices are considered high, service tends
'to blow hot and cold', and a largely French wine list includes some classy
bottles, plus eight house wines between £8.50 and £14.50.

CHEF: Erik Michel   PROPRIETORS: Erik and Karen Michel   OPEN: Tue to Fri and Sun L 12.30 to
1.30, Tue to Sat D 7.30 to 9 (7 to 9.30 Sat)   CLOSED: early Jan, 2 weeks Aug   MEALS: alc (main
courses £19 to £23). Set L Tue to Fri £14 (2 courses) to £18, Set L Sun £21, Set D Tue to Fri £30
(inc wine)   SERVICE: not inc   CARDS: Amex, Delta, MasterCard, Switch, Visa   DETAILS: 50
seats. Private parties: 12 private room. Car park. No cigars/pipes in dining room. Wheelchair
access (not WC). No music

ROADE Northamptonshire   map 5

▲ Roade House ⁵✶

16 High Street, Roade NN7 2NW
TEL: (01604) 863372   FAX: (01604) 862421   COOKING 5
off A508, 4m S of Northampton   COST £24–£42

Restructuring of the premises is all over and done with, we are told – upstairs
there are nine bedrooms now – and downstairs the restaurant is now kitted out
in pale yellow and deep red. Menus typically contain one or two plain starters
such as smoked salmon, or a plate of fruit, to balance against busier ones in
which eggs or pastry may feature: a 'simple but effective' broccoli and stilton tart,
perhaps, or one reporter's poached egg on a croûton with tomato concasse, oyster
mushrooms and chorizo, described as 'a rich, slightly bizarre but gorgeous
mixture'. Fish laudably includes the humble sardine as well as posher halibut
and tuna, and is generally dealt with sympathetically, from a smoked haddock

fish cake 'full of flavour' served with a spicy tomato salsa, to a moist, well-timed piece of cod with a dollop of tapénade and a cylinder of saffron mash.

Game usually features in season – roast partridge with a 'cairn' of cranberries in a light jus that 'went down a treat' – and some dishes (pheasant or rabbit perhaps) are obligingly served with a sausage of the leg meat. There is a degree of comfort about the food, and reassurance about the cooking, as it deals in red-blooded calf's liver, or fillet of beef with a wild mushroom sauce and a relish of beetroot and horseradish. Desserts are all the better for being straightforward, whether a simple pairing of crème brûlée and fresh raspberries, or a 'classic seventies' chocolate marquise with good custard. A serviceable wine list centred on France and the antipodes starts with house red and white at £10.75.

CHEFS: Christopher Kewley and Steven Barnes PROPRIETORS: Christopher and Susan Kewley OPEN: Tue to Fri and Sun L 12.30 to 1.45, Mon to Sat D 7 to 9.30 (10 Sat) MEALS: alc D (main courses £14 to £17). Set L £14.50 (2 courses) to £16.50 SERVICE: net prices, card slips closed CARDS: Amex, Delta, MasterCard, Switch, Visa DETAILS: 45 seats. 12 seats outside. Private parties: 58 main room. Car park. Children's helpings. No smoking in dining room. Wheelchair access (also WC). Occasional music. Air-conditioned ACCOMMODATION: 9 rooms, all with bath/shower. TV. Phone. B&B £50 to £75. Rooms for disabled

---

ROCHDALE Greater Manchester   map 8

After Eight ⚟✳

2 Edenfield Road, Rochdale OL11 5AA   COOKING 4
TEL: (01706) 646432   COST £28–£42

At their imposing and comfortable stone house, set in pretty gardens, Anne and Geoff Taylor run a tight yet convivial ship, delivering a sensibly restrained menu, based on familiar and often local ingredients. The cooking is founded on classical techniques and combinations (cream and alcohol are used without demur), but Geoff more than tips his hat to current thinking. Take for example Lancashire hotpot parcels with mint and red wine jus as a starter; or main-course roast chicken with an almond and tarragon crust, served with a pepper salsa; or indeed three-nut (cashew, chestnut and walnut) pithiviers from the vegetarian menu, which comes with an orange, redcurrant and port sauce. Enticing desserts might include pecan and butterscotch pudding, Italian-style pear tartlet with Amaretto ice cream, or meringue layered with cream and strawberries. A straightforward wine list deals in some good names (Australia's Henschke for instance) and manages to stay mostly below £20. House French is £9.90.

CHEF: G.P. Taylor PROPRIETORS: G.P. and A. Taylor OPEN: Tue to Sat D only 7 to 9.30
CLOSED: 25 and 26 Dec, 1 Jan MEALS: alc (main courses £12.50 to £16) SERVICE: not inc
CARDS: Amex, Delta, Diners, MasterCard, Switch, Visa DETAILS: 45 seats. Private parties: 30 main room. Vegetarian meals. Children's helpings. No smoking in dining room. Music (£5)

⚟✳ *indicates that smoking is either banned altogether or that a dining-room is maintained for non-smokers. The symbol does not apply to restaurants that simply have no-smoking areas.*

ROMALDKIRK   Co Durham   map 10

▲ *Rose & Crown* ⁵⋇

Romaldkirk DL12 9EB
TEL: (01833) 650213   FAX: (01833) 650828
EMAIL: hotel@rose-and-crown.co.uk   COOKING 2
on B6277, 6m NW of Barnard Castle   COST £20–£39

As a base for walking, this Teesdale village inn is a comfortable, reasonably
priced place to stay, offering bar meals of baked halibut, roast belly pork, or
steak and kidney pie, as well as four-course set-price dinners. Prime materials
include game from local shoots, and lamb from Teesdale Fell, perhaps served
innovatively with wild mushroom and potato broth and black pudding crostini.
Dishes are 'well-balanced and interesting', presentation 'pleasingly unpretentious'. A meal that begins with pork and rabbit terrine with apple aïoli might
finish with crème caramel and poached apricots. A wide-ranging list of wines at
fair prices includes over two dozen half-bottles, and eight by the glass. House
Chilean is £9.50.

CHEFS: Christopher Davy and Dawn Stephenson   PROPRIETORS: Christopher and Alison Davy
OPEN: Sun L 12 to 1.30, Mon to Sat D 7.30 to 9   CLOSED: Christmas and 31 Dec eve   MEALS: Set
L £13.50, Set D £25. Bar L and D available all week   SERVICE: not inc, card slips closed   CARDS:
MasterCard, Switch, Visa   DETAILS: 24 seats. 24 seats outside. Private parties: 30 main room.
Car park. No smoking in dining room. No music   ACCOMMODATION: 12 rooms, all with
bath/shower. TV. Phone. B&B £62 to £98. Rooms for disabled (*The Which? Hotel Guide*)   £5

ROMSEY   Hampshire   map 2

Old Manor House ▮

21 Palmerston Street, Romsey SO51 8GF   COOKING 6
TEL: (01794) 517353   COST £34–£52

In 2000 the Bregolis chalk up twenty years at this brick and timber house in the
centre of Romsey, where the small lounge has been enlarged at the expense of a
dining room which now has only six tables. Two decades of gutsy and often
uncompromising Italian cooking have shown Mauro Bregoli to be something of
a pig supremo, specifically a man who makes salami and other cured pork
products as others might knock up a bowl of custard or a pastry case. The beauty
of Italy is that this sort of thing is common, the sadness of England is that it is
rare, all the more reason to celebrate the milestone with a plate of coppa on a bed
of winter salad, or equally home-made cotechino sausage with lentils.

Although some items appear familiar – Tuscan bean soup, boned and stuffed
porchetta, or baked aubergine with Parma ham and mozzarella – this is about as
far from a high street Italian trattoria as you can get. Wild mushrooms now seem
to be everywhere, but this kitchen was using them with a passion long before
most, another sign of its resolute Italian identity: they might appear (collected
from the New Forest) with chicken breast or in a creamy sauce with pasta.
Typical of puddings are classic zuppa inglese or zabaglione with strawberries.
Service has been the only weak link, but the wine list continues to be the

438

linchpin. Given the cuisine, it would seem churlish not to pick one of the many starry Italians, but if mature, top-class claret or venerable Burgundy (white or red) is a must, then you won't be disappointed. Naturally, such rare and prestigious bins come at a price, but there is also a reasonable choice under £20, starting with Chilean Sauvignon Blanc and Merlot at £11.50 each.

CHEF: Mauro Bregoli   PROPRIETORS: Mr and Mrs Mauro Bregoli   OPEN: Tue to Sun L 12 to 2, Tue to Sat D 7 to 9.30   MEALS: alc (main courses £14.50 to £17.50)   SERVICE: not inc, card slips closed   CARDS: Amex, Delta, Diners, MasterCard, Switch, Visa   DETAILS: 20 seats. Private parties: 20 main room. Car park. No cigars/pipes in dining room. No music

---

ROSS-ON-WYE Herefordshire   map 5

Le Faisan Doré ▮ ⅍✖

52 Edde Cross Street, Ross-on-Wye HR9 7BZ   COOKING 3
TEL: (01989) 565751   COST £34–£50

Apart from Eileen Brunnarius herself, it is all change at what used to be Pheasants. The colour scheme is now aubergine and gold, white tablecloths have gone, bare tables are in. The aim is a more relaxed atmosphere and format. In place of the fixed-price meal, a carte now deals in a wide-ranging mix of dishes from chicken liver terrine, via sautéed squid with red peppers and linguine, to braised salt-cured Trelough duck with buttered cabbage. Greater flexibility is apparent in that some dishes can be taken as either first or main courses. The *Guide* had no feedback on the new style before going to press, but since the chef's approach to global country cooking appears not to have altered significantly, and since she is still doing the cooking, standards look set to continue. Reports, naturally, are welcome. Whether the new arrangement will put paid to the long waits that have befallen a couple of reporters remains to be seen, but if not, the time will be well spent enjoying the continuing delights of the wine list. Claret buffs will search in vain, but other oenophiles will find much that impresses and intrigues. Bottles are helpfully arranged by style then grape variety and include many below £20, while a commendable number of wines by the glass are suggested as 'starter partners', 'pudding partners' or 'cheese partners'.

CHEF/PROPRIETOR: Eileen Brunnarius   OPEN: Tue to Sat D only 7 to 10   CLOSED: 24 Dec to 4 Jan, 1 to 8 June   MEALS: alc (main courses £13.50 to £16)   SERVICE: not inc   CARDS: Amex, Diners, MasterCard, Switch, Visa   DETAILS: 22 seats. Private parties: 24 main room. Vegetarian meals. Children's helpings. No smoking in dining room. Wheelchair access (not WC). Music (£5)

'The only criticism is why, being a specifically French restaurant, they don't get their menu French proof-read. Surely the local sixth form could oblige.' (On eating in Shropshire)

All details are as accurate as possible at the time of going to press, but chefs and owners often change, and it is wise to check by telephone before making a special journey. Many readers have been disappointed when set-price bargain meals are no longer available. Ask when booking.

ROWDE Wiltshire   map 2

George & Dragon ✦❋

High Street, Rowde SN10 2PN   COOKING 6
TEL: (01380) 723053   FAX: (01380) 724738   COST £18–£46

'What a find!' exclaimed one visitor to this tiny pub in the middle of Wiltshire. While luxuries may be conspicuous by their absence, the cheerful, idiosyncratic décor – much of it wood – is in good taste, and the place certainly pulls in the crowds. That is hardly surprising given that meals are unhurried, and the blackboard menu is deemed 'amazing value'. For over a decade the Withers have been wowing landlocked customers with seafood main courses that might run from Thai fish curry, via steamed skate with salsa verde, to grilled Cornish lobster with herb butter. Straightforward grills are mixed with more enterprising ideas, such as cod in beer batter with chilli soy sauce, all of which appear to work equally well: what impressed one seasoned observer, a supporter of the 'simple as possible' school of fish cookery, was that 'it's possible to do as much with fish as with anything else'.

Starters (or snacks) may be along the same lines – provençale fish soup, salmon fish-cakes – but also provide variety in the shape of goats' cheese and onion marmalade tart, or pheasant risotto. A short list of simple, traditional puddings might include crème brûlée, brown sugar meringues or rhubarb crumble. Obliging and courteous staff are 'outstandingly well informed' about the food and convey the feeling that 'all they want is for you to have a very pleasant evening'. The compact wine list doesn't go out of its way to specialise in whites but does pick up some extremely good bottles, which it offers at reasonable prices, starting with house Vin de Pays d'Oc at £9.50.

CHEFS: Tim Withers, Hannah Seal and Kate Phillips   PROPRIETORS: Tim and Helen Withers
OPEN: Tue to Sat 12 to 2, 7 to 10   CLOSED: 25 Dec to 2 Jan   MEALS: alc (main courses £8 to £16).
Set L £8.50 (2 courses) to £10   SERVICE: not inc, card slips closed   CARDS: Delta, MasterCard,
Switch, Visa   DETAILS: 35 seats. 20 seats outside. Private parties: 12 main room. Car park.
Children's helpings. No smoking in dining room. No music

RYE East Sussex   map 3

Landgate Bistro £

5–6 Landgate, Rye TN31 7LH   COOKING 4
TEL: (01797) 222829   COST £20–£36

Nick Parkin and Toni Ferguson-Lees will have notched up twenty years here in 2000, their continuity a testament to satisfied repeat custom. A generous carte and a short set-price menu cover a range from spicy chickpea fritters with avocado and cucumber salsa, to a thin, crisp leek and pecorino tart with dressed salad leaves. Fish is a strong suit – crunchy-crumbed salmon and salt-cod fish cakes with lemony parsley sauce, or simply grilled Dover sole – and the kitchen also subscribes to the view that there is more to life than simple steaks and chops, making use of lambs' kidneys and sweetbreads, wild rabbit, and slowly cooked leg and 'juicy' breast of partridge with a 'classic' bread sauce. As to vegetables, take advice from staff, since main courses come in different sizes.

Seasonal dishes are part of the appeal, from asparagus risotto in May, to fruity desserts of summer pudding in August and 'tart but luxurious' damson fool in October. Good in-house bread and smooth service (note the net prices) enhance the experience, while around sixty wines accommodate all tastes from conservative to adventurous, sporting some good names at fair prices. Seven house wines (starting at £8.90) also come by the glass.

CHEF: Toni Ferguson-Lees PROPRIETORS: Nick Parkin and Toni Ferguson-Lees OPEN: Tue to Sat D only 7 to 9.30 (10 Sat) CLOSED: 2 weeks Christmas, 1 week summer MEALS: alc (main courses £9 to £12). Set D Tue to Thur £15.90 SERVICE: net prices, card slips closed CARDS: Amex, Delta, Diners, MasterCard, Switch, Visa DETAILS: 30 seats. Children's helpings. No cigars/pipes in dining room. Music (£5)

ST IVES Cornwall   map 1

Alfresco   NEW ENTRY

Harbourside, Wharf Road, St Ives TR26 1LF   COOKING 4
TEL: (01736) 793737   COST £24–£45

St Ives has lost the Pig 'n' Fish since the 1999 *Guide* was published, but Mike Gill's seafood restaurant looks well placed to fill the gap. The name comes into its own in clement weather when the glass frontage opens up to allow an unmediated view of the beach and harbour. Colourful modern art brightens the already light interior, paper tablecloths indicating that the focus is on the quality of what you eat rather than what you eat it off. As befits a place close to the source of the catch, daily blackboard specials are as extensive as the printed menus and may include John Dory with red peppers, crab claws, and scallops with sauce vierge. Crab and mussels go into a Thai-inspired soup with coriander, ginger and enough chilli to give warmth without scalding the palate, and the robust style is also evident in skate with salsa verde, and chargrilled sea bass with pickled fennel. There are meat options too, while puddings might turn up summer fruits and candied orange with mascarpone cream. A list with almost as many red wines as white reflects the gutsiness of many of the dishes, and selections are sound. Four house wines from South Africa and Chile are £9.

CHEF: Grant Nethercott PROPRIETOR: Mike Gill OPEN: all week 12 to 3, 7 to 9.30; reduced opening Oct to Dec and Feb to Apr CLOSED: 5 Jan to 24 Feb MEALS: alc (main courses L £8 to £15.50, D £11 to £17) SERVICE: not inc, card slips closed CARDS: Delta, MasterCard, Switch, Visa DETAILS: 26 seats. 6 seats outside. Private parties: 30 main room. Vegetarian meals. Children's helpings. Wheelchair access (not WC). Music

---

'When I finally was ready to order wine, I asked about one of the house wine selections. The wine waiter replied, "Well, frankly sir, that is the sort of wine you want to chuck down your throat pretty quickly."' (On eating in Cambridgeshire)

ST KEYNE Cornwall	map 1

▲ *Well House* ¶ ⬗

St Keyne PL14 4RN
TEL: (01579) 342001 FAX: (01579) 343891
EMAIL: wellhse@aol.com
on B3254, 3m S of Liskeard; at end of village near   COOKING 5
church follow sign to St Keyne Well   COST £38–£54

A tea planter built Well House at the turn of the century in order to avail himself of the curative waters of St Keyne's Well. It is a grey-stone edifice with gracefully pitched roof, deep in the tranquil Looe Valley, with garden views adding soft-focus charm to a pastel yellow dining room. Despite several changes of chef in recent years, standards seem to fluctuate only slightly, and the format remains a fixed-price menu of up to four courses, with cheese an option after the main. John Lyons has slipped easily into refined country-house mode, and has a penchant for some unusual combinations: pink squab pigeon and langoustine, for example, paired in a starter with shellfish and rocket risotto, or well- timed beef fillet accompanied by half a dozen frogs' legs in a Beaujolais-based sauce.

Main courses typically incorporate an Italian element – red mullet with truffle ravioli, or roast halibut with potato gnocchi – and the style ranges from a substantial starter of cabbage-wrapped foie gras with morteau sausage, to a light main course of turbot fillet with onion tart and wild mushrooms. Stylishly novel presentations continue with desserts of apple crème brûlée with apple sorbet, or a perhaps a deconstructed tiramisù that arrives as four individual items: chocolate-crusted mousse, firmly set coffee cream, vanilla sponge moistened with alcohol, and an almond biscuit. Nick Wainford oversees service, and dispenses knowledgeable advice about the wine list, which, while centred in France, features some astute selections from the New World. Prices are fair at all levels, with Chilean, French and Australian house wines all at £9.95.

CHEF: John Lyons PROPRIETORS: Nick Wainford and Ione Nurdin OPEN: all week 12.15 to 1.30, 7 to 9 MEALS: Set L and D £21.95 (2 courses) to £30.50 SERVICE: not inc, card slips closed CARDS: Amex, Delta, Diners, MasterCard, Switch, Visa DETAILS: 32 seats. 18 seats outside. Private parties: 24 main room. Car park. Vegetarian meals. No children under 8 at D. No cigars/pipes in dining room. Wheelchair access (also WC). No music ACCOMMODATION: 9 rooms, all with bath/shower. TV. Phone. B&B £70 to £160. Swimming pool (*The Which? Hotel Guide*)

⬗ indicates that there has been a change of chef since last year's Guide, and the Editor has judged that the change is of sufficient interest to merit the reader's attention.

Net prices *in the details at the end of an entry indicates that the prices given on a menu and on a bill are inclusive of VAT and service charge, and that this practice is clearly stated on menu and bill.*

ST MARGARET'S AT CLIFFE   Kent

map 3

▲ Wallett's Court ⁵⊁

West Cliffe, St Margaret's at Cliffe CT15 6EW
TEL: (01304) 852424   FAX: (01304) 853430
EMAIL: wallettscourt@compuserve.com
on B2058, off A258 Dover to Deal road, 3m NE of
Dover

| NEW CHEF |
COST £30–£72

This large old farmhouse on the brow of a hill is 'all beams, exposed bricks and white plaster', its enormous barn converted to a health spa. The cooking has traditionally taken a rather elaborate, mainly Anglo-French, line, focusing on local ingredients: from 'garden of England' fruits and veg, to game, to organic beef and pork. After nearly a quarter of a century, Chris Oakley is retiring, leaving newcomer Stephen Harvey in charge. The same style is likely to continue – game consommé with quail's eggs, poached turbot with langoustines, raspberry sablé – and we welcome reports on progress. The mainly French wine list is reasonably priced, with house white £14, red £15.

CHEF: Stephen Harvey   PROPRIETORS: the Oakley family   OPEN: all week 12 to 2, 7 to 9
CLOSED: 31 Dec to 4 Jan   MEALS: alc (main courses £17 to £22.50). Set L £17.50, Set D £27.50
SERVICE: not inc   CARDS: Amex, Delta, Diners, MasterCard, Switch, Visa   DETAILS: 60 seats.
Private parties: 40 main room, 40 private room. Car park. Vegetarian meals. Children's helpings.
No children under 8 after 8pm in dining room. No smoking in dining room. Occasional music
ACCOMMODATION: 16 rooms, all with bath/shower. TV. Phone. B&B £65 to £130. Baby facilities.
Swimming pool   (£5)

ST MARTIN'S   Isles of Scilly

map 1

▲ St Martin's Hotel ⁵⊁

Lower Town, St Martin's TR25 0QW
TEL: (01720) 422092   FAX: (01720) 422298

COOKING 5
COST £38–£45

An intrepid frame of mind is called for to visit St Martin's, since the journey might involve light aircraft, a mini-bus and a ferry. En route it becomes apparent that 'this is perhaps somewhere special', and if the hotel doesn't quite live up to the magical setting, it is none the less comfortable and welcoming. In the dark blue and orange dining room, guests who stay long enough get a turn by the window to enjoy the sea views. Not surprisingly, menus have a fishy feel – crab bisque or roast scallops to start, perhaps turbot, red mullet or John Dory to follow – but meat is by no means neglected.

Menu descriptions are to the point, the cooking quite complex and demanding, yet despite a certain busyness on the plate, flavours are clear and well balanced. A 'first-class' fillet of turbot has come on saffron-braised fennel with two sauces, and a 'fabulous' piece of John Dory has arrived with an assembly of tomato confit, mushroom duxelles, creamed celeriac, bacon stuffed with goats' cheese, and chicken jus, all the different elements 'adding sharpness and richness on demand'. Desserts of red berry tartlet with crème brûlée, and apricot and almond financier, are strong on both technique and presentation. House wine on the predominantly French list is £13.50.

CHEF: Patrick Pierre Tweedy   PROPRIETORS: Peter and Penny Sykes   OPEN: all week D only 12.30 to 2, 7 to 10   CLOSED: Nov to Feb   MEALS: Set D £25. Bar L available   SERVICE: not inc, card slips closed   CARDS: Amex, Delta, Diners, MasterCard, Switch, Visa   DETAILS: 60 seats. Private parties: 100 main room. No children under 12 in dining room. No smoking in dining room. Occasional music   ACCOMMODATION: 30 rooms, all with bath/shower. TV. Phone. D,B&B £85 to £220. Rooms for disabled. Swimming pool (*The Which? Hotel Guide*)

ST MAWES   Cornwall

map 1

▲ *Tresanton Hotel* 🛏

27 Lower Castle Road, St Mawes TR2 5DR
TEL: (01326) 270055   FAX: (01326) 270053

COOKING 5
COST £30–£50

'This must be *the* perfect seaside hotel,' reckoned one visitor, and indeed the set-up meets with universal approval: a waterside location, with St Anthony's lighthouse turned into a logo for everything from napkins to menus, and a fine-weather terrace with table-top heaters. Inside, it is 'well-bred nautical', with light, space, clean lines, bright blue and pale yellow fabrics, and an understanding of the elusive 'cosset factor'.

Seafood – sourced from local fishermen and Newlyn Market – is a strong suit, producing a 'frilly mobcap' of pasta filled with chopped scallop (including coral), served with a cauliflower velouté, and strips of Dover sole in a velvety sauce, with slices of artichoke heart and sprue-sized asparagus. Fussy garnishes are conspicuous by their absence, and 'they can do meat as well as fish', according to one who enjoyed creamy-textured, intensely flavoured parfait of foie gras with Madeira jelly, followed by pink roast loin of tarragon-flavoured Cornish lamb.

Portions are well judged, making desserts a realistic possibility. They range from simple but impressive pistachio and coconut ice creams, to a 'memorable' moulded, seed-speckled, passion fruit mousse. 'Deft, unobtrusive' service is directed by 'friendly but not familiar' management, and the sommelier knows her stuff. She oversees a high-quality list, with prices to match, that starts with a decent selection by the glass. House Italian is £11.

CHEF: Barry Zonfrillo   PROPRIETOR: Olga Polizzi   OPEN: all week 12.30 to 2.30, 7 to 10 CLOSED: 4 Jan to 12 Feb   MEALS: Set L £15 to £20, Set D £24.50 to £30   SERVICE: not inc, card slips closed   CARDS: Amex, Delta, MasterCard, Switch, Visa   DETAILS: 48 seats. 60 seats outside. Private parties: 50 main room, 50 private room. Car park. Children's helpings. Wheelchair access (not WC). Occasional music   ACCOMMODATION: 26 rooms, all with bath/shower. TV. Phone. B&B £127.50 to £250. Baby facilities (*The Which? Hotel Guide*)

Several sharp operators have tried to extort money from restaurateurs on the promise of an entry in a guidebook that has never appeared. The Good Food Guide *makes no charge for inclusion.*

The Guide *office can quickly spot when a restaurateur is encouraging customers to write recommending inclusion. Such reports do not further a restaurant's cause. Please tell us if a restaurateur invites you to write to the* Guide.

SAINT MICHAEL'S ON WYRE Lancashire   map 8

Mallards

Garstang Road, St Michael's on Wyre PR3 0TE   COOKING 1
TEL: (01995) 679661   COST £18–£35

The ground floor of this detached town house has been opened up to make one room, the bar separated from the rest by a screen. Walls are white, or papered in a small floral design, tables are well spaced and the mallard theme predominates, in every shape and size, pot and bronze. An Anglo-French theme runs through the repertoire, producing at inspection a 'beautifully poached' pear stuffed with Stilton and port, served with a lightly curried mayonnaise, and an equally successful pancake of smoked haddock and prawns with a vermouth cream sauce. The range extends from standards of salmon (served plain or with a cream sauce), via fillet steak with a well-judged red wine sauce, to slghtly more exotic Barbary duck with oriental lemon and lime sauce with ginger. Desserts in similar vein run from raspberry crème brûlée to coconut ice cream with banana and toffee sauce. Service is competent but can be leisurely. The wine list plays safe with success and there is a good selection of half-bottles. House wines are £8.95.

CHEF: John Steel   PROPRIETORS: Ann and John Steel   OPEN: Sun L 12 to 2.15, Mon to Sat D 7 to 9 (9.30 Sat)   CLOSED: 1 week Jan,1 week July, 1 week Oct   MEALS: Set L Sun £11.50, Set D £16.50 (2 courses) to £19.95   SERVICE: not inc, card slips closed   CARDS: Delta, MasterCard, Switch, Visa   DETAILS: 24 seats. Private parties: 30 main room. Car park. Children's helpings. Wheelchair access (also WC). Music (£5)

SALE Greater Manchester   map 8

Hanni's £

4 Brooklands Road, Sale M33 3SQ   COOKING 2
TEL/FAX: (0161) 973 6606   COST £23–£40

Cuisine from the eastern Mediterranean is extensively covered and well priced at Hanni's. The popular restaurant occupies a mock-Tudor shopping parade and features maroon décor, gold stars on walls and ceiling, and Middle Eastern music 'burbling away happily in the background'. Dishes range from couscous, kebabs and grills to banquet meals and a host of starters. One reporter recommends the meze, particularly falafel and bean salad, and also vouches for chicken chawourma (in an onion and pepper sauce), and vegetable couscous with its 'chunky pieces of root vegetables and celery'. Desserts include halva and a compote of dried fruits. Service is skilful, and wines from Israel, Lebanon, Turkey and Greece feature on the global list. House wines are £11.50 per litre.

CHEF: Mr Hoonanian   PROPRIETOR: Mohamed Hanni Al-Taraboulsy   OPEN: Mon to Sat 6 to 10.30 (11 Fri and Sat)   CLOSED: 25 and 26 Dec, Good Fri, Easter Mon, last 2 weeks Aug   MEALS: alc (main courses £8.50 to £13.50)   CARDS: Amex, Delta, MasterCard, Switch, Visa   DETAILS: 50 seats. Private parties: 50 main room. Vegetarian meals. Children's helpings. Wheelchair access (not WC). Music. Air-conditioned

445

SANDGATE Kent   map 3

▲ *Sandgate Hotel* ♟ ⁵⨯

Wellington Terrace, The Esplanade,
Sandgate CT20 3DY   COOKING 7
TEL: (01303) 220444   FAX: (01303) 220496   COST £33–£72

After five years this seaside hotel restaurant is 'still as good as ever'. One of the
best places to eat in Kent – and handy for both tunnel and ferry – it has a small but
attractively furnished dining room with flowers, comfortable seating, and a view
of the Channel, even France on a good day. Its fiercely French identity, coupled
with serious cooking, produces food that is as easy to understand as it is to enjoy,
provided you don't mind a few luxuries: 'out-of-this-world' duck foie gras from
Landes, for example, served warm with a pear and kumquat confit. Shellfish
make up most of the other first courses, maybe scallops on truffled potato purée,
or langoustines and artichoke heart in a sauce combining Pineau des Charentes
and peppermint.

Well-sourced materials include Romney Marsh or Highgrove lamb, and local
fish, which gets star billing among main courses, ranging from turbot with a
frothy champagne sauce to a fricassee de petites anguilles ('little hills' if you
believe the menu's translation) with garlic potatoes. Set-price meals are
considered good value, particularly the more expensive version which yields
four courses plus an appetiser and mid-meal sorbet: one reporter's lunch
included a 'perfectly judged' starter of foie gras on shredded duck confit with
Puy lentils, 'impressive' red mullet and John Dory on a bed of celeriac and
fennel, and 'divine' caramel soufflé with a prune and armagnac ice cream.
Cheeses are from Philippe Olivier across the water, or there may be a Valrhona
chocolate dessert with coffee ice cream. Service is professional but sufficiently
relaxed, welcoming and friendly: staff are 'extremely attentive but not suffocat-
ingly so'. If the sight of all the lovely Burgundies, top clarets and fine Rhône
wines on the predominantly French list isn't enough to prime the palate, then
the accompanying tasting notes will certainly set the taste buds tingling in
anticipation. Prices are very fair, starting at £13.50 for house white or red.

CHEF: Samuel Gicqueau   PROPRIETORS: Zara and Samuel Gicqueau   OPEN: Tue to Sun L 12.15
to 1.30, Tue to Sat D 7.15 to 9.30   CLOSED: first week Oct, Jan   MEALS: alc (main courses £16
to £24.50). Set L and D Tue to Fri £20.50, Set L Sat and Sun and D Sat £29.50   SERVICE: not
inc   CARDS: Amex, Delta, Diners, MasterCard, Switch, Visa   DETAILS: 24 seats. Private parties:
26 main room. Car park. Children's helpings. No smoking in dining room. Wheelchair access
(not WC). Music   ACCOMMODATION: 15 rooms, all with bath/shower. TV. Phone. B&B £44 to
£74. Baby facilities (*The Which? Hotel Guide*)

'*For £8 you can have a glass of wine each, sit in the lovely tranquil garden, and stuff down
more nuts more quickly than a hamster with a train to catch.*'
(On eating in the West Country)

The Guide *is totally independent, accepts no free hospitality, and survives on the number
of copies sold each year.*

SAWLEY Lancashire   map 8

▲ *Spread Eagle* ✱✶ £

Sawley BB7 4NH   COOKING 3
TEL: (01200) 441202   FAX: (01200) 441973   COST £16–£37

Steven Doherty is back to cooking full-time at the Punch Bowl (see entry, Crosthwaite), so no longer has to perform a 50-mile dash from one kitchen to another. He has left the Spread Eagle in the capable hands of Greig Barnes, who continues to serve European dishes overlaid with North Country heartiness. The dining room is 'a serious affair', with splendid river views and menus from prestigious restaurants on the walls. Yet there's a pleasant informality about the whole operation, helped along by friendly but unobtrusive service. Those with appetites sharpened by a brisk walk will find plenty to satisfy in the keenly priced set lunches: 'well-flavoured' home-baked ham with lentil sauce, perhaps, or braised shoulder of lamb. Vegetables are 'cooked long enough to soften them without spoiling them'. Puddings designed to insulate against the cold (sticky date and ginger sponge, warm chocolate fudge brownie) are supplemented by real raspberry jelly, and an 'intense' dark and white chocolate terrine. 'It's nice to be offered tisanes without feeling a health freak,' noted one reporter. Argentinian house wine from the short but sensible list is £9.

CHEF: Greig Barnes   PROPRIETORS: Steven and Marjorie Doherty   OPEN: all week 12 to 2, 6 to 9 (6.30 to 9.30 Sat)   CLOSED: 25 Dec, 2 weeks Nov   MEALS: alc (main courses £7.50 to £10.50). Set L Mon to Fri £7.95 (2 courses) to £9.50, Set L Sun £9.25 (2 courses) to £11.95   SERVICE: not inc, card slips closed   CARDS: Amex, MasterCard, Switch, Visa   DETAILS: 60 seats. Private parties: 80 main room, 30 and 80 private rooms. Car park. Vegetarian meals. Children's helpings. No smoking in dining room. Wheelchair access (inc WC). No music ACCOMMODATION: 10 rooms, all with bath/shower. TV. Phone. B&B £37.50 to £60. Rooms for disabled (*The Which? Hotel Guide*)

SAXTON North Yorkshire   map 9

Plough Inn ✱✶

Headwell Lane, Saxton LS24 9PB
TEL: (01937) 557242   FAX: (01937) 557655   COOKING 3
off A162, between Tadcaster and Sherburn in Elmet   COST £20–£36

A friendly, Victorian pub that caters for drinkers and eaters in equal measure, the Plough has a tiny snug with a fire where lunchtime snacks are served, from sandwiches to pork and leek sausage with mash and onion gravy, and a dining room with polished tables and a wide-ranging menu. Europe is the focus of attention – braised lamb shank on Tuscan beans, escalope of veal on spring onion risotto – with potted shrimps and black pudding from closer to home. Fish comes well reported, from 'home done' gravlax to seafood parcel with lobster sauce, while meats (local venison, or duck breast with Chinese vegetables) are cooked 'as requested, pink'. Comforting desserts typically offer dark chocolate tart or crème brûlée, and sixty-odd varied wines achieve a high level of interest at fair prices, mostly under £20.

CHEF: Simon Treanor   PROPRIETORS: Simon and Nicky Treanor   OPEN: Tue to Sun L 12 to 2, Tue to Sat D 6.30 to 9.30   CLOSED: 25 and 26 Dec, 1 to 16 Jan   MEALS: alc Tue to Sat L and D (main courses £10 to £12.50). Set L Sun £13.95. Bar menu Tue to Sat L only   SERVICE: not inc, card slips closed   CARDS: Delta, MasterCard, Switch, Visa   DETAILS: 65 seats. 20 seats outside. Private parties: 70 main room. Car park. Vegetarian meals. Children's helpings. No smoking in dining room. Wheelchair access (also women's WC). Music

---

SCARBOROUGH North Yorkshire   map 9

Lanterna £

33 Queen Street, Scarborough YO11 1HQ   COOKING 3
TEL/FAX: (01723) 363616   COST £24–£38

At a time when many restaurants seem to be clones of each other, and menus bring on bouts of *déjà vu*, it is good to find that individuality still prospers. The Alessios combine an old-style Italian approach – serving chicken four ways, veal five, steak seven – with three more distinctive and endearing practices. First, they make their own pasta, turning out spaghetti carbonara and salmon-filled ravioli, as well as cooking three kinds of risotto. Second, they use 'local' produce, which happens to be seafood: scallops in lemon sauce, or simply grilled turbot, halibut or Dover sole, according to availability. Third, they use seasonal produce, the most exciting of which is white truffle (October to January), shaved for best effect on to pasta or mushroom risotto. It would be churlish not to finish with zabaglione, tiramisù or pannacotta, just as it makes sense to drink one of the thirty well-chosen Italian wines. A friendly atmosphere and good service add to the appeal.

CHEF: Giorgio Alessio   PROPRIETORS: Giorgio and Rachel Alessio   OPEN: Mon to Sat D only 6.30 to 11   CLOSED: 2 weeks end Oct, 25 and 26 Dec, 1 Jan   MEALS: alc (main courses £9.50 to £16)   SERVICE: not inc, card slips closed   CARDS: Delta, MasterCard, Switch, Visa   DETAILS: 30 seats. Private parties: 35 main room. Vegetarian meals. Children's helpings. No children under 2. Wheelchair access (not WC). Music. Air-conditioned

---

SEAFORD East Sussex   map 3

Quincy's ▮ ⅝✳

42 High Street, Seaford BN25 1PL   COOKING 3
TEL: (01323) 895490   COST £36–£43

Dawn and Ian Dowding's pretty restaurant in old Seaford is unpretentious in its fresh, bookish décor, low lighting, and (mostly) attentive, well-timed service. Ian offers seven choices at each stage of his imaginative set meals. Warm haddock and quail's eggs may come with new potatoes and aïoli or in a kedgeree, while soup may be beetroot, accompanied by little pastries. Indeed, pastry is a major theme: filo encloses feta cheese and tomatoes, and puff contains devilled crab (both starters), while smoked cheese pastry might accompany mushroom cassoulet as a main course. Osso buco, the day's fish, or perhaps roast breast of duck with raisin and Madeira sauce come with interesting vegetables, such as mashed parsnip cakes with cumin and parsley. Ice cream is another talent, so you may be lured by a honey one to complement nectarines in

Amaretto sauce, or a white chocolate one for chocolate soufflé. The wine list is similarly attractive, with plenty of half-bottles, as well as quietly enthusiastic choices under £15. Most come from France, but Quincy's also champions Breaky Bottom wines from just down the road. House French is £9.75, Chilean £10.25.

CHEF: Ian Dowding   PROPRIETORS: Dawn and Ian Dowding   OPEN: Sun L 12 to 2, Tue to Sat D 7 to 10   CLOSED: first week Jan   MEALS: Set L and D £21 (2 courses) to £25.50   SERVICE: not inc   CARDS: Amex, Diners, MasterCard, Visa   DETAILS: 30 seats. Private parties: 30 main room. Vegetarian meals. Children's helpings. No smoking in dining room. Music

---

SEATON BURN Tyne & Wear   map 10

▲ Horton Grange ⚡✱

Seaton Burn NE13 6BU
TEL: (01661) 860686   FAX: (01661) 860308
EMAIL: andrew@horton-grange.co.uk
from A1 take A19 exit; at roundabout take first exit;
after 1m turn left, signposted to Brenkley and   COOKING 6
Dinnington; hotel 2m on right   COST £44–£52

The conservatory dining room – with white walls, modern paintings, trickling water and smartly set tables overlooking a Japanese garden – has proved a hit. 'Conservatories can be a bit of a bore,' wrote one visitor, 'but this is a really stylish, well-designed modern building, which is such a contrast to the stone-built house that it ends up working magnificently.' It is the setting for ambitious-sounding four-course dinners (plus appetisers and coffee) in modern British mould, which makes a virtue of sweet fruity accompaniments such as Parma ham with poached pear and plums in a passion fruit and citrus coulis, or honey-roast breast of duck with mango and an orange liqueur sauce.

If there sounds to be a lot going on in some of the dishes, the food itself, much to its credit, does not appear fussy. Priorities are as they should be, resulting, for example, in a first course of pink, gamey pigeon served with a smooth quenelle of garlic and spring onion mash, before a 'superior' gazpacho soup with intense tomato and garlic flavour, refreshing acidity, and proper texture. Main courses have produced marinated medallions of venison with forest mushrooms and Madeira sauce, and crisply herb-crusted halibut fillet, 'moist within', served with a restrained cream and butter chive sauce. Well-kept cheeses, delivered to table at room temperature, offer a viable alternative to baked American cheesecake or caramel cream custard with sweet biscuits. Service is 'pleasant and knowledgeable', and nearly all the wines on the short, well-annotated list are available by the glass; five 'house selections' are £10.90 a bottle, £2.50 a glass.

CHEF: Steven Martin   PROPRIETORS: Andrew and Sue Shilton   OPEN: Mon to Sat D only 7 to 8.30   CLOSED: Christmas and New Year   MEALS: Set D £34   SERVICE: not inc, card slips closed   CARDS: Amex, Delta, MasterCard, Switch, Visa   DETAILS: 50 seats. Private parties: 70 main room. Car park. No smoking in dining room. Wheelchair access (also WC). Music ACCOMMODATION: 9 rooms, all with bath/shower. TV. Phone. B&B £59 to £90. Rooms for disabled. Fishing   (£5)

SHAFTESBURY Dorset   map 2

La Fleur de Lys ▼

25 Salisbury Street, Shaftesbury SP7 8EL	COOKING **4**
TEL: (01747) 853717	COST £31–£52

The wood-panelled dining room, overlooking a courtyard, occupies a converted loft and is reached along a passageway and up a flight of stairs. Down below, the busy kitchen services a long carte (with a required 'minimum spend' of £22), plus a set-price dinner menu. The cooking has a traditional country slant to it, taking in pan-fried pork tenderloin with an apple and cranberry chutney, veal sweetbreads on celeriac purée with tarragon sauce, and beef fillet with Stilton and port sauce. This being Dorset, albeit the northern reaches, seafood makes a significant appearance. Scallops, langoustines and prawns are assembled into a tartlet, and grilled Dover sole fillets have been served with a lemon butter sauce.

Desserts span a range from simple strawberries and raspberries with clotted cream, to a chocolate box filled with prune and Muscat liqueur ice cream, served with marinated prunes and a sabayon sauce. The wine list opens with a stylish selection from France before moving on to cover most of the key points on the wine compass. Quality is high and mark-ups comparatively low. House red and white from South Africa are £11, from France £11.50.

CHEFS: D. Shepherd and M. Preston   PROPRIETORS: D.M. Griffin, D. Shepherd and M. Preston   OPEN: Tue to Sun L 12 to 2.30, Mon to Sat D 7 to 10 (9.30 Mon to Wed)   CLOSED: Mon D Jan to Mar, 2 weeks Jan   MEALS: alc (main courses L £11.50 to £13, D £14.50 to £18.50). Set D £19.50 (2 courses; Mon to Thur only) to £23.50   SERVICE: not inc   CARDS: Amex, Delta, Diners, MasterCard, Switch, Visa   DETAILS: 40 seats. Private parties: 40 main room. Vegetarian meals. Children's helpings. No smoking before 10pm at D. Occasional music   £5

SHEFFIELD South Yorkshire   map 9

Milano   NEW ENTRY

Archer Road, Millhouses, Sheffield S8 0LA	COOKING **3**
TEL: (0114) 235 3080 FAX: (0114) 235 3010	COST £30–£62

Despite its name, this fresh, airy, converted police station done out in pastel shades is not an Italian restaurant. It takes inspiration from a wide variety of sources, turning out nettle gnocchi, tuna sashimi, and roast monkfish with crab and okra gumbo tart. Materials are particularly impressive, judging by an inspector's 'brilliantly fresh', lightly cooked scallops, and 'superb-quality' pink loin of lamb. Spicing can be appealing too, producing an interesting combination of flavours in Moroccan fish couscous with chermoula dressing, and careful cooking has yielded other first-rate fish, from crisp-skinned John Dory on crushed Jersey Royals, to firm steamed sea bass in a bouillabaisse sauce.

On the downside, saucing could be improved, and dinner prices appear rather out of line, but lunch offers less expensive 'small plates' and 'big plates' of duck confit with peppered pineapple vinaigrette, lamb patties flavoured with coriander and cumin, and salt-cod and chickpea casserole. Desserts have included chocolate tart with Turkish delight ice cream, and lime and ginger brûlée with cumin shortbread. Close on 50 wines are arranged by style, starting with house Vin de Pays des Côtes du Tarn at £9.25.

CHEF: Jason Fretwell   PROPRIETORS: Bohan & Brady Partnership   OPEN: all week L 12 to 2.30 (3.30 Sun), Mon to Sat D 6.30 to 10   MEALS: alc (main courses L £7.50 to £11, D £11 to £19). Set D Mon to Thur £19.95. Tapas menu Mon to Sat 5 to 7   SERVICE: not inc   CARDS: Delta, Diners, MasterCard, Switch, Visa   DETAILS: 56 seats. 50 seats outside. Private parties: 25 main room. Car park. Vegetarian meals. Wheelchair access (also WC). Music. Air-conditioned

Rafters

220 Oakbrook Road, Nether Green, Sheffield S11 7ED   COOKING 4
TEL/FAX: (0114) 230 4819   COST £34–£43

An unobtrusive dark green door and a few steps announce the presence of the Bosworths' unexpectedly spacious restaurant in an appealing residential sector of Sheffield. Italian designer lights, and a terracotta and pale yellow colour scheme, lend a bit of class, and the format is a simple one: fixed-price menus, dinners only. There is no shortage of imagination in the kitchen, and few contemporary ingredients that don't find a home somewhere. A pizza starter has come topped with duck confit, Brie and plum sauce, for example, while loin of lamb has been accompanied by a burger of pork and apple, black pudding and a calvados sauce. More straightforward dishes are well rendered too – chargrilled asparagus with shaved Parmesan, a poached egg and pesto – and accurate timing has made a success of olive-crusted cod in a well-judged creamy, herby broth strewn with broad beans. Presentation is carefully attended to throughout, and the generally earthy and hearty style does not preclude a delicate touch when required: in poached pear with champagne jelly and cinnamon ice cream, for instance, which rounded off a satisfying inspection meal. Incidentals, including bread and petits fours, have got the thumbs up, and a modestly serviceable wine list starts with house French at £8.90.

CHEFS/PROPRIETORS: Wayne and Jamie Bosworth   OPEN: Mon and Wed to Sat D only 7 to 10 CLOSED: bank hols, first 2 weeks Aug   MEALS: Set D £23.95   SERVICE: not inc   CARD: Amex DETAILS: 44 seats. Private parties: 44 main room. Vegetarian meals. Children's helpings. No children under 4. Music

Smith's of Sheffield ⁵✸

34 Sandygate Road, Sheffield S10 5RY   COOKING 5
TEL: (0114) 266 6096   COST £26–£42

Canvas adorns the walls and ceiling of this five-year-old restaurant, occupying a converted shop in a suburban terrace. Some combinations on the carte may appear 'trendy', others 'interesting' or even 'American', indicating that Richard Smith seems to enjoy the challenge of discovering new partnerships: perhaps sesame-crusted sea bream with spring onion potato purée, chilli syrup, and an oriental salsa verde is one of them. More familiar ideas typically form the backbone, however, from baked tomato tart with mozzarella, tapénade and pesto, to grilled Aberdeen Angus fillet with roast winter root vegetables and red wine sauce. 'We are currently introducing the use of rare and traditional breeds of meat on to our menus', writes Richard Smith, who already makes use of

451

organic vegetables. Not all reporters are equally pleased with the results (timing and temperatures can be variable, for example) but careful sourcing pays dividends in terms of flavour. A traditional selection of desserts might include brioche bread-and-butter pudding, or lemon meringue pie. Variety is a welcome characteristic of the wine list, which is also sympathetically priced. French house wine is £9.50, but why not try Willi Opitz's McLaren Welschriesling Kabinett 1995 from Austria (at a grand prix of £25.75), for a formula wine with a difference?

CHEF: Richard Smith   PROPRIETORS: Richard and Victoria Smith, and Sallie Tetchner   OPEN: Tue to Sat D only 6.30 to 10   CLOSED: 25 Dec   MEALS: alc (main courses £14.50). Set D Tue to Fri £15.50 (2 courses) to £18.50   SERVICE: not inc   CARDS: Amex, Delta, MasterCard, Switch, Visa   DETAILS: 44 seats. Private parties: 50 main room, 12 private room. Children's helpings. No smoking in dining room. Wheelchair access (not WC). Music   £5

SHELF West Yorkshire   map 8

Bentley's ⁵⅟✻ £

12 Wade House Road, Shelf HX3 7PB	COOKING 3
TEL: (01274) 690992 FAX: (01274) 690011	COST £16–£39

Shelf is an industrial village between Bradford and Halifax, and Pam and Paul Bentley's English bistro was once a two up, two downer, still with its flagstone floors and open fire, and decorated with grandparental furniture and pictures. The set-price lunch (also available in the upstairs bar) appeals to visitors, as does the Yorkshire brand of friendly service, although the popularity of the place may at times make a meal seem rushed. Starters picked out for praise include generous goujons of haddock and salmon in crisp batter, and 'terrific' crab cakes; many are salady, such as chicken and smoked duck with a sesame seed dressing. From the eight or so main courses you might choose flash-fried halibut with tomato and red pepper sauce and fettucine, or braised lamb shank with root vegetables and dumplings. A good way to finish might be rhubarb and ginger tiramisù with Belgian chocolate, or Grandma Bentley's malt loaf with Cheddar and Stilton. Breads, pastas, ice creams and petits fours are all Bentley-made. Three dozen affordable wines are displayed on an approachable card with unaffected notes; two of each colour come by the glass or 'soup bowl' and from £9.50 by the bottle.

CHEFS: Paul Bentley and Anthony Bickers   PROPRIETORS: Paul and Pam Bentley   OPEN: Tue to Fri L 12 to 2, Tue to Sat D 6.30 to 9.30   CLOSED: 24 to 30 Dec   MEALS: alc (main courses £9 to £13). Set L £6.75 (2 courses) to £7.95   SERVICE: not inc, card slips closed   CARDS: Delta, MasterCard, Switch, Visa   DETAILS: 48 seats. Private parties: 24 main room. Vegetarian meals. Children's helpings. No smoking in dining room. Music   £5

'The lurid orange prawns, glowing like some left-over special effect from a Dr Who *episode, is a sight I won't forget in a hurry.'* (On eating in London)

SHEPTON MALLET   Somerset   map 2

Blostin's ✦ £

29 Waterloo Road, Shepton Mallet BA4 5HH   COOKING 2
TEL/FAX: (01749) 343648   COST £22–£37

Blostin's remains, in the view of one reporter, pretty much what it has always
been: an unpretentious, honest restaurant with rustic, cottagey décor, serving
seriously prepared Anglo-French food at reasonable prices. Local materials play
an increasing role – 'we have found this is what people want', writes Nick Reed –
from Cheddar strawberries and asparagus to, naturally enough, cheese. The
country style of cooking embraces salmon fish cakes with watercress sauce, loin
of venison with wild mushrooms and game sauce, and vegetarian options such
as grilled Somerset goats' cheese with brioche and salad. Desserts might include
hot chocolate sponge, or caramelised pears with meringue and vanilla ice cream.
Service is 'shyly pleasant', and around forty varietally arranged wines are fairly
priced, starting with house French at £8.95.

CHEF: Nick Reed   PROPRIETORS: Nick and Lynne Reed   OPEN: Tue to Sat D only 7 to 9.30 (10
Sat)   CLOSED: 2 weeks Jan, 2 weeks Aug   MEALS: alc (main courses £11 to £13). Set D £13.95
(2 courses) to £15.95   SERVICE: not inc, card slips closed   CARDS: Delta, MasterCard, Switch,
Visa   DETAILS: 50 seats. Private parties: 32 main room, 18 private room. Vegetarian meals.
Children's helpings. No smoking in dining room. Wheelchair access (not WC). Occasional
music £5

▲ Bowlish House ▮ ✦

Wells Road, Shepton Mallet BA4 5JD
TEL/FAX: (01749) 342022   COOKING 4
on A371 to Wells, ¼m from town centre   COST £23–£39

The fabric may be looking forward eagerly to its next refurbishment at this pale
Georgian mansion on the edge of town, but what comes out of Linda Morley's
kitchen is 'a great deal bolder and better balanced than much of the food served
up in slicker establishments'. Her three-course meals (five choices per course)
are not complex, and contain few surprises – smoked salmon mousse with
watercress and avocado cream, or Cheddar cheese and chive soufflé to begin –
but that does not mean they are lacking in refinement.
    Ingredients are well chosen and the cooking sure-footed, taking in upbeat
main courses of plump, rosy slices of lamb with a thin covering of crispy fat,
served with a garlic-flavoured butter-bean purée; and a fine piece of brill, given a
jaunty provençale feel with cherry tomatoes, red pepper and black olive.
Desserts range from a 'substantial but not heavy' sticky toffee pudding, to
passion fruit semifreddo – with delicate texture and tart flavour – served with
raspberry coulis. Bob Morley runs front-of-house affably and enthusiastically,
and his wine list demonstrates an unerring eye for good producers, and a sense of
fair play when it comes to prices. Classic and modern bins from the major regions
are introduced without pretension, dessert wines and half-bottles are taken
seriously, and nine house wines (including two from England) are all £9.95 a
bottle, £1.95 a glass.

CHEF: Linda Morley   PROPRIETORS: Bob and Linda Morley   OPEN: L first Sun in month 1.30 to 2, all week D 7 to 9   CLOSED: 1 week spring, 1 week autumn   MEALS: Set L Sun £14.50, Set D £22.50   SERVICE: not inc, card slips closed   CARDS: Amex, Delta, MasterCard, Switch, Visa   DETAILS: 24 seats. Private parties: 40 main room. Car park. Vegetarian meals. No smoking in dining room. Occasional music   ACCOMMODATION: 3 rooms. TV. B&B £48 to £58 (*The Which? Hotel Guide*)

▲ *Charlton House, Mulberry Restaurant* ⁵⚹

Charlton Road, Shepton Mallet BA4 4PR
TEL: (01749) 342008   FAX: (01749) 346362   COOKING 5
EMAIL: reservations-charltonhouse@btinternet.com   COST £26–£83

'A visual feast' awaits at this highly rated country house, which is an elaborate shop window for the Mulberry brand of 'fabrics, furnishings and tableware', all set out with impressive flair and attention to detail. The food has a contemporary European feel to it, pairing Cornish red mullet with baby artichoke in a sauce vierge, and making a croustade of duck confit using birds from a local farm, although it seems pernickety to charge supplements for some dishes (£5 for a salad of marinated tuna, crab and papaya, for example, or £6 for veal sweetbreads) given the already hefty price of dinner. Supplements appear against a number of items at lunch too, which offers a choice of around five dishes at each course: perhaps saffron risotto with scallops to start, then braised shank of lamb with rosemary and mustard, followed by redcurrant crème brûlée.

Somerset cheeses make an appearance, and workmanship extends to desserts of poached William pear on an almond sablé tart, and an assiette of banana. Those who intend to stay a few days may like to note that the menu is relatively unchanging. Service is 'young, intelligent, friendly and impeccably dressed', and an enterprising array of wines is grouped by style, though there are not many options under £20. House Pinot Gris from South Africa is £14, Syrah from Argentina £14.50.

CHEF: Adam Fellows   PROPRIETORS: Mr and Mrs Roger Saul   OPEN: all week 12.30 to 2.30, 7.30 to 9.30 (10 Sat)   MEALS: Set L £10 (2 courses) to £14.50, Set D £35 to £43   SERVICE: not inc   CARDS: Amex, Delta, Diners, MasterCard, Switch, Visa   DETAILS: 60 seats. 20 seats outside. Private parties: 84 main room, 24 to 34 private rooms. Car park. Vegetarian meals. Children's helpings. No smoking in dining room. Wheelchair access (also WC). Music   ACCOMMODATION: 16 rooms, all with bath/shower. TV. Phone. B&B £90 to £300. Baby facilities. Swimming pool. Fishing (*The Which? Hotel Guide*)

SHERE Surrey   map 3

Kinghams ⁵⚹

Gomshall Lane, Shere GU5 9HE
TEL: (01483) 202168   COOKING 4
just off A25 Dorking to Guildford road   COST £29–£48

Set in a picturesque village in a wealthy commuter belt, with a 'chocolate box' exterior, Kinghams feels like a converted country pub, with low ceilings, dark beams, 'characterful fireplaces', small rooms and close-together tables. Despite some mainstream materials (lamb cutlets, chicken breast, fillet of salmon), Paul

Baker still finds room on his menus – daily fish offerings are listed on a board – for variety in the shape of spider crab (with Newburg sauce), wild rabbit (in a terrine), and a salady starter incorporating slices of ostrich meat with small heaps of juniper berries. He has a deft touch and an eye for some unusual combinations – a rösti-type fish cake surrounded by little piles of smoked fish (eel, trout and salmon) with dollops of horseradish – but also successfully turns out more traditional marinated saddle of venison with red cabbage and a gamey red wine sauce. Desserts likewise range from simple chocolate pudding with vanilla sauce, to an inventive but effective combination of pineapple treacle tart with clotted cream and strawberries. Those with an eye to value should seize on the set-price meals. Service has veered from 'inexperienced' on one occasion to 'bright and attentive' on another, and the wine list is concise but far-reaching, starting with Chilean and French house wines at £10.95.

CHEF/PROPRIETOR: Paul Baker   OPEN: Tue to Sun L 12 to 2.30, Tue to Sat D 7 to 9   CLOSED: 25 Dec to 2 Jan   MEALS: alc (main courses £10 to £15). Set L £10.95 (2 courses), Set D Tue to Thur £12.50 (2 courses)   SERVICE: not inc   CARDS: Amex, Delta, Diners, MasterCard, Switch, Visa DETAILS: 46 seats. 20 seats outside. Private parties: 30 main room, 18 and 30 private rooms. Car park. Vegetarian meals. Children's helpings. No smoking in dining room. Wheelchair access (not WC). Occasional music   £5

SHINFIELD Berkshire   map 2

L'Ortolan

The Old Vicarage, Church Lane, Shinfield RG2 9BY
TEL: (0118) 988 3783   FAX: (0118) 988 5391
EMAIL: l'ortolan@shinfields.freeserve.co.uk   COOKING 8
off A33, S of M4 junction 11   COST £46–£135

Up a winding country lane, with a garden, fountain, and tables outside for summer drinking, the extended brick vicarage sports a succession of rooms: a compact but comfortable bar, a dining room with dragged apricot and yellow walls, and two conservatories, one with a barrelled ceiling for eating, another with stuffed sofas for coffee. Arrive in time to deliberate over the menus, for there is a lot to take in, not least the 'seriously expensive' prices: à la carte starters are in the region of £25 to £30, and there is a supplement of £7 for cheese on the £28 lunch menu, which begins to make the £160-for-two 'menu gourmand' (five-courses plus extras) sound reasonable after all.

But then just look at the workmanship involved in servicing a carte of around twenty elaborate savoury dishes, where luxury materials are marshalled on stage like so many extras in a play with a complex plot. Ravioli of salmon is topped with scallop mousseline and given a smoked chicken jus; a three-way oyster starter includes beignet (with sweet-and-sour sauce), a flan (with cucumber and butter sauce) and fresh (with caviare). This is an extreme form of cooking that takes a disciplined brigade and focused director to make it as successful as it is. Timing varies within a whisker either side of ideal, but not enough to spoil enjoyment: at one meal, properly undercooked salmon wrapped in bacon with a potato crust, followed by 'red, rather than pink as requested' noisettes of lamb with a herb crust in a light meat jus.

Desserts are no less industrious in composition and presentation: light apple soufflé encased in apple skin, surrounded by plum sauce and fresh fruits in syrup, or runny chocolate fondant, with raisins, white chocolate ice cream and sauce, and a biscuit trellis. Appetisers are of a high order, and it is a tribute to both their substance and appeal that 'my wife could not face a starter after the nibbles'. Meals are served by a 'veritable army of waiters and sommeliers', the latter overseeing a dauntingly aristocratic list with which there is not a thing wrong except for its high prices. The sommelier's selection of around a dozen starts at £20.

CHEF: John Burton-Race   PROPRIETOR: Burton-Race Restaurants plc   OPEN: Tue to Sun L 12 to 2.30, Tue to Sat D 7 to 10   MEALS: alc (main courses £33 to £38). Set L £28 to £44, Set D Tue to Fri £44, menu gourmand D £160 for 2   SERVICE: not inc, card slips closed   CARDS: Amex, Delta, Diners, MasterCard, Switch, Visa   DETAILS: 60 seats. Private parties: 30 main room. Car park. Vegetarian meals. Children's helpings. Wheelchair access (also WC). No music   £5

SHIPHAM Somerset   map 2

▲ *Daneswood House* £✳

Cuck Hill, Shipham BS25 1RD
TEL: (01934) 843145   FAX: (01934) 843824
S of Bristol off A38 towards Cheddar; hotel is on left as   COOKING 2
you leave the village   COST £25–£49

On the western edge of the Mendips, well sited at the top of a drive, with a conservatory extension and trees around, this turn-of-the-century 'bourgeois' country-house hotel serves set-price meals in busy modern style. Cajun-spiced sea bass samosas come with chilli and mango jam, for example, and 'scorched' breast of chicken is served with asparagus risotto and a mushroom cappuccino sauce. Lunch tends to be less exotic, eliciting praise for lemon fish cakes with red onions and capers, flavourful game terrine, and roast beef with Yorkshire pudding. Baked rhubarb and lemon tart is safely paired with stem ginger ice cream, and 'Dorchester-style' bread-and-butter pudding has been 'feather light and delectable' for one reporter, 'too sickly sweet' for another. The atmosphere is one of formal service and 'hushed tones', and a very traditional wine list starts with a dozen or so house recommendations between £10 and £16.

CHEFS: Julian Prosser and Heather Matthews   PROPRIETORS: David and Elise Hodges   OPEN: all week 12.15 to 1.45, 7 to 9.30 (8 Sun)   CLOSED: 26 Dec to 4 Jan   MEALS: Set L Mon to Sat £15.95 to £29.95, Set L Sun £13.95 (2 courses) to £17.95, Set D £23.95 to £29.95   SERVICE: not inc, card slips closed   CARDS: Amex, Delta, Diners, MasterCard, Switch, Visa   DETAILS: 60 seats. Private parties: 36 main room, 10 to 36 private rooms. Car park. Vegetarian meals. Children's helpings. No smoking in dining room. Wheelchair access (also WC). Occasional music   ACCOMMODATION: 12 rooms, all with bath/shower. TV. Phone. B&B £65 to £125. Baby facilities   £5

'Crispy quail with tamarind sauce seemed to be either two small birds or one with extra legs.' (On eating in London)

SHREWSBURY Shropshire   map 5

Sol 💥

82 Wyle Cop, Shrewsbury SY1 1UT	COOKING 5
TEL: (01743) 340560 FAX: (01743) 340552	COST £29–£49

Despite its name and Mexican-inspired colour scheme – either 'brash', or like 'being suddenly transported to a warmer clime', according to taste – this is not a Central American restaurant. Instead, a backbone of fine English produce is subjected to contemporary global treatment, yielding Thai-spiced smoked haddock fish cake, Cornish brill with ravioli of Tuscan vegetables, and chargrilled local venison with balsamic jus.

John Williams's cooking is more sophisticated than the casual-looking interior might imply. Clever garnishes provide what some reporters consider to be unnecessary elaboration, but there's plenty of substance too. Duck confit has been well received, as have seared gravad lax with tomato tian and horseradish cream, and guinea fowl with wild mushroom butter sauce. Puddings usually include a hot soufflé, such as plum or pineapple; or try chocolate fondant served with mint or pistachio ice cream. Value is considered good for such accomplished cooking, a sentiment that extends to a well-rounded wine list, which starts with house wines at £9.95.

CHEF: John Williams   PROPRIETORS: John and Debbie Williams, Clare Cadwallader and Simon Cousins   OPEN: Tue to Sat 12 to 1.45, 7 to 9.30   CLOSED: 1 week winter, 1 week summer   MEALS: alc L (main courses £11.50). Set L £19.50, Set D £27.50 to £32   SERVICE: not inc, card slips closed   CARDS: Amex, Delta, MasterCard, Switch, Visa   DETAILS: 45 seats. Private parties: 20 main room, 20 private room. Vegetarian meals. No smoking in dining room. Wheelchair access (not WC). Music

SHURDINGTON Gloucestershire   map 2

▲ The Greenway 🍷 💥

Shurdington GL51 5UG	
TEL: (01242) 862352 FAX: (01242) 862780	COOKING 3
on A46, 2½m S of Cheltenham	COST £41–£70

'You move into a different world of peace and tranquillity, luxury and comfort,' reckoned one visitor to this well-proportioned sixteenth-century manor house built of Cotswold stone. Elegant, spacious, uncluttered, it nevertheless remains low key – 'no one is overwhelmed by the style of the place' – and staff put visitors at ease. Meals are unhurried, and the kitchen's sourcing of materials is taken seriously. Lamb is English or Welsh, beef Scottish (perhaps served with a foie gras sausage), and seafood generally Cornish: lobster salad, perhaps, or tortellini of crab. Peter Fairclough aims for an elaborate style, which may explain why some dishes (quail stuffed with wild mushrooms, or roast cannon of lamb with sarladaise potatoes) remain more or less unchanged.

There is variety and balance to the menus, however, vegetables are organic, and local resources include game and Stinking Bishop cheese. It is difficult, though, to resist finishing with hot banana soufflé and lavender ice cream, or vanilla parfait with chocolate and orange ravioli. The wine list opens with a leisurely stroll through the classic regions of France, nips across to Germany for some fine Rieslings, then takes a quick jaunt round the rest of the world. Vintage ports remain a high point (allow time for decanting) and house wines are still a lowly £13.50.

CHEF: Peter Fairclough   PROPRIETORS: David and Valerie White   OPEN: Sun to Fri L 12.30 to 2, all week D 7.30 (7 Sat) to 9.30   CLOSED: L bank hols   MEALS: alc D (main courses £14 to £21.50). Set L £5.50 (1 course) to £21.50, Set D £27.50 to £35   SERVICE: not inc, card slips closed   CARDS: Amex, Diners, MasterCard, Switch, Visa   DETAILS: 55 seats. 16 seats outside. Private parties: 64 main room, 14 and 24 private rooms. Car park. Vegetarian meals. Children's helpings. No children under 7 in dining room. No smoking in dining room. Wheelchair access (also women's WC). Music   ACCOMMODATION: 19 rooms, all with bath/shower. TV. Phone. B&B £95 to £240. Rooms for disabled. No children under 7 in accommodation (*The Which? Hotel Guide*)   £5

SKIPTON North Yorkshire   map 8

Le Caveau ✸ £   NEW ENTRY

86 High Street, Skipton BD23 1JJ	COOKING 2
TEL/FAX: (01756) 794274	COST £20–£39

Where felons were once incarcerated, guests now eat untroubled at well-spaced tables beneath the vaulted stone barrel ceiling of this bare-walled cellar. Lunch and the mid-week set dinner represent sound value, and dishes on the printed carte, plus a half-dozen blackboard specials, also come in at fair prices. Interesting English/French starters that don't venture too far out on a limb include goats'-cheese tartlet, and smoked haddock rarebit, while soup might be parsnip and orange. To follow, rack of lamb, its skin crisp from a minty breadcrumb coating, has arrived on mashed potato stirred through with crunchy cabbage, and Toulouse sausage is served with bubble and squeak. Fish specials might call on tuna, swordfish or sea bass, and plentiful vegetables come buttered. The sparkle continues at pudding stage: lemon-curd tartlet with lime marmalade ice cream and orange caramel sauce, for example, or pear tartlet with a squidgy cinnamon frangipane. Service is 'knowledgeable and obliging'. All the wines apart from the fizz are under £22 and present a good-value collection. House French is £8.95.

CHEFS: Richard Barker and Carol Denison   PROPRIETORS: Brian Womersley and Richard Barker   OPEN: Tue to Sat 12 to 1.45, 7 to 9.30   CLOSED: 1 week Feb, 2 weeks Aug/Sept   MEALS: alc (main courses £7 to £14). Set L £6.95 (2 courses), Set D Tue to Thur £11.95   SERVICE: not inc   CARDS: Delta, MasterCard, Switch, Visa   DETAILS: 28 seats. Private parties: 30 main room, 16 private room. Vegetarian meals. Children's helpings. No smoking in dining room. Music   £5

The 2001 Guide will be published before Christmas 2000. Reports on meals are most welcome at any time of the year, but are particularly valuable in the spring (no later than June). Send them to The Good Food Guide, *FREEPOST, 2 Marylebone Road, London NW1 4DF. Or email your report to guidereports@which.co.uk.*

SNAPE Suffolk   map 6

▲ *Crown Inn* £

Bridge Road, Snape IP17 1SL   COOKING 1
TEL: (01728) 688324   COST £22–£39

Although this is still technically a pub – and a venerable five centuries old at that
– most of the tables are usually laid for food. A blackboard menu serves both the
L-shaped bar, with its prominent settle, and the dining room, offering a good
selection of meat, fish and vegetable options, and a potentially wide range of
flavours, from Thai seafood salad, via razor clams in lemon oil, to calf's liver with
mustard mash. Highlights have included well-flavoured butternut squash soup,
wild boar steak, and chocolate Amaretto cheesecake. Proximity to the Maltings
brings pre- and post-concert supper deals on request. The style is informal – the
barmaid acts as head waitress – and over sixty wines from the Adnams list
combine interest with value. House Spanish is £9.50.

CHEF/PROPRIETOR: Diane Maylott   OPEN: all week 12 to 2, 7 to 9 (pre- and post-concert
bookings on request)   CLOSED: 25 Dec, 26 Dec D   MEALS: alc (main courses £8 to £12.50)
SERVICE: not inc, card slips closed   CARDS: Delta, MasterCard, Switch, Visa   DETAILS: 50
seats. 50 seats outside. Private parties: 28 main room. Car park. Vegetarian meals. No children
under 14 in dining room. Wheelchair access (also WC). No music   ACCOMMODATION: 3 rooms,
all with bath/shower. B&B £35 to £50. No children under 14 in accommodation

SOUTHALL   Greater London   map 3

Brilliant

72–76 Western Road, Southall UB2 5DZ
TEL: (0181) 574 1928, changing to (020) 8574 1928   COOKING 3
FAX: (0181) 574 0276, changing to (020) 8574 0276   COST £20–£52

Brilliant has taken the bold step of doubling in size this year, its capacity
increased to 240, so even more people can enjoy the high-quality northern
Indian/Punjabi food on offer. The style has gone upmarket, as have the prices
(some increasing by 50 per cent or more), though one enthusiastic regular felt it
still represented good value for money when compared with some of its
competitiors. Despite all this, there are not many changes (other than cosmetic)
to the menu: it is now a large, colourfully printed sheet. Innovations include
paneer tikka, filo-wrapped prawns, and chicken tikka masala. All the old
favourites remain, including butter chicken, jeera chicken and palak lamb in
portions for up to five people. House wine is £9.

CHEF: D.K. Anand   PROPRIETORS: K.K. and D.K. Anand   OPEN: Tue to Fri L 12.15 to 2.30, Tue to
Sun D 6.15 to 11   CLOSED: 3 weeks Aug   MEALS: alc (main courses £6 to £10). Set L £12.50, Set
D £15   SERVICE: 10%, card slips closed   CARDS: Amex, Delta, Diners, MasterCard, Switch,
Visa   DETAILS: 240 seats. Private parties: 120 main room, 80 private room. Car park. Vegetarian
meals. Children's helpings. Wheelchair access (also WC). Music. Air-conditioned

*Occasional music in the details at the end of an entry means live or recorded music is played
in the dining room only rarely or for special events. No music means it is never played.*

Gifto's Lahore Karahi £

162–164 The Broadway, Southall UB1 1NN
TEL: (0181) 813 8669, changing to (020) 8813 8669
FAX: (0181) 574 1630, changing to (020) 8574 1630   COOKING 1
EMAIL: gifto@virgin.net   COST £12–£30

Choose from the menu if you must in this teeming, neon-lit eating house (Lahore Karahi & Tandoori in last year's *Guide*), but far better simply to ask the waiter to feed you. Prices remain rock-bottom for well-cooked dishes, particularly the straightforward grills – lamb tikka, chicken wings, seekh kebab, and so on – and breads from the tandoor. Stray from these and your hit rate may well fall. Chicken tandoor comes three ways: whole, breast or leg, and the tandoor treatment is also applied to fish, lamb, quail and prawns. Drink salted lassi, delicately flavoured with coriander. Otherwise, bring your own wine or beer: there is no licence, or corkage.

CHEF: Mohammad Muslim   PROPRIETOR: Asif Rahman   OPEN: all week 12 to 11.30 (12 Sat and Sun)   MEALS: alc (main courses £1.60 to £8)   SERVICE: not inc, net prices   CARDS: Amex, Delta, Diners, MasterCard, Switch, Visa   DETAILS: 350 seats. Private parties: 350 main room, 100 and 300 private rooms. Car park. Vegetarian meals. Wheelchair access (also WC). Music

---

SOUTH MOLTON Devon   map 1

▲ *Whitechapel Manor* ⁙✖

South Molton EX36 3EG   COOKING 5
TEL: (01769) 573377   FAX: (01769) 573797   COST £43–£60

Lights beckon through the stone mullioned windows on a winter's evening, and the gardens of this 'truly wonderful' old house are a delight in summer. A carved rood screen, huge flower arrangements and heavy period furniture combine to make the Great Hall feel like a 'National Trust-type stately home', while the dining room's floral paintings and well-spaced tables give it a more 'cool and modern' air. Matthew Corner's three-course dinners (a separate vegetarian menu is available on request) reflect good supplies and real expertise: for example, an intensely flavoured mushroom soup made with good stock and aromatised with a little truffle oil, or sea bass fillet laid over a pile of plump-grained risotto 'pungent with Parmesan'.

Saucing is generally sparse: a small puddle of red pepper coulis with a starter of duck leg confit, or a modest amount of lightly mustardy gravy to partner roast pork tenderloin and its accompanying crisp pastry tart of juicy, glazed apple chunks. Vegetables are wisely kept simple, while puddings are 'a joy', at least judging by an assiette of passion fruit consisting of a tiny tart brûlée, a hot mini-soufflé, a scoop of sorbet, and a seed-speckled mousse. If this is indicative of the workmanship the kitchen is capable of, so too are bread, canapés and petits fours. Cheese is a pre-selected trio, locally sourced. Service is 'friendly, helpful, deft and well trained', and wines offer fair choice under £20 alongside some superior bottles, but value is remarkably variable. House French white is £10.75, red £10.50.

CHEF: Matt Corner   PROPRIETORS: Margaret Aris and Charles Brown   OPEN: all week D only 7 to 8.45   MEALS: Set D £34 to £40   SERVICE: not inc, card slips closed   CARDS: Amex, Delta, Diners, MasterCard, Switch, Visa   DETAILS: 24 seats. Private parties: 24 main room. Car park. Children's helpings. No smoking in dining room. No music   ACCOMMODATION: 10 rooms, all with bath/shower. TV. Phone. B&B £70 to £170. Baby facilities (*The Which? Hotel Guide*)   £5

SOUTHWATER West Sussex map 3

Cole's ✻

Worthing Road, Southwater RH13 7BS	COOKING 4
TEL: (01403) 730456	COST £25–£51

It may be set in a 'characterless conurbation', but this ancient beamed barn, once the village tea room, charms with a huge old brick fireplace in the dining room and a 'spick and span' feel. In among the prawn cocktail, chilled melon and plainly grilled fillet steak are to be found a more contemporary salad of goats' cheese and roast peppers, and sea bass with a lime and coriander sauce. Materials are fresh, and timing at inspection was 'irreproachable': lightly seared scallops in a thicket of frisée leaves, good-sized sole meunière, and flavourful duck served 'well done and crispy'. Carefully cooked vegetables (from dauphinois potatoes to carrot and turnip purée spiced with cumin) are singled out for praise. Opinions on desserts vary from unexciting to 'excellent' lemon posset. A rather cool 'old-fashioned' atmosphere prevails, but a Spanish waiter delivers generally efficient service, and the southern hemisphere makes a decent contribution to the French-dominated wine list. House wine is £10.95.

CHEF: Elizabeth Cole   PROPRIETORS: the Cole family   OPEN: Tue to Fri and Sun L 12 to 2, Tue to Sat D 7 to 9   CLOSED: 1 week after Christmas, 2 weeks summer   MEALS: alc L Tue to Fri and D Tue to Sat (main courses £12 to £20). Set L Tue to Fri £12.95 (2 courses) to £15, Set L Sun £15   SERVICE: not inc   CARDS: Amex, Delta, Diners, MasterCard, Switch, Visa   DETAILS: 36 seats. Private parties: 36 main room, 10 private room. Car park. Vegetarian meals. Children's helpings. No smoking in dining room. Wheelchair access (also WC). Music   £5

SOUTHWOLD Suffolk map 6

▲ The Crown ▮ ✻

High Street, Southwold IP18 6DP	COOKING 4
TEL: (01502) 722275 FAX: (01502) 727263	COST £23–£36

Popular with locals and visitors alike – 'we very much like the atmosphere' – this old coaching inn offers informal eating around the bar (duck liver parfait, grilled mackerel fillets), with slightly more serious stuff in the bright, sunny dining room. Décor and furnishings are sparse, simple and understated, conveying the feel of 'a basic hostelry' that welcomes all comers. Seafood is a strong suit, from scallops with bacon, via red mullet with saffron linguini, to sea bass on wilted spinach leaves, a dish praised by many reporters. Some incidentals may crop up more than once (parsnip crisps, or a herb dressing), and the food may not always sing with a great deal of passion, but it is technically sound and well presented: 'exactly seared' liver maybe, or a dramatic 'Persil-white' goats' cheese on rich red roast beetroot with green salad leaves.

461

Cheeses are kept in good condition, and desserts have included an orange and chocolate mousse, and poached pears with blackcurrant ice cream. Service from 'unstressed' young staff is 'friendly, helpful and efficient'. The Jewel in The Crown is its wine list, an inspired collection from some of the world's best producers. Its sensible layout aids the selection process while the fair pricing policy means that good-value drinking can be had at all levels, and that includes below £10. Twenty wines by the glass from a featured country change every month.

CHEF: Craig Dunn PROPRIETOR: Adnams Hotels OPEN: all week 12.15 to 2, 7.15 to 9 CLOSED: 1 week Jan MEALS: Set L £14 (2 courses) to £17, Set D £19 (2 courses) to £23. Bar food available SERVICE: not inc, card slips closed CARDS: Amex, Delta, Diners, MasterCard, Switch, Visa DETAILS: 22 seats. 15 seats outside. Private parties: 22 main room, 30 private room. Car park. Vegetarian meals. Children's helpings. No children under 5 in dining room. No smoking in dining room. No music. Air-conditioned ACCOMMODATION: 12 rooms, 9 with bath/shower. TV. Phone. B&B £47 to £98 (*The Which? Hotel Guide*)

STADDLEBRIDGE North Yorkshire   map 9

▲ *McCoy's Bistro*

The Cleveland Tontine, Staddlebridge DL6 3JB
TEL: (01609) 882671 FAX: (01609) 882660   COOKING 5
6m NE of Northallerton, at junction of A19 and A172   COST £21–£51

'If only there were more places like this,' sighed one visitor, charmed by the dining room's potted palms, dim lights, idiosyncratic furnishings, '40s pop music, and 'the house cat occupying the best armchair in front of the fire'. Add serious food, colourful rooms, great breakfasts, and relaxed, friendly owners who maintain high professional standards, and it is easy to see why it makes for 'a comforting and amusing stopover'. The dining room is open two nights only, serving dishes more or less interchangeable with those in the basement bistro, although choice in the latter is generous to a fault. By turns rustic and sophisticated, this is food that satisfies: squab pigeon with lentils, cod in batter with pea purée and chips, sausage with Yorkshire pudding and onion gravy, or rack of lamb with fondant potato and béarnaise.

Fish has included tuna with Israeli couscous, sea bass with fennel confit and sauce antiboise, and roasted salmon with 'a nice contrast between crust and succulence', served with samphire. Desserts tend to be indulgent, along the lines of black cherry sponge, crème brûlée with fruit compote, or white chocolate cheesecake with malted chocolate ice cream. The Bistro's fifty-strong wine list offers a little more choice than the dining room's, but styles and prices cover a wide range in both. House wine is £10.95 (£12.95 in the dining room).

CHEF: Marcus Bennett PROPRIETORS: the McCoy brothers OPEN: restaurant Fri and Sat D only 7 to 9.30; bistro all week 12 to 2, 7 to 9.30 CLOSED: 25 and 26 Dec, 1 Jan MEALS: restaurant Set D £28. Bistro alc (main courses £12 to £18). Set L £9.95 (2 courses) to £11.95, Set D before 8 £17 (2 courses) to £28 SERVICE: not inc CARDS: Amex, Delta, Diners, MasterCard, Switch, Visa DETAILS: 80 seats. Private parties: 50 main room, 12 to 50 private rooms. Car park. Vegetarian meals. Children's helpings. Music. Air-conditioned ACCOMMODATION: 6 rooms, all with bath/shower. TV. Phone. B&B £75 to £90

STAITHES North Yorkshire   map 9

▲ *Endeavour* ✝✳

| 1 High Street, Staithes TS13 5BH | COOKING 2 |
| TEL: (01947) 840825 | COST £26–£46 |

Named after the ship once sailed by Staithes resident Captain Cook, Endeavour
is a 'friendly, Yorkshire fisherman's sort of place,' occupying a pretty cottage near
the quayside. Blue-checked curtains and tablecloths, and nautical memorabilia
and paintings, indicate rich pickings for fish lovers: crab and cod fish cakes with
coriander, or local sea bass topped with a crust of olives and herbs. The entire
menu of the day is chalked up on a blackboard and has produced, for one
reporter, creamy, herby fish soup, followed by an 'enormous steak' of high-
quality swordfish on a bed of lettuce with bitter orange chutney. There is praise,
too, for cinnamon-flavoured Moroccan lamb stew with 'lots of tomatoey juices'.
The house speciality of crème brûlée with raspberries receives many compliments, while other desserts capitalise on seasonal fruits made into tarts and
crêpe fillings. Friendly service is performed by 'local ladies', and the nicely
chosen French house wines cost £8.60 per bottle.

CHEF/PROPRIETOR: Lisa Chapman   OPEN: Tue to Sat 12 to 2, 6.45 to 9, and bank hol Sun D
CLOSED: Nov, 25 and 26 Dec, mid-Jan to mid-Mar   MEALS: alc (main courses £9.50 to £18)
SERVICE: not inc   CARDS: none   DETAILS: 45 seats. Private parties: 30 main room, 12 and 16
private rooms. Vegetarian meals. No smoking in dining room. Occasional music
ACCOMMODATION: 3 rooms, 2 with bath/shower. TV. B&B £42 to £55 £5

STANDLAKE Oxfordshire   map 2

Bell £   NEW ENTRY

21 High Street, Standlake OX8 7RH	
TEL: (01865) 300784	COOKING 3
off A415, 5m SE of Witney	COST £21–£40

The Bell is a dyed-in-the-wool contemporary gastro-pub where good eating is
accorded equal prominence with hand-pumped ales and a grown-up wine list. It
occupies a red-brick building in the middle of a charming Thames Valley village,
the décor an unpretentious mix of plain wood tables and half-timbered walls.
Choice in both bar and restaurant areas is wide, chalked up on blackboards that
may take some time to peruse. Seafood options have included Cornish crab with
a Chinese dressing, and paupiettes of salmon and sea bass stuffed with olives
and herbs, while offal has produced lightly fried lamb sweetbreads (served in
clear cooking juices incorporating garlic, lemon juice and parsley), and, at
inspection, chicken livers with bacon and pine nuts in a marsala sauce.
'Shiveringly light' white chocolate cheesecake on dark chocolate sauce was a
memorable summer dessert, or there may be traditional sherry trifle, or
gooseberry meringue pie. Service may sometimes seem stretched, but copes, and
value for money has been praised. Wines – equitably spread between Europe
and the southern hemisphere – are fairly priced (starting at £8.95 a bottle), and
many are available by the glass (from £1.75).

CHEFS/PROPRIETORS: Barbara Colaço and Nicholas Heaney   OPEN: Sun L 12 to 2, Tue to Sat D 6.30 to 9.30 (also open for reservations only bank hol Sun and Mon D 7 to 9)   CLOSED: 26 Dec, 1 Jan   MEALS: alc D (main courses £8 to £15). Set L Sun £12.95. Bar L available Tue to Sat   SERVICE: not inc, card slips closed   CARDS: Delta, MasterCard, Switch, Visa   DETAILS: 35 seats. Private parties: 40 main room. Car park. Vegetarian meals. Children's helpings. No-smoking area. Music

---

STANTON Suffolk   map 6

Leaping Hare Vineyard Restaurant

Wyken Vineyards, Stanton IP31 2DW   COOKING 1
TEL: (01359) 250287   FAX: (01359) 252256   COST £29–£44

This vineyard and farm includes numerous gardens, 'ancient woodlands' and a 'nuttery', and its great barn houses a shop selling Wyken wines. At its other end is the rustic, airy restaurant, where Peter Harrison has been cooking since early 1999. The carte (six choices per course) is largely English, but stretches to serving ratatouille with Norfolk lamb, and home-made focaccia with several dishes, including an inspector's first-rate pigeon terrine, and moist, crisp-skinned chicken confit. Scrupulously sourced ingredients include cream from one named supplier, and ice cream from two. No bookings are taken at the new Leaping Hare Café, which offers snacks as light as smoked salmon blinis or as satisfying as faggots and mash with onion gravy. Wines include five whites and one red from the Wyken vineyard plus a few 'guest wines'. The Wyken Bacchus 1996 (£15.50) is highly recommended to those who like Marlborough-style Sauvignons.

CHEF: Peter Harrison   PROPRIETORS: Kenneth and Carla Carlisle   OPEN: Wed to Sun L 12 to 2.30, Fri and Sat D 7 to 9.30   CLOSED: 2 weeks Christmas   MEALS: alc (main courses £9 to £14)   SERVICE: not inc, card slips closed   CARDS: Delta, MasterCard, Switch, Visa   DETAILS: 45 seats. 16 seats outside. Private parties: 50 main room. Car park. Vegetarian meals. Children's helpings. No smoking in dining room. Wheelchair access (also WC). No music £5

STOCKCROSS Berkshire   map 2

▲ Vineyard at Stockcross

Stockcross RG20 8JU
TEL: (01635) 528770   FAX: (01635) 528398
EMAIL: general@the-vineyard.co.uk   COOKING 5
just off A4, 2m W of Newbury   COST £33–£112

The Vineyard has every imaginable extravagance (and a few more besides) but no vineyard. Named in honour of millionaire proprietor Sir Peter Michael's Californian winery, it is set in a building that reporters consider more appropriate to Marbella or the Caribbean than somewhere just off the Newbury by-pass. Outside, flames shoot up from a shallow lake, liveried doormen beckon and greet, then valet-park the car. Others escort you indoors, bid good evening, urge enjoyment of the meal, then serve it in an elegant split-level dining room graced by a private art collection. The whole operation (including dome waving) is impressively choreographed, but staff are friendly too.

Billy Reid's admirably restrained repertoire of updated French classics includes some expected luxuries but doesn't scorn simpler dishes of velvety celeriac soup, or a black pudding beignet with shallots and potato. Although a couple of items repeated themselves during the course of an inspection meal, variety of materials and treatments is generally good, taking in salads – of langoustine, or grilled goats' cheese – followed by roast squab pigeon with foie gras. Seafood gets sympathetic treatment, from a well-composed salad of scallops and Jerusalem artichokes, to 'full-flavoured and firm' red mullet on wild mushrooms with olive oil mash. Puddings have included an 'exquisitely presented' assiette of chocolate, and apple tart on paper-thin pastry with caramel sauce and vanilla ice cream. Lunchtime menus are surprisingly reasonable.

All those addicted to fine Californian wines, and who can afford to feed their habit, will think they have died and gone to heaven when they see Sir Peter Michael's unique list, which includes several samples from his own vineyard. To avoid the headache of selecting from the bejewelled international wine book, seek the advice of head sommelier Edoardo Amadi. If some prices seem high, this is a reflection of quality and rarity value; choice is excellent under £20 too.

CHEF: Billy Reid   PROPRIETOR: Sir Peter Michael   OPEN: all week 12 to 2, 7 to 10   MEALS: alc (main courses £17.50 to £23). Set L £20, Set D Sun to Thur £39, Set D Fri and Sat £75   SERVICE: not inc   CARDS: Amex, Delta, Diners, MasterCard, Switch, Visa   DETAILS: 70 seats. 20 seats outside. Private parties: 100 main room, 40 private room. Car park. Vegetarian meals. Children's helpings. No smoking in 1 dining room. Wheelchair access (also WC). Music. Air-conditioned ACCOMMODATION: 33 rooms, all with bath/shower. TV. Phone. B&B £135 to £185. Rooms for disabled. Baby facilities. Swimming pool. Fishing (£5)

STOKE HOLY CROSS   Norfolk   map 6

Wildebeest Arms

Norwich Road, Stoke Holy Cross NR14 8QJ
TEL: (01508) 492497   FAX: (01508) 494353
from Norwich take A140 Ipswich road; directly after
roundabout take the left turn signposted Stoke Holy   COOKING 1
Cross   COST £21–£43

Combining the roles of pub and restaurant, this idiosyncratic African animal is a casual and unpretentious place with a rough-and-ready air to the décor. The theme is promoted with the help of spears, wooden face masks and bongo drums, and to say the tables are made of wood is an understatement: they are just big chunks of tree resting on tubular steel legs. The food has a cosmopolitan feel, ranging from salmon ceviche, via wild pigeon terrine with candied green bean salad, to roast duck breast with cranberry gravy. There are some evident skills – leek and Parmesan tart with a properly poached egg at one meal – but a piece of unfresh cod let the side down at inspection. Finish with crème brûlée, caramelised bananas with vanilla ice cream, or, as one reporter did, with a light, creamy 'citrus moose (I hope the spelling was deliberate)'. France and the New World share the bulk of the wines between them. House red and white are £9.95.

CHEF: Paul Hatch   PROPRIETORS: Henry Watt and Andrew Wilkins   OPEN: all week 12 to 2 (12.30 to 2.30 Sun), 7 to 10 (9 Sun)   CLOSED: 25 and 26 Dec   MEALS: alc (main courses £9 to £14). Set L £9.95 (2 courses) to £12.95   SERVICE: 10% (optional), card slips closed   CARDS: Amex, Delta, Diners, MasterCard, Switch, Visa   DETAILS: 60 seats. 30 seats outside. Private parties: 100 main room. Car park. Vegetarian meals. Children's helpings. No smoking in 1 dining room. Wheelchair access (not WC). Music   (£5)

STOKESLEY   North Yorkshire   map 10

▲ *Chapters* ⁵⅟✳

27 High Street, Stokesley TS9 5AD   COOKING 3
TEL: (01642) 711888   FAX: (01642) 713387   COST £25–£49

Low lighting, dark walls, and blues Muzak create a rather subdued atmosphere in this long, narrow dining room, but don't be put off: 'the food shines'. Dave Connelly, who arrived in 1998, has now taken full charge of the kitchen, and although the bulk of the menu resides in mainland Europe – marinated grilled vegetables, and chicken liver parfait with prune chutney are typical – occasional forays to the East bring back Thai fish cake with bok choy and red curry sauce; or spring roll of lobster and Asian greens with curry oil. Main courses at inspection impressed: bouillabaisse, from the daily specials board, comprised a pot piled high with fresh fish and shellfish in a rich gravy; while properly braised lamb shank with moist pea and mint risotto 'was superb in every respect'. Desserts might include tropical fruit pavlova with saffron and lime syrup, or warm banana bread sandwich with butterscotch sauce and hazelnut tuille. Service is 'bright-eyed and quite knowledgeable', and the eclectic wine list offers value for adventurous and conservative tastes alike. House French is £11.

CHEF: Dave Connelly   PROPRIETORS: Alan and Catherine Thompson   OPEN: Mon to Sat 12 to 2.30, 6.30 to 9.30   CLOSED: 25 Dec, 1 Jan   MEALS: alc (main courses L £5.50 to £13.50, D £9.50 to £17)   SERVICE: not inc   CARDS: Amex, Delta, Diners, MasterCard, Switch, Visa   DETAILS: 100 seats. 40 seats outside. Private parties: 50 main room. Vegetarian meals. Children's helpings. No smoking in 1 dining room. No cigars/pipes in dining room. Wheelchair access (not WC). Music   ACCOMMODATION: 13 rooms, all with bath/shower. TV. Phone. B&B £44 to £69. Baby facilities   (£5)

STON EASTON   Somerset   map 2

▲ *Ston Easton Park* ♟ ⁵⅟✳

Ston Easton BA3 4DF
TEL: (01761) 241631   FAX: (01761) 241377
EMAIL: stoneastonpark@stoneaston.co.uk   COOKING 5
on A37, 12m S of Bristol   COST £29–£78

Set in landscaped gardens (extensive enough to land a helicopter), this imposing Palladian mansion has been impeccably restored, though in rather more chintzy style than might be expected. Its grand and formal manner is tempered by 'friendly and unstuffy' staff who go out of their way to be helpful. Though it is not a place for cutting-edge cuisine, menus are thoughtful and well-balanced, relying on classic treatments of 'scrupulously sourced' raw materials for impact.

Starters have generally impressed more than main courses: a 'moist' game terrine, for example, with satisfying chunks of rare meat, or just-cooked sweet scallops served with a refreshing lemon grass butter sauce. Flavours may sometimes appear muted, but accurate timing extends to 'tender and moist' pork fillet, with honey glaze and cider sauce.

Rich, classic desserts might include crème brûlée, chocolate fondant or tarte Tatin. An 'excellent' cheeseboard and a prettily presented platter of sorbets and ice creams make tempting alternatives. Bargain set lunches come with 'all the trimmings', including a generous plateful of canapés to start and petits fours to follow. The lengthy wine list contains many high-quality bottles, and while majoring on French classics it does shine light into other regions too. Prices tend to reflect the grandeur of the surroundings, although an introductory selection stays mostly under £20 and includes Wairau River Sauvignon Blanc 1997, Marlborough, New Zealand at £17.

CHEF: Mark Harrington   PROPRIETORS: Peter and Christine Smedley   OPEN: all week 12.30 to 2, 7 to 9.30 (10 Fri and Sat)   MEALS: alc (main courses L £14.50 to £16, D £20 to £26). Set L £11 (2 courses) to £16, Set D £39.50   SERVICE: not inc, card slips closed   CARDS: Amex, Delta, Diners, MasterCard, Switch, Visa   DETAILS: 38 seats. 24 seats outside. Private parties: 50 main room, 16 to 30 private rooms. Car park. Vegetarian meals. No children under 7 in dining room. Jacket and tie. No smoking in dining room. Wheelchair access (not WC). No music   ACCOMMODATION: 21 rooms, all with bath/shower. TV. Phone. Room only £155 to £405. No children under 7 exc babes in arms in accommodation. Baby facilities (*The Which? Hotel Guide*)   (£5)

STORRINGTON West Sussex   map 3

Fleur de Sel   NEW ENTRY

Manleys Hill, Storrington RH20 4BT   COOKING 6
TEL: (01903) 742331   FAX: (01903) 740649   COST £28–£54

The Perrauds, who were in Haslemere, bought what used to be Manleys and opened up at the beginning of 1999, renaming it after their original restaurant. They have effected an attractive refit, making it all feel 'lighter and prettier' than before, with flowers and sumptuous curtain fabrics. Menus – in 'modern classical French' mould – resort to farandoles, bouquets, aumonières and darnettes, but translations are straightforward enough, and the most expensive version offers particularly generous choice.

Fine-quality ingredients lay a firm foundation, ambition is high, and at its best the food is characterised by balance and 'definition', succeeding better with simpler dishes than 'when it seeks to impress and embellish'. Good command of technical skills at inspection resulted in a difficult to improve mixture of well-timed red mullet, John Dory, sea bass and salmon, assembled in a light creamy vermouth sauce. An astute approach to flavouring has produced a large tureen of 'serious' and deeply tasty fish bisque, and slices of accurately cooked calf's liver, piled over a thick bed of spinach, in an unlikely-sounding but well-judged apricot brandy sauce: an assured and well-conceived dish.

On-plate vegetables, which may appear sparse but add up to a decent portion, have included potatoes sculpted rather unnecessarily into mushroom shapes; though not the other way round. The kitchen is adept at desserts of cherry-filled

ENGLAND

chocolate sponge with ginger ice cream, and well-risen raspberry soufflé with fromage blanc sorbet spooned into the centre. A couple of reporters have questioned value for money, but service has been 'intelligent and attentive', and the mainly French wine list errs towards the grander end of the scale: more bottles under £20 might be appreciated. House Côtes de Duras white and Costières de Nîmes red are £12.50.

CHEF: Michel Perraud PROPRIETORS: Bernadette and Michel Perraud OPEN: Tue to Fri and Sun L 12 to 2, Tue to Sat D 7 to 10 CLOSED: 2 weeks Jan MEALS: Set L Tue to Fri £12.50 (2 courses) to £31, Set L Sun £16.50 (2 courses) to £20.50, Set D Tue to Thur £16.50 (2 courses) to £31, Set D Fri and Sat £26 to £31 SERVICE: 12.5% (optional), card slips closed CARDS: Amex, Delta, MasterCard, Switch, Visa DETAILS: 50 seats. Private parties: 20 main room. Car park. Vegetarian meals. No children under 12. No cigars/pipes in dining room. Occasional music

Old Forge ♟

Church Street, Storrington RH20 4LA
TEL: (01903) 743402 FAX: (01903) 742540   COOKING 4
EMAIL: contact@oldforge.co.uk   COST £22–£45

'Like an Elizabethan doll's house', the impeccably kept Old Forge is black, white and cottagey, its two tiny rooms so pressed for space that a table has been shoehorned into the fireplace. The atmosphere is 'unpretentious but deeply involved', a reflection of Cathy Roberts's warm welcome and hands-on approach. While finding room for tuna and lime pickle terrine, or mint and asparagus tabbouleh, the cooking adopts a generally Francophile approach, typified by a smoked haddock version of brandade, and pink best end of lamb, served with garlic-infused potato cakes (crisp outside, 'immaculately puréed within') and a generous amount of red wine sauce.

The cooking is skilful, presentation is appealing, and dishes are well balanced: crostini of blue Fourme d'Ambert cheese and aubergine purée is laced with good olive oil, and a main course of black bream fillets in filo pastry comes with a rich, winey, cream-enhanced sauce. Lyonnaise potatoes and celeriac purée might feature among accompanying vegetables. Cheeses, many of them British, are impressive, while dark chocolate torte with orange pistachio ice cream is 'everything that a dessert should be'. A compact but sharply chosen wine list displays a decided partiality for the New World; mark-ups are admirably low – house wines start at £11.75 – and dessert wines by the glass are inviting.

CHEF: Clive Roberts PROPRIETORS: Cathy and Clive Roberts OPEN: Wed to Fri and Sun L 12.15 to 1.15, Wed to Sat D 7.15 to 9 CLOSED: Christmas to 31 Dec, 2 weeks spring, 2 weeks autumn MEALS: Set L Wed to Fri £8.50 (1 course) to £28, Set L Sun £15 (2 courses) to £18, Set D £18 (2 courses) to £28 SERVICE: not inc, card slips closed CARDS: Amex, Delta, Diners, MasterCard, Switch, Visa DETAILS: 34 seats. Private parties: 14 main room. Vegetarian meals. Children's helpings. No smoking while others eat. Music (£5)

'The chef uses salt in a unique way, as if the basic measure were not a pinch but a cup.' (On eating in London)

STRETE Devon   map 1

Laughing Monk

Blackawton Road, Strete TQ6 0RN
TEL: (01803) 770639   COOKING 2
5m S of Dartmouth, just off A379   COST £19–£41

Trudy Rothwell is instrumental in creating a sense of welcome and warmth at this converted schoolhouse. An L-shaped dining room is done out in terracotta and scarlet, with pine tables, settles, and black pans full of spiky greenery hanging from the ceiling. David's good-value provender includes Dartmoor venison and local seafood: gingered crab cakes with lemon and capers, perhaps, or three large rare scallops in a fluted pastry case, topped with hollandaise and herby breadcrumbs. Cooking was slightly erratic at inspection, but included first-rate beef fillet with wild mushrooms, and crisp duck breast with a sweet plum glaze. Vegetables arrive tiered on a wrought-iron stand, the quality in no way inferior to the presentation, and puddings, made by Trudy Rothwell, might include lemon pavlova or strawberry almond flan. Fifty or so sensibly chosen wines are grouped by style rather than region. House wine is £9.25.

CHEF: David Rothwell   PROPRIETORS: David and Trudy Rothwell   OPEN: Sun L on last Sun of month 12 to 1.30, Tue to Sat D 7 to 9.30   MEALS: alc D (main courses £11 to £14.50). Set L Sun £12.50   SERVICE: not inc, card slips closed   CARDS: Delta, Diners, MasterCard, Switch, Visa DETAILS: 50 seats. Private parties: 65 main room, 36 private room. Car park. Children's helpings. Music

---

STUCKTON Hampshire   map 2

▲ Three Lions ♈ ⅚✳

Stuckton Road, Stuckton SP6 2HF
TEL: (01425) 652489   FAX: (01425) 656144
½m SE of Fordingbridge, off A338 but not signposted
from it: take the turn just S of Fordingbridge and   COOKING 7
follow a sign down a narrow country lane   COST £32–£56

This converted pub, with scrubbed pine tables and starched napkins, is run professionally but with charm and warmth by the Womersleys. It is a homely place, with fresh flowers, potted plants, and a central fire that warms both bar and dining room. The philosophy, according to one observer, seems to be 'good-quality ingredients, precise cooking, and good sauces', while another calls it 'brilliant, unfussy food'. The menu – six or seven choices per course – is chalked on a tall narrow blackboard, its starting point 'the best produce I can source', according to Mike Womersley. Fish (from local dayboats) is a particularly strong suit, its 'crisp, clean flavours' generally matched by light sauces: perhaps briefly seared scallops (corals and all) with a tarragon beurre blanc, or an accurately timed thick skinless fillet of brill topped with braised fennel in a cream sauce. There is a welcome absence of frills and decoration on the plate, too.

Meat is by no means neglected. Indeed, the kitchen makes good use of game (from the New Forest), fowl and offal in particular: pink lambs' kidneys with braised apricots, sesame-roasted duck with mango, or six thick slices of pink venison in a gamey wine sauce. Local small growers provide vegetables (charged separately, but adapted to the dish) and fruit: maybe fanned poached pear with a delicate verbena ice cream. Hot chocolate pudding, 'firm on the outside, runny inside', comes in for praise, or there may be a posh version of banana and custard. Prices, though not cheap, are fair for the context, and the two-course lunch is considered good value.

Wines encompass a broad sweep of flavours from all over the globe. One reporter found the mark-ups so reasonable that he was tempted 'to spend that bit more for something better', and plenty of good drinking can be had for under £20, including a dozen house wines starting at £11.75.

CHEF: Michael Womersley PROPRIETORS: Mr and Mrs Michael Womersley OPEN: Tue to Sun L 12 to 2, Tue to Sat D 7 to 9.30 (10 Sat) CLOSED: last 2 weeks Jan, first week Feb MEALS: alc (main courses £12.50 to £16.50). Set L £13.50 (2 courses) SERVICE: not inc CARDS: Delta, MasterCard, Switch, Visa DETAILS: 60 seats. Private parties: 60 main room. Car park. Vegetarian meals. Children's helpings. No smoking in dining room. Wheelchair access (not WC). No music ACCOMMODATION: 3 rooms, all with bath/shower. TV. B&B £65 to £85. Rooms for disabled (£5)

STURMINSTER NEWTON Dorset   map 2

▲ *Plumber Manor*

Sturminster Newton DT10 2AF
TEL: (01258) 472507 FAX: (01258) 473370
EMAIL: plumbermanor@btinternet.com
A357 to Sturminster Newton, take first left to   COOKING 3
Hazelbury Bryan, on left- hand side after 2m   COST £25–£50

It is perhaps not surprising that this attractive old house still has the air of another age about it, since the Prideaux-Brune family has lived here for centuries. Orders are taken with a flourish, nibbles eaten, and aperitifs drunk in front of a big log fire, before dinner in a more modern blue and gold dining room. Straightforward in tone, the food occupies an Anglo-French niche exemplified by moules marinière, duck liver pâté, and loin of pork stuffed with prunes or apricots. A degree of accomplishment is apparent in, for example, a 'wobbly' scallop mousseline in a creamy saffron-flecked sauce, pink roast lamb with a minty stock-based sauce, and first-rate custard to pour over plum and almond Bakewell tart, although an inspection meal found that flavours and seasoning were generally rather shy. Ask for vegetables with the main course and you get a plate of seven. Wines are predominantly French, including house Vin de Pays d'Oc Chardonnay and Cabernet-Syrah at £10.

CHEF: Brian Prideaux-Brune PROPRIETOR: Richard Prideaux-Brune OPEN: Sun L 12.30 to 2, all week D 7.30 to 9 CLOSED: Feb MEALS: Set L Sun £17.50, Set D £19.50 (2 courses) to £29.50 SERVICE: not inc CARDS: Amex, Diners, MasterCard, Switch, Visa DETAILS: 65 seats. Private parties: 40 main room, 22 private room. Car park. Vegetarian meals. Children's helpings. Wheelchair access (also WC). No music ACCOMMODATION: 16 rooms, all with bath/shower. TV. Phone. B&B £75 to £140. Rooms for disabled. Baby facilities (*The Which? Hotel Guide*)

map 6

Brasserie Four Seven £

47 Gainsborough Street, Sudbury CO10 6ET	COOKING 1
TEL/FAX: (01787) 374298	COST £20–£35

Church pew seating and padded chairs are the form at this inexpensive brasserie just inside the Suffolk border. Wooden partitions divide the room up, watercolours decorate the walls, and daily specials are chalked on a blackboard over the open-plan kitchen, supplementing a menu (a cross between set price and à la carte) of around eight choices per course. Starters – smoked mackerel and spring onion fish cake, or duck confit and bacon salad – come with good French bread, while main courses make use of pheasant (with a bourguignon sauce), grilled liver (with chips) and baked cod (on creamy leeks). Desserts, meanwhile, run to roasted bananas with caramel sauce, and lemon tart. Home-made fudge comes with unlimited coffee, and a short, modest wine list (nothing over £20 apart from champagne) starts with house VDQS at £7.95.

CHEF: Fraser Green PROPRIETORS: Fiona and Fraser Green OPEN: Tue to Sat 12 to 2, 7 to 9.45 CLOSED: 24 Dec to 4 Jan MEALS: alc (main courses £7 to £12) SERVICE: not inc, card slips closed CARDS: Amex, Delta, Diners, MasterCard, Switch, Visa DETAILS: 56 seats. Private parties: 25 main room, 25 private room. Vegetarian meals. Children's helpings. No smoking in 1 dining room. Wheelchair access (not WC). No music. Air-conditioned (£5)

Red Onion Bistro £

57 Ballingdon Street, Sudbury CO10 6DA	COOKING 2
TEL: (01787) 376777 FAX: (01787) 883156	COST £14–£33

Unfussy décor and an easy-going atmosphere help to make this a local favourite. A change in the kitchen has seen Craig Formoy move up the ranks (the Fords still cook on his days off), but the same combination of variety and value is the draw. Most of the menus change daily, the evening carte every couple of weeks, but the repertoire runs along classic bistro lines of grilled langoustines with garlic breadcrumbs, Normandy rabbit casserole, and twice-baked cheese soufflé. Shellfish shows up in the form of whole crabs and half-lobsters, and puddings (the province of Claire Humphries) might include apple and rhubarb crumble, or chocolate and coffee marquise. Service is prompt and friendly. House vin de pays is £7.75.

CHEFS: Craig Formoy and Claire Humphries PROPRIETORS: Gerry and Jane Ford OPEN: Mon to Sat 12 to 2, 6.30 to 9.30 CLOSED: Christmas to New Year, bank hol Mons MEALS: alc (main courses £6.50 to £10.50). Set L £6.25 (2 courses) to £8.25, Set D Mon to Thur £8.25 (2 courses) to £10.25 SERVICE: not inc, card slips closed CARDS: Delta, MasterCard, Switch, Visa DETAILS: 75 seats. 30 seats outside. Private parties: 25 main room. Car park. Vegetarian meals. Children's helpings. No cigars/pipes in dining room. Wheelchair access (not WC). No music

The Guide's *top-rated restaurants are listed near the front of the book.*

SUNDERLAND Tyne & Wear   map 10

Brasserie 21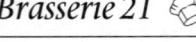

Wylam Wharf, Sunderland SR1 2AD	COOKING 3
TEL: (0191) 567 6594 FAX: (0191) 510 3994	COST £23–£50

This particular arm of Terence Laybourne's north-eastern operations (see also 21 Queen Street, Newcastle upon Tyne; Café 21, Ponteland; and Bistro 21, Durham) is to be found on a redeveloped wharf a mile from the city centre, opposite the National Glass Centre, where small boats float at anchor on the Wear. Modern décor – walls adorned with blown-up shots of cutlery – is in keeping with the cooking style. Andrew Richardson, who took over in late 1998, cooks a traditional brasserie menu, printed on a long, sectioned card. Seafood is as reliable as it ought to be with the fish quay scarcely 200 yards away: palpably fresh crab mayonnaise is served simply with slices of toasted baguette, and an inspector commended sautéed king prawns with peppers and ginger and a pyramid of sticky rice. Other crowd-pleasers are calf's liver with apples, onions and bacon, and duck confit with potatoes roasted in garlic and thyme on a red wine sauce. Baked Alaska with hot cherries might appear among the tarts and ice creams on the dessert list. Young and keen waiters are dressed French-style: in black with white apron fronts. France and the New World represent the principal poles of the wine selection. House Duboeuf is £10.

CHEF: Martin Horsley   PROPRIETORS: Terence and Susan Laybourne   OPEN: Mon to Sat 12 to 2, 5.30 to 10.30   CLOSED: 31 Dec, bank hols   MEALS: alc (main courses £9.50 to £16.50). Set L £12.50 (2 courses) to £14.50   SERVICE: not inc   CARDS: Amex, Delta, Diners, MasterCard, Switch, Visa   DETAILS: 64 seats. 20 seats outside. Private parties: 48 main room. Car park. Vegetarian meals. Children's helpings. Wheelchair access (also WC). Music

---

SUTTON GAULT Cambridgeshire   map 6

▲ Anchor Inn ♥ ⁵⁄✳

Sutton Gault CB6 2BD	
TEL: (01353) 778537 FAX: (01353) 776180	
EMAIL: anchor-sutton-gault@compuserve.com	
off B1381 Sutton to Earith road, just S of Sutton,	COOKING 2
6m W of Ely	COST £23–£44

Looking across the Ouse Washes and RSPB territory, this brick-built, rickety-floored seventeenth-century inn is considered a 'food pub' in today's terminology. For one Cambridge reporter 'it is the first place I think of in the area for a quiet meal and friendly reception'. Sourcing of materials – fish from Grimsby, local game – extends to rare-breed meats, such as Norfolk Horn lamb, which might be simply served with rösti and redcurrant sauce. Traces of the exotic, such as ostrich (with creamed spinach) or crispy hoisin-marinated quail with rice vermicelli, are balanced by more homely renderings of steak, kidney and Guinness pie, or chicken, leek and bacon crumble. Finish with banana pudding and custard, or Bennet's ice cream, and note the special deals for children and 'paupers'. Monthly specials, typically around £11 to £13, take the place of house wines on a helpful, varied and good-value list, and a real ale is usually on offer.

CHEFS: Geoff Moyle, Richard Bradley and Jonathon Dunckley   PROPRIETORS: Robin and Heather Moore   OPEN: all week 12 to 2, 7 to 9 (6.30 to 9.30 Sat)   CLOSED: 26 Dec   MEALS: alc (main courses £9.50 to £15). Set L Mon to Fri (exc bank hols) £7.50 (2 courses), Set L Sun £15.50, Set D Mon and Tue Oct to Mar £15.50   SERVICE: not inc   CARDS: Amex, Delta, MasterCard, Switch, Visa   DETAILS: 70 seats. 40 seats outside. Private parties: 35 main room. Car park. Vegetarian meals. Children's helpings. No very young children after 8. No smoking in dining room. Wheelchair access (also WC). No music   ACCOMMODATION: 2 rooms, both with bath/shower. TV. Phone. B&B £50 to £85   (£5)

SWAFFHAM Norfolk   map 6

▲ *Strattons* ⁵✗

4 Ash Close, Swaffham PE37 7NH   COOKING 4
TEL: (01760) 723845   FAX: (01760) 720458   COST £40–£48

'Don't overdress,' advised one visitor to this unstuffy, family-run Queen Anne villa set in its own grounds just off the market square. Drinks and orders are taken in the first-floor lounges – heavily decorated in Victorian fashion with family photographs and 'collections of odd things' – while the ground-floor dining room is neat and smart. A handwritten menu concentrates on light salady or vegetable-based starters, perhaps aubergine and ricotta muffins, or an upturned red pepper mousse with an interesting collection of leaves and a few slices of smoked duck breast. As a result of a long-running egg saga in the early months of 1999, which involved a dispute over their use raw – for example in mayonnaise (the local Environmental Health Office recommended using liquid pasteurised egg) – Vanessa Scott emerged triumphantly self-sufficient in bantam hens, whose eggs, now never more than two days old, might appear poached as part of a celeriac, bacon and frisée salad.

Three main courses offer a fish, a meat and a vegetarian option: perhaps mackerel with artichoke and tomato salsa, Norfolk asparagus soufflé, or stuffed roast rack of lamb. 'Almost everything purchased is now local and organic': game is from a nearby country estate (maybe rabbit terrine with elderberry chutney), and wild mushrooms might turn up with pink fir apple potatoes in a herb salad with chicken livers.

Puddings are announced by Les Scott: perhaps a rhubarb spin on bread-and-butter, or a rich chocolate tart with a dribble or orange sauce, while a small selection of British cheeses comes with home-made biscuits. A few reporters have found the service slow, but those who stay reckon that breakfast, which includes first-rate Cley kippers and a good vegetarian selection, 'is worth a special mention'. Les's enthusiasm for wine is evident, both in the handwritten notes on the illustrated list and his ability to talk knowledgeably about specific vineyards. The wines themselves offer a wide range of styles and flavours at fair prices (Spanish house red is £7.98), but note that not all bottles on the 100-plus list are always available.

CHEFS: Vanessa Scott, Margaret Cooper and Hannah Scott PROPRIETORS: Les and Vanessa Scott OPEN: all week D only 7 to 8.30 (8 Sun, 1 sitting) CLOSED: 24 to 26 Dec MEALS: Set D £32.50 SERVICE: not inc, card slips closed CARDS: Amex, Delta, MasterCard, Switch, Visa DETAILS: 20 seats. 4 seats outside. Private parties: 12 main room. Car park. Vegetarian meals. Children's helpings. No smoking in dining room. Occasional music ACCOMMODATION: 7 rooms, all with bath/shower. TV. Phone. B&B £70 to £140. Baby facilities (*The Which? Hotel Guide*) £5

SWANAGE Dorset   map 2

Galley

9 High Street, Swanage BH19 2LN	COOKING 3
TEL: (01929) 427299	COST £30–£36

Decked out with nets, storm lanterns and seaside pictures, this small high-street place is the setting for well-sourced local materials, principally fish, lamb and game. A pair of regulars, who have eaten their way through most things in the repertoire, return for mainstays of fish soup (served in a jug, with garlic bread and grated cheese), Lulworth Bay scallops (pehaps griddled with hop shoots and bacon), venison steak with chestnuts, and lamb with roast garlic and mint pesto. Menus change slowly – 'it is amazing how customers cling to certain dishes,' writes Nick Storer, while a reporter hankers after 'something new' – but the range takes in dressed crab with locally smoked salmon, razor clam chowder, and skate in black butter. Meals are executed 'efficiently and well', and 'sauces, though simple, are spot on'. Accurate timing is a feature too: making the best of Poole Bay cod with parsley sauce. Tables soon become 'awash with side dishes of vegetables', and a retired master baker is now producing fruit tarts, frangipane, and Dorset apple cake. Service is informed and friendly, and the short wine list – appropriate and mostly under £25 – is arranged by style. House wine is £8.50.

CHEF: Nick Storer PROPRIETORS: M.G. and N.D. Storer OPEN: all week D only 6.30 to 9.30 (10 Sat) CLOSED: 3 weeks Nov, 1 Jan to 14 Feb MEALS: Set D £21.50 SERVICE: not inc, card slips closed CARDS: MasterCard, Visa DETAILS: 34 seats. Private parties: 30 main room. Vegetarian meals. Children's helpings. Wheelchair access (not WC). Music. Air-conditioned

---

TADCASTER North Yorkshire   map 9

▲ *Hazlewood Castle, Restaurant 1086* ⁵✶

Paradise Lane, Hazlewood, Tadcaster LS24 9NJ	
TEL: (01937) 535353 FAX: (01937) 530630	COOKING 4
off A64, 3½m SW of Tadcaster	COST £25–£68

The brochure for this medieval-castle-turned-hotel promises 'a distinctly different experience' and it is indeed quite extraordinary, even as castles go. There are 77 acres of grounds, plus a State Drawing Room, a Great Hall, and a dining room that combines Greek mythology with oriental style, and still manages to be 'airy and relaxing'. The avowed aim is to dispense with the pomp and formality normally associated with fine dining, but the menus (christened

Elementary, Indulgence and Extravaganza) are not without affectation: 'stir-fry of the day to inspire you'; vegetables served 'where we feel it is appropriate'. The food itself, however, is refreshingly lacking in pretension, with stylish but sensible combinations such as roast sea bass with saffron and fennel pasta, or pearl barley risotto with braised shin beef. One diner enjoyed a 'simple but good' salad of herbs with charred new potatoes and green beans, followed by moist fillet of gurnard with wilted bok choy and a well-flavoured Thai broth. 'Light and fluffy' praline and hazelnut cheesecake rounded things off nicely. Service lacks co-ordination, according to one reporter, although another found staff 'pleasant and attentive'. French house wine is £12.50.

CHEFS: John and Matthew Benson-Smith   PROPRIETOR: Hazlewood Castle Hotel   OPEN: Tue to Fri and Sun L 12 to 2.30, Mon to Sat D 6 to 9.30   MEALS: Set L £15 to £45, Set D 6 to 8 (9 Mon) £15, Set D all evening £29.50 to £45   SERVICE: not inc, card slips closed   CARDS: Amex, Delta, Diners, MasterCard, Switch, Visa   DETAILS: 80 seats. Private parties: 14 main room, 30 to 120 private rooms. Car park. Vegetarian meals. Children's helpings. No smoking in dining room. Wheelchair access (also WC). Music   ACCOMMODATION: 21 rooms, all with bath/shower. TV. Phone. B&B £95 to £165 (£5)

Singers ⅃✳ £

16 Westgate, Tadcaster LS24 9AB	COOKING 3
TEL: (01937) 835121	COST £20–£32

Although there is only one performance a day in this musically themed town house, early arrivals at the stage door can get in mid-week at a concessionary price. A welcoming tone, echoed in a warm greeting and helpful service, forms the backdrop to a breezy modern menu that might start with tomato tarte Tatin, warm goats'-cheese salad, and chargrilled tuna steak with spicy lentils (one of the few dishes to attract a supplement), followed by a choice of six or seven main courses. Materials have included calf's liver and brill fillets, while dishes run to pork steak with sage mash, and duck breast on stir-fried vegetables with soy, honey and sesame sauce. Finish (assuming you have a Yorkshire appetite) with dark chocolate tart, baked treacle sponge and custard, or caramelised rice pudding. Value extends to two dozen wines, starting with house Duboeuf at £8.95.

CHEFS: David Lockwood and Richard Thompson   PROPRIETORS: Philip Taylor and Guy Vicari   OPEN: Tue to Sat D only 6 to 9.30   CLOSED: 25 and 26 Dec, 1 week Feb, 1 week Aug   MEALS: Set D before 7pm Tue to Fri £11.95, Set D Tue to Thu £13.50 (2 courses) to £16.50, Set D Fri and Sat £16.50   SERVICE: not inc, card slips closed   CARDS: Delta, MasterCard, Switch, Visa   DETAILS: 38 seats. Private parties: 38 main room. Vegetarian meals. No smoking in dining room. Wheelchair access (not WC). Music (£5)

'We initially thought the head of house was Welsh but when he later took our order, we realised he was French, or at least trying to be French. Did I just imagine I heard him greeting someone with "Ça va, boyo?"' (On eating in Wales)

TADWORTH Surrey	map 3

Gemini ⁵⁄✱

28 Station Approach Road, Tadworth KT20 5AH	COOKING 3
TEL/FAX: (01737) 812179	COST £24–£44

'Tastefully decorated' with a pleasant, relaxing atmosphere, Gemini serves its
local constituency with 'good ingredients cooked well'. Dinner is the main
business, and Robert Foster has an eye for appealing and sometimes unusual
combinations. Start, perhaps, with wild mushroom and dolcelatte soup with
parsnip crisps, followed by calf's liver with haggis champ, or best end of lamb
served with hummus and a broad-bean café au lait sauce. A 'particularly good
risotto of mushrooms with shavings of Parmesan' got one reporter's meal off to a
good start, and 'excellent' desserts finished it: fresh pineapple in Grand Marnier
with coconut and Amaretto ice cream, and a chocolate sponge fondant with light
and dark chocolate sauce and ginger ice cream. Service has been 'friendly and
attentive'. Forty-odd wines, which major on France, include eight house wines
in the £10 to £13 range.

CHEF/PROPRIETOR: Robert Foster   OPEN: Tue to Sun L 12 to 2.30, Tue to Sat D 7 to 9.30
CLOSED: 2 weeks Christmas, 2 weeks summer   MEALS: Set L £9.50 (1 course) to £15.50, Set D
Tue to Thur £22 (2 courses) to £27, Set D Fri and Sat £27   SERVICE: not inc   CARDS: Amex,
Delta, Diners, MasterCard, Switch, Visa   DETAILS: 52 seats. 12 seats outside. Private parties: 42
main room. Vegetarian meals. Children's helpings L. No children under 12 at D. No smoking in
dining room. Wheelchair access (not WC). Music

TAPLOW Berkshire	map 3

▲ Cliveden, Waldo's ⁵⁄✱

Taplow SL6 0JF	
TEL: (01628) 668561 FAX: (01628) 661837	NEW CHEF
off A4, 2m N of Taplow on Cliveden Road	COST £68–£115

Designed by Sir Charles Barry, architect of the Houses of Parliament, Cliveden is
a sprawling, imposing, Victorian mansion with acres of woods, formal gardens,
and a stretch of the River Thames to call its own. What it didn't have, as the *Guide*
went to press, was a fully operational kitchen brigade to call its own. Gary Jones
left to work with Raymond Blanc at Le Manoir aux Quat' Saisons (see entry,
Great Milton), and John Wood, from Chapters One (in Farnborough) and Two
(in Blackheath) was about to take over as executive chef of the whole outfit. A
brief summer closure was anticipated, to settle the new team and prepare menus,
and re-opening was scheduled for October 1999. Reports are, of course,
particularly welcome. Wine buffs, meanwhile, can enjoy plenty of top-quality
bottles from the classical French appellations, but those searching for wines
under £20 will find they can count the whites on the fingers of one hand and the
reds on, er, one finger.

See inside the front cover for an explanation of the symbols used at the tops of entries.

CHEF: John Wood PROPRIETOR: Cliveden plc OPEN: Tue to Sat D only 7 to 10.30 CLOSED: 24 Dec to 17 Jan MEALS: Set D £58 to £84 SERVICE: net prices, card slips closed CARDS: Amex, Diners, MasterCard, Switch, Visa DETAILS: 28 seats. Private parties: 12 to 54 private rooms. Car park. Vegetarian meals. Children welcome. Jacket and tie. No smoking in dining room. Wheelchair access (also WC). Music. Air-conditioned ACCOMMODATION: 38 rooms, all with bath/shower. TV. Phone. Room only £270 to £775. Rooms for disabled. Children welcome. Baby facilities. Swimming pool. Fishing

---

TAUNTON Somerset   map 2

Brazz £

| Castle Bow, Taunton TA1 1NF | NEW CHEF |
| TEL/FAX: (01823) 252000 | COST £22–£51 |

As the *Guide* went to press, Phil Vickery left Brazz's parent operation the Castle Hotel (see Round-ups, Taunton) after nine distinguished years, and no replacement had been appointed, which is why it appears in the Round-up section this year. Andy Knight also departed the trendy, design-conscious Brazz, but his second-in-command was able to step straight into his shoes. Given the carefully constructed, user-friendly menu – prawn cocktail, ribeye steak and burger, crispy won tons with smoked chicken mayonnaise, and steamed jam roll with custard – it is unlikely that the style will change radically. But we have no feedback, so reports are particularly welcome. A short wine list stays mostly under £20, starting with house vin de pays at £9.50.

CHEF: Matthew Eke PROPRIETORS: the Chapman family OPEN: all week 11.30 to 3, 6.30 to 10.30 (11 Fri and Sat) CLOSED: 25 Dec MEALS: alc (main courses £7 to £15) SERVICE: not inc, card slips closed CARDS: Amex, Delta, Diners, MasterCard, Switch, Visa DETAILS: 150 seats. Private parties: 100 main room. Vegetarian meals. Children's helpings. Wheelchair access (also WC). Music. Air-conditioned (£5)

TAVISTOCK Devon   map 1

▲ *Horn of Plenty* ⁙✴

Gulworthy, Tavistock PL19 8JD
TEL/FAX: (01822) 832528
3m W of Tavistock on A390, turn right at   COOKING 6
Gulworthy Cross   COST £31–£58

There has been a change of ownership at this peaceful restaurant-with-rooms, and if new proprietors Paul and Andie Roston are counting their blessings, the fact that Peter Gorton remains as chef must be uppermost among them. The country-house atmosphere remains, and with it the general impression of 'comfort and elegance'. On fine evenings, drinks can be taken on the vine-covered terrace with its sweeping views of the Tamar Valley; in winter a big log fire is lit in the comfortable bar. 'Friendly and efficient' service ensures that everything runs smoothly.

Peter Gorton's cooking takes in influences from the Orient, France and the Mediterranean, but his sense of adventure is tempered by a keen palate and sound judgement, so that combinations are never novel purely for the sake of it.

Strong flavours of cumin, garlic and lime have enhanced a starter of guinea fowl, and fillet of beef has been complemented by a 'dark, spicy but not overpowering' oriental sauce, plus accompaniments of sweet potato, asparagus and hollandaise. Top-of-the-range fish, meanwhile, have included turbot and sea bass ('a resounding success'). Desserts such as passion fruit mousse are well up to standard, as are canapés, coffee and petits fours. Well-chosen French wines are supplemented by a decent selection from the New World, and eight house wines start at £13.25.

CHEF: Peter Gorton   PROPRIETORS: Paul and Andie Roston   OPEN: all week 12 to 2, 7 to 9.30   CLOSED: 25 and 26 Dec   MEALS: Set L £14.50 (2 courses) to £21.50, Set D £35   SERVICE: not inc   CARDS: Amex, Delta, MasterCard, Switch, Visa   DETAILS: 50 seats. Private parties: 60 main room, 15 private room. Car park. Vegetarian meals. Children's helpings. No children under 13 at D. No smoking in dining room. Wheelchair access (not WC). No music   ACCOMMODATION: 8 rooms, all with bath/shower. TV. Phone. B&B £80 to £225. Rooms for disabled. Baby facilities (The Which? Hotel Guide) £5

TEFFONT EVIAS Wiltshire   map 2

▲ Howard's House 🕏✳

Teffont Evias SP3 5RJ
TEL: (01722) 716392   FAX: (01722) 716820
EMAIL: paul.firmin@virgin.net
off B3089, W of Dinton and 9½m W of Salisbury,   COOKING 3
signposted Chicksgrove   COST £27–£40

A meal at Howard's House is a calm, English sort of experience. Outside are gardens of box hedges, lawns and a fountain, while the dining room is cool and comfortable, decorated in the palest of greens, with white-clothed tables, and flower arrangements in front of a grand antique mirror. Staff are quietly welcoming. Paul Firmin puts a modern British stamp on some traditional favourites – marinated loin of lamb with roast winter vegetables and mint salsa – but the half-dozen choices per course also turn up fine examples of repertoire standards, such as feuilleté of seafood with a fennel-flavoured cream and white wine sauce, and corn-fed chicken stuffed with tarragon and sun-dried tomatoes. Finish, perhaps, with a light, hot, orange soufflé pancake with bitter chocolate sauce, or iced passion-fruit parfait. The wine list runs to a hundred or so bottles from classic areas, including a good few halves and enthusiastically recommended unusual wines, but prices are on the high side if you step beyond house wines, which start at £9.95.

CHEF: Paul Firmin   PROPRIETORS: Paul Firmin and Jonathan Ford   OPEN: Sun L 12.30 to 2, all week D 7.30 to 9.30   CLOSED: 30 Dec to 2 Jan   MEALS: Set L £19.50, Set D £22 (2 courses) to £25   SERVICE: not inc, card slips closed   CARDS: Amex, Delta, Diners, MasterCard, Switch, Visa   DETAILS: 30 seats. Private parties: 40 main room. Car park. Children's helpings. No smoking in dining room. Occasional music   ACCOMMODATION: 9 rooms, all with bath/shower. TV. Phone. B&B £75 to £145. Baby facilities (The Which? Hotel Guide) £5

▲ *means accommodation is available.*

THAME Oxfordshire   map 2

▲ *Old Trout* 🌢✹

29–30 Lower High Street, Thame OX9 2AA
TEL: (01844) 212146   FAX: (01844) 212614   COOKING 2
EMAIL: mj4trout@aol.com   COST £28–£46

A thatched roof, bulging walls, a rabbit warren of rooms and alcoves: this double cottage oozes ancient character. Although the menu takes in chargrilled and roasted vegetables with pesto, and lunchtime bangers and mash, fish is the leading player. One diner delighted in the silver salver of sea bass, red mullet, mussels, a langoustine and a crayfish that was laid before her, while starters that have pleased include a risotto, and a chowder of seafood served with good chunky bread. Judging by the busy weekends in particular, it seems that people enjoy the basic simplicity of the food, evident in crispy duck salad, and rack of lamb with a red pepper sauce. After the generous main courses, a scoop or two of ice cream – ginger or cinnamon perhaps – might be a good way to finish. Much of the varietally grouped wine list can be had for less than £20, including half a dozen house selections around £13 chalked on a blackboard.

CHEFS: Mark Jones   PROPRIETORS: Mr and Mrs M.E. Jones   OPEN: Mon to Sat 12 to 2.30, 6.30 to 10   CLOSED: 2 weeks Christmas   MEALS: alc (main courses £8.50 to £15.50). Set L £10.50 (2 courses)   SERVICE: not inc, card slips closed   CARDS: Diners, MasterCard, Switch, Visa DETAILS: 68 seats. 24 seats outside. Private parties: 25 main room. Car park. No smoking in 1 dining room. Occasional music   ACCOMMODATION: 8 rooms, all with bath/shower. TV. Phone. B&B £55 to £75 (*The Which? Hotel Guide*)

TITLEY Herefordshire   map 5

▲ *Stagg Inn* ✹🌢 £   [NEW ENTRY]

Titley HR5 3RL
TEL: (01544) 230221   FAX: (01544) 231390   COOKING 4
on B4355, NE of Kington   COST £16–£39

This tall, two-storey building on the edge of Titley is well patronised by locals both as a pub and restaurant. The bar area, with tables for eating, is quite separate from the main dining room with its pubby carpet, terracotta-coloured walls and darker curtains. Steve Reynolds's cooking relies on sourcing good ingredients, organic where possible, and keeping dishes straightforward and simple. An inspection meal started with diver-caught scallops with creamed leeks and black pepper oil, 'the combination of flavours quite brilliant', and went on to a 'thick, generous and supple' fillet of Herefordshire beef with whisky sauce. Other successes have included smoked haddock with mustard mash, and guinea fowl breast with lemon and tarragon. Vegetables, served separately, are well timed and attractively presented. Welsh and border cheeses are kept in good condition, and desserts might run to lemon tart with orange-curd ice cream, or soft chocolate cake with coffee sauce and whipped cream. Service, headed by Nicola Holland, is both relaxed and hard-working.

The fairly priced wine list scans the world, coming up with a good selection of half-bottles in the process. Six house wines are £8.95.

CHEFS: Steve Reynolds, Adam Davidson and Elaine Smith   PROPRIETORS: Steve Reynolds and Nicola Holland   OPEN: Tue to Sun L 12 to 2, all week D 6.30 (7 Sun) to 10   MEALS: alc exc Sun L (main courses £6.50 to £13.50). Set L Sun £9 to £14   SERVICE: not inc, card slips closed CARDS: Delta, MasterCard, Switch, Visa   DETAILS: 50 seats. 40 seats outside. Private parties: 30 main room, 20 and 30 private rooms. Car park. Vegetarian meals. Children's helpings. No smoking in 1 dining room. No music   ACCOMMODATION: 2 rooms, both with bath/shower. TV. B&B £25 to £40   £5

TORQUAY Devon   map 1

Table

135 Babbacombe Road, Torquay TQ1 3SR
TEL/FAX: (01803) 324292   COST £36–£44

As the Guide *went to press, this restaurant was sold*

CHEF/PROPRIETOR: Julie Tuckett   OPEN: Tue to Fri L 12.15 to 1.45, all week D 7.30 to 9.30 CLOSED: first 2 weeks Feb, last 2 weeks Mar   MEALS: Set L £9.50 (1 course) to £27.50, Set D £7.50   SERVICE: not inc, card slips closed   CARDS: Amex, Diners, MasterCard, Visa   DETAILS: 20 seats. Private parties: 20 main room. No children under 10. No smoking while others eat. Wheelchair access (not WC). No music   £5

TUNBRIDGE WELLS Kent   map 3

▲ *Hotel du Vin & Bistro*

Crescent Road, Tunbridge Wells TN1 2LY
TEL: (01892) 526455   FAX: (01892) 512044   COOKING 5
EMAIL: reception@tunbridgewells.hotelduvin.co.uk   COST £30–£47

Sharing an enviable formula with its sister operation in Winchester (see entry), this is a lively, informal bistro within a Georgian town house hotel, serving 'classy comfort food' and first-rate wines: a trompe l'oeil mural in the bar depicts the owners and friends in a convivial drinking scene. The restaurant feels comfortable and well worn, despite its newness, with bare floorboards, panelled walls in 'a sort of nicotine yellow', and masses of framed adverts and wine paraphernalia.

Despite a change of chef, the food still demonstrates a knack for effective combinations: grilled cod with chorizo, clams and parsley sauce, for instance, or green apple risotto with blue cheese and walnut wafers, a marriage of flavours that owes something to Caesar. Other dishes lean towards cuisine grand-mère: perhaps 'tender, lean' loin of pork stuffed with prunes and served with 'soft, moist and buttery mash'.

Vegetables have included 'bright-green, crisp and fat' sugar-snap peas, 'lovely, earthy' aubergine purée and 'authentically French' frites. For pudding, try an indulgent chocolate brownie with cinnamon ice cream, or perhaps pannacotta with blackberries or poached apricots. Efficiency and attention to detail are watchwords of the service, with green-aproned staff ensuring that everything runs smoothly at a well-judged pace. The widely-travelled 'Screwpull Cellar' wine list is priced to encourage experimentation (it boasts bottles from Morocco, Greece and Israel alongside those from more familiar territories), and quality and interest are high wherever you look. A varying selection of ten house wines is also offered by bottle or glass from around £10 to £18/£3 to £6. As the *Guide* went to press there were plans to open a third hotel in Bristol.

CHEF: Sam Mahoney   PROPRIETOR: Alternative Hotel Company   OPEN: all week 12 to 1.45, 7 to 9.45   CLOSED: 2 days Christmas   MEALS: alc (main courses £10 to £13.50)   SERVICE: not inc   CARDS: Amex, Delta, Diners, MasterCard, Switch, Visa   DETAILS: 80 seats. Private parties: 10 main room, 12 and 80 private rooms. Car park. Vegetarian meals. Children's helpings. No cigars/pipes in dining room. Wheelchair access (also WC). No music   ACCOMMODATION: 32 rooms, all with bath/shower. TV. Phone. Room only £79 to £119. Baby facilities (*The Which? Hotel Guide*)

Thackeray's House ♥ ⁵✳

| 85 London Road, Tunbridge Wells TN1 1EA | COOKING 6 |
| TEL/FAX: (01892) 511921 | COST £35–£43 |

Bruce Wass is expanding. The Jolly Sportsman (see entry, East Chiltington) now joins his portfolio, along with this old, three-storeyed, green and white, former novelist's property overlooking the common on the edge of town. Walls are covered with paintings, the floor with plush carpets, and well-spaced tables with starched linen, while a genial welcome from staff makes a good impression. The varied approach to cooking is well illustrated by fish, which might show up as monkfish ceviche, smoked haddock croustade, a mini-bouillabaisse (all first courses), or coriander-crusted cod with pasta and mussels.

Some eyebrow-raising combinations – preserved-duck salad with roast scallops and tamarind dressing – sit alongside more mainstream grilled wood pigeon breasts with pea risotto, but the feel is of a kitchen at home with a wide spectrum of ideas and treatments, from simple leek and almond soup to a macho roast haunch of hare with prunes, sweet potato and two types of cabbage. The search for flavour compatibility continues into desserts of chocolate espresso truffle with griotte cherries and coffee sauce, and roast spiced pear with grilled panettone and ginger ice cream. Wines on the slimmed-down list are now presented by grape variety, but otherwise follow no particular order (not of region, vintage or price). However, some good – even great – bottles are still to be found. Prices begin at £12.75 for house French but soon rise above £20.

CHEF/PROPRIETOR: Bruce Wass   OPEN: Tue to Sun L 12.30 to 2, Tue to Sat D 7 to 10   CLOSED: 10 days Christmas   MEALS: Set L and D £13.50 (2 courses) to £23.50   SERVICE: not inc; 10% for parties of 9 or more   CARDS: Delta, MasterCard, Switch, Visa   DETAILS: 50 seats. 30 seats outside. Private parties: 45 main room, 12 to 24 private rooms. Vegetarian meals. Children's helpings. No smoking in 1 dining room. Wheelchair access (not WC). No music

---

TWICKENHAM   Greater London   map 3

McClements

2 Whitton Road, Twickenham TW1 1BJ
TEL: (0181) 744 9610, changing to (020) 8744 9610   COOKING 6
FAX: (01784) 252967   COST £28–£67

McClements is visible almost as you soon as you emerge from the railway station. It looks surprisingly small and weathered for a place that put Twickenham on the gastro-map – though as the *Guide* went to press there were plans to open a large new extension at the back – and it has since spawned a sibling establishment, TW1 (see entry below).

John McClements seems to be cooking up a storm. The main fixed-price menu is accompanied by a six-course tasting menu with pre-selected wines for each course. Both offer much to tempt. Appetisers set the tone: perhaps a demi-tasse of seafood bisque containing a single whole scallop, immediately followed by mini-brochettes of seafood and a little disc of smoked salmon on a potato pancake. Masterly handling of seafood continues with a first course combining grilled scallops painted with sesame oil, seared tuna sliced into centimetre-thick collops, and light dim sum of lobster, the whole thing power-dressed with chilli and soy. Artful main-course compositions have included a dual guinea fowl presentation, the breast gently cooked and served with dauphinoise, the leg incorporated into an otherwise textbook coq au vin. At inspection, the package of '5 little puddings' yielded pear tarte Tatin, tiramisù, chocolate sponge with a warm chocolate sauce, apricot and passion fruit charlotte, and mango ice-cream, each 'perfectly executed'. Service is confident and unobtrusive. The wine list favours France but features some canny New World selections. House claret is £10, or for £1,200 you can have a bottle of Ch. Lafite 1919.

CHEF/PROPRIETOR: John McClements   OPEN: Mon to Sat 12 to 2.30, 7 to 11   MEALS: Set L £16 (2 courses) to £19, Set D £25 (2 courses) to £45   SERVICE: 10% (optional), card slips closed CARDS: Amex, MasterCard, Switch, Visa   DETAILS: 45 seats. Private parties: 200 main room. Car park. Vegetarian meals. No-smoking area. Wheelchair access (also WC). No music. Air-conditioned   £5

Prices quoted in the Guide *are based on information supplied by restaurateurs. The prices quoted at the top of each entry represent a range, from the lowest meal price to the highest; the latter is inflated by 20 per cent to take account of likely price rises during the year of the* Guide.

TW1

108 Heath Road, Twickenham TW1 4BN
TEL: (0181) 891 0008, changing to (020) 8891 0008
FAX: (01784) 240 593

COOKING 3
COST £21–£41

John McClements relaunched this second venue (originally Chez Clements) in early 1999 with a new chef, Stephen Blakemore, whose previous employers have included Marco Pierre White. It is a small restaurant with tables packed pretty close either side of a central screen. Fixed-price lunches supplement the main carte, with some dishes common to both. Oriental seasonings are much in favour, producing a plate of mixed hors d'oeuvres that encompass tuna sushi, mini won tons of lobster, 'fiercely seared' sesame scallops dressed in ginger and soy, and a crab cake. Technique is both sound and novel, as evidenced by a crisp deep-fried cake of wild mushroom risotto with a 'vibrant' basil dressing. More mushrooms – ceps in an earthy cream sauce – and boulangère potatoes make sturdy accompaniments to sea bass, while peppered duck breast is given textural contrast with dauphinois potatoes, red onion confit and caramelised chicory. Puddings tend to be rich and sticky: hot chocolate soufflé with coffee sauce, or pear tarte Tatin. Service is willing enough, but can give the impression of chasing its own tail at a busy session. Stylistically arranged wines start with Chilean Sauvignon Blanc at £9.50.

CHEF: Stephen Blakemore   PROPRIETOR: John McClements   OPEN: all week L 12 to 3 (5 Sun), Mon to Sat D 6.30 to 11.30   MEALS: alc (main courses £11.50 to £14). Set L £12.50   SERVICE: 10% (optional), card slips closed   CARDS: Delta, MasterCard, Switch, Visa   DETAILS: 70 seats. 15 seats outside. Private parties: 100 main room. Vegetarian meals. Children's helpings. Wheelchair access (also WC). No music. Air-conditioned   (£5)

ULLSWATER Cumbria

map 10

▲ *Sharrow Bay* ▮ ⁵⁕

Ullswater CA10 2LZ
TEL: (017684) 86301   FAX: (017684) 86349
EMAIL: enquiries@sharrow-bay.com
2m from Pooley Bridge on E side of lake, signposted
Howtown and Martindale

COOKING 7
COST £45–£67

'The late Francis Coulson, Brian, Nigel and all the staff, would like to welcome you.' So begins the menu, not in the least bit ghoulish; just a simple recognition that fifty years of unassuming dedication cannot be wiped out by mere mortality. The décor hasn't altered – 'cherubs are still doing unspeakable things on the ceiling' – the food-with-a-view combination is as good as any in England, Brian Sack continues the bread rounds, and there is still a 'generosity of spirit' about the place. But Bay watchers hunting for tell-tale signs of change claim to have noticed a new 'lightness of touch' in the cooking, and less creamily rich saucing. Even the renowned fish course has been simplified, shorn of its soufflé and flaky pastry. Smaller portions are available to those who ask: 'this is a *big* change noted one reporter, pleased to be able to get through a whole meal at last.

Given the amount of food it turns out, the kitchen must be the size of Wembley Stadium: afternoon teas are a draw, lunching here is 'one of life's delights', and menus offer a choice of some twenty-five dishes, from a dainty mound of dressed crab that looked and tasted 'a treat', to pig's trotter stuffed with ham shank and chicken mousseline on pease pudding. Many of the essentials remain (Johnnie Martin and Colin Akrigg started in the kitchen in the 1960s), among them fillet steak with oxtail, calf's liver with red onion marmalade, and pink herb-crusted lamb fillet: perhaps on crisp rösti with plump asparagus tips, another time on ratatouille with fried polenta. The display of cold desserts at the entrance to the dining room might take in an individual 'pie' of raspberry and lemon bavarois, while the defiantly 'original' sticky toffee pudding is a 'light and sweet-tooth-decaying luxury'.

You can set your watch by the service – 9pm is main-course time – and 'you never have to ask for anything'. Sharrow Bay is 'the ultimate in coddling its customers', who 'pay quite a lot, but somehow you do not mind'. Equally, the whole experience may be stylised, but 'everybody forgives them'. The wine list is an extensive collection that casts its net wide, in terms of both geography and pricing, and catches shoals of top-quality bottles. Over thirty wines by the glass mean that 'it would be quite possible for a couple to have a different wine with each course and different wines from each other'. House French is £14.75.

CHEFS: Johnnie Martin and Colin Akrigg   PROPRIETORS: Brian Sack and Nigel Lightburn   OPEN: all week 1 to 1.45, 8 to 8.30   CLOSED: 4 Dec to 4 Mar   MEALS: Set L £37.25, Set D £48.25   SERVICE: net prices, card slips closed   CARDS: Delta, MasterCard, Switch, Visa   DETAILS: 65 seats. Private parties: 12 main room. Car park. Vegetarian meals. No children under 13 in dining room. No smoking in dining room. Wheelchair access (also WC). No music. Air-conditioned   ACCOMMODATION: 26 rooms, 24 with bath/shower. TV. Phone. D,B&B £125 to £390. No children under 13 in accommodation (*The Which? Hotel Guide*)

ULVERSTON   Cumbria   map 8

▲ *Bay Horse Hotel* ▼ ⅝✳

Canal Foot, Ulverston LA12 9EL
TEL: (01229) 583972   FAX: (01229) 580502
EMAIL: reservations@bayhorse.furness.co.uk
off A590; just before centre of Ulverston, follow signs   COOKING 5
to Canal Foot   COST £26–£48

What used to be an old coaching inn – horses would stop en route across Morecambe Bay – retains its old world charm with much timber, gleaming brassware, padded wall-bench seating and an open fire. Informal lunches are served in the bar – perhaps smoked haddock and sweetcorn chowder, or a puff pastry pie of braised lamb with apricots and ginger – while a more elaborate menu operates in the conservatory. The food still has the 'Tovey touch' (John of that ilk is part-owner) with busy dishes and flamboyant sauces: perhaps pan-fried calves' sweetbreads and strips of ox tongue, with wild mushrooms in a sour cream and marsala sauce. Among seafood options, crab mousse with avocado pear on hot buttered toast might start the ball rolling, while John Dory has been successfully partnered with crispy leeks, water chestnuts and prawns in a creamy herb sauce. Vegetarians have a separate menu, and desserts come in for praise: brandy and chocolate roulade, say, or 'quite splendid' poached peach with butterscotch sauce. The agreeably priced wine list (£12.95 is the starting point) betrays the buyer's partiality for Chardonnay, and for New World producers. Otherwise there are hand-pumped real ales.

CHEFS: Robert Lyons and Esther Jarvis PROPRIETORS: John Tovey and Robert Lyons OPEN: Tue to Sat L 12 to 1.30, all week D 7.30 for 8 (1 sitting) MEALS: alc (main courses £16 to £18). Set L £16.75. Bar L available SERVICE: 10%, card slips closed CARDS: Delta, MasterCard, Switch, Visa DETAILS: 50 seats. Private parties: 50 main room, 20 and 30 private rooms. Car park. Vegetarian meals. No children under 12 in dining room. No smoking in dining room. Wheelchair access (also WC). Music ACCOMMODATION: 7 rooms, all with bath/shower. TV. Phone. D,B&B £85 to £160. No children under 12 in accommodation (*The Which? Hotel Guide*)

UPPER SLAUGHTER Gloucestershire   map 5

▲ *Lords of the Manor* ⸘✳

Upper Slaughter, nr Bourton-on-the-Water GL54 2JD
TEL: (01451) 820243 FAX: (01451) 820696
EMAIL: lordsofthemanor@btinternet.com   COOKING 6
turn W off A429, 3m S of Stow-on-the-Wold   COST £29–£90

Originally a seventeenth-century rectory, set in eight acres of parkland on the edge of a Cotswold village, Lords of the Manor is confidently adding more rooms and eventually a bistro to its armoury. Old fireplaces abound in the atmospheric stone house, and enormous flowers and heavy curtains decorate the low-ceilinged dining room, where John Campbell's technically accomplished food straddles the contemporary Anglo-French divide. Dishes are described simply, and the kitchen is a busy one, for example making an unfatty, peppery black pudding to serve on a disc of green mashed potato with dribbles of balsamic and mustard sauces.

First-rate thin pasta has been called on to wrap a whole scallop, served as a starter in a frothy white sauce strewn with asparagus tips, and to encase an expertly fashioned lobster mousse at inspection, which sat on a seared fillet of sea bass – towers are a favourite method of presentation – in turn underpinned by finely diced ratatouille. Accurate timing can be taken as read, and materials are both fresh and tasty: rare roast chump of lamb has proved these points, served thinly sliced with a properly reduced, stock-based, rosemary-flavoured sauce. Workmanship continues into desserts of hot banana soufflé, and a simply designed but effective rhubarb and champagne jelly accompanied by a white chocolate and mascarpone ice cream. Young, international service is generally professional, and while an enthusiastic sommelier and fifteen wines by the glass indicate a commitment to ordinary drinkers, many prices on the extensive, largely French list pull in the opposite direction. House wine is £14.95.

CHEF: John Campbell PROPRIETOR: Empire Ventures Ltd OPEN: all week 12 to 2 (2.30 Sun), 7 to 9.30 MEALS: alc (main courses £19.50 to £26.50). Set L £11.95 (2 courses) to £59, Set D £59 SERVICE: not inc L, 12.5% D; card slips closed CARDS: Amex, Delta, Diners, MasterCard, Switch, Visa DETAILS: 50 seats. 25 seats outside. Private parties: 50 main room. Car park. Vegetarian meals. No children under 10 at D. No smoking in dining room. No music ACCOMMODATION: 27 rooms, all with bath/shower. TV. Phone. B&B £98 to £295. Baby facilities. Fishing (*The Which? Hotel Guide*)

VIRGINSTOW Devon   map 1

▲ Percy's at Coombeshead 🗲✳

Virginstow EX21 5EA
TEL: (01409) 211236 FAX: (01409) 211275
EMAIL: percyscoombes@compuserve.com
follow signs to Percy's at Coombeshead from Gridley
corner on A388, or from B3218 at Metherell Cross   COOKING 5
junction   COST £32–£38

The Bricknell-Webbs are refugees from suburban North London and give every impression of having made a life-enhancing decision in decamping to this farm conversion not far from Launceston. West Country produce is of course the speciality, there is extensive use of organic and free-range materials, and they are the proud possessors of a licence to bid at the Looe fish auction. Visitors who stay over in the converted stable block report back with tales of comfort and tranquillity.

Deceptively simple-sounding menus may not prepare you for the complexity of many dishes, but, as one reader points out, the balance among protein, vegetables and carbohydrate is always carefully managed. Rapidly sautéed squid on mixed salad leaves is a triumph of timing, as is red mullet marinated in olive oil, sea salt, black pepper and lime juice, then flashed under a grill. The quality of meats is equally formidable: lamb stroganoff with a boozy Madeira sauce, or beef fillet, accompanied by spaghetti lengths of shredded parsnip, with roast garlic in the sauce. Desserts veer towards the sweeter end of the spectrum – steamed chocolate and Grand Marnier pudding with marmalade ice cream and chocolate sauce – although straightforward ice creams (perhaps rosemary flavoured) are highly rated. Service is as helpful as can be, but prepare for a leisurely pace. The shortish wine list is informatively annotated. Prices soon jump above £20, although the bidding opens at £9.95.

CHEF: Tina Bricknell-Webb PROPRIETORS: Tony and Tina Bricknell-Webb OPEN: all week D only 6.30 to 9.30 CLOSED: Nov MEALS: Set D £24 SERVICE: 10% (optional), card slips closed CARDS: Amex, Delta, MasterCard, Switch, Visa DETAILS: 34 seats. Private parties: 20 main room, 14 and 20 private rooms. Car park. No children under 12 in dining room. No smoking in dining room. Wheelchair access (not WC). Music ACCOMMODATION: 8 rooms, all with bath/shower. TV. B&B £59.50 to £99.50. Rooms for disabled. Baby facilities (*The Which? Hotel Guide*) (£5)

WALKINGTON East Riding of Yorkshire   map 9

▲ Manor House

Northlands, Newbold Road, Walkington HU17 8RT
TEL: (01482) 881645 FAX: (01482) 866501   COOKING 2
off B1230 towards Beverley from Walkington   COST £29–£54

A Victorian retreat in the Yorkshire Wolds overlooking horse paddocks and parkland, the Manor House is a hotel run very much as a family home. Fixed-price dinner in the attractive conservatory comes as four courses plus coffee, with soup or sorbet before the main, and there is a cheaper three-course alternative from Monday to Friday. Derek Baugh's daring sleights of hand have produced confit of salmon with 'Mexican beurre blanc', and a salsa of tomatoes that have been dried by wind rather than sun (this is Yorkshire). Otherwise expect 'zonkingly good' smoked haddock and prawn fish cakes, or an impressive dish of guinea fowl with leeks and bacon in Madeira sauce. Finish with bread-and-butter pudding with bramble sauce, perhaps, or have a look at the vast cheeseboard. The wine list majors in the French classic regions at fairly brisk prices. There are lashings of halves, though, and the house range starts at £11.95.

CHEF: Derek Baugh   PROPRIETORS: Derek and Lee Baugh   OPEN: Mon to Sat D only 7 to 9.15
CLOSED: 25 and 26 Dec, 1 Jan, bank hol Mons   MEALS: Set D Mon to Fri £18.50 to £30, Set D Sat
£30   SERVICE: not inc, card slips closed   CARDS: MasterCard, Switch, Visa   DETAILS: 56 seats.
Private parties: 40 main room, 24 private room. Car park. No cigars/pipes in dining room.
Music   ACCOMMODATION: 7 rooms, all with bath/shower. TV. Phone. Room only £65 to £100
(£5)

WAREHAM Dorset   map 2

▲ *Priory Hotel* ▮ ⅝✳

| Church Green, Wareham BH20 4ND | COOKING 4 |
| TEL: (01929) 551666 FAX: (01929) 554519 | COST £26–£72 |

Next to the church, with four acres of gardens extending down to the River Frome, this sixteenth-century stone-built priory – 'an attractive set of rambly buildings' – is a restful spot. The old cellar, with flag floor, wooden pillars and beams, has been converted into an atmospheric dining room with 'something of the refectory' about it. Stephen Astley likes his oriental flavourings, judging by a creamy Thai soup of tiger prawns, coconut and chilli, and by a large, crisp, puff pastry circle – filled with ratatouille mixture, strewn with scallops – the whole infused with freshly ground pungent spices.

Not everything is quite so exotic, as the repertoire also includes rich celery and Stilton soup, and pink roast loin of lamb (accurately timed and properly rested) served with two wild mushroom 'pithiviers' and a stock-based herby thyme sauce. Vegetables might be improved, although portions are generally big enough without them. That generosity extends to desserts: for example a 'rich and filling' slice of layered chocolate cake, served with crumbled pistachios in a thick crème anglaise. 'Uncertain' service could be sharper. Classic regions of France and Germany are accorded due reverence on a list that is none the less sufficiently enlightened to include some good-quality, modern wines from Italy and the New World. House Chardonnay and Pinot Noir from Dom. Laroche are £12.50, and prices remain fair throughout.

CHEF: Stephen Astley   PROPRIETORS: Stuart and John Turner   OPEN: all week 12.30 to 2, 7.30
to 10   MEALS: alc (main courses £19.50 to £23). Set L Mon to Sat £13.95 (2 courses) to £19.95,
Set L Sun £19.95, Set D Sun to Fri £26.50, Set D Sat £31.50   SERVICE: not inc, card slips
closed   CARDS: Amex, Delta, Diners, MasterCard, Switch, Visa   DETAILS: 45 seats. 40 seats
outside. Private parties: 45 main room, 25 and 45 private rooms. Car park. Vegetarian meals. No
children under 8 in dining room. No smoking in dining room. Music   ACCOMMODATION: 19
rooms, all with bath/shower. TV. Phone. B&B £80 to £240. No children under 8 in
accommodation. Fishing (*The Which? Hotel Guide*)

WARMINSTER Wiltshire
map 2

▲ *Bishopstrow House* 🏨✷

Warminster BA12 9HH
TEL: (01985) 212312 FAX: (01985) 216769
EMAIL: reservations@bishopstrow.co.uk
on B3414, SW of Warminster

COOKING 2
COST £26–£65

'There were quite a lot of diners: casually dressed, some with wet hair,' observed one visitor, which is perhaps only to be expected in a country house that boasts two swimming pools as part of its health and beauty package. Although Chris Suter's menu might include a rocket and watercress salad, tuna carpaccio, and a 'tulip' of sorbets, it is not designed specifically for slimmers. Instead it offers a generous run of sometimes indulgent dishes from duck confit and lentils with chilli and coriander, via wild mushroom risotto, and saddle of venison with sarladaise potatoes, to chocolate tart with cappuccino ice cream. Service (for which a 15 per cent charge is levied) has registered a few longueurs and lapses, and high prices generally put a question mark over the value, not helped by a wine list that struggles to find much of interest under £20. House Argentinian is £13.50.

CHEF: Chris Suter PROPRIETORS: Simon Lowe, Andrew Leeman and Howard Malin OPEN: all week 12 to 2.15, 7.30 to 9.30 MEALS: alc L Mon to Sat (main courses £7 to £14). Set L Sun £19.50, Set D £35 SERVICE: 15% (optional), card slips closed CARDS: Amex, Delta, Diners, MasterCard, Switch, Visa DETAILS: 80 seats. 50 seats outside. Private parties: 65 main room, 22 private rooms. Car park. Vegetarian meals. Children's helpings. No smoking in dining room. Wheelchair access (not WC). Music ACCOMMODATION: 31 rooms, all with bath/shower. TV. Phone. B&B £90 to £320. Rooms for disabled. Baby facilities. Swimming pool. Fishing (*The Which? Hotel Guide*) (£5)

WARWICK Warwickshire
map 5

Findons
NEW ENTRY

7 Old Square, Warwick CV34 4RA
TEL: (01926) 411755 FAX: (01926) 400453

COOKING 3
COST £31–£57

'Very sophisticated,' summed up one visitor to this elegant Georgian town house, appreciative of the well-spaced, white-clothed tables decorated with fresh flowers, the classic jazz, and service that is 'attentive without being overpowering'. Michael Findon is an adherent of the modern British school, producing for example a warm salad of goats' cheese with apple and onion marmalade, and a spicy dish of scallops and prawns incorporating saffron, masala and chickpeas. Meat and fish reflect well on both supplier and chef, if reports of duck breast with cherries and cinnamon, and cod with fennel are anything to go by. 'Artistry without fuss' is another aim that the restaurant seems to be achieving, evident in the 'minimal' and prettily cut vegetables adorning main courses. A lunchtime 'rapide' menu offers lighter options of chicken breast in curry sauce or brioche with wild mushroom and coriander cream. Desserts include traditional crème brûlée or slightly more adventurous cinnamon-apple brioche with calvados ice cream. The wine list concentrates on France but offers one or two bottles from most other wine regions, including England; prices are fair, starting with house French red and Spanish white at £10.95.

CHEFS: Sean Rouse and Michael Findon   PROPRIETOR: Findon & Williams Ltd   OPEN: Mon to Fri L 12 to 2, Mon to Sat D 7 to 9.30   CLOSED: bank hols   MEALS: alc (main courses £13 to £20). Set L £4.95 (1 course) to £15.95 (2 courses), Set D £15.95 (2 courses)   SERVICE: not inc, 10% for parties of 8 or more   CARDS: Amex, Delta, Diners, MasterCard, Switch, Visa   DETAILS: 50 seats. 20 seats outside. Private parties: 36 main room, 14 and 36 private rooms. Vegetarian meals. No children under 8 at D. Wheelchair access (not WC). Music

WATERHOUSES   Staffordshire   map 5

▲ *Old Beams* 🍾 ✸

Leek Road, Waterhouses ST10 3HW
TEL: (01538) 308254   FAX: (01538) 308157 — COOKING 6
on A523, 7m SE of Leek — COST £33–£68

In a 'wild and isolated' part of the country, Old Beams straddles the road, restaurant on one side, accommodation on the other. Inside, the beamed dining room has been extended by a modern conservatory, where a mural features Romeo and Juliet types in a heavily stylised garden. Ann and Nigel Wallis are celebrating their twentieth year here and, if there's a feeling that they haven't moved with the times in culinary terms, there's no doubt that what they do they do extraordinarily well. Nigel Wallis's grasp of technique is unquestioned, and at best his cooking is 'immaculately accomplished'.

The lunchtime set menu may take in starters of red mullet with roast red pepper coulis, and fricassee of mussels with pearl barley, followed by noisettes of pork with black pudding ravioli on a grain mustard sauce. Evenings are à la carte, with a scattering of luxury ingredients – langoustines, foie gras and truffles – and prices to match. An inspector was impressed by the skilful champagne sauce accompanying her starter of scallops and langoustines, but bowled over by a flavourful confit duck leg that came with the breast and 'interesting' couscous: 'copybook stuff; the sort that spoils you for all future confits'. 'Amazingly intense' chocolate sorbet was a winner too, although its accompanying chestnut mousse didn't quite match up in terms of flavour. Quality rather than quantity is the philosophy behind a wine list that majors in the French classic regions but also features more modern styles from some highly respected producers. Prices are fair, half-bottles are plentiful, and house Beaujolais (red and white) is £15.95.

CHEF: Nigel Wallis   PROPRIETORS: Nigel and Ann Wallis   OPEN: Wed to Fri and Sun L 12 to 1.30, Tue to Sat D 7 to 9 (9.30 Sat)   CLOSED: Jan   MEALS: alc D (main courses £18.50 to £20.50). Set L £16.95 (2 courses) to £22   SERVICE: not inc, card slips closed   CARDS: Amex, Delta, Diners, MasterCard, Switch, Visa   DETAILS: 45 seats. 15 seats outside. Private parties: 60 main room, 10 private room. Car park. Children's helpings. No smoking in dining room. Occasional music ACCOMMODATION: 5 rooms, all with bath/shower. TV. Phone. B&B £75 to £120 (double rooms). Rooms for disabled. Baby facilities. Fishing (*The Which? Hotel Guide*)   £5

🍾 *denotes an outstanding wine cellar;* 🍷 *denotes a good wine list, worth travelling for.*

WATERMILLOCK   Cumbria   map 10

▲ *Rampsbeck Hotel* ♥ ⅚✶

Watermillock, Ullswater CA11 0LP
TEL: (017684) 86442   FAX: (017684) 86688   COOKING 3
on A592 Penrith to Windermere road   COST £34–£55

The lakeside setting, with fine views of the fells, induces a sense of calm and
relaxation, helped along by open fireplaces, antique furniture and a candlelit
dining room. An Anglo-French approach has produced pot-au-feu of spring
lamb, and Barbary duck breast with a fruity griottine sauce and creamy
dauphinois potatoes, while an inspection meal, which confirmed reports that
standards are not what they once were, showed up some impressively fresh fish
to start: brill fillet with a subtle but distinctive curried dressing, and 'firm,
brilliantly undercooked' red mullet between layers of pasta with a ratatouille
dressing. Portions tend to be on the small side, but materials are well sourced,
and presentation is given a high priority: one reporter's rhubarb mousse was
considered 'a work of art', sitting on jellied rhubarb on a disc of shortbread,
topped with blood orange ice cream and accompanied by a ginger sauce. Concise
tasting notes on each bin make for a user-friendly list in which diverse wines are
grouped according to acidity, fruit, oak and tannin levels (thus explaining why a
Canadian Chardonnay is placed next to a Spanish Sauvignon Blanc). Prices are
reasonable, with house wines starting at £11.25.

CHEF: Andrew McGeorge   PROPRIETORS: Mr and Mrs T.I. Gibb, and Mrs M.J. MacDowall
OPEN: all week 12 to 1, 7 to 8 (booking essential L)   CLOSED: early Jan to early Feb   MEALS: Set
L £25, Set D £26 to £36. Bar L available   SERVICE: not inc, card slips closed
CARDS: Delta, MasterCard, Switch, Visa   DETAILS: 40 seats. Private parties: 60 main room, 12
private room. Car park. Vegetarian meals. No children under 8. No smoking in dining room. No
music   ACCOMMODATION: 20 rooms, all with bath/shower. TV. Phone. B&B £60 to £180 (*The
Which? Hotel Guide*)

WATH-IN-NIDDERDALE   North Yorkshire   map 8

▲ *Sportsman's Arms* ⅚✶

Wath-in-Nidderdale HG3 5PP
TEL: (01423) 711306   FAX: (01423) 712524   COOKING 4
off B6265, 2m NW of Pateley Bridge   COST £25–£48

The stone building looks pubby enough from outside, and functions as such
with a big fire in the congenial bar, but it has a pink and grey dining room, too,
that 'felt like a French railway station restaurant' to one reporter. The same menu
is served throughout, supplemented by a blackboard of daily specials, and fish
features prominently, typically Scarborough woof topped with Wath rarebit in
caper sauce, or roast salmon with ginger and spring onions. Ray Carter's homely
but up-to-date style yields starters of black pudding in a spicy chorizo and
tomato sauce, and smoked Nidderdale trout with creamed horseradish. A hearty
streak runs through, in the form of Toulouse sausage and mash in a red onion
and butter bean gravy, while simple desserts have included notable summer
pudding with pouring cream. Staff move effortlessly between lounge, bar and

dining room and apparently miss nothing but on occasion can be slow. Fair pricing characterises the intelligent wine list, which opens with a page of house recommendations from around £10.

CHEF: Ray Carter   PROPRIETORS: Ray and Jane Carter   OPEN: Sun L 12 to 2, all week D 7 to 9   CLOSED: 25 Dec   MEALS: alc (main courses £8 to £16). Set L Sun £17   SERVICE: not inc, card slips closed   CARDS: MasterCard, Switch, Visa   DETAILS: 60 seats. Private parties: 55 main room, 12 private room. Car park. Vegetarian meals. Children's helpings. No smoking in dining room. Wheelchair access (not WC). No music   ACCOMMODATION: 13 rooms, 11 with bath/shower. TV. Phone. B&B £35 to £100. Rooms for disabled. Fishing (*The Which? Hotel Guide*) £5

WELLS Somerset   map 2

Ritcher's

5 Sadler Street, Wells BA5 2RR   COOKING 4
TEL/FAX: (01749) 679085   COST £15–£38

Look for a little passageway off Wells's main thoroughfare. At the end is a small courtyard and the two-storey Victorian building that houses Ritcher's. Brick-surrounded arches, dark rust-coloured drapes, and Chinese vases filled with false flowers lend character to the ground-floor dining room, while the wood-panelled bar reminded one well-travelled reporter of 'an Andalusian bodega'.

'Devoid of gimmicks or pretention', the food takes a sensible approach with generally familiar ideas, from a straightforward, balsamic-dressed salad of mozzarella, plum tomatoes and basil, to a rich and creamy oyster mushroom stuffing for tortellini. Despite an occasional daring leap – partnering stuffed guinea fowl breast with a smoked salmon croûte – it is the 'simple, unshowy' things that seem to work best: duck and foie gras pâté with blackcurrant chutney, for example, or simply grilled halibut with a throughly professional beurre blanc. Desserts display 'real skill', from crème brûlée to the rich dense flavours of chocolate tart with honey ice cream. Locally produced breads and fine espresso flesh out the details. France dominates the fairly priced wine list, while a good run of vintage ports draws things to an elegant conclusion. House wines start at £8.95.

CHEFS: Nick Hart and Danielle Barton   PROPRIETORS: Nick Hart and Kate Ritcher   OPEN: all week 12 to 2, 7 to 9.30 (10 Sat, 6 to 10 in summer)   CLOSED: 1 Jan   MEALS: Set L £5.50 (1 course) to £7.50, Set D £14.95 (2 courses) to £17.95   SERVICE: not inc, card slips closed   CARDS: MasterCard, Switch, Visa   DETAILS: 40 seats. 12 seats outside. Private parties: 22 main room. Vegetarian meals. Children's helpings. No cigars/pipes while others eat. Wheelchair access (not WC). Music

---

'My friend chose the soufflé of Swiss cheese with casserole of shellfish and Kirsch, because he couldn't believe that anything that sounded so awful could be any good. And he was right.'
(On eating in Wiltshire)

Card slips closed *in the details at the end of an entry indicates that the total on the slips of credit cards is closed when handed over for signature.*

WEST BAY   Dorset   map 2

Riverside Restaurant £

West Bay DT6 4EZ
TEL: (01308) 422011   COOKING 2
off A35, 1m S of Bridport   COST £21–£66

The atmosphere at this waterside establishment is warm and casual, helped by rules being 'kept to a minimum', although booking has now become essential. Unfussy, unpretentious cooking is what draws customers in to the double-glazed multi-windowed dining room, and fish – 'really fresh and cooked correctly' – provides the main focus: a hearty starter of mussels steamed with tomato, garlic, onion and coriander, or grilled fillet of brill with crispy spinach and sorrel sauce. A specials menu, a carte and a blackboard mean that getting to grips with what you want to eat can take a little time, but non-fish eaters and vegetarians will not be disappointed, and orders are taken with 'unfailing cheerfulness and charm'. Locally made ice creams feature among puddings, and children's portions are available at 20 per cent reduction in price. The largely white wine list kicks off with litres of French at £12 and then moves on to specified growers from around the world.

CHEFS: Mike Mills and Nic Larcombe   PROPRIETORS: Arthur and Janet Watson   OPEN: Tue to Sun L 12 to 2.30, Tue to Sat D 6.30 to 9; also open Sun and Mon bank hols; possible variations at D in Mar and late Oct/Nov: phone to check   CLOSED: 1 Dec to 1 Mar   MEALS: alc (main courses £7 to £25)   SERVICE: not inc, card slips closed   CARDS: Amex, Delta, MasterCard, Switch, Visa   DETAILS: 80 seats. 20 seats outside. Private parties: 70 main room, 12 to 20 private room. Vegetarian meals. Children's helpings. No cigars/pipes in dining room. Wheelchair access (not WC). Occasional music

---

WEST ILSLEY   Berkshire   map 2

Harrow Inn ¾✕ | NEW ENTRY |

West Ilsley RG20 7AR
TEL: (01635) 281260   FAX: (01635) 281139   COOKING 3
1½m off A34, 10m N of Newbury   COST £25–£40

A little to the north of West Ilsley on the Winchester to Oxford road, opposite a cricket pitch and thickly populated duck pond, is a seventeenth-century inn of considerable charm. Newbury racecourse isn't far away, which explains the equestrian prints, but menus indicate that time has not stood still. 'Everything that goes by, you wish you had ordered,' commented one who had a good nosey at other people's plates, and the choice is indeed extensive. Cornish king scallops with Caesar salad is just one of several dishes that may be taken as starter or main, and satisfies either way, as is squid tempura with onion and herbs. Moist venison has come with a convincing rendition of wild mushroom risotto, while another reporter heartily commended breast and confit leg of duck. Traditionalists will rejoice in fine steak and kidney pudding, while Peasemore cream should be relished at dessert stage (it comes from a local herd of just eight Jerseys), whether dolloped on to caramelised orange tart or 'lovely' sticky toffee pudding. Service has been judged 'observant, sensible and pleasant'. Wines are serviceable rather than thrilling, but a broad house selection is commendably pegged at £10 throughout.

CHEF: Scott Hunter   PROPRIETORS: Scott Hunter and Emily Hawes   OPEN: all week 12 to 1.55, 7 to 9   CLOSED: D Sun and Mon Dec to Jan   MEALS: alc (main courses £8.50 to £12.50) SERVICE: not inc, card slips closed; 10% for parties of 8 or more   CARDS: Delta, MasterCard, Switch, Visa   DETAILS: 60 seats. 60 seats outside. Private parties: 22 main room. Car park. Vegetarian meals. Children's helpings. No children under 12 Fri and Sat D. No smoking in dining room. No music

---

WEST TANFIELD   North Yorkshire   map 9

▲ Bruce Arms

West Tanfield HG4 5JJ   COOKING 4
TEL: (01677) 470325   FAX: (01677) 470796   COST £19–£38

Log fires and blackboard menus are the form at this ivy-covered, stone-built bistro-pub in Uredale, where Geoff Smith's cooking embraces many traditional ideas. Twice-baked Wensleydale cheese soufflé might start the ball rolling, followed by braised lamb shank with parsley mash and red wine gravy. Fish extends from roast salmon with red cabbage to classical smoked haddock with spinach, poached egg and hollandaise, and while vegetarians might opt for cashew nut curry, lovers of red meat (of whom there are a few in Yorkshire) can choose between pan-fried pigeon and calf's liver with bacon. 'Light lunches' might take in Cumberland sausage and mash, or smoked salmon with scrambled egg, while desserts range from lemon posset to treacle tart and custard. Around three dozen wines, mostly well below £20, include nine by the large or small glass.

CHEF: Geoff Smith   PROPRIETORS: Amanda Donkin and Geoff Smith   OPEN: Tue to Sun L 12 to 2 (2.30 Sun), Tue to Sat D 6.30 to 9.30   MEALS: alc (main courses £9 to £14.50). Set L Sun £9.95 (2 courses) to £11.50; light L available Tue to Sat   SERVICE: not inc, card slips closed   CARDS: Delta, MasterCard, Switch, Visa   DETAILS: 42 seats. 16 seats outside. Private parties: 26 main room, 26 private room. Car park. Vegetarian meals. No children under 14. Music ACCOMMODATION: 3 rooms, all with bath/shower. TV. B&B £30 to £50. No children under 14

WETHERSFIELD   Essex   map 6

Dicken's ▼

The Green, Wethersfield CM7 4BS   COOKING 5
TEL/FAX: (01371) 850723   COST £23–£45

Overlooking a small green, this attractive, pink-washed, bay-windowed building boasts two dining rooms, one with Regency striped wallpaper, foodie pictures and dried flowers, the other larger with a minstrels' gallery. They are the setting for some bright-sounding dishes, from steamed local rabbit and onion pudding, to crispy king prawn tempura with a spicy chilli dip, by way of Aldeburgh cod meunière on Moroccan lentils. The two-course 'lunch for a tenner' (considered a steal by supporters) has yielded creamy Mediterranean fish soup with rouille and croûtons, followed by braised lamb shank.

Judging by discrepancies in reports, standards appear to vary considerably, ranging from 'the crispest, tenderest, most flavoursome confit of duck I have eaten in years' to poor saucing at an inspection meal, one of whose highlights was a strongly peppery dish of penne with a generous amount of undyed smoked haddock. Desserts have included simple baked apple and rhubarb tart, as well as an unusual, lightly spicy, winter fruitcake parfait drizzled with caramel. John Dicken's personal selection of wines priced between £10.50 and £22.50 opens an interesting, quality-filled list that is helpfully arranged by style, with a discernible penchant for France.

CHEF/PROPRIETOR: John Dicken   OPEN: Wed to Sun L 12.30 to 2, Wed to Sat D 7.30 to 9.30   CLOSED: 24 to 26 Dec, 1 Jan, bank hols   MEALS: alc (main courses £11 to £15). Set L Wed to Sat £10 (2 courses), Set L Sun £19.50   SERVICE: not inc   CARDS: Delta, MasterCard, Switch, Visa   DETAILS: 60 seats. 12 seats outside. Private parties: 36 main room, 10 and 18 private rooms. Car park. Vegetarian meals. Children's helpings. Wheelchair access (also WC). Occasional music
£5

WHITBY North Yorkshire

map 9

Magpie Café £

14 Pier Road, Whitby YO21 3PU
TEL: (01947) 602058 and 821723
FAX: (01947) 601801

NORTH YORKS
2000
FISH 'N' CHIPS

COOKING 2
COST £16–£46

Queues at this 'delightfully unsophisticated and unpretentious' fish 'n' chip restaurant are standard, 'even at 4pm but it was well worth it'. A three-storey merchant's house overlooking the harbour, it used to open only in the summer months but now runs all year. Menus are numerous, portions huge. Start with locally smoked kippers, perhaps, or crab, smoked salmon or lobster, then move on to cod, haddock, plaice, sole or skate, all with chips, or you can have a small portion of each. Sole and halibut also come with lemon and butter, grapes and potatoes, but generally nothing more elaborate than that, the focus clearly on the fish. Not that carnivores are left out: sausages, ham, turkey and steak get straightforward, no-nonsense treatment. Desserts are split into hot and cold, from sticky toffee to sherry trifle. Service is pleasant and polite, and around thirty wines from Bibendum start at £7.95 for vins de pays.

CHEF: Ian Robson   PROPRIETORS: Ian Robson and Alison McKenzie-Robson, and Ian and Sheila McKenzie   OPEN: all week 11.30 to 9   CLOSED: 22 to 25 Dec, 1 Jan, 1 month from 9 Jan   MEALS: alc (main courses £5 to £17). Set L and D £9.95 to £15.95   SERVICE: not inc, card slips closed   CARDS: Delta, MasterCard, Switch, Visa   DETAILS: 100 seats. Private parties: 50 main room. Vegetarian meals. Children's helpings. No smoking in dining room. Occasional music. Air-conditioned £5

£ *means that it is possible to have a three-course meal, including coffee, half a bottle of house wine and service for £25 or less per person, at any time the restaurant is open, i.e. at dinner as well as lunch. It may be possible to spend considerably more than this, but by choosing carefully you should find £25 or less achievable.*

WHITCHURCH Hampshire   map 2

Red House ✸ £ | NEW ENTRY |

21 London Street, Whitchurch RG28 7LH   COOKING 2
TEL: (01256) 895558   COST £19–£33

To help find the Red House in the small town of Whitchurch, remember that it is
not red but white. A busy bar occupies one half, the other given over to a
magnolia-painted dining room with wooden floors, its walls hung with huge
mirrors. Shelves are enthusiastically stacked with home-made pickles, oils and
preserves, and cheerful service backs up the sense of commitment. Printed
menus and blackboard specials between them point to diverse, even 'inspi-
rational', ideas, from duck leg with pineapple and chilli salsa, to Asian lamb
salad with cashews and roasted peppers. Portions tend to be large: a 'massive'
salad of warm potato with black pudding and chorizo; or one of four plump
breasts of roast pigeon set on various leaves with mild red onion in an oily
dressing. Desserts come generously portioned too: pavlova, perhaps, or 'trem-
blingly wobbly' Key lime pie. The wine list is limited but fairly priced, with six
house wines starting at £7.99.

CHEF: Shannon Wells PROPRIETORS: Shannon and Caroline Wells OPEN: all week 12 to 2, 6.30
(7 Sun) to 9.30 MEALS: alc (main courses £7 to £13.50) SERVICE: not inc, card slips closed
CARDS: Delta, MasterCard, Switch, Visa DETAILS: 28 seats. 60 seats outside. Private parties:
30 main room. Car park. Vegetarian meals. Children's helpings. No children under 14 at D. No
smoking in dining room. Occasional music

WHITSTABLE Kent   map 3

Whitstable Oyster Fishery Co

Royal Native Oyster Stores, The Horsebridge,
Whitstable CT5 1BU   COOKING 1
TEL: (01227) 276856 FAX: (01227) 280257   COST £26–£64

As an idea this is hard to beat. A run-down oyster store beside the pebble beach
is converted (with minimal attention to peeling paint) into a large dining room,
where fish straight from the boats – cod, lobster, skate, dabs, whiting and
gurnard among them – are simply cooked and unceremoniously presented.
Reality is less rosy – choice may be limited, for example, and the blackboard
menu rigidly insists that starters cannot be taken as main courses – but enough
visitors enjoy the food to report positively on it. Native Whitstable oysters are
£12.60 for half a dozen, smoked eel comes with creamy horseradish on toast, and
grilled plaice is served with new potatoes and broad beans. Thick chunks of
brown bread accompany, unassuming desserts include rhubarb cobbler, and
Muscadet seems a popular choice on the very short wine list.

CHEFS: Chris Williams, Joe Trivelli and Steve Harris PROPRIETOR: Whitstable Oyster Fishery
Co OPEN: Tue to Sun L 12 to 2, Tue to Sat D 7 to 9, and Mon L and Sun and Mon D in summer
MEALS: alc (main courses £8.50 to £22). Set L and D £22.50 SERVICE: not inc, 10% for parties of
6 or more CARDS: Amex, Delta, Diners, MasterCard, Switch, Visa DETAILS: 150 seats. Private
parties: 30 main room. Children's helpings. Wheelchair access (not WC). Occasional music (The
Which? Hotel Guide)

WICKHAM Hampshire   map 2

▲ Old House Hotel and Brasserie 🍴✱ | NEW ENTRY |

The Square, Wickham PO17 5JG   COOKING 4
TEL: (01329) 833049   FAX: (01329) 833672   COST £28–£50

Some readers may remember the Ruthven-Stuarts from Old Chesil Rectory in
Winchester (see entry), which they ran until the autumn of 1998. The dining
room of their newly acquired, brick-built, creeper-clad property on Wickham's
market square has been converted from an old barn and overlooks a garden.
Despite the casual approach of hand-written menus and a brasserie format, the
kitchen gives firm direction to the operation, its style embracing 'deep flavours
without fussy garnishes'. The confident cooking shows in, for example, a
generous mound of ochre-brown crab risotto in a shellfish bisque, its 'definitive
crabbiness' indicative of a chef who 'understands shellfish'.

The repertoire runs from familiar smoked haddock fish cakes to a main course
trio of fillets (beef, lamb and pork) in a port and rosemary sauce, and a range of
cooking techniques is sensibly and appropriately applied. A dish of crisp-
skinned Gressingham duck, for example, has produced roast breast, with a confit
leg deriving a rich tang from its salty cure. Vegetables are part of the dish: in this
case precisely cooked sugar snap peas and smooth celeriac purée. The English,
French and Italian strands continue into desserts of raspberry shortbread, prune
and armagnac ice cream, and a sweet, creamy, vanilla-infused pannacotta, well
complemented by a chocolate mousse and a passion fruit and mango sorbet.
Smooth service is well paced, and the forty-five-strong wine list is stylistically
arranged, France contributing the lion's share. House vin de pays is £10.95.

CHEF: Nicholas Ruthven-Stuart   PROPRIETORS: Nicholas and Christina Ruthven-Stuart   OPEN:
Tue to Sat L 12 to 2, Mon to Sat D 7 to 9.30   CLOSED: 2 weeks Christmas   MEALS: alc L (main
courses £10 to £17.50). Set L £13.50 (2 courses) to £17.50, Set D £26 (2 courses) to £30
SERVICE: not inc, 12.5% for parties of 6 or more   CARDS: Amex, Delta, Diners, MasterCard,
Switch, Visa   DETAILS: 40 seats. 10 seats outside. Private parties: 40 main room, 14 private
room. Car park. Children's helpings. No smoking in dining room. Wheelchair access (not WC).
No music   ACCOMMODATION: 8 rooms, all with bath/shower. TV. Phone. Room only £65 to £90.
Baby facilities

WILLITON Somerset   map 2

▲ White House 🍷 🍴✱

11 Long Street, Williton TA4 4QW   COOKING 6
TEL: (01984) 632777   COST £45–£54

Painted stark white, with French shutters at the windows, a palm tree at the front
and a mimosa to the side, this small Georgian town house – not far from the
coastal path than runs along Bridgwater Bay – takes on a different character
inside. There are palms here too, but dark stone walls, and old tea chests pressed
into service as tables in the bar, combine with antiques and modern paintings to
produce a 'relaxed and unpretentious' atmosphere. The format may indicate that
the Smiths have other interests – they are open for only half the year, and then
only for dinner – but there is nothing half-hearted about their approach to food.
They source materials well, and treat them intelligently.

496

The style is a personal one that might have had its origins in Elizabeth David – the Smiths have been cooking here since 1967 – but is certainly not old-fashioned. It includes steamed asparagus (from nearby Withycombe) with hollandaise, and roast pesto-crusted monkfish with olive oil potato purée. Wild salmon and sea trout have featured among main courses, alongside rare wood pigeon breast thinly sliced on to hot beetroot. The food is distinguished by its 'freshness and simplicity', and meals might begin with a tartlet of Brixham crab and prawns or soufflé Suissesse, and finish with an apple and calvados pancake, or chocolate marquise with praline. The choice of French growers on the highly interesting wine list reveals an unerring eye for quality that doesn't lose focus when it switches its gaze elsewhere. Ten dessert wines by the glass include nuts 'n' raisins-like Scholz Hermanos Solera 1885 Malaga (£2.90): taste it while you still can for it is no longer produced. House French is £14.

CHEFS/PROPRIETORS: Dick and Kay Smith   OPEN: all week D only 7 to 8.30   CLOSED: Nov to mid-May   MEALS: Set D £31.50   SERVICE: not inc   CARDS: none   DETAILS: 22 seats. Private parties: 6 main room. Car park. Children's helpings. No smoking in dining room. Wheelchair access (not WC). No music   ACCOMMODATION: 10 rooms, all with bath/shower. TV. Phone. B&B £44 to £98. Rooms for disabled. Baby facilities

---

WILMINGTON East Sussex   map 3

▲ *Crossways* 🌟

Lewes Road, Wilmington BN26 5SG
TEL: (01323) 482455   FAX: (01323) 487811
EMAIL: crossways@fastnet.co.uk   COOKING 4
on A27, 2m W of Polegate   COST £36–£44

Walkers may like to note that both the South Downs Way and Weald Way pass only about half a mile from this white-painted, green-shuttered, 'delightfully run' Georgian house in the Cuckmere Valley, not far from the chalk figure of the Long Man of Wilmington. With a proprietorial presence in both kitchen and dining room it is 'a very hands-on place' where, amid Queen Anne chairs and floral drapes, a sensibly balanced, weekly-changing, four-course menu is served five nights out of seven.

A degree of spicing is applied to main courses such as lamb chump chops with orange and ginger, or wild boar Cajun style. There may also be guinea fowl or duck, as well as the regular (surcharged) fillet steak. Seafood pancake, and Stilton and leek noodle bake, are among traditional starters to expect, followed by a soup course, while desserts typically range from ginger spotted dick with custard to seasonal fruits in muscat jelly. Of interest on the seventy-strong and otherwise mainstream list are a trio of organic wines and four English ones, including house Hidden Springs white at £10.25. The red (same price) is from Chile.

CHEFS: David Stott and Juliet Anderson   PROPRIETORS: David Stott and Clive James   OPEN: Tue to Sat D 7.30 to 8.45   CLOSED: 24 Dec to 24 Jan   MEALS: Set D £27.95   SERVICE: not inc   CARDS: Amex, Delta, MasterCard, Switch, Visa   DETAILS: 24 seats. Private parties: 6 main room. Car park. No smoking in dining room. Wheelchair access (not WC). Occasional music   ACCOMMODATION: 7 rooms, all with bath/shower. TV. Phone. B&B £48 to £76. No children under 12 in accommodation

WILMSLOW Cheshire   map 8

Bank Square

4 Bank Square, Wilmslow SK9 1AN   COOKING 4
TEL: (01625) 539754   COST £35–£55

The appeal of this centrally sited restaurant, according to one visitor, is 'well-presented food in stylish surroundings at moderate prices'. Music, noise and smoke drift up from the downstairs bar, as the place tries to please more than one constituency, but alcoves in the sedate split-level dining room promote a feeling of privacy, and smartly set tables point to an orderly concern for the food's context. It may be ostensibly brasserie food, but it takes some effort to service a menu of seven starters and seven mains when, for example, a roast fillet of snapper requires both a fennel confit and a provençale stew of clams and mussels, or when chargrilled beef is accompanied by a fricassee of Portobello mushrooms, celeriac crisps, and a horseradish emulsion. Not all reporters have gone away happy, but the kitchen is adept at timing – both searing and slowly cooking – and produces some robust flavours. Desserts offer an indulgent-sounding tripartite chocolate plate alongside perhaps pear and blueberry tart with almond milk sorbet. Wines on the fifty-strong list start off firmly in France, then take a trot through the 'rest of the world'. Eleven wines are available by the glass; house South African is £12.50 per bottle.

CHEF: Michael Dodds   PROPRIETORS: Janet and David Rivett   OPEN: Mon to Sat 12 to 2.30, 6.30 to 10.30   MEALS: alc (main courses £13 to £18). Set L £9.95 (2 courses), Set D 6.30 to 7.30 £10.95 (2 courses), Set D Mon to Fri 7.30 to 10.30 £13.50 (2 courses)   SERVICE: not inc, 10% for parties of 6 or more   CARDS: Amex, Delta, Diners, MasterCard, Switch, Visa   DETAILS: 50 seats. Private parties: 55 main room. Vegetarian meals. Children's helpings. Occasional music. Air-conditioned (£5)

WINCHCOMBE Gloucestershire   map 5

▲ Wesley House ▼ ⬜ ⁵⋇

High Street, Winchcombe GL54 5LJ   COOKING 3
TEL: (01242) 602366   FAX: (01242) 602405   COST £23–£55

Step straight off the main street into the lounge-bar of this ancient half-timbered restaurant-with-rooms, where aperitifs are taken and a blackboard of daily specials is hawked around to supplement the carte. Ahead is the split-level dining area with white plaster walls, dark old beams and exposed stone. Dinner is the main meal, and while many dishes sound ordinary enough – brill with leeks and scallops, duck breast with calvados sauce – there is usually a bit more excitement on offer, perhaps in the form of salmon marinated in kalamansi and lemon grass, garnished with cheese beignets. Lunch offers less choice but no less interest: perhaps Chinese crab, tomato and sweetcorn soup, followed by steamed venison pudding.

Timing and judgement of some savoury dishes have been called into question, but one couple ended on a high note with cheese and a plate of sorbets and ice creams; otherwise there may be dark chocolate sponge, blueberry crème brûlée or coconut mousse. Service is decently paced, and quality is maintained on the wine front. South Africa is the favoured country and the Stellenbosch region supplies a specially recommended white and red: 1997 Saxenburg Private Collection Chardonnay (£19.50) and 1993 Rust-en-Vrede Estate 1993 (£23) Those who prefer their wines from outside Africa will find plenty that appeals. House wines start at £12.50.

CHEF: James Lovatt   PROPRIETOR: Matthew Brown   OPEN: all week L 12 to 2, Mon to Sat D 6.45 to 9.15 (9.30 Sat)   CLOSED: mid-Jan   MEALS: Set L £8.95 (2 courses) to £12.50, Set D £15.50 (2 courses) to £28.50   SERVICE: not inc, card slips closed   CARDS: Amex, Delta, Diners, MasterCard, Switch, Visa   DETAILS: 55 seats. 16 seats outside. Private parties: 65 main room. Children's helpings. No smoking in dining room. Occasional music   ACCOMMODATION: 6 rooms, all with bath/shower. TV. Phone. B&B £48 to £75. Baby facilities (*The Which? Hotel Guide*) (£5)

WINCHESTER Hampshire   map 2

▲ *Hotel du Vin & Bistro* ▮

Southgate Street, Winchester SO23 9EF
TEL: (01962) 841414   FAX: (01962) 842458   COOKING 6
EMAIL: admin@winchester.hotelduvin.co.uk   COST £29–£49

Satisfied customers are ten a penny at this big old house on one of Winchester's main streets: 'if I were a cat I would purr for the remainder of the day,' admitted a lunchtime visitor. With old bare wood, hops garlanded around windows, small tables, and 'bottles everywhere', it provides an amenable setting for bistro food as it should be: calf's liver on creamy polenta, rump of lamb with borlotti beans, or 'perfectly done' skate wing on mustard mash with anchovy and caper sauce. Portions can be generous, and results range from 'top notch' to 'so so', with strong endorsement for such simple dishes as 'fresh-tasting' chilled tomato soup in summer, or a year-round 'assembly' starter of wild rocket salad with Parmesan.

The well-judged contemporary repertoire might also include Mediterranean vegetable terrine, langoustine tempura, and venison with pearl barley risotto, finishing perhaps with apple jelly and fresh berries, or properly crusted crème brûlée. 'Lots of different people serve you' but the food comes 'hot and prompt'. Wine service is all it should be and more, extending to guided tours of the cellar for hotel guests. The main list is a veritable cornucopia of vinous treasures offered at realistic prices. New in 1999 was the quartet of Hotel du Vin own-label wines sourced from Dom. St-Hilaire in the Languedoc, offering great-value drinking from £11.50. A regularly changing list by the glass at £3 and upwards includes dedicated pudding wines.

CHEF: Andy Clark   PROPRIETOR: Alternative Hotel Company   OPEN: all week 12 to 1.45, 7 to 9.45   MEALS: alc (main courses £12 to £15). Set L Sun £21.50   SERVICE: not inc, card slips closed   CARDS: Amex, Delta, Diners, MasterCard, Switch, Visa   DETAILS: 65 seats. 20 seats outside. Private parties: 48 main room, 12 and 48 private rooms. Car park. Vegetarian meals. Children's helpings. No cigars/pipes in dining room. Wheelchair access (not WC). No music   ACCOMMODATION: 23 rooms, all with bath/shower. TV. Phone. Room only £85 to £185. Rooms for disabled (*The Which? Hotel Guide*)

Hunters ✸✖

5 Jewry Street, Winchester SO23 8RZ	COOKING 2
TEL: (01962) 860006	COST £23–£41

Small, tightly packed tables with candles and flowers give this busy, noisy town-centre restaurant a bistro feel. Keenly priced set menus are a big draw, and dishes run the gamut from pork and chilli sausages with warm potato salad, to tagliatelle with wild mushrooms and blue cheese. A vibrant oriental seam, meanwhile, produces tea-smoked chicken with sesame dressing, duck breast on a noodle and spring onion pancake with plum jus, and much appreciated Thai fish cakes with pickled cucumber. Puddings continue the theme with lemon grass brûlée, or there might be good old apple crumble, or steamed banana and cinnamon sponge. Service is efficient, though can be overstretched. The wine list centres on France but dips into most other wine-producing nations too. House wine is £9.95.

CHEF: Jon Perrett   PROPRIETOR: David Birmingham   OPEN: Mon to Sat 12 to 2, 6.30 to 10 CLOSED: 24 Dec to 3 Jan, bank hols   MEALS: alc (main courses L £6 to £9, D £13). Set D Mon to Fri £9.95 (2 courses) to £12.95   SERVICE: not inc, 10% for parties of 6 or more   CARDS: Amex, Delta, Diners, MasterCard, Switch, Visa   DETAILS: 65 seats. Private parties: 16 main room, 25 private room. Vegetarian meals. No smoking in 1 dining room. Music   £5

Old Chesil Rectory ✸✖

1 Chesil Street, Winchester SO23 0HU	COOKING 5
TEL: (01962) 851555 FAX: (01962) 869704	COST £33–£52

The 'old' in the name means just that. Winchester's most ancient house, dating from 1459, appreciably retains much of its original structure, its beamed façade rising to elegant twin peaks; even candles in the dining room on a summer lunchtime seem 'only right and proper' for the feel of the place. Philip Storey was chef under the previous owners (who have moved to Wickham, see entry), so he hasn't needed a settling-in period, and the contemporary British slant to the cooking continues as before.

Meals offer two- or three-course deals, and lunch flexibly allows the possibility of opting out of a main course. Soups range from highly praised langoustine bisque, via quail consommé, to the only disappointment at inspection, an under-flavoured vichyssoise with scallops. But materials are well sourced and dishes typically well balanced, for example a highly rated fillet of Newlyn cod served on purées of aubergine and courgette, with crisp-fried Parma ham and balsamic dressing. Among local and seasonal produce (some of it organic) has been an intriguing suet pudding of March hare with roast saddle and cabbage. Meals are distinguished by 'lightness and finesse', from a twice-baked Roquefort soufflé to deeply flavoured champagne jelly with white peach coulis, and vanilla bavarois with cherries and strawberries. Agreeable service completes the picture. The modestly proportioned wine list is arranged by style to suit the food, and is supplemented by a slate of posher options. House selections start at £13.95.

CHEF: Philip Storey PROPRIETORS: Philip and Catherine Storey OPEN: Tue to Sat 12 to 2, 7 to 9 (9.30 Sat) CLOSED: 2 weeks Christmas (exc 31 Dec), 2 weeks Aug MEALS: Set L £15 (2 courses) to £20, Set D £27.50 (2 courses) to £30 SERVICE: not inc, 12.5% for parties of 6 or more CARDS: Delta, Diners, MasterCard, Switch, Visa DETAILS: 60 seats. Private parties: 40 main room, 10 and 14 private rooms. Vegetarian meals. Children's helpings. No smoking in 1 dining room. Music (£5)

▲ Wykeham Arms ♥ ⁵⋇

75 Kingsgate Street, Winchester SO23 9PE COOKING 2
TEL: (01962) 853834 FAX: (01962) 854411 COST £20–£38

A visit to this unspoiled pub just south of the cathedral is a very English experience, with resonances of royalty, military history, Trollope and the college next door. Three log fires cheer the rooms, and no music thumps the ear, just a civilised buzz of conversation. Lunch for the tourists, business people and locals who sit cheek by jowl is a matter of various platters or sandwiches, cottage pie, or the 'Wyk' rarebit, plus some interesting specials: lamb and redcurrant casserole, say, or celeriac and potato dauphinois. Candlelit evening meals (for which booking is essential) might be a simple steak, or ever-popular rack of Hampshire lamb with honey-roasted celeriac and parsnip chips. Among a half-dozen puddings may be iced ginger terrine, or chocolate truffle tart. George Gale owns the pub, so handpumped ales are a real alternative to the attractively priced wines, which show some seasonal variation. The devotion to Burgundy of Graeme Jameson (former proprietor who still consults on wines) is a constant. His ebullient introduction to the list points novices in the right direction, while twenty wines by the glass aid those who like to pick 'n' mix. Four house wines are £10.95 each.

CHEF: Belinda Watson PROPRIETOR: George Gale & Co. OPEN: Mon to Sat 12 to 2.30, 6.30 to 9 CLOSED: 25 and 26 Dec MEALS: alc (main courses L £5 to £12, D £10 to £13) SERVICE: not inc, card slips closed CARDS: Amex, Delta, Diners, MasterCard, Switch, Visa DETAILS: 75 seats. 30 seats outside. Private parties: 8 main room. Car park. Vegetarian meals. No children under 14 in dining room. No smoking in 3 dining rooms. No music ACCOMMODATION: 13 rooms, all with bath/shower. TV. Phone. B&B £45 to £117.50. No children under 14 in accommodation (*The Which? Hotel Guide*)

WINDERMERE Cumbria map 8

▲ Gilpin Lodge ♥ ⁵⋇

Crook Road, Windermere LA23 3NE
TEL: (015394) 88818 FAX: (015394) 88058
EMAIL: hotel@gilpin-lodge.co.uk COOKING 5
on B5284, 2m SE of Windermere COST £25–£54

Even by Lake District standards, this comfortably appointed, well-decorated country house is high in the charm stakes, with real fires, homely but smart furnishings, and a general air of ease. Lunch offers a good range of dishes, some in two sizes, from salmon and crab cakes (served with poached egg and hollandaise), via charred pineapple and bacon rarebit, to calf's liver and champ with a sage, onion and ale sauce. Dinner is a more serious four-course affair (five

501

if you count a mid-meal sorbet) that might start with smoked trout fritters, followed by risotto of Flookburgh shrimps, and a main course of lamb cutlets with mint and pea couscous. Local materials include pheasant from Holker Hall and fish from Fleetwood, perhaps poached halibut in a mussel and saffron sauce.

To finish, cheese and savouries are up against the stiff competition of warm chocolate and sour cherry tartlet, or steamed plum sponge. At its best the 'beautifully prepared, cooked and presented' food pleases reporters, although it does have embarrassing lapses of timing and taste, as one couple found at a Sunday dinner in October. For those who stay, breakfast comes highly recommended. Concise yet apt tasting notes reveal a sound mind behind the wine list, and one that is as open to quality and variety as it is closed to outrageous mark-ups. Seven house wines from six countries start at £12.50 a bottle, £3 a glass.

CHEFS: Christopher Davies and Christine Cunliffe   PROPRIETORS: John and Christine Cunliffe
OPEN: all week 12 to 2.30, 7 to 9   MEALS: alc L Mon to Sat (main courses £7.50 to £9). Set L Sun £16.50, Set D £29.50   SERVICE: not inc   CARDS: Amex, Delta, Diners, MasterCard, Switch, Visa   DETAILS: 55 seats. 20 seats outside. Private parties: 28 main room, 13 and 22 private rooms. Car park. Vegetarian meals. No children under 7 in dining room. No smoking in dining room. Wheelchair access (not WC). Music   ACCOMMODATION: 14 rooms, all with bath/shower. TV. Phone. B&B £60 to £180. Rooms for disabled. No children under 7 in accommodation (*The Which? Hotel Guide*)   £5

▲ Holbeck Ghyll 🍴 ⁵✳

Holbeck Lane, Windermere LA23 1LU
TEL: (015394) 32375   FAX: (015394) 34743
EMAIL: accommodation@holbeck-ghyll.co.uk
off A591, take Holbeck Lane 3m N of Windermere   COOKING 5
signposted Troutbeck; hotel ½m on left   COST £27–£59

There are fine views over Lake Windermere and Langdale Fells and a homely atmosphere in this nineteenth-century hunting-lodge turned country-house hotel. It has two dining rooms, one with oak panelling, bare wooden tables and giraffe-decorated curtains, the other equally comforting with French windows leading out on to a terrace for al fresco dining, weather permitting. After the appointment early in 1999 of Stephen Smith, previously head chef at Gordleton Mill (see entry, Lymington), the style of cooking remains in contemporary European mould, exemplified by cappuccino of bouillabaisse with red mullet, or braised pig's trotter stuffed with ham hock, pork knuckle and foie gras.

Output is founded in high quality and sometimes luxurious raw materials, ranging from lobster (in a velouté), and foie gras (with Szechaun pepper and Jurançon jelly) to veal sweetbreads (casseroled with girolles and truffle as a starter). Pasta also makes its presence felt, perhaps as an open ravioli of squab pigeon. Dishes are cooked professionally, yielding for example crisp-skinned sea bass in a sauce vierge made with basil oil, although the anticipated flair was absent from an inspection meal. Anglo-French cheeses come with a spicy chutney, while desserts embrace crème vanille with raspberries, and a classically styled tarte fine aux pommes with vanilla ice cream and caramel sauce. Incidentals, from an appetiser soup to freshly baked bread rolls, come in for praise, and service is professional and knowledgeable. The reasonably priced wine list is strongest in France, although the USA also gets good billing. Eight house wines start at £13.95.

CHEF: Stephen Smith   PROPRIETORS: David and Patricia Nicholson   OPEN: all week 12 to 2, 7 to 9   MEALS: Set L £10.50 (1 course) to £17.95, Set D £32.50 to £37.50   SERVICE: not inc, card slips closed   CARDS: Amex, Delta, Diners, MasterCard, Switch, Visa   DETAILS: 50 seats. 20 seats outside. Private parties: 40 main room, 20 private room. Car park. Vegetarian meals. No children under 8 in dining room. No smoking in dining room. Wheelchair access (not WC). No music   ACCOMMODATION: 20 rooms, all with bath/shower. TV. Phone. B&B £75 to £190. Rooms for disabled. Baby facilities (The Which? Hotel Guide)   (£5)

Jerichos ⁵⊁

Birch Street, Windermere LA23 1EG	COOKING 5
TEL/FAX: (015394) 42522	COST £28–£47

In a quiet street off the main shopping area, with its name (nearly an anagram of owners Chris and Jo) on a dark red awning, Jerichos is reached up a short, steep flight of broad stone steps. With purple décor, striking artificial flower arrangements, and a view of the kitchen, the place exudes a sense of 'thriving progress'. The menu reads appealingly – 'I felt in good hands,' commented a visitor – and the cooking is confident within a manageable repertoire. A soup is usually on offer (pea and ham, or more exotic roasted coriander with parsnip, celeriac and grated Lancashire cheese), and duck leg confit makes a regular appearance, perhaps on mustard-glazed neeps, or in a salad with ginger, pine nuts and walnut oil.

Highly rated chargrilled beef fillet – with curried butter, well-done French fries, grilled tomatoes and mushrooms – is a main-course fixture, as is a vegetarian dish: perhaps a 'sludgy, flavoursome' risotto of aubergine, red pepper and olives topped with pecorino shavings. Desserts tread the familiar ground of runny chocolate sponge, rice pudding, baked custard, and an apple charlotte that 'made me want to try to re-create this at home'. Relaxed, friendly but smart service from Jo Blaydes is appreciated, and wines eschew traditional heavy-weights in favour of New World interest and fair pricing. Eight varied house wines are £10.75 each.

CHEFS: Chris Blaydes and Sarah Connolly   PROPRIETORS: Chris and Jo Blaydes   OPEN: Tue to Sun D only 6.45 to 10   CLOSED: 4 weeks in winter   MEALS: alc (main courses £10 to £16)   SERVICE: not inc   CARDS: Delta, MasterCard, Switch, Visa   DETAILS: 38 seats. Private parties: 22 main room. Vegetarian meals. No children under 12. No smoking in dining room. Music   (£5)

▲ Miller Howe ♚ ⁵⊁

Rayrigg Road, Windermere LA23 1EY	
TEL: (015394) 42536 FAX: (015394) 45664	
EMAIL: lakeview@millerhowe.com	COOKING 6
on A592, between Windermere and Bowness	COST £25–£57

The policy of gradual change initiated by the Garsides last year continues. The dark colour scheme has been replaced by pastel blues in one dining room, sandy tones in the other, with full-length wall-width mirrors doing much to increase the perception of scale. There is still a feeling of opulence in the leather-clad drawing rooms; views from the conservatory and dining room remain a match for any; and the sense of theatre continues as lights are dimmed for the evening's performance. Three-course lunches consist of three choices per course, four-course dinners (although set out unconventionally) of four, with a no-choice fish course before the main, and Susan Elliott maintains the refined country-style impetus established by her mentor, John Tovey.

Multi-layered dishes are a feature, and sauces are a strong suit. Those accompanying meat typically consist of a stock reduction with alcohol: Madeira-based to partner a generously truffled, chargrilled beef fillet and its mini foie gras mousse; or red wine-based, and lightly cinnamoned, in the case of rich, seared, marinated turkey liver. Fish typically gets lighter treatment, perhaps a fennel sauce for monkfish, or an intense red pepper jus and herb oil for firm fillet of brill.

Desserts tend to fly the home flag in the form of a subtler-than-usual sticky toffee pudding with matching sauce, or a flavourful pavé of rhubarb with a sharp fruit sorbet and a 'truly nectar-ish' apple juice. Owner and chef do the rounds, and the senior staff are as friendly as ever. There is plenty of flag-waving, too, by Australia, New Zealand, South Africa and the USA on a wine list that concentrates on quality at affordable prices, although a separate short list of European wines still does enough to cause a traditionalist's heart to flutter. House wines are £16.50 for Australian Chardonnay and £16 for a South African red; three wines by the glass change nightly.

CHEF: Susan Elliott   PROPRIETORS: Charles Garside and Iain Garside   OPEN: all week 1 and 8 (each 1 sitting)   CLOSED: 3 Jan to mid-Feb   MEALS: Set L £9.99 (2 courses) to £18.50, Set D £35   SERVICE: not inc, card slips closed   CARDS: Amex, Diners, MasterCard, Switch, Visa DETAILS: 64 seats. Car park. Vegetarian meals. No children under 8 in dining room. No smoking in dining room. Occasional music. Air-conditioned   ACCOMMODATION: 12 rooms, all with bath/shower. TV. Phone. D,B&B £70 to £250. No children under 8 in accommodation (*The Which? Hotel Guide*) (£5)

WINKLEIGH Devon   map 1

Pophams ⁑✳ £

Castle Street, Winkleigh EX19 8HU   COOKING 5
TEL: (01837) 83767   COST £24–£41

With just three tables, this qualifies as one of the smallest restaurants in the *Guide*, but if good things come in small packages then Pophams is a very good thing indeed. Marathon lunchtime sessions (it's closed in the evening) can turn into 'a relaxed party': 'it's a little like eating in your own kitchen,' write proprietors Melvyn Popham and Dennis Hawkes, and customers could hardly be closer to the action. Melvyn chats to them as he cooks, while Dennis waits at table and acts as kitchen assistant. Yet there's nothing remotely amateurish about the operation; cooking sensibly keeps within the operating limitations, but a combination of efficiency and culinary flair ensures highly polished results.

The daily-changing blackboard menu might offer carrot and artichoke soup, or chicken liver terrine with Cumberland sauce to start, followed by good-quality (sometimes local) meats or fish served with well-judged sauces: perhaps roast salmon with red pepper and vermouth, or beef with oyster mushrooms and Madeira. Accompanying vegetables have included little skewers of aubergine, tomato, courgette and mushroom baked in foil. For dessert, sticky toffee pudding with clotted cream is considered 'ambrosial', but a stem ginger version with ginger wine and brandy sauce may also prove hard to resist. The premises are unlicensed, but customers' wine is treated 'knowledgeably and with care' and no corkage is charged.

CHEF: Melvyn Popham   PROPRIETORS: Melvyn Popham and Dennis Hawkes   OPEN: Wed to Sat L only 12 to 1.30   CLOSED: Feb   MEALS: alc (main courses £12 to £16.50). Unlicensed but BYO (no corkage)   SERVICE: not inc, card slips closed   CARDS: MasterCard, Visa   DETAILS: 10 seats. Private parties: 10 main room. No children under 14. No smoking in dining room. Wheelchair access (not WC). Music. Air-conditioned

---

WINSFORD Somerset   map 1

▲ *Savery's at Karslake House* 🍴✳

Halse Lane, Winsford TA24 7JE   COOKING 5
TEL/FAX: (01643) 851242   COST £40–£51

The welcome is warm at this fifteenth-century house in the middle of Exmoor National Park, with service overseen by Patricia Carpenter, who seems to strike just the right balance between homeliness and efficiency. John Savery's cooking hits a similar note, making use of prime, often locally sourced ingredients which are carefully handled to yield full-flavoured, comforting dishes. There is a relaxing lounge for drinks, while the dining room has a light, airy feel. The kitchen has delivered well-executed starters of king prawns and courgettes in tempura batter on a mango salsa, and terrine of pork and pickled pistachios, served with a tangy pickle of apricot, mango and lime. Main courses might include roast rack of lamb served off the bone along with bubble and squeak, black pudding, roast chestnuts and a herb jus – a dish with 'lots of flavour' – or praiseworthy fillet of beef, served with shallots and mushrooms cooked in red wine. For dessert there may be light-textured sticky toffee pudding, or perhaps 'rich and creamy' rice pudding with caramelised bananas flavoured with Drambuie. Incidentals such as bread and petits fours do not let the side down, either. The wine list is short, largely French and well priced, with a batch of house wines around £12.50.

CHEFS: John Savery and Nikki Plumb   PROPRIETORS: Patricia Carpenter and John Savery   OPEN: Mon to Sat D only 7 to 9.15 (9.30 Sat)   CLOSED: Feb   MEALS: Set D £27.50   SERVICE: not inc, card slips closed   CARDS: Delta, MasterCard, Switch, Visa   DETAILS: 30 seats. Private parties: 36 main room. Car park. No smoking in dining room. No children under 15 in dining room. No music   ACCOMMODATION: 7 rooms, all with bath/shower. TV. B&B £45 to £95. Rooms for disabled. No children under 15 in accommodation (*The Which? Hotel Guide*)

'Service was far too slick, and one cheeky young man, when I said I was not happy, said, "Do you wish to make a formal complaint, or are you just joking?"'
(On eating in Yorkshire)

▲ *Winteringham Fields* ♀ ⁵⋇

Winteringham DN15 9PF
TEL: (01724) 733096   FAX: (01724) 733898   COOKING 9
EMAIL: euroannie@aol.com   COST £36–£92

'The standard never goes downhill,' reckoned one visitor to this converted
farmhouse near the Humber. One of the first things to strike reporters is service
that is 'totally correct' while still putting most people at their ease, overseen by a
relaxed and natural Annie Schwab MBE. Next to impress are the waves of
pre-meal nibbles, taken either in a chintzy lounge or amid the 'riot of plants and
furnishings' in the conservatory. Reporters are borne along on a train of
cromesquis of lobster eggs, and small cups of deeply shellfishy scallop
consommé, to the newly marble-floored dining room with extravagant ostrich
egg table decorations.

Although undeniably a 'contemporary' chef, Germain Schwab is no slave to
fashion. Nor is this a kitchen that boringly perfects a few 'signature' dishes,
rather one that applies considerable skill to a continuous stream of interesting
ideas, among them a ballottine of oak-smoked skate wing filled with pike
mousse on a cider sauce, and pot au feu of scallops with pan-fried duck foie gras
in a galangal and vegetable broth. 'You have to recognise the fact that the chef
does like to experiment,' reckoned one diner, but a sound classical background
helps to pull everything together.

The 'wow' factor is further enhanced by strong visual appeal: for example,
three different-coloured pasta tubes filled with chicken mousse and langoustine
flesh, with a sweet yellow corn sauce and leek fritters for crispness and crunch.
Above all it is the skill of making simple things taste good that marks out this
cooking, be it a fricassee of lambs' sweetbreads with soft-boiled quails' eggs and
quartered artichoke hearts, or a smooth hazelnut mousse encased in chocolate on
a nougatine sauce.

Cheeses are in tiptop condition, and the trolley and its driver come in for praise
for making this course a joy, 'even for children'. Prices are considered fair in view
of the 'quiet perfection', but if money is an issue, try the fixed-price lunch. For
those who stay (a listed cottage and Dovecot have recently been added) there is
the prospect of a breakfast that is 'an object lesson to many more expensive
British hotels'. Classy French wines abound on the lengthy list, which also
sports some famous names from Italy and the New World (and a lesser-known
octet of producers from Switzerland). But you don't have to pay a huge sum for a
wine to match the fine cuisine: Amity Gewürztraminer 1995 from Oregon's
Willamette Valley is £22 and would be a perfect partner for the scallops and foie
gras. House wines are £14.

CHEF: Germain Schwab   PROPRIETORS: Annie and Germain Schwab   OPEN: Tue to Sat 12 to
1.30, 7 to 9.30   CLOSED: 2 weeks from 24 Dec, 1 week March, 1 week Aug, bank hols   MEALS:
alc (main courses £25.50 to £27). Set L £22, Set D £29 to £54   SERVICE: not inc, card slips
closed   CARDS: Amex, Delta, MasterCard, Switch, Visa   DETAILS: 46 seats. Private parties: 10
main room, 10 private room. Car park. No smoking in dining room. Wheelchair access (not WC).
No music   ACCOMMODATION: 10 rooms, all with bath/shower. TV. Phone. Room only £70 to
£150. Rooms for disabled. No children under 8 exc babes in arms in accommodation (*The
Which? Hotel Guide*)

WITHERSLACK Cumbria   map 8

▲ *Old Vicarage* ♟ ⁵⭑

Church Road, Witherslack LA11 6RS
TEL: (015395) 52381   FAX: (015395) 52373
EMAIL: hotel@oldvicarage.com   COOKING 3
off A590, take first left in village to church   COST £22–£49

'Well away from the touristy tat', this roughly rendered Georgian house is
decorated with chintz curtains, heavily patterned wallpaper and candlelit tables.
After twenty years Stanley Reeve has retired, and co-chef James Brown has
taken charge of the kitchen. At the same time, the old set price menu has been
replaced by a carte, allowing those who still want four courses to carry on as
before (for about the same price), while giving smaller appetites the option of
fewer courses. The style continues in similar Anglo-French country-house vein,
however, offering meunière of Morecambe Bay flukes, brown shrimps and
capers, and parsley-crusted saddle of Mansergh Hall lamb with dijonnaise
potatoes. Careful sourcing extends to roast fillet of Tunstall organic outdoor
pork, wrapped in Waberthwaite air-cured ham, and vegetables are an integral
part of main courses.

Traditional desserts, such as steamed orange sponge with custard, share the
billing with slightly more cosmopolitan amaretti semifreddo or dark chocolate
tart. Carefully selected British farmhouse cheeses are served in good condition at
the right temperature. Enthusiastic promotion of interesting wines at fair prices
is exemplified by the page of Italian house specialities. Puglian house wines are
£9, a good number of half-bottles helps those who like to ring the changes, and
there are beers from Cumbrian brewery Jennings (£2.90 a bottle).

CHEFS: James Brown and Chris Foley   PROPRIETORS: Jill and Roger Brown, and Irene and
Stanley Reeve   OPEN: Sun L 12.30 to 1, all week D 7 to 9   MEALS: alc (main courses £13.50 to
£16.50). Set L Sun £15.50, Set D £32.50   SERVICE: not inc, card slips closed   CARDS: Amex,
Delta, MasterCard, Switch, Visa   DETAILS: 40 seats. Private parties: 20 main room, 12 and 28
private rooms. Car park. Vegetarian meals. Children's helpings. No smoking in dining room.
Music   ACCOMMODATION: 14 rooms, all with bath/shower. TV. Phone. D,B&B £80 to £200.
Rooms for disabled. Baby facilities (*The Which? Hotel Guide*) (£5)

WOKINGHAM Berkshire   map 3

Rose Street ⁵⭑ | NEW ENTRY |

6 Rose Street, Wokingham RG40 1XU   COOKING 4
TEL: (0118) 978 8025   FAX: (0118) 989 1314   COST £27–£52

'Simplicity sums up the style' of John Read's restaurant. Part of a picturesque
row of tiny red-brick cottages converted to various businesses, it has a 'faintly
Victorian' air, with ancient floorboards, beamed ceilings, and simple wooden
tables. Paul Scott's cosmopolitan credentials are not hard to find, in a menu that
deals in foie gras with grape chutney and Sauternes jelly, and in pepper-dusted
seared scallops (the timing 'spot on') in an emulsified cappuccino of white
haricot beans and truffle oil.

His is generally confident cooking, with accurate timing applied to pink, garlic-rubbed rump of lamb, and to roast breast of duck, sauced with honey and ginger, served with fondant potatoes and stock-braised Puy lentils. There is a generosity about the food, too, from sauces that lap the rim of the plate, to a substantial tian of crab, plump langoustines and potato with an abundance of rocket. Vegetarian dishes are accorded the same inventive pains as the rest of the menu, while desserts, although less successful at inspection, have produced sumptuously textured Bailey's crème brûlée. 'Casual but friendly' is what most people would ask of service. The compact wine list does its principal business in France, with only cursory offerings from elsewhere: the food deserves a more enterprising approach. House selections start with French vins de table at £10.95.

CHEF: Paul Scott   PROPRIETOR: John Read   OPEN: all week L 12 to 2.30 (12.30 to 3 Sun), Mon to Sat D 7 to 10   MEALS: alc (main courses £11 to £16). Set L £13.95 (2 courses) to £17.95 SERVICE: not inc, 10% for parties of 8 or more   CARDS: Amex, Delta, MasterCard, Switch, Visa DETAILS: 36 seats. 4 seats outside. Private parties: 18 main room. Vegetarian meals. No smoking in 1 dining room. Wheelchair access (also women's WC). Music (£5)

WOODBRIDGE Suffolk

map 6

Captain's Table ⁵⁜ £

| 3 Quay Street, Woodbridge IP12 1BX | COOKING 4 |
| TEL: (01394) 383145 FAX: (01394) 388508 | COST £21–£38 |

'An excellent, simple restaurant', summed up one visitor to this trio of plainly decorated, interconnecting, low-beamed dining rooms near the quayside. Dishes are well balanced, helpings generous, and the ingredients mostly high quality. Simplicity is indeed the watchword, with starters of rock oysters, crab mayonnaise, and a plate of charcuterie with gherkins, the food capturing the mood of the times with its generally light and unfussy approach. Main courses of pasta with pesto, or chicken breast with black-bean salsa, take their place beside a range of fish options, from seared salmon with lime and coriander to steamed sea bass filled with fish mousse in a herby sauce.

Some dishes might appear as either a first or main course – perhaps salade niçoise with fresh tuna, or a garlic, lemon and parsley risotto with scallops – and daily specials are chalked on a board. Desserts tend to explore the toffee and chocolate end of the spectrum, but there may also be an unusual rhubarb crumble ice cream. While service may sometimes lack warmth, 'young, attentive and polite staff' in Captain's Mate T-shirts generally cope well. Some fifty wines are well varied in terms of style and origin and, as with the food, fairly priced. House French red and Australian white are £8.95.

CHEF: Pascal Pommier   PROPRIETORS: Jo Moussa and Pascal Pommier   OPEN: Tue to Sun and bank hol Mon L 12 to 2 (3 Sun), Tue to Sat and bank hol Mon D 6.30 to 9.30 (10 Fri and Sat) CLOSED: 2 weeks Jan   MEALS: alc (main courses £7 to £13)   SERVICE: not inc, card slips closed   CARDS: Delta, MasterCard, Switch, Visa   DETAILS: 50 seats. 30 seats outside. Private parties: 34 main room, 19 to 34 private rooms. Car park. Vegetarian meals. No smoking in 1 dining room. Wheelchair access (not WC). No music

WOODSTOCK Oxfordshire   map 2

▲ Feathers Hotel 🏠✖

Market Street, Woodstock OX20 1SX
TEL: (01993) 812291   FAX: (01993) 813158   COOKING 7
EMAIL: enquiries@feathers.co.uk   COST £33–£69

It took four seventeenth-century houses to produce this attractive, red-brick and custard-yellow inn near the entrance to Blenheim Palace, which explains the series of little rooms with deep sofas and flagstone floors, where drinks and bar meals are available. The dining room is the one with foodie oil paintings, yellow and blue furnishings, frills and tie-backs. A generous carte uses consistently top-class materials, and a degree of originality in the cooking makes dishes appear 'endlessly interesting'. Chicken and lobster are set in a clear basil and Muscadet jelly, foie gras comes with a split pea casserole, and risottos are generally accompanied by a deep-fried vegetable: a crab version with carrot, for example.

Dishes look 'classy' (main courses come on 'whopping' plates), and are marked by a high degree of technical accomplishment. Even the 'bits and bobs' (of which there are usually quite a few in a dish) taste 'seriously interesting and to the point'. Half a dozen scallops, for instance, are roasted to 'wobbly nuttiness' and set around a mound of white haricot beans (some whole, some purée) with a trickle of truffle oil; each scallop is decorated with a deep-fried sage leaf, the haricots with baked sticks of salsify, all of which worked 'brilliantly'. More classically inclined dishes have included pink, honey-roast Gressingham duck breast in a claret and stock glaze, served with fine olive oil mashed potatoes.

'Sophisticated, subtle, and clear tasting,' is one of many enthusiastic endorsements, applied to a round tart of first-class shortcrust pastry with a sliced, fanned pear embedded in an 'almond mash' filling, served with an intense honey ice cream. Extras, including appetiser, bread, and petits fours (priced separately from coffee) are a 'positive revelation'. Service continues to lag behind the rest of the operation, despite an 'optional' 15 per cent charge that also applies to some ambitious prices – Hamilton Russell Pinot Noir 1996 at £49.95, for example – on the high-quality wine list. House Duboeuf is £11.75.

CHEF: Mark Treasure   PROPRIETORS: Andrew Leeman, Simon Lowe and Howard Malin   OPEN: all week 12.30 to 2.15, 7.30 to 9.15 (9.45 Fri and Sat)   CLOSED: D 25 Dec   MEALS: alc D (main courses £17 to £22). Set L Mon to Sat £17.50 (2 courses) to £21, Set L Sun £20.50, Set D £44   SERVICE: 15% (optional), card slips closed   CARDS: Amex, Delta, Diners, MasterCard, Switch, Visa   DETAILS: 60 seats. 60 seats outside. Private parties: 60 main room. Vegetarian meals. Children's helpings. No smoking in dining room. Music. Air-conditioned   ACCOMMODATION: 22 rooms, 21 with bath/shower. TV. Phone. B&B £88 to £275. Baby facilities (*The Which? Hotel Guide*)

Restaurateurs justifiably resent no-shows. If you quote a credit card number when booking, you may be liable for the restaurant's lost profit margin if you don't turn up. Always phone to cancel.

All entries, including Round-ups, are fully indexed at the back of the Guide.

WORCESTER Worcestershire map 5

Brown's

24 Quay Street, Worcester WR1 2JJ COOKING 3
TEL: (01905) 26263 FAX: (01905) 25768 COST £24–£48

Tall ceilings, cream-painted brick walls, and a view of the Severn through windows lushly framed with greenery, recall Brown's former life as a mill. Seemingly coccooned in a world of their own, the dining room's crisp pink cloths, fresh flowers and colourful modern pictures convey a 'safe and comforting' air: 'we left feeling pampered and well fed' remarked one couple. On offer from the kitchen is essentially Anglo-French cooking with occasional Italian input: perhaps coq au vin, devilled kidneys on grilled polenta, or grilled squid with avocado salsa. The style may be familiar rather than exciting, but the kitchen still turns out properly poached egg in red wine sauce, and 'fishily aromatic' crab ravioli in crab bisque. Effective partnerships have included pink breast and confit leg of duck given a zestful foil of sweet mango purée dotted with green peppercorns. Among the simple and traditional desserts might be rhubarb compote with vanilla sorbet, and a 'light and refreshing' trio of ice creams. Service from efficient, apron-clad staff adds to the sense of ease and confidence. The largely French wine list is well chosen, although mark-ups can be high. French and Italian house wines are £11.95.

CHEFS: W.R. Tansley and L. Jones PROPRIETORS: W.R. and P.M. Tansley OPEN: Tue to Fri and Sun L 12.30 to 1.45, Tue to Sat D 7.30 to 9.45 CLOSED: 24 to 31 Dec, bank hols MEALS: Set L £18.50, Set D £34.50 SERVICE: net prices, card slips closed CARDS: Amex, Delta, MasterCard, Switch, Visa DETAILS: 100 seats. Private parties: 22 main room. Vegetarian meals. No children under 8. Wheelchair access (also WC). No music

WORFIELD Shropshire map 5

▲ *Old Vicarage Hotel*

Worfield WV15 5JZ
TEL: (01746) 716497 FAX: (01746) 716552
EMAIL: admin@the-old-vicarage.demon.co.uk COOKING 4
2m N of A545, 3m E of Bridgnorth COST £31–£64

This comfortable red-brick hotel in quiet rural surroundings dates from 1905 and retains something of an Edwardian aura: décor, considered the opposite of exciting, is on the dark side with lots of prints. Visitors don't just get a menu to read before dinner, but a sheet grandly titled 'Philosophy of The Old Vicarage', which says a word or two about wines, staff achievements and suppliers: vegetables and herbs from a Victorian walled garden, and Bobbington wild boar among them.

The style is a lively one. Shetland salmon has been served with couscous and a lime and chive sauce, and local pork with an attention-grabbing apple polenta cake and sun-dried tomato relish. One reporter who took advantage of a short break found 'little variation in the menu from day to day', that 'portion control rules', that service could have been sharper, and that prices were a bit steep, while another proclaimed that beef – perhaps fillet, with shallot confit and a truffle and mushroom sauce – 'is well worth the £1.50 extra'. Among desserts to shine is a hot apple dumpling in apple soup, and cheeses are recommended. Burgundy lovers are particularly well served by a wine list that strongly favours the Old World (although it is by no means immune to the attractions of the New). A commendably high number of half-bottles assists those who like to pick 'n' mix, and French house wines are £14.50.

CHEFS: Richard Arnold and Blaine Reed   PROPRIETORS: Peter and Christine Iles   OPEN: Sun to Fri L 12 to 1.45, all week D 7 to 8.45   MEALS: Set L £17.50, Set D £25 to £35   SERVICE: not inc CARDS: Amex, Diners, MasterCard, Visa   DETAILS: 62 seats. Private parties: 38 main room, 10 to 38 private rooms. Car park. Vegetarian meals. Children's helpings. No smoking in dining room. Wheelchair access (also WC). Music   ACCOMMODATION: 14 rooms, all with bath/shower. TV. Phone. B&B £70 to £170. Rooms for disabled. Baby facilities (*The Which? Hotel Guide*)   £5

WORLESTON Cheshire   map 5

▲ *Rookery Hall* ⚡✸

Main Road, Worleston CW5 6DQ
TEL: (01270) 610016   FAX: (01270) 626027   COOKING 4
on B5074, 2½m N of Nantwich   COST £31–£70

Built for a sugar-planter, William Hilton Cooke, in 1816, the hall is an imposing Georgian pile of grey stone, with balustraded roof and panelled interiors, enjoying 38 acres of wooded parkland by the edge of the River Weaver. It is the kind of place that wouldn't be complete without a spot of haunting, and spook-hunters may like to sniff the air for a floral waft announcing the proximity of the Grey Lady, who had a fatal fall while hanging curtains. But the main and altogether cheerier attraction is Craig Grant's cooking, which tackles the full-dress country-house style with panache. It manoeuvres skilfully through some complexities, for example in a terrine of ham hock, Puy lentils and spinach, served with parsley vinaigrette and a salad of pickled oyster mushrooms. Main-course choices are balanced equally between fish and meats: herb-crusted salmon suprême is served with a chive-flecked sabayon, rosette of beef fillet comes with parsley purée and a sauce enriched with foie gras. Desserts mobilise mousses, parfaits and pastry to complete the sense of being gently coddled, or there are British and Irish cheeses. The wine list, oddly, has half as many whites again as reds, and prices reflect the expected corporate business. The starting-point is £16.

CHEF: Craig Grant   PROPRIETOR: Arcadian International   OPEN: Sun to Fri L 12 to 2, all week D 7 to 9.30   MEALS: alc L (main courses £13 to £15.50). Set L Mon to Fri £12.99 (2 courses), Set L Sun £20, Set D £45   SERVICE: not inc   CARDS: Amex, Delta, Diners, MasterCard, Switch, Visa DETAILS: 40 seats. Private parties: 66 main room, 14 to 36 private rooms. Car park. Vegetarian meals. Children's helpings. Jacket and tie. No smoking in dining room. Wheelchair access (also WC). No music   ACCOMMODATION: 45 rooms, all with bath/shower. TV. Phone. B&B £120 to £140. Rooms for disabled. Baby facilities. Fishing   £5

'I didn't understand how they could make a "confit" of chocolate mousse, and neither did the waiter apparently. "It's just a chocolate mousse," he said, and it was.'
(On eating in Somerset)

WRIGHTINGTON Lancashire map 8

High Moor

High Moor Lane, Wrightington WN6 9QA
TEL: (01257) 252364   FAX: (01257) 255120
off A5209, between M6 junction 27 and Parbold; take
Robin Hood Lane at crossroads W of Wrightington
Hospital, then next left

COOKING 2
COST £21–£40

Well placed for the M6 and Lancashire conurbations, High Moor is white-painted and stone-flagged, with a long, low dining room of wooden tables and upholstered banquettes. Lunch can be as simple as soup and a sandwich, or a heartier two- or three-course meal from either the carte or set-price menu. A wide range of popular favourites takes in potato pancake with poached smoked haddock in a creamy sauce, and black pudding with Welsh rarebit on toasted Italian bread. Indeed the list of dishes seems almost endless, but varied cooking methods bring diversity, from chargrilling (beef fillet with onion rings), to braising (shank of lamb), to deep-frying (fish and chips with mushy peas). Desserts can be 'very sweet' judging by one visitor's gingerbread pudding with butterscotch sauce and ice cream. Staff are welcoming and efficient, and the wine list draws in bottles from far and wide, offering eight of each colour by the glass. House Australian is £9.95.

CHEFS: Darren Wynn and Ken Lea   PROPRIETORS: John Nelson and Jim Sines   OPEN: all week 12 to 2, 5.30 to 10 (8.30 Sun)   CLOSED: 26 Dec, 1 Jan   MEALS: alc (main courses L £5.50 to £13.50, D £9 to £14). Set L £11 (2 courses) to £13, Set D 5.30 to 7 £11 (2 courses) to £13 SERVICE: not inc   CARDS: Amex, Delta, Diners, MasterCard, Switch, Visa   DETAILS: 100 seats. 20 seats outside. Private parties: 140 main room. Car park. Vegetarian meals. Children's helpings. Wheelchair access (also WC). Occasional music

WYE Kent map 3

▲ Wife of Bath

4 Upper Bridge Street, Wye TN25 5AW
TEL: (01233) 812540   FAX: (01233) 813630
EMAIL: ali@w-o-b.demon.co.uk
just off A28, Ashford to Canterbury road

COOKING 3
COST £24–£45

The link with Chaucer, factual or imaginative, is faint, and the two intercon-necting dining rooms appear more like the front room of somebody's house. In keeping with that, the welcome is 'friendly, with sound service and good cooking', according to one reporter. Robert Hymers's simple style converts good raw materials into balanced dishes, whether they involve mallard, pré-salé lamb, or venison 'just as high as it should be'. The well-focused menu deals in crab cakes with lime and ginger hollandaise, and confit of duck on a potato pancake, while main courses embrace 'soft and creamy' calf's liver with caramelised onion and sage, and sea bass from nearby Hythe, with coriander and cucumber dressing: 'head, tail and all arrived, the skin black, the flesh moist and very fresh.' Of desserts, both brown bread ice cream and chocolate brûlée come in for praise. Front-of-house is well paced, and the wine list is well travelled and sensibly priced, with house wines starting at £12.75.

CHEF: Robert Hymers   PROPRIETOR: John Morgan   OPEN: Tue to Sat 12 to 2, 7 to 10   CLOSED: 1 week from 25 Dec   MEALS: alc L (main courses £10.50 to £14). Set L £10 (2 courses) to £13.75, Set D £23.75   SERVICE: not inc   CARDS: Amex, Delta, Diners, MasterCard, Switch, Visa   DETAILS: 50 seats. Private parties: 50 main room. Car park. Children's helpings. No pipes in dining room. Wheelchair access (not WC). No music   ACCOMMODATION: 6 rooms, all with bath/shower. TV. Phone. B&B £40 to £80. Rooms for disabled (*The Which? Hotel Guide*)   £5

YARM Stockton-on-Tees　　　　　　　　　　　　　　　　　map 10

Chadwick's ⅙✳

104B High Street, Yarm TS15 9AU　　　　　　　　　COOKING 4
TEL: (01642) 788558　　　　　　　　　　　　　　COST £21–£48

The food is as lively as food gets, in this high-ceilinged brasserie with marble-topped tables, handsome fat pillars, and walls covered in a wide assortment of pictures. Styling itself a 'licensed Continental café' – there is no booking – it aims to be all things to all comers, offering a generous carte that ranges from sandwiches and pasta dishes at lunchtime to heartier grilled ribeye of beef with fries and béarnaise at dinner. Hardly a culinary stone is left unturned on the weekly-changing menu, which might take in herb risotto with scallops, Thai fish curry with sticky coconut rice, grilled pork cutlet with black pudding hash and plum chutney, or wood pigeon with wild mushroom and lentil salad. Fish arrives daily from Hartlepool, and locally shot game appears in season. Some forty wines stay mostly under £20, starting with house Duboeuf at £10.50, and 'usually any on the list can be served by the glass'.

CHEF/PROPRIETOR: David Brownless   OPEN: Tue to Fri and Sun L 12 to 2.30, Tue to Fri D 6 to 9.30, Sat 12 to 9.30   CLOSED: 1 week Oct, 25 and 26 Dec, bank hol Mons   MEALS: alc (main courses L £5 to £11, D £7.50 to £15). Set D Tue to Fri before 7pm £10.95   SERVICE: not inc   CARDS: Amex, Delta, MasterCard, Switch, Visa   DETAILS: 70 seats. Private parties: 70 main room. Vegetarian meals. Children's helpings. No smoking in 1 dining room. Music

---

YARMOUTH Isle of Wight　　　　　　　　　　　　　　map 2

▲ George Hotel ♟

Quay Street, Yarmouth PO41 0PE
TEL: (01983) 760331   FAX: (01983) 760425　　　COOKING 6
EMAIL: res@thegeorge.co.uk　　　　　　　　　　COST £44–£53

With an enviable location, and 'magnificent' views across lawns to the harbour and beyond, the George makes a favourable impression on visitors. In fact the light, modern brasserie has the best of the view, and serves up smoked haddock and spinach tart with hollandaise, braised ox cheek, and escabèche of cod with a parsley dressing. The kitchen's main thrust, however, is a three-course dinner menu, served in a 'serious and formal' dining room with panelled walls in maroon and mallard green. This goes in for more complex dishes, some of which have more than one centre of gravity: a well-crafted trio of duck, for example – richly flavoured rillettes, ravioli, and fiercely seared foie gras on a Madeira sauce

– or one of passion fruit delivering a lively 'classic' tart in biscuity pastry, a clean-tasting sorbet, and a chiffon pie.

Such combinations are generally 'sound', according to one who tried several, but for skilful cooking and 'impeccable' flavours, seafood seems to shine brightest: juicy, just-cooked, poached oysters 'full of sea flavours' served with chive butter, or a fillet of sweetly fresh sea bass, on a bed of samphire surrounded by girolles in a frothy shellfish sauce. For 'supreme lightness', try a white chocolate bavarois, neatly complemented by the richer sweetness of a Valrhona ice cream. Service could be sharpened up: at an inspection meal, for example, wine had to be requested several times. The list, though, is well chosen, offering a good range of styles while keeping quality high. It is mostly grouped by price, opening at £11.50, and finishes with a string of fine clarets stretching back to 1937.

CHEF: Kevin Mangeolles   PROPRIETORS: Jeremy and Amy Willcock, and John Illsley   OPEN: Tue to Sat D only 7 to 10   MEALS: Set D £38.75. Brasserie menu available all week L and D   SERVICE: none, card slips closed   CARDS: Amex, Delta, MasterCard, Switch, Visa   DETAILS: 40 seats. 100 seats outside. Private parties: 60 main room, 25 private room. Children's helpings. No children under 10 in dining room. No cigars/pipes. No music. Air-conditioned   ACCOMMODATION: 16 rooms, all with bath/shower. TV. Phone. B&B £70 to £175. No children under 8 in accommodation. Baby facilities (*The Which? Hotel Guide*)

YATTENDON Berkshire   map 2

▲ *Royal Oak* ⚡✳

The Square, Yattendon RG18 0UG
TEL: (01635) 201325   FAX: (01635) 201926   COOKING 5
off B4009, 5m W of Pangbourne   COST £24–£52

This old inn on the village green is all things to all comers: a pub, an informal eating space of wood and brick with a large fireplace, where one course is as normal as three, and a sunny yellow dining room with floral pictures. After a brief absence, Robbie Macrae has returned to the stoves, overseeing a carte and a three-course set-price menu which between them cover a lot of ground. This is 'cosmopolitan cooking with a sense of style and purpose' that takes in bresaola and mozzarella with rocket and truffle dressing, oyster tempura with vichyssoise cream, and warm wood pigeon salad with celeriac rémoulade.

The impression is of fresh materials, sound technique ('expertly cooked' roast fillet of beef) and food that is 'full of flavour', including a rich, silky textured, well-balanced foie gras and chicken liver parfait served with onion marmalade. Another plus is that the food doesn't get too complicated, helping to make a success of a slab of 'juicy' griddled swordfish on a bed of crushed waxy new potatoes mixed with fragrant, herby pesto. 'Visually delightful' presentation extends to desserts of deep-flavoured blackcurrant soufflé with a sharp elder-flower sorbet, and a crispy-topped chocolate bread-and-butter pudding. Service is efficient and friendly, although perhaps not always as sharp as it might be. A new wine list was in preparation as the *Guide* went to press.

See inside the front cover for an explanation of the symbols used at the tops of entries.

CHEF: Robbie Macrae PROPRIETOR: The Restaurant Partnership/Regal Corus Group OPEN: Sun L 12 to 2.30, Mon to Sat D 7 to 9 (9.30 Fri and Sat) MEALS: alc (main courses £9.50 to £12.50). Set L £12.50 (2 courses) to £15, Set D £32.50 SERVICE: not inc CARDS: Amex, Delta, Diners, MasterCard, Switch, Visa DETAILS: 65 seats. 28 seats outside. Private parties: 24 main room, 8 private room. Car park. Children's helpings. No smoking in dining room. No music ACCOMMODATION: 5 rooms, all with bath/shower. TV. Phone. Room only £95 to £125. Baby facilities (*The Which? Hotel Guide*) £5

YORK North Yorkshire   map 9

Melton's ♀ ✻

7 Scarcroft Road, York YO23 1ND   COOKING 5
TEL: (01904) 634341   FAX: (01904) 635115   COST £21–£40

Redecoration with blue 'linen-look' chair covers and deep coral walls ushers in the start of the Hjorts' second decade. 'I like the idea of prices including mineral water, bread, coffee and service,' summed up one visitor on behalf of several, a practice all the more welcome in the face of 'top-quality ingredients, excellent timing, and great flavour combinations', exemplified perhaps by a salad with chunks of lobster flesh, halved baby artichoke hearts, rocket, fresh herbs, and a drizzle of olive oil. Vegetarian options are also well received, taking in 'innovative' courgette waffles laced with mint, a fragrant Thai lentil curry, and regularly appearing goats'-cheese gnocchi (baked rather than poached) with pesto and oven-dried tomatoes.

Fish, also a strong suit, ranges from mackerel escabèche with ginger and coriander to seafish kebab with rice and vegetable relish, while slow-cooked meats have included braised ox-tongue, and roast shoulder of pork. Not all reporters have room for dessert, a pity because roast peaches with caramel sauce was 'the dish of the evening' for one party; or there may be ginger sponge with hot sherry custard. Warm, friendly service from enthusiastic staff is intelligent and well informed. Wines on the user-friendly list carry a maximum mark-up of £10, a policy that gives good value to the more expensive wines, but neither are drinkers on a budget by any means neglected. Seven wines by the glass are all £2.75.

CHEFS: Michael Hjort and Adam Holliday PROPRIETORS: Michael and Lucy Hjort OPEN: Tue to Sun L 12 to 2, Mon to Sat D 5.30 to 10 CLOSED: 3 weeks Christmas, 1 week August MEALS: alc (main courses £10.50 to £14.50). Set L £15, Set D £15 (5.30 to 6.15) to £19.50 SERVICE: net prices, card slips closed CARDS: Delta, MasterCard, Switch, Visa DETAILS: 40 seats. Private parties: 33 main room, 16 private room. Vegetarian meals. Children's helpings. No smoking in 1 dining room. Wheelchair access (not WC). Music £5

▲ Middlethorpe Hall ♀ 🍴 ✻

Bishopthorpe Road, York YO23 2GB
TEL: (01904) 641241   FAX: (01904) 620176   COOKING 3
EMAIL: info@middlethorpe.u-net.com   COST £27–£65

For anyone who likes comfort in an opulent historical setting, this is the place. Historic House Hotels have an impressive track record in their treatment of a few choice properties (including Bodysgallen Hall, Llandudno, Wales, and Hartwell

House, Aylesbury – see entries), and this large seventeenth-century country house, about a mile and a half from the city, is no exception. Its well-maintained grounds include a walled garden, and it goes in for chandeliers, moulded and painted ceilings, antiques and traditional wood-panelled dining rooms (there are three). It all strikes a rather serious note, as do Martin Barker's menus, which add a few supplements to the already substantial price of dinner: for poached oysters, beef fillet, even roast Goosnargh duck breast, perhaps because of its accompanying 'torte' of foie gras and artichoke.

At their best, materials have included tender fillet of lamb, with provençale vegetables and red wine sauce, and first-rate barely cooked scallops (just two, as a starter) well combined with foie gras and an oily dressing. Indeed, saucing is a strength: red mullet comes with freshly made pesto as well as a moist, flavourful mussel risotto. Puddings are less successful, but wines are of good character, whether they hail from the classical French regions or were raised in the New World. Mark-ups reflect the luxury of the location, although a number of bottles under £20 can be found, starting with house French at £13.

CHEF: Martin Barker   PROPRIETOR: Historic House Hotels Ltd   OPEN: all week 12.30 (12 on race days) to 1.45, 7 to 9.45   CLOSED: 25 Dec and 31 Dec (exc for residents) ((??))   MEALS: Set L £14.50 (2 courses) to £17.50, Set D £32   SERVICE: net prices, card slips closed   CARDS: Delta, MasterCard, Switch, Visa   DETAILS: 60 seats. Private parties: 50 private room. Car park. Vegetarian meals. No children under 8 in dining room. Jacket and tie. No smoking in dining room. No music   ACCOMMODATION: 30 rooms, all with bath/shower. TV. Phone. Room only £99 to £250. No children under 8 in accommodation. Swimming pool (*The Which? Hotel Guide*)

Scotland

ABERDEEN Aberdeen   map 11

Faraday's

---

2 Kirk Brae, Cults, Aberdeen AB15 9SQ
TEL/FAX: (01224) 869666   COOKING 2
on A93, 3m from city centre   COST £20–£56

The décor has not changed since John Inches opened this former electricity
substation as a restaurant a dozen years ago. It still has 'the welcoming air of an
old friend', makes no attempt to be trendy, and is appreciated for its total lack of
pretence. Although lunches might take a more Scottish approach, with pan-fried
oatmeal haddock, or steak mince with skirlie and peas, the weekly-changing
menu has no centre of gravity other than its own wide-ranging interests: from
oven-baked Scandinavian-style salmon fillet, via stir-fried king prawns with
chilli jam, to pork wiener schnitzel. Simplicity is the key to success, in a dish of
smoked haddock and rice en cocotte, or salmon and leek rissoles that are 'light
and full of flavour', accompanied by 'first-class' roast potatoes with caraway, and
buttered cabbage. Finish, perhaps, as one reporter did, with a 'rich and creamy'
bread-and-butter pudding. A serviceable wine list includes house French at
£13.90.

CHEF: Dorothy Skene   PROPRIETOR: John Inches   OPEN: Tue to Sat 12 to 2, 7 to 9.30   MEALS:
alc L and D Tue to Thur (main courses L £6 to £13.50, D £9 to £15.50). Set D Fri and Sat £26.95
SERVICE: 10%, card slips closed   CARDS: Amex, Delta, MasterCard, Switch, Visa (2.5%
surcharge on credit cards)   DETAILS: 40 seats. Private parties: 36 main room. Car park.
Vegetarian meals. Children's helpings. No smoking before 2pm L and 10pm D. Wheelchair
access (also WC). Music. Air-conditioned

Silver Darling

Pocra Quay, North Pier, Aberdeen AB11 5DQ   COOKING 4
TEL: (01224) 576229   FAX: (01224) 791275   COST £26–£53

Last year's refurbishment, which opened up the first floor as a dining room, has
met with further approval. Climb a black-metal spiral staircase to the glass
rooftop extension for all-round views of beach, promenade and ships coming
and going at the harbour entrance. The backbone of the operation is barbecued
fish 'in French style', exemplified by tuna and swordfish marinated in olive oil
and provençale herbs, served with oven-dried tomatoes, roasted aubergine and
olives.

Weightier dishes such as a 'cassoulet' of salmon and chorizo are balanced by oriental-sounding steamed halibut and seaweed with a lemon grass and coconut emulsion, while starters range from scallop salad to mussel and langoustine soup with sorrel and aïoli. There are token meat options for those who must, and desserts of warm apple tart, chocolate terrine, or iced Drambuie soufflé. For those who lunch, a set-price menu offers four to six choices at each stage, perhaps Mediterranean fish soup, followed by pan-fried sea bass with black olive tapénade, finishing with iced raspberry soufflé. White wines understandably predominate on the mainstream and almost exclusively French list, starting with house red and white from Haut-Poitou at £9.70.

CHEF: Didier Dejean   PROPRIETORS: Catherine Wood and Didier Dejean   OPEN: Mon to Fri L 12 to 2, Mon to Sat D 7 to 9.30   CLOSED: 25 and 26 Dec, 1 to 6 Jan   MEALS: alc (main courses £14 to £18). Set L Mon to Fri £18.50   SERVICE: not inc, card slips closed   CARDS: Amex, Delta, Diners, MasterCard, Switch, Visa   DETAILS: 58 seats. Private parties: 20 private room. No smoking while others eat. Wheelchair access (also WC). Music

---

ABERFELDY   Perthshire & Kinross   map 11

▲ *Farleyer House* 🍴✳

Aberfeldy PH15 2JE
TEL: (01887) 820332   FAX: (01887) 829430
EMAIL: reservations@farleyer.com
on B846, Aberfeldy to Kinloch Rannoch road, 1½m W   COOKING 3
of Weem   COST £25–£45

What started as a humble croft overlooking the Tay has been enlarged and refashioned over the centuries into an imposing group of turreted white buildings, somewhere in the middle of which the mustard yellow and dark green Glen Lyon dining room (routes to it are not signposted) is covered with vibrantly coloured modern paintings. Scottish materials pepper the menu, from Skye scallops and traceable Highland beef to pink, boned loin of Perthshire lamb with wild mushrooms. Even snow hare has turned up among game dishes, along with more usual roe deer and Tay salmon, and hot and cold smoking is done on the premises.

The cooking is sound, and while flavours at inspection were rather shy, and timing variable, the kitchen is nevertheless adept at many things: making appealingly thick, crumbly pastry for a warm Cullen skink tartlet, or a fine, fruity apricot and date chutney to accompany pheasant and hare terrine, as well as a dark basin-shaped sticky toffee pudding served with a golf ball of caramel-coloured ice cream and streaks of toffee sauce. Aspects of housekeeping and service are in need of improvement, and mark-ups on the aristocratic, 200-strong wine list are likely to raise an eyebrow, although ten house recommendations come in under £20.

CHEF: Kieran Grant   PROPRIETOR: Janice Reid   OPEN: all week 12 to 2.30, 6 to 9.30   MEALS: alc (main courses £8.50 to £16)   SERVICE: not inc   CARDS: Amex, Delta, Diners, MasterCard, Switch, Visa   DETAILS: 110 seats. 20 seats outside. Private parties: 60 main room, 30 and 40 private rooms. Car park. Vegetarian meals. Children's helpings. No smoking in 1 dining room. Wheelchair access (also WC). Music   ACCOMMODATION: 19 rooms, all with bath/shower. TV. Phone. D,B&B £125 to £220. Rooms for disabled. Baby facilities. Fishing (£5)

7 The Square ⚡✶   NEW ENTRY

7 The Square, Aberfeldy PH15 2DD   COOKING 5
TEL/FAX: (01887) 829120   COST £29–£35

Richard Lyth, who used to work at nearby Farleyer House (see entry above), opened this 'café and bistro' in mid-1998. It sits at the end of a short lane off the main square, quietly and simply decorated, lit by candles and spotlights, with an occasional glimpse of the chef at work. His menus are short – three starters, two mains, and two desserts plus cheese – and don't give much away, although smart, cheerful and informative service from Kirsteen Lyth soon fills in any gaps. Sea bream with asparagus butter, for example, turns out to be a compilation of nine or so ingredients, 'not one of which was superfluous', among them two crisp-skinned fillets, courgette 'spaghetti', sliced fennel and tomato, and a sauce full of the sappy, grassy flavour of asparagus.

The food is attractive to look at and a pleasure to eat: a salad of livery-tasting duck magret, for example, dressed with a sweetly acid balsamic and oil mix, with finely sliced cucumber to counter any bite. 'We applaud chefs who take the trouble to make compatible vegetables an integral part of each dish rather than merely supply a separately served random selection,' noted an inspector, prompted by a piece of purple-red beef fillet sitting on creamy potato and celeriac mash, accompanied by expertly cooked shallots, beetroot cubes and a wedge of braised chicory. Desserts are equally accomplished, judging by a 'real wow' of a pistachio ice cream with 'sublime, squishy' nougat in a pool of pleasantly sharp redcurrant coulis. Around thirty wines (including six halves) are mostly French, and prices start at £10.50.

CHEF: Richard Lyth   PROPRIETORS: Richard, Peter and Kirsteen Lyth   OPEN: Tue to Sat 7 to 9.15 (10 high season)   CLOSED: 1 week Oct, Christmas, Feb   MEALS: Set D £19.50. Light L available   SERVICE: not inc   CARDS: Delta, MasterCard, Switch, Visa   DETAILS: 28 seats. 10 seats outside. Private parties: 30 main room. Vegetarian meals. No smoking in dining room. Wheelchair access (also WC). Occasional music

---

ABOYNE Aberdeenshire   map 11

▲ White Cottage ⚡✶

Dess, Aboyne AB34 5BP
TEL/FAX: (013398) 86265   COOKING 4
on A93 2½m E of Aboyne.   COST £25–£47

'No, it's not white,' observed one visitor, except for the Victorian porch, which leads straight into a low-ceilinged dining room whose central feature is 'a wrought-iron spiral staircase going nowhere'. Lunch offers the option of Caesar salad, a giant BLT in a baguette, a cheese platter with oatcakes and fruit, or more substantial fillet of beef with wild mushrooms and shallots. Three-course dinners run to four choices at each stage, and flavourings range from tried and tested – locally reared chicken with sherry vinegar and tarragon – to slightly more exotic mango, carrot and cardamom soup. Well-sourced materials have included Pittenweem scallops, roast rack of Perthshire lamb with organic root vegetables, and a spinach roulade made from goose eggs, served with ratatouille. Deeside strawberries dressed with sugar and lemon juice might accompany a baked cheesecake, and passion-fruit tart has been served with sugared-nut ice cream. A handful of sherries feature among aperitifs on a fifty-strong wine list, which starts with six house wines available by the glass and bottle. South African Colombard and Cabernet Sauvignon are £12.80/£2.10.

CHEF: Laurie Mill   PROPRIETORS: Laurie and Josephine Mill   OPEN: Tue to Sat 11.30 to 2.45, 7 to 9   CLOSED: 1 week Oct, 26 to 30 Dec, 1 week Easter, 1 week summer   MEALS: alc L (main courses £8.50 to £14.50). Set D £29.50   SERVICE: not inc   CARDS: Diners, MasterCard, Switch, Visa   DETAILS: 60 seats. 16 seats outside. Private parties: 45 main room, 20 private room. Car park. Vegetarian meals. Children's helpings. No smoking in 1 dining room. Wheelchair access (also WC). Occasional music   ACCOMMODATION: 1 room with bath/shower. B&B £26 (£5)

ACHILTIBUIE Highland   map 11

▲ *Summer Isles Hotel* 🍷 ✳

Achiltibuie IV26 2YG
TEL: (01854) 622282   FAX: (01854) 622251
take A835 to Drumrunie, 10m N of Ullapool, then
single-track road for 15m; hotel 1m past Achiltibuie   COOKING 5
on left   COST £43–£51

Even those used to the West Coast are struck by how stunning the view is from the light, bright and 'beautifully decorated' dining room: how fortunate that dinner so often coincides with sunset. A friendly atmosphere prevails, and the one-sitting house-party approach results in an informal and relaxed feel. Meals are essentially simple five-course affairs (the last cheese), with no choice before dessert, although 'allergies and dislikes are coped with very well'. This is not cooking to set the pulse racing; rather to enjoy for its straightforward way with materials, many of them local: inevitably so, given Achiltibuie's out-on-a-limb location. Seafood naturally plays an important role, turning up as smoked haddock flan, crab ravioli, or well-timed halibut in butter sauce, and a typical menu might start with smoked eel salad with gooseberry sauce, followed by carpaccio of Aberdeen Angus beef, then lobster with a buttery fish sauce. Plainly cooked vegetables accompany.

Sweets trolleys, according to one reporter, are 'usually a culinary hazard to be wary of', but not here, where it might be loaded with lemon ice cream, chocolate mousse tart and strawberry pavlova: 'I had a helping of all three, cheerily and generously dispensed.' Not every dish that comes out of the kitchen is fault-free, but the hit rate is good enough to enthuse most reporters. As to service, 'nobody seems particularly "trained", yet all are attentive, discreet and extremely competent'. Wines have been chosen to suit all palates and pockets (assuming the latter are elastic enough to stretch from £9.50 for a Chilean Chardonnay to £1,500 for the exalted Ch. Pétrus 1982), drawing mainly on classical France but keeping quality high when venturing outside. Half-bottles are numerous, and six table wines are offered by the glass from £2.30, with one extra each night specifically to match the first course.

'It was certainly a tasty wine, though light. [It] had a good cherry flavour with undertones of freshly worn ladies' nylon tights.' (On eating in Sussex)

CHEF: Chris Firth-Bernard   PROPRIETORS: Mark and Gerry Irvine   OPEN: Mon to Sat light L 12 to 2, all week D 8 (1 sitting)   CLOSED: mid-Oct to Easter   MEALS: Set D £36.50   SERVICE: net prices, card slips closed   CARDS: MasterCard, Switch, Visa   DETAILS: 28 seats. Private parties: 8 main room. Car park. Vegetarian meals. Children's helpings. No children under 6 in dining room. No smoking in dining room. No music   ACCOMMODATION: 13 rooms, all with bath/shower. Phone. B&B £55 to £200. No children under 6 in accommodation. Fishing (*The Which? Hotel Guide*)

ALEXANDRIA   Dumbarton & Clydebank   map 11

▲ *Cameron House, Georgian Room* ♟ ⁵⨯

Loch Lomond, Alexandria G83 8QZ
TEL: (01389) 755565   FAX: (01389) 759522
EMAIL: devere.cameron@airtime.co.uk   COOKING 6
off A82, ½m N of Balloch roundabout, 1m S of Arden   COST £34–£96

The 100-acre estate has bagged itself a prime spot overlooking Loch Lomond, allowing plenty of room for expansion of the baronial style house to include gym, swimming pools and squash court. It may be decorated in rather unimaginative hotel style, but the view, service, wine and food easily make up for that. The dining room's opulence and comfort are matched by some of Peter Fleming's materials – pan-fried foie gras, a host of wild mushrooms, casserole of lobster and Mull scallops – all subject to sympathetic and broadly European treatment. Precision timing is characteristically applied to pan-fried sea bream served on buttery, herby, mashed ratte potatoes, balanced by a slightly acidic cucumber fish cream, and the prime quality of ingredients also impressed an inspector, who was 'enchanted' by crisp crusted noisettes of new season lamb 'brilliantly accompanied' by a zinging sweet-sour redcurrant and lime jus.

Soufflés – sweet and savoury – are handled with deft assurance, including a 'frothy and delectable' one of spinach and smoked salmon, with a dollop of velvety coriander cream, and another of strawberry with a 'tongue-tingling' champagne sorbet. Accompaniments such as these are 'exquisitely judged' to complement and contrast with the main components of the dish; likewise a 'moreish' chocolate fondant set off by an orange and tea ice cream and a necklace of lime and pistachio sauce. A lavish cheeseboard, good bread and petits fours, and informed service add to the appeal. The wine list, which is full of fine bottles, is aimed at those who are happy to pay that bit extra for quality rather than those looking for something cheap and cheerful. There are no house wines, but a few bins come in under £20, and eleven wines by the glass are between £4.50 and £6.95.

CHEF: Peter Fleming   PROPRIETOR: De Vere Hotels   OPEN: Mon to Fri L 12 to 1.45, all week D 7 to 9.45   MEALS: alc (main courses £24 to £33). Set L £17.50 (2 courses) to £21.50, Set D £38.50   SERVICE: not inc   CARDS: Amex, Delta, Diners, MasterCard, Switch, Visa   DETAILS: 480 seats. Private parties: 200 main room, 16 to 40 private rooms. Car park. Vegetarian meals. Children's helpings. Jacket and tie. No smoking in dining room. Music. Air-conditioned ACCOMMODATION: 98 rooms, all with bath/shower. TV. Phone. B&B £180 to £450. Rooms for disabled. Baby facilities. Swimming pool (£5)

The Guide *always appreciates hearing about changes of chef or owner.*

521

ALYTH   Perthshire & Kinross

map 11

WOOD-FIRED 2000 WONDER

▲ Drumnacree House   £

St Ninians Road, Alyth PH11 8AP
TEL: (01828) 633355   FAX: (01828) 632194
EMAIL: allan.cull@virgin.net
turn off A926 Blairgowrie to Kirriemuir road to Alyth;
take first left after Clydesdale Bank; hotel entrance is
300 metres on right

COOKING 4
COST £18–£35

A lot has changed at this welcoming hotel since the last edition of the *Guide*. The Culls have converted their bar-lounge into a bistro, in the process turning part of it back into the quarry-tiled kitchen it used to be when it was a private house. Their new pride and joy is an igloo-shaped wood-burning oven ('the only one north of Edinburgh,' they claim), ideal for fast cooking (bread and pizzas particularly), but also for slow roasting. This is not the first time Allan Cull has changed culinary direction (traces of his love affair with Cajun dishes, gumbos and dirty rice remain), but his shifts do at least appear to stem from genuine enthusiasm for the food itself. The open-to-view oven turns out thin-based pizzas for lunch, alongside more substantial baked salmon, braised lamb shank and roasted vegetables in the evening.

Residents, meanwhile, can opt for a set-price meal in their own dining room: perhaps Arbroath smokie mousse, chicken on onion confit with mustard sauce, and chocolate pot or French apple tart. There is little choice here, but preferences are discussed when booking, and the repertoire might also include frogs' legs in garlic and herb sauce, peppered wild venison with brandy cream sauce, and syrup sponge. Scottish cheeses are another new departure: perhaps Bonchester, Lanark blue (ewe's milk) and Bonnet (goats'). A tiny wine list starts with house French at £9.

CHEF: Allan Cull   PROPRIETORS: Allan and Eleanor Cull   OPEN: Tue to Sun 12 to 2, 6.30 to 9.30 (open all week for residents)   CLOSED: 27 Dec to 3 Jan   MEALS: alc (main courses £5 to £12.50). Set D (residents only) £20   SERVICE: not inc   CARDS: Amex, MasterCard, Switch, Visa DETAILS: 50 seats. Private parties: 22 main room, 12 and 30 private rooms. Car park. Vegetarian meals. Children's helpings. No pipes in dining room. Wheelchair access (also women's WC). Music   ACCOMMODATION: 6 rooms, all with bath/shower. TV. B&B £44 to £80. Baby facilities
£5

ANSTRUTHER   Fife

map 11

Cellar

24 East Green, Anstruther KY10 3AA
TEL: (01333) 310378   FAX: (01333) 312544

COOKING 6
COST £26–£47

Little seems to have changed during the eighteen years that Peter Jukes has been serving up fresh fish to locals and visitors alike at his stone-built restaurant on the east coast. Start in the small bar, then move to the single dining room – the sewing machine tables are still there, along with 1970s lamps and log fire – where first-class fish and shellfish are treated simply and effectively. Peter Jukes notes that seafood has its own seasons, following an unchanging annual cycle that gives structure to his menus: simply grilled halibut, served with Jersey Royals and local asparagus, will be just as good in May this year as it will next year, and the year after. But that still leaves plenty of room for variety: at one lunchtime crayfish bisque, quiche of lobster and smoked sea trout, and seared tuna with niçoise dressing.

Apart from freshness of supplies, it is the ability of these dishes to tread a fine line between interesting treatment and necessary restraint that makes them appealing: for example, roast cod with greens, pine nuts, bacon and pesto, or roast scallops and langoustine tails with sweet chilli, crème fraîche and a few leaves. Among non-fishy items might be wild mushroom risotto, and token desserts such as iced hazelnut praline parfait with cassis. Fish-friendly wines at pocket-friendly prices hold sway on a list that embraces very fine bins from Burgundy and Alsace as well as some classy New World whites. Wine 'carnivores' need not despair as a number of good meaty reds are also provided. House wines from South Africa and France are £13.50.

CHEF/PROPRIETOR: Peter Jukes OPEN: Fri and Sat L 12.30 to 1 (light L until 1.30), Tue to Sat D 7 to 9.30 (open Tue to Sat L and Mon to Sat D Easter to end Oct) MEALS: Set L £16.50, Set D £28.50. Light L available SERVICE: not inc CARDS: Amex, Delta, Diners, MasterCard, Switch, Visa DETAILS: 30 seats. Private parties: 32 main room. Children's helpings. No smoking in dining room. No music

---

ARCHIESTOWN Moray — map 11

▲ *Archiestown Hotel*

Archiestown AB38 7QL — COOKING 2
TEL: (01340) 810218 FAX: (01340) 810239 — COST £25–£52

Judith and Michael Bulger run their solid granite hotel in a tiny Speyside village with character and conviviality, catering mainly for sporting types with serious appetites 'stimulated by the river, moor or loch'. 'Jeans and tiaras are equally welcome' at the bare wooden tables in the junkshop atmosphere of the bistro, its shelves heaving with antique and modern curios. Judith's wholesome country cooking with flair but no frills might produce 'thick, sweet' cabbage and apple soup, 'tender' devilled kidneys, a slab of creamy fish pie, and meringue with butterscotch sauce. Items are listed on the blackboard menu in no-nonsense fashion with plenty for those on a budget (hare pâté, beef and aubergine curry) or those with a bit more to spend (langoustines mayonnaise, Arctic char baked with samphire). The wine is mostly French and includes a page each of vintage clarets, miscellaneous magnums and ports; house selections start at £12.

CHEF: Judith Bulger PROPRIETORS: Judith and Michael Bulger OPEN: all week 12.30 to 2, 6.30 to 9 CLOSED: 1 Oct to 9 Feb MEALS: alc (main courses £6.50 to £17.50) SERVICE: not inc, card slips closed CARDS: MasterCard, Visa DETAILS: 35 seats. 12 seats outside. Private parties: 25 main room, 20 private room. Car park. Children's helpings. No children under 16 after 8pm. No music ACCOMMODATION: 9 rooms, 7 with bath/shower. TV. Phone. B&B £37.50 to £90
(£5)

'The menu is a blackboard and the writing seems to have got bigger, but more likely the choice has diminished.' (On eating in Kent)

523

ARISAIG Highland   map 11

▲ *Arisaig House* ⭐✳

Beasdale, by Arisaig PH39 4NR
TEL: (01687) 450622   FAX: (01687) 450626
EMAIL: arisaighse@aol.com   COOKING 5
on A830, 3m E of Arisaig   COST £38–£62

Built in 1864, this 'civilised' house is a stone's throw from the lochside, with splendid views from the formal gardens and plenty of opportunities for walks. Comfortably and tastefully furnished, with no hint of ostentation, it has a well-groomed appearance that 'combines elegance with warmth'. While the set-lunch menu offers two choices at each stage – perhaps gravad lax with fennel and Arran mustard, followed by poached monkfish in star anise bouillon, and ending with pistachio, pineapple and apricot mousse with coffee sauce – dinner is four courses, the second a choice between soup (Cullen skink, perhaps), sorbet and salad. Waiting staff are knowledgeable about what goes on in the kitchen and where raw materials come from: according to Ruth Smither, some 75 per cent is locally produced or sourced.

The cooking, however, centres on a contemporary interpretation of largely European ideas, taking in warm asparagus with a morel and coriander dressing, terrine of lamb sweetbreads with gribiche dressing, and a 'navarin' of seafood in a prawn and saffron consommé. Fish, a strong suit, is sensibly treated – poached turbot fillet with cauliflower mousseline, for example – and a vegetarian option (such as couscous) takes its place alongside maybe roast squab pigeon with root vegetables, while puddings run to 'really tasty' nougat parfait with redcurrants. Classy claret features prominently on the largely French wine list, where prices favour those with more than £20 to spend, but two red and three white house wines cost £14.50 each.

CHEF: Duncan Gibson   PROPRIETORS: Ruth, John and Andrew Smither, and Alison Wilkinson
OPEN: all week 12.30 to 2, 7.30 to 8.30   CLOSED: Nov to Mar   MEALS: Set L £25, Set D £39.50.
Light L available   SERVICE: not inc, card slips closed   CARDS: MasterCard, Switch, Visa
DETAILS: 30 seats. 20 seats outside. Car park. Vegetarian meals. No children under 10 in dining room. No smoking in dining room. No music   ACCOMMODATION: 12 rooms, all with bath/shower. TV. Phone. B&B £80 to £275. No children under 10 in accommodation

AUCHMITHIE Angus   map 11

But 'n' Ben ⭐✳ £

Auchmithie DD11 5SQ
TEL: (01241) 877223   COOKING 2
on coast, 3m NE of Arbroath, off A92   COST £17–£40

Two cottages knocked into one provide a bar area and restaurant with views over a 'spectacular' inlet and all-day dining, from morning coffee through high teas (excellent value, according to one reporter) to dinner. Service is friendly and understated, with a distinctly homely atmosphere. Seafood and fish are the things to go for, particularly anything involving Arbroath smokies, which come from just down the coast and turn up in pancakes, or plainly and simply with butter. At inspection, partan bree had 'rich crab flavours', and mussels, marinière style, were 'fresh and tasty'. Old-fashioned meat stalwarts also feature – mince with tatties and skirlie, or Angus steak mince pie, the latter 'a real treat' – alongside more modern dishes of peppered liver with spicy tomato sauce. Desserts, 'mostly of the big cake with lots of cream inside variety', arrive on a trolley. Wines on the short list start at £9.50 and, apart from champagne, prices never rise beyond the £20 mark.

CHEFS: Angus and Margaret Horn   PROPRIETORS: Margaret, Iain and Angus Horn   OPEN: Wed to Mon L 12 to 3, Mon and Wed to Sat 7 to 9.30   CLOSED: 26 Dec, 1 and 2 Jan   MEALS: alc (main courses £5.50 to £13.50)   SERVICE: not inc, card slips closed   CARDS: Amex, Diners, MasterCard, Switch, Visa   DETAILS: 40 seats. Private parties: 50 main room. Vegetarian meals. Children's helpings. No smoking in dining room. Wheelchair access (also WC). No music   £5

AUCHTERARDER   Perthshire & Kinross   map 11

▲ *Auchterarder House* ▼ 🗒 ⁂

Auchterarder PH3 1DZ   COOKING 2
TEL: (01764) 663646   FAX: (01764) 662939   COST £27–£63

Built as a family home in 1832, this lavish baronial pile seems to be 'heaving with history', thanks to its oak panelling, portraits of luminaries from Ronald and Nancy Reagan to Sir Winston Churchill, and its scale: the dining room feels more like a banqueting hall. Lunch is three courses, dinner four (five if you count coffee) with, typically, two choices at each stage. Traditional, if predictable, ways have a lot to recommend them: French onion soup with Parmesan straws, for example, while simple 'unambitious' dishes have included 'hot and creamy' butternut squash soup, and a starter of asparagus wrapped in Parma ham with a lemon oil dressing and a shower of tarragon and chives. An 'assiette' is a common vehicle for main courses: perhaps a mix of local seafood with fennel sauce, or chunky pieces of beef, game and lamb in a smooth creamy gravy. Finish with iced banana parfait, or strawberries with butterscotch ice cream. The wine list likewise has a traditional emphasis on claret and Burgundy, although selected New World bins are provided for modernists. House wines from Louis Latour are £16.50.

CHEF: William Deans   PROPRIETOR: Wren's Hotel Group   OPEN: all week 12.30 to 2, 7 to 9   MEALS: Set L £16.50, Set D £39.50   SERVICE: not inc   CARDS: Amex, Delta, Diners, MasterCard, Switch, Visa   DETAILS: 30 seats. Private parties: 70 main room, 15 and 30 private rooms. Car park. No children under 12 in dining room. Jacket and tie. No smoking in dining room. Occasional music   ACCOMMODATION: 15 rooms, all with bath/shower. TV. Phone. B&B £120 to £400   £5

'One waiter walked smartly up to the table, wiped off a bottle with a clean cloth, and with a polished turn of the wrist presented for my inspection the label of a Holsten Export lager. This would have been fine but we had ordered a bottle of Châteauneuf-du-Pape.'
(On eating in Wales)

AULDEARN Highland   map 11

▲ Boath House ⁵⅍

Auldearn IV12 5LE
TEL: (01667) 454896   FAX: (01667) 455469   COOKING 5
on A96, 2m E of Nairn   COST £22–£59

Rooms are spacious and attractive, the view 'superb', at this listed, restored
Georgian mansion built of pink granite and set in 20 acres. Dinner is the main
meal, and although there are only three choices per course, menus are well
balanced. Starters typically include a soup (such as beetroot and plum tomato
with pigeon dumplings), a terrine or parfait (foie gras and chicken liver with
apricot chutney) and a warm salad or pasta (ravioli of lobster and scallops in a
shellfish bisque). Native supplies play an essential role in the kitchen's success,
from Moray Firth lobsters to soft fruit from the farm next door, but it is the
kitchen's industry that gives the food its identity and character: steamed cod on
smoked salmon brandade, served with langoustines and basil purée with a
caviare velouté, for example.

Besides fish, main courses also run to a game or poultry option (quail with
boudin blanc on sweet potato purée), plus a conventional meat dish such as roast
marinated lamb with kidneys and asparagus. Four Scottish cheeses, changed
monthly – perhaps Inverloch goats', Dunsyre blue, Old Kelso Cheddar, and
Baby Pentland – take their place alongside apricot crème brûlée, lemon tart with
raspberry sorbet, or nougat glacé with bitter chocolate ice cream. Although there
is more of interest above £20 on the wide-ranging wine list, decent drinking is
possible for less, starting with six house wines: vin de pays is £9.50.

CHEF: Charles Lockley   PROPRIETORS: Don and Wendy Matheson   OPEN: Thur to Sun L 12 to 2,
Wed to Sun D 7 to 9   MEALS: alc (main courses L £9 to £11, D £15 to £22). Set L £15.50
SERVICE: not inc   CARDS: Amex, Delta, Diners, MasterCard, Switch, Visa   DETAILS: 35 seats.
Private parties: 30 main room, 8 private room. Car park. Vegetarian meals. Children's helpings.
No smoking in dining room. Wheelchair access (also WC). Music   ACCOMMODATION: 7 rooms,
all with bath/shower. TV. Phone. B&B £80 to £175. Rooms for disabled. Baby facilities. Fishing
(£5)

AYR South Ayrshire   map 11

Fouters Bistro ⁵⅍

2A Academy Street, Ayr KA7 1HS
TEL: (01292) 261391   FAX: (01292) 619323   COOKING 3
EMAIL: laurie@fouters.demon.co.uk   COST £19–£50

It is easy to miss, along a narrow lane, down a flight of steps to a series of tiny
cellar rooms connected by arched doorways, 'where money has not been wasted
on décor'. Totally unpretentious, as a bistro should be (although it now styles
itself 'bistro restaurant'), Fouters sets a 'noble example' of the art of serving
unfussy food using good ingredients. Laurie Black (now with an assistant in the
kitchen) notes an increasing awareness among customers about the origin of
produce: some is organic, much is sourced locally or from within Scotland, for
example roast loin of Carrick Hill lamb and venison, or carpaccio of Ayrshire
beef with an oriental salad. The carte is a model of simplicity and clarity, with

a line in seafood that includes haddock goujons, sole mousse with lobster sauce, and seared west coast scallops with couscous and vanilla velouté. Finish with crème brûlée (perhaps an 'egg nog' version with Advocaat liqueur), steamed sponge pudding, or dark chocolate terrine, and drink from a 45-strong dependable list starting with house French at £12.50.

CHEFS: Laurie Black and Lee Williamsen   PROPRIETORS: Laurie and Fran Black   OPEN: Tue to Sat 12 to 2, 6.30 to 10.15   CLOSED: 25 to 27 Dec, 1 to 3 Jan   MEALS: alc (main courses L £5 to £10, D £9 to £15)   SERVICE: not inc   CARDS: Amex, Diners, MasterCard, Switch, Visa   DETAILS: 38 seats. Private parties: 24 main room. Children's helpings. No smoking in 1 dining room. Music. Air-conditioned (£5)

BALLATER Aberdeenshire   map 11

▲ *Balgonie Country House* ✻ | NEW ENTRY |

Braemar Place, Ballater AB35 5NQ   COOKING 3
TEL/FAX: (013397) 55482   COST £41–£49

Impeccable housekeeping and a cheerful welcome from John and Priscilla Finnie linger in visitors' memories as much as the views from this Edwardian house over to Glen Muick. Amid furnishings and décor sympathetic to the age of the place, guests eat well on local produce cooked without gimmicks. Four-course dinners might start with a terrine of chicken livers with Cumberland sauce, or a 'well-balanced' leek and potato soup, followed by a no-choice fish course of, for example, warm fillet of sea trout with horseradish crème fraîche. Then back to three items for the main event: roast black-faced lamb with a sweet confit of shallots, tender duck breast on braised red cabbage, or more fish ('always inventively handled'), perhaps salmon accompanied by bacon and spring onion mashed potatoes with pesto. The mostly traditional approach continues with puddings that might include lemon cream with frosted grapes, or chocolate soufflé with a 'beguiling' rhubarb, orange and ginger sauce. Eighty or so wines, wide-ranging and with a good few half-bottles, are fairly priced, starting at around £14. There are no house selections but plenty of choice under £20.

CHEF: John Finnie   PROPRIETORS: John and Priscilla Finnie   OPEN: all week D only 7 to 9 CLOSED: 5 Jan to 10 Feb   MEALS: Set D £29.50   SERVICE: not inc, card slips closed   CARDS: Amex, Delta, Diners, MasterCard, Switch, Visa   DETAILS: 30 seats. Private parties: 30 main room. Car park. Children's helpings. No children under 7 in dining room (high tea available). No smoking in dining room. No music   ACCOMMODATION: 9 rooms, all with bath/shower. TV. Phone. B&B £65 to £120. Baby facilities (*The Which? Hotel Guide*) (£5)

▲ *Darroch Learg* ♟ ✻

Braemar Road, Ballater AB35 5UX   COOKING 6
TEL: (013397) 55443   FAX: (013397) 55252   COST £22–£53

Visitors to this substantial and comfortable Victorian hotel on the outskirts of Ballater are welcomed 'in a Jeevesian fashion that we find beguiling'. Its elegant lounges and tastefully furnished dining room are a fitting backdrop for food with a 'generosity of flavour'. Dishes are well designed, with interesting pairings and partnerships: deep-fried snails have come with pea purée, Swiss chard and truffle, and ravioli of foie gras and Parma ham might be served with onion jam, crispy potatoes and Parmesan cream. Industry extends to home-made black pudding, and home-smoked salmon served with poached egg, caviare and a chive velouté, while native materials also play their part, from loin of lamb with a tian of vegetables, to saddle of 'rare and tender' local venison.

Classic lemon tart is one of the kitchen's signature dishes, or there may be iced banana and pistachio parfait, or hot chocolate tart with blueberry ice and a Highland whisky sauce. Lunch is a lighter affair, incorporating for one party spicy carrot soup, open roast beef sandwich, smoked salmon ravioli, vegetable pancakes, and a plate of Scottish cheeses. Service from attentive staff is appreciated, as are net prices: 'significantly, the management refused any additional tips; they said that their staff were well paid.' The wine list continues to improve, and this year sees the welcome introduction of Ridge, Phelps and Mondavi to an expanded Californian section, although Bordeaux and Burgundy lovers can rest assured that their needs are also well catered for. House wines from Chile and South Africa are £14.90, but the fixed mark-up policy means that it is worth taking a look at the more expensive bottles.

CHEF: David Mutter   PROPRIETORS: the Franks family   OPEN: all week 12.30 to 2, 7 to 9 CLOSED: Christmas, 3 weeks Jan   MEALS: alc L Mon to Sat (main courses £6.50 to £16.50). Set L Sun £17.50, Set D £31.50   SERVICE: net prices, card slips closed   CARDS: Amex, Diners, MasterCard, Switch, Visa   DETAILS: 48 seats. Private parties: 62 main room. Car park. Children's helpings. No smoking in dining room. Wheelchair access (not WC). No music ACCOMMODATION: 18 rooms, all with bath/shower. TV. Phone. D,B&B £68 to £196. Rooms for disabled. Baby facilities (*The Which? Hotel Guide*) (£5)

▲ Green Inn ▼

9 Victoria Road, Ballater AB35 5QQ   COOKING 6
TEL/FAX: (013397) 55701   COST £39–£47

The homely exterior may not give much clue that there is a talented chef at work, but the menu on display certainly hints at it. A small squarish dining room with a pine-clad bar is tastefully decorated in pastel shades of blue and pink, with matching china, and the food proclaims itself as modern Scottish: seared scallops and halibut with rhubarb butter, or a 'gâteau' incorporating lemon-flavoured crowdie and salmon smoked over oak chips from a whisky barrel. Vivid, sometimes fiery spicing ('like listening to music that is all fortissimo') can occasionally compete with the item it is partnering, as in a chilli-rich tomato salsa that came with an otherwise 'beautifully made' ballottine of chicken and lobster, but the kitchen's skills generally enable it to combine multiple tastes well.

Among highlights, freshly baked flaky pastry 'bridies' filled with cream cheese have accompanied a velvety and 'outstandingly good' tomato and basil soup with langoustines to good effect, and accurate timing extends to wafer-thin slices of salmon draped over a mound of hot new potato and smoked salmon. One reporter was 'stunned' by his basil ice cream with peppercorn syrup; alternatively there may be aniseed parfait, chocolate terrine, or rice pudding with a compote of pineapple in vanilla butter. Service is efficient, and the food would be good value even without all the little extras of a mini smoked haddock mousse appetiser, walnut bread and so forth. Breakfast is appreciated by those who stay. A few choice bottles cannily selected from the major wine-growing countries – along with a good selection of cask-strength single malts – feature on the list; house French is £10.95.

CHEF: Jeffrey Purves   PROPRIETORS: Jeffrey and Carol Purves   OPEN: all week D only 7 to 9.30   CLOSED: Sun and Mon Oct to Mar, 1 week Christmas, 2 weeks Oct   MEALS: Set D £24 (2 courses) to £28.50   SERVICE: not inc, card slips closed   CARDS: Amex, Diners, MasterCard, Switch, Visa   DETAILS: 30 seats. Private parties: 8 main room. Vegetarian meals. Children's helpings. No smoking while others eat, no cigars/pipes in dining room. Wheelchair access (not WC). Music. Air-conditioned   ACCOMMODATION: 3 rooms, all with bath/shower. TV. D,B&B £64 to £115. Baby facilities (£5)

BALQUHIDDER Stirling   map 11

▲ *Monachyle Mhor*

Balquhidder FK19 8PQ	COOKING 3
TEL: (01877) 384622 FAX: (01877) 384305	COST £27–£45

Part of a large working estate that offers deerstalking, grouse shooting and salmon fishing, Monachyle Mhor is a slate-roofed, pink-washed house with hills behind and a loch on either side. Meat is local or 'semi-local', fish comes from the West Coast, a walled garden supplies half the kitchen's vegetables and herbs, and fungi such as ceps, chanterelles and blewits are picked nearby, perhaps appearing alongside pan-fried breasts of Glen Dochart grouse for dinner. Although Tom Lewis takes inspiration from all over (a hot- and cold-smoked salmon starter comes with a beetroot, lime and ginger salsa), his classical leanings steer him towards butter bean and truffle oil soup, or calf's liver with caramelised red onions in a grainy mustard sauce.

Seafood dishes have included diver-caught scallops in a saffron beurre blanc, and among other meatless options might be a risotto of Mull Cheddar with spinach and chives. Simple vegetable accompaniments make 'perfect complements' to main courses, while desserts might run to bread-and-butter soufflé, or seasonal fruit crumble. Around sixty sensibly chosen wines are offered at fair prices, starting with house French Chardonnay and Merlot at £10.50.

CHEF: Tom Lewis   PROPRIETORS: Jean, Rob and Tom Lewis   OPEN: all week 12 to 2, 7.30 to 9   MEALS: Set L £10.50 (2 courses) to £19.50, Set D £29   SERVICE: not inc, card slips closed   CARDS: MasterCard, Switch, Visa   DETAILS: 42 seats. Private parties: 42 main room. Car park. Vegetarian meals. No children under 12 in dining room. Jacket and tie. No smoking in dining room. Wheelchair access (also WC). No music. Air-conditioned   ACCOMMODATION: 10 rooms, all with bath/shower. TV. Phone. B&B £70 to £90 (double room). No children under 12 in accommodation except babies. Baby facilities. Fishing (*The Which? Hotel Guide*)

Prices quoted in the Guide *are based on information supplied by restaurateurs. The prices quoted at the top of each entry represent a range, from the lowest meal price to the highest; the latter is inflated by 20 per cent to take account of likely price rises during the year of the* Guide.

BLAIR ATHOLL Perthshire & Kinross   map 11

Loft ⁵✳ | NEW ENTRY |

Blair Atholl, by Pitlochry PH18 5TE   COOKING 2
TEL: (01796) 481377   FAX: (01796) 481511   COST £22–£43

The Loft is a well-run complex, modern in style and flexible in approach, with facilities that include a swimming pool, steam room and mini-gym. Dining options take in light meals in the conservatory or al fresco on the terrace, and more formal ones in the first-floor dining room, plus morning coffee and afternoon tea. Imaginative use of good ingredients is shown in 'pink and tender' saddle of venison with a spiced red cabbage compote and a game and chocolate jus; stir-fried marinated Gressingham duck breast given a boost of colour and taste by mango and snow peas; and orange and Cointreau parfait on a ginger biscuit with rich caramel sauce. The conservatory menu follows similar lines with prawn and roast yellow pepper salad, and lambs' liver with black pudding and apple. About thirty wines, mostly under £20, kick off with house Australian at £9.50.

CHEF: Kevin Graham   PROPRIETOR: Marise Richardson   OPEN: all week 12 to 2.30, 7 to 9
MEALS: alc (main courses L £8 to £11, D £10 to £15)   SERVICE: not inc, card slips closed
CARDS: Amex, Delta, Diners, MasterCard, Switch, Visa   DETAILS: 55 seats. 20 seats outside.
Private parties: 34 main room. Car park. Vegetarian meals. Children's helpings. No children
under 12. No smoking in dining room. Music. Air-conditioned (£5)

BLAIRGOWRIE Perthshire & Kinross   map 11

▲ *Kinloch House* ♥ ⁵✳

by Blairgowrie PH10 6SG
TEL: (01250) 884237   FAX: (01250) 884333
EMAIL: kinlochhouse@compuserve.com   COOKING 4
on A923, 3m W of Blairgowrie towards Dunkeld   COST £26–£64

The kitchen of this well-maintained, ivy-covered, wood-panelled, early-Victorian house sets appropriate store by its materials. Many supplies come from within a 20-mile radius, including a few from their own walled vegetable garden and greenhouses. The upshot is free range eggs and poultry, a range of game (fillet of hare with Savoy cabbage) and seafood (Kyle of Lochalsh scallops with a dill and mushroom sauce). The pattern is bar lunches (except Sunday) in the conservatory, and four-course dinners in the dining room: ravioli of rabbit mousseline, followed by oyster and chanterelle risotto, then cod with a tomato and black olive sauce. Supplements are applied to a variety of well-hung Aberdeen Angus steaks from accredited herds, and to several ways with Scottish lobster, including 'Nell Gwyn', with a dash of orange in the vermouth and parsley sauce. Vegetarians have their own menu, and a savoury (creamed smoked haddock on toast) provides a viable alternative to busy desserts of, for example, warm gingerbread with glazed bananas and a dark chocolate and Jack Daniels ice cream. Clarets dating back to 1961 are a feature of a wine list that gives France serious consideration before turning its attention to the New World.

Half-bottles and bottles under £20 are plentiful, and house wines from France and South Africa begin at £15.50.

CHEF: Bill McNicoll   PROPRIETORS: David and Sarah Shentall   OPEN: Sun L 12.30 to 2, all week D 7 to 9.15   CLOSED: 18 to 29 Dec   MEALS: Set L Sun £15.95, Set D £29.90. Bar L available all week   SERVICE: net prices, card slips closed   CARDS: Amex, Delta, Diners, MasterCard, Switch, Visa   DETAILS: Private parties: 10 main room, 16 private room. Car park. Vegetarian meals. Children's helpings. No children under 7 in dining room. Jacket and tie. No smoking in dining room. Wheelchair access (not WC). No music   ACCOMMODATION: 21 rooms, all with bath/shower. TV. Phone. D,B&B £93 to £235. Rooms for disabled. Baby facilities. Swimming pool. Fishing (*The Which? Hotel Guide*)

BOWMORE Argyll & Bute   map 11

▲ *Harbour Inn* ⅚✳

The Square, Bowmore PA43 7JR
TEL: (01496) 810330   FAX: (01496) 810990   COOKING 2
EMAIL: harbour@harbour-inn.com   COST £17–£56

Fish is, unsurprisingly, the major pre-occupation at this three-storeyed white-painted hotel in the 'centre' of Bowmore; in fact, Bowmore is so small that almost everywhere in it can claim that geographical distinction. Despite an occasional interloper, such as spiced pork kebab with vegetable samosa, the drive is firmly towards native ideas and materials, in the form of Islay sirloin steak, loin of local hare, and Islay crabmeat with a cheese soufflé topping, a dish that one impressed reporter is still trying to emulate at home. Loch Gruinart oysters are served fresh or baked, lobster is fashioned into ravioli, and sea trout is peat-smoked. Finish perhaps with steamed apple sponge, and drink from a serviceable and sensibly priced wine list that starts with house Côtes du Roussillon red and white at £8.90. Those who stay and breakfast may like to note that Scott Chance holds the World Porridge Making title.

CHEF: Scott Chance   PROPRIETORS: Scott and Wendy Chance   OPEN: Mon to Sat L 12 to 2.30, all week D 6 to 9   MEALS: alc (main courses L £5 to £10, D £10.50 to £25)   SERVICE: not inc CARDS: Amex, Delta, MasterCard, Switch, Visa   DETAILS: 44 seats. Private parties: 40 main room. Vegetarian meals. Children's helpings. No smoking in dining room. Wheelchair access (also WC). No music   ACCOMMODATION: 4 rooms, all with bath/shower. TV. Phone. B&B £35 to £60   £5

CAIRNDOW Argyll & Bute   map 11

Loch Fyne Oyster Bar 🍴 ⅚✳ £

Clachan Farm, Cairndow PA26 8BH
TEL: (01499) 600236   FAX: (01499) 600234   COOKING 3
on A83, at head of Loch Fyne   COST £21–£66

A handy stopping-off place for people on their way to or from the West Coast, the oyster bar is an open-all-day extension of the smoking business, whose shop carries a difficult-to-resist display of salmon in its increasingly varied guises. An information sheet in the restaurant explains about the organic, free-range and sustainable wild resources used: this multipurpose venture embodies an intelligent response to its environment and circumstances. There is no set pattern for eating, just a generous selection of hot and cold seafood items. Salmon, for example, comes hot smoked, heavily or lightly cold smoked, as gravad lax, or as a superior smoked Kinglas fillet served sushi-style with wasabi. Oysters, although generally best eaten fresh on ice, also come baked and grilled, and a few platters assemble a variety of shellfish and crustaceans. Grilled steak, a few cheeses, and token desserts complete the picture. An annotated list of some two dozen wines includes eight by the glass. House white is £8.95, red £11.60. Branches in England include one in Elton and one in Cambridge (see Round-up entries).

CHEF: Greta Cameron   PROPRIETOR: Loch Fyne Oysters Ltd   OPEN: all week 9am to 9pm (6pm weekdays end Oct to third week Mar, exc Christmas to New Year)   CLOSED: 25 and 26 Dec, 1 Jan   MEALS: alc (main courses £5 to £30)   SERVICE: not inc   CARDS: Amex, Diners, MasterCard, Switch, Visa   DETAILS: 100 seats. 20 seats outside. Private parties: 40 main room. Car park. Vegetarian meals. Children's helpings. No smoking in dining room. Wheelchair access (also WC). Occasional music   (£5)

CANONBIE Dumfries & Galloway   map 11

▲ *Riverside Inn* ♥ ⁵✳ £

Canonbie DG14 0UX
TEL: (013873) 71295 and 71512   COOKING 1
just off A7, just over the border   COST £19–£32

'We've been here for twenty-five years and are still trying new recipes with enthusiasm,' writes Susan Phillips, who with her husband Robert champions the traditional in the kitchen. Simply treated, good raw materials are the hallmark of their comfortable and carefully run seventeenth-century inn across the road from the River Esk in a peaceful village. The same menus now operate in the split-level beamed bar, adorned by stuffed birds, and in the more formal dining room (undergoing millennial refurbishment). You may find grilled garlic oysters, Cumbrian air-dried ham and melon, or something potted – guinea fowl or shrimps – to start, followed by chicken pot-au-feu, braised rabbit, or plenty of fish: maybe poached haddock with parsley and egg sauce, or Aga-roast cod with cheese. Old-fashioned puddings might include walnut tart, date pudding with toffee sauce or rhubarb and ginger tansy. Sixty-odd wines, virtually all under £20, offer reasonable choices wherever your predilections lie. House wine is £9.75.

CHEFS/PROPRIETORS: Robert and Susan Phillips   OPEN: all week L 12 to 2, Tue to Sat D 7.30 to 8.30   MEALS: alc (main courses £7 to £11). Set L Sun £11.95, Set D £19.50   SERVICE: not inc, card slips closed   CARDS: Delta, MasterCard, Switch, Visa   DETAILS: 30 seats. 30 seats outside. Private parties: 30 main room. Car park. Vegetarian meals. Children's helpings. No smoking in dining room. No music   ACCOMMODATION: 7 rooms, all with bath/shower. TV. B&B £55 to £78

---

⁵✳ *indicates that smoking is either banned altogether or that a dining-room is maintained for non-smokers. The symbol does not apply to restaurants that simply have no-smoking areas.*

COLBOST Highland   map 11

▲ *Three Chimneys* ♥ ✾

Colbost, by Dunvegan, Isle of Skye IV55 8ZT
TEL: (01470) 511258   FAX: (01470) 511358
EMAIL: eatandstay@threechimneys.co.uk   COOKING 4
on B884, 4m W of Dunvegan   COST £25–£66

Shirley and Eddie Spear attract a buzz of contented custom to their remote crofters' cottages on the shore of a sea loch by dint of good cheer and fine, simple cooking. Shirley takes traditional recipes and turns them out in a fresh style, for example bedding lobster on a salad next to a cucumber and lime crème fraîche dip, or setting a pearl barley risotto beside breast of wood pigeon. Straight-forward presentation gets the best out of materials, for example in the 'grand seafood platter' of lobster, langoustines, oysters, mussels, squatties, crab claws and velvet crabs, a feast for two to share. The Spears have created a small snug bar this year and opened the House Over-By, thus becoming a restaurant-with-rooms, which may well suit those who, having dined on 'rich, creamy' lobster and crab bisque, 'wonderful' fish pie and 'scrumptious and light' cranachan, don't feel up to the drive back along Skye's single-track roads. Wines are worth lingering over too, whether they be from France, Italy or the New World. Quality is high and mark-ups refreshingly low, with eight house wines available by the glass or bottle from £3.20/£12.95.

CHEF: Shirley Spear   PROPRIETORS: Eddie and Shirley Spear   OPEN: Mon to Sat L 12.30 to 2.30, all week D 6.30 to 9.30   CLOSED: mid-Jan to mid-Feb   MEALS: alc (main courses £18 to £27.50). Set L £11.95 (2 courses) to £16.50, Set D £22.50 (2 courses) to £27.50   SERVICE: not inc   CARDS: Delta, MasterCard, Switch, Visa   DETAILS: 32 seats. 6 seats outside. Private parties: 18 main room. Car park. Vegetarian meals. No children under 8 at D. No smoking in dining room. Wheelchair access (also WC). No music   ACCOMMODATION: 6 rooms, all with bath/shower. TV. Phone. B&B £120 to £140. Rooms for disabled. Baby facilities (£5)

CUPAR Fife   map 11

Ostlers Close ♥

25 Bonnygate, Cupar KY15 4BU   COOKING 6
TEL: (01334) 655574   FAX: (01334) 654036   COST £25–£53

Although this small, stone-built cottage conversion feels relaxed and informal, it treats its food, particularly the rigorously sourced ingredients, with an appropriate degree of seriousness. A local organic farm supplies bespoke vegetables and herbs, eggs and poultry are free-range, fish arrives from nearby Pittenweem market, and crabs and lobsters come and go with the tide, often appearing as a supplement to the written menu, lobster perhaps served with chanterelles and a saffron sauce. Indeed, fungi are a passion: 'every available spare minute is spent on the hunt,' writes Amanda Graham, who tracks them through the seasons from St George's mushrooms in May to main-season ceps, puffballs and blewits, to winter chanterelles.

533

These and other materials translate into a frequently changing menu which, despite a few nods to modern trends, stays mostly with tried-and-tested flavour combinations: beef fillet with horseradish, or saddle of roe deer and wood pigeon with wild mushrooms. But James Graham really shines when it comes to fish and has the confidence to cook sometimes simple combinations 'so perfectly that one would drive many miles to eat it again': steamed halibut and seared scallops, for example, have a champagne butter sauce, while salmon fillets are accompanied by a leek tartlet. Sticky toffee pudding is a regular among desserts that may also include a chocolate trio (mousse, tart and sorbet) or steamed apricot and syrup sponge with custard. Prices are considered reasonable, especially when the extras are taken into account, and, fittingly, mark-ups on the wines are not at all greedy. Just over a hundred bottles from around the globe provide a good choice without being overwhelming, and a fair number of halves include some luscious dessert wines. Chilean house wines are £10.50 and £11.50 for white and red respectively.

CHEF: James Graham   PROPRIETORS: James and Amanda Graham   OPEN: Tue, Fri and Sat L 12.15 to 1.45, Tue to Sat D 7 to 9.30   CLOSED: 25 and 26 Dec, 1 Jan, 2 weeks Jan, 2 weeks May to June   MEALS: alc (main courses L £9.50 to £12, D £15.50 to £18.50)   SERVICE: not inc, card slips closed   CARDS: Amex, Delta, MasterCard, Switch, Visa   DETAILS: 28 seats. Private parties: 28 main room. Vegetarian meals. Children's helpings. No children under 6 at D. No smoking while others eat. No music   £5

DALRY North Ayrshire   map 11

Braidwoods ⁵⭐

Drumastle Mill Cottage, Dalry KA24 4LN
TEL: (01294) 833544   FAX: (01294) 833553   COOKING 6
1m off A737 on Dalry to Saltcoats road   COST £24–£48

Set in rolling fields, where grazing sheep add to the tranquil atmosphere, this is a place for 'respite dining': wear anything from acid power suits to comfortable tweeds and old sweaters. It is a small restaurant – two rooms with bare stone walls, done in cool blues and creams – that can get busy, so booking is advisable. The Braidwoods are 'dedicated professionals' who administer impeccably well-informed service and take their sourcing seriously: vegetables, for example, are grown at the farm across the way. Dinner, the main meal, offers two or three items at each stage, perhaps taking in a herby risotto with scallops, loin of red deer, and a warm dark chocolate and maple tart to finish.

Precise timing and a degree of flair characterise Keith Braidwood's cooking, producing a juicily gamey, bronze-skinned duck leg confit, with well-judged stir-fried shredded vegetables, and 'a trencherman's serving' of pink loin of lamb, with a scant pile of couscous studded with red pepper and parsley. Fish is well handled too: perhaps a thick slice of turbot fillet with a 'silky' lobster sauce. Flavourings may be understated, preferring a 'ladylike pinch' of herbs and spices to bold handfuls, but this can work to great advantage in, for example, an 'exquisitely creamy' armagnac parfait that came at inspection with rough-textured prunes. France and the New World share roughly equal billing on the keenly priced wine list, starting with house French at £11.95.

534

CHEF: Keith Braidwood   PROPRIETORS: Keith and Nicola Braidwood   OPEN: Wed to Sun L 12 to
1.45, Tue to Sat D 7 to 9   CLOSED: 25 Dec, first 3 weeks Jan, last week Sep, first week Oct
MEALS: Set L Wed to Sat £14 (2 courses) to £16, Set L Sun £18, Set D £27.50 to £30   SERVICE:
not inc, card slips closed   CARDS: Amex, Delta, Diners, MasterCard, Switch, Visa   DETAILS: 24
seats. Private parties: 14 main room. Car park. Children's helpings. No smoking in dining room.
No music

DERVAIG Argyll & Bute   map 11

▲ *Druimard Country House* ⁵⁄✳

Dervaig, Isle of Mull PA75 6QW   COOKING 4
TEL/FAX: (01688) 400345   COST £38–£45

'If you have made it to the Isle of Mull, you have already seen some wild and
beautiful scenery,' wrote one visitor. But the last stretch to this comfortable, if
'quirky', Victorian house, with views over the Glen and River Bellart is
outstanding even by west coast standards. Dinner time depends on whether or
not the theatre is playing, and a slight change since last year means that there is
now only one fixed-price menu of five courses with no choice before dessert. A
typical meal might start with fish cakes or a seafood terrine, followed by sorbet
(or sometimes soup), before the main business: maybe Aberdeen Angus with
caramelised shallots and wild mushrooms in a red wine sauce.

   Wendy Hubbard's food matches the homeliness of the surroundings, taking in
twice-baked onion soufflé, and carrot and coriander soup, while her French
leanings might produce a main course of halibut (from Oban or Mallaig) with
fennel in a bouillabaisse sauce. 'Very good' soft chocolate cake has been among a
trio of desserts, alongside an iced Glayva and honey soufflé. The last course
brings a selection of Howgate Brie, Mull Cheddar, Inverloch goats', Strathdon
blue and other regional cheeses. Fair prices are a feature of the straightforward
forty-strong wine list, starting with house Côtes de Duras at £8.95.

CHEF: Wendy Hubbard   PROPRIETORS: Haydn and Wendy Hubbard   OPEN: all week D only 7
(6.30 when theatre playing) to 8.30   CLOSED: Nov to Mar   MEALS: Set D £27.50   SERVICE: not
inc   CARDS: Delta, MasterCard, Visa   DETAILS: 28 seats. Private parties: 20 main room. Car
park. Children's helpings. No smoking in dining room. Music   ACCOMMODATION: 7 rooms, all
with bath/shower. TV. Phone. D,B&B £72 to £150. Baby facilities (*The Which? Hotel Guide*)

DORNOCH Highland   map 11

▲ *2 Quail* ⁵⁄✳

Castle Street, Dornoch IV25 3SN   COOKING 4
TEL: (01862) 811811   COST £34–£41

The scale of everything is small, the approach simple. No more than about ten
people can eat in each of the two warmly decorated rooms of this terraced house,
a couple of hundred yards from the thirteenth-century cathedral. The weekly-
changing menu (dinner only) offers a choice of three items per course, and the
Carrs do everything themselves: he single-handed in the kitchen, she maitre d',
sommelier and waitress all in one. Quail, understandably, has appeared on the
menu, in a ragoût with asparagus on a potato galette, and there is typically a good

showing of fish: smoked haddock and saffron risotto, or salmon tataki to start, and perhaps a cioppino of west coast seafood to follow. Native materials figure prominently, and an unfussy approach to cooking yields pot roast rump of lamb with a parsnip and onion Tatin, and bitter chocolate marquise with a cinnamon-flavoured coffee sauce. Wines are sharply chosen and keenly priced (look at the whites between £15 and £20), starting with house vin de pays at £11.50.

CHEF: Michael Carr   PROPRIETORS: Michael and Kerensa Carr   OPEN: Tue to Sat D only 7.30 to 9.30   MEALS: Set D £25   SERVICE: not inc   CARDS: Amex, Delta, MasterCard, Switch, Visa   DETAILS: 20 seats. Private parties: 8 and 10 private rooms. Car park. Vegetarian meals. No smoking in 1 dining room. Occasional music   ACCOMMODATION: 3 rooms, all with bath/shower. TV. B&B £25 to £80. No children under 10 in accommodation

---

DUMFRIES   Dumfries & Galloway   map 11

Wisharts

Roberts Burns Centre, Mill Road, Dumfries DG2 7BE   COOKING 6
TEL: (01387) 259679   COST £30–£46

'Stylish cooking served in simple surroundings' is a fair summing up of what is on offer in this L-shaped room next to the cinema, where Mark Wishart surveys diners from his see-through kitchen. 'The ingredients are the stars, not me,' he writes, sourcing locally grown vegetables, traditional breeds of meat, and hand-dived scallops, perhaps paired with endive marmalade. He brings a cosmopolitan assurance to bear on them, serving an oval scoop of rich and creamily smooth chicken liver and foie gras parfait with triangles of brioche and a lightly gingery raisin chutney. The menu is sensibly limited to three or four items per course, and dishes are unfussily presented: maybe a moist roast breast and thigh of corn-fed chicken with braised chicory in a lively sauce of tomato, onion, tarragon and chilli.

Technically expert cooking, fine judgement and some creative combinations add up to dishes that 'please the senses', for example a 'perfectly cooked' salmon fillet wrapped in crisp Parma ham, with wilted cos lettuce and roasted red pepper, a main course that looked attractive, smelled appetising, contrasted textures, and successfully balanced basic tastes of acidity, sweetness, saltiness and bitterness. The simple but classic approach extends to desserts of pears with vanilla cream, and bitter chocolate mousse. 'We think it very good value for such a high standard of cooking,' reckoned one couple, who might have included the compact thirty-strong wine list in the equation. House wines are £9.75 and six other recommendations are available by the glass.

CHEF: Mark Wishart   PROPRIETORS: Mark and Ian Wishart   OPEN: Sun L 1 to 2.30, Tue to Sat D 7 to 10   CLOSED: Christmas and New Year, first 2 weeks Jan, first 2 weeks July   MEALS: alc (main courses £13 to £16). Set L Sun £12.50 (2 courses)   SERVICE: not inc, card slips closed   CARDS: Delta, MasterCard, Switch, Visa   DETAILS: 36 seats. Private parties: 36 main room. Car park. Children's helpings. Wheelchair access (also WC). Occasional music

---

'When we asked what was in the trio of chocolate desserts the waiter said, "Does it matter?"' (On eating in London)

DUNKELD   Perthshire & Kinross   map 11

▲ Kinnaird 🍷 ✸

Kinnaird Estate, Dunkeld PH8 0LB
TEL: (01796) 482440   FAX: (01796) 482289
EMAIL: enquiry@kinnairdestate.demon.co.uk
from A9 2m N of Dunkeld, take B898, signposted   COOKING 6
Kinnaird, for 4½m   COST £36–£73

Still privately run by a member of the Ward family, this imposing country house hotel stands in 9,000 acres of wooded grounds in the Tay Valley and boasts a dining room with Arcadian Italian frescoes, gleaming chandeliers and views over terraced lawns to the toy-like, silent cars on the road below. Despite such grandeur it is 'surprisingly cheerful and homely'. The output of Trevor Brooks's kitchen is deemed 'very professional indeed', making the best of such prime ingredients as warm Kinnaird smoked salmon, Skye scallops, Loch Linnhe prawns and home-cured bresaola. Sometimes dishes strike their consumers as 'rather heavily seasoned', but they are rarely less than interesting. Braised shoulder of Perthshire lamb has been served as three turrets of 'very tender, tasty meat', topped with capers in a creamy sauce with asparagus tips and beans.

Similarly, desserts hit home with big flavours and luxurious textures, eliciting superlatives along the way, from an intensely flavoured chocolate marquise with poached pears and vanilla sauce, to an old-fashioned suet pudding 'oozing with richness and ginger' and drenched in butterscotch sauce. Service is attentive 'but unstuffy'. Make no mistake, however: men are required to wear jacket and tie, and in a further quaint perpetuation of old-fashioned restaurant etiquette, female diners are presented with unpriced menus. Classic French wines take up the bulk of the hefty list, with Italy, California and Australia providing extra weight. Many bottles carry country house-style price tags: look to Chile, the Loire or vins de pays for those under £20. However, a good number of half-bottles helps those who like to ring the changes with their courses.

CHEF: Trevor Brooks   PROPRIETOR: Constance Ward   OPEN: all week 12.30 to 1.45, 7.15 to 9.30   CLOSED: Mon to Wed in Jan and Feb   MEALS: Set L £19.50 (2 courses) to £24, Set D £45   SERVICE: not inc, card slips closed   CARDS: Amex, MasterCard, Switch, Visa   DETAILS: 35 seats. Private parties: 20 main room, 20 and 30 private rooms. Car park. Children's helpings. No children under 12 in dining room. Jacket and tie. No smoking in dining room. Wheelchair access (also WC). No music   ACCOMMODATION: 9 rooms, all with bath/shower. TV. Phone. B&B £255 to £350. Rooms for disabled. No children under 12 in accommodation. Fishing (*The Which? Hotel Guide*)

'There was no room for pushing stuff around the plate, taking a bit of this with a bit of that. You had to eat certain things first in order to get at the substrata underneath. A bit like munching through a geological fault.' (On eating in Somerset)

The Guide *office can quickly spot when a restaurateur is encouraging customers to write recommending inclusion. Such reports do not further a restaurant's cause. Please tell us if a restaurateur invites you to write to the* Guide.

DUNVEGAN Highland   map 11

▲ Harlosh House ⁵⁕

Dunvegan IV55 8ZG
TEL/FAX: (01470) 521367
EMAIL: harlosh.house@virgin.net   COOKING 4
off A863, 3m S of Dunvegan   COST £39–£47

Built around 1750, Harlosh House faces Loch Bracadale and the distant Cuillin
Hills. It is a 'homely' restaurant-with-rooms, one of which is a cottage-like
beamed dining room, where the format is four courses with no choice before
pudding. Seafood understandably predominates, and locally caught shellfish is
fresh and plentiful: crab on toasted brioche with smoked goats' cheese, or half a
plain grilled lobster with a salad of leaves grown at nearby Glendale (Peter
Elford is 'moving towards' organic produce). The second course is typically soup
– pea, mint and lettuce, or cream of watercress – followed by a bright fishy
centrepiece such as chargrilled halibut with lemon and parsley risotto, or roast
sea bass with lime, coriander, capers and fried garlic. Puddings may not always
reflect seasonally available produce – chocolate terrine, and caramel profiteroles
in July – but year-round comfort food is not such a bad thing on Scotland's
Atlantic coast. White wines, and a few light reds, mostly young, make
appropriate seafood partners. Prices start at £12.50.

CHEF/PROPRIETOR: Peter Elford   OPEN: all week D only 7 to 8.30   CLOSED: mid-Oct to Easter
MEALS: Set D £27.50   SERVICE: not inc, card slips closed   CARDS: Delta, MasterCard, Switch,
Visa   DETAILS: 16 seats. Private parties: 4 main room. Car park. Children's helpings. No children
under 8. No smoking in dining room. Music   ACCOMMODATION: 6 rooms, all with bath/shower.
B&B £52.50 to £105. Baby facilities (The Which? Hotel Guide)   (£5)

EDINBURGH Edinburgh   map 11

Atrium ▼

10 Cambridge Street, Edinburgh EH1 2ED   COOKING 4
TEL: (0131) 228 8882   FAX: (0131) 228 8808   COST £26–£54

Its location, on the ground floor of the Traverse Theatre complex, next to Usher
Hall, makes this a handy venue for early and late evening nourishment. The
minimalist 'industrial chic' design includes recycled railway sleepers, and
lighting is dim enough to make reading the menu and bill a bit of a trial, but Alan
Mathieson's ambitious cooking is high-wattage stuff, taking in seared peppered
tuna with pig's cheek ravioli, and roasted sea bass with langoustine and
coriander risotto. Ideas are widely sourced – roast rump of lamb with sesame
chickpea purée, or halibut with wasabi mash, tomato crostini and sweet chilli
sauce – but a lack of punchy flavours, and a few irregularities in temperature,
including cod on cold couscous, and well-flavoured, crisp-skinned chicken on
cold boiled potatoes, took the shine off an inspection meal. Well-balanced
menus might end with iced banana parfait, cinnamon crème brûlée, or chocolate
tart with orange compote. Service is 'business-like' and wines are aimed more at
those armed with a corporate credit card than an equity card. An imaginative

range extends beyond the expected French classics to embrace Italy, Austria and California. French house white is £10.50, the red £11.50.

CHEF: Alan Mathieson   PROPRIETOR: Andrew Radford   OPEN: Mon to Fri L 12 to 2.30, Mon to Sat D 6 to 10.30   CLOSED: 24 to 30 Dec   MEALS: alc D (main courses £14 to £18.50). Set L £14 (2 courses) to £18   SERVICE: not inc, 10% (optional) for parties of 6 or more   CARDS: Amex, Delta, Diners, MasterCard, Switch, Visa   DETAILS: 70 seats. Private parties: 100 main room. Vegetarian meals. Children's helpings. Wheelchair access (also WC). No music. Air-conditioned

▲ Balmoral, Number One

Princes Street, EH2 2EQ   COOKING 6
TEL: (0131) 557 6727   FAX: (0131) 557 8740   COST £33–£76

The bar gleams, the spacious dining room is 'simple, elegant, unfussy', and Jeff Bland's sharp, modern cooking is divided between a carte and a set-price 'market' menu, plus a tasting menu of six light courses for £50 (available after 9.30). Scottish materials – seafood, beef, game, lamb – are supplemented by a few imports: chickens and pigeons come from Bresse, the former perhaps marinated in red wine and herbs, and served with garlic potato purée and glazed shallots. Although the food owes much to classical ways – chunky venison terrine, and Roquefort and Parmesan soufflé have been well received – an individual stamp is evident. Loin of lamb, for example, comes with tomato boulangère and beetroot jus, and osso buco with foie gras and woodland mushrooms.

Even a simple salad of endive, avocado and cherry tomatoes, not normally a dish to make a fuss about, impressed one reporter thanks to its 'positively bouffant' thatch of greenery 'in first-class condition', while another praised hot pear and chocolate soufflé, served with vanilla ice cream sandwiched between two discs of chocolate. Loaves of 'top-quality bread' are sliced on demand, and staff are 'friendly, attentive and informative'. 'Expensive but good value' sums up the food's impact on the wallet, although when wines enter the equation it can be a different story. Sommelier David Harvey, mentioned in dispatches for his sound advice, presides over a top-quality list, though with not much for ordinary drinkers. A varied selection of house recommendations weighs in between £15 and £25. Hadrian's, also on the premises, offers 'contemporary' food in a bistro atmosphere.

CHEF: Jeff Bland   PROPRIETOR: Sir Rocco Forte   OPEN: Mon to Fri L 12 to 2, all week D 7 to 10 (10.30 Fri and Sat)   CLOSED: first 2 weeks Jan   MEALS: alc (main courses £19.50 to £22.50). Set L £15.95 (2 courses) to £50, Set D £33.50 to £50   SERVICE: not inc;12.5% for parties of 6 or more   CARDS: Amex, Delta, Diners, MasterCard, Switch, Visa   DETAILS: 60 seats. Private parties: 60 main room, 25 and 40 private rooms. Car park. Vegetarian meals. Children's helpings. Music. Air-conditioned   ACCOMMODATION: 180 rooms, all with bath/shower. TV. Phone. Room only £150 to £950. Rooms for disabled. Baby facilities. Swimming pool   £5

'Bread was brought to table in a basket, and when we asked for an itemisation the waitress said, "This one's white, that one's brown, and this one's home-made." When I volunteered to sample the latter, she seemed to think it was a bold move on my part.'
(On eating in Shropshire)

Blue Bar Café £ | NEW ENTRY |

| Cambridge Street, Edinburgh EH1 2ED | COOKING 3 |
| TEL: (0131) 221 1222   FAX: (0131) 228 8808 | COST £20–£47 |

Under the same ownership as Atrium (see entry), and located directly above it, this is a cheaper, more informal, light and airy alternative. It occupies a long, echoing room with lots of wood and glass, and although customers may be on the young and noisy side, 'at 72 I still enjoyed it!' Well-prepared, modern and imaginative dishes are its forte, from tomato and dolcelatte tart, via pigeon with black pudding and mushroom risotto, to a choice of sausages: beef with Cheddar, or pork with leek and apple. Value is good, and despite the pitch towards affordable prices it manages to produce a convincingly deep-flavoured wild mushroom soup with truffle oil.

Some dishes were more accurately timed and flavourful than others at inspection; among recommendations are a well-dressed salad of asparagus with deep-fried Parma ham and Parmesan, and a balanced main course of cod with a leek crust on young spinach. Some items are available all day, from sandwiches to simple desserts of plum ice cream or tiramisù. Service by 'young and chirpy' staff is friendly and knowledgeable, and a brief but state-of-the-art wine list includes around fifteen by the glass, champagne at only £4.75. Bottles of Argentinian house wine are £9.75.

CHEF: David Haetzman   PROPRIETORS: Andrew and Lisa Radford   OPEN: all week 12 to 3, 6 to 11 (12 Fri and Sat)   CLOSED: 1 week Christmas   MEALS: alc (main courses L £8.50 to £9.50, D £8.50 to £15). Set L £9 (2 courses) to £12   SERVICE: not inc, 10% for parties of 8 or more   CARDS: Amex, Delta, Diners, MasterCard, Switch, Visa   DETAILS: 120 seats. Private parties: 120 main room. Vegetarian meals. Children's helpings. Wheelchair access (also WC). Music. Air-conditioned

▲ *The Bonham* | NEW ENTRY |

| 35 Drumsheugh Gardens, Edinburgh EH3 7RN | COOKING 4 |
| TEL: (0131) 226 6050   FAX: (0131) 226 6080 | COST £24–£38 |

A long, bright dining room combines old-fashioned stained-wood floors with modern fittings at this stylishly renovated West End hotel. The food claims Californian inspiration (Pelham Hill has worked there), perhaps in the shape of sweet potato and pecan pie with lemon grass and chive crème fraîche. A crispy, spicy black pudding and bacon beignet with gazpacho dressing, however, can only be described as of no fixed culinary abode, a crowded address it shares with smoked haddock and chorizo kedgeree, and venison with chocolate couscous. Generally the fusion works well, as in an inspector's crisp-skinned, moist-fleshed chicken with clapshot, a 'simple but effective' combination lifted by a spicy harissa dressing.

Various breads make light work of the sandwich idea: a brioche and pink roast duck version, for example, or a highly flavoured minute steak in 'light and fluffy' foccacia with aïoli and salad. Even the Bonham burger in a toasted roll is 'a winning combination of flavours and textures'. Dishes are attractively presented, and first courses at lunch can easily be converted to mains, and vice versa. Around fifty savvy wines play off Europe against the New World, starting with six enterprising house wines from £13 to £15.

CHEF: Pelham Hill   PROPRIETOR: Peter Taylor   OPEN: all week 12 to 2.30, 6.30 to 9.30 (10 Fri and Sat)   CLOSED: 26 Dec to 9 Jan   MEALS: alc L (main courses £6 to £7). Set L £9.50 (2 courses) to £12.50, Set D £17.50 (2 courses) to £21.50   SERVICE: not inc   CARDS: Amex, Delta, Diners, MasterCard, Switch, Visa   DETAILS: 65 seats. Private parties: 75 main room, 20 private room. Vegetarian meals. No-smoking area. Music   ACCOMMODATION: 48 rooms, all with bath/shower. TV. Phone. B&B £125 to £185. Rooms for disabled. Baby facilities (*The Which? Hotel Guide*)   (£5)

Café St-Honoré ⁙✳

34 N.W. Thistle Street Lane, Edinburgh EH2 1EA	COOKING 1
TEL: (0131) 226 2211	COST £23–£47

It's not easy to find this atmospheric bistro, down a little lane between Hanover and Frederick Streets. The interior is 'more fin-de-siècle France than contemporary Edinburgh', but the cooking attempts to combine the best of both worlds: on the busy menu, bistro staples (steak au poivre) rub shoulders with more extravagant combinations of perhaps a warm salad of squid, chorizo and scallops, or wild mushroom samosa with pesto. Reports indicate that classic dishes are the more successful, such as a chicken liver pâté or an inspector's 'traditional, well-made and tasty' ham and mushroom crêpe. For dessert, apple and calvados parfait has been praised for its well-judged flavours and 'impressively smooth texture'. Service succeeds in negotiating the fine line between watchful and obtrusive. Although the short wine list turns mainly to France for inspiration it also includes some appealing modern choices. House wine is £9.50.

CHEFS: Chris Colverson and Phil White   PROPRIETORS: Chris and Gill Colverson   OPEN: Mon to Fri L 12 to 2.15, Mon to Sat D 5 to 10   CLOSED: 3 days Christmas, 3 days New Year, 2 weeks Easter, 1 week Oct   MEALS: alc (main courses L £7.50 to £12.50, D £13.50 to £17.50). Set D 5 to 7 £9 (2 courses) to £18   SERVICE: not inc, 10% for parties of 8 or more   CARDS: Amex, Delta, Diners, MasterCard, Switch, Visa   DETAILS: 52 seats. Private parties: 38 main room, 12 to 24 private rooms. Children's helpings. No smoking in 1 dining room. Wheelchair access (not WC). Music

Fishers ♟ £

1 Shore, Leith, Edinburgh EH6 6QW	COOKING 2
TEL: (0131) 554 5666	COST £21–£43

Once a pub at the end of the Leith waterfront, this informal bistro – the bar dark, the other room light and airy, if a bit cramped – offers food all day. A few meaty and vegetarian inventions are hidden among the fishy glories of the menu, which staff take turns to write out, as it changes daily to reflect what has been brought ashore. Start with prawn, rocket and spring onion samosa with ginger yoghurt, perhaps, or smoked salmon and asparagus tart with a sweet pepper dressing, and proceed to chargrilled swordfish and marinated crevettes with beetroot and orange risotto, or grilled halibut with lime, cashew nut and basil pesto. To keep it simple, just ask for seafood soup or salad or platter. Puddings revert to the straightforward, such as apple and plum crumble, and lemon and lime tart. Service is charming and attentive, and the wines are a classy collection that, stylistically, creeps into every vinous nook and cranny. Prices start at £8.95 for house French and remain fair even when reaching three figures in the 'finer and rarer' section.

CHEFS: Mary Walker, Brendan Sugars, Ruth O'Hara and Glynn Sommerville   PROPRIETORS: James Millar and Graeme Lumsden   OPEN: all week noon to 10.30   CLOSED: 25 and 26 Dec, 1 Jan   MEALS: alc (main courses £9 to £15)   SERVICE: not inc; 10% for parties of 8 or more   CARDS: Amex, Diners, MasterCard, Switch, Visa   DETAILS: 45 seats. 20 seats outside. Private parties: 35 main room. Wheelchair access (not WC). No music

Haldanes 🍴✳

39A Albany Street, Edinburgh EH1 3QY	COOKING 4
TEL: (0131) 556 8407 FAX: (0131) 557 2662	COST £26–£57

Opulently furnished like a country house, Haldanes in fact occupies basement premises of the Albany Townhouse Hotel, a Georgian building in the city centre. It is a relaxed, friendly spot overlooking a walled garden; a few tables are put outside in fine weather. More often, drinks are taken by the open fire in a sitting room, then diners choose from an extensive menu featuring several Scottish specialities in the attractive, light restaurant. George Kelso's cooking makes good use of native ingredients, though his creations often have broader influences: witness croustade of marinated goats' cheese and wild mushrooms with an onion, tomato and courgette salsa. The set-price menu (with surcharges for some dishes) might begin with smoked haddock and spring onion cake with steamed mussels and tomato and chive coulis, and go on to a 'tasty, good-sized portion' of saddle of venison with wild mushroom mousse and a celeriac and port sauce. Desserts range from classics such as strawberry pavlova with exotic fruit compote to the 'dark flavours' of sticky toffee pudding. Wines are split between Old and New Worlds with a pleasing number of half-bottles. House wines start at £12.75.

CHEF: George Kelso   PROPRIETORS: Michelle and George Kelso   OPEN: Mon to Fri L 12 to 1.45, all week D 6 to 10.30 (11 Sat)   MEALS: alc L (main courses £9.50 to £13). Set D £22 (2 courses) to £25   SERVICE: not inc   CARDS: Amex, Delta, Diners, MasterCard, Switch, Visa   DETAILS: 40 seats. 8 seats outside. Private parties: 40 main room, 16 private room. Vegetarian meals. Children's helpings. No children under 6 at D. No smoking in dining room. No music   (£5)

Kalpna 🍴✳ £

2–3 St Patrick Square, Edinburgh EH14 1AJ	COOKING 2
TEL: (0131) 667 9890 FAX: (0131) 443 9523	COST £11–£43

A small, simple but spruce place, with pink walls enlivened by ethnic hangings, Kalpna offers varied and inexpensive Indian meat-free dishes. The menu encompasses snacks such as samosas, kachoris and pakoras for starters, diverse dosas and thalis, traditional combinations such as palak paneer, plus rich specialities including khoa kaju (cashew nuts in reduced cream) and khumb masala (mushrooms in coconut milk with tomatoes, onion and coriander). Though spicing tends to be tempered to local tastes, flavours can be complex and pleasing, such as in bhindi masala, the okra invigorated by the tang of tamarind. For dessert, mango kulfi has been praised for its 'creamy texture' and 'intense mango flavour'. Service comes from civil staff who offer sensible advice. The concise wine list is moderately priced, with the New World prominent. House wine is £8.50.

CHEF/PROPRIETOR: Ajay Bhartdwaj   OPEN: Mon to Fri L 12 to 2, Mon to Sat D 5.30 to 10.30 (11 in summer)   CLOSED: 25 and 26 Dec, 1 Jan   MEALS: alc D (main courses £4 to £10.50). Set L £5, Set D Wed £8.95   SERVICE: 10%, card slips closed   CARDS: MasterCard, Visa   DETAILS: 65 seats. Private parties: 65 main room, 30 private room. Vegetarian meals. No smoking in dining room. Wheelchair access (not WC). Music

Martins ♥ ⁵✳ 🦐

70 Rose Street North Lane, Edinburgh EH2 3DX	COOKING 3
TEL: (0131) 225 3106 FAX: (0131) 220 3040	COST £28–£56

David Romanos worked at Martin and Gay Irons' bright and welcoming backstreet restaurant for more than a year before taking full charge of the kitchen in summer 1999, and continues the formula of menus that are short and to the point, with just a few more choices at lunch than in the evening. Pastry is good, perhaps in cheese, apple and tarragon appetisers, or in a monkfish and leek tartlet, and meats are well handled: 'immaculately cooked' loin of lamb, or tender guinea fowl breast, moist inside, crisp outside, with an excellent herby risotto. Sauces sometimes underplay their key ingredient, but vegetables are tailored to the dish, such as faintly gingered crunchy white cabbage and courgette slivers for the lamb. Breads are interesting, perhaps rye with a chive dip at the outset, or, at the end, apricot and walnut as an alternative to oatcakes to go with an outstanding collection of Scottish and Irish cheeses, for which Martin can cite chapter and verse on the makers and even breed of cow. Alternatively, finish with pineapple and mango crumble, or a warm date pudding with toffee sauce. Local merchant Raeburn Fine Wines supplies many of the gems on the cannily chosen wine list in which France rules the roost in the Old World section and the USA just wins by a nose in the New. House wines from Portugal and Italy are £11.80.

CHEF: David Romanos   PROPRIETORS: Martin and Gay Irons   OPEN: Tue to Fri L 12 to 2, Tue to Sat D 7 to 10 (open Mon L 12 to 2, D 6.30 to 11, during Festival)   CLOSED: 1 week Oct, 4 weeks from 24 Dec, 1 week May/June   MEALS: alc (main courses L £9.50 to £11, D £18 to £20.50) SERVICE: not inc, 10% (optional) for parties of 6 or more   CARDS: Amex, Delta, Diners, MasterCard, Switch, Visa   DETAILS: 48 seats. Private parties: 30 main room, 8 and 18 private rooms. No children under 8. No smoking in dining room. No music

Restaurant Martin Wishart   `NEW ENTRY`

54 The Shore, Leith, Edinburgh EH6 6RA	COOKING 5
TEL: (0131) 553 3557 FAX: (0131) 467 7091	COST £21–£49

'A star is born,' ran one enthusiastic endorsement of this small, brightly coloured restaurant down by the water (and now the Royal Yacht Britannia) in Leith. In an area where competition on price is fiercer than on quality, Martin Wishart – no relation to the Wisharts in Dumfries (see entry) – has set out a confident stall. Choice at lunch is limited to two items per course, at dinner only slightly more, but it still manages to span a range from crisp but richly battered beignets of soft squid with a tomato and avocado salsa, to a 'deeply flavoured classic French dish' of thinly sliced rump of beef with 'wonderful' Lyonnaise potatoes and a 'brilliant' red wine sauce.

'If you are looking for big flavours, look elsewhere,' commented one reporter, and indeed the subtlety of a celeriac and saffron soup sharpened with lemon was one of the things that impressed an inspector. The tight menu control pays off in terms of timing and presentation, and the kitchen is able to get the balance of flavours, textures and seasoning right, as in 'perfectly cooked' sole with roast fennel and richly flavoured langoustine sauce, or in rice pudding, its creaminess cut by the acidity of preserved strawberries. Service is keen, and wines are on a scale to match the rest of the operation: some thirty sharply selected and reasonably priced bottles, starting with house French red and organic white at £11.

CHEF/PROPRIETOR: Martin Wishart   OPEN: Tue to Fri L 12.30 to 2.30, Tue to Sat D 7 to 10 (10.30 Fri and Sat)   MEALS: alc D (main courses £12.50 to £16). Set L £11.50 (2 courses) to £13.50, Set D tasting menu by arrangement   SERVICE: not inc   CARDS: Delta, MasterCard, Switch, Visa   DETAILS: 30 seats. Private parties: 35 main room. No smoking before coffee. Wheelchair access (also WC). Music

Shore ⁵⁄* £

3–4 The Shore, Leith, Edinburgh EH6 6QW
TEL/FAX: (0131) 553 5080   COOKING 2
off A199 on Firth of Forth, 2m E of city centre   COST £22–£45

The appeal of this predominantly fish restaurant overlooking the Water of Leith is as direct as the cooking is straightforward. The plain, high-ceilinged dining room is quieter than the smoky bar, but the place does not set out to impress with smart décor, or indeed trimmings of any kind. Rather it goes in for starters of poached mussels, grilled sardines with thyme and tomatoes, or squid in coriander and lime sauce, followed by meatier fish for main course, but still simply treated: roast monkfish with smoked bacon, or grilled sea bass in pesto. Game is the second string – roast saddle of venison with beetroot and port, say – and vegetarian options have included an aubergine, mushroom and Brie tart. Desserts tend to be homely, along the lines of plum and almond tart, tiramisù, or marmalade-flavoured bread-and-butter pudding. Friendly staff are 'right for the venue', as are the predominantly white wines, most of which stay comfortably below £20, including house Côtes du Roussillon at £9.90.

CHEFS: Alison Bryant and Innes Gibson   PROPRIETOR: Stuart Linsley   OPEN: all week 12 to 2.30 (12.30 to 3 Sun), 6.30 to 10   CLOSED: 25 and 26 Dec, 1 and 2 Jan   MEALS: alc (main courses £8.50 to £16). Set L Mon to Sat £6.95 (2 courses), Set L Sun £10.50 (2 courses) to £13.50   SERVICE: not inc; 10% for parties of 8 or more   CARDS: Amex, Diners, MasterCard, Switch, Visa   DETAILS: 36 seats. 12 seats outside. Private parties: 36 main room. Vegetarian meals. Children's helpings. No smoking in dining room. Wheelchair access (not WC). Occasional music
£5

If you have access to the Internet, you can find The Good Food Guide *online at the Which? Online web site (http://www.which.net).*

Skippers

1A Dock Place, Leith, Edinburgh EH6 6LU	COOKING 2
TEL: (0131) 554 1018 FAX: (0131) 553 5988	COST £22–£37

New owners have taken over this fish bistro 'full of quirky trinkets' in Leith, but the low-key convivial atmosphere continues, and the kitchen team remains in place, its aims unchanged: 'it's mainly fish and it's mainly simple,' summed up one visitor. Expect to come across potted crab, scallops with horseradish mash, and sea bass with red pepper relish, whether lunching or dining. An inspector judged the house fish cakes, and a slab of crusted halibut with a pear and plum compote, underwhelming, although a lightly textured and subtly flavoured trout mousse won approval. Finish perhaps with orthodox bread-and-butter pudding, or an indulgent banana and toffee pie with whipped cream. A free-ranging wine list keeps its centre of gravity commendably under £20, starting with house Duboeuf at £9.25.

CHEFS: Kerr Marrian and Neil Wright   PROPRIETORS: Gavin Ferguson and Karen Miller   OPEN: Mon to Sat 12.30 to 2, 7 to 10   CLOSED: 24 to 27 Dec, 31 Dec to 2 Jan, 1 week Mar, 2 weeks Sept   MEALS: alc L (main courses £7 to £15.50). Set D £18 (2 courses) to £21.50   SERVICE: not inc   CARDS: Amex, Delta, MasterCard, Switch, Visa   DETAILS: 58 seats. 12 seats outside. Private parties: 24 main room. Wheelchair access (also WC). Music

Tower Restaurant ⬤✻

NEW ENTRY

Museum of Scotland, Chambers Street,	
Edinburgh EH1 1JF	COOKING 2
TEL: (0131) 225 3003 FAX: (0131) 247 4220	COST £21–£54

This stand-alone restaurant on the top floor of the new pink sandstone museum (there is a lift) is designed to take advantage of its setting, with an enviable view of the castle. A five-minute walk from Parliament's temporary location in the Assembly Hall, it is contemporary, spacious, relaxing, and open long hours. There is a feeling that, in trying to please all comers, the food has yet to find its own identity: prawn cocktail is offered, alongside a light yet 'elegantly rich' duck liver parfait, and a 'good peasanty soup' of potato and leek. But the range of options allows anything from half a dozen oysters, via sushi and salads (perhaps feta, coriander and roast red pepper), to 'simple, comforting' chargrilled chicken with roast root vegetables.

Despite inedible braised lamb shank, an inspector emerged tolerably happy, thanks not least to a successful cheesecake with a topping of 'freshly cooked, not-too-sweet' blueberries, while others have found tarte Tatin and sticky toffee pudding well above the norm. Service is friendly and attentive, and wines run the gamut of styles and prices from Chilean Sauvignon Blanc (£14.95) to Ch. Latour 1990 (£670); a useful 'under £20' section may come in handy, as may a dozen house wines starting at £9.95 (£1.75 a glass).

CHEF: Steven Adair   PROPRIETOR: James Thomson   OPEN: all week L 12 to 6, D 6 to 11   CLOSED: 25 Dec, D 26 Dec   MEALS: alc (main courses L £5 to £13.50, D £10 to £18)   SERVICE: not inc CARDS: Amex, Delta, Diners, MasterCard, Switch, Visa   DETAILS: 78 seats. 70 seats outside. Private parties: 78 main room. Vegetarian meals. No smoking in dining room. Wheelchair access (also WC). Music. Air-conditioned

Tuscan Square £ | NEW ENTRY |

30 Grindlay Street, Edinburgh EH3 9AX
TEL: (0131) 229 9859   FAX: (0131) 221 9515

COOKING 3
COST £18–£34

Glasgow-born Iain McMaster worked at several addresses in the city, most recently Yes and Puppet Theatre, before moving to Edinburgh to open his own show in the spring of 1999. Its location next to the Lyceum Theatre, a few minutes' walk from the Usher Hall and Traverse Theatre, naturally gears it to early and late evening trade. A bright ground-floor bar in suitably Mediterranean yellows serves light meals all day, while the upstairs dining room aims to bridge the gap between northern Italy and America's west coast, with the help of native Scottish produce.

This brings an appealing mix of dishes from Caesar salad to strong-tasting chicken liver pâté with sweet-sharp balsamic onions, from grilled ribeye steak with fries to a dessert crostini of chocolate, banana and walnuts. An early reporter was taken with 'first-class risotto and wonderful Italian breads', another by simply but carefully prepared chicken breast with fettucine carbonara, and sole with a side dish of pesto mash that apparently came directly from heaven. Service may have been 'all over the place' for an inspector, but the compensation was a 'very satisfying' dinner of 'astonishing value'. Five of the twenty wines are available by the glass; house Chilean is £10.95/£2.50.

CHEF/PROPRIETOR: Iain McMaster   OPEN: Tue to Sat 12 to 2.30, 5 to 11 (open all week during Festival and Dec)   CLOSED: 25 and 26 Dec, 1 and 2 Jan   MEALS: Set L £7.95 (2 courses) to £9.95, Set D £10.95 (2 courses) to £14.95, Set pre- and post-theatre D £8.95 (2 courses) to £10.95   SERVICE: not inc   CARDS: MasterCard, Switch, Visa   DETAILS: 60 seats. 40 seats outside. Private parties: 70 main room, 50 private room. Vegetarian meals. Children's helpings. Wheelchair access (also WC). Music. Air-conditioned

Valvona & Crolla Caffè Bar ▮ ✳ £

19 Elm Row, Edinburgh EH7 4AA
TEL: (0131) 556 6066   FAX: (0131) 556 1668
EMAIL: caffe@valvonacrolla.co.uk

COOKING 2
COST £20–£36

The Continis are old-fashioned Italian grocers, importing much of their produce direct from Italy – a van arrives weekly from Milan market – to supplement the Aberdeen Angus beef, west coast seafood and organic vegetables that appear on the daily-changing carte. The long-established delicatessen is 'as bewitching as ever', while the bright first-floor caffè bar serves a range of dishes from assaggini (appetisers) via panetella (warm bread with a choice of filings) to pasta, frittata and a 'satisfying, traditional pizza'. Other options might include fried squid and prawns in a salad, Tuscan chickpea soup, or chunks of spicy sausage on grilled polenta. 'They are doing some serious cooking,' reckoned an inspector, though 'not all of it successful'. Among the triumphs is 'the ultimate lemon thrill': a crumbly torta di limone with an 'incredibly sharp' filling made from unwaxed Amalfi lemons. Popularity, in conjunction with a complex menu of dishes cooked to order, means there can be long waits. Fortunately, the time can be passed happily perusing the shop's excellent wine list, which features one thousand bottles from the top to toe of Italy, any of which can be drunk in the caffè for a £3 corkage. All the star names are here: Gaja, Antinori, Conterno, *et al*, but at down-to-earth prices; a monthly-changing house selection of ten wines starts at £7.99 a bottle, £2.75 a glass.

CHEF: Carina Contini   PROPRIETORS: the Contini family   OPEN: Mon to Sat breakfast 8 to 11, all-day menu 11 to 5, L 12 to 3 (also open D during Festival 6 to 9)   CLOSED: 25 and 26 Dec, 1 and 2 Jan   MEALS: alc (main courses L £6.50 to £9)   SERVICE: not inc   CARDS: Amex, Delta, MasterCard, Switch, Visa   DETAILS: 80 seats. Private parties: 80 main room, 40 private room. Vegetarian meals. Children's helpings. No smoking in dining room. Wheelchair access (also WC). Music. Air-conditioned

Vintners Rooms ♦ ✳

The Vaults, 87 Giles Street, Leith,
Edinburgh EH6 6BZ   COOKING 4
TEL: (0131) 554 6767   FAX: (0131) 467 7130   COST £24–£53

In the eighteenth century, when the wine trade reigned supreme in Leith, this was the auction room of the Edinburgh Vintners' Guild. If it was designed as a reflection of the merchants' success, they'd certainly done pretty well for themselves. A magnificent rococo ceiling is covered with an elaborate vine-leaf motif and sports an outsized gilded chandelier, while stucco cherubs adorn the stone fireplace. It is a memorable setting for some distinctly modern cuisine that has a firm French foundation but borrows from Italy here and there too.

Starters vary from a simple plate of Parma ham with Parmesan and truffle oil to more complex langoustine ravioli with langoustine broth, while sauces ('a delight') are a recurring theme in reports: salmon in filo with sauce Messine, venison with redcurrant and honey sauce, or lamb with leek and Merlot. Appropriately enough, wine is a popular flavouring: Muscadet with baked monkfish, apple Muscat purée with boudin noir, and marsala with chicken livers and polenta. Desserts stick to old favourites, such as prune and armagnac parfait, and sticky toffee pudding, and service is 'relaxed . . . with no pretensions'. The wine list is also grounded in classical France but has some thoroughly modern touches. While prices aren't knockdown, they are certainly fair. Seven of the nine house wines are offered by the glass from £2.80 (£12 a bottle).

CHEFS: A.T. Cumming and J. Baxter   PROPRIETORS: A.T. and S.C. Cumming   OPEN: Mon to Sat 12 to 2, 6.30 to 10   CLOSED: 2 weeks Christmas and New Year   MEALS: alc D (main courses £15 to £19). Set L £11 (2 courses) to £14.50   SERVICE: not inc   CARDS: Amex, Delta, MasterCard, Switch, Visa   DETAILS: 65 seats. Private parties: 36 main room. Car park. Vegetarian meals. Children's helpings. No smoking in dining room. Wheelchair access (not WC). No music

Winter Glen

3A1 Dundas Street, Edinburgh EH3 6QG   COOKING 4
TEL: (0131) 477 7060   FAX: (0131) 624 7087   COST £26–£44

The cobbled streets of the New Town, a few minutes from the city centre, are home to Blair Glen and Graham Winter's 'modern Scottish' restaurant: down a flight of steps in a cellar, it exudes a 'dignified' atmosphere. They define the style partly by what it is not (i.e. not porridge and haggis with tatties and neeps) and concentrate instead on such items as roast salmon, Aberdeen Angus beef with whisky sauce, or a rich seasonal game casserole with basil and butter dumplings. Native dishes often have an element of comfort – haddock with poached egg and a cheesy parsley sauce, for example – which does not seem at odds with more contemporary imported ideas such as red onion and thyme tartlet with goats' cheese, or wild mushroom and roast pepper risotto. For afters, there's warm chocolate truffle cake, or seared bananas on brioche with fudge sauce. Service comes in for regular praise. There are more wines over £20 than under among the three dozen bins, but four French house wines have a ceiling of £12.50.

CHEF: Graham Winter   PROPRIETORS: Graham Winter and Blair Glen   OPEN: Mon and Wed to Sat 12 to 2, 6.30 to 10 (10.30 Fri and Sat)   CLOSED: 25 and 26 Dec, first week Jan   MEALS: Set L £15 (2 courses) to £17.50, Set D Mon and Wed to Fri £25 (2 courses) to £27.50, Set D Sat £27.50   SERVICE: not inc   CARDS: Amex, Delta, MasterCard, Switch, Visa   DETAILS: 60 seats. Private parties: 60 main room, 14 private room. Vegetarian meals. No children under 14 at D. No smoking before 2 at L, before 9 at D. Music. Air-conditioned

---

EDNAM Borders   map 11

▲ *Edenwater House* ❧ | NEW ENTRY |

Ednam TD5 7QL
TEL/FAX: (01573) 224070   COOKING 5
on B6461, 2m N of Kelso   COST £35–£42

Since they last appeared in the *Guide* (in 1997 at their eponymous Edinburgh restaurant), the Kellys have moved to an elegant, attractive former manse, next to the church in a small tranquil village. Tastefully decorated in restful colours, with large windows looking out over the garden and River Eden, it is open for only three sessions a week (except for residents and private parties). Jeff is a 'stylish and friendly host-cum-waiter', and Jacqui cooks meals of four carefully constructed courses that revolve around two main-course choices, perhaps roast saddle of hare with foie gras, or pork fillet with a ginger and honey glaze. Superfluous flourishes are usually conspicuous by their absence: cubes of monkfish fillet crusted with basil and coriander in a simple beurre blanc, for example, although a main-course beef fillet at inspection was outshone by its lively accompaniments of caramelised onions on a crisp filo pastry base in a sweetly rich Madeira sauce.

Sometimes a fish course precedes the main, at other times a cheese or savoury appears before dessert: on one occasion a memorable variation on rarebit incorporating lightly caramelised apple, oozing local Doddington and vigorously flavoured goats' cheese, and a salty Parmesan crisp. Dishes are artistically arranged, for example quartered strawberries under a lightly glazed sweet sabayon, with raspberries and a dusting of caster sugar on top, all on a clean-flavoured strawberry sauce. Evident skill has also produced a hot chocolate soufflé that was 'an airy delight . . . a real pleasure'. A forty-strong international wine list emphasises quality, starting with house French at £10.

If a restaurant is new to the Guide *this year (did not appear as a main entry in the last edition),* NEW ENTRY *appears opposite its name.*

CHEF: Jacqui Kelly   PROPRIETORS: Jeff and Jacqui Kelly   OPEN: Thur to Sat only 7.30 to 8
CLOSED: 25 and 26 Dec, 1 to 14 Jan, last 2 weeks in May   MEALS: Set D £27.50   SERVICE: net
prices   CARDS: none   DETAILS: 16 seats. Private parties: 18 main room. Car park. No smoking
in dining room. Wheelchair access (not WC). No music   ACCOMMODATION: 3 rooms, all with
bath/shower. TV. B&B £55 to £75. No children under 10 in accommodation   (£5)

ERISKA   Argyll & Bute   map 11

▲ *Isle of Eriska* ♥ ⅚✳

Ledaig, Eriska PA37 1SD
TEL: (01631) 720371   FAX: (01631) 720531
EMAIL: bbs@eriska-hotel.co.uk   COOKING 7
off A828, 12m N of Oban   COST £46–£56

Designed by Hippolyte Blanc, the imposing house of formal grey granite and
warm red sandstone was built in 1884, but it is the seventeen-year tenure of the
Buchanan-Smiths that has turned it into a welcoming island retreat for visitors
in search of comfort and cossetting. The setting, welcome, tasteful decoration
and hands-on owners are part of the 'all-round' appeal. Indoor and outdoor
sports cater for more active souls, although even wildlife watchers will be kept
busy, and all can enjoy the 'superb standard' of Robert MacPherson's highly
accomplished six-course dinners.

'Top-quality fish' is perhaps to be expected in these parts, but it takes
sympathetic handling to impress reporters so thoroughly. It is possible to surf
through most of the meal on a wave of seafood: starting, for example, with a 'trio
of cod' served with pickled samphire and a tapénade-dressed winter salad,
followed by John Dory on wild leek risotto (with vanilla essence and pimento
syrup), then a main course of scallop ravioli with langoustines and a crab sauce.
No reports, so far, of jellyfish for pudding.

This 'skilful and innovative' cooking takes a range of different and sometimes
complex dishes in its stride, from a terrine of pork knuckle with foie gras and
lentils wrapped in cabbage, served with caramelised beetroot and warm
Sauternes jus, to simply 'some of the best roast beef I've ever eaten'. Surprisingly, given the integrity of main courses, a separate plate of vegetables is
also served. Desserts of apple tart with cinnamon anglaise, or hot peach soufflé
with kiwi fruit coulis, are followed by a savoury, then finally a selection of
cheeses in good condition. The wine list stands out for its pricing, with many
bins below £20 that would be above elsewhere: Cloudy Bay Sauvignon Blanc
1998 at £16.70, to name but one. More than half the bottles are French, including
a quartet of vins de pays that stay usefully under £9, and there is a good choice of
half-bottles.

CHEF: Robert MacPherson   PROPRIETORS: the Buchanan-Smith family   OPEN: all week D only
8 to 9   CLOSED: Jan   MEALS: Set D £37.50   SERVICE: not inc, card slips closed   CARDS: Amex,
MasterCard, Switch, Visa   DETAILS: 40 seats. Private parties: 20 main room. Car park. Jacket
and tie. No smoking in dining room. Wheelchair access (not WC). No music   ACCOMMODATION:
17 rooms, all with bath/shower. TV. Phone. B&B £170 to £250. Rooms for disabled. Swimming
pool. Fishing (*The Which? Hotel Guide*)

FORT WILLIAM Highland   map 11

Crannog 🎋✱ £

Town Pier, Fort William PH33 7NG	COOKING 1
TEL: (01397) 705589	COST £22–£44

The single most important contributor to a good fish restaurant is fresh fish, so it makes sense for a group of fishermen to join forces and take control of supplies. This Crannog did a decade ago. Subsequent expansion was marred by complications, and with red tape, licences and quotas making fishing more difficult, the Fort William original is now the focus of a new 'seafood marketing initiative', involving other fishermen's associations, which may take it in new directions. For the time being, it continues to offer 'honest, simple cooking', from langoustines in garlic butter to skate wing in black butter, by way of potted crab, or a generous quantity of gravad lax with 'an excellent balance between sweet and sour'. One reporter who ate here twice in one day found staff 'as happy to serve me with just a plate of moules for lunch as they were to provide a three-course meal for five people in the evening'. Service is swift, young and friendly, and around twenty wines fit the bill, starting with house white at £9.95.

CHEF: Annie Mackinnon   PROPRIETOR: Crannog Ltd   OPEN: all week 12 to 2.30, 6 to 10 (9 in winter)   CLOSED: 25 and 26 Dec, 1 and 2 Jan   MEALS: alc (main courses £6.50 to £15)   SERVICE: not inc, card slips closed   CARDS: MasterCard, Switch, Visa   DETAILS: 65 seats. 20 seats outside. Private parties: 40 main room. Vegetarian meals. Children's helpings. No-smoking area. Wheelchair access (also WC). Music

---

▲ Inverlochy Castle 🍷 🎋✱

Torlundy, Fort William PH33 6SN
TEL: (01397) 702177   FAX: (01397) 702953
EMAIL: info@inverlochy.co.uk   COOKING 6
3m N of Fort William on A82   COST £40–£83

The impressive situation below Ben Nevis and the landscaped grounds dropping to the wooded lake below tend to inspire a succession of superlatives in first-time visitors. Inside, the spectacle continues as a wander down a corridor reveals some of the eccentricities and luxuries to be expected from a castle: grand furniture, brocade, cherubs, heavy gold mirrors and vast flower arrangements.

In the 'Victorian Gothic' dining room, with its table settings of gleaming wood, white damask napkins and highly polished silver, four-course set dinners are also extravaganzas of presentation. Appetisers arrive on a tiered cake stand: tiny monkfish and pepper brochettes and a Parmesan tuile, perhaps. Although one reporter found a starter of pavé of home-smoked salmon excessively salty, crab with potato tuiles at the same meal was 'excellent, subtle and interesting in texture', and the soup course (cream of artichoke) was 'rich, balanced and full of flavour'. Next might come a pot au feu of pigeon – no peasant dish this – the pink and tender meat accompanied by discs of cabbage in three colours and asymmetric wedges of Toulouse sausage. 'You could say it was over the top, but it was delicious and entertaining to eat.' The frolic continues with lime mousse in a tall tower on a green glass plate. Staff dressed in Black Watch tartan are abundant and can be 'almost overpowering' in their attentiveness.

Cru classé clarets stretching back to 1966 and mature Burgundies (white and red) are the meat and gravy of a lengthy wine list, with other major wine regions supplying a number of interesting side dishes. Prices reflect the high quality, but bottles under £20 are scattered throughout: look to the New World or the final page of house wines, which includes Vins de Pays d'Oc at £9 and Justerini & Brooks claret and white Burgundy at £16 each. Half-bottles are liberally distributed too.

CHEF: Simon Haigh   PROPRIETOR: Inverlochy Castle Ltd   OPEN: all week 12.30 to 1.45, 7.15 to 9.15   CLOSED: 3 to 31 Jan   MEALS: Set L £23 (2 courses) to £33, Set D £45 to £55   SERVICE: not inc, card slips closed   CARDS: Amex, Delta, MasterCard, Switch, Visa   DETAILS: 34 seats. Private parties: 34 main room, 15 private room. Car park. Vegetarian meals. Children's helpings. Jacket and tie. No smoking in dining room. Wheelchair access (not WC). No music ACCOMMODATION: 17 rooms, all with bath/shower. TV. Phone. B&B £180 to £450. Baby facilities. Fishing (*The Which? Hotel Guide*)

GLASGOW Glasgow   map 11

Buttery   NEW ENTRY

652 Argyle Street, Glasgow G3 8UF   COOKING 4
TEL: (0141) 221 8188   FAX: (0141) 204 4639   COST £25–£60

The Buttery, which returns to the *Guide* on the strength of its new chef Ian Fleming, opened in 1869, and an Old World atmosphere prevails: decorative plaster ceilings, a mirrored mahogany bar, and wooden booths are equally well suited to discreet business lunches and intimate dinners. Dishes can be both inventive and elaborate, and some items, such as wild mushrooms, may well appear in both first and main courses: the mushroom cake partnering an accomplished fillet of beef, with whisky oil and a chilli-edged sauce at inspection, was judged 'exquisite'. Precise timing makes the best of such materials, including rare, gamey Perthsire venison served with an 'exemplary' reduction incorporating blaeberries.

Side-plated vegetables (and nibbles and coffee) might be improved, but desserts have yielded a 'wicked' chocolate truffle cake with a light coffee cream sauce, and a 'winner' of sliced apple marinated in red wine, with a sharp calvados sorbet. Despite white gloves and domes, service is both 'droll and well informed'. Wines are biased towards France, and quite a few are on the pricey side. House French at £12.50 is the only wine available by the glass (£2.95).

CHEF: Ian Fleming   PROPRIETOR: Allied Domecq Restaurants   OPEN: Sun to Fri L 12 to 2.30, Mon to Sat D 7 to 10.30   CLOSED: 25 Dec, 1 Jan   MEALS: alc D (main courses £13.50 to £18). Set L £16.85   SERVICE: 10% (optional)   CARDS: Amex, Delta, Diners, MasterCard, Switch, Visa   DETAILS: 54 seats. Private parties: 48 main room, 10 private room. Car park. Vegetarian meals. Music

---

'Although the menu claims that vegetables are integrated into the dish, "thrown in at random" would sometimes seem a more accurate description.'
(On eating in Yorkshire)

Café Gandolfi £

64 Albion Street, Glasgow G1 1NY	COOKING 2
TEL: (0141) 552 6813	COST £21–£32

A cross between a 1960s bistro, an Irish pub and an American diner, Café Gandolfi has dark wooden panels, heavy furniture and stained glass. The 'honest, rough-and-ready food' runs through the day, from a 'good morning' menu of eggs en cocotte, croissants, scones and sandwiches, to light meals of Caesar salad with bacon, or linguine with red pepper, roasted pine nuts and Gorgonzola. More substantial dinners run the gamut from smoked venison with gratin dauphinoise to New York pastrami. Dishes from the seasonal menu have included beef goulash with herb dumplings, then apple crumble with cream. The small wine list is well focused and fairly priced, starting at £9.95 a bottle; or go for a Bavarian wheat beer.

CHEF: Margaret Clarence   PROPRIETOR: Seumas MacInnes   OPEN: all week 9am to 11.30pm (noon to 11.30pm Sun)   CLOSED: 25 and 26 Dec, 1 and 2 Jan   MEALS: alc (main courses £7.50 to £10)   SERVICE: not inc; 10% for parties of 6 or more   CARDS: Delta, MasterCard, Switch, Visa   DETAILS: 65 seats. Vegetarian meals. No children after 8.30pm. No-smoking area. Wheelchair access (not WC). Music

Lux

1051 Great Western Road, Glasgow G12 0XP	COOKING 3
TEL: (0141) 576 7576 FAX: (0141) 576 0162	COST £37–£45

'Miles up the Great Western Road', near the entrance to Gartnavel Hospital, is this two-part Victorian station conversion. Ground-floor Stazione is a less expensive, informal brasserie serving 'hearty meals from big bowls and plates', while upstairs Lux is spacious, decked out with candles, mirrors and modern prints: an appropriate setting for some bright contemporary cooking. Stephen Johnson doesn't stray too far from bedrock ideas to produce charred monkfish with a caper and red onion compote, or pigeon with wild mushroom couscous, but he generally achieves a good balance: for example in spoonfuls of warm salmon mousse on a 'nicely seasoned' smoky cream sauce.

Vegetables could be improved, but among desserts of Malibu parfait and Bakewell tart it was raspberry crème brûlée that pleased one reporter on all levels: 'nice top, good middle and not too sweet bottom.' Service is 'chatty'. Temperature-controlled storage helps to make the most of a cosmopolitan selection of wines arranged by style, and inert gas improves the chances of a good wine by the glass, of which there are ten. House Touraine Sauvignon and Anjou Gamay are £15 and £16 a bottle respectively.

CHEF: Stephen Johnson   PROPRIETORS: David Maguire and Ronnie Somerville   OPEN: Tue to Sat D only 6 to 10.30 (later on request)   CLOSED: 25 and 26 Dec, 1 and 2 Jan   MEALS: Set D £19 (2 courses; Tue to Thur only) to £25   SERVICE: not inc; 10% for parties of 6 or more   CARDS: Delta, MasterCard, Switch, Visa   DETAILS: 65 seats. Private parties: 65 main room, 14 private room. Car park. Vegetarian meals. No cigars/pipes in dining room. Music. Air-conditioned
(£5)

▲ *Nairns* 🍞

13 Woodside Crescent, Glasgow G3 7UP
TEL: (0141) 353 0707   FAX: (0141) 331 1684   COOKING 4
EMAIL: info@nairns.co.uk   COST £29–£49

Booking may involve more than just picking up the phone and reserving a table – time limits and credit card numbers are an increasingly frequent facet of cosmopolitan eating – but those who secure a place find a comfortable terraced Victorian house with a basement in 'battleship grey', a first-floor dining room that reflects some of the house's original features, and 'a touch of utility' about the furnishings. The food remains an expression of Nick Nairn's passion for subjecting predominantly Scottish produce to a range of varied treatments, from a mix of 'nicely cooked' langoustine, scallop, mussel and red mullet with fettuccine, via baked pheasant with brussel sprout purée, to braised shin of beef with veal sweetbreads.

Neil Forbes, who cooked at Braeval in Aberfoyle (sold by Fiona Nairn, now a tea shop), took over as head chef in May 1999. He makes a good job of many dishes, particularly starters and desserts at inspection: a chicken liver and foie gras pâté that was 'full of flavour', an accomplished crème brûlée, and an 'intense, sharp' lemon tart with good pastry and an effectively sharp accompanying raspberry sorbet. At its best service has been 'prompt and friendly', although it has not always been at its best. The majority of wines now tip the scales at £20 or more, but take in some good names. House South African varietals from Neil Ellis are £14.50.

CHEF: Neil Forbes   PROPRIETORS: Nick and Christopher Nairn   OPEN: all week 12 to 2, 6 to 10
CLOSED: 25 and 26 Dec, 1 and 2 Jan   MEALS: Set L £13.50 (2 courses) to £17, Set D £27.50
SERVICE: not inc, 10% for parties of 8 or more, card slips closed   CARDS: Amex, Delta, Diners,
MasterCard, Switch, Visa   DETAILS: 75 seats. Private parties: 30 main room. Vegetarian meals.
No smoking before coffee. No cigars/pipes in dining room. Wheelchair access (not WC).
Music   ACCOMMODATION: 4 rooms, all with bath/shower. TV. Phone. Room only £90 to £125.
Baby facilities

▲ *One Devonshire Gardens* 🍴✳

1 Devonshire Gardens, Glasgow G12 0UX
TEL: (0141) 339 2001   FAX: (0141) 337 1663   COOKING 5
EMAIL: markcalpin@btconnect.com   COST £45–£81

This trio of converted town houses, part of a Victorian terrace in the city's West End, offers a warm welcome and congenial atmosphere. It is spacious and comfortable, and one who hadn't visited in a while found the dining room lighter and much improved. The set-price four-course dinner has gone, and the kitchen's energy now seems concentrated in a fairly generous carte. While the hotel's sights may be set on an upmarket international clientele, Andrew Fairlie's contemporary cooking, given direction and purpose by a sound classical background, is more appealing than is often the case in such circumstances.

Luxuries are incorporated – foie gras parfait with spiced fig chutney, or home-smoked lobster in a lime and herb butter sauce – but are not the main point. More importantly, dishes are clearly focused: 'sushi-style' dressed crab and avocado salsa, or grilled sea bass with roasted aubergine purée and sauce vierge. This apparently simple yet sophisticated approach ends with Grand Marnier soufflé, or hot chocolate pudding with amaretti ice cream. Service is 'quiet, timely, accurate', although the aristocratic wine list holds little comfort for those of modest means. House wine is £19.

CHEF: Andrew Fairlie   PROPRIETOR: Ken McCulloch   OPEN: Sun to Fri L 12 to 1.45, all week D 7.15 to 9.45   CLOSED: 30 and 31 Dec   MEALS: alc D (main courses £16.50 to £22.50). Set L £21 (2 courses) to £27.50   SERVICE: not inc   CARDS: Amex, Delta, Diners, MasterCard, Visa DETAILS: 40 seats. Private parties: 8 main room, 12 to 32 private rooms. Car park. Vegetarian meals. Children's helpings. No smoking in dining room. Music   ACCOMMODATION: 27 rooms, all with bath/shower. TV. Phone. Room only £130 to £230. Rooms for disabled. Baby facilities (*The Which? Hotel Guide*)

La Parmigiana

447 Great Western Road, Glasgow G12 8HH
TEL: (0141) 334 0686

COOKING 2
COST £15–£47

Gilt-framed prints line this long, narrow dining room, where the food has been described as 'fresh, well-prepared, perhaps slightly old fashioned, but good'. A more recent visitor, however, found that the style of menu and cuisine had changed. Not all dishes are new, but a generally more contemporary approach admits courgette risotto, 'pink, juicy' calf's liver in agrodolce, and venison on a polenta croûton. Start with 'perfectly cooked' lobster ravioli in creamy basil and tomato sauce, or terrine of roasted sweet red peppers with salty, garlicky bagna cauda, and finish with chocolate and almond tart or appley crème brûlée. Generous portions and prime materials contribute to the sense of 'excellent value', as does the forty-strong Italian wine list; house red and white are £10.20 a litre.

CHEF: Sandro Giovanazzi   PROPRIETORS: Angelo and Sandro Giovanazzi   OPEN: Mon to Sat 12 to 2.30, 6 to 11   CLOSED: 25 Dec, 1 Jan, bank hols   MEALS: alc (main courses £11.50 to £16). Set L Mon to Fri £8.30   SERVICE: not inc   CARDS: Amex, Delta, Diners, MasterCard, Switch, Visa   DETAILS: 55 seats. Private parties: 60 main room. Vegetarian meals. Children's helpings. No pipes in dining room. Wheelchair access (not WC). Music. Air-conditioned   £5

Puppet Theatre ⚡

11 Ruthven Lane, Glasgow G12 9BG
TEL: (0141) 339 8444   FAX: (0141) 339 7666

NEW CHEF
COST £25–£53

Considered 'one of the most relaxed places to eat out in Glasgow', this lavishly decorated restaurant – with four dining rooms, plus a modish Gaudí-style conservatory at the back – acquired a new chef too late for us to inspect for the current edition of the *Guide*. Hervé Martin's lively two- and three-course modern menus, however, take in items such as scallop carpaccio with lemon grass and Sauternes dressing, or crisp guinea fowl confit, along with a vegetarian roast chickpea and basil gâteau, and desserts such as spicy pineapple tarte Tatin. A cannily chosen wine list, arranged in no particular order, incorporates a good variety of styles. House Chilean is £14. Reports please.

CHEF: Hervé Martin PROPRIETORS: Ron McCulloch and George Swanson OPEN: Tue to Fri and Sun L 12 to 2.30, Tue to Sun D 7 to 10.30 CLOSED: 1 and 2 Jan, bank hols MEALS: Set L £12.95 (2 courses) to £14.50, Set D £24.95 (2 courses) to £29.50 SERVICE: not inc CARDS: Amex, Delta, MasterCard, Switch, Visa DETAILS: 65 seats. Private parties: 27 main room, 8 to 27 private rooms. Car park. Vegetarian meals. No children under 12. No smoking in 1 dining room. Wheelchair access (not WC). Music. Air-conditioned

Rogano

11 Exchange Place, Glasgow G1 3AN COOKING 4
TEL: (0141) 248 4055 FAX: (0141) 248 2608 COST £27–£56

Art deco surroundings, a friendly milieu, and 'excellent' service are part of the appeal at this old stager, as is the wide-ranging menu, which has a bias towards fish. 'Superb cuisine, impeccably presented,' summed up one visitor, who could not resist a refill of fish soup with rouille and croûtons. Plain dishes abound, with plenty of grilling, baking and steaming, and some straightforward saucing: Guinness and grain mustard for halibut, meunière for lemon sole, mayonnaise for lobster. Richer dishes might take the form of Aberdeen Angus tournedos with foie gras and Madeira, or chocolate mascarpone cheesecake with fruit, nuts and crème fraîche, while vegetarians get their own menu: a choice of three items per course that might include poached egg on toasted brioche with tarragon beurre blanc, followed by seared polenta with herbs and wild mushrooms. Only a handful of wines on the varied list stay below £20, including house French at £11.

CHEF: William Simpson PROPRIETOR: Allied Domecq OPEN: all week 12.30 to 2.30, 6.30 to 10.30; café all week 12 to 11 (12 Fri and Sat) CLOSED: 25 Dec, 1 Jan MEALS: alc (main courses £17.50 to £30). Set L £16.50 SERVICE: 12.5% (optional), card slips closed CARDS: Amex, Delta, Diners, MasterCard, Switch, Visa DETAILS: 60 seats. 32 seats outside. Private parties: 70 main room, 16 and 20 private rooms. Vegetarian meals. No smoking before 2 L and 10 D. Wheelchair access (not WC). Music. Air-conditioned (£5)

78 St Vincent ⁵✳

78 St Vincent Street, Glasgow G2 5UB
TEL: (0141) 248 7878 FAX: (0141) 248 4663 COOKING 2
EMAIL: mconyers@leonardo.demon.co.uk COST £22–£44

A convivial atmosphere prevails at the restored Phoenix Assurance building, its uncluttered space set off by an original marble staircase, some 'arresting' metalwork, and a mural by Glasgow artist Donald Macleod. Andrew Crawford's broadly based 'bistro-style' cooking extends from pheasant terrine with thyme jelly, via Peking duck spring roll with teryaki sauce, to spiced lamb sausage with coriander mash. Good-quality ingredients are the backbone, and treatments are generally straightforward: roast scallops, for example, come with tapénade and yellow pepper coulis. A vegetarian menu might list leek and mozzarella tart or spiced couscous, while desserts take in cinnamon-flavoured apple and peach strudel, or Tia Maria parfait. Service is 'charming', and around forty wines start with eight either by the large or enormous glass. House French is £10.95.

CHEF: Andrew Crawford   PROPRIETOR: Michael Conyers   OPEN: Mon to Sat L 12 to 3, all week D 5 (4.30 Sun) to 10.30 (10.45 Fri and Sat)   CLOSED: 25 Dec, 1 Jan   MEALS: Set L £9.95 (2 courses) to £12.95, Set D £17.50 (2 courses) to £21   SERVICE: not inc, 10% (optional) for parties of 7 or more   CARDS: Amex, Delta, Diners, MasterCard, Switch, Visa   DETAILS: 120 seats. Private parties: 64 main room, 16 and 36 private rooms. Vegetarian meals. Children's helpings. No smoking in 1 dining room. Wheelchair access (also WC). No music   £5

Stravaigin

26 Gibson Street, Glasgow G12 8NX   COOKING 5
TEL: (0141) 334 2665   FAX: (0141) 334 4099   COST £32–£39

A door next to the pub, in a part of the city not far from the university, leads down a short flight of steps to a brightly coloured, modern dining room. Colin Clydesdale takes his 'modern Scottish' approach seriously, starting with a wide range of native ingredients, among them sea urchins from Minch, monkfish landed at Uig, and breast of Perthshire wood pigeon: either in a starter salad or, more ambitiously, sitting on a cabbage and pumpkin 'raft' with a chocolate and port sauce.

As that dish suggests, he is not short of ideas: a spin on a Chilean version of chicken soup incorporates Stornaway black pudding, and loin of ostrich comes on shredded cabbage. A Vietnamese train of thought has produced pigs' trotters with yam, chestnut and tamarind, as well as a coconut dessert with lemon-grass syrup; otherwise there might be rum baba, or highly rated cheeses from Iain Mellis. A global wine list is distinguished by an enterprising collection of grape varieties and sympathetic pricing; some half a dozen are available in two glass sizes.

CHEF/PROPRIETOR: Colin Clydesdale   OPEN: restaurant Fri and Sat L 12 to 2.30, all week D 5 to 11; café-bar all week 11 (12.30 Sun) to 10.30   CLOSED: 25 and 26 Dec, 1 and 2 Jan   MEALS: restaurant Set L and D £13.95 (1 course) to £23.95. Bar menu available in restaurant Mon to Sat L 12 to 2.30, Mon to Thur D 5 to 7, and in café-bar all week 11 (12.30 Sun) to 10.30. 'All-day breakfast' menu available in café-bar Sun 12.30 to 3.30   SERVICE: not inc   CARDS: Amex, Diners, MasterCard, Switch, Visa   DETAILS: 80 seats. Private parties: 80 main room. Vegetarian meals. Children's helpings. No smoking before 10pm. Music. Air-conditioned   £5

Ubiquitous Chip ▮

12 Ashton Lane, Glasgow G12 8SJ   COOKING 4
TEL: (0141) 334 5007   FAX: (0141) 337 1302   COST £33–£63

'I was amused that it was a chip-free zone,' wrote one visitor to this Glasgow landmark, 28 years in the *Guide*. The cobbled courtyard, with bare wooden tables and much greenery, still exerts a pull: 'we finally got here,' wrote one determined couple, well into their 'third decade of foodyism in Scotland'. The ambition remains to use native produce – Argyllshire venison, Ayrshire guinea fowl, Perthshire duck and wood pigeon – and put Scottish home cooking into a restaurant setting, serving up haggis (venison or vegetarian), Aberdeen Angus fillet with stovies, oatmeal ice cream, and cheeses from Dunsyre Blue (cows' milk) to Ayrshire Bonnet (goats') and Galloway Cairnsmore (ewes').

Despite the use of whisky to marinate salmon and perk up a burnt cream, it goes beyond heritage cooking by, in one reporter's words, 'keeping up with contemporary food trends while not following fashion just for fashion's sake', which explains such items as coriander-flavoured chickpea fritters with a sweet carrot and orange salad, and ling served with a 'crunchy yet moist' noodle pancake. Upstairs at the Chip is a less expensive bistro with plenty of choice, and wines offer good value on both floors. Mature bottles from Bordeaux and Burgundy are just one of the strengths of the intelligently chosen main list. Germany and Italy also make a strong contribution (try Jermann's Pinot Grigio 1996, £26, if full-flavoured whites are your weakness), while the New World selection proves its producers can flex their muscles with the best of them.

CHEF/PROPRIETOR: Ronnie Clydesdale   OPEN: all week 12 to 2.30 (12.30 to 3.30 Sun), 5.30 to 11   CLOSED: 25 Dec, 1 Jan   MEALS: Set L £18.95 (2 courses) to £23.95, Set D £26.95 (2 courses) to £31.95; bistro alc (main courses £4.50 to £15.50)   SERVICE: not inc   CARDS: Amex, Delta, Diners, MasterCard, Switch, Visa   DETAILS: 80 seats. 60 seats outside. Private parties: 80 main room. Vegetarian meals. Children's helpings. Wheelchair access (also WC). No music

Yes

22 West Nile Street, Glasgow G1 2PW   COOKING 4
TEL: (0141) 221 8044   FAX: (0141) 248 9159   COST £29–£52

Ferrier Richardson's colourful cosmopolitan bar, brasserie and restaurant is now five years old, and the basement dining room's blond wood and deep purple carpets convey an air of well-being and confidence. As Iain McMaster moved to open his own restaurant (see Tuscan Square, Edinburgh), Steven Caputa took charge of the kitchen, continuing the broadly international theme in which Scotland, the Mediterranean and Far East rub shoulders more or less happily. Judge for yourself, from a repertoire that includes gâteau of haggis with turnips and potatoes, oriental duck broth, and seafood brochette with lemon and herb couscous.

Among dishes that have impressed are a light and delicate wild mushroom ravioli with an intense Madeira and tarragon reduction, sharing the plate with a tower of balsamic-dressed rocket and Parmesan crisps, and a strongly flavoured chocolate mousse topped with frothy cappuccino, accompanied by a first-rate pistachio ice cream. Fifty-plus wines seem geared to match the surroundings as much as the food, starting with house vin de pays at £13.95.

CHEF: Steven Caputa   PROPRIETOR: Ferrier Richardson   OPEN: Mon to Sat 12 to 2.30, 7 to 11   CLOSED: 25 and 26 Dec, 1 and 2 Jan, bank hols   MEALS: Set L £13.95 (2 courses) to £16.95, Set D £23.95 (2 courses) to £30.50   SERVICE: not inc   CARDS: Amex, Delta, Diners, MasterCard, Switch, Visa   DETAILS: 120 seats. Private parties: 120 main room, 23 private room. Vegetarian meals. Children's helpings. Music

All details are as accurate as possible at the time of going to press, but chefs and owners often change, and it is wise to check by telephone before making a special journey. Many readers have been disappointed when set-price bargain meals are no longer available. Ask when booking.

GULLANE   East Lothian

map 11

▲ Golf Inn Hotel, Daniel's Restaurant £

NEW ENTRY

Main Street, Gullane EH31 2AB
TEL: (01620) 843259   FAX: (01620) 842066

COOKING 5
COST £20–£38

Lisa Saddler's parents have owned this small ivy-covered pub-with-rooms, in a place that is no stranger to quality restaurants, for over twenty years. In what sounds like a sensible move, her boyfriend Dan Hall, who has cooked at Nairns and Braeval, took charge of the kitchen as the last edition of the *Guide* came out, transforming a basic pub menu of haddock and chips (still available, but now with a beer batter) and steak pie, into something considerably more interesting. His long menu – around thirty regular items plus half a dozen or more daily-changing specials – has a penchant for Italian ideas: 'great' asparagus simply grilled with Parma ham, rocket and truffle oil, or 'light and fluffy' gnocchi with roast pepper and plum tomatoes.

That still leaves room for Thai chicken curry, and the 'sharp, distinct flavours' of lamb confit with Toulouse sausage in a deeply tasty sauce. Portions are hearty but those who make it to dessert are rewarded with a 'uniformly excellent' array, in which flavours and textures triumph over mere visual effect, from sharp lemon and coconut tart with 'brilliant' pastry, to a Valrhona chocolate mousse with pistachio ice cream. The food warrants sharper service but is backed up by thirty reasonably priced wines from around the world. Four house wines start at £8.90.

CHEFS: Dan Hall and Will Hay   PROPRIETORS: Tom and Kathleen Saddler   OPEN: all week 12 to 2.30, 5.30 to 9.30   MEALS: alc (main courses £6 to £10.50). Set D £14 (2 courses) to £17.50
SERVICE: not inc   CARDS: Amex, MasterCard, Switch, Visa   DETAILS: 50 seats. Private parties: 40 main room, 100 private room. Vegetarian meals. Children's helpings. No smoking before 10pm. Wheelchair access (also WC). Music   ACCOMMODATION: 16 rooms, all with bath/shower. TV. Phone. B&B £35 to £50. Baby facilities

▲ Greywalls

Muirfield, Gullane EH31 2EG
TEL: (01620) 842144   FAX: (01620) 842241
on A198, at W end of Gullane

COOKING 5
COST £26–£54

If one requirement of country house hotels is that they should seem like permanent fixtures, then Greywalls certainly qualifies. Giles Weaver's parents turned the Lutyens-designed house into a hotel just after the war (it passed its fiftieth anniversary milestone in 1998) and its high level of old-fashioned comfort – sofas and wood panelling in an assortment of lounges, drawing rooms and a library – is the kind that comes only with mature houses. The food is fairly described as modern British, in that it makes use of much native material (Highland roe deer, peat-smoked Shetland salmon), and sets it in the context of bright global flavourings. Fish, for example, might include North Berwick halibut on a tomato and ginger compote, or roast codling with chorizo and aubergine caviare.

The second of four courses at dinner is soup or salad, and luxuries are not neglected: foie gras might be seared and served with Sauternes sauce as a first course, while ravioli of lobster, lemon and truffle have come in an asparagus and ginger broth. Lunches tend to consist of more straightforward options. Farmhouse cheeses, or grilled crottin on garlic bread, provide a savoury alternative to a warm fruit gratin, or blueberry and pear jelly with lemon cream. The wine list caters equally for those who like (and can afford) grand old wines – Ch. Haut-Brion 1934 and Ch. d'Yquem 1943, or Vega Sicilia Unico 1974, for example – and those who like something more unusual, such as a Mexican Barbera or a Late Harvest Vidal from Canada. Ten house wines start at £12.50 a bottle or £2.60 a glass, and there is much that appeals at every price point.

CHEF: Simon Burns   PROPRIETOR: Giles Weaver   OPEN: all week 12.30 to 1.45, 7.30 to 9.15   CLOSED: Nov to Mar   MEALS: Set L Mon to Sat £15 (2 courses) to £17.50, Set L Sun £20, Set D £35. Bar L available Mon to Sat   SERVICE: not inc, card slips closed   CARDS: Amex, Delta, Diners, MasterCard, Switch, Visa   DETAILS: 50 seats. 15 seats outside. Private parties: 35 main room, 20 private room. Car park. Jacket and tie at D. No smoking in dining room. Wheelchair access (also WC). No music   ACCOMMODATION: 23 rooms, all with bath/shower. TV. Phone. B&B £100 to £200. Rooms for disabled. Baby facilities (*The Which? Hotel Guide*)   £5

La Potinière 🍷 ⅚✳

Main Street, Gullane EH31 2AA
TEL/FAX: (01620) 843214
on A198, 4m SW of North Berwick

COOKING 8
COST £31–£51

Anyone looking for one of the best restaurants in Britain could be forgiven for failing to find this modest 'shed-like' building on the main street where, in 2000, the Browns celebrate twenty-five years. Inside, it is 'as tiny as a vestry in a Nonconformist chapel', but the conversational buzz of expectation before meals seems to confirm its French name: a 'gossiping place'. The menu is written in French (the Browns are dedicated Francophiles) and the fact that there is only one copy for the whole dining room does not matter a jot, for there is no choice whatever. This is less an indication of parsimony than a statement that the meal as it stands will be well-balanced.

Daily-changing dishes are culled from a repertoire that regulars are familiar with, but which is broad enough to deliver variety. The food looks simple and straightforward, yet combines depth, intensity and subtlety of flavour, and is careful with textures. Soups have included potage St Germain, and a smooth, lightly spiced combination of carrot, apple and apricot. A fish course follows. Franglais speakers will appreciate the gâteau de smokies, served with a sauce vierge, while crisp-skinned, moist-fleshed salmon, perhaps accompanied by fennel and a vanilla sauce, is enduringly popular.

Game and poultry tend to dominate main courses, where the lack of frills exposes the quality of ingredients for what they are, from a satisfyingly 'rustic' breast of guinea fowl, to a pink-fleshed, gamey-tasting breast of wood pigeon sitting on a mound of tarragon-flavoured lentils intensified by morels. Dauphinoise potatoes accompany, and the ordinary-sounding salad that follows – a variety of leaves combined with asaparagus, peas and slices of pear, with a walnut oil dressing – impressed an inspector as 'simply the best salad I've had'. Cheese is typically unpasteurised Brie de Meaux 'in perfect condition', and dessert ranges from a light pannacotta, via chocolate in some form, to a 'sensual' tarte au citron.

David Brown generally wears a concentrated look. His preoccupied style of service doesn't suit all reporters – one found himself wineless for two courses – but the majority view is of a 'first-class' operation led by 'a fount of information', especially when it comes to wines: his own recommendations (usually below £20 or £30) are well worth following. The list was in a state of flux as we went to press, but mature champagnes, clarets and Burgundies, fine Italians and good-quality wines from south-west France and South Africa (both regions in which the Browns have a particular interest) will all be offered at very reasonable prices. House wine red and white are £13.75.

CHEF: Hilary Brown   PROPRIETORS: David and Hilary Brown   OPEN: Thu and Sun L 1pm (1 sitting), Fri and Sat D 8pm (1 sitting)   MEALS: Set L £21.50, Set D £32.50   SERVICE: not inc CARDS: none   DETAILS: 26 seats. Private parties: 26 main room. Car park. No smoking in dining room. Wheelchair access (not WC). No music

---

INVERNESS Highland   map 11

▲ *Culloden House* ⁵⁕

Culloden, Inverness IV2 7BZ
TEL: (01463) 790461 and (0800) 980 4561
FAX: (01463) 790461
EMAIL: reserv@cullodenhouse.co.uk
from Inverness take A96 to Nairn, turn right after 1m,   COOKING 2
then left at Culloden House Avenue   COST £32–£60

It may have seen better days, but this Adam-style Georgian mansion is built on an impressive scale. Given the manicured lawn, high ceilings, chandeliers, plaster reliefs and marble fireplaces, you half expect a banquet. Instead, what you get is friendly, down-to-earth service, an à la carte, plus four courses for a set price at dinner. Good raw materials are at the heart of it, including a 'fine piece of pink Aberdeen Angus steak' at one meal, and 'tender, moist' chicken breast in a creamy green peppercorn sauce with a pastry case of wild mushrooms. Start perhaps with warm smoked salmon in dill butter, or a 'wholesome, chunky, smoky' lentil soup containing carrots, turnips, barley and ham, and finish with a straightforward sticky toffee pudding or crisp meringue with strawberry and coconut ice creams. An ambitious wine list provides for most eventualities, including those with a £20 ceiling. House wines are Justerini & Brooks claret (£12.60) and white Burgundy (£16.80).

CHEF: Michael Simpson   PROPRIETOR: North American Country Inns   OPEN: all week 12.30 to 2.30, 7 to 9   MEALS: alc L (main courses £10.50 to £18.50). Set D £35   SERVICE: not inc, card slips closed   CARDS: Amex, Delta, Diners, MasterCard, Switch, Visa   DETAILS: 60 seats. Private parties: 76 main room, 30 private room. Car park. Vegetarian meals. Children welcome by arrangement in dining room. Jacket and tie. No smoking in dining room. Occasional music ACCOMMODATION: 28 rooms, all with bath/shower. TV. Phone. B&B £135 to £270. Children welcome by arrangement in accommodation. Baby facilities (£5)

▲ *means accommodation is available.*

▲ *Dunain Park* ⁵⁄✳

Inverness IV3 8JN
TEL: (01463) 230512 FAX: (01463) 224532
EMAIL: dunainparkhotel@btinternet.com
on A82, 2m from Inverness

COOKING 2
COST £36–£48

This family-run hotel is domestic rather than baronial in scale, with 'tasteful and comfortable furnishings' ranged around an open fire in the lounge. 'Natural fresh ingredients are the order of the day,' observed one visitor, who also noted the lack of pretension on a menu that combines Scottish and French input in almost equal measure. Results extend from the relatively familiar (honey-roast duck breast), via a comforting risotto of peas (from the walled garden) topped with poached egg and hollandaise, to a more enterprising ballottine of salmon with pickled mussels, and pan-fried pigeon breast with black-pudding fritter. Steaks (from Aberdeen Angus accredited herds) are a big feature, served with a choice of sauces, while puddings are self-service from the buffet. A worldly spread of nearly one hundred bins opens with a quartet of house wines at £12.50, and in a country where extensive malt whisky collections are not unknown, this one stands out.

CHEF: Ann Nicoll PROPRIETORS: Ann and Edward Nicoll OPEN: all week D only 7 to 8.30 CLOSED: 3 weeks Jan/Feb MEALS: alc (main courses £15.95) SERVICE: not inc, card slips closed CARDS: Amex, Delta, MasterCard, Switch, Visa DETAILS: 36 seats. Private parties: 12 main room. Car park. Vegetarian meals. No smoking in dining room. Wheelchair access (not WC). No music ACCOMMODATION: 13 rooms, all with bath/shower. TV. Phone. B&B £138 to £198. Rooms for disabled. Baby facilities. Swimming pool (*The Which? Hotel Guide*) £5

KILLIECRANKIE Perthshire & Kinross   map 11

▲ *Killiecrankie Hotel* ⁵⁄✳

Killiecrankie PH16 5LG
TEL: (01796) 473220 FAX: (01796) 472451
off A9, 3m N of Pitlochry

COOKING 3
COST £41–£49

Here in this old manse beside the steep gorge that is the Killiecrankie Pass, close to woodlands and an RSPB reserve, substantial Scottish-international cooking is the draw; four courses plus coffee is the format. Smoked fish is likely to appear in some guise as a starter – Arbroath smokie mousse wrapped in smoked salmon, for example – perhaps alongside broccoli and almond soup, or a warm salad of grilled goats' cheese and avocado with herb croûtons and balsamic dressing. Grilling, roasting and pan-frying are favoured cooking methods, applied to medallions of venison, served with a potato and beetroot galette; to guinea fowl, accompanied by apple and walnut stuffing and Madeira sauce; or to monkfish, which might come with Lyonnaise potatoes, brunoise vegetables and a Meaux mustard sauce. Baked peaches in pistachio caramel sauce and orange crème brûlée show the style of the sweets, and meals end with a selection of Scottish and international cheeses. Service is 'professional but friendly'. Of the seventy-plus wines, about half are French and sixteen are half-bottles; eight house wines start at £10.60.

CHEF: Mark Easton   PROPRIETORS: Colin and Carole Anderson   OPEN: all week D only 7 to 8.30   CLOSED: 3 Jan to 4 Feb   MEALS: Set D £31. Bar L and D available   SERVICE: not inc, card slips closed   CARDS: Delta, MasterCard, Switch, Visa   DETAILS: 34 seats. Car park. Children's helpings. No children under 5. No smoking in dining room. No music   ACCOMMODATION: 10 rooms, all with bath/shower. TV. Phone. D,B&B £63 to £168. Baby facilities (*The Which? Hotel Guide*)

KINCLAVEN Perthshire & Kinross   map 11

▲ *Ballathie House* ⁵✳

Kinclaven, Stanley PH1 4QN
TEL: (01250) 883268   FAX: (01250) 883396
EMAIL: email@ballathiehousehotel.com   COOKING 2
off B9099, take right fork 1m N of Stanley   COST £22–£50

An air of tranquillity suffuses this attractively furnished and tastefully decorated house, whose lofty dining room windows overlook the River Tay. Menus change daily: bar lunches during the week give way to a three-course spread on Sunday, while dinner is four courses (with a sorbet, or perhaps a lively, spice-infused carrot soup in the middle). Materials include salmon and cod from Shetland, and Perthshire lamb and beef. The kitchen takes pains over presentation – adding a decorative salad to a smooth, creamy-textured pâté of goose and duck liver, for example, or making chocolate and fruit flower patterns for a dessert of vanilla terrine – although our inspector was left to wonder at the errors in timing and seasoning of a dinner for two. As the menu advises, meats are served pink and vegetables crisp, unless otherwise requested. Well-trained staff are 'swift and pleasant', and a catholic selection of largely affordable wines is well supported by half-bottles and around a dozen by the glass. House Dalwood from Australia is £10.50.

CHEF: Kevin MacGillivray   PROPRIETOR: Ballathie House Hotel Ltd   OPEN: all week 12.30 to 2, 7 to 9   MEALS: alc L Mon to Sat (main courses £6 to £8.50). Set L Sun £18.50, Set D £29.90 to £33   SERVICE: not inc   CARDS: Amex, Delta, Diners, MasterCard, Switch, Visa   DETAILS: 65 seats. Private parties: 60 main room, 16 and 32 private rooms. Car park. Vegetarian meals. No smoking in dining room. Wheelchair access (also WC). No music   ACCOMMODATION: 27 rooms, all with bath/shower. TV. Phone. D,B&B £95 to £260. Rooms for disabled. Baby facilities. Fishing £5

'[One diner at] this small and friendly restaurant . . . got quite drunk (the wine glasses were very large) and made rather a nuisance of himself, asking for the recipe for each course and trying to order combinations not listed on the menu, although the restaurant was self-evidently too busy to be able to accommodate his increasingly bizarre requests. When the desserts arrived, which were beautifully assembled and presented, the staff had stuck a raw parsnip in the middle of his.' (On eating in Gloucestershire)

Report forms are at the back of the book; write a letter if you prefer; or email us at guidereports@which.co.uk.

KINGUSSIE Highland  map 11

▲ *The Cross*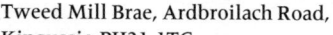

Tweed Mill Brae, Ardbroilach Road,
Kingussie PH21 1TC
TEL: (01540) 661166 FAX: (01540) 661080
EMAIL: fabulousfood@thecross.co.uk

COOKING 6
COST £45–£54

'A charming hotel in an idyllic situation' is how one visitor sums up this converted tweed mill beside the tumbling brae. The dining room is expansive, the atmosphere relaxed, but the Hadleys have a committed approach and strong views on a number of issues. Smokers who put salt on everything and love French wines should tread carefully: windows (in the lounge, where smoking is permitted) may be flung open to dispel the fug; salt and pepper are not supplied at table; and French wines are conspicuous by their absence from the list (a protest against that country's nuclear testing programme in the Pacific). On the other hand, Kingussie spring water is free, the 'corkage' charge for wine is a small taste, and supplies are given serious attention: the Hadleys take the trouble to visit the farms that provide the materials for their Highland style of food.

Diver-caught scallops from the West Coast might be served with Thai-dressed noodles to start, and an intermediate course of Shetland salmon (smoked in-house a few hours before) has come with Puy lentils. Five courses are the norm: a fish dish precedes soup, another follows it, and game features prominently among main courses, perhaps saddle of mountain hare, or venison fillet with redcurrants and port. Wild mushrooms appear occasionally, and breast of Ayrshire guinea fowl has come with a sauce of Lanark blue cheese and rosemary. The only choice is between two main-course items, and either of two desserts (baked lime cheesecake or strawberry shortcake perhaps) or cheese.

If the lack of French wines leaves some drinkers nervous of exploring virgin territory, they needn't worry, for Tony is an enthusiastic and expert guide. It is no surprise that New World wines now form the bulk of his fine list, but the Old World maintains a worthy presence, bolstered by the reintroduction of a few Italian bins. A satisfying number of bottles cost less than £15, half-bottles are abundant, and wines by the glass are constantly changing.

CHEFS: Ruth Hadley and Becca Henderson PROPRIETORS: Tony and Ruth Hadley OPEN: Wed to Sun D only 7 to 9 CLOSED: 1 to 26 Dec, 5 Jan to 25 Feb MEALS: Set D £35 SERVICE: not inc, card slips closed CARDS: Delta, MasterCard, Switch, Visa DETAILS: 28 seats. Private parties: 28 main room. Car park. No children under 12 in dining room. No smoking in dining room. Wheelchair access (also WC). No music ACCOMMODATION: 9 rooms, all with bath/shower. Phone. D,B&B £95 to £190. No children under 12 in accommodation (*The Which? Hotel Guide*)

'*We asked how an Italian summer pudding differed from an English one, and the waitress couldn't really say, adding that, funnily enough, somebody had asked her that very same question only the night before, and she didn't know then either.*' (On eating in London)

denotes an outstanding wine cellar; denotes a good wine list, worth travelling for.

KINLOCHMOIDART Highland   map 11

Kinacarra £※

Kinlochmoidart PH38 4ND
TEL: (01967) 431238   COOKING 4
on A861, at head of Loch Moidart   COST £19–£37

Out on a limb west of Fort William, overlooking a sea loch, Angus and Frances
MacLean's unassuming stone-built restaurant offers a generous carte under the
circumstances, with half a dozen main courses to choose from. The cooking holds
few surprises, indeed some dishes hark back a long way – duck with morello
cherry sauce, or pork fillet with mushrooms and soured cream – but more
contemporary flavours find their way into the repertoire too: turkey kofta with
lime and coriander, or fried halloumi cheese with capers. Scottish sirloin steak is
a regular feature, and seafood might include spicy baked monkfish, or sauté
scallops with spring onions and crème fraîche. Expect homely desserts along the
lines of chocolate roulade, ginger figgy pudding, or profiteroles. Eighteen wines,
sourced solely from the New World, start with house Chilean red and South
African white at £11.

CHEF: Frances MacLean   PROPRIETORS: Angus and Frances MacLean   OPEN: Tue to Sun L 12
to 2, Tue to Sat D 7 to 8.30   CLOSED: end Oct to Easter   MEALS: alc (main courses L £4.50 to £7,
D £10 to £13)   SERVICE: not inc   CARDS: none   DETAILS: 24 seats. 6 seats outside. Car park.
Vegetarian meals. Children's helpings. No smoking in dining room. Wheelchair access (also
WC). No music

LINLITHGOW West Lothian   map 11

▲ Champany Inn 🍾

Champany Corner, Linlithgow EH49 7LU
TEL: (01506) 834532   FAX: (01506) 834302   COOKING 6
2m NE of Linlithgow at junction of A904 and A803   COST £29–£78

The ban on serving beef on the bone has hit many places hard, none more so than
this specialist in beef cuisine. Aberdeen Angus, hung for three weeks in an
ionised chill room, is the core of the business, showing up as pope's eye, strip
loin, ribeye, or fillet with a choice of three sauces, plus other cuts available by
weight. 'If you want a light meal, this is not the place to come,' advised one
visitor, who rated his charcoal-grilled fillet steak above the accompanying chips
and onion rings. Seafood provides a counterpoint, however, in the form of Loch
Gruinart oysters, spicy prawn piri-piri, west coast scallops or Shetland salmon
trout.

The above description (and the score) applies to the great round stone-built
dining room. Those who have lunched in the less expensive, tightly packed chop
and ale house, which majors in generously sized burgers, find it 'an excellent
pub lunch' and good value into the bargain. The inn now boasts a 32,000-bottle
wine cellar that includes practically every kind of red one would wish to partner
with beef, from mature Burgundy to Châteauneuf-du-Pape to Pinotage (the
range of South African reds is exceptional). White wine lovers can relax in the
knowledge that they are also well looked after. Mark-ups reflect the high cost of

keeping such a huge stock, but wines under £20 can be found, starting at £14.50 for the house South Africans.

CHEF: Clive Davidson PROPRIETORS: Clive and Anne Davidson OPEN: Mon to Fri L 12.30 to 2, Mon to Sat D 7 to 10 CLOSED: 25 Dec, 1 and 2 Jan MEALS: alc (main courses £15.50 to £27.50). Set L £16.75 SERVICE: 10%, card slips closed CARDS: Amex, Delta, Diners, MasterCard, Switch, Visa DETAILS: 50 seats. 20 seats outside. Private parties: 16 main room, 40 private room. Car park. Vegetarian meals. No children under 8. Wheelchair access (also WC). No music ACCOMMODATION: 16 rooms, all with bath/shower. TV. Phone. B&B £120 to £135. Rooms for disabled

LOCHINVER Highland map 11

▲ *The Albannach*

NEW ENTRY

Baddidarroch, Lochinver IV27 4LP COOKING 5
TEL: (01571) 844407 FAX: (01571) 844285 COST £39–£46

Set in the extreme north-west of Scotland near the fishing port of Lochinver, which supplies much of its fish, The Albannach is 'a great hidden find'. The atmosphere is Scottish 'without the tweeness that often accompanies the tartan', the welcome warm, and views across the bay to the Assynt mountains are spectacular. A lack of pretension coupled with meticulous attention to detail characterise the running of both hotel and restaurant. Dinner is an intelligently constructed, no-choice, five-course affair, served in a wood-panelled dining room where a stag's head peers at diners from above a well-stoked log fire. Dressed in kilt, sporran and leather waistcoat, co-proprietor Colin Craig waits at table with 'a certain panache'. He and partner Lesley Crosfield describe their food as 'contemporary Scottish', which is to say they source the best local materials and allow flavours to shine. Seafood is a dominant theme, in simple dishes of grilled langoustines with mustard mayonnaise, for example, but meat is also given its due in Highland beef with Madeira sauce, tarragon mash and skirlie. An inspection meal was notable for 'richly flavoured' crab and prawn bisque, followed by a well-conceived dish of 'outstanding' Lochinver halibut with hollandaise, its 'cooked but crisp' vegetables providing a good foil to the voluptuous fish and sauce. A 'perfectly executed' warm tartlet of apples with calvados ice cream made a fitting finale.

Bread is well made, and farmhouse cheeses, served with 'excellent' home-made oatcakes, are in tiptop condition. Colin is an enthusiastic guide to a 150-strong wine list that offers a good mix of modern bottles for adventurous palates and classic bins for traditional tastes. Prices are reasonable, starting at £10 for Chilean Sauvignon Blanc, and four wines by the glass change daily to match the menu.

CHEFS/PROPRIETORS: Colin Craig and Lesley Crosfield OPEN: all week D only 8 (1 sitting) CLOSED: 27 Dec to 15 Mar MEALS: Set D £30 SERVICE: not inc, card slips closed CARDS: Delta, MasterCard, Switch, Visa DETAILS: 17 seats. Private parties: 22 main room. Car park. No children under 12 in dining room. No smoking in dining room. Occasional music ACCOMMODATION: 5 rooms, all with bath/shower. Phone. D,B&B £67 to £150. No children under 12 in accommodation (*The Which? Hotel Guide*)

SCOTLAND

MILNGAVIE East Dunbartonshire   map 11

Gingerhill £

1 Hillhead Street, Milngavie G62 8AF
TEL: (0141) 956 6515   COOKING **2**
off A81, 4m N of Glasgow   COST £16–£40

Climb the steep outside staircase, and walk along a tight corridor into a small, bright dining room with big windows and close-together tables. It is ten years since Carol Thomson and Heather Gorman opened their reasonably priced, informal and unpretentious café-style restaurant in a well-heeled Glasgow suburb, and their commitment to small local suppliers is holding up well despite a decline in their numbers. Links to the west coast, particularly the Isle of Gigha, yield a blackboard of seafood specials from paella to monkfish thermidor, balancing vegetarian items and chargrilled beef on the carte. Generous portions take precedence over presentation, and 'you don't get stylish or sophisticated cuisine, but you do get homely, honestly prepared, hearty food'. Snacks of stuffed croissants and baked potatoes also appear at lunchtime, along with an array of cakes, bakes and pastries. There is no drinks licence, and no corkage charge for BYO.

CHEFS: Heather Gorman and Carol Mercer   PROPRIETOR: Carol Thomson   OPEN: Mon to Sat L 11.30 to 3, Thu to Sat D 7.30 (1 sitting)   CLOSED: 1 Jan   MEALS: alc (main courses L £5 to £10.50, D £8.50 to £18.50). Unlicensed, BYO (no corkage)   SERVICE: not inc, card slips closed   CARDS: MasterCard, Visa   DETAILS: 26 seats. 14 seats outside. Private parties: 14 main room, 12 and 14 private rooms. Vegetarian meals. Children's helpings. No smoking while others eat. Occasional music

---

MOFFAT Dumfries & Galloway   map 11

▲ *Well View* ♥ ⅝✳

Ballplay Road, Moffat DG10 9JU   COOKING **3**
TEL: (01683) 220184   FAX: (01683) 220088   COST £20–£43

'I always enjoy eating here,' remarks one of several regular visitors to this Victorian house on the leafy edge of Moffat. Service from John Schuckardt is attentive, and the atmosphere relaxed. Lunch is three courses, dinner six, with no choice before dessert, but this doesn't appear to be a problem for anyone. After generous canapés in the lounge might come smoked chicken salad with tarragon dressing, then a mousseline of plaice and smoked salmon. At dinner a soup (perhaps carrot and apricot) or citrus sorbet precedes the main course: lamb with spicy couscous, or beef with roasted vegetables. Meats are served pink and vegetables crisp unless requested otherwise. Endorsements have included lightly grilled salmon in a buttery sauce, and pheasant breast with pearl barley risotto, while favoured desserts – after a good selection of cheeses with home-made chutney – run to chocoloate mousse, and caramelised lemon cream with butterscotch sauce. A briefly annotated wine list offers good choice from France and Germany and a few bins from other major wine countries, although reporters have been more than happy with the one white and one red recommended on the day's menu. House French is £11.

566

CHEF: Janet Schuckardt PROPRIETORS: Janet and John Schuckardt OPEN: Sun to Fri 12.15 to 1.15, all week D 6.30 to 8.30 (booking essential L and D) MEALS: Set L £13, Set D £27 SERVICE: none, card slips closed CARDS: Amex, Delta, MasterCard, Switch, Visa DETAILS: 24 seats. Private parties: 6 private room. Car park. No children under 5 at D. No smoking in dining room. No music ACCOMMODATION: 6 rooms, all with bath/shower. TV. B&B £50 to £100. Baby facilities (*The Which? Hotel Guide*) £5

MUIR OF ORD Highland   map 11

▲ *The Dower House* ▓ ✣

Highfield, Muir of Ord IV6 7XN
TEL/FAX: (01463) 870090
EMAIL: thedowerhouse@compuserve.com   COOKING 3
on A862, 1m N of Muir of Ord   COST £40–£48

This small one-storey house, done in Victorian 'cottage orné' style, is furnished with antiques, polished mahogany tables, assorted ornaments, and old pictures in elaborate frames, all of which manage to stay 'the correct side of tasteful'. 'We felt totally relaxed,' volunteered one couple. Robyn Aitchison's cooking reminded another visitor of 'a very good amateur dinner party', partly perhaps because there is no choice (other than cheese or dessert). The style is appealingly simple, and meals might begin with red wine risotto, cheese and tomato tart, or a warm salad (maybe salmon), followed by a contrasting main course: respectively fillet of beef with Mediterranean vegetables, turbot with saffron sauce, and lamb with spinach and flageolet beans. Desserts have included warm raspberry soufflé, 'nicely gooey' pear and apple tarte Tatin, and 'very light' bread-and-butter pudding. There are no appetisers, and coffee incurs an extra charge. The wine list happily ranges from traditional to new wave to downright unusual. Australian Durif or Canadian Baco Noir, anyone? Don't forget to check the four pages of bin-ends before making your final selection. House French is £13 a bottle, £3.20 a glass.

CHEF: Robyn Aitchison PROPRIETORS: Robyn and Mena Aitchison OPEN: all week D only 8 to 9.30 (L by arrangement) CLOSED: 25 Dec MEALS: Set D £30 SERVICE: not inc, card slips closed CARDS: MasterCard, Visa DETAILS: 26 seats. 8 seats outside. Private parties: 28 main room. Car park. Children's helpings. No children under 5. No smoking in dining room. Wheelchair access (also WC). No music ACCOMMODATION: 5 rooms, all with bath/shower. TV. Phone. B&B £65 to £150. Baby facilities (*The Which? Hotel Guide*)

NAIRN Highland   map 11

▲ *Clifton House* ▐ ✣

Viewfield Street, Nairn IV12 4HW
TEL: (01667) 453119 FAX: (01667) 452836
EMAIL: macintyre@clara.net   COOKING 4
W of town roundabout on A96   COST £34–£52

'What an extraordinary place!' exclaimed one visitor. Another called it 'individual, idiosyncratic and charming'. J. Gordon Macintyre has lived in this civilised Victorian town house all his sixty-eight years, and it bears his personal stamp, from objets d'art and paintings to musical and theatrical performances, to the drawing room wallpaper, originally designed by Pugin for the Robing Room of the Palace of Westminster (ask how it came to cover the walls of Clifton House). Menus are written in French because they always have been, and in any case a word of explanation provides a point of contact over aperitifs. This is not ambitious or imaginative French food – eggs mayonnaise, mushrooms à la grecque, Parmentier soup – but it does use good raw materials well, producing blanc de volaille au citron from free-range corn-fed chickens, or filet de boeuf maître d'hôtel from Highland beef.

Simple and effective treatment drew an inspector's endorsement for wild salmon served 'very pink' with beurrre blanc, and 'extremely tasty' lamb chops, briefly griddled and served with fortified pan juices, tomatoes and mushrooms. Puddings tend to be more international, along the lines of sherry trifle, or an intense dark chocolate terrine in chocolate sauce with whipped cream. While the cellar doesn't have any wines in their sixties it does have some first-class clarets from the 1960s, and many more venerable bottles from the rest of France and beyond. Prices are eminently fair despite all the famous names flying around, and there is good drinking to be had under £15.

CHEFS: J. Gordon Macintyre and Charles Macintyre PROPRIETOR: J. Gordon Macintyre OPEN: all week 12.30 to 1, 7 to 9.30 CLOSED: mid-Dec to mid-Jan MEALS: alc (main courses £13 to £17) SERVICE: none, card slips closed CARDS: Amex, Diners, MasterCard, Visa DETAILS: 40 seats. Private parties: 60 main room, 12 private room. Car park. Vegetarian meals. Children's helpings. No smoking in 1 dining room. Music ACCOMMODATION: 12 rooms, all with bath/shower. B&B £60 to £107 (*The Which? Hotel Guide*) £5

NEWTON STEWART Dumfries & Galloway   map 11

▲ *Kirroughtree Hotel* 🐟✗

Newton Stewart DG8 6AN
TEL: (01671) 402141 FAX: (01671) 402425   COOKING 2
off A712, just outside Newton Stewart   COST £22–£49

Acres of landscaped gardens make a fine backdrop to this eighteenth-century house just off the main road, and décor and service are equally impressive. The kitchen's attention is directed primarily at four-course dinners, which centre around vegetable-inclusive main courses of, for example, guinea fowl with potato rösti, Puy lentils, garlic confit and Albufera sauce, or salmon on celeriac purée with aubergine caviare, braised leeks, red pepper ragoût and basil oil. Before that might come cod brandade with roast scallops, curried apple soup, or Thai pork appetiser. Scottish cheeses, served with bannocks, are an alternative to desserts of prune and almond tart, or iced coffee parfait. Supporters think it should score more, others feel it is over-rated: perhaps fourteen mealtimes a week make consistency difficult. An extensive wine list finds room for some decent drinking under £20, starting with house Vin de Pays d'Oc at £13.75.

All entries in the Guide *are re-researched and rewritten every year, not least because restaurant standards fluctuate. Don't rely on an out-of-date* Guide.

CHEF: Ian Bennett   PROPRIETOR: McMillan Hotels Ltd   OPEN: all week 12 to 1.30, 7 to 9
CLOSED: 3 Jan to mid-Feb   MEALS: alc (main courses £10.50 to £13). Set L £13.50, Set D £30
SERVICE: not inc, card slips closed   CARDS: Delta, MasterCard, Switch, Visa   DETAILS: 50
seats. Private parties: 20 main room. Car park. Vegetarian meals. No children under 10 in dining
room. Jacket and tie. No smoking in dining room. Occasional music   ACCOMMODATION: 17
rooms, all with bath/shower. TV. Phone. B&B £75 to £200. No children under 10 in
accommodation. Garden

PEAT INN Fife   map 11

▲ *Peat Inn* 🍶 ✳

Peat Inn KY15 5LH
TEL: (01334) 840206   FAX: (01334) 840530   COOKING 6
at junction of B940 and B941, 6m SW of St Andrews   COST £30–£61

This former coaching inn at the village crossroads is a restaurant with quite
luxurious rooms. Preliminaries take place in a comfortable, boldly coloured
lounge with an open log fire, meals in three small 'rustic' dining rooms with
rough-plastered walls, mock black beams and high-backed chairs. Lunch is
three courses (no choice), while dinner offers an à la carte, a menu of the day, and
a six-course tasting menu (for the whole table only), all with a degree of overlap,
but amounting to a generous choice from a small kitchen. Good, locally sourced
materials – notably game, such as pigeon, or venison liver and kidney on onion
marmalade, and a range of seafood – are the bedrock of the kitchen's activity and
are generally treated with care.

Seafood tends towards the luxury end of the spectrum, perhaps monkfish and
chunks of lobster with ceps and artichoke heart, and dishes impress for their lack
of frilly presentation, as in crisp-roasted halibut fillet with a moist vegetable
risotto surrounded by a well-made lobster sauce. Reports indicate that standards
continue to vary, but technical accomplishment can be high, producing good
textural contrasts, for example in a colourful dish of roast scallops, slices of crisp
artichoke heart, soft leek and crunchy bacon bits on a sweet-tasting pea purée.
Meals might finish with lemon parfait in a sea of intensely fruity orange coulis,
or with a 'wonderful balance of flavours' in an orange sorbet topped with lemon
rind steeped in Grenadine, surrounded by caramelised orange segments.

Top-quality wines from France, Germany and the New World are introduced
in an informative yet straightforward fashion and are served with a similar lack
of fuss: reds will be decanted at table only on request. Mark-ups are realistic too,
designed to encourage – and reward – the adventurous. House wines cost £15
and change regularly.

CHEF: David Wilson   PROPRIETORS: David and Patricia Wilson   OPEN: Tue to Sat 12.30 for 1 (1
sitting), 7 to 9.30   CLOSED: 25 Dec, 1 Jan   MEALS: alc D (main courses £16 to £19.50). Set L
£19.50, Set D £28   SERVICE: not inc, card slips closed   CARDS: Amex, Diners, MasterCard,
Switch, Visa   DETAILS: 48 seats. Private parties: 24 main room, 12 private room. Car park.
Vegetarian meals. Children's helpings. No smoking in dining room. Wheelchair access (also
WC). No music   ACCOMMODATION: 8 rooms, all with bath/shower. TV. Phone. B&B £75 to £145.
Rooms for disabled (*The Which? Hotel Guide*)

PEEBLES Borders   map 11

▲ *Cringletie House* 🍴✳

Eddleston, Peebles EH45 8PL
TEL: (01721) 730233   FAX: (01721) 730244   COOKING 5
on A703, 2½m N of Peebles   COST £25–£51

The setting for chef Gregg Russell's 'classic-style cuisine with a modern accent'
is gracious: a pink sandstone mansion in the Scottish baronial style, with a
dining room characterised by grand oil portraits, antiques and an ornately
carved fireplace. According to approving guests, he continues to source his
superb raw materials from the local area, including vegetables, fruit and herbs
from Cringletie's pretty walled garden. One regular visitor attributed a
'somewhat impersonal' atmosphere to corporate ownership, while another
appreciated 'courteous service' and 'an element of homeliness'. Most praise is
reserved for the main courses: 'melting' pink medallions of venison with an
intense port sauce on mashed potato and wild mushrooms; perfectly cooked
guinea fowl in a 'rich, sweet, yet creamy Madeira sauce' flavoured with ginger.
An inspector thought starters of almond and broccoli soup, and ravioli of chicken
and mushroom could have packed more punch on the seasoning front, but
praised ambitious desserts of 'subtle' iced honey and whisky parfait, and a
panaché of tropical and dried fruits with lemon sorbet and pan-fried pineapple.
The wine list offers comfort with a selection of good-value bottles from around
the world (from £10.95), as well as a traditional focus on French vineyards.

CHEF: Gregg Russell   PROPRIETOR: Wren's Hotel Group   OPEN: all week; 12.30 to 2, 7 to 9
MEALS: Set L £17, Set D £29.50 to £32.50   SERVICE: not inc, card slips closed   CARDS: Amex,
Delta, MasterCard, Switch, Visa   DETAILS: 60 seats. Private parties: 60 main room, 20 private
room. Car park. Vegetarian meals. Children's helpings. No smoking in dining room. No music
ACCOMMODATION: 13 rooms, all with bath/shower. TV. Phone. B&B £65 to £160. Rooms for
disabled. Baby facilities

PERTH   Perthshire & Kinross   map 11

▲ *Kinfauns Castle Hotel* 🍴✳ | NEW ENTRY |

Perth PH2 7JZ
TEL: (01738) 620777   FAX: (01738) 620778
EMAIL: email@kinfaunscastle.co.uk   COOKING 3
on A90 Dundee road, 1½m from Perth   COST £26–£55

This gigantic, castellated, pink sandstone pile is set high among the hills in 26
acres of park and landscaped garden. Walk through long rooms with huge doors,
past Far Eastern artefacts, traditional baronial paintings and modern artworks,
into an elegant, understated, Muzak-filled dining room where service is
remarkably affable and friendly. The lunch menu is short and reasonable value
in view of the prime materials it deals in, a fixed-price dinner of three or five
courses offers slightly more choice, and there is a carte as well.

Native materials naturally extend to Aberdeen Angus beef: perhaps fillet on a
bed of creamy clapshot spiked with spring onions in a rich mushroom and red
wine sauce. Starters might include game terrine with tomato chutney, or scallops

with lardons, croûtons and a 'perfect' poached egg. Under-seasoning and subdued flavours were a feature of a 'patchy' inspection meal, but banana tart (made with good pastry) combined well with a banana and toffee ice cream to finish. Nearly 150 wines range from posh to negoçiant, with France in the ascendancy, and there are bottles to be had under £20. House Patriarche varietals are £13.95.

CHEF: Jeremy Wares   PROPRIETOR: James Smith   OPEN: all week 12 to 1.30, 7 to 8.45   MEALS: alc (main courses £9.50 to £20). Set L Mon to Sat £18.50, Set L Sun £20.50, Set D £32 to £35   SERVICE: not inc, card slips closed   CARDS: Amex, Delta, Diners, MasterCard, Switch, Visa   DETAILS: 50 seats. 20 seats outside. Private parties: 50 main room, 12 and 14 private rooms. Car park. Vegetarian meals. No children under 12 at D. Jacket and tie. No smoking in dining room. Occasional music   ACCOMMODATION: 16 rooms, all with bath/shower. TV. Phone. B&B £100 to £280. No children under 8 in accommodation. Fishing   £5

Let's Eat/Let's Eat Again

77 Kinnoull Street, Perth PH1 5EZ
TEL: (01738) 643377   FAX: (01738) 621464
33 George Street, Perth PH1 5LA   COOKING 3
TEL: (01738) 633771   FAX: (01738) 621464   COST £22–£42

Concerns that the opening of a second branch in George Street might compromise the original 'have not in our experience been borne out', according to one observer. Both offer a standard of cooking and delivery that stand out locally. Popular and informal, Let's Eat is a purveyor of hearty, vibrantly flavoured food, and an enthusiast for contemporary international ideas from Thai crab cake to smoked Rannoch venison with Pecorino, from banana-stuffed chicken breast with curry sauce to 'fabulous' cod in brioche crumbs served with creamy mash, aïoli and tapénade. Daily blackboard specials are what Tony Heath says he would like most of his regulars to eat: 'thankfully most of them take the hint', including a reporter who finds them a reliable repository for seasonal items and whatever fish happens to be available. Those intent on dessert should leave plenty of room for baked chocolate pudding with orange curd ice cream, or poached pear in mascarpone with a nutty crumble and honey ice cream. A generally youthful wine list packs in plenty of interest under £20, and half a dozen house wines under £11.

The substantial bistro-style cooking on offer at Let's Eat Again has taken in Arbroath smokie chowder, and a 'simple and well done' plate of chargrilled vegetables with mozzarella and pesto to start, followed by ribeye steak with good frites. 'We allow people to snack as well as have three courses,' writes Tony Heath, a flexibility encouraged by a range of familiar items from Caesar-style salad with chicken to simple pasta dishes, from fish cakes to braised lamb shank. Dessert lovers can just pop in for sticky toffee pudding or dark and white chocolate terrine if they like. Wines, from all over the place, are nearly all in the £10–£20 bracket.

£5 *indicates that the restaurant has elected to participate in the* **Good Food Guide** *voucher scheme. For full details, see page 6.*

CHEFS: Tony Heath, Lewis Pringle, Graeme Pallister and Richard Paton (Let's Eat); Neil Simpson, Colin Christie and Michael Pallister (Let's Eat Again) PROPRIETORS: Tony Heath and Shona Drysdale OPEN: Tue to Sat 12 to 2, 6.30 to 9.45 (6 to 9.30 Let's Eat Again) CLOSED: 25 and 26 Dec, 2 weeks Jan, 2 weeks July MEALS: alc (main courses £7 to £15) SERVICE: not inc, card slips closed CARDS: Amex, Delta, MasterCard, Switch, Visa DETAILS: 70 seats (Let's Eat), 40 seats (Let's Eat Again). Private parties: 70 main room (Let's Eat); 40 main room (Let's Eat Again). Vegetarian meals. Children's helpings. No-smoking area (Let's Eat). Wheelchair access (also WC) (Let's Eat). Music (£5)

PORT APPIN Argyll & Bute   map 11

▲ *Airds Hotel* ▮ ⁵✳

Port Appin PA38 4DF
TEL: (01631) 730236   FAX: (01631) 730535
EMAIL: airds@airds-hotel.com   COOKING 7
2m off A828, on E shore of Loch Linnhe   COST £59–£70

Airds has 'such an unfair advantage in its location that I would imagine it is hard not to have a wonderful evening here,' wrote one visitor, intoxicated by the air, seabirds' cries, and a dining room view of the sun setting over the Lismore hills, just a short boat ride away from the nearby jetty. The keynote of this old-fashioned, white-painted, immaculately maintained hotel is 'understated luxury', its comfortable sitting room given a Scottish stamp with Highland pictures, and an antlered stag over the fireplace. A similar sentiment applies to the food, which treats native materials indulgently: Aberdeen Angus fillet with truffled leeks and wild mushrooms, for instance.

'One feels in safe hands when eating here,' observed one visitor, summing up the combination of prime materials and skilful treatment that has produced guinea fowl 'tender and full of flavour' with chanterelles, and pink duck in Madeira gravy, served with celeriac purée, al dente vegetables, and 'melting' shallots and prunes. Graeme Allen is equally sure-footed when it comes to seafood – large, 'very fresh', lightly poached Lismore oysters with smoked salmon and chopped champagne jelly – and is adept at partnering flavours, as in roast salmon fillet on a bed of sweet-sour aubergine.

Herbs are well used, our inspector noted: in a dish of sweet roasted scallops, served with strips of red pepper and deep-fried squid in a bouillabaisse sauce, the whole perfumed with basil, sweet cicely and aniseed. Likewise a cream of tomato and mint soup (the second of four courses) was considered 'an inspiration', so effective a combination that 'it should be a classic dish'. Well-kept cheeses are served at the proper temperature, and desserts aim for simplicity: orange and grapefruit segments in Grand Marnier jelly, or steamed date pudding of a texture 'which can only described as heavy yet light' served plain without cream or custard.

Meals 'have a strong sense of occasion but are none the less very relaxed', and service is friendly, unfussy, yet highly professional. The already strong Burgundy section has expanded on the Eurocentric wine list, and the North American contingent has also been fortified. Fans of super-Tuscans, however, can rest assured that this has not been at their expense. Half-bottles, which at the time of going to press numbered around forty, were also due to increase. House wines start at £12.

CHEFS: Graeme Allen and Steve McCallum   PROPRIETORS: the Allen family   OPEN: all week D only 7.30 to 8.30   CLOSED: 20 to 27 Dec, 6 to 29 Jan   MEALS: Set D £40   SERVICE: not inc, card slips closed   CARDS: Delta, MasterCard, Switch, Visa   DETAILS: 36 seats. Private parties: 36 main room. Car park. Children's helpings. No children under 8 at D. No smoking in dining room. No music   ACCOMMODATION: 16 rooms, all with bath/shower. TV. Phone. B&B £45 to £210. Baby facilities. Fishing *(The Which? Hotel Guide)*   £5

▲ *Pierhouse* ⁵⋇

Port Appin PA38 4DE
TEL: (01631) 730302   FAX: (01631) 730400
EMAIL: pierhouse@btinternet.com
off A828, on E shore of Loch Linnhe, opposite   COOKING 3
Lismore ferry   COST £26–£52

It's hard to get much closer to the source of supply than this seafood restaurant: 'we actually watched the chef walk down to the pier and retrieve a basket of oysters.' Rita Thomson continues to deliver food that draws plaudits from reporters: from a cocktail of Loch Linnhe langoustines to Inverawe smoked salmon and prawn parcels, from 'succulent' cold lobster salad to 'superb' seared scallops, their 'toasted surfaces contrasting wonderfully with moist, barely cooked interiors'. Carnivores are catered for with venison, steak and chicken, and the less formal lunchtime menu offers open sandwiches, risotto and pasta, as well as salmon fish cakes and lobster thermidor. For dessert choose from the likes of crème brûlée, apple and raisin slice or chocolate roulade. Service has come in for some criticism, as have poor incidentals such as mayonnaise and salads, but an off-duty inspector concluded, 'For wonderful, fresh shellfish cooked to perfection we know of nowhere on mainland Britain that rivals the Pierhouse.' Wines, supplied by Lay & Wheeler, provide global choice and a decent number of half-bottles. House wines start at £12.50.

CHEFS: Rita Thomson and Simon Harper   PROPRIETORS: David and Liz Hamblin   OPEN: all week 12.30 to 2.30, 6.30 to 9.30   CLOSED: 25 Dec   MEALS: alc (main courses L £7.50 to £13, D £11.50 to £17)   SERVICE: not inc   CARDS: Delta, MasterCard, Switch, Visa   DETAILS: 52 seats. 28 seats outside. Private parties: 60 main room, 20 private room. Car park. Vegetarian meals. Children's helpings. No smoking in dining room. Wheelchair access (also WC). Music ACCOMMODATION: 12 rooms, all with bath/shower. TV. Phone. B&B £45 to £75. Rooms for disabled. Baby facilities

---

ST MARGARET'S HOPE Orkney   map 11

▲ *The Creel* ⁵⋇

Front Road, St Margaret's Hope KW17 2SL
TEL: (01856) 831311   COOKING 7
off A961, 13m S of Kirkwall, on South Ronaldsay   COST £34–£45

Joyce and Alan Craigie, in the process of upgrading their restaurant-with-rooms, will celebrate fifteen years at this 'lonely gastronomic outpost' in 2000. Like all island restaurants, it takes a bit of effort to reach from the

573

mainland, but this delivers more than most, resting its appeal on a combination of fine local materials, enterprising ideas and skilful handling. Alan Craigie is described as an unassuming but determined perfectionist who works like an alchemist, producing 'world-class' full-bodied soups generously endowed with fish and shellfish, plus a wide range of 'breathtaking seafare' served with simple but effective accompaniments: roast red pepper relish with halibut, white bean cassoulet with hake, or spiced brown lentils with salmon.

Orcadian fish stew is a regular main course but needs another name, according to one visitor, who felt this was no way to describe 'an elegant tower of perfectly cooked fish fillets' surrounded by a fish broth delicately flavoured with tomato and basil. Mediterranean and other flavours abound – Orkney beef with onion and chilli marmalade, or wolf fish and hake with a salad of roasted red peppers, capers, olives and herbs – although one observer felt that, particularly when it comes to fish, native partnerships work better: that same wolf and hake duo, for example, served in a rich, subtle crab and cockle broth. Likewise, North Ronaldsay lamb shows to good effect accompanied by baby haggis and pearl barley risotto.

Those who stay several days are divided in their assessments: one felt the range (usually three or four choices per course) to be rather narrow; another found consistently high standards 'night after night, dish after dish' thanks to the fact that Alan Craigie is a totally hands-on chef. Desserts may not be in quite the same league as the rest of the operation, although they have produced a good vanilla parfait layered between home-made cloutie dumpling. 'Irresistible' beremeal bannocks and soda bread are enthusiastically devoured. The minuscule twenty-strong wine list starts with Australian Chenin Blanc at £8.50 and Chilean Cabernet Sauvignon at £9.60.

CHEF: Alan Craigie   PROPRIETORS: Joyce and Alan Craigie   OPEN: all week D only 7 to 9.30
CLOSED: 2 weeks Oct, Jan and Feb   MEALS: alc (main courses £15.50 to £17.50)   SERVICE: not inc, card slips closed   CARDS: MasterCard, Visa   DETAILS: 36 seats. Private parties: 36 main room. Car park. Children's helpings. No smoking in dining room. Wheelchair access (also WC). No music   ACCOMMODATION: 3 rooms, all with bath/shower. TV. B&B £40 to £70.

SPEAN BRIDGE Highland   map 11

▲ *Old Pines* ⊱✳

Spean Bridge PH34 4EG
TEL: (01397) 712324   FAX: (01397) 712433   COOKING 4
EMAIL: goodfood.at.oldpines@lineone.net   COST £33–£43

'It probably helps if you like a family atmosphere,' wrote one visitor to this Scandinavian 'chalet' surrounded by big old pine trees just north of Fort William. It is a family home, and feels like it; children are 'especially welcome' and the younger ones are served high tea, after which they retire to the playroom, leaving dinner (three or five courses) free for grown-ups. One strength is the use of local produce, which the Barbers now actively source, including organic fruit and veg from a dedicated local smallholder, fungi, venison (maybe roast haunch with fresh pineapple, thyme and juniper), and fish and shellfish landed at Mallaig: scallops, squat lobster and mussels are combined with spinach in an orange sauce, and roast cod with ratatouille and garlic mayonnaise.

In addition to making their own bread, pasta, ice cream and preserves, the Barbers go in for home-smoking, serving smoked trout pâté with smoked salmon and a quince and crab apple jelly. Scottish farmhouse cheeses follow a dessert such as lemon feather cake with cardamom ice cream, and for those who stay, breakfast is 'several cuts above the average best'. There is still no corkage charge for those who prefer to bring their own wine, but the Barbers now have a drinks licence and a short but varied list that opens at £10.50 for house French, and stays mostly below £20.

CHEF: Sukie Barber   PROPRIETORS: Bill and Sukie Barber   OPEN: all week D only 8pm (1 sitting, occasionally 7.30 in winter, May to Sept Sun D residents only)   MEALS: Set D £23.50 to £27.50. Light meals available all day   SERVICE: not inc, card slips closed   CARDS: Delta, MasterCard, Switch, Visa   DETAILS: 30 seats. 10 seats outside. Private parties: 30 main room. Car park. Vegetarian meals. Children's helpings. No babies or small children in dining room. No smoking in dining room. Wheelchair access (also WC). No music   ACCOMMODATION: 8 rooms, all with bath/shower. D,B&B £60 to £130. Rooms for disabled. Baby facilities (*The Which? Hotel Guide*)
(£5)

STEIN Highland   map 11

▲ *Lochbay* ⁵✳ £

1–2 Macleod Terrace, Stein, Isle of Skye IV55 8GA   COOKING 1
TEL/FAX: (01470) 592235   COST £18–£49

At her tiny gleaming white fisherman's cottage Margaret Greenhalgh serves the freshest of fish and seafood straightforwardly and in abundance. A blackboard points the way to the day's specials, but the printed menu has plenty to entice: hearty fish soup or gravad lax for starters, say, or 'cephalopods' – squid, octopus and cuttlefish – marinated in olive oil. Main-course plates overflow with Loch Bay king prawns, grilled and dressed lobster, scallops in orange sauce, or other seafood plainly treated. Everything comes with chips or baked potatoes and veg or salad. Finish with chocolate bread-and-butter pudding or cloutie dumpling. Don't automatically go for one of the wines on the short list (although dry Silver Birch, apparently a cure for baldness and Prince Albert's favourite, might find its takers), but consider an ale such as gooseberry Grozet or elderberry Ebulum. House wine is £9.50.

CHEF/PROPRIETOR: Margaret Greenhalgh   OPEN: Mon to Fri 12 to 3, 6 to 9   MEALS: alc (main courses £7 to £25)   SERVICE: not inc, card slips closed   CARDS: MasterCard, Visa   DETAILS: 24 seats. 12 seats outside. Private parties: 6 main room. Car park. Children's helpings. No smoking in dining room. Music   ACCOMMODATION: 2 rooms, both with bath/shower. TV. B&B £28 to £44. Baby facilities

---

'Lemon mousse came in a brandy-snap bracelet which I could not resist slipping on to my wrist after the mousse was eaten. There was nothing else to do with it. It was inedible.'
(On eating in Hampshire)

All entries, including Round-ups, are fully indexed at the back of the Guide.

STONEHAVEN Aberdeenshire	map 11

Tolbooth

Old Pier, Stonehaven AB39 2JU
TEL/FAX: (01569) 762287   COOKING 3
on A90, 15m S of Aberdeen   COST £24–£46

This is the kind of place that visitors love to stumble across in any fishing port. Climb the stone steps to a first-floor dining room with its view of the harbour, and prepare for a carte of bright, modern seafood dishes: chargrilled squid with a honey, mint and chilli dressing, or blackened salmon fillet with Cajun spices, avocado salsa and red pepper vinaigrette. Locally landed shellfish is a highlight of the colder months, producing a bisque with crab raviolo and basil rouille, or a terrine of lobster with smoked salmon and leek. More far-flung species might include shark, blue-nose bass, or swordfish, and simple roasting and char-grilling are typical and effective ways of dealing with these and the day's other specials, which may also include cod on saffron risotto. There are still smoked haddock fish cakes for traditionalists, and fillet of Glenbervie Aberdeen Angus beef for a change. Ice creams or sorbets figure among desserts, as do cheesecakes: perhaps a port and Stilton version with bramble coulis and a poached pear. A serviceable international list of mostly white wines starts at £9.50.

CHEFS: Jean-François Meder and Andrew Ritchie   PROPRIETORS: Jean-François Meder and Chris McCarrey   OPEN: Tue to Sun D only 6.30 to 9 (9.30 Fri and Sat)   CLOSED: first 2 weeks Jan   MEALS: alc Tue to Sat (main courses £9 to £18). Set D Sun £18.95   SERVICE: not inc CARDS: Delta, MasterCard, Switch, Visa   DETAILS: 44 seats. Private parties: 40 main room. Vegetarian meals. Children's helpings. No children under 8. No cigars/pipes in dining room. Music   (£5)

STRONTIAN Highland	map 11

▲ Kilcamb Lodge 🍷 ⅹ

Strontian PH36 4HY
TEL: (01967) 402257   FAX: (01967) 402041   COOKING 3
on A861, by N shore of Loch Sunart   COST £21–£47

Nature lovers who can take their eyes off the vista of sea and hills will find much to absorb them. Twenty-eight acres, and half a mile of private shoreline bordering Loch Sunart, provide a good base from which to observe seals, pine martens, wild flowers and golden eagles. Light lunches are available, but an early dinner (orders by 6pm) is the main meal at this family-run restored former hunting lodge. Neil Mellis operates a daily-changing menu that incorporates regional produce from Grampian pork and Highland lamb to loin of Argyll venison, perhaps served on a mozzarella, spinach and potato rösti with a chocolate-enriched game sauce. Seafood runs to squat lobster casserole, red mullet with risotto, and baked cod with pea and pimento mash in a saffron butter sauce, while native cranachan takes its place alongside more European desserts of Swiss meringue roulade or chocolate marquise. Wine lovers will find plenty that appeals in a cosmopolitan collection that has prices to suit all pockets (eleven house wines start at £9.75) and an easy-to-use style guide for novices.

CHEF: Neil Mellis   PROPRIETORS: the Blakeway family   OPEN: all week 12 to 2, 7.30 (1 sitting D)   CLOSED: 25 Dec   MEALS: alc L (main courses £4.50 to 6.50). Set D £29.50   SERVICE: not inc, card slips closed   CARDS: Delta, MasterCard, Switch, Visa   DETAILS: 26 seats. Private parties: 26 main room. Car park. Vegetarian meals. Children's helpings. No children under 6 in dining room. No smoking in dining room. Wheelchair access (also men's WC). No music   ACCOMMODATION: 11 rooms, all with bath/shower. TV. D,B&B £60 to £200. Baby facilities. Fishing (*The Which? Hotel Guide*)

SWINTON Borders   map 11

▲ *Wheatsheaf Hotel* ⁑✳ £

Main Street, Swinton TD11 3JJ
TEL: (01890) 860257   FAX: (01890) 860688   COOKING 3
on A6112, Coldstream to Duns road   COST £19–£44

A domestic air prevails amid the chintz, log fire, flowers and stuffed pheasants of this well-loved pub-cum-restaurant: 'booking is essential, even for lunch,' reckons one visitor. Flexibility is built into the system, with bar snacks at lunchtime, a free-ranging carte from which a starter and pudding can make a light meal, and options for vegetarians and vegans. Local materials include lobster from Eyemouth market, expertly prepared in a salad with new potatoes; loin of border lamb, served with a bubble and squeak cake; and fillet of roe deer from a nearby estate that comes with root vegetables and pearl barley. For one reporter, summer pudding 'perfectly rounded off a cold summer luncheon on a warm summer day'; the shortbread served with coffee has also been praised. Service, by polite young waiters who ensure customers are relaxed and satisfied, is 'especially commendable'. A fairly priced, wide-ranging wine list starts with six house wines under £10 and ends with nearly twenty half-bottles. New accommodation with wheelchair access will be available from mid-2000.

CHEF: Alan Reid   PROPRIETORS: Alan and Julie Reid   OPEN: Tue to Sun 11.45 to 2, 6 to 9.30   CLOSED: Sun D Nov to Mar, 25 and 26 Dec, 1 Jan   MEALS: alc (main courses L £5.50 to £13, D £8 to £15.50)   SERVICE: not inc, card slips closed   CARDS: Delta, MasterCard, Switch, Visa   DETAILS: 56 seats. 18 seats outside. Private parties: 26 main room, 16 and 26 private rooms. Car park. Vegetarian meals. Children's helpings. No smoking in dining room. Wheelchair access (not WC). No music   ACCOMMODATION: 6 rooms, all with bath/shower. TV. B&B £47 to £98. Baby facilities (*The Which? Hotel Guide*)

'As the cheese was served the [smoking] waitress came and plonked down butter and said, "This is your butter," salt and said, "This is your salt", fork and said, "This is your fork", celery and said, "This is your celery". Well, a potential script writer for "Eastenders", I would say.' (On eating in Somerset)

The 2001 Guide *will be published before Christmas 2000. Reports on meals are most welcome at any time of the year, but are particularly valuable in the spring (no later than June). Send them to* The Good Food Guide, *FREEPOST, 2 Marylebone Road, London NW1 4DF. Or email your report to guidereports@which.co.uk.*

TROON South Ayrshire   map 11

▲ *Lochgreen House* ♥ ⁵✕

Monktonhill Road, Southwood,
Troon KA10 7EN   COOKING 5
TEL: (01292) 313343   FAX: (01292) 318661   COST £27–£46

Set in precisely measured and manicured grounds, Lochgreen is tastefully
furnished, with wood panelling, comfortable sofas, capacious armchairs and
'stunning' flower arrangements. Lunch is three courses, dinner the same but for a
mid-meal soup or sorbet (both include coffee), and the cooking seems to be on an
upward trajectory. Among starters, duck confit has appeared with pearl barley
risotto, and in a well-judged terrine with a sliver of foie gras, while accurate
timing and intelligent flavouring have shown to good effect in seared sea bream
with delicately Thai-spiced noodles, where the oriental approach 'worked a
treat'.

  Main courses come complete (the lack of extra vegetables is considered a plus)
which might involve a risotto here, a fricassee of vegetables there, and among
successes has been a richly flavoured, crusty brown medallion of beef (rare as
requested) on a crisp potato galette. Treatment of fish has ranged from poached
halibut 'unsullied by seasoning', served with asparagus and peas in a red wine
sauce, to salmon marinated in lime and coriander, with a fresh and expertly
glazed oyster.

  Desserts maintain interest, for example in an unctuously rich, liquid, dark
chocolate mousse with a scoop of apricot ice cream, or a revival of a nursery
classic, caramelised rhubarb and ginger rice pudding accompanied by caramelised banana. Staff are 'ultra-smart and polite' yet smiling, friendly and
responsive, and wines are a wide-ranging mix of the venerable and appealingly
youthful. Six house wines from four countries start at £14.50. Or relax in the
'Malt Room' with a tumbler or two of whisky from the 120-strong list. William
Costley also owns and runs Highgrove House (Old Loans Road, Troon, tel.
(01292) 312511) which opens all week and serves a lengthy brasserie-style
menu.

CHEF: Andrew Costley   PROPRIETOR: Costley and Costley Hoteliers Ltd   OPEN: all week 12 to 2,
7 to 9   MEALS: Set L £19.95, Set D £29.95   SERVICE: not inc, card slips closed   CARDS: Amex,
Delta, MasterCard, Switch, Visa   DETAILS: 80 seats. Private parties: 45 main room, 15 to 45
private rooms. Car park. Vegetarian meals. Children's helpings L. No children at D. No smoking
in dining room. Wheelchair access (also WC). Music   ACCOMMODATION: 15 rooms, all with
bath/shower. TV. Phone. B&B £140 per couple. Rooms for disabled. No children in
accommodation (*The Which? Hotel Guide*)

MacCallums' Oyster Bar   NEW ENTRY

The Harbour, Troon KA10 6DH   COOKING 3
TEL/FAX: (01292) 319339   COST £20–£42

'A real discovery!' exclaimed one explorer who chanced on this converted pump
house by the harbour with its varnished wood, nautical prints, and display of
Scottish-built yachts that have competed in the America's Cup. Part of a seafood
business, MacCallums' (or simply the 'Oyster Bar' to locals) is able to source a

good variety of materials from near and far: their tanks next door can hold two tons of live seafood. Not only oysters and lobster, but mussels, sea bass, and salmon fish cakes with leek sauce are 'all as fresh as imaginable' and simply cooked 'with care and precision'. Large grilled langoustines come halved in a light garlic butter, and Chardonnay mussels are 'large juicy specimens'. Look out for the day's whole grilled fish to follow. Token meat dishes and perfunctory puddings (crème brûlée, chocolate parfait) are hardly the point. Enthusiasm is such that even 'amateurish' service cannot stop reporters planning to return. A short and predominantly white wine list (mostly under £20) starts with house Chilean Chardonnay at £9.50.

CHEFS: Douglas Smith and Nick Wright   PROPRIETORS: Joan and James MacCallum   OPEN: Tue to Sun L 12 to 2.30 (4 Sun), Tue to Sat D 2.30, 7 to 9   CLOSED: 2 weeks at Christmas   MEALS: alc (main courses £7.50 to £18.50)   SERVICE: not inc, card slips closed   CARDS: Delta, MasterCard, Switch, Visa   DETAILS: 42 seats. Private parties: 30 main room. Car park. Wheelchair access (not WC). Music

UIG   Western Isles

map 11

▲ Baile-na-Cille ⁵✱

Timsgarry, Uig, Isle of Lewis HS2 9JD
TEL: (01851) 672242   FAX: (01851) 672241
EMAIL: randjgollin@compuserve.com
B8011 to Uig, then right down track on to shore

COOKING 1
COST £28–£34

'There cannot be a better beach-side location than this in Scotland,' writes a supporter of Richard Gollin's unique enterprise. The hotel sits on a grassy bank above a stretch of white sand, a magnet for families, and serves simple three-course dinners along the lines of tomato and basil soup, roast duck with mangoes, and hot caramelised pears. The food is generous (second helpings are offered) and a few local materials find their way on to the menu, from lamb and 'excellent' venison casserole to salmon and bacon smoked in the village. Joanna Gollin has not always been there when reporters have visited, and she is, after all, the main chef, so one or two disappointments have been registered. Wines, mostly from Robin Yapp (there is no list), have remained at two prices – £8.50 and £12.50 – 'since we were given our liquor licence in 1985'.

CHEFS/PROPRIETORS: Joanna and Richard Gollin   OPEN: all week D only 7 (1 sitting)   CLOSED: 16 Oct to 14 Mar   MEALS: Set D £24   SERVICE: net prices, card slips closed   CARDS: MasterCard, Visa   DETAILS: 30 seats. Private parties: 30 main room. Car park. Children's helpings. No smoking in dining room. No music   ACCOMMODATION: 12 rooms, all with bath/shower. B&B £24 to £78. Baby facilities. (*The Which? Hotel Guide*)

Net prices *in the details at the end of an entry indicates that the prices given on a menu and on a bill are inclusive of VAT and service charge, and that this practice is clearly stated on menu and bill.*

Occasional music *in the details at the end of an entry means live or recorded music is played in the dining room only rarely or for special events. No music means it is never played.*

ULLAPOOL Highland

map 11

▲ *Altnaharrie Inn* 🍶 ✱

Ullapool IV26 2SS	COOKING **9**
TEL: (01854) 633230	COST £90–£108

'It is hard to believe that so remote a place can offer some of the very best cooking in the British Isles'. Being collected by boat from Ullapool jetty is the only way to get there, and on arrival Fred Brown gives a two minute pep-talk about routines; later he announces the evening's dishes, collects wine orders (by 6pm), and recites a long list of well-kept cheeses. His quiet service is 'flawless', 'charming' and carried out with 'sheer professionalism'. He and the 'totally invisible' Gunn preside over a house of consummate good taste with objects of interest at every turn, including a dining room of dark wooden tables, high-backed Jacobean-style chairs, candles, and gleaming silver and crystal.

Gunn Eriksen's unique style is 'neither traditional nor cutting-edge', according to one observer, yet reporters repeatedly refer to dishes as 'one of the best I have ever tasted'. Five-course dinners (the second soup, the fourth cheese) offer no choice before dessert, but one of the attractions is that diners don't repeat dishes: a couple who stayed three nights, for example, ate nine different savoury dishes, from salmon in champagne aspic to squab pigeon with foie gras. Some reports of individual dishes are longer than this entry, so it is difficult to do justice to them in detail. Suffice to say that, for most, the apparent complexity produces harmonious results: for example, scallop and crab mousseline enclosed in 'eggshell thin' pastry, its three accompanying sauces generating 'sequential revelations': a smear of coral sauce, a meat jus, and an intense, Barsac-sweetened shellfish reduction.

All this magic is spun from an economic range of luxurious materials featuring crab, lobster, salmon or turbot, alongside pigeon, roe deer and foie gras. First-course shellfish is typically presented through the medium of pasta, mousse or aspic, while sauces alternate between a simple jus and a highly concentrated and intense reduction, champagne and Burgundy being the preferred alcoholic constituents. Presentation, a hallmark of the whole place, is a forte, although when it comes to conceptualisation, an inspector felt that some of the expensive flourishes rang a little hollow given that combinations did not always make the best of individual components – langoustines in a peppery morel soup, for example – and a few misjudgements in execution also took the shine off.

Three desserts are the norm, and among the best have been an 'electric' combination of dark chocolate and blackcurrant formed into a trio of mousse, ice cream and sauce, and a simple galette of hot puff pastry filled with firm, sweet juicy plum halves beside a scoop of peach liqueur ice cream. Although the package requires an overnight stay, making a meal relatively expensive, most reporters consider it good value, helped by fairly modest mark-ups on wines. Venerable Burgundies and mature clarets dominate, but there is still plenty of choice for Francophobes. Fourteen house wines are priced between £11.50 and £28.50, and half-bottles are numerous.

CHEF: Gunn Eriksen   PROPRIETORS: Fred Brown and Gunn Eriksen   OPEN: all week, D only 8pm (1 sitting)   CLOSED: late Oct to Easter   MEALS: Set D £75   SERVICE: none, card slips closed   CARDS: Amex, Delta, MasterCard, Switch, Visa   DETAILS: 18 seats. Private parties: 16 main room. Car park. No children under 8 at D. No smoking in dining room. No music   ACCOMMODATION: 8 rooms, all with bath/shower. D,B&B £165 to £410. No children under 8 in accommodation (*The Which? Hotel Guide*)

WALLS Shetland   map 11

▲ *Burrastow House* ⚓✳

Burrastow, Walls ZE2 9PD
TEL: (01595) 809307   FAX: (01595) 809213
EMAIL: burr.hs.hotel@zetnet.co.uk
at Walls drive to top of hill, turn left, then follow road   COOKING 3
for 2m to Burrastow   COST £20–£46

At this isolated and friendly hotel right by the sea, Bo Simmons's starting point is good local produce, including lobsters from the voe, locally smoked salmon, and vegetables and herbs from the garden. These she magics into unfussy and clear-tasting dishes that can be eaten in the oak-panelled, fire-warmed dining room if the winds howl and the rains lash, or the bright conservatory, with a view, if you are lucky, of otters diving for their sunset supper. Praise has come in for insalata of squid, lobster, scallops and tiger prawns in a red pepper dressing, duck breast with plum and ginger sauce, three-fish stew, and 'quite the best turbot we have ever eaten', served with a buttery saffron and chive sauce. To finish, there might be simple baked apple stuffed with dates and honey. The wine list is 'well thought out, with some adventurous spots', and includes plenty of organic bottles; house wine is £9.25 and seven are offered by the glass.

CHEF: Bo Simmons   PROPRIETORS: Bo Simmons and Henry Anderton   OPEN: Wed to Sun L 12 to 2.30, Tue to Sat D 7.30 to 9   CLOSED: 1 week Oct   MEALS: alc (main courses L £6.50 to £9.50, D £13 to £16.50)   SERVICE: not inc   CARDS: Amex, MasterCard, Switch, Visa   DETAILS: 30 seats. Private parties: 15 main room, 26 private room. Car park. Vegetarian meals. Children's helpings. No smoking in dining room. Wheelchair access (also WC). No music   ACCOMMODATION: 5 rooms, all with bath/shower. D,B&B £74 to £168. Rooms for disabled. Baby facilities. Fishing (*The Which? Hotel Guide*)

Wales

▲ *Penhelig Arms Hotel* 🍷 ⁑✳

Terrace Road, Aberdovey LL35 0LT
TEL: (01654) 767215   FAX: (01654) 767690
EMAIL: penheligarms@saqnet.co.uk
on A493 Tywyn to Machynlleth road, opposite   COOKING 2
Penhelig station   COST £19–£45

'The welcome is always warm and the food interesting' at this black-and-white seaside inn, which seems to accommodate unlimited numbers (from locals to second-home owners and visiting golfers) without becoming overcrowded; refurbishment with a new colour scheme and modern paintings has brightened up the dining room. The cooking style may be straightforward, but the ambitious menu typically offers two dozen items, with a distinct preference for locally sourced fish: battered haddock with tartare sauce, or roast monkfish in sweet-and-sour sauce. A fair bit of dairy produce is used: cheese with smoked haddock pancakes, and a cucumber and yoghurt dressing for 'beautifully fresh' fillet of cod in tikka spices; and puddings are yet to come. Still, the diet is varied, taking in goose liver parfait, Cajun-spiced chicken, and desserts of white chocolate cheesecake and lemon tart. Reasonable prices make it all 'extraordinary value', and this applies to the wines too. Hughes's enthusiasm for his frequently changing, varied list is infectious and adds to imbibers' enjoyment. Ten appealing house wines are mostly £10 a bottle, £2.50 a glass, and champagne is £3.50 a glass.

CHEF: Jane Howkins   PROPRIETORS: Robert and Sally Hughes   OPEN: all week 12 to 2, 7 to 9.30   CLOSED: 25 and 26 Dec   MEALS: alc L Mon to Sat (main courses £6 to £12). Set L Sun £12.95, Set D £20. Bar meals available   SERVICE: not inc, card slips closed   CARDS: Delta, MasterCard, Switch, Visa   DETAILS: 34 seats. Private parties: 18 main room. Car park. Vegetarian meals. Children's helpings. No smoking in dining room. No music ACCOMMODATION: 10 rooms, all with bath/shower. TV. Phone. B&B £40 to £79 (*The Which? Hotel Guide*) £5

'Dover sole was served in a silver dish and filleted at the table if desired. My wife, having trained as a surgeon, declines this service and dissects the fish herself, putting to good use all those years of expensive medical training.' (On eating in London)

ABERSOCH Gwynedd   map 7

▲ *Porth Tocyn Hotel* ░✳

Abersoch LL53 7BU
TEL: (01758) 713303   FAX: (01758) 713538
on minor road 2m S of Abersoch through hamlets of   COOKING 4
Sarn Bach and Bwlchtocyn   COST £26–£47

The Fletcher-Brewers migrate during winter, returning each spring to throw
open the doors of their 'cottagey' hotel on the Lleyn Peninsula for another
season: they have notched up an entry in each *Guide* since 1957. Views across
Cardigan Bay to mountainous Snowdonia combine with a family-friendly
atmosphere to provide a relaxed setting: 'I am always made welcome,' writes a
regular. Dinner is either two courses or five (why not three or four?), and light
weekday lunches give way to an 'endless' crowd-pleasing Sunday buffet.
Dubbed 'modern British cookery without ostentation' by one visitor, the food
might take in crab cakes with lime hollandaise and carrot crisps, and a
red-blooded roast of venison or beef fillet. Fish has turned up as grilled sea bass
with roast red peppers and Pernod beurre blanc, although plainer treatments of
any dish are readily available on request. Cheese, the last of the five courses,
might follow strawberry vacherin or chocolate brandy cake. Nine house
recommendations, starting around £11, head up an attractively varied wine list.

CHEFS: Louise Fletcher-Brewer and David Carney   PROPRIETORS: the Fletcher-Brewer family
OPEN: all week 12 to 2, 7.15 to 9   CLOSED: mid-Nov to Easter   MEALS: Set buffet L Sun £17.50
(children £9), Set D all week £22.75 (2 courses) to £30. Light L Mon to Sat   SERVICE: not inc, card
slips closed   CARDS: MasterCard, Switch, Visa   DETAILS: 50 seats. 30 seats outside. Private
parties: 50 main room. Car park. Vegetarian meals. Children's helpings. No children under 7. No
smoking in dining room. No music   ACCOMMODATION: 17 rooms, all with bath/shower. TV.
Phone. B&B £48 to £116. Rooms for disabled. Baby facilities. Swimming pool (*The Which? Hotel
Guide*)

BASSALEG Newport   map 4

Junction 28 ▼ £

Station Approach, Bassaleg NP1 9LD
TEL: (01633) 891891   FAX: (01633) 895982
from M4 junction 28 take A468 towards Caerphilly,   COOKING 2
turn right at Tredegar Arms and take first left   COST £17–£46

With over forty items on the carte, plus the early evening 'flyer' menu, dishes 'on
the side' and desserts to attend to, it is amazing that the kitchen manages to
produce such robust and good-looking food as consistently as it does. Under Jon
West's direction, the menu moves freely from a trio of lamb (breast meat,
kidneys in a vol-au-vent, and grilled fillet) through fish (grilled sea bass with
truffle tagliatelle), to 'a bit of both' (halibut with smoked duck breast); and from
comforting (pan-seared foie gras with black pudding), to vegetarian (asparagus
with wild mushrooms and scrambled eggs). The restaurant itself also defies
categorisation: a former railway station transformed beyond recognition into a
smart, bright, colonial-style dining room, with bamboo screens to break up the
space. Staff are friendly and efficient. Just like the menu, the wine list leaps

around the world, as the bins are simply split by colour then arranged in ascending order of price. Quality and variety seem to be the prime considerations as mark-ups are very fair. House French is £9.95.

CHEF: Jon West PROPRIETORS: Richard Wallace and Jon West OPEN: all week L 12 to 2 (4 Sun), Mon to Sat D 5.30 to 9.30 CLOSED: 26 Dec, 1 Jan, first week July, last week Aug MEALS: alc (main courses £4 to £15). Set L Sun £9.95 (2 courses) to £11.95, Set D before 7pm £11.95 SERVICE: not inc, card slips closed CARDS: Delta, MasterCard, Switch, Visa DETAILS: 160 seats. Private parties: 50 main room, 12 and 50 private rooms. Car park. Vegetarian meals. No cigars/pipes in dining room. Wheelchair access (also WC). Occasional music. Air-conditioned

---

BEAUMARIS Isle of Anglesey   map 7

▲ *Ye Olde Bulls Head* ♥ ✣

Castle Street, Beaumaris LL58 8AP   COOKING 3
TEL: (01248) 810329 FAX: (01248) 811202   COST £20–£48

This ancient hostelry (built in 1617, and counting Dr Johnson and Charles Dickens among its visitors) is going through a period of change. A new conservatory-style brasserie extension, which blends well with the original, thanks to open stonework, hefty wooden beams, slate floor and lots of glass, serves sandwiches, pasta, and chargrills of fish and meat. The first-floor restaurant, meanwhile, was scheduled for refurbishment as the *Guide* went to press, and its style of food may change too, as a new chef was due to be appointed under the direction of Keith Rothwell, but the kitchen has ably demonstrated its sourcing of fine ingredients and precise, confident cooking.

Fierce searing has brought out the best from both fish and meat: 'ultra rare' juicy tuna on a base of mineral-packed seaweed (wakame and laver), given depth by Chinese oyster sauce, and a partnership of venison loin and whole crisp-skinned quail in a well-reduced sauce. Vegetables are served separately, and desserts have included a rhubarb and stem ginger variant on tiramisù. Much to the management's credit, everything happens 'without any fuss or pomp'. The wide-ranging restaurant wine list is full of interest, sharp on quality and fair on prices. Four house wines from France and Argentina are £13.75 a bottle, £3 a glass. The brasserie offers a short list of appealing bins under £20.

CHEF: Keith Rothwell PROPRIETOR: Rothwell and Robertson Ltd OPEN: brasserie all week 12 to 2, 6 to 9; restaurant Mon to Sat D only 7 to 9.30 CLOSED: 25 and 26 Dec MEALS: brasserie alc (main courses £5 to £8); restaurant Set D £27.50 SERVICE: not inc CARDS: Amex, Delta, MasterCard, Switch, Visa DETAILS: 45 seats. Private parties: 45 main room. Vegetarian meals. Children's helpings. No children under 7 in restaurant. No smoking in restaurant; no-smoking area in brasserie. No music ACCOMMODATION: 15 rooms, all with bath/shower. TV. Phone. B&B £51 to £94. Baby facilities (*The Which? Hotel Guide*)

'I did suggest that they needed a new chef, and this was not a welcome piece of feedback.'
(On eating in Cheshire)

The Guide *is totally independent, accepts no free hospitality, and survives on the number of copies sold each year.*

BROAD HAVEN Pembrokeshire   map 4

▲ *Druidstone* £

Druidston Haven, Broad Haven SA62 3NE
TEL: (01437) 781221   FAX: (01437) 781133
from B4341 at Broad Haven turn right at sea; after 1½m   COOKING 3
turn left to Druidston Haven; hotel ¾m on left   COST £17–£32

Druidstone is different: an easy-going, what-you-see-is-what-you-get kind of place, with a marvellous view over the cliffs and a rare sense of individuality. What it may lack in sophistication it more than makes up for in directness, honesty and wholesomeness. One couple, finding a large party completely occupying the dining room, were content to eat in the staff kitchen: 'this is Druidstone, and we love it.' Meals might begin with soup – lamb and leek, or turkey broth – or green-lipped mussels with lemon grass and ginger. Despite lamb chops, chicken breast and fillet steak, fish and vegetable main courses are a prominent fixture: mullet with dried basil leaves and sliced olives, scallops baked in cream and Pernod, or a pancake filled with courgettes, spinach and feta cheese. Finish with profiteroles, St Clements soufflé, or the highly rated cheesecake. Service is youthful and friendly, wines (around three dozen) varied and fairly priced. House Vin de Pays du Gers is £7 a bottle, £10 a litre.

CHEFS: Rod and Jane Bell, Donna Banner, Angus Bell and John Lewis   PROPRIETORS: Rod and Jane Bell   OPEN: Sun L 1 to 2, Mon to Sat D 7.0 to 9.30   CLOSED: Mon to Thur from 1st week Nov to 2nd week Dec and 1st week Jan to 2nd week Feb   MEALS: alc (main courses £6 to £12). Bar menu available all week L and D   SERVICE: not inc, card slips closed   CARDS: Amex, Delta, MasterCard, Switch, Visa   DETAILS: 36 seats. 40 seats outside. Private parties: 36 main room, 12 private room. Car park. Vegetarian meals. Children's helpings. No smoking while others eat. Wheelchair access (also WC). No music   ACCOMMODATION: 9 rooms. B&B £31 to £74. Baby facilities (*The Which? Hotel Guide*)

CAPEL GARMON Conwy   map 7

▲ *Tan-y-Foel* ♥ ✾

Capel Garmon, nr Betws-y-Coed LL26 0RE
TEL: (01690) 710507   FAX: (01690) 710681
take turning marked Capel Garmon and Nebo from
A470 about halfway between Betws-y-Coed and   COOKING 4
Llanrwst   COST £32–£44

Being 'beautifully quiet with fabulous views' is a big draw at this family-run rural retreat in Snowdonia National Park. The sixteenth-century stone-built farmhouse belies a comfortably furnished, sophisticated interior which, after refurbishment, boasts a 'very modern and minimalistic' sitting room, plus a breakfast/lunch room for residents. Another change is an extension to three choices per course at dinner, served in the pale green dining room at the back with its wood-burning stove and conservatory addition. Local materials (including rack of Welsh lamb, perhaps with leek and potato pancakes) play an integral part in proceedings, and a degree of cosmopolitan refinement pervades the cooking: from white bean soup with frizzled onions to crisp-coated turbot with curried pea purée. Welsh cheeses or a plate of fresh fruit offer viable alternatives to panettone bread-and-butter pudding or baked egg custard with blackberry compote. The wine list travels around the world picking up some appealing bins wherever it touches down. Six house wines start at £10.20 a bottle; all are £3.85 a glass.

CHEF: Janet Pitman   PROPRIETORS: Peter and Janet Pitman   OPEN: all week D only 7 to 8.15   MEALS: Set D £24 (2 courses) to £28. Light L menu (residents only)   SERVICE: not inc, card slips closed   CARDS: Amex, Delta, Diners, MasterCard, Switch, Visa   DETAILS: 16 seats. Car park. No children under 7 in dining room. No smoking. No music   ACCOMMODATION: 7 rooms, all with bath/shower. TV. Phone. B&B £70 to £150. No children under 7 in accommodation (*The Which? Hotel Guide*)

CARDIFF Cardiff map 4

Armless Dragon ✱ £

97 Wyeverne Road, Cathays, Cardiff CF2 4BG
TEL/FAX: (01222) 382357, changing to   COOKING 2
(029) 2038 2357   COST £16–£38

Two terraced houses joined together, fresh flowers, and cream, terracotta and green walls provide a bright, clean setting for this well-established bistro. The formula is an unchanging laminated menu, offering steak several ways, duck or chicken, plus various treatments for daily-changing fish on the blackboard, which also lists at least six starters, and eight meat main courses: hunter's pie perhaps, or roast wild rabbit with tarragon and mustard. The retro style may lack obvious excitement but the Armless Dragon consistently turns out simple, unpretentious dishes and remains popular with locals. Vegetarians are not sold short, given such offerings as stuffed aubergine with chestnuts, or pine nuts and peperonata, and desserts bring no surprises. The wine list favours France, but not to the exclusion of the rest of the world. House wines are £7.90.

CHEF/PROPRIETOR: David Richards   OPEN: Tue to Fri L 12 to 2.15, Tue to Sat D 7 to 10.15 (post-theatre D by arrangement)   CLOSED: 25 Dec   MEALS: alc (main courses £9 to £14). Set L £7.90 (2 courses) to £9.90   SERVICE: not inc   CARDS: Amex, Delta, Diners, MasterCard, Switch, Visa   DETAILS: 50 seats. Private parties: 50 main room. Vegetarian meals. Children's helpings. No smoking in dining room. Wheelchair access (not WC). Music £5

Le Cassoulet

5 Romilly Crescent, Canton, Cardiff CF1 9NP
TEL/FAX: (01222) 221905, changing to   COOKING 5
(029) 2022 1905   COST £25–£48

Small and decorated with reminders of France, from posters to bottles of armagnac, Le Cassoulet is run by the 'delightful and charming' Viaders. Their kitchen tends to deal in classic dishes, not all as weighty as the eponymous cassoulet toulousain, and despite having its centre of gravity in south-west France it is happy to branch out into poached egg florentine, tagliatelle with pistou, and salmon with couscous. The concise à la carte – in French with simple translations – might take in a terrine of fish or game, duck foie gras with apple chutney, and roast best end of Welsh lamb with a herb crust and rosemary sauce, while the set-price lunch, for one visitor, was 'an eye opener' that began with warm goats'-cheese salad before boeuf bourguignon, and ended with a chocolate and nut mousse with ice cream. Desserts are, if anything, more firmly in French mould, with pain perdu or nougat glacé alongside crème brûlée and chocolate soufflé. Wines are exclusively French (apart from a lone Californian red called Viader) and include some big names at reasonable prices. House Vin de Pays du Gers is £10.95.

CHEF: Gilbert Viader   PROPRIETORS: Gilbert and Claire Viader   OPEN: Tue to Sat 12 to 2, 7 to 10 (late D Sat by arrangement)   CLOSED: 2 weeks Christmas, 3 weeks Aug   MEALS: alc (main courses £12.50 to £16). Set L £12.50 (2 courses) to £15   SERVICE: not inc   CARDS: Amex, Delta, Diners, MasterCard, Switch, Visa   DETAILS: 35 seats. Private parties: 35 main room. Vegetarian meals. Children's helpings. No cigars/pipes in dining room. Occasional music

Gilby's ┆✳

NEW ENTRY

Old Port Road, Culverhouse Cross, Cardiff CF5 6DN
TEL: (01222) 670800, changing to (029) 2067 0800   COOKING 3
FAX: (01222) 594437, changing to (029) 2059 4437   COST £20–£50

'A welcome addition to Cardiff' (one of four new entries this year) was one visitor's judgement of this converted stable block on the western outskirts of the city. Its 'mock-rustic' style, floral brocade and abstract prints give it the feel of 'a large, upmarket, high-turnover pub dining room', but it assembles good materials into a wide range of dishes. A big printed menu touches base with everyday globe-trotting ideas such as plaice tempura with wasabi mayonnaise, wild mushroom risotto, and chargrilled tuna with tabbouleh-style couscous, and offers a short glossary of terms for those unfamiliar with rocket, polenta and tapénade.

It takes seafood seriously enough to offer oysters three ways, whole Pembrokeshire crab with noodles in a bouillabaisse-style broth, and three 'meaty, moist and fresh' scallops with coriander dressing. Balancing this might be a 'satisfying' starter of black pudding with bacon, high-quality breast of Gressingham duck with choucroute, or fillet steak 'cooked as requested' with a choice of three sauces (all, like bread and vegetables, charged extra). Puddings of crème brûlée or lemon tart with pistachio ice cream seem to elicit less excitement. Service is 'unfailingly friendly' and so prompt on one occasion that 'plates were removed before we had finished eating from them'. A short wine list offers around ten by the glass. House French is £10.95.

CHEFS: Anthony Armelin and Gareth Silcock   PROPRIETOR: Anthony Armelin   OPEN: Tue to Sun L 2 to 2.30, Tue to Sat D 6 to 10.30   CLOSED: 10 days Christmas, bank hols   MEALS: alc (main courses £9 to £14.50). Set L Tue to Sat £7.95 (2 courses), Set D Tue to Fri before 7 £11.95 SERVICE: not inc   CARDS: Amex, Delta, MasterCard, Switch, Visa   DETAILS: 110 seats. 28 seats outside. Private parties: 20 main room. Car park. Vegetarian meals. No children under 7. No smoking in dining room. Wheelchair access (not WC). Music   (£5)

'Beware – do not enter into a light-hearted conversation with the owner, you will be verbally disembowelled.' (On eating in Yorkshire)

Le Monde

60 St Mary Street, Cardiff CF1 1FE
TEL/FAX: (01222) 387376,
changing to (029) 2038 7376   COOKING 1
EMAIL: chefuk@globalnet.co.uk   COST £17–£43

The set-up is as simple and informal as can be. There is sawdust on the floor, no bookings are taken (except for large parties), and there is no menu or wine list. Meat and fish dishes are chalked on a board, ingredients are stored in chill cabinets, and the chargrill works overtime. Join the queue and order from a long list of options. Start with provençale fish soup, baked mussels, or shrimps in garlic butter, and buy your fish by the pound: halibut and Dover sole at the top end, hake and salmon for two thirds the price. Dessert is crêpes Suzette, take it or leave it, and house wine is £9.45. Adjoining Champers (tel. (01222) 373363, changing to (029) 2037 3363) and La Brasserie (tel. (01222) 372164, changing to (029) 2037 2164) are under the same ownership and run along similar lines, the former with more of a Spanish theme, the latter with more steak than fish.

CHEFS: David Legg and Paul Barnes   PROPRIETOR: Benigno Martinez   OPEN: Mon to Sat 12 to 2.30, 7 to 12   CLOSED: 25 and 26 Dec   MEALS: alc (main courses £7 to £20). Set L Sat £6 (2 courses)   SERVICE: not inc, card slips closed   CARDS: Amex, Delta, Diners, MasterCard, Switch, Visa   DETAILS: 180 seats. Private parties: 50 main room, 100 private room. Vegetarian meals. Music. Air-conditioned (£5)

Pied-a-Terre   [NEW ENTRY]

5 Pontcanna Street, Cardiff CF1 9HQ   COOKING 4
TEL: (01222) 232616, changing to (029) 2023 2616   COST £25–£46

In a popular part of the city for cafés and restaurants, a relatively conservative-looking frontage identifies the very French Pied-a-Terre. Cream walls, tall glasses and white napery contribute to its elegant feel, and the front-of-house approach – 'correct' rather than lively – confirms that the food is going to be 'very serious'. Its contemporary spin on classical ideas demands a lot of skill to bring off, but Simon Thomas (who returned to Cardiff after working in France) is certainly up to it. A range of techniques has produced fiercely seared, well-rested duck magret with crisp skin and pink flesh, and 'hefty chunks' of pot-roasted leg of lamb.

Those who believe that size isn't everything will be best placed to enjoy a starter of three small slices of briefly seared white scallop meat, surrounded by a green 'gazpacho' tasting of mint and fennel. Accomplished saucing also shows in a rich red wine version accompanying rare ribeye of beef 'on a mash of roots'. Unpasteurised French cheeses are kept in good condition, and desserts (ordered at the beginning) have ranged from a 'light, clean fresh' poached peach, via textbook raspberry soufflé, to a wedge of dark and rich chocolate tart served with armagnac-soaked prunes. Wines are as French as the rest of the establishment, with around forty bins offering a reasonable choice above and below £20. House vin de pays is £11.

CHEF/PROPRIETOR: Simon Thomas   OPEN: Tue to Fri and Sun L 12.30 to 2, Tue to Sat D 7.15 to 9.30   CLOSED: 26 to 30 Dec, last week Aug, first week Sept   MEALS: alc L Tue to Fri, D Tue to Sat (main courses L £8, D £10 to £15). Set L Sun £15.95   SERVICE: net prices, card slips closed   CARDS: Delta, MasterCard, Switch, Visa   DETAILS: 36 seats. Private parties: 30 main room. Vegetarian meals. Children's helpings. No cigars/pipes in dining room. Music

---

▲ St David's Hotel & Spa ▮ ⁵⁂   **NEW ENTRY**

Havana Street, Cardiff Bay, Cardiff CF10 5SD
TEL: (01222) 454045, changing to (029) 2045 4045
FAX: (01222) 487056, changing to (029) 2048 7056   COOKING 4
EMAIL: reservations@fivestar-htl-wales.com   COST £32–£55

Sir Rocco Forte's waterfront hotel, built just in time for the opening of the Welsh Assembly, is shaped like an ocean liner, with a sail-like dome, balconies aping decks, and a maritime theme prevailing throughout the minimalist interior, from wavy lines and shades of blue to 'lighthouse' cruet sets. Martin Green's experience includes time at the Connaught, but there is strong Welsh input not only among his team, but also in well-sourced raw materials treated with respect: 'tender, rare, pink' slices of Mountain venison in a rich port and blackcurrant sauce, or Black beef 'of the highest quality' on creamy parsley mash.

This is not traditional Welsh cooking, however, given strong Mediterranean leanings in the shape of red mullet with bouillabaisse sauce and saffron potatoes, and an occasional 'crossover' dish such as sliced foie gras on a savoury currantless Welshcake (a contradiction, perhaps, for traditionalists) served with caramelised endive in a rich balsamic sauce. An absence of fussy presentation is welcome, sauces and purées are full of verve without overwhelming – for example a tian of crab with diced tomato and an avocado and coriander salsa – and puddings of lemon tart, and exotic fruit salad with coconut and pineapple sorbet, have 'a particular intensity of taste'. Efficient, unstarchy service helps to make everything run smoothly. The vast wine list has much for the well-heeled, whether they have a penchant for top red Burgundy (all six Domaine de la Romanée-Contis from 1989) or white (domaines Leflaive and Louis Jadot), first-growth clarets (dating back to 1961) or Super-Tuscans. The needs of cost-conscious drinkers are also catered for by a good, international range under £20. House French is £15.

CHEF: Martin Green   PROPRIETORS: Sir Rocco Forte and Family Cardiff Bay Ltd   OPEN: all week 12 to 2.30, 6.30 to 10.30   MEALS: alc (main courses £11 to £16.50). Set L £14.50 (2 courses) to £19.50   SERVICE: net prices   CARDS: Amex, Delta, Diners, MasterCard, Switch, Visa   DETAILS: 120 seats. 20 seats outside. Private parties: 220 main room, 12 to 220 private rooms. Car park. Vegetarian meals. Children's helpings. No smoking in dining room. Wheelchair access (also WC). Occasional music. Air-conditioned   ACCOMMODATION: 136 rooms, all with bath/shower. TV. Phone. Room only £160 to £500. Rooms for disabled. Baby facilities. Swimming pool ⑤£5⑤

£5 *indicates that the restaurant has elected to participate in the* **Good Food** **Guide** *voucher scheme. For full details, see page 6.*

Woods Brasserie

NEW ENTRY

Pilotage Building, Stuart Street, Cardiff Bay,
Cardiff CF1 5BW
TEL: (01222) 492400, changing to (029) 2049 2400   COOKING 4
FAX: (01222) 230002, changing to (029) 2023 0002   COST £25–£52

Transplanted from Llantrisant, Woods occupies a Grade II-listed building (formerly Scott's Brasserie) in 'up-and-coming' Cardiff Bay. Décor is modern and sophisticated, with stainless steel, glass walls and black marble – 'it felt like eating in a rather noisy Habitat' – and there is a generous menu to match. Its essence is simple, fresh ingredients given a stylish lift with a few apposite (sometimes exotic) accompaniments: perhaps lightly cooked scallops with intensely flavoured roast tomatoes stuffed with garlic and herbs, or chunks of battered and deep-fried 'Japanese' chicken with a sweet-and-sour dipping sauce and a pile of saffron-soaked noodle-like strands of Chinese radish.

A clear focus and confident delivery make the most of flavour combinations and textural contrasts: for example, slices of pink-roasted rump of Welsh salt-marsh lamb, on a pile of pale green creamed flageolet beans with roast garlic cloves and crisp-fried sage leaves. First-rate vegetables are (like bread) charged extra, but may not be necessary, and relatively conventional desserts might include 'perfectly executed' crème brûlée, or a rich, dense, chocolate truffle parfait. Deborah Peters runs a friendly and capable front-of-house team, and a forty-strong international wine list offers good variety under £20. House Chilean is £10.50.

CHEF: Martyn Peters   PROPRIETORS: Martyn and Deborah Peters   OPEN: Mon to Sat 12 to 2, 6.30 to 10   CLOSED: 1 week autumn, Christmas, 1 week spring, bank hols   MEALS: alc (main courses £7 to £16)   SERVICE: not inc, 10% for parties of 8 or more, card slips closed   CARDS: Amex, Delta, Diners, MasterCard, Switch, Visa   DETAILS: 86 seats. 30 seats outside. Private parties: 60 main room, 30 private room. Vegetarian meals. Children's helpings. Wheelchair access (also WC). Music. Air-conditioned

---

CLYTHA Monmouthshire   map 2

▲ Clytha Arms 🍴✳

Clytha NP7 9BW
TEL/FAX: (01873) 840206
off old Abergavenny to Raglan road, S of A40, 6m E of   COOKING 4
Abergavenny   COST £22–£44

There is a 'slight colonial air' to this superior pub, a pale pink building graced by a wrought iron verandah and green lawns, situated in ancient Clytha Park. Inside, a dartboard, real ales and two large resident dogs set an informal tone. Cooking is a family affair, with owner Andrew Canning as chef and his daughter Sarah an able support, turning out Welsh-influenced dishes noted for their 'sheer generosity and lack of pretentiousness'. A recent visitor concluded that they have 'taken great strides in the right direction in the last few years', specifying the quality of produce used, excellent timing and great value for money (including wines). On the other hand, criticisms have been made of the service, which, though normally effected by very young, but 'extremely well-informed' women, occasionally deteriorates when staff are in short supply. Other reporters assert that the cooking 'is worth waiting for' and heap praise on 'spankingly fresh scallops with classically made pesto' or 'exceptionally mature, well-hung, classy beef' served simply with a huge tomato stuffed with wild mushrooms. Cinnamon and almond cake is served warm in a rough wedge, with 'full flavoured and creamy' honey ice cream. Some classy contributions from the New World add to the attractions of the largely French wine list. House wine is £8.75.

CHEFS: Andrew and Sarah Canning   PROPRIETORS: Andrew and Beverley Canning   OPEN: all week L 12.30 to 2.15, Tue to Sat D 7 to 9.30   CLOSED: 25 Dec   MEALS: alc Mon to Sat L, Tue to Sat D (main courses £10 to £15.50). Set L Sun £13.95. Bar meals available   SERVICE: not inc, card slips closed   CARDS: Amex, Delta, Diners, MasterCard, Switch, Visa   DETAILS: 60 seats. 60 seats outside. Private parties: 45 main room, 20 private room. Car park. Vegetarian meals. Children's helpings. No smoking in dining room. No music   ACCOMMODATION: 4 rooms. TV. B&B £45 to £70 (The Which? Hotel Guide) £5

COLWYN BAY Conwy   map 7

Café Niçoise £

124 Abergele Road, Colwyn Bay LL29 7PS   COOKING 4
TEL: (01492) 531555   COST £22–£43

From the narrow frontage on the high street, the dining room of this intimate French restaurant stretches back some way. Walls are painted with a terracotta wash and hung with Parisian paintings to reinforce the theme. Lynne Swift handles front-of-house, where there is a 'real buzz' about the service, while Carl Swift mans the stoves with deftness and precision. At lunchtimes and weekday evenings a menu touristique offers additional choice to the well-focused, monthly-changing carte. Start perhaps with baked goats' cheese in filo pastry with a 'very generous' smoked bacon salad, enhanced by olives, capers, pine nuts and small tomatoes. Main courses lack frippery, the focus very much on sourcing good ingredients and handling them well, as evidenced by an inspector's assiette of seafood with a light vermouth sauce, comprising salmon, sea bass, monk, bream and mussels, all 'in super condition'. The assiette of desserts solves any difficulty in choosing from chocolate nemesis with mocha sauce, lemon tart, or pineapple crème brûlée. A well-chosen wine list is good on half-bottles; house selections start at £7.95.

CHEF: Carl Swift   PROPRIETORS: Carl and Lynne Swift   OPEN: Wed to Sat L 12 to 1.45, Mon to Sat D 7 to 10   CLOSED: 1 week Jan, 1 week June   MEALS: alc (main courses £7.50 to £15). Set L Wed to Sat and D Mon to Fri £12.75 (2 courses) to £14.95   SERVICE: not inc, card slips closed CARDS: Amex, Delta, MasterCard, Switch, Visa   DETAILS: 32 seats. Private parties: 30 main room. Vegetarian meals. Children's helpings. No children under 5 at D. No-smoking area. Music £5

'The fish came with "coconut emulsion", which sounded like a new addition to the Dulux range.' (On eating in London)

CREIGIAU Cardiff   map 4

Caesar's Arms £

Cardiff Road, Creigiau CF4 8NN
TEL: (01222) 890486, changing to (029) 2089 0486   COOKING 1
FAX: (01222) 892176, changing to (029) 2089 2176   COST £21–£47

The setting is an old white stone pub outside Cardiff with solid furniture and a
bustling atmosphere. Service is efficient, and helpful staff explain the drill to
first-timers: check in at the counter, find your table, then return to the counter to
pick the raw material for your meal. Reporters like the system for its value both
in terms of money and entertainment: watch your food being cooked if your
table has a view of the open kitchen. Meat, fish and shellfish are simply grilled,
fried or poached and served with a choice of sauces and self-service salads. There
may be steaks, marinated pork kebabs, monkfish, hake, or whole sewin baked
in salt to choose from. Start with provençale fish soup or spicy chicken winglets,
and finish with pavlova or cheesecake. There are also daily specials, and two or
three roasts on Sundays. Around 100 wines are listed on blackboards; house
French is £9.45.

CHEF: Earl Smikle   PROPRIETOR: Steadychance Ltd   OPEN: all week L 12 to 2.30 (3 Sun), Mon to
Sat D 7 to 10.30   CLOSED: 25 Dec   MEALS: alc (main courses £5 to £17)   SERVICE: not inc, card
slips closed   CARDS: Amex, Delta, Diners, MasterCard, Switch, Visa   DETAILS: 180 seats. 40
seats outside. Private parties: 50 main room, 60 private room. Car park. Vegetarian meals.
Wheelchair access (also WC). Music

CRICCIETH Gwynedd   map 7

Tir-a-Môr ♥

1–3 Mona Terrace, Criccieth LL52 0HG   COOKING 3
TEL: (01766) 523084   COST £27–£50

'A magic find,' wrote one visitor of this large-windowed informal brasserie.
Clare and Martin Vowell are committed to local suppliers, particularly for fish,
which are listed on daily-changing blackboards, as well as game, wild
mushrooms, Lleyn rose beef and salt-marsh lamb, perhaps accompanied by
minted samphire. Clare's style is modern, the range of ingredients wide, her
repertoire continually evolving, taking in prawn and ricotta filo pie, baked
mullet with a warm potato salad, and scallop and langoustine ravioli. Italy is
another passion – as shown in the 'asides' of tigelle (flat bread with pesto or
tapénade), and dishes such as stincotto (pork with butterbeans, served in a
portion large enough for two). Martin has put together a globe-trotting
collection of seventy or so attractively priced wines helpfully presented by style.
Look out for some interesting bottles and glasses on the specials board, too.
House whites are £9.95, the red is £10.95.

CHEF: Clare Vowell   PROPRIETORS: Clare and Martin Vowell   OPEN: Mon to Sat D 7 to 9.30
CLOSED: Fri and Sat Nov to Mar, 1 month from last weekend before Christmas   MEALS: alc (main
courses £10 to £18)   SERVICE: not inc, card slips closed   CARDS: Delta, MasterCard, Switch,
Visa   DETAILS: 35 seats. Private parties: 25 main room. Vegetarian meals. No children under 7.
Wheelchair access (not WC). Music

CRICKHOWELL Powys   map 4

▲ *Bear Hotel*

High Street, Crickhowell NP8 1BW
TEL: (01873) 810408   FAX: (01873) 811696
EMAIL: bearhotel@aol.com   COOKING 3
on A40, 6m NW of Abergavenny   COST £21–£45

The Bear retains much of its original fifteenth-century charm, with all the low
ceilings, creepers and flowery tubs that any self-respecting coaching-inn must
have. Run by the Hindmarshes for over twenty years, it gives the impression of
being the hub of this small market town. There are two dining areas to choose
from, one rustic, stone-walled and flagstone-floored, the other more of a
Victorian parlour. Among more traditional items on the blackboard menu might
be a tart of delicate shortcrust pastry with a robust filling of salmon, leeks and
lentils, or a 'filling and fulfilling' game casserole, but chef Denver Dodwell
occasionally spreads his wings to come up with spicy beef won tons, and wild
mushroom and artichoke ravioli, always basing dishes on good local produce.
The hotel's signature rum and banana bread-and-butter pudding with a scoop of
'grainy, creamy' brown bread ice-cream impressed at inspection; alternatively,
finish with Welsh cheeses. Service is cheerful and efficient, and the wine list is
short and to the point; house wine is £8.50.

CHEF: Denver Dodwell   PROPRIETORS: Stephen and Judy Hindmarsh   OPEN: Sun L 12 to 2,
Mon to Sat D 7 to 9.30   MEALS: alc (main courses £9.50 to £17). Set L Sun £14.95. Bar/bistro
menu available all week L and D   SERVICE: not inc   CARDS: Amex, Delta, MasterCard, Switch,
Visa   DETAILS: 175 seats. 50 seats outside. Private parties: 60 main room, 25 to 60 private
rooms. Car park. Vegetarian meals. Children's helpings. No children under 7 in dining room.
No-smoking area. Wheelchair access (also WC). Music   ACCOMMODATION: 34 rooms, all with
bath/shower. TV. Phone. B&B £45 to £110 (*The Which? Hotel Guide*)

Nantyffin Cider Mill Inn ▼ ⁵✗

Brecon Road, Crickhowell NP8 1SG
TEL/FAX: (01873) 810775   COOKING 2
1½m W of Crickhowell at junction of A40 and A479   COST £24–£46

Aiming to be a 'destination restaurant', like its nearby sister establishment, the
Manor Hotel, this old drovers' pub in the picturesque Usk Valley was indeed a
cider mill until the '60s – the press is still visible in the dining area, formerly the
apple store. Sean Gerrard devises contemporary menus using local and organic
produce, perhaps brill tempura, tender chargrilled squid, or a plain warm fresh
crab. Bar menu, evening set menu and chalked specials all offer 'impressive,
imaginative choices' of vegetarian, fish and meat dishes, many displaying an
Eastern, North African or Mediterranean influence: rabbit tagine with couscous,
or chargrilled Black beef on saffron potatoes with chorizo and mozzarella, for
example. Real ales, traditional ciders and home-made lemonade are offered,
while the wine list, once entirely American, has broadened its scope to include
bottles from Australia and New Zealand, all listed in price order, all described
with enthusiasm and with many under £20. House Chilean and Australian are
£10.95/£12.95.

CHEF: Sean Gerrard   PROPRIETORS: Sean Gerrard and Glyn Bridgeman   OPEN: Tue to Sun 12 to 2 (2.30 Apr to Sept), 6.30 to 9.30   CLOSED: Sun D in winter   MEALS: alc (main courses £7.50 to £15). Set L £12.95 to £14.95   SERVICE: not inc, card slips closed   CARDS: Amex, Delta, MasterCard, Switch, Visa   DETAILS: 120 seats. 50 seats outside. Private parties: 50 main room. Car park. Vegetarian meals. Children's helpings. No smoking in dining room. Wheelchair access (also WC). No music

---

DOLGELLAU Gwynedd   map 7

Dylanwad Da ♥ ⅙✷ £

2 Ffôs-y-Felin, Dolgellau LL40 1BS   COOKING 2
TEL: (01341) 422870   COST £24–£37

Dylan Rowlands plans few changes at his popular bistro although his embrace of local produce now extends to some slate candle holders. The wine-red frontage gives way to apricot walls and well-spaced tables with fresh flowers, and the music, like the customers, is loud and cheerful. Healthy and straight-forward menus always include a salady starter, maybe of hot smoked venison, and an interesting vegetarian number such as Shropshire Blue and port cheesecake. Main courses all come with the same robust cornucopia of fresh and tasty vegetables, including an inspector's Thai chicken and coconut, which had clear and strong flavours and well-balanced spicing. 'Chunky and intense' coffee and walnut ice cream may turn up at dessert stage. Extras, such as bread, have disappointed, but prices throughout are kind, and service from smiley young women is willing and friendly: 'this is what bistro eating should be all about.' Mr Rowlands has put together a short, impressive and informed wine list, simply arranged by price. As well as house wines (£9 a bottle/£1.80 a glass), he now offers a duo of classy wines of the month at the same ungrasping mark-up.

CHEF/PROPRIETOR: Dylan Rowlands   OPEN: Thur to Sat (Tue to Sun summer, all week Easter and Whitsun) D only 7 to 9   CLOSED: 6 weeks Feb/Mar   MEALS: alc (main courses £9 to £13.50)   SERVICE: not inc   CARDS: none   DETAILS: 30 seats. Private parties: 30 main room. Vegetarian meals. Children's helpings. No smoking in dining room. Wheelchair access (not WC). Music (£5)

EGLWYSFACH Powys   map 7

▲ *Ynyshir Hall* ♥ ⅙✷

Eglwysfach SY20 8TA
TEL: (01654) 781209   FAX: (01654) 781366
EMAIL: info@ynyshir-hall.co.uk   COOKING 5
off A487, 6m SW of Machynlleth   COST £31–£56

Sheltered, secluded and peaceful this white-painted house may be, but there is no lack of colour to it. Presentation is given pride of place throughout, from deep turquoise walls and flower-patterned fabrics in the dining room, to the calligraphic menu (four choices per course) with a colour reproduction of one of Rob Reen's bold paintings, to the food itself. While a culinary phrase book might help to decipher beetroot arancini (served with roast squab pigeon), and sauce Albufera (with saddle of Brecon venison), and a degree of faith may be required to order a dish consisting of roast cod, rocket soufflé, Parma ham, lemon pickle and garlic butter, raw materials and technical skills are not in question.

If some of the ideas and treatments are rather ambitious, at the expense of clarity of flavour, others work thanks to prime ingredients: for example, 'superb-quality' beef 'excellently timed' on a bed of fresh pasta. Likewise a 'very professional' hot lime soufflé presented in a copper saucepan scored highly for dexterity and skill, less so for its accompanying 'cigar' of white chocolate and lemon grass sorbet. 'Superabundant' extras extend from a silver salver of appetisers, via a pre-meal soup (frothy green parsley with a warmed oyster), and half a dozen 'fresh and yeasty' in-house breads to 'comparatively restrained' petits fours. The cheeseboard offers an interesting selection of Welsh farmhouse cheeses, including smoked merlin and Caerphilly with leek and garlic. The owners are charming, and staff 'seriously well trained'. Mature Bordeaux and Burgundies lend their weight to the 'hefty bound tome' that is the wine list, and prices can be on the heavy side too (look to southern France for lighter fare, with bottles starting at £11). Thirteen wines by the glass from £3 display imagination.

CHEF: Chris Colmer   PROPRIETORS: Joan and Rob Reen   OPEN: all week 12.30 to 1.30, 7 to 8.30   CLOSED: 5 to 23 Jan   MEALS: Set L £21, Set D £35. Bar menu available Mon to Sat L   SERVICE: not inc, card slips closed   CARDS: Amex, Diners, MasterCard, Switch, Visa   DETAILS: 35 seats. Private parties: 28 main room, 18 private room. Car park. Vegetarian meals. No children under 9 in dining room. No smoking in dining room. Music   ACCOMMODATION: 10 rooms, all with bath/shower. TV. Phone. B&B £85 to £195. No children under 9 in accommodation (*The Which? Hotel Guide*)

FISHGUARD Pembrokeshire   map 4

▲ *Three Main Street* ※

3 Main Street, Fishguard SA65 9HG   COOKING 5
TEL: (01348) 874275   COST £35–£42

This smart Georgian town house, just off the market square, is 'obviously organised and run by ladies who have good taste'. It is in pristine condition, with plenty of natural light, rich fabrics and crisp napery, yet relaxed and completely unfussy: a sign of the owners' dedication and confidence (developed over a decade) which also characterises the food. 'Local, fresh and organic' materials are actively sought, from free-range poultry and eggs to vegetables and herbs. Fish landed nearby adds to the appeal, and the kitchen moves easily from traditional partnerships such as asparagus salad with smoked bacon, or leek and watercress soup, to duck confit with ginger and soy.

First-class delivery matches the high quality of materials, producing seared scallops ('as good as one could possibly get,' according to an inspector) accompanied by a small salad dressed with sweet chilli sauce, and sweet, pink, spring lamb with 'creamy, crispy fat' on a mound of spring greens with a racily flavoured basil and tomato sauce. Vegetables are served separately (perhaps new potatoes and chicory gratin), and desserts have included a light, sharp rhubarb mousse neatly paired with crunchy almond thins. Lunch (unless by prior arrangement) is a lighter affair, and the place functions as a coffee house from 10.30am to 2pm. A sensibly chosen, briefly annotated, fair-value wine list begins with a dozen recommendations under £15, including house French at £10.50.

CHEFS: Marion Evans and Simon Gulliver   PROPRIETORS: Marion Evans and Inez Ford   OPEN: Tue to Sat 12 to 2, 7 to 9 (booking essential L; phone to check opening during winter months) CLOSED: 25 Dec   MEALS: Set L and D £21 (2 courses) to £25. Light L available   SERVICE: not inc   CARDS: none   DETAILS: 35 seats. Private parties: 22 main room, 14 and 22 private rooms. Vegetarian meals. Children's helpings. No smoking in dining room. Wheelchair access (not WC). No music   ACCOMMODATION: 3 rooms, all with bath/shower. TV. B&B £35 to £70 (*The Which? Hotel Guide*)

GANLLWYD Gwynedd   map 7

▲ *Plas Dolmelynllyn* ♟ ⅝✳

Ganllwyd LL40 2HP
TEL: (01341) 440273   FAX: (01341) 440640
EMAIL: dolly@ganllwyd.freeserve.co.uk   COOKING 2
on A470, 5m N of Dolgellau   COST £33–£39

The grey stone used to build this old house is entirely in keeping with the 'awesome grandeur' of the surrounding mountains. It may be out of the way but, as the favourite in the area for one reporter, it charms with its conservatory overlooking the garden, its panelled walls, flowers, sideboard full of silver, and artistic furnishings that are 'absolutely right for it'. Well-balanced menus incorporate traditional ideas – loin of Welsh lamb with braised leeks – alongside more contemporary spiced chicken goujons with yoghurt and coriander mayonnaise, and sensible combinations are the norm, from baked roulade of pork with watercress and bitter orange gravy, to dark chocolate and hazelnut bread-and-butter pudding served with marmalade sauce. Jon Barkwith is happy to proffer advice on his globetrotting wine list, which manages to keep a satisfactory 30 per cent of bottles under £12. Several of the wines are organic – the Reuilly 1997, Dom. Henri Beurdin (£13.75), for instance – but hardly any are highlighted as such: an easily amendable oversight. Half-bottles are liberally scattered throughout the list; wines by the glass are £2 and £2.50.

CHEF: Jo Reddicliffe   PROPRIETORS: Jonathan Barkwith and Jo Reddicliffe   OPEN: all week D only 7 to 8.30   CLOSED: Nov to Feb   MEALS: Set D £24.50   SERVICE: not inc, card slips closed   CARDS: Amex, Delta, Diners, MasterCard, Switch, Visa   DETAILS: 20 seats. Private parties: 50 main room. Car park. Vegetarian meals. Children's helpings. High teas for children under 8. No smoking in dining room. Wheelchair access (not WC). No music   ACCOMMODATION: 10 rooms, all with bath/shower. TV. Phone. B&B £40 to £115. Children under 8 by arrangement. Fishing (*The Which? Hotel Guide*)   (£5)

Several sharp operators have tried to extort money from restaurateurs on the promise of an entry in a guidebook that has never appeared. The Good Food Guide *makes no charge for inclusion.*

Not inc in the details at the end of an entry indicates that no service charge is made and any tipping is at the discretion of the customer.

HARLECH Gwynedd   map 7

▲ Castle Cottage 🍴

Pen Llech, Harlech LL46 2YL   COOKING 2
TEL/FAX: (01766) 780479   COST £30–£36

Pictures of Welsh pastoral scenes and Mediterranean islands cover the walls, shelves are stacked with ornaments, and pigs range from fluffy to comely pot figures in this ancient, low-beamed house just a couple of hundred yards from the castle. Glyn Roberts makes use of Welsh resources in the form of locally landed sea bass, salt-marsh lamb, Brecon venison, and Black beef steaks (sirloin, fillet, ribeye), which are a constant on the weekly-changing menu. Partnerships are as simple as rosemary and garlic for the lamb, or a coriander and lime tartare sauce for grilled lemon sole, while starters might run from Cardigan Bay prawns with mayonnaise to a tandoori chicken salad with mango and bacon. Finish with lemon posset or treacle tart, and drink the Australian sweetie, Brown Brothers' Orange Muscat & Flora 1997 (£11.50 a half-bottle). To begin at the beginning, a dozen attractive wines are offered under £15 (the lowest is £9.75), while the main list continues the good-value theme.

CHEF: Glyn Roberts   PROPRIETORS: Glyn and Jacqueline Roberts   OPEN: all week D only 7 to 9.30   CLOSED: 2 weeks Jan   MEALS: Set D £22.50   SERVICE: not inc   CARDS: Delta, MasterCard, Switch, Visa   DETAILS: 45 seats. Private parties: 45 main room. Vegetarian meals. Children's helpings. No smoking in dining room. Wheelchair access (not WC). Occasional music   ACCOMMODATION: 6 rooms, 4 with bath/shower. B&B £27 to £58. Baby facilities (*The Which? Hotel Guide*) £5

HAY-ON-WYE Powys   map 4

The Pavement £

The Pavement, Hay-on-Wye HR3 5BU   COOKING 4
TEL: (01497) 821932   COST £17–£43

Easy to find on the corner of a square in the centre of Hay, The Pavement (formerly Nino's, but with the same chef and owners) is simply but attractively decorated with a few portraits on white-painted brickwork. Its warmth emanates from informed, attentive service – genuinely anxious to please and to involve everybody in proceedings – and the whole approach, from the kitchen as well, seems confident and skilful. Ingredients, some sourced locally, 'could not be fresher', and the cooking successfully captures their quality, as in a 'whole, really soft' chargrilled baby squid, or a thick fillet of poached cod served with lots of mussels in a light tarragon cream sauce. Eastern flavourings, Thai in particular, figure prominently in the repertoire, perhaps mixed into crisply fried fish cakes served with a sweet dipping sauce, or added to sea bass baked in foil.

Presentation is attractive, helpings are generous, and results are consistent, whether a 'rich and satisfying' lentil soup, or an 'accomplished' dish of Brecon venison on a bed of Savoy cabbage with a chocolate-enriched sauce. A blackboard supplements the carte and lists desserts, such as creamy iced nougat with a sharp contrasting raspberry coulis. An annotated list of around thirty agreeable wines stays mostly below £20, and four house wines cost £9.50

CHEF: Rod Lewis   PROPRIETORS: Mr and Mrs C.A. Letts   OPEN: Wed to Sun 12 to 2, 7 to 9.30 (10 Sat)   CLOSED: 25 and 26 Dec   MEALS: alc (main courses L £5 to £8, D £9 to £16). Set L £8.95 (2 courses)   SERVICE: not inc, card slips closed   CARDS: Delta, MasterCard, Switch, Visa   DETAILS: 26 seats. 9 seats outside. Private parties: 30 main room, 30 private room. Vegetarian meals. Children's helpings. Music

---

LLANARMON DYFFRYN CEIRIOG   Wrexham   map 7

▲ West Arms ⁵✳

Llanarmon Dyffryn Ceiriog LL20 7LD
TEL: (01691) 600665   FAX: (01691) 600622
off A5 LLangollen to Oswestry road at Chirk, then   COOKING 2
follow B4500 for 11m   COST £19–£32

Built in 1580 in the Berwyn foothills and progressively extended to include several outbuildings as well as the one-time drovers' inn, West Arms feels as ancient as it sounds, with an abundance of beams and rafters (it is 'not for the tall') and massive inglenook fireplaces. The food's Welsh theme is tempered by cooking 'in the French style', producing roast rack of lamb with a Burgundy sauce, and local beef fillet served with an olive-flavoured pesto. Local game (perhaps pheasant in pastry) puts in an appearance, but fish is a particular strength, from a 'seriously composed' salad with plentiful crab – 'a real pleasure' for its reporter – to brill and crayfish tails in a soured-cream sauce. A savoury usually figures among desserts of, for example, warm cherry tart, or chocolate and banana bread pudding. Anything over £20 is a rarity on a wine list that starts with house French at £8.95.

CHEFS: Grant Williams and David Smart   PROPRIETORS: R.J.W. and M.A. Evans   OPEN: Sun L 12 to 2.15, all week D 7 to 9   MEALS: Set L Sun £12.50, Set D £19.50; bar food available   SERVICE: not inc, card slips closed   CARDS: Delta, MasterCard, Switch, Visa   DETAILS: 90 seats. 100 seats outside. Private parties: 35 main room, 20 to 60 private rooms. Car park. Children's helpings. No smoking in dining room. Wheelchair access (also WC). Music   ACCOMMODATION: 15 rooms, all with bath/shower. TV. Phone. B&B £42.50 to £75. Baby facilities. Fishing (The Which? Hotel Guide)   £5

LLANBERIS   Gwynedd   map 7

Y Bistro ⁵✳

43–45 High Street, Llanberis LL55 4EU
TEL/FAX: (01286) 871278
EMAIL: ybistro@nwi.co.uk   COOKING 2
off A4086, at foot of Mount Snowdon   COST £27–£41

'I wish to recommend this restaurant as a potential new entry into the Guide,' wrote a 'trauma surgeon', who would presumably be shocked to discover that it has been in every edition since 1982. The corner site, originally a shop, has three well-kept dining rooms where Nerys Roberts and her son-in-law serve 'fresh and innovative food'. They do not pretend to follow fashion (lamb is not cooked pink, even on request), but they deploy plump Caernarfon Bay cockles with enthusiasm – on a seafood risotto cake, or with baked fillet of herb-crusted trout – and are happy to gather hedgerow dandelions and primroses to garnish a marinated goats' cheese starter. It can be 'hefty stuff' with gratin toppings and rich sauces, but this is walking country. In any case, what counts is taste: 'the flavour of pork that's long been forgotten,' for example. Homely desserts of brown sugar meringues, or suet pudding, might be balanced by lime cheesecake with toasted coconut. A short, modestly priced wine list starts with a trio each of Welsh and house wines, the latter at £8.95.

CHEFS: Nerys Roberts and Sion Llwyd Elis PROPRIETORS: Danny and Nerys Roberts OPEN: Mon to Sat (and bank hol Sun) D only 7.30 to 9.45 CLOSED: Mon and Tue in winter MEALS: Set D £20 (2 courses) to £26.50 SERVICE: not inc, card slips closed CARDS: Delta, MasterCard, Switch, Visa DETAILS: 52 seats. Private parties: 50 main room, 8 and 22 private rooms. Vegetarian meals. Children's helpings. No smoking in dining room. Wheelchair access (not WC). No music (£5)

LLANDDEINIOLEN Gwynedd   map 7

▲ Ty'n Rhos ⁵✱

Seion, Llanddeiniolen LL55 3AE
TEL: (01248) 670489 FAX: (01248) 670079
EMAIL: bookings@tynrhos.co.uk
off B4366, 5m NE of Caernarfon on road   COOKING 4
signposted Seion   COST £22–£42

Not least of the attractions at this immaculate small hotel are the views – Snowdonia on one side and, on the other, acres of rolling farmland leading to the Menai Straits and Anglesey – which can be enjoyed over pre-dinner drinks from the light and airy conservatory. A no-choice table d'hôte is supplemented by a more ambitious and slightly more expensive version with half a dozen choices at each course, and both are built around a commitment to local produce, including, naturally enough, Welsh lamb, while the kitchen garden supplies fruit and vegetables. Carys Davies's confident cooking strikes a good balance between traditional and modern, perhaps in a nage of mullet and brill with saffron coulis and deep-fried curly kale, or local skate on tomato, dill and caper-infused olive oil. The 'excellent' cheeseboard majors on Welsh cheeses, including a 'delightfully creamy' Harlech with horseradish, and is served with oatcakes and bara brith. Puddings tend to be old favourites with an interesting twist, such as tiramisù with blackcurrant sauce. The wine list offers a modestly priced international selection divided by style, with ten house wines all at £9.50.

CHEFS: Carys Davies and Ian Cashen PROPRIETORS: Lynda and Nigel Kettle OPEN: Tue to Sun L 12 to 1.45, Mon to Sat D 6.45 to 8.45 CLOSED: 2 weeks Christmas, 1 week Jan (open to residents only), 1 week Aug MEALS: alc L (main courses £7 to £13). Set L Mon to Thur £19.50 (2 courses, Set L Sun £14.95, Set D £22.50 to £27 SERVICE: not inc, card slips closed CARDS: Amex, Delta, MasterCard, Switch, Visa DETAILS: 35 seats. Private parties: 30 main room, 20 private room. Car park. Vegetarian meals. Children's helpings. No children under 6 in dining room. No smoking in dining room. No music ACCOMMODATION: 14 rooms, 12 with bath/shower. TV. Phone. B&B £49 to £96. Rooms for disabled. No children under 6 in accommodation. Fishing (*The Which? Hotel Guide*)

The Good Food Guide *is a registered trade mark of Which? Ltd.*

LLANDEGLA Denbighshire
map 7

▲ *Bodidris Hall* ⚡✳

Llandegla LL11 3AL
TEL: (01978) 790434   FAX: (01978) 790335
on A5104, 9m SE of Ruthin

COOKING 3
COST £24–£47

The setting is full of character – a stone-built Tudor house, with atmospheric props including an inglenook fireplace and a suit of armour – indicating that this is a place to linger over meals: three courses, extended to five by virtue of a mid-meal sorbet and coffee. The food is not old-fashioned, though, and Kevin Steel is full of ideas, from a provençale vegetable and lamb terrine, via wild mushroom parfait, to monkfish with lemon grass and ginger sauce. He runs a busy kitchen, prepared to serve a starter of seared tuna on a warm niçoise salad with pesto and an oyster glazed with elderflower sabayon. 'Consistently good throughout' was how one reporter summed up a lunch that began with langoustine and crab soup, and finished with a chocolate pancake layered with Grand Marnier ice cream. A varied, reasonably priced wine list begins with nine house wines under £12.

CHEF: Kevin Steel   PROPRIETOR: W.J. Farden   OPEN: all week 12 to 2, 7 to 9.15   MEALS: Set L £16, Set D £30   SERVICE: not inc, card slips closed   CARDS: Amex, Delta, Diners, MasterCard, Switch, Visa   DETAILS: 40 seats. 24 seats outside. Private parties: 65 main room, 22 private room. Car park. No children on Sat. Jacket and tie. No smoking in dining room. Music ACCOMMODATION: 9 rooms, all with bath/shower. TV. Phone. B&B £80 to £140. Fishing (£5)

LLANDEILO Carmarthenshire
map 4

▲ *Cawdor Arms* ⚡✳

Rhosmaen Street, Llandeilo SA19 6EN
TEL: (01558) 823500   FAX: (01558) 822399
EMAIL: cawdor.arms@btinternet.com

COOKING 3
COST £22–£38

This Georgian inn, with flagstones, antiques and a welcoming fire, makes an attractive setting for appreciative visitors: 'we returned to Cawdor Arms each day looking forward to dinner. We were not disappointed.' The kitchen's priority is Welsh produce – including Brechfa trout and St David's duckling – which Rod Peterson uses in some inventive ways: cannon of Camarthenshire lamb with a ewes'-milk-cheese mousseline on smoked-bacon risotto, for example, or grilled Welsh beef fillet with bean sprouts, ginger, onion and chilli. 'Superb' Towy sewin and cockle mousse pleased one lunchtime visitor, while another (two-and-a-half years old) enjoyed two 'beautifully cooked free-range eggs and a plateful of buttered soldiers'. Rhubarb custard crumble and fudge crème brûlée are comforting ways to finish, while 'formal but friendly' service, and fair prices, help to send most reporters away happy. Light à la carte lunches are served in the sitting room. 'The wine list enables you to drink well at reasonable prices', starting with a trio of house wines under £10.

To find a restaurant in a particular area use the maps at the centre of the book.

CHEF: Rodney Peterson   PROPRIETORS: John and Sylvia Silver   OPEN: all week 12 to 2, 7.30 to 9   MEALS: Set L £13.50, Set D £21. Bar L available   SERVICE: not inc, card slips closed   CARDS: Amex, Delta, MasterCard, Switch, Visa   DETAILS: 60 seats. 30 seats outside. Private parties: 110 main room, 18 and 26 private rooms. Car park. Vegetarian meals. Children's helpings. No smoking in dining room. Wheelchair access (also women's WC). Music   ACCOMMODATION: 17 rooms, all with bath/shower. TV. Phone. B&B £45 to £75. Baby facilities (*The Which? Hotel Guide*) (£5)

LLANDEWI SKIRRID   Monmouthshire   map 4

Walnut Tree Inn ▮

Llandewi Skirrid NP7 8AW
TEL: (01873) 852797   COOKING 7
on B4521, 3m NE of Abergavenny   COST £34–£60

Everything about the Walnut Tree is unpretentious. It is a white-painted former pub on a quiet country road, with pine furniture, close-together tables, a flag-floored bar and non-bookable bistro; beyond is the dining room, distinguished only by a carpet, tablecloths and a display of kitchen pottery. Its casual, functional approach is helped by staff who are friendly and courteous but do not stand on ceremony. This may all seem happily accidental, but in fact it makes an important statement: that eating good food should be a normal part of everyday business. The genius of Franco and Ann Taruschio has been to produce hearty, generous food in open and hospitable fashion, plainly designed for enjoyment and appreciated as such; for this reason alone they should be considered a national treasure.

To have done this for thirty-seven years is a tribute to their dedication, their sense of mission and purpose, which in any case are immediately apparent on reading the handwritten menu of fifteen to twenty choices per course: few other kitchens are as busy and enthusiastic as this. Lady Llanover's salt duck and vincisgrassi maceratese, both old recipes and old stalwarts, neatly express the food's individuality and Welsh-Italian foundation, as perhaps does a dish of roast monkfish and scallops with prawns in a laverbread sauce.

Well-sourced materials have included a 'tip-top' tournedos of mature fillet steak, accurately timed, full of flavour, and with enough texture 'to get your teeth into', in a well-made stock-based sauce scattered with wild mushrooms. Skilful treatment has also produced a well-judged risotto primavera containing asparagus, broad beans, peas and broccoli. Seafood is abundant, although more than one reporter has experienced a less than successful brodetto, complaining of components that were not as pristine as anticipated in a restaurant of this quality; it is significant, however, that support for the enterprise rarely diminishes in the face of occasional disappointment. Desserts run along simple and traditional lines, from fresh strawberries with mascarpone, via banana parfait, to dolce torinese and Malakofftorte. A string of fine Italian wines opens the list, leaving France to play second fiddle with a none the less impressive collection of bins. A small but perfectly formed selection from other major wine-growing countries completes the range, and a good number of bottles cost under £20, including house Italian at £12.50.

CHEF: Franco Taruschio   PROPRIETORS: Franco and Ann Taruschio   OPEN: Tue to Sat 12 to 3, 7 to 10.15   CLOSED: 1 week Christmas, 2 weeks Feb   MEALS: alc (main courses £8 to £17). Cover £1   SERVICE: not inc   CARDS: none   DETAILS: 102 seats. 36 seats outside. Private parties: 46 main room. Car park. Vegetarian meals. Children's helpings. Wheelchair access (also WC). No music. Air-conditioned

---

LLANDRILLO Denbighshire   map 7

▲ *Tyddyn Llan* ⁵⁊✳

Llandrillo LL21 0ST
TEL: (01490) 440264   FAX: (01490) 440414
EMAIL: tyddnllanhotel@compuserve.com | NEW CHEF |
on B4401, 4½ miles S of Corwen   COST £24–£53

Rough stone walls and overhanging gables greet the eye at this extended Georgian country house in rural Wales; inside, Peter Kindred's paintings (he also runs courses) form part of the décor, along with gilt cherubs and Victorian prints. Jason Hornbuckle has left after four years, but Sean Ballington, who arrived just as the *Guide* went to press, looks set to continue the mix of Mediterranean, cosmopolitan and traditional ideas. Expect seared tuna with warm niçoise salad, chicken suprême filled with coriander mousseline, and steamed jam roly-poly. Reports please. Wines cover a good range of styles and prices, starting with a dozen or so sensibly recommended house wines from £12.50 upwards.

CHEF: Sean Ballington   PROPRIETORS: Peter and Bridget Kindred   OPEN: Tue to Sun L 12.30 to 2, all week D 7 to 9   MEALS: Set L £13 (2 courses) to £15, Set D £25 (2 courses) to £27. Light L available   SERVICE: not inc, card slips closed   CARDS: Amex, Delta, Diners, MasterCard, Switch, Visa   DETAILS: 50 seats. 20 seats outside. Private parties: 50 main room, 25 private room. Car park. Vegetarian meals. No smoking in dining room. Wheelchair access (also men's WC). Music   ACCOMMODATION: 10 rooms, all with bath/shower. TV. Phone. B&B £65 to £134. Baby facilities. Fishing (*The Which? Hotel Guide*) (£5)

LLANDUDNO Conwy   map 7

▲ *Bodysgallen Hall* ♥ ⁵⁊✳

Llandudno LL30 1RS
TEL: (01492) 584466   FAX: (01492) 582519
EMAIL: info@bodysgallen-net.com   COOKING 2
off A470, 2m SE of Llandudno   COST £24–£69

The 'magnificent stone house' surrounded by gardens and rolling acres is a gem: 'if I could afford it, I would lodge there permanently,' vowed one supporter. It is a restful place, with open fires, dark wood panelling, antiques and squashy sofas, and a kitchen that applies good ideas to sound ingredients, often involving quite a bit of workmanship. Seafood might be fashioned into a sausage and served in mussel broth, 'spot-on' boned roast poussin has been stuffed with cardamom mousse, and pesto noodles have accompanied pan-fried loin of veal. Partnerships also help to keep up interest: poached pear and tomato salsa with asparagus mousse, or coconut ice cream with chocolate and macadamia nut tartlet. One or two items (such as plain grilled fish or fillet steak) carry a supplement, service is 'attentive and discreet', and wines blend classic styles of the Old World with fresh, bright flavours of the New. Mark-ups can reflect the magnificence of the setting, but there is a decent choice under £20 and a fair number of half-bottles. House French is £12.75.

CHEF: Mike Penny   PROPRIETOR: Historic House Hotels   OPEN: all week 12.30 to 1.45, 7 to 9.30   MEALS: Set L £14.50 (2 courses) to £16.50, Set D £32.50   SERVICE: net prices, card slips closed   CARDS: Delta, MasterCard, Switch, Visa   DETAILS: 60 seats. Private parties: 40 main room, 40 private room. Car park. Vegetarian meals. No children under 8 in dining room. Jacket and tie. No smoking in dining room. Wheelchair access (also WC). Occasional music. Air-conditioned   ACCOMMODATION: 35 rooms, all with bath/shower. TV. Phone. Room only £99 to £225. Rooms for disabled. No children under 8 in accommodation. Swimming pool (*The Which? Hotel Guide*)   £5

▲ *Martin's*

11 Mostyn Avenue, Craig-y-Don,
Llandudno LL30 1YS   COOKING 3
TEL: (01492) 870070   FAX: (01492) 876661   COST £23–£54

The spacious dining room, old fashioned in terms of furnishings and ornaments, stretches from front to back of this modest house in a street of shops set back from the promenade. Chef Martin James, previously at Bodysgallen Hall (see entry above), cooks in firmly classical mode, evident in a 'light and moist' trout mousse (wrapped in smoked salmon and served with queen scallops and a cucumber, green bean, tomato and dill salad), or a beef tomato stuffed with avocado mousse and topped with fresh Conwy crab meat. Portions are generous and flavours can veer towards richness, as in an inspector's main course of five cutlets of Welsh lamb with onion marmalade in a red wine jus, though execution throughout is 'thoroughly professional'. Desserts such as 'rich and luxuriant' dark and white chocolate mousses with Tia Maria sauce have been praised, and Welsh cheeses are served 'in good condition'. Service is 'friendly and open'. The wine list holds few surprises but is well priced. House wines start at £10.50.

CHEF: Martin James   PROPRIETORS: Martin James and Jan Williams   OPEN: Mon to Sat 12 to 2, 5 to 9.30   CLOSED: last 2 weeks Jan   MEALS: alc D (main courses £13 to £19.50). Set L £10.50 (2 courses) to £12.95, Set D before 7 £15.95 (2 courses) to £17.95   SERVICE: not inc, card slips closed   CARDS: Amex, Delta, MasterCard, Switch, Visa   DETAILS: 30 seats. Private parties: 36 main room. Vegetarian meals. Children's helpings. No-smoking area. No smoking before coffee is served. Wheelchair access (not WC). Music   ACCOMMODATION: 4 rooms, all with bath/shower. TV. B&B £30 to £58. No children in accommodation   £5

Richard's

7 Church Walks, Llandudno LL30 2HD   COOKING 2
TEL: (01492) 877924 and 875315   COST £26–£45

This 'warm and friendly' Victorian terraced house offers a relaxed ground-floor room with bare pine tables, and a more dimly lit formal dining area upstairs, both sharing the same menu. A few daily specials combine with the carte to produce a fair choice, and Richard Hendey 'evidently cares greatly about the

LLANDUDNO

ingredients he uses'. 'I've rarely tasted better halibut,' reckoned an inspector, although the sheer number of flavours in a dish, and sometimes the combinations themselves (apple, chicory, pesto and strawberries to accompany first-rate seared salmon, for instance) can militate against success; a pity, since ambition and effort are not in question. Hot and spicy flavours are characteristic: cauliflower and mustard soup with tomato salsa, or salad of beef fillet with a Thai sauce. Butterscotch cheesecake with fruit salad was 'the best part of the meal' for one reporter. A standard, sixty-strong wine list, mostly under £20, begins with house wine at around £10.

CHEFS: Richard Hendey, Gordon McQueen and Chris Jones   PROPRIETOR: Richard Hendey
OPEN: all week D only 5.30 to 11   CLOSED: 25 and 26 Dec   MEALS: alc (main courses £11 to £15)   SERVICE: net prices, card slips closed   CARDS: Amex, Delta, Diners, MasterCard, Switch, Visa   DETAILS: 50 seats. Private parties: 30 main room. Vegetarian meals. Children's helpings. Music

▲ St Tudno Hotel 🍷 ❄✳

Promenade, Llandudno LL30 2LP
TEL: (01492) 874411   FAX: (01492) 860407   COOKING 3
EMAIL: sttudnohotel@btinternet.com   COST £24–£68

Martin and Janette Bland have been at their Victorian promenade hotel opposite the pier for nearly thirty years, and David Harding in the kitchen for ten, and it seems they have got what their customers want down to a fine art. In the sunny Garden Room, hanging baskets, wicker chairs and crisp linen (and harp music on Saturday evenings) provide the setting for fine dishes cooked with flair. The seasonal gourmet menu is supplemented by a daily one to offer some flexibility, and diners can dip and dive between the two. Most raw materials have not had to travel far before being spun into crab and laverbread tart, Conwy mussel risotto, lamb shank with garlic mashed potato, or Herefordshire duckling with tomato compote. A vegetarian dish of the day could well involve ratatouille. 'Celtic' cheeses make an attractive alternative to iced coconut parfait or pineapple and strawberry fritters. Six pages of wines from Willi Opitz (Austria), d'Arenberg (McLaren Vale), Lawson's Dry Hills (Marlborough) and Ch. Musar (Lebanon) get the wine list off to a flying start, and those who feel the need to explore further will find that the combination of quality and interest is maintained. House French is £9.50 or £11.50.

CHEF: David Harding   PROPRIETORS: Martin and Janette Bland   OPEN: all week 12.30 to 1.45, 7 to 9.30 (9 Sun)   MEALS: Set L £16.95, Set D £24 (2 courses) to £32.50   SERVICE: not inc, card slips closed   CARDS: Amex, Delta, Diners, MasterCard, Switch, Visa   DETAILS: 60 seats. Private parties: 70 main room. Car park. Vegetarian meals. Children's helpings. No babies/toddlers at D. No smoking in dining room. Wheelchair access (not WC). Occasional music. Air-conditioned   ACCOMMODATION: 19 rooms, all with bath/shower. TV. Phone. B&B £65 to £250. Baby facilities. Swimming pool (*The Which? Hotel Guide*) (£5)

❄✳ *indicates that smoking is either banned altogether or that a dining-room is maintained for non-smokers. The symbol does not apply to restaurants that simply have no-smoking areas.*

LLANFIHANGEL NANT MELAN Powys

map 4

▲ *Red Lion Inn* ¦✗ £

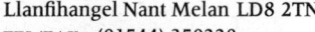

Llanfihangel Nant Melan LD8 2TN
TEL/FAX: (01544) 350220
on A44 Rhayader to Kington road, 3m W of
New Radnor

COOKING 4
COST £17–£35

Friendly owners at this simple, remote, sixteenth-century, no-frills pub beside
the A44 oversee a beamed bar and conservatory-style dining room, where
Gareth Johns's commendable use of Welsh produce yields soused Mumbles
mackerel, black beef with onion relish, and Powys pork with sauerkraut; an 'old
favourites' board of scampi, gammon, and steak speaks for itself. The house pâté
is a smooth, smoky, gamey, herb-flavoured triumph, bread is tiptop, and,
although salads might be improved upon, 'attention to our personal tastes was
gratifying', according to a garlic-guzzler.

Citrus syrup tart with blackcurrants might feature among desserts, along with
chocolate mousse cake or banana and toffee shortbread. Reporters don't expect
sophisticated accommodation, which is just as well, although they do get 'a good
fry-up' for breakfast (thick-cut bacon, 'old-fashioned' sausages), as well as lots
of hospitality and 'discreetly cheerful courtesy'. Indeed, service is universally
considered one of the strengths, as are the very fair prices, which also apply to a
short wine list, starting with four house wines under £7.

CHEF: Gareth Johns PROPRIETORS: Keith, Elizabeth and Gareth Johns OPEN: Sun L 12 to 2,
Wed to Mon D 7 to 9 (9.30 Sat) CLOSED: 1 week Nov, D 25 Dec, 26 Dec MEALS: alc (main
courses £6 to £13) SERVICE: not inc, card slips closed CARDS: Delta, MasterCard, Switch,
Visa DETAILS: 40 seats. 16 seats outside. Private parties: 24 main room, 20 and 24 private
rooms. Car park. Vegetarian meals. Children's helpings. No smoking in 1 dining room. No
music ACCOMMODATION: 3 rooms, all with bath/shower. B&B £20 to £40

LLANGAMMARCH WELLS Powys

map 4

▲ *Lake Country House* � ¦✗

Llangammarch Wells LD4 4BS
TEL: (01591) 620202 FAX: (01591) 620457
EMAIL: lakehotel@ndirect.co.uk
off B483 at Garth, 6m W of Builth Wells

COOKING 4
COST £26–£53

A house more of size than character, Lake sits in 50 acres, with lawns running
down to a river; inside, where oil portraits hang on walls and floral fabrics
abound in the dining room, the scale is just as grand. Jeremy Medley deals in
mostly simple but well-considered ideas. After a soup appetiser (such as apple
and celery with walnut and herb dumplings) might come a puff pastry quail pie,
or Cornish scallops with tomato compote and fried onions, before a choice of five
main courses. A degree of restraint helps to keep things in focus, as in Brecon
venison with potato galette and plum chutney, or pot-roast pork with black
pudding and vanilla, while desserts might typically include a hot soufflé, and
maybe warm chocolate tart or steamed carrot and cardamom sponge. Service has
been 'slick and professional'. The highlight of a lengthy wine list has to be the

long line of clarets stretching back to 1959, including a number of first growths and 'super seconds' at remarkably good prices. Fans of other French classics and those with a fondness for Spain are not neglected. A worldly collection of 'special recommendations' opens at £9.75.

CHEF: Jeremy Medley PROPRIETORS: Mr and Mrs J.P. Mifsud OPEN: all week 12.30 to 2, 7.30 to 9 MEALS: Set L £18.50, Set D £32.50 SERVICE: not inc, card slips closed CARDS: Amex, Delta, Diners, MasterCard, Switch, Visa DETAILS: 40 seats. Private parties: 80 main room, 20 to 50 private rooms. Car park. Vegetarian meals. Children's helpings. No children under 7 at D. Jacket and tie. No smoking in dining room. Wheelchair access (not WC). No music ACCOMMODATION: 19 rooms, all with bath/shower. TV. Phone. B&B £80 to £210. Rooms for disabled. Baby facilities. Fishing (*The Which? Hotel Guide*) £5

LLANRHIDIAN Swansea   map 4

Welcome to Town ⁵⧉

Llanrhidian SA3 1EH
TEL: (01792) 390015
on B4295, 10m W of Swansea

COOKING 1
COST £25–£36

Standing on the village green opposite the church, this low whitewashed building with views over the estuary was clearly once a pub. Now it is an informal country bistro, run by the Allen family, with Sheila at the stoves and Robert ensuring the 'welcome'. The style is modern Welsh, using local produce in traditional and more innovative dishes. Starters may include onion and olive tart, or the party piece, Llanrhidian bun, a brioche stuffed with cockles, laverbread, leek and bacon. Smoked duck breast as a main course may come sliced on a bed of red cabbage: 'so moist that no sauce was required'. Sheila's heart is in her baking and patisserie, so for dessert try something like apple and blackcurrant crumble tart. Like the menus, the short wine list changes monthly, and most choices are under £12; house Chilean is £10.

CHEF: Sheila Allen PROPRIETORS: Robert, Sheila and Tim Allen OPEN: Tue to Sat 12.30 to 2, 7 to 8.30 CLOSED: Oct, bank hols MEALS: alc (main courses £9.50 to £12) SERVICE: not inc, card slips closed CARDS: Amex, Delta, MasterCard, Switch, Visa DETAILS: 36 seats. 20 seats outside. Private parties: 8 main room. Car park. Vegetarian meals. No children under 14 at D. No smoking in dining room. Wheelchair access (not WC). Music £5

LLANSANFFRAID GLAN CONWY Conwy   map 7

▲ Old Rectory ▮ ⁵⧉

Llanrwst Road, Llansanffraid Glan Conwy,
nr Conwy LL28 5LF
TEL: (01492) 580611 FAX: (01492) 584555
EMAIL: oldrect@aol.com
on A470, ½m S of junction with A55

COOKING 6
COST £44–£60

Panoramic views towards the Conwy estuary greet visitors to this simple country-house hotel, and 'the gardens are worth mentioning' too. Interesting paintings and antiques decorate the house, curtains hang in swathes, the atmosphere is 'friendly and homely', and Michael Vaughan is a courteous and 'indefatigable' host. Everybody gathers in the panelled lounge in time for the single sitting: in a spacious dining room with polished tables and bone-handled cutlery. There is no choice before dessert (unless arranged when booking), and the pace tends to be leisurely.

Wendy Vaughan's food consists of 'excellent ingredients precisely cooked'. The first course is typically fish or vegetarian, the second fowl, or perhaps loin of Welsh mountain lamb, and dishes are kept relatively simple and thus coherent: for example, guinea fowl stuffed with cabbage and pearl barley, served with rösti and a flavourful jus. Results generally triumph: one reporter's starter of warm goats' cheese with a nut topping, sauté potatoes, mixed herbs and tomato coulis 'sounded complex, but was a super blend of simple flavours, well executed'. Combinations can be inventive – lemon grass and chanterelles to accompany chicken breast with artichoke and celeriac mash – and presentation is attractive. Desserts might include strawberry cheesecake with wine jelly, bread is freshly baked, and cheeses (some Welsh) are 'served at their peak'. France is still the star of the benevolently priced list, but bottles from Germany, Italy, Iberia and the New World make the most of their supporting roles. Half-bottles impress both for their number and range. House French is £14.90.

CHEF: Wendy Vaughan   PROPRIETORS: Michael and Wendy Vaughan   OPEN: all week D only 7.30 for 8 (1 sitting)   CLOSED: 2nd week Nov, 20 Dec to 1 Feb   MEALS: Set D £29.90   SERVICE: not inc, card slips closed   CARDS: Delta, MasterCard, Switch, Visa   DETAILS: 16 seats. Private parties: 12 main room. Car park. No children under 5 in dining room. No smoking in dining room. Wheelchair access (not WC). No music   ACCOMMODATION: 6 rooms, all with bath/shower. TV. Phone. B&B £99 to £149. No children under 5 in accommodation (*The Which? Hotel Guide*)

LLANWRTYD WELLS Powys   map 4

▲ *Carlton House* ▼ ✳

Dolycoed Road, Llanwrtyd Wells LD5 4RA   COOKING 6
TEL: (01591) 610248   FAX: (01591) 610242   COST £22–£52

In what claims to be the smallest town in Wales, this four-storeyed Victorian villa, 'now a rather fetching shade of red', is a 'mildly eccentric' restaurant-with-rooms. The south-facing dining room, with original nineteenth-century wooden panelling, is where residents get specially tailored set menus (as well as an impressive breakfast), and there is a short daily-changing carte. Most ingredients, Mary Ann Gilchrist informs us, are now either free-range or organic, with increasing input from local producers, which brings in its wake a greater sense of seasonality: peppered Black beef fillet might appear in a warm summer salad with tarragon and caper sauce or, in spring, with mash and buttered cabbage.

For a restaurant so far from the sea, fish is considered 'noteworthy': perhaps halibut with squid ink pasta in a lemon butter sauce. To start, variations on a mixed-leaf salad have included a version with quail's eggs, Carmarthen ham and lentil dressing, and one with baked goats' cheese and apple croustade; to finish there is usually a plate of Celtic cheeses, a savoury rarebit, or perhaps profiteroles with butterscotch sauce. 'What we ate was simple, but very well done,' concluded one reporter. Meals are helped along by Alan Gilchrist's 'quiet professionalism and invariable good humour'. Wines have been chosen for their quality and individuality – Canada and Mexico provide a white and red respectively – and mark-ups are kept sensibly low (Chilean house wines from Concha y Toro are £9.95). Concise tasting notes aid selection, though Alan will gladly advise. Dom. de Triennes supplies an impressive trio of French varietals from the Vin de Pays du Var: Viognier £16.25, Merlot £16.25, and Syrah £14.50.

CHEF: Mary Ann Gilchrist   PROPRIETORS: Alan and Mary Ann Gilchrist   OPEN: Tue to Sat L 12.30 to 1.45, Mon to Sat D 7 to 8.30   CLOSED: Christmas   MEALS: alc (main courses £13.50 to £18). Set L £9.95 (2 courses) to £12.50, Set D £16.50 (2 courses) to £19.95   SERVICE: not inc, card slips closed   CARDS: Delta, MasterCard, Switch, Visa   DETAILS: 14 seats. Private parties: 14 main room. Vegetarian meals. No smoking in dining room. No music   ACCOMMODATION: 7 rooms, all with bath/shower. TV. B&B £30 to £70 (*The Which? Hotel Guide*)

LLYSWEN Powys   map 4

▲ *Griffin Inn* ₹✳

Llyswen LD3 0UR
TEL: (01874) 754241   FAX: (01874) 754592   COOKING 1
EMAIL: info@griffin-inn.freeserve.co.uk   COST £20–£41

This creeper clad sporting inn (bedrooms are named after salmon flies and lures) on the main road from Builth to Brecon has been steadily refurbished over the decade and a half that it has been in the Stockton family. Its strength is well-sourced materials: free-range eggs, herbs from the garden, and seafood from south and west Wales, including mussels, crab, cockles, plaice, sole and sewin. Seasonal poultry and game run from Michaelmas goose to pheasant, partridge, grouse, woodcock and snipe from local shoots, while rabbit, hare and venison make regular appearances. Slow roasts and casseroles are the kitchen's mainstay: braised shank of Radnorshire lamb, or pot-roast Black beef, preceded by simple starters of soup or garlic mushrooms. Desserts embrace treacle tart, fruit pavlovas and crumbles. Poor service marked one visitor's stay, but real ales are a draw, and over a dozen wines are available by the glass.

CHEFS: Richard Stockton and Andrew Addis Fuller   PROPRIETORS: Richard and Di Stockton   OPEN: Sun L 12 to 2, Mon to Sat D 7 to 9   CLOSED: 25 and 26 Dec   MEALS: alc (main courses L £6 to £9, D £10 to £15)   SERVICE: not inc, card slips closed   CARDS: Amex, Delta, Diners, MasterCard, Switch, Visa   DETAILS: 80 seats. 16 seats outside. Private parties: 40 main room, 16 private room. Car park. Vegetarian meals. Children's helpings. No smoking in dining room. No music   ACCOMMODATION: 7 rooms, all with bath/shower. TV. Phone. B&B £45 to £80. Fishing (*The Which? Hotel Guide*)   £5

▲ *Llangoed Hall* ₹✳

Llyswen LD3 0YP
TEL: (01874) 754525   FAX: (01874) 754545
EMAIL: 101543.3211@compuserve.com   NEW CHEF
on A470 2m NW of LLyswen   COST £34–£57

Dating back to 1632, the restored house operates on a grand scale: set in 17 acres on the banks of the River Wye, it is filled with antiques and Laura Ashley fabrics (Sir Bernard has owned it for ten years). Joseph Croan arrived from London just as the *Guide* went to press, and indications are that his repertoire will include vichyssoise soup, salmon with spinach and a chive velouté, and calf's liver with Lyonnaise potatoes, with desserts of warm chocolate fondant with praline ice cream. Set-price dinner menus offer no choice. Reports please. The aristocratic wine list seems largely directed towards expense accounts, although it includes a few under £20, including a quartet of house wines.

CHEF: Joseph Croan   PROPRIETOR: Sir Bernard Ashley   OPEN: all week 12.15 to 2, 7.15 to 9.30   MEALS: Set L £18.50 (2 courses) to £24.50, Set D £35   SERVICE: not inc, card slips closed   CARDS: Amex, Delta, Diners, MasterCard, Switch, Visa   DETAILS: 100 seats. 40 seats outside. Private parties: 50 main room, 16 to 50 private rooms. Car park. Vegetarian meals. No children under 8 in dining room. No smoking in dining room. Wheelchair access (also WC). Occasional music   ACCOMMODATION: 23 rooms, all with bath/shower. TV. Phone. B&B £155 to £425. No children under 8 in accommodation. Fishing (*The Which? Hotel Guide*)   £5

MATHRY Pembrokeshire   map 4

Ann FitzGerald's Farmhouse Kitchen ▼ £

Mabws Fawr, Mathry SA62 5JB
TEL: (01348) 831347   COOKING 2
off A487, 6m SW of Fishguard   COST £19–£43

The setting, at the end of a long narrow lane, can seem perplexing, with a collection of cottages, a yard, and the farmhouse itself: walk through a kitchen store, straight to table (there is no bar) in a large beamed dining room that would make a decorator's mouth water. The choice is enormous: a balanced carte of around thirty items from which set-price options are extracted, plus a separate vegetarian menu. Seasonal items include braised sewin, game pâté and roast grouse with port sauce, and portions can be generous: a starter of large spicy fish cakes with soy and ginger would have satisfied one diner as a main course. Sauces at inspection tended to overpower: a chilli-hot chicken Bumbu Bali, for example, and 'fresh, juicy, meaty' lobster with a brandy and cream sauce. For one couple, the cheeseboard alone was worth the visit, while desserts have included tangy lemon tart, and bread-and-butter pudding with whisky custard. France fills most of the cellar, although a few choice bottles from other countries can also be found on the racks. Prices are fair, beginning at £10 for house wines from France, Italy and Germany.

CHEFS/PROPRIETORS: Ann and Lionel FitzGerald   OPEN: all week 12 to 2, 6 to 9   MEALS: alc (main courses L £6 to £14, D £12 to £15). Set L £12, Set D £17   SERVICE: not inc, card slips closed   CARDS: MasterCard, Visa   DETAILS: 30 seats. 12 seats outside. Car park. Vegetarian meals. Children's helpings. Wheelchair access (also WC). Music   £5

The 2001 Guide *will be published before Christmas 2000. Reports on meals are most welcome at any time of the year, but are particularly valuable in the spring (no later than June). Send them to* The Good Food Guide, *FREEPOST, 2 Marylebone Road, London NW1 4DF. Or email your report to guidereports@which.co.uk.*

The Guide *relies on feedback from its readers. Especially welcome are reports on new restaurants appearing in the book for the first time. All letters to the* Guide *are acknowledged.*

NANTGAREDIG Carmarthenshire   map 4

▲ *Four Seasons*

Cwmtwrch Farm Hotel, Nantgaredig SA32 7NY
TEL: (01267) 290238   FAX: (01267) 290808   COOKING 3
on B4310, ½m N of Nantgaredig   COST £30–£40

In a quiet rural spot off the Nantgaredig to Brechfa road, this collection of 'tidy
and tasteful' stone buildings houses a light and airy white-walled restaurant
that is the essence of 'rural modernity'. Tables are sensibly spaced, the
atmosphere is relaxed, and helpful staff cope well even when busy, serving four
courses from a balanced menu. Local produce is the foundation – beef is Welsh
Black, smoked salmon comes from five miles up the road, Camarthen ham is off
the market, herbs are from the garden – yet ideas are lively and most un-Welsh:
salt-marsh lamb has come with aubergine caponata, Towy salmon with spring
onion couscous, and local shellfish has produced a starter of crab cakes with red
pesto dressing. Desserts of strawberry pavlova or pear and almond tart have a
more traditional bias, and Welsh cheeses might include Llanboidy and
Penybont. The small wine company that operates from the premises yields an
intelligent, manageable and fairly priced list, starting with a trio of house wines
at £9.50.

CHEFS/PROPRIETORS: Charlotte Pasetti and Maryann Wright   OPEN: Tue to Sat D only 7.30 to
9.30   CLOSED: 25 Dec   MEALS: Set D £22.50   SERVICE: not inc, card slips closed   CARDS:
Delta, MasterCard, Switch, Visa   DETAILS: 45 seats. 6 seats outside. Private parties: 60 main
room. Car park. Vegetarian meals. Children's helpings. Wheelchair access (not WC). Music
ACCOMMODATION: 5 rooms, all with bath/shower. TV. B&B £40 to £60. Baby facilities. Swimming
pool (*The Which? Hotel Guide*) £5

NEWPORT Pembrokeshire   map 4

▲ *Cnapan* ⚡✳

East Street, Newport SA42 0SY   COOKING 2
TEL: (01239) 820575   FAX: (01239) 820878   COST £16–£36

Cnapan is a large, comfortable listed townhouse, run by two generations of the
Lloyd/Cooper family, their treasures displayed on walls and dressers
throughout. The men are welcoming and efficient front-of-house, while mother
and daughter prepare the food, mostly using locally sourced produce, including
cheese, beef, lamb and organic vegetables. Seafood depends on the catch,
perhaps turning up simple moist salmon with piquant herby mayonnaise.
Attractive choices at good prices on the evening carte range from lamb with
puréed pea and leek to a fruit and spice stuffed pepper topped with goats' cheese,
while lighter weekday lunches tend to include wholesome dishes such as
faggots with onion gravy, or oat-based carrot and cashew nut flan. A 'perfect'
meringue with raspberry sauce has been an enthusiastically reported dessert.
Yet more local produce – Welsh Monnow Valley – appears in the short and
modestly priced wine list; house wines are £8.75.

▲ *Beech Hill Country House, Ardmore Restaurant* 🍴✹

32 Ardmore Road, Londonderry BT47 3QP
TEL: (01504) 349279, changing to (028) 7134 9279
FAX: (01504) 345366, changing to (028) 7134 5366
EMAIL: info@beech-hill.com
turn off A6 Londonderry to Belfast road at Faughan
Bridge and proceed to Ardmore chapel; hotel is | NEW CHEF |
opposite chapel   COST £25–£63

Once again Beech Hill – an elegant early-Georgian pile standing in 32 acres of
lush parkland awash with ponds and waterfalls – changed chefs just as the *Guide*
went to press. Anthony McTrew moved up from second chef, and, if he
continues in like vein his menus will include quite a bit of up-to-the-minute
mixing and matching of culinary idioms: perhaps chicken raviolo with truffled
Puy lentils and spinach, followed by roast pork with sauerkraut and Toulouse
sausage, then lemon tart with orange ice cream and raspberry coulis. Plenty of
New World flavours crop up on the broadly based wine list, which opens with
six house selections including Chilean Merlot and Chardonnay at £11.90.

CHEF: Anthony McTrew   PROPRIETOR: Mr S. Donnelly   OPEN: all week 12 to 2.30, 6 to 9.45
CLOSED: 24 and 25 Dec, L 26 Dec   MEALS: alc (main courses £15 to £18). Set L £16.95, Set D
£24.95 to £41.95   SERVICE: not inc, card slips closed   CARDS: Amex, MasterCard, Switch,
Visa   DETAILS: 60 seats. Private parties: 80 main room, 15 to 80 private rooms. Car park.
Vegetarian meals. Children's helpings. No smoking in dining room. Wheelchair access (also
WC). Music   ACCOMMODATION: 27 rooms, all with bath/shower. TV. Phone. B&B £57.50 to
£125. Rooms for disabled. Baby facilities

Ramore ♟

The Harbour, Portrush BT56 8BN
TEL: (01265) 824313, changing to (028) 7082 4313   COOKING 4
FAX: (01265) 823194, changing to (028) 7082 3194   COST £28–£45

This bright, first-floor room in an unprepossessing building has views out over
the small harbour. An open-plan kitchen adds to the genial atmosphere, the
black-and-white décor and background jazz setting a laid-back and informal
tone. George McAlpin's menu scans the world for inspriation, running from
goats' cheese quesadillas with sour cream, black-bean salsa and Mexican salad,
to chicken fillet stuffed with garlic butter on white truffle pomme purée. An
inspection meal started with a visually stunning prawn cocktail: a small
mountain of salad leaves topped with coriander and red onion, boiled eggs and
'plenty of fish', served on a large, dramatic, transparent blue plate. Fish of the day
– written along with other specials on a blackboard above the kitchen – might be
monkfish on puff pastry with lobster, shiitake mushrooms and truffle cream,
while the regular menu has turned up rack of lamb with gnocchi, grilled
vegetables and pesto. Desserts are 'all familiar items' but with 'some nice
touches': peach Melba comes with peach schnapps, lemon tart with mascarpone,

CHEF: Judith Cooper PROPRIETORS: Michael and Judith Cooper, and John and Eluned Lloyd
OPEN: Wed to Mon L 12 to 2, Mon and Wed to Sat D 6.45 to 9 (Sun D by arrangement) CLOSED:
25 and 26 Dec, Jan and Feb MEALS: alc (main courses L £5 to £6.50, D £11.50 to £13.50)
SERVICE: not inc, card slips closed CARDS: Delta, MasterCard, Visa DETAILS: 36 seats. 30
seats outside. Private parties: 36 main room. Car park. Vegetarian meals. Children's helpings.
No smoking in dining room. Wheelchair access (also WC). Occasional music
ACCOMMODATION: 5 rooms, all with bath/shower. TV. B&B £28. Baby facilities (*The Which? Hotel
Guide*)

PEMBROKE Pembrokeshire   map 4

Left Bank ₅⋇

63 Main Street, Pembroke SA71 4DA   COOKING 2
TEL: (01646) 622333   COST £17–£38

Bold Parisian street scenes cover the walls, café-style tables are simply set, and
Andrew Griffith's enthusiasm for combining Welsh produce with more voguish
ingredients produces a spirited modern menu. He takes in sturdy dishes of
Welsh Black beef with parsnips, alongside lamb 'steak' on dauphinoise potato,
with a well-reduced stock sauce. There might also be a homely soup of creamy,
mildly savoured leek and potato with an indulgent twirl of truffle oil, or more
ambitious items such as ravioli of lobster and cockles.

   The food is generally tasty and well presented, if patchy in execution, but has
produced a lively smoked mozzarella and tomato risotto, a chunky, crunchy,
salmon fish cake with a creamy curry sauce, and a beautifully presented
caramelised lemon tart with vanilla ice cream and raspberry coulis. Lunches are
lighter and reasonably priced, and a serviceable, drinker-friendly wine list starts
with five house wines under £10.

CHEF: Andrew Griffith PROPRIETOR: Gareth Griffith OPEN: Tue to Sat 12 to 2.30, 7 to 9.30
CLOSED: 25 and 26 Dec, first 2 weeks Jan MEALS: alc L (main courses £2.50 to £5). Set L and D
£19 (2 courses) to £23 SERVICE: not inc, card slips closed CARDS: Delta, MasterCard, Switch,
Visa DETAILS: 30 seats. Private parties: 30 main room, 40 private room. Vegetarian meals.
Children's helpings. No smoking in dining room. Wheelchair access (not WC). Music.
Air-conditioned £5

PONTFAEN Pembrokeshire   map 4

▲ *Tregynon Farmhouse* ₅⋇

Pontfaen SA65 9TU
TEL: (01239) 820531 FAX: (01239) 820808
EMAIL: tregynon@uk-holidays.co.uk
at junction of B4313 and B4329, take B4313 towards   COOKING 2
Fishguard, then take first right, and first right again   COST £29–£50

This sixteenth-century converted farmhouse in the Gwaun Valley, with thick
stone walls, wooden beams and an inglenook fireplace, serves three-course
dinners in its brace of small dining rooms. The Heards have made the rotating
menu something of an art form and, for the sake of those who stay two weeks,
never repeat a starter or main course (or even a vegetable cooked the same way)

during a fifteen-day period. Given that canapés are on a seven-day rotation, and supplementary dishes on a three-day rotation, it is quite likely the Heards could calculate the trajectory of an interplanetary space probe using only the back of an envelope. The food needs to be ordered well in advance too, which not all reporters are comfortable with. Starters might feature cheese (grilled goats'-cheese muffins), soups have included mulligatawny, and mains typically take in fish (plaice fillets in a garlic mushroom sauce), meat (turkey escalopes schnitzel style) and vegetarian options (cauliflower and broccoli roulade). Desserts such as chocolate and orange pudding, or tiramisù, make a regular appearance, and around forty wines are, like much else, extensively annotated; house Touraine is £11.45.

CHEFS/PROPRIETORS: Peter and Jane Heard OPEN: all week D only 7.30 to 8.30 CLOSED: 31 Dec to 3 Jan MEALS: Set D £20.95 (£19.95 for residents) SERVICE: not inc CARDS: Delta, MasterCard, Switch, Visa DETAILS: 24 seats. Private parties: 14 main room, 10 private room. Car park. Vegetarian meals. No children under 6 in dining room. No smoking in dining room. Music ACCOMMODATION: 6 rooms, all with bath/shower. TV. Phone. B&B £60 to £77. No children under 6 in accommodation (*The Which? Hotel Guide*)

PORTHGAIN Pembrokeshire   map 4

Harbour Lights 🍴✹

Porthgain, nr St David's SA62 5BL
TEL: (01348) 831549   FAX: (01348) 831193
EMAIL: harblights@aol.com   COOKING 4
off A487 at Croesgoch, 4m W of Mathry   COST £33–£40

'We are almost a fish restaurant,' writes Annie Davies, who still aims to provide for meat eaters (and vegetarians too, with prior notice). Their achievement, aided by husband, partner, mother-in-law and son, is 'admirable use of fine local and organic produce', professionally and informally served. Visitors are charmed first by the remarkable setting: three bayside cottages knocked into one, high cliffs and imposing lime kilns towering above. Inside, the walls are dark terracotta, the tables wooden, the decoration supplied by wild flowers, candles and local artists' works. Then the food charms too: an inspector rated laverbread and spinach gratin with cockles and bacon a 'superb' combination of textures and tastes (the sisters gather the laver themselves). Praise has also come the way of rich onion soup, steamed Dover sole fillets with a buttery, lemony parsley sauce, and vegetables that may include pommes Anna and creamed cabbage with tarragon. Well-kept local cheeses are served with apple and chicory; alternatively, finish with 'perfect, golden' raspberry meringue with fruit compote. Organic wines feature in the short, well-annotated list; house wine is £9.75.

CHEFS: Anne Marie Davies and Bernadette Lomax PROPRIETOR: Anne Marie Davies OPEN: summer Wed to Sun and winter Fri and Sat (other days in winter by arrangement) D only 6.30 to 9.30; L by arrangement only CLOSED: Christmas MEALS: Set D £14.95 (1 course) to £24 SERVICE: not inc CARDS: Delta, MasterCard, Switch, Visa DETAILS: 50 seats. 20 seats outside. Private parties: 25 main room, 15 private room. Car park. Children's helpings. No smoking in dining room. Wheelchair access (not WC). Music

---

PORTMEIRION Gwynedd   map 7

▲ *Hotel Portmeirion* ▮ ⅖✳

Portmeirion LL48 6ET
TEL: (01766) 770000   FAX: (01766) 771331
EMAIL: hotel@portmeirion-village.com   COOKING 2
off A487, signposted from Minffordd   COST £17–£53

Designed by Sir Clough Williams Ellis, long before Disneyland, this secluded, fairy-tale Italianate village is a riot of steeples, rotundas, loggias, castles and gateways. The hotel – blinding white and trade-mark sea green – is 'absolutely charming', with a huge, theatrical, semi-circular dining room that overlooks the estuary. Colin Pritchard makes use of local suppliers and is developing an on-site vegetable garden, but results are mixed: an inspection meal was 'full of contradictions', from a poorly conceived trio of fish with cucumber noodles and vanilla butter, via a disappointing duck main course, to a 'quite gorgeous and very well-made' white chocolate dessert (soft mousse in a hard shell) with slivers of poached fig and pear in a spicy red wine sauce. The kitchen may be on firmer ground when serving plainer dishes: highlights of one winter meal were smoked Welsh salmon, beef tournedos and tarte Tatin. Both menu and plentiful staff are bilingual, as is the wine list. The *Bwrgwyn gwyn* (white Burgundy) section, like most of the rest of the list, is high on quality, and the number of attractive bins at £15 or under speaks volumes about sommelier Brian Walshe's ability to combine low prices with palatability.

CHEFS: Colin Pritchard, Billy Taylor and Olivier Piffaudat   PROPRIETOR: Portmeirion Ltd   OPEN: Tue to Sun L 12.30 to 2, all week D 7 to 9.45   CLOSED: 9 Jan to 4 Feb   MEALS: Set L Tue to Sat £10.50 to £13.50, Set L Sun £15, Set D £35   SERVICE: not inc, card slips closed   CARDS: Amex, Delta, Diners, MasterCard, Switch, Visa   DETAILS: 100 seats. Private parties: 100 main room, 12, 30 private rooms. Car park. Vegetarian meals. Children's helpings. No smoking in dining room. No music   ACCOMMODATION: 40 rooms, all with bath/shower. TV. Phone. Room only £84 to £200. Baby facilities. Swimming pool (*The Which? Hotel Guide*)

PWLLGLOYW Powys   map 4

Seland Newydd ⅖✳

Pwllgloyw LD3 9PY
TEL: (01874) 690282   COOKING 2
on B4520, 4m N of Brecon   COST £27–£42

Neatness is not the prime concern at this long, pale yellow roadside pub in the heart of Wales, but there is 'a certain bare-bones charm' to its well-used bar and long narrow dining room. Maynard Harvey serves up blackboard bar meals and a printed carte at both lunch and dinner, the latter taking in stir-fry chicken in filo pastry with a sweet-and-sour sauce, a mould of rather solid smoked trout 'mousse' wrapped in smoked salmon, and a huge, tender beef fillet tournedos with vegetables and potato rösti. Desserts have combined coffee and Baileys in a cheesecake, and white chocolate and passion fruit in a liquidy mousse encased in a brandy-snap biscuit. The food at inspection was rather more ambitious and complex than the kitchen was able to deliver successfully, but the wine list includes a covetable Hunter's Sauvignon Blanc from Freya Harvey's native New Zealand. House French is £8.75.

CHEF: Maynard Harvey PROPRIETORS: Maynard and Freya Harvey OPEN: all week 12 to 2, 7 to 9 MEALS: alc (main courses £11 to £14). Bar L and D available SERVICE: not inc, card slips closed CARDS: Delta, MasterCard, Switch, Visa DETAILS: 70 seats. 40 seats outside. Private parties: 35 main room. Car park. Vegetarian meals. Children's helpings. No smoking in dining room. Wheelchair access (not WC). Music

PWLLHELI Gwynedd WELSH 2000 STAR map 7

▲ *Plas Bodegroes*

Nefyn Road, Pwllheli LL53 5TH
TEL: (01758) 612363 FAX: (01758) 701247 COOKING 7
on A497, 1m W of Pwllheli COST £23–£52

Separated from the main road by rhododendrons and an avenue of ancient beech trees, Plas Bodegroes is a white-painted Georgian manor house with a dining room of 'cool restfulness', thanks to its hardwood floor, sea-green walls, and well-lit modern Welsh paintings. 'Very stylish' is how it appears, and the elegant surroundings are matched by experienced and professional service from Gunna Chown and helpers. Back in the kitchen after an extended sabbatical, Chris Chown now puts the polish on what was already a very accomplished operation under Shaun Mitchell. The food combines both classical and adventurous streaks – from fillet of Welsh Black beef with parsley dumpling and braised oxtail, to Thai fish cakes with coriander beurre blanc – and 'excellent raw materials go without saying'.

Flavour combinations are striking, as shown in the clean, sharp directness of a thick slab of tuna, seared so briefly that it amounted to raw tuna with a crust, then cooled and thinly sliced, which came on ribbons of cucumber with a blob of wasabi and a sesame oil dressing. Presentation is notably spare – 'this is the last place where you'd find anything non-essential in a dish' – yet flavours and textures combine in 'almost flamboyant brilliance'. Slices of duck breast buttressing a mound of finely sliced red cabbage were partnered at inspection by a roughly shaped cake of layered duck confit and wafer-thin potato, each item 'perfectly prepared'. 'And I shan't forget the surrounding sauce in a hurry': an intense and sophisticated reduction of stock, port and orange.

Admirable technical skills are also evident in pastrywork: take, for example, the 'stunning simplicity' of a warm tart of mixed nuts (Brazils, pine nuts and pistachios among them) in butterscotch sauce with a creamy scoop of mascarpone. Extras, in the form of nibbles, appetisers, bread and petits fours are as impressive as everything else. When it comes to wines, the Chowns continue to laud the food-matching abilities of those from Alsace; indeed, the Tokay-Pinot Gris Reserve 1995, Rolly-Gassmann (£26) would be a perfect partner for tuna. However, those wary of Alsatians will find bottles of good breed from other key regions. Prices begin at £12 for house vins de pays.

denotes an outstanding wine cellar; denotes a good wine list, worth travelling for.

CHEFS: Christopher Chown and Shaun Mitchell PROPRIETORS: Christopher and Gunna Chown OPEN: Sun L 12 to 2, Tue to Sun D 7 to 9.30 CLOSED: Dec to Feb MEALS: alc D (main courses £15 to £18). Set L £12.50 SERVICE: not inc CARDS: Delta, MasterCard, Switch, Visa DETAILS: 35 seats. Private parties: 40 main room, 16 private room. Car park. No smoking in dining room. Wheelchair access (also WC). Music ACCOMMODATION: 11 rooms, all with bath/shower. TV. Phone. B&B £35 to £120. Baby facilities (£5)

REYNOLDSTON Swansea

map 4

▲ *Fairyhill* ▮ ⁵✱

Reynoldston SA3 1BS	COOKING 4
TEL: (01792) 390139 FAX: (01792) 391358	COST £28–£54

This eighteenth-century country-house hotel offers 'everything you might expect' of it, from a wood-panelled entrance hall to comfortable sofas and log fires. 'I was much impressed by the ambience,' wrote one who began with a drink and fresh cockles in the comfortable sitting room, before taking up residence at one of the well-spaced tables in the dining room. The 'modern Welsh' tag that seems to suit the cooking might involve laverbread roulade on a gazpacho coulis, or an unusual starter of lamb's liver with an avocado salsa and lime and sage butter. While flavours do not always shine clearly, recommendations have included 'excellent' Welsh lamb cutlets 'cooked in Welsh style so they were not too rare', and tasty pigeon breast with Puy lentils. Monthly-changing menus incorporate some local ingredients – Welsh cheese soufflé, Black beef Wellington, or juniper-coated Bwlch venison – and Fairyhill's own walled garden and orchard provide herbs and fruit: perhaps for an apple and tarragon tart. Service is 'friendly, helpful and efficient'. Superstar Meursault producer Jean-François Coche-Dury, and the stellar Henschke from Australia's Adelaide Hills, are awarded their own pages on the massive wine list, but many other renowned growers from both hemispheres are found throughout. Do note that there are more bottles under £20 than those highlighted at the front. House wines start at £12.50.

CHEFS: Paul Davies, Adrian Coulthard and Bryony Jones PROPRIETORS: Peter and Jane Camm, Andrew Hetherington and Paul Davies OPEN: Mon to Sat 12.30 to 1.45, 7.30 to 9, Sun 12.30 to 2.15, 7.30 to 8.30 CLOSED: 26 Dec to 6 Jan MEALS: Set L £14.50 (2 courses) to £17.50, Set D £25 (2 courses) to £32 SERVICE: not inc, card slips closed CARDS: Amex, Delta, MasterCard, Switch, Visa DETAILS: 60 seats. 20 seats outside. Private parties: 52 main room, 40 and 52 private rooms. Car park. Vegetarian meals. Children's helpings No children under 8 at D. No smoking in dining room. Wheelchair access (not WC). Music ACCOMMODATION: 8 rooms, all with bath/shower. TV. Phone. B&B £95 to £160. No children under 8 in accommodation (*The Which? Hotel Guide*)

'Waitress: *"Everything all right, sir?"* Myself: *"Well, we've had two nights of bland, tasteless food but now it's much better. What's happened?"* Waitress: *"Actually, it's the chef's night off."'* (On eating in North Yorkshire)

Report forms are at the back of the book; write a letter if you prefer; or email us at guidereports@which.co.uk.

ROSEBUSH Pembrokeshire   map 4

Tafarn Newydd ⁵⊁ £

Rosebush SA66 7RA
TEL: (01437) 532542   FAX: (01437) 532926
EMAIL: tafarn.newydd@usa.net   COOKING **2**
on B4313, 8m SE of Fishguard   COST £21–£43

The New Tavern was new once: in the seventeenth century. Its 'potpourri of
furniture and styles' takes in flagstones, beams, stone walls and wooden tables,
and a relaxed atmosphere pervades the pub's various rooms: bar, informal eating
space and restaurant. Organic meat makes an appearance, along with local
seafood and cheeses, resulting in a range of items from a half-pint of prawns, via
a dish of cockles, bacon, wild garlic and laver pesto, to lamb shank with
chickpeas, flavoured with cinnamon, paprika, cumin and honey. Meatless
options are equally appealing, as in marinated local goats' cheese with roast
pepper, pistachio oil and spiced tomato chutney. Puddings are 'nothing fancy',
but there is fair choice and they are well made: perhaps lime posset, chocolate
roulade or pistachio tart. Drink real ale, or a wine from the enterprising
thirty-strong list, where prices start at £10.

CHEF: Diana Richards   PROPRIETOR: Tafarn Newydd Ltd   OPEN: Wed to Mon L 12 (12.30 Sun)
to 2, Mon and Wed to Sat D 7 to 9   CLOSED: 2nd week Nov, 25 Dec, 2 weeks mid-Jan   MEALS:
alc (main courses £6 to £17)   SERVICE: not inc, card slips closed   CARDS: Delta, MasterCard,
Switch, Visa   DETAILS: 42 seats. 10 seats outside. Private parties: 25 main room. Car park.
Vegetarian meals. Children's helpings. No smoking in dining room. No music

ST DAVID'S Pembrokeshire   map 4

Morgan's Brasserie ⁵⊁

20 Nun Street, St David's SA62 6NT   COOKING **3**
TEL: (01437) 720508   COST £25–£41

The most westerly Welsh restaurant in the *Guide*, on the road out to Fishguard, is
a neat, well-run, stone townhouse where fresh seafood, one of the delights of
Pembrokeshire, is a strength. A blackboard lists the day's offerings, from bass to
sole to swordfish, and treatment is appropriately straightforward: 'the best way
with such good fish,' according to one who enjoyed a 'moist, perfectly fresh'
skinned tail fillet of sewin served with 'earthy, sweet' new potatoes and
hollandaise. Spicy flavours are well controlled: a mild and creamy coconut curry
sauce accompanies chunks of salmon, monk and hake. A starter of dressed crab
featured (disappointingly for our inspector) only white meat, but came with
fanned avocado at the peak of ripeness. Meat, either organic or from pedigree
stock, also comes from the region: loin of lamb with garlic and rosemary, or Black
beef tournedos Rossini. Desserts and cheese elicit less excitement. Two dozen
reasonably priced wines start with house French at £9.50.

The Guide's *longest-serving restaurants are listed near the front of the book.*

CHEF: Ceri Morgan   PROPRIETORS: Ceri and Elaine Morgan   OPEN: D only 7 to 9 as follows: Nov and Dec Fri and Sat, Mar and Apr Wed to Sat, May to Oct Mon to Sat   CLOSED: Jan and Feb   MEALS: alc (main courses £9 to £15)   SERVICE: not inc, card slips closed   CARDS: Amex, MasterCard, Switch, Visa   DETAILS: 32 seats. Private parties: 20 main room. Vegetarian meals. No smoking in dining room. Occasional music

---

ST GEORGE Conwy   map 7

Kinmel Arms ⁵✳ £

St George LL22 9BP   COOKING 3
TEL/FAX: (01745) 832207   COST £21–£35

Built of grey slate, on the edge of an estate that supplies it with game, this seventeenth-century inn still operates as a pub, but also has a discreetly refurbished split-level dining room that opens five nights a week. The well-balanced menu ranges from prawn cocktail to duck confit with hoisin sauce, but generally focuses on more traditionally minded black pudding with mustard sauce, smoked haddock tartlet, or pot roast shank of Welsh lamb with garlic and rosemary. The food indicates 'a sound style of cooking and presentation', and meals might end with chocolate marquise and orange sabayon, or Amaretto-flavoured crème brûlée. Service is correct but unfussy, and a short wine list starts with three house recommendations at £8.50.

CHEF: Gary Edwards   PROPRIETORS: Gary Edwards and Dermot McGee   OPEN: Tue to Sat D only 7 to 9   CLOSED: 25 Dec   MEALS: alc (main courses £9 to £12.50). Set D Tue to Fri £13.50. Bar meals available L and D all week   SERVICE: not inc   CARDS: Delta, MasterCard, Switch, Visa   DETAILS: 70 seats. Private parties: 40 main room, 20 private room. Car park. Vegetarian meals. Children's helpings. No smoking in dining room. Wheelchair access (not WC)

SWANSEA Swansea   map 4

La Braseria £

28 Wind Street, Swansea SA1 1DZ   COOKING 1
TEL: (01792) 469683   FAX: (01792) 470816   COST £18–£44

Beyond the smart blue neon sign is a huge mock bodega with sawdust on the floor, Rioja labels everywhere, and a noisy, jostly atmosphere. There are no bookings for small parties (under six), so it pays to arrive early. Having found a table, start perhaps with fish soup, poached scallops or stuffed mushrooms, then choose your red mullet, marinated swordfish, rump steak or lamb kebab from the well-stocked chill cabinet. Most items are chargrilled and served with little adornment, but there are some sauces, and baked dishes notably include sea bass in rock salt. Chips are good, and 'you know exactly what you are going to get, year in, year out' even down to the salads and dressings. Puddings, bread and coffee are not highlights, service from a superfluity of staff is 'fast and impersonal', and half a dozen house wines are served by the glass for around £2.

If you have access to the Internet, you can find The Good Food Guide *online at the Which? Online web site (http://www.which.net).*

CHEF: I. Wing   PROPRIETOR: Manuel Tercero   OPEN: Mon to Sat 12 to 2.30, 7 to 11.30 CLOSED: 25 and 26 Dec, D 31 Dec, 1 Jan   MEALS: alc (main courses £4 to £15.50). Set L £6.75 (2 courses)   SERVICE: not inc, card slips closed   CARDS: Amex, Delta, Diners, MasterCard, Switch, Visa   DETAILS: 170 seats. Private parties: 100 main room. Vegetarian meals. Wheelchair access (also WC). Music. Air-conditioned

Hanson's   NEW ENTRY

Pilot House Wharf, Trawler Road, Swansea Marina,
Swansea SA1 1UN   COOKING 3
TEL: (01792) 466200   FAX: (01792) 201774   COST £17–£40

Opened in November 1998, at the end of the marina where trawlers tie up, Hanson's is a bright attractive room above a fishing tackle shop. Lobster pots and pictures of old Swansea decorate the spiral staircase, wooden tables are laid with gold cloths, and a blackboard lists the day's fish and good-value set-price lunch options. Andrew Hanson is 'choosing some of the best local produce and cooking it with some flair', according to an inspector. There are some interesting fusion items – for example, 'light, non-greasy' samosas filled with cockles, laverbread and bacon – but nods to other culinary worlds do not obscure the primacy of main materials. The food is marked by clean, fresh flavours, which accompaniments only help to enhance, as in pink, tasty chicken livers with a thick juice of Indian spices and a moat of yoghurt and mint sauce, or good-quality, well-timed chicken breast on ratatouille that is 'full of the proper tastes'. Simple desserts of strawberries and cream, or bread-and-butter pudding, bring up the rear, and around twenty wines start with house French at £9.25.

CHEF: Andrew Hanson   PROPRIETORS: Andrew Hanson and Helen Tennant   OPEN: all week L 12 to 2.30, Mon to Sat D 6.30 to 10   CLOSED: 25 and 26 Dec   MEALS: alc (main courses £8 to £14). Set L £8.25 (2 courses) to £9.95   SERVICE: not inc   CARDS: Delta, MasterCard, Switch, Visa   DETAILS: 50 seats. Private parties: 50 main room. Vegetarian meals. Children's helpings. Music (£5)

TALSARNAU Gwynedd   map 7

▲ *Maes-y-Neuadd* ♦ ⁙✱

Talsarnau LL47 6YA
TEL: (01766) 780200   FAX: (01766) 780211
EMAIL: maes@neuadd.com   COOKING 4
off B4573, 1m S of Talsarnau   COST £20–£50

An air of gracious living permeates the chintzy sitting room, the bar with beams and leather chesterfields, and the 'cream lace' dining room of this old, low-ceilinged stone house. Dinners are an elaborate affair in terms of number of courses, although choice is limited to two starters and four mains, one of them vegetarian, the other not entirely unexpected in serious lamb country: a 'distinguished' navarin the night our inspector called. Vegetables, understandably minimal in the context, are from the Victorian walled garden, and are 'sweet, delicious and beautiful to behold'.

Start maybe with tuna tartare, or glazed poached egg and spinach, add a soup and/or fish course according to mood, and end with a trio of Welsh cheeses or a 'grand finale' of three puddings (sticky toffee, ice cream, pineapple fritter) or as many as appetite permits. Lunch is a much less grand event, organised around a daily-changing main course: fish goujons and tartare sauce on Tuesdays, cottage pie on Thursdays, and so on. Bread in various guises and flavours is 'remarkably good', and young waitresses are 'charming and extremely helpful'. A suggested trio of wines by the glass at £12.80 solves the dilemma of finding a bottle to match the meal, but those who relish the challenge will find plenty of tempting bins both in the major European regions and the New World. French house white is £9.75, the red £12.15.

CHEF: Peter Jackson   PROPRIETORS: Michael and June Slatter   OPEN: all week 12 to 1.45, 7 to 9   MEALS: Set L Mon to Sat £9.50 (1 course) to £13.75, Set L Sun £15.50, Set D £26 to £33 SERVICE: not inc, card slips closed   CARDS: Amex, Delta, Diners, MasterCard, Switch, Visa DETAILS: 60 seats. 12 seats outside. Private parties: 60 main room, 12 private room. Car park. Vegetarian meals. No children under 7 at D. No smoking in dining room. Wheelchair access (also WC). Occasional music   ACCOMMODATION: 16 rooms, all with bath/shower. TV. Phone. D,B&B £84 to £230. Rooms for disabled. Baby facilities (*The Which? Hotel Guide*) £5

WELSH HOOK Pembrokeshire   map 4

▲ *Stone Hall*

Welsh Hook, Wolf's Castle SA62 5NS
TEL: (01348) 840212   FAX: (01348) 840815
1½m off A40, between Letterston and Wolf's Castle,   COOKING 1
W of Welsh Hook   COST £24–£40

The façade may not look particularly imposing, but Stone Hall has six centuries of Welsh history locked up in its walls, beams, flagged floors and wood panelling, and quite a bit of Gallic culinary history stored in its bilingual menu. 'The fact that our most popular main course is cassoulet seems to confirm that traditional French cuisine is alive and well,' writes Alan Watson, and there is no shortage of other dishes to back up the contention: frogs' legs in garlic butter, turbot with a creamy sorrel sauce, and roast lamb provençale. Seasonal input – leek and potato soup, roast partridge – turns up either on the daily-changing set menu or as a 'special', while among desserts the familiar territory of crème brûlée and chocolate profiteroles is occasionally invaded by a more ambitious cara-melised fennel tart with anise sorbet. A predominantly French wine list stays mostly below £20, starting with house Sauvignon and Gamay from Touraine at £10.50.

CHEFS: Martine Watson and Jean-Yves Poujade   PROPRIETORS: Alan and Martine Watson OPEN: all week D only 7 to 9.30   MEALS: alc (main courses £9.50 to £14). Set D £18 to £19 SERVICE: not inc   CARDS: Amex, Diners, MasterCard, Visa   DETAILS: 34 seats. Private parties: 45 main room, 20 private room. Car park. Vegetarian meals. Children's helpings. No cigars/pipes in dining room. No music   ACCOMMODATION: 5 rooms, all with bath/shower. TV. B&B £48 to £72. Baby facilities £5

WHITEBROOK   Monmouthshire   map 2

▲ *The Crown at Whitebrook* ❦ ⁵⨯

Whitebrook NP5 4TX
TEL: (01600) 860254   FAX: (01600) 860607   COOKING 4
5m S of Monmouth, between A466 and B4293   COST £26–£50

Set in the deep Wye Valley, at the edge of the village, the Crown thinks of itself as
an 'auberge', which is to say it has accommodation and a penchant for French
cooking. Plaster walls, black painted beams and sofas decorate the lounge, while
meals are eaten at 'refectory tables'. Although France is the inspiration, it is by no
means the whole story. Expect chicken liver parfait with raspberry vinaigrette
by all means, along with carré d'agneau and sablé de fraises, but the food is
'adapted to British tastes'. Welsh goats' cheese appears in a tart topped with herb
and nut crumble, and pork has come in three guises on one plate: stuffed fillet,
crisp belly, and sausage with apple and apricot compote.

Soufflés might appear in savoury form – a wild mushroom version to start – or
as apple and calvados soufflé tart for dessert, a course which also calls on alcohol,
in the form of Grand Marnier, for flaming pancakes and adding to custard.
Service has varied from 'attentive' and 'prompt' to 'indifferent'. Value for money
is the wine list's *raison d'être*, and while it mostly tells a French tale, it is by no
means blind to the virtues of producers from other countries. House wines are
£9.95 a bottle, £1.95 a glass.

CHEFS: Sandra Bates and Mark Turton   PROPRIETORS: Rodger and Sandra Bates   OPEN: Tue
to Sun L 12 to 1.45, Mon to Sat D 7 to 9   CLOSED: 25 Dec, first 2 weeks Jan   MEALS: Set L
£16.50, Set D £28.95. Light L available Tue to Sat   SERVICE: not inc   CARDS: Amex, Delta,
Diners, MasterCard, Switch, Visa   DETAILS: 34 seats. 12 seats outside. Private parties: 24 main
room, 12 private room. Car park. Vegetarian meals. Children's helpings. No smoking in dining
room. No music   ACCOMMODATION: 10 rooms, all with bath/shower. TV. Phone. D,B&B £70 to
£130. No children under 14. Swimming pool. Fishing (*The Which? Hotel Guide*)

WOLF'S CASTLE   Pembrokeshire   map 4

▲ *The Wolfe* ⁵⨯   **NEW ENTRY**

Wolf's Castle SA62 5LS   COOKING 1
TEL: (01437) 741662   FAX: (01437) 741676   COST £18–£45

New owners have brought a welcome breath of fresh air to this beamed,
stone-walled, roadside pub. Three distinctively renovated dining rooms –
conservatory, hunting lodge and Victorian room – reflect a personal touch, and
the menu speaks both Italian (minestrone soup, or salami and ham with pesto
and mozzarella) and a form of Welsh, offering best end of lamb with garlic and
tarragon hollandaise, and Black beef tournedos. Daily additions to the short
menu are described by Gianni di Lorenzo. Judging by one visitor's generous
brace of monkfish tails in a large quantity of cream and chive sauce, restraint is
not a characteristic of portion control; meals also come with a selection of six
vegetables on a side plate. Finish with fresh fruit pavlova, or chocolate
cheesecake. Drinks include real ales, coffees, liqueurs, malt whiskies and a
range of Italian wines, plus sixteen available by the glass. House French is £7.40.

CHEFS: Mike Lewis and Simon Periam   PROPRIETORS: Gianni and Jackie di Lorenzo   OPEN: all week L 12 to 2, Mon to Sat D 7 to 9   CLOSED: 26 to 28 Dec   MEALS: alc (main courses L £4.50 to £12, D £9.50 to £16)   SERVICE: not inc, card slips closed   CARDS: Delta, MasterCard, Switch, Visa   DETAILS: 75 seats. 16 seats outside. Private parties: 28 main room, 25 private room. Car park. Vegetarian meals. Children's helpings. No smoking in dining room. Wheelchair access (also women's WC). Occasional music   ACCOMMODATION: 3 rooms, 1 with bath/shower. TV. B&B £28 to £45 (£5)

Channel Islands

Jersey Pottery Restaurant | NEW ENTRY |

Gorey JE3 9EP   COOKING 1
TEL: (01534) 851119   FAX: (01534) 856403   COST £26–£53

This large garden restaurant in a glass-roofed conservatory has wooden tables, green trellis work and burgeoning vegetation. Thick brown tableware is a reminder that it is part of a pottery, but courteous, attentive service suits a restaurant in its own right. Most local of the indigenous seafood dominating the menu are oysters from Grouville Bay, a mile down the road. The menu displays originality without extremism, though some may think the 'Mediterasian' platter of feta and spinach spring roll, spicy vegetable samosa, and roasted pepper filled with goats' cheese has blown a fusion. Simple dishes showing off the freshness of ingredients are recommended: crab cakes, fried 'pottery prawns' (real ones, actually), baked cod, and roast fillet of sea bass are 'expertly cooked', and fruity desserts are highly praised. The longish, moderately priced wine list starts with house wines at £11.50.

CHEF: Tony Dorris   PROPRIETOR: the Jones family   OPEN: Mon to Sat L only 12 to 3   CLOSED: 10 days Christmas   MEALS: alc (main courses £10 to £27.50)   SERVICE: net prices, card slips closed   CARDS: Amex, Delta, Diners, MasterCard, Switch, Visa   DETAILS: 200 seats. 130 seats outside. Private parties: 290 main room. Car park. Vegetarian meals. Children's helpings. No-smoking area. Wheelchair access (also WC). Music

---

Suma's | NEW ENTRY |

6 Gorey Hill, Gorey JE3 6ET   COOKING 6
TEL: (01534) 853291   FAX: (01534) 851913   COST £20–£45

Opened in May 1997, the 'baby sister' of island heavyweight Longueville Manor (see entry, St Saviour) lost no time in building an enthusiastic clientele with a taste for impeccably fresh fish and modern English-cum-Mediterranean cuisine. Built into a hillside, its bare wooden floors, and white walls punctuated by colourful modern art give it a fresh and lively feel, enhanced by sparkling views of the harbour and the castle. Interesting ideas abound on the menu, for example a pairing of plump grilled scallops and pork rillettes surrounding a chilli salad. Combinations work effectively, whether a relatively conventional breast of guinea fowl with bubble and squeak, braised leeks and morel ravioli, or a more unusual mille-feuille of seared salmon served with 'spicy, warm and creamy' baba ganoush and a yoghurt and mint dressing.

As befits any seaside eatery, seafood – 'all beautifully fresh' – features strongly, yet vegetarians are also well catered for in dishes such as risotto with shiitake mushrooms and wok-fried greens, or roasted vegetables with noodles, rocket and Parmesan. Desserts are just as inventive as everything else: banana fritters are served with coconut and chilli ice cream ('with the chillies adding a hot note, the whole dish was heaven with horns'), and trifle is made with lychees, champagne and almond biscuits. Service is relaxed and professional, and the brief wine list has been described as 'interesting', at prices ranging from £8.75.

CHEF: Mark Anderson   PROPRIETORS: Malcom Lewis and Susan Dufty   OPEN: all week L 12 to 3, Mon to Sat D 6.30 to 10   CLOSED: 22 Dec to 24 Jan   MEALS: alc (main courses £5 to £16.50). Set L £11.25 (2 courses) to £13.75   SERVICE: net prices, card slips closed   CARDS: Amex, Delta, Diners, MasterCard, Switch, Visa   DETAILS: 45 seats. 14 seats outside. Private parties: 45 main room. Vegetarian meals. Music. Air-conditioned

Village Bistro

Gorey JE3 9EP   COOKING 6
TEL: (01534) 853429   COST £20–£47

Pass through the patio garden and enter a bright square room with blue and yellow carpet, bare tables, and 'very unusual décor', noted a reporter, commenting on the suns, moons and stars that are all over the place. David Cameron's approach is a global one that keeps its feet on the ground, producing terrine of ham hock with piccalilli, braised oxtail in red wine, and fillets of beef or lamb. Fish understandably pops up in a number of guises, from brandade of cod with smoked salmon and deep-fried oysters, via roast scallops on a warm apple and ginger puree, to monkfish fillet and crab won tons in a Thai sauce. A short 'options' menu helpfully offers dishes in two sizes: roast salmon salad with a sweet pepper chilli dressing perhaps, or deep-fried cod with tartare sauce and chips. Desserts are 'rich and varied', ranging from port-roasted figs with cinnamon fritters and mascarpone, or chocolate tart with lime syrup and lemon sorbet, to vanilla crème brûlée. Service is 'charming' and 'attentive'. France gets star billing on the wine list, with the New World trailing behind. House wines are £7.50.

CHEF: David Cameron   PROPRIETORS: Sandra Dalziel and David Cameron   OPEN: Fri to Sun and bank hol Mon L 12 to 2 (3 Sun), Tue to Sun and bank hol Mon D 7 to 10 (9.30 Sun)   CLOSED: 25 and 26 Dec   MEALS: alc (main courses £12.50 to £16.50). Set L Tue to Sat £13.50, Set L Sun £14.95   SERVICE: not inc; 10% for parties of 10 or more   CARDS: MasterCard, Switch, Visa   DETAILS: 40 seats. 25 seats outside. Private parties: 42 main room. Children's helpings. No cigars/pipes in dining room. Wheelchair access (not WC). Music

The 2001 Guide *will be published before Christmas 2000. Reports on meals are most welcome at any time of the year, but are particularly valuable in the spring (no later than June). Send them to* The Good Food Guide, FREEPOST, 2 Marylebone Road, London NW1 4DF. Or email your report to guidereports@which.co.uk.

ST BRELADE Jersey	map 1

▲ *Sea Crest*

La Route du Petit Port, St Brelade JE3 8HH
TEL: (01534) 746353   FAX: (01534) 747316
EMAIL: seacrest@super.net.uk

COOKING 4
COST £21–£73

A roadside setting and plastic garden furniture reminded one visitor of those restaurants in France where 'the outward appearance of the place gives no indication of the culinary talents within'. Roger White's more than competent cooking deploys some fine ingredients, and although dishes may appear complex – timbale of Jersey crab bound with shallots, herbs and crème fraîche with roasted king prawns and gazpacho sauce, for example – this is more a case of an overwritten menu than tricksy food combinations. Among successful seafood items, scallops have been served on a creamy herb risotto to start, and as part of a main course alongside fillet of sea bass with a salad of roasted vegetables: a 'dream fish dish' for its reporter. 'Flavour combinations are well thought out,' affirmed an inspector, whose meal ended with a tower-like mille-feuille of dark, bitter chocolate mousse sandwiched between layers of coconut tuile in a sweet sauce of orange and Grand Marnier. Owners and staff are 'welcoming, highly professional and knowledgeable'. Wines have been chosen by someone who knows how to please all palates and pockets, and although France supplies the bulk of the bottles, other wine-producing regions make some useful contributions, including the Australian house wines from Rosemount at £12.50.

CHEF: Roger White   PROPRIETORS: Julian and Martha Bernstein   OPEN: Tue to Sun 12.30 to 2, 5.30 to 10   MEALS: alc (main courses £16 to £28). Set L Tue to Fri £13.50, Set D Tue to Fri £19.50   SERVICE: not inc, card slips closed   CARDS: Amex, Delta, MasterCard, Switch, Visa DETAILS: 60 seats. 24 seats outside. Private parties: 80 main room. Car park. Vegetarian meals. Children's helpings. No cigars/pipes in dining room. Music. Air-conditioned   ACCOMMODATION: 7 rooms, all with bath/shower. TV. Phone. B&B £67 to £120. Baby facilities. Swimming pool £5

ST SAVIOUR Jersey	map 1

▲ *Longueville Manor* ⁵⅄✖

St Saviour JE2 7WF
TEL: (01534) 725501   FAX: (01534) 731613
EMAIL: longman@itl.net

COOKING 6
COST £25–£90

Country house in style and setting, with deep carpets, oak panelling and open fires, the manor's welcome is warm, friendly and relaxed. It is not short of space, with gardens for summer use, a number of sitting rooms, nooks and crannies, and two dining rooms: the non-smoker more intimate, the other light and functional. Andrew Baird's style is decidedly formal, but his focus on local suppliers and prime ingredients, combined with a light touch, produces food that 'stays as good as ever', according to a regular and long-standing visitor. Menus are generous in their offerings, and while the classically based cooking shows in pot roast poulet noir with a fricassee of woodland mushrooms, or a nage of lobster, crab, langoustines and scallops, it is also happy to cross a few culinary borders. A warm salad of duck and duck confit comes with spring onions and plum sauce, for example, and starter of seared tuna and grilled red mullet has been served with an aromatic herb noodle salad and sweet pepper compote. So enthusiastic is Mr Baird about his vegetables that a vegetarian menu has been introduced, perhaps offering Brie tortellini on a French bean salad, and lasagne of asparagus and wild mushrooms flavoured with truffle. Desserts run from plain-sounding rhubarb and custard to chocolate gâteau with ginger and chocolate chip cookies. House Vin de Pays d'Oc is £9 for the white, £9.50 for the red, and a decent choice is offered by the large glass.

CHEF: Andrew Baird   PROPRIETORS: Malcolm Lewis and Susan Dufty   OPEN: all week 12.30 to 2, 7.30 to 9.30   MEALS: alc D (main courses £21 to £24). Set L £16 (2 courses) to £20, Set D £55 to £75 (both inc wine)   SERVICE: net prices, card slips closed   CARDS: Amex, Delta, Diners, MasterCard, Switch, Visa   DETAILS: 65 seats. 25 seats outside. Private parties: 70 main room, 16 and 20 private rooms. Car park. Vegetarian meals. Children's helpings. No smoking in 1 dining room. Wheelchair access (not WC). No music   ACCOMMODATION: 32 rooms, all with bath/shower. TV. Phone. B&B £147 to £225. Rooms for disabled. Baby facilities. Swimming pool

Northern Ireland

BALLYCLARE Co Antrim   map 16

Ginger Tree

29 Ballyrobert Road, Ballyclare BT36 4TL
TEL: (01232) 848176, changing to (028) 9084 8176   COOKING 4
FAX: (01232) 840777, changing to (028) 9084 0777   COST £23–£50

This pleasant nineteenth-century farmhouse is a Japanese enclave deep in rural
Antrim. The menu makes some concessions to local tastes, though it is still
authentic enough to attract visiting Japanese. Grilled eel was the high point of a
reporter's meal which also included pan-fried chicken teriyaki, vegetable
sukiyaki and age dofu (fried bean curd), all well received. With raw fish
available only at week-ends, and even then limited to salmon, sushi use only
vegetables or pickles, although a wider range can be ordered for parties. Set
menus, offering virtually everything on the carte, are a good introduction to the
cuisine. Desserts include Japanese-style variations of profiteroles and banoffi,
and more typically Japanese green tea ice cream. A final untraditional touch is
that they offer 'pleasant' coffee. House wines are £10.50 and there are some other
respectable bottles under £20.

CHEF: Shotapo Obana PROPRIETORS: Shotapo Obana and Elizabeth Wylie OPEN: Mon to Fri L
12 to 2, Mon to Sat D 7 to 8.30 MEALS: alc D (main courses £9 to £12.50). Set L £7.40 to £10.75,
Set D Mon to Fri £14.95, Set D £19.50 to £22 SERVICE: not inc, card slips closed CARDS:
Amex, Diners, MasterCard, Visa DETAILS: 60 seats. Private parties: 65 main room. Car park.
Vegetarian meals. Children's helpings. Music. Air-conditioned

---

BANGOR Co Down   map 16

Shanks ♥

The Blackwood, 150 Crawfordsburn Road,
Bangor BT19 1GB
TEL: (01247) 853313, changing to (028) 9185 3313   COOKING 6
FAX: (01247) 852493, changing to (028) 9185 2493   COST £29–£66

'Much use of made of local seafood, game, and organic vegetables' at this
modern, minimal, Conran-designed restaurant. Shirley Millar adds that venison
from the Marchioness of Dufferin and Ava's Clandeboye Estate (on which the
restaurant is located) is a winter speciality. Indeed, seasonality is a strong feature
of Robbie Millar's cooking: summer brings lobster salad niçoise, while autumn
sees roast squab pigeon and foie gras arrive on a gratin of lentils with smoked

bacon and thyme. The style is in modern European mould in its broadest sense, producing chicken with morels, pheasant tart with a salad of wild mushrooms, and loin of lamb with couscous. Luxuries are scattered throughout, resulting in a few supplements for materials such as foie gras, seared scallops, steamed turbot, and beef fillet, perhaps served with salsify chips and béarnaise.

Dishes are well designed, with enough going on to maintain interest, yet not so much as to obscure their purpose: grilled sea bass, for example, comes with white beans, fennel salsa, and shiitakes with truffle oil. Desserts typically arrive with an ice cream: apple tarte Tatin with a cinnamon version, or warm chocolate tart with vanilla. The cheeseboard (another supplement) is a monster, with twenty to thirty varieties on offer at any given time: and not just Irish, but French, Swiss and Italian too. The wine list offers a judicious mix of styles from both hemispheres at surprisingly pocket-friendly prices given the plethora of famous names. House French is £12.50.

CHEF: Robbie Millar PROPRIETORS: Robbie Millar and Shirley Millar OPEN: Tue to Fri L 12.30 to 2.30, Tue to Sat D 7 to 10 CLOSED: 25 and 26 Dec, 1 Jan, 2 weeks July MEALS: Set L £13.95 (2 courss) to £17.95, Set D £29.50 SERVICE: not inc, 10% (optional) for parties of 6 or more CARDS: Amex, MasterCard, Switch, Visa DETAILS: 80 seats. 25 seats outside. Private parties: 12 main room, 30 private room. Car park. Vegetarian meals. Children's helpings. No cigars/pipes in dining room. Occasional music

---

BELFAST Co Antrim   map 16

La Belle Epoque £

61 Dublin Road, Belfast BT2 7HE
TEL/FAX: (01232) 323244, changing to   COOKING 2
(028) 9032 3244   COST £19–£40

This lively brasserie-style eatery is near both Queens University and the BBC, and seemingly benefits from the custom of both constituencies. Exposed brick walls painted with hazy pseudo-Impressionist murals, together with bare wooden tables and swagged drapes, give the place an idiosyncratic decorative air. Menus are written firstly in French for no evident reason, as the cooking style is by no means exclusively Gallic. Fine chicken liver pâté with armagnac and raisins is a clever essay in flavours, right down to the armagnac jelly covering the surface, while sea bass on a red wine fish fumet offers 'firm, yet succulent fish and a glossy, well-reduced sauce'. Vegetables, charged separately, include an oriental stir-fry with garlic and ginger, or potato galette with spring onions. Among puddings, cinnamon-scented apple crumble comes with an impressive combination of butterscotch ice cream and raspberry coulis. Service can be very casual. Vintages are strangely absent from the wine list, which favours France, then Spain and the New World, although prices seem reasonable. House vin de pays is £9.50.

CHEF: Alain Rousse PROPRIETORS: J. Delbart, Alain Rousse and G. Sanchez OPEN: Mon to Fri L 12 to 11, Sat 6 to 11 CLOSED: 25 and 26 Dec MEALS: alc (main courses £7 to £11.50). Set L £5.95 to £10.95 (both 2 courses), Set D Mon to Fri £15 SERVICE: not inc CARDS: Amex, Delta, Diners, MasterCard, Switch, Visa DETAILS: 84 seats. Private parties: 40 main room. Vegetarian meals. Music

▲ Crescent Townhouse, Metro   [NEW ENTRY]

Lower Crescent, Belfast BT7 1NR
TEL: (01232) 323349, changing to (028) 9032 3349
FAX: (01232) 320646, changing to (028) 9032 0646   COOKING 2
EMAIL: info@crescenttownhouse.com   COST £17–£46

Five minutes walk from the city centre, this small hotel's brasserie is a modern, pleasantly intimate room. Its well-spaced, marble and wooden topped tables, without cloths, are set against warm terracotta walls. In the main, menus offer local specialities, such as cockles steamed in cabbage and bacon broth, or roast cod with colcannon potatoes and sauce vierge, but oriental and Mediterranean influences are strong. Sunday set meals of 'tapas' ('sample dishes rather than authentic Spanish tapas') offer a good cross-section of the range: springy, yeasty bread with herb oil and onion jam precedes the kitchen's selection, perhaps including feta cheese fried in batter; Thai crab omelette; then 'main tapas' which might include deep-fried turbot; juicy grilled lemon chicken; and beef, olive and feta salad. A dessert plate included a rich chocolate mousse, and 'tangy' lemon sorbet. House wines £9.

CHEF: Tony O'Neill   PROPRIETOR: Wine Inns Ltd   OPEN: Sun to Fri L 12 to 2.30, Mon to Sat 6 to 9.30 (10 Fri and Sat)   CLOSED: 25 and 26 Dec, 1 Jan, 12 and 13 July   MEALS: alc Mon to Fri L, Mon to Sat D (main courses L £6 to £7.50, D £9 to £13). Set L Sun £9.95, Set D before 7.30pm £9.95 (2 courses) to £12.50   SERVICE: not inc, 10% for parties of 8 or more, card slips closed   CARDS: Amex, Delta, MasterCard, Switch, Visa   DETAILS: 65 seats. Private parties: 70 main room. Vegetarian meals. Children's helpings. No cigars in dining room. Wheelchair access (also WC). Music. Air-conditioned   ACCOMMODATION: 11 rooms, all with bath/shower. TV. Phone. B&B £55 to £110. Baby facilities

Deane's

34–40 Howard Street, Belfast BT16 1YR
TEL: (01232) 331134, changing to (028) 9033 1134   COOKING 6
FAX: (01232) 560001, changing to (028) 9056 0001   COST £47–£57

The reception area at Deane's is 'all gentleman's club': polished wood floors, wood-panelled walls and luxuriously upholstered chairs with copies of *The Times* (both the British and Irish versions) for those who wish to dawdle. A magnificent sweeping staircase leads to the dining room, where hushed opulence reigns, and huge vases of lilies everywhere make one wonder at the flower bill. The main menu deals in voguish combinations utilising sound ingredients in a thought-provoking style. Hot and sour scallops with spinach and foie gras were one eye-catching main course in May.

Fish dishes appear to be where the kitchen's finest skills are honed: for example a raviolo of monkfish (like a 'flaccid frilly mobcap') cooked al dente, filled with an appetisingly rich fish mixture, and garnished with black caviare as well as aubergine stewed in olive oil. Halibut has been lightly brushed with curry oil and roasted to exterior crispness, presented on fanned pommes Anna with morels in a chive cream sauce. Pre-desserts anticipate the arrival of such temptations as an assortment of red fruit items that included brilliant raspberry mousse on a biscuit base with an almond tuile stuck in it. Menu descriptions may give only an approximate idea of what turns up, but when it stretches itself this is a kitchen indubitably capable of aiming for the stars. The wine list offers a good blend of sunny flavours from the New World with more traditional styles from the Old. Sixteen house wines begin at £12.95, and six are also available by the glass from £2.25.

CHEF: Michael Deane   PROPRIETORS: Michael Deane, and Brian and Lynda Smith   OPEN: Tue to Sat D only 7 to 9.30   CLOSED: 24 to 26 Dec, 1 Jan, 1 week July   MEALS: Set D £27 (2 courses) to £55   SERVICE: not inc; 10% for parties of 6 or more   CARDS: Amex, Delta, MasterCard, Switch, Visa   DETAILS: 40 seats. Private parties: 40 main room. Vegetarian meals. No cigars/pipes in dining room. Music. Air-conditioned

Nick's Warehouse ▮ £

35 Hill Street, Belfast BT1 2LB
TEL: (01232) 439690, changing to (028) 9043 9690   COOKING 5
FAX: (01232) 230514, changing to (028) 9023 0514   COST £17–£40

Down a cobbled alley behind St Anne's Cathedral, Nick Price's immensely popular wine bar and restaurant occupies a former Bushmills whiskey warehouse now extended and decked out in neo-industrial style. Enter through the wine bar, with its high counters and bare brick walls, and go into the restaurant area, newly constructed in similar style. Here, well-spaced polished beech tables rest on wooden floors, and a plate-glass window reveals the chefs at work. The menu changes daily, but 'expect the contemporary, a fusion of Mediterranean, Californian and Irish'. A meal starts with high-quality breads baked on the premises and might continue with smoked bacon risotto with Parmesan and pesto (a 'nice combination of tastes'), or a 'palate-attacking' salad of oven-dried tomatoes, pickled cucumber, roast fennel and scallions. Main courses have included chargrilled swordfish with roast sesame, soy and chilli ('excellent' fish, 'beautifully caramelised' sauce); vegetables, charged extra, often include champ. Desserts may lack similar inspiration, but a reporter enjoyed the 'creamy pleasant texture' of chocolate pudding with ice cream. Business diners take up residence at lunchtimes, while an unstuffy but well-dressed mix of folk come in the evenings. Nick's is usually leisurely, with polite, unflappable staff, but glitches in service can occur at weekends, when the place gets crowded and the noise level reaches a crescendo. The wine list may be short but it is long on value for money, with a round-the-world selection featuring some highly respected producers and a handful of luscious dessert wines. House wines start at £7.95 a bottle, £1.95 a glass.

CHEFS: Nick Price, Simon McCance and Alan Montgomery   PROPRIETORS: Nick and Kathy Price   OPEN: Mon to Fri L 12 to 3, Mon to Sat D 6 to 9.30   CLOSED: 25 and 26 Dec, 1 Jan, Easter Mon and Tue, 12 July   MEALS: alc (main courses £5.50 to £14)   SERVICE: not inc; 10% for parties of 5 or more   CARDS: Amex, Delta, Diners, MasterCard, Switch, Visa   DETAILS: 180 seats. Private parties: 45 main room. Vegetarian meals. Wheelchair access (also WC). Occasional music. Air-conditioned

The text of entries is based on unsolicited reports sent in by readers, backed up by inspections conducted anonymously. The factual details under the text are from questionnaires the Guide *sends to all restaurants that feature in the book.*

Roscoff ▼

7 Lesley House, Shaftesbury Square, Belfast BT2 7DB
TEL: (01232) 331532, changing to (028) 9033 1532   COOKING 7
FAX: (01232) 312093, changing to (028) 9031 2093   COST £27–£75

'Roscoff is two shopfronts with frosted windows so you do not feel you are in a goldfish bowl,' claimed one visitor, rather understating the elegance and glamour of this smart city-centre restaurant. Its white, black and chrome are offset by modern paintings (for sale), while well-trained staff, wearing hand-painted silk ties and long white starched aprons, are all 'friendly, helpful and knowledgeable'. Reporters sense they are in for a good time even before they pick up a knife and fork, and the food does not disappoint.

The Rankins are at the culinary cutting edge, dusting shiitake powder over snail and chicken dumplings, and spicing up crispy fried skate with aïoli and chilli oil, but the feeling is of a purposeful kitchen rather than a merely experimental one. This is invention that carries the conviction of sound judgement. Whether a simple starter of peppers, courgettes and aubergines with tomato coulis, or a more adventurous apple and ginger soup with cockles and mussels, ideas and flavours have obviously been carefully worked out. Even though the Mediterranean and Pacific might meet in the same dish (perhaps ravioli of prawns with a chilli and coriander jus), a clear identity prevails, and impressive materials underscore the enterprise: for example, a thick piece of 'the best cod for many a day' with a dark brown tapénade crust, served with rösti and sauce antiboise.

Desserts typically include a hot raspberry soufflé, something chocolatey (a custard tart flavoured with Grand Marnier perhaps) and maybe a variation on rice pudding: coconut-flavoured, served with roast spiced pineapple. Like the food, wines from regions adjoining the Mediterranean or Pacific meet in the same list, together with some from more landlocked areas. Bright flavours are to the fore, not least in the baker's dozen of house wines priced from £12.95, with eight available by the glass from £2.95.

CHEFS/PROPRIETORS: Paul and Jeanne Rankin   OPEN: Mon to Fri L 12.30 to 2.30, Mon to Sat D 6.30 to 10.30   CLOSED: 25 and 26 Dec, Easter Mon and Tue, 12 and 13 July   MEALS: alc (main courses £15 to £26). Set L £17.50, Set D Mon to Thur £25.50   SERVICE: 10% (optional), card slips closed   CARDS: Amex, Delta, Diners, MasterCard, Switch, Visa   DETAILS: 65 seats. Private parties: 14 main room. Vegetarian meals. Children's helpings. Wheelchair access (also WC). Music. Air-conditioned

---

HOLYWOOD   Co Down   map 16

Fontana ▼   **NEW ENTRY**

61A High Street, Holywood BT18 9AE
TEL: (01232) 809908, changing to (028) 9080 9908   COOKING 2
FAX: (01232) 422475, changing to (028) 9042 2475   COST £20–£47

A local reporter was delighted with the advent of this bright and buzzy restaurant located above a shop on the main street of Holywood. Apparently small, but deep, the dining room is characterised by lemon yellow walls, uncovered wooden tables and modern art hangings. Colleen Bennett's new wave menu spans the globe, starting with risotto of peas, fava beans, courgette, asparagus, basil and Parmesan, or salmon teriyaki on wilted bok choy, and finishing on pecan pie, or a polenta cake flavoured with lemon and almond. Main courses are reckoned to be the stars of the show, with chargrilled loin of lamb – accompanied by roasted red peppers, new potatoes and baba ganoush – rated 'surprisingly delicate'; praise is also lavished on roast haunch of venison with celeriac gratin. Wines on the short but well-chosen and favourably priced list are sourced from some starry producers from around the globe. Prices begin at £9.95, although the Jim Barry Watervale Riesling 1997 from South Australia's Clare Valley would be well worth a try at £11.50.

CHEF: Colleen Bennett   PROPRIETORS: Colleen Bennett and Stephen McAuley   OPEN: Tue to Sun L 12 to 2.30, Tue to Sat D 6.30 to 10   CLOSED: 25 and 26 Dec   MEALS: alc (main courses L £4 to £10, D £7 to £14)   SERVICE: not inc, 10% for parties of 6 or more, card slips closed   CARDS: Delta, MasterCard, Switch, Visa   DETAILS: 71 seats. 14 seats outside. Vegetarian meals. Children's helpings. No cigars in dining room. Wheelchair access (also WC). Music (£5)

LIMAVADY Co Londonderry   map 16

The Lime Tree £

60 Catherine Street, Limavady BT49 9DB   COOKING 2
TEL: (015047) 64300, changing to (028) 7776 4300   COST £14–£40

'Plain cooking using fresh ingredients well' is the draw in this large ground-floor dining room. Family-run by friendly owners, it is a 'soothing and relaxing' place, with a cosmopolitan menu mixing home-grown and far-flung ideas in more or less equal measure: start with country game terrine and Cumberland sauce, or crab cakes with Thai-style dressing, followed perhaps by hot-smoked salmon steak with warm Mediterranean vegetable dressing. Finish maybe with a dessert combining choux bun with vanilla ice cream, bananas and toffee. A few themed evenings throughout the year offer more experimental dishes which, if successful, might appear on the regular menu. Fair prices increase the appeal of a short, sharp wine list, which starts with half a dozen house wines around £9.

CHEF: Stanley Matthews   PROPRIETORS: Stanley and Maria Matthews   OPEN: Wed to Sun 12 to 2, 6 to 9, and Mon and Tue D during summer   CLOSED: 1 week Nov, 1 week Mar, 1 week July   MEALS: alc (main courses L £5 to £8, D £9 to £14.50). Set L Wed to Sat £6.95, Set L Sun £11.95, Set D 6 to 7 Wed to Fri and Sun £12.95   SERVICE: not inc   CARDS: Amex, Delta, MasterCard, Switch, Visa   DETAILS: 30 seats. Private parties: 34 main room. Vegetarian meals. Children's helpings. Wheelchair access (also WC). Music

---

NEW CHEF *is shown instead of a cooking mark where a change of chef occurred too late for a new assessment of the cooking.*

Dining rooms where music, either live or recorded, is never played are signalled by No music *in the details at the end of an entry.*

---

and ginger cake with lime cream. Service is young, attentive and well-trained. Wines are a pleasing blend of Old World favourites and New World gems, Chilean red Seña 1995 being a particularly welcome addition. House wines start at a lowly £7.95.

CHEF: George McAlpin   PROPRIETORS: George and Jane McAlpin   OPEN: Tue to Sat D only 6.30 to 10.30   CLOSED: 24 to 26 Dec, 1 Jan   MEALS: alc (main courses £10 to £14)   SERVICE: not inc   CARDS: Delta, MasterCard, Switch, Visa   DETAILS: 70 seats. Private parties: 70 main room. Car park. No children after 9pm. Music

Republic of Ireland

We have not given marks for cooking for the Republic of Ireland entries because of a shortage of reports; please do give us feedback should you visit. To telephone the Republic from mainland Britain, dial 00 353 followed by the number listed, but dropping the initial 0. Prices are quoted in Irish punts.

ADARE Co Limerick   map 16

▲ *Adare Manor* ⁵✳

Adare
TEL: (061) 396566   FAX: (061) 396124   COST £37–£78

The coronet heading the menu and every page of the 'wine book' hints at the manorial style of this 'wonderful house and its superb setting'. Absorb the atmosphere and admire the views over drinks in the library before dinner in the conservatory. Foie gras terrine with pigeon, quail and truffled new potatoes is a luxurious starter, while soups might be more homely classical French onion. Colcannon and black pudding appear in a garnish for fillet of beef, and interesting vegetables include couscous and ratatouille with roast cannon of lamb, and carrot and courgette tagliatelle with piccata of veal. Irish salmon is smoked and served with griddled scallops as a starter, or roasted with prawns and accompanied by herb risotto as a main course. The cheese platter is said to be excellent, or there might be traditional bread-and-butter pudding with honey ice cream. France dominates the wine list, which is notable for some distinguished producers and good vintages ? at a price. House wines are £21.

CHEF: Gerard Costello   PROPRIETOR: Mr and Mrs Kane   OPEN: all week 12.30 to 2, 7 to 10 MEALS: alc D (main courses £19 to £25). Set L £21.50, Set D £36.50   SERVICE: 15%   CARDS: Amex, Delta, Diners, MasterCard, Visa   DETAILS: 60 seats. Private parties: 50 main room, 140 private room. Car park. Jacket and tie. No smoking in 1 dining room. Wheelchair access (not WC). Music   ACCOMMODATION: 63 rooms, all with bath/shower. TV. Phone. Room only £145 to £240. Rooms for disabled. Baby facilities. Swimming pool. Fishing

---

All details are as accurate as possible at the time of going to press, but chefs and owners often change, and it is wise to check by telephone before making a special journey. Many readers have been disappointed when set-price bargain meals are no longer available. Ask when booking.

AHAKISTA Co Cork

map 16

Shiro ✥

Ahakista
TEL: (027) 67030 FAX: (027) 67206   COST £56–£67

This must be one of the more divertingly picturesque places in Cork, a Japanese restaurant reached via a steep drive through overhanging trees, the grounds a riot of flowers and statuary, the interiors a blend of Japanese aesthetics in an Irish country-cottage ambience. What's more, it looks out over a broad sweep of Dunmanus Bay. The structure of meals follows a Western paradigm of hors d'oeuvre, then soup, a sorbet (of green tea), followed by a main course, then ice cream to finish. Chef Kei Pilz helpfully explains the zensai starters, which may take in crunchy rice-coated squid, tiny pieces of sushi, and spicy shiitake and lotus-root paste. Deep-fried tempura items are highly recommended, as are the sashimi that come with the approved condiments of chopped ginger, wasabi and soy sauce. Dessert is presented on a lacquer tray, with home-made ice cream garnished with fresh fruits and a little basket of macaroons. Saké, served hot in two carafes at £16, heads up a French wine list, which opens at £13.

CHEF: Kei Pilz PROPRIETORS: Kei and Werner Pilz OPEN: all week D only 7 to 9 CLOSED: Christmas and New Year MEALS: Set D £42 SERVICE: 10% CARDS: Amex, Diners, MasterCard, Visa DETAILS: 16 seats. Private parties: 7 main room. Car park. Vegetarian meals. No smoking in 1 dining room. Music

BALLINA Co Mayo

map 16

▲ *Mount Falcon Castle* ✥

Ballina
TEL: (096) 21172 FAX: (096) 71517
EMAIL: info@mountfalconcastle.com   COST £47–£56

Join fellow guests at eight for dinner, which follows a set pattern. First hors d'oeuvre, such as avocado vinaigrette, or mushrooms à la crème; then soup, often a vegetable cream. Main dishes include a roast, usually traditionally garnished and sauced, but alternatives might be baked salmon with mustard sauce, a casserole, or chicken curry. Game in season could produce jugged hare soup or roast woodcock. Then comes Irish cheese followed by a choice of desserts: simple rice pudding or fruit salad, or more elaborate crème de menthe mousse. Coffee is served in the drawing room. House wine is £12.

CHEF: Mary Loughney PROPRIETORS: the Aldridge family OPEN: all week D only 8pm (1 sitting) CLOSED: Christmas, Feb, Mar MEALS: Set L £15, Set D £25 (booking essential) SERVICE: not inc, card slips closed CARDS: Amex, Diners, MasterCard, Visa DETAILS: 30 seats. 10 seats outside. Private parties: 50 main room, 25 and 50 private room. Car park. Children's helpings. No smoking in dining room. No music ACCOMMODATION: 9 rooms, all with bath/shower. Phone. B&B £50 to £120. Baby facilities. Fishing

If you have access to the Internet, you can find The Good Food Guide *online at the* Which? *Online web site (http://www.which.net).*

BALLYDEHOB Co Cork   map 16

Annie's

Main Street, Ballydehob
TEL: (028) 37292   COST £31–£42

Nothing much changes from year to year at Annie's. The drill for dinner is still to take your menus over to the pub across the road for aperitifs, and then repair to the restaurant when your first courses are ready. Those might be a smart salad of fresh seafood, or baked avocado with crabmeat, and be followed by fried monkfish tail with a choice of lemon sauce or garlic butter, or – for those who prefer flesh to fish – pork medallions sauced with apples and Cointreau. Homely puddings include blackberry and apple sponge with custard, or hot chocolate fudge cake with cream. The shortish wine list shows off some good growers and opens with half a dozen house wines, all at £12.50.

CHEFS/PROPRIETORS: Dano and Anne Barry OPEN: Tue to Sat D only 7 to 9.30 CLOSED: Oct to Nov, 24 to 27 Dec MEALS: alc (main courses £14 to £16). Set D £22 SERVICE: not inc CARDS: MasterCard, Visa DETAILS: 24 seats. Private parties: 24 main room. Children's helpings. No cigars/pipes in dining room. Occasional music

---

BALLYLICKEY Co Cork   map 16

▲ Ballylickey Manor, Le Rendez-Vous ⚡✖

Ballylickey, Bantry Bay
TEL: (027) 50071   FAX: (027) 50124   COST £28–£66

A Georgian manor house at the head of Bantry Bay has been home to the Graves family (as in *I, Claudius*) since 1946. Immense old trees stand in the grounds, and the Rendez-Vous dining room is in the old pool house. The kitchen, in French hands, majors in a classical style of cooking with the odd nouvelle flourish. Broccoli and spinach soup in which the two flavours were 'absolutely distinct', as one reporter found, is quite an achievement. Turbot is robustly roasted with garlic and thyme, while beef fillet is gratinated with bone marrow. A sense of refinement is brought to bear in desserts such as pear poached in Muscat wine, or the heartily endorsed crème brûlée flavoured with rosemary. Wines are as French as the cooking, exclusively so, with prices opening at £16.

CHEF: Thierry Laurier PROPRIETORS: Mr and Mrs Graves OPEN: Thur to Tue L 12.30 to 2, all week D 7 to 9 MEALS: alc (main courses £13.50 to £19). Set L £15, Set D £30 SERVICE: 10%, card slips closed CARDS: Amex, MasterCard, Visa DETAILS: 30 seats. 15 seats outside. Private parties: 40 main room. Car park. No children under 8 in dining room. Jacket and tie. No smoking in dining room. Occasional music ACCOMMODATION: 11 rooms, all with bath/shower. TV. Phone. B&B £100 to £200. Baby facilities. Swimming pool. Fishing

---

Prices quoted in the Guide *are based on information supplied by restaurateurs. The prices quoted at the top of each entry represent a range, from the lowest meal price to the highest; the latter is inflated by 20 per cent to take account of likely price rises during the year of the* Guide.

BALLYVAUGHAN Co Clare   map 16

▲ Gregans Castle ▼ 🦑

Ballyvaughan
TEL: (065) 7077005   FAX: (065) 7077111
EMAIL: res@gregans.ie
on N67, 3½m S of Ballyvaughan   COST £52–£62

The castle is set amid the limestone terrain of the Burren, where Alpine and Arctic flowers exotically mingle, and megalithic tombs of Ireland's oldest indigenous peoples dot the landscape. A new chef, John Hughes, was appointed in 1999 to serve the refurbished dining room, and early indications are of exciting things going on in the weekly-changing fixed-price menus. Smoked local eel with grain mustard sauce, gravad lax served with deep-fried oysters, and a pastry parcel of quail and bacon stuffed with mushroom duxelles give an idea of the range of choice among starters alone. A reporter thought his lamb cutlets with apricot and sage mousse was a bold idea that worked well, while fruit timbale with a Kirsch sabayon was a distinguished way to finish. Wines are an astute blend of Old World favourites and more modern styles from the New World, and include six that are produced organically. The house selection starts at £14.50.

CHEF: John Hughes   PROPRIETORS: the Haden family   OPEN: all week D only 7 to 8.30 CLOSED: 16 Oct to 31 Dec, 1 Jan to 13 Apr   MEALS: Set D £25 (2 courses) to £36. Bar L available   SERVICE: not inc, card slips closed   CARDS: Amex, MasterCard, Visa   DETAILS: 50 seats. Private parties: 70 main room, 30 private room. Car park. Vegetarian meals. Children's helpings. No-smoking area. Wheelchair access (not WC). Music   ACCOMMODATION: 22 rooms, all with bath/shower. Phone. B&B £100 to £280. Baby facilities

---

BANTRY Co Cork   map 16

▲ Larchwood House   NEW ENTRY

Pearsons Bridge, Bantry
TEL: (027) 66181   COST £34–£41

The dining room of this creeper-covered, stone-built house has views of the garden from some of its widely spaced, pink-and-grey-clothed tables. The 1970s rococo dècor makes a change from '90s minimalism, and even more surprising are the successful combinations of tastes and textures achieved in the five-course menu. So generous are the portions that a reporter thought his starter of smoked salmon and citrus relish with fresh, nutty, brown soda bread would have made a fine lunch on its own. Second-course soups might be 'unusual and interesting' rhubarb and lettuce, followed perhaps by John Dory with sesame seeds in a creamy buttery sauce. The chef's skills are also evident in accompanying vegetables: a crunchy mixture of grated courgettes and carrots, for example. Six scoops of good praline ice cream with butterscotch sauce may be too much for some after the large portions that have gone before, but a lighter option might be highly original carrageen moss with rhubarb sauce. Service, while aiming to please, is not over-fast. House wines are £12.

CHEF: Sheila Vaughan   PROPRIETORS: Sheila and Aidan Vaughan   OPEN: Mon to Sat D only 7 to 10   CLOSED: 5 days Christmas   MEALS: Set D £25   SERVICE: not inc, card slips closed   CARDS: Amex, Diners, MasterCard, Visa   DETAILS: 27 seats. Private parties: 12 main room. Vegetarian meals. Children's helpings. Wheelchair access (not WC). Music   ACCOMMODATION: 4 rooms, all with bath/shower. Room only £25 to £50

BLACKLION Co Cavan   map 16

▲ MacNean Bistro 🍷✳

Blacklion
TEL: (072) 53022   FAX: (072) 53404   COST £19–£61

The name 'bistro' must be negative blarney for this restaurant-with-rooms in a 'one-street town' near the border. Organically grown vegetables, herbs and free-range products are used, although not specified in a menu that incorporates many exotic ideas and ingredients. One dinner menu included, among five starters, grilled quail with truffle risotto, balsamic vinegar, celeriac and Parmesan; and chicken, crab and chilli won tons with black beans. On the same menu were main dishes of cannon of lamb with herb couscous, tapénade and red wine; and monkfish tempura with aromatic rice and chilli jam. Desserts are pretty fancy, too, especially spicy apple parfait with apple lasagne and cider amber, or 'roast pineapple fancier cake with a poppy seed parfait'. The short but interesting wine list has white from £10.20, red from £11.

CHEF: Neven Maguire   PROPRIETORS: Vera and Joe Maguire   OPEN: Sun L 12.30 to 3.15, Tue to Sun D 6 to 9   CLOSED: 24 to 27 Dec   MEALS: alc D (main courses £13.50 to £15). Set L Sun £12, Set D £26 to £39   SERVICE: not inc   CARDS: MasterCard, Visa   DETAILS: 40 seats. Private parties: 40 main room, 15 private room. Car park. Vegetarian meals. Children's helpings. No smoking in dining room. Wheelchair access (not WC). Music   ACCOMMODATION: 6 rooms, all with bath/shower. TV. Phone. B&B £23 to £46. Baby facilities

---

CASHEL Co Tipperary   map 16

Chez Hans 🍷 🍲 ✳

Moor Lane, Cashel
TEL: (062) 61177   COST £34–£48

Jason, son of Hans, has taken over in the kitchen of the family business, whose home is a former church at the foot of Cashel Rock. While the style of the cooking remains largely unchanged, some up-to-date ideas have been introduced to the menu, with starters as 'modern Irish' as coriander, coconut and ginger in a seafood chowder, or Knocklara feta cheese salad with tapénade and home-dried tomatoes. Appealing main dishes include roast scallops with cider butter sauce, cassoulette of seafood, and herb-crusted rack of Tipperary lamb with pea purée and sauce paloise. A dozen well-chosen wines all priced at £12 a bottle (£2.50 a glass) open a list that concentrates on the classic regions of France but also takes in some interesting bins from elsewhere.

See inside the front cover for an explanation of the symbols used at the tops of entries.

CHEF: Jason Matthiae   PROPRIETOR: Hans-Peter and Jason Matthiae   OPEN: Tue to Sat D only 6.30 to 10   CLOSED: 6 Jan to 1 Feb   MEALS: alc (main courses £15 to £17.50). Set D £25 SERVICE: not inc, card slips closed   CARDS: MasterCard, Visa   DETAILS: 80 seats. Private parties: 80 main room. Car park. Vegetarian meals. Children's helpings. No smoking in 1 dining room. Wheelchair access (also WC). Occasional music

---

CASTLEBALDWIN Co Sligo   map 16

▲ *Cromleach Lodge* ⁵⁄*

Castlebaldwin, via Boyle
TEL: (071) 65155 FAX: (071) 65455
EMAIL: cromleac@iol.ie.   COST £37–£61

Less like a country house than a striking modern conservatory, Cromleach Lodge offers splendid views across Lough Arrow to the Carrowkeel Cairns. The cuisine, described as modern Irish, includes fine local ingredients such as Atlantic turbot, Sligo beef and free-range duck. A typically straightforward main dish is loin of lamb scented with rosemary and garlic on barley risotto. More adventurous starters might be poached John Dory and basil pesto, or quail breasts with smoked duck mousse and armagnac sauce. On the gourmet menu soup follows starters before a main course of something along the lines of veal escalopes with grain mustard sauce. The dessert menu ('Tonight's Delights') might include ginger and coffee mousse gâteau on whiskey caramel sauce; iced almond and apricot nougat; or a florentine cone of marinated tropical fruits; while the undecided can opt for the tasting selection. The list of 100 wines is strong in the New World for bottles up to £20, while classics, especially claret, include some distinguished bins. House recommendations are £12.95.

CHEF: Moira Tighe   PROPRIETORS: Christy and Moira Tighe   OPEN: all week D only 6.30 to 9 CLOSED: Nov to Feb   MEALS: alc (main courses £17). Set D £35   SERVICE: not inc, card slips closed   CARDS: Amex, Diners, MasterCard, Visa   DETAILS: 40 seats. Private parties: 24 main room, 6 and 24 private rooms. Car park. Children's helpings. No children under 7 after 7 in dining room. No smoking in dining room. Wheelchair access (not WC). No music   ACCOMMODATION: 10 rooms, all with bath/shower. TV. Phone. B&B £89 to £179. Baby facilities

---

CORK Co Cork   map 16

Crawford Gallery Café 🍴 £

Emmet Place, Cork
TEL: (021) 274415   COST £19–£34

There is now a no-smoking area in this offshoot of Ballymaloe House (see entry, Shanagarry), where you might be tempted by fish of the day 'landed at Ballycotton Pier last night'. New chef Nina Sisk joined just as the *Guide* went to press, but if she continues in similar vein to what has gone before menus might well feature dishes along the lines of pasta primavera, spinach and mushroom pancake, minute steak with champ, and chicken pie Massachusetts. Be sure to try the Ballymaloe breads. The set lunch consists of soup, a choice of main course and dessert; and morning coffee and afternoon tea are also offered. House wines are £10 a bottle, £2 per glass.

CHEF: Nina Sisk   PROPRIETOR: Crawford Art Gallery   OPEN: Mon to Sat 10 to 5   CLOSED: bank hols   MEALS: alc (main courses £6.50 to £8.50). Set L £12   SERVICE: not inc, card slips closed   CARDS: MasterCard, Visa   DETAILS: 80 seats. Vegetarian meals. No-smoking area. Wheelchair access (also WC). Occasional music

---

DINGLE   Co Kerry   map 16

Beginish ♥ ⅙✳

Green Street, Dingle
TEL: (066) 915 1588   FAX: (066) 915 1591
EMAIL: patmoore@tinet.ie   COST £30–£52

Beautiful gardens form a suitably relaxing backdrop, viewed from a conservatory attached to this Georgian terraced house. There is an elegant, relaxed air, reinforced by welcoming and efficient service. The menu deals mainly, but not exclusively, in fish, and straightforward descriptions herald well-prepared food that concentrates on ingredients rather than frippery: crab salad with a spicy avocado and chilli mayonnaise; smoked salmon with shallots, capers and horseradish cream; or Caesar salad. Main courses might be as simple as sole meunière, or crab claws with garlic butter, but there are also more complex items: fillet of beef with blue cheese polenta, red onion marmalade and brandy cream sauce, for example. Desserts tend towards the likes of sticky toffee pudding, and triple chocolate treat. The reasonably priced wine list leans towards the Old World, but also takes in the New, and the house selection starts at £11 a bottle, £3.20 a glass.

CHEF: Pat Moore   PROPRIETORS: John and Pat Moore   OPEN: Tue to Sun 12.30 to 2.15, 6 to 10   CLOSED: 25 Dec.   MEALS: alc (main courses £11.50 to £20)   SERVICE: not inc, card slips closed   CARDS: Amex, Diners, MasterCard, Visa   DETAILS: 52 seats. Private parties: 20 main room. Vegetarian meals. Children's helpings. No smoking in 1 dining room. Wheelchair access (not WC). Music. Air-conditioned

▲ *Half Door* ♥ ⅙✳

3 John Street, Dingle
TEL: (066) 51600   FAX: (066) 51883   COST £24–£66

Dingle, the most westerly place in this *Guide*, is on a peninsula poking into the Atlantic and is thus surrounded by fish and crustacea, many of which find their way through the half-door. Lobster, prawns, crab and mussels are in Teresa's shellfish selection, oysters are offered 'nature', as is oak-smoked salmon, although that delicacy may also appear in the form of a mousse with garlic toast. In main courses, traditional ways with shellfish include moules marinière, and lobster thermidor. Fish might include roast fillet of cod, medallions of monkfish, and certainly salmon, perhaps baked in pastry, or steamed with sole in a prawn sauce. Steaks, duck, and chicken cater for carnivores, and to finish there is pear and apple crumble or Belgian chocolate cake. House wines run from £13 to £16.50, and another 120 bottles include some excellent producers and good vintages.

641

CHEF: Denis O'Connor PROPRIETORS: Denis and Teresa O'Connor OPEN: Mon to Sat 12.30 to 2, 6 to 10 CLOSED: Jan and Feb MEALS: alc (main courses £8 to £28) SERVICE: not inc CARDS: Amex, MasterCard, Visa DETAILS: 50 seats. Private parties: 20 main room. Vegetarian meals. Children's helpings. No smoking in 1 dining room. Wheelchair access (not WC). Occasional music. Air-conditioned ACCOMMODATION: 7 rooms, all with bath/shower. TV. Phone. B&B £25 to £60

DONEGAL Co Donegal　　　　　　　　　　　　　　　　　　map 16

▲ *Harvey's Point* ⁵⋇

Lough Eske, Donegal
TEL: (073) 22208 FAX: (073) 22352
EMAIL: harveyspoint@tinet.ie　　　　　　　　　　　　　COST £20–£48

This Irish country hotel in the style of a Swiss chalet sits on the edge of Lough Eske beneath a skyline shaped by the Blue Stack Mountains. Marc Gysling imaginatively handles local produce, as in a starter of half a dozen Donegal Bay oysters, three cold and dressed with shallots, and three gratinated with dill. Black sole is fried on the bone and served simply with pommes vapeur and spinach, or there's speciality house tournedos done in a whiskey sauce, or escalope of Atlantic salmon on a bed of purée turnips and carrots with beurre blanc. Pear feuilleté with vanilla ice cream, and raspberry and vanilla bavarois are typical desserts. The wine list includes a listing of 'everyday easy drinking' suggestions, as well as showcase Burgundies and clarets. House French and Spanish are £12.50.

CHEF/PROPRIETOR: Marc Gysling OPEN: all week 12.30 to 2.30, 6.30 to 9.30 CLOSED: Nov to Mar exc Christmas and New Year MEALS: alc (main courses L £8.50 to £10, D £13.50 to £18.50). Set L £10 (2 courses) to £12.50, Set D £30 SERVICE: net prices, card slips closed CARDS: Amex, Diners, MasterCard, Visa DETAILS: 80 seats. Private parties: 80 main room, 80 to 400 private rooms. Car park. Vegetarian meals. Jacket and tie. No smoking in 1 dining room. Wheelchair access (also WC). Music. Air-conditioned ACCOMMODATION: 20 rooms, all with bath/shower. TV. Phone. B&B £64 to £110

DOUGLAS Co Cork　　　　　　　　　　　　　　　　　　map 16

Lovetts ♥ ⁵⋇

Churchyard Lane, off Well Road, Douglas
TEL: (021) 294909 and 293604 FAX: (021) 294024　　　　COST £24–£67

The Lovetts announce that their style of cooking continues to emphasise the strengths of local producers and that, although European trends are acknowledged, they are made to complement rather than dominate what is offered. Crab baked with champ and given a salsa of watercress and tomato is one such example, while venison from a specialist butcher in Mitchelstown is served with a walnut and potato croquette and sauced with apricot brandy. A separate vegetarian menu takes in such novelties as a layered cake of couscous and poppadoms with a sauce of 'scorched' tomatoes, and the less formal brasserie might offer smoked fish hash, marinated beef stir-fry, or pan-fried lambs' kidneys. Wines are a fascinating mix of the new, the old and the downright ancient: the Greek red Limnio is mentioned in the works of Aristotle. Lovetts own-label house wines (from Daumas de Gassac) are £12.75.

CHEFS: Marie Harding and Margaret Lovett PROPRIETORS: the Lovett family OPEN: Tue to Fri L 12.30 to 2, Tue to Sat D 7 to 9.30 CLOSED: 1 week Christmas, first week Aug MEALS: alc (main dishes £13 to £17), Set L £15.50, Set vegetarian D £15.50 (2 courses). Brasserie menu available SERVICE: not inc, card slips closed CARDS: Amex, Diners, MasterCard, Visa DETAILS: 70 seats. Private parties: 50 main room, 24 and 50 private rooms. Car park. Vegetarian meals. Children's helpings. No smoking in dining room. Wheelchair access (not WC). Music

---

DUBLIN Co Dublin map 16

▲ *Clarence, Tea Room*

6–8 Wellington Quay, Dublin 2
TEL: (01) 6707766 FAX: (01) 6707833
EMAIL: clarence@indigo.ie COST £28–£62

When Irish supergroup U2 began diversifying from platinum discs and saving the planet, they opened this smart hotel in the dynamic Temple Bar district of the capital. Michael Martin is the chef charged with bringing cutting-edge cuisine to the ironically named Tea Room restaurant, fulfilling his mission with considerable aplomb and much metaphorical shifting of culinary terminology. Crab forms the basis of a simple starter salad that includes little gems, Parmesan and black vinegar, duck livers the principal component of a more complex one taking in fried artichoke and fennel and a dressing of truffled Madeira. A 'roast cushion' might seem a diverting main course, especially when it turns out to be veal with a 'brandade' of potato and cabbage. Bright ideas among puddings have been cider-flavoured crème brûlée with an apple and raisin won ton, or pineapple Tatin with Malibu ice cream. Pedigree wines abound on a list that eschews geographical demarcations but opens with house French at £14.

CHEF: Michael Martin PROPRIETOR: Brushfield Ltd OPEN: Mon to Fri L 12.30 to 2.20, all week D 6.30 to 10.20 (10 Sun) MEALS: alc (main courses £15 to £19). Set L £13.50 (2 courses) to £17 SERVICE: not inc CARDS: Amex, Diners, MasterCard, Visa DETAILS: 90 seats. Private parties: 90 main room. Vegetarian meals. Wheelchair access (also WC). Music ACCOMMODATION: 50 rooms, all with bath/shower. TV. Phone. Room only £180 to £195. Rooms for disabled. Baby facilities

---

Commons

Newman House, 85–86 St Stephen's Green, Dublin 2
TEL: (01) 4780530 FAX: (01) 4780551 COST £34–£84

The entrance to the Commons, down a flight of granite steps, is not overly impressive, but, inside, the sense of space is surprisingly generous. The back of the restaurant looks out over a paved courtyard with well-established borders where you can eat, weather permitting. Staff are a mixture of French and Irish and service is good and attentive. Sebastien Masi's style is classical, with Eastern influences making fleeting appearances: Asian-style chicken bouillon with prawns, for example, or star anise coulis with a tart of asparagus and Gorgonzola. An inspection meal included pan-fried foie gras with ginger breadcrumbs on

Puy lentils, the ginger well judged, the breadcrumbs providing contrast; and open ravioli of curried scallops with basmati rice and coconut cream, consisting of three scallops on a bench of rice covered with a blanket of spinach ravioli. A pre-main-course savoury might be 'delicious' tomato and herb-infused soup with mini-ravioli, while main courses themselves could run from 'almost textbook' tournedos Rossini, through 'superb' magret of duck flavoured with honey and spices and served with fennel cream, to sea bream baked in puff pastry with lemon grass stock. Desserts might be a mille-feuille of coffee and caramel with Irish cream sauce, or chocolate tart with fromage blanc. France makes up the bulk of the largely expensive wine list. House French and Argentinian are respectively £18 and £20.

CHEF: Sebastien Masi PROPRIETOR: Michael Fitzgerald OPEN: Mon to Fri 12.30 to 2.15, 7 to 10.15 CLOSED: 1 week Christmas, bank hols MEALS: alc (main courses £20 to £24). Set L £22, Set D £55 SERVICE: not inc CARDS: Amex, Diners, MasterCard, Visa DETAILS: 60 seats. Private parties: 74 main room, 26 and 60 private rooms. Vegetarian meals. Children's helpings. No-smoking area. Music. Air-conditioned

Le Coq Hardi 🍾 ⁵✳

35 Pembroke Road, Dublin 4
TEL: (01) 6689070 FAX: (01) 6689887   COST £37–£95

Here is Irish cooking in the grand manner. John Howard, long a promoter of the finest that Ireland can produce, delivers recognisable, classy and generous dishes and the finest of wines in the most sumptuous and graceful of houses – Georgian, of course – on the corner of Pembroke and Wellington Roads. The lunch menu is a trimmed or slightly adapted version of the evening full fig, perhaps a warm terrine of Clonakilty black and white puddings with an apple and calvados compote, then pot-roast quail, stuffed with cabbage, wild mushrooms and foie gras and served with Toulouse sausage. If you yearn for a plain garlic-grilled lobster, or a fillet of Irish beef with champ, this is the place, but modern ingredients like bok choy and balsamic vinegar also figure in the lavish scheme of things. This is also the place to come if you have a penchant for really old first-class claret, and the funds to indulge your fancy. A string of Mouton-Rothschilds stretching back to 1870 are among the many delights from Bordeaux, Burgundy and beyond. House French is £18.

CHEF: John Howard PROPRIETORS: John and Catherine Howard OPEN: Mon to Fri L 12.30 to 2.30, Mon to Sat D 7 to 11 CLOSED: 2 weeks Christmas, 2 weeks Aug, bank hols MEALS: alc (main courses £20.50 to £26). Set L £24.50, Set D £39 SERVICE: 12.5%, card slips closed CARDS: Amex, Diners, MasterCard, Visa DETAILS: 50 seats. Private parties: 50 main room, 2 to 35 private rooms. Car park. Vegetarian meals. Jacket and tie. No smoking in 1 dining room. Occasional music. Air-conditioned

⁵✳ *indicates that smoking is either banned altogether or that a dining-room is maintained for non-smokers. The symbol does not apply to restaurants that simply have no-smoking areas.*

L'Ecrivain

109 Lower Baggot Street, Dublin 2
TEL: (01) 6611919   FAX: (01) 6610617   COST £18–£51

In his 'small, but well-planned' restaurant first-floor dining room named for its collection of portraits of Irish writers, Derry Clarke offers a menu full of modern ideas that span the globe, from crisp spring roll of aromatic duck, mango and dill salsa with hoisin, to classic pan-fried foie gras with brioche or, closer to home, leek and potato soup. Follow with a fillet of sea bass with cured ham and mille-feuilles of aubergine, 'excellent' roast hake with a herb and tomato crust, or breast of wild duck with confit and sauerkraut. A good way to finish would be 'wonderful' crème brûlée. The wine list was undergoing major changes as the *Guide* went to press. Note that the 10% service charge is not applied to drinks.

CHEF: Derry Clarke   PROPRIETORS: Sallyanne and Derry Clarke   OPEN: Mon to Fri L 12.30 to 2, Mon to Sat D 7 to 11   CLOSED: 25 Dec, bank hols   MEALS: alc (main courses L £8.50, D £20). Set L £14.50 (2 courses) to £16.50, Set D £27 to £31.50   SERVICE: 10%   CARDS: Amex, Diners, MasterCard, Visa   DETAILS: 66 seats. 20 seats outside. Private parties: 60 main room, 10 private room. Vegetarian meals. Children's helpings. No-smoking area. Music. Air-conditioned

Ernie's

Mulberry Gardens, Dublin 4
TEL: (01) 2693300   FAX: (01) 2693260
off Morehampton Road in Donnybrook village   COST £26–£67

A windswept Irish mountainscape adorns the menu at the Evanses' restaurant in the Donnybrook district of the capital. Over 200 paintings offer a visual feast, and John Sultan does his conscientious best to provide the real one. In a dining room that overlooks a patio garden with ornamental fountain, you will eat roast wood pigeon on a potato galette with caramelised onions and port sauce, perhaps, or saffron-scented seafood chowder. The best of the day's catch is treated to lively combinations such as fennel and ginger fondue and red pepper sauce for seared turbot fillets, while meat eaters might opt for beef tournedos on herb rösti with black olive blinis and sauce bordelaise. Populist desserts include sticky toffee pudding served with crème fraîche. Eight French house wines start at £15.50.

CHEF: John Sultan   PROPRIETORS: the Evans family   OPEN: Tue to Fri L 12.30 to 2, Tue to Sat D 7.30 to 10   CLOSED: 2 weeks Christmas   MEALS: alc (main courses £13 to £20). Set L £14.95, Set D £25   SERVICE: 12.5%   CARDS: Amex, Diners, MasterCard, Visa   DETAILS: 60 seats. Private parties: 60 main room. Vegetarian meals. Children's helpings. No children under 12. No-smoking area. Wheelchair access (not WC). No music. Air-conditioned

Les Frères Jacques

74 Dame Street, Dublin 2
TEL/FAX: (01) 6794555   COST £23–£69

New chef Eddi Smittarello arrived at this small part of France not far from Dublin Castle just as the *Guide* went to press. If he should continue in his predecessor's style, on offer will be fresh fish and shellfish of the day, plus dishes along the lines of rack of veal with light oriental flavours, or perhaps pork shank pie with foie gras and wild mushrooms, and desserts of apple tart or baked passion fruit custard. The largely French wine list offers good hunting at fair prices, starting at £11.

CHEF: Eddi Smittarello   PROPRIETOR: Jean-Jacques Caillabet   OPEN: Mon to Fri L 12 to 2.30, Mon to Sat D 7 to 10.30 (11 Fri and Sat)   CLOSED: 24 Dec, 2 Jan, bank hols   MEALS: alc D (main courses £17 to £26). Set L £13.50, Set D £21   SERVICE: 12.5% (optional)   CARDS: Amex, Diners, MasterCard, Visa   DETAILS: 65 seats. Private parties: 40 main room, 20 and 40 private rooms. Children's helpings. No smoking in 1 dining room. Wheelchair access (not WC). Music. Air-conditioned (£5)

Kapriol

45 Lower Camden Street, Dublin 2
TEL: (01) 4751235   FAX: (01) 4753770
EMAIL: kapriol@indigo.ie   COST £30–£65

Kapriol has enjoyed a well-nigh unassailable reputation for quality Italian cooking in Dublin for close on a quarter of a century. Those just being initiated into the experience are enjoined to begin with the signature dish, prawns Kapriol: jumbo specimens grilled in their shells and anointed with a textbook potion of wine, butter, garlic and herbs. Bruschetta Toscana, with Parma ham, salami and black olives, acknowledges that today's patrons have caught up with a more contemporary strand in Italian cooking, but there are also vitello alla this and that, chicken involtini, and seasonal game for the traditionalists. Card slips are left open, in case you wish to add another layer of gratuity to the 12.5 per cent that is automatically applied. The Franco-Italian wine list opens with house Merlot and Pinot Bianco from the Veneto at £13.

CHEFS: Ronan Flanagan and Maura Hughes   PROPRIETOR: Ronan Flanagan   OPEN: Tue to Sat D only 6.30 to 12   CLOSED: 24 Dec to 2 Jan   MEALS: alc (main courses £10 to £20). Set D Tue to Fri 6.30 to 8.30 £16.95 (2 courses) to £19.95   SERVICE: 12.5%   CARDS: Amex, MasterCard, Visa   DETAILS: 36 seats. Private parties: 40 main room. Children's helpings. Wheelchair access (not WC). Music

Lloyds Brasserie   **NEW ENTRY**

20 Upper Merrion Street, Dublin 2
TEL: (01) 6627240   FAX: (01) 6627243   COST £27–£53

A new venture from Conrad Gallagher, who also owns Peacock Alley (see entry below), offers what the management describes as 'minimalist chic and urban modernist cooking'. It's a basement venue approached down a black-walled stairway past troughs of flowers. Chrome and strident colours set the tone in the dining area, and the menus look equally vivid. Sautéed scallops with pancetta, potato mousseline and garlic butter get things off to a good start. Presentations are carefully worked on to effect maximum dazzle, as in a multi-sauced kebab of spiced lamb served on pitta with hoisin and chilli, bean sprouts and alfalfa. A thoroughgoing treatment of rabbit brings on saddle, leg, kidney and liver, with correctly timed pumpkin polenta and rosemary sauce: a kind of 'reinvented rustic Sunday dinner', thought one who ordered it.

Fruit-based puddings include lemon and raspberry cheesecake, or apple and banana crumble. The well-chosen wine list is arranged by grape variety and opens at £14.

CHEF: Lorcan Cribbin   PROPRIETOR: Conrad Gallagher   OPEN: all week 12.30 to 2.30, 6 to 11 (12 Sat and Sun)   MEALS: alc (main courses £9 to £17). Set L £12.50 (2 courses) to £15.50 SERVICE: not inc, 12.5% for parties of 8 or more   CARDS: Amex, Delta, Diners, MasterCard, Switch, Visa   DETAILS: 130 seats. Private parties: 130 main room, 15 private room. Vegetarian meals. Children's helpings. Music. Air-conditioned

Mermaid Café | NEW ENTRY |

69–70 Dame Street, Dublin 2
TEL: (01) 6708236   FAX: (01) 6708205   COST £22–£54

'Clapboard beach house with a touch of Martha's Vineyard' is how an inspector described this bright corner site with its white walls, varnished wooden floor and old-fashioned pine tables. Service by white-shirt staff is both relaxed and enthusiastic. Starters might include salmon fish fingers with couscous crust and basil mayonnaise, roast veal sweetbreads and confit shallots on toasted brioche, and an Irish take on an Italian theme in asparagus, rocket and oven-dried vine tomatoes with shaved Gabriel cheese. An inspection lunch started with well-flavoured mussel and smoked fish chowder, and crab cakes with piquant mayonnaise, and continued with main courses of seafood tart with baby spinach salad, the filling rich and of the sea, and a colourful dish of grilled polenta with Gabriel cheese, tapénade and grilled vegetables. Desserts might be rhubarb, mascarpone and crêpe terrine, or pecan pie with maple ice cream. The wine list is keen on the New World but doesn't forget the Old. Five house wines vary from £12.95 to £15.50.

CHEF: Ben Gorman   PROPRIETORS: Mark Harrell and Ben Gorman   OPEN: all week 12.30 to 2.30 (3.30 Sun), 6.30 to 11 (5.30 to 9 Sun)   CLOSED: Christmas, 31 Dec, 1 Jan   MEALS: alc (main courses L £6 to £11, D £11 to £18)   SERVICE: not inc, 10% for parties of 5 or more   CARDS: MasterCard, Visa   DETAILS: 50 seats. Private parties: 65 main room, 24 private room. Vegetarian meals. Children's helpings. Wheelchair access (also WC). Music. Air-conditioned

Patrick Guilbaud

21 Upper Merrion Street, Dublin 2
TEL: (01) 6764192   FAX: (01) 6610052   COST £32–£98

Sited at the Merrion Hotel, Patrick Guilbaud's elegant French restaurant enjoys what one reporter called a 'curiously cathedral-like' feel. 'Extremely inventive and varied' is how the cooking was characterised by a regular, a description that seems borne out by hermit crab served warm and accompanied by coriander gnocchi, lemon confit, rocket and a vinaigrette crustacé. A thick piece of griddled foie gras on a bed of marinated red cabbage was a memorable first course at an October lunch, and main courses of some substance have included Challans duck roasted in honey, lemon and soy, and venison fillet poached in mulled wine with celeriac and horseradish. Sea bass might be roasted, partnered with fondant potatoes, and sauced with an infusion of orange juice and sage. Typical desserts are hot rhubarb soufflé with lemon ice cream, and highly rated crème brûlée. A wine list was unavailable, but house Burgundy is £3.50 a glass.

CHEF: Guillaume Lebrun   PROPRIETOR: Patrick Guilbaud   OPEN: Tue to Sat 12.30 to 2.15, 7.30 to 10.15   MEALS: alc (main courses £24 to £29). Set L £20, Set D £65   SERVICE: not inc CARDS: Amex, Diners, MasterCard, Visa   DETAILS: 85 seats. 20 seats outside. Private parties: 85 main room, 25 private room. Car park. Vegetarian meals. No-smoking area. No music. Air-conditioned

Peacock Alley ✸✖

Fitzwilliam Hotel, St Stephen's Green, Dublin 2
TEL: (01) 6770708   FAX:)01) 4787043   COST £36–£83

Conrad Gallagher's restaurant, designed by Sir Terence Conran, is a luxuriously large space with subdued lighting, some vivid modern art and stunning views over the park. The carte unrolls in confident length, and the range of culinary reference is wide indeed. Chestnut soup incorporates pieces of roasted pheasant, salsify, cognac and crème fraîche, while langoustines are wrapped in pasta and presented with stewed peppers, chorizo and a chillied tomato consommé. To some, the style may appear to involve a lot of lily-gilding, but the end results are usually worth it. Fillet of beef, for example, arrives in the company of watercress purée, celeriac spaghetti, tomato confit, goats'-cheese ravioli and 'shoestring' potatoes – something for everyone. Finish with a cylinder of bitter chocolate filled with pistachio ice cream, or the likes of lemon tart with raspberry sorbet. Alternatively, abdicate all choice and go for the £65 menu gourmand of eight courses plus coffee. A high-flier's dream wine list is offered: have your £5,000 ready for the '45 Latour – or £17 for one of the well-selected house wines. Conrad Gallagher has now opened Lloyds Brasserie in Upper Merrion Street (see entry).

CHEF/PROPRIETOR: Conrad Gallagher   OPEN: Mon to Sat 12.30 to 2.30, 6 to 11   MEALS: alc (main courses £19 to £27). Set L £23, Set D £45 to £65   SERVICE: not inc   CARDS: Amex, Diners, MasterCard, Visa   DETAILS: 110 seats. Private parties: 120 main room, 20 private room. Car park. Vegetarian meals. No children. No smoking in 1 dining room. Music. Air-conditioned

Roly's Bistro

7 Ballsbridge Terrace, Dublin 4
TEL: (01) 6682611   FAX: (01) 6608535   COST £19–£44

This large establishment spread over two floors provides 'excellent atmosphere, service and prices', according to a reporter who was smitten by 'superb' venison with mashed swede. The menu is eclectic in its approach, moving from salmon and sole terrine wrapped in leeks with saffron mayonnaise, to crispy chicken won ton, bean sprouts, ginger and sesame seed with hoisin sauce. In the main, however, Europe is the guiding light, as in linguine with black olives and basil, and mushroom soup with rosemary. Main courses might be Kerry lamb pie with roasted parsnips, or monkfish with peppers and balsamic vinegar. Desserts show spirit: cardamom-scented crème brûlée, perhaps, or tiramisù made with apricots and orange flower water. The wine list is succinct and fairly priced. House wine is £9.95, and a house selection of a further ten bottles is £10.95 each.

CHEFS: Colin O'Daly and Paul Cartwright   PROPRIETORS: Roly Saul, John O'Sullivan and Colin O'Daly   OPEN: all week 12 to 3, 6 to 10 (10.30 Fri and Sat)   CLOSED: 25 and 26 Dec, Good Fri   MEALS: alc D (main courses £9.50 to £15). Set L £12.50   SERVICE: 10% (optional), card slips closed   CARDS: Amex, Diners, MasterCard, Visa   DETAILS: 160 seats. Private parties: 12 main room. Vegetarian meals. No-smoking area. Wheelchair access (also WC). Occasional music

Thornton's 🍷 ⚡✗

1 Portobello Road, Dublin 8
TEL: (01) 4549067   FAX: (01) 4532947   COST £35–£90

The corner terraced house conversion, in an out-of-town area by the canals of Dublin 8, is 'elegant but understated', with strong blocks of solid colour in carpets and sofas, rough beige silk curtains, and one-inch-square tiles decorated with modern designs. The ambience is calm but not staid, and the black-uniformed staff, mostly young and French, take pride in their work and offer helpful advice on the menu. The choice is not easy, although there are only eight starters and eight main dishes; there is also a six-course tasting menu for the whole table only. Pressed terrine of goats' cheese with yellow tomato and pesto jus, wrapped in fried aubergine skin, makes a rich but not heavy way to begin, while an inspector has been in raptures about a 'sensational' starter of seared foie gras with sliced scallops, tiny heaps of celeriac topped with thin slices of truffle and 'opulent, almost decadent' cep jus. Perfectly cooked turbot is covered with golden potato 'scales' and served with an unctuous saffron sauce, baby fennel adding 'a crunchy textural complexity'.

Praise comes in too for 'excellent' breads, pre-dessert vanilla-scented milk pudding – followed by the visual treats of nougat pyramid with glazed fruits and orange sauce, or 'delicious' Valrhona chocolate pavé – and strong coffee and petits fours. The wine list boasts many big names and superior vintages from Bordeaux, Burgundy and beyond, with Spain, Italy, Australia and California in particular supplying some highly prized bottles. Six house wines start at £15.

CHEF: Kevin Thornton   PROPRIETORS: Kevin and Muriel Thornton   OPEN: Fri L 12.30 to 1.45, Tue to Sat D 7 to 10.30   CLOSED: 1 week Christmas, bank hols   MEALS: alc (main courses £23 to £29). Set L £24, Set D £59   SERVICE: 12.5%   CARDS: Amex, Diners, MasterCard, Visa   DETAILS: 45 seats. Private parties: 35 main room, 15 private room. Vegetarian meals. Children's helpings. No smoking in 1 dining room. Music. Air-conditioned

---

DURRUS   Co Cork   map 16

▲ Blairs Cove

Durrus
TEL: (027) 61127   FAX: (027) 61487
EMAIL: blairscove@tinet.ie
1½m out of Durrus on Barleycove to Goleen road   COST £41–£49

A Georgian manor house in four acres, Blairs Cove is built around a cobbled courtyard complete with a lush garden and lily pond. The dining room has a high-ceilinged chapel-like ambience, but is bright and airy and features a wood-burning grill where the meats are flamed. Mix and match your starters from the buffet table (perhaps home-made brawn, ceviche or curried courgettes) before ordering main courses at table. These take in steamed brill with sauce américaine, or grilled chicken breast stuffed with goats' cheese, served with chilli jam and marinated peppers. After mains, stretch your legs again for desserts, which are set out on top of the grand piano and might include two-tone chocolate terrine, Bakewell tart, crème caramel, and more. The wine list displays a decided partiality for France, although the presence of an Irish Reichensteiner shows some loyalty to the home country. House wines are £12.50.

CHEFS/PROPRIETORS: Philippe and Sabine De Mey   OPEN: Tue to Sat (and Mon July and Aug) D only 7 to 9.30   CLOSED: Nov to Mar   MEALS: Set D £29   SERVICE: not inc, card slips closed   CARDS: MasterCard, Visa   DETAILS: 75 seats. Private parties: 40 main room, 35 private room. Car park. Vegetarian meals. Children's helpings. No-smoking area. Wheelchair access (not WC). Music   ACCOMMODATION: 4 rooms, all with bath/shower. TV. Phone. B&B £35 to £60

GOREY Co Wexford   map 16

▲ *Marlfield House* 🍴 ✳

Courtown Road, Gorey
TEL: (055) 21124   FAX: (055) 21572
EMAIL: marlf@iol.ie   COST £32–£71

Grand this certainly is, with a conservatory dining room, 14 acres of gardens and enough thick carpet to keep the brigade of staff as busy as bees. The brochure says the aim is for 'keeping the standards of yesterday today', and the impression is certainly that standards are high. A change of chef since the last edition of the *Guide* means that, while the style remains global, there is perhaps less emphasis on leaping across continents in search of inspiration. A starter of Asian-style smoked duck breast, wrapped in brick pastry and served with coriander salsa, shows that things have not all changed, but chicken liver parfait with asparagus and green beans, and scallops niçoise with tomato oil and rocket are perhaps more illustrative of the overall focus. Main courses, too, tend towards the likes of roast rack of lamb with mint mash and a ragoût of garden vegetables – very likely picked from outside the back door – or fillet of hake with mixed seafood brandade. Desserts swing from simple lemon posset to gratin of banana with Malibu sabayon and chocolate ice cream. The wine list is serious and pricey, although the adventurous will be rewarded. Six house wines are all £16.

CHEF: Henry Stone   PROPRIETORS: Mary and Ray Bowe   OPEN: Sun L 12.30 to 1.45, all week D 7 to 9 (9.30 Sat)   CLOSED: mid-Dec to end Jan   MEALS: Set L Sun £21 to £23, Set D £36 to £41. Light L available Mon to Sat   SERVICE: not inc, card slips closed   CARDS: Amex, Diners, MasterCard, Switch, Visa   DETAILS: 65 seats. Private parties: 20 main room, 20 private room. Car park. Vegetarian meals. Children's helpings. No children under 10 at D. Jacket and tie. No smoking in dining room. Wheelchair access (also WC). No music. Air-conditioned ACCOMMODATION: 20 rooms, all with bath/shower. TV. Phone. B&B £80 to £490. Rooms for disabled. Baby facilities

---

Not inc *in the details at the end of an entry indicates that no service charge is made and any tipping is at the discretion of the customer.*

HOWTH   Co Dublin

map 16

▲ *King Sitric*

East Pier, Howth
TEL: (01) 8325235   FAX: (01) 8392442
EMAIL: info@kingsitric.ie   COST £33–£74

The MacManuses' seafood restaurant, in a two-storeyed house that was once the home of the local harbourmaster, sits on Balscadden Bay, an improbably short distance from Dublin city centre. As the *Guide* went to press it was undergoing refurbishment, with a wine bar and lounge planned for downstairs and with views of the harbour promised for diners in the upstairs restaurant. Fast nearing thirty years of gastronomic service to Howth, Aidan MacManus's cooking shows no sign of flagging in terms of either imagination or indeed commitment to making use of the freshest of seafood. Monkfish is marinated in lime and served with a tomato ice cream, or opt for more traditional moules marinière, or fish quenelles au gratin. Proceed to seafood couscous, or a fashionable pairing of grilled scallops with Clonakilty black and white puddings. Banoffi pie, or perhaps rhubarb crumble, might lure the sweet of tooth; otherwise, Ireland's celebrated farmhouse cheeses await. An English pair on a summer visit sang the praises of the 'welcoming, friendly and helpful' approach. The commendable wine list includes some excellent Burgundies among a host of seafood-friendly whites from France and the rest of the vinous globe. Red wine lovers are also well catered for, and all oenophiles will be gladdened by very fair prices. House French is £12.50.

CHEF: Aidan MacManus   PROPRIETORS: Aidan and Joan MacManus   OPEN: all week D only 6.30 to 10.30   CLOSED: Christmas, 2 weeks Jan   MEALS: alc (main courses £14.50 to £30). Set D £30. Light L available in summer   SERVICE: not inc   CARDS: Amex, Diners, MasterCard, Laser, Visa   DETAILS: 65 seats. Private parties: 65 main room, 24 private room. Vegetarian meals. Children's helpings. No smoking in 1 dining room. Wheelchair access (also WC). Occasional music. Air-conditioned   ACCOMMODATION: 8 rooms, all with bath/shower. TV. Phone. B&B £70 to £110. Rooms for disabled. Baby facilities (£5)

KANTURK   Co Cork

map 16

▲ *Assolas Country House*

Kanturk
TEL: (029) 50015   FAX: (029) 50795
signposted from N72, NE of Kanturk, 8m W of Mallow   COST £39–£47

The summer and autumn of 1999 marked the thirty-third season for Assolas, which has evolved into a full-dress country-house hotel in that time. Fish from the Cork auctions, local free-range poultry and their own fruits and vegetables, herbs and salads form the backbone of the Bourkes' approach, and Hazel is a confident and inventive chef. English guests on a gastronomic sweep through Ireland wrote in praise of a meal that took in a brochette of superb prawns with a chive beurre blanc, tomato and basil soup, a generous serving of baked monkfish tail topped with mushrooms and herbs, and desserts from the trolley. The front of the menu announces that tipping is not expected – and they mean it. France,

Spain and Italy are the focus of the wine list, which leads with Guigal's benchmark Côtes du Rhône in all three colours at £14.50 the bottle, £3 the glass.

CHEF: Hazel Bourke   PROPRIETORS: the Bourke family   OPEN: all week D only 7 to 8.30 CLOSED: 1 Nov to 1 Apr   MEALS: Set D £32   SERVICE: none, card slips closed   CARDS: Amex, MasterCard, Visa   DETAILS: 20 seats. Private parties: 12 main room, 20 private room. Car park. Vegetarian meals. Children's helpings. No children under 8 at D. No cigars/pipes in dining room. Wheelchair access (not WC). No music   ACCOMMODATION: 9 rooms, all with bath/shower. Phone. B&B £65 to £168. Baby facilities. Fishing

---

KENMARE   Co Kerry   map 16

▲ Park Hotel Kenmare

Kenmare, Co Kerry
TEL: (064) 41200   FAX: (064) 41402
EMAIL: phkenmare@iol.ie   COST £52–£85

The 100-year-old grand country house overlooking the Beara Peninsula and the Caher Mountains is very much on the well-heeled international circuit. Oils and antiques abound, a superb team of waitresses flies in formation, and a 'hushed but not reverential solemnity' pertains in the dining room. In the kitchen Joe Ryan has been promoted to head chef and is producing innovative and accomplished dishes using plenty of tiptop local – and not so local – ingredients. One diner's appetiser exemplifies the style in microcosm: a little pot with a tiny piece of faintly curried braised lamb on a bed of aubergine, laid across with a single chive. Florid dish descriptions can be difficult to imagine, not least for the breadth of ingredients, but come together in taste, texture and prettiness on the plate, such as two fair-sized scallops in half-crown slices, with welcome spiciness from guacamole and roughness from rocket, and a sliver of deep-fried aubergine.

Book an early table if you are set on lobster; others with an eye to sodium, cholesterol and calorie intake may pitch into a mid-course gin and tonic sorbet, to be followed by turbot fillet 'injected with parsley essence' with steamed baby cos lettuce, and later by St Tola goats' cheese on a walnut salad (one of a trio of cheese dishes), rather than a substantial and complicated dessert. France has the edge over the rest of the world on quantity, but quality is high wherever you look on the hefty yet easy-to-follow wine list. House Bordeaux from André Lurton is £17.50.

CHEF: Joe Ryan   PROPRIETOR: Francis Brennan   OPEN: all week D only 7 to 9   CLOSED: 1 Nov to 23 Dec, 3 Jan to mid-Apr   MEALS: alc (main courses £19.50 to £24). Set D £39.50   SERVICE: not inc, card slips closed   CARDS: Amex, Diners, MasterCard, Visa   DETAILS: 80 seats. 30 seats outside. Private parties: 120 main room, 35 private room. Car park. Vegetarian meals. Children's helpings. No children after 8pm in dining room. Jacket and tie. No-smoking area. Wheelchair access (not WC). Music   ACCOMMODATION: 49 rooms, all with bath/shower. TV. Phone. B&B £126 to £284. Rooms for disabled. Baby facilities

---

indicates that there has been a change of chef since last year's Guide, and the Editor has judged that the change is of sufficient interest to merit the reader's attention.

▲ Sheen Falls Lodge, La Cascade ¦

Kenmare
TEL: (064) 41600   FAX: (064) 41386
EMAIL: info@sheenfallslodge.ie
follow signs for Glengariff from Kenmare; hotel
signposted after about ½m   COST £55–£66

The modern building, which is both hotel and leisure complex, sits somewhat oddly in the surrounding verdant countryside of Kenmare Bay. Not that your attention is likely to be swayed for long, however, as both menu and wine list require serious contemplation. Take for example first-course sauté of foie gras, ravioli of smoked bacon and oyster mushrooms with asparagus, and then choose loin of venison with braised salsify with beetroot and caraway essence, or breast of corn-fed chicken with polenta croûton and asparagus, caper and tarragon cream. Desserts might be sugar-glazed lemon tart with raspberry sorbet, or champagne mousse with marinated seasonal fruits. The wine list is a grand collection of clarets, Burgundies and Rhônes of good breed, backed up by some pedigree productions from Spain, Italy and the New World. Prices can be high, but careful hunting will reveal a few bottles under £20.

CHEF: Fergus Moore   PROPRIETOR: Bent Hoyer   OPEN: all week D only 7.15 to 9.30   CLOSED: 30 Nov to 23 Dec, 3 Jan to 5 Feb   MEALS: Set D £37.50   SERVICE: not inc, card slips closed   CARDS: Amex, Diners, MasterCard, Visa   DETAILS: 80 seats. Private parties: 120 main room, 20 to 60 private rooms. Car park. Children's helpings. No-smoking area. Wheelchair access (also WC). Music   ACCOMMODATION: 61 rooms, all with bath/shower. TV. Phone. Room only £168 to £258. Rooms for disabled. Baby facilities. Swimming pool. Fishing

---

KILKENNY   Co Kilkenny   map 16

▲ Lacken House

Dublin Road, Kilkenny
TEL: (056) 61085   FAX: (056) 62435
EMAIL: lackenhs@indigo.ie   COST £35–£51

Diners at Eugene and Breda McSweeney's restaurant and guesthouse have a pleasingly wide choice in the set dinner and in the short carte. Largely traditional ingredients are deployed in imaginative combinations: cappuccino of seafood soup, glazed stuffed fillets of sole with samphire and tarragon butter, warm salad of lambs' kidneys with garlic croûtons, and confit of Callan bacon with Puy lentils and crab apple jelly. The 1990s idiom appears in a starter of grilled goats' cheese on beetroot bread, and in a main course of pan-fried fillet of plaice with chilli jam and pepper salsa. Vegetables are all organic. Breda McSweeney's list of sixty wines includes choice bottles from New Zealand, Australia, Italy and Spain, as well as French classics, and house wines from the McGuinness estate in the Côtes du Ventoux are from Domaine des Anges.

CHEF: Eugene McSweeney   PROPRIETORS: Breda and Eugene McSweeney   OPEN: Tue to Sat D only 6.30 to 10.30   CLOSED: Christmas   MEALS: alc (main courses £17). Set D £25   SERVICE: not inc, card slips closed   CARDS: MasterCard, Visa   DETAILS: 30 seats. Private parties: 35 main room, 15 private room. Car park. Vegetarian meals. Children's helpings. No music. Air-conditioned   ACCOMMODATION: 9 rooms, all with bath/shower. TV. Phone. B&B £36 to £60

KINVARA   Co Galway   map 16

▲ *Merriman*

Kinvara
TEL: (091) 638222   FAX: (091) 637686   COST £20–£49

The Merriman rose from the ashes of a previous hotel that burned down in the 1980s. Perched on Kinvara Bay, its prominent architectural feature is a thatched roof of 1,800 square metres, so extravagantly large that the builders had to resort to Turkish water-reed to finish it, having exhausted Ireland's supply. Breton chef Mathias Salesses aims to make an equally diverting impression in the Quilty Room restaurant, named after a local painter. Smoked salmon comes with cauliflower parfait and a sauce of yoghurt, herbs and almonds, and fish cookery is as bracing as one would expect for the location. Monkfish and clams, for example, are pot-roasted with cabbage, smoked bacon and red wine. A pudding combining apples, prunes and walnuts in a roulade with spiced prune coulis offers a true whiff of Brittany. The wine list nips around the world, picking up a couple of bottles from each region, and opening at £10.50 for house wines.

CHEF: Mathias Salesses   PROPRIETORS: Padraic and Hillary Burke   OPEN: Sun L 12.30 to 2.30, all week D 7.15 to 9.30   MEALS: alc (main courses £9 to £18.50). Set L Sun £12.50, Set D £21   SERVICE: not inc, card slips closed   CARDS: Amex, Diners, MasterCard, Visa   DETAILS: 65 seats. Private parties: 65 main room, 30 private room. Car park. Vegetarian meals. Children's helpings. No-smoking area. Wheelchair access (also WC). Music. Air-conditioned   ACCOMMODATION: 32 rooms, all with bath/shower. TV. Phone. B&B £30 to £70. Rooms for disabled

---

LETTERFRACK   Co Galway   map 16

▲ *Rosleague Manor* 🍞 ⁵⁄✳

Letterfrack, Connemara
TEL: (095) 41101   FAX: (095) 41168
on N59 to Westport, 7m NW of Clifden   COST £27–£65

In the 'timeless' setting diners gaze on 'magical' views of the Connemara coast. Ross Lee, who was co-chef with Rosie Curran for part of the past year, now has charge of the kitchens. If the repertoire continues along similar lines, lunches will remain light affairs: just crab or smoked trout salad, or an 'intensely flavoured' soup such as celery with a Parmesan and blue cheese croûton. The style at dinner has been more elaborate, delivering 'thick, tender' beef fillet that comes blackened and rare if you want it to, Connemara lamb with garden herbs, and roast monkfish with crispy capers. Puddings have included dark chocolate and Bailey's terrine, crêpes suzette, and almond pie. The short wine list is fairly priced, with house Chilean £12.50.

CHEF: Ross Lee   PROPRIETORS: Patrick and Anne Foyle   OPEN: all week D only 8 to 9.30   CLOSED: Nov to Easter   MEALS: alc (main courses £8.50 to £20). Set D £29. Light L available   SERVICE: not inc   CARDS: Amex, MasterCard, Visa   DETAILS: 60 seats. Private parties: 60 main room. Car park. Vegetarian meals. Children's helpings. No children under 10 at D. No smoking in dining room. No music   ACCOMMODATION: 20 rooms, all with bath/shower. TV. Phone. B&B £50 to £150. Rooms for disabled. Baby facilities   (£5)

LISDOONVARNA   Co Clare   map 16

▲ *Sheedy's* ⚐✗   NEW ENTRY

Lisdoonvarna
TEL: (065) 7074026   FAX: (065) 7074555
EMAIL: cmv@indigo.ie   COST £24–£48

Happy marriages of opposites start with the one between the Georgian house
with old fireplaces and ceiling mouldings, and the London-converted-ware-
house-style of the restaurant in the front extension. The bar looks like unaltered
1960s, but the restaurant's bare brickwork and purple and terracotta paint return
us to the 1990s. The cooking offers equally pleasing contrasts, imaginatively
employing spices and exotic flavours with locally sourced, largely organic
ingredients. A tiny bowl of Irish stew as an appetiser might be followed by
'nicely smoky and fresh' house-cured salmon on marinated aubergine, red
peppers and tomato, all crowned by a grilled scallop. Carnivores can choose
between, say, rack of lamb with white bean purée, and slow-roasted duck with
potato and sage stuffing and apple sauce, while roast fillet of monkfish in a
mildly curried parsley crust with mussel cream sauce may be among fish
options. Chocolate mud cake, 'moist, with a deep black chocolate taste',
enhanced by whiskey cream, makes a rich ending to a meal. Local goats' cheese
appears both as a starter of twice-baked soufflé with pears and as a final course
with home-made relishes. The wine list offers thirty carefully chosen bottles,
with house recommendations at £12.50 and nothing above £29.

CHEF: John Sheedy   PROPRIETORS: Martina and John Sheedy   OPEN: all week D only 6 to 9
CLOSED: Oct to Easter   MEALS: alc (main courses £13 to £18.50). Set D 6 to 7 £15.95. Bar food
available   SERVICE: not inc, card slips closed   CARDS: Amex, MasterCard, Visa   DETAILS: 35
seats. Private parties: 35 main room. Car park. Vegetarian meals. Children's helpings. No
smoking in dining room. Wheelchair access (not WC). Music. Air-conditioned
ACCOMMODATION: 11 rooms, all with bath/shower. TV. Phone. B&B £40 to £65

MALLOW   Co Cork   map 16

▲ *Longueville House* ⚐✗

Mallow
TEL: (022) 47156   FAX: (022) 47459
EMAIL: info@longuevillehouse.ie
3m W of Mallow on N72 Killarney road   COST £42–£69

A rambling manor house set in 500 acres of working farmland, Longueville is a
tribute to the self-sufficiency principle. Mr O'Callaghan senior even makes his
own white wine on the estate. Son William is a bold, accomplished chef working
in a thoroughly contemporary idiom seemingly never short of good ideas. Oil
portraits of former Irish presidents look down from the walls of the dining room,
in which you may well eat roasted scallops in a risotto with leek crisps and
chervil vinaigrette, and then sliced duck magret with red cabbage and apple, a
parsnip pancake and cinnamon sauce, before finishing with passion fruit parfait.
Classic wines from France lead the list, but selections throughout are sound.
House French is £15.

CHEF: William O'Callaghan PROPRIETORS: the O'Callaghan family OPEN: all week D only 6.30 to 9 CLOSED: 20 Dec to mid-Feb MEALS: Set D £31 to £45. Bar L available SERVICE: not inc, card slips closed; 10% for parties of 8 or more CARDS: Amex, Diners, MasterCard, Visa DETAILS: 50 seats. Private parties: 40 main room, 14 and 16 private rooms. Car park. Children's helpings. No smoking in 1 dining room. Occasional music ACCOMMODATION: 20 rooms, all with bath/shower. TV. Phone. B&B £60 to £180. Baby facilities. Fishing

---

MIDLETON Co Cork   map 16

Farmgate

Coolbawn, Midleton
TEL/FAX: (021) 632771   COST £17–£45

Máróg O'Brien says she has been running Farmgate since birth, by which she presumably means the birth of the restaurant. She and David Doran use daily fish deliveries, free-range poultry and locally reared beef and lamb to telling effect in what is an honest and direct style of cooking. A meal might trace a course from a balsamic-dressed salad of black pudding with brioche and Gorgonzola, through roasted monkfish with chargrilled red peppers and mussels, to arrive at something like lemon tart or a farmhouse cheese platter. The wine list is a bit light on detail but at least keeps prices at a reasonable level. House Spanish is £11.

CHEFS: Máróg O'Brien and David Doran PROPRIETOR: Máróg O'Brien OPEN: Mon to Sat L 12 to 4, Wed to Sat D 6.30 to 9.45 CLOSED: Christmas, bank hols MEALS: alc (main courses L £5 to £8, D £8 to £17.50) SERVICE: not inc CARDS: Diners, MasterCard, Visa DETAILS: 70 seats. 20 seats outside. Private parties: 50 main room. Children's helpings. Wheelchair access (also WC). Music

---

MOYCULLEN Co Galway   map 16

Drimcong House ♥ ✳

Moycullen
TEL: (091) 555115 and 555585   FAX: (091) 555836
EMAIL: drimcong@indigo.ie
on Galway to Clifden road, 1m W of Moycullen   COST £35–£97

Drimcong is a well-kept seventeenth-century manor house about a mile to the west of Moycullen itself. Gerry Galvin's cooking style is an enterprising one, making for seafood sausage with banana chutney and citrus dressing, roast pigeon with a venison rissole, red cabbage, beetroot and apple sauce, or the rarely encountered mutton, served as the rack with garlic and parsley cream. Irish farmhouse cheeses sit proudly alongside the likes of mango mousse cake at meal's end, and more cake is served with coffee. Wines are arranged by style on a list that favours France but clearly has a soft spot for the New World too. House wines start at £12.50.

All entries in the Guide *are re-researched and rewritten every year, not least because restaurant standards fluctuate. Don't rely on an out-of-date* Guide.

CHEF: Gerry Galvin PROPRIETORS: Gerry and Marie Galvin OPEN: Tue to Sat D only 6.30 to 10.30 CLOSED: Christmas to Mar, bank hols MEALS: alc (main courses £19.50 to £25). Set D £23 to £27 SERVICE: not inc, 10% for parties of 10 or more CARDS: Amex, Diners, MasterCard, Visa DETAILS: 50 seats. Private parties: 50 main room, 10 to 30 private rooms. Car park. Vegetarian meals. Children's helpings. No smoking in dining room. Wheelchair access (also WC). Music

---

NEWPORT Co Mayo   map 16

▲ *Newport House* 🍾 ⁵✳

Newport
TEL: (098) 41222 FAX: (098) 41613
EMAIL: kjt1@anu.ie   COST £42–£51

Thelma and Kieran Thompson's Regency mansion is an elegant retreat on the west coast of Mayo, and popular not least for its salmon fishing rights. Lunch is a matter of soup and cold meats or home-smoked salmon, leaving the main business of the day to be discussed over John Gavin's six-course dinners. There is plenty of fish and seafood, always in some sort of sauce. Pace yourself through gravlax with its traditional dill-mustard accompaniment, or a plate of smoked fish with horseradish sauce, then oysters, if they are available, before a soup, followed by a main course of perhaps brill with celeriac purée, or chicken breast stuffed with Cashel Blue on noodles, or a simple piece of sirloin with sauce béarnaise. At the end, Irish farmhouse cheeses precede fruity desserts, such as home-made blackcurrant ice cream with pineapple and nectarine timbale, or strawberry shortbread with fruit coulis. The impressive wine list covers Bordeaux thoroughly in terms of châteaux, age and price, before switching its gaze to Burgundy and the Rhône. Italy and Australia provide the odd vinous delight too. House wines include Guigal Côtes du Rhône, red and white, at £16.

CHEF: John Gavin PROPRIETORS: Thelma and Kieran Thompson OPEN: all week D only 7 to 9.30 CLOSED: 5 Oct to 18 Mar MEALS: Set D £32. Light L available SERVICE: not inc, card slips closed CARDS: Amex, Diners, MasterCard, Visa DETAILS: 38 seats. Private parties: 12 main room. Car park. Children's helpings. No smoking in dining room. Wheelchair access (also WC). No music ACCOMMODATION: 18 rooms, all with bath/shower. Phone. B&B £75 to £156. Rooms for disabled. Baby facilities. Fishing (£5)

OUGHTERARD Co Galway   map 16

▲ *Currarevagh House* ⁵✳

Oughterard, Connemara
TEL: (091) 552312 and 552313 FAX: (091) 552731
4m NW of Oughterard on Hill of Doon Lakeshore road   COST £29–£34

The format is fixed: everyone dines at 8pm in this Victorian house set amid the wilds of Connemara. In true dinner-party style, seconds are offered and you are encouraged to help yourself. One reporter, returning after thirty-seven years (Harry Hodgson's parents were then in charge), was enthusiastic about the good, no-frills approach evident in seafood soup, and 'excellent' roast mutton. Five courses is the norm: perhaps walnut and Gorgonzola strudel, baked local trout,

657

roast goose with potato stuffing, then white chocolate terrine followed by a selection of Irish cheeses. There's no choice, but June Hodgson will offer alternatives and take account of dietary requirements if given advance notice. The wine list is largely French, fairly priced and with a good half-bottle selection. House wines are £10.20 and £11.20.

CHEF: June Hodgson   PROPRIETORS: Harry and June Hodgson   OPEN: all week D only 8 (1 sitting)   CLOSED: 18 Oct to 1 Apr   MEALS: Set D £21   SERVICE: 10%   CARDS: none   DETAILS: 30 seats. Private parties: 10 main room. Car park. No smoking in dining room. No music   ACCOMMODATION: 15 rooms, all with bath/shower. B&B £53 to £110. Fishing

---

SCHULL   Co Cork   map 16

▲ Restaurant in Blue £✳

Gubbeen, Schull
TEL/FAX: (028) 28305   COST £36–£44

Blue used to be an unusual colour for a restaurant, but the rest of the civilised world has now caught up with Schull. This restaurant is rather bigger than the small entrance suggests, and there is a conservatory too. Some French has sneaked into the otherwise English-language menu: note vermouth 'nage' with sea trout, and 'caviare d'aubergine' with Caerphilly sausage. There are other unexpected touches in grilled scallops on spiced avocado with chilli and lime, or crispy duck with apricot and ginger sauce. More homely is tomato and lovage soup, but Yorkshire pudding with prawns and sauces of both parsley and garlic might raise an eyebrow in Leeds. Another pudding, rice, becomes a luxury with caramelised apple and raisins. The ambience is relaxed and friendly, and the short, fairly priced wine list starts with Spanish and Argentinian house wines at £11 and £11.50.

CHEF: Burvill Evans   PROPRIETORS: Burvill Evans and Christine Crabtree   OPEN: Wed to Sun D only 6.30 to 9.30 (7 to 9.15 in low season)   CLOSED: Nov to Mar   MEALS: Set D £26   SERVICE: not inc   CARDS: MasterCard, Visa   DETAILS: 50 seats. Private parties: 40 main room, 25 to 40 private rooms. Car park. Vegetarian meals. Children's helpings. No children under 9 in dining room. No smoking in 1 dining room. Music   ACCOMMODATION: 2 rooms, both with bath/shower. B&B £35 to £60   £5

SHANAGARRY   Co Cork   map 16

▲ Ballymaloe House £✳

Shanagarry, nr Midleton
TEL: (021) 652531   FAX: (021) 652021
EMAIL: bmaloe@iol.ie
2m outside Cloyne on Ballycotton road   COST £46–£61

The Allens' 400-acre farm supplies much of the produce for what is one of the longer-standing stalwarts of the Irish gastronomic scene, its walled gardens and glasshouses supplementing the exemplary seafood that comes from a fishing village about four miles away. True respect for the seasons is implicit in everything the kitchen puts out, whether wild watercress soup, braised hogget with wild garlic and scallions, or gooseberry and elderflower compote. Roast goose is a favourite meat, and vegetarian dishes show imagination too. The wine list tries to offer something for everyone in its geographical scope; prices are not of the cheapest, but there is a stimulating choice of half-bottles. House Duboeuf is £14.

CHEF: Rory O'Connell   PROPRIETORS: the Allen family   OPEN: all week D only 7 to 9.30 CLOSED: 23 to 26 Dec   MEALS: Set D £34.50   SERVICE: not inc, card slips closed   CARDS: Amex, Diners, MasterCard, Visa   DETAILS: 100 seats. Private parties: 20 main room, 15 and 20 private rooms. Car park. Vegetarian meals. Children's helpings. No children under 7 in dining rooms. No smoking in 1 dining room. Wheelchair access (not WC). No music ACCOMMODATION: 33 rooms, all with bath/shower. Phone. B&B £80 to £160. Rooms for disabled. Baby facilities. Swimming pool

---

WATERFORD   Co Waterford   map 16

Dwyers 🍴✕

8 Mary Street, Waterford
TEL: (051) 877478   FAX: (051) 877480
EMAIL: dwyerest@tinet.ie   COST £24–£43

The Dwyers have now clocked up their first decade at their modestly proportioned restaurant not far south of Waterford Bridge. They are 'charming and friendly hosts', according to visitors who ate there on a Monday and felt compelled to return on the Friday. Spiced carrot soup, elderflower sorbet, chicken stuffed with white pudding and pistachios, and roast cod with mussels and turmeric were the sorts of dishes that impressed them. In addition to the main carte, an early-evening fixed-price deal is offered, incorporating a vegetarian option such as baked onion stuffed with couscous, toasted almonds and dill. Finish with pear and almond tart, or three-coloured chocolate marquise. The wine list leads with France, with one or two selections from elsewhere. Prices start at £11.75 for Muscadet de Sèvre-et-Maine sur lie.

CHEF: Martin Dwyer   PROPRIETORS: Martin and Sile Dwyer   OPEN: Mon to Sat D only 6 to 10 CLOSED: 1 week Christmas, bank hols   MEALS: alc (main courses £11 to £15.50). Set D 6 to 7 £15   SERVICE: not inc   CARDS: Amex, Diners, MasterCard, Visa   DETAILS: 32 seats. Private parties: 24 main room, 8 private room. Vegetarian meals. Children's helpings. No smoking in 1 dining room. No cigars/pipes while other eat. Wheelchair access (also WC). Music (£5)

WICKLOW   Co Wicklow   map 16

▲ Old Rectory 🍴✕

Wicklow
TEL: (0404) 67048   FAX: (0404) 69181
EMAIL: mail@oldrectory.ie   COST £36–£50

The setting is 'surprisingly secluded' despite the proximity of a supermarket, thanks to a curtain of tall trees. In the attractive dining room, where bright chandeliers complement pastel-shaded ceilings and plasterwork covings, dinner is taken at eight o'clock. The carte offers four simple but interesting dishes at each course: perhaps spicy parsnip and bean soup, or cheese fondue, followed by salmon, or venison with girolles and Gewurztraminer. But most diners choose the daily-changing gourmet menu of five courses plus coffee. Its signature flourish is in the use of flowers, in such delicacies as herb consommé with sage flower fritters, or crab with melba toast and wild garlic flower butter. The less floral main dish might be 'expertly cooked' Wicklow Bay salmon trout with tomato sauce, followed perhaps by cheesecake with orange sauce. For £18 you can drink six wines to accompany the gourmet menu. The well-chosen wine list includes a page of exceptional Spanish bottles, mostly Rioja, plus Spanish red and Chilean white house wines at £14 and £13 respectively.

CHEFS: Linda Saunders and Linda O'Sullivan PROPRIETORS: Paul and Linda Saunders OPEN: all week D only 8 (1 sitting) CLOSED: 1 Jan to end Feb MEALS: alc (main courses £16 to £19). Set D £30.50 SERVICE: none, card slips closed CARDS: Amex, MasterCard, Visa DETAILS: 24 seats. Private parties: 16 main room. Car park. Vegetarian meals. Children's helpings. No smoking in dining room. Wheelchair access (not WC). Music ACCOMMODATION: 8 rooms, all with bath/shower. TV. Phone. B&B £78 to £104. Baby facilities (£5)

Round-ups

Looking for a suitable place to eat can be a lottery, especially if you are travelling around the country with no set plans in mind. The Round-up section is intended to provide some interesting gastronomic possibilities, whether you find yourself in a strange city centre or the northern outposts of Scotland. Pubs are becoming increasingly valuable as sources of high-quality food, but the listings also include modest family-run enterprises in country towns, lively café/bars and ethnic restaurants in big cities, and a sprinkling of hotel dining rooms in all parts of the land. Dip into this section and you are almost bound to find somewhere that suits your needs and pocket. Entries are based on readers' recommendations supported by inspectors' reports. Sometimes restaurants appear in the Round-ups instead of the main entry section because seasonal closures or weekly openings limit their usefulness, or because there are changes in the air, or because positive feedback has been thin on the ground. Reports on these places are especially welcome, as they help to broaden our coverage of good eating places in the UK. Round-up entries (outside London) are arranged alphabetically by locality within England, Scotland, Wales, the Channel Islands and Northern Ireland.

England

● **ALDEBURGH** (Suffolk)
152 152 High Street, (01728) 454152. Small high street restaurant offering good-value modern cooking, including daily specials majoring on fish. After red pepper mousse, or a salad of pan-fried scallops and bacon, try perhaps asparagus, pea and mint risotto with griddled prawns, or Aldeburgh skate wing with salsa verde. Finish with raspberry and mascarpone tart. Influences from further afield are apparent in Thai fish cakes, and a tagine of roasted root vegetables with Moroccan spices. The short wine list is from Adnams. Open Tue to Sun (also Mon in summer).

● **AMERSHAM** (Buckinghamshire)
Gilbey's 1 Market Square, Old Amersham, (01494) 727242. Under same ownership as Gilbey's in Ealing (see entry London Round-ups), this red-brick, ivy clad restaurant has pine floors and furniture. Wines at shop prices are the star attraction. Start with rabbit terrine or carrot and coriander soup, followed by salmon ballottine, rich tender Aylesbury duck or 'superb' squid brochette, and finish with 'first-class' lemon tart and 'fab' fine apple tart. Open all week.

● **ARDINGTON** (Oxfordshire)
Boar's Head Church Street, (01235) 833254. Bruce Buchan, formerly at the Bear & Ragged Staff in Cumnor, has taken over the kitchen at this family-friendly country pub. A summer menu shows he has not lost his penchant for colourful, modern fish cookery, taking in warmed oysters with creamy mash and Guinness dressing, seared swordfish with potato bahjee, and tempura of Cornish scallops with chilli jam. Non-fish dishes might be crispy lamb and five-spice salad or beef fillet with rösti. Closed Sun D.

● **BARHAM** (Kent)
Old Coach House Dover Road, (01227) 831218. Expect a warm welcome from the French chef/patron in this small roadside restaurant close to the Channel. Starters might be sardine provençal or freshly cooked langoustines, followed by grilled lamb steak or local wild goose ('cooked to perfection'). Also available are local game in season, a casserole and fish of the day, and maybe spit roast pig. Open all week D, lunch for parties of 6 or more by arrangement.

● **BARNARD CASTLE** (Co Durham)
Blagraves House The Bank, (01833) 637668. The attic of this seventeenth-

century house, built for the Blagrave family, was used as a meeting place by the followers of John Wesley. A warmly furnished first-floor dining room offers a set-price dinner menu and carte. Typical dishes might be fillet of turbot with a mussel and saffron sauce, saddle of hare with hazelnuts and orange, or leg of guinea fowl with a 'subtle' thyme stuffing. Desserts run to raspberry and honeycomb parfait or chocolate and rum bread-and-butter pudding. Tue to Sat D.

● **BARNSTAPLE** (Devon)
Lynwood House Bishop's Tawton Road, (01271) 343695. Long-standing family-run restaurant-with-rooms in a 'Victorian gentleman's residence' about 1 mile south of the town centre. Fish tops the bill on both main and 'lighter meal' menus: chunky fish soup with maybe ten different varieties of fish, poached skate wing with capers, or prawn omelette. Meat eaters and vegetarians will also find a few options, and puddings include 'excellent' crème caramel. Closed Sat L and all day Sun.

● **BARTON-UPON-HUMBER** (North Lincolnshire)
Elio's 11 Market Place, (01652) 635147. 'We have been called an Italian fish restaurant,' writes Elio Grossi. Not an unfair description, considering a menu that runs through the repertoire from pizza Margherita to saltimbocca alla romana, and a more inviting daily specials board offering lots of locally landed fish, cooked simply and served plain or sauced: fennel for sea bass, provençale for halibut, and salsa verde for tuna. Desserts are old Italian favourites.

● **BASLOW** (Derbyshire)
Cavendish Hotel Baslow, (01246) 582311. Country-house hotel in the heart of the Peak District National Park with views over the Chatsworth Estate; oak beams, open fires and antique furniture set the tone within. Start with hot canapés, followed by fresh asparagus strudel with walnut mayonnaise, and then chargrilled fillet of beef with wood-roasted beetroot and aubergine pâté (a dish 'full of nicely blending flavours').

Light meals are served in the Garden Room. Accommodation available. Open all week.

● **BATH** (Bath & N.E. Somerset)
Firehouse Rotisserie 2 John Street, (01225) 482070. Stylish, airy Californian/Italian restaurant in a Georgian building serving up good-quality pizzas – Tuscan roasted vegetables with goats' cheese and thyme, for example, or spicy Baja chicken with salsa, avocado and sour cream – from a brick-fired oven, and rotisserie dishes. Otherwise, there's Caesar salad, fillet of cat-fish seared in Creole spices, or smoked salmon fish cakes. Mandarin and lemon sorbet might be a good way to finish. Closed Sun.

Rendez Vous Provençal 2 Margarets Buildings, (01225) 310064.
Small Gallic bistro on two floors in a pedestrianised street close to Royal Crescent. Grilled wild boar sausage, and casserole of duck breast in mustard sauce have been recommended; finish with a selection of cheeses with a glass of port. Vegetarians might be offered baked lentils, aubergines and sweet potato topped with cheese. A daily three-course menu looks good value and on some days there is a special crêpe menu. Closed Sun.

● **BEVERLEY** (East Riding of Yorkshire)
Cerutti 2 Beverley Station, (01482) 866700. Cheerful 1920s décor creates a pleasant atmosphere in which to enjoy good fish cooking at this family-run restaurant. Devilled crab, Chinese-style scallops, deep-fried monkfish, and goujons of haddock and smoked salmon have been endorsed. There is also plenty for non-fish eaters such as warm chicken liver salad or rack of lamb, and puds are reckoned to be 'very good'. The original Cerutti is at 10 Nelson Street, Hull, (01482) 328501. Closed Sun.

● **BILBROUGH** (North Yorkshire)
Three Hares Bilbrough, (01937) 832128. In a pretty, leafy-laned village, this attractively furnished old-beamed coaching inn offers modern, well-presented food at reasonable prices. Reporters have praised seared scallops – served perhaps with banana relish, or in a

light, creamy sauce – as well as chicken liver parfait, breast of duck with wild mushroom risotto, and medallions of lamb in a red wine sauce. Desserts too get the thumbs-up: 'excellent' tarte Tatin, and bread-and-butter pudding. Mainly New World wines feature on the list, with about ten by the glass. Open Tue to Sun.

● **BIRMINGHAM** (West Midlands)
Berlioz Burlington Hotel, 126 New Street, (0121) 633 1737. In a swish hotel, this is a 'plush, dignified place, with an air of opulence', offering cooking based in France but with occasional Eastern overtones: cumin cream, for example, garnishing a rich parsnip soup. Recommended dishes have included 'sweet' French onion soup, tomato tarte Tatin, and a cassoulet with 'meltingly-cooked chunks' of belly pork with broad and kidney beans. Desserts might include strawberry cheesecake or warm banana strudel. Open all week.

Café Ikon Ikon Gallery, Oozells Square, Brindley Place, (0121) 248 3226. A former school converted into a contemporary art gallery is now home to this bright, airy, high-ceilinged café with large glass doors and views of sculptures. A Spanish menu of tapas and raciones is joined by five varieties of paella (minimum 2 people). Recommended dishes have included artichoke hearts with garlic butter and Manchego cheese, and 'moist' monkfish bruschetta. Toasted sandwiches are available at lunchtime and the café stays open until 11pm from Wednesday to Saturday. Closed Mon.

San Carlo 4 Temple Street, (0121) 633 0251. A light, modern Italian restaurant with plenty of greenery and a menu of just under 150 dishes, running through most of the traditional repertoire: antipasti, pasta, pizzas and main courses. Among more interesting options are avocado with crab, apple, raisins and celery, and a new wave 'healthy' pizza topped with salmon, yoghurt and dill. A further selection of daily fish is advertised on a blackboard, perhaps simply grilled Dover sole or swordfish, or lobster Thermidor with tagliolini. Open all week.

Sfizio Arcadian Centre, (0121) 622 7009. Set in a shopping centre well placed for Birmingham's theatres and main cinema, this new Italian restaurant has pleased locals with its simple traditional cooking. Décor is stylish, in a black, grey and silver theme, but the food is more rustic, ranging from spaghetti carbonara with lots of chunky pancetta to robustly flavoured chicken stuffed with lobster. Supplies from the city's fish market appear in abundance on the specials board, perhaps scallops with white wine and garlic, or monkfish with a peppercorn sauce. Closed Sun.

● **BLACKPOOL** (Lancashire)
Kwizeen 47–49 King Street, (01253) 290045. This new Blackpool bistro follows no prescribed style, defining its own unaffected version of modern European cooking. Some up-to-the-minute ideas are incorporated sensibly alongside more traditional ones, producing, for example, venison glazed with Madeira and blueberries, marinated lamb on couscous pie, Welsh rarebit of halibut with hot chutney, and ravioli of Dublin Bay prawns with ginger and spring onions. Vegetarians might be tempted by ginger and parsnip crumble, and a bargain set-price lunch menu (£4.95 for 2 courses) looks reason enough to visit. Closed Sun.

● **BLEWBURY** (Oxfordshire)
Blewbury Inn London Road, (01235) 850496. A country pub offering inventive food in relaxed surroundings. The owner/chef comes from Brittany and produces dishes along the lines of spicy carrot and Jerusalem artichoke soup with coriander, medallions of beef fillet with a Stilton crust and spinach fondue, and 'excellent' rhubarb and apricot tartlet with elderflower sorbet. Light L available Mon to Sat; closed Sun D and all day Mon.

● **BOSTON SPA** (West Yorkshire)
Spice Box 152 High Street, (01937) 842558. This former chemist's shop on the main street still retains some of the original fittings. The owners have been described as having 'tremendous enthusiasm and flair' and have put

together an unusual wine list. Specials might include fresh oysters, whole lobster, mussels or fresh sardines, while the main menu offers starters of smoked duck or sweetcorn chowder, followed by pan-seared tuna loin or roasted duck breast. Finish with apple tart or ginger spice, or an excellent selection of cheeses. A vegetarian menu is also available on request. Closed Mon L, Sun D.

● **BRADFORD** (West Yorkshire)
Mumtaz Paan House 390 Great Horton Road, (01274) 571 861. Order by the pound or half-pound from a long list of karahi dishes at this basic Pakistani eatery a few miles from the city centre. Familiar names include chicken dopiaza, korma, and tikka, but less familiar are king prawn nariyal, cod anari (with pomegranates), the suffixes indicating which spices and vegetables are used. The usual starters are offered together with vegetarian delicacies such as bel puri. Absolutely no alcoholic drinks are permitted, so drink lassi – plain, salted, sweet or with fruit – from brass pitchers. Open all week.
Symposium 7 Albion Street, Idle, (01274) 616587. This red-fronted, neighbourhood restaurant is run by chef Nick Turner. Typical dishes are grilled goats' cheese on green bean and olive salad, or a terrine of confit rabbit, ham and black pudding to start, followed by wild boar sausages on Stilton mash or fish cakes with stir-fried vegetables. Finish with hot chocolate pudding or crème brûlée with raspberries. Bread has come in for high praise. Closed Sun and Mon.

● **BRIGHOUSE** (West Yorkshire)
Brook's 6–8 Bradford Road, (01484) 715284. Open only for dinner (and not on Sundays), this small bistro with its drawing- and doodle-lined walls offers a weekly-changing menu plus 'favourite specials'. Try pan-fried mackerel sausage on a mixed leaf salad followed by hare fillets with braised Puy lentils, or fried yam with red onion and lime salad. Floating islands or hazelnut cheesecake bring up the rear. Open L in Dec by arrangement.

● **BRIGHTON** (East Sussex)
Bushby's Brasserie 24 Ship Street, (01273) 321233. A small, comfortable converted shop in the centre of town with a frontage that opens on to the pavement in warm weather. A recent reporter enjoyed an 'excellent' platter of smoked fish, followed by nicely pink rack of lamb with tomatoes, onions and black olives, ending with a peach schnapps crème brûlée. Closed Sun D.

● **BRINKWORTH** (Wiltshire)
Three Crowns Brinkworth, (01666) 510366. Popular country pub on the village green, with low ceilings, log fires and antique rustic furniture. Unusual ingredients might include ostrich, kangaroo and crocodile. Reporters, commenting on the generous portions, have enjoyed delicately flavoured salmon suprême, and a dish of monkfish, prawns and mussels in a creamy tarragon sauce. Puddings run to banana pancakes, and chocolate and Grand Marnier mousse. Lunchtime bar snacks embrace jacket potatoes with a variety of garnishes. Staff are friendly and attentive. Open all week.

● **BRISTOL** (Bristol)
Tico Tico 24 Alma Vale Road, (0117) 923 8700. Part of a terrace of shops in a quiet side street in the lively Whiteladies area, this brasserie with bright yellow walls, stripped pine floor, framed prints and artificial flowers offers 'modern rustic cooking' with Eastern leanings. Recommended dishes have included chargrilled lamb chops with lightly curried sautéed potatoes, and pork chop with pear and blue cheese salsa. Finish with a Swiss pear and almond tart, or cinnamon and raspberry shortcake. Expect a friendly welcome, good service, and a reasonably priced non-run-of-the-mill wine list. Open Tue to Sat D only.

● **BROMFIELD** (Shropshire)
Cookhouse Bromfield, (01584) 856565. This roadside restaurant on the A49 north of Ludlow meets your culinary needs all day long. Take breakfast from 9 to 11, lunch in the café from 11 to 6.30, and dinner in the main restaurant. An 'In and

Out' lunch of starter and main course served in under an hour is handy for a quick stop, and a carte and set three-course menu is available in the restaurant for those with more time. A reporter enjoyed garlic mushrooms and a prawn and asparagus salad in the bistro, and a 'handsome' slice of tuna with a warm niçoise salad in the restaurant. Desserts include lemon tart and a 'light' bread-and-butter pudding. Open all week.

● **BROXTON** (Cheshire)
Frogg Manor Nantwich Road, (01829) 782629. John Sykes is 'clearly an eccentric host with a passion for life'. Witness the ubiquitous froggy theme (the creatures appear everywhere except on the menu, unless you count 'toad not in the hole'), plus the fact that he seems to run his smartly refurbished Georgian manor house as a one-man-band, and an eclectic menu (priced in guineas) that veers from old-fashioned steak pie to Singapore-style roast duck breast.

● **BURGH LE MARSH** (Lincolnshire)
Windmill 46 High Street, (01754) 810281. Frank Fleischer, resplendent in chef's whites, personally greets guests to his 'cottagey' restaurant, just a few miles from Skegness. A broad menu catering for all tastes is founded on good supplies: herbs from the garden, meat from a local butcher, fish from Grimsby, and 'excellent' bread, made with flour produced at the eponymous windmill next door to the restaurant. Reporters have enjoyed feta salad with a spicy dressing, crisp roast duckling in Cointreau sauce, halibut with hollandaise, and pecan pie.

● **BURNHAM MARKET** (Norfolk)
Hoste Arms The Green, (01328) 738777. A large seventeenth-century inn on the village green with a bar area for casual drinkers though most space is given over to eating. Local fish and seafood supplies feature, among them Burnham Creek oysters and Cromer crab, the latter perhaps served with cucumber noodles and crème fraîche. Otherwise, the wide-ranging cooking style takes in niçoise salad with sardines and pesto, best end of

lamb with chorizo and globe artichokes, and stir-fried chilli chicken with noodles. Open all week.

● **BURPHAM** (West Sussex)
George and Dragon Burpham, (01903) 883131. Walkers will appreciate this eighteenth-century South Downs inn – a marked route starts and ends here – but leave muddy boots outside the smart bar, noted for its well-kept local real ales and above-average pub grub. The more formal restaurant (dinner only) makes good use of local produce in game risotto, venison in mulled wine and blackberry sauce, and rump of lamb with caraway and mustard dumplings.

● **BURY ST EDMUNDS** (Suffolk)
Ravenwood Hall Rougham Green, (01359) 270345. A Tudor country house-hotel with extensive grounds and animals in the paddocks. The 'delightful ambience' has pleased reporters, as has roast beef with all the trimmings. Otherwise try crispy baked wild salmon cakes or Dover sole with lobster butter, finishing with lemon and treacle tart or white chocolate brûlée. Open all week.

● **BUSHEY** (Hertfordshire)
St James 30 High Street, (0181) 950 2480. The global larder has been scoured to put together a menu as diverse as it is long at this venue of note in an area not overly blessed with good eateries. Dishes can be complex: beef fillet with rösti, spinach, horseradish and asparagus sauce; chargrilled swordfish with courgettes, aubergines and a spicy Moroccan sauce; and tomato gnocchi with a basil and pine kernel sauce are typical. The modern dining room is brightened by a large mural, and obliging staff make sure the show runs smoothly. Closed Sun.

● **BUXTON** (Derbyshire)
Columbine 7 Hall Bank, (01298) 78752. Handy for supper before or after the opera (by arrangement only), this small, informal restaurant has no frills in the décor but more than compensates with 'friendly' service and 'great' value. Typical of the style are shellfish soup flavoured with ginger and lemon grass,

crisp roast Aylesbury duckling with wild mushrooms, and pork cutlets with Stilton and cognac sauce. Vegetarian menu also available.

● **BYTHORN** (Cambridgeshire)
White Hart Bythorn, (01832) 710226. Whitewashed pub serving large portions of food and good Greene King beer in a relaxed and friendly environment. Seafood pasta has been particularly recommended; otherwise try game and Guinness casserole, wild boar sausage with mash, or fish and chips with mushy peas. Puddings described as 'Your Just Desserts' might be Amaretto parfait or toasted fruit sabayon. Closed Sat L, Sun and Mon.

● **CAMBRIDGE** (Cambridgeshire)
Loch Fyne The Little Rose, Trumpington Street, (01223) 362433. Newly opened branch of this chain of fish restaurants opposite the Fitzwilliam Museum. Spacious room with 'charming and attentive' service, plus a seafood shop. Usual choices of Bradon Orach (strongly smoked salmon) or gravadlax to start, good seafood platters and a fish of the day. Steak or sausages for non-fish eaters; finish with chocolate nut tart or caramelised apple crumble. Open all week.
Sala Thong 35 Newnham Road, (01223) 323178. For more than ten years now Supannee Taylor has been providing students, tourists and locals with straightforward, authentic Thai cooking at her family-run restaurant just ten minutes from the city centre. The menu covers everything from soups (hot and sour banana blossom, mushrooms and coconut) and salads (spicy king prawn) to curries (yellow chicken), stir-fries (chicken with chillies and basil) and grills (honey-roasted duck with ginger pickle). Closed Mon.

● **CAMPSEA ASHE** (Suffolk)
Old Rectory Campsea Ashe, (01728) 746524. 'It feels like the home everybody would like in the countryside,' wrote one visitor to this former Georgian rectory with its creeper-clad exterior and 'charming', well-furnished, country-

house-style interior. Dinner is a set-price no-choice menu that might take in warm pastry tartlets of seaweed and scallops, marinated fillet of roast beef in a rich mustard and red wine sauce, and apple caramel or 'yummy' hot ginger pudding. Accommodation available. Open D only Mon to Sat.

● **CASTLE CARY** (Somerset)
Bond's Ansford Hill, (01963) 350464. An extensively renovated bistro with rooms. Light meals are available at lunchtime, while dinner might start with fish soup (including fiery rouille and croûtons) or herb-roasted vegetables with goats' cheese. Main courses of rack of lamb with field mushroom risotto, or roast fillet of salmon with tomatoes and basil, are followed by toffee apple flan or a selection of cheeses: five are offered. Closed Mon and Tue L, Sun and Mon D.

● **CHELTENHAM** (Gloucestershire)
Beaujolais 15 Rotunda Terrace, (01242) 525230. A smart restaurant in a Regency street of shops, with blue woodwork, white tablecloths and framed cartoons of the Beaujolais area on the walls. Typical starters might include feta cheese on a bed of roasted peppers, or crab, avocado and ginger strudel, followed by pan-fried calf's liver on a potato rösti, or grilled halibut with a lemon hollandaise. Hot lemon sponge pudding or iced chocolate parfait round things off. Closed Mon L and Sun.
Daffodil 18–20 Suffolk Parade, (01242) 700055. The 'awe-inspiring' setting is a vast converted cinema with a high ceiling, an art deco theme and aquamarine and cream colour scheme. An open kitchen, positioned where the screen used to be, provides the visual entertainment these days, and Oscar-worthy turns have come in the shape of seared scallops with crispy shredded leeks and red pepper coulis, a provençale-style tart of aubergine, pepper and sun-dried tomato, and honey mousse with tangy orange sauce.

● **CHETTLE** (Dorset)
Castleman Hotel Chettle, (01258) 830051/830096. This converted dower

house on a family-owned estate is decorated with traditional oil paintings. A frequently changing menu might offer lightly spiced aubergine and cream cheese pâté or local crab to start, followed by 'succulent' boned and roast quail stuffed with rice, spinach and pine nuts. Be transported 'out of this world' by warm chocolate pudding. Open Sun L, all week D.

● **CHICHESTER** (West Sussex)
Comme Ça 67 Broyle Road, (01243) 788724. Children are offered Sunday lunch at half-price at this French-style former roadside pub, and pre- and after-theatre menus are available from Tuesday to Saturday. Recommended dishes have included a crusty filo pastry parcel of three cheeses, and chicken pâté with Armagnac to start, followed by charcoal-grilled lamb with deep-fried leeks and a garlic and herb sauce. A selection of desserts is served from the trolley. Closed Sun D and Mon.

● **CHILLESFORD** (Suffolk)
Froize Inn The Street, Chillesford, (01394) 450282. This upmarket pub, built of distinctive local red bricks, dates back to 1490. Fish – caught locally and from Lowestoft market – is a speciality, perhaps fillet of griddled bonito with mango compote. Meat dishes include beef and beer pie, or loin of venison with red onion and juniper berries, while coffee cheesecake or apple and toffee crumble bring up the rear. There is a good choice of wines by the glass, or drink local Naughty Novice or Nun-Chaser beers brewed in nearby Sudbury. Closed Mon.

● **CHIPPING CAMPDEN** (Gloucestershire)
Eight Bells Church Street, (01386) 840371. This old Cotswold stone pub is worth knowing about, not least because it is set in one of the prettiest of Cotswold villages and is itself full of 'Olde English' charm. Add to this the temptation of a blackboard menu offering a mix of hearty pub annuals and some more cosmopolitan dishes, and it makes for an attractive package. Cep risotto, duck braised with bok choy, and summer

pudding have all demonstrated the kitchen's accomplishment.

● **CHIPPING NORTON** (Oxfordshire)
Morel's 2 Horsefair, (01608) 641075. Reporters visiting this small restaurant with its bright, fresh interior and well-spaced tables have been impressed by a number of dishes: among them a tart of scallops with spinach and caramelised onions, noisette of lamb on polenta and goats' cheese, and quail that was a 'delight'. Banana beignet with a toffee soufflé might bring things to a close. A vegetarian menu is also available. Open Tue to Sat.

● **CHITTLEHAMHOLT** (Devon)
Highbullen Chittlehamholt, (01769) 540561. Owned by the Neils since 1963, Highbullen is a large Gothic house set in 200 acres of grounds complete with an 18-hole golf course. Light snacks are available at lunchtime, including ploughman's, sandwiches and meat platters, while the set-dinner menu might offer pan-fried black pudding followed by seafood risotto and finishing with chocolate roulade.

● **CLACTON ON SEA** (Essex)
Wendle's 3 Rosemary Road, (01255) 426316. Owner Bernard Jinadasa cooks everything to order at this simply decorated, comfortable restaurant, where set-price menus might start with chicken livers on a bed of red cabbage, followed by salmon stuffed with crab mousse, then apricot-filled pancakes. A selection of tropical and local seafood (red snapper, dorade, lobster) is always available on the carte, accompanied by 'your choice' of sauce: Creole perhaps, or lemon butter. Open for dinner only, Tuesday to Sunday, but regular themed evenings are held.

● **COGGESHALL** (Essex)
Baumann's Brasserie 4–6 Stoneham Street, (01376) 561453. Opposite the clock tower in this old market town, the brasserie inhabits a sixteenth-century building, with oil and pastel paintings on its walls. A fixed-price three-course menu (weekdays only) includes coffee, and a frequently changing carte is also available. Typical of the output are confit

of pressed guinea fowl, or potted crab to start, followed by griddled veal cutlet, or one of the day's market fish from Billingsgate. An apple, pear and sultana roulade is one way to finish. Closed Sat L, Sun D and all day Mon.

● **COLCHESTER** (Essex)
North Hill Exchange Brasserie 19 North Hill, (01206) 769988 Occupying one of Colchester's finest Georgian properties (look for the famous listed kettle hanging outside) this spacious brasserie deals in modern European food with a few Eastern overtones. The format is good-value two- or three-course set menus (weekdays only) plus a carte (vegetarian and fish dishes are listed separately). Choose perhaps Isle of Wight crab, or Indonesian chicken satay, then honey-roast breast of duck with apricots, or roasted Mediterranean vegetables with basil pasta and olives. End perhaps with ice cream, or chocolate and pear tart with almonds and crème anglaise. Closed Sat L and all day Sun.

● **CONSTANTINE** (Cornwall)
Trengilly Wartha Nancenoy, (01326) 340332. It is worth making the effort to find this remote inn, perched on the side of a wooded valley. A regular bar menu of pub staples is enhanced by blackboard specials of cassoulet, smoked haddock risotto, or navarin of lamb, while more formal meals in the restaurant might run to warm smoked trout and crab with cumin crisps, and wood pigeon on black pudding, finishing with lightly battered deep-fried apricot or good local cheeses. Open all week.

● **COPPULL MOOR** (Lancashire)
Coppull Moor 311 Preston Road, (01257) 792222. For six nights a week (not Mondays), diners at this small former pub sit down together at eight for five ambitious and elaborate courses, including soup and fish before the main event, plus coffee and petit fours at the end. The cooking is as traditional as the format, taking in medallions of beef with horseradish flavoured mash, honey-roast Gressingham duck, and sea bass steamed

in white wine with lemon and herbs. Sunday lunch is four courses but follows similar lines.

● **CORBRIDGE** (Northumberland)
Valley Old Station House, (01434) 633434 The station used to be a real one, and it is still possible to arrive by special train at this Indian restaurant (phone for details), open for dinner only from Monday to Saturday. There are kebabs, tikkas, soups and more to start, then perhaps Shahjhani Pasanda (lamb cooked in cream, yoghurt and almonds), or, for those who like it hot, Ceylon chicken with 'lots of coconut'. Baburchi Ke Pasand is a seven-course surprise dinner for two or four people. A second branch, Valley Junction 347, is at the Old Station, Jesmond, tel (0191) 281 6397.

● **CUDDINGTON** (Buckinghamshire)
Annie Bailey's Ale & Eating House Cuddington, (01844) 291215. A country pub in a picturesque village popular with walkers, Annie Bailey's has a tasteful ambience, enthusiastic staff, and a menu that takes in black pudding, fish cakes, or aubergine and goats' cheese gâteau to start, followed by knuckle of ham on braised celery and leeks or seafood crumble. Its traditional leanings extend to puddings of treacle sponge or chocolate truffle cake. Closed Sat L, Sun D, Mon.

● **DEDHAM** (Essex)
Fountain House Dedham Hall, Brook Street, (01206) 323027. Set in six acres of Constable country, this fifteenth-century cottage offers a weekly-changing menu covering a good mix of traditional and modern English cuisine. Choose a starter of watercress soup, or fish cakes with provençale sauce, and then decide between Beef Wellington, and mixed fish kebab with scallops. For pudding there could be lemon cheesecake, or mixed fruit vacherin with strawberry coulis. A well-priced wine list includes plenty of half-bottles plus a bin-end list. Open Tue to Sat D only.

● **DENSHAW** (Greater Manchester)
Rams Head Ripponden Road, (01457) 874802. An enviable location on

Saddleworth Moor is reason enough to visit this pub/restaurant, but it is also worth stopping to eat. Blackboard menus reveal ambitions well above the local competition, with starters of Greek squid stew or home-made fish cake with chunky tartare sauce, while main courses run to red snapper with garlic, ginger and black-bean sauce, or rack of new season's lamb with a lavender sauce. Desserts include rich cool coffee cheesecake and sticky toffee pudding. Closed Mon L.

● **DODDISCOMBSLEIGH** (Devon)
Nobody Inn Doddiscombsleigh, (01647) 252394. This fifteenth-century inn in an obscure location is well worth the journey through narrow lanes. Typical dishes might be Nobody soup with locally made bread, traditional pork sausages with mash, or hot three cheese and basil 'panini'. It boasts a fantastic selection of around forty cheeses (mainly from Devon), along with a few other local treats: clotted cream fudge cake or organic honeycomb toffee ice cream. The extensive wine list is a big draw. Open all week.

● **EAST STOKE** (Dorset)
Kemps East Stoke, (01929) 462563. The conservatory dining room of this country hotel, overlooking the garden, offers a range of menus covering a lot of ground – and sea. Among dishes enjoyed from the daily-changing lunch menu have been mille-feuille of salmon, smoked haddock, crab and prawns; calf's liver with pancetta, spiced sausage and black pudding; and a vegetarian pasta parcel of spinach and mozzarella cheese. The fresh fish board might offer blue-nose bass, red snapper on squid ink linguini, or salmon with a saffron and dill sauce.

● **ELTON** (Cambridgeshire)
Loch Fyne Oyster Bar The Old Dairy, (01832) 280298. Expect simple décor, and prompt and friendly service at this, one of a quartet of seafood restaurants related to the original in Cairndow (see main entry, Scotland). Choose good oysters, 'small and all the better for it', gravadlax, Loch Fyne kippers or fish of the day from the blackboard. Non-fish

eaters are offered sausages or steak, and everybody can finish with ice cream, sorbet or a selection of Scottish cheeses. Closed Sun D.

● **EVERSHOT** (Dorset)
Acorn Inn Fore Street, (01935) 83228. Under the same ownership as the Fox in Corscombe (see main entry) this stone-built sixteenth-century listed inn was immortalised by Thomas Hardy as the *Sow & Acorn* in his novels. The intimate upmarket panelled restaurant offers Cullen skink to start, followed by whole Megrim sole with anchovy butter or venison casserole with juniper. Banana cheesecake or poached pears with caramel sauce are typical ways to finish. The bar menu ranges from soup, fish and chips to pies and sausages. Vegetarians might be offered green herb risotto or stuffed marrow. Open all week.

● **EVESHAM** (Worcestershire)
Evesham Hotel Coopers Lane, (01386) 765566. Built in 1540 as a Tudor farmhouse and modernised in 1810, this long-standing family-run hotel has pleasant gardens that include six mulberry trees and a Cedar of Lebanon planted in 1809. Recommended dishes have included crab cocotte and ostrich in a Madeira sauce, as well as 'tender' walnut lamb cutlets, and marmalade ice-cream; children have their own menu. A pleasant ambience – including the jokey menus – and good service are appreciated; an extensive wine list covers the world minus France and Germany. Open all week.

● **FAWLEY** (Buckinghamshire)
Walnut Tree Fawley, (01491) 638360. Follow the long single track road to this friendly, welcoming country pub-restaurant. The blackboard menu in the bar is the same as the printed one in the (non-smoking) conservatory. Reports praise baked crab with prawns in cream sauce glazed with Parmesan; confit of poussin in brandy, apple and cream sauce; accurately grilled Dover sole; and desserts such as sticky toffee pudding with 'superior' vanilla ice cream. Open all week.

● **FELSTED** (Essex)
Rumbles Cottage Braintree Road,
(01371) 820996. Joy Hadley has been
cooking for sixteen years at this white-
painted, sixteenth-century cottage in the
heart of Essex. She grows many of the
vegetables and is keen to experiment to
the extent of featuring a 'guinea pig'
menu of new dishes. Dishes are based on
the best produce available on any given
day, and might include duck pâté or king
prawn and pawpaw salad to start,
followed by gingered beef or salmon
teriyaki. Earl Grey tea fruit salad, and
white chocolate brandy Alexander are
among desserts. Service is efficient and
polite. Open Tue to Sat D and Sun L.

● **FLITWICK** (Bedfordshire)
Flitwick Manor Church Road, (01525)
712242. A Georgian manor house in a
peaceful, secluded setting (only three
miles from the M1) with an elegant and
comfortable interior. A nice array of
appetisers might be followed by 'smooth'
roasted sweetcorn and jalapeño broth, or
smoked haddock fish cakes, and main
courses of pan-fried chicken suprême in a
morel cream, or baked salmon fillet on
beurre blanc. Extensive wine list.
Convenient for Woburn, Whipsnade and
Luton Hoo. Open all week.

● **FORTON** (Lancashire)
El Nido Whinney Brow Lane, (01524)
791254. Lancashire may be the location
but the menu is almost entirely Spanish
and in Spanish. For example chanquetes
(local name whitebait), to conejo Santa
Cruz (rabbit with wine, vegetables and
chorizo) or paella (paella). Most of the
long menu also appears in the £15.50
three course table d'hôte and the early
birds' menu, even better value at £10.95.
Some brasserie dishes are more
international such as Mexican influenced
taco hotpot, oriental style pollo ahumado
and 'exotic fish'n'chips'. Open Sat and
Sun L, Tue to Sun D.

● **FOTHERINGHAY** (Northamptonshire)
Falcon Inn Fotheringhay, (01832)
226254. The most recent addition to the
Hunstbridge stable (see main entries at

Great Yeldham, Keyston and Madingley,
and a Round-up in Huntingdon), the
Falcon Inn is still very much a local,
situated in the heart of the village
overlooking the impressive church. Chef/
patron Ray Smikle cooks contemporary
food: chilled gazpacho or grilled salmon
and leek terrine to start, and main courses
of sea bass with ratatouille, saffron mash
and spinach, or a salad of penne, roast
peppers, cannellini beans, rocket and
chilli. Blueberry, mascarpone and
Amaretti tart makes an interesting finish.
The flexible approach receives many
plaudits: there is a single menu
throughout the pub, eat only a single
course if you wish, and small portions are
available for children. Closed Mon L.

● **FROME** (Somerset)
Croft's 21 Fromefield, (01373) 472149.
Authentic Thai home cooking is one of
the attractions at this small, 'slightly
rustic' restaurant run by a husband and
wife team: the regular menu is
occasionally replaced by a no-choice
three-course option that takes in deep-
fried stuffed chicken wings, and beef
curry with peanuts and tamarind. At
other times expect more familiar fare
along the lines of salmon fish cakes,
chicken baked with Parma ham and
goats' cheese, and caramel cheesecake.

● **FUNTINGTON** (West Sussex)
Hallidays Watery Lane, (01243)
575331. A charming, pretty, thatched,
family-run village restaurant, with a
warm and restful atmosphere. Reporters
have recommended pork with prunes,
salmon with monkfish and banana
pancakes, and raspberry crème brûlée.
From the set lunch menu, or the carte,
also consider tiger spring rolls, confit of
duck with girolles, or fillets of lemon sole
and red mullet. Closed Mon, Sat L, Sun D.

● **GEDNEY DYKE** (Lincolnshire)
Chequers Main Street, (01406) 362666.
A bright, well-kept Fenland pub with a
warm and friendly welcome, Chequers
goes in for modern eclecticism. Start with
warm goats'-cheese salad, or tian of fresh
crab with gazpacho sauce, and move on

to stuffed Gressingham duck breast in marsala sauce, or herb-crumbed monkfish tails with a red pepper salsa; vegetarians are also offered a good choice. Adnams provide beers and a list of around sixty wines. Open all week.

● **GILLAN** (Cornwall)
Tregildry Hotel Gillan, (01326) 231378. Stunning views, an attractive dining room with prettily laid, well-spaced tables, and 'professional, friendly and obliging service' are all pluses at this clifftop hotel. Fish dishes have been particularly praised: spicy tiger prawns in soy and ginger, salmon fillet with a vermouth and mint sauce, and crab cakes. Crème brûlée has been recommended for pudding. Accommodation available. Open D only.

● **GOSFIELD** (Essex)
Green Man The Street, (01787) 472746. A lively, friendly Greene King pub, offering a tempting daily-changing blackboard menu of traditional English country cooking, with a few contemporary twists. Expect to find avocado with crab and prawns, pheasant casseroled in red wine, steak and kidney pudding, or an oriental king prawn platter with sweet-and-sour sauce. A pair of regulars praised consistency, recommending roast lamb and beef, and 'beautifully cooked' tongue with a port and cranberry sauce. Service is 'faultless'. No food Sun D.

● **GRAMPOUND** (Cornwall)
Eastern Promise 1 Moor View, (01726) 883033. The exotic connotations of the name may seem at odds with the location in a small village on the River Fal, but the menu combines the virtues of the Far East and Cornwall with a good selection of fish and seafood done up in traditional Szechuan and Cantonese style. Crab braised with ginger and spring onion, deep-fried oysters, and stir-fried fillet of Dover sole are typical; there are also plenty of meat and vegetable options. Open Thur to Mon D only.

● **GREAT WHITTINGTON** (Northumberland)
Queen's Head Great Whittington, (01434) 672267. Hidden away in a tiny, remote village overlooking lovely countryside, this traditionally decorated old whitewashed inn offers better-than-average pub grub. It aims to satisfy all tastes with old-fashioned regional and hearty dishes and some modern thinking. Traditionalists might opt for steamed leek pudding, or pot-roasted guinea-fowl with bacon and mushrooms, while the fashion-conscious might prefer braised scallops on balsamic-dressed salad, or fried black pudding with beetroot relish.

● **GREAT YARMOUTH** (Norfolk)
Seafood Restaurant 85 North Quay, (01493) 856009. This recently refurbished family-run restaurant is thoroughly focused on fish. Service has been described as 'attentive but unobtrusive' and the menu offers Dover sole in a Dublin Bay prawn sauce, mixed fish and shellfish platters, scampi in a garlic sauce, and fresh lobsters from the tank. Non-fish eaters can enjoy steaks or beef stroganoff. Closed Sat L, Sun and bank hols.

● **GRIMSTHORPE** (Lincolnshire)
Black Horse Inn Grimsthorpe, (01778) 591247. Accommodation, real ales and bar 'brasserie' meals are offered at this traditionally decorated eighteenth-century coaching inn, but the focus is on the ambitious restaurant. Its industrious kitchen actively seeks out local produce as well as making all its own bread, pasta and ice cream. Cooking aims high and results are elegantly presented, typically including fillet of Lincoln Red steak (with sweet potato and parsnip purée, lentils and red wine sauce), or baked sea bass (with wilted leaves, pan-fried chorizo, rösti and vanilla 'cappuccino' jus). Closed Mon.

● **GRIMSTON** (Norfolk)
Congham Hall Lynn Road, (01485) 600250. The long-standing owners of this Georgian country house hotel are trying to sell the property, and a new chef arrived just as the *Guide* was going to

press. James Parkinson lists stints at the Aubergine (see entry, London) and L'Ortolan (see entry, Shinfield) on his CV, so expectations are high. The style of food to date has seen a terrine of ham knuckle and foie gras followed by fillet of sea bass, then baked honey cheesecake. Light lunches and snacks are also available. Open all week. Reports please.

● **GUILDFORD** (Surrey)
The Gate 3 Milkhouse Gate, (01483) 576300. Former chef Keith Russell is now the owner of this two-storey restaurant off the high street and it was under refurbishment as we went to press, so more reports please. The new menu offers goats' cheese ravioli with tomato and herb coulis or a marinated brochette of king prawns and monkfish to start, followed by roast guinea fowl with salardaise potatoes, or glazed pork with mustard mash and apple jus. Puddings veer towards traditional pear and almond tart or rhubarb and gooseberry crumble. Closed Sun.

● **HARROGATE** (North Yorkshire)
Bettys 1 Parliament Street, (01423) 502746. 'I always think of this place as somewhere for tea and cakes, but they also do excellent light lunches,' wrote a reporter who enjoyed a salad of avocado, bacon and Parmesan, and a Mediterranean tart with rösti. This is the original version of what is now a highly popular mini-chain with branches across North Yorkshire. Open all week.
Oliver's 24 24 King's Road, (01423) 568600. Part of a Victorian terrace carefully converted into a light, bright and modern restaurant. Expect brasserie style food with a distinctly global flavour: Thai spiced fish cakes, roast scallops and panzanella salad with chargrilled foccacia to start, followed by salt roast cod or cajun seared chicken breast. Finish with warm fig tart or iced treacle sponge pudding. Attentive and informal service. Closed Sun.
Rick's Just for Starters 7 Bower Road, (01423) 502700. A compact bistro with a relaxed atmosphere, pleasant service and bargain prices. Most dishes on the printed

menu can be taken as either starter or main course, and (as the name suggests) a meal can be based on starters only; a daily blackboard lists further main courses. Typical of the fairly traditional style are salmon and dill fish cakes, crêpe Alfredo, oyster mushroom box, or Thai chicken with ginger, lemon grass and bok choy. Desserts range from hot sticky toffee pudding to warm pear and almond tart. Closed Sun L.

● **HARROW** (Greater London)
Golden Palace 146–150 Station Road, (0181) 863 2333. A good neighbourhood Chinese restaurant, evidently the hub of the local Chinese community, also attracts others who appreciate the friendly atmosphere and consistent, authentic cooking at 'Chinatown prices'. A regular has praised dim sum such as siu mai, deep-fried sesame prawn dumplings, fried rice noodles packed with pork, chicken, squid and vegetables, and 'fantastic' steamed baby octopus in curry gravy. Open all week.

● **HARVINGTON** (Hereford & Worcester)
Mill at Harvington Anchor Lane, (01386) 870688. This Georgian house, standing in eight acres of woodland, with 200 feet of river frontage and a 1750s malting mill behind, is now a hotel and restaurant. In 1998 a flood destroyed everything, but it has been fully restored with the addition of a daytime eaterie, The Chestnut Tree, serving light lunches of black pudding with potato cake and an apple and sage sauce, or baked fish crumble. In the main restaurant try carpaccio of monkfish, or chicken liver salad, followed by lamb argenteuil or fillets of red mullet on a bed of braised aubergine. Open all week.

● **HEREFORD** (Hereford)
Café at All Saints High Street, (01432) 370415. Fresh and organic produce is the foundation for good-value vegetarian lunches and all-day take-aways in a medieval working church. Eat anything from a sandwich or a piece of cake with a cappuccino to a hot meal of goats'-cheese gratin, or chilli bean casserole, or choose from the summer salad selection. Desserts

might be pecan pie or ginger cake. Drink local apple juice, cider, beer or house wines. Lunch 12 to 2.30 Mon to Sat; take-aways 8.30 to 5.30.

● **HOUGHTON CONQUEST** (Bedfordshire)
Knife & Cleaver The Grove, (01234) 740387. A converted pub with a conservatory-style dining room and rear patio garden, offering a good value lunch menu, plus a carte. The bar menu and specials board might offer smoked parsnip soup, daube of shin of beef with black olives, and puddings of apple and Amaretti meringue sponge, or crème brûlée tart. A wide range of fish is on offer including whole fresh lobsters, a medley of seafood, 'excellent' steamed sturgeon, or red snapper. Extensive wine list with two dozen by the glass. Closed Sun D.

● **HUNTINGDON** (Cambridgeshire)
Old Bridge Hotel 1 High Street, (01480) 452681. This handsome eighteenth-century hotel overlooking the River Ouse is part of the Huntsbridge group (see main entries at Great Yeldham, Keyston and Madingley, and a Round-up in Fotheringhay), whose modern attitude in traditional surroundings is something of a hit. A new chef this year is producing a menu that might start with jellied eel terrine, or Caesar salad, and move on to baked halibut with fennel or rare calf's liver. Finish with passion fruit mousse or lemon polenta cake. The same menu is available in the terrace or the main restaurant. Closed Sun D.

● **ILKLEY** (West Yorkshire)
Bettys 34 The Grove, (01943) 608029. Branch of a popular mini-chain of tea shops spread throughout North Yorkshire. As well as the famed cakes, breads and teas, there are also more substantial dishes such as club sandwich, pan-fried salmon salad or sausages with rösti. Open all week.

● **KELSALE** (Suffolk)
Hedgehogs Kelsale, (01728) 604444. This small sixteenth-century 'country cottage' restaurant, attractive inside and out, caters for hearty Suffolk appetites with a good-value three-course menu

that offers something for everyone: from crispy confit duck with green beans and mushrooms, and fillet of Scotch salmon with seafood and tarragon, to chilli beef samosa, Chinese-style glazed pork hock, and roast pigeon breast with chorizo and roast parsnips. Closed Sat L and Mon.

● **KING'S LYNN** (Norfolk)
Riverside King's Lynn Arts Centre, 27 King Street, (01553) 773134. Enjoy the view over the river from this light and airy restaurant in the Arts Centre complex, while studying the menus: light lunch, full lunch, evening carte, or vegetarian. Light dishes are represented by pasta, or spinach and mushroom pancake, main courses by pan-fried salmon, or venison and wild mushroom pie. More elaborate evening main courses take in braised fillet of black sea bass with Pastis, and honey roast duck with roast parsnips and apples. Closed Sun.

● **KINTBURY** (Berkshire)
Dundas Arms 53 Station Road, (01488) 658263. Traditional old pub between the Kennet & Avon canal and the river, with tables on the terrace for summer eating. Recommended dishes have included a 'masterly' ham hock terrine, smoked cod's roe with pipérade, bang bang chicken, 'tender, lightly gamey' roast partridge, and slices of venison in a rich onion sauce. Well-presented desserts run to sticky toffee pudding and frozen coffee and praline mousse; huge wine list. Closed Sun and Mon D.

● **KNIGHTWICK** (Worcestershire)
Talbot Knightwick, (01886) 821235. This large, comfortable, white-painted fourteenth-century pub, quietly situated on the banks of the River Teme, is well known for its local sourcing of materials, including organic produce from its own gardens, meats from its own farm animals, and beer brewed from its own hops. Inside are exposed beams, log fires, comfortable chairs and well-set tables, plus 'very welcoming, but unobtrusive' service. Recommended dishes have included spiced venison, goose cassoulet, steak and mushroom pudding, and chicken basquaise. Damson and rosemary

ice cream, and pear and frangipane tart both show 'a precise touch with ingredients'. Accommodation available. Open all week.

● **KNUTSFORD** (Cheshire)
Belle Epoque 60 King Street, (01565) 633060. Art nouveau-style dining room in a historic building run by the Mooneys for over a quarter of a century. Typical starters of black pudding with curried apple and onion compote, or Cheshire cheese sausage, are followed by gammon with pineapple salsa, or fish of the day such as braised monkfish with mash. For afters crème brûlée with liqueur-soaked oranges has been 'tasty and well executed'. Accommodation available. Closed Sat L and all day Sun.

● **LANGTOFT** (East Riding of Yorkshire)
The Old Mill Mill Lane, (01377) 267284. Surrounded by open countryside, the Old Mill was originally an eighteenth-century farmhouse with a corn mill (which still stands behind the hotel). The menu offers a variety of local produce and fresh fish from the nearby coast. Typical are seared king prawns with a Thai-dressed salad, roast rack of lamb with garlic mash, and warm chocolate and frangipane tart. Vegetarians might head for red onion tart, or tagliatelle in a creamy Stilton sauce with asparagus and wild mushrooms. Accommodation available. Open Sun L and all week D.

● **LAVENHAM** (Suffolk)
Swan High Street, (01787) 247477. 'A wonderful old building of ancient beams and odd angles meandering its way along the sloping main street in the picturesque medieval village of Lavenham,' wrote a reporter in lyrical mood. Beams and leaded windows continue the traditional theme inside, while the menu adds a modern note with open ravioli of cured salmon with beurre blanc, and asparagus and pea risotto topped with crostini of Parmesan, olives and sun-dried tomatoes. Desserts might include baked Bramley apple or treacle tart. Open all week.

● **LEEDS** (West Yorkshire)
Bibis Minerva House, (0113) 243 0905. Long-standing Italian trattoria with a large menu, plus blackboard dishes ranging from halibut to kangaroo. Visitors have enjoyed 'perfect' seared scallops, 'fresh' sea bass with king prawns in a 'very good' white wine and lemon sauce, and 'lovely, tender, massive' tuna steak. Or choose pasta, pizza, saltimbocca, or scaloppa di vitello. Open all week.

Olive Tree Oaklands, 55 Rodley Lane, Rodley, (0113) 256 9283. A Victorian house on the city's outer ring road is an unlikely site for a Greek Cypriot taverna, but there it is. The owner's warm welcome and farewell add to the sympathetic ambience. Prices are modest for the traditional array of meze including a full range of dips and 'beautifully moist and spiced' keftedes (meat balls). The house dessert stafidhoppita incorporates orange liqueur as a welcome balance for its honey-sweetness. Open all week.

Paris Calverley Bridge, (0113) 258 1885. Under the same ownership as Leodis (see main entry), this spacious air-conditioned modern restaurant is in an old Victorian building, with pleasant unobtrusive service from friendly staff. Choose chargrilled salmon with olives and mash, or generous duck confit with good vegetables, followed by lemon tart or chocolate marquise. An extensive, well-priced wine list includes two dozen half-bottles. Closed Sat L.

● **LICHFIELD** (Staffordshire)
Chandlers Corn Exchange, (01543) 416 688. A spacious brasserie with stained-glass windows and subdued, tasteful décor on two floors of the old Corn Exchange, Chandlers presents ambitious 'Euro-mix' menus with some Eastern overtones. Reporters have praised calves' liver with buttery sage and pancetta, monkfish with salsa, and 'perfect' crème brûlée; or you might opt for lemon grass and coriander couscous with seared chicken suprême. Dishes on the carte have been more successful than on set menus. Brisk, professional service. Open all week.

● **LITTLE ECCLESTON** (Lancashire)
The Smithy Cartford Lane, (01995) 670485. Some attractive old buildings

have been sensitively converted into a country restaurant, its décor defined by horse brasses and green and white table settings. Typical of the homely cooking style are fettucini with cream and mushroom sauce, potted chunks of salmon with hollandaise and a dash of caviare, and 'well-judged' poached chicken à la crème with a brandy cream sauce. With early-bird specials, excellent value set-price and children's menus, it has been described as 'a real find'. Open Sun L, Tue to Sat D.

● LITTLE WALSINGHAM (Norfolk)
Old Bakehouse 33 High Street, (01328) 820454. Recent visitors to this partly Georgian house in a medieval village have enjoyed warm tartlet of goats' cheese with a walnut and redcurrant dressing, pan-fried breast of Barbary duck with a honey and ginger glaze, and home-made salmon fish cakes with a lemon butter sauce. Typical of desserts might be bramble sorbet or brandy apricot mousse. Vegetarians have their own menu, and on Thursday evenings a limited choice menu is offered, often featuring new dishes. Open Wed to Sat D and once a month for Sun L.

● LIVERPOOL (Merseyside)
Number Seven Café 7 Falkner Street, (0151) 709 9633. Under the same ownership as Ziba (see main entry, Liverpool), this modern shop conversion, much patronised by students, also has a deli and an art gallery behind. Start with breakfast and go on to soup or a full lunch: Greek feta salad, chicken fricassee with wild mushrooms, and sticky toffee pudding perhaps. After tea and cakes in the afternoon tuck into a three-course dinner. Menus are half-vegetarian, and meats on the other half we are told are partly sourced from the owners' own 'in transition to organic' farm. A short, useful wine lists has some interesting choices. Closed Sun D.
Taste Albert Dock, (0151) 709 7097. Located within the Tate Gallery, Taste is considered an 'exceptionally pleasant environment'. It functions as a café-bar by day, offering a range of salads,

sandwiches, burgers, plus such things as penne with goats' cheese, and bangers & mash, then at 6pm becomes a bistro, enhancing the repertoire with the likes of grilled Barnsley chop with mint and red wine jus, or lemon-marinated pork sautéed with fennel. Closed Sun D.

● LONGDON GREEN (Staffordshire)
Red Lion Inn Longdon Green, (01543) 490250. Tastefully converted red-brick pub overlooking the village green. Lunchtime bar snacks include soup, sandwiches, and maybe stuffed mushrooms or steak and kidney pie. The main menu might offer smoked Barbary duck breast with raspberry vinaigrette, followed by rack of lamb with black cherry sauce, or pan-fried halibut steak with pesto. Finish on tarte au citron and a 'very calorific' 'death by raspberry and white chocolate'. Closed Mon L.

● LONG MELFORD (Suffolk)
Chimneys Hall Street, (01787) 379806. Sixteenth-century timbered restaurant in a historic town, with exposed beams and inglenook fireplaces. A lunchtime set menu and evening carte offer carrot and coriander soup, or deep-fried Brie fritters with tomato chutney, followed by baked fillet of salmon, or roast poussin stuffed with ricotta and sage. Finish with apple and sultana strudel, or blackcurrant bavarois. Regular speciality evenings cover topics such as 'the delights of the Mediterranean' or 'the taste of Burgundy'. Closed Sun.

● LOOE (Cornwall)
Trawlers Buller Quay, (01503) 263593. Fish is not surprisingly the mainstay at this 'very pleasant quayside restaurant' offering a friendly welcome and good service. The influence of the American chef shows up in 'subtly spiced' Cajun crab fish cakes, while 'superb' fish soup comes in a tureen large enough for a triple helping. Main-course John Dory poached in cider has been 'outstanding', and recommended puddings include crêpes Suzette, and profiteroles filled with ice cream. Open Tue to Sat D only (also Mon D June through Aug).

● **LOWER ODDINGTON**
(Gloucestershire)
Fox Inn   Lower Oddington, (01451)
870555. This creeper-covered pub in the
main street of a pretty village is only a five
minute drive from Stow on the Wold. Sit
in the Green Room alongside pictures of
Queen Victoria and her family, while a
welcoming owner provides 'wholesome'
home-cooked meals in a 'friendly, buzzy'
atmosphere. On offer might be
Gloucestershire pie, or salmon goujons
with tartare sauce, followed by sticky
toffee pudding or lemon crunch. Wash it
all down with one of the real ales on
offer. Open all week.

● **LOW LAITHE**   (North Yorkshire)
Carters Knox Mill   Summer Bridge,
(01423) 780607 Originally a silk mill,
Knox Manor dates from around 1750 and
is set in beautiful Nidderdale countryside.
Typical dishes served in the large upstairs
dining room might be a parcel of Brie
with crab and spinach, roast best end of
Nidderdale lamb with a herb crust, and
banana and blueberry bread-and-butter
pudding. Carters Knox Trio is half a
lobster, sole and salmon in a vermouth
sauce. A bar/bistro is downstairs.
Accommodation available. Open all
week.

● **LYMINGTON**   (Hampshire)
Old Bank House   68 High Street, (01590)
671128. 'Well-prepared and -presented'
food is served by 'friendly and entusiastic'
staff in this unpretentious converted bank
with a vine-covered patio; bargain-price
weekday lunches are a draw. Expect
warm pigeon breast, or shredded crispy
duck on Thai fried noodles, followed by
roast monkfish wrapped in Parma ham,
or honey roast lamb noisette on spinach
and goats' cheese. Closed Sat L and all day
Sun.

● **MANCHESTER**   (Greater Manchester)
Café Exchange   Royal Exchange Theatre,
St Ann's Square, (0161) 932 6666. The
rather bleak split-level theatre café
becomes quite handsome at night, with
black cloths on the tables to match the
leather seats. Subtly illuminated wooden
reliefs of cultural icons from Chaucer to

Nureyev line the walls. A run of
recommendations from the short menu
has included red mullet and saffron soup,
moules marinières, roasted Provençale
vegetables, roast cod on ratatouille, duck
confit, crème brulée and chocolate truffle
cake. Friendly informed service with last
orders at 1.30am. Closed Sun.
Market Restaurant   104 High Street,
(0161) 834 3743. This small, friendly
restaurant celebrates its twentieth
birthday in 2000. Recommended dishes
have included twice-baked courgette
soufflé with goats' cheese, breast of
Barbary duck on a sorrel pancake, and
chocolate amaretti mousse. Or be brave
and try 'patatas brava', proceed to
peppered fillet of beef with red wine
gravy, and cap it all with English cheeses
and home-made chutney. Good selection
of beers and wines. Open Wed to Sat D
only.
Pearl City   33 George Street, (0161) 228
7683.This well-established restaurant in
the heart of Manchester's Chinatown is a
sound choice for traditional Cantonese
cooking. A comprehensive menu runs
through all the old favourites, and one
reporter considered duck with prawn-
meat stuffing 'as good as you'd get
anywhere'. Dim sum have been
recommended, as have the various set
menus, which offer good value and
generous flexibility in choice. Open all
week.
Sanam   145–151 Wilmslow Road, (0161)
224 1008. Lavishly decorated Indian
'sweet house and restaurant' that has
been attracting crowds of locals, including
many Asian families, for 30 years. The
menu runs through a familiar range of
reasonably priced curries, and a few less-
familiar items (karahi heart and kidneys
being a notable example), but the range
of home-made traditional Indian sweets
(ras malai, gulub jamun, kulfi and 20
different versions of burfi) are what to
look forward to. Open all week.

● **MAWGAN**   (Cornwall)
Yard Bistro   Trelowarren, (01326)
221595. Trevor Bayfield has been doing

his best to support local produce and suppliers at his converted stable block bistro since long before it became fashionable to do so, and he maintains a defiantly individual approach. The blackboard menu turns up plenty of fish – home-pickled wild salmon in cognac, and fried monkfish fillets with chives and sun-dried tomatoes, for example – plus Cornish lamb, beef and game, all served in a lively, friendly atmosphere.

● **MELMERBY** (Cumbria)
Village Bakery Melmerby, (01768) 881515. The Village Bakery only uses organic ingredients for its breakfasts, light meals, sandwiches, lunches and teas, to make home-made soups, quiches, pies and fresh scones. More substantial dishes run to grilled rainbow trout wrapped in bacon, or pasta with sun-dried tomatoes and pesto. The upstairs gallery has baking equipment and books for sale; breadmaking courses are also held, making use of their wood-fired brick oven.

● **MERLEY** (Dorset)
Les Bouviers Oakley Hill, (01202) 889555. The good value lunch menu in this comfortable conservatory dining room features its 'renowned' poached egg on brioche with smoked salmon and hollandaise sauce, as well as duck and orange parfait, followed by braised chicken chasseur with mushrooms and tarragon, or seared fillet of cod with sage. A menu gourmand and a surprise menu are also available (minimum two people) and might offer hot cheese soufflé followed by boned and roasted quail filled with couscous in a sweet-and-sour sauce.

● **MILBORNE PORT** (Somerset)
Old Vicarage Sherborne Road, (01963) 251117. This Victorian vicarage, mainly offering bed and breakfast, is open to non-residents for pre-booked dinners on Friday and Saturday. Set-price two- to four-course menus list five choices ranging from starters of wild mushrooms in puff pastry, and Thai-spiced beef cabbage rolls with sweet chilli sauce, to mains of duck breast with kumquat and port sauce, or halibut with spring onion

and black bean sauce. Desserts might feature tiramisù, or lemon, almond and gin tart.

● **MILTON KEYNES** (Buckinghamshire)
Metro's 315–325 Upper Fourth Street, (01908) 231323. Competing with better-known chain restaurants in the 'theatre district' of Milton Keynes, this new brasserie, a 'dramatic, modern space' with dark blue and orange décor and loud pop music, stands out for fresh ingredients, good timing and value for money. Fashionable flavours abound on the lively menu, from spicy chicken with peanut and cucumber salad, to chargrilled tuna with a tomato, saffron and coriander sauce and black noodles.

● **MONTACUTE** (Somerset)
Milk House The Borough, (01935) 823823. Listed fifteenth-century hamstone house in the village square. Three-course menus use organic produce wherever possible and offer three choices per course (one of them vegetarian) perhaps starting with home-made country pâté or spiced parsnip soup. Mains might include seafood medley with a creamy coriander sauce or lamb daube à l'avignonnaise. Finish with apple tart or blackberry trifle. Open D only (L by arrangement) Wed to Sun from April to September.

● **MOUSEHOLE** (Cornwall)
Cornish Range Chapel Street, (01736) 731488. This tiny restaurant, only open for dinner, has recently changed hands but held on to its chef. In a picturesque coastal village it has bright window boxes and small orange trees either side of the entrance. Local produce features strongly including Newlyn crab salad or Cornish goats' cheese bruschetta among the starters, and local fish, perhaps in a pie as a main course. Try Cornish ice cream or west country cheeses to finish. Open all week D.

● **NAYLAND** (Suffolk)
White Hart 11 High Street, (01206) 263382. As the *Guide* went to press, this 'very civilised' old coaching inn was closed for major refurbishment, due to re-open as a restaurant-with-rooms in

late summer 1999. Signs are promising: new chef Neil Bishop is a protégé of Michel Roux, and we are told that a Mediterranean influence will be apparent on the menu. Reports on the new set-up are welcome. Closed Mon.

● **NEWARK** (Nottinghamshire)
Café Bleu 14 Castle Gate, (01636) 610141. A French café-style interior, with a relaxed and informal atmosphere, provides the backdrop to live music most evenings and some lunchtimes. Huge oil paintings by a local artist are displayed in the restaurant and in a gallery on the first floor. Competent cooking of good quality fresh ingredients has produced 'plump and juicy' tiger prawns, duck liver parfait with orange and apple chutney, and mains of roast rack of lamb or a parcel of sea trout with prawn mousse; finish perhaps with lemon tart or bread-and-butter pudding with butterscotch sauce. Closed Sun.

● **NEWCASTLE UPON TYNE**
(Tyne & Wear)
Leela's 20 Dean Street, (0191) 230 1261. Reputed to be the only South Indian restaurant in the north-east. Leela Paul is dedicated to healthy eating, and cooks dishes from her native Kerala: pork pattichularthithu (stir-fried with spices), lamb biriyani, or batham kozhi (marinated chicken breast cooked in almond sauce). A sprinkling of fish dishes is available, and vegetarians have a good choice. Finish with 'fruity angels' or kulfi. Closed Sun.

● **NEWENT** (Gloucestershire)
Three Choirs Restaurant Newent, (01531) 890223. Beautiful views over surrounding vineyards, friendly and efficient staff and, of course, the estate's own wines are among the attractions, along with some appealing modern cooking. Recommendations have come in for bacon hock terrine with mustard chutney, Tia Maria cheesecake, and home-baked bread. Otherwise, try salad of poached pear with goats' cheese and walnuts, followed by braised beef with onions and grain mustard mash. Vegetarians might be offered marinated

vegetables with white beans and a tomato vinaigrette. Open all week L, Thu to Sat D.

● **NEW POLZEATH** (Cornwall)
Cornish Cottage Hotel New Polzeath, (01208) 862213. The hotel stands in a beautiful location on a remote headland, and inside you will find a bric-à-brac-filled dining room where the emphasis is on fresh local produce and good value: beef and venison feuilleté, and rack of lamb among them, followed by pineapple upside-down pudding, and chocolate marquise. Service is pleasant. A new chef, Gareth Eddy, was appointed just as the *Guide* went to press, so more reports please. Accommodation available. Open Sun L and D all week.

● **NORTHALLERTON** (North Yorkshire)
Bettys 188 High Street, (01609) 775154. First-class teas, pastries, breads and cakes are the draw at this branch of a mini-chain of tea rooms famed throughout North Yorkshire. Those looking for more of a meal will also find Swiss macaroni, Betty's Yorkshire rarebit, or warm chicken and bacon salad. Open all week.

● **NORTH BOVEY** (Devon)
Blackaller Hotel North Bovey, (01647) 440322. This simply furnished converted farmhouse is in 'a delightful spot' on the edge of Dartmoor 'with nobody else within 500 metres'. Just five tables in a 'spotless' room, and a welcoming atmosphere set the scene for good ingredients 'perfectly cooked without too much fuss', as in bacon and mushroom tart, salmon with a crunchy pesto topping, and 'super' lemon tart. Open Mon to Sat D only.

● **NORTH HUISH** (Devon)
Brookdale House North Huish, (01548) 821661. A Grade II-listed Tudor-style house offering a high standard of service. Recommended dishes have included starters of goats' cheese and onion tartlet, and a dariole of crab mousse, followed by herb-crusted pheasant, and peppered loin of lamb. Otherwise start with griddled scallops, before going on to roast Lunesdale duck, and end with sticky toffee pudding or chocolate nemesis.

Accommodation available; open all week.

● **NORWICH** (Norfolk)

The Aquarium 22 Tombland, (01603) 630090. Close to the Cathedral, this trendy, airy restaurant fetches up ideas from East, West and all over to present dishes such as spring chicken noodle laksa with crab won ton, deep-fried feta parcels, and chermoula-grilled tuna loin, served with warm chickpea and roast vegetable salad. But it's not above offering a side order of chips for £1.95. Complete your meal with apple relish and crème fraîche. Closed Sun.

Brasted's 8–10 St Andrews Hill, (01603) 625949. Down cobbled lanes in the heart of old Norwich, somewhere between the castle and the cathedral, Brasted's occupies a corner site. John Brasted has been producing his brand of traditional dishes with some contemporary flashes since the mid-eighties. Expect dishes of the day – soup and a grilled fish – and traditional offerings like steak and kidney pie, lambs' sweetbreads in puff pastry, or sea bass with lemon butter sauce. A table d'hôte menu is good value at £14.95 for three courses. Service has been described as attentive and polite. Closed Sat L and all day Sun.

● **NOTTINGHAM** (Nottinghamshire)

Saagar 473 Mansfield Road, (0115) 962 2014/969 2860. Tastefully decorated Indian restaurant with a warm ambience a mile or two out of the city centre on the main Mansfield road at Sherwood. From the tandoor come a variety of dishes based on chicken, prawn and lamb, staple meats that also appear in birianis and Punjabi and rogan josh dishes. The house special meal includes Kashmiri kofta balls, Malai chicken or lamb (with creams, almonds, mushrooms and coriander), and mixed vegetables, paneer (cheese) nan, rice and mushroom bajia. Takeaways also available. Closed Sun L.

Sonny's 3 Carlton Street, (0115) 947 3041. A new chef was arriving and the restaurant was undergoing refurbishment as we went to press, so more reports please. It is a busy neighbourhood restaurant with light, spacious surroundings using much organic and locally grown produce. Typical dishes have been red pepper and chilli soup described as 'a winner', and a fat filo parcel packed with aubergines, peppers and Gruyère on lemony cabbage. Open all week.

● **ODIHAM** (Hampshire)

Grapevine 121 High Street, (01256) 701122. Lunchers are drawn to this attractive terraced house at the end of the high street by the prospect of a good-value set-price deal, a range of tapas, and light options such as smoked salmon and scrambled eggs, or an open sandwich of chargrilled chicken. In the evening, the menu runs to roast monkfish and pepper brochette with fennel purée, roast rack of lamb (with mash, spiced berries, and a cinnamon and clove jus), and warm bourbon and pecan pie.

● **ORFORD** (Suffolk)

Butley-Orford Oysterage Market Hill, (01394) 450277. This smokehouse, shop and café rolled into one is set in a picturesque village. Oysters are recommended again (this year with black pepper and tabasco), along with smoked eel on toast, fillet of cod with parsley sauce, skate with capers, and a pair of Dover soles. Finish with 'pleasing' rum pudding. Winter opening times are limited to lunchtime and dinner on Fridays and Saturdays. Open all week summer.

● **OSWESTRY** (Shropshire)

Walls Welsh Walls, (01691) 670970. Large former school building rescued from a dilapidated state in 1995. The menu is mostly traditional in style, aptly divided into 'Foundation course' (starters) and 'Bricks and mortar' (mains). Start perhaps with goose rillettes with kumquat marmalade, or smoked fish and prawn pot, going on to pork belly with beans and Chinese spices, or fillet of salmon with a crunchy herb topping. The last course (for bricklayer and diner alike) might take in vanilla cheesecake or French apple puff with cream. Sunday lunch is a carvery. Closed Sun D.

● **Oxford** (Oxfordshire)
Fishers 36–37 St Clements Street, (01865) 243003. Blackboard dishes done with 'flair', and friendly, willing service by young staff, are pluses at this nautically decorated fish restaurant with an all-glass frontage. Go for grilled queen scallops with oyster mushrooms and asparagus, then perhaps chargrilled marlin, or a house selection of deep-fried cod, bass, tiger prawns and squid, ending with hot choux-pastry fritters with sliced figs on a raspberry coulis. Closed Mon L.
Gee's 61A Banbury Road, (01865) 553540. A Victorian conservatory, not far from the city centre, makes an attractive and unusual setting. Friendly service, hundreds of plants, and tightly-packed tables with bamboo chairs enhance a lively, informal atmosphere that attracts locals and tourists alike. Influences from the Mediterranean and beyond are apparent on the suitably upbeat menu: typical are mussels steamed with coriander and chilli, pan-fried duck breast with smoked aubergine and polenta, and roast cod with chickpea purée and tomato dressing.
Restaurant Elizabeth 82 St Aldate's, (01865) 242230. After a ten-year absence a visitor was delighted to find this long-standing restaurant, upstairs 'in a fine old house' opposite Christ Church, 'back to its old excellent standards'. Recommended have been 'beautifully light and full-flavoured' quenelles de saumon with sauce Nantua, beef stroganoff with excellent vegetables, and desserts 'of admirable quality' that included crème brûlée, raspberry sorbet, and candied chestnuts in Kirsch. Closed Mon.

● **Padstow** (Cornwall)
Bistro No.6 6 Middle Street, (01841) 532093. Close to the famous Rick Stein establishments, this light and airy double-fronted cottage offers two and three-course set-price dinner menus. Among recommended dishes have been grilled goats' cheese with a broad bean salad, pan-fried tuna steak with roasted

vegetables, and chocolate pithiviers with ice cream. Closed Tue.

● **Penrith** (Cumbria)
A Bit on the Side Brunswick Square, (01768) 892526. Small, cheerful, cheekily named restaurant with a dedicated and ever-present chef/proprietor. Begin with broccoli and blue cheese soup, or choose a selection of starters, before going on to roast grey mullet, or pan-fried calf's liver with black pudding. Vegetarians are offered spinach and ricotta gnocchi or sun-dried tomato and cheese tortelloni. Dark chocolate soufflé has been described as 'historic'. Closed Sat and Tue L, all day Mon.

● **Petworth** (West Sussex)
Soanes Grove Lane, (01798) 343659. Only open for dinner at one sitting from Tuesday to Saturday (plus Sunday lunch once a month), this family-run restaurant in a sixteenth-century farmhouse is modestly decorated, with a conservatory extension and views to the South Downs. A 'quite expensive' carte provided one reporter with 'wonderful' twice-baked cheese soufflé, followed by pigeon breasts with an intense port and thyme reduction, sticky toffee pudding and 'excellent' petit fours.

● **Polperro** (Cornwall)
Cottage Restaurant The Coombes, (01503) 272217. 'At the harbour quay each morning' is where you will find chef/co-owner Dave Foster buying fresh fish for the day's menus at this tiny cottage dating back to 1691; at least in summer, for the restaurant is not open during winter. Inside are beams, copper kettles, horse brasses, 'swirly carpets', and 'friendly and competent service' overseen by wife Pam. Reporters have praised seared scallops, lobster and prawn ravioli, grilled John Dory, and monkfish provençale, as well as desserts of hot chocolate brioche, and strawberry crème brûlée. Non-fish eaters can plump for steaks or Cornish chicken, and vegetarians for cannelloni with ricotta and spinach. Accommodation available. Closed Sat L and Sun D.

● **ROCKBEARE** (Devon)
Jack in the Green Rockbeare, (01404) 822240. Welcoming pub on the A30, five miles from Exeter, with excellent service and well-presented food. Try grilled goats' cheese, or smoked fish roulade, followed by loin of pork, chicken suprême, or beef stew with dumplings; finish with sticky toffee pudding, or poached pears and Chantilly cream stack. Set-price and bar-snack menus available. Open all week.

● **ROYDHOUSE** (West Yorkshire)
Three Acres Inn Roydhouse, (01484) 602606. Former coaching inn enjoying panoramic Pennine views and boasting a seafood bar, restaurant and deli. Starters might be soup, chicken liver parfait on toasted brioche, or a tempura of king prawns and baby squid. Consider mains of coq au vin or salmon fish cakes with vegetable ribbons, or lash out on a fruits de mer platter at £25. Puddings are traditional. Open all week.

● **SAFFRON WALDEN** (Essex)
Old Hoops 15 King Street, (01799) 522813. Ray and Sue Morrison have run this friendly, first-floor, oak-beamed restaurant serving a good-value classical repertoire since 1984. Set menus, available at both lunch and dinner, might offer lentil and bacon soup, then poached skate wing with prawns and mushrooms, ending with rhubarb crumble. Or from the carte choose oriental chicken, followed by spiced pork fillet served with mushroom and cherry brandy sauce. Closed Sun and Mon.

● **ST IVES** (Cornwall)
Porthminster Beach Café Porthminster Beach, (01736) 795352. Seafood restaurant on the beach, overlooking St Ives Bay, offering Mediterranean-style cooking with Pacific Rim influences: 'simple but excellent food served with panache'. Recommended dishes span the range from baked St Ives mackerel on couscous, to tuna on linguini, to monkfish dahl. Puddings are based on traditional ideas: glazed lemon tart with Cornish clotted cream, or 'superb' saffron bread-and-butter pudding. Open from Easter till November only; closed Sun D.

● **SAMLESBURY** (Lancashire)
Campions Samlesbury, (01772) 877641. Owned by Jennings Brewery, Campions is open all week for set-price lunches and à la carte dinners. Under the heading 'Birds and things with hooves' try Goosnargh chicken breast or double thick pork chop. 'Deep sea and fresh water dwellers' offers fillet of red snapper or pan-fried black tiger prawns; while 'sweet concoctions' applies to apple Charlotte and raspberry meringue.

● **SEAVIEW** (Isle of Wight)
Priory Bay Hotel Priory Drive, (01983) 613146. Opened in 1998 by Andrew Palmer, founder of the New Covent Garden Soup Company and owner of the Roussillon restaurant (see entry, London), this tastefully refurbished, imposing country-house hotel overlooks Spithead and the Channel, and has its own beach, including a seafood café on the cliffs. Menus have included Bembridge crab ravioli, rack of lamb with wild garlic, and 'silky' chocolate fondant with caramelised banana. A new chef was about to be appointed as the *Guide* went to press, so reports please. Accommodation available. Open all week.
Seaview Hotel High Street, (01983) 612711. Stylish restaurant in a small hotel close to the sea. Reporters have enjoyed spinach and cream cheese mousse with a shellfish sauce; flash-fried Cajun prawns with mushrooms, potato and courgette; and knuckle of lamb with shredded beetroot. Tipsy red berry trifle is one way to finish. Attentive service. Closed Sun D.

● **SHEFFIELD** (South Yorkshire)
Greenhead House 84 Burncross Road, (0114) 246 9004. On the northerly outskirts of Sheffield, this large family house has a homely atmosphere, and a lounge for pre-meal drinks. There is a light lunch menu, while four-course dinners are priced according to the main dish: best end of lamb (£29), medallions of beef fillet (£31.50), or casserole of fresh

lobster (£33). Starters include some non-meat options – smoked Ribblesdale goats'-cheese mousse, or warm lentil and onion patties – as indeed do desserts such as chocolate tart with a cappuccino ice-cream. Friendly, efficient service. Open only for L Thur and Fri and D Wed to Sat.

● **SINNINGTON** (North Yorkshire)
Fox and Hounds Sinnington, (01751) 431577. The oak-beamed dining room of this eighteenth-century stone-built former coaching inn has ancient wood panelling, log fires, and is candlelit in the evening. Reporters have commended the welcoming atmosphere, attentive service and food ranging from home-made pies, cod and chips or steaks on the bar menu, to specials such as oven-baked sea bass (with chillies, ginger and lemongrass), and chargrilled wild boar steak on wild mushroom risotto. Desserts run to strawberry mille-feuille or pineapple and mango tart. Open all week.

● **SISSINGHURST** (Kent)
Rankins' Restaurant The Street, (01580) 713964. Long-established small shop conversion, open for lunch on Sunday and dinner from Wednesday to Saturday. Traditional set-price menus are not cheap, but offer salad starters such as cod and crevette with pickled cucumber, and mains of roast lemon and basil chicken, or griddled ribeye of beef; finish with chocolate nemesis, ice-creams or sorbets.

● **SPEEN** (Buckinghamshire)
Old Plow Inn Flowers Bottom Lane, (01494) 488300. This comfortable country inn, with a relaxed atmosphere and pleasant garden in the heart of the Chilterns, is surrounded by fine walking country. Start perhaps with goats' cheese tart with pine kernels, or iced gazpacho with prawns, before going on to grilled sea bass with a red wine sauce or loin of lamb with a fruity sauce. Those who have already been for a walk may finish with Grand Marnier parfait or chocolate mousse with créme anglaise. Closed Mon, Sat L and Sun D.

● **STOCKLAND** (Devon)
Kings Arms Inn Stockland, (01404) 881361. Long whitewashed thatched pub in a small Devon village offering light dishes or a full carte. Portuguese sardines, or mushroom and mozzarella gratin, might be followed by Membury trout or king prawn Madras, with meat courses of guinea fowl breast or ostrich fillet. Vegetarian choices run from pasta to stroganoff, while desserts take in apple and treacle crumbly, and coffee and chocolate parfait glacé. Closed Sun L.

● **STOKE BRUERNE** (Northamptonshire)
Bruerne's Lock The Canalside, (01604) 863654. Recent renovations have seen the addition of a cellar bar and a terrace overlooking the canal; the restaurant has been redecorated in Regency stripes. Recommended dishes have included a light but tasty leek tartlet and an 'excellent' Stilton soufflé to start, followed by good steak and breast of Gressingham duck. Finish with banana brûlée or baked apple and vanilla crumble. Service is knowledgeable and helpful. Closed Mon, Sat L and Sun D.

● **STOWMARKET** (Suffolk)
Tot Hill House Tot Hill, (01449) 673375. Christopher and Mary Bruce have made the transition from dining pub (they used to own the Bull at Blackmore End) to fully-fledged restaurant. Their new venture, an attractive, creeper-covered building on the A14, has an upmarket feel, with flowers, polished silver and crisp white linen. Typical of their country house cooking style are smoked haddock and Parmesan in a puff pastry box, lamb rack and kidneys with rosemary mash, and guinea fowl with wild mushroom ravioli and Madeira sauce. Booking essential, closed Mon and Tue.

● **STRATFORD-UPON-AVON** (Warwickshire)
Boathouse Swan's Nest Lane, (01789) 297733. Stylish restaurant above a working boatyard, with a balcony looking across the Avon to the RSC. A short menu is mainly French with global twists, and there are pre-theatre dinners. Start with Devon blue cheesecake with a walnut

dressing or tempura of cod with a potato galette, before going on to Deben duck breast in a liquorice jus, or braised fillet of brill with oyster mushrooms and leeks. A well-priced wine list includes specially imported bottles from the Languedoc-Roussillon. Closed Sun, Mon L and Sat L.

Desports 13–14 Meer Street, (01789) 269304. This yellow and blue restaurant on the first floor of a 16th-century building majors in English and Mediterranean cuisine with Eastern influences. From a menu sub-titled Earth, Land, Sea and Heaven, recommended dishes have included grilled sea bass with a potato and pumpkin cake, and apple tart with sorbet and caramel sauce. Service is helpful and charming. Closed Sun and Mon.

No. 6 Restaurant 6 Union Street, (01789) 269106. Fish is the mainstay at this French bistro-style side-street restaurant: perhaps 'plump and firm' baby halibut with basil and almonds, or chargrilled tuna steak with olive oil, red onion, chili and garlic. For one reporter Scottish mussels with shallots, cream and a white wine sauce were 'the best ever eaten'. The non-piscatorial might want to try warm chicken salad dressed with a raspberry vinaigrette which has 'loads of flavour'. Staff are 'warm and helpful'. Closed Sun.

Russons 8 Church Street, (01789) 268822. Open from Tuesday to Saturday for lunch, pre-theatre meals and dinner, this tiny restaurant still manages a separate eating room for non-smokers. Try goats'-cheese salad, chicken satay, or baked seafood crêpe, followed by half a roast Norfolk duck, or paupiettes de boeuf. Or, if in the mood for something more down to earth, go for 'Mr Barry the Butcher's' pork and smoked bacon sausages with mash, or beer-battered haddock and chips.

● **STRETTON** (Leicestershire)
Ram Jam Inn Great North Road, (01780) 410776. A useful inn open all day on the A1, mid-way between London and Yorkshire, offering bistro and à la carte menus plus children's dishes.

Choose from fried potato cakes with poached eggs, prawn open sandwich, Rutland sausage, and salmon fish cakes, and finish with lime and basil cheesecake. Specials embrace spicy prawn quesadillas, Polish sausage, and chicken pasta. Accommodation available.

● **STROUD** (Gloucestershire)
Fischer's Restaurant 169 Slad Road, (01453) 759950. In a large house on the road from Stroud to Slad (of *Cider with Rosie* fame), Fisher's consists of two rooms joined by an arch and a snug bar. Fixed-price (£12 for two courses, £15 for three) and à la carte menus offer well-presented dishes which might include 'perfectly sautéed' scallops with aubergine salad, tartlet of feta cheese and mixed vegetables, and guinea fowl in its own conserve with leeks and squash. Hot chocolate sponge and orange soufflé sound like good ways to finish. Closed Sun D and all day Mon.

● **STUDLAND** (Dorset)
Shell Bay Ferry Road, (01929) 450363. Newly refurbished restaurant now with scrubbed pine tables and aluminium bistro-style chairs, plus wonderful views over Poole Harbour. A new chef has arrived since the last *Guide,* so more reports, please. The bias remains towards fish, and a typical meal might consist of Shell Bay seafood broth, followed by tuna steak with stir-fried vegetables, then chocolate and lime cake. Vegetarians might be offered a nut roast with sun-dried tomato sauce, and meater eaters fillet steak 'as you like it'. Open all week high season, Thur to Sun (not Sun D) low season.

● **SUTTON COLDFIELD** (West Midlands)
La Truffe 65 Birmingham Road, (0121) 355 5836. Named after the truffle-hunting pig shown on its logo, this French restaurant offers classic cuisine such as warm salad of chicken livers, or venison terrine, followed by loin of wild boar on a bed of apples with a port sauce, or fillet of pastry-topped oven-roasted lamb with garlic mushrooms. Desserts are typically Gallic too: crêpes Suzette or nougat glacé. Both a carte and set menus

are offered, including a six-course menu gastronomique. Closed Sat L and all day Sun and Mon.

● **SWANAGE** (Dorset)
Cauldron Bistro 5 High Street, (01929) 422671. Simple décor with polished wooden tables and settle seating are the backdrop for an unpretentious menu offering generous portions. Expect warm goats' cheese salad, or wild boar and apple sausages, followed by blackened chicken cooked on hot coals, or coquille St Jacques. Puddings run to chocolate truffle cake and a selection of ice creams. Closed Mon (exc bank hols), Tue L and Wed L.

● **TAUNTON** (Somerset)
Castle Hotel Castle Green, (01823) 272671. After nearly ten distinguished years in the kitchen, Phil Vickery has left to pursue other activities. As the *Guide* went to press a new chef had yet to be appointed, but the Castle has a reputation for employing rising stars of modern British cookery (this is where Gary Rhodes started) and we can only hope that the new incumbent will be from the same mould. Open all week.

● **TAVISTOCK** (Devon)
Neil's 27 King Street, (01822) 615550. Tiny restaurant (converted from an old farmhouse) using local organic and free-range produce. Reporters have endorsed seafood in puff pastry, and sautéed chicken livers with shallots, followed by 'excellent' main courses of venison on a potato galette, and fillet of beef with creamed celeriac in a Marsala sauce. Desserts might take in carrot cake pudding, or lemon and mascarpone ice cream. Reasonably priced wine list. Open Tue to Sat D only.

● **TIRRIL** (Cumbria)
Queens Head Tirril, (01768) 863219. Spacious pub occupying a Grade II-listed house once owned by the Wordsworth family. A bar snack menu at lunchtime offers baguettes, jacket potatoes, ploughman's, scampi, pasta and steak. Blackboard specials veer towards fish: Thai fish cakes, perhaps, or Solway salmon. Meat offerings on the printed menu might include medallions of pork, or Cumberland tattie pot, while puddings take in sticky toffee or maybe chocolate dipped pear. Country wines from Lindisfarne add interest to the short wine list. Open all week.

● **TORQUAY** (Devon)
Mulberry House 1 Scarborough Road, (01803) 213639. Lesley Cooper's restaurant-with-rooms, a white stucco villa not far from the sea, was deemed by one reporter 'the only civilised way to visit Torquay'. 'Beautifully furnished' rooms and 'immaculate' fittings make for a comfortable stay, and the food is another reason to come: grilled yam with spicy mayonnaise, whole grilled lobster with garlic and herbs, game pie, chicken breast stuffed with fruit, and crème brûlée with home-made ice cream have all been praised.

● **TRESCO** (Isles of Scilly)
Island Hotel (01720) 422883. Owned by the Dorrien-Smith family for nearly thirty years, this cluster of buildings makes for a hotel with spectacular views over the sea to St Martin's. Among recommended dishes have been a generous portion of roast sea bass on tomato couscous, noisettes of lamb, and crème brûlée. Five-course set menus include coffee and petit fours; otherwise go for the cold seafood platter. The hotel is closed from Nov to early March. Open all week.

● **TRURO** (Cornwall)
Oliver's Frances Street, (01872) 273028. In the basement of the Wig and Pen Inn below the Law Courts, Oliver's is an informal restaurant decorated in blue and yellow. Daily-changing set-price menus use local produce and might offer salmon and crab cakes with dill and caper oil, saddle of West Country lamb on a rösti potato, and iced lemon parfait or farmhouse cheeses. Closed Sun.
Saffron 5 Quay Street, (01872) 263771. Opened in early 1999 by Nik Tinney, who has worked at various London restaurants, Saffron has a cheerful yellow interior and makes good use of local produce, which finds its way into a weekly-changing menu, a pre-theatre

two-course dinner (including a glass of house wine) for £7.50, and a Saturday brunch menu. Sandwiches and cakes are also available until 5pm.

Recommendations have included soups – rich mushroom with smoked garlic, and crab and sweetcorn chowder – as well as seared scallops with black pudding, ribeye steak with peppered vegetables, and saffron bread-and-butter pudding. Closed Mon D and all day Sun.

● **TUNBRIDGE WELLS** (Kent)
Sankey's Fish House 39 Mount Ephraim, (01892) 511422. Spacious rooms in this large house are decorated with fishy paintings by local artists. As well as the restaurant, there's an oyster bar and a cellar wine bar, plus summer eating on the terrace or in the patio garden. The main business is fish: Cornish cock crab, seafood thermidor, smoked cod and prawn fish cakes, seared shark. Otherwise there's honey roast duck, or Cumberland sausage ring with onion gravy and garlic mash. The wine list is carefully chosen, with a fair number by the glass. Closed Sun.

● **TWICKENHAM** (Greater London)
Fishermans Hut 175 Hampton Road, (0181) 255 6222. A pub conversion done out in nautical style – fishing nets on the ceiling laden with crab and scallop shells – sets the tone for a traditional maritime menu of skate wing with capers and butter sauce, oysters baked in a creamy sauce, moules marinière, and bouillabaisse piled high with good seafood. Carnivores won't be disappointed, though, given such offerings as calf's liver topped with black pudding on herbed mash. Closed Mon L.

● **WELWYN GARDEN CITY** (Hertfordshire)
Auberge du Lac Brocket Hall, (01707) 368888. Set in the beautiful grounds of Brocket Hall, this expensive restaurant offers modern French cuisine with Asian influences; new chef Pascal Breant arrived as we went to press, so more reports please. The new menu offers starters of braised sweetbreads or a crab and mango salad, followed by panaché of

seafood or braised chicken gigot. Twenty wines by the glass range from £4.50 to £9.50. Closed Sun D and Mon.

● **WEMBLEY** (Greater London)
Sakonis 127–129 Ealing Road, (0181) 903 9601. Large-scale vegetarian restaurant catering for the Asian community of Wembley. Décor is basic but the quality of the food puts the vast majority of curry houses to shame, and prices are 'absurdly low'. Snacks (or 'Bites') include various pooris, chats and samosas, while the 'Eats' section of the menu offers more substantial dhosas, biryani, and even uttapa sandwich. There are also plenty of Chinese dishes 'prepared Indian style' and a good range of home-made sweets. Open all week.

● **WESTFIELD** (East Sussex)
Wild Mushroom Westfield Lane, (01424) 751137. A recently built conservatory annexe with an attractive bar has added to the comfort of this small restaurant, which offers a genuinely warm welcome. One party enjoyed a 'fine meal' that included bouillabaise, fillet of beef with potato galette, pigeon breasts with creamed leek and potato cake, and an iced parfait of pineapple, mango and sweet ginger, served with hot dark chocolate and rum sauce. Try English wines from the local Carr Taylor and Breaky Bottom vineyards. Open Sun L and Tue to Sat D.

● **WEYBOURNE** (Norfolk)
Gasche's The Street, (01263) 588220. Small thatched-roof restaurant offering weekly-changing set-price menus. Start with avocado with prawns, or pâté maison, proceed to strips of wild boar and venison with red onions, or baked herb crusted cod, and finish with steamed marmalade sponge, or pavlova with strawberries and cream. Sunday lunch and à la carte menus are also available. Closed Sun D and all day Mon.

● **WEYMOUTH** (Dorset)
Perry's 4 Trinity Road, (01305) 785799. A 'friendly, buzzy' atmosphere pervades this popular fish restaurant in a narrow cobbled street on the harbour's edge. Keep an eye out for the large board in the

entrance with pictures of every fish imaginable. From blackboards choose perhaps 'light and tasty' gratin of crabmeat with a Chablis and Parmesan sauce, or grilled lemon sole 'cooked just right', accompanied by a basket of crisp, fresh bread. Service is 'cheery and helpful'.

● **WHIMPLE** (Devon)
Woodhayes Whimple, (01404) 822237. 'A relaxing, comfortable place for a holiday with a good evening meal thrown in,' concluded one visitor to this elegant Georgian country house. Under new owners Eddie and Lynda Katz, it is first and foremost a hotel, with limited restaurant service for non-residents (no lunches, booking essential), but is worth visiting for Lynda Katz's well-balanced and skilfully executed no-choice five-course 'dinner party' menu that typically offers salmon and broccoli in flaky pastry, roast venison with tomato concassé, and mint chocolate mousse followed by local cheeses.

● **WILLINGTON** (Co Durham)
Stile 97 High Street, (01388) 746615. Converted former mine-owner's cottage using local game and fish. The owners' visits to France add a Gallic flavour to the repertoire, yielding grilled goats' cheese on roast Mediterranean vegetables, spatchcocked spring chicken, and orange liqueur pancakes or chocolate and brandy marquise. An extensive wine list covers the globe but also majors on France. A conservatory is available for private parties and wine tastings. Open D only Tue to Sat.

● **WINGFIELD** (Suffolk)
De La Pole Arms Wingfield, (01379) 384545. Peaceful sixteenth-century pub opposite the village church, tastefully modernised with beamed ceilings, log-burning stoves and stripped wood tables. The separate restaurant is big on fish, bowls of seafood served with crusty bread being a speciality. Otherwise try 'very enjoyable' stuffed and battered mushrooms, or monkfish in Parma ham with a tomato and kiwi fruit salsa. Maple cheesecake and spiced apple pie have also

been recommended. Part of St Peter's Brewery chain, so try their ales or fruit and wheat beers. Open all week.

● **WOBURN** (Bedfordshire)
Paris House Woburn Park, (01525) 290692. In an idyllic setting in Woburn Park, the house was originally built for the 1878 Paris exhibition and re-erected piece by piece on the Woburn Estate. Set meals range from £28.50 (lunch only) to a £50 five-course gastronomique menu. Try perhaps a crab salad basket, followed by breast of duck with apples and calvados, or fillet of beef in a green peppercorn sauce, finishing with a Grand Marnier soufflé. An extensive, but expensive, wine list complements it all. In summer take drinks on the patio; regular themed evenings and cookery demonstrations are also on offer. Closed Sun D and all day Mon; and Feb.

● **WOOLTON HILL** (Hampshire)
Hollington House Woolton Hill, (01635) 255100. Delightful Edwardian country house in gardens designed by Gertrude Jekyll. Another new chef as we went to press, so more reports please. Typical dishes in the past have been a tian of scallops or a terrine of chicken and ceps to start, followed by suprême of salmon or cannon of lamb on a potato rösti. Desserts have included wild strawberry cheesecake and iced tiramisù. Excellent antipodean wine list. Open all week.

● **YORK** (North Yorkshire)
Bettys 6–8 St Helen's Square, (01904) 659142. At the height of the tourist season there are likely to be endless queues outside this famous tea shop, one of a mini-chain spread throughout the north. The crowds come for exemplary teas, pastries, cakes and breads, as well as things like cheese and herb paté, coronation chicken salad or goujons of lemon sole. Open all week.
Grange Hotel Clifton, (01904) 644744. There is a choice of eating places in this town-house hotel in the city centre. The Ivy Restaurant, done out in rich reds, offers French and modern British cuisine along the lines of pressed pork knuckle and foie gras terrine followed by crisp

breast and confit leg of duck, ending with pannacotta with pear and ginger syrup. It has a small wine list and friendly, unobtrusive service. The more informal

cellar Brasserie is open all week; also try the Seafood Bar. Ivy and Seafood Bar closed Sat L.

Scotland

● **ABERDEEN** (Aberdeen)
Courtyard 1 Alford Lane, (01224) 213795. A first floor restaurant offers modern Scottish cooking with mostly European and a few Eastern influences. Try goats'-cheese salad with apple chutney, followed by a trio of market fish in a pool of mussel and bacon sauce with a pastry lattice, and finish with poached pear covered with Grand Marnier sabayon. Martha's Bistro on the ground floor displays a blackboard of less expensive dishes. Closed Mon D and all day Sun.

● **ARDUAINE** (Argyll & Bute)
Loch Melfort Hotel Arduaine, (01852) 200233. Lovely location next to the National Trust gardens, with views across Asknish Bay. On offer are bar lunches, five-course dinners, and a new café-bistro called 'The Skerry' with lots of fish, plus cassoulet, Speyside lamb and steak. The main dinner menu might start with shellfish bisque or confit of duck, followed by roast topside of Angus beef or poached Ardmaddy salmon. Puddings run to white chocolate mousse or fresh figs in Pernod. Open all week.

● **BIGGAR** (South Lanarkshire)
Culter Mill Coulter Village, (01899) 220950. This converted mill was lovingly restored by chef/proprietor Douglas Collins in 1990. He and his team cook an eclectic menu, taking inspiration from Scotland and, well, just about everywhere else. Expect to find haggis (in a risotto, or more traditionally with neeps and tatties), and Scottish salmon (either as gravadlax or seared and served with hollandaise and asparagus). Chicken satay is marinated in saké, coriander and soy sauce, and lasagne is served with

French fries. Open Wed to Sun (summer only).

● **BROADFORD** (Highland)
Creelers Seafood Bistro Broadford, (01471) 822281. New owners have taken over since the last *Guide* at this tiny restaurant with wonderful views over Broadford Bay. Specials might include venison in bramble and red wine jus, steak Diane, or shelled squat lobster sautéed in garlic butter and white wine. Otherwise try Princess scallops, or the house speciality: seafood gumbo. Children are offered fish fingers, beefburgers or sausages, all with beans and chips. Takeaway dishes available.

● **CRIEFF** (Perthshire & Kinross)
Bank Restaurant 32 High Street, (01764) 656575. Spacious town-centre bistro in a listed building once housing the British Linen Bank, offering modern Scottish cooking in a welcoming atmosphere. Reporters have enjoyed wild mushroom and butter bean soup with truffle oil, fillet of sea bass with scallops and a shellfish sauce, lemon tart with crème fraîche, and 'fantastic' Glayva cream. Closed Mon and Sun D

● **CRINAN** (Argyll & Bute)
Crinan Hotel Crinan, (01546) 830261. This white-painted hotel in the heart of the village has breathtaking views of Argyll's rugged coastline. Bar lunches offer Loch Etive mussels with garlic and vermouth cream sauce, braised sausages or Arbroath smokie. The two restaurants (Loch 16 and Westward) are more expensive. Lock 16 offers a no choice menu of freshly landed seafood simply cooked, while in the Westward restaurant you might expect cappuccino of wild mushroom soup with porcini powder and winter truffle, followed by boudin of corn

fed chicken with morel cream. A new chef has been appointed, so reports please. The restaurants have different opening times, so phone to check. Open all week.

● **DARVEL** (East Ayrshire)
Scoretulloch House Darvel, (01560) 323331. Down a narrow track in the rolling Ayrshire hills, Scoretulloch is a beautifully restored mill cottage. Visitors have enjoyed red mullet broth with a saffron infusion, roulade of foie gras and duck confit, followed by fillet of turbot, and new season's Ayrshire lamb with 'tasty' sweetbreads and basil mousse. Finish with mascarpone and white chocolate cheesecake. Open all week.

● **DRYBRIDGE** (Moray)
Old Monastery Drybridge, (01542) 832660. Converted Benedictine monastic retreat with panoramic views over the Moray Firth, under new ownership this year, though some of the kitchen staff have remained. Typical of the straightforward cooking style might be cheese soufflé, or salmon and potato terrine to start, followed by medallions of venison, or mushroom samosa with tempura vegetables, finishing with a tangy lemon tartlet or tiramisù. Six house wines are available by the glass. Reports please. Closed Sun and Mon.

● **EDINBURGH** (Edinburgh)
Fitz Henry 19 Shore Place, (0131) 555 6625. The décor has been described as 'warehouse baroque' with wall hangings and a diverse collection of paintings. Recommended dishes have included mussels in Laksa broth, duck confit with red cabbage and Madeira jus, and daube of lamb avignonaise. Finish with poached pear with pistachio parfait. Closed Sun.
Howies 208 Bruntsfield Place, (0131) 221 1777. One of three reasonably priced restaurants under the same ownership; other branches are at 63 Dalry Road and 75 St Leonard's Street. Its buzzy atmosphere, interesting food, tremendous value and friendly service have featured among recent appreciative reports. Try a warm salad of bacon and pine kernels with a 'first-class' Meaux

mustard sauce, then breast of pink-fleshed, crisp-skinned Barbary duck with wild Scottish mushrooms. Open all week.
Siam Erawan 48 Howe Street, (0131) 226 3675. Little alcoves in whitewashed rough stone walls make this basement 'an intimate setting for a romantic meal'. Friendly service is led by the owner, Miss Chinnapong, who is proficient at explaining the menus: a reasonably priced set lunch with plenty of choice, or a long à la carte. They include traditional spicy-hot tom yam soup; tempura prawns with white fish and vegetables; chicken wings; and various Thai curries and noodles. Closed Sun L.

● **FAIRLIE** (North Ayrshire)
Fins Fencefoot Farm, (01475) 568989. This informal and trendy restaurant squeezed into a converted byre has a bustling atmosphere and is popular with tourists. It offers a mainly seafood menu, taking in a cold seafood platter, hot smoked salmon, and queen scallops provençale. Finish with home-made puddings, ice creams or cheese. A separate smokehouse, farm shop and specialist cookshop are also part of the set-up. Closed Sun D and all day Mon.

● **GATTONSIDE** (Borders)
Hoebridge Inn Gattonside, (01896) 823082. An old coaching inn in a great countryside location on the banks of the River Tweed with a friendly and relaxed atmosphere. Among many recommended dishes have been red mullet soup with two fillets on top, 'fantastic' suprême of venison and pigeon breasts, and king prawns in a sweet potato batter with a sweet-and-sour chilli sauce. A selection of Scottish cheeses provides an alternative to poached pear in orange syrup with chocolate and Cointreau ice cream. Open Tue to Sun D only.

● **GLASGOW** (Glasgow)
Gamba 225A West George Street, (0141) 572 0899. As the name suggests, fish and seafood are the specialities in this modern basement restaurant. Interesting and unusual treatments include tartare of halibut, fish soup with gingered crab and cod dumplings, and red snapper on

scallops and artichoke with a thyme cream sauce. Grilled lemon sole is available for those who like to keep it simple, and Angus beef teriyaki with wasabi and chips caters for non-piscivores. Closed Sun.

Killermont Polo Club 2022 Maryhill Road, (0141) 946 5412. An 'oasis of calm in bustling Maryhill', with colonial décor and a polo theme evoking a Raj atmosphere: this is no ordinary curry house. The 'dum pukht' (meaning 'covered with life') style of cooking originated in the food courts of seventeenth-century Moghul emperors, and produces rich, aromatic, slow-cooked dishes such as chicken stuffed with pomegranate, mint, cheese and onions, and lamb simmered with poppy seeds, cashews and saffron. Closed Sun L.

Mitchells/Mitchells West End 157 North Street, (0141) 204 4312, and 35 Ashton Lane, (0141) 339 2220. Popular neighbourhood brasserie-style restaurants offering lunch and dinner cartes and pre-theatre menus; bring your own wine Monday to Thursday for a small corkage charge. Typical items include West Coast sea-fish chowder to start, followed by seared fillet of salmon or roast haunch of Inverness venison. End traditionally with steamed lemon and ginger pudding or macerated fruits with ice cream. Closed Sat L and Sun (North Street), closed Mon to Sat L and Sun (Ashton Lane).

Two Fat Ladies 88 Dumbarton Road, (0141) 339 1944. This small restaurant is nothing to do with celebrity chefs (but note the Round-up entry in Haddington below). It deals largely (but not exclusively) in fish, with the kitchen open to view and a blackboard of daily specials. One diner enjoyed mackerel followed by sea bream teriyaki, finishing with Scottish cheeses, while the short lunch menu might offer pan-fried herrings followed by sauté chicken with lentils. Pre-theatre meals are also available. Service is 'knowledgeable and friendly'. Open Fri and Sat L, Tue to Sat D.

● **GLENDEVON** (Perthshire & Kinross)
Tormaukin Hotel Glendevon, (01259) 781252. Eighteenth-century drovers' inn on an isolated road in the Ochil hills offering an eclectic range of dishes far above the usual pub norm. At dinner you might start with venison terrine with Cumberland sauce before moving on to smoked salmon fish cakes with a dill crème fraîche dressing, or lamb chops with minted aïoli. Then it could be sizzling lemon pancakes, or boozy cherry crème brûlée. Children have their own selection, and snacks available L. Open all week; accommodation.

● **HADDINGTON** (East Lothian)
Clarissa's Lennoxlove House, (01620) 823720. TV chef Clarissa Dickson-Wright's restaurant is on the Duke of Hamilton's estate in an attractive and peaceful setting. 'Restrained' décor sets the scene for a short blackboard menu. A recent meal started with caramelised onions with balsamic and Parmesan, followed by 'flavoursome' lamb chops with port and marmalade sauce. Other recommended dishes have included a 'light' salmon and blue cheese terrine, 'perfectly seared' scallops on a bed of roast peppers, and fillets of halibut with a creamy gremolata topping; finish with rhubarb pavlova or hot chocolate pudding with vanilla ice cream. Open Tue to Sat L (Wed to Sat D by arrangement).

● **KILCHRENAN** (Argyll & Bute)
Taychreggan Kilchrenan, (01866) 833211/366. There was a change of chef at this converted drovers' inn on the edge of Loch Awe as we went to press, so more reports please. Three-course lunches and five-course dinners might deal in rabbit and spinach ravioli, then roast duck on a potato cake with caramelised onions, finishing with a banana and treacle rum baba with toffee sauce, or Tayberry délice. Snacks are available in the bar. Open all week.

● **MELROSE** (Borders)
Burts Hotel The Square, (01896) 822285. Market-town hotel built in 1722

for a local dignitary, now with an attractively laid-out restaurant and efficient but unobtrusive service. Visitors have enjoyed a tian of smoked prawns with avocado and tomatoes, and a parfait of venison and quail, followed by seared fillet of salmon on a shellfish stir-fry, and a trio of Border lamb chops. Desserts take in sticky toffee pudding and plum and frangipane tart. Open all week.

● **MOFFAT** (Dumfries & Galloway)
Beechwood Country House Hotel
Harthope Place, (01683) 220210. Overlooking the Annan valley and set, appropriately enough, in a dozen acres of beech trees, this Victorian country-house hotel is open all week for dinner, and Friday to Sunday for lunch. All-inclusive set-price menus might offer venison and cranberry terrine, or leek and potato cake topped with a poached egg, followed by breast of chicken, or pan-fried scampi. Blackcurrant crumble tart makes a homely alternative to chocolate and Amaretto mousse, or there is cheese. Service is attentive.

● **OBAN** (Argyll & Bute)
Knipoch Hotel Knipoch, (01852) 316251. This informal, relaxed hotel enjoys an attractive setting by Loch Feochan, not far from Oban. There is a 'Scottish heritage' feel about the three- or five-course dinner menus, which regularly employ whisky, Aberdeen Angus beef, Scottish cheeses and local fish and seafood, including the speciality: home-smoked Loch Creran salmon. Water is provided by the hotel's own spring.

● **SHIELDAIG** (Highland)
Tigh an Eilean Shieldaig, (01520) 755251. Converted waterfront croft with friendly owners, enthusiastic staff and an attractive dining room. The draw is outstanding locally caught fish and seafood: Torridon crab dijonnaise, or Kinlochbervie plaice bonne femme, for example. Meat-eaters might choose between Barbary duckling with bigarade sauce and roast loin of beef. Try the local cheeses, or a simple dessert such as raspberry pavlova or lemon flan. Open for dinner only from Easter to mid-October (the adjoining pub under the same ownership serves bar meals all year round).

● **TURNBERRY** (South Ayrshire)
Turnberry Hotel Turnberry, (01655) 331000. Spectacular views across the Firth of Clyde can be enjoyed from the restaurant of this huge and imposing golfing hotel. Chef Stewart Cameron has been cooking here for nearly twenty years, making good use of luxury ingredients and local produce: Argyll scampi and seared scallops might come with ginger cream and orange poppy seed 'confit', and marinated and smoked Scottish salmon with beluga caviare. Main courses have seen Ayrshire lamb paired with forest mushrooms, and sea bass served with black pepper polenta, lemon grass oil and balsamic vinegar. Finish with a baked tart of figs or chocolate temptation. The Terrace Brasserie offers an alternative to the formality of the main restaurant. Both open all week D and Sun L.

Wales

● **ABERSOCH** (Gwynedd)
Riverside Hotel Abersoch, (01758) 712419. 'We think that we are slightly traditional but with some interesting variations,' writes Wendy Bakewell, who ought to be a good judge after 32 years in charge of this small hotel together with husband John. The statement is borne out by a set-price dinner menu that typically offers courgette mousse on saffron sauce, poached monkfish with grain mustard and tarragon cream sauce, and pecan meringues served with summer fruits under a Baileys sabayon.

● **CARDIFF** (Cardiff)
Buffs 8 Mount Stuart Square, (01222) 464628, changing to (029) 2046 4628.

Open weekdays from 11 to 7, this relaxed but stylish wine bar with its terracotta walls and church pew seating is in a listed building in the old docks. Recommended on the good-value, innovative menu (supplemented by daily specials) have been deep-fried goats' cheese with an onion marmalade, and 'very satisfying' home-made mushroom soup; or try venison sausage with mash, or a club sandwich. A pancake with cream, calvados and sautéed apples might be a good way to finish. A restaurant, open the same hours, offers more expensive meals incorporating baked stuffed red snapper, or lemon chicken.

De Courcey's Tyla Morris Ave, Pentyrch, (01222) 892232, changing to (029) 2089 2232. A fifteen minute walk from the city centre, De Courcey's offers set-price menus and a gourmet *carte* listing dishes such as roulade of salmon and herbs, pan-fried scallops with squid-ink sauce, and pan-fried breast of guinea-fowl. Desserts might include hot rhubarb soufflé or dark chocolate tart. Open Sun L and Thur to Sat D only; owners say 'no jeans or denims'.

Le Gallois 6–8 Romilly Street, (01222) 341264, changing to (029) 2034 1264. Popular with locals in an arty part of Cardiff, this family-run, split-level restaurant with fresh, minimalist décor is now run by Graham and Anne Jones with son Padvig heading the kitchen. 'Good breads', 'excellent' fish cakes and tarte Tatin have been recommended, or try wild mushroom medley, herbed chicken with bubble-and-squeak, and vanilla crème brûlée. Attentive and friendly staff; wide-ranging pocket-friendly wine list. Closed Sun and Mon.

Metropolis 60 Charles Street, (01222) 344300, changing to (029) 2034 4300. Mauves and yellows contribute to the décor's 'mad eclecticism' (helped by photos of skyscrapers, and sculpted busts straight out of Picasso paintings), all of which sets the scene for some 'civilised' francophone cooking. Consistency may not be the strongest suit, but a number of dishes have earned praise, among them

light salmon and herb fish cakes, rack of Welsh lamb with honey-glazed shallots, and poached pears with mulled wine syrup.

● **CARMARTHEN** (Carmarthenshire)
Quayside Brasserie The Quay, (01267) 223000. This barn-like restaurant has a large balcony from which you can enjoy views over the river Towy. Game, poultry, meat and fish are all displayed on a counter, and the kitchen is open to view. A good value two-course lunch might offer seafood gratin, followed by stir-fried beef, while the blackboard menu runs to pan-fried cockles or Pembrokeshire duck with honey and black peppercorns. Puddings might include bara brith with celtic ice cream. Closed Sun.

● **CHEPSTOW** (Monmouthshire)
Wye Knot 18A The Back, (01291) 622929. This modern restaurant in a row of terraced cottages, with views at high tide of fishing boats bobbing at their moorings, offers a concisely described menu that shows a confident diversity of style and ingredients. Terrine of duck, pork and pheasant comes with an onion and orange marmalade, and fusion touches appear in the form of crab ravioli with fried king scallops and a mild chilli sauce.

● **CHURCH BAY** (Isle of Anglesey)
Lobster Pot Church Bay, (01407) 730588. This family business was established over 50 years ago by Mr Wilson senior who now, in his nineties, grows (organically) most of the salads and vegetables: four of them are served with main dishes. Andrew Wilson, lobster and crab exporter, supplies specimens from ponds in the garden, which also has a few tables from which to enjoy the sea view. The mainly seafood menu looks abroad for paella or salmon and scallop filo purses; and looks back to such classics as lobster Thermidor and scallop Mornay. Staff are local Welsh speakers, décor recalls the '60s, and wines are very reasonably priced. Open Tue to Sat (Sun in Aug and bank hol weekends).

691

● **CRICKHOWELL** (Powys)
Gliffaes Country House Hotel (01874) 730371/ 0800 730463. 'Gloriously green' are the views down to the valley from this late-nineteenth-century grey-stone Italianate country house; set above the Usk in 33 acres of grounds, it has been owned by the same family for over fifty years. Lunches (except on Sunday) tend to be light affairs, while set-price three-course dinner menus offer salad of home-smoked quail to start, followed by seared fillet of cod with potted shrimps and a red wine sauce, ending with lime chiffon pie with a compote of raspberries and a chocolate sorbet. Buffet-style afternoon teas.

● **GLANWYDDEN** (Conwy)
Queen's Head Glanwydden, (01492) 546570. A pleasing country pub and restaurant, with a wood burning stove in the bar. Local ingredients are used in the highly praised seafood platter; other fish specialities include monkfish and bacon kebab on saffron couscous, and mussels sautéed in garlic butter topped with local cheese. Carnivores may find local lamb and beef. A mahogany dresser displays 'superb' blackberry cheesecake, and chocolate brandy trifle, while hot desserts have included treacle tart and bread-and-butter pudding. Short well chosen wine list. Open all week.

● **LAUGHARNE** (Carmarthenshire)
The Cors Laugharne, (01994) 427219. Built in the 1830's, this recently refurbished house has two conservatories overlooking landscaped gardens bordered by the river Corran. The weekly-changing carte uses fine ingredients prepared with care and flair and might consist of bruschetta with grilled goats' cheese, or potato and dill pancake, followed by pan-fried noisettes of Welsh spring lamb or roast fillet of sea bass. Open Thur to Sat D, Sun L.

● **LLANABER** (Gwynedd)
Llwyndu Farmhouse Llanaber, (01341) 280144. Lovely old farmhouse described as 'even more comfy than home'. A typical menu might offer naturally smoked haddock in a lightly curried sauce, or a salad of avocado, olives and feta cheese to start, with main courses of casseroled organic Welsh Black beef or salmon with laverbread and couscous. Indulgent desserts have included toffee rhubarb pudding, and butterscotch banana pancakes. Open Mon to Sat D.

● **LLANFYLLIN** (Powys)
Seeds 5 Penybryn Cottages, High Street (01691) 648604. A deeply rural location, and flagstones within, set the scene for short, weekly-changing set-price menus offering perhaps potted shrimps, pan-seared salmon, and rack of Welsh lamb. Vegetarians might try roast Mediterranean vegetables with couscous, or wild mushroom and spring onion risotto. Finish with treacle tart or lemon posset. Closed Sun D and Mon L.

● **LLANGOLLEN** (Denbighshire)
Gales 18 Bridge Street, (01978) 860089. Small town-house hotel serving a daily-changing menu in its wine bar, using locally grown produce. Choices might include anchovy and sardine cream pâté followed by strips of fillet steak in a Stilton sauce or Burgundy chicken. Round things off with rich chocolate cheesecake or home-made ice creams. Visitors may like to note that the Llangollen Railway and Canal Wharf are a short walk away. Closed Sun.

● **LLANWDDYN** (Powys)
Lake Vyrnwy Hotel Lake Vyrnwy, (01691) 870692. After a day's fishing, walking, birdwatching, or pursuing one of the many other sporting activities available on the 26,000-acre estate, enjoy fine lake views from the conservatory dining room of this Victorian hotel. Seasonal menus take produce from the garden, trout from the lake and game from the estate, and run from a daily roast (Black beef with Yorkshire pudding) to a seafood medley containing tuna carpaccio and risotto-stuffed squid, or Barbary duck with beetroot sauce.

● **PENMAENPOOL** (Gwynedd)
Penmaenuchaf Hall Penmaenpool, (01341) 422129. Penmaenuchaf has had

a rather high turnover of new chefs in recent years, and as the *Guide* went to press, another new face was arriving: Mohammedali Bashir from the Cawdor Arms in Llandeilo (see entry). Local materials have always played a significant role at this relaxed and elegant Victorian country-house hotel with its 'magical' views, and will doubtless continue to do so: the sea is only six miles away, nearby butchers supply Welsh Black and Lleyn Rose beef, Mark Watson is an avid collector of fungi, and there is a kitchen garden to raid. Open all week.

● **SOLVA** (Pembrokeshire)
Old Pharmacy 5 Main Street, (01437) 720005. Informal, family-friendly bistro-cum-coffee-shop run by two local brothers, who offer morning coffee, simple lunches, afternoon teas and more ambitious dinners. The accent of the long, eclectic evening menu is mainly on local seafood, and the robust cooking style might produce Thai king prawns, salad niçoise, or halibut in a horseradish butter sauce. Non-fish dishes include Welsh lamb leg steak and good vegetarian options.

● **SWANSEA** (Swansea)
L'Amuse 93 Newton Road, (01792) 366006. Expect friendly and helpful service, a cheerful but intimate ambience in bistro-like surroundings, and a sensible wine list. The food is attractively presented, quality is consistent, and recommendations have included starters of 'fine' onion tart and carpaccio of monkfish, and main courses of pork fillet with caramelised apples and calvados, and seared salmon with sauce vierge. To finish, frangipane tart comes with chocolate and pears, and cheeses are from the Alps. Closed Mon and Sun D.
Annie's 56 St Helen's Road, (01792) 655603. Open for dinner only from Tuesday to Saturday, Annie's offers cheaper menus in the Cellar restaurant – mixed seafood grill, or cassoulet of pork, for example – and set-price two- or three-course meals in the main restaurant. These might start with a Roquefort soufflé and go on to roast guinea fowl,

finishing with cinnamon mousse and poached pears.
P.A.'s Wine Bar 95 Newton Road, (01792) 367723. A typical long, narrow wine and food bar in the centre of Mumbles offering a set lunch of, say, creamy mint and potato soup followed by baked fillet of halibut mornay. The more extensive carte of things like sauté wild rabbit, and grilled medallions of ostrich, is supplemented by a daily-changing fish board, perhaps offering shellfish paella, and chargrilled swordfish steak. Closed Sun D.

● **TALYLLYN** (Gwynedd)
Minffordd Hotel Talyllyn, (01654) 761665. New owners took over this charming small hotel at the foot of Cader Idris early in 1999 and have scaled down the operation to cater mainly for residents. Dinner is served at 7.30 in the relaxed dining room with old oak furniture and log fires, and sensibly limited menus make good use of local produce in dishes ranging from the old-fashioned (grilled grapefruit, beef in ale) to the modern (deep-fried avocado with a 'racy' chilli salsa).

● **TENBY** (Pembrokeshire)
Mews Bistro The Mews, Upper Frog Street, (01834) 844068. There are tables outside for summer eating at this large restaurant (open only for dinner), where the chef/owner produces unusual combinations with great success. Among recommendtions have been 'fresh and tasty' mushrooms and leeks cooked en papillote with fresh herbs, prime loin of Welsh lamb served with a rich mixed bean and red wine cassoulet, and fillet of Teifi salmon filled with green herb butter in a light pastry coracle. An 'excellent' whole cob loaf with bread knife is served to each table.

● **TREDUNNOCK** (Monmouthshire)
Newbridge Inn Tredunnock, (01633) 451000. Variously a pub and restaurant in the past, this imposing old building, under new ownership since late 1998, has been thoroughly and stylishly refurbished inside and out, and now combines those roles. The setting is

'spectacular', and the modern bistro menu offers much to tempt. An early visit turned up excellent salmon fish cakes, and 'tender and tasty' pink roast rump of lamb with roasted vegetables that showed much promise. Reports please. Closed Mon L.

Channel Islands

● **ST PETER PORT** (Guernsey)
La Frégate Les Cotils, (01481) 724624. Classic French food with a good showing from the sea is what's on offer at this former manor house, now a hotel decorated in traditional style and with spectacular views over the harbour. Besides crêpes filled with crabmeat and prawns in a creamy sauce, or poached sea bass with spinach, there may be smoked duck breast with cranberry and Cointreau sauce, or perhaps 'beautiful' steak tartare. End with marbled chocolate terrine, or rum and raisin ice cream. Menu gourmand available. Open all week.
Le Nautique Quay Steps, (01481) 721714. This former warehouse overlooking the harbour and with good views of the castle 'feels very French'. It specialises in fish dishes from gratin of crab and prawns, to brill with lobster sauce, although there are ample choices 'pour les végétarians' (gratin of curried eggs and avocado) and for those hankering after 'les viandes' (veal with Gruyère). For dessert there might be 'excellent' pistachio ice cream, or crème brûlée. Closed Sat L and all day Sun.

Northern Ireland

● **BELFAST** (Co Antrim)
Strand 12 Stranmillis Road, (01232) 682266, changing to (028) 9068 2266. In the Malone district, close to the heart of the city, the Strand offers 'modern, eclectic but simple' food. The room is decorated in Rennie Mackintosh style and can create 'quite a buzz' when full. A 'Lite Bite' menu is served from 12 to 7, while the main carte offers the likes of caramelised shallot and wild mushroom bruschetta, or steamed scallops with a soy, chilli and ginger sauce. Main courses have included half a roast duck with a bitter orange glaze, and darne of salmon with coriander and horseradish mash. Vegetarians are well catered for. Open all week.

The Good Food Club 1999

Many thanks to all the following people who contributed to this year's *Guide* . . .

Dr Sidney Abrahams
Mrs P. Abrahamsen
Wilhelm Ackermann
Mike and Barbara Adams
Nick Adams
Robert Adams
Stephen C.F. Adams
Peter Adcock
Karen Addington
John Ainsworth
Hilary Akenhead
R.H. Alcock
Lawrence Alexander
Mr and Mrs Alexander
Harry Allen
Mr and Mrs Allom
Catherine Allwood
Sir Anthony Alment
Mrs B. Alsford
Ginny Anderson
Prof J.C. Anderson
Margaret Anderson
Mark and Victoria Andrew
Gwen and Peter Andrews
Kim Andrews
Lee Andrews
Mr T. Appleton
Adrian Appley
Cynthia Archer
Mr P.F. Arden
Fiona Arghebant
J.N. Arkell
Ruth Armitage
John Arnold
Dr P.D. Arnold
Mrs H.G. Ashburn
Carole Ashby
Geoffrey Ashworth
Brian Atkinson
Nicholas Atkinson
Iain Baillie
Lorna Bailliro
Capt Ian Baird
Mr and Mrs J. Baird
Marion Baker
Philippa and Stephen Baker

Susan Baker
Hanon Baldoch
Graham Balfry
Dr C.B. Ballinger
Colin Barker
John Barker
Col. Keith Barker
Glenice Barnard
David Barnes
Mr K.J. Barnes
Richard Barnes
Erica Barnett
Jean Barrett
Janet Barron
Tony Barrow
Ian Barrron
Mr M.D. Bartlett
Mrs R.A. Barton
Mr and Mrs M.J. Bastin
Stanley Bates
Mrs M.G. Bateson
Diana Baum
Michael and Helen Baws
Dr R.W. Baxter
Conrad Bayliss
E.P. Bazalgette
T.H. Beale
B. and H. Beaumont
Mrs M. Bebo
Mr F.R. Beckett
Andrew Bell
Mrs H. Bell
Mrs Ruth Bell
Mr T. Bendhem
Nonnie Benkert
Bruce Bennett
William Bentsen
Mr and Mrs H.I. Berkeley
Mr and Mrs Berlin
Gabriele Berneck
R. Berresford
Miss C. Berry
Mr and Mrs E. Berry
Mrs A.W. Berryman
Mr W.J. Best
Constance Bibby
J.N. Bickerton
Jeff Bidwell
Mrs V.A. Bingham

Betty and Chris Birch
Mr E.R. Birch
Dr J.M. Bird
Mr R.G. Birt
Joyce Black
Anne Blackburn
Mr C.T. Blackburn
Roger Blackburn
Mrs Blackshow
Natasha Blair
Diana Blake
Mrs J.A. Blanks
Nina Blathwayt
Mrs H.B. Blazey
Edward Blincoe
Mr and Mrs S. Bliss
Mr and Mrs Bloomfield
J. Boait
Mr J. Bolt
Christopher Bolton
Richard Bond
Rowland Bonham
Elizabeth Bonython
Mrs J. Booker
Graham Booth
P.A. Boothman
Michael Bordeaux
Mr and Mrs D. Borton
Robin Bourne
Mr A.J. Bowen
J.J. Bowes
Mr and Mrs W. Bowman
P.J Bowyer
Ken and Janet Bracey
Lawrence Brackstone
Anthony Bradbury
Mr M. Brady
Barry Brahams
H. Bramwell
Beatrice Brandon
D. Brandon
Nial Brannigan
Mr B. Brears
Michael Brett
Mr and Mrs Edwin Brew

Mrs Jonica Bridge
Mr and Mrs John Brierley
Steven Briggs
B.J. Britton
Roy Bromell
Mr and Mrs Graham Brooker
Mrs C. Brooks
Dr S.R. Brooks
Mr T.C. Broomfield
Mrs A.M. Brown
Dr and Mrs D.G. Brown
Mrs J.A. Brown
R. Brown
Steve Brown
Tim Brown
Nick Browne
Hugh Browton
Charles Brune
Mr and Mrs S.G. Brunning
Ron Brush
Isobel Bryan
Mr and Mrs Edgar Bryant
M. Bryden
E.M. Buchan
Mr and Mrs H.G. Buck
Mrs F.A. Buckley
Daphne Bullock
Mr and Mrs Peter Burnstone
Rosemary Burpitt
Mr M.H. Burr
Tony Burrows
David Busby
A.K.S. Bush
Mr and Mrs Butler
Mr D. Butterfield
Mr and Mrs J.M. Butterfield
I. Buttress
Maurice and Leslie Buxton
Peter Byworth
Prof Robert Cahn
Mr G.S. Cairns
Mrs G.P. Callagher
N.K. Campbell

Prof Linda Cardozo
Julia Carling
Nikki Carmody
Mr C. Carr
Patricia Carr
Peter Carr
Mr K. Carslaw
Mr D. Carter
Mr N. Carter
Mr P.E. Carter
Simon Carter
Mr J.A.H. Cartwright
Richard Cashmore
Dr R.E. Catlow
Mr and Mrs Tom Caulcott
Mr and Mrs Caulton
Judy Cave
George Cernoch
Mr P.D. Cetti
Helen Chalmers
B. and I. Chandler
Mr A.W.T. Chapman
Mr and Mrs F.S. Chapman
Mr H. Chapman
P. and H. Chapman
Roger Chater
Peter Cheetham
Mrs E. Cherry
Mr W.J. Chesneau
Fay Chester
A.J. Chivers
P.A. Church
Grace Ciappara
Lesley Clare
Dr and Mrs A. Clark
Mrs A. Clark
Patricia Clark
Mrs A. Clarke
D. Clarke
Donald Clayton
Pat Clayton
R.S. Clayton
Dr D.F.G. Clegg
Kenneth Cleveland
Sonia Cohen
Dr Vivienne Cohen
Mr and Mrs Cole
Mr and Mrs Roger Colebrook
Denise Coles
Janet Collett
Dr Joe Collier
Garth Colling
Mrs A. Collins
Mr G. Collins
Mrs Hannah Colton
Sara Colville
Mr R.T. Combe
Mr M. Comninos
Brian Congreve

Sean Connolly
Mr and Mrs Conry
James Cook
Catherine Cooke
Robert Cooper
A.J. Coote
Sir Patrick Cormack
Debbie and Neville Cornforth
Stephen Court
N.A. Coussmaker
Mr J.S. Coward
Janet Coward
Pip Cowley
Mrs Diane Cox
D.T. Crabtree
David and Christina Cramb
Mr and Mrs Peter Crane
Mr and Mrs Justin Crawford
Michael Crick
Sir Julian Critchley
Tom Crompton
Mr J.D. Crosland
Rodney Cross
Dr J.M. Crossley
David Cubey
Mrs E. Cuzner
Dr Stan da Prato
Mr and Mrs P.F. Dakin
I. Daly
Mrs S.T. Daly
Mr and Mrs Dalzell
Mr M. Daneshvar
Chris and Rachael Daubney
Mr and Mrs P. Davey
Mr and Mrs D.W.M. Davidson
Mr W.H. Davidson
Duncan Davies
Mr and Mrs Davies
Mr and Mrs John Davies
Prof and Mrs R.J. Davies
A.E. Davis
Mr and Mrs Geoff Daw
Dr and Mrs R.P.R. Dawber
Mr M.J. Day
Timothy James de Lay
Mr and Mrs F.C. de Paula
Leopold de Rothschild

Mr and Mrs J.I. de Villiers
Brian Dean
C.B. Dean
Mrs J. Dean
N.C. Dee
Nicola Delis
Gerald Della-Porta
Hugh Dempster
C. Derby
Mr and Mrs Dewar
Kay and Mark Dewsbury
Norma Dickens
Rebecca Dickinson
Ian Dickson
Mrs J. Dinham
Mr G.M. Dobbie
M.L. Dodd
Mr Dodman
Susy Dowse
A. Dubash
Laleh Dubash
John Ducker
Jonathan Duffy
Ian Dunbar
Mr A. Dunn
Dr Andrew Dunn
Denis Durno
G.R. Eagle
Dr and Mrs Lindsay Easton
Dr S. Eden
Mr R. Edmonds
Mrs E.H. Edward
Aileen Edwards
Bryan Edwards
D.E. Edwards
Mrs G.F.J. Edwards
G.M. Edwards
Malcolm Edwards
William Edwards
John Elder
Mr T.M. Eldrid
Mr G. Elflett
Simon Elliot
Mr A.C.R. Elliott
John Elliott
Roy Elliott
John Elvidge
Rosalind Ereira
Dr Stephen Erskine
Mr and Mrs John Ette
Mrs Evans
Peter Evans
John Ewan
J. Ewart
Liz Eyre
Gerry Fairweather
Mrs Jane Falloon

Dr and Mrs I.K. Farquhar
Ann Farrow
J.F. Fawcett
Mr G.D. Fearnehough
Catherine Feeny
Doanld Feinstein
Mr G.A. Fenn
John Field
Dr and Mrs Finer
J. Fines
John and Moira Firth
Linda Fisher
Valerie Fisher
Maureen Fitz-Henry
Susan Fleming
Mr A.T.R. Fletcher
R.F. Flower
Prof Peter Fookes
Angela Ford
William Fordham
Mrs P.L. Forrest
Mr B.W. Forster
Graham Foster
S.R. Foster
Mr R. Frankenburg
Dr M.L. Franks
Justin Fraser
Alken Freer
Mrs L. Frishwasser
Malcolm Fyfe
Michael Gabb
Mr K.F. Gabbertas
Roger and Pam Gadsby
Mr H. Gale
Mr Iain Galloway
Mr D.A Gamble
Judge Michael Garner
Christopher Garrand
Michael Garrison
S.R. Gascoigns
Dr Ian Gavin
Vera George
Colin Gershinson
Mr J.W. Gibbon
J. Gibbs
Mr P. Gibbs
Richard Gibson
Kathryn Gilbert and Ben Nichols
Tim Giles
Mr D.A. Gilmour
D.F. Gimber
Mr E. Glennon
Mrs P.M. Glover
Mr and Mrs Jim Godfrey

Peter Row and
Lawrence
Goldberg
Alan Golding
Joy and Raymond
Goldman
Jennie Goldrei
Rebecca Goldsmith
Tom Gondris
Steve Goodacre
Kate Goodchild
G.R. Goodson
Kate Gordon
Mr M. Gordon-
Russell
Mr R.L. Gorick
Terry Gorman
Mr and Mrs David
Gostyn
Lorraine Gough
Mr and Mrs
Raymond Gough
Robert Gower
Suzanne Gower
Mr M.B. Gowers
Janet Graham
Mr and Mrs
Gransden
David Grant
Julio Grau
J.A. Gray
Mr T.C. Gray
Alison Green
David Green
John Greene
Mr R.R.F. Greene
Mr and Mrs
Greenhow
Jim Greenwood
Mr W.N. Greenwood
Conal Gregory
Janet and John
Gregory
Prof K.J. Gregory
Mr and Mrs Peter
Gregory
Mr R.F. Grieve
C.J. Griffin
Mr J.R. Griffin
Brian Griffiths
Mr D.R. Griffiths
T.J. Griffiths
Rev William Griffiths
William Grime
Mr N.M. Grimwood
Nigel Grisswood
Lieut K.R. Groves
Captain A.C.
Grunert
Mr B.G. Gunary
A.F. Gwynedd
Dr Bryan Hall

Hazel Hall
J. Hall
Joyce Hall
Mr and Mrs P.J. Hall
Patrick Hall
Robin and Shiona
Hall
Mr and Mrs Michael
Hallsworth
Barry Hancock
Gordon Hands
Mr R. Harding
N.G. Hardy
Dr B. Hargrove
Christopher Harlowe
Danny Harman
Tim Harper
Mr R.W. Harries
T.R.R. Harries
R.E. Harris
Raymond Harris
Frank Harris-Jones
Dr B.D.W. Harrison
Duncan Harrison
Mr G.W. Harrison
Ms M. Harrison
Mr and Mrs Colin
Hart
Sir Graham Hart
Sharon Hart
Ms W. Hart
J.V. Hartley
Mavis Hawkins
Richard Hawkins
Margaux Haynes
T.D. Hazell
Peter Hazelton
Dr and Mrs Healy
John Hearle
K.T. Heather
Mrs A. Henley
Mr N.F. Henshaw
R.A. Hepher
Mr R.E. Hepple-
Wilson
Dr Andrew
Herxheimer
Mr and Mrs Peter
Heslop
Gad Heuman
Allan Hewitt
Mrs M.J. Hewitt
P.W.G. Heywood
Kay Hickman
Jennifer Hicks
John Hicks
Julia Higgs
J.E. Hilditch
Joan Hildith
Mr G. Hill
Mrs M.H. Hill

Rupert and Nicola
Hill
Wendy Hillary
Mr P.C. Hillier
L. Hillman
Hindle Zinkin
Mr and Mrs R. Hinds
Dr E. Hiscock
Mrs E. Hoare
Mr and Mrs P.A.
Hoare
B.J. Hodges
Bob and Gina
Hodges
Mrs D.J. Hogbin
William Hogg
Margot Holbrook
Margaret Holden
Roger Hole
David Holes
Mr J.F. Holman
Mr Holmes
Mr and Mrs R.
Holmes
Fred Homer
Mrs I.P. Honeywood
Betty Hooper
Dr R.J. Hopkins
Lt Col and Mrs
Hopkinson
Susan Hopps
Ralph Hopton
Mr and Mrs R.H.
Horncastle
A. Hoskins
Julian Hoskins
Matthew Hoskins
Mrs C.E. Housle
Mr S. Howard
Wendy Howard
Lord Howe
Mr D.P. Howell
Mr and Ms Howells
Mr M.R. Howes
Dianne Howlett
Mr and Mrs P.N.
Hubbard
Mrs M. Hubner
Lynn Hudd
David Hudson
Mr C. Hughes
Cheryl Hughes
Gwilym Hughes
Jon Hughes
P.H.O. Hughes
Mr and Mrs Hume
B.E.and D.R. Hunt
Mrs Sheila Hunt
Dr Tim Hunt
D. Hunter
D.E. Hunter
Mr C.J. Hurd

Roger Huxtable
Penny Hyatt
Mr and Mrs David
Hyman
Mr T.J. Hypher
Mrs Rosemary Inge
Mr J.C. Ison
Vivienne Ivry
Dr H.R.S. Jack
Mrs A. Jackson
Mr P. Jackson
Mr A.L. Jacobs
Geoffrey Jacobs
K.G. James
Bruce Jamieson
Brenda Jeeves
Alan Jeffery
Ms N. Jeffery
Sarah Jeffery
Valerie Jenkins
Peter Jenks
E.D. Jennings
Paul Jerome
David Jervois
Stephen Jessel
Mr and Mrs Brian
Jobson
Mr B.M. Joce
Sandra John
Barbara Johnson
Brian Johnson
D. Johnson
Mr H.G. Johnson
Madeleine Johnson
P. Johnson
Mr and Mrs Jones
Anthony Jones
Ian Jones
Iris Jones
Mrs M. Jones
Mark Jones
Paul Joslin
Mr and Mrs M.
Joyce
Mr M.R Judd
Mr and Mrs Kane
Dr Leon Kaufman
E.R. Kaylor
Dr J.W. Keeling
Sheila Keene
Tatiana Keeran
Dr E.W. Kellerman
Mr A. Kellett-Long
Geoffrey Kemp
Henry Kemp
Mr P.G. Kemp
E.A. Kennington
Mr W.J. Kent
Mr R.B. Kenyon
Dr L.W. Kerr
J.S. Kerridge
Mrs S.J. Kettell

T.A. Smith
Mrs J.C. Smye
Paul Snape
Mr and Mrs Timothy Spall
Wg Cdr R.M. Sparkes
Dennis Speight
Mrs J.M. Spencer-Wort
Mr T. Spickett
Dr and Mrs W.B. Spry
Louise Spurrier
Jeffrey and Wendy Stackhouse
Mrs R. Stanton
Mike and Gillian Staples
P.M. Steeples
Mrs G.M. Stein
Mrs Stephens
Anthony Stern
Mr and Mrs P.N. Stevens
Alastair Stevenson
Dr Andrew Stevenson
Andrew Stevenson
Capt and Mrs J.S. Stewart
Michael Stewart
Terry Stewart
K.M.S. Stimpson
Mrs Stockham
Gwyneth Stokes Kimble
Mr and Mrs C.M. Stooke
Anne Storm
P.N. Stott
Mr and Mrs Strong
Len Stuckey
Mrs L.J. Sugden
A.J. Sunderland
Mr W.M. Sutton
Audrey and Harry Swales
Erica Swift
Mr P.J. Swindlehurst
Brenda Symes
Godfrey and Jo Talbot
David Tanner
John Tarrant
Mr and Mrs Tate
Dr and Mrs P.H. Tattersall
Dr D.M. Taub
Mrs A.C. Taylor

Barry Taylor
George Taylor
Jean Taylor
M.L. Taylor
Mr and Mrs Steven Taylor
Mr H. Tebbutt
A.J. Telford
Alison Telling
Jack Temple
Edward Thackray
Russell Thersby
Sue Thody
Mr A.D. Thomas
Alan Thomas
Dr Margaret Thompson
N.J. Thompson
Angela Thomsett
Mr and Mrs J. Thorburn
Dr A.G. Thornton
Mr and Mrs G.N. Thornton
Myles Thornton
Roger Thornton
Samantha and Darren Thorpe
Mr and Mrs Thurlow
Dr A.C. Thurlow
Judge David Ticehurst
Jeanne and Ken Tichbon
Sean Timmins
Mr G.G. Tiramani
Roberta Tish
Julian Tobin
F. Tomlin
C. and D. Tomlinson
Michael Townson
Sylvia Trench
S.R. Tromans
Inge Trott
John Trueman
Maria Trygger
Mr B.W.B. Turner
David Turner
Stuart Turner
Curzon Tussaud
Gary Twynam
Elizabeth Tylor
Mrs F. Tyndall
J.R. Tyrie
Prof and Mrs Edward Ullendorff
Mr P.G. Urben
Kenneth Van Barthold
Margaret Van Veelen

Mr J. Vanderbilt-Sloane
Gloria Varley
R.G. Veasey
Eileen Vielvoye
Gerald Vinestock
The Hon Mrs A.M. Viney
Stephen Vokes
Michael Wace
Mr P.H. Wainman
Mr R.T. Wainwright
Christopher Waite
Lilian Wakefield
Christine Walby
Anthony Walker
F. Walker
Tony Walker
Val Walker-Dendle
Prof Helen Wallace
James Waller
Dr Robert Waller
Janet Wallington
Dr Graham Wallis
P.J. Walpole
Michael Walsh
Mrs P.A. Ward
Stella Wardell
Mr A.J. Wardrop
P.J. Warland
Roger Warshaw
Mr R.A. Wartnaby
A. Washbourn
R.S. Watkins
A.R. Watson
Mr and Mrs J. Watson
Doreen Webb
John Webb
Peggy and John Webb
Richard Webb
Stewart Webster
John Wedge
Libby Weir-Breen
Roger Weldhen
M. Wensley
I.E. West
Mr J.F.M. West
M.J. West
Mr M.J. West
Charles Weston
Mrs M. Weston-Smith
Mrs C. Whalley
S.E. Wharton
Julia Whatley
Kate Wheeldon
Mr and Mrs John Wheeler

Paul Whitaker
Mrs J. Whitbread
N.H. White
Roger White
Sandra Whitham
D.J. Whiting
David Whiting
M.C Whiting
Lesley Whittaker
Paul Whittard
Mr D.N. Whyte
Mrs P.D. Wiffen
D.T. Wiggins
Giles Wigoder
Mr and Mrs J. Wildman
R.C. Wiles
John Wilkin
Prof Wilks
Mr P. Willer
Donald Williams
Dr Elinor Williams
J.J.B. Williams
M.E. Williams
Mr N. Williams
Mr R.B. Williams
Mr and Mrs R.W. Williams
Stephen Williamson
Drs A. and C. Wilson
C.H. Wilson
Mr and Mrs Ian Wilson
Prof P.N. Wilson
D.R. Windsor
Mr E.C. Winter
L.M. Wise
A. Wiseman
Sandra Witham
Mr and Mrs Withers
Dr N.P. Woffenden
David Wolff
Virginia Woodgate
Diana Woodward
Mrs V. Woolf
Alan Worsdale
J. and S. Worth
Mr and Mrs Wright
Mr and Mrs Derek Wright
Dr Harold Wright
Helen Wright
Paul and Anne Marie Wright
Anthony Wyld
Mr J. Yardley
Michael York-Palmer

Index of entries

Index of entries

Names in bold are main entries. Names in italics are Round-ups.

703

Launceston Place, London W8 116
Laurent, London NW2 116
Lavender, London SW11 205
Lawn, London SE3 117
Leaping Hare Vineyard Restaurant, Stanton 464
Leatherne Bottel, Goring 316
L'Ecrivain, Dublin 645
Lee Fook, London W2 117
Leela's, Newcastle upon Tyne 678
Left Bank, Pembroke 612
Leftbank, Birmingham 237
Leith's, London W11 118
Leith's at Dartmouth House, London W1 205
Leith's Soho, London W1 118
Lemonia, London NW1 205
Lemon Tree, Oxford 416
Leodis, Leeds 357
L'Escargot, London W1 89
L'Estaminet, London WC2 90
Let's Eat/Let's Eat Again, Perth 571
Lettonie, Bath 228
Lewtrenchard Manor, Lewdown 361
Lighthouse, Aldeburgh 213
The Lime Tree, Limavady 632
Lime Tree, Manchester 386
Lincoln, Manchester 387
L'Incontro, London SW1 108
Lindsay House, London W1 119
Linthwaite House, Bowness-on-Windermere 243
Little Barwick House, Barwick 224
Little Yang Sing, Manchester 387
Livebait, London SE1 and WC2 120
Llangoed Hall, Llyswen 609
Lloyds Brasserie, Dublin 646
Llwyndu Farmhouse, Llanaber 692
Lobster Pot, Church Bay 691
Lobster Pot, London SE11 120
Lochbay, Stein 575
Loch Fyne, Cambridge 666
Loch Fyne Oyster Bar, Cairndow 531
Loch Fyne Oyster Bar, Elton 669
Lochgreen House, Troon 578
Loch Melfort Hotel, Arduaine 687

Lodge Hotel, Huddersfield 338
Loft, Blair Atholl 530
Lola's, London N1 121
Lomo, London SW10 121
London Hilton, Windows Rooftop Restaurant, London W1 205
Longueville House, Mallow 655
Longueville Manor, St Saviour 625
Lords of the Manor, Upper Slaughter 485
Lou Pescadou, London SW5 122
Lovetts, Douglas 642
Lower Slaughter Manor, Lower Slaughter 371
Lucknam Park, Colerne 280
Lundum's, London SW7 123
Lux, Glasgow 552
Lygon Arms, Broadway 257
Lynwood House, Barnstaple 662
MacCallums' Oyster Bar, Troon 578
MacNean Bistro, Blacklion 639
Maes-y-Neuadd, Talsarnau 619
Magno's, London WC2 123
Magpie Café, Whitby 494
Magpies, Horncastle 334
Maharaja, Birmingham 238
Maison Bleue at Mortimer's, Bury St Edmunds 263
Maison Novelli, London EC1 124
Mallards, Saint Michael's on Wyre 445
Mandalay, London W2 205
Mandarin Kitchen, London W2 124
Le Manoir aux Quat' Saisons, Great Milton 320
Manor House, Castle Combe 268
Manor House, Walkington 486
Manor House Inn, Carterway Heads 266
Mansion House, Poole 426
Mantanah, London SE25 125
Manzi's, London WC2 206
Marco's, Norwich 411
Margot's, Padstow 419
Market Restaurant, Manchester 676
Markwicks, Bristol 253
Marlfield House, Gorey 650
Marquis, London W1 206

Notes

Notes

Notes

Report Form   **2000**

To the Editor *The Good Food Guide*
FREEPOST, 2 Marylebone Road, London NW1 4DF

Or send your report by electronic mail to: *guidereports@which.co.uk*

From my personal experience the following establishment should/should not be included in the *Guide* (please print in BLOCK CAPITALS):

_____

_____

Telephone_____

I had lunch/dinner/stayed there on (date) _____ 19____

I would rate this establishment _____ out of ten.

please continue overleaf

My meal for _____ people cost £ _____ *attach bill where possible*

☐ Please tick if you would like more report forms

Reports received up to the end of **May 2000** will be used in the research of the 2001 edition.

I am not connected in any way with management or proprietors, and have not been asked by them to write to the *Guide*.
Name and address (BLOCK CAPITALS, please)

_____

_____

Signed _____

As a result of your sending us this report form, we may send you information on **The Good Food Guide** and **The Which? Hotel Guide** in the future. If you would prefer not to receive such information, please tick this box [   ].

Report Form   2000

To the Editor *The Good Food Guide*
FREEPOST, 2 Marylebone Road, London NW1 4DF

Or send your report by electronic mail to: *guidereports@which.co.uk*

From my personal experience the following establishment
should/should not be included in the *Guide* (please print in BLOCK
CAPITALS):

_____

_____

                              Telephone_____

I had lunch/dinner/stayed there on (date) _____ 19___

I would rate this establishment _____ out of ten.

please continue overleaf

My meal for _____ people cost £ _____ *attach bill where possible*

☐ Please tick if you would like more report forms

Reports received up to the end of May 2000 will be used in the research of the 2001 edition.

I am not connected in any way with management or proprietors, and have not been asked by them to write to the *Guide*.
Name and address (BLOCK CAPITALS, please)

_____

_____

Signed _____

Report Form

To the Editor *The Good Food Guide*   **2000**
FREEPOST, 2 Marylebone Road, London NW1 4DF

Or send your report by electronic mail to: *guidereports@which.co.uk*

From my personal experience the following es...
should/should not be included in the *Guide* (please print ...ent
CAPITALS):

_____

_____

                                    Telephone_____

I had lunch/dinner/stayed there on (date) _____ 19___

I would rate this establishment _____ out of ten.

please continue overleaf

My meal for ____ people cost £ _____ *attach bill where possible*

☐ Please tick if you would like more report forms

Reports received up to the end of **May 2000** will be used in the research of the 2001 edition.

I am not connected in any way with management or proprietors, and have not been asked by them to write to the *Guide*.
Name and address (BLOCK CAPITALS, please)

_____

_____

Signed _____

As a result of your sending us this report form, we may send you information on **The Good Food Guide** and **The Which? Hotel Guide** in the future. If you would prefer not to receive such information, please tick this box [   ].

Report Form   **2000**

To the Editor *The Good Food Guide*
FREEPOST, 2 Marylebone Road, London NW1 4DF

Or send your report by electronic mail to: *guidereports@which.co.uk*

From my personal experience the following establishment should/should not be included in the *Guide* (please print in BLOCK CAPITALS):

_____

_____

Telephone_____

I had lunch/dinner/stayed there on (date) _____ 19____

I would rate this establishment _____ out of ten.

please continue overleaf

My meal for _____ people cost £ _____ *attach bill where possible*

☐ Please tick if you would like more report forms

Reports received up to the end of **May 2000** will be used in the research of the 2001 edition.

I am not connected in any way with management or proprietors, and have not been asked by them to write to the *Guide*.
Name and address (**BLOCK CAPITALS**, please)

_____

_____

Signed _____

As a result of your sending us this report form, we may send you information on **The Good Food Guide** and **The Which? Hotel Guide** in the future. If you would prefer not to receive such information, please tick this box [　].

Report Form

2000

To the Editor *The Good Food Guide*
FREEPOST, 2 Marylebone Road, London NW1 4DF

Or send your report by electronic mail to: *guidereports@which.co.uk*

From my personal experience the following establishment should/should not be included in the *Guide* (please print in BLOCK CAPITALS):

_____

_____

Telephone_____

I had lunch/dinner/stayed there on (date) _____ 19____

I would rate this establishment _____ out of ten.

please continue overleaf

My meal for ____ people cost £ _____ *attach bill where possible*

☐ Please tick if you would like more report forms

Reports received up to the end of May 2000 will be used in the research of the 2001 edition.

I am not connected in any way with management or proprietors, and have not been asked by them to write to the *Guide*.
Name and address (BLOCK CAPITALS, please)

_____

_____

Signed _____

As a result of your sending us this report form, we may send you information on **The Good Food Guide** and **The Which? Hotel Guide** in the future. If you would prefer not to receive such information, please tick this box [   ].

Report Form

2000

To the Editor *The Good Food Guide*
FREEPOST, 2 Marylebone Road, London NW1 4DF

Or send your report by electronic mail to: *guidereports@which.co.uk*

From my personal experience the following establishment should/should not be included in the *Guide* (please print in BLOCK CAPITALS):

_____

_____

Telephone_____

I had lunch/dinner/stayed there on (date) _____ 19____

I would rate this establishment _____ out of ten.

please continue overleaf

My meal for ____ people cost £ _____ *attach bill where possible*

☐ Please tick if you would like more report forms

Reports received up to the end of **May 2000** will be used in the research of the 2001 edition.

I am not connected in any way with management or proprietors, and have not been asked by them to write to the *Guide*.
Name and address (BLOCK CAPITALS, please)

_____

_____

Signed _____

As a result of your sending us this report form, we may send you information on **The Good Food Guide** and **The Which? Hotel Guide** in the future. If you would prefer not to receive such information, please tick this box [ ].